THEOLOGICAL DICTIONARY

OF THE

NEW TESTAMENT

Volume X
INDEX VOLUME

compiled by
RONALD E. PITKIN

WM. B. EERDMANS PUBLISHING COMPANY
GRAND RAPIDS, MICHIGAN

Portions Translated and Adapted
by
Geoffrey W. Bromiley
from
THEOLOGISCHES WÖRTERBUCH ZUM NEUEN TESTAMENT
Zehnter Band: Register, herausgegeben von Gerhard Friedrich
Published by
W. KOHLHAMMER VERLAG
Stuttgart, Germany

Library of Congress Cataloging in Publication Data

Kittel, Gerhard, 1888-1948, ed.
  Theological dictionary of the New Testament.
  Vol. 5-9 edited by Gerhard Friedrich; vol. 10: Index
volume, compiled by R. E. Pitkin.
  1. Greek language, Biblical—Dictionaries—English.
2. Bible. N.T.—Dictionaries. I. Bromiley, Geoffrey
William, ed. and tr. II. Friedrich, Gerhard, 1908-
ed. III. Title. IV. Pitkin, Ronald E., 1942-
PA881.K513   225.3   64-15136

ISBN 0-8028-2323-8

to
the faculty of
Bethel Theological Seminary,
St. Paul, Minnesota

CONTENTS

PREFACE

It is not at all unreasonable to wonder why a busy parish minister would undertake such a massive task as this Index Volume to the *Theological Dictionary of the New Testament*. In retrospect, I would ask myself the same question; for when I began this project I suspected neither the amount of labor and personal sacrifice it would entail nor the problems I would encounter in the course of its completion.

At the outset my purpose was simple: to provide a ready reference that would make the use of the *Theological Dictionary* a more economical investment of time and money. Each feature of the Index is designed with that purpose in mind; and, taking into account one's abilities or disabilities in Greek and Hebrew, to the degree that the various indexes are used interdependently the volume should accomplish it. While the *Index* is designed with the needs of busy ministers in mind (and, for that matter, of anyone finding himself frustratingly unable to give the time necessary to use the *Dictionary* properly), it should also prove useful in the scholar's work.

The life-situation of this book's conception and birth has been the Church; and it is not without realization of that fact that I bring my work on the Index to a close. The *Theological Dictionary of the New Testament* has enriched and deepened my ministry; and to the extent that this volume opens it to others, my efforts will have been well invested.

RONALD E. PITKIN

INDICES
OF THE
THEOLOGICAL DICTIONARY
OF THE
NEW TESTAMENT

INDEX OF ENGLISH KEYWORDS

The keywords below are based primarily on usage in the King James and Revised Standard versions of the New Testament. They are indexed as an aid to locating in the *Dictionary* discussions of the Greek words they translate. They should not be taken as representing necessarily the meanings endorsed in the articles themselves; nor are all the renderings listed below discussed in the articles.

For minor renderings not listed, consult the INDEX OF BIBLICAL REFERENCES under specific passages.

in vain	II:380-381; IV:523-524
incentive	V:816-823
inclose, to	VII:744-747
incontinency	II:339-342
incontinent	II:339-342
incorruptible	IX:93-106
incorruption	IX:93-106
increase, to	VI:263-266; 279-283;
	730-719; VIII:167-168; 517-519
independent	II:487-502
indicate, to	II:61-62; VII:262-265
indifferent things	IX:62-64
indignant, to be	VI:948-950
indolent	V:166-167
indulge in immorality, to	VI:579-595
indulgence	VI:131-134
self-indulgence	II:339-342
infant	V:636-654
inferior	IV:648-659
be inferior, to	VIII:592-601
infirmity	I:490-493
inform, to	IX:7
inherit, to	III:767-785
inheritance	III:767-785
give as an	
inheritance, to	III:767-785
obtain an	
inheritance, to	III:764-765
iniquity	I:153-157; 161-163;
	IV:1085-1086; 1090
injure, to	I:157-161
injurious	VIII:295-307
injury	VIII:295-307
injustice	I:153-157
ink	IV:549-551
inn	IV:328-335; 338
inner	II:698-699
innocent	I:209-210
inquire carefully, to	II:655-657
inscrutable	I:358-359
insight	IV:968-971; IX:220-235
insincerity	VIII:559-570
act insincerely	
with, to	VIII:559-570
insolent	VIII:295-307
inspired by God	VI:453-455
installment	
first installment	I:475
instantly	II:464
instead of	I:372-373
instinct	
by instinct	IX:251-277
instruct, to	II:135-148; III:638-640;
	IV:828; 1019-1022; V:596-625
	VII:527-528; 763-766; IX:480-482
instructed	II:165

instruction	II:160-163; 163-165;
	IV:1019-1022; VIII:246-259
instructor	V:596-625
instrument	V:292-294; VII:358-367
insubordinate	VIII:47
insult, to	III:468; VIII:295-307;
	cf. VI:973-976
insurrection	VII:568-571
insurrectionist	IV:257-262
intellect	IV:951-960
intelligible	II:770
intend, to	VIII:164-167
intent	IV:968-971
intention	I:636-637
intercede	VIII:242-244
intercession	VIII:244-245
make intercession, to	VIII:242-244
interpose	IV:598-624
interpret, to	II:661-666
interpretation	II:661-666;
	IV:328-335; 337; 338
interpreter	II:661-666
into	II:420-434; 537-543; 698-699
intoxicated, to become	IV:545-548
intrude into, to	II:535-536
investigate, to	I:215-216
investigation	II:893-894
invisible	V:368-370
invite, to	III:487-491; 496; V:773-799
invite in return, to	III:496
irksome	V:166-167
irrational	IV:141
irreproachable	I:356-357; IV:9
irrevocable	IV:626-629
irritable, to be	V:857
Israel	III:356-391
Israelite	III:356-391
it is necessary	II:21-25
it must be	II:21-25
Jacob	III:191-192
jailor	I:561-563
Jambres	III:192-193
jangling	
vain jangling	IV:524
Jannes	III:192-193
jealous, to be	II:882-888
jealousy	II:877-882
Jeremiah	III:218-221
Jerusalem	VII:292-338
people of Jerusalem	VII:292-338
Jesus	III:284-293
Jew	III:356-391
live as a Jew, to	III:356-391
Jewish	III:356-391
Judaism	III:356-391

to be II:459-460
out of season III:462
out of the synagogue VII:848-852
out of trouble IV:593
outrage, to VIII:295-307
outside II:575-576
outsider III:215-217
over, to be VI:700-703
overcome, to IV:9-10; 942-945
overextend, to II:465
overflow, to VI:58-61; 263-266
overseer II:608-620
overshadow, to VII:399-400
oversight, to exercise II:599-605
overtake IV:9-10; 14-15
overthrow, to VII:715-717
overthrowing VII:715-717
overturn, to VII:715-717
owe, to V:559-564
own I:727
one's own VI:57-58
owner II:44-49

pain
cause pain, to IV:313-322
take pains, to I:494-496
pangs IX:667-674
suffer birth pangs, to IX:667-674
parable V:744-761
Paraclete V:800-814
paradise V:765-773
pardon, to I:509-512
Parousia V:858-871
part IV:555-568; 594-598
partake (of), to I:675-677; II:830-832;
III:797-809; IV:10-11
partaker II:830-832; III:797-809
partaker of afflictions,
to be V:936-938
partaker with II:830-832
partiality III:953; VI:779-780
one who shows
partiality VI:779-780
shows partiality, to VI:779-780
without partiality III:950-951
participate with, to III:797-809
participation III:797-809
partner II:830-832; III:797-809
party I:180-184
pass, to I:523; II:676; 681-682;
VIII:523-524
come to pass, to I:681-682
pass away, to I:129-130; II:681-682
pass by, to I:129-130; II:681-682
pass through, to II:676
passing over I:509-512

passion V:447-448; 926-930; 930-935
of like passions V:938-939
passover V:896-904
past
time past V:717
pastor VI:485-499
patience III:619-620; IV:374-387;
581-588
have patience, to IV:374-387
patient III:486-487; IV:374-387
be patient, to IV:374-387
patiently IV:374-387; 387
wait patiently, to II:56
pattern VIII:246-259
pay, to II:167-169
pay attention to, to V:559
without pay II:167
peace II:400-417
be at peace, to II:417-418
live in peace, to II:417-418
make peace, to II:419-420
peaceable II:418-419; IV:527-528
live peaceably, to II:417-418
peaceful II:418-419
peacemaker II:419
pearl IV:472-473
peculiar VI:57-58
peddle, to III:603-605
penalty IV:695-728
Pentecost VI:44-53
people II:63; 372; IV:29-57;
V:582-590; VI:279-283
people of Jerusalem VII:292-338
people to lead by the hand IX:435
perceive, to I:187-188; 689-714;
IV:9-10; 948-951; V:379-381
perceive clearly, to V:379-381
perdition I:396-397
perfect I:475-476; VIII:67-78
perfect, make
perfect, to I:475-476;
VIII:61-62; 79-84
perfect health III:767
perfect soundness III:767
perfecter VIII:86-87
perfection;
perfectness VIII:78-79; 84-86
perform, to VIII:61-62
perform the services of
priest, to III:248-249
performance VIII:84-86
perish, to I:394-396
perishable IX:93-106
imperishable IX:93-106
perjurer V:466
permission I:716-717

feel sensuous impulses, to	III:631	sharp disagreement	V:857
sentence	III:622-623; 945-946	sharper	VIII:181-186
separate, to	V:454-455; 455-456	sharply	VIII:106-109
sepulchre	IV:679-680; 680-681	sharpness	VIII:106-109
sergeant (serjeant)	VI:971	shatter, to	VII:919-925
serious	I:556-558; VII:191-196	shed, to	II:467-469
serpent	V:566-582	shed blood, to	II:467-469
servant	II:88-93; 261-279; III:132;	shedding the blood	I:176-177
	IV:229-231; V:636-654;	sheep	VI:689-692
	VIII:530-544	sheepskin	IV:637-638
become a servant, to	II:279	shepherd	VI:485-499
fellow servant	II:261-279	chief shepherd	VI:485-499
hired servant	IV:695-728	shield	V:312-314
servant of God	V:654-717	shift from, to	III:720
servant of the Lord	V:654-717	shine, to	I:507-508; IV:16-28;
serve, to	II:81-87; 261-279;		VII:665-666; IX:1-2; 310-358
	III:128-131; IV:58-65; 215-229;	shine around, to	IV:16-28
	VIII:530-544	shine forth, to	I:507-508; IV:16-28
serve in the army, to	VII:701-713	shipwreck	
service	II:87-88; III:155-159;	suffer shipwreck, to	IV:891
	IV:58-76; 215-229; 231	shod with, to be	V:310-312
eye-service	II:280	shoe	V:310-312
perform the services of		shorten, to	III:823-824
priest, to	III:248-249	grow short, to	VII:596-597
set, to	II:318; III:654; VII:638-653	should suffer	V:924
set apart, to	V:454-455	shout	III:656-659; 898-903
set aside	VIII:158-159	shout, to	I:625-628
set aside, to	I:452-454	show, to	I:56-58; 61-64; 69-70;
set before, to	VIII:162-164		70-72; II:25-30; 30;
set before, to be	III:656		VII:262-265; 896-898
set beside, to	III:656	make a show of, to	II:31-32
set forth in order, to	VIII:32-33	one who shows	
set free, to	II:487-502; VI:998-1003	partiality	VI:779-780
set over, to	III:444-446	show forth, to	I:56-58; 69-70
settle, to	IV:328-335; 337	show hospitality, to	V:1-36
seven; seven times	II:627-635	show mercy, to	II:477-485
seven thousand	II:627-635	show partiality, to	VI:779-780
seventh	II:627-635	show piety, to	VI:175-185
seventy; seventy times	II:627-635	show respect, to	II:908-909
severity	VIII:106-109	show zeal, to	II:882-888
shadow	VII:394-398; 399	showing	II:31
overshadow, to	VII:399-400	make a good showing, to	VI:779
shake, to	VII:65-70; 196-200	shrink	
be shaken, to	VII:54-56	those who shrink back	VII:599
shame	I:189-191	shrub	IV:65-67
shame, put to		Sicarii	VII:278-282
shame, to	I:189-191; II:32	sick	I:490-493
shamefacedness	I:169-171	be sick, to	I:490-493; IV:1091-1098
shameful	I:189-191	be sick of a fever, to	VI:956-959
treat shamefully, to	VIII:295-307	sickness	I:490-493; IV:1091-1098
shape	II:373-375	side	
share	II:830-832; III:758-764	by the side	V:727-736
share, to	II:830-832; III:797-809;	fight at my side, to	I:167-168
	IV:10-11	many-sided	VI:485
sharer	III:797-809	sift, to	VII:291-292
sharing (with)	II:830-832; III:797-809	sigh, to	VII:600-603

unwashed	IV:947-948
unwillingly	II:469-470
unwise	IV:961-962
unworthily	I:379-380
unworthy	I:379-380; IV:519-522
up	I:376-377
be up, to	I:351-352
upbraid, to	V:239-240
upon	II:420-434
upright	V:449-450
walk uprightly, to	V:451
uproot	VI:991
upward	I:376-377
urge, to	I:344-347; II:828
urgent, to be	III:655
Uriah	
the wife of Uriah	III:1-3
use, to	
use force, to	I:609-613
use sorcery, to	IV:359
use vain repetitions, to	I:597
useless	I:452
uttermost	
to the uttermost	VIII:66-67
vain	III:659-660; IV:519-522
become vain, to	IV:523
in vain	II:167; 380-381; IV:523-524
use vain repetitions, to	I:597
vain discussion	IV:524
vain jangling	IV:524
vain talker	IV:524
vainglory	III:662
demons of vain glory	III:662
value	VIII:169-180
be of more value, to	IX:62-64
value, to	VIII:169-180
vanity	IV:523
variety	I:184-185
various	VI:484-485; IX:62-64
vaunt oneself, to	VI:93-95
vegetable	IV:65-67
veil	III:558-560; 628-630
vengeance	II:178-182; 445-446
do vengeance, to	II:442-443
verily	I:335-338
very	
very attentive, to be	III:915-921
very bold, to be	VIII:181-186
very earnest	VII:559-568
very highly	VI:61-62
very pitiful	VII:548-559
very unhappy	IV:323
vessel	VII:358-367
victory	IV:942-945
win a most glorious	

victory, to	IV:942-945
win a victory, to	III:397-402
vigilant	IV:939-941
villainy	VI:972-973
vindicate, to	II:442-444
vindication	II:178-182; 445-446
vine	I:342-343
vinegar	V:288-289
violate the law, to	IV:1091
violation	V:739-740
violence	V:467-472
suffer violence, to	I:609-613
violent	I:613-614
enter violently, to	I:609-613
run violently, to	V:467-472
viper	II:815-816
virgin	V:826-837
virtue	I:457-461
visible	V:368-370
invisible	V:368-370
vision	V:370-371; 371-372; 372-373
visit, to	II:599-608; III:391-396
voice	IX:278-301
void, to make	III:661-662; 1099-1100
vote	IX:604-607
votive offering	I:354-355
vow	II:775-806
vow, to	II:775-806
wages	V:591-592
wail, bewail, to	I:227-228;
	III:830-852; VI:40-43
wailing	II:725-726
waist	V:495-496
wait for, to	II:56; 57-58; IV:578-579;
	VI:725-727
wait patiently, to	II:56
wake, to	VIII:545-556
walk, to	V:940-945; VI:566-578;
	VII:666-669
walk in, to	V:940-945
walk uprightly, to	V:451
wall	
dividing wall	IV:625
wander about, to	II:682-683
wandering	VI:228-253
want	VIII:592-601
want, to	I:629-633; III:44-52;
	VIII:592-601
wanton against, to become	III:631
war	VI:502-515
prisoner of war	I:195-197
war, to	VII:701-713
make war, to	VI:502-515
warfare	VII:701-713
warn, to	IV:1019-1022

INDEX OF GREEK KEYWORDS

The numbers at the left of the Greek words are those of the system that is being used increasingly in New Testament reference works.

163	αἰχμαλωτίζω	I:195-197	286	ἀμνός	I:338-340
164	αἰχμάλωτος	I:195-197	288	ἄμπελος	I:342-343
165	αἰών	I:197-208	298	ἀμώμητος	IV:831
166	αἰώνιος	I:208-209	299	ἄμωμος	IV:830-831
167	ἀκαθαρσία	III:427-429	305	ἀναβαίνω	I:519-522
169	ἀκάθαρτος	III:427-429	312	ἀναγγέλλω	I:61-64
170	ἀκαιρέω	III:462	313	ἀναγεννάω	I:673-675
171	ἄκαιρος	III:462	314	ἀναγινώσκω	I:343-344
172	ἄκακος	III:482	315	ἀναγκάζω	I:344-347
175	ἄκαρπος	III:616	316	ἀναγκαῖος	I:344-347
176	ἀκατάγνωστος	I:714-715	318	ἀνάγκη	I:344-347
178	ἀκατάκριτος	III:952	320	ἀνάγνωσις	I:343-344
179	ἀκατάλυτος	IV:328-335; 338-339	322	ἀναδείκνυμι	II:30
181	ἀκαταστασία	III:446	323	ἀνάδειξις	II:31
182	ἀκατάστατος	III:447	326	ἀναζάω	II:872-873
185	ἀκέραιος	I:209-210	331	ἀνάθεμα	I:354-355
189	ἀκοή	I:221-222	332	ἀναθεματίζω	I:355-356
190	ἀκολουθέω	I:210-215	334	ἀνάθημα	I:354-355
191	ἀκούω	I:216-221	340	ἀνακαινίζω	III:451-452
192	ἀκρασία	II:339-342	341	ἀνακαινόω	III:452-453
193	ἀκρατής	II:339-342	342	ἀνακαίνωσις	III:453
203	ἀκροβυστία	I:225-226	343	ἀνακαλύπτω	III:560-561
204	ἀκρογωνιαῖος	I:792	345	ἀνάκειμαι	III:654-655
208	ἀκυρόω	III:1099-1100	346	ἀνακεφαλαιόομαι	III:681-682
210	ἄκων	II:469-470	349	ἀνακράζω	III:898-903
212	ἀλαζονεία	I:226-227	350	ἀνακρίνω	III:943-944
213	ἀλαζών	I:226-227	351	ἀνάκρισις	III:943-944
214	ἀλαλάζω	I:227-228	353	ἀναλαμβάνω	IV:7-9
217	ἅλας	I:228-229	354	ἀνάλημψις	IV:7-9
218	ἀλείφω	I:229-232	356	ἀναλογία	I:347-348
225	ἀλήθεια	I:232-247	359	ἀνάλυσις	IV:328-335; 337
226	ἀληθεύω	I:251	360	ἀναλύω	IV:328-335; 337
227	ἀληθής	I:247-249	361	ἀναμάρτητος	I:333-335
228	ἀληθινός	I:249-250	364	ἀνάμνησις	I:348-349
236	ἀλλάσσω	I:251-252	365	ἀνανεόω	IV:899-901
238	ἀλληγορέω	I:260-263	370	ἀνάξιος	I:379-380
239	ἀλληλουϊά	I:264	372	ἀνάπαυσις	I:350-351
241	ἀλλογενής	I:266-267	373	ἀναπαύω	I:350
243	ἄλλος	I:264-265	378	ἀναπληρόω	VI:305-306
244	ἀλλοτρι(ο)επίσκοπος	II:620-622	386	ἀνάστασις	I:371-372
245	ἀλλότριος	I:265	388	ἀνασταυρόω	VII:583-584
246	ἀλλόφυλος	I:267	390	ἀναστρέφω	VII:715-717
249	ἄλογος	IV:141	391	ἀναστροφή	VII:715-717
253	ἄλυπος	IV:323	392	ἀνατάσσω	VIII:32-33
264	ἁμαρτάνω	I:267-316	393	ἀνατέλλω	I:351-352
265	ἁμάρτημα	I:267-316	394	ἀνατίθημι	I:353-354
266	ἁμαρτία	I:267-316	395	ἀνατολή	I:352-353
268	ἁμαρτωλός	I:317-333	399	ἀναφέρω	IX:60-61
269	ἄμαχος	IV:527-528	403	ἀνάψυξις	IX:664-665
273	ἄμεμπτος	IV:571-574	404	ἀναψύχω	IX:663-664
275	ἀμέριμνος	IV:593	407	ἀνδρίζομαι	I:360-363
278	ἀμεταμέλητος	IV:626-629	410	ἀνέγκλητος	I:356-357
279	ἀμετανόητος	IV:1009	414	ἀνεκτός	I:359-360
280	ἄμετρος	IV:632-634	415	ἀνελεήμων	II:487
281	ἀμήν	I:335-338	448	ἀνέλεος	II:487
283	ἀμίαντος	IV:647	419	ἀνεξερεύνητος	I:357

646	ἀποστασία	I:513-514	778	ἀσκέω	I:494-496
649	ἀποστέλλω	I:398-406	782	ἀσπάζομαι	I:496-502
651	ἀποστολή	I:446-447	783	ἀσπασμός	I:496-502
652	ἀπόστολος	I:407-445	784	ἄσπιλος	I:502
654	ἀποστρέφω	VII:719-722		ἄσπλαγχνος	VII:548-559
656	ἀποσυνάγωγος	VII:848-852	790	ἀστατέω	I:503
657	ἀποτάσσω	VIII:33-34	792	ἀστήρ	I:503-505
662	ἀποτολμάω	VIII:181-186	793	ἀστήρικτος	VII:653-657
663	ἀποτομία	VIII:106-109	796	ἀστραπή	I:505
664	ἀπότομος	VIII:106-109	798	ἄστρον	I:503-505
664	ἀποτόμως	VIII:106-109	801	ἀσύνετος	VII:888-896
669	ἀποφθέγγομαι	I:447	803	ἀσφάλεια	I:506
677	ἀπρόσκοπος	VI:745-758	804	ἀσφαλής	I:506
678	ἀπροσωπολήμπτως	VI:779-780	805	ἀσφαλίζω	I:506
683	ἀπωθέω	I:448	806	ἀσφαλῶς	I:506
684	ἀπώλεια	I:396-397	810	ἀσωτία	I:506-507
685	ἀρά	I:448	811	ἄσωτος	I:506-507
691	ἀργέω	I:452	812	ἀτακτέω	VIII:47-48
692	ἀργός	I:452	813	ἄτακτος	VIII:47-48
699	ἀρεσκεία	I:456	814	ἀτάκτως	VIII:47-48
700	ἀρέσκω	I:455	826	αὐγάζω	I:507-508
701	ἀρεστός	I:456	829	αὐθάδης	I:508-509
703	ἀρετή	I:457-461	837	αὐξάνω	VIII:517-519
704	ἀρήν	I:340	841	αὐτάρκεια	I:466-467
705	ἀριθμέω	I:461-464	842	αὐτάρκης	I:466-467
706	ἀριθμός	I:461-464	843	αὐτοκατάκριτος	III:952
713	ἀρκετός	I:464-466	845	αὐτόπτης	V:373
714	ἀρκέω	I:464-466	859	ἄφεσις	I:509-512
717	Ἁρ Μαγεδών	I:468	861	ἀφθαρσία	IX:93-106
720	ἀρνέομαι	I:469-471	862	ἄφθαρτος	IX:93-106
721	ἀρνίον	I:340-341		ἀφθορία	IX:93-106
725	ἁρπαγμός	I:473-474	863	ἀφίημι	I:509-512
726	ἁρπάζω	I:472-473	865	ἀφιλάγαθος	I:18
728	ἀρραβών	I:475	868	ἀφίστημι	I:512-513
737	ἄρτι	IV:1106-1123	871	ἀφομοιόω	V:198
738	ἀρτιγέννητος	I:672	873	ἀφορίζω	V:454-455
739	ἄρτιος	I:475-476	874	ἀφορμή	V:472-474
740	ἄρτος	I:477-478	877	ἀφροσύνη	IX:220-235
743	ἀρχάγγελος	I:87	878	ἄφρων	IX:220-235
744	ἀρχαῖος	I:486-487	879	ἀφυπνόω	VIII:545-556
746	ἀρχή	I:479-484		ἀφυστερέω	VIII:592-601
747	ἀρχηγός	I:487-488	884	ἀχάριστος	IX:372-402
749	ἀρχιερεύς	III:265-283	886	ἀχειροποίητος	IX:436
750	ἀρχιποίμην	VI:485-499	893	ἀψευδής	IX:594-603
752	ἀρχισυνάγωγος	VII:844-847		ἄψευστος	IX:594-603
757	ἄρχω	I:478-479	897	Βαβυλών	I:514-517
758	ἄρχων	I:488-489	899	βάθος	I:517-518
763	ἀσέβεια	VII:185-191		βαίνω	I:518
764	ἀσεβέω	VII:185-191	903	Βαλαάμ	I:524-525
765	ἀσεβής	VII:185-191	905	βαλλάντιον	I:525-526
766	ἀσέλγεια	I:490	906	βάλλω	I:526-527
767	ἄσημος	VII:267	907	βαπτίζω	I:529-545
769	ἀσθένεια	I:490-493	908	βάπτισμα	I:545
770	ἀσθενέω	I:490-493	909	βαπτισμός	I:545
771	ἀσθένημα	I:490-493	910	βαπτιστής	I:545-546
772	ἀσθενής	I:490-493	911	βάπτω	I:529-545

915	βάρβαρος	I:546-553	1062	γάμος	I:648-657
916	βαρέω	I:558-561	1067	γέεννα	I:657-658
922	βάρος	I:553-556	1070	γελάω	I:658-662
926	βαρύς	I:556-558	1071	γέλως	I:658-662
928	βασανίζω	I:561-563	1074	γενεά	I:662-663
929	βασανισμός	I:561-563	1075	γενεαλογέω	I:665
930	βασανιστής	I:561-563	1076	γενεαλογία	I:663-665
931	βάσανος	I:561-563	1078	γένεσις	I:682-684
932	βασιλεία	I:564-593	1081	γένημα	I:685
934	βασίλειος	I:564-593	1080	γεννάω	I:665-672
935	βασιλεύς	I:564-593	1081	γέννημα	I:672
936	βασιλεύω	I:564-593	1084	γεννητός	I:672
937	βασιλικός	I:564-593	1085	γένος	I:684-685
938	βασίλισσα	I:564-593	1089	γεύομαι	I:675-677
940	βασκαίνω	I:594-595	1093	γῆ	I:677-680
941	βαστάζω	I:596	1096	γίνομαι	I:681-682
945	βατταλογέω	I:597	1097	γινώσκω	I:689-714
946	βδέλυγμα	I:598-600	1100	γλῶσσα	I:719-726
947	βδελυκτός	I:598-600	1103	γνήσιος	I:727
948	βδελύσσομαι	I:598-600	1106	γνώμη	I:717-718
949	βέβαιος	I:600-603	1107	γνωρίζω	I:718
950	βεβαιόω	I:600-603	1108	γνῶσις	I:689-714
951	βεβαίωσις	I:600-603	1110	γνωστός	I:718-719
952	βέβηλος	I:604-605	1111	γογγύζω	I:728-735
953	βεβηλόω	I:605	1112	γογγυσμός	I:735-736
954	Βεελζεβούλ	I:605-606	1113	γογγυστής	I:737
955	Βελίαρ	I:607	1114	γόης	I:737-738
956	βέλος	I:608-609	1119	γόνυ	I:738-740
971	βιάζομαι	I:609-613	1120	γονυπετέω	I:738-740
973	βιαστής	I:613-614	1121	γράμμα	I:761-769
975	βιβλίον	I:617-620	1122	γραμματεύς	I:740-742
976	βίβλος	I:615-616	1124	γραφή	I:749-761
979	βίος	II:832-872	1125	γράφω	I:742-749
980	βιόω	II:832-872	1127	γρηγορέω	II:338-339
987	βλασφημέω	I:621-625	1128	γυμνάζω	I:775
988	βλασφημία	I:621-625	1129	γυμνασία	I:775-776
989	βλάσφημος	I:621-625	1131	γυμνός	I:773-775
991	βλέπω	V:315-367	1132	γυμνότης	I:775
994	βοάω	I:625-628	1135	γυνή	I:776-789
996	βοήθεια	I:628-629	1136	Γὼγ καὶ Μαγώγ	I:789-791
997	βοηθέω	I:628	1137	γωνία	I:791-792
998	βοηθός	I:628		κεφαλὴ γωνίας	I:792-793
1012	βουλή	I:633-636	1139	δαιμονίζομαι	I:19-20
1013	βούλημα	I:636-637	1140	δαιμόνιον	II:1-19
1014	βούλομαι	I:629-633	1141	δαιμονιώδης	II:20
1017	βραβεῖον	I:638-639	1142	δαίμων	II:1-19
1018	βραβεύω	I:637-638	1147	δάκτυλος	II:20-21
1023	βραχίων	I:639-640	1138	Δαυίδ (υἱὸς Δ.)	VIII:478-488
1025	βρέφος	V:636-654	1162	δέησις	II:40-41
1027	βροντή	I:640-641	1163	δεῖ	II:21-25
1030	βρυγμός	I:641-642	1165	δειγματίζω	II:31-32
1031	βρύχω	I:641	1166	δείκνυμι	II:25-30
1033	βρῶμα	I:642-645	1172	δειπνέω	II:34-35
1035	βρῶσις	I:642-645	1173	δεῖπνον	II:34-35
1051	γάλα	I:645-647	1175	δεισιδαιμονία	II:20
1060	γαμέω	I:648-657	1174	δεισιδαίμων	II:20

1440	ἑβδομήκοντα	II:627-635
1441	ἑβδομηκοντάκις	II:627-635
1442	ἕβδομος	II:627-635
1444	Ἑβραϊκός	III:356-391
1445	Ἑβραῖος	III:356-391
1446	ἑβραΐς	III:356-391
1447	ἑβραϊστί	III:356-391
1448	ἐγγίζω	II:330-332
1449	ἐγγράφω	I:769-770
1450	ἔγγυος	II:329
1451	ἐγγύς	II:330-332
1453	ἐγείρω	II:333-337
1454	ἔγερσις	II:337-338
1457	ἐγκαινίζω	III:453-454
1573	ἐγκακέω	III:486
1458	ἐγκαλέω	III:496
2744	ἐγκαυχάομαι	III:653
1462	ἔγκλημα	III:496
1463	ἐγκομβόομαι	II:339
1464	ἐγκοπή	III:855-857
1465	ἐγκόπτω	III:855-857
1466	ἐγκράτεια	II:339-342
1467	ἐγκρατεύομαι	II:339-342
1468	ἐγκρατής	II:339-342
1469	ἐγκρίνω	III:951
1473	ἐγώ	II:343-362
1476	ἑδραῖος	II:362-364
1477	ἑδραίωμα	II:362-364
1479	ἐθελοθρησκεία	III:155-159
1482	ἐθνικός	II:372
1484	ἔθνος	II:364-372
1485	ἔθος	II:372-373
2397	εἰδέα	II:373-375
1492	εἶδον	V:315-367
1491	εἶδος	II:373-375
1493	εἰδωλεῖον	II:379
1494	εἰδωλόθυτον	II:378-379
1496	εἰδωλολάτρης	II:379-380
1495	εἰδωλολατρία	II:379-380
1497	εἴδωλον	II:375-378
1500	εἰκῇ	II:380-381
1504	εἰκών	II:381-397
1505	εἰλικρίνεια	II:397-398
1506	εἰλικρινής	II:397-398
1510	εἰμί	II:398-400
1514	εἰρηνεύω	II:417-418
1515	εἰρήνη	II:400-417
1516	εἰρηνικός	II:418-419
1517	εἰρηνοποιέω	II:419-420
1518	εἰρηνοποιός	II:419
1519	εἰς	II:420-434
1520	εἷς	II:434-442
1522	εἰσακούω	I:222
1523	εἰσδέχομαι	II:57
1525	εἰσέρχομαι	II:676-678
1528	εἰσκαλέω	III:496

1529	εἴσοδος	V:103-109
1531	εἰσπορεύομαι	VI:578
1533	εἰσφέρω	IX:64-65
	ἑκατὸν τεσσεράκοντα	
	τέσσαρες	II:321-328
1544	ἐκβάλλω	I:527-528
1551	ἐκδέχομαι	II:56
1553	ἐκδημέω	II:63-64
1556	ἐκδικέω	II:442-444
1557	ἐκδίκησις	II:445-446
1558	ἔκδικος	II:444-445
1562	ἐκδύω	II:318
1567	ἐκζητέω	II:894-895
1568	ἐκθαμβέομαι	III:4-7
1569	ἔκθαμβος	III:4-7
1571	ἐκκαθαίρω	III:430
1574	ἐκκεντέω	II:446-447
1577	ἐκκλησία	III:501-536
1581	ἐκκόπτω	III:857-860
1582	ἐκκρέμαμαι	III:915-921
1584	ἐκλάμπω	IV:16-28
1586	ἐκλέγομαι	IV:144-176
1588	ἐκλεκτός	IV:181-192
1589	ἐκλογή	IV:176-181
1592	ἐκμυκτηρίζω	IV:796-799
1594	ἐκνήφω	IV:941
1595	ἑκούσιος	II:470
1598	ἐκπειράζω	VI:23-36
1601	ἐκπίπτω	VI:167-169
1603	ἐκπληρόω	VI:307-308
1604	ἐκπλήρωσις	VI:308
1606	ἐκπνέω	VI:452-453
1607	ἐκπορεύομαι	VI:578-579
1608	ἐκπορνεύω	VI:579-595
1609	ἐκπτύω	II:448-449
1610	ἐκριζόω	VI:991
1611	ἔκστασις	II:449-458
1614	ἐκτείνω	II:460-463
1616	ἐκτένεια	II:464
1617	ἐκτενέστερον	II:463-464
1618	ἐκτενής	II:463-464
1626	ἔκτρωμα	II:465-467
1632	ἐκχέω	II:467-469
1632	ἐκχύν(ν)ω	II:467-469
1635	ἐκών	II:469-470
1637	ἔλαιον	II:470-473
1640	ἐλάττων	IV:648-659
1646	ἐλάχιστος	IV:648-659
1650	ἐλεγμός	II:476
1649	ἔλεγξις	II:476
1650	ἔλεγχος	II:476
1651	ἐλέγχω	II:473-475
1653	ἐλεέω	II:477-485
1654	ἐλεημοσύνη	II:485-487
1655	ἐλεήμων	II:485
1656	ἔλεος	II:477-485

1957	ἐπιμαρτυρέω	IV:508-510	2084	ἑτερόγλωσσος	I:726-727
1964	ἐπιορκέω	V:466-467	2085	ἑτεροδιδασκαλέω	II:163
1965	ἐπίορκος	V:466	2086	ἑτεροζυγέω	II:901
1967	ἐπιούσιος	II:590-599	2087	ἕτερος	II:702-704
1977	ἐπιρίπτω	VI:991-993	2090	ἑτοιμάζω	II:704-706
1978	ἐπίσημος	VII:267-268	2091	ἑτοιμασία	II:704-706
1980	ἐπισκέπτομαι	II:599-605	2092	ἕτοιμος	II:704-706
1981	ἐπισκηνόω	VII:386-387	2097	εὐαγγελίζομαι	II:707-721
1982	ἐπισκιάζω	VII:399-400	2098	εὐαγγέλιον	II:721-736
1983	ἐπισκοπέω	II:599-605	2099	εὐαγγελιστής	II:736-737
1984	ἐπισκοπή	II:606-608	2100	εὐαρεστέω	I:456-457
1985	ἐπίσκοπος	II:608-620	2101	εὐάρεστος	I:456-457
1988	ἐπιστάτης	II:622-623	2106	εὐδοκέω	II:738-742
1989	ἐπιστέλλω	VII:593-595	2107	εὐδοκία	II:742-751
1991	ἐπιστηρίζω	VII:653-657	2108	εὐεργεσία	II:654-655
1992	ἐπιστολή	VII:593-595	2110	εὐεργέτης	II:654-655
1994	ἐπιστρέφω	VII:722-729	2120	εὐκαιρία	III:462
1995	ἐπιστροφή	VII:722-729	2121	εὔκαιρος	III:462
1997	ἐπισυναγωγή	VII:841-843	2124	εὐλάβεια	II:751-754
2002	ἐπισωρεύω	VII:1094-1096	2125	εὐλαβεῖσθαι	II:751-754
2003	ἐπιταγή	VIII:36-37	2126	εὐλαβής	II:751-754
2005	ἐπιτελέω	VIII:61-62	2127	εὐλογέω	II:754-763
2007	ἐπιτίθημι	VIII:159-161	2128	εὐλογητός	II:764
2008	ἐπιτιμάω	II:623-626	2129	εὐλογία	II:754-763
2009	ἐπιτιμία	II:627	2132	εὐνοέω	IV:971-973
2014	ἐπιφαίνω	IX:7-10	2133	εὔνοια	IV:971-973
2015	ἐπιφάνεια	IX:7-10	2134	εὐνουχίζω	II:765-768
2016	ἐπιφανής	IX:7-10	2135	εὐνοῦχος	II:765-768
2017	ἐπιφαύσκω	IX:310-358	2137	εὐοδόω	V:109-114
2020	ἐπιφώσκω	IX:310-358	2144	εὐπρόσδεκτος	II:58-59
2026	ἐποικοδομέω	V:147-148	2146	εὐπροσωπέω	VI:779
2028	ἐπονομάζω	V:282	2147	εὑρίσκω	II:769-770
2029	ἐποπτεύω	V:373-375	2150	εὐσέβεια	VII:175-185
2030	ἐπόπτης	V:373-375	2151	εὐσεβέω	VII:175-185
2032	ἐπουράνιος	V:538-542	2152	εὐσεβής	VII:175-185
2033	ἑπτά	II:627-635	2154	εὔσημος	II:770
2034	ἑπτάκις	II:627-635	2155	εὔσπλαγχνος	VII:548-559
2035	ἑπτακισχίλιοι	II:627-635	2158	εὐσχήμων	II:770-772
2038	ἐργάζομαι	II:635-652	2165	εὐφραίνω	II:772-775
2041	ἔργον	II:635-652	2167	εὐφροσύνη	II:772-775
2045	ἐρευνάω	II:655-657	2168	εὐχαριστέω	IX:407-415
2047	ἐρημία	II:657-659	2169	εὐχαριστία	IX:407-415
2048	ἔρημος	II:657-659	2170	εὐχάριστος	IX:407-415
2049	ἐρημόω	II:657-659	2171	εὐχή	II:775-806
2050	ἐρήμωσις	II:660	2172	εὔχομαι	II:775-806
2052	ἐριθεία	II:660-661	2175	εὐωδία	II:808-810
2058	ἑρμηνεία	II:661-666	2178	ἐφάπαξ	I:383-384
	ἑρμηνευτής	II:661-666	2189	ἔχθρα	II:815
2059	ἑρμηνεύω	II:661-666	2190	ἐχθρός	II:811-814
2064	ἔρχομαι	II:666-675	2191	ἔχιδνα	II:815-816
2065	ἐρωτάω	II:685-687	2192	ἔχω	II:816-827
2068	ἐσθίω	II:689-695	2198	ζάω	II:832-872
2072	ἔσοπτρον	I:178-180; II:696	2200	ζεστός	II:876-877
2078	ἔσχατος	II:697-698	2204	ζέω	II:875-876
2080	ἔσω	II:698-699	2205	ζῆλος	II:877-882
2083	ἑταῖρος	II:699-701	2206	ζηλόω	II:882-888

2207	ζηλωτής	II:882-888		2323	θεραπεύω	III:128-131
2209	ζημία	II:888-892		2324	θεράπων	III:132
2210	ζημιόω	II:888-892		2325	θερίζω	III:132-133
2212	ζητέω	II:892-893		2326	θερισμός	III:133
2214	ζήτησις	II:893-894		2334	θεωρέω	V:315-367
2218	ζυγός	II:896-901		2342	θηρίον	III:133-135
2219	ζύμη	II:902-906		2343	θησαυρίζω	III:138
2220	ζυμόω	II:902-906		2344	θησαυρός	III:136-138
2222	ζωή	II:832-872		2346	θλίβω	III:139-148
2223	ζώνη	V:302-308		2347	θλῖψις	III:139-148
2224	ζώννυμι	V:302-308		2348	θνήσκω	III:7-21
2224	ζωννύω	V:302-308		2349	θνητός	III:21-22
2225	ζωογονέω	II:873-874		2354	θρηνέω	III:148-155
2226	ζῷον	II:873		2355	θρῆνος	III:148-155
2227	ζωοποιέω	II:874-875		2356	θρησκεία	III:155-159
2233	ἡγέομαι	II:907-908		2357	θρῆσκος	III:155-159
2237	ἡδονή	II:909-926		2358	θριαμβεύω	III:159-160
2240	ἥκω	II:926-928		2362	θρόνος	III:160-167
2243	Ἡλ(ε)ίας	II:928-941		2372	θυμός	III:167-168
2244	ἡλικία	II:941-943		2374	θύρα	III:173-180
2250	ἡμέρα	II:943-953		2375	θυρεός	V:312-314
2269	Ἠσαῦ	II:953-954		2378	θυσία	III:180-190
2278	ἠχέω	II:954-955		2379	θυσιαστήριον	III:180-190
2283	Θαμάρ	III:1-3		2380	θύω	III:180-190
2284	θαμβέω	III:4-7		2382	θώραξ	V:308-310
2285	θάμβος	III:4-7		2384	Ἰακώβ	III:191-192
2288	θάνατος	III:7-21		2386	ἴαμα	III:194-215
2289	θανατόω	III:21		2387	Ἰαμβρῆς	III:192-193
2292	θαρρέω	III:25-27		2389	Ἰαννης	III:192-193
2293	θαρσέω	III:25-27		2390	ἰάομαι	III:194-215
2295	θαῦμα	III:27-42		2392	ἴασις	III:194-215
2296	θαυμάζω	III:27-42		2395	ἰατρός	III:194-215
2297	θαυμάσιος	III:27-42		2397	ἰδέα	II:373-375
2298	θαυμαστός	III:27-42		2399	ἰδιώτης	III:215-217
2300	θεάομαι	V:315-367		2403	Ἰεζάβελ	III:217-218
2301	θεατρίζομαι	III:42-43		2405	ἱερατεία	III:251
2302	θέατρον	III:42-43		2406	ἱεράτευμα	III:249-251
2304	θεῖος	III:122-123		2407	ἱερατεύω	III:248-249
2305	θειότης	III:123		2405	ἱερατία	III:251
2307	θέλημα	III:52-62		2408	Ἰερεμίας	III:218-221
2308	θέλησις	III:62		2409	ἱερεύς	III:257-265
2309	θέλω	III:44-52			ἱερόθυτος	III:252-253
2310	θεμέλιον	III:63-64			ἱεροκῆρυξ	III:683-696
2310	θεμέλιος	III:63-64		2411	ἱερόν (τὸ ι.)	III:230-247
2311	θεμελιόω	III:63-64		2412	ἱεροπρεπής	III:253-254
2312	θεοδίδακτος	III:121		2413	ἱερός	III:221-230
	θεοκρατία	III:905-910		2414	Ἰεροσόλυμα	VII:292-338
2313	θεομαχέω	IV:528		2415	Ἰεροσολυμίτης	VII:292-338
2314	θεομάχος	IV:528		2416	ἱεροσυλέω	III:255-256
2315	θεόπνευστος	VI:453-455		2417	ἱερόσυλος	III:256-257
2316	θεός	III:65-119		2419	Ἰερουσαλήμ	VII:292-338
	παῖς θεοῦ	V:654-717		2420	ἱερωσύνη	III:247-248
2317	θεοσέβεια	III:123-128		2424	Ἰησοῦς	III:284-293
2318	θεοσεβής	III:123-128		2425	ἱκανός	III:293-296
2320	θεότης	III:119		2426	ἱκανότης	III:293-296
2322	θεραπεία	III:131		2427	ἱκανόω	III:293-296

2428	ἱκετηρία	III:296-297	2555	κακοποιός	III:485-486
2431	ἱλαρός	III:297-300	2556	κακός	III:469-481
2432	ἱλαρότης	III:297-300	2557	κακοῦργος	III:484
2433	ἱλάσκομαι	III:301-318	2559	κακόω	III:484
2434	ἱλασμός	III:301-318	2560	κακῶς ἔχω	IV:1091-1098
2435	ἱλαστήριον	III:318-323	2564	καλέω	III:487-491
2436	ἵλεως	III:300-301	2567	καλοδιδάσκαλος	II:159-160
2443	ἵνα	III:323-333	2570	καλός	III:536-556
2446	Ἰορδάνης	VI:608-623	2571	κάλυμμα	III:558-560
2447	ἰός	III:334-336	2573	καλύπτω	III:556-558
2449	Ἰουδαία	III:356-391	2574	κάμηλος	III:592-594
2450	ἰουδαΐζω	III:356-391	2578	κάμπτω	III:594-595
2451	Ἰουδαϊκός	III:356-391	2583	κανών	III:596-602
2453	Ἰουδαῖος	III:356-391	2585	καπηλεύω	III:603-605
2454	Ἰουδαϊσμός	III:356-391	2588	καρδία	III:605-613
2462	ἵππος	III:336-339	2589	καρδιογνώστης	III:613
2463	ἶρις	III:339-342	2590	καρπός	III:614-616
2465	ἰσάγγελος	I:87	2592	καρποφορέω	III:616
2470	ἴσος	III:343-355	2594	καρτερέω	III:617
2471	ἰσότης	III:343-355	2597	καταβαίνω	I:522-523
2472	ἰσότιμος	III:343-355	2602	καταβολή	III:620-621
2474	Ἰσραήλ	III:356-391	2604	καταγγελεύς	I:70-73
2475	Ἰσραηλίτης	III:356-391	2605	καταγγέλλω	I:70-73
2476	ἵστημι	VII:638-653	2606	καταγελάω	I:658-662
2477	ἱστορέω	III:391-396	2607	καταγινώσκω	I:714-715
	ἱστορία	III:391-396	2613	καταδικάζω	III:621-622
2478	ἰσχυρός	III:397-402		καταδίκη	III:622-623
2479	ἰσχύς	III:397-402	2615	καταδουλόω	II:279
2480	ἰσχύω	III:397-402	2652	κατάθεμα	I:354-355
2487	ἴχνος	III:402-406	2653	καταθεματίζω	I:355-356
2495	Ἰωνᾶς	III:406-410	2617	καταισχύνω	I:189-191
2506	καθαίρεσις	III:412-413	2619	κατακαλύπτω	III:561-563
2507	καθαιρέω	III:411-412	2620	κατακαυχάομαι	III:653-654
2508	καθαίρω	III:413-426	2621	κατάκειμαι	III:655-656
2511	καθαρίζω	III:413-426		κατακληρονομέω	III:767-785
2512	καθαρισμός	III:429-430	2631	κατάκριμα	III:951-952
2513	καθαρός	III:413-426	2632	κατακρίνω	III:951-952
2514	καθαρότης	III:413-426	2633	κατάκρισις	III:951-952
2516	καθέζομαι	III:440-444	2634	κατακυριεύω	III:1098
2518	καθεύδω	III:431-437	2635	καταλαλέω	IV:3-5
2520	καθήκω	III:437-440	2636	καταλαλιά	IV:3-5
2521	κάθημαι	III:440-444	2637	κατάλαλος	IV:3-5
2523	καθίζω	III:440-444	2638	καταλαμβάνω	IV:9-10
2525	καθίστημι	III:444-446	2640	κατάλειμμα	IV:194-214
2529	καθοράω	V:379-381	2641	καταλείπω	IV:194-214
2535	Κάϊν (Ἄβελ-Κάϊν)	I:6-8	2642	καταλιθάζω	IV:267-268
2537	καινός	III:447-450	2643	καταλλαγή	I:258
2538	καινότης	III:450-451	2644	καταλλάσσω	I:254-258
2540	καιρός	III:455-462	2646	κατάλυμα	IV:328-335; 338
2545	καίω	III:464-467	2647	καταλύω	IV:328-335; 338
2549	κακία	III:482-484	2648	καταμανθάνω	IV:414-415
2550	κακοήθεια	III:485	2649	καταμαρτυρέω	IV:508-510
2551	κακολογέω	III:468	2657	κατανοέω	IV:973-975
2552	κακοπάθεια	V:936-938	2658	καταντάω	III:623-625
2553	κακοπαθέω	V:936-938	2659	κατάνυξις	III:626
2554	κακοποιέω	III:485-486	2660	κατανύσσω	III:626

2661	καταξιόω	I:380	2749	κεῖμαι	III:654
2662	καταπατέω	V:940-945	2752	κέλευσμα	III:656-659
2663	κατάπαυσις	III:628	2754	κενοδοξία	III:662
2664	καταπαύω	III:627	2755	κενόδοξος	III:662
2665	καταπέτασμα	III:628-630	2756	κενός	III:659-660
2666	καταπίνω	VI:158-159	2758	κενόω	III:661-662
2667	καταπίπτω	VI:169-170	2759	κέντρον	III:663-668
2671	κατάρα	I:449-451	2768	κέρας	III:669-671
2672	καταράομαι	I:448-449	2770	κερδαίνω	III:672-673
2673	καταργέω	I:452-454	2771	κέρδος	III:672-673
2675	καταρτίζω	I:475-476	2776	κεφαλή	III:673-681
2676	κατάρτισις	I:475-476		κεφαλὴ γωνίας	I:792-793
2677	καταρτισμός	I:475-476	2782	κήρυγμα	III:714-717
2681	κατασκηνόω	VII:387-389	2783	κῆρυξ	III:683-696
2684	κατασκοπέω	VII:416-417	2784	κηρύσσω	III:697-714
2685	κατάσκοπος	VII:417	2786	Κηφᾶς	VI:100-112
2687	καταστέλλω	VII:595-596	2795	κινέω	III:718-719
2689	καταστολή	VII:595-596	2798	κλάδος	III:720-722
2690	καταστρέφω	VII:715-717	2799	κλαίω	III:722-725
2691	καταστρηνιάω	III:631	2800	κλάσις	III:726-743
2692	καταστροφή	VII:715-717	2801	κλάσμα	III:726-743
2696	κατασφραγίζω	VII:939-953	2805	κλαυθμός	III:725-726
2699	κατατομή	VIII:109-111	2806	κλάω	III:726-743
2704	καταφθείρω	IX:93-106	2807	κλείς	III:744-753
2705	καταφιλέω	IX:114-146	2812	κλέπτης	III:754-756
2706	καταφρονέω	III:631-632	2813	κλέπτω	III:754-756
2707	καταφρονητής	III:632	2814	κλῆμα	III:757
2709	καταχθόνιος	III:633-634	2816	κληρονομέω	III:767-785
4785	καταψηφίζομαι	IX:604-607	2817	κληρονομία	III:767-785
2712	κατείδωλος	II:379	2818	κληρονόμος	III:767-785
2715	κατεξουσιάζω	II:575	2819	κλῆρος	III:758-764
2716	κατεργάζομαι	III:634-635	2820	κληρόω	III:764-765
2722	κατέχω	II:829-830	2821	κλῆσις	III:491-493
2723	κατηγορέω	III:637	2822	κλητός	III:494-496
2724	κατηγορία	III:637	2836	κοιλία	III:786-789
2725	κατήγορος	III:636	2839	κοινός	III:789-797
2725	κατήγωρ	III:636	2840	κοινόω	III:809
2727	κατηχέω	III:638-640	2841	κοινωνέω	III:797-809
2728	κατιόομαι	III:334-336	2842	κοινωνία	III:797-809
2729	κατισχύω	III:397-402	2843	κοινωνικός	III:809
2730	κατοικέω	V:153-155	2844	κοινωνός	III:797-809
2732	κατοικητήριον	V:155-156	2847	κόκκινος	III:812-814
	κατοικίζω	V:156	2848	κόκκος	III:810-812
2734	κατοπτρίζομαι	II:696-697	2849	κολάζω	III:814-816
2736	κάτω	III:640		κολακεύω	III:817-818
2737	κατώτερος	III:640-642	2850	κολακία	III:817-818
2736	κατωτέρω	III:640	2851	κόλασις	III:816-817
2738	καῦμα	III:642-643	2852	κολαφίζω	III:818-821
2739	καυματίζω	III:643	2853	κολλάω	III:822-823
2740	καῦσις	III:643	2856	κολοβόω	III:823-824
2741	καυσόομαι	III:644	2859	κόλπος	III:824-826
2744	καυστηριάζομαι	III:644-645	2867	κονιάω	III:827
2742	καύσων	III:644	2870	κοπετός	III:830-852
2744	καυχάομαι	III:645-653	2872	κοπιάω	III:827-830
2745	καύχημα	III:645-653	2873	κόπος	III:827-830
2746	καύχησις	III:645-653	2875	κόπτω	III:830-852

2878	κορβᾶν	III:860-866	3003	λεγιών	IV:68-69
2878	κορβανᾶς	III:860-866	3004	λέγω	IV:69-136
2885	κοσμέω	III:867	3005	λεῖμμα	IV:194-214
2886	κοσμικός	III:897-898	3006	λεῖος	IV:193
2887	κόσμιος	III:895-896	3008	λειτουργέω	IV:215-229
2888	κοσμοκράτωρ	III:913-914	3009	λειτουργία	IV:215-229
2889	κόσμος	III:868-895	3010	λειτουργικός	IV:231
2896	κράζω	III:898-903	3011	λειτουργός	IV:229-231
2899	κράσπεδον	III:904	3013	λεπίς	IV:232-233
2900	κραταιός	III:912	3014	λέπρα	IV:233-234
2901	κραταιόω	III:912-913	3015	λεπρός	IV:233-234
2902	κρατέω	III:910-912	3017	Λευ(ε)ί	IV:234-239
2904	κράτος	III:905-910	3018	Λευ(ε)ίς	IV:234-239
2905	κραυγάζω	III:898-903	3019	Λευ(ε)ίτης	IV:239-241
2906	κραυγή	III:898-903	3021	λευκαίνω	IV:241-250
2910	κρέμαμαι	III:915-921	3022	λευκός	IV:241-250
2910	κρεμάννυμι	III:915-921	3023	λέων	IV:251-253
	κρεμάω	III:915-921	3025	ληνός	IV:254-257
2917	κρίμα	III:942	3027	ληστής	IV:257-262
2919	κρίνω	III:921-941	3030	λίβανος	IV:263-264
2920	κρίσις	III:941-942	3031	λιβανωτός	IV:263-264
2922	κριτήριον	III:943	3032	Λιβερτῖνοι	IV:265-266
2923	κριτής	III:942-943	3034	λιθάζω	IV:267-268
2924	κριτικός	III:943	3035	λίθινος	IV:268-280
2925	κρούω	III:954-957	3036	λιθοβολέω	IV:267-268
2926	κρύπτη	III:957-1000	3037	λίθος	IV:268-280
2927	κρυπτός	III:957-1000	3039	λικμάω	IV:280-281
2928	κρύπτω	III:957-1000	3042	λιμός	VI:12-22
	κρυφαῖος	III:957-1000	3048	λογεία	IV:282-283
2931	κρυφῇ	III:957-1000	3049	λογίζομαι	IV:284-292
2936	κτίζω	III:1000-1035	3050	λογικός	IV:142-143
2937	κτίσις	III:1000-1035	3051	λόγιον	IV:137-141
2938	κτίσμα	III:1000-1035	3052	λόγιος	IV:136-137
2939	κτίστης	III:1000-1035	3053	λογισμός	IV:284-292
2941	κυβέρνησις	III:1035-1037	3054	λογομαχέω	IV:143
2950	κύμβαλον	III:1037-1039	3055	λογομαχία	IV:143
2952	κυνάριον	III:1104	3056	λόγος	IV:69-136
2959	κυρία	III:1095	3058	λοιδορέω	IV:293-294
2960	κυριακός	III:1095-1096	3059	λοιδορία	IV:293-294
2961	κυριεύω	III:1097	3060	λοίδορος	IV:293-294
2962	κύριος	III:1039-1095	3067	λουτρόν	IV:295-307
2963	κυριότης	III:1096-1097	3068	λούω	IV:295-307
2964	κυρόω	III:1098-1099	3074	λύκος	IV:308-311
2965	κύων	III:1101-1104	3075	λυμαίνομαι	IV:312
2975	λαγχάνω	IV:1-2	3076	λυπέω	IV:313-322
2979	λακτίζω	IV:3	3077	λύπη	IV:313-322
2980	λαλέω	IV:3-5; 69-136	3083	λύτρον	IV:328-335; 340-349
2983	λαμβάνω	IV:5-7	3084	λυτρόω	IV:328-335; 349-351
2985	λαμπάς	IV:16-28	3085	λύτρωσις	IV:328-335; 351
2986	λαμπρός	IV:16-28	3086	λυτρωτής	IV:328-335; 351
2989	λάμπω	IV:16-28	3087	λυχνία	IV:324-327
2992	λαός	IV:29-57	3088	λύχνος	IV:324-327
2995	λάρυγξ	IV:57-58	3089	λύω	II:60-61; IV:328-337
2999	λατρεία	IV:58-65	3095	μαγεία	IV:359
3000	λατρεύω	IV:58-65	3096	μαγεύω	IV:359
3001	λάχανον	IV:65-67	3097	μάγος	IV:356-359

3098	Μαγώγ (Γὼγ καὶ Μ.)	I:789-791	3202	μεμψίμοιρος	IV:571-574
3100	μαθητεύω	IV:461	3306	μένω	IV:574-576
3101	μαθητής	IV:415-460	3308	μέριμνα	IV:589-593
3102	μαθήτρια	IV:460-461	3309	μεριμνάω	IV:589-593
3105	μαίνομαι	IV:360-361	3313	μέρος	IV:594-598
3106	μακαρίζω	IV:362-370	3315	μεσιτεύω	IV:598-624
3107	μακάριος	IV:362-370	3316	μεσίτης	IV:598-624
3108	μακαρισμός	IV:362-370	3320	μεσότοιχον	IV:625
3111	μάκελλον	IV:370-372	3326	μετά	VII:766-797
3112	μακράν	IV:372-374	3327	μεταβαίνω	I:523
3113	μακρόθεν	IV:372-374	3331	μετάθεσις	VIII:161-162
3114	μακροθυμέω	IV:374-387	3333	μετακαλέω	III:496
3115	μακροθυμία	IV:374-387	3334	μετακινέω	III:720
3116	μακρόθυμος	IV:374-387	3335	μεταλαμβάνω	IV:10-11
3116	μακροθύμως	IV:387	3336	μετάλημψις	IV:10-11
3119	μαλακία	IV:1091-1098	3337	μεταλλάσσω	I:259
3126	μαμωνᾶς	IV:388-390	3338	μεταμέλομαι	IV:626-629
3129	μανθάνω	IV:390-413	3339	μεταμορφόω	IV:755-759
3131	Μάννα	IV:462-466	3340	μετανοέω	IV:975-1008
3134	μαραναθά	IV:466-472	3341	μετάνοια	IV:975-1008
3135	μαργαρίτης	IV:472-473	3344	μεταστρέφω	VII:729
3140	μαρτυρέω	IV:474-508	3345	μετασχηματίζω	VII:957-958
3141	μαρτυρία	IV:474-508	3346	μετατίθημι	VIII:161-162
3142	μαρτύριον	IV:474-508	3348	μετέχω	II:830-832
3143	μαρτύρομαι	IV:510-512	3349	μετεωρίζομαι	IV:630-631
3144	μάρτυς	IV:474-508	3352	μετοχή	II:830-832
3145	μασάομαι	IV:514-515	3353	μέτοχος	II:830-832
3146	μαστιγόω	IV:515-518	3354	μετρέω	IV:632-634
3147	μαστίζω	IV:515-518	3356	μετριοπαθέω	V:938
3148	μάστιξ	IV:518-519; 1091-1098	3358	μέτρον	IV:632-634
3150	ματαιολογία	IV:524	3359	μέτωπον	IV:635-637
3151	ματαιολόγος	IV:524	3374	μηλωτή	IV:637-638
3152	μάταιος	IV:519-522	3376	μήν	IV:638-642
3153	ματαιότης	IV:523	3384	μήτηρ	IV:642-644
3154	ματαιόω	IV:523	3392	μιαίνω	IV:644-646
3155	μάτην	IV:523-524	3393	μίασμα	IV:646-647
3162	μάχαιρα	IV:524-527	3394	μιασμός	IV:647
3163	μάχη	IV:527-528	3398	μικρός	IV:648-659
3164	μάχομαι	IV:527-528	3401	μιμέομαι	IV:659-674
3167	μεγαλεῖον	IV:541	3402	μιμητής	IV:659-674
3168	μεγαλειότης	IV:541-542	3403	μιμνήσκομαι	IV:675-678
3169	μεγαλοπρεπής	IV:542-543	3404	μισέω	IV:683-694
3170	μεγαλύνω	IV:543	3405	μισθαποδοσία	IV:695-728
3172	μεγαλωσύνη	IV:544	3406	μισθαποδότης	IV:695-728
3173	μέγας	IV:529-541	3407	μίσθιος	IV:695-728
3174	μέγεθος	IV:544	3408	μισθός	IV:695-728
3178	μέθη	IV:545-548	3409	μισθόω	IV:695-728
3180	μεθοδεία	V:102-103	3411	μισθωτός	IV:695-728
3182	μεθύσκομαι	IV:545-548	3417	μνεία	IV:678-679
3183	μέθυσος	IV:545-548	3418	μνῆμα	IV:679-680
3184	μεθύω	IV:545-548	3419	μνημεῖον	IV:680-681
3189	μέλας	IV:549-551	3420	μνήμη	IV:679
3192	μέλι	IV:552-554	3421	μνημονεύω	IV:682-683
3196	μέλος	IV:555-568	3425	μόγις	IV:735-736
3198	Μελχισεδέκ	IV:568-571	3428	μοιχαλίς	IV:729-735
3201	μέμφομαι	IV:571-574	3429	μοιχάω	IV:729-735

3430	μοιχεία	IV:729-735	3550	νομοθέτης	IV:1089
3431	μοιχεύω	IV:729-735	3551	νόμος	IV:1022-1085
3432	μοῖχος	IV:729-735	3552	νοσέω	IV:1091-1098
3433	μόλις	IV:735-736	3553	νόσημα	IV:1091-1098
3435	μολύνω	IV:736-737	3554	νόσος	IV:1091-1098
3436	μολυσμός	IV:737	3559	νουθεσία	IV:1019-1022
3437	μομφή	IV:571-574	3560	νουθετέω	IV:1019-1022
3438	μονή	IV:579-581	3562	νουνεχῶς	II:816-827
3439	μονογενής	IV:737-741	3563	νοῦς	IV:951-960
3444	μορφή	IV:742-752	3565	νύμφη	IV:1099-1106
3445	μορφόω	IV:752-754	3566	νυμφίος	IV:1099-1106
3446	μόρφωσις	IV:754-755	3568	νῦν	IV:1106-1123
3448	μόσχος	IV:760-762	3571	νύξ	IV:1123-1126
3453	μυέω	IV:828	3576	νωθρός	IV:1126
3454	μῦθος	IV:762-795	3578	ξενία	V:1-36
3456	μυκτηρίζω	IV:796	3579	ξενίζω	V:1-36
3462	μυρίζω	IV:800-801	3580	ξενοδοχέω	V:1-36
3464	μύρον	IV:800-801	3581	ξένος	V:1-36
3466	μυστήριον	IV:802-827	3586	ξύλον	V:37-41
3468	μώλωψ	IV:829	3591	ὄγκος	V:41
3470	μῶμος	IV:829-830	3594	ὁδηγέω	V:97-102
3471	μωραίνω	IV:832-847	3595	ὁδηγός	V:97-102
3472	μωρία	IV:832-847	3598	ὁδός	V:42-96
3473	μωρολογία	IV:832-847	3600	ὀδυνάομαι	V:115
3474	μωρός	IV:832-847	3601	ὀδύνη	V:115
3475	Μωυσῆς	IV:848-873	3602	ὀδυρμός	V:116
3479	Ναζαρηνός	IV:874-879		ὀδύρομαι	V:116
3480	Ναζωραῖος	IV:874-879	1492	οἶδα	V:116-119
3485	ναός	IV:880-890	3609	οἰκεῖος	V:134-135
3489	ναυαγέω	IV:891	3611	οἰκέω	V:135-136
3498	νεκρός	IV:892-894	3613	οἰκητήριον	V:155
3499	νεκρόω	IV:894	3614	οἰκία	V:131-134
3500	νέκρωσις	IV:895	3616	οἰκοδεσποτέω	II:49
3561	νεομηνία	IV:638-642	3617	οἰκοδεσπότης	II:49
3501	νέος	IV:896-899	3618	οἰκοδομέω	V:136-144
3507	νεφέλη	IV:902-910	3619	οἰκοδομή	V:144-147
3509	νέφος	IV:902-910		οἰκοδόμος	V:136
3510	νεφρός	IV:911	3620	οἰκονομία	V:151-153
3515	νηπιάζω	IV:912-923	3623	οἰκονόμος	V:149-151
3516	νήπιος	IV:912-923	3624	οἶκος	V:119-131
3521	νηστεία	IV:924-935	3625	οἰκουμένη	V:157-159
3522	νηστεύω	IV:924-935	3628	οἰκτιρμός	V:159-161
3523	νῆστις	IV:924-935	3629	οἰκτίρμων	V:159-161
3524	νηφάλιος	IV:939-941	3627	οἰκτίρω	V:159-161
3525	νήφω	IV:936-939	3631	οἶνος	V:162-166
3528	νικάω	IV:942-945	3636	ὀκνηρός	V:166-167
3529	νίκη	IV:942-945	3645	ὀλεθρεύω	V:167-168
3534	νῖκος	IV:942-945	3639	ὄλεθρος	V:168-169
3538	νίπτω	IV:946-947	3640	ὀλιγοπιστία	VI:174-228
3539	νοέω	IV:948-951	3640	ὀλιγόπιστος	VI:174-228
3540	νόημα	IV:960-961	3641	ὀλίγος	V:171-173
3544	νομικός	IV:1088	3642	ὀλιγόψυχος	IX:665-666
3545	νόμιμος	IV:1088-1089	3644	ὀλοθρευτής	V:169-170
3547	νομοδιδάσκαλος	II:159	3647	ὁλοκληρία	III:767
3548	νομοθεσία	IV:1089	3648	ὁλόκληρος	III:766-767
3549	νομοθετέω	IV:1090	3649	ὀλολύζω	V:173-174

3872	παρακαταθήκη	VIII:162-164	
3873	παράκειμαι	III:656	
3874	παράκλησις	V:773-799	
3875	παράκλητος	V:800-814	
3876	παρακοή	I:223	
3877	παρακολουθέω	I:215-216	
3878	παρακούω	I:223	
3879	παρακύπτω	V:814-816	
3880	παραλαμβάνω	IV:11-14	
3887	παραμένω	IV:577-578	
3888	παραμυθέομαι	V:816-823	
3889	παραμυθία	V:816-823	
3890	παραμύθιον	V:816-823	
3891	παρανομέω	IV:1091	
3892	παρανομία	IV:1090	
3893	παραπικραίνω	VI:125-127	
3894	παραπικρασμός	VI:125-127	
3895	παραπίπτω	VI:170-172	
3900	παράπτωμα	VI:170-172	
3904	παρασκευή	VII:1-34	
3906	παρατηρέω	VIII:146-148	
3907	παρατήρησις	VIII:148-151	
3908	παρατίθημι	VIII:162-164	
3918	πάρειμι	V:858-871	
3919	παρεισάγω	V:824-826	
3920	παρείσακτος	V:824-826	
3922	παρεισέρχομαι	II:682	
3927	παρεπίδημος	II:64-65	
3928	παρέρχομαι	II:681-682	
3929	πάρεσις	I:509-512	
3933	παρθένος	V:826-837	
3935	παρίημι	I:509-512	
3936	παριστάνω	V:837-841	
3936	παρίστημι	V:837-841	
3939	παροικέω	V:841-853	
3940	παροικία	V:841-853	
3941	πάροικος	V:841-853	
3942	παροιμία	V:854-856	
3945	παρομοιάζω	V:199	
3946	παρόμοιος	V:198-199	
3947	παροξύνω	V:857	
3948	παροξυσμός	V:857	
3949	παροργίζω	V:382-447	
3950	παροργισμός	V:382-447	
3952	παρουσία	V:858-871	
3954	παρρησία	V:871-886	
3955	παρρησιάζομαι	V:871-886	
3956	πᾶς	V:886-896	
3957	πάσχα	V:896-904	
3958	πάσχω	V:904-924	
3960	πατάσσω	V:939-940	
3961	πατέω	V:940-945	
3962	πατήρ	V:945-1014	
3965	πατριά	V:1015-1019	
3967	πατρικός	V:1021-1022	
3971	πατρῷος	V:1014-1015	
3975	παχύνω	V:1022-1025	
3980	πειθαρχέω	VI:9-10	
3981	πειθός	VI:8-9	
3982	πείθω	VI:1-7	
3982	πειθώ	VI:8-9	
3983	πεινάω	VI:12-22	
3984	πεῖρα	VI:23-36	
3985	πειράζω	VI:23-36	
3986	πειρασμός	VI:23-36	
3987	πειράω	VI:23-36	
3988	πεισμονή	VI:9	
3992	πέμπω	I:398-406	
3993	πένης	VI:37-40	
3996	πενθέω	VI:40-43	
3997	πένθος	VI:40-43	
3998	πενιχρός	VI:40	
4005	πεντηκοστή	VI:44-53	
4006	πεποίθησις	VI:7-8	
4012	περί	VI:53-56	
4022	περιέρχομαι	II:682-683	
4024	περιζώννυμι	V:302-308	
4024	περιζωννύω	V:302-308	
4027	περικάθαρμα	III:430-431	
4029	περίκειμαι	III:656	
4030	περικεφαλαία	V:314-315	
4034	περιλάμπω	IV:16-28	
	περίλειμμα	IV:195-214	
4036	περίλυπος	IV:323	
4037	περιμένω	IV:578-579	
4041	περιούσιος	VI:57-58	
4043	περιπατέω	V:940-945	
4045	περιπίπτω	VI:173	
4050	περισσεία	VI:63	
4051	περίσσευμα	VI:63	
4052	περισσεύω	VI:58-61	
4053	περισσός	VI:61-62	
4054	περιστερά	VI:63-72	
4059	περιτέμνω	VI:72-84	
4061	περιτομή	VI:72-84	
4065	περιφρονέω	III:633	
4067	περίψημα	VI:84-93	
4068	περπερεύομαι	VI:93-95	
4073	πέτρα	VI:95-99	
4074	Πέτρος	VI:100-112	
4077	πηγή	VI:112-117	
4081	πηλός	VI:118-119	
4082	πήρα	VI:119-121	
4456	πηρόω	V:1022-1024; 1025-1028	
4457	πήρωσις	V:1022-1024; 1025-1028	
4087	πικραίνω	VI:122-125	
4088	πικρία	VI:122-125	
4089	πικρός	VI:122-125	
4091	πίμπλημι	VI:128-131	
4095	πίνω	VI:135-145	
4097	πιπράσκω	VI:160	
4098	πίπτω	VI:161-166	

4100	πιστεύω	VI:174-228	4188	πόμα	VI:145-148
4102	πίστις	VI:174-228	4189	πονηρία	VI:562-566
4103	πιστός	VI:174-228	4190	πονηρός	VI:546-562
4104	πιστόω	VI:174-228	4198	πορεύομαι	VI:566-578
4105	πλανάομαι	VI:228-253	4202	πορνεία	VI:579-595
4105	πλανάω	VI:228-253	4203	πορνεύω	VI:579-595
4106	πλάνη	VI:228-253	4204	πόρνη	VI:579-595
4106	πλάνης	VI:228-253	4205	πόρνος	VI:579-595
4107	πλανήτης	VI:228-253	4213	πόσις	VI:145-148
4108	πλάνος	VI:228-253	4215	ποταμός	VI:595-607
4110	πλάσμα	VI:254-262	4216	ποταμοφόρητος	VI:607-608
4111	πλάσσω	VI:254-262	4221	ποτήριον	VI:148-158
4112	πλαστός	VI:262	4222	ποτίζω	VI:159-160
4121	πλεονάζω	VI:263-266	4224	ποτόν	VI:145-148
4122	πλεονεκτέω	VI:266-274	4224	πότος	VI:145-148
4123	πλεονέκτης	VI:266-274	4228	πούς	VI:624-631
4124	πλεονεξία	VI:266-274	4229	πρᾶγμα	VI:638-640
4128	πλῆθος	VI:274-279	4230	πραγματεία	VI:640-641
4129	πληθύνω	VI:279-283	4231	πραγματεύομαι	VI:641-642
4134	πλήρης	VI:283-286	4233	πράκτωρ	VI:642
4135	πληροφορέω	VI:309-310	4234	πρᾶξις	VI:642-644
4136	πληροφορία	VI:310-311	4238	πράσσω	VI:632-638
4137	πληρόω	VI:286-298		πραϋπάθεια	V:939
4138	πλήρωμα	VI:298-305	4239	πραΰς	VI:645-651
4139	πλησίον	VI:311-318	4240	πραΰτης	VI:645-651
4140	πλησμονή	VI:131-134	4243	πρεσβεύω	VI:681-683
4145	πλούσιος	VI:318-332	4245	πρέσβυς	VI:651-680
4147	πλουτέω	VI:318-332	4244	πρεσβυτέριον	VI:651-680
4148	πλουτίζω	VI:318-332	4245	πρεσβύτερος	VI:651-680
4149	πλοῦτος	VI:318-332	4246	πρεσβύτης	VI:683
4151	πνεῦμα	VI:332-451	4253	πρό	VI:683-688
4152	πνευματικός	VI:332-451	4254	προάγω	I:130-131
4154	πνέω	VI:452		προβάτιον	VI:689-692
4155	πνίγω	VI:455-458	4263	πρόβατον	VI:689-692
4156	πνικτός	VI:455-458	4267	προγινώσκω	I:715-716
4157	πνοή	VI:453	4268	πρόγνωσις	I:715-716
4160	ποιέω	VI:458-484	4270	προγράφω	I:770-772
4161	ποίημα	VI:458-484	4274	πρόδρομος	VIII:235
4162	ποίησις	VI:458-484	4308	προεῖδον	V:381-382
4163	ποιητής	VI:458-484	4276	προελπίζω	II:534-535
4164	ποικίλος	VI:484-485	4279	προεπαγγέλλομαι	II:586
4165	ποιμαίνω	VI:485-499	4282	προετοιμάζω	II:704-706
4166	ποιμήν	VI:485-499	4283	προευαγγελίζομαι	II:737
4167	ποίμνη	VI:499-502	4284	προέχομαι	VI:692-693
4168	ποίμνιον	VI:499-502	4285	προηγέομαι	II:908-909
4170	πολεμέω	VI:502-515	4286	πρόθεσις	VIII:164-167
4171	πόλεμος	VI:502-515	4288	προθυμία	VI:697-700
4172	πόλις	VI:516-535	4289	πρόθυμος	VI:694-697
4174	πολιτεία	VI:516-535	4291	προΐστημι	VI:700-703
4175	πολίτευμα	VI:516-535	4292	προκαλέω	III:496
4176	πολιτεύομαι	VI:516-535	4293	προκαταγγέλλω	I:70-73
4177	πολίτης	VI:516-535	4295	πρόκειμαι	III:656
4183	πολλοί	VI:536-545	4296	προκηρύσσω	III:717-718
4180	πολυλογία	VI:545-546	4297	προκοπή	VI:703-719
4182	πολυποίκιλος	VI:485	4298	προκόπτω	VI:703-719
4184	πολύσπλαγχνος	VII:548-559	4299	πρόκριμα	III:953

4541	Σαμαρίτης	VII:88-94	4654	σκοτίζω	VII:423-445
4542	Σαμαρῖτις	VII:88-94	4655	σκότος	VII:423-445
4547	σανδάλιον	V:310-312	4656	σκοτόω	VII:423-445
4550	σαπρός	VII:94-97	4757	σκύβαλον	VII:445-447
4559	σαρκικός	VII:98-151	4658	Σκύθης	VII:447-450
4560	σάρκινος	VII:98-151	4659	σκυθρωπός	VII:450-451
4561	σάρξ	VII:98-151	4662	σκωληκόβρωτος	VII:456-457
4567	σατανᾶς	VII:151-165	4663	σκώληξ	VII:452-456
4570	σβέννυμι	VII:165-168	4666	σμύρνα	VII:457-458
4573	σεβάζομαι	VII:172-173	4669	σμυρνίζω	VII:458-459
4574	σέβασμα	VII:173-174	4672	Σολομών	VII:459-465
4575	Σεβαστός	VII:174-175	4678	σοφία	VII:465-526
4576	σέβομαι	VII:169-172	4679	σοφίζω	VII:527-528
4578	σεισμός	VII:196-200	4680	σοφός	VII:465-526
4579	σείω	VII:196-200	4687	σπείρω	VII:536-547
4586	σεμνός	VII:191-196	4689	σπένδομαι	VII:528-536
4587	σεμνότης	VII:191-196	4690	σπέρμα	VII:536-547
4591	σημαίνω	VII:262-265	4697	σπλαγχνίζομαι	VII:548-559
4592	σημεῖον	VII:200-261	4698	σπλάγχνον	VII:548-559
4593	σημειόω	VII:265-266	4701	σπορά	VII:536-547
4594	σήμερον	VII:269-275	4702	σπόριμος	VII:536-547
4595	σήπω	VII:94-97	4703	σπόρος	VII:536-547
4597	σής	VII:275-278	4704	σπουδάζω	VII:559-568
4598	σητόβρωτος	VII:275-278	4705	σπουδαῖος	VII:559-568
4607	σικάριος	VII:278-282	4710	σπουδή	VII:559-568
4614	Σινᾶ	VII:282-287	4714	στάσις	VII:568-571
4615	σίναπι	VII:287-291	4716	σταυρός	VII:572-580
4617	σινιάζω	VII:291-292	4717	σταυρόω	VII:581-583
4622	Σιών	VII:292-338	4722	στέγω	VII:585-587
4624	σκανδαλίζω	VII:339-358	4724	στέλλω	VII:588-590
4625	σκάνδαλον	VII:339-358	4726	στεναγμός	VII:600-603
4632	σκεῦος	VII:358-367	4727	στενάζω	VII:600-603
4633	σκηνή	VII:368-381	4728	στενός	VII:604-608
4634	σκηνοπηγία	VII:390-392	4729	στενοχωρέω	VII:604-608
4635	σκηνοποιός	VII:393-394	4730	στενοχωρία	VII:604-608
4636	σκῆνος	VII:381-383	4731	στερεός	VII:609-614
4637	σκηνόω	VII:385-386	4732	στερεόω	VII:609-614
4638	σκήνωμα	VII:383-384	4733	στερέωμα	VII:609-614
4639	σκιά	VII:394-398	4735	στέφανος	VII:615-636
4640	σκιρτάω	VII:401-402	4737	στεφανόω	VII:615-636
4641	σκληροκαρδία	III:613-614	4739	στήκω	VII:636-638
4642	σκληρός	V:1022-1024; 1028	4740	στηριγμός	VII:653-657
4643	σκληρότης		4741	στηρίζω	VII:653-657
		V:1022-1024; 1028-1029	4742	στίγμα	VII:657-664
4644	σκληροτράχηλος		4744	στίλβω	VII:665-666
		V:1022-1024; 1029	4747	στοιχεῖον	VII:670-687
4645	σκληρύνω		4748	στοιχέω	VII:666-669
		V:1022-1024; 1030-1031	4749	στολή	VII:687-691
4646	σκολιός	VII:403-408	4750	στόμα	VII:692-701
4647	σκόλοψ	VII:409-413	4752	στρατεία	VII:701-713
4648	σκοπέω	VII:414-416	4753	στράτευμα	VII:701-713
4649	σκοπός	VII:413-414	4754	στρατεύομαι	VII:701-713
4650	σκορπίζω	VII:418-422	4755	στρατηγός	VII:701-713
	σκορπισμός	VII:418-422	4756	στρατιά	VII:701-713
4652	σκοτεινός	VII:423-445	4757	στρατιώτης	VII:701-713
4653	σκοτία	VII:423-445	4758	στρατολογέω	VII:701-713

4760	στρατόπεδον	VII:701-713
4762	στρέφω	VII:714-715
4765	στρουθίον	VII:730-732
4769	στῦλος	VII:732-736
4772	συγγένεια	VII:736-742
4773	συγγενής	VII:736-742
4774	συγγνώμη	I:716-717
4776	συγκαθίζω	VII:766-797
4777	συγκακοπαθέω	V:936-938
4779	συγκαλέω	III:496
4780	συγκαλύπτω	VII:743
4785	συγκαταψηφίζομαι	IX:604-607
4788	συγκλείω	VII:744-747
4789	συγκληρονόμος	
	III:767-785;	VII:766-797
4790	συγκοινωνέω	III:797-809
4791	συγκοινωνός	III:797-809
4793	συγκρίνω	III:953-954
4796	συγχαίρω	IX:359-372
4800	συζάω	VII:766-797
4802	συζητέω	VII:747-748
4803	συζήτησις	VII:748
4804	συζητητής	VII:748
4805	σύζυγος	VII:748-750
4806	συζωοποιέω	VII:766-797
4807	συκάμινος	VII:758
4808	συκῆ	VII:751-757
4809	συκομορέα	VII:758
4810	σῦκον	VII:751-757
4811	συκοφαντέω	VII:759
4815	συλλαμβάνω	VII:759-762
4818	συλλυπέομαι	IV:323-324
4821	συμβασιλεύ	
	I:564-593;	VII:766-797
4822	συμβιβάζω	VII:763-766
4827	συμμαθητής	IV:460
4828	συμμαρτυρέω	IV:508-510
4830	συμμέτοχος	II:830-832
4831	συμμιμητής	IV:659-674
	συμμορφίζω	VII:766-797
4832	σύμμορφος	VII:766-797
4834	συμπαθέω	V:935-936
4835	συμπαθής	V:935-936
4841	συμπάσχω	
	V:925-926;	VII:766-797
4845	συμπληρόω	VI:308-309
4846	συμπνίγω	VI:455-458
4850	συμπρεσβύτερος	VI:651-680
4851	συμφέρω	IX:69-78
	σύμφορος	IX:69-78
4854	σύμφυτος	VII:766-797
4856	συμφωνέω	IX:304-309
4857	συμφώνησις	IX:304-309
4858	συμφωνία	IX:304-309
4859	σύμφωνος	IX:304-309
4860	συμψηφίζω	IX:604-607

4862	σύν	VII:766-797
4864	συναγωγή	VII:798-841
4866	συναθλέω	I:167-168
4869	συναιχμάλωτος	I:195-197
4870	συνακολουθέω	I:216
4873	συνανάκειμαι	III:654-655
4874	συναναμείγνυμι	VII:852-855
4878	συναντιλαμβάνομαι	I:375-376
4880	συναποθνῄσκω	
	III:7-21;	VII:766-797
4883	συναρμολογέω	VII:855-856
4886	σύνδεσμος	VII:856-859
4888	συνδοξάζω	
	II:253-254;	VII:766-797
4889	σύνδουλος	II:261-279
4891	συνεγείρω	VII:766-797
4892	συνέδριον	VII:860-871
4893	συνείδησις	VII:898-919
4901	συνεπιμαρτυρέω	IV:508-510
4903	συνεργέω	VII:871-876
4904	συνεργός	VII:871-876
4905	συνέρχομαι	II:684
4907	σύνεσις	VII:888-896
4908	συνετός	VII:888-896
4912	συνέχω	VII:877-885
4916	συνθάπτω	VII:766-797
4920	συνίημι	VII:888-896
4921	συνιστάνω	VII:896-898
4921	συνίστημι	VII:896-898
4894	σύνοιδα	VII:898-919
4925	συνοικοδομέω	V:148
4928	συνοχή	VII:886-887
4930	συντέλεια	VIII:64-66
4931	συντελέω	VIII:62-64
4933	συντηρέω	VIII:151
4937	συντρίβω	VII:919-925
4938	σύντριμμα	VII:919-925
4942	συνυποκρίνομαι	VIII:559-570
4953	σύσσημον	VII:269
4954	σύσσωμος	VII:1024-1094
4957	συσταυρόω	VII:766-797
4958	συστέλλω	VII:596-597
4959	συστενάζω	VII:600-603
4960	συστοιχέω	VII:669
4961	συστρατιώτης	VII:701-713
4967	σφαγή	VII:935-938
4969	σφάζω	VII:925-935
4972	σφραγίζω	VII:939-953
4973	σφραγίς	VII:939-953
4976	σχῆμα	VII:954-956
4977	σχίζω	VII:959-963
4978	σχίσμα	VII:963-964
4982	σῴζω	VII:965-1003
4983	σῶμα	VII:1024-1094
4984	σωματικός	VII:1024-1094
4987	σωρεύω	VII:1094-1096

4990	σωτήρ	VII:1003-1021
4991	σωτηρία	VII:965-1003
4992	σωτήριος	VII:1021-1024
4993	σωφρονέω	VII:1097-1104
4994	σωφρονίζω	VII:1104
4995	σωφρονισμός	VII:1104
4997	σωφροσύνη	VII:1097-1104
4998	σώφρων	VII:1097-1104
5001	τάγμα	VIII:31-32
5011	ταπεινός	VIII:1-26
5012	ταπεινοφροσύνη	VIII:1-26
	ταπεινόφρων	VIII:1-26
5013	ταπεινόω	VIII:1-26
5014	ταπείνωσις	VIII:1-26
5015	τάσσω	VIII:27-31
5040	τεκνίον	V:636-654
5043	τέκνον	V:636-654
5046	τέλειος	VIII:67-78
5047	τελειότης	VIII:78-79
5048	τελειόω	VIII:79-84
5050	τελείωσις	VIII:84-86
5051	τελειωτής	VIII:86-87
5055	τελέω	VIII:57-61
5056	τέλος	VIII:49-57
5057	τελώνης	VIII:88-105
	τέμνω	VIII:106
5059	τέρας	VIII:113-126
5064	τέσσαρες	VIII:127-135
5062	τεσσεράκοντα	VIII:135-139
	ἑκατὸν τεσσεράκοντα	
	τέσσαρες	II:321-328
5063	τεσσερακονταετής	VIII:135-139
5066	τεταρταῖος	VIII:127-135
5067	τέταρτος	VIII:127-135
5083	τηρέω	VIII:140-146
5084	τήρησις	VIII:146
5087	τίθημι	VIII:152-158
5091	τιμάω	VIII:169-180
5092	τιμή	VIII:169-180
5111	τολμάω	VIII:181-186
5112	τολμηρός	VIII:181-186
5113	τολμητής	VIII:181-186
5117	τόπος	VIII:187-208
5132	τράπεζα	VIII:209-215
5140	τρεῖς	VIII:216-225
5143	τρέχω	VIII:226-233
5151	τρίς	VIII:216-225
5154	τρίτος	VIII:216-225
5167	τρυγών	VI:63-72
5176	τρώγω	VIII:236-237
5177	τυγχάνω	VIII:238-242
	τυπικός	VIII:246-259
5179	τύπος	VIII:246-259
5180	τύπτω	VIII:260-269
5185	τυφλός	VIII:270-294
5188	τυφλόω	VIII:270-294

5195	ὑβρίζω	VIII:295-307
5196	ὕβρις	VIII:295-307
5197	ὑβριστής	VIII:295-307
5198	ὑγιαίνω	VIII:308-313
5199	ὑγιής	VIII:308-313
5204	ὕδωρ	VIII:314-333
5206	υἱοθεσία	VIII:397-399
5207	υἱός	VIII:334-397
	υἱὸς Δαυίδ	VIII:478-488
	ὁ υἱὸς τοῦ ἀνθρώπου	
		VIII:400-477
5214	ὑμνέω	VIII:489-503
5215	ὕμνος	VIII:489-503
5217	ὑπάγω	VIII:504-506
5218	ὑπακοή	I:224-225
5219	ὑπακούω	I:223-224
5221	ὑπαντάω	III:625-626
5222	ὑπάντησις	III:625-626
5228	ὑπέρ	VIII:507-516
5232	ὑπεραυξάνω	VIII:517-519
5233	ὑπερβαίνω	V:743-744
5234	ὑπερβαλλόντως	VIII:520-522
5235	ὑπερβάλλω	VIII:520-522
5236	ὑπερβολή	VIII:520-522
5240	ὑπερεκπερισσοῦ	VI:61-62
5240	ὑπερεκπερισσῶς	VI:61-62
5239	ὑπερεκτείνω	II:465
5242	ὑπερέχω	VIII:523-524
5243	ὑπερηφανία	VIII:525-529
5244	ὑπερήφανος	VIII:525-529
5245	ὑπερνικάω	IV:942-945
5247	ὑπεροχή	VIII:523-524
5248	ὑπερπερισσεύω	VI:58-61
5250	ὑπερπλεονάζω	VI:263-266
5251	ὑπερυψόω	VIII:606-613
5255	ὑπήκοος	I:224-225
5256	ὑπηρετέω	VIII:530-544
5257	ὑπηρέτης	VIII:530-544
5258	ὕπνος	VIII:545-556
5261	ὑπογραμμός	I:772-773
	ὑπογράφω	I:772-773
5262	ὑπόδειγμα	II:32-33
5265	ὑποδέω	V:310-312
5266	ὑπόδημα	V:310-312
5267	ὑπόδικος	VIII:557-558
5271	ὑποκρίνομαι	VIII:559-570
5272	ὑπόκρισις	VIII:559-570
5273	ὑποκριτής	VIII:559-570
5274	ὑπολαμβάνω	IV:15
	ὑπόλειμμα	IV:194-214
5276	ὑπολήνιον	IV:254-257
5278	ὑπομένω	IV:581-588
5280	ὑπόμνησις	I:348-349
5281	ὑπομονή	IV:581-588
5282	ὑπονοέω	IV:1017-1019
5283	ὑπόνοια	IV:1017-1019

5287	ὑπόστασις	VIII:572-589		5438	φυλακή	IX:241-244
5288	ὑποστέλλω	VII:597-598		5442	φυλάσσω	IX:236-241
5289	ὑποστολή	VII:599		5443	φυλή	IX:245-250
5292	ὑποταγή	VIII:46-47		5446	φυσικός	IX:251-277
5293	ὑποτάσσω	VIII:39-46		5447	φυσικῶς	IX:251-277
5296	ὑποτύπωσις	VIII:246-259		5449	φύσις	IX:251-277
5299	ὑπωπιάζω	VIII:590-591		5455	φωνέω	IX:301-303
5302	ὑστερέω	VIII:592-601		5456	φωνή	IX:278-301
5303	ὑστέρημα	VIII:592-601		5457	φῶς	IX:310-358
5304	ὑστέρησις	VIII:592-601		5458	φωστήρ	IX:310-358
5305	ὕστερον	VIII:592-601		5459	φωσφόρος	IX:310-358
5306	ὕστερος	VIII:592-601		5460	φωτεινός	IX:310-358
5310	ὕψιστος	VIII:614-620		5461	φωτίζω	IX:310-358
5311	ὕψος	VIII:602-606		5462	φωτισμός	IX:310-358
5312	ὑψόω	VIII:606-613		5463	χαίρω	IX:359-372
5313	ὕψωμά	VIII:613-614		5479	χαρά	IX:359-372
5316	φαίνω	IX:1-2		5480	χάραγμα	IX:416-417
5318	φανερός	IX:2-3		5481	χαρακτήρ	IX:418-423
5319	φανερόω	IX:3-6		5483	χαρίζομαι	IX:372-402
5321	φανέρωσις	IX:6		5485	χάρις	IX:372-402
5324	φαντάζω	IX:6		5486	χάρισμα	IX:402-406
5326	φάντασμα	IX:6		5487	χαριτόω	IX:372-402
5330	Φαρισαῖος	IX:11-48		5495	χείρ	IX:424-434
5336	φάτνη	IX:49-55		5496	χειραγωγέω	IX:435
5342	φέρω	IX:56-60		5497	χειραγωγός	IX:435
5348	φθάνω	IX:88-92		5498	χειρόγραφον	IX:435-436
5349	φθαρτός	IX:93-106		5499	χειροποίητος	IX:436
5351	φθείρω	IX:93-106		5500	χειροτονέω	IX:437
5356	φθορά	IX:93-106		5502	χερουβίν	IX:438-439
5358	φιλάγαθος	I:18		5503	χήρα	IX:440-465
5359	φιλαδελφία	I:144-146		5505	χιλιάς	IX:466-471
5361	φιλάδελφος	I:144-146		5507	χίλιοι	IX:466-471
5363	φιλανθρωπία	IX:107-112		5513	χλιαρός	II:876-877
5364	φιλανθρώπως	IX:107-112		5517	χοϊκός	IX:472-479
5368	φιλέω	IX:114-146		5536	χρῆμα	IX:480
5384	φίλη	IX:146-171		5537	χρηματίζω	IX:480-482
5369	φιλήδονος	II:909-926		5538	χρηματισμός	IX:482
5370	φίλημα	IX:114-146		5541	χρηστεύομαι	IX:491-492
5373	φιλία	IX:146-171		5542	χρηστολογία	IX:492
5381	φιλοξενία	V:1-36		5543	χρηστός	IX:483-489
5382	φιλόξενος	V:1-36		5544	χρηστότης	IX:489-491
5384	φίλος	IX:146-171		5545	χρῖσμα	IX:493-580
5385	φιλοσοφία	IX:172-188		5546	Χριστιανός	IX:493-580
5386	φιλόσοφος	IX:172-188		5547	Χριστός	IX:493-580
5399	φοβέομαι	IX:189-219		5548	χρίω	IX:493-580
5399	φοβέω	IX:189-219		5550	χρόνος	IX:581-593
5401	φόβος	IX:189-219		5567	ψάλλω	VIII:489-503
5409	φορέω	IX:83-84		5568	ψαλμός	VIII:489-503
5411	φόρος	IX:78-83		5569	ψευδάδελφος	I:144-146
5412	φορτίζω	IX:86-87		5570	ψευδαπόστολος	I:445-446
5413	φορτίον	IX:84-86		5571	ψευδής	IX:594-603
5424	φρήν	IX:220-235		5572	ψευδοδιδάσκαλος	II:160
5426	φρονέω	IX:220-235		5574	ψεύδομαι	IX:594-603
5427	φρόνημα	IX:220-235		5576	ψευδομαρτυρέω	IV:513-514
5428	φρόνησις	IX:220-235		5577	ψευδομαρτυρία	IV:513-514
5429	φρόνιμος	IX:220-235		5575	ψευδόμαρτυς	IV:513-514

INDEX OF HEBREW AND ARAMAIC WORDS

עֶלְיוֹן	VIII:615-619		רָעֵב	VI:14-17
עַלְמָה	V:831-834		רָצוֹן	II:743-745
עַם	II:364-369; IV:32-37		רָשָׁע	I:320-327
עמד	VII:641-646		שָׂחַק	I:659-662
עָנָה	VIII:6-15		שְׂחֹק	V:627-629
עָנִי	VI:888-902		שָׂטָן	II:73-79
עשׂה	III:1005-1028; VI:459-472		שׂמח	IX:362-366
עָתַר	II:785-800		שָׂנֵא	IV:685-689
פִּדְיוֹן	IV:329-335		שָׂעִיר	II:10-16
פֶּה	VII:695-698		שֵׂעָר	III:29-36
פחד	IX:203-208		שֹׂק	VII:57-61
פלט	IV:196-209; VII:970-989		שָׂרַף	V:571-579
פָּלַל	II:785-800		שׂרר	IV:196-209
פָּנִים	VI:771-775		שָׁאוֹל	I:146-148
פעל	III:1005-1028		שׁאר	IV:196-209
פְּקֻדָּה	II:606-607		שְׁאָר	VII:105-124
פְּרִישַׁיָּא	IX:12-35		שֵׁבֶט	IX:246-249
פשׁע	I:268-293		שָׁבַע	V:459-461
פֶּתֶן	V:571-579		שׁבר	VII:920-922
צבא	VII:705-707		שַׁבָּת	VII:1-20
צדק	II:212-214		שׁגה	I:268-293
צָדוּקִי	VII:35-51		שׁוּב	IV:984-999; VII:723-726
צְדָקָה	II:174-178; 195-198		שׁוֹפָר	VII:76-85
צום	IV:927-931		שׁחה	II:788-800; VI:760-763
צִיּוֹן	VII:293-327		שׁחט	VII:929-933
צלח	V:110-112		שׁחת	IX:96-100
קדשׁ	I:89-100		שָׁלוּחַ	I:413-420
קָהָל	III:527-531		שָׁלוֹם	II:402-410
קוה	IV:583-585; VI:193-202		שָׁלַח	I:400-403
קוֹל	IX:280-290		שָׁלִיחַ	I:413-420
קום	VII:641-646		שְׁלֹמֹה	VII:459-463
קָחָל	VII:802-828		שֵׁם	V:252-270
קינה	III:150-152		שֵׁם יהוה	V:255-258
קִנְאָה	II:878-880		שָׁמַיִם	V:502-513
קנה	III:1005-1028		שׁמם	III:29-36
קרא	III:700-702		שׁמר	IX:237-239
קָרְבָּן	III:860-864		שֹׁרֶשׁ	VI:985-988
קֶרֶן	VII:76-85		שֵׁרֵת	IV:219-225
רָאָה	V:324-340		תּוֹלֵעָה	VII:453-455
רַבּוּנִי	VI:961-963		תּוֹרָה	IV:1036-1059
רַבִּי	VI:961-963		תּוֹשָׁב	V:8-28
רַבִּים	VI:536-540		תַּלְמִיד	IV:426-441
רוּחַ	VI:359-389		תעה	VI:233-236
רוּחַ (ה)קֹּדֶשׁ	I:103-106		תְּפִלָּה	II:785-800
רָחַץ	IV:300-302		תָּקוֹעַ	VII:76-85
רַע	III:476-479; VI:549-554		תְּרוּעָה	VII:76-85
רֵעַ	VI:312-315			

87

INDEX OF BIBLICAL REFERENCES

Explanation: Biblical references are based on the Revised Standard Version; where the Masoretic Text and Septuagint (here abbreviated as M and S, for reasons of space) differ from the RSV enumeration, that fact is noted in parentheses. Footnotes are designated by the letter "n"; a reference in parentheses indicates that the footnote merely illustrates a statement made in the body of the page, whereas one without parentheses refers to a footnote that includes further discussion. References in **bold type** are meant to indicate substantive discussion.

GENESIS

Title III:874

1 II:392; 648; 943; III:1009n70; **1010-1015** (1011n76; 1012n80); IV:99; 132; 1043; V:514n128; VII:429; 434n89, n90; 609; 1053; VIII:72; 471n477; 519; IX:320n65; **321-322** (321n72); 334n177; 591

1f IX:475; 661n4

1ff VII:256n371

1-11 IV:780

1:1 I:482n21; 666; II:566n28; 572n63; III:1008; 1012, n80; 1015, n91; 1016; 1017, n107, n108; 1018n109; 1020n125, n132, n133; 1027; IV:43; 71; **131-132;** 135; 1057; V:504(n55); 890; VI:386n306; 876n30; VII:116; 499n215; VIII:319; IX:184n106; 320; 327n117; 584

1:1f III:877; 1012

1:1ff III:881; 1005; IV:998; V:894

1:1-5 III:877

1:1-2:3 VI:459

1:1-2:4 IX:586n26

1:1-2:4a V:509; VII:485

1:1-2:4b II:390

1:1-12:9 V:574n92

1:2 III:1012; 1016; 1017; 1018n109; 1072n183; V:368; 514n128; 515n128; 835; VI:66; 340; 363, n149; 366; 373; 375; 384; 386, n306; 387, n307; 392; 396n393; 421n585; VII:116; 429; 897(n4); IX:288n41; 322n73; 323n83; 628

1:3 III:587; 1018n112; IV:22; 25; 132; VII:441n162;

VIII:602n7; IX:326n113; 327; 346n292

1:3-5 IX:321n72

1:4 III:544; 553; IV:132; V:325

1:5 I:204; II:943; 947; III:886n65; IV:171n106; 1123; V:252n84; VII:424n5

1:6 III:196n3; V:515n128; VI:611n36

1:6f III:1008

1:6-8 IV:610

1:6ff VI:603n69; VII:897(n4); VIII:319

1:7 III:114n346;1008

1:8 III:1016; V:253; 325; 502; 510n89

1:9 II:408; V:510; VII:805; VIII:193n44, n45; 319

1:10 III:544; VII:374

1:11 III:1012n79; V:189; VI:471; IX:661n4

1:12 III:544; 1031; V:189; VII:539

1:14 III:87; 459; V:503; 510n89; VII:209n59; 211; 221; 222n154; 227; VIII:38, n8; IX:318; 590; 676n7

1:14f III:1008

1:16 II:572n63; IV:529; 640; V:586; IX:318

1:16f III:1008

1:17 VII:809; VIII:154

1:18 III:544

1:20 III:1008; VII:745; 746; VIII:403n19

1:21 II:849n116; 873; III:544; 1008; V:572; 576

1:22 II:756; VI:263; 280; 282; 287

1:24 II:849n116; III:1008; 1012n79; VI:258

1:25 III:544; 1008

1:26 I:379; **II:390-392** (390n52, n60,

	n65, n68); 572n63;	2:5f	VII:758n4; VIII:319
	III:86n106; 87; 113n337; 351;	2:5-5:5	VIII:409n55
	1008n59; 1021; 1022n148;	2:6	VI:51n44; 771; 780
	IV:602; 753; V:190; 191;	2:7	I:2n9; 142; 143, n13; 206;
	503(n46); 891; VI:387, n307;		365n10; 666; II:337;
	461; 464; VII:500n218; 676;		390(n51); 392; 394; 395; 396;
	677; 872; 1052; VIII:40;		437; 536(n2); 629; 844;
	410n66, n68; 473n484;		849n114; 850(n126); 852,
	IX:637; 662		n156; 855n172; 858n207; 860;
1:26f	I:142; II:392; 394; 395;		III:452n1; 1007; 1014; 1016;
	III:1014; 1077; VII:788,		1021; 1022n153; V:528, n251;
	n100; IX:420; 421; 422, n31;		529; VI:118(n11); 256; 258;
	475; 477; 661n4		260, n30; 303n44; 335n2; 341;
1:26-30	VIII:369n247		364; 366, n164; 370; 373; 377;
1:27	I:143, n13; 362; 484n32; 666;		378, n239; 380n249; 396n396;
	782; II:394, n78; 395; 396;		436n696; 442n752; 452; 453;
	III:679; 1008, n59; 1021, n147;		771; VII:434n89; 698;
	1027; IV:751n53; V:528n251;		734n21; 1053; 1086, n563;
	529n255; VI:260; 262; 459,		1087; 1093; VIII:328; 472;
	n10; 461; 463; 464; VII:1083;		IX:29; 125; 184; **472;** 473, n6;
	1093; VIII:423n185;		475, n30; 477, n52; 478; **620;**
	473n484; IX:29; 476n37; 477,		629; 636; 661, n3, n4; 662
	n46; 661	2:7a	VII:1086
1:28	I:648; II:390; 626n20; 756; 757;	2:7b	VII:1086; IX:662
	767; 850n134; III:1013; 1098;	2:7f	IV:752f
	V:503(n46); 645; VI:280,	2:8	I:352; III:1007; IV:750n43;
	n11; 282; 287; VIII:519;		V:766n6; 768; VI:256; 258
	536n56	2:8f	III:1008n60
1:28f	VIII:411n76	2:8-10	V:766
1:29	VII:374; 539; VIII:406n32	2:9	II:860n224; III:543; V:38; 370;
1:29f	VII:121n187		371; 769(n40); VI:551; 604;
1:30	II:852; III:1014; IV:66;		IX:228; 229
	V:503(n46)	2:10	I:481; V:454; 766n6;
1:31	I:676; II:648; 920n67; III:544;		VIII:131n47; 496n51
	1014; 1022; IV:997; V:772	2:10ff	IV:27(n39); VI:596; 604;
2	II:422n7; 637; III:81; VI:532;		VIII:318
	VII:429; 1053; VII:471n477	2:10-14	V:483; VIII:131; 319
2f	V:404; 766	2:13	V:252; VI:612n43; IX:287
2:1	III:880; 1019n120; 1021n140;	2:14	VI:599, n34
	V:506; VII:4n16; 675n39;	2:15	II:648; V:766, n12; VI:256,
	VIII:63; 65; IX:289n52		(n15); 258; IX:237; 238
2:1-3	VII:5	2:16	II:545; 551(n21); 692; V:766
2:2	II:637; 640; III:627; 628;	2:17	II:844n85; III:21n2; VI:550,
	IV:100; VII:5n25; 27n213;		n29; 551; 604; IX:228
	31, n243; 34; 265; VIII:63;	2:18	III:1072n183; VI:258; 461n17;
	64; IX:434; 471; 584		VIII:43n23; 282n91
2:2f	III:435; 1011; VII:3; 4n16; 7	2:19	II:392n66; 852; III:1007; 1008;
2:3	I:82n49; 91; 111; 747; II:246;		1014; V:325; 891; VI:256;
	637; 640; 756; 757; III:362;		258; VII:118n161
	1008; VII:6n34, n37; 31;	2:19f	V:253; V:503(n46)
	IX:184n106	2:20	V:252; 253; VII:873n11
2:4	I:683; II:197n25; 247; 393(n72);	2:21	I:529; II:450; III:434;
	III:326n32; 1008; 1015n91;		VI:51n44; 306; 308; 820n270;
	1018n112; 1020n130;		VII:119n168; 507n297;
	1021n139; V:504(n55); 751;		VIII:550n41
	VII:156n25; VIII:596n21;	2:21f	VI:258
	IX:526	2:22	I:654n41; 781; V:974n158;
2:4b	III:81n69; 1005n44		VI:51n44; 258; 461n17
2:4f	VII:946	2:22f	VIII:43n23
2:4-11:9	**IV:708**	2:23	VII:106; 137n293; 873n11
2:4bff	III:1005	2:23f	IX:622
2:5	II:648; III:811n2; 1084	2:24	I:142, n9; 648; 655; 656n50;

12:13	II:69; IX:598	15:1	IV:93; 697; V:313; 333n93; 371; 586; 684n213; VI:803; IX:203; 232n71
12:14	III:543		
12:15	V:120		
12:16	IV:760; V:10; 283	15:1ff	II:47n19
12:17	II:580n32; V:120; VII:745; IX:164n152	15:1-6	IX:169n185
		15:2	II:45; 46; 47; III:81n71; 889; 1059; IV:328n3; V:645; 657n10; VI:570n30; VII:738; VIII:504n4
12:18	VI:468		
12:19ff	V:10		
12:20	II:545; IV:166n98; VII:772		
13:1	VII:772	15:2f	VI:324
13:2	II:238; VI:323	15:3	VIII:345
13:3	VII:369; 374; VIII:193	15:3f	III:776
13:4	II:786; III:499; 701n18; V:255; 262; VII:390n5	15:4	VI:803; IX:290
		15:5	II:576; III:192
13:5	VII:772	15:5f	VII:547
13:8	VI:127	15:6	I:659; II:177n11; 201; 219; 434; IV:166; 285; **289-292** (289n20; 291n28, n29); V:305; VI:187; 191n130; 197; 198, n153; 202; 285; VII:876; VIII:82; IX:168
13:10	IV:879; V:766		
13:11	IV:149; 168		
13:12	VI:523; VII:377; 385		
13:13	I:322; VI:551		
13:14	VIII:131; 193		
13:14ff	VII:547	15:6a	IV:289
13:14-17	III:769	15:6b	IV:289
13:15	III:784; VII:374	15:7	III:777
13:16	II:757; VII:538; IX:169n185	15:7-21	IX:169n185
13:17	I:368	15:8	II:45; 46; 47; 116; III:81n71; 1059; IV:289; 527
13:18	VII:385n5; IX:170n199		
14	III:275; 1005; 1007; IV:568n1; 569; VII:299; 302n68; VIII:196n63; 616; 618	15:8ff	II:116; III:1100n1
		15:9	II:116; VI:67n46; VIII:217; IX:391n138
14:1	IV:650; V:689n263; VIII:99n115; IX:287	15:9ff	IV:289
		15:10	I:184; II:108n18; 116; V:459; VI:313n11
14:1ff	VII:222		
14:1-15:4	VII:114n133	15:11	VII:787; 1045, n274; 1048n293
14:2	VI:467	15:12	II:116; 450; 453; III:434; VII:507n297; VIII:550n41
14:3	III:800; V:766n9; IX:307		
14:4	I:512	15:13	I:753; II:279; V:8; 27; 846; 851; VI:731; VIII:6; 7; IX:290
14:7	VI:114		
14:9	II:756; V:515n130		
14:10	IV:197	15:14	IV:530; V:269n179
14:11-23	VI:324	15:15	II:402n17; 407; 843(n80); VI:572(n33); VII:772
14:12	IV:389		
14:13	II:107n2; 112n31; III:359; 373; VII:978	15:16	I:117n7; IV:1107; VI:185; 306; VIII:132
14:14	VI:609, n8; VII:580; 671; VIII:225	15:17	II:116; IV:22; 26; 749; V:861; VI:937
14:17-20	IV:570	15:18	II:116; 126; III:769; VI:597; 599; 604; 610n28; IX:525; 526
14:18	III:116n363; 275; 277n54; IV:568; 569; V:789; VII:299; 301; 320; VIII:620		
		15:18b	VI:597n16
		15:19f	VII:485
14:18-20	IV:237	15:19-21	IX:526
14:19	II:758; III:1005; 1007; 1027; IV:41; 569; V:504; VIII:618	15:21	VII:301n61
		16	I:55
		16:2	VI:384n284; VII:744; 880; 881n42; VIII:227n11; 344; IX:287
14:19f	II:761; 764		
14:19-22	VIII:616		
14:20	II:764; IV:569	16:3	VI:686
14:21	IX:622n63	16:4f	V:325
14:22	III:1005; 1007; 1027; V:459n19; 504	16:4ff	I:781
		16:5	I:781; II:197n26; 434; III:824; 923; IX:182
14:23	III:303n12; VI:323		
14:24	VII:768	16:6	V:964(n108); VII:263; VIII:6
15	II:117, n49; V:1005; VII:564	16:7	VI:113; 116n21

19:12-14	VIII:194; 203n115	21:1f	V:833
19:13	V:261	21:2	VII:761n17; VIII:341
19:14	II:233; V:630	21:2f	VII:760n6
19:15	I:368; II:11(n79); IV:1085	21:3f	VI:82n73
19:16	III:911	21:6	I:659, n4; V:254; 628n11
19:17	V:332; VII:540	21:7	II:715n80; VIII:341; 345
19:17-22	VII:980	21:8	II:54(n2); V:638; VI:467;
19:18	III:1061n118		VIII:517
19:19	II:174; 195; 479(n33); 769;	21:9	I:659, n1; V:628, n11
	III:477n29; IV:543; V:479;	21:10	I:528
	VI:563; IX:380n60; 382;	21:12	II:488; V:253
	389n116	21:14	VI:234(n33)
19:20	VII:970n16	21:14f	VIII:318
19:21	III:30; VI:780	21:15	VI:992
19:22	VI:638	21:16	IV:372; VIII:71; IX:281
19:24	I:378n4; V:505; 532(n283);	21:17	I:78n17; IV:171n106; IX:203
	VI:936; 942	21:17ff	I:77
19:24f	VI:946	21:18f	VIII:285
19:24ff	VI:948	21:19	VI:114
19:26	I:217; V:290; 332; VII:725	21:20	VII:779; VIII:517
19:27	I:739; VII:643; VIII:193	21:22	II:923; VII:706; 779
19:29	IV:675	21:23	II:174; 195; 479(n33); V:177;
19:30ff	IV:165n94		261, n138; VI:468; 469;
19:31	III:439; V:48; 891; VI:654;		VII:540; 772n35; IX:382;
	873n10		598n42
19:32	I:368; VII:543	21:26	VII:270(n7)
19:32-35	VII:772	21:27	II:117n51; 126; IV:760
19:33	IX:671	21:28	I:601
19:33f	VI:873n10	21:28f	VII:641
19:34	I:368; VI:654	21:30	II:117n51; IV:485; V:728
19:36f	VII:760n6	21:31	V:261; 264; 459; VIII:195; 196
19:37	VI:873n10	21:32	I:368; II:126; 793
19:37f	III:1072n182; IV:1107n15;	21:33	I:200; 201; 204n23; 208;
	VII:270		III:499; 882; V:262; 766n9;
20	IV:166n98		VI:901n145; VII:1013n58
20:1	V:843	21:34	V:843
20:3	II:676; V:221; 231; 333n93;	22	II:795; IV:588; VIII:71; 82;
	861; VII:366; VIII:550		196n60
20:4	I:115	22:1	IV:93; 95
20:5	II:175; III:607; VI:469	22:1ff	VI:34n57
20:5f	VII:910	22:1-13	IX:201
20:6	I:510; 700; II:432; V:229;	22:1-14	VIII:354n116
	333n93; VIII:550	22:1-19	**VI:25**
20:6f	V:229	22:2	III:1084; IV:225; 739, n7, n10;
20:7	III:249; V:809; VI:54; 803; 811;		V:372n2; 481; 646; VI:571;
	IX:505		875; VII:819; VIII:354;
20:8	V:546; 547		368n240; 603n14; IX:286;
20:9	I:273; II:645; VI:469		298n98
20:10	I:171	22:3	III:338n8; V:283; 285; VII:959;
20:11	III:124; V:609n75; VI:183n86;		VIII:193
	IX:201, n63	22:3f	VIII:202
20:12	VI:186n103	22:4	IV:372
20:13	II:174; 195; 479(n33); VI:468;	22:5	II:789; V:283; VI:761(n33)
	VIII:193	22:6	IV:525; VI:994; VIII:159
20:14	IV:760; V:657n5	22:7	II:76n23; 624n7; VI:689
20:16	III:302; VII:772; VIII:172;	22:7f	IX:286; 298n98
	IX:467	22:7ff	II:789n166
20:17	II:793(n197); III:203; V:809	22:8	IV:147
20:17f	VII:745	22:9	I:82, n48; VIII:159; 193; IX:61
20:18	VII:744; VIII:342	22:9f	III:183; VII:931; IX:169n185
21	II:795	22:10	IV:525; VII:930; 931
21:1	II:602; 603n16	22:11	I:78n17

25:12ff	I:55n1
25:13	VI:872
25:14	IX:482
25:16	VII:370n8
25:17	IV:33
25:18	VI:772
25:19	III:192n4
25:20	VIII:137
25:21	II:785n115; 793(n200); V:833; VII:760n6
25:21ff	III:571
25:22	VI:193n139; VII:401; 402
25:23	III:363; 571; IV:179; VIII:523; 524
25:24	II:947; III:786; VI:288
25:25	III:1072n182; V:254; VI:872
25:26	III:1072n182; V:254
25:27	I:697(n32); VII:370n7; VIII:517
25:29	I:605n7
25:29ff	VI:873; 875
25:29-34	VIII:343
25:30	V:254; VI:952
25:31	II:337
25:31ff	VII:271(n14)
25:31-34	VI:875
25:32	VIII:504n4
25:33	VII:271(n13)
25:33f	VI:875
25:34	VI:875
26	IV:166n98
26:2	V:333; 338; 849
26:3	II:757; V:843; 851; VI:293; VII:539n7; 642; 775; IX:526
26:3f	VII:539n7
26:3-5	III:769
26:4	II:368; IV:166; VII:539n7
26:5	I:701n55; II:220; IV:710n64; 1046, (n92)
26:7	VIII:194; 203n115; IX:200
26:8	I:659n1; V:628n11; 629; 815; VII:772; IX:585n17
26:10	I:117n7; 280n38; V:561n13; VII:772
26:11	IV:33
26:13	VIII:606
26:14	II:883
26:15	IX:585
26:16	V:734n60
26:18	V:263; 264
26:18f	VIII:318
26:19	VI:113; 116n20
26:20	I:269
26:21	II:73
26:22	VIII:517
26:24	IV:166; 1125; V:333; 338; 663(n43); VII:775; IX:203
26:25	III:499; V:255; 262; VII:369; 377
26:27	IV:685
26:28	II:116; 128; V:325
26:28f	VII:779
26:29	II:402n17; 407; 764; III:477n29; VI:469; 552n35; 563; VII:772
26:30	II:54(n2); 117n51
26:31	II:408; VII:772; 971
26:32	VIII:318
26:33	VI:132, n3; VII:270
26:34	VI:383n274; VIII:137
26:35	VI:361; 368; IX:629n85
27	VIII:344
27:1	II:197n25; IV:530; VI:875n28; VIII:279n66; 283; 284; 285
27:1ff	II:756
27:4	I:23n15; IX:125
27:9	IX:125
27:11	IV:193
27:12	III:632; V:631; 971
27:13	I:499n22; VI:570
27:14	IX:125
27:16	I:640n1
27:19	III:441; VI:875
27:20	III:1075
27:22	II:330; IX:281
27:23	I:704; IV:998
27:25	**IX:620**
27:26f	IX:126; 127; 141n243
27:27	V:493; 768n30; IX:16n19
27:28	V:162
27:28f	II:761
27:29	II:789n165; III:1058; 1068; V:961n94
27:30	V:105
27:32	VI:872
27:33	II:450; 459; VIII:538
27:33f	II:954n6
27:34	IV:530; VI:122
27:35	IX:428
27:36	III:1072n182; V:254; VI:875
27:37	III:1058; V:162
27:38	IX:281
27:40	II:850(n132); 897
27:41	III:837
27:41-45	III:304(n14)
27:42	I:400(n15)
27:44	VII:772
27:44f	V:395
28	II:795; III:1080n213
28:3	II:757n7; III:528; VII:803, n26
28:4	III:770; 778
28:7	IV:666
28:10ff	II:421; III:434; V:229; 230; 329; 504; VIII:550
28:11	III:675; VIII:196; 202
28:11f	V:229
28:11ff	IV:610; V:229
28:11-19	VIII:195
28:12	I:78n22; 80n27; 521; II:421; III:675; 787; 987; V:530; VII:655; VIII:403n18; 469, n465; 550n38
28:12ff	V:231
28:13	III:769n5; IV:95; V:333n93; 861; IX:198; 203; 207

28:13f	I:677; VIII:196	30:15	III:295n8
28:13ff	V:229	30:16	IV:697; VII:270(n7)
28:13-16	V:333n92; VIII:196	30:17	II:796
28:14	III:779; IX:246	30:18	IV:697; IX:411n40
28:15	V:64; VII:719; 775	30:20	IV:1114n57
28:16	VIII:196; 550n38	30:22	II:796; IV:675; 681
28:17	II:745; III:176; 177; 179n80;	30:24	IV:406
	V:120; 254; 530n266;	30:25	VIII:194
	VIII:196; IX:200n60	30:27	V:104
28:17b	V:530	30:28	IV:697
28:18	IV:273; 279; V:861; VII:641;	30:30	VI:276n13; 626n31; VIII:517
	VIII:196; IX:501; 580n547	30:31	VI:384n284; 468
28:19	V:120, (n7); 254; VIII:196	30:32	IV:243; VII:270(n6)
28:20	VI:570; VII:777	30:32f	IV:549; 697
28:20ff	II:795n220	30:33	III:754
28:21	II:408; 784n104; VII:971	30:35	IV:243; 549
28:22	II:36; V:120(n7); VI:96n17, n19	30:36	V:49; VIII:217
29	I:38	30:37	IV:244
29f	V:962n96	30:37ff	VI:967
29:2	IV:273; VIII:218	30:38	IV:254; VI:689; VIII:318
29:2f	IV:278n83	30:39f	IV:243
29:3	VIII:194	30:40	IV:549
29:6	II:402(n14); 408; VIII:310	30:40f	VI:689
29:7	IX:676	30:41	IV:254
29:11	IX:126, n127; 138n227	30:42	VII:267; 268
29:13	IX:126, n126	30:43	V:657n5; VI:323
29:14	VII:106; 772; IX:622	31	VI:728n12
29:14-31:16	VI:324	31:1	II:238
29:15	IV:697	31:2	V:325; VI:771
29:17	II:373; III:543	31:3	III:770; VII:775
29:18	I:24n20; II:266	31:4	I:400(n19)
29:19	VII:772	31:5	V:325; VII:777
29:20	I:24n20	31:7	III:485; VI:728n12
29:21	I:776; IV:1099(n5); VI:288	31:7f	IV:697
29:22	I:648; VI:467	31:8	IV:243
29:26	VI:873n10	31:10	IV:243; V:229; 329
29:27	V:731; VI:306; VIII:63	31:10f	VIII:550
29:27f	VIII:63n3	31:10ff	V:229
29:28	VI:306	31:11	V:329n76
29:30	I:24n20; 25n27	31:11f	V:229
29:31	I:24; IV:685; 689; V:833;	31:11-13	VI:490
	983n237; VI:591n72; 902;	31:11ff	I:77; V:229; 231
	IX:129n157	31:12	IV:243; VII:222
29:31f	V:325; VII:761n17	31:13	I:229; II:795n220; V:333, n92;
29:31-30:24	V:254		334; VII:775; IX:501;
29:32	I:24n20;VIII:6; 11		580n547
29:32-35	VII:760n6	31:14	III:759; 770n6; 777
29:33	I:24; IV:685; V:983n237;	31:15	IV:285; V:8; VI:160
	IX:129n157	31:16	VI:323
29:34	IV:1114n57	31:17	VIII:345
29:35	VII:641; VII:496	31:17ff	III:593
30:1	II:883; VIII:282n86; 345	31:19	II:377(n15); III:754; IV:754n2
30:1f	VIII:342	31:20	III:606; IX:627
30:2	III:614; V:395n83	31:20f	III:972
30:3	VIII:344; 345n65	31:21	V:469; VI:596n13; 599
30:6	II:796	31:22ff	V:19
30:8	VII:760	31:23	V:49
30:8ff	VII:760n6	31:24	I:14n12; IV:1125; V:229;
30:9	VII:641		333n93; VIII:550
30:11	V:967n119; **VIII:240-241**	31:25	II:113; III:917(n14); VII:370
	(240n18)	31:27	VII:772; 872
30:13	IV:364; 365; IX:249	31:28	VI:634; IX:126

	392	41:33	V:328; VII:477(n89); 484
39:23	I:699n42; V:111; 328; VII:779	41:34	II:615; IV:162n91
40	V:231	41:36	VIII:162
40:1	I:272	41:37f	V:638
40:1f	V:395	41:38	II:819n25; VI:362; 406n473
40:2	V:394(n73)	41:38f	VII:493
40:3	VIII:193; IX:243	41:39	II:29; V:229; VI:362;
40:4	IV:219; 220n17; V:838		VII:477(n89)
40:5	IV:1125; V:221; 329; 370	41:40	III:162; IV:33; 34; VIII:523
40:5ff	III:435; V:229	41:41	VII:271(n12); 689
40:6	V:393	41:41-43	VII:942n41
40:7	VI:771; VII:270(n5); 271(n12);	41:42	VII:689; 945
	451	41:43	III:694; 700, n14; V:960n83
40:8	II:663; III:954(n4); IV:328;	41:44	V:695n305
	337n1, n2; V:229; 329	41:45	IV:1102; V:254
40:8ff	V:229	41:47	VI:471
40:9	VIII:550	41:49	II:284
40:13	I:481; III:925n12	41:50	IV:1102
40:14	II:479n22; IV:676	41:52	VIII:11; 517; 606
40:15	III:359(n23); 754	41:55	III:898; IV:33; VI:15
40:16	I:185; III:675; 954(n4)	41:56	VI:772
40:17	V:510	42f	VI:874n16
40:19	III:918; V:510	42-44	VII:58n13
40:20f	I:481	42:1	I:179; V:325; VI:383n279
40:22	III:918; 954(n4)	42:4f	VII:772
41	V:231	42:5	VIII:348n88
41ff	VI:323	42:6	II:789n165; VI:761(n28), n38;
41:1	VII:272		IX:79
41:1ff	III:435; V:221; 229; VI:596	42:8	I:704
41:2	III:543; IV:145	42:9	IV:974
41:2f	VII:106	42:9-34	VII:417
41:4	II:334; IV:145	42:11	VI:381n259; 384n284
41:5	IV:145	42:11-34	II:418
41:6	IX:98	42:13	VII:270(n6)
41:7	II:334; IV:145	42:15	V:177
41:8	I:400(n19); IV:328; 337n1;	42:15f	V:185n86
	V:226; VI:361; 368; VII:480;	42:16	I:234; 251; IV:93; V:177
	483; 495; IX:180n74; 617;	42:18	IX:201n63
	641n150	42:20	IV:93; VI:184
41:9	I:272; II:73; VII:270(n5)	42:21	I:273n20; III:140; 142; VII:908;
41:10	V:638		IX:379
41:11	IV:1125	42:22	I:158; 273
41:12	III:359(n22); 954(n4); IV:328;	42:23	II:662; IV:602
	337n1	42:25	V:49; VII:58
41:13	III:918; 954(n4); V:234	42:27	IV:328; VII:58, n13
41:14	I:400(n19); VI:195n145;	42:28	III:606
	VII:689	42:30	VII:417
41:15	III:954(n4)	42:32	VII:270(n6)
41:16	II:408; 663; V:229; VII:493;	42:35	VII:58; IX:200
	1022	42:37	V:963n106
41:17	VIII:550	42:38	II:76n31; IV:197; 318; IX:624
41:18	IV:145	43:2	VIII:63
41:19	VI:563; 888	43:3	V:325; VI:776
41:20	IV:145	43:5	V:325; VI:570; 776
41:21	III:786	43:9	I:273; VII:641
41:22	V:329; VIII:550	43:11	IV:553; IX:79
41:24	V:226; IX:180n74	43:12	I:115; 271n13
41:25	II:29; III:1080	43:14	I:467n6; II:479n34
41:26f	II:714	43:16	VII:772; 930n25
41:29	VI:132	43:18	VII:759n2; IX:200
41:30	VI:132	43:23	II:408; III:300
41:32	I:601	43:24	VIII:320

	IX:626n72	49:26	II:756; III:675; IV:879; V:482;
49:7	I:508; V:411; 1030; VI:152n39		VII:81
49:8	II:789n165; VIII:341; 496	49:27	III:1084n233; IV:309; VI:382;
49:8ff	I:567		384n281
49:9	III:595; IV:160n85; 252;	49:29	IV:33; VI:572(n33); VII:772
	253n21; VIII:427n211	49:33	II:527n74, n76; III:627; IV:33;
49:10	II:365n6; 368; III:1073n192;		VI:572(n33); 969n22
	IV:857n111; 1014; V:862;	50:1	III:150; 722; VI:771; IX:126
	VI:726; VIII:481n16;	50:2	III:201
	IX:525n203; 526	50:3	III:150; 838
49:10f	VIII:481	50:3f	III:837
49:11	I:176; III:337n4; **V:284-285**	50:4	III:837; 842n83
	(285n9); VI:155n71; 960, n8;	50:7	VI:656n37
	988; VIII:340; 342;	50:8	V:1021
	353(n114); IX:524; 526	50:10	III:150; 152; 831n3; 837; 838;
49:11ff	V:284		842; 843; 845n99; 847n116;
49:12	IV:250n67; VI:135n4		V:686
49:13	III:407n9	50:11	III:837; IV:529
49:14	V:10n62; 283	50:13	II:847; IV:680
49:15	V:915n83; IX:80n9	50:14	IV:865n206; VIII:138
49:16	IV:33	50:15	III:477n29
49:16-18	VI:162	50:17	II:51; V:659n22; 673n111;
49:17	V:63; 571; 572, n77; 573;		VI:550(n26); VIII:342
	IX:248	50:19	I:27; IV:689
49:18	II:522n30; IV:578; VII:374	50:19f	I:17n19
49:21	I:446	50:20	III:325(n24); IV:34; 285n3;
49:22	I:746n18; VIII:340; 342;		1014; V:616n118;
	403n14; 517		VII:271(n10)
49:23	III:1058n97	50:21	I:374; V:778; 798n185
49:24	III:906; 1061; VI:487(n17),	50:23	VIII:345, n65
	n18; VII:922	50:24	II:602; 606; III:770
49:25	II:756; V:507; VIII:319n33	50:24f	II:607
49:25f	II:756	50:25	II:602; 606

EXODUS

1	II:636	1:15-21	IX:201
1:1	VI:578	1:16	III:359(n22); IV:914;
1:5	II:634; V:252		VIII:345n65; 353(n114);
1:7	VI:281; VIII:519n16		IX:644; 669
1:8	I:697n31; VI:281	1:17f	II:874
1:8ff	III:987	1:19	III:359(n23); V:981n225;
1:9	IV:33n15; VI:277		VIII:310n20; IX:671
1:9ff	IV:870n237	1:20	VI:280
1:10	VII:484; 527n2; VIII:168	1:22	II:874; IV:33; 34; 870n237, n238;
1:11	II:623; 636; VI:889n26;		914; VI:596; VIII:353(n114)
	VII:277n10	2	III:192n4
1:11f	VIII:6	2:1	II:817n5; III:1065n131
1:12	VIII:7	2:1ff	IV:235; 849n5
1:13	V:632	2:2	III:554; VII:760n6;
1:14	V:632; VII:772		VIII:353(n114)
1:15	III:192n2; 193n9, n10	2:3	III:958; IV:1107n15; VI:326n72

2:4	IV:400; 401n88; VII:417	3:13f	IV:612; V:257
2:5	IV:300; 946n10; V:734; IX:426	3:13ff	VII:212
2:6	III:359(n22)	3:14	II:344; 345; 352; 398, n2; 399;
2:7	III:359(n23)		III:90n113; 110n306; 1040;
2:8	V:831		1067; 1069n159; **1071-1073;**
2:9	IV:697		V:255; 264; VII:283;
2:10	IV:850n15; 860, n144; VIII:344;		VIII:223n52
	IX:672	3:14b	III:1073
2:11	IV:529; 531n9; 865n206; 974	3:15	III:80; 1063n123; 1071; IV:682;
2:11ff	VIII:291n153		V:264; 269
2:11-14	VIII:261n12	3:15f	III:191n1
2:12	III:959; IV:866n211; V:940;	3:16	II:606; V:324; 331; VI:655;
	964n110; VI:647n15		660(n52)
2:13	I:157; 161; V:354n192; VI:316;	3:17	I:646; III:141; 770; IV:552;
	VIII:375n298		VII:301n61
2:14	III:444; 923; 924n8; 942n1;	3:18	II:710n29; III:359(n23); V:49;
	IV:865n206; IX:200		VI:570; 655; 660(n52);
2:15	III:193n13; 441; V:851;		VII:765n17; 930
	VI:115n11	3:19f	IX:427
2:16	I:781	3:20	III:35
2:17	VI:1001; VII:971n21	3:21	IX:379; 380; 389
2:18	III:260; 1066; VII:271(n15)	3:22	V:728; VI:313n14; VII:385n6
2:19	VI:1001	4	VII:764
2:20	II:689	4-10	IV:60
2:21	III:260	4:1	V:324; 331; VI:186; 187; 197
2:22	V:31n208; 846; 849; VI:731	4:1ff	VII:222n150; 260
2:23	I:626; II:786; VII:600; 601	4:2	VI:967
2:24	II:126; III:191n1; IV:675;	4:2ff	V:575
	VII:600	4:4	VI:967
3	**III:1065-1066;** 1071; IV:749;	4:5	V:324; 331; VI:197n149
	V:265; VII:285; VIII:122	4:6	VII:255
3:1	III:1066; 1071n180; IV:856n105;	4:6f	III:824
	V:172; VI:489n42; 490;	4:7	I:387; VII:106
	VII:282(n5); 283n9	4:8	VII:210; 212; 215
3:1f	VII:285	4:8f	VI:186; 187; 191; 197; 215n314
3:1ff	I:218; IV:612	4:9	VI:197n149
3:2	I:80n32; 81; 83, n63; III:191;	4:10	III:132n1; 698; IV:865;
	IV:22; V:331; 336; VI:934;		V:659n25; 674; 681n183
	936; 942; 944; IX:284	4:10ff	IV:431; VII:212
3:2ff	I:77; IV:749; 753; V:338; 861	4:11	V:327; VIII:279; 280; 281;
3:3	III:40; V:371, n3; 372; VII:734		IX:230
3:4	IV:95; V:328; 331	4:12	III:1023n159; IV:430n119;
3:4b	III:1071n180		VII:763
3:4ff	V:351; VI:936	4:13	II:933n38; IV:154n47; VI:862
3:5	I:90; 91; II:330; III:1066; IV:328;	4:14	III:260; 612n22; V:398
	437n172; V:311n2; VI:627;	4:15	VI:469; VII:763
	631; VII:641; 648; VIII:191;	4:15f	VII:696n44
	202	4:16	II:663n3; 664; III:96; IV:612;
3:6	I:217; 752; II:752; III:98n200;		852n62; VI:803
	191, n1, n2; 1070; 1071n180;	4:17	VI:471; 967; VII:209n59;
	V:331; 332; 333; 337; IX:200		212n73; VIII:118n32; 119
3:7	I:221; IV:54; V:325; 341	4:18	VIII:310
3:7f	III:770; VII:603	4:19	IV:870; VI:846; VIII:282n86
3:8	I:646; II:421; IV:552; V:861;	4:20	III:109; 338n8; IV:860; 863;
	VII:301n61; VIII:194		V:284; VI:967
3:9	III:140; 141; 142; IX:89	4:21	III:607; V:1030; VI:471;
3:9-14	III:1071n180		VII:210n66; VIII:118, n32;
3:10	I:402n25; II:425		119
3:12	I:433; III:1065; IV:60; 63;	4:21ff	IV:1014
	VII:220; 228; 229; 231(n213);	4:22	I:31n61; IV:41, n50; 739;
	775; VIII:204n132, n134		V:966; 973; VI:810; 873;
3:13	IV:615; V:961		874n14; 875; 881n62;

	VIII:351; 355; 360; 368n241; 377n314
4:22f	VIII:352
4:23	I:631n16; III:1065; IV:32n12; 60; VIII:353, (n114)
4:24	II:74n15; III:109; 1070; V:398
4:24f	V:402
4:24ff	**VI:76**
4:25	I:226; VI:73; 74; 76n21; 95n6; IX:605, n10
4:25f	II:115n44; IX:98
4:26	VI:74
4:27	IX:126; 287; 288, n40; 296n86
4:28	VII:209n59
4:29	IV:612; VI:655, n24; 660(n52)
4:30	VI:471
4:30f	VII:212
4:31	I:739; II:602; 789n170; III:141; 142; VI:761(n33); VII:228
5	II:636
5ff	IV:431
5:1	I:419; IV:612; V:261; VIII:353
5:2	II:855n172, n173; III:1084n227; VIII:121
5:3	III:359(n23); VI:996n24; VII:765n17
5:4	IV:240n17; VII:718
5:7	VII:270; VIII:218
5:8	II:334; III:898
5:9	III:659; IV:590
5:13	III:439; VI:642n5; VIII:63
5:14	II:623; IV:515; VII:270; VIII:63
5:16	I:158; 272n18; IV:515; V:562n15; 674
5:19	III:439
5:21	I:598; V:493
5:22f	III:484; V:261; IX:158
5:23	V:262; VI:1001
6:1	I:527; 640, n1; V:851
6:2	I:237; IV:602; 615; V:255
6:2f	III:1071; VII:283
6:3	II:61; III:81; 1064; V:331
6:4	II:126; V:843; VII:641
6:5	IV:675; VII:600
6:6	I:640; IV:333; V:851; VI:1000; VII:249
6:7	IV:5; 147
6:8	I:401n23; III:759; 770; V:459n19; IX:426
6:9	VI:361; 368; IX:629, n85; 666
6:12	I:226; IV:141; IX:292n66
6:14	V:1016, n2
6:16	VII:737
6:17	V:120; 1016
6:18	II:884n6; 933n38; 934n44
6:19	V:120; 1016; VII:737
6:20	III:1065; IV:235; V:960
6:25	V:1016
6:26	VII:770
6:27	II:94
6:30	VI:80n56

7	III:193; 1068n148
7-9	IV:34
7-11	II:36
7:1	II:664; III:90n115; 96; IV:612; 852n62; VI:803; IX:97
7:3	III:607; V:1030; VI:280; VII:210(n65); 218n130; 242; 260n405; VIII:123
7:3-5	VII:215n97
7:4	I:529; VII:769n14; VIII:118; IX:427
7:5	I:401n23; IV:36
7:6	VI:471
7:7	VIII:137
7:8ff	III:990; V:575; VIII:123n65
7:9	II:893n6; III:32, n24; 1102; V:567n5; VII:209; 218n121; 219; 220; 229; VIII:117; 118; 119; 123
7:9f	V:572
7:9ff	VI:967
7:9-12	VI:967
7:11	I:433; III:192n2, n6; 193n10; VII:480; 483; 497n202; 527; IX:180n74
7:11ff	III:193
7:12	III:193n11; V:572
7:13	III:607
7:14	I:558n1; 559, n2
7:14ff	VI:598
7:16	III:359(n23); IV:36; 60
7:17	II:939; IV:863n189; 909n44; VII:715; VIII:268n64; 325
7:17ff	I:176
7:18	II:284
7:19	II:939; IV:909n44; V:940; VI:115; VII:715; 897
7:19f	IV:863n189
7:20	II:939; V:940
7:22	I:433; V:1030; IX:180n74
7:23	IV:953; VII:725
7:25	V:940; VI:306
8:1 (7:26, M/S)	IV:36; 60; VIII:354
8:2 (7:27, M/S)	VIII:261; 268, n64
8:4 (7:29, M/S)	I:10n6
8:5-32 (8, M/S)	IV:36
8:7 (8:3, M/S)	IX:180n74
8:8 (8:4, M/S)	II:785n115; IV:60
8:9 (8:5, M/S)	II:785n115
8:10 (8:6, M/S)	V:324
8:13 (8:9, M/S)	VI:460
8:15 (8:11, M/S)	I:559n2; III:607; V:325; IX:664, n3
8:16f (8:12f, M/S)	V:940
8:17 (8:13, M/S)	VI:967
8:18 (8:14, M/S)	II:284
8:18f (8:14f, M/S)	IX:180n74
8:19 (8:15, M/S)	II:21; V:1030; IX:91n26
8:20 (8:16, M/S)	IV:36; 60; VIII:354
8:21 (8:17, M/S)	I:631n16; IV:36
8:22 (8:18, M/S)	III:33n27
8:22f (8:18f, M/S)	**VII:215,** n97

8:23 (8:19, M/S)	IV:36; VII:215n94; 592
8:24 (8:20, M/S)	VI:278; IX:96; 99
8:26 (8:22, M/S)	IV:165n95
8:28 (8:24, M/S)	II:785n115
8:29 (8:25, M/S)	II:785n115; 796(n225)
8:30 (8:26, M/S)	II:785n115; 796(n225)
8:32 (8:28, M/S)	I:559n2; VII:215
9:1	III:359(n23); IV:36; 60; 223n23; VIII:354
9:3	III:336; IV:529
9:4	III:33n27; IV:36
9:5	I:677n2; IV:482
9:7	I:559n2; III:607
9:8	VI:300n9; 978n10
9:10	I:123; VI:978n10
9:10f	VI:554n52
9:11	IX:180n74
9:12	V:1030
9:13	III:359(n23); IV:36; 60; 223n23; 998; VII:641; VIII:354
9:14	I:677n2; IV:1114n57; V:891
9:14f	IV:1112
9:15	I:401; V:940
9:16	I:68, n12; 677n2; II:286; 338; III:324(n6); 325(n20); 329; V:257; 271; **IX:59**
9:17	IV:36; VIII:302
9:18	II:239n23; III:1027; IX:676
9:21	I:510
9:23	IX:280; 290
9:23f	V:532(n283); IX:283n22
9:24	VI:935; 936; 943
9:27	I:276n26; IV:33; 1108n17
9:28	II:785n115; VI:935; IX:280
9:29	II:790(n182); 793(n193); 796(n225); V:506; 509; IX:280
9:31	V:839; VII:539
9:33	II:790(n182); 796(n225); V:506
9:33f	IX:280
9:34	I:559n2
9:35	V:1030
10	III:338
10:1	I:559n2; V:1030, n4
10:1f	VII:212; 215, n97
10:2	V:547; 631; VIII:343
10:3	IV:36; 60; VIII:354
10:5	IV:196; V:379; VI:62; VII:978n49
10:6	IV:1107n14; 1108n16; V:960
10:7	IV:60; VII:341
10:8	II:796(n225); IV:60
10:9	VII:770
10:10	VI:552n35
10:11	I:361
10:13	V:509; VI:360; 967; IX:628
10:17	II:51n8; 785n115
10:18	II:785n115
10:19	VI:360
10:20	V:1026n5
10:21ff	VII:431n54; 440n151, n153

10:22	VII:428n40
10:24	IV:60
10:25	VI:470
10:26	IV:60
10:27	V:1026n5
10:28f	V:325
10:29	VI:772
11:2	V:728; VI:313, n14
11:3	V:836n66; IX:379; 380
11:4f	VIII:120n41
11:5	III:162; 442; VI:872
11:7	III:33n27; IV:36
11:8	VI:761(n37); VII:772
11:9	III:32; VI:280
11:9f	VII:209; 220; VIII:117; 118; 119; 123
11:10	III:32
12	V:168; 902, n52
12:1	III:191n2; V:586; 978n206; VIII:538n73
12:1f	III:452n3; 1023n159; IV:998; V:480n66; VIII:373n283
12:1-14	V:962
12:2	I:654n40; 746n17; II:20; IV:41; 42; VI:927n59
12:3	I:339(n3); V:1016n2; VII:804
12:4	II:138n20; III:803; VI:313n11; VII:760; 772
12:5	I:339(n3); V:898; VIII:72; 347
12:6	III:529; V:331n84; 898; 962; VI:277; VII:931; IX:388
12:6f	VII:804
12:6ff	III:181n2
12:7	I:177; V:898, n21; VII:661n33; IX:580n547
12:7ff	VII:221
12:8	II:903(n8); 904; 906; V:331n84; VI:934
12:8f	III:992n144; V:898
12:9	III:675; VI:626; VII:771
12:10	VI:935; VII:921
12:11	II:138n20; III:5; IV:318n25; V:304; 306; 496; 614; 896n2; VII:562; 772
12:12	I:82n49; III:86; V:439; 696n311; 811; 940; VI:872; 875; 938
12:12f	VI:872
12:13	I:177; IV:636; V:328; VII:211n68; 214; 219; 661n33; IX:96
12:14	I:349; IV:682
12:15	II:903(n8); 906; V:603
12:15ff	II:906
12:16	I:107n60; III:495; 496; VI:470
12:17	III:1020n131; VI:470; IX:240n19
12:18	II:902; 943
12:19	II:906; V:603; 849n39; VI:731; 736n89; VII:804
12:20	II:902; V:155
12:21	III:181; V:897n8; VI:655, n21;

	660(n52)
12:21-28	V:962
12:22	IV:946n10
12:22f	I:176; 177; V:168n3
12:22-27	V:898
12:23	I:489n4; 510; II:11(n79); V:167; 168n3; 170n4; 328; 940
12:25	III:770; IV:61
12:26	IV:61; V:604
12:26f	V:963; VIII:343
12:27	I:739; II:789n170; V:896n2; 940
12:28	VI:469
12:29	II:77n39; III:162; 442; IV:110n169; V:802; 811; 940; VI:872; IX:364; 365
12:32	IV:7
12:33	VII:562
12:34	II:902; 906
12:36	IX:379; 380
12:39	II:902; 906
12:40	I:756n31; IX:52n26
12:41	VII:987; IX:364n39
12:42	IV:857n107; VI:838; VII:987; VIII:147; 149; 151n19
12:43	I:266; II:580n35; V:845; VI:728; VII:663
12:43ff	VI:77n29
12:44	V:657(n9); VI:73
12:45	IV:697; V:8; 844; 845; VI:731
12:46	VII:921, n13; 923; 924n28
12:46f	VII:804
12:47	VII:804
12:48	V:11n66; 897n7; VI:73; 470; 729n16; 739
12:48a	V:845
12:48b	V:845
12:48f	VI:77n29
12:49	V:845, n18; VI:728
12:50	IV:817; VI:469; VII:662n38
12:51	VII:770
13	VI:876
13:2	I:111; V:841; VI:872; 875; 876; VIII:362n188
13:2ff	III:488
13:3	II:266; 906; III:98n200; IV:682; V:120; IX:427
13:3f	VII:271(n13)
13:5	III:770; IV:61; VI:470
13:6f	II:902; 906
13:7	II:906; IV:1101n21; V:48; 719
13:8	VI:460; 578; VIII:343
13:8ff	VII:492n188
13:9	IV:636n3, n5; 682; 1045 (n85); VII:214; 215, (n95); 218n131; 219; 227; 660; 697
13:12	VI:876
13:12-15	V:841
13:13	IV:331; 333; 349; V:841n14; VI:690
13:14	I:323n46; II:266; V:120; 604; IX:427
13:15	IV:331; 333

13:16	IV:636n3, n5; VII:68n17; 215(n95); 218n131; 219; 660; IX:427
13:17	I:762; IV:627; V:98; VII:156n25
13:19	II:602; 606; V:461n29; 465n8; VII:772
13:20	VII:706
13:21	IV:22; 908; V:98; VIII:331
13:21f	I:211; IV:905; VI:936; VII:733; 736n36
14	IV:852
14:2	VII:706
14:3	IV:110n170; VI:234(n33); VII:744
14:4	I:704; 707; II:254; V:696n311; 1030; VI:508(n45)
14:5	II:266; IV:60; VII:729
14:6	IV:34
14:7f	II:254
14:8	V:1030; VI:578; VII:655; IX:428
14:9	III:336
14:9ff	V:575n100
14:10	II:786; VII:705n24; 706; IX:200
14:10ff	VII:257n383
14:11	IV:37
14:12	I:509; IV:60
14:13	III:26; VI:460; VII:270(n3); 271(n10); 636; 637; 641; IX:203; 287; 585
14:13f	VII:271(n9), (n12), (n13)
14:14	VI:508(n35)
14:15	I:82n56; 782; II:76n31; IV:42; V:684n213; VI:908n216
14:15-31	VI:827
14:16	VI:967; VIII:123n64
14:16b	VIII:319
14:16ff	III:406n20
14:17	V:1030; VII:611n21; 627
14:18	III:572; VI:508(n45)
14:19	I:77; VII:733n11
14:19ff	IV:905
14:20	IV:47; 902; VII:519n376
14:21	VI:360; VI:960; VIII:504; IX:628
14:21b	VIII:319
14:21f	V:49
14:22	VIII:319; 331
14:24	III:193n14; IV:22; VI:936; VII:733n11; IX:243
14:25	VI:772; VII:772
14:27b	VIII:319
14:28	I:237; II:285; III:557
14:29	III:32n24
14:30	II:713; III:13n56; VI:1000
14:30f	VI:510n66
14:31	II:294; III:900; IV:853n65, n77; 872; V:663; 664n46; 674; VI:187; 188; 191; 197; 199n161; IX:201n62; 427
15	III:772; 1065n129; IV:872;

16:24	IV:463; VII:453
16:25	I:790n4; IV:437n173; VI:59; VII:270(n5); IX:672
16:26f	VII:7
16:27	IV:463n5
16:27-30	IV:463n15
16:28	I:631n16; IV:1046, (n92)
16:29	VII:5; 13; VIII:193n44; 195n51
16:29f	IV:463n5
16:30	I:790; VII:7
16:31	IV:462; 463n5; 553, n15; V:129
16:31a	IV:463
16:31b	IV:463
16:32	IV:462; 463n6, n13; VII:265n26
16:32a	IV:463n6
16:32f	IV:462
16:32-34	IV:463n6; 464
16:33	II:934n50; IV:462; 464n22; 466; VI:59; 300n9; 970
16:33f	IV:464n20
16:34a	IV:463n6
16:35	IV:462; 463n14; VIII:136
16:35a	IV:463, n5
16:35b	IV:463n6
17	VI:97
17:1	II:66
17:1f	VII:804; VIII:132
17:1ff	I:733; V:575n100
17:1-7	V:575; VI:27; 32
17:2	I:730; VI:27; 126
17:2-7	VIII:318
17:3	I:730; II:227
17:4	II:786; IV:267
17:5	VI:655; 967
17:6	III:991; IV:272; 278; 463(n12); VI:95; 97, n29; 136(n8); 146(n10); 289; VII:282(n5); 283n9; 518n376; 643; 644; VIII:463n430
17:7	IV:293; V:1030; VI:126; 127, n12; VIII:196
17:8	III:326n32; VI:97n29
17:8ff	V:575; VI:915; VIII:121
17:8-13	II:463
17:9	II:795; III:260; 285; VI:967
17:9f	V:481
17:11	II:793(n193); 795; V:578n138
17:11f	IV:825; 873
17:12	II:795; III:441; IV:279; VI:184n91, n93; VII:655
17:13	IV:34; 525n12
17:14	I:193; 487n2; 617(n7); 618n13; 619n21; III:285n5; IV:682; 714; V:253; 546; 547; 550; 554n100, n105; VIII:393; IX:207
17:15	II:403n24; III:1065n132; V:252; VII:209n49; IX:364
17:15f	III:98n199
17:16	I:547; III:1065n132; VI:508n39; VIII:393; IX:426
18	III:260; VI:656n28; VII:764

18:1	I:41n106; II:297
18:1ff	III:1066
18:3	V:846; VI:731
18:7	I:498; II:408; VI:761, n39, n40; VII:370; IX:126
18:8	V:49n26
18:9	I:14; II:459
18:9-11	IX:363
18:10	II:764n2
18:11	III:86; IV:538; V:734; 891; VIII:160; 301
18:12	I:219; III:110n305; 889; IV:534n25; VI:655; 888; VII:772; VIII:495
18:13	VII:787
18:13ff	VI:656
18:15	V:728
18:16	IV:1045(n85); 1046, n92; VII:763, n6; 764
18:18	IX:100
18:19	VII:779; IX:60
18:20	II:198n30; III:546n31; 843, n91; IV:512; 1045(n85); 1046, n92; V:50; VI:469; 570; VII:263
18:21	I:179n7; 233n2; II:182; III:125; IV:147; 389; 686n13; 687; VI:270; VIII:526; IX:201
18:22	I:375; III:942, n6; IV:530; IX:60, 677
18:23	II:402n17; VIII:194
18:25	IV:149; 861
18:26	IX:60; 677
18:27	II:921
19	II:120; III:90n110; IV:152; 1038; V:398; 401; 407; VI:47n19; 49; 935; VII:80; 373; IX:284, n26
19f	V:338; 339; IX:287
19-24	VII:282
19-Numbers 10	VII:282
19:1	IV:1102n28; V:104; VI:49
19:1f	VII:282(n4)
19:1ff	III:249, n3; VI:47n19
19:2	IX:287, n39
19:3	III:109; 249; V:510; VI:817n250
19:3f	III:1066
19:3ff	IV:612
19:4	I:133; IV:7; 36
19:4ff	III:572; 574
19:4-7	IV:35
19:5	II:365n6; 366; III:250; 772; IV:33n15; 35; 55; 164; 710n64; V:891; VI:57, n7; 58, n16; IX:237; 284n27
19:5f	I:324; III:1014; IV:54; V:901n42
19:6	I:91; 94; 100; 106; 107n63; 570n28; 591; II:366; III:249; 250, n7; 264, n30, n31; IV:33; V:142; IX:296

21:6	I:132; III:96; 109; IV:60; V:546, n26; VII:660; 661
21:7	II:266; V:674; 963
21:8	IV:33n15; 331; 335; 351n1; VIII:158
21:9	II:220; V:963; VI:468; VIII:343n56
21:10	VII:107; 108; IX:623n67
21:11	V:964
21:12	IV:1036(n39); V:939f; 964n110; VI:313; 975
21:12-14	III:21n4
21:12ff	III:21
21:13	II:470; VIII:536n47
21:14	II:138n21; IV:883; V:724(n15); 725(n17); VI:313(n17); VIII:160; 301
21:15	V:962n96; 964, (n110); 975; VI:313; VIII:268n66
21:15-17	IV:1036(n39)
21:16	III:468; IV:643; V:982n233; VI:313; 314n24
21:17	II:548; III:754; V:962n96; 964; n110; 965; 975n172
21:18	VI:313(n17); 915
21:19	V:942; VI:967
21:20	II:174; 181; V:674; VI:967
21:20f	V:964
21:21	V:657n5; 963n105
21:22	I:361; II:465n4; 889n10; IV:962n1
21:23f	III:853
21:24	IV:525n12; V:377: VIII:280
21:25	IV:829
21:26	V:618; VIII:279; 280
21:26f	II:271; V:657(n6); 674; 964
21:29	IV:512; VIII:218
21:30	III:303; IV:329; 331; 389
21:31	VI:468
21:32	III:439; V:674
21:33	V:287(n25)
21:35	V:14n91; VI:313(n17); 315n30
21:36	IV:483
22:1 (21:37, M/S)	II:631; III:754; VII:930n25; 932; 933; VIII:105n154; 132
22:2-31 (22, M/S)	III:1058n97; VIII:162
22:2 (22:1, M/S)	III:755n4
22:3 (22:2, M/S)	III:754; VI:160
22:3ff (22:2ff, M/S)	III:754
22:4 (22:3, M/S)	V:287(n25)
22:6 (22:5, M/S)	VI:934; VIII:240n13
2:7 (22:6, M/S)	VI:313(n17); VIII:162
22:7f (22:6f, M/S)	III:754
22:7-13 (22:6-12, M/S)	VIII:162
22:8 (22:7, M/S)	I:162; III:96; 754; VI:313(n17)
22:8ff (22:7ff, M/S)	III:96
22:9 (22:8, M/S)	I:117n7; III:86n103; V:460; VI:313(n17)
22:10 (22:9, M/S)	VI:313(n17); VIII:162
22:11 (22:10, M/S)	I:699n42; V:460; VI:313(n17); 314n21
22:12 (22:11, M/S)	IV:389
22:14 (22:13, M/S)	IV:697; VI:313(n17)
22:16 (22:15, M/S)	VI:585n36
22:16f (22:15f, M/S)	I:781
22:19 (22:18, M/S)	II:874n5
22:19f (22:18f, M/S)	IV:1036(n39)
22:20 (22:19, M/S)	VI:732n37
22:21 (22:20, M/S)	I:39; III:140; 141; V:8; 9; VI:731; 738; 890; IX:207
22:21f (22:20f, M/S)	IX:445
22:21ff (22:20ff, M/S)	VI:728, n7
22:22 (2:21, M/S)	V:488; VIII:6; IX:445
22:22-24 (22:21-23, M/S)	IX:446
22:22ff (22:21ff, M/S)	I:626; IX:445
22:23 (22:22, M/S)	I:626; 627; III:899; VIII:6
22:24 (22:23, M/S)	V:398n119; 409
22:25 (22:24, M/S)	VI:40; 313n18; 314n21; 647n11; 888; 890; VII:721; IX:445
22:25c (22:24c, M/S)	VI:891
22:26 (22:25, M/S)	V:542; VI:313(n17)
22:26f (22:25f, M/S)	III:434
22:27 (22:26, M/S)	II:485; VI:313n18; 890n33; IX:378(n53)
22:28 (22:27, M/S)	IV:981
22:29 (22:28, M/S)	I:622; IV:254n4; VIII:594n14
22:29f (22:28f, M/S)	VI:873
22:30 (22:29, M/S)	VI:888
22:31 (22:30, M/S)	VI:457
23	IV:99
23:1	I:151; 273n21; IV:483; 522
23:2	VI:278; 537; VIII:8; IX:289
23:3	III:30; VI:38
23:4	II:812; IV:1101(n25); V:287(n25); VI:234
23:4f	**I:26;** 39
23:5	VII:25n198; 26n203; 786; IX:85
23:6	III:929n24; 942(n7); VI:39; 890; VII:718
23:7	I:276n26; II:212; IV:110n167; VII:187
23:8	IV:312; V:327; 376; VIII:285
23:9	III:140; 141; V:10; VI:728n7; 729; 731; 890
23:10f	II:628; VI:890; VII:6
23:11	I:510; VI:314n21; 891
23:12	V:1060; VI:564n8; **729;** 737n104; VII:2; 3n5; 4; IX:618; 664, n3
23:13	III:1063n123
23:14	VIII:218
23:14f	II:902
23:15	II:902; 906; III:659; IX:364
23:16	V:105; VI:45, n4; VII:803; VIII:65, n5
23:17	III:1061; VIII:218
23:18	II:904; 906
23:19	I:485
23:20	I:77; 83n58; 610; II:705; 936n65; IV:46n82; V:50; 70n96, n97; VI:387n311; 684; 772; VIII:193n44; 195; 356; IX:237

23:20f	**V:256;** 257	24:15ff	II:239; 240; IV:905; 908; V:326;
23:20-23	III:290; 291		VII:429; IX:320
23:20-33	III:770	24:15-18	VIII:419n151
23:21	V:256; VI:10n1	24:16	II:237; 245; IV:869n228;
23:22	I:591; II:812; III:140; 249;		VII:282(n4); 283n6;
	IV:33; 54; V:891; VI:57, n7		IX:332n157
23:24	II:645; 789n168; III:411; 412;	24:17	I:292n78; II:245; 246; IV:22;
	IV:60; VI:761(n34), (n36)		749; V:326; VI:936
23:25	IV:60; 225; VII:720; VIII:318	24:18	II:676; IV:869n228; VII:286;
23:26	VI:306		VIII:137
23:27	II:459	25	IV:327; VII:690n24; 733n8;
23:27f	VI:508(n44)		VIII:256; 257; IX:505n57
23:30	III:778	25-30	VI:468
23:31	VI:610n28	25-31	VII:282
23:32f	II:118n54	25-37	VII:96n19
23:33	IV:60; VI:470; 747; 748; 749;	25:2	IV:1057; VI:696; 698(n5)
	751	25:2f	I:485; IV:5
24	IV:152; 851; VI:656; 982n29,	25:4	III:812; VII:453, n8
	n30, n31, n32; VII:379	25:6	IX:498
24:1	II:789n170; IV:372; 869n228;	25:7	VI:299n8; VIII:85n6
	V:331; VI:655; 656; 761(n33)	25:8	II:26; 33; IV:580; VI:468;
24:1ff	III:802		VII:372n27
24:3	II:676; VI:470; IX:282	25:9	V:508; VII:372; VIII:249; 256
24:3ff	IV:761	25:10	IV:486; VII:397; VIII:603
24:3-8	VI:980n22; 892; 893n43	25:11	III:414
24:4	I:744; IV:99	25:12	VIII:132
24:4-8	I:91	25:15	IV:485
24:5	II:122n68; VI:739; 982n29;	25:15ff	IV:486
	VII:1023	25:16	III:319; 320; IV:485
24:6	I:176; II:132; 468, n2	25:16-21	III:319
24:6-8	IV:111n177	25:17	III:319; 320
24:6ff	II:132; III:454	25:17-22	III:318
24:7	I:617, n8; II:122; III:1079;	25:17-23	III:319
	IV:99; V:546; 547	25:18	IX:438
24:8	I:174; II:105; 115; 120; 133;	25:18-20	IX:438
	468, n2; 545; III:731; IV:99;	25:19	IX:438, n3
	111n177; VI:980, n22; 982	25:30	III:318; IV:485
24:9	IV:869n228; VI:655; 660n52	25:21	III:319; IV:485
24:9f	II:381; VI:656	25:22	II:240n26; III:318; 321; IV:482;
24:9-11	II:121; V:505; IX:290		485; 486; 1042; IX:438
24:9ff	III:802; IV:749	25:23	VIII:603
24:9-18	IV:869; VII:379	25:23-30	VIII:165
24:10	II:245; n48; 422; III:109; 414,	25:26	VIII:132
	n3; V:331; 337; VI:627; VII:	25:29	VII:531n22
	610n10; 643; VIII:199n86;	25:30	VIII:165n3
	202, n104; IX:54n56; 624	25:31ff	IV:325n11
24:10a	V:336	25:31-35	IV:324
24:10f	**V:331-332;** 333; VIII:199n86	25:34	VIII:132
24:10ff	V:861	25:37	IX:1n4
24:11	II:122n68; 250; 690; III:109;	25:37a	IX:127n136; 139n233
	802; V:331; 332; 337;	25:40	II:25; 26; 33; III:278; V:363;
	VI:136(n14); VIII:199n86		508; VI:468; 476; 939;
24:11a	V:333		VII:286n37; 372; 375; 398;
24:11b	V:336		VIII:35; 246; 248; 249;
24:12	I:744; 770; II:546; IV:269;		**256-259**
	1045(n85); VI:454	26	I:751; II:36; VII:733
24:12f	IV:869n228	26-40	IV: 324
24:12ff	V:331	26:1	III:812; VII:453
24:13	IV:219; 427(n94); V:838	26:2	VIII:132
24:15	IV:869n228	26:3	VII:880
24:15f	III:557; IV:869n228;	26:4	III:800
	VIII:369n249	26:6	III:800

26:7	VII:57n11; 394n10
27:8	VIII:132
26:10	III:800
26:12	VI:264; VIII:523
26:13	VIII:523
26:14	III:558n1
26:15-25	VII:733
26:17	IX:427
26:19	IX:427
26:24	III:344
26:30	II:26; III:240; VII:372
26:31	III:812; IV:285n3; VII:453
26:31-35	III:629; IV:885n21
26:32	VIII:132
26:33	I:90; V:77n124
26:33f	IV:486
26:34	I:90; III:319; 561
26:36	III:812; VII:453
26:37	III:629
27	II:36
27:1	VIII:217
27:2	III:557; 669
27:8	VII:372
27:13	IX:653
27:16	III:558n1; 812; VII:453
27:17	I:22n8
27:19	II:636
27:20	II:471; 472; VII:324n187
27:21	II:106; 126; III:629
28	III:269n22; 307; IX:500
28-39	IV:219
28:1	I:3n1; II:615; VII:37n14
28:1f	VIII:175
28:1-4	III:249
28:2	VII:690; VIII:172; IX:398n214
28:3	I:188; III:607; IV:965; VI:129; 361; 362; 369; VII:476n88; 484; 493; 497n202
28:4	V:304
28:5	III:812; VII:453n8
28:5f	VII:453
28:7	I:476; III:800; VII:880
28:8	III:812; VI:471; VII:453
28:10	V:252
28:15	III:812; VII:453; 945
28:17	VI:299
28:21	VII:945
28:24	VI:123
28:25	IV:635
28:26	I:65n9
28:29f	IX:626
28:30	II:176; IV:237; VI:578
28:32	V:309; IX:127n136; 139n233
28:33	III:812; VII:453
28:34	I:111
28:35	IV:219; 220; IX:281
28:36	I:94; VII:661; 945
28:38	IV:635
28:39	VIII:613
28:41	IX:426; 497(n21); 501
28:42	IV:27n40; VI:107; VII:108n86; IX:622

28:43	IV:221; VI:578
29	III:269n22; 307; VIII:58
29:1	I:237; 450(n6); IV:830
29:2	IX:502
29:3ff	VI:596
29:4	I:132; IV:300; VIII:320
29:5	V:304
29:7	IX:498; 500n39; 510
29:8	I:132
29:9	III:251; V:304; VIII:80; 81n11; IX:426
29:10	I:131; III:675; VII:655; VIII:160; IX:428
29:10-14	IV:760
29:12	I:176; V:733; VII:533
29:13	IV:911
29:14	I:270n7
29:15	VIII:160; IX:428
29:17	II:225; IV:557, (n21); VI:626; VIII:320
29:18	IX:60
29:19	IX:428
29:20	V:548; VI:627n36
29:20f	I:175
29:21	I:111; VI:979; 980; VII:690; IX:498; 510
29:22	III:561; IV:911; VIII:85n7
29:23	VIII:165
29:24	V:455
29:25	IX:60
29:26	V:455; VIII:85
29:27	VIII:85
29:28	VII:1023
29:29	VIII:80, n9; 81n11; IX:498; 500n39
29:30	IV:220; IX:500n39
29:31	III:670; VIII:83
29:32f	III:992n144
29:33	I:111, n3; 266; III:302; 307; 1102; V:8; 80; 81n11; 82n20
29:34	VI:935; VIII:85
29:35	VIII:80; 81n11
29:36	I:111, n3; II:947; III:302; 414; 429; VI:470; IX:497 (n19); 501
29:36f	III:307
29:37	III:302; 414
29:38ff	III:862n12
29:38-41	V:162; VII:532
29:40	VII:531
29:42	I:699
29:43	I:91; 111; 699; II:240(n27); 245; VIII:28
29:43f	II:240n26; VII:372n27
29:45	IV:580
30:1	III:183
30:6	II:240n26; III:319; 629; IV:486
30:8	II:66
30:9	V:8n48; 10; VII:531, n22; 532; 533
30:10	I:381; III:302; 309; 414; 429, (n4)

30:11ff	IV:283	32:4	II:813n12; IV:760; VI:257
30:12	II:601; 606; III:303; IV:329;	32:5	III:700
	340; VI:508(n41)	32:5a	VI:805n169
30:12-16	VI:88n57	32:6	I:659, nl; II:921n75; III:182;
30:13	VII:351		441; IV:53; V:628; 629;
30:13f	IV:861		V:630; VIII:85n2; 210
30:15	III:305	32:7	III:362; VI:817n248; IX:96
30:16	III:305; 634; IV:221n19	32:8	V:51; 92; 737
30:17-21	VII:320	32:9	V:1029; IX:625
30:18	II:467	32:11	I:640n1; II:76n31; 77n39; 291;
30:18f	IV:946		785n124; 786(n128); IV:539;
30:19	VI:627n36		615; V:811
30:19f	VIII:321	32:11f	V:406
30:19-21	IV:947	32:11ff	IV:612; 615
30:20	IX:60	32:11-14	II:796; V:809
30:21	VII:240n284	32:12	I:350; III:109; IV:989; V:400;
30:23	IV:145; 182; VII:457; 458n7		406; 409; VI:563; 564(n8);
30:24	III:340, n5		VII:715; 772
30:25	IV:800; IX:498	32:13	III:770; 775; IV:675; V:184n73;
30:26	IX:497(n21); 501		460n21; 663; 674
30:29	I:111; IX:497(n21)	32:14	III:315; VI:564(n8); VII:715
30:30	IX:497(n19); 501	32:15	I:744; 745n15; IV:486
30:31	IX:498	32:16	I:749; VI:454; VIII:75n41
30:32	VI:468; IX:510	32:17	III:898, (n5); IX:280
30:34	III:343; VII:858	32:18	IX:281
30:34f	IV:263; VII:676	32:19	V:394, n72; 629; VI:647n15;
30:35	I:228		992
30:36	IV:486	32:22	V:394; 470
30:37	VI:468	32:25	V:263n143
31:1f	III:703n28; 1020n136	32:25ff	III:260
31:2	III:490; IV:148; V:262;	32:25-29	IV:235
	IX:449n76	32:26	IV:151
31:2f	VI:373	32:27	II:330; V:964; VI:313n11;
31:2ff	VI:259		VIII:154
31:3	I:706n69; VI:129; 363; VII:484;	32:27f	IV:237n23
	493; 497n202	32:29	VII:270(n3)
31:4	III:812	32:30	III:304; V:671n98
31:6	VII:476n88; 484; 493; 497n202	32:30f	I:295n87
31:7	II:106; 126; 132n103; III:319;	32:30ff	IV:612; 615
	VII:390n5	32:31f	II:796; 864(n283); V:406
31:9	II:883	32:32	I:355; 510; 744; II:845n89;
31:10	IV:224; 231		III:121(n7); IV:853, n80;
31:11	IX:498		869n230; V:446n433;
31:12	I:213		532n295; 809; IX:158
31:12-17	VII:2	32:32f	I:619, (n21); V:253; 281n244
31:13	VII:5; 211; 215n97; 219	32:34	II:602; V:97; VI:708; 772;
31:13f	VII:7		VIII:193n48
31:14	V:603; VIII:452n367	33:1-3	V:761
31:14f	IV:1036(n39); VII:5	32:2f	I:78
31:16	I:208; II:126; VI:470; VII:5	33:3	III:613; IV:554n29; V:1029, n2;
31:17	III:1018; VII:5; 211; 219;		IX:625
	IX:618	33:4	IV:249n52; VI:550(n27)
31:18	I:744; 745n15; 770; II:20; 244;	33:5	II:29; III:613; 880; V:1029;
	IV:269; 486; VI:454;		IX:625
	VII:282(n4); IX:91n26; 434	33:5ff	IV:612
32	III:193, n15; 260;	33:6	III:880; VII:263; 282(n5)
	IV:430(n118); V:398(n117);	33:7	VII:373
	403; VI:805n169	33:7ff	VII:391n8
32:34	VII:282	33:7-11	III:260
32:1	III:192n4; 528; VI:468; VII:897	33:8	IV:974; VII:415; 641
32:2f	V:546	33:9f	IV:905
32:2-6	VIII:49	33:10	II:789n170

35:12	III:319; 629
35:12f	III:629
35:15	III:629; IX:498
35:19	III:251; 266; IV:220
35:20	VII:804n27
35:21	III:634; VI:361; 368; 696; 698n5; IX:617; 629f
35:22	IV:965; VI:696n24; VII:359; 943; 945; IX:57
35:23	VII:57n11; 453, n8
35:25	III:812; IV:965; VII:453; 476n88
35:25f	VII:484
35:26	IV:965; VII:57n11; 497n202
35:27	VI:300; VIII:85n6
35:28	II:472; IX:498
35:29	II:66; VI:696; 698, (n5); VII:804n27
35:30	III:490; IV:148; V:262
35:31	I:706n69; VI:129; 363; VII:484; 493; 497n202
35:32	IV:284
35:33	III:634; VI:468; VII:944
35:35	III:607; 812; IV:965; VII:453, n8; 484; 497n202; 944
36:1	III:439; IV:965; VII:477(n91)
36:1f	VII:476n88; 484; 493; 497n202
36:2	I:631(n21); III:607
36:4	VII:484
36:5	VI:277
36:6	I:485; III:695n82; 700; VIII:38; IX:281
36:8	VII:453; 476n88; 484; 497n202
36:14	VII:57n11
36:22	IX:427
36:24	IX:427
36:33	IV:220
36:35 (37:3, S)	III:812; VII:453
36:35ff (37:3ff, S)	III:629
36:37 (37:5, S)	VII:453
36:37f (37:5f, S)	III:629
36:39 (37:7, S)	I:742; 761; 767n17
37:6 (38:5, S)	III:319
37:6-9 (38:5-8, S)	III:319
37:7 (38:6, S)	IX:438
37:7-9 (38:6-8, S)	IX:438
37:7ff (38:6ff, S)	IX:438n3
37:19 (38:16, S)	IV:324
37:27 (no S)	IV:54
37:29 (38:25, S)	IX:498
38:4 (38:23, S)	VII:359
38:8 (38:26, S)	I:178n2; 786; IV:929; V:962n97; VII:705
38:17 (37:15, S)	I:22n8

38:18 (37:16, S)	III:629; VII:453
38:21 (37:19, S)	II:66
38:23 (37:21, S)	VII:453
38:24 (39:1, S)	I:485; III:634
38:25 (39:2, S)	IX:467
38:27 (39:4, S)	III:629
38:28 (39:5, S)	I:22n8
39 (36:8-38 or 39:12-23, S)	IX:500
39:1 (36:8 or 39:12, S)	III:266; IV:220; 231; VII:453
39:1-3 (36:8-10 or 39:12, S)	VII:453
39:2 (36:9, S)	III:812
39:3 (36:10, S)	III:812; VIII:106n2
39:4 (36:11, S)	VII:880
39:5 (36:12, S)	III:812; VII:453
39:6 (36:13, S)	VII:945
39:14 (36:21, S)	I:770; VII:945
39:23 (36:30, S)	V:309
39:24 (36:31, S)	III:812; VII:453
39:29 (36:36, S)	V:304; VII:453
39:30 (36:37, S)	I:742; 761
39:32 (36:11, S)	IX:526
39:35 (39:14, S)	II:106; 126; III:319
39:36 (39:17, S)	VIII:165n3; 211
39:37 (39:16, S)	III:643
39:38 (39:15, S)	II:106; 132n103; IX:498
39:40 (39:19, S)	III:629
39:41 (39:18, S)	III:251
40	VIII:154
40:2	II:950; VII:641
40:3	III:629
40:4	VIII:165
40:5	III:183; 558n1; 629; IV:486
40:6	VII:931
40:9	IX:498; 501
40:10	II:933n34; IX:501
40:11	IX:497(n21); 501; 509n71
40:12	I:132; IV:300; VIII:320
40:12-14	VII:37n14
40:13	I:229; VII:690; IX:497n21; 500n39
40:15	I:229; III:249; 251; IX:497(n21); 498; 501; 510
40:17f	VII:641
40:20	IV:486
40:21	IV:486
40:21-26	III:629
40:23	VIII:165
40:29	VII:931
40:34	II:245; IV:905
40:34f	II:240; VI:128; VII:399
40:35	IV:908; VI:290n17; VII:400
40:36f	IV:905

LEVITICUS

1	III:308	4:3	I:489n3; II:229n2; 409; III:202;
1ff	III:309; V:891		266; IV:32n13; 34; 830;
1-7	III:261		1094n15; VI:376n218;
1:1	I:82; 178; IV:612; 655n33;		IX:500; 502; **505;** 510, n72
	VI:381n259	4:3ff	IV:760
1:2	III:861n6; V:684n213; VI:689;	4:4	VII:931; IX:428
	798n126; VIII:407n36	4:5	III:266; VIII:81, n11; 82;
1:3	I:131; II:59; IV:830; VII:931		IX:500; 502; **505;** 510
1:4	III:308; VII:931; VIII:160;	4:5ff	I:419
	IX:428	4:6	I:90; 535; III:629; (n15);
1:5	I:4; 176; VII:931; 932n32		IV:946n10; VI:977n3, n5;
1:6	II:225; IV:557, (n21)		979
1:7	VIII:160	4:7	I:176; III:182; 183; VII:533;
1:7ff	VI:934		VIII:160
1:8	IV:557n21	4:9	IV:911
1:9	III:787; 861n6; V:494; VI:626;	4:11	VII:109n88; 771
	VIII:320	4:12	III:417; VI:935
1:11	I:176; VII:931	4:13	I:115; 274; 280; IV:99;
1:12	I:184; IV:557(n21)		V:561n13; VII:802n21; 804
1:13	III:861; V:494; VI:626;	4:14	I:131; III:529; VII:802n21
	VIII:320	4:15	VII:802n21; 804; 931; IX:428
1:14	VI:67; VIII:346	4:16	III:266; IX:500; 502; **505;** 510
1:16	VIII:198	4:17	I:535; III:629; (n15);
1:17	V:494		IV:946n10; VI:977n3; 979
2	III:308	4:18	I:176; VII:533
2:1	III:181; 755n3; 861n5, n6;	4:20	I:510; III:307
	1084n225; VI:902n146	4:21	III:529; VII:802n21
2:1ff	III:860; 861n5	4:22	I:280; II:470; IV:32n13;
2:2	VI:299n9		V:561n13
2:3	II:690; III:1102; IV:433	4:23	I:295n87
2:4	IX:502	4:24	VII:931; VIII:198; IX:428
2:4f	II:906	4:25	I:176; VII:533
2:6	III:728	4:26	III:307
2:7ff	III:181	4:27	II:470; IV:32n13; 34;
2:11	II:906; IV:553		IX:648n195
2:12	V:494	4:29	VII:929n24; 931; IX:428
2:13	I:228; III:181	4:30	I:176; VII:533
2:14	VI:934	4:31	III:305(n22); 307
3	III:308	4:33	VII:931; IX:428
3:1	VII:1023; IX:409n20	4:34	I:176; VII:533
3:2	VII:931; VIII:160; IX:428	4:35	III:307; VII:85n2
3:3	I:131	5:1	II:129; 855n173; III:695n82;
3:3ff	IV:911		IV:483; V:467; 811; VI:389;
3:4	IV:911; VI:191n131		VII:825; IX:164n152; 281;
3:5	III:305n22		288n41
3:8	VIII:160; IX:428	5:1-6	III:306
3:10	IV:911; VI:191n131	5:2	I:280; VI:638; VII:1045
3:11	I:90	5:3	III:427; IV:645(n12)
3:13	VII:931; VIII:160; IX:428	5:4	VI:469
3:14	IX:60	5:6	I:295n87; VIII:383n362
3:15	IV:911; VI:191n131	5:7	I:268n2; VI:67(n48); 891n46;
3:16	VII:931		VIII:353(n114)
3:17	I:173; IV:516; VI:458	5:7-13	III:307
4	III:307	5:9	IV:197; VI:978n10; 979
4-7	V:603	5:10	I:295n87; 510; III:439
4:1	I:291; IV:612	5:11	VI:67(n48); 891n46;
4:1-5	I:270		VIII:383n362
4:2	I:274; 280; II:470; III:277; 309;	5:11-13	III:307
	VI:378n234	5:12	VI:299n9

5:13	I:295n87; 510; II:690
5:14	IV:612
5:14-16	III:307
5:15	I:280; III:277; 307; IV:830; V:739; VIII:172
5:16	III:309
5:17	II:21; 22; 197n26; 437n10; V:696; 891; VIII:410n66
5:17-19	III:307
5:18	I:115; 117; 280; II:470; IV:334; 335(n20); VIII:172
6:1ff (5:20ff, M/S)	VIII:103; 105n154
6:1-7 (5:20-26, M/S)	III:306; 307
6:2 (5:21, M/S)	I:159; III:306; 800; 808n73; IV:603; VIII:162
6:2f (5:21f, M/S)	IX:598
6:2ff (5:21ff, M/S)	II:218; V:467
6:4 (5:23, M/S)	VIII:162
6:5 (5:24, M/S)	II:473
6:6 (5:25, M/S)	II:218; IV:334; 335(n20)
6:8 (6:1, M/S)	IV:612
6:9 (6:2, M/S)	IV:1045(n89); VI:934
6:9ff (6:2ff, M/S)	VIII:162
6:10 (6:3, M/S)	VII:106; 107; 1045
6:11 (6:4, M/S)	VII:689; 690; VIII:198
6:12 (6:5, M/S)	VIII:85n2
6:12f (6:5f, M/S)	VII:166
6:13 (6:6, M/S)	VI:934
6:14 (6:7, M/S)	IV: 1045(n89)
6:16 (6:9, M/S)	I:90; VIII:198
6:16ff (6:9ff, M/S)	II:690
6:17 (6:10, M/S)	II:906; IV:334; 335(n20); V:561n13
6:19-23 (6:12-16, M/S)	III:280n62
6:20 (6:13, M/S)	II:66; IX:498(n22); 500n39
6:21 (6:14, M/S)	III:728; 861n6
6:22 (6:15, M/S)	VIII:61; IX:502; **505**; 510
6:24ff (6:17ff, M/S)	III:307
6:25 (6:18, M/S)	IV:1045(n89); 1070n210; VIII:198
6:26 (6:19, M/S)	III:992n144; VIII:198; IX:60
6:26ff (6:19ff, M/S)	I:90
6:27 (6:20, M/S)	IV:946n10; VI:977; 979; VIII:198
6:27b (6:20b, M/S)	VI:977n3
6:28 (6:21, M/S)	VII:920
6:29 (6:22, M/S)	IX:510
6:30 (6:23, M/S)	VI:55
7	III:184
7:1	IV: 335(n20); 1045(n89)
7:1ff	III:307
7:4	IV:911
7:6	I:131; II:470; 777; VIII:198
7:8	II:53
7:9	II:690
7:10	III:343
7:11	III:1102; IV:1045(n89)
7:12	III:181; IV:436; VIII:496; IX:61; 409; 502
7:18	I:30n54; II:53; 738; IV:285; 286; 646

7:19	III:414; IX:622
7:20	V:603
7:21	III:427; V:603; VI:639
7:23-27	VII:931
7:25	V:603
7:26f	I:173
7:27	V:603
7:29	VIII:85n2
7:29ff	II:690
7:34	IX:390n134
7:35	IV:542
7:36	IX:501
7:37	IV:334; 335(n20); 1045(n89); VI:55; 299n8; VIII:85; 383n362
7:38	VII:282(n4); 283n6
8	III:307; VI:627n36; VIII:86
8:1	III:312n40; V:686n226
8:2	IV:997; IX:498
8:2ff	IV:760
8:3	III:527; VII:803; 804
8:3f	VII:804
8:4	VII:803
8:5	IV:99
8:6	IV:300; 946n10; VIII:320; IX:65
8:7	V:304
8:7-9	VIII:160
8:8	II:319
8:10	IX:497(n21); 498; 501
8:10f	VII:376
8:11	VI:979; IX:501
8:11f	IX:497(n19)
8:12	IX:498; 500n39
8:13	V:304
8:14	VII:655; IX:428
8:15	I:176; III:414; VII:376
8:18	VII:655; IX:428
8:19f	IV:557(n21)
8:21	VI:626; VIII:320
8:22	VII:655; VIII:85; IX:428
8:22ff	V:529n49
8:23f	V:546n25; VI:627n36
8:24	I:132
8:26	VIII:85
8:27	IX:60
8:28	VIII:85
8:29	VIII:85
8:30	VI:979; 980; IX:498
8:31	VIII:85; 198
8:32	II:538
8:33	VI:287; 288; 299n8; VIII:80; 81n11; 85
8:33f	VIII:80n7
8:36	IV:99
9	III:307
9:1	I:654n40; III:283; VI:660(n52); VII:507n292; 811; 821n138
9:2f	VIII:383n362
9:3	VI:660(n52)
9:4	VII:271(n12); VIII:85n2
9:5	II:545; VII:643; 804

9:5f	VII:804	11:44f	I:94
9:6	II:240(n27); 249; IV:99; V:326	11:46	IV:1045(n89); V:891
9:7	III:307	11:47	II:873
9:9	I:176; IV:946n10	12	III:308; 416(n11), (n13);
9:12	I:176		VI:130; VIII:60
9:13	IV:557(n21)	12:1ff	VIII:137
9:14	III:787; VI:626; VIII:320	12:1-5	IV:645n10
9:17	III:439; VIII:80n8	12:2	I:291; III:621n3; VI:387n307;
9:22	I:186(n2); VII:1023		VIII:410n68
9:22f	II:758	12:3	I:226; VI:73; 77; VII:14; 28;
9:23	V:326		105; 107
9:23f	II:240(n27); IV:22; VI:937	12:4	II:947; VIII:137
9:24	II:459; VII:676; VIII:419n151	12:5	III:427
10	VII:764	12:6	VI:67n46; 69n66; 306;
10:1	I:529; V:8; 10; VI:934; VIII:38		VIII:346; 347; 383n362
10:1f	V:403n150	12:6ff	V:841n14
10:2	V:603; VI:936; 940	12:7	III:414; VI:116n18
10:3	I:91; 111; II:213; 253;	12:8	III:414; VI:67(n48); 69n66,
	III:1070n174; VII:804		(n67); 891n46;VIII:383n362
10:4	V:960	13	I:270; IV:243
10:6	V:396; 398, (n118); 403n150;	13f	IV:233; 503n75
	409; VII:804	13:2	IV:232; 634n11; VI:382n265;
10:7	IX:498		817n251; VIII:407n36
10:8-10	IV:937; 940; V:615n104	13:2ff	IV:519n5; VII:105
10:9	IV:940n6; VI:136n12; 145n2;	13:3	IV:645; VIII:9
	VII:373	13:4	VIII:9
10:10	I:604n3; III:414; 427; 791	13:4f	III:419; V:455
10:11	II:66; VII:763; 764	13:6	IV:946n3
10:12f	II:690	13:7	I:108; IV:232
10:13	VIII:198	13:8	V:744
10:14	VIII:198	13:9	IV:519n5
10:15	V:455	13:10	II:852
10:16	V:394	13:10ff	VII:105
10:17	I:186n8; II:51; III:307;	13:11	III:427; V:455
	VIII:198	13:12	V:370
10:18	VIII:198	13:12f	IV:244
10:19	VII:270(n5)	13:13	III:414; VII:106
11	II:690; III:416(n14);	13:14	IV:654n10
	IV:645n11; V:187	13:15f	VIII:311n26
11-15	III:418n34; VIII:320	13:16	I:387
11:1	III:362n37; IV:110n161; 612	13:18	VII:106
11:1ff	III:427	13:19	VIII:195n53
11:9	IV:232	13:20	IV:233; 519n5; VIII:9
11:9ff	VI:599	13:21	III:419; V:455; VIII:9
11:10	II:849n116; IV:232	13:24	IV:243
11:12	IV:232	13:24ff	I:507
11:16	VII:731	13:25	IV:519n5; VIII:9
11:25	IV:946n10	13:26	III:419; V:455; VIII:9
11:28	IV:946n10	13:27	IV:519n5
11:29	V:544n9	13:28	IX:420
11:29f	III:416n15	13:31	IV:549; 550; V:455
11:32	I:535; III:416(n19); VIII:320	13:31-33	III:419
11:33	VI:149(n10); VII:359; 920	13:32	IV:550
11:33f	VI:145n2	13:33	V:455
11:34	VI:136	13:36	II:601; VI:689n6
11:35	III:411	13:37	I:351; IV:549
11:36	VI:115n15; 145n2; VII:803; 805	13:38f	I:507
11:37	VII:542	13:46	III:427
11:40	IV:300; 946n10	13:49	II:26; III:264; VII:359
11:42	III:787; V:573	13:49ff	III:201
11:43	I:598	13:52	VI:935
11:44	IV:36	13:52f	VII:359

16:15	VI:772; 977; 979; IX:61		VI:588n47; VII:106; 108;
16:15ff	II:631		VIII:71; IX:623n67
16:16	I:162; 278; III:427; 1027;	18:6ff	III:577
	VI:980	18:6-18	VI:593
16:17	III:273; 308; VIII:71	18:8	I:776
16:18	VI:980	18:10	II:893n6
16:19	III:416(n18); VI:978n10; 980	18:11	I:776; V:960
16:20	III:309; VI:980; VIII:63	18:12	IV:195; IX:623n67
16:21	I:278; 289; III:992n145; V:891;	18:12f	V:134; VII:108
	IX:428	18:14	V:960; VII:738
16:21f	V:40; 923; IX:61n6	18:15	IV:1099n2; V:891
16:21ff	III:308; 309n27; 417(n21)	18:17	IV:195; VII:105n58; 108n82;
16:22	IV:6		VIII:341
16:23	III:983	18:21	I:605; IV:61; V:255; VIII:343
16:23f	VII:689	18:24a	IV:1058
16:23ff	III:416(n18)	18:30	I:598
16:24	III:421n59; VII:1045; VIII:198	19:2	I:92; 101; 324; III:352n45;
16:26	I:510; VII:1045		IV:36; 403; V:623; VI:708;
16:27	III:992n144; VI:55; 87n48; 922;		VII:805; 829n201;
	IX:64		VIII:74n36
16:29	II:794n218; IV:927; VIII:7, n19	19:3	V:962n97; 974; VII:2; 7;
16:29f	III:414n2		IX:199; 200
16:29ff	IV:928	19:4	II:377, (n19)
16:30	III:309; 312; 414	19:5	II:59; 743
16:31	II:794n218; IV:927; VIII:7, n19	19:7	II:53; 738
16:32	III:249; VII:689; VIII:80, n9;	19:9f	VI:39; 891
	81n11; IX:497(n19)	19:10	VI:40; 731; 736; 740; 888
16:33	VII:804	19:11	III:754; VII:759n2; IX:598n42
16:34	III:309	19:12	I:605; V:178; 255, n101; 260;
17	VI:593		459; 467
17-26	I:92; 97; III:417n22; IV:1043	19:13	IV:697; 698; VI:313n19
17:2	IV:99	19:14	V:99n14; VI:751; VII:341; 345;
17:3	V:845; VI:314; VII:816n110;		356; VIII:155n3; 280, n69;
	VIII:284; IX:289n52		285; IX:202n67
17:3f	VII:931	19:15	II:175n1; 286; III:30; IV:530;
17:3-9	VII:932		V:741n5; VI:888
17:4	I:175; IV:285; 286; VII:929n24;	19:15ff	IV:1043
	1022	19:16	VI:313n19; 314; 571; 573;
17:5	VII:929n24		VIII:565
17:7	II:11; 12n86; IV:521n4;	19:16-18	**VI:314-315**
	V:292n15; VI:584; 587	19:17	I:25(n29); 270n10; II:474;
17:10	I:173; III:307; VI:773		IV:685; 688; 965; VI:314
17:10-14	VII:931	19:18	I:22n13; **25-26;** 29; 38; 753;
17:11	I:173; II:850(n125); III:307;		II:83; 442n1; 548; 549; 550;
	VI:458; VII:106; 109; 533;		III:1022n151; IV:535; 685n6;
	931; **IX:619;** 622; 632		688; 690; V:10n61; 15;
17:12	V:8		395n88; 411; VI:313n19;
17:13	VII:533		314; **315;** 316: VIII:60;
17:13f	VI:457		147n5; IX:130; 134n193
17:14	I:173; II:115; 844(n84);	19:19	II:901; VI:585; VII:442n173;
	850(n125); VI:314; 458;		IX:63
	VII:106; 109; IX:619	19:20	II:606; VI:689n6
17:15	VI:457	19:20ff	IV:730n3
17:16	VII:1045	19:23	I:212; 226; IV:402; 569;
18	VI:593; 740		VI:74n7; VII:507n293
18:1ff	IV:1043	19:23f	**VI:75**
18:3	IV:44; V:51; 269n179; VI:571;	19:23-25	VIII:132
	VIII:479	19:24	II:760; VIII:133
18:4	VI:469; 470	19:25	VI:969n22
18:5	II:854; IV:870; 1058; 1072;	19:26	VII:931
	VI:469; 470; 480; 718	19:27	VII:215; IX:98n17
18:6	I:573n51; IV:195; V:134;	19:28	I:761; III:854; VII:660; 661;

	n41; VIII:7	25:25	IV:330; 332; 335, n21; VI:380;
23:33ff	III:862		891; VII:48; 738; VIII:7n20;
23:34	VII:370; 390		IX:636n112
23:34-36	VII:390	25:26	IV:330; 335(n20); 341
23:35	III:495	25:27	IV:285; VII:1045n273;
23:36	III:495; VI:47n14		VIII:523
23:37	III:495; VII:532	25:29	IV:332; 335, (n20); VI:287;
23:39	IV:53; VIII:65		VIII:282
23:39-43	VII:390	25:29f	VI:288
23:40	II:385; VII:371	25:30	I:602; III:1098; IV:332
23:42	V:11n66	25:31	IV:285; 335
23:42f	VII:370; 390n8	25:32	IV:335
24:1	I:505(n4)	25:33	IV:332
24:2	II:470; 472; III:810n1	25:34	VI:160
24:3	III:629	25:35	II:285; V:844; 848
24:5-9	III:264; VIII:165	25:35ff	IV:1043
24:6	I:100; VIII:160	25:36	VI:277; IX:202n67
24:7	I:349	25:37	VI:277; VII:721
24:8	I:208; II:126; VII:5; 16; 22;	25:39	I:526; II:196n12; 393;
	VIII:165		III:298n4; 635; V:657n3;
24:9	VI:19; VIII:198		VI:160; 894, n74; 902n148;
24:10	I:5; 41n107; V:985n248		VIII:7, n20
24:10-16	I:622	25:40	IV:697; V:657n3; 844
24:11	I:622; III:1070; V:263; 264;	25:41	V:1022
	268; 269	25:42	V:657; VI:160
24:11-23	VIII:302	25:43	V:632; IX:202n67
24:12	VII:591n4	25:44	V:674
24:14	VI:87n48, n53; 921(n5); 922;	25:45	VII:738; VIII:346
	VII:655; 804; VIII:160;	25:46	III:775; V:632
	IX:429n26	25:46-53	V:632
24:15	I:270n10; II:51; 828n2	25:47	V:10n62; 844; 848; 850n54;
24:16	IV:1036(n39); V:255n101; 263;		VI:741n149
	268; 269, n177; 585; VII:804	25:47f	VI:160
24:17	VI:975	25:48	IV:330; 335
24:19f	IV:830	25:48f	IV:332; 350
24:20	III:853; V:377; VIII:280	25:48ff	IV:330
24:22	II:223; V:11n66	25:49	V:959; VI:588n47; VII:106;
24:23	VI:921(n5)		108; IX:246; 623n67
25	I:510; III:774; V:657n3	25:50	IV:285; 698
25:1	VII:282(n4); 283n6	25:51	IV:341
25:1ff	II:628	25:51f	IV:330
25:1-7	VII:6	25:52	IV:197; 285; 341
25:3	II:788; III:614; VIII:106(n2)	25:53	III:635; IV:697
25:4	II:788; VII:6; VIII:106(n2)	25:55	V:659n23
25:6	IV:697; V:844; VI:731; VII:6	26:1	II:383; 789; VII:821n137;
25:8	VII:7n40		IX:436
25:8f	VII:80	26:2	VII:2; IX:200
25:8ff	VI:891	26:3	II:922n81; 950n43; IV:213;
25:8-55	VII:6		VI:383; VIII:133; IX:75
25:9	I:68; VII:78	26:3ff	II:757
25:10	I:510	26:3-6	II:408
25:10f	VI:44	26:4	II:167; III:459; VI:59n3; IX:24
25:11	I:111n3	26:4f	VI:59; IX:526
25:14	III:140; 141; IX:79	26:5	VI:5n14; 132
25:17	III:140; 141; IX:202n67	26:6	II:404; VI:549; VII:922n16;
25:18	VI:470		IX:198
25:19	VI:132	26:7	VI:996n24
25:21	VI:471	26:9	II:126; VI:280; VII:641; IX:526
25:22	V:718	26:10	IV:897; V:718; IX:487n19
25:23	I:602; 680n12; V:27; 462n33;	26:11	II:126; IV:580; VII:372n27;
	847; 848; VI:160; 731		641, n8
25:24	IV:330; 341	26:11-13	VII:641

NUMBERS

6:15	IX:502	8:22	IV:220
6:18	I:97; II:341n3; VI:935	8:23	IV:220
6:19	II:777	8:24	II:653; IV:221, n19; V:838n5;
6:21	I:123; VII:697		VII:705
6:22	II:246; IV:464n27	8:25	IV:221
6:22ff	II:760	8:26	IX:238; 243
6:22-27	II:758	9:1	VII:282(n4)
6:24	II:633; VI:379; IX:237	9:2	V:897n2; IX:677
6:24-26	I:336; V:255n100; VIII:218	9:2-14	V:897n7
6:25	I:706n69; IV:23; VI:772; 778;	9:3	III:459
	IX:9; 378	9:5	VII:282(n4)
6:25f	IX:320	9:6	III:427; IX:620
6:26	I:527; II:297; 408; 409; n43,	9:7	III:459; VIII:594
	n46; 410n49; 561n1; 633;	9:10	IV:372; IX:620
	VI:772; VII:266n6	9:12	VII:921
6:26b	III:780	9:13	I:270n10; II:138; III:459; V:49;
6:27	V:255n100; IX:378		VIII:594
7	III:309	9:14	V:845, n18
7:1	VI:943n78; VII:375n38;	9:14b	V:845
	IX:497(n21); 501	9:15	IV:486; V:120n6; VII:641
7:2	II:606	9:15f	III:557
7:3ff	III:861	9:15ff	IV:905
7:5	I:378n3; IV:231	9:17	VII:641
7:8	II:66	9:19f	V:398(n118)
7:9	IV:221n18	9:20	IX:290
7:10	IX:498(n22); 501	9:22	VI:264
7:10f	III:454	9:23	II:66
7:12ff	III:860	10:1ff	VII:802n20
7:13	IV:240n17; 272; IV:509n71	10:2	II:246n55; 247; VII:76; 804
7:15	I:341n2	10:2ff	VII:79
7:18	VII:507n296	10:3	VII:802n21
7:19	I:2	10:3f	VII:81
7:24f	VII:507n296	10:3ff	VII:81
7:41f	VII:745	10:5	VII:78
7:48	II:708n7; 726n46; III:986n103;	10:5f	VII:78; 81
	VII:507n294; IX:509n71;	10:6	VII:78
	526; 527	10:7	III:528; VII:78; 81; 263n9;
7:54	II:952		802n21
7:78	III:883; VII:675n39	10:8	VII:72; 76; 78
7:84	III:454; IX:498(n22); 501	10:9	I:346; 563n13, n15; 790;
7:88	III:454; IX:498(n22); 501		III:700n13; VII:78; 79; 263;
7:89	III:318; 319; IV:486; 1042;		970; 976
	IX:282; 288n45; 438	10:10	I:348; 572n43; IV:639; VII:79;
8:2	IV:23; IX:327		84; 532n31
8:2f	VII:985	10:11	IV:486
8:4	II:20; 26	10:12	VII:282n4; 641
8:5-22	III:307	10:12-28	IX:248
8:6	VI:979	10:13	VII:803; VIII:35n10; IX:290
8:6f	VI:979	10:14ff	VIII:31
8:7	I:124; VI:977; 978; 979; VII:	10:29	I:172; III:3; 260; VIII:193; 195
	1045; VIII:320	10:29ff	I:14
8:8	VI:55n17	10:33	I:350; II:132n103
8:9	I:132; III:528; VII:803; 804	10:33ff	I:212
8:10	I:132; VII:655; VIII:160;	10:34	III:172; IV:905
	IX:428n25	10:35	I:172; 377n4; 732; II:334; 633;
8:11	III:232		III:115n354; 1065; IV:686
8:12	IX:428	10:35f	I:92; VII:229(n206)
8:15	III:232; 416(n17)	10:36	I:172; 377n4; IV:905
8:16-19	III:308n24	11	III:169; V:406; VI:655n27; 656;
8:19	III:232; IV:239(n8); VIII:82n18		n30; 657; 797n113
8:20	VII:804	11:1	I:729; 730; 733, n23;
8:21	I:123; VIII:320		V:398(n117); 400; 402;

14:15f	V:406
14:16	VII:411n20; 930
14:17	VIII:606
14:18	II:483n96; IV:376(n18); 377n30; V:405, n171; 406; VIII:132; 218; 291(n150); 343, n58; 344n58; IX:383, n81
14:19	I:510; II:480n47; IV:1110; V:565n1
14:21	II:242; 244; V:177n9; 263; 460; VI:129
14:21-23	V:460
14:22	V:326; 327; VI:27; VII:211; 212, n73; 220n137; 257
14:22f	IX:593
14:23	I:14n12; III:770; IV:898n16; VI:277n14
14:24	III:778; V:661n29; 664n44; 674; VI:118(n119); 362
14:27	I:730; 735; VI:551; VII:804; 805; IX:426n9
14:28	V:177; 460; 549
14:29	I:730; II:606
14:30	V:459n19; VII:388; IX:426
14:31	III:777
14:32	I:730; VIII:136
14:33	VI:587; IX:60
14:33f	VIII:136
14:34	II:601; IV:572
14:34ff	V:439
14:35	VI:460; VII:804; 805
14:36	I:730, n9
14:37	VI:550(n26)
14:40	VIII:193
14:41	V:112; 737; VII:696
14:42	VI:772; VII:777
14:43	VII:719
15	II:809
15:2-15	V:162
15:3	III:32; IV:543; VI:689, n8
15:4ff	III:984
15:5	VII:531
15:7	II:809; III:54; 187n28
15:8	III:32; IV:543; VII:1022
15:14	V:845; VI:738n121
15:15	VII:805
15:15f	V:845; VI:729n15
15:17-21	VI:988
15:20f	I:485
15:21	I:648
15:22	I:280; 290
15:22-24	I:115
15:22ff	III:309
15:24	VIII:342
15:25	II:470
15:25f	I:510
15:27	IX:648n195
15:29	VI:471
15:30	I:275; 280; 292; 622; III:277; 309; V:845n18; VI:471; VIII:221; 526; 527; 528;

	IX:426
15:30f	I:622
15:31	I:98; 280; 622; II:129; 218; 952; III:110n301; 313n45; IV:750
15:32	VII:3n10; VIII:240n13
15:32-36	VII:5
15:34	VII:265n27
15:35	VI:922
15:35f	VI:921(n5); VII:24
15:36	VII:804
15:37-41	I:219; II:801; 901; VII:17
15:38	II:921; IV:110n167
15:38f	III:904, n2
15:39	I:218n16; III:606; IV:559n39; 965; 966; VI:584; VII:137; 141(n318); 718; VIII:284n102
15:39f	IV:675
15:40	I:94; IV:36
15:41	I:125; II:880n11; IV:350; 1058; V:679n166
16	IV:865n203; VII:571
16:1ff	VII:802n20; 805
16:2	V:261; VII:804
16:3	III:249n2; IV:35; VII:802n21; 805; 897
16:4	VI:163n15; 772
16:5	I:94; 133; 700; 706; II:601n5; 739
16:5-7	IV:155n51
16:7	I:94; II:739; IV:155; 168
16:9	I:133; IV:60n2; 219; 220; 221; V:838; VII:804
16:10	I:133; III:249
16:11	I:730n9, n10; VII:803
16:14	III:759; 770
16:15	I:764; III:861n6; V:809
16:16	II:706
16:18	I:529
16:19	II:245; III:528; V:326
16:21	V:400; VII:805; 960
16:22	II:850(n127); V:891; 1014n412; VI:163n15; 361; 362; 368; 375n214; 393n353; 772; VII:106; 109; IX:629
16:24	VII:805
16:25	VI:655
16:26	VII:960
16:26f	VII:370; 371n18
16:27	VII:370n10; 371; 383
16:28	III:607; IX:627
16:29	II:606
16:30	I:679; II:26; III:1007; 1008; V:857n2; VI:158; 159n5; VII:370; 695
16:31ff	V:1031
16:32	VI:158; 159n5; VII:370n10; 373
16:33	III:529n90; 751n75; VII:804n27
16:33f	VII:804
16:34	VI:158
16:35	I:2; II:692; III:986; IV:22; 863n189; VIII:137, n21; 175n32; 284; IX:289n52;

	509n71		IX:52n28
16:37 (17:2, M/S)	I:111	18:20ff	III:770
16:38 (17:3, M/S)	I:111; IV:232; VII:211; 214; 215(n95)	18:21	III:776n14; IV:220; 237
		18:22	I:270n10
16:39 (17:4, M/S)	IV:466	18:24	III:759; 776n14; V:455
16:40 (17:5, M/S)	I:266; VII:214; 803; VIII:82n18	18:26	III:776n14; IV:897
16:41 (17:6, M/S)	I:730	18:27	IV:254n4; 285
16:41ff (17:6ff, M/S)	V:575n100; VII:802n20	18:28	IV:5
16:41-46	V:405	18:30	IV:254n4; 285
(17:6-11, M/S)		18:31	IV:697; VII:194
16:41-50	III:306; V:170; 402	19	IV:300n21; 762; VI:612; 978;
(17:6-15, M/S)			979n14; 980, 982, 984;
16:42 (17:7, M/S)	II:240(n27); IV:905; V:326; 469		VII:938; VIII:225; 321
16:44ff (17:9ff, M/S)	V:406n176	19:2	III:313n51; IV:762n7; 1045n90;
16:45 (17:10, M/S)	V:400; VII:211; 802n21; 805		V:286; 578n124; VI:952;
16:45ff (17:10ff, M/S)	IV:612		VII:593; VIII:403n19
16:46 (17:11, M/S)	II:679; V:396; 398(n118);	19:2-10	VI:979
	399n126; 400; 407; VII:803;	19:3	VIII:198
	805	19:4	VI:977n5; 979; 982n32
16:46ff (17:11ff, M/S)	IV:1042	19:6	III:812, n2; 813; 992n145;
16:47 (17:12, M/S)	VII:802n21; VIII:229		VI:980n17; 982n30; VII:453;
16:48 (17:13, M/S)	III:273		580
16:49 (17:14, M/S)	V:401(n141)	19:7f	IV:300; VII:1045
17:1ff (17:16ff, M/S)	IV:466; VII:951	19:9	VI:978; VIII:198; 320
17:1-11	I:3; VI:969	19:9ff	III:417n20
(17:16-26, M/S)		19:11	III:416(n12); 419n44; 421
17:2 (17:17, M/S)	V:1016; VI:967	19:11-22	III:418n34
17:5 (17:20, M/S)	I:730; 736; IV:169	19:12	I:123
17:6 (17:21, M/S)	VIII:348n88	19:13	III:427; VI:977, n3; 978; 979;
17:7 (17:22, M/S)	IV:486		VIII:320; IX:620; **621**
17:7ff (17:22ff, M/S)	III:309	19:14	VIII:407n36
17:8 (17:23, M/S)	IV:486	19:15	V:615
17:10 (17:25, M/S)	I:3; 736; IV:612; VI:970;	19:16	II:847(n107); VI:738
	VIII:346	19:17	II:467; VII:359; 676; VIII:320
17:12f (17:27f, M/S)	IV:612	19:18	VI:977n3; 978; 979; 980n17
17:13 (17:28, M/S)	VIII:52	19:18f	VIII:320
18:1	I:3n1; III:251; VII:37n14	19:19	VI:977n3; 978; 979
18:2	IV:486; IX:246n11	19:20	VI:977, n3; 978; 979; VIII:320
18:2ff	IV:239(n8)	19:20f	VIII:320
18:3	III:863n16; V:689n263;	19:21	VI:977n3; 978; VIII:320
	VIII:82n18	19:22	III:427; 802n38
18:4	II:683; IV:221	20	VI:97, n29
18:5	III:308n24; V:396; 398(n118);	20:1	VII:802n21; 804
	400	20:1ff	VII:802n20
18:6	IV:221	20:2	VII:802n21
18:7	III:629; VII:37n14	20:2ff	V:575n100
18:8	IX:364	20:2-5	V:1030
18:8ff	III:182	20:2-13	V:575
18:8-12	I:485	20:4	III:528; VII:802n21; 804; 805
18:8-19	III:1102	20:5	VI:136(n8); 549; VII:752n15
18:9	I:268n2; VI:934	20:6	II:240(n27); V:326;
18:10	I:90		VII:802n21; VIII:419n151
18:15	I:485; IV:331; VI:872; 875;	20:7ff	IV:272
	VII:106	20:7-11	VI:146(n10); VIII:318
18:15-17	IV:333	20:7-13	VII:518n376
18:15ff	VI:873	20:8	III:527; VII:802n21; 803
18:16	III:303; IV:335	20:8f	VI:967
18:17	II:809	20:10	IV:840; VI:10(n2) VII:802n21;
18:18	II:138n18; 669n18		803
18:19	I:228, n6; II:114n39; IV:235	20:11	III:991; IV:860; VI:136(n8);
18:20	I:157n16; 191n11; II:823;		VII:802n21; 804
	III:759; 776n14; VII:628;	20:12	I:111; V:671n98; VI:187; 191;

	V:329; 370; VIII:550, n32, n41
24:5	VII:375
24:6	V:766n3; VII:375
24:6b	VII:541
24:7	I:575; 791n14; V:864; VI:540; VIII:318; 404n24; 410n67; 517; IX:510; 520
24:8	II:244; III:81n73; V:98
24:9	III:595
24:10	V:395; VIII:217
24:11	VIII:195; 594n14
24:13	VI:300n9; 550n27; IX:627
24:14	II:698; 947; IV:33; VIII:53; 195
24:15	V:329n74; 749; VIII:340
24:15ff	II:454
24:15-19	VI:797
24:16	III:81n73; 577; IV:94; 137; V:329; 370; VIII:550, n32, n41
24:17	I:352; 353; 505, n19; 640; II:29; 330, n1; 659; 932n29; IV:364; 366; 616n68; V:338n113; 481n71; VI:824; VIII:410n67; IX:510; 523, n189; 527
24:17a	IX:513
24:17ff	IX:524
24:18	V:404
24:20	IV:162; 365n33; VII:540
24:20-23	V:749
24:21	V:263
24:22	V:724n13; 725n18
24:23	I:524n5; III:81n73
25	III:305f; 917; IV:854; V:403
25:1	I:524, n1; III:802; VI:584; VII:344n31
25:1f	VII:345; VIII:506
25:1ff	I:524n1; IV:165n94; VI:594
25:1-5	V:407
25:2	II:377(n22)
25:3	IV:814; V:398(n117); VIII:58; 59
25:4	II:32; III:917; V:398(n117); 410; VII:720
25:5	IV:814; 828; VIII:59
25:5ff	II:884n7
25:5-11	II:885
25:6	I:132
25:6-11	V:407
25:6-13	II:878
25:7ff	VI:698
25:7-13	V:398(n118)
25:8	II:446
25:9	V:401(n141); IX:469n25
25:9-11	V:405
25:11	II:879; 884; V:407n183
25:11-13	III:306
25:12	II:408; 933n37, n38
25:12f	II:126; IX:511; 512; 519
25:13	II:884; III:251; V:686, n234; VII:534

25:17	III:140
26	II:601
26:2	VII:804
26:2-51	VI:508(n38)
26:5-51	IX:247; 248
26:9	VII:805
26:9f	VII:805
26:10	II:692; VI:158; VII:209; 220
26:18	II:606
26:22	II:606
26:43	II:606
26:47	II:606
26:52ff	III:759; 771
26:52-56	III:770
26:54	VI:264
26:55	III:759(n6)
26:56	III:759(n6)
26:61	V:10
26:62	III:770
26:64	VII:282n4
27	III:771; IX:433n55
27:1-3	VIII:342
27:1ff	III:770
27:1-11	III:775; V:253; VIII:343n56
27:2	VII:641
27:3	VII:805
27:5	I:132
27:7	III:760
27:8	I:781; III:778
27:11	III:776; VII:108; IX:246
27:12	I:515n3; III:989n112; V:532n292
27:13	VI:572(n33)
27:14	I:111; V:417n249; VI:126; VIII:318
27:15ff	IV:428
27:15-23	IX:429n28; 433n55
27:16	II:602; 605; 615; 844(n88); 850n126; III:137n13; V:891; 1014n412; VI:361; 362; 368; 375n214; 393n353; 490; VII:106; 109; IX:433n55; 629
27:17	III:528; VI:489n45; 490; 500; 690; VII:805
27:18	II:540; 819n25; III:889; VI:363; 406n473; 433n670; VII:655; VIII:160; IX:429n28; 433n55
27:18-20	IX:429; 625
27:19	VII:641; IX:433n55
27:20	II:246, n54
27:21	IV:237
27:21-33	IX:429
27:22	VII:641
27:23	VII:655; VIII:160; IX:433n55
28	II:809; III:309; VI:45n4; 47n22
28f	II:66; 467
28:2	I:764
28:4	VI:470
28:6	VII:282n4
28:7	VII:531n22
28:7-10	VII:532
28:8	II:809; III:187n28; VI:470

28:9	IV:1059	31:23	I:536n34; VI:399n418; 935; 978
28:9f	VII:5; 16; 23; 532	31:27	VII:804
28:10	VII:7n39	31:28	I:764; VIII:51; 52; 99n115;
28:11	IV:639		IX:79
28:14	VII:532	31:28ff	VI:689
28:14f	VII:532	31:35	I:697
28:15	III:309(n31)	31:36	VII:705
28:16f	II:902; V:898(n16)	31:37	VIII:99n115
28:22	III:309, (n31)	31:37-41	VIII:52; IX:79
28:24	VII:532	31:48-54	III:305
28:25	III:495	31:50	VIII:240n13
28:26	VI:45; 46	32:1	II:38; VIII:199
28:27ff	VI:46n7	32:1a	VI:277
28:30	III:309, (n31)	32:1b	VI:277
28:31	VII:532	32:6	VI:570
29	II:809; III:309	32:7	VII:718
29:1	VII:78; 80	32:8f	IV:974
29:5	III:309, (n31)	32:10-14	V:398(n118)
29:6	VII:532	32:11	I:14n12; VI:188(n119);
29:7	II:794n218; IV:927, n18; 928;		VIII:136
	IX:640n141	32:13	VI:551; VIII:136
29:7-11	III:992n144	32:14	IV:434; V:409
29:11	III:309(n31)	32:14ff	VIII:136
29:11ff	VII:532	32:15	VII:719
29:16	III:309(n31)	32:16	VI:523; IX:51n23
29:19	III:309(n31)	32:17f	VIII:195, n51
29:22	III:309(n31)	32:18	III:759
29:25	III:309(n31)	32:18f	III:770
29:28	III:309(n31)	32:19	III:759
29:31	III:309(n31)	32:24	VI:523; 579; IX:51n23
29:34	III:309(n31)	32:26	VI:523
29:35	I:754n20; VI:47n14	32:32	III:778
29:36-39	VII:532	32:34	VI:523
29:38	III:309(n31)	32:36	IX:51n23
29:39	VII:1022; 1023	32:38	VI:523
29:40 (30, M/S)	V:452n2	32:39	III:778
30:2 (30:3, M/S)	V:178, n17; 467	32:42	V:262; VI:522; 523
30:2f (30:3f, M/S)	III:864n23; 866	33:4	V:940; VIII:268
30:2-15	IX:622n64	33:8f	VI:123
(30:3-16, M/S)		33:15f	VII:282n4
30:3 (30:4, M/S)	V:467	33:16	III:170
30:4 (30:5, M/S)	IV:575	33:17	III:170
30:4f (30:5f, M/S)	VII:641n6	33:21	I:568
30:6 (30:7, M/S)	II:777; VII:593	33:38	V:104; VI:312; VII:698;
30:7 (30:8, M/S)	VII:641n6		VIII:136
30:9 (30:10, M/S)	IX:446f	33:50-54	III:770
30:11 (30:12, M/S)	VII:641n6	33:52	II:377(n14); III:778
30:12 (30:13, M/S)	III:1099n1	33:53	III:778
30:13 (30:14, M/S)	IV:927n18; 928; IX:640n141	33:53f	III:759
30:13f (30:14f, M/S)	VI:293; VII:641n6	33:53ff	III:759
31:2	II:443; 445	33:54	III:759(n6); 771; 778; V:262
31:3	II:446	33:55	III:140; VII:411, n16
31:8	I:524, n8	34	V:109
31:10	VI:523	34:2	III:759; 770; 778; VI:578
31:14	II:614; V:394	34:6	V:452
31:16	I:524, n9; III:528; V:417n250;	34:6f	IV:529
	VI:594; VII:345; 804; 805	34:10ff	VI:610
31:18	I:697	34:13	III:759(n6); 771
31:19-24	III:418n34	34:14f	III:759
31:20	VII:57n6, n7	34:14-18	III:770
31:21	IV:1045n90	34:17	III:776
31:22ff	III:417n20	34:29	III:770

DEUTERONOMY

2:21	II:365n6	4:13	I:744; II:126; IV:98
2:25	V:261; IX:199; 204	4:14	III:771; IV:401
2:26	II:407n37; 418	4:15	V:331; 332n85; VI:361;
2:29	III:771		VII:282(n5)
2:30	III:607; V:1023; 1026n5; 1030;	4:15f	II:382
	VI:362; IX:630, n86	4:16	V:191; VI:468; IX:96; 98
2:34	IV:195; 196; 996	4:16ff	II:383; V:191
2:37	VII:4n17	4:17	II:33
3:1	V:48	4:18	VI:598
3:3	IV:195; 196; 198; VII:540n14	4:19	II:292; 365n6; III:880; IV:35;
3:5	VI:523		60; 164; 640; V:506; 966;
3:11	IV:197		VI:235; 761(n34), (n36);
3:13	IV:284n2		VII:705
3:18	III:771; VI:772; VIII:346	4:20	II:292; III:772; IV:35; 36; 164;
3:20	III:627; 771		VIII:53
3:21	V:326	4:21	III:771
3:23	II:785(n121); III:751n75;	4:21f	VI:812
	IV:105n143; 437; 1056;	4:23	II:105; 126; VII:4n17
	VIII:479; IX:379; 388n110	4:24	I:212; III:88; IV:22; V:660;
3:23ff	IV:612		VI:937; 945; VII:678n51
3:24	I:469n2; 640; II:26; 292;	4:25	V:403(n152); VI:551
	301n62; 640; III:174n12; 397;	4:25f	VII:270(n4)
	887n68; IV:627n7; 854n89;	4:26	III:771; IV:511; V:510
	856n105; V:513n119;	4:27	IV:36; 204; V:172
	659n25; 680n179; 686, n227;	4:27f	VII:419
	VI:539n17; IX:427	4:28	II:377(n25); 645; IV:60; 269n9;
3:25	IX:207		V:324
3:26	I:465n2; 466, n6; III:295, n13;	4:29	II:790n186; III:141; 142;
	989n112; V:671n98;		VI:193n139; IX:628n81; 633
	VII:324n179; 815	4:30	II:947; VII:725; IX:284
3:28	I:481n13; III:771; 777;	4:31	II:126; IV:36
	V:777n17; 778	4:32	I:679; II:947; III:1008; 1027;
3:29	III:449n13; 1023n159		V:503; 516; 604
4	IV:35	4:32ff	IV:333; 1040
4:1	II:106n5; 147; 220; 678n6;	4:33	V:332n85; IX:284
	III:771; VII:271	4:34	I:640, n1; II:676; III:32; 572;
4:1f	V:561; VII:271(n13)		IV:36; V:371; VII:4n17;
4:2	VI:293n44; VII:270(n2);		210(n65); 211; 212; 218;
	IX:239; 241n31		IX:201; 427
4:3	I:211; V:291; 326; 891	4:34f	VII:215n97
4:4	VII:271, (n13); 764n13	4:35	II:352n82; III:82; 1080
4:5	II:27; 29; 106n5; 136, n12; 220;	4:36	V:256; 506(n72); 607; 611;
	III:771; VII:4n17		IX:284; 292
4:6	I:706n69; VI:469;	4:36-40	VII:271(n11)
	VII:477(n89), (n90); 486	4:37	II:291; IV:35; 163; 539;
4:6ff	IV:165		IX:134n191; 625
4:7	II:330	4:38	III:771
4:7ff	IV:36	4:39	I:698; III:887n68; IV:965;
4:8	II:220		V:507; 513n119; VII:271(n9)
4:9	V:326; 647; VII:492n188; 764;	4:40	II:220; III:771; IX:585n17
	VIII:343; IX:628n81	4:41	V:454; 455
4:9f	VII:764	4:41ff	IV:301
4:10	II:137; 546; III:527; IV:401;	4:42	IV:685
	427n90; VI:411; VII:282(n5);	4:44	II:810n13; IV:99; 1046;
	643; VIII:345; IX:201		VIII:162
4:11	III:967; IV:902; V:509;	4:45	IV:99; 486
	VII:428n40, n42	5	II:36; VI:313; VII:3
4:11f	IX:284	5:1	III:1080; IV:401; 427n90;
4:12	IV:746n17; V:191; 331; 332n85;		V:547
	335; IX:284; 292; 295n80;	5:1ff	II:628; IV:430(n118)
	296, n88; 297	5:2	VII:282(n5)
4:12f	IX:284	5:2f	IV:165

	IV:36; 1041; VI:185; IX:238; 383, n80, n82; 468
7:10	IV:685; 687; VI:771
7:11	II:220
7:12	II:480(n37); IX:383n82
7:12ff	IV:1040
7:13	I:33; 38; III:771; VI:689
7:14	I:28; III:857n14; V:482n78
7:15	IV:686; 1091; VI:550; VIII:160; 310n17
7:16	IV:60; VI:510n73; 749n28; VII:342
7:18	IV:675; 678; VII:4n17; 215; IX:200
7:18f	VII:214
7:19	I:640, n1; II:365n6; VI:29n35; VII:4n17; 210(n65); 211; 212; 218; VIII:119n40; 123
7:20	IV:197
7:21	III:912
7:25	IV:164; VI:883; 935; VII:341n16
7:25f	III:255; 256; VI:510n73
7:26	I:354; VIII:304
8:1	II:546; III:771
8:2	II:546; 658; IV:675; V:50; VI:25; VII:4n17; VIII:136
8:2f	VI:19(n50); VIII:9
8:2-6	V:607n61
8:3	I:644; II:845; 850, (n132); III:315; IV:462; 463n9; 860n152; VI:16; 19; 579; VII:696; 698; VIII:71; 81; 431n234
8:3b	VI:35
8:4	V:718; VIII:136
8:5	I:34; 698; IV:166, n97; V:607; 608; 611; 970; VIII:352; IX:138n222
8:6	II:546; V:51; 52; VI:571; IX:201
8:7	VI:115n17; 579; VIII:318
8:8	II:471; IV:553n15
8:9	VI:889; 891
8:9-17	II:756
8:10	II:758; 760; III:771; VI:136n9
8:11	II:546
8:14	III:606; VIII:607
8:15	II:227; V:572; 575; VI:97n28; VII:420; VIII:318; IX:200
8:16	II:948n23; IV:462; VIII:9
8:16f	VI:509(n58)
8:17	III:612; 906; IV:539
8:17f	II:293
8:18	II:126; IV:675; VII:4n17; 271(n13); 641
8:19	I:211n10; II:789n169; IV:60; V:510; VI:761(n36); VII:270(n4)
8:20	IX:284
9	V:406
9:1	III:778; 1080; V:811; VI:389;

	523; VII:271(n9); IX:97
9:2	I:697n31; VI:772
9:3	VI:937; 945; VII:271(n10); 720
9:3ff	VII:270(n4); 271(n13)
9:4	III:612; 771
9:5	II:106; 126; 128; III:607; 771; IV:35; 99; 165; 1040; V:493; VI:772; VII:642
9:6	III:613; IV:35; 165; V:1029; IX:625
9:7	IV:675; V:857n2; VI:10n1; VII:4n17; VIII:194
9:8	V:398(n119); 400; 857n2; VII:282(n5)
9:8f	IV:612
9:9	II:132n103; 658; 690; IV:871; 927; 931; VI:136; 846; VIII:137; 318
9:10	I:513; 744; 745n15; II:20; III:504; 527; 529n90; VI:411
9:11	II:126; 132n103
9:12	V:51; 52; 737; IX:99
9:13	I:381; III:613; V:1029; IX:625
9:14	V:171; 252
9:15	II:107; IV:486n30; V:509; IX:284
9:16	IV:760; V:51; 325; 737
9:18	II:658; IV:871; V:403(n152); VI:136; 846; VIII:137; 318
9:18ff	VI:812
9:19	III:974; V:396; 400; 406; 409; 857n3; IX:198; 297n92
9:20	V:398; 406
9:21	IV:760; VI:992
9:22	III:170; V:857n2; VI:27; 126
9:23	II:432; VI:187; 191; 197
9:23f	VI:10n1
9:24	I:697n31; IV:148
9:25	V:400; VIII:137
9:26	I:107; 639; II:291; 777; III:397; 402; 772; IV:148; 331; 333; VII:4n17; IX:427
9:26ff	IV:612
9:26-29	II:796n226
9:27	I:293; III:191n1; IV:675; V:663; 1029
9:29	I:639; II:291; III:402; 760; 772; VII:4n17
10:1	II:198n31; 938n78; IV:615; 853n80; 855n96; VIII:304
10:3	VII:96n19
10:4	I:749; III:529n90; IV:98
10:6	III:249
10:8	II:132n103; 758; IV:148; 220; 235; 237; V:260; 838
10:9	II:823; III:759; 776n14; IV:237
10:10	III:47(n34); VIII:137; IX:98
10:11	III:771; 778
10:12	I:28n39; 29; 191; IV:60; 61; 1041; VI:571; IX:201; 628n81
10:12f	IV:62; V:51
10:12ff	IV:61; 65

10:13	II:546	11:21	III:771; IV:1054; V:503
10:14	V:502; 503(n48); 507; 511; 512; 890	11:22	I:28n41; 29; 60; 753n13; III:789n18; IV:1057; V:51;
10:14-16	I:28		52; 980, n220; IV:571;
10:14ff	I:33		VIII:141; IX:678n19
10:15	I:22n8; IV:163; 169; 170	11:23	I:527; III:778
10:16	I:226; 540; III:607; 612n21;	11:23ff	VI:509(n58)
	613; V:1028; 1029; 1030;	11:24	III:405; V:941; VI:599n33;
	1031; VI:73; 77n32; IX:628		610n28; 626, n33; VIII:193
10:17	III:30; 86; IV:379; 538; V:273;	11:25	III:32n21; 771; VI:772; IX:199;
	VI:779; 780; IX:201		200; 204
10:17f	VI:732	11:26	IV:1058; V:59, n49, n51, n52;
10:18	I:30(n57); II:580n35; III:927;		94; VII:270(n3), (n4)
	930; V:10; 14n89; 488n4;	11:26ff	II:757
	VI:732; 738; IX:445; 446	11:28	I:120; IV:60, n2; V:51; 52;
10:18f	V:5n25; 10; 16		59n51; 86; VI:235; 236(n41),
10:19	I:26n32; III:930; V:21; VI:315;		(n42)
	731	11:29	III:771; V:479; 481
10:20	IV:60; 1041; V:177n8; 459;	11:30	V:48n23; VIII:603n14
	IX:201	11:31	III:771
10:21	III:646; 648; IV:531n10; IX:201	12	III:802; V:255n97; VII:932
10:22	VI:276n13; 277	12:1	III:771
11:1	I:29n49; IV:61; IX:134n191;	12:2	III:88; 777; IV:60; VIII:197
	385	12:2-9	V:482
11:2	I:698; IV:541; V:607; 611;	12:5	I:92; II:739; IV:610; V:256;
	VII:4n17; 1100; IX:427		264; 506(n73); VI:524;
11:2f	VII:215n97		VIII:197
11:2ff	VII:271(n12), (n13)	12:5-7	VIII:197n66
11:3	II:640, n18; IV:1059; VI:460;	12:5ff	II:794n208
	VII:212n73; 226n177;	12:5-26:2	IV:169
	VIII:119	12:6	V:204; VI:689
11:4	IV:1108n16	12:6f	IX:363
11:5	VIII:194	12:7	I:529; III:802; IX:363
11:6	VII:370; VIII:580; 582n102;	12:8	VII:271(n14)
	583	12:9	I:107; III:771; IV:1107
11:7	II:640; V:326	12:9f	VII:34
11:9	III:771	12:10	III:771; VI:5n14
11:10	I:141n1; IV:66; 1056;	12:11	II:793; IV:182; V:256; 263;
	V:976n180; VI:578;		506(n73); VI:524; VIII:197
	VII:507n290	12:12	I:781; 786; III:802; V:657(n9);
11:10f	VIII:318		VII:4n18
11:10-17	VI:15	12:13	VIII:197n65
11:11	V:542n2; VI:138; VIII:318	12:14	II:739; IV:163n92; VIII:97n65,
11:12	I:29; II:602; III:787; V:376;		n66
	VIII:65	12:15	III:1102; IX:621
11:13	I:29; 43n117; II:142; III:187;	12:15f	VII:932
	611; 919; IV:143; 225; 403;	12:16	VI:457; VII:533; VIII:322
	V:52; IX:628n81	12:17	II:471; V:204
11:13-21	I:218; II:801; 901; VII:17	12:18	I:529; III:802; V:657(n9); 845;
11:14	IX:676		VII:4n18
11:16	II:789n169; 921; III:607; IV:60;	12:19	IX:585
	V:270n182; 417n248	12:20	III:169n21; 609; VII:404n8;
11:16f	V:403		IX:632
11:17	III:614; V:398n119; VII:879;	12:20ff	IX:621
	880	12:20-25	VII:932
11:18	I:291; II:924; IV:636n5;	12:21	III:169n21; V:506(n73)
	VI:684n1; VII:153; 155; 219;	12:23	I:173; II:115; 850(n125);
	661n30; 1095n5; IX:632		III:307n23; V:879; VI:457;
11:19	II:137; III:1022n154; V:646;		**IX:619-620** (620n55); 622;
	647; VIII:71		636
11:19ff	VII:492n188	12:23-13:19	V:403
11:20	I:744; VIII:343	12:24	VII:533; VIII:322

12:25	VI:470
12:26	V:263; VIII:197n66
12:27	VII:533
12:28	I:558n5; III:544
12:29	III:777; VI:509(n58)
12:30	II:154; VII:341n16
12:31	IV:686; VI:935; VIII:343
12:32 (13:1, M/S)	IX:239
13:1 (13:2, M/S)	IV:99; VI:234; VII:210; 241; VIII:123
13:1f (13:2f, M/S)	VI:234; 241; VII:210(n65), (n66); 216n103; 218; VIII:119n38; 123
13:1ff (13:2ff, M/S)	V:230; VIII:551
13:1-5 (13:2-6, M/S)	VI:807
13:2 (13:3, M/S)	I:120; VII:212n74
13:3 (13:4, M/S)	I:23; 29; IX:628n81
13:4 (13:5, M/S)	I:211; 212; V:291; VI:571; VIII:168
13:4f (13:5f, M/S)	VI:813, n211
13:5 (13:6, M/S)	IV:60; 331; 333; V:51; VI:234; 236;(n42); 550(n30); VII:4n17
13:6 (13:7, M/S)	I:776; III:347; 824; 825n3; V:777n17; 817n5; 961n94; 964n109; VI:313, n18; 315n32; IX:152n54; 154; 156
13:6ff (13:7ff, M/S)	IV:834; 1040
13:6-18 (13:7-19, M/S)	VII:280
13:7 (13:8, M/S)	I:679; IV:372; V:516
13:8 (13:9, M/S)	VI:469
13:9 (13:10, M/S)	V:963n106
13:9f (13:10f, M/S)	IV:1037
13:11 (13:12, M/S)	IX:200
13:13 (13:14, M/S)	I:607, n4; VIII:346
13:14 (13:15, M/S)	I:233
13:15 (13:16, M/S)	I:356; IV:525n12
13:16 (13:17, M/S)	V:175n2; VI:934; 935
13:17 (13:18, M/S)	I:354; II:481, (n54); V:406; VII:720
13:18 (13:19, M/S)	IX:284
14	V:187
14:1	I:31n61; II:847(n105); III:854; IV:41, n50; 42; 225; V:652; 970; 971; VII:948n77; VIII:110, n7; 351; 352; 354; 355; 359
14:1f	VII:661
14:2	I:107n63; III:249n2; 772; IV:35; 43, n61; 55; 159; 168; 169; V:891; VI:57, (n6); 58; 772
14:3ff	II:690
14:4ff	IV:645n11
14:7ff	III:416(n14)
14:8	VII:1045
14:9	IV:232
14:10	IV:232
14:13	II:758
14:15	VII:731
14:21	III:249n2; IV:35; 43n61; V:8;

	14n89; 844; 845n22; VI:457; 522; 728; 731
14:22f	IV:66; IX:201
14:23	III:109; IV:163n92; 401; V:256; VIII:197n66
14:23f	V:263; 506(n73)
14:24	IV:372; V:256; VI:524; IX:60
14:24ff	IV:1041
14:25	VIII:197n66
14:27	V:845n22
14:29	II:649(n46); V:9; VI:735, n85; 900; IX:447
15:1	VII:6; VIII:53n28
15:1ff	I:510; VI:891
15:2	V:14n91; 560; 565; VI:313n18; IX:31
15:2f	I:194; IV:1041; VI:642
15:2-11	VII:6
15:3	VI:728; 899n120
15:4	III:771; 796; VI:891; 895; 896
15:5	IX:284
15:7	IV:1041; VII:721n10
15:7-11	VI:891
15:8	VIII:594
15:9	I:272n17; 607; IV:1041; VII:19; 721n10; IX:239
15:10	II:649(n46); III:606
15:11	VI:39, n13; 888; 895
15:11f	IV:1041
15:12	IV:60; VI:160
15:12ff	VI:891
15:13	I:406
15:14	VI:689
15:15	IV:331; 333; 675; VII:4n17
15:16f	VII:660
15:17	I:209; V:546, n26
15:18	IV:60; 697
15:19ff	VI:873
15:20	IV:163n92; 610; VIII:197n66
15:21	IV:830; VI:549; VIII:280, n71, n73
15:23	VII:533; VIII:322
16	V:898n12; VI:47n19
16:1	V:897n2, n7
16:1-8	II:902
16:2	III:181; V:263; 897n8; VI:689; VIII:197n66
16:3	II:903n10; 904; III:5; 733, n41; IV:675; VII:4n17; 562
16:3f	II:902; 906
16:5f	III:181; V:897n8
16:5-7	V:898
16:6	V:263
16:6f	III:181n2
16:8	VI:46n9; 47n14
16:9	III:766; VI:45, n4
16:9ff	VI:47n19
16:10	VI:45
16:10f	VI:729
16:11	V:256; 263; 845n22; VI:45; IX:447
16:11f	VII:4n18

	VI:313n18	21:19	VIII:193n44; 194
19:15	I:272; 293; IV:483; 490, n49 452, 498; 500; VII:641n6; 648; 698; **VIII:221,** n36	21:21	V:900; 964n107; 971; VI:550; IX:200
		21:22	I:272; III:917; V:39, n12
19:15-21	I:272	21:22f	VII:574; VIII:303; 509
19:16	VII:187	21:23	I:450; II:847(n107); III:771;
19:16ff	IV:483		917; 918; V:39; VII:574;
18:17	I:272n16; 421		1045; VIII:307n85
19:18	IV:483	21:23f	IV:685
19:18f	IV:1041	22:1	VI:234
19:19	VI:550	22:1-4	**I:26**
19:20	IX:200	22:3	II:284
19:21	III:853; V:377; VIII:280	22:4	VII:25n198; 26n203
20:1	IV:34; VII:775	22:5	VII:359; 687n2; 689n16; IX:238
20:2-4	VII:976n40	22:6	II:758
20:3	III:606; 1080	22:6f	VIII:342
20:3f	VII:976n40	22:7	II:758
20:4	VI:508(n42); VII:775; 970; 976	22:8	VI:469; VIII:536n57
20:5	III:454; VI:657; VIII:132n58	22:9	I:111; 685; IX:63
20:5ff	VII:725	22:10	II:538; V:284; 287(n25);
20:8	III:606; VI:657; IX:200; 201n64		VII:442n173
20:10	II:403(n21); III:490; 530	22:12	III:904, n2; VIII:132
20:11	II:418; 769	22:13	IV:685; VI:591n72
20:13	IV:525n12	22:13ff	I:24
20:15	IV:372; VI:460	22:13-19	IV:516
20:16	III:771; VI:364; 368; 452; IX:618	22:13-21	VI:657
		22:14	V:252; VI:549; 552n34
20:16f	VI:509(n58)	22:15	VI:657
20:17	I:356; III:412n7; VII:4n17	22:16	IV:685
20:18	VI:468; 509(n59); 510n73	22:18	V:604n45; 608
20:19	III:858; VII:879n25; IX:97	22:19	II:889n10; V:270n189; VI:549; 552n34; IX:585
21:1	III:771; 778		
21:1ff	IV:1037	22:20	I:233
21:1-9	VI:657	22:21	VI:469; 550; 585; IX:227
21:2	VI:657	22:22	IV:1100n8; VI:550, (n30); VII:366
21:3	V:286		
21:5	II:758; IV:155; 219; V:262; 838	22:22ff	IV:730
21:6	IV:946; VIII:320	22:23	V:832
21:6-8	VII:272	22:23f	I:363
21:6ff	III:417n22	22:23ff	I:781; VI:585n36
21:6-9	III:812n2	22:24	I:776; IV:1099(n5); 1100n8; VI:550; 921(n5); VIII:7
21:7	VI:382; VII:533		
21:7f	IV:1041; VI:382	22:26	I:272n17
21:8	III:302; 304; IV:331; 333; VI:388n313	22:27	VII:987
		22:28	V:637; 832
21:8a	VI:382	22:29	VIII:7; IX:585
21:8b	VI:382	23 (23:2-26, M/S)	III:528
21:11	I:22n8	23:1 (23:2, M/S)	III:853; 854; 855; IX:98
21:13	III:722; VII:366	23:1f (23:2f; M/S)	VI:588
21:14	I:22n6; III:45n10; VII:7	23:1ff (23:2ff, M/S)	III:527; 529n90; V:11
21:15	IV:685; VI:591n72	23:1-8 (23:2-9, M/S)	II:766; VI:585n38
21:15f	IV:689; IX:124n115	23:2 (23:3, M/S)	IV:433n143; 732; VI:585
21:15-17	IV:690, n23; VI:588; VIII:343; IX:129n157	23:4 (23:5, M/S)	IV:697; IV:578
		23:4f (23:5f, M/S)	I:524
21:15ff	I:24; 34n72; IV:685, n7	23:5 (23:6, M/S)	I:33n69; II:756; VII:729
21:16	III:771; 775; 777; VI:875	23:6 (23:7, M/S)	II:402(n19); 418; IX:74
21:17	I:103; III:439; VI:872n8; 875; VIII:343	23:7 (23:8, M/S)	V:844; VI:728; 731
		23:7f (23:8f, M/S)	V:846
21:18	I:223; IV:840; V:604n45; 616; 971	23:8 (23:9, M/S)	VIII:218
		23:9 (23:10, M/S)	VI:551
21:18ff	IV:916; V:975	23:9ff (23:10ff, M/S)	I:92
21:18-21	V:613; 963; VI:657; VIII:343	23:11 (23:12, M/S)	IV:300; 946n10; VII:1045n273

23:13 (23:14, M/S)	V:551		25:12	III:859
23:14 (23:15, M/S)	I:92; V:942		25:13	IV:649
23:15 (23:16, M/S)	V:657(n8); VIII:168		25:14	III:984n91
23:16 (23:17, M/S)	III:140; 141		25:14f	IV:632
23:17 (23:18, M/S)	I:92; IV:814; VI:584, n28; 586;		25:15	II:184(n5)
	VII:858; VIII:58; 59		25:17	V:50; VII:4n17
23:17f (23:18f, M/S)	VI:586		25:18	VI:15; IX:201n64
23:18 (23:19, M/S)	II:561n3		25:19	III:771; V:261; VII:34
23:19 (23:20, M/S)	VI:891; VII:721		26	V:506
23:20 (23:21, M/S)	VI:728		26:1	III:771
23:21 (23:22, M/S)	I:272n17; II:277		26:1f	VIII:197n66
23:21ff (23:22ff, M/S)	III:864n23; V:178		26:2	I:485; V:263; 506(n73); VII:280
23:23 (23:24, M/S)	VI:469; 579		26:3	III:771; VII:271(n11)
23:24f (23:25f, M/S)	III:864n25; VI:313n18; 891		26:3-10	VI:47
23:25 (23:26, M/S)	VII:21		26:5	VI:277
24:1	I:617; 783; IV:105; 733; VI:591;		26:5ff	II:794; **VII:216-217**
	592n72; 639; VII:366; IX:380		26:5-8	VII:217
24:1ff	I:24		26:5-11	VIII:496n50
24:3	I:617; IV:685, n7; VI:592n72		26:6	III:484; V:506(n73); VIII:7;
24:4	III:771			160
24:5	VI:638; 767; VII:705		26:7	III:141; VIII:10; IX:281; 282
24:6	VI:891		26:8	I:640; II:291; III:32; 402;
24:7	III:754, n1; VI:314n24; 550,			V:371; VII:4n17; 210(n65);
	(n30)			211; 212; 218; VIII:123;
24:8	III:262; IV:519n5			IX:201; 427
24:9	V:50; VII:4n17		26:9	III:771
24:10	V:560n7; 565; VI:313n18		26:10	I:485; III:771; VI:761(n33)
24:11	VII:641		26:11	V:506(n73)
24:12	VI:647n11; 888		26:12	VI:900; VIII:63; IX:447
24:12f	III:434; IX:447n59		26:12f	IX:447
24:13	II:196; 485f; 486n10		26:13	I:90; III:430; VI:732; IX:448
24:14	IV:697; VI:728n9; 888		26:13ff	II:794
24:14f	VI:39		26:14	II:847(n105); III:416(n12);
24:14ff	VI:891			V:115; 967; IX:284
24:15	I:272n17; 626; II:522; IV:697;		26:15	III:771; V:256; 379; 506
	698; VI:888		26:16	IV:1041; IX:289; 628n81
24:16	VIII:343; 513n31		26:16-18	VII:271(n12)
24:17	III:929n24; V:488; IX:445; 447		26:17	IV:150; VI:571n31; IX:284
24:18	IV:331; 333; 675; VII:4n17		26:17f	II:122; 783n95
24:19-21	IX:447		26:17-19	VII:271
24:20	IV:675		26:18	I:180; II:546; III:772; IV:35;
24:21	VI:731			VI:57, (n6)
24:22	IV:675; VII:4n17		26:18f	IV:35
25:1	I:714; II:177n9; 212; 683;		26:19	I:91; III:249n2; 646; IV:43n61;
	VII:187			V:252; 261
25:1-3	IV:516		27:1	VI:657; VIII:38
25:2	VI:657; VII:187; VIII:340; 347;		27:2	III:771; 827; VII:641
	353(n114)		27:3	I:743; III:771; IV:1046
25:2f	IV:515; 516n10		27:4	III:827; VII:641
25:3	IV:516; VII:12n80; VIII:137		27:6	III:766; V:175n2; 980n215
25:4	III:990		27:7	III:181; VII:1022, n3;
25:5	V:8; VII:540; VIII:353(n114)			VIII:85n2
25:5f	I:746		27:8	IV:279; 1046
25:5ff	I:369; 781; II:630		27:9	III:262; 1080
25:5-10	V:253; VI:657; IX:447		27:9ff	II:757
25:6	VI:872		27:10	II:546; IX:284
25:7	VI:657		27:12f	V:481
25:8f	VI:774		27:14	IV:530; IX:281; 282
25:9	VI:626n33		27:14ff	I:233n1
25:9f	V:311n3		27:15	II:381n1; 383; III:961; 968
25:11	VIII:303		27:15ff	I:335; IV:93
25:11f	III:853		27:15-26	IV:1036(n40); VI:186, n104

27:16	III:468, n4; V:982n233	28:43f	III:675
27:17	VIII:161	28:44	III:675; VI:987n14
27:18	V:99n14; VI:234; VIII:279;	28:45	IX:284
	280; 282; 285; 286	28:46	VII:210(n65); 216n103; 218;
27:19	II:929n24; V:488n4; VI:735;		VIII:123, n61
	IX:445; 446	28:47	III:606; IV:60; 965; VII:909
27:24	VIII:261	28:47f	VI:15
27:25	VIII:261	28:47ff	III:142
27:26	I:450; 451; 617; III:918; IV:577;	28:48	I:775; II:897; IV:60; VI:15;
	VI:293; VIII:509		VIII:538n74
29	**IV:710**; VI:523	28:49	IV:1071n219; V:469; 471;
28:1	VII:816n110; 827; IX:284		IX:290
28:1-13	II:757	28:50	III:30; IX:377n43; 625
28:1-14	VI:324	28:52	III:140; 411; VI:191; 523
28:3	VI:522	28:53	III:140; 141; 142; VII:605;
28:3f	II:762		607n20
28:4	III:786	28:53ff	III:141
28:4-11	VIII:342	28:54	I:595; III:824; V:376
28:6	II:764	28:55	III:140; 141; 142; VII:605
28:7	VII:922n16	28:56	I:518; 595; III:824; IV:5; V:376
28:8	III:771	28:57	III:140; 141; 142; VII:605
28:9	III:249n2; IV:36; 43n61	28:58	I:617n8; 748; III:33; 1070;
28:10	IX:200		IX:201
28:11	III:786; VI:281	28:58f	IV:516
28:12	II:756; III:137n9; 177n51; 459;	28:58-61	IX:202
	750n63; IV:681; V:537;	28:59	III:31; 33; IV:1091n1; VI:184;
	IX:426		550; VIII:310n17
28:13	II:675; **676**; VI:987n14;	28:61	I:617n8; IV:1046; VIII:310n17
	VII:1077n489	28:62	IV:204; VI:276n13; 277
28:14	V:62; 63n59; 737	28:63	II:773n14, n15; III:771
28:15	IX:284	28:64	IV:60; 269n9; V:516; VII:419
28:16	VI:522	28:65	III:405; VII:570; VIII:280n66
28:18	V:1023; VIII:342	28:65ff	IX:204
28:19	VI:578; 579	28:66	III:921; VI:187n109
28:20	II:624(n5); VI:551	28:66f	IX:197
28:21	III:771	28:67	V:371
28:21ff	VIII:267n59	28:68	VII:719
28:22	VI:940n65; **957**; 996n24;	29:1 (28:69, M/S)	II:126; VII:282(n5); 642
	VIII:268	29:2-29 (29, M/S)	IV:1046
28:25	II:99, n3; 606; VI:746; 748; 749;	29:3 (29:2, M/S)	V:548n48; VI:29n35;
	VII:539		VII:210(n65); 218;
28:26	IV:892(n9); IX:198		VIII:119n40; 123
28:27	VII:295n15	29:4 (29:3, M/S)	III:606; 626; IV:1107n15;
28:28	II:450, n1; III:5; 607; IV:360n4;		V:327; 378; 557; VII:273;
	965; V:368n3		IX:478n58
28:28f	VIII:281	29:5 (29:4, M/S)	V:718; VIII:136
28:29	I:159; V:111; VII:424n10;	29:5f (29:4f, M/S)	VI:136(n8)
	425n16; 428; VIII:279	29:6 (29:5, M/S)	I:698; II:689; VI:16
28:31	VII:930n25; 932	29:7 (29:6, M/S)	VIII:194
28:32	III:83n81, n82; V:327n68;	29:8 (29:7, M/S)	V:396
	IX:625	29:9 (29:8, M/S)	IV:516
28:33	I:159	29:10 (29:9, M/S)	VI:657; VII:643
28:34	IV:360n4; V:327n68; 371	29:10-15	VI:729
28:35	III:405; VI:550; 554n52;	(29:9-14, M/S)	
	VIII:310	29:11 (29:10, M/S)	V:10n62
28:36	II:377(n25); IV:269n9	29:11f (29:10f, M/S)	I:786
28:37	V:748(n20); 752n54	29:12 (29:11, M/S)	II:108n16; 126
28:38	V:172	29:14 (29:13, M/S)	II:126
28:38ff	II:471	29:16-18	V:403
28:39	III:634; VII:453	(29:15-17, M/S)	
28:40	II:471; IX:496n3; 510	29:17 (29:16, M/S)	II:377(n17), (n25); III:431n5;
28:43	III:675		IV:269n9

29:18 (29:17, M/S)	III:607; 675n2; IV:60; 965; V:586n19; VI:123; 124, n13; 125, n13; 987; 990; IX:665	31:10ff	II:628	
		31:11	IV:1036n43; V:547; 550; VIII:197, n66	
29:19 (29:18, M/S)	I:286; 320n31; 334; II:228; III:606; 607; V:491; VIII:483n35	31:12	III:527; V:845n22	
		31:12f	IV:401	
		31:14	I:213, n24; 292; II:36n9; III:497n4; 695n85; IV:437n173; 856n106; 866n210; V:416n241; VI:325n60; VII:265; IX:127; 646n173	
29:20 (29:19, M/S)	I:617n8; II:879; V:399n128; 403n162; 410			
29:20ff (29:19ff, M/S)	V:398n119			
29:21 (29:20, M/S)	I:617n8; IV:1091; VI:728; VIII:345			
29:23 (29:22, M/S)	V:404	31:15	IV:905; VII:641; 733n12	
29:25 (29:24, M/S)	II:126	31:16	VI:587	
29:25c (29:24c, M/S)	V:966n115	31:17	III:140; 141; V:446; VII:720	
29:27 (29:26, M/S)	I:617n8	31:17f	III:477	
29:28 (29:27, M/S)	V:857	31:18	VI:470; VII:719; 720	
29:29 (29:28, M/S)	III:960; 967; 969; VI:470	31:19	II:137; IV:483; 485; VII:696	
30	IV:1046	31:20	III:771; 1099n1; V:857n2	
30:1	II:52; VI:772	31:21	III:140; 771; IV:483; VI:564(n12); VII:271(n14); 696	
30:1ff	II:757			
30:2	IV:989; IX:628n81			
30:3	I:287; 388; II:481(n56); III:203; IV:1094	31:22	II:137	
		31:24	VIII:52; 85	
30:4	I:679; II:99; 933n34; 934n44; V:510; 516; VIII:450	31:25f	II:126	
		31:26	I:617n8; IV:485; 503; 1046	
30:5	III:771; 778	31:26f	VII:271(n8)	
30:5ff	VIII:551	31:27	V:1029; VI:126n4; IX:625	
30:6	I:29; 540; III:612n21; VI:74; 77n32; VII:910; IX:628, n81	31:28	III:527; IV:512; V:510; VI:657	
		31:29	V:51; VI:470; VIII:53; IX:99; 426	
30:7	IV:686			
30:8	II:546; VII:993n119; IX:284	31:30	V:547; VIII:52	
30:9	II:755n3; 773n15	32	II:345; III:772; V:674; 968; VII:16n122; VIII:347n77; 495; 496; 497, n52; 617n21	
30:9f	II:774; IX:366n57			
30:10	I:617n8; 748; IV:989; IX:284; 628n81			
		32:1	III:54; V:512; VII:697; IX:52n28	
30:11	III:32; IV:99; 373; 861n154; V:525n224			
		32:2	IV:135; VI:378n233, n237	
30:11ff	I:557; IV:99	32:3	III:54; IV:544; VI:411n514; IX:636	
30:11-14	I:521			
30:12	I:520; IV:861n154; V:503; 525n224; VIII:304	32:4	I:153; II:176; 186, n32; 195; 213; 642; 715n80; III:930; 931; V:55; 91; 490; 491; 771; 968; VI:95(n8), n9; 153n40; 750; IX:184n106; 486	
30:12-14	V:158n2; VI:472n77			
30:14	II:331; III:610; 612; IV:93; 99; V:209; VII:697; 700; 908; 993n119			
		32:4-6	VII:406n17	
30:15	I:14; V:59n51	32:5	I:663; IV:831; VII:404; 406; 407n26; 484; 718; VIII:261; 351	
30:15ff	II:757			
30:15-20	II:845; 851(n149); VII:270			
30:16	I:29, n51; II:175; 220; 757; III:771; V:51; 59n51; VI:571n31	32:5f	VIII:352; 355	
		32:6	I:34n70; 276; III:1007; 1012; 1027; IV:148n16; 833; 834; 837; 846n114; V:968; 972; 978, n206, n207; VI:256; 257; VII:483; 487; 507n290; VIII:351; 352	
30:17	VI:235; 236(n41)			
30:19	II:844n82; IV:149n20; 168; 512; V:59; n51, n52; 94; 510			
30:20	II:823n44; III:771; IV:1041; VII:141n320; IX:284			
		32:7	IV:675; VIII:343	
31:2	VI:579; VII:270(n7)	32:8	I:601; II:104; 367; 368; 634; III:81n72; 760; 772; 891n85; IV:35; 40n41; VI:411n514; VIII:39; 346; 347, n77; 348; 354; 617n21	
31:6	I:363n14; 367; VII:777			
31:7	III:771			
31:8	VII:777			
31:9	VI:657			
31:10	I:510; **VII:390-391**; 393	32:8b	VIII:355	

32:8f	III:760; **IV:40;** 41, n47; **V:965;** VI:873; VIII:347n77; 617n21	32:39	I:252n2; II:352; 399; 844(n88); 850; 852; 873n3; III:1011; IV:1014; V:337; 940; VII:487; IX:645n171
32:8ff	IV:35		
32:9	I:107; III:772; 889; V:965	32:39ff	II:344
32:10	I:573n50; V:516n145; 579; VI:767; VIII:47	32:40	I:185; 201; V:177; 459n19; 506; IX:426
32:11	II:57n2; IV:7; 36	32:41	II:174; 181; III:304; IV:687; V:416, n245
32:12	III:88; V:15; VII:777		
32:13	II:471; IV:553, n15; VI:97n28	32:42	I:608; III:304; IX:622
32:14	I:176; IV:760; 911; VII:507n290	32:43	I:174; 207; 627n13; II:174; 181; 367n11; 442n1; 774;
32:15	I:512; 513; 663; III:86; 1012; IV:3; V:1025; VI:95(n8); 750;VII:976f; 1013; VIII:62; 299n41; 301		III:97n181; 302; 304; 430n1; IV:52; 54; 687; V:510; 533; 674; VI:880; VIII:347n77; 355; 617n21
32:15c	V:972	32:44	V:547
32:16	II:883n3; V:6n33; VI:125n2, n4	32:46	IV:512; 1045; VII:271(n8); VIII:343
32:17	II:11; 13n100; 378; III:86; 181; 448; VI:157n88; 767	32:47	II:845; 851(n149)); III:448; IV:138; VII:285
32:18	I:33n67; V:968; 972; VI:95(n8); 750; VII:272; VIII:351; 352; IX:669	32:50	VIII:410n66
		32:51	VI:126; VIII:318
32:18f	VIII:352	33	VIII:84
32:18-20	VIII:355	33:1	I:364; 365; II:78n42; VI:809
32:19	II:884; V:417n248; 857n3; 968; VIII:351	33:1ff	II:758
		33:2	I:83; 291; II:38, n3; 927;
32:19f	V:446		III:957; 1066; IV:618;
32:20	I:663; II:947; 948n23; VI:188n116; 190n126; 773; VII:257n382; 719n6; 720; VIII:51n15		866n210; 1057; V:861; 877; VI:938; 951n2; VII:118; 282n5; 283; 796; IX:7, n1; 9; 10n19; 288n40; 319
32:20f	V:403	33:3	I:22; 34; 51n103; 112; II:51; VI:379n240
32:21	II:377(n20); 881; V:410; 415n233; 419; VII:895n64	33:4	V:233; VII:805
32:22	V:399; 412; 417n252; 480; VIII:55	33:5	I:568; IV:152; V:861
		33:6	III:751n75
32:23	I:608; VI:15	33:7	IX:281
32:23f	VI:15	33:7-11	II:796
32:24	II:13n100; V:392; 411; 573	33:8	III:260; IV:237; V:490; VI:126; 127; 152n39; VIII:318
32:25	III:747n42; 748n48; V:832; VII:420	33:8-11	III:260; IV:236
32:27	III:324(n5)	33:9	I:698(n36); II:534n5; IV:91; 137; 237; 240n16; V:964n108
32:28	I:633; II:232n2; IV:47		
32:29	II:52; VII:485; IX:586	33:9-11	IV:235
32:30	III:720; VI:95(n8), n9; 160n6	33:10	II:176; IV:1036n43; 1046n92
32:31	IV:962, n1; VI:95(n8); VII:610n16	33:11	II:53; 738; IV:686; V:496
		33:12	I:30(n52); VII:372n25; 388; IX:168n184
32:32	I:487; VI:123		
32:32f	V:578n134, n136	33:13	V:507; VI:115n17; VIII:319n33
32:33	III:675n2; V:437n384; 571; 572; 573; 577	33:15	V:482
		33:15b	IX:677
32:34	IV:151; VII:944	33:16	II:757n8; IV:879; VI:300; IX:624; 677
32:35	II:169; 345n19; 445; 446; V:861; VI:626n31	33:17	III:554; 669; 670n11; IX:527n233
32:35f	II:195		
32:36	III:891n85; 930; V:674; 680n169; 778n25; VII:880, n33	33:18	VII:383
		33:19	II:193
		33:21	I:485; II:196, n7, n8, n9; 203; III:925; IV:162n88; 463n13; 856; V:686; VI:460
32:37	VI:95(n8); 193		
32:37f	VI:157n88		
32:38	VII:523n24	33:22	V:469

JOSHUA

4:3	VII:706; VIII:581n87	6:23	III:444; VII:417
4:6	VII:214; 215n94; 219; 948n77	6:24	III:137; VI:935; VII:768n13
4:6f	VII:492n188	6:25	III:958; V:1021
4:6ff	VII:211	6:26	VI:875; VII:970n18
4:7	II:61; III:406n20: VI:601; VII:211; 214	6:27	V:261; VII:779
		7	V:398; 408n190
4:8	VIII:65	7:1	III:754n1; V:402; 407; 409; VII:373
4:9	VI:609; VII:270		
4:11	VIII:63	7:5	VI:510(n64); VIII:322
4:14	IV:428; VIII:517; IX:200; 585	7:6	VI:655
4:16	II:106	7:8	II:812
4:18	V:469; VIII:193n44; 218; 319	7:9	V:252; 253; 257(n110)
4:20	VII:641	7:11	II:105; 126; III:754; V:737; IX:597
4:21	VII:492n188		
4:21ff	VII:211	7:11ff	I:354
4:23	VIII:319	7:12	VII:775
4:23f	II:292	7:13	I:91; 111
4:24	II:646; III:109; VII:171; IX:585	7:14	V:961
5:1	IV:966n17; VI:362; 368; 601; IX:224	7:15	VI:470; 935
		7:16-18	VI:655n23
5:2	**VI:76,** n23; 99	7:17	V:961
5:2f	IV:279; 525; VI:76n21	7:19	II:758n12; III:968; V:219; VII:270(n4); VIII:345
5:2-8	VI:73		
5:3	I:226; V:481; VI:99	7:20	VI:186n103
5:4	VI:74, n9	7:21	III:968; VII:689n16
5:6	IV:552; VI:74, n9; VIII:136; IX:284	7:21f	VII:373
		7:21ff	VII:370
5:8	VI:75n17; VIII:310n17	7:22	I:400(n17); III:968
5:8f	**VI:76,** n23	7:23	VIII:154
5:9	VI:75n19; VIII:195; 196	7:24f	VIII:343
5:10	V:896n2; 897n2, n7	7:25	III:754n1; VII:270(n4)
5:12	IV:462	7:25f	V:407
5:13	I:78n21; 80n27; V:333n91	7:26	V:264; VII:1095
5:13-15	VI:627	8:1	IX:426
5:14	I:87; II:45, n14; 46; 47n23; 48; 789(n173); IV:1112; 1113; V:506; VI:760n23; VII:705; VIII:348n89	8:3	IV:34
		8:10	II:601; VI:655
		8:11	VI:570
		8:17	IV:197
		8:18	V:297
5:15	I:90; 91; IV:328; V:311n2	8:20	V:328
6	I:92; VI:510; 523	8:21	V:509
6:1	VII:744	8:22	IV:196; 198
6:1ff	II:630	8:24	II:427; VI:994; VIII:52
6:2	VI:508(n36); IX:426	8:26	V:297
6:4	VII:77, n39; 87(n57)	8:29	III:411; 917; 918n23; VI:992; VII:1095
6:5	III:898; V:469; VI:162; VII:77; 78		
		8:31 (9:4 or 9:2b, S)	I:748; III:766; V:175n2; 663; VII:1023; VIII:85n2
6:5ff	VII:77		
6:6	VII:77	8:32 (9:5 or 9:2c, S)	I:743; IV:1046; 1047n97
6:7	V:762	8:33 (9:6 or 9:2d, S)	V:481; VI:657
6:8	I:215; III:226; 227; VII:77; 87(n57); 263n7	8:34 (9:7 or 9:2e, S)	I:748; 749; IV:1046
		8:35 (9:8 or 9:2f, S)	V:548n45
6:9	I:211n14	9	VI:736
6:10	I:68; III:700n13	9:1	IV:855n95
6:13	I:211n14; V:290; 584n11; 585; VII:72; 77; 87(n57)	9:4	V:718; 724(n13); 725n18; VII:58
6:16	III:700n13; 898, (n2); VI:508(n36); 827	9:5	V:718
		9:6f	II:115n42
6:17	VI:584	9:8f	V:674
6:17f	I:354	9:9	V:257; 261; 262; 276
6:19	III:137	9:11	V:658n16; 674; VI:656n37
6:20	VI:162; VII:76; 79	9:13	II:115n42; V:718; 720
6:22ff	III:3		

9:14	VII:697	12:7ff	VI:523
9:15	II:115n42; 403(n23)	12:9	VI:312
9:15f	II:105	12:10	VII:301n65
9:18	I:730; 735n3; VII:804	13-19	IX:247n15
9:20	V:396	13-21	III:771
9:22	II:115n42	13:1	III:771; IV:197
9:22ff	V:10n62	13:5	V:104
9:23	V:658; 674	13:7	III:771
9:24	IX:200	13:12	IV:197
9:25 (9:31, S)	II:233	13:14	III:776n14
9:27	IV:169; VIII:197	13:15ff	VI:610
10:1	IV:879; VII:295; 301n65	13:19	VII:294n1
10:1ff	VII:307	13:21	VII:294n1; 532(n24)
10:2	VI:522	13:22	I:524
10:3	IV:879; VII:301n65	13:27	V:452
10:5	IV:32, n12; VII:301n65	13:33	III:776n14
10:6c	V:297n11	14:2	III:759(n6); 771
10:7	IV:34	14:5	V:400
10:8	IX:426	14:6	VI:809
10:10	II:459	14:7	II:268; IV:953; V:675n119;
10:11	V:297; VI:508(n44); 991		VII:417; VIII:137
10:12	II:795; III:290; IV:857n110;	14:8	IV:965
	VII:641	14:9	I:215; VI:626
10:12f	IX:320	14:10f	VII:271(n8)
10:13	II:795; VII:570; VIII:52	14:10ff	IV:1109
10:14	VI:508(n35)	14:12	VI:523
10:15	IV:34	14:14	I:215
10:17	III:285	15-19	V:109
10:19	VII:637n5; IX:426	15:1	III:771
10:20	VIII:52	15:4	VI:570
10:21	II:408; VIII:311	15:8	I:657; VII:296; 301, n61
10:23	VII:301n65	15:9	VI:116n21
10:24	VI:626; IX:625	15:12	V:452
10:26	III:917	15:13	V:960
10:27	III:411; VI:992	15:18	I:192; 657; V:104
10:28	IV:196; 198; IX:620; 622n63	15:32	VI:522
10:28ff	II:849(n116)	15:34	VI:522
10:28-40	VI:452	15:63	III:778; VII:301, n61
10:30	IV:196; IX:622n63	16:1	III:771; VIII:317
10:33	IV:34; 196	16:9	V:454; 455
10:35	IX:622n63	16:9a	V:297n11
10:37	IV:196; IX:622n63	16:9c	V:297n11
10:39	IV:196; VI:522; IX:622n63	16:10	II:446; III:778
10:40	II:852n155; IV:196; VI:364;	17:4	III:759
	368; VII:970n16; IX:618	17:11	I:468
10:42	VI:508(n35)	17:14	III:285; 776; IV:34
11	IV:5	17:15	III:430, n1
11:3	VII:301n61	17:18	III:430n1; V:480
11:4	VI:276n13; 277	18:1	I:92; III:528; 635; VII:391n8;
11:5	V:186n2; VIII:317		803
11:6	IX:676	18:1ff	III:759
11:7	VIII:317	18:3	III:778
11:8	IV:196	18:4f	I:184
11:11	V:891; VI:364; 368; 452;	18:6	III:759; 771; VII:166
	IX:618; 620; 622n63	18:7	III:251; 776n14
11:12	VI:523	18:8	III:759
11:14	V:891; VI:364; 368; 452;	18:9	I:744
	IX:618	18:10	III:759
11:16	VIII:9	18:11	III:759
11:20	V:1026n5; IX:379	18:14	V:327
11:23	III:760; VII:963	18:16	I:657; VII:301, n61
12:6	III:759; V:674	18:20	IV:595; V:452

18:28	VII:296; 300; 301n61
19:1	III:760
19:8f	I:185
19:12	IV:877n14
19:14	III:82
19:15	V:9
19:26	VII:294n1
19:33	V:109
19:38	III:82
19:40ff	III:772
19:47 (19:48, S)	V:261; 941

Special S Additions

19:47a	I:559
19:48a	IX:80

Back to RSV and M Text

19:48 (19:47, S)	VI:570
19:49	II:535; III:771
19:50	I:192
19:51	I:184; II:535; VII:391n8
20:3	I:274; II:470; IV:330
20:5	IV:330; 685; VII:744
20:6	III:266; VII:804
20:9	II:470; IV:330; V:845n17; VII:804
21:1	III:675n2; V:960
21:4	III:262
21:8	III:759(n6)
21:9	V:258
21:21ff	VI:522
21:27	VII:166
21:28	IV:877n14
21:36	VI:522
21:40	I:192
21:42	VII:34

Special S Additions

21:42a	VIII:63
21:42b	I:192
21:42d	IV:525; VI:73; 76n21

Back to RSV and M Text

21:44	VII:34
21:45	IV:93; VI:169
22	IV:485
22:4	IV:1106n2; 1121
22:5	I:29; II:546; III:607; IV:965; V:51; VI:469; IX:628n81
22:8	IX:480
22:9	III:777
22:9-34	V:396n102; VII:811n74
22:12	III:528
22:13	III:266
22:16	I:513; VII:719
22:16f	VII:805
22:16ff	VII:271(n14)
22:17	VII:804
22:17f	VII:804
22:18	V:396; 398n119; VII:719
22:18f	I:512
22:19	I:513; III:772
22:20	V:396, n102; 398; 400; 402; 409

22:22	I:513; III:81; 88
22:23	I:512
22:24	II:752
22:25	VII:171
22:27	IV:60; 61; VII:1022
22:29	VII:719; 1022
22:31	VII:777
23:2	VI:655; 657
23:4	III:771; IV:197
23:5	III:778
23:6	I:617n8; 749
23:7	IV:197; V:263; 668n78
23:10	VI:508(n35)
23:11	I:29
23:12	VII:719; VIII:168
23:13	VI:749n28; VII:342; 345; 346n43
23:14	V:50; VI:164; IX:628n81
23:15	VI:55n27
23:16	II:126; V:403; VI:570
24	II:120; III:357; 1073; IV:151n29; 152; 156; **IX:247**
24:1	VI:655; 657; VII:643
24:2f	III:1064
24:3	IV:147; 151; V:98; VI:280
24:4	III:759; 760
24:5	III:484
24:7	IV:902; VI:508(n44)
24:9f	I:524
24:11	III:290; 291; 412
24:12	III:1073; V:404
24:13	II:120; III:828
24:14	I:233; II:175; 199; IV:60; 151; VI:188, n120; VIII:72n22
24:14f	II:120; III:1073; 1074; IV:60
24:14-24	IV:60
24:14b-23	IV:150n26
24:15	II:120; III:1062; IV:60; 146; 149; 150; 151; 174; V:961; 963
24:16	III:300n3; IV:151
24:16ff	III:1065
24:17	II:120; VII:212n73
24:18	V:891
24:19	I:293f; 367; II:884; III:88; 1070n174; IV:61; 151; V:660
24:20	VI:460
24:21ff	II:126
24:22	II:121; IV:146; 149, n20; **150-152** (151n29); 170; 174; 483
24:23	V:10; 970
24:24	IV:150n26; IX:284
24:25	II:109n19; 121; 126; IV:99
24:26	I:744; II:121
24:26f	IV:279
24:27	II:113n36; 786n129; IV:151; 485; 503; IX:598
24:28	III:771; VIII:195n54
24:29 (24:30, S)	II:268; V:663n44; 674
24:30 (24:31, S)	III:759; 771
24:31 (24:29, S)	II:640; IV:60; IX:585

	Special S Additions		**Special S Additions**
24:31a	IV:525; VI:73; 76n21	24:33b	III:1098; VII:171

	Back to RSV and M Text
24:32	II:847; III:771; IV:680; V:960; VIII:463n427
24:33	III:266

JUDGES

Ref	References	Ref	References
1:3	III:771		V:403(n152); 409
1:5ff	IV:879	2:15	VI:587n46
1:6	II:602	2:16	II:334; VII:974; 975; 1012
1:6f	III:852; VII:301n65	2:17	II:789; V:51; VI:587
1:7	VII:302n65; VIII:212n28	2:18	II:334; 812; III:140; V:777n25; VII:779; 974; 975; 1012; IX:426
1:8	VI:994; VII:302n65		
1:12	II:531		
1:14	I:192; 731; V:104	2:19	II:789; IV:60; V:53; VI:571; VII:719; IX:99
1:15	VIII:9		
1:16	III:1066	2:20	II:480(n46); VI:570
1:18	I:287; III:777; 778	2:21	VI:509n59
1:19	II:955; VII:591n5; 779	2:22	V:51; VI:25; 570; IX:237
1:19b	III:778	2:23	I:510
1:20	III:294n3	3:1	I:510
1:20f	I:467	3:1f	VI:509n59
1:21	III:294n3; VII:301, n61	3:2	IV:280; VIII:67
1:21ff	III:778	3:4	II:546
1:24	VI:468; IX:382	3:5	VII:301n61
1:24f	II:25	3:7	IV:61
1:26	VI:523	3:8	II:266; 459; IV:60; V:403(n152)
1:27	VII:449	3:9	II:334; 786n131; III:899; V:406n179; VII:974; 975; 1012; VIII:377
1:28	IX:80		
1:29ff	IX:80		
1:35	I:559	3:10	III:923; V:861; VI:363; 366
1:36	VI:95	3:11	VIII:136
2:1	II:126	3:13	III:776
2:1ff	I:77; 78n18	3:14	II:266; IV:60
2:2	II:118n54; IX:284	3:15	II:334; 786n131; III:861n5; 899; VII:974; 975; 1012; VIII:377
2:3	VI:749n28; VII:342; 886		
2:4	IX:282	3:15ff	IX:79
2:5	VIII:196	3:16	IV:525n4; 527n26; VI:997n26
2:6	III:771	3:17f	III:861; IX:65
2:7	I:699n42; II:640; IV:60; 539	3:18	VIII:63
2:8	II:268; V:663n44; 674	3:19	IV:96
2:9	III:771	3:20	IV:96
2:10	II:640	3:24	VI:627n35
2:11	II:601n6; IV:61	3:25	IV:579; 583
2:11ff	IV:1043	3:26	VII:980
2:11-23	VI:708	3:27	VII:78; 79; 770
2:12	I:211; II:789; V:291; VI:571	3:28	VI:508(n36); IX:426
2:13	IV:61	3:29	VII:979
2:14	I:535; II:812; III:441;	3:30	VIII:136

3:31	VII:974	5:22	V:469
4:1ff	III:443	5:23	VI:508; VII:708
4:2	IX:426	5:24	II:762; VII:370
4:3	III:140; 899; 906	5:25	III:861; VI:135(n3); IX:65
4:4	II:454; III:923; VI:804	5:26	V:907n21
4:5	I:368; III:441; V:766n9	5:28	IV:414n4; V:815, n8; VI:626
4:6f	VI:804	5:28b	VI:382
4:7	I:252; VI:277; IX:426	5:28-31	VI:382
4:8	V:111	5:29	VI:382; VII:485
4:9	I:699	5:30	II:284; IX:155; 156
4:10	I:368; V:762	5:31	I:28n46; II:246; 286; 305n75;
4:11	III:260; 1066; VI:269, n7;		IV:160; 164n93; V:104; 891;
	VII:370		VIII:136
4:14	VI:508(n42); IX:426	5:31a	VI:382
4:14-16	VI:508n33	6:1	IX:426
4:15	II:459	6:2	V:480; VI:954n9
4:16	III:824	6:4	II:853n164; IX:96; 98
4:17	II:420n20; 406	6:5	III:593; VI:276n13; 277;
4:17b	II:115n42		VII:370
4:17f	VII:370	6:6	II:786n131; III:899; VI:888
4:17ff	V:19n140	6:7	II:786n131; III:899
4:18	I:683; III:2; 1060; VII:743;	6:7-10	VI:802
	IX:203	6:8	I:402n25
4:20	VII:370	6:9	I:527; III:140; 142; VI:1000
4:21	III:917(n14); VII:370	6:10	III:444; IX:284
4:22	II:25; IV:892n7	6:11	VI:971
4:23	VII:921; VIII:8	6:11ff	I:77; V:333n91
4:24	V:1030; VI:570; IX:426	6:11-24	V:861
5	VI:728n5	6:12	I:499; VII:775; 776
5:1	II:788	6:13	III:35
5:2	II:758; III:356n2; VI:508(n37);	6:13f	IX:426
	695n5; 698n9	6:14	I:402n25
5:2-31	VII:198	6:14ff	VII:975
5:3	VIII:493	6:15	IV:649; VIII:9
5:4	II:239; III:1066; VII:199	6:16f	VII:775; 776
5:4f	I:505n5; III:1006; IV:905;	6:17	I:433; II:769; V:376;
	V:861; VII:198; 283		VII:212n73
5:5	III:1066n139; V:480;	6:18	II:400; IX:57
	VII:282n4, n6	6:19-21	VII:931
5:6	V:49; 54n34; VI:570;	6:20	II:903n10
	VII:404n5; 718	6:21	VI:936; 937; 967
5:7	V:962n97	6:22	VI:771; 773
5:7ff	III:356n2	6:22f	V:332; 333n91
5:8	II:120n65; IV:149, n24; 170;	6:23	I:217; II:407; V:332n90; IX:203
	V:296	6:24	II:123; 403(n24)
5:9	II:758; VI:508(n37); 695n5;	6:25	IV:761; V:333n93
	696n23	6:25ff	VI:803
5:10	II:787; III:337n4; IV:243, n13	6:26	V:37; 333
5:11	II:176; III:1064; IV:159;	6:29	VI:639
	VI:511n79; VIII:517; IX:281	6:31	I:374n6; III:89; VII:974
5:11f	VI:508n33	6:34	II:286; 319; VI:363; 366;
5:13	IV:195n5; 543; VIII:8; 11n25		VII:79; 689n18; IX:198n47
5:14	VI:967	6:35	I:400(n17)
5:15	I:185; 403n34; II:97	6:36f	VII:975
5:16	I:185; III:607; IV:487(n25)	6:36ff	III:571
5:17	V:109n25; VII:385	6:36-40	II:796
5:17a	V:844	6:38	VI:299n9
5:17b	V:844	6:39	I:382n6; V:409
5:18	VIII:603	7:2	III:646; VII:975
5:19	I:468; IV:389; VI:269; VIII:317	7:2ff	VI:508(n40)
5:20	I:78n21; V:506; VI:508(n44)	7:3	V:469; IX:198n47; 199; 200
5:20f	VII:922n15	7:4	III:430; VII:769n15

7:5	III:595
7:6	III:595
7:7	VII:975; VIII:194; 195n54
7:8	VII:370
7:9	IX:426
7:9f	IX:200
7:9ff	VII:424n11
7:10f	VII:707n30
7:12	III:593; VI:276n13; 277
7:13	V:221; VI:162; VII:373
7:13ff	V:229
7:15	IX:426
7:16	IV:16; VII:77
7:18ff	VII:79
7:19	II:337
7:20	IV:16
7:21	VII:263
7:24	I:400(n17)
7:25	VII:706
8:1	II:94; 95
8:3	V:411; VI:361
8:4	IX:666
8:4f	VI:15
8:5ff	IV:879
8:8f	VI:954
8:9	V:591; VII:725
8:10	V:296
8:11	VII:370n7; 385
8:12	II:459; III:911
8:14	I:743n4; V:261; VI:523; 656n37; VIII:343
8:16	VI:656n37
8:17	VI:954
8:18	IV:746; VIII:341
8:19	II:874; V:459; VIII:341
8:20	IX:200
8:21	II:286; III:593; IV:640
8:22	VI:324; VII:975; IX:426
8:23	IV:157n61; VI:324
8:24	I:191; 193, n2, n7
8:26	I:8(n7); 191; IV:640
8:27	VI:587; 749n28; VII:342; 344
8:28	VII:496; VIII:136
8:30	VI:655n26; VIII:343
8:31	VI:584n30; VIII:160
8:32	II:843(n80)
8:33	II:119; 121; VII:719
8:34	III:140; VI:1000; 1002; IX:426
8:35	VI:297n72
9	IV:707; 708
9:1-6	IV:157
9:2	III:1097; VI:523; 655n26; 656n37; VII:106; IX:622
9:2ff	VI:523
9:4	I:212; III:5; 84n87; 659; IV:697; VIII:302
9:5	VI:655n26
9:6	IV:156; VII:570
9:7	III:722(n1); 723; V:480; IX:281
9:7-15	VII:752; 754n29; IX:498; 499
9:8-15	IV:157n60; V:749
9:13	III:86; V:162; 792n148
9:15	I:243; II:531n101; VI:193; VII:395; IX:497(n20)
9:16	VIII:78
9:17	VI:1001
9:18	I:361; VI:523; VII:271n8; VIII:341
9:19	VIII:78
9:23	II:11(n80); VI:363; 367; VIII:158
9:23f	IV:707; V:1026n5; IV:523
9:24	IX:625
9:25	III:675
9:28	II:614; IV:60; 162n91
9:29	VI:280
9:30	VI:523
9:31	I:400(n17)
9:33	VI:549
9:34	VIII:132
9:36	III:675; VII:395
9:37	VII:318n125
9:38	IV:60
9:45	III:411
9:46	II:118; 119; III:84n87
9:48f	IX:85
9:49	I:212
9:51	VI:954n9
9:51f	VI:954
9:52	II:330
9:53	III:728
9:54	II:446; VII:359
9:55	VIII:194
9:56	VI:564(n9); VII:720; 723
9:56f	III:483
9:57	I:499n22; III:675; VI:564(n9); VII:723
10:1	VII:974
10:4	III:337n4; V:283; 284; 287n23; VI:960; VIII:343
10:6	II:267
10:6a	IV:60
10:6b	IV:60
10:6-16	III:142
10:7	V:403(n152); IX:426
10:8	III:140; 141
10:8f	III:141
10:9	III:140
10:10	I:288; 626; II:267; IV:60
10:12	III:140; 899
10:12-14	VII:976
10:12ff	VII:974
10:13	II:267; IV:60; 151
10:14	III:89; 140; 141; IV:149, n22; 151
10:16	II:268; IV:60; V:10; IX:619
10:18	III:675
11:1	VI:584; 585; VIII:344n64
11:2	III:775; 776; V:963; VI:584; 585n34
11:3	III:659; IV:841
11:3-11	VI:656n37
11:5	VI:657
11:7	III:140; IV:685

	VIII:280n75; IX:435	19:10f	VII:296; 300
16:27	V:328; 628	19:11	VII:296
16:28	I:382n6; II:443; 793(n198); 796;	19:11f	VII:301
	III:722(n1); 723; IV:675	19:11ff	VI:315n29
16:29	VII:655	19:13	VIII:194
16:30	II:849, (n115); IX:621n61	19:15	V:49
17	V:15; 17	19:16	VIII:194
17f	III:772; V:962; VI:510	19:19	V:638; VI:638
17:2	II:114n40; 764; V:464	19:19f	VIII:595
17:3	I:113	19:20	II:402(n13)
17:5	IV:754n2; V:120; VI:287, n3	19:22	I:607; III:954; VII:909;
17:5f	III:260		VIII:346
17:6	VI:470	19:22f	III:1058n97
17:7-9	V:843	19:23	VI:469
17:8	V:49; 69n89; VI:467;	19:24	V:832; VI:469; VIII:7
	VIII:193n48	19:25	II:739; V:631; 632; VIII:302
17:9	VIII:193n48	19:29	I:117n49; 225; IV:557, n22;
17:10	I:665n3; V:962; VIII:343n57		VI:993; 994
17:11	II:739; V:844	19:30	V:324; 325; VII:210n61;
17:12	VI:287		VIII:154
17:13	IV:235	20	II:601
18	VI:191	20:1	III:528; IV:162n89; VII:803
18.1	III:772	20:2	III:527; 529n90
18.2	IV:594; VIII:346	20:3	VI:564(n9)
18:2f	V:15	20:5	III:46n18; V:632; VIII:7; 302
18:3	I:704; IX:281	20:6	II:225; III:772; IV:557n22;
18:4	IV:697		IX:225
18:5	V:111; 112; 113; VI:510	20:7	VIII:154
18:5f	V:50	20:12	VI:564(n9)
18:6	II:407; V:113; VI:570	20:13	I:607; II:739; VI:564(n9)
18:7	II:523n36; III:926n14; IV:372;	20:13a	I:607
	VI:191; VII:388	20:15	IV:149; 182
18:9	V:166; 942	20:16	I:271
18:10	II:523n36; VII:388; VIII:595	20:21	IX:98
18:11	VII:359; 360	20:22	VI:866n7; VIII:193
18:12	VIII:196	20:26	IV:925; 928; VII:1022, n3;
18:13	VIII:193n48		VIII:72
18:14	I:697(n33)	20:28	V:838
18:15	I:498n15; II:407	20:31	VIII:261
18:17	III:776; VII:359	20:32	VI:163n15; 746; 748
18:19	V:962; VIII:343n57	20:33	V:721n1; VIII:195
18:20	VII:909	20:34	I:559; IX:89
18:21	I:553	20:36	VI:191
18:22	III:898, (n5); IV:10; 32, n12	20:37	V:469
18:24	III:87n107	20:38	IV:482; VII:209n50; 220; 269
18:25	VI:122	20:39	VI:163n15; 167; VIII:261
18:27	II:523n36; VI:191; VII:388	20:40	VII:269; VIII:65
18:29	V:258	20:41	VI:564(n9)
18:30	III:260; IX:248	20:42	IX:89
18:31	V:120	20:44	VII:770n24
19	V:9; VI:728n6	20:46	VII:770n24
19f	IV:1038n50	20:47	VIII:132
19-2!	III:772; VI:510	20:48	VI:934
19:2	VIII:132	21	II:601; VII:1022
19:3	I:253	21:2	I:185; IX:281
19:4	II:689; VIII:550	21:3	II:602
19:5	III:728; VII:655; IX:626	21:4	VII:1022; VIII:72
19:6	I:478n2; 589n2	21:6	V:777n25
19:8	II:947; VII:655; 705, n24;	21:7	VI:62
	IX:626	21:10	VII:804; VIII:61
19:9	III:606; IV:574	21:11	V:832
19:10	II:739	21:12	I:697; V:832

RUTH

I SAMUEL

1	II:786; 793		616; IX:502; 503; 517
1-3	VI:802	2:11	IV:220
1:1	V:270	2:12	I:607; 698; II:220
1:2	V:645	2:16	VI:868; IX:621
1:4	III:182; V:647	2:17	III:305; 861n5; VIII:158
1:4f	I:786	2:18	IV:221; V:304
1:5	I:24n21; 781	2:18ff	V:647
1:5ff	I:781	2:19	IX:60
1:6	I:731; III:140; 142; V:411	2:20	II:758
1:7	III:722	2:21	II:602; VI:713
1:8	I:24n21; V:734n61; VIII:262; 343; 515n46; IX:627	2:22	V:838n5; 962n97; VII:391n8; 705; 769n14
1:9	IV:400n87; 882	2:24	II:265
1:10	IX:621; 629n85	2:25	I:631(n23); III:305; IV:962n1; V:1026n5; IX:97
1:10ff	II:796		
1:11	II:603n16; 795(n219); IV:675; VI:136; VII:540; VIII:11; 21; 342	2:26	VI:570; 713, n71; VII:514; 780n73; IX:392n151
		2:27	II:454; III:577
1:12	VI:280; VIII:147	2:27ff	VI:809
1:13	IV:285; IX:281	2:28	III:249; IV:155; 169; VI:934; IX:246n12
1:13f	IV:546		
1:15	II:786; VI:361; 368; VII:535; IX:620; 629	2:29	IV:3; VIII:301
		2:32	II:654
1:16	I:174; 607; IV:1107; V:411; VI:276n13	2:33	VI:59
		2:34	VII:212n74; 220; 231(n213)
1:17	I:193; II:434; 758; VI:570; VIII:504	2:35	I:369; III:607; V:121; 943; VI:184; 185; IX:502
1:18	IV:338n7	2:36	III:251
1:19	IV:675; VI:570	3:1	VI:713; 802
1:20	III:459; 489; V:254; IX:671	3:1ff	III:434; IV:95; V:230; VI:802
1:21	IX:497n4	3:1-19	V:646
1:22ff	V:647	3:2	I:559n2; V:327; VIII:280n66
1:24	VIII:197	3:3	IV:882; VII:166
1:24ff	VII:931	3:4f	IV:95
1:25	VII:929n24; 931	3:5	VIII:229
1:26	I:739; II:790; 849n118; 852; V:460	3:6	VIII:345
		3:7	III:577; IV:95; 96; V:549n49
1:27	I:193	3:8	VII:527
1:28	II:789; V:647; VI:760n23; IX:671	3:9	IV:95
		3:10	IV:95; V:333n93; 861
2	II:798n253, n254	3:11ff	V:460
2:1	II:787(n147); III:606; VII:610; 976; VIII:606; IX:627	3:12	VIII:61
		3:13	IV:1020
2:1f	IX:363	3:14	III:305
2:1-10	II:796; V:202; VI:18n43; VIII:496n50	3:15	IX:200
		3:16	VIII:345
2:2	II:185; VI:95(n8)	3:17	II:117n50; V:548n45
2:2f	III:646	3:18	VI:460
2:3	I:700; VII:493; VIII:302	3:19	III:575; VI:164; VII:779
2:5	VI:16; 284	3:19f	VI:801
2:6	II:873; III:21; VI:925n44; VIII:526n12; IX:645n171	3:20	IV:162n89; VI:185; 802
		3:21	III:577; IV:95; V:53; 891; VI:551; 802
2:7	VI:889; VIII:8; 526n12; 607		
2:7f	III:660	4	III:774
2:8	II:334; 777; III:161; 777; 1009; VI:888; 889; 891n50	4-6	VII:308
		4:2	VI:883
2:8ff	III:1005n47	4:3	VI:657; 883; VII:976
2:9	VI:626n31; IX:386n97; 625	4:4	III:161n13; 441; IX:438
2:10	I:374; 520; V:510; VI:323; VII:890; VIII:224n61; 607;	4:5	II:955; III:700n13
		4:5f	VII:78

4:6	III:359(n22); IX:280		VIII:65
4:6f	V:861	8:4	VI:657
4:7	II:927; VII:270; VIII:218;	8:5	III:444; IV:158; V:51
	IX:200n60	8:6	VI:550; 551; VIII:527
4:8	V:940	8:7	IV:156
4:9	III:359(n22); 913	8:9	II:220; IV:512
4:10	VI:883; VII:383; VIII:31	8:14f	V:658n13
4:13	III:5; 606; IV:400n87; VII:415	8:15	III:853; VII:539n9
4:14	IX:280; 281	8:18	IV:151(n30); 156; 169
4:15	VIII:280n66	8:19	I:631n16
4:16	VII:270(n6); 271(n9), (n11);	8:20	III:924
	VIII:345	8:21	V:549
4:17	II:707; 712	8:22	VI:523
4:18	III:923; VIII:136n12	9	VI:809
4:19	I:60; III:595; IV:1099;	9f	IX:503
	VII:760n7	9:2	V:252
4:20	III:459; IV:949; V:838n5;	9:6	I:66; II:254; V:50; 861
	VIII:342	9:6ff	II:454; III:571
4:22	II:245	9:6-10	VI:809
5	I:92	9:7	VIII:580n78; 581n86
5:3	I:559; II:334; VIII:194	9:8	I:66; V:50
5:3f	VI:163n15	9:9	IV:95; V:327; VI:193n139; 809
5:4	IV:197	9:11	V:327; VI:809; VIII:240n13;
5:5	V:743		318
5:6	I:559	9:12	VII:270(n6); VIII:613
5:6ff	VII:295n15	9:12ff	V:481, n76
5:11	III:441; VII:527	9:13	II:758; VI:802
6	I:92; III:306	9:15	V:547
6:2	I:718; II:454	9:15ff	III:571
6:3	I:562	9:16	I:626; VII:974; 975; VIII:10;
6:4	I:10n6; 562		IX:497(n20); 498; 499; 502
6:4f	VII:295n15	9:18	V:327; VI:809
6:5	IX:99	9:19	I:66; II:690; V:327; 481, n76;
6:6	I:559n2; V:631		VI:809; IX:627
6:7	V:286; VI:874	9:19f	VII:270(n7)
6:8	I:562	9:19ff	III:182
6:9	IV:1014; VII:215	9:20	III:606; VII:270; VIII:154
6:10	VI:874	9:21	IV:649; IX:246n12
6:12	V:65n64	9:22	IV:338n7; VIII:199
6:12ff	I:212	9:23f	VII:930n27; 931
6:14	III:284; 285; VII:959	9:24	IV:195; 197; 482; 483
6:14f	IV:279	9:25	V:481, n76
6:15	III:181	9:27	IV:95; VII:271(n8)
6:17	I:562	10	IV:157; VI:799
6:18	III:285; VI:523	10:1	III:772; IV:158; VII:220;
6:19	V:398; 400; 401(n141); 402		970n16; IX:126; 497, (n20);
6:20	I:92		498; 499; 502
6:21ff	VIII:196	10:1f	VII:231n213
7:1	V:481; 665n57	10:1ff	VII:224n165
7:2	VI:280	10:2	II:769; VII:270(n3)
7:3	IV:989; V:10	10:3	IV:182; VII:532n30
7:5	VI:54	10:4	I:485; II:407
7:6	II:467; 794n218; IV:928; 981,	10:5	II:503; V:482; VI:800n134;
	(n22); VII:51		VIII:496n48
7:8f	V:809	10:5f	VI:797
7:9	II:786n131; VII:770	10:5ff	I:724; II:454
7:10	VI:883; IX:280; 282; 283	10:6	V:469; VI:68n56; 362; 366;
7:12	IV:279		VII:714; IX:628
7:13	VIII:8	10:7	VII:212n74; 779
8	III:924; V:670n92	10:8	I:718; III:181
8:2	V:969	10:9	VII:212n74; 729
8:3	IV:389; V:51; VI:270; 570;	10:10	V:469; VI:68n56; 362; 366;

	VIII:348n88; IX:628	12:21	III:87; IX:73
10:10ff	IV:428; VI:797	12:22	I:448; II:589; IV:15; 147;
10:11	I:697n31; VI:797n112		V:252; 257(n110)
10:12	V:747, n19	12:23	II:27; V:52; 53; 809; VIII:111
10:13	VI:797n111; VIII:63	12:24	I:243; III:607; 609
10:17	V:763	12:25	IV:156
10:17ff	**IV:157-158**	13:1	VIII:138n30
10:18	VI:810	13:2	IV:168; VII:383
10:18f	VI:324; VII:975	13:3	I:267; VII:78; 79
10:18ff	III:142	13:6	VII:605
10:19	III:140; 141; IV:151n28;	13:8	IV:482; VI:194
	152n34; V:891; VII:641; 1012	13:9	VII:1022
10:19-21	IX:246n12	13:10	II:759
10:19ff	IV:158n73; 1014	13:11	IV:482; VIII:34
10:20f	III:761n10; 764n1; IV:155n51	13:12	II:786
10:21	II:769; IX:246n12	13:13	II:546; 705; IV:523
10:22	IV:157; VII:359	13:14	III:607; 612; VII:641
10:23	VIII:606	13:15	II:601; IV:195
10:24	I:699n41; III:701n20;	13:17	IX:98; 99
	IV:156n54; 157; 169	13:17f	V:48
10:25	I:744; VIII:194	13:19	III:359(n22)
10:26	II:284	13:21	VIII:580(n78); 581
10:27	I:607	13:23	VII:570n7; VIII:580(n78);
11	II:121n66; IV:156		581n87; 582n102
11:1	V:573n83	14:1	VII:359; 570n7; VIII:580n78;
11:2	II:108n16; VIII:154; 280		581n87
11:3	VI:523; VII:974	14:1-20	I:413
11:4	I:91; IX:281	14:4	IV:879; VIII:580(n78); 581n87;
11:5	V:665n57		582n102
11:5-10	VI:656n37	14:6	I:413; 414; V:171; VI:76n27;
11:6	V:394; 409; 861; VI:68n56; 363;		508(n40); VII:879; 880; 975;
	366		VIII:581n87
11:7	II:117n49; 225; 450; IV:152;	14:10	VII:220; 231(n213)
	557(n22); VI:578; IX:204	14:11	III:359(n22); VIII:581n87
11:8	II:601; III:357(n6); IV:162n91;	14:12	I:697
	VIII:353(n114)	14:15	III:5; 7n17; VI:508(n44);
11:9	VII:974		VIII:581n87; IX:98
11:10	V:665n57	14:15a	II:450
11:11	IV:197; VIII:261	14:15b	II:450
11:12-14	IV:158n73	14:16	VII:414
11:13	VII:976	14:17	II:601; VII:359
11:14	III:453	14:19	VI:281
11:15	IV:158(n73); VII:1023	14:21	III:359; VIII:218
12:2	VII:716	14:23	VII:976
12:3	I:157; III:303; IV:330; 389;	14:24	I:675; II:443; IV:928;
	860n140; IX:502; 503		VI:140n50; VII:271(n16)
12:5	VII:271(n10), (n15); IX:502;	14:25f	IV:553n11
	503; 511	14:26	IX:200
12:5f	IV:483; IX:446n53	14:27	IX:318; 625
12:6	VI:460	14:28	VII:271(n16)
12:7	I:66; II:175; 213; VI:511n79	14:28ff	VII:271(n15)
12:8	III:72; VIII:7; 195	14:29	I:252; IX:318
12:12	I:569; IV:156	14:32	VII:931, n30
12:13	IV:151(n30); 156; 159; 169	14:32-34	VII:771; 930
12:14	IX:284	14:32ff	I:173
12:14f	VII:696	14:34	VII:931, n30
12:16ff	IV:1014	14:37ff	III:571
12:17	V:325; VII:271(n15)	14:39	VII:976
12:17f	VII:271(n16); IX:280; 283n22	14:41	III:260; 764; IV:1014
12:18	IX:200	14:42	I:427
12:19	V:809	14:42a	III:764n1
12:20	III:607; 609	14:42b	III:764n1

	IX:156		
18:1-4	IX:156n88	20:7	III:483; VII:270; VIII:63
18:3	I:24; II:112, (n30); 849; IX:156	20:8	II:112, (n30); 479; IX:382
18:3f	IX:156	20:9	II:233; V:729; VIII:63
18:4	II:112; V:305	20:11	VI:570
18:5	II:267; V:657(n12)	20:12	V:459; 547n34
18:6	III:1037	20:13	II:117n50; VII:779; VIII:504
18:7	V:627; IX:468	20:14-17	I:156n89
18:8	VI:550	20:15f	V:253
18:10	II:11(n80); VI:164n17; 363;	20:16	V:129; 261
	367; 549; **IX:629**	20:16f	IX:156
18:10f	VI:797	20:17	I:24; IX:156
18:11	V:296	20:19	II:602
18:13	VI:578	20:20	I:400(n15), n16
18:14	V:5; VII:779	20:23	IV:483; IX:446n53
18:15	II:752	20:24	VIII:210
18:17	I:781; III:1065; VIII:346	20:25	II:602; VIII:199
18:19	I:781	20:27	II:602; VIII:199; 209
18:20	IX:124n115	20:28	I:195
18:21	VII:341; 342; 346n43;	20:29	VII:970n18; 980; VIII:209;
	VIII:351n102		IX:246n12
18:22	I:22n6; II:738; III:45n13	20:30	IV:146, n6; V:395
18:23	III:216; VI:889; VIII:9	20:31	I:570; VIII:347
18:24	II:443	20:33	V:729; VIII:63
18:25	I:226; 631n22	20:35	IV:482
18:27	I:226; 781; VI:288	20:41	II:700; VI:761n40; VIII:65;
18:28	VII:779		IX:126
18:29	II:752	20:42	II:407; IV:483; V:177; 255; 260;
18:30	II:267		262; IX:446n53
19	VI:799	20:42d-21:9	V:121
19:1	I:22n6; IX:156	(21:1-10, M/S)	
19:3	IX:426	21:1-6 (21:2-7, M/S)	VI:19; VII:21
19:4	I:272; II:267	21:2 (21:3, M/S)	VIII:195, n52
19:5	I:273; II:167; VIII:154	21:3ff (21:4ff, M/S)	III:416(n13)
19:8	VI:772	21:4 (21:5, M/S)	VII:22n170
19:9	II:11(n80); VI:363; 549;	21:4f (21:5f, M/S)	I:89; 604
	VIII:493	21:4-6 (21:5-7, M/S)	I:90
19:10	VI:772; VII:970n18; 979	21:5 (21:6, M/S)	VI:510; VII:360; 880
19:11	VII:980	21:6 (21:7, M/S)	III:264; IV:1059; VI:774;
19:12	VII:979		VIII:165n3; 211
19:13	III:557; IV:754n2; VII:57	21:7 (21:8, M/S)	V:658n14; VI:487(n29);
19:14	VIII:310n17		VII:880
19:16	VII:57	21:8 (21:9, M/S)	VII:562
19:17f	VII:979	21:8f (21:9f, M/S)	VI:994
19:18	VII:970n16, n18	21:9 (21:10, M/S)	VI:994
19:18ff	VI:797	21:10 (21:11, M/S)	VI:772
19:18-24	VI:800	21:12 (21:13, M/S)	III:612n19; IX:199; 200
19:19	VI:800n134	22:1	VII:979
19:19ff	II:503	22:2	VII:605; IX:629n85
19:19-22	VIII:218	22:3f	V:10
19:20	III:527; 529; IV:428; V:861;	22:4	V:776n16; 777n24
	VI:362; 797n112; IX:628	22:5	VI:801, n136
19:20ff	I:724; II:454; IV:428	22:6f	V:674n113
19:23	VI:362	22:7	V:658(n13); VII:706; VIII:28
19:24	VI:626n29	22:8	II:108n16; III:577; V:674; 925
20	I:38	22:9	V:657(n12)
20:1	I:162; 268	22:10	VI:994
20:2	III:577; V:547	22:13	VII:154; IX:413n72
20:3	V:460n20	22:14	V:674n113; 762n16; VI:185
20:5	III:441; VIII:210	22:15	IX:413n72
20:6	I:195; II:601; VI:523; VIII:229;	22:17	I:288; III:577; VIII:229
	IX:246n12	22:19	IV:915; VI:523
		22:20	VII:21n167; 979n54

28:21	VIII:154		VII:752(n12) IX:629
28:24	III:181	30:13	IV:1092; V:674n112; VII:270;
29f	V:10		VIII:310n17
29:3	III:359(n22)	30:14	IV:595
29:3f	VII:706	30:17	III:593; VII:970n15, n16; 979
29:4	I:22n7; 253; II:73; IV:318;	30:21	II:407n38; 686
	V:394(n74); 395n83;	30:22	I:607; VI:551
	VIII:194	30:23	IX:237
29:6	V:104	30:26	VI:313; 657
29:7	VI:469; 570	30:26-31	VI:656n37
29:8	II:812	30:31	VIII:194
29:9	I:77	31:1	VI:772
30:2	IV:531n7	31:3	I:559
30:4	IX:281	31:4	V:631; IX:200n59
30:6	III:25n2; 142; 913n3;	31:4f	VI:994
	VI:508(n43); IX:621; 629n85	31:9	II:318; 377(n11); 707(n6); 708;
30:9	VI:62		710n25; 712(n60); VII:359
30:10	VIII:580n80	31:10	VII:583; 1045
30:11f	VIII:318	31:12	VI:935n43; VII:116n150; 1045
30:12	III:728; VI:361; 368;	31:13	III:838; 848; IV:927; 928

II SAMUEL

1:1	VIII:261		498
1:3f	VII:979	2:6	II:479n35; VI:469
1:4	IV:105	2:7	IV:156; VIII:346; IX:497(n20);
1:6	V:479; VI:173; VII:655		**498**
1:9	II:849(n115); VII:428n39	2:8f	IV:157
1:10	II:712(n59)	2:10	VIII:137
1:11f	III:839n72	2:12	V:657(n12)
1:11ff	III:838	2:13	V:657(n12)
1:12	III:837; 838; 846; 848; 850n126;	2:14	V:628n10
	IV:927; 928; V:129	2:15	V:657(n12)
1:13	V:844; VI:731	2:16	VI:994
1:14	IX:96; 200n59; 502	2:17	V:657(n12); VI:883
1:15f	II:721	2:21	V:296
1:16	I:174; III:675; IX:502; 624	2:23	VIII:261
1:17f	III:150	2:24	V:262
1:17ff	III:838	2:25	III:675
1:17-27	III:150	2:25f	V:480
1:18	I:617(n2); 748n27	2:26	II:692; IV:943
1:19	VIII:603	2:28	VII:79
1:19-27	III:151	2:30	II:602
1:20	II:787(n152); V:104	2:32	IX:318
1:21	V:297; 479; IX:497; 501n48;	3:1	VI:570; 704n6
	502n49, n51; 510, n72	3:6	V:1017n6
1:22	III:659; V:296	3:8	II:479n22
1:23	III:913	3:10	III:162; V:1017n6
1:24	III:812; 838; 880; 881	3:13	I:192; II:105
1:26	I:24n23; II:114n41; III:31; 839;	3:14	I:226
	IX:125n118; 156	3:15	V:728n3
2:1-4	IV:159n77	3:17	VI:657
2:4	IV:156; VII:302; IX:497(n20);	3:18	IV:158n66; V:664; 703n370;

	VII:975
3:21	VI:570
3:24	II:408
3:25	V:104
3:29	III:625n5
3:31	III:839n72; V:305; VII:59
3:31f	III:850n124
3:31ff	III:838
3:32	III:722; IX:281
3:33f	III:150
3:34	I:155; III:150; 839
3:35	I:675; II:107; III:848; IV:927; 928
3:39	VI:470; VII:738; IX:497; 498n25; 502n50; 510; 624
4:1	I:509
4:3	V:843
4:4	I:60; V:604n44; VI:183
4:6	VII:980
4:8	II:445
4:9	IV:331; 333
4:10	II:707; 709; 712(n59); 721; 725
4:11	II:895
4:12	III:823; 853; 917
5:1	VII:106
5:2	IV:54; 158n66; VI:488n30; 494n84
5:3	IV:156; VI:657; VII:302; IX:498
5:4f	VIII:136
5:5	VIII:136n13
5:5ff	VII:307
5:1-I Kings 11:42	VII:295
5:6	VII:301n61; VIII:280n70, n74
5:6-8	VII:302; VIII:280n74
5:7	VI:522; VII:293; 294
5:8	IV:685; V:747n19; VII:301n61; VIII:261; 280n70, n71, n74; 287n120
5:8a	VIII:280n74
5:9	VI:299; 522
5:9-11	VII:302
5:10	VI:570; VII:779
5:12	II:705; IV:155; VIII:607
5:14	VIII:482n31
5:15	**IV:152-153**
5:19	IX:413n72
5:20	VIII:317; 322
5:24	VI:508(n42); IX:280
5:25	VI:469
6	I:92; 781; II:794, n209; 796; VII:302; 308
6:2	III:161n13; 441; 498; V:253; IX:438
6:3	V:481
6:3f	VII:771
6:5	III:1037; V:627; VIII:496n48
6:6	I:401
6:7	V:398; 399n126; 401, n144; 402; 405; VIII:261; 268
6:8	V:394n72; 395; VIII:196
6:9	V:861

6:10	I:631(n17)
6:10ff	VII:294n3
6:12	VIII:196; IX:363n30
6:14	V:627n9; VI:772
6:14-16	V:627
6:15	II:796n229; VII:76; 77; 79; IX:281; 283
6:16	V:861; VII:402n8
6:17	VIII:196
6:17f	VII:1022
6:18	II:758; V:255; 260; 262
6:19	I:786
6:20	VII:271n8; VIII:171
6:21	II:796n229; IV:156n54; 168; V:627
6:23	VIII:342
7	I:566; 567; V:664; 676n127; 968n126; VI:802; 810; **VIII:349-350** (349n95); 362; 480
7:1ff	VI:801; 803; VIII:196
7:1-7	VIII:349
7:2	VI:808n183; VII:370
7:3	VII:779
7:4	IV:96; V:333n93; 861; VI:810; 836
7:5	VI:571; 810; VII:371
7:5f	VII:370n10; 371
7:6	V:942; VII:371; VIII:197
7:7	VI:487(n29)
7:8	VI:810; VIII:369n245
7:8ff	VI:810
7:8-16	V:491; VII:308; VIII:349; **350**
7:9	V:252; 257n110; 261; 264n144; 891; VII:775; VIII:350
7:10	I:155; IV:590; VI:985; VII:385n6; 387n2; 388; VIII:7; 195; 197
7:10-14	VIII:361
7:11	I:350; V:120; VIII:28
7:11-16	II:757; IX:519
7:12	II:947; III:14n60; 786; IV:270n19; VII:542; VIII:349; 367n233; IX:569n483
7:12f	VIII:367n233; IX:512; 568n481
7:12-14	VIII:366n228
7:12ff	III:162; 164; VIII:366
7:12-16	VIII:480
7:13	V:143; 253; 256; VIII:267n233; 361n177; 370n255
7:14	I:30n53; II:345n20; IV:611; V:966n118; 1006n365; 1014; VI:880, n58; 881n58; 967; VIII:349; **351;** 355; 359; **360-362** (361n177); 370n255; 389n400; IX:516n126
7:14a	VIII:361
7:14f	V:971
7:14b-15	VIII:349
7:16	I:570; III:162; V:121; VI:184; VIII:267n233; 361n177;

	370n255; 478; IX:503; 569n483	11:12	VII:270; 271n8
7:17	VIII:349	11:13	IV:546; V:658n14
7:18	I:22n2	11:14	I:617(n5)
7:18-29	II:796; VII:308; VIII:349; 350	11:15	VIII:261
7:19	IV:373	11:20	II:330
7:20	IV:148	11:21f	III:728
7:21	V:659n25	11:23	III:913
7:23	II:366; IV:333; V:98; VI:382;	11:25	VI:550
	460; VII:384n3; IX:9; 201	11:26	III:837; 838; 850n126
7:24	II:705	11:27	III:837; V:376; VI:550; 551
7:25	VI:293	12	VI:801
7:25-27	VIII:369n245	12:1	V:233; VI:323
7:26	IV:543	12:1ff	II:454; VI:836
7:27	II:769; III:577; 606; IV:965n7;	12:1-4	V:749; VI:39
	V:547	12:1-7a	VI:802n143
7:28	I:237; IV:93	12:1-15a	VI:802
7:29	II:400	12:2	VI:323
8:1	III:814; IX:80n9	12:3	III:824; VI:67n52; 889; IX:51;
8:2	VI:728n5; 967; IX:57; 80n9		502
8:4	III:336	12:4	V:19; VI:323
8:6	VII:976; IX:57	12:5	V:394; IX:502
8:6f	V:676n127	12:6	II:631; VIII:132
8:7	V:296	12:6b	V:749
8:7-I Kings 11:42	VII:307	12:7	V:749; VI:810; 1000;
8:10	II:407n38; 686		IX:497(n20); 498; 499
8:13	V:252	12:7ff	III:573; VI:810
8:14	VII:976	12:8	III:824
8:15	II:196n14; 200n41; V:310	12:10	IX:641n153
8:15ff	I:740n4	12:11	VI:313; 810
8:16	IV:679n5	12:13-15a	VI:802n143
8:16-18	IX:247f	12:14	I:622; II:812; III:1n5
8:17	III:268(n13)	12:14f	VIII:342
9:2	V:658n14; 674n112, n113	12:15ff	III:201; IV:983(n38); V:646
9:7	VIII:212; IX:203	12:16	II:790n186; IV:925;
9:8	III:1101; v:658n18		VI:193n139
9:9	V:658n14	12:16ff	IV:928
9:10	V:674n112; VIII:343	12:17	II:107; 334
9:11	VIII:341	12:18	VI:470; IX:200
9:12	V:674n112	12:18f	V:674
10:1f	I:416	12:19	IV:949; VII:890
10:2	V:788, n123; 820	12:20	I:229; II:472; IV:300; V:120;
10:2f	V:778		VI:195n145
10:2-4	V:658n14	12:21	IV:927
10:2ff	V:664	12:23	VI:572; VII:716, n3
10:3	II:253; VII:417; VIII:172n17	12:24	III:1n5; V:778
10:6	IV:697	12:25	I:30n53; IX:168n184
10:8	V:731	12:27	VI:522
10:9	II:707(n6); IV:145n4; 182	12:28	III:498n8; V:253; 263
10:11	VII:974	12:30	VII:624
10:12	I:363; III:913; VI:524	12:31	II:225
10:15	VI:883	13:1	IX:125n118
10:19	V:658; 674; VI:883; VII:974;	13:1-22	I:24
	IX:200	13:2	III:32; 142; V:832
11:2	III:169; IV:300; 946n10; V:942	13:3	VI:313; VII:484
11:4	I:93; III:416(n13); 427; IV:300	13:4	VI:888; VIII:341
11:5	II:400	13:5	II:107
11:7	II:407; VIII:310n18	13:5f	V:325
11:8	VI:627n35; VIII:320	13:6	II:107
11:9	V:658n14; 731	13:7	II:107
11:11	V:460; VII:370	13:10	II:107
11:11ff	VI:627n35; VII:370	13:12	VI:469; VIII:7
		13:14	VIII:7

I KINGS

6:20	VII:744; VIII:211	8:25	III:442; V:51; IX:237
6:22	VIII:65	8:26	IV:93; VI:185
6:23	IV:544; IX:438	8:27	II:421; V:124; 256; 503(n48);
6:23-32	IX:438		507; 511; 512; VI:186n103;
6:25	VIII:65		290, n15; 303; 439(n723);
6:28	I:743; IX:438		VII:309; 464n33; 777
6:29	I:743	8:28	VII:271(n17)
6:36	III:629; 634	8:28ff	II:421
7	II:36; VI:468	8:29	V:121; VIII:197n70
7:2ff (7:39ff, S)	VII:733	8:29f	VIII:197
7:4 (7:41, S)	V:815n7	8:29ff	VIII:197
7:7 (7:44, S)	III:162	8:30	V:506n70; 521; 664n47;
7:9ff (7:46ff, S)	IV:269n5		VIII:199; IX:379
7:14 (7:2, S)	VI:287; VII:477(n91), (n93);	8:31	V:459
	482; 484; 497n202	8:31f	V:460
7:19 (7:7, S)	VI:225n362	8:32	II:177n10; 212; III:675; V:50;
7:21 (7:9, S)	VII:641; 734n19		51; 521
7:22 (7:10, S)	VIII:81	8:33	II:785(n121) V:204; VI:883;
7:23 (7:10, S, sic.)	VI:947		IX:379
7:29 (7:16, S)	IV:251	8:33-35	VII:724
7:31f (7:17, S)	VI:471	8:33ff	IV:980n17; 982
7:32f (7:18f, S)	IX:427	8:34	III:772; IV:33n15; V:680n175
7:33 (7:19, S)	VI:641	8:35	V:204; 507; VII:720; 721n12;
7:35 (7:21, S)	III:673		880; VIII:8
7:36 (7:22, S)	IV:251	8:35f	VIII:9
7:47 (7:32, S)	VI:276n13	8:36	II:61; III:772; V:52; 53; 664n47
7:48 (7:34, S)	VIII:211	8:36b	IV:33n15
7:50 (7:36, S)	IV:882n7	8:37	III:140; 141; VI:15
7:51 (7:37, S)	III:137	8:37-43	V:891
8	III:318; 930; VIII:197	8:38	II:793(n195); V:891; VII:815;
8:1	III:527; VI:657; VII:293n1;		908
	294; 296n17; 299	8:39	III:613; V:53; 155; IX:627
8:3	VI:657	8:39b	V:891
8:4	III:262; VII:383	8:41	V:253
8:5	VII:769n15; 804; IX:605	8:41-43	IV:37; V:10
8:6f	VIII:196; IX:438	8:42	II:927
8:8	V:327; VI:772; VIII:523	8:43	V:155; 263; 891
8:9	I:4n5; IV:466; VII:282n5	8:44	V:48n23; VI:524; VII:815
8:10	V:861	8:45	II:220; VI:460
8:10f	IV:905; VI:128	8:47	I:158; II:785(n121); III:607;
8:11	II:245; IV:888; VII:637		VII:724; VIII:224n62;
8:12	II:240n25; 382, (n3) III:967;		IX:379
	1005n46; V:506n71; VII:383;	8:48	III:772; VII:724; 815;
	385; 429		IX:628n81
8:12f	V:256; VII:304; 309	8:49	III:930; V:155
8:13	I:92; II:363; V:155	8:50	II:480n51; 481; III:930;
8:14	II:758; III:527; VI:771; VII:643		V:160(n18)
8:14ff	III:529n90; V:256	8:51	III:772
8:15	II:764; VI:288; VII:271(n17)	8:52	V:664n47
8:15ff	V:338	8:53	I:617(n2); III:772; V:663; 891
8:16	IV:156n54; 168; 169; V:262	8:53a	I:748n27; III:451; 1005; V:510;
8:17	III:607; V:256; 263		VII:429
8:19	IX:626	8:54	I:739; II:789(n180); 790(n183);
8:20	V:263; VI:293; VII:384		793(n193); III:595; VIII:63
8:21	II:126	8:55	II:758; III:527; VII:643;
8:22	II:790, (n182); 793(n193);		IX:281; 282
	III:527	8:55f	VII:829n201
8:23	II:479(n35); 480(n37); III:351;	8:56	III:575; 628; V:663; VII:34;
	V:513n119; VI:571; IX:238;		271(n17)
	383n82; 398n216	8:57	VII:720; 777
8:23-53	II:796	8:58	II:546; III:606; VI:571n31;
8:24	VI:288		IX:238

8:58f	III:930
8:59	II:220; 785(n121); IV:33n15;
	V:664n47; 674n114; IX:379
8:60	V:891
8:61	III:930; VI:188(n118); 571; 575;
	VII:909; VIII:72; IX:627
8:63	III:181; 454
8:64	II:284; VII:1022
8:65	III:527; VI:597
8:66	VII:383
9:1	I:22n8; VI:641
9:2	V:333
9:3	II:785(n121); V:256;
	VI:524n50; VIII:154; IX:379
9:4	V:493; VI:188n120; VII:909
9:5	III:161
9:6	VII:719
9:7	III:772; V:256; 747n14; 891
9:11	IV:531n7
9:16	I:446, n2
9:19	I:22n8; VI:641; VII:384n3
9:20	VII:301n61
9:20f	V:10n62
9:22	V:656n2
9:27	I:697(n32)
10:1	V:261; VI:24; VII:481
10:1-10	VII:460; 465
10:1-13	VII:516
10:2	III:593; VII:296n20
10:4	VII:481(n130)
10:4-8	VII:488
10:5	IV:230; VI:361; IX:629
10:6	I:234; IV:93
10:6-8	VII:481(n130)
10:7	III:441; IV:93; VI:186; 197
10:8	I:216; IV:365; V:838
10:9	I:30n55; II:764; III:45n13;
	VI:469; VII:641
10:10	VI:276n13
10:12	V:325; VII:210n61;
	VIII:496n48
10:13	I:192; III:45(n8); VII:460
10:15	VII:570; VIII:40; IX:80
10:16	V:313
10:16f	V:312
10:17	V:293
10:18	VI:136n14
10:18-20	III:162
10:18ff	III:442
10:19f	IV:251
10:21	VI:148, n5; VII:359

Special S Additions

10:22a	VI:641
10:22c	VI:638

Back to RSV and M

10:23	VII:459; 488
10:23f	VII:481(n130)
10:24	I:216; VII:460; 493
10:25	III:336; IX:79
10:26	IX:50

10:27	IV:270n17; VI:276n13; VII:758
10:28f	V:104
10:29	III:336
11:1-3	I:24n20
11:1-8	VII:43n54
11:1-13	VII:460
11:2	II:377(n22); III:822; V:291
11:3	VII:461
11:4	III:459; VI:188(n118); VII:779;
	909; VIII:72; IX:627
11:5 (11:6, S)	II:377(n18); III:86; VI:550; 571
11:6 (11:8, S)	VI:188(n119)
11:7 (11:5, S)	II:377(n18); V:484n102
11:7f (11:5, 7, S)	III:88; V:10
11:8 (11:7, S)	II:377(n22); III:181
11:9	III:606; V:333
11:10	VI:571; VII:110n104; VIII:72
11:11	II:107
11:13	V:664n45; 703n370; VII:308;
	310
11:14	II:334
11:14ff	II:73(n14)
11:18	VIII:34
11:19	IV:530
11:20	VIII:341; 344
11:23	II:334
11:26	V:658n14; VI:584n30
11:27	VII:299
11:28	I:553n1
11:29ff	VI:812
11:29-39	VI:802
11:30f	VII:959n2
11:31	VI:801
11:32	IV:169; V:664n45; 703n370;
	VII:308; 310
11:33	II:377(n22); V:51; 52; VI:470;
	760n23; VIII:348n82
11:34	V:664; 703n370; VI:14
11:36	IV:325n17; V:256n106; 263;
	664n45; 681n184; VI:524n50;
	VII:296; 310
11:38	V:51; 52; 121; VI:184; 470;
	VII:775
11:39	V:907n21; IX:512n89
11:41	I:617(n2); 748n27; IV:93;
	VI:468; VII:481(n130); 488
11:42	VIII:136
11:43	II:847
12:4	I:556n9
12:5	VIII:218
12:7	II:267
12:8	I:633
12:10	V:747n19
12:11	III:664n9; IV:518; 1020(n7);
	V:604n46
12:12	VII:218
12:14	I:556n9; III:664n9; IV:518;
	V:604n46
12:14f	I:269
12:15	V:1026n5; VI:293; VII:642;
	729; VIII:35n10
12:16	III:759; V:129; VII:383

12:18	IX:88	14:7ff	VI:836
12:18–2 Kings		14:7-16	VI:802
24:18	VII:296; 307	14:8	I:211; V:291; 681n184; 1017n6;
12:19	I:273		VI:571
12:20	VII:804	14:9	VI:992; VII:1045, n268; 1046
12:21	III:357(n9); 527; V:129;	14:10	I:748; VII:445n3; 880, n33;
	VII:805n30		VIII:81
12:22	I:364; VI:809	14:10f	III:483
12:23	III:357(n9)	14:11	III:1001, n2; V:510
12:24	I:455n4; II:543; III:759; 838,	14:13	III:837; 838; 840
	n64; IV:96; 195; V:510	14:14	I:369
		14:15	III:772; IV:281n6; V:403(n152)

Special S Additions

		14:18	III:837; 838; 840; V:665
12:24b	VI:584n30	14:19	I:618n11; VI:62
12:24c	IX:198	14:20	V:638
12:24d	I:193	14:21	V:263; VII:310
12:24m	VII:880n33	14:22	VI:550
12:24r	IV:515	14:23	V:481n75
12:24t	VII:383	14:24	II:366; VI:468; 585; 586, (n44);
			VII:858

Back to RSV and M

		14:25f	VII:304n79
12:26ff	VII:303n71	14:26	III:137
12:27	VII:296; IX:60	14:29	IV:93
12:28	VI:409(n499)	15:1	IX:589
12:31	V:120	15:3	VI:188(n118); VII:779; VIII:72
12:32	III:263; V:839	15:4	IV:196n8; 325n17; VII:296n17
12:33	VI:256; 258; IX:627	15:12	IV:814n107; VI:586;
13	VI:802; 809		VII:854n14; 858; VIII:59;
13:1	I:364; II:454; IV:96		132
13:1ff	VI:809	15:14	VI:188(n118); VIII:72
13:1-5	VIII:118	15:15	VII:733n9
13:1-6	VII:24n192	15:18	III:137
13:2	III:497n4; IV:96; V:129;	15:19	II:112n31; 126
	1017n6; VII:931	15:20	VII:706
13:2f	VI:802	15:22	V:762
13:3	VII:216; VIII:123	15:23	III:459
13:5	IV:96; VII:216; VIII:123	15:26	V:51; VI:570
13:6	II:786(n128)	15:29	IV:96; V:665; VI:364; 453;
13:7	IX:161n123		IX:618
13:8	VIII:194	15:30	V:410
13:9	IV:96	15:32	VII:72
13:13	III:843	15:34	V:51
13:14	III:441	16:1ff	VI:836
13:16	VIII:194	16:1-4	VI:801; 802
13:17	IV:96	16:2	IV:33n15; 521n4; V:51;
13:18	IV:96		680n175; VIII:606
13:19	VII:769n15	16:4	III:1101
13:20	IV:96; VIII:210	16:7	II:645; VI:470; 801
13:21	IV:93; VI:126	16:9	V:149; 658n14
13:22	VIII:194	16:11	III:162; IV:198
13:26	IV:93; VI:126; VII:920	16:12	IV:96; VI:801
13:29f	III:837	16:18f	VIII:512n25
13:30	III:838, n64; VII:1045	16:19	V:51
13:30f	III:845n99; VIII:262	16:24	V:252
13:31	VII:970n16; VIII:154	16:26	V:51
13:32	IV:96	16:27	III:907n11
13:33	IV:989; VI:287	16:28b	V:51
14:1ff	II:454	16:31	III:88; 217; 295n8
14:2	VI:801	16:33	V:403(n152); 410
14:4	VIII:280n66	16:34	III:284; IV:96; VI:523
14:6	IX:280	17	IV:882n7; IX:446
14:7	VIII:496n48	17:1	II:934; 939; III:441n12; 573;

	VII:643; IX:284
19:14	II:884; III:183; VI:800; 803; 834n348; IX:482
19:15	VI:571; IX:497n16; 498
19:15f	IX:497(n20); 499; 511
19:15ff	IV:1014
19:15-18	VI:510(n64)
19:16	IV:429; V:668n79; IX:498; 501; 505
19:16b	IX:511
19:17	VII:980
19:18	I:739; II:629; 935; III:595; IV:36; 202; 203; 205; 211; VI:760(n26); IX:123n95; 124n112; 469; 482
19:19	II:936n70; IV:428; 637
19:19-21	IX:511
19:19ff	IV:428; 429
19:20	I:211; IX:126
19:20f	I:213; V:982n235; VIII:33
19:21	I:368; IV:220; 428
20 (21, S)	VI:801
20:1ff (21:1ff, S)	III:336; VII:224
20:3 (21:3, S)	VI:810
20:5 (21:5, S)	VI:810
20:6 (21:6, S)	VII:141n318; IX:676
20:7f (21:7f, S)	VI:657
20:11 (21:11, S)	III:646; V:304; 305; 747n19
20:12 (21:12, S)	VII:370
20:13 (21:13, S)	V:584n13; VI:802; 810
20:13f (21:13f, S)	VI:801
20:15 (21:15, S)	II:601; VI:160n6
20:20 (21:20, S)	VI:160n6; VII:979
20:22 (21:22, S)	VI:801; VII:723
20:23 (21:23, S)	V:482
20:24 (21:24, S)	VIII:195n53
20:26 (21:26, S)	II:601
20:27 (21:27, S)	II:601
20:28 (21:28, S)	VI:508(n36); 801, n137; 802; 809; 810
20:28f (21:28f, S)	V:482
20:30 (21:30, S)	VI:162
20:31 (21:31, S)	II:874; VI:627n39; **IX:382;** 643n164
20:31f (21:31f, S)	VII:58; 60, n34
20:32 (21:32, S)	V:304; 305; 658n16
20:34 (21:34, S)	II:106n1; V:104
20:35 (21:35, S)	VIII:346
20:35ff (21:35ff, S)	VI:799, n130; VII:227
20:35-43 (21:35-43, S)	VII:948n77
20:38 (21:38, S)	IV:636n3; VI:800
20:38-42 (21:38-42, S)	VI:802
20:39 (21:39, S)	VII:641
20:40 (21:40, S)	II:175n1
20:40f (21:40f, S)	VII:661
20:41 (21:41, S)	IV:636n3; VI:800
20:42 (21:42, S)	VI:800; 810
20:43 (21:43, S)	V:393; 395
21 (20, S)	III:775
21:1 (20:1, S)	IV:882n7
21:2 (20:2, S)	I:252; IV:66
21:3 (20:3, S)	III:775
21:4 (20:4, S)	V:393; 395n83
21:5 (20:5, S)	VI:361
21:5ff (20:5ff, S)	III:217
21:6 (20:6, S)	I:631(n22)
21:7 (20:7, S)	III:611
21:8 (20:8, S)	I:617(n5); V:259; 262; VI:657; VII:944
21:9 (20:9, S)	IV:925; 928
21:10 (20:10, S)	I:607; II:759; IV:510
21:11 (20:11, S)	VI:657
21:12 (20:12, S)	III:675
21:13 (20:13, S)	I:607; II:759; IV:510
21:15-19 (20:15-19, S)	III:776; 778
21:17ff (20:17ff, S)	II:454; III:573; VI:836
21:19 (20:19, S)	III:1101; IV:300
21:19ff (20:19ff, S)	I:626
21:20 (20:20, S)	VI:160
21:21 (20:21, S)	VII:880
21:24 (20:24, S)	III:1101
21:25 (20:25, S)	VI:160
21:26 (20:26, S)	I:211; 598
21:27 (20:27, S)	IV:928; 981(n19); VI:627n39; VII:60; 106; 1045
22	VI:797; 799; 800
22:2	VII:610
22:2-28	VI:235
22:4	III:336
22:5	VI:799; 801; VII:271(n17)
22:5ff	II:404; III:575
22:6ff	III:571
22:7	VI:799; 801
22:8	III:477n29; IV:685; VI:193n139; 798; 799
22:8ff	III:154
22:9	III:853
22:10	III:162; VI:797; 799
22:11	III:669; VI:797; 799; 812
22:12	V:111; VI:797; 799
22:15	V:111
22:16	I:234n8; V:262; 464; 465n8
22:17	VI:499n8; VII:728n33
22:17ff	VI:811
22:17-23	VI:802
22:18	III:477n29; VI:798; 799
22:19	I:78n21; 568; II:38; III:88; 162; V:330; 506; 538n21; VI:668; VII:705
22:19ff	II:74; 75n17; III:574; V:665n53; VI:367; IX:243
22:19-22	III:163; V:505, (n67)
22:20f	I:384; V:402
22:21	VI:364; 370n184
22:21f	VII:643
22:21ff	II:11(n80); **IX:629**
22:22	VI:799
22:22f	VI:799; VII:696n46; IX:599
22:23	III:477n29; VI:799
22:24	III:819n5; VI:362; 799; VIII:263n22, n24

22:26f	VIII:341	22:43a (22:43, M/S)	V:51
22:27	III:141; VI:834n348; VIII:318;	22:44 (22:45, M/S)	II:417
	IX:243	22:45 (22:46, M/S)	I:769; III:907n11; VI:865
22:30	VII:689n16; 743	22:46 (22:47, M/S)	VI:62
22:34	V:305; 309n7; VIII:240n14	22:47 (22:48, M/S)	VI:586
22:35	III:824	22:52 (22:53, M/S)	I:268; V:51
22:38	III:1101; IV:300; VI:589	22:53 (22:54, M/S)	VI:761(n34)
22:39	I:748n27		

II KINGS

1:2	I:605; 606n5; III:86	2:13	II:936n70
1:2f	VI:193n139	2:13f	IV:637; VII:63n54
1:2ff	IV:708	2:14	II:936n70; VI:614n61
1:3	I:77; 605; 606n5	2:15	II:302n68; IV:429; 434; VI:362;
1:4	V:790		761(n39)
1:6	I:605; 606n5; VI:193n139	2:16	VI:362; 409
1:7	III:925n12	2:17	VIII:218
1:8	II:936n70; 937n70; III:593;	2:19	VI:549
	IV:637; V:304; 496;	2:19-22	VII:535
	VI:969n22; VII:63, n54	2:21	V:109; VI:800; 992
1:9	III:441; V:482; VII:706	2:23	V:631
1:9-12	IX:284n26	2:23f	V:646
1:9-13	VI:809	2:23-25	II:170
1:10	II:935; V:510; 532(n283); VI:936;	2:24	V:255; 260; 739
	942; 943; 945; VIII:218	3:6	II:601
1:12	II:935; V:510; 532(n283); VI:935;	3:11	IV:428; VI:801; VIII:328n93
	942; VIII:218	3:11ff	IV:429
1:13	I:739; III:595; IX:379	3:12	VII:389
1:15	I:77	3:14	V:839
1:16	VI:193n139	3:15	VIII:493; IX:427
1:17	IV:96	3:16	VI:800
2	**VI:800**	3:17	VI:800
2-9	VI:799	3:19	IV:145; 146; VI:523
2:1	VI:800n134; VII:197	3:21	V:305
2:1ff	II:424; IV:429; 905; 909n44	3:22	VI:952
2:2ff	V:460n20	3:24	VIII:261
2:3	IV:437n174; VI:799; 800n134;	3:25	IV:197
	VII:271(n12); VIII:346	3:27	III:88; 1074; IV:627, (n4);
2:5	II:454; VI:799; 800n134;		V:393n65; 397n108
	VII:271(n12)		VIII:343
2:8	II:936n70; IV:637; VI:614n61;	4:1	VI:800
	VII:63n54; VIII:319	4:1ff	IX:445n45
2:9	I:103; V:668n79; VI:362	4:1-7	I:229
2:9f	II:848n111; VI:142	4:2	VII:359
2:9-11	IV:8	4:3ff	VI:287
2:9ff	IV:429	4:4	II:254; 850(n132)
2:10	V:1031; VII:408n32	4:7	II:947
2:11	I:520; II:930; 931n19; 939n91;	4:8	III:575
	III:336; IV:8; V:506; 508;	4:8ff	IX:450n93
	VI:572; 937; VII:197	4:8-37	I:93; 103
2:12	I:665; V:963; VI:508;	4:9	III:441; VIII:210n6
	VIII:343n57	4:10	IX:54n46
		4:10f	

15:19	VII:769n15	18:18	V:149
15:23	VI:44	18:19	IV:529; VI:5n14; 7
15:27	VI:44	18:20	I:633; IV:1108; VI:191
15:28	II:58	18:21	VI:191; 967; VII:655
16:3	I:657; II:366; III:88; IV:982;	18:23	III:336
	V:51; VI:935	18:24	II:523(n37); V:658; VI:191;
16:5	VII:304n79		VII:720
16:6	VII:723	18:25	IV:160n84; VIII:197; IX:99
16:7	II:267; V:658n16; 660; 971;	18:26	III:359n25
	VII:974; VIII:345	18:27	VI:627n35
16:9	VII:760	18:28	IX:281
16:13	VII:531n22; 532n30; 1022	18:30	VI:191
16:13-15	VII:532n24	18:31	VII:752(n18)
16:15	VI:689n6; VII:532n30	18:32	IV:553n15; VI:1000
16:17	III:411; VII:744	18:33	VI:1001
16:18	V:104	18:35	III:97n179
17:3	IX:80n9	18:37	V:149
17:3f	IX:79; 80n8	19:1	VII:60
17:6	IX:248	19:1ff	VI:801
17:7	IX:199	19:2	III:262; V:149; VII:60n36
17:8	VI:571	19:3	III:140; 141; 142; V:410;
17:9	VI:522; 954		430n340; IX:670
17:12	II:377(n17); IV:60	19:4	I:621; II:850, (n138); IV:195;
17:13	II:546; IV:512; 1044; V:53; 329;		197; 205n36
	665(n52); VI:551; 802, n146;	19:6	I:621
	809n194; VII:719, n1	19:6f	VI:802
17:13-15	IV:486	19:7	I:60; VI:361; 362; VII:304n80
17:14	V:1029; 1030; VI:187; 191; 197	19:8f	VII:304n80
17:15	II:107; 126	19:12	IX:99
17:16	II:292; V:506(n69)	19:14	V:506n71
17:17	V:403(n152); VI:160; 935	19:14f	II:240n25
17:18	IV:197	19:15	III:161n13; 441; 1012; V:891;
17:19ff	IV:989		IX:438
17:20	VI:991; VII:66	19:15-19	II:797(n236)
17:21	V:1017n6	19:16	V:324
17:23	II:268; V:665(n52); VI:802	19:17	VI:186n103
17:24	III:776; VII:88	19:18	II:645; IV:269n9
17:24ff	V:847	19:20-34	VI:802
17:24-28	III:926	19:21	III:718; IV:796; 797; V:629;
17:25f	VI:736		VII:294; 296
17:27	V:670n92	19:22	I:93; 621; 622; VIII:603; 607;
17:29	VII:88		IX:281
17:30	IV:251; VII:88	19:23	IV:145; 146; V:480; 658n14;
17:30f	VIII:91		VIII:51
17:32	III:263	19:24	III:405; VI:598; 626;
17:33	III:926; IV:60n2		VII:886(n7)
17:34	V:253	19:25	III:1006; IV:373; V:456n2;
17:36	I:640; II:291		VI:257
17:37	I:746	19:25ff	IV:1014
18f	VII:304	19:26	V:942
18:4	V:576n103	19:27	I:700; V:104
18:6	III:823n7	19:28	III:631; VII:944
18:7	VII:779	19:29	VII:220; 231(n213); 539
18:8	VI:954	19:30	III:357(n9); IV:196; VII:970
18:9	VIII:132	19:30f	VII:978(n51); 979
18:10	VII:760; VIII:51	19:31	II:879; IV:196; 197; 198; 203;
18:11	IX:248		204; 205; VI:460; VII:296;
18:12	II:126; V:663; 737; IX:284		315; 970; 973n30
18:13	VII:760	19:34	V:664n45; 703n370; VIII:580n4
18:14	I:272; VII:720; VIII:160	19:35	I:77; II:11(n79); VII:304n80;
18:16	VI:184n88		1045
18:17	VI:961; VIII:318	19:37	VII:970n16; 980

20:1	VI:802	22:16-20	VIII:197
20:1ff	III:200	22:17	II:645; V:403(n152); VII:167
20:1-11	**VIII:118**	22:18	VI:193n139
20:2	II:777; 793(n201)	22:18-20	VI:802
20:2f	II:797(n236)	22:19	III:723
20:3	I:242; 455n2; III:607; 723;	22:19f	III:723
	IV:675; V:943; 945n25;	22:20	II:402n17; VII:295n17
	VI:188n118; 284; 575n55;	23:1-3	VIII:350
	VII:909	23:2	I:617n8; VI:800n133
20:5	V:324; VIII:218	23:2f	IV:99
20:5f	III:723; VI:802; 810	23:3	I:211; II:546; V:291; VI:293;
20:6	V:664n45; 703n370		VII:642; 733
20:7	VII:752(n11), (n13); VIII:160	23:4f	II:292; V:506(n69)
20:8	VII:219	23:5	IV:640
20:9	VI:460; VII:220; 231(n213);	23:6	IV:886; V:14; VI:992; VIII:346
	395; IX:677n15	23:7	VI:586; VII:689n16; 858
20:10	VII:395	23:8	II:11n77; III:284; 285;
20:11	VII:395		VIII:603, n14
20:13	II:471; 564	23:9	IV:239(n6)
20:16-18	VI:802	23:10	I:657; IV:645n11
20:17	III:138	23:11	III:337n3; VI:935
20:19	II:402(n18); VI:184n90	23:12	VI:992
20:20	VII:304; 317n121; 333	23:13	III:88; VII:459n1
21:2	II:366	23:15	VI:802; VII:720
21:3	II:292; III:1074; V:506(n69);	23:16-18	VI:802; 809
	VII:719	23:18	VII:980n58
21:4	V:256n106; 261; 263;	23:20	VII:931
	VI:524n50; VII:310	23:21	I:617n8; IV:99; V:897n7
21:5	II:292; V:506(n69)	23:21-23	V:898
21:6	I:657; II:10n73; IV:982;	23:24	I:748; II:10n73; 377(n17);
	VI:280; 365; 368; 919(n16),		VI:293; 365; 368; 919(n16),
	(n21); 935; VIII:198n78		(n21); VII:642
21:7	III:960; IV:169; 886; V:256;	23:25	III:397; IV:966; 989; VII:726
	263; VII:310	23:26	V:398; 400; 409; VII:720
21:8	III:772; IV:1047n97; VI:626;	23:30	IV:159(n76); IX:497(n21); 498;
	VII:66		499
21:9	II:366; VI:234	23:33	IX:79; 80n7
21:10	V:665(n52); VI:802	23:34	V:254
21:10-15	VI:802	23:35	VI:642
21:11	II:377(n17); VI:551	24:1ff	II:267
21:11f	III:477	24:2	V:665(n52); VI:802
21:13	II:465; IV:632	24:4	III:47(n34); 315
21:14	III:772; IV:195	24:10	VII:886(n7)
21:16	V:403(n152)	24:12	III:853
21:21	II:377(n17); IV:60; V:51	24:13	VII:312
21:22	V:51	24:14	IV:197; VII:888
21:23	VII:304n79	24:15	III:85n91; 853
21:24	IV:159(n76)	24:17	V:254
22:2	V:51	24:20	VI:991; VII:312
22:4	III:266	25:1f	VI:954
22:7	IV:285	25:2	VII:886(n7)
22:8	I:617n8; III:266; IV:1046	25:3	VI:15
22:8ff	III:723	25:6	III:925n12
22:8-10	IX:678n19	25:7	VII:930; VIII:279; 280
22:11	I:617n8; III:723; IV:1046	25:8	VI:961; VII:650n29
22:12	V:658; 674	25:9	VI:814
22:13	I:749; V:399n127; 410;	25:10	IV:329
	VI:193n139; 801	25:11	IV:197; 205n36; VI:62
22:14	VII:304	25:12	IV:197; VI:888
22:14-20	VI:801	25:13ff	VII:733
22:16	I:617n8; IV:96; 98	25:14	IV:220
22:16f	III:477; VI:802	25:17	I:729; IV:274n51; 275n64

25:18	III:266; VI:865	25:22	IV:197; 205n36
25:19	II:623; 766; III:853n9; V:325;	25:23	III:407; VII:944
	VI:771; IX:22n58	25:27	III:675

I CHRONICLES

1-9	I:266n4	6:19 (6:4, M/S)	V:1016
1:5	I:791	6:49 (6:34, M/S)	III:232; 309; V:659n22
1:6	VII:448	6:50-53 (6:35-38, M/S)	III:268n13
1:14	VII:301n61	6:72 (6:57, M/S)	IV:877n14
1:17	IV:879	7:2	VII:299n51
1:53	IV:879	7:4	IV:257n1; V:1022
2-9	IX:248	7:7	V:1022
2:1	V:261	7:11	V:1016
2:3	VI:551	7:17	VIII:353
2:26	VII:626n65	7:22	V:778
2:38	III:285	7:23	VII:760n6
2:47	III:285	7:27	III:284; 285
2:53	IV:434	7:35	VIII:341n46
2:55	IV:429; 434	7:40	IV:145
3:5	VII:296, n21; VIII:482n31	9	VI:184n93
4:3	VII:541n16	9:2	III:262
4:10	I:700; II:785(n119); VI:280; 460;	9:13	III:232; IV:221
	VIII:8	9:19	IV:221
4:12	V:573n83	9:22	IV:145; 182; V:327; VI:184n93;
4:22	V:573n83		191n129; 809; 812
4:23	IV:225	9:24	VIII:131
4:27	V:1018n15; VI:264	9:25	III:459
4:29	II:341n3	9:26	VI:184n93; 191n129; VIII:131
4:32	VI:522	9:27	III:233
4:38	VI:276n13; 281	9:28	IV:221
4:40	II:408	9:29	IV:263
4:41	I:744	9:31	VI:184n93; 191n129
4:43	IV:196; 197; VII:978n49	9:32	VII:5; 16; VIII:165n3
5:1	I:664n5; 665; VI:875	10:3	III:559
5:4	I:791	10:4	II:446; V:631; IX:200n59
5:12	III:675n2	10:9	II:377(n11); 707(n6); 712(n59)
5:18	IV:400	10:12	II:334; III:838; IV:925; 927;
5:19	VII:286n33		VII:116; 1045
5:20	VII:384n3	10:13	VI:365; 919(n16), (n21)
5:21	III:593	10:14	VII:723
5:23	VI:264	11:1	VII:106
5:24	V:252; 261	11:1-3	IV:159n77
5:25	VI:584; 587	11:2	VI:488n30
5:26	VI:362; IX:629	11:3	IX:497(n20); 498
6:3ff (5:29ff, M/S)	III:268n13	11:4	VII:300; 318
6:3-8 (5:29-34, M/S)	VII:37	11:5	VII:293; 294; 295n15
6:3-15 (5:29-41, M/S)	III:268n13	11:6	V:586; VII:706
6:4 (5:30, M/S)	IX:512n87	11:9	VII:779
6:8 (5:34, M/S)	IX:512n87	11:11	III:459n31; 675n2; VI:993
6:10 (5:36, M/S)	III:249	11:13	IV:34; VI:284
6:14f (5:40f, M/S)	VII:37n12	11:14	VII:641
6:15 (5:41, M/S)	VII:308	11:16	VIII:261

11:18	VII:532
11:19	IX:619n54; 620
11:20	III:459n31; VI:993
11:22	VII:300
11:23	V:368; VI:967
12:1	VII:880
12:9	VI:771
12:16	VI:287
12:18	II:52n10; 286; 402n20; 407
12:19	I:634; VI:363
12:24	V:262n140; VII:723
12:29	V:1021
12:31	V:252; 261
12:32	V:263
12:33	III:458
12:34	IX:627
12:38	II:418
12:39	IV:197; IX:617; 627; 641n152
12:41	VII:752(n12)
13:2	III:527; V:110; 112
13:3	VII:303n71
13:5	III:527
13:6	III:441; IX:438
13:8	II:286; III:1037; V:627; VII:77; 79; VIII:496n48
13:10	V:398
13:11	VIII:196
14:2	II:705; VIII:517; 603
14:4	VIII:482n31
14:8	III:625; IX:497(n20); 498
14:11	VIII:196; 322
14:12	VI:935
14:17	IV:655n33
15f	VII:318
15:1	VII:390n5; VIII:196n64
15:2	IV:155; 169
15:3	III:527; VIII:196n64
15:12	I:123
15:14	I:123; III:266
15:15	I:750
15:16	II:788n157; n164; VIII:496n48; 603; IX:302
15:19	II:788n157, n164; III:1037
15:20	V:831
15:22	IV:877
15:24	IV:877; VII:77; 78; 79; 87(n57)
15:27	V:304; VII:689n15
15:28	II:788n164; VII:77; 79; 81; VIII:496n48; IX:303n7
15:29	V:627; 815; VII:401n5; IX:617
16	II:794n209; 797; V:1016n5
16:4	I:177; II:787; 797; V:214n43; VIII:28
16:4f	IX:303n7
16:5	II:788n164; VIII:496n48
16:7	II:797n233
16:7-10	I:164
16:8	I:718; III:499; IV:682; V:214n43; 262
16:8ff	IX:504n56
16:8-36	II:797; VIII:495, n45
16:9	III:35; V:891; VIII:493
16:9-22	VIII:495
16:10	I:91; II:744; V:262
16:12	II:35; IV:682; VII:696; VIII:118
16:13	IV:155; 183; V:663n43
16:14	V:891
16:18	II:319
16:22	VI:808; IX:502
16:23	II:712; V:891; VII:1022n2
16:23-29	VIII:495
16:23-33	V:1016
16:24	III:35
16:25	II:786(n135)
16:26	II:366; 377(n19); III:88
16:27	II:244; 587; 588; V:129n40; VIII:199
16:27f	III:646
16:28	I:201; II:244; V:1016
16:30	III:1009; VI:772; VII:67; IX:198n47; 669n22
16:30a	VII:66
16:30-33	VIII:495
16:31	V:510
16:32	VII:768n13
16:33	III:647
16:34	I:14; V:214n43; IX:385
16:35	I:91; VII:971n19; 1013n55
16:36	I:177; 233n1; 335; 336; VI:186
16:37	IV:220
16:39	V:481, n76; VII:371
16:40	I:749; IV:1046
16:41	IV:145; 196; 197; VIII:495n45
16:42	II:788n164; VII:78; IX:303n7
17	V:676n127
17:1	VI:808, (n183)
17:2	VII:779; IX:617
17:3	V:333n93
17:4	V:676n127
17:4f	VII:370n10
17:6	V:942; VI:487(n29)
17:7	V:676n127
17:8	IV:529; 532n12; VII:775
17:9	IV:590; VIII:7; 155
17:10	VIII:8; 517, n6
17:11	VIII:353(n114)
17:11ff	III:162
17:13	IV:32n12; VIII:349
17:14	I:569; 570
17:16	I:22n2; III:442
17:17	V:370; VIII:606
17:20	III:351
17:21	II:366; IV:35; 333; V:98; IX:9
17:23	IV:93
17:23f	VI:185
17:25	V:676n125
17:26	V:676n125
18:6f	V:676n125
18:10	II:407n38; 811
18:16	III:285
19:2f	V:778, n123
19:3	VII:417
19:6f	IV:697

28:20	VII:779	29:15	I:680n12; III:992n147; IV:583;
28:21	III:262n20; VI:641; 694;		V:27; 843; 847; VI:194n141;
	VII:484; 497n202		731; VII:396
29:1	I:184; II:739; IV:156n54;	29:16	V:847; VI:277
	VII:308n94	29:17	I:387n3; II:175; VI:694n2;
29:1ff	VI:694		696n23; IX:627
29:2	II:286; VI:300; VIII:85n6	29:18	III:612; 613; IV:965; 966
29:3	I:90; II:738	29:19	IV:486; VI:188n118; VII:909;
29:4	II:255; III:233		VIII:52; IX:240n19
29:5	VI:287; VII:271(n17)	29:20	I:739; II:787; 789; 797(n240);
29:9	III:607; VI:188n118; 284		III:595
	694n2; 696n23	29:21	VI:276n13
29:10	V:981; 1007n370; 1009n384	29:22	III:248; IX:497(n20); 498;
29:10-12	II:294		499n32; 500, n39
29:10-19	II:797(n240)	29:23	I:569; 570; II:738; III:162;
29:11	II:286; III:397; 646; IV:943;		V:110n6; 664n46
	V:513n119; 891; VIII:178n51	29:24	II:286; VIII:40
29:11f	II:294	29:27	VIII:136
29:12	II:565; V:891	29:28	VI:284; 324; VII:459n1
29:13	V:214n43	29:29	V:327; VI:808; 809; 810; 812
29:14	V:847; IX:413(n68)		

II CHRONICLES

1:1	VII:779; VIII:603	4:8	VIII:211n22
1:1-9:31	VII:460	4:19	VII:359
1:2	III:924n8	5:2	III:527; V:1016; VII:294; 295n15
1:3	V:481; 663	5:6	IV:284n2; V:850n51; VI:276,
1:6	IX:57		n13; VII:804; IX:198; 207
1:7	V:333	5:9	V:327n68; VI:772; VIII:523
1:9	IV:93; V:262; VI:185	5:10	IV:466n32
1:10	VII:481(n130); 484; 890	5:11	VIII:34
1:12	VII:481(n130); 493	5:12	II:788n157; VII:77; 79; 643;
1:13	V:107n13; 481, n76		689n15; VIII:496n48
2:4 (2:3, M/S)	IV:639; VII:4n22; 5n27; 7n39;	5:12f	VII:77; 78
	30n234; 462n20	5:13	I:14; II:788n157, n164; 797n235;
2:5 (2:4, M/S)	IV:538		V:214n43; VI:129; VII:80;
2:6 (2:5, M/S)	V:503(n48); 511; VI:290, n15		VIII:494n42; 495n45; IX:281;
2:7 (2:6, M/S)	VII:308; 484		282; 303n7; 385
2:10 (2:9, M/S)	II:636	5:13f	IV:905; VII:79
2:11 (2:10, M/S)	I:30n55; 750; VII:481(n130)	5:14	VI:129; VII:643
2:13f (2:12f, M/S)	VII:484	6:1	III:967; VII:385; 429
2:14 (2:13, M/S)	VI:467	6:1f	VII:388
2:17 (2:16, M/S)	VI:728	6:2	I:200n10; V:263
2:18 (2:17, M/S)	V:10n62; 584n12	6:3	III:527; V:839
3:1	V:483	6:4	VI:288
3:2	VIII:132	6:5	IV:156n54
3:6	III:867	6:6	IV:156n54; VII:308n94; 310; 318
3:14	III:629	6:7	V:263
4:2	VI:947	6:8	V:263
4:4	V:327	6:9	V:263; 496; 497
4:6	IV:946	6:10	VI:293
4:7	I:65n1; VIII:211n22	6:11	V:332n85

6:12	II:790(n183); VII:643	8:7	VII:301n61
6:12f	III:527	8:9	VI:638
6:13	I:739; II:789n179; III:233; 595;	8:11	V:861
	VI:163n15	8:12	IV:882
6:14	III:351	8:13	II:906; VI:45; 46; VII:5n27;
6:14ff	IX:238		370; 462n20; VIII:218
6:15	VI:288	8:14	I:185; 364; III:262n20; VI:809;
6:16	V:51		VII:641
6:17	IV:93; VI:185	8:15	II:681
6:18	V:124; 503(n48); 511;	8:16	VIII:81
	VI:186n103; VII:464n33	9:1	V:261; VI:24; IX:617
6:19	VII:271(n17)	9:1-9	VII:465
6:20	V:263	9:3	VII:481(n130)
6:20f	VIII:197	9:4	IV:230; VII:570
6:21	V:521; IX:379	9:5	I:234; IV:93
6:22	V:459	9:5-7	VII:481(n130)
6:23	V:50; 51; 510; 511; 521	9:6	IV:93; VI:186; 277
6:24	V:214n43; VII:724; IX:379	9:7	IV:365; V:838
6:25	V:521; VII:719	9:8	I:30n55; 569; 570; III:45(n17);
6:26	VII:724; 880; VIII:8		162; IV:147; VI:469
6:27	II:61; V:52; 521	9:11	V:325
6:28	III:140; VI:15	9:12	III:53
6:29	I:562n8	9:14	VIII:40; IX:80n10
6:30	III:203; 315; V:53	9:15	V:313
6:32	I:640; IV:372; V:521	9:15f	V:312; 313
6:32f	VII:318	9:17	II:255
6:33	III:498	9:17-19	III:162
6:34	II:793(n195); IV:168; V:521;	9:18f	IV:251
	VII:308n94; 815	9:20	IV:285; 287n11; VI:148n5
6:35	II:220	9:21	VI:290
6:36	V:521	9:22f	VII:481(n130)
6:37	I:158; VIII:224n62; IX:379	9:25	III:336; IX:50; 51n22
6:38	IV:168; VI:524; VII:308n94; 815	9:29	I:748; IV:196; 197; V:329;
6:40	VII:197, n70		VI:808; 810; 812
6:41	V:490n16; 491; VII:977, n43;	9:30	VIII:136
	IX:386n97	10:4	I:557; V:1031
6:41-42a	VII:977n43	10:4ff	II:897
6:42	II:480n36; IV:675; V:491;	10:7	VII:271(n11)
	VII:720; IX:502; 503; 504n55	10:11	IV:518; 1020(n7); V:604n46
7:1	V:532(n283); VI:937	10:14	IV:518; 897; V:604n46
7:1f	VI:128	10:15	VI:293; VII:729
7:1-3	IV:888	10:16	III:759; VII:383
7:1ff	VII:318	11:2	VI:809
7:3	II:789; 797n235; VI:761n29;	11:12	VI:277
	VIII:495n45; IX:385	11:14	IV:220; VII:318; 384n3
7:5	III:454	11:15	II:11; IV:521n4
7:6	V:214n43; VII:78; 79;	11:16	VII:318
	VIII:493; 495n45; IX:385	11:17	VI:51; VI:570
7:9	III:454; VI:47n14	11:21	VIII:343
7:10	IV:34; VII:383	11:23	VI:276n13; 277; VIII:517
7:11	III:46n18; V:111; IX:617	12:1-7	V:403n153
7:11b	IX:503	12:2	I:287
7:12	IV:1125; V:333; VIII:197, n67	12:3	VI:277
7:13	VII:880	12:5	VI:808
7:14	III:498; V:253; 263; VII:720	12:6	I:189
7:15	VIII:197n70	12:7	VII:971; 973; 978(n50); 979
7:16	VII:308n94; 310	12:12	II:427; VII:720; VIII:52;
7:17	VI:570		IX:91n23
7:18	II:105; III:161	12:13	V:263; 264; VI:524n50;
7:19	IV:60; VII:720		VII:308n94; 310
7:20	VII:720	12:14	VI:470
8:6	I:22n8; VI:523	12:15	V:329; VI:643; 808; 810; 812

20:30	II:417
20:32	V:51
20:34	III:285
20:35f	III:801
20:37	II:284; VI:799; IX:155; 156n86; 157
21:3	V:293; VI:873
21:7	IV:325n17; VI:550
21:8	I:512
21:9	II:334; VII:383
21:11	V:481n75; VI:235; 468; 584; 585; 587; VII:296
21:12	I:750; VI:808
21:12-19	II:929
21:13	VI:584; 587
21:15	III:786
21:16	VI:362; IX:629
21:16f	VII:304n79
21:17	IV:197; VIII:342
21:19	II:667; III:722n1
21:20	II:587
22:6	V:327
22:7	IX:497(n19); 498; 499
22:8	IV:220
22:10	II:334
23:1	II:107
23:3	II:26
23:8	V:105
23:9	V:293; 313
23:10	V:293
23:11	IX:498; 499n33
23:12	V:214n43; IX:280
23:13	I:177; II:788n157; 797n235; VII:76; 77; 78; 79; 374; 570
23:17	II:377(n14); VII:921
23:18	II:636; IV:1046
23:20	II:284
24	IV:883, n11; V:124n24
24:1	VIII:136
24:6	II:601; IV:486; V:663; 665n55; 676
24:9	III:700; V:659n22
24:10	VI:287
24:11	III:266; 675n2; IV:530; V:711n445; VI:264; VIII:194
24:12	IV:697
24:13	VII:570
24:14	IV:196; 224; 231; VIII:63
24:15	VI:284; VIII:353(n114)
24:16	VI:297n72; 469
24:18	II:377(n11); V:396; 398
24:19	IV:512
24:20	II:319; V:111; VI:362; 808
24:20f	I:756
24:20-22	III:220
24:21	VI:834n348; VIII:160
24:23	VIII:65
24:25f	VIII:160
24:27	I:749; 754
25:1	VII:296
25:2	VI:188n118; 284
25:4	II:106

25:5	II:284; VII:295n17
25:7	VI:809; VII:777
25:9	VI:809
25:14	VII:641
25:14-18	V:403n153
25:15f	VI:808
25:16	IV:515
25:17	V:325
25:18	V:941
25:19	I:558
25:21	V:325
25:22	VII:383
25:24	VII:854n15
25:27	VIII:160
26:5	V:111; IX:198n49
26:9	VII:304, n75
26:10	VI:954
26:12	III:675n2; V:960
26:14	V:296; 309; 314
26:15	I:527; III:31
26:16	I:158; VIII:607; IX:99n26
26:16-21	VII:37n14
26:19	I:351; IV:264; V:393; 394n72; 395
26:19f	IV:635
26:20	II:473; VI:865
26:22	I:748; VI:808
27f	IV:1043
27:2	IX:99n26
27:3	VII:295n15; 304
27:7	VI:643
28:2	III:1058
28:3	VIII:341n46
28:5	VIII:261
28:7	VIII:341
28:9	V:511; 519; VI:808; IX:89
28:10	IV:483
28:13	I:117; V:397; VIII:165n2; 168
28:15	I:229; 774; III:444; V:310; IX:496n3
28:18	I:747
28:19	VIII:8
28:22	III:140
28:23	III:88; VIII:261
28:26	VI:643
28:27	VII:296n17
29:1	V:969
29:5	I:123; 599n7
29:6	VII:720
29:7	IV:882; VII:166
29:8	V:396; 398; 409; 410n201; 632n10
29:10	VII:720
29:11	IV:155; VII:308n94; 643
29:15	I:123; III:416(n18)
29:16	II:676; V:891
29:17	IV:882; VIII:63
29:18	I:123; VIII:211
29:19	I:513
29:21	IX:60n2
29:22c	VI:978n10
29:23	IX:428

35	V:896n2	35:21f	IV:711
35:1	V:897n7, n8; 898, (n16);	35:22	I:468; VII:695; 696
	VII:930n26	35:24	III:837
35:3	IV:220; 222	35:24f	III:838
35:4	I:750; IV:542	35:25	I:478; II:788(n154); III:218;
35:5	I:185		838; 839; 845n103; 847;
35:5f	VII:931		850n126
35:6	V:897n8; VII:930n26	35:26	I:748; II:522
35:10	I:185; II:546; VII:570	35:27	VI:634n6
35:11	V:897n8; 898; VII:930n26; 931	36:1	II:30; IX:510
35:12	I:185; 617n8; 748; II:704n2;	36:3	IX:80
	V:1016	36:10	VII:723
35:13	V:110; 112; VI:934; VIII:229	36:12	III:218; VI:808; VII:695;
35:14	I:145n7		696(n42)
35:14f	V:897n8	36:13	V:465n8; 1023; 1029; 1030;
35:15	VI:810; 812; VII:570		VIII:158
35:16	II:546; IV:221; IX:57	36:14	II:366; VI:280; 669n107
35:16-18	V:897n7	36:15	I:77n12; 400(n18); IV:990n71;
35:17	II:902; V:898(n16)		VI:812
35:19	I:748; V:891	36:15f	I:58n8
		36:16	I:58(n12); IV:796; 797; 798;
Special S Additions			V:400; 631; VI:808; VIII:302
35:19a	VI:293; 919n16	36:19	VI:953n7; VIII:63
35:19c	V:410; VII:720	36:20	IV:197; 205n36
35:19d	IV:169	36:21	VI:308; VII:5; 6n31
		36:21f	III:218; VI:288; VII:696
Back to RSV and M		36:22	I:746; III:700, (n16); V:763;
35:20	VI:570		VI:287; 362; IX:281; 629
35:21	VII:777n60	36:23	V:516n144; VII:779

EZRA*

*The S references for Ezra are from 2 Esdras,
same numeration.

1:1	I:746; III:218; VI:362; VIII:58;	2:43ff	IV:239(n12)
	IX:281; 589	2:55	V:659n21
1:1f	IX:591	2:58	V:659n21
1:2	II:602; V:510; 516n144	2:61	V:263; VIII:346
1:2f	VII:307	2:61-63	I:665
1:3	VII:310; 779	2:62	I:750; III:251; IV:334n17;
1:4	VIII:193; 194		1044n81
1:5	VI:362	2:63	II:319; VIII:72
1:8	IV:158n71	2:68	II:470
1:11	V:763	2:70	VI:523
2	V:659n21; IX:248	3:1	IX:89
2:1	III:357(n10); V:843, n9;	3:2	I:749; VI:809
	VI:523; VIII:346	3:4	I:749; VII:370
2:36	III:285, n5	3:5	II:470; IV:639
2:40	III:285; 290n42; IV:239(n9);	3:6	II:950
	V:643n45	3:7	II:471
2:41	IV:239(n10)	3:8	IV:197
2:42	IV:239(n11)	3:9	V:643n45

3:10	VII:78; 79	6:16f	III:454
3:10f	I:177	6:17	III:309
3:10ff	II:797n235	6:18	I:185; 753; 754; VII:297n26
3:11	II:788n159; V:204; VII:263;	6:19	V:897n7
	VIII:495n45; IX:385	6:19-22	V:898(n16)
3:11f	I:14	6:20	III:416(n17); VII:931; VIII:346
3:12	III:722; V:585; VI:658n40;	6:21	II:693n31; 903n8; III:427;
	IX:281		V:897n8
3:13	III:700n13; IX:281	6:22	II:906; III:606; VII:729; IX:625
4:3	IV:196; 197	7-10	VII:37n13
4:6	I:743n5; II:73; VII:296; 307	7:1ff	VII:37n13
4:7	II:662; IV:196; 197; VII:770n24	7:5	III:266; VI:866
4:8	VII:297n26	7:6	I:740n5; IV:1046
4:11	VIII:36; 402	7:10	III:607; 705n42
4:12	VII:297n26	7:11	I:617n8; 740n5; II:546; VII:531
4:13	III:485(n1); IX:79; 80	7:12	IV:1046n93; V:507n77;
4:14	I:400(n15); II:560		513n115; 516n144; VIII:58;
4:15	I:617n3; II:601; III:485(n1);		IX:22
	IX:585	7:12-26	I:740n5
4:16	II:408	7:13-17	VII:297n26
4:19	I:186; II:601; VIII:154	7:14	II:601; IV:1046n93; IX:155
4:20	IV:595; VII:297n26; IX:79; 80	7:15	VII:310; 388
4:21	VIII:154	7:19	IV:221; 223n23; VII:297n26
4:22	VI:281	7:21	V:507n77; 516n144; IX:22
4:23	III:336; V:585n15; VII:562	7:22	I:750
4:23f	VII:297n26	7:23	V:423; 507n77; 516n144;
4:24	I:452; IX:589		VIII:341
5:1	V:259n126; VI:799	7:24	II:574; IV:223n23; 230; IX:79;
5:1f	VI:808; VII:297n26		80
5:5	VII:862n5	7:25	VII:476; 489; 821n139
5:7	I:497; 747; II:402n13;	7:25f	IV:1046n93
	VI:283n26	7:26	V:608
5:8	IV:145; V:110; 111; 112n12	7:28	II:479n34
5:9	VI:658; VII:862n5	8:1	V:97
5:11	II:421; III:1017n104;	8:1-14	VI:658; VII:37n13
	V:516n144; 659n22;	8:2	VII:37n13
	675n123; 678	8:6	I:186n1
5:11f	V:507n77; 510; 513n115	8:8	II:137n14
5:12	I:287; II:421; IV:328; 338n1;	8:12	IV:649
	V:516n144; VI:126n3	8:16	VII:300
5:14-17	VII:297n26	8:21	IV:927, n18; 928; VIII:7
5:15	VIII:198	8:22	I:189; 192; II:790n186; III:906;
5:15ff	VII:311		V:440n402; 450n1
5:16	VIII:58	8:23	II:794; IV:928
5:17	I:400(n15); II:601	8:24	VI:669n107
6:1	II:601	8:25	I:485
6:3	III:227; VII:297n26; VIII:198	8:27	IV:243n13; VII:665; IX:63
6:5	VII:297n26; VIII:198	8:28	II:470; IV:35n20; 37
6:7	VI:658; VIII:198	8:29	III:262n20; VI:669n107;
6:7f	VII:862n5		VIII:141
6:8	VI:658; IX:80	8:31	II:811; VI:1000
6:9	V:516n144; VII:297n26;	8:32f	VIII:132; 218
	VIII:342; 595	8:33	VII:641
6:9f	II:421; V:507n77; 510; 513n115	8:34	IX:675n4
6:10	V:516n144; VIII:341	8:34b	IX:675n4
6:11	III:918; 1099n1; VIII:402;	8:35	III:309; V:843; VII:539n8;
	610n38		VIII:346
6:12	V:263; VII:297n26	9f	IV:1044; V:11
6:13	VII:872	9:1	VII:301n61; VIII:58
6:14	VI:658; 808; 812; VII:862n5	9:2	VII:540, n14; 542
6:15	VIII:58	9:3ff	IV:929
6:16	VIII:346	9:4	II:230

9:5	I:739; II:789(n180); 793(n193); IV:927, n18; VIII:11	9:14f	VII:970; 978(n51)
		9:15	I:249; II:185; IV:196; 197; 205
9:5ff	II:793(n202); IV:1043	10:1ff	II:797
9:6	III:675; V:519	10:2	I:288; II:368; IV:583
9:6ff	IV:981; VI:986	10:3	I:288; IX:198
9:6-15	II:797	10:5	VI:669n107
9:7	II:366	10:6	III:407; VI:42; VIII:318
9:8	IV:196; 197; 205; V:376; VI:986; VII:971; 973; 978(n51); 979; VIII:197, n69; 198; IX:379; 625	10:7	IX:281
		10:7-17	**VI:658**
		10:8	V:455; VI:658n40; VII:862n5
		10:9	II:543
9:8f	II:874	10:11	II:368; V:204
9:9	II:479(n34)	10:12	IX:281
9:10ff	IV:878n16	10:13	VI:280
9:11	II:366; 367n12; IV:34; V:665(n52); 675n123; VI:233n32; 808	10:14	V:396; 400; VI:658, n40; IX:586n18
		10:16	VI:658
9:12	III:769; 776	10:17	II:950; VIII:58
9:13	II:645; IV:197; 204; 205; VI:551; VII:971; 973; 978(n50)	10:18	VI:658
		10:23	IX:248
		10:31	IX:248
9:13-15	VI:986	10:35	VIII:353
9:13ff	VII:979	10:42	IX:248
9:14	IV:196; 197; 204; VII:973n30; VIII:65	10:44	VIII:344n64

NEHEMIAH*

*Numbers in parenthesis refer to 2 Esdras, S.

1(11):2	IV:196; 197; 205; VII:970; 978(n51); 979	2(12):8	V:766n2, n9; VII:306
		2(12):10	VI:550; 563
1(11):3	III:141; 357(n10); IV:197; 205; V:241; VI:563	2(12):13	V:573n83; VI:115n13; 194n143; VII:317n121; 921
1(11):4	II:794; 797(n241); IV:928; V:516n144	2(12):14	VIII:199
		2(12):15	VI:194n143; VII:921
1(11):5	I:29n49; V:516n144; IX:201; 238; 383n82; 398n216	2(12):16	VI:658; VII:706; 862n6
		2(12):20	V:111; 516n144; VII:309
1(11):5ff	IV:981	3(13):1	VII:306; 332n262
1(11):5-11	II:797(n241)	3(13):7	III:162
1(11):7f	V:676	3(13):8	VIII:346, n72
1(11):8	IV:676	3(13):10	I:717
1(11):9	II:99; IV:169; V:263; 510; VII:388; VIII:197	3(13):15	VI:115n13
		3(13):25	IX:243
1(11):10	II:292; IV:333	3(13):26f	VII:295n15
1(11):11	II:480n51; 766; III:46(n30); V:111; 160(n18); 676; VII:720	3(13):28	III:337
		3(13):31	VIII:346n72
		3(13):32	VII:332n262
2(12):2	III:606; VI:550; 563; VII:451; IX:200	4:1 (3:33, M; 13:33, S)	V:394(n73)
		4:3 (3:35, M; 13:35, S)	VIII:197n68
2(12):4	II:797(n241); V:516n144	4:4 (3:36, M; 13:36, S)	IV:798; V:631; VII:723
2(12):5	I:400(n15)	4:4f (3:36f, M;	
2(12):6	V:864n33; IX:678n18	13:36f, S)	II:797(n241)

4:5 (3:37, M; 13:37, S) III:304n18
4:10 (4:4, M; 14:4, S) V:584n12; VII:921
4:11 (4:5, M; 14:5, S) V:325
4:12 (4:6, M; 14:6, S) VIII:194
4:13 (4:7, M; 14:7, S) VIII:195
4:14 (4:8, M; 14:8, S) VI:658; VII:862n6; IX:201
4:15 (4:9, M; 14:9, S) I:633; 699n42
4:16 (4:10, M;
  14:10, S)   V:309
4:18 (4:12, M;
  14:12, S)   V:305; VII:78; 79
4:19 (4:13, M;
  14:13, S)   VI:658; VII:862n6
4:20 (4:14, M;
  14:14, S)   VIII:193
4:21 (4:15, M;
  14:15, S)   I:633
5(15):2   V:963n105
5(15):3   VI:15
5(15):4   IX:80
5(15):5   III:79; 83n81; VII:106
5(15):6   V:394
5(15):7   III:527; IV:527; VI:658;
           VII:862n6
5(15):9   III:124
5(15):11   VII:723
5(15):13   I:232n1; 335; 336; VI:186; 293;
           VII:642
5(15):14   VII:306
5(15):15   III:124; VIII:137
5(15):17   VI:658
5(15):18   IV:145; VI:277; 689
5(15):19   II:346(n34); 797(n241); IV:676
6(16):2   VI:563
6(16):3   VIII:81
6(16):4   VIII:132
6(16):7   IV:158n67; VI:808; VII:641
6(16):8   IX:598; 627
6(16):9   IX:198; 199
6(16):10   VII:879; 880; 884
6(16):10-13   IX:200
6(16):12   IV:697; V:585; VI:812
6(16):12f   V:585
6(16):13   V:263; VI:549
6(16):14   II:797(n241); IV:676; VI:808;
           IX:198
6(16):15   VIII:58
6(16):16   VI:164; VIII:81; IX:198, n47
6(16):18   II:114n39
6(16):19   IX:198
7(17)   V:659n21
7(17):1   II:602; 605
7(17):1-3   VII:307
7(17):2   I:233n2; 248; VI:537; VII:306
7(17):3   II:338
7(17):4-72a   VII:307
7(17):5   I:617n3; III:612; VI:658;
           VII:862n6
7(17):5f   I:620
7(17):6   III:357(n10)
7(17):6-65   VI:658
7(17):6-73   IX:248

7(17):7   II:266
7(17):34   VIII:353(n114)
7(17):43   V:643n45
7(17):57   V:659n21
7(17):60   V:659n21
7(17):63   V:263
7(17):64   I:620; 750; IV:334n17
7(17):71   IV:197
7(17):72   III:226n19
7(17):73 (7:72, M)   IX:89
8(18)   IV:1046; VII:805n28
8(18):3   I:617n8
8(18):4   VI:953; VII:819n128
8(18):4-6   VII:811n76
8(18):5   I:618n11; VII:819n128
8(18):6   I:186n1; 233n1; 335; 336;
           II:789; 797n235, (n241);
           VI:186
8(18):7   VII:570
8(18):7f   VII:811n76
8(18):8   I:617n8; VII:819n128
8(18):9   II:944; III:724n17; VI:42n9
8(18):9ff   III:723
8(18):10   IV:283; VI:169; IX:363
8(18):11   VI:169
8(18):12   I:718; IV:283
8(18):13   V:891
8(18):14   I:748
8(18):14-17   VII:370
8(18):15   I:749; VII:79; 371
8(18):15-17   VII:390
8(18):16   VI:468
8(18):17   III:284
8(18):18   VI:47n14
9(19)   II:797; III:772; IV:981; 982;
           VI:369n177; 808
9(19):1   IV:928; 981(n19), (n20); VII:60
9(19):1ff   II:794; IV:928; 981(n22)
9(19):2   V:11
9(19):3   II:789; V:204; VII:570
9(19):4   IX:281
9(19):4f   V:643n45
9(19):5   II:760n15; 797n235;
           VIII:603n11; 606
9(19):6   II:874; III:884; 887; 1011; 1012;
           V:503(n48); 511; 515n129;
           VII:570
9(19):7   IV:154; 166; 169
9(19):8   II:126; 769; III:607; 772;
           IV:154; VI:185; 293; 1001;
           VII:301n61
9(19):9   VIII:10
9(19):10   IV:34; VII:210(n65); 212;
           221n142; VIII:301; 526n5
9(19):11   V:471; VIII:319
9(19):12   V:98; VI:936; VII:733n11
9(19):13   I:14n11; 236; VII:282n4; 283n6
9(19):14   I:90; V:676
9(19):15   I:477; II:277; III:772;
           VI:15n23; 97n28
9(19):16   VIII:301
9(19):16f   V:1029; 1030

9(19):17	I:481; III:35; 86n100; IV:376(n18); VII:724; IX:378(n52); 383	11(21):9	II:615
		11(21):14	II:615
		11(21):18	I:90
9(19):18	IV:760; V:410	11(21):20	IV:196; 197
9(19):19	V:98; VI:936; VII:733n11	11(21):21	VII:295n15
9(19):20	II:227; IV:462; VI:363; VIII:594n14	11(21):22	II:615
		11(21):25	VI:522
9(19):21	V:718; VIII:136	11(21):26	III:285
9(19):23	III:772	12(22)	II:794
9(19):24	II:743; IV:34	12(22):1-7	III:262
9(19):25	III:778	12(22):7	I:488; III:285n5
9(19):26	IV:512; VI:808; 834n348; 992; VII:1045; 1046	12(22):8	V:643n45
		12(22):12	V:1016
9(19):26f	III:142	12(22):12-21	III:262
9(19):27	II:483n96; III:140; 141; VII:975; 1012; 1013n55	12(22):24	I:177; V:643n45; VI:809; VIII:493
9(19):28	VI:551; VII:724	12(22):27	III:454; 1037n3; V:219; IX:367n69
9(19):29	IV:984; 989; V:1029; 1030; VI:10n1; VIII:301	12(22):28	II:788(n157); VIII:346
9(19):29f	IV:510n1	12(22):29	II:788(n157)
9(19):30	IV:34; VI:363; 808	12(22):31	I:181n2; II:787
9(19):31	VIII:65; IX:378(n52)	12(22):35	VII:78; 79
9(19):32	III:912; VI:808; IX:238; 383n82; 398n216	12(22):36	VI:809
		12(22):38	I:181n2; II:787
9(19):33	I:236; VI:460	12(22):39	VII:332n262
9(19):34	IV:512	12(22):40	I:181(n2); II:787
9(19):35	III:772; VI:551	12(22):41	VII:78; 79; 87(n57)
9(19):36	III:772	12(22):42	II:601n5; 788(n157), n164
9(19):37	II:743; VII:1045; 1046n275	12(22):43	II:787
9:38 (10:1, M; 20:1, S)	II:108n16; VI:190	12(22):44	I:485n8
10(20)	IX:248	12(22):46	VIII:493
10:1 (10:2, M; 20:2, S)	VII:945	13(23):1	III:527
10:2-8 (10:3-9, M; 20:3-9, S)	III:262	13(23):2	I:524; II:756; IV:697; VII:714
		13(23):4	II:480(n44); VII:294n1
10:9 (10:10, M; 20:10, S)	V:643n45	13(23):4-9	VII:309
		13(23):5	I:485n8
10:28 (10:29, M; 20:29, S)	IV:197; V:11; 891	13(23):6	VIII:51
		13(23):8	II:346n33; VI:550
10:29 (10:30, M; 20:30, S)	V:459; 659n22	13(23):11	IV:527; VII:570
		13(23):13	VI:185
10:30 (10:31, M; 20:31, S)	II:368	13(23):14	I:619n21; II:346(n34); 479n22; 645; 797(n241); IV:676; IX:386
10:31 (10:32, M; 20:32, S)	I:90; II:368; III:603n2; V:560n7; 728; VII:5; 6n31; 18n140		
		13(23):15	IV:254; 510n1; V:941; IX:85
		13(23):15-22	VII:5
10:32f (10:33f, M; 20:33f, S)	IV:283	13(23):16ff	III:603n2
		13(23):17	IV:93; 527
10:33 (10:34, M; 20:34, S)	IV:639; VII:4n22	13(23):17f	I:605
		13(23):18	V:397; 403n150
10:34 (10:35, M; 20:35, S)	III:759; 761; IX:586, n18	13(23):21	IV:510n1; 512
		13(23):22	II:346(n34); 480n36; 797(n241); IV:676, n4; VI:276, n13
10:36 (10:37, M; 20:37, S)	I:748		
10:36ff (10:37ff, M; 20:37ff, S)	I:485	13(23):24	III:359n25
		13(23):25	II:346n33; IV:527; V:464
10:39 (10:40, M; 20:40, S)	IV:230	13(23):26	I:30; VI:537
		13(23):27	VI:470; 563
11(21):1	I:90; III:759; IV:196; 197; VI:524; VII:296; 310	13(23):28	IV:1099
		13(23):29	III:251; IV:334n17; 676
11(21):2	VI:695n5	13(23):31	II:346(n34); 645; 797(n241); IV:676; IX:586
11(21):3	III:357(n10); V:659n21		

ESTHER

1:1	IV:48; VIII:99n115; 564n23; IX:79

Special S Additions

1:1a	V:329
1:1aff	V:232
1:1b	III:129; 361n35; 365n59
1:1d-k	VI:248n121
1:1e	V:576; 721n1
1:1g	III:142; VII:605
1:1h	IX:198
1:1k	VIII:607
1:1n	IV:590
1:1s	III:911

Back to RSV and M

1:3	II:54(n2);367
1:4	IV:1100n9; VI:323
1:5	VI:306; VII:384
1:6	VI:256(n22); 258
1:7	VII:359n4
1:8	II:743; III:47n43; 53; V:149 VI:961
1:8ff	IV:1046n93
1:10	II:91; IV:219; 231n8; VII:361; IX:155n79
1:12	IV:259; V:394(n75); 395
1:12b	IX:226
1:13	VII:483, n146
1:14	II:330; V:325; VI:865; IX:155n79
1:15	IV:43n62
1:16	II:367
1:18	V:393; VIII:182
1:19	VI:313
1:20	I:326n66; VIII:172
1:21	II:766
1:22	VIII:132; IX:198n49
2:2	II:91; IV:219; 231n8; V:832n44; IX:97n13
2:5	III:361n35; 363, n43, n45; 364n53; VI:901n143
2:6	VII:296; 307n91
2:7	V:604n44; 960; 1019; 1020; VI:183; VIII:344
2:9	II:479(n34); IX:386
2:11	II:601; V:942
2:12	II:471; 472; VI:306; VII:458
2:14	I:22n6; V:261; 264n144
2:15	V:960; VI:306; VIII:344; IX:380n59; 586
2:17	II:479(n34); IX:380n59; 381n64; 386; 389n115
2:18	I:510; 648
2:19	III:129
2:20	I:129; VI:184; IX:198
2:22	V:259; 261; IX:7
2:23	IV:973
3:1	II:253
3:2	VI:760; 762(n41)

3:3	I:223
3:5	V:394(n73); VI:760; 762(n41)
3:6	IV:276; 281n10
3:7	VI:164
3:8	I:223; IX:74
3:9	II:231
3:10	VII:945
3:12	V:259; 262; VII:944, n59
3:13	I:402n34; II:589; IV:916
3:13f	VIII:28

Special S Additions

3:13a	VIII:40
3:13b	IV:900; VI:539; 647; VIII:40
3:13c	IV:973; IX:63
3:13d	IV:1048; V:12
3:13e	IV:1048; V:12; 27; VIII:240
3:13g	VIII:52; IX:586

Back to RSV and M

4:1f	VII:60; 62n48
4:2	II:561
4:3	I:763; III:837; 847n116; 850n124; IV:928; 981(n20); VI:42n9; 537; VII:58, n14; 61n47; 62n48; VIII:193
4:4	VI:3; IX:669n22
4:5	IV:400; 401n88
4:7	II:579; V:838n5; VII:769n14
4:8	I:195; 763; II:231; VI:881; VIII:10; IX:379, n55
4:11	VI:967; VII:972n27
4:13	IX:622n63
4:14	I:223; III:325; 458
4:15	II:580n35
4:16	II:690; IV:928; 981; VIII:218
4:17	II:823; VI:123

Special S Additions

4:17b	III:365n59; VII:970n16
4:17bc	III:1012
4:17b-d	V:891
4:17c	III:35; 1019, n124
4:17cd	III:1019
4:17d	VI:116; VII:971; VIII:302; 526; IX:126, n132
4:17h	III:315; 760
4:17i	III:365
4:17i-z	V:205
4:17k	III:365n59; VII:60n36; 605; VIII:526
4:17m	III:365n59
4:17p	III:30; VII:110
4:17s	IV:253n20; VIII:65
4:17u	I:460n19
	(Alternate reference, C. 21)
4:17w	V:372; VIII:526
4:17z	IX:198

JOB

1	I:78(n19); II:72; V:330; IX:544n333	2:13	III:832n19
1f	I:194; II:74; VII:292	3:4	I:378; V:531
1:1	II:175; 375n19; III:125; IV:572; VII:487, n160; IX:202	3:5	III:5; IV:334n17; VI:123n7; VII:395; 396
1:2	VIII:217n16; 343; IX:573n507	3:8	II:283; IV:530; V:572; 576
1:3	IV:530; V:284; VI:960; VIII:535	3:9	I:352; IV:583; 1125; VI:194
1:5	I:91; III:606; IV:965; VII:496n197; VIII:63; IX:65n2	3:10	I:252
		3:11	III:786; V:402n149
1:6	III:81; 97(n181); V:510; 838; 942; VI:668; VIII:347; 354	3:11-26	II:850
		3:12	VIII:345, n65, n68
1:6ff	I:374; III:636; V:505(n67); 533(n307); VI:367; IX:243	3:13	VIII:551n44
		3:16	II:465; III:1072n183; IV:915; V:324; VI:579; IX:320
1:6-12	V:505; 809; VIII:348	3:17	V:409; 410; VII:1046n276, n280
1:7	V:510; 942	3:17f	II:851
1:8	II:175; 375n19; III:125; IV:572; V:665; 666; 675n121; VIII:72n22; IX:202	3:18	VI:642n5; IX:80n9
		3:19	II:851; III:1063n121; IV:532; 653n25
1:9	IV:712; VII:171	3:20	II:850(n142); VI:123; IX:629n85
1:10	II:649(n46); IV:390	3:21	V:176, n1
1:11	II:74; 759; VII:496n197	3:22	VIII:240
1:12	VI:772	3:23	III:969; V:50
1:13	VI:872	3:24	VII:881; IX:198n49
1:13ff	VIII:132	3:25	II:752; IX:198
1:14	V:284	3:25f	IX:204
1:15ff	VII:980	3:26	II:417; V:409
1:16	V:532(n283); VI:935	4:3	IV:1020; V:777n17, n24
1:18	VI:872	4:4	II:285
1:19	VI:360	4:5	IV:1106n2; VII:562
1:20	II:789(n173); VI:163n13	4:6	IV:583n9; V:53; VI:191n131; VII:487n160
1:21	I:773; II:759; 764; III:786; 787; VII:716n3	4:7	III:414; 417; V:313n7
		4:8	III:132; V:115
1:21f	IV:588	4:9	V:394; 411; VI:360; 363; 364; IX:125n123; 629
1:22	IV:571; VII:496n197		
2	II:72; IX:544333	4:10	IV:252n11; IX:281
2:1	II:667; V:838; VI:668; VIII:347; 354	4:11	IV:252n11; VIII:342; 353(n114)
		4:12	II:51; IV:100
2:1ff	I:374	4:12ff	IV:749; V:332n90
2:1-6	VIII:348	4:12-16	IV:95
2:2	V:510; 942	4:12-21	VII:493
2:3	II:175; III:125; 482; 659; IV:572; V:665; 666; IX:202	4:13	IX:198n49
		4:13ff	V:230
2:4	II:74; 843; 850(n141)	4:14	IX:203; 624
2:5	I:401; II:759; VI:772; VII:107; 496n197	4:15	VI:360; 370n184; VII:106n61; 109; IX:623
2:7	III:675; VI:550	4:16	I:718; IV:746; 751n53; V:378; VI:684n1; IX:284n26
2:8ff	III:443		
2:9	II:759; III:617; 828n7; VII:97n23; 496n197; IX:586; 670	4:17	II:644; IV:572; V:404n167
		4:17ff	VII:121
2:9a	II:58; VII:971	4:17-21	VII:495
2:9a-d	VII:881n47	4:18	I:79; V:664n49; 665; 700; VI:187; 197n149; VII:381n3; 406; 408
2:9c	VII:454		
2:9d	II:58; VI:233n31; 234, (n33); VII:881; 882n53	4:19	V:132; VI:118(n11); VII:276n8; 277; 278; 381n3; IX:472; 473n7
2:10	II:50; 51n7; III:478; VII:496n197		
2:11	V:766n9; 778; 820, n23; VI:313; VII:480; VIII:193n44; 194; 218	4:21	II:536n3; IV:195n7; VII:485
		5:1	I:79, (n24); 90; V:333n91; 809;
2:12	VI:978n10; IX:281		

9:2	I:270n4; III:82; VI:186n103	10:22	VII:427
9:3	I:631(n21)	11:2	I:672
9:4	IV:584; 965; VII:476n88; 488; 489	11:2f	V:395
		11:3	I:672; V:631
9:5	V:480; 718; 720n2	11:4	II:644; IV:572; VII:488
9:5ff	III:574; IV:610; 1013	11:5	VII:695n39
9:6	V:510; VII:66; 197; 733	11:6	VII:489; 493; 494
9:7	VII:406	11:7	III:406n20; 1011; VII:518n372
9:7ff	IV:22	11:8	III:635
9:8	III:1008; V:942; VIII:323n60	11:9	IV:632
9:9	VII:276n8; 277	11:10	V:891; VI:460
9:10	I:358; II:294; III:33	11:11	II:645
9:11	V:333; 743	11:12	I:276n25; III:606n1; IV:141; V:284; VI:960, n12
9:12	I:252; VI:260		
9:13	III:1009; V:400; 510; 576; VII:720; VIII:418	11:13	III:31; 607; VII:910n41
		11:13b	III:31n17
9:14	IV:146	11:13ff	II:797n242
9:15	II:213; 785(n121)	11:15	IX:98
9:16	II:797(n245); VI:197n149	11:16	III:828
9:18	VI:123; 129; 360; 368	11:17	II:853; VIII:581n90
9:18-22	V:407	11:18	II:408; 522(n29); IV:590, n13; VI:5n14; 191; 194n141
9:19	III:906		
9:20	IV:572; VII:406; VIII:72n22	11:19	II:41
9:21	I:698(n36)	11:20	VI:194n141; VII:971; IX:619
9:22	III:1076	12:2	III:1080n212; VI:186n103; VII:488
9:23	II:175		
9:24	II:77; III:302; VI:552	12:3	IX:627
9:25	VIII:229n30	12:3ab	V:547n37
9:28	IV:557	12:3-11	V:547n37
9:30	IV:300	12:4	II:797n244; IV:572; VIII:72n22
9:31	VII:689; IX:99	12:5	VIII:28; IX:586; 625
9:33	IV:601; 611	12:6	III:83n82; V:393; 410
9:34	I:252; V:400n137; VI:967	12:9	III:1008; V:891
10:1	VI:123; VII:881, n49	12:9f	V:547n37
10:2-22	II:797(n246)	12:9-11	V:548
10:3	II:636; 637; 638	12:10	II:844(n88); 850n126; III:137; V:891; VI:361; 362; 369; VII:106; 108
10:4	V:327n68; 328; 376; VII:107		
10:4a	V:379		
10:4b	V:379	12:11	I:675; IV:953; V:546n30; 547, n37, n38
10:7	II:565		
10:8	IV:990n71; VI:256; 257	12:12	VII:492; IX:586
10:8ff	IV:1014	12:12aa	IX:586n21
10:9	IV:675; VI:256; 257; VII:716n3; IX:472	12:12ba	IX:586n21
		12:12f	VII:477(n91)
10:10	VII:117	12:13	II:293; VII:488; 489; 514n342; 890(n19)
10:11	II:319; III:1009		
10:12	II:606; IV:1013; 1014; VI:361; 362; VIII:154; IX:237	12:13ff	IV:1014
		12:16	**I:274;** II:293; III:397; 906
10:13	V:891	12:17ff	III:660
10:14	VII:108; IX:237	12:18	V:305n13; 604n46
10:15	II:213; VI:284	12:19	III:412
10:16	III:33; IV:252n11; 253n19; 990n71; VII:935	12:20	I:253; 676n4; VI:185n99
		12:21	III:203; V:304; VIII:10; 11n25
10:17	IV:482(n25); V:393; VI:25; VII:705, n25	12:22	VII:395; 396; 429; IX:320
		12:23	VI:233n32; 234
10:18	V:402n149	12:24	I:253; V:62; VI:234; 236(n42)
10:19	I:252	12:25	VI:233n32; 234; VII:424n10; 430n48
10:20	V:171; IX:585		
10:20-22	**VII:428**	13:1	V:324
10:20ff	VII:425n13	13:3	IV:611
10:21	VI:572; VII:716	13:4	IV:141
10:21f	I:146; VII:395	13:5	VII:485

13:7	IX:598n43	15:15	I:79, (n24); 90; 502; III:414; VI:187; 197n149; VIII:421n169
13:10	III:30		
13:11	IX:204		
13:12	IV:898n16; V:748; VII:1046	15:16	I:598; VI:139
13:13-22	V:407	15:17	VII:492
13:14	I:627; II:849(n123); VI:368; VII:107; VIII:154	15:19	V:8
		15:19f	VII:492
13:15	II:523; VI:194	15:20	V:892
13:16	VII:974	15:20-22	VII:495
13:18	III:942(n7); VII:597	15:20ff	VIII:302
13:20	III:968	15:21	II:233; 417; IX:204; 281
13:20-14:22	II:797(n246)	15:22	VII:430n48
13:24	III:969; V:402n149	15:22ff	VII:427n39; 430
13:25	VI:168n3	15:23	VI:169; VII:430n48
13:27	II:637; VI:985; IX:237	15:24	III:5; 141; 142; VII:706
13:28	V:718; VII:96n21; 276, n8; 277, n12	15:25	V:1025n5
		15:25-27	VIII:302
14	V:407	15:26	V:1025n1, n5; VIII:229
14:1	I:672; VI:284; VIII:383n358	15:27	V:1025, n5
14:1-4	V:404	15:29	IV:575
14:1-6	V:407	15:30	VI:168; 360
14:2	VI:168; VII:395; 396	15:31	II:233; IV:584
14:5	V:743; IX:586	15:32	IX:97
14:6	II:738; IV:697	15:33	VI:168
14:7	III:993; VI:194n141	15:34	IV:483; VII:803n25; VIII:564, n26
14:7-9	VI:986		
14:8	VI:985	15:35	III:786; V:115; VII:761n8
14:9	V:493	16:2	I:269; V:777n20; 788; 801; 805n39
14:11	IX:586; 593n70		
14:12	V:509; 718; VIII:551; IX:237n8	16:3	V:632; VI:360; 369n179; IX:628
14:13	III:969; V:410; VI:460; VIII:28; IX:237; 586		
		16:4	III:718; V:927n4
14:13-15	V:666	16:7	IV:836; VII:96
14:14	I:687; IV:579n2; 583; 585; VI:194; VII:705; IX:237n8	16:8	II:898; IV:9; IX:598
		16:9	I:641; V:402; VI:25
14:15	II:638	16:10	I:641; VIII:263n24; 265n40
14:17	I:525; 526; II:470; VII:944; 945; 1096	16:11	IV:914
		16:12	I:150; VII:414
14:18	V:718; VIII:200; 206n150	16:13	II:417; IV:911
14:19	IV:583; 585; VIII:322	16:14	II:284; VIII:229
14:20	II:426; VIII:51	16:15	III:669; VII:60
14:22	V:907n21; VII:107n73	16:16	VII:395
15:2	VI:360; 369n180; VII:486	16:17	II:797n244
15:3	III:659; IX:73	16:18	VII:108n84
15:4	V:395; VII:482n139; 487n160	16:18ff	I:626; IV:611
15:5	IV:146; 149; 168; V:724(n15); 725(n17)	16:19	IV:483; V:510; VIII:617; IX:446n53
		16:19-22	V:809
15:6	II:473; IV:510	16:20	II:786; 797n244; V:802; 809n67, n68; VI:313
15:7	III:1009		
15:7a	VI:865	16:20f	V:408
15:7b	VI:865	16:21	II:797n244; VI:313n13; IX:164n152
15:7f	VII:491; 493; VIII:411n76		
15:8	IV:814n113; VI:865; VII:489; 518n372	16:22	I:147; V:50; VI:572
		17:1	II:40; VI:361; VIII:420; IX:98
15:9	IV:949	17:2	V:632
15:10	VII:492; IX:586n21	17:2ff	II:797(n246)
15:11	I:288; IV:515; V:172; 777n20; VIII:520	17:4	VII:493
		17:6	I:659; V:747n14
15:12	VIII:182	17:7	IV:557n21; V:393; 1026
15:13	VI:360	17:8	II:175; 185; III:31; VIII:564n25
15:14	I:672; II:213; IV:572	17:9	IV:7; V:51
15:14ff	VII:121		

17:11	IX:225	20:4	I:200
17:12f	VII:425n15; 429	20:4-29	VII:481n135
17:13	IV:583; 585	20:5	VIII:564, n25
17:14	VII:96n21; 97n23; 453	20:5f	III:184
17:15	II:522n29; IV:583n9; 1010;	20:6	IV:903
	VI:194n141	20:6ff	III:660
17:16	VI:924; 925; IX:472; 473	20:7	II:233; VII:445n3; VIII:51
18:4	V:395; 480; 510; VIII:200	20:8	III:33; V:229; 230; IX:6
18:5	VI:934; VII:166	20:9	VIII:199
18:5a	VII:430n53	20:10	I:22n7; V:115; VII:481n135;
18:5-21	VII:481n135		495
18:6	IV:325; VII:430n48	20:11	V:739; VI:129; IX:472
18:7	I:633	20:12	VI:563
18:8	I:403n34; V:593	20:12-16	III:334
18:11	VII:605	20:14	III:334; V:573; VI:127
18:12	VI:16n29	20:15	III:79
18:13	II:692; IV:253n21; 557n21;	20:16	V:571; 572; VII:481n135
	VI:876n31	20:18	III:660; 828
18:14	I:565	20:19	II:285
18:15	VII:370n10; 1046	20:20	VII:971; 980
18:15ff	VII:430	20:21	IV:195
18:16	VI:985	20:22	II:233; VI:287
18:17	V:252	20:23	V:400; VI:287
18:18	VII:430n48	20:24	V:309; VII:972
18:19	V:842n7; VII:495; 540n13	20:24f	VII:481n135
18:20	III:31	20:25	V:942; VI:127; VII:1045; 1046
18:21	I:698; V:117n7; VIII:199	20:26	VII:430
19:2	III:855n1	20:27	V:509
19:3	I:699; IV:3	20:28	V:405; 410; 430n340; VIII:52
19:4	I:271n13; 275; VI:235; 236	20:29	II:614; III:775
19:4a	VI:233n31; 235	21:2	V:778
19:4f	VI:186n103	21:4	II:473; III:823n2; VI:361; 368;
19:5	V:239		IX:629n85
19:6	I:699; V:591	21:5	III:31; IX:426
19:7	II:797(n245); III:942(n7)	21:6	III:5; VII:492; 562; IX:623
19:8	VII:428	21:7	II:846(n101); VI:325;
19:9	II:243; VII:626; 689n21		VIII:311n22
19:10	III:858; VI:194n141	21:8	IV:518; VII:539
19:11	V:402	21:9	II:408; V:400n137; IX:204
19:12	VI:25	21:10	II:466; VI:894; VII:936; 970
19:13	II:487n2; IV:147	21:11	IV:914; 915; VII:401n5
19:14	V:262; 324	21:12	VIII:494; IX:281, n13
19:15	V:134	21:13	V:718; VIII:63
19:16	IX:379	21:14	V:55
19:17	III:817, n2; VI:360; VIII:341;	21:15	III:294n3; VII:494; IX:73
	IX:377n37	21:16	II:644; 645; VII:97n23
19:18	IV:914	21:17	IV:325; IX:97; 670
19:20	VII:96; 106	21:17f	VII:430; IX:323n79
19:21	IX:377	21:18	VI:360
19:22	VII:107	21:19ff	VI:894
19:25	II:848; 854; IV:328; 330; 334;	21:20	V:396; 399; VI:139n38; 167n2;
	611; IX:472; 631n89		VII:972n27
19:25-27	V:809; IX:290	21:21	III:53
19:25ff	I:369	21:22	II:136; 151(n30); IX:73n8
19:26	I:218n10; II:708n7;	21:23	III:906
	VII:107n73; 1046n277; 1048;	21:24	VI:284n4; IX:626n75
	VIII:63	21:25	II:692; VI:123
19:26f	I:218; 334	21:26	VII:96n21; 453; IX:472
19:27	III:109; 825; IV:911n3; V:347	21:27	III:172n2; IV:970n7; 971n16
19:28	II:229	21:29	V:48; VII:211; 213; 218n127;
20	VI:325		219
20:3	V:606; VI:361; 369, n179	21:30	V:405, n168; 430n340

21:31	V:50
21:32	VII:1095
21:33	II:675n2
21:34	III:627; V:789
22:2	II:137; 151(n30); IV:712; IX:73n8
22:2f	VII:494; IX:73
22:3	II:214; 645; III:53; 672; IV:572; V:51
22:4	IV:102; VII:487n160
22:6	I:774
22:7	VI:16n31; VIII:318
22:8	III:30
22:9	IX:445; 446n51
22:10	V:594n5; VII:562
22:10f	VII:428
22:11	VII:430n48; VIII:322
22:11ff	VII:430
22:12	VIII:8; 11n25; 302
22:13f	IV:905; V:507
22:14	V:324; 502n44
22:15	V:942
22:16	VII:760
22:17	V:55
22:18	I:633
22:19	IV:798
22:20	IV:196; VIII:580, n84; 582n102; 583
22:21	IV:584
22:22	IV:7; 1045n91; 1047n97; VII:696; 697
22:23	I:269
22:23-27	V:876
22:25	VI:949; VII:494
22:26	III:298; V:510; 876
22:27	II:776; 795; 797n243
22:28	IV:91
22:28ff	II:347n49
22:29	VII:977
22:30	VI:1000; 1001; VII:980; VIII:580n78
23:2	II:473; VII:600
23:3	VIII:52
23:4	VI:129
23:5	I:188
23:7	VIII:51
23:9	V:333; 334
23:10	V:50
23:11	V:51; 52; VI:361; 626n31; IX:237
23:12	VII:695n39; 696
23:13	III:47n33; VI:460
23:15	IV:1020; VII:562; IX:204
23:15a	IV:974
23:16	VII:562
23:17	VII:428
24:1	IX:677
24:2	V:743
24:3	IX:445; 447n59
24:4	II:285; V:52; 53; VI:647; 894
24:4-11	VI:16n31
24:5	III:635; IV:897n14; VI:643

24:5-8	VII:485
24:8	VI:192n136
24:9	VI:168; 647n11; 894
24:11	V:52
24:12	IV:836; 916n24
24:13	II:199; V:52
24:14	II:645; III:755; IV:1125; VI:647n11; 894
24:14-16a	VII:485
24:14ff	VII:424n11
24:15	IV:730; 732; 1010; IX:625
24:16	III:755, n4; VII:944; IX:353(n356)
24:17	VII:395
24:19	II:228n11
24:20	VII:453
24:22	VI:187n109; 197n149
24:23	IV:1091
24:24	VIII:613
24:25	IX:597
25:2	II:403; VIII:617; IX:204
25:3	VI:25
25:4	I:672; V:646
25:4ff	VII:121
25:5	III:414
25:6	VII:97n23; 453; 454
26:2	VII:974
26:3	IV:539; VII:486
26:4	VI:364
26:5	I:146; IV:528
26:6	I:4; 396; III:746n33
26:7	III:916; 1008; IX:320n68
26:8	IV:906
26:9	III:162
26:10	VII:429n45; VIII:65; IX:320n68
26:11	II:624; III:5; 34n35; V:502; VII:733; IX:320n68
26:12	V:576; VII:429; 489; VIII:418
26:13	II:281n4; 283; III:746n33; V:572; 576; VI:360; VIII:418
26:14	IV:595; V:55; 56; IX:284
27:1	V:747n14
27:2	VI:123; IX:621f; 629n85
27:3	VI:361; 363; 364; 368; 453; IX:629
27:5	I:252
27:6	VI:634; 693; VII:909
27:8	VI:5; 194n141; 269; VII:970n16; VIII:564n25
27:9	III:126; 141
27:9f	V:875
27:11	IX:598; 601n70
27:13	III:775
27:14	VII:495; 935
27:15	II:850; III:839; VIII:603, n14; IX:450n94; 452n108
27:17	V:891
27:18	VII:276, n8; 277
27:20	VII:277n11; VIII:322; IX:237n6
27:21	IV:280

32:7	IV:923; VII:492; IX:585		V:546n30; 547, n37
32:7-10	VII:493	34:4	IV:146n5; 149n20
32:8	I:700n46; VI:361; 362; 363;	34:5	I:252
	364; 369, n177; 453	34:6	I:608; IX:595n6
32:9	III:942(n7)	34:7	IV:798; V:631; VI:139;
32:10	VII:493; 494n191		VIII:322
32:11	II:51	34:8	III:801; IV:798; V:53; VI:470;
32:13	II:769; VII:484		VII:187(n5)
32:14	VII:494n191	34:9	II:606n2; VI:364n159; VII:494;
32:15	V:718		IX:73
32:16	IV:579n2; 583	34:10	III:606; IX:627
32:17	VII:493	34:12	II:187(n18); VI:186n103
32:18	VI:361; 369	34:12f	III:1013
32:18-20	VII:494n191	34:13	V:510
32:19	II:875; IV:897(n12); VI:364	34:14	VI:363; 364; 366; IX:629
32:21	I:171	34:14f	II:850(n127), n130; III:1011;
32:22	III:30; VII:277n11		IX:631
33:3	I:700n46; VII:493	34:15	VI:256(n21); 257; 258; VII:106;
33:4	I:700n46; VI:363; 364; 366;		716n3; IX:472
	369n177; 453; IX:629	34:16	IV:1020
33:6	IX:472	34:17	IV:687
33:7	III:5	34:18	I:607
33:9	II:645; IV:572	34:19	I:171; III:30; VI:894; VIII:172;
33:10	IV:572; IX:99		IX:427
33:11	II:637; IV:962n1; V:39; IX:237	34:21	II:637; V:328
33:13-24	VII:495	34:22	III:967; VII:395; 429; IX:320
33:15	IX:198n49	34:23	V:374; 891
33:15f	V:230(n39)	34:24	I:358; IV:10
33:16	III:561; IV:953; V:546; 547n33,	34:25	I:718; II:645
	n37; 606n52; VII:721n12;	34:26	V:368; VII:167
	IX:198n49, n50	34:27	II:220
33:17	II:637; VI:1000; 1001; VII:720;	34:28	VI:39; 894
	721n12; 1046; 1048	34:29	III:622; 969; V:334
33:18	II:849(n117)	34:29b	V:334
33:19-25	V:809	34:29-31	IV:401n90
33:20	II:850(n136)	34:30	VII:341; 408n32; VIII:564
33:21	VII:96; 106	34:32	II:27
33:22	I:79; II:849(n117); IX:99	34:33	IV:146; 170
33:23	I:79; 82n54; IV:572; 602; 949;	34:34	IV:401n90; VII:488
	962; 963n2; V:802; 809, n67;	34:35	IV:401n90; VII:493n190
	811	34:36	IV:400n87; 401n90; V:971n141
33:23f	II:78n41; V:809	34:37	I:278
33:23-30	V:811	35:3	VII:494; IX:73
33:24	III:303; IV:900; VII:1046;	35:5	IV:414; 903
	IX:377n37, n41	35:6-8	VII:494
33:25	IV:916	35:9	VI:276n13; 278n18; VIII:300
33:26	I:30n54; II:59; III:298; V:325;	35:12	VI:550; VIII:300
	334	35:13f	V:328; 334; IX:290
33:26-28	**V:202-203**	35:14	V:333; 334; VII:973; VIII:63
33:27	II:788n155; IV:571	35:15	II:602
33:27f	V:203	35:16	I:118; VII:493n190
33:28	II:849(n117); 850(n142); 853;	36:3	III:1008; VII:493
	IV:331; V:324; VII:972n27;	36:4	VI:186n103; VII:493;
	IX:320		IX:601n73
33:29	II:637; V:49; VIII:218	36:5	III:482
33:30	II:850(n142); 853; V:324;	36:6	II:874; III:929n24; VI:894
	IX:320; 351n338	36:7	VIII:607
33:31	II:352n83	36:8	VII:881
33:32	II:214	36:9	II:645; VI:170
33:33	VII:485	36:10	IV:990; V:547n33; 606
34:2	VII:477(n92); 488	36:12	IV:1020; V:117n7;
34:3	I:675; II:256; IV:149n20; 953;		VII:493n190; 970n18

36:13	III:607; VIII:563; 564, n25	38:8f	VII:429n45; IX:320
36:14	II:849(n117); VI:586	38:8ff	IV:1013
36:15	II:285; III:140n2; VI:647, n11; 894; VIII:564n25	38:9	IV:906
		38:10	I:147; VI:924n32; VIII:154
36:16	VII:695	38:10f	VIII:319n38
36:17	VIII:594	38:11	III:1012; V:743; VII:924n31
36:18	III:303; V:410	38:12	VIII:193n45; 200
36:19	II:470; IV:953; IX:198n49	38:13	I:679
36:21	IV:146; VI:634	38:14	VI:256, (n16); 257
36:22	III:913	38:15	III:859; VIII:301; 526; IX:353(n356)
36:23	II:637; VI:634		
36:24	I:478; II:642; IV:530	38:16	V:942; VI:115n17
36:27	V:503	38:17	I:147; III:745n22; VII:425n13; 695n35; IX:198n49
36:27f	IV:906; VIII:319		
36:27-37:13	VII:485	38:17a	VI:924, n29; 925n43
36:28b	VII:1046	38:17b	V:326n63; VI:924; 925n36
36:29	IV:572; 906; VII:372; 489; 890	38:18	IV:974n7; 1020; V:510
36:29f	VII:372n24	38:19	V:48; VIII:200
36:30	VI:985	38:19f	IX:321n72
37:1	III:612	38:21	IX:585n17
37:2	V:409; VII:695	38:22	III:137; V:503
37:2-5	IX:283	38:23	IX:676; 678
37:3	I:679; V:510; IX:319	38:24	V:510
37:4	IX:282	38:25	II:704; V:49; VII:591n4; IX:280
37:5	III:35		
37:5f	III:1012	38:27	V:104
37:6	III:1068	38:28	VII:886; IX:356n388
37:9	V:503	38:28ff	III:1009n70
37:10	II:536n3; VI:364; 453	38:30	VII:880n35
37:11	IV:145; 183; 906	38:31	I:699
37:12	V:503	38:32	III:459; VII:276n8; 277; VIII:342, n50
37:14	III:32; IV:974n8; 1020; VII:643		
37:15	II:639; VII:429n45; IX:320	38:33	IV:1013; V:503(n53); 510
37:15-18	VII:485	38:34	V:469; VIII:233; IX:281
37:16	III:33; 949; IV:906; VII:489; 493	38:36	IV:836; 969n5; VII:477(n90); 483; 493
37:18	III:1009; VII:610n9	38:36f	VII:499n215
37:20	V:838n5	38:37	IV:906; V:503; VII:489; VIII:318
37:21	III:41; V:368		
37:22	IV:530	38:39	II:850(n136); VI:129
37:23	VIII:8	38:40	VII:369
37:24	III:606; VII:476n88; 487	38:41	III:898n1; VI:234; VIII:342n49
38	III:574; VII:427n33; 429n43, n45	39	III:574
		39:1	III:459; IX:237; 669
38f	III:1009	39:2	IV:328; VI:284; 877n40; IX:673n54
38ff	I:218n11; II:47n19; V:395; VII:481n134		
		39:3	IV:337; VIII:342n49; IX:198; 670
38-41	V:890		
38:1	IV:905; V:334; VII:197	39:4	VIII:342
38:2	I:634; VII:881	39:5	IV:328
38:3	V:304	39:5ff	V:284
38:4	III:881	39:5-8	V:284
38:4-8	V:968n129	39:7	IV:572; VI:642n5; IX:80n9
38:4-11	VIII:319	39:9	IX:51; 52n27
38:4-39:30	VII:485	39:11b	II:636
38:5	III:596; IV:632	39:12	VI:187n109
38:6	I:527; VI:96; VII:733, n7	39:15	VII:484
38:6f	III:1009n70; 1011	39:17	VII:477(n90); 484
38:7	I:79, n23; II:787(n149); III:81; 97n181; VIII:347; 348; 354	39:18	I:659; III:458
		39:19	II:319
38:8	III:1009; V:721n1; VI:579; 924n32	39:19-25	III:336
		39:20	V:296

39:21	V:309	41:17 (41:9, M/S)	V:907n18; VII:880
39:22	IX:204	41:18ff (41:10ff, M/S)	IV:22
39:24	VII:66; 67; IX:281	41:19 (41:11, M/S)	IV:26; VII:972n25
39:24f	VII:79	41:20 (41:12, M/S)	VI:950
39:26	V:379	41:21 (41:13, M/S)	VII:1095
39:29	VII:415	41:22 (41:14, M/S)	VIII:229
40:2	III:294n3; V:604n47; VIII:563n22	41:23 (41:15, M/S)	VII:106; 109
		41:24 (41:16, M/S)	IV:269n10; IX:627
40:3	II:214	41:25 (41:17, M/S)	IX:198
40:4	I:640; IV:1020	41:26 (41:18, M/S)	VI:993
40:4f	VII:496	41:27 (41:19, M/S)	IV:285
40:6	VII:197	41:28 (41:20, M/S)	VIII:345
40:7	V:304; 496	41:29 (41:21, M/S)	IV:285
40:9	I:640; VII:974; IX:283	41:32 (41:24, M/S)	IV:285; V:942
40:10	VII:689(n20); VIII:172; 603	41:34 (41:26, M/S)	VIII:301; 346
40:11	V:396; VIII:8	42	I:287
40:12	VII:96; 167; VIII:526	42:1f	IV:1014
40:13	VI:129	42:1-6	III:1011
40:14	V:204; VII:975	42:2	II:285; 306; VI:25
40:15-24	VII:485	42:2f	VII:496
40:17	V:960	42:2-6	II:797
40:18	I:188	42:3	I:634; III:31; 32; 35; IV:530; VII:493
40:19	II:52; V:48; VI:258; 460; VII:934	42:5	V:324; 334; 347; 376
40:22	VII:395	42:5f	VII:496
40:23	II:523n36; VI:191	42:6	I:715; V:395; IX:472n4
40:24	VII:341	42:7	I:287; II:700; III:109; V:411
41:1 (40:25, M/S)	V:572	42:7f	V:406; 665; 666; VII:496
41:1ff (40:25ff, M/S)	V:629n16	42:8	I:287; II:51n8; IV:798; V:675n121
41:1-34 (40:25-41:26, M/S)	VII:485	42:9	I:287; IV:328; 336n8
41:3 (40:27, M/S)	III:297n9	42:10	I:287; VIII:517
41:4 (40:28, M/S)	II:109n23	42:11	III:30; V:778; 788; 820; VII:267
41:5 (40:29, M/S)	V:629, n17	42:12	V:284
41:5a (40:29a, M/S)	VII:731n14	42:13	VIII:217n16; 343
41:5b (40:29b, M/S)	VII:731n14	42:15	III:775; 777; V:510; 973n149; VIII:343n56
41:6 (40:30, M/S)	III:800	42:17	II:843(n81); VI:284
41:8 (40:32, M/S)	VII:675n38; 1046		
41:9 (41:1, M/S)	III:33; IX:597	**Special S Additions**	
41:11 (41:3, M/S)	IV:584; 585; V:510; 890		
41:12 (41:4, M/S)	IX:389n116	42:17a	I:747
41:13b (41:5b, M/S)	V:309n8	42:17b	I:617(n2); II:662
41:15 (41:7, M/S)	VII:858; 1046	42:17b-d	V:262
41:16 (41:8, M/S)	I:361; VI:360		

PSALMS

1	I:321; IV:711n66; V:46n12; 748n22; VIII:499n77; IX:339n224	1:1f	IV:365; V:55n38
		1:1-5	VI:399n425
1-57	I:321n33	1:2	III:53; 434; IV:365n32; 578n4; 1046; IX:203; 363
1:1	I:286; 321; 633; IV:365; 366n36; 572; 898n16; V:53; 54; 93; VI:571; VIII:225	1:3	III:459; V:108n19; 109, n24; 112; VII:580; VIII:317; 322
		1:4	VI:778

204

7:7 (7:8, M/S) | V:424n302; VII:803; VIII:606; IX:14n10

7:8 (7:9, M/S) | III:703n27

7:9 (7:10, M/S) | II:212; III:612; 613; IV:911; VI:563

7:10 (7:11, M/S) | III:607; 613; V:313

7:10ff (7:11ff, M/S) | V:297

7:11 (7:12, M/S) | II:176; IV:377(n31); V:393(n67); 407n184

7:11f (7:12f, M/S) | IV:378n34

7:12 (7:13, M/S) | IV:990; VII:665

7:12f (7:13f, M/S) | V:297

7:13 (7:14, M/S) | I:608; V:314n10; VI:950; VII:359

7:14 (7:15, M/S) | VII:760, n8; 761n8; IX:670

7:16 (7:17, M/S) | III:675; IV:761; IX:99

7:17 (7:18, M/S) | II:786n138; V:214n43; 257; VIII:494; 616n17

8 | I:143; II:392; III:551; 574; 1011; 1015; 1069n160; IV:254n3; VIII:41n9; 411n76; **464;** 471

8:1 (8:2, M/S) | III:32; 35; 1061; IV:542

8:2 (8:3, M/S) | I:177; 476; II:444; III:140; 242; IV:914; 915; 920, n44; 921, n48; V:646; VII:697; VIII:41n9; IX:684

8:3 (8:4, M/S) | II:20; 638; III:1008; 1009; IV:22

8:4 (8:5, M/S) | I:364n1; II:602; 605; III:1076; IV:148; VIII:346; 404n24; 405; 407n38; 423n185; 464; 471; 477

8:4-6 (8:5-7, M/S) | IV:676; VII:633; VIII:41n9; 175; 464

8:4ff (8:5ff, M/S) | III:1089

8:5 (8:6, M/S) | II:243; V:728n1; 735; VII:626

8:5a (8:6a, M/S) | VIII:41n9

8:5f (8:6f, M/S) | II:391; VIII:42

8:6 (8:7, M/S) | II:638; III:444; 881; 884n60; 1089; V:891; 894; 895; VI:629; VII:1078n499; VIII:40; 41, n7, n9; 42; 172; 371; 405; 464; IX:427

8:6b (8:7b, M/S) | VIII:42; 471

8:6-8 (8:7-9, M/S) | II:648

8:7f (8:8f, M/S) | VII:485

8:9 (8:10, M/S) | III:32; 35; 1061

9:1 (9:2, M/S) | III:35; V:214n43

9:2 (9:3, M/S) | II:787(n147); VIII:494; 498n66; IX:363; 366n57

9:3 (9:4, M/S) | VI:745; 748; 750

9:4 (9:5, M/S) | II:174; 180; 196; III:163

9:5 (9:6, M/S) | I:396; II:624

9:5f (9:6f, M/S) | IV:682

9:6 (9:7, M/S) | I:396; VIII:51; IX:91n23

9:7 (9:8, M/S) | III:163; IV:575

9:8 (9:9, M/S) | III:891; V:158n7; VIII:612n47

9:9 (9:10, M/S) | III:141; 143; 462; V:591; IX:184n106

9:10 (9:11, M/S) | I:698; V:257; VI:193n139

9:11 (9:12, M/S) | I:79(n25); II:787; VII:309;

VIII:494

9:12 (9:13, M/S) | II:895; VI:39; 892

9:13 (9:14, M/S) | III:141; V:325; VI:924; 925; 926; VIII:11; 287; 612n47; IX:377n44; 378, n45

9:14 (9:15, M/S) | I:70; II:787(n145); VIII:606; 607

9:15 (9:16, M/S) | V:593; IX:99; 625

9:15ff (9:16ff, M/S) | I:326

9:16 (9:17, M/S) | VI:460; VII:341n16

9:16f (9:17f, M/S) | V:401

9:17 (9:18, M/S) | I:326; VII:716n3

9:17b (9:18b, M/S) | VIII:51

9:18 (9:19, M/S) | II:522n30; IV:583; 584; VI:39; 892; IX:91n23

9:18a (9:19a, M/S) | VIII:51

9:20 (9:21, M/S) | III:32n21; IV:1089

10:1 (9:22, M/S) | II:95; III:141; 462; IV:372

10:2 (9:23, M/S) | IV:368; VI:892; VII:760

10:3 (9:24, M/S) | II:759; IV:389; VI:269

10:4 (9:25, M/S) | I:321; III:120; 1074; IV:970n7; V:55; 410; 857n2; VI:278; IX:625

10:4ff (9:25ff, M/S) | VII:908

10:5 (9:26, M/S) | I:605n1

10:6 (9:27, M/S) | VII:67

10:7 (9:28, M/S) | I:321; 448; III:968; VI:123; 125; 127n11; 290; VII:701

10:7f (9:28f, M/S) | V:368

10:7ff (9:28ff, M/S) | VII:428

10:8 (9:29, M/S) | III:961; 968; VI:889; IX:184n106

10:9 (9:30, M/S) | VI:892; VII:369

10:10 (9:31, M/S) | III:969; V:327; VI:897n94; VIII:7

10:11 (9:32, M/S) | VII:720; VIII:51

10:12 (9:33, M/S) | VIII:606

10:13 (9:34, M/S) | IV:974; V:327; 374n5; 488n4; VI:892

10:14 (9:35, M/S) | V:374n5; VI:889

10:15 (9:36, M/S) | VI:550

10:16 (9:37, M/S) | VI:39; 892

10:17 (9:38, M/S) | V:487n2; VI:892; VIII:6; 165

10:17f (9:38f, M/S) | VIII:9

11:1 (10:1, S) | V:480; VII:731

11:2 (10:2, S) | III:613; 635; VII:428; 909

11:3 (10:3, S) | II:636n6

11:4 (10:4, S) | III:162; V:507; 522n188, n192

11:5 (10:5, S) | I:23n15

11:5f (10:5f, S) | V:401

11:5-7 (10:5-7, S) | IV:711n66

11:6 (10:6, S) | V:594; VI:150, (n19), n23; 152(n38); 360; 944

11:7 (10:7, S) | II:176n7; V:325

12:1 (12:2, M) (11:2, S) | IV:193n2; V:491; VII:976(n39); IX:682

12:2 (12:3, M) (11:3, S) | I:721; III:607; VIII:563; IX:627

12:3 (12:4, M) (11:4(3), S) | I:721; II:46n18; 47n24; V:171

12:4 (12:5, M) (11:5, S) | III:1060; IV:543

12:5 (12:6, M) (11:6(5), S) | V:877; VI:39; 914; VII:971n19;

	VIII:154; 462	16:8 (15:8, S)	V:381; VII:67; 69
12:6 (12:7, M)		16:8-11 (15:8-11, S)	III:747; V:85; 772; VII:29n226;
(11:7(6), S)	I:122; II:256; VI:949		389; VIII:483n33;
12:7 (12:8, M)(11:8, S)	VIII:151n4; IX:237		IX:534n282; 646
12:8 (12:9, M)(11:9, S)	VIII:603	16:9 (15:9, S)	I:21; 721; II:238n22; 532; 775;
13 (12, S)	IV:981n26		III:607, n4; 612; VII:107;
13:1 (13:2, M)(12:2, S)	VI:773; VII:720; VIII:52		115; 388; 389n9; IX:363;
13:2 (13:3, M)			626n72; 627
(12:3(2), S)	IV:590n12; 965; V:115;	16:9c (15:9c, S)	VII:389
	VIII:607; IX:318; 320n64;	16:9f (15:9f, S)	II:848; 849(n123)
	627	16:10 (15:10, S)	I:396; III:202; V:85; 326; 342;
13:3 (13:4, M)			VI:308; VIII:367n233; 483;
(12:4(3), S)	V:376; VIII:551n44		IX:99; 632; 655n227
13:4 (13:5, M)		16:11 (15:11, S)	I:706n68; 718; II:775;
(12:5(4), S)	III:140; 143; V:262; IX:384		792(n188); 845n94;
13:5 (13:6, M)			851(n150); 854; 864n279;
(12:6(5), S)	II:479(n28); 522n30, (n31);		V:52; 53; 85; VI:132; 287;
	523(n39)		772; 777; VII:780; VIII:52;
13:6 13:7, M)			IX:363
12:7(6), S)	II:654; V:263	17 (16, S)	II:785
14:1 (13:1, S)	I:598; II:917; III:612; IV:834,	17:1 (16:1, S)	V:559
	n21; VI:469; VII:908; IX:96;	17:2 (16:2, S)	II:175n1; V:325; 326n61;
	99; 490		VI:772
14:1f (13:1f, S)	I:276	17:3 (16:3, S)	II:257; 601; 769; IV:162n91;
14:1-3 (13:1-3, S)	II:191		VI:949; VII:695n39; IX:97;
14:1ff (13:1ff, S)	III:120		627
14:2 (13:2, S)	V:328; 522n192; VII:895n64	17:3ff (16:3ff, S)	II:645
14:3 (13:3, S)	I:174; III:334; IV:58n2;	17:4 (16:4, S)	V:51; 52; 53; 741; IX:237
	VI:123n5; 125n14; 290;	17:5 (16:5, S)	I:476; VII:67
	IX:198; 490	17:6 (16:6, S)	III:82; 499; 899; V:549
14:4 (13:4, S)	I:153; II:692; III:499	17:7 (16:7, S)	II:37; 522n31; III:31; IV:583;
14:6 (13:6(5), S)	II:522n31; 529n91; 788n155;		VI:193; VIII:118; IX:384;
	IV:368		385n86
14:7 (13:7, S)	I:388; II:35; 787(n145), (n153);	17:8 (16:8, S)	VII:395; IX:237
	VII:310; 327; 721; 722; 724;	17:10 (16:10, S)	VIII:526
	IX:363; 526	17:11 (16:11, S)	IV:364
15 (14, S)	II:678n6; III:919; V:25; 604;	17:12 (16:12, S)	IV:253n19; V:368
	661n30	17:13 (16:13, S)	VI:1000; 1001; IX:89
15:1 (14:1, S)	V:25; 27; 844; VII:310; 383	17:13f (16:13f, S)	II:792
15:2 (14:2, S)	I:235; II:645; IV:830; VIII:73	17:13ff (16:13ff, S)	II:792(n189)
15:3 (14:3, S)	II:330; IX:598	17:14 (16:14, S)	II:244; 853n164; IV:915;
15:4 (14:4, S)	VI:315n33; IX:203		VIII:581n90
15:5 (14:5, S)	VII:67	17:15 (16:15, S)	I:218n10; II:792, (n188);
16 (15, S)	II:775; 823; V:85; 381; 492,		III:1063; IV:751n53; V:325;
	n25; VI:198n155; VII:69;		327; 331; 333; 334; 340n125,
	782; VIII:483n33; IX:103		n129; IX:290
16:1 (15:1, S)	III:82; IV:583; VI:193;	17:15a (16:15a, S)	V:325; 333
	VII:7n20; IX:237	18 (17, S)	II:796n230; IV:685n8; 905;
16:2 (15:2, S)	I:99n38		V:407; VIII:307
16:3 (15:3(2), S)	III:31; 32; 53	18 (Title) (18:1, M)	
16:4 (15:4, S)	VII:531n22; 532; 805	(17:1(Title), S)	V:675n122; VI:1002
16:5 (15:5, S)	I:388; III:759; 774; 775;	18:1 (18:2, M)	
	VI:150n23; 151; 152(n38);	(17:2(1), S)	I:22n3; 28n42; III:397
	VII:977	18:2 (18:3, M)	
16:5f (15:5f, S)	III:760	(17:3(2), S)	III:89; 669; 670; V:313;
16:5ff (15:5ff, S)	IV:1014		VI:6n20; 193; VII:610
16:5bf (15:5bf, S)	III:777	18:2-5 (18:3-6, M)	
16:6 (15:6, S)	III:774; 775; VI:164	(17:3-6, S)	VII:614n53
16:7 (15:7, S)	II:758; IV:911; V:605; IX:626;	18:3 (18:4, M)(17:4, S)	I:276n28; II:786(n135); IX:670
	632n94	18:4 (18:5, M)	
16:7f (15:7f, S)	VII:908	(17:5(4), S)	I:607; III:5; 406n20; IV:337;
16:7-11 (15:7-11, S)	VIII:367		IX:670; 671; 672; 674

19:5 (19:6, M)
  (18:6(5), S)
I:679; III:810n1; V:968;
VII:1092; VIII:229

19:6 (19:7, M)
  (18:7(6), S)
III:959; IV:1013; V:49; 96; 104;
108; IX:320n68

19:7 (19:8, M)
  (18:8(7), S)
I:276n25; IV:482; 830; 917;
VI:185; VII:486; 517n364;
527; 724

19:7-14 (19:8-15, M)
  (18:8-15, S)
IX:203

19:8 (19:9, M)
  (18:9(8), S)
II:773; IV:1046; V:376; IX:318;
319; 320n64; 322; 625

19:9 (19:10, M)
  (18:10(9), S)
I:236; 249; II:214; VI:183n86;
IX:199

19:10 (19:11, M)
  (18:11(10), S)
IV:553

19:11 (19:12, M)
  (18:12, S)
II:268n45; IX:237

19:12 (19:13, M)
  (18:13(12), S)
I:271; III:968; VI:170

19:12f (19:13f, M)
  (18:13f(12f), S)
III:414

19:13 (19:14, M)
  (18:14, S)
II:268n45

19:14 (19:15, M)
  (18:15(14), S)
I:671n33; II:743; 744; 786n129;
IV:137; 335; 351; VII:610n15

20f (19f, S)
I:566

20:1 (20:2, M)
  (19:2(1), S)
III:141; 192n4; V:258

20:2 (20:3, M)
  (19:3, S)
VII:294; 311

20:5 (20:6, M)
  (19:6, S)
I:20; VI:543; V:258; 259n126;
260; VIII:350

20:5f (20:6f, M)
  (19:6f(5f), S)
VI:287

20:6 (20:7, M)
  (19:7(6), S)
II:37; IX:502

20:7 (20:8, M)
  (19:8(7), S)
III:337; 499; V:260

20:9 (20:10, M)
  (19:10, S)
VII:976(n39); IX:682

21:1 (21:2, M)
  (20:2, S)
VII:974

21:2 (21:3, M)
  (20:3(2), S)
III:62; 606; VIII:350; IX:617

21:3 (21:4, M)
  (20:4, S)
VII:625; 628; VIII:350; IX:490

21:4 (21:5, M)
  (20:5, S)
II:785(n119); VIII:350

21:5 (21:6, M)
  (20:6, S)
IV:542

21:6 (21:7, M)
  (20:7, S)
IV:433; VII:780

21:6f (21:7f, M)
  (20:7f, S)
IV:798

21:7 (21:8, M)

  (20:8, S)
IV:798; IX:384

21:8 (21:9, M)
  (20:9(8), S)
II:37

21:8-12 (21:9-13, M)
  (20:9-13, S)
IX:505

21:9 (21:10, M)
  (20:10(9), S)
II:692; III:458; VI:935;
VIII:154

21:9f (21:10f, M)
  (20:10f, S)
IV:686

21:11 (21:12, M)
  (20:12(11), S)
II:95; IV:970n7

21:13 (21:14, M)
  (20:14(13), S)
I:164; II:294; 788n160;
VIII:494; 606

22 (21, S)
I:627n14; III:552; 901n12;
1101; V:202; VII:998;
IX:294n76

22:1 (22:2, M) (21:2(1),
  S)
II:786; 935; III:7; 102n244; 678;
IV:373; V:240; 701n349;
VII:439; IX:294, n76

22:2 (22:3, M) (21:3(2),
  S)
III:500; 900; IV:962

22:3 (22:4, M) (21:4(3),
  S)
II:522n30; 587; 713; III:42;
VIII:493

22:4 (22:5, M) (21:5, S) II:529n91

22:4f (22:5f, M)
  (21:5f(4f), S)
II:522(n31)

22:5 (22:6, M) (21:6(5),
  S)
II:786n131; III:499; 899;
VI:1001; VII:980

22:6 (22:7, M) (22:7(6),
  S)
VII:453; 454

22:6f (22:7f, M) (21:7f,
  S)
VI:892n57

22:6-8 (22:7-9, M)
  (21:7-9(6-8), S)
III:551; VII:455

22:7 (22:8, M) (21:8(7),
  S)
III:718; IV:796; V:367; VII:719

22:8 (22:9, M) (21:9(8),
  S)
I:570n29; II:522; III:47;
102n242; VI:6, n20; VIII:378

22:9 (22:10, M)
  (21:10(9), S)
VI:191n132; 1001; 1002; IX:670

22:9f (22:10f, M)
  (21:10f, S)
IV:1014

22:10 (22:11, M)
  (21:11(10), S)
III:89; 787; IV:643; VI:192;
VIII:349n90

22:13 (22:14, M)
  (21:14(13), S)
IV:252

22:14 (22:15, M)
  (21:15, S)
VIII:322

22:15 (22:16, M)
  (21:16(15), S)
VII:422; VIII:82

22:16 (22:17, M)
  (21:17(16), S)
II:226n1; III:528; 1101, n2;
VII:803n25; 830n209

22:17 (22:18, M)
  (21:18(17), S)
IV:974; VII:803

22:18 (22:19, M)
  (21:19(18), S)   II:759; IV:1; V:286;
                VII:923n27; 962

22:20 (22:21, M)
  (21:21(20), S)   III:1101, n2; IV:738; VI:998;
                1000

22:21 (22:22, M)
  (21:22(21), S)   III:513; 669; IV:253, n20, n21;
                VII:695; 976(n39);
                VIII:11n25

22:22 (22:23, M)
  (21:23(22), S)   I:67; III:513; 970; V:213n42;
                214; 218; 272n197; VI:537;
                VII:802n22; 829n201;
                VIII:464; 493; 502

22:22f (22:23f, M)
  (21:23f(22f), S)   I:177; VI:892n60; IX:203
22:23 (22:24, M)
  (21:24, S)   IX:198n47; 203
22:24 (22:25, M)
  (21:25(24), S)   II:40; III:899; 969; VI:773;
                VII:720

22:25 (22:26, M)
  (21:26(25), S)   II:587; 787; 794(n210); VI:537;
                VII:802n22; IX:203

22:25f (22:26f, M)
  (21:26f, S)   II:794
22:26 (22:27, M)
  (21:27(26), S)   II:850n139; III:607; 609; VI:39;
                892, n57; VIII:6; IX:626

22:27 (22:28, M)
  (21:28(27), S)   I:707; V:1016; VI:892; VII:725
22:28 (22:29, M)
  (21:29(28), S)   I:569(n24); 570n28; II:47
22:29 (22:30, M)
  (21:30(29), S)   III:595; VI:761n29; IX:472
22:30 (22:31, M)
  (21:31, S)   II:667
22:30f (22:31f, M)
  (21:31f, S)   I:63
22:31 (22:32, M)
  (21:31, S)   V:309
23 (22, S)   II:792(n188); VI:121n20; 487;
                VIII:496n50
23:1 (22:1, S)   V:98; VI:487n18; 489;
                VII:680n62; VIII:496n51;
                594
23:1-4 (22:1-4, S)   VI:487(n27); 499(n8)
23:2 (22:2, S)   VI:117n25; 487(n22), (n23);
                VII:388; 897(n4); VIII:322
23:2f (22:2f, S)   V:100; VIII:325
23:3 (22:3, S)   II:193; V:98; 253; 257;
                VI:487(n20); VII:724;
                IX:632
23:4 (22:4, S)   III:477n30; V:102n27; 789;
                VI:487(n24); 967; VII:395;
                396; 777; IX:200
23:5 (22:5, S)   II:470; III:140; 143; IV:801n6;
                V:25; VI:150n23; 151;
                VIII:209
23:6 (22:6, S)   IX:384
24 (23, S)   II:678n6; V:661n30; VII:611;

VIII:495
24:1 (23:1, S)   I:679; II:379; 760; III:884;
                V:88; 149; 158; 890; VI:299;
                309; VII:7; 915
24:1f (23:1f, S)   III:1012; VI:598n24
24:2 (23:2, S)   III:1009; VIII:328
24:3 (23:3, S)   VII:310; VIII:197, n69
24:3f (23:3f, S)   VII:643
24:3-6 (23:3-6, S)   V:604
24:4 (23:4, S)   II:486; 757; III:414; 607; 614;
                IV:368; VII:909; 910
24:5 (23:5, S)   II:196; 486n5; VII:977
24:6 (23:6, S)   II:790n186; 893; V:160n17;
                VI:193n139
24:7 (23:7, S)   I:208
24:7ff (23:7ff, S)   I:569n22; II:244; V:861
24:8 (23:8, S)   II:241; 293; III:912
24:10 (23:10, S)   III:552
25 (24, S)   III:452n1
25:1 (24:1, S)   IX:640n143
25:1ff (24:1ff, S)   II:522
25:2 (24:2, S)   II:522n30; IV:583; VI:192; 193;
                196
25:2f (24:2f, S)   II:522n30
25:3 (24:3, S)   II:51n6; 58; IV:578n1; 583; 584;
                V:891; VI:196; 726
25:4 (24:4, S)   I:718; V:53
25:5 (24:5, S)   I:236; IV:578n1; 583; 584;
                V:98; 100; 102n27;
                VI:190n127; 196; VII:404n5;
                1013
25:6 (24:6, S)   II:479n22, (n31); 480n48;
                IV:675; V:160n17; IX:384;
                385n86
25:6f (24:6f, S)   II:480(n36)
25:6ff (24:6ff, S)   III:930
25:7 (24:7, S)   I:117n7; IV:675; V:1008n378;
                IX:384, (n84), n84; 490
25:8 (24:8, S)   I:271; 321, (n34); V:53; IX:486
25:9 (24:9, S)   III:929n24; IV:401; V:53; 88;
                98; VI:647
25:10 (24:10, S)   IV:135; V:55; 891; IX:384
25:11 (24:11, S)   III:315
25:12 (24:12, S)   IV:150; 168; 169; V:53
25:14 (24:14, S)   II:61; IV:921; V:262; VI:196;
                IX:203
25:15 (24:15, S)   V:376
25:16 (24:16, S)   IV:739n7; VI:892; IX:378
25:17 (24:17, S)   III:141; VII:886
25:17f (24:17f, S)   III:141
25:18 (24:18, S)   I:510; III:828; V:325; 891;
                VIII:11
25:19 (24:19, S)   IV:686; VI:281
25:20 (24:20, S)   II:522n30; VI:193; 196; 1000;
                IX:237
25:21 (24:21 S)   IV:583; VI:196
25:22 (24:22, S)   III:358n17; IV:333;
                VI:560(n97)
26 (25, S)   VI:26n19
26:1 (25:1, S)   VI:192; 571; VII:67
26:2 (25:2, S)   II:257; VI:26; 27; 949; IX:626
26:3 (25:3, S)   I:236; 455; V:943n7;

	VI:190n127; 192; IX:384
26:4 (25:4, S)	III:441; VII:772; 861
26:5 (25:5, S)	IV:687n14; VII:772
26:6 (25:6, S)	IV:946; V:627; VIII:320n42
26:7 (25:7, S)	II:787(n140); III:35
26:8 (25:8, S)	VII:383; 825; VIII:197n69
26:9 (25:9, S)	II:268n45; III:407n9, n13; VII:772; IX:450n91
26:10 (25:10, S)	IV:970n7
26:11 (25:11, S)	IV:333; VI:560(n97); IX:378
26:12 (25:12, S)	III:527; VI:537; VII:643
27 (26, S)	V:970
27:1 (26:1, S)	II:850(n142); VI:954n9; VII:433n75; 1013; 1014n59; IX:200; 319
27:2 (26:2, S)	II:330; 692; III:140; VII:107; 343
27:3 (26:3, S)	VI:191; IX:200
27:4 (26:4, S)	I:95; II:601; 785(n119); 792(n188); III:553; 1070n170; V:328; VI:689n6
27:5 (26:5, S)	II:948; III:968; IV:909; VII:369; 372; 383; 610n18; VIII:198n77
27:6 (26:6, S)	II:788n155, n160; 794; III:184; VII:372; VIII:493; 498n67; 499
27:7 (26:7, S)	III:899; IX:282
27:8 (26:8, S)	II:790n186; 893; V:398; VI:193n139; 774
27:9 (26:9, S)	V:446; VII:1013
27:10 (26:10, S)	IV:15; V:962n96; 971; 974; VIII:349n90; 352
27:11 (26:11, S)	IV:1090; V:53; 98
27:12 (26:12, S)	III:140; IV:483; VII:869n66; IX:621
27:13 (26:13, S)	V:326
27:14 (26:14, S)	II:522n30, (n31); III:607; 913, n2; IV:584; VII:610n18
28 (27, S)	II:792(n189)
28:1 (27:1, S)	III:499; 899; V:189; 747n16; VII:610n6
28:2 (27:2, S)	I:90; II:785(n122); 790n185; 793(n192), (n194); III:202; IX:281; 379; 426
28:3 (27:3, S)	III:478; 635, n3; VI:312n6; VII:772
28:4 (27:4, S)	III:635; V:401; VI:643
28:5 (27:5, S)	II:642; III:411; 635; V:137; VI:643; VII:890
28:6 (27:6, S)	II:785(n122); IX:281; 379
28:7 (27:7, S)	II:522n30; 787n146; III:53; 992n142; V:214n43; 313; 591; VI:954n9
28:8 (27:8, S)	IV:155; IX:502; 504
28:9 (27:9, S)	II:757n7; III:774; VI:487(n27); 499(n8); VII:976(n39); IX:682
29 (28, S)	II:239; 292; III:574; 1011(n77); VIII:347, n78; 348; **IX:283;** 288n40; 320
29:1 (28:1, S)	III:81; 86n101; V:966;

	VIII:172; 347
29:1f (28:1f, S)	II:241(n33); 244; V:1016; IX:57
29:2 (28:2, S)	II:789; V:257n113; VI:761(n33)
29:3 (28:3, S)	II:244; VIII:317; 319
29:3ff (28:3ff, S)	IX:283n20
29:3-9 (28:3-9, S)	II:633
29:4 (28:4, S)	II:292; IV:542
29:6 (28:6, S)	VII:401n5; 402n8; VIII:342
29:7 (28:7, S)	VI:935
29:8 (28:8, S)	IX:669
29:9 (28:9, S)	II:244; IX:669
29:9b (28:9b, S)	IX:283
29:10 (28:10, S)	V:505
29:11 (28:11, S)	II:297
30 (29, S)	V:202
30:1 (30:2, M) (29:2, S)	II:787(n144); VIII:606
30:2 (30:3, M) (29:3(2), S)	III:202; 203
30:3 (30:4, M) (29:4, S)	II:874n5
30:4 (30:5, M) (29:5(4), S)	I:114; IV:679n5; V:214n43; VIII:494
30:5 (30:6, M) (29:6(5), S)	II:743; III:53; V:401; 408
30:6 (30:7, M) (29:7, S)	VII:67
30:7 (30:8, M) (29:8, S)	II:46n18; 743; III:53; VI:773; VII:67
30:8 (30:9, M) (29:9, S)	II:785(n121); III:499; IX:379
30:9 (30:10, M) (29:10(9), S)	I:63; 64; 236; III:672; V:214n43; IX:472
30:10 (30:11, M) (29:11, S)	II:847(n108); IX:378n45
30:11 (30:12, M) (29:12(11), S)	II:242(n36); III:154; 837; 841; V:305; VII:57n5; 58n13; 60; 714
30:12 (30:13, M) (29:13(12), S)	II:238n22; 786n138; III:626; IX:626n72
31 (30, S)	VI:446n787
31:1 (31:2, M) (30:2, S)	VI:193; 1002
31:2 (31:3, M) (30:3, S)	V:591; VI:954n9; VII:610n16
31:3 (31:4, M) (30:4(3), S)	II:479(n30); V:98
31:4 (31:5, M) (30:5(4), S)	V:593
31:5 (31:6, M) (30:6(5), S)	I:236; 242; IV:333; VI:361; 370; VII:439; VIII:163; IX:294; 431; 630
31:6 (31:7, M) (30:7(6), S)	I:233; II:66; 522n30; III:88; IV:663; VI:192
31:6a (31:7a, M) (30:7a, S)	II:814

31:7 (31:8, M)
(30:8(7), S) I:698n36; III:141; VIII:11;
                IX:363; 384
31:8 (31:9, M)
(30:9, S)   VII:643; IX:625
31:9 (31:10, M)
(30:10(9), S) III:142; VII:428; 744; IX:378,
                n45; 625n71; 641n150
31:10 (31:11, M)
(30:11(10), S) I:493; II:786n132, (n133);
                IV:590n12; V:115; VII:343;
                600; 605; IX:623
31:11 (31:12, M)
(30:12(11), S) I:490; 697n31; 718; VII:341n16
31:12 (31:13, M)
(30:13(12), S) IV:892(n8); VII:359
31:13 (31:14, M)
(30:14(13), S) V:875n12; 877n19
31:14 (31:15, M)
(30:15(14), S) II:522n30; III:761
31:15 (31:16, M)
(30:16(15), S) II:229; 944
31:16 (31:17, M)
(30:17(16), S) II:268n45; VII:976(n39); IX:9;
                318; 320; 384(n84)
31:17 (31:18, M)
(30:18(17), S) III:499
31:18 (31:19, M)
(30:19, S)   VIII:302; 496n51; 526
31:19 (31:20, M)
(31:20(19), S) II:637; III:969; VI:277; IX:490
31:20 (31:21, M)
(30:21(20), S) II:32; III:961; 968; VI:193;
                VII:372
31:21 (31:22, M)
(30:22(21), S) III:31; 858; IX:384; 403
31:22 (31:23, M)
(30:23(22), S) II:450; 785(n122); 786; III:7;
                899; VI:992; VII:67; IX:281;
                379
31:23 (31:24, M)
(30:24(23), S) I:29n51; III:7n19; V:491(n18);
                VI:62; 187n112; VIII:526
31:23f (31:24f, M)
(30:24f, S)   VI:892n60
31:24 (31:25, M)
(30:25(24), S) I:363; III:613; 913, n2; IV:579;
                VII:610n18
32 (31, S)   I:275; II:792(n187); III:200;
                968; IV:1093n11; VI:708;
                IX:363n31
32:1 (31:1, S) I:280; 511; II:205; IV:366
32:1f (31:1f, S) I:295; IV:369
32:1-5 (31:1-5, S) III:968
32:2 (31:2, S) IV:286; **292**; 366; VI:362
32:3 (31:3, S) II:786; V:718; IX:623
32:3f (31:3f, S) III:202; VII:908
32:4 (31:4, S) I:559; III:434; IX:79n13
32:5 (31:5, S) I:278; 510; 718; III:557; 573;
                IV:1085

32:5ff (31:5ff, S) VII:908
32:6 (31:6, S) II:330; III:625n5; V:491;
                VIII:322
32:7 (31:7, S) III:141; 143; IV:332; 333
32:8 (31:8, S) V:53; VII:655; 764
32:9 (31:9, S) III:338
32:10 (31:10, S) IV:518; VI:192; VII:689n21
32:11 (31:11, S) III:646; VII:909; IX:363;
                366n57
33 (32, S)   III:574; 931n26; IV:100;
                IX:363
33:1 (32:1, S) IX:363
33:2 (32:2, S) V:203; VII:671; VIII:493
33:3 (32:3, S) III:448; 449n11; VIII:499n71
33:4 (32:4, S) II:642; 650
33:4f (32:4f, S) III:1013
33:5 (32:5, S) II:196; 485; III:546; 930(n25);
                942; VI:276; 284; 285n6; 363;
                366; 386n304; IX:384
33:6 (32:6, S) II:295; III:1012; 1018;
                V:504(n55); 510; VI:360;
                VII:610, n10; 696; 697
33:6ff (32:6ff, S) III:1009; 1013
33:7 (32:7, S) V:503; VIII:154; 319
33:8 (32:8, S) V:158; 412; VI:196; VII:66
33:9 (32:9, S) III:1010; 1012; 1027; V:839n10;
                968(n129); IX:591
33:10 (32:10, S) I:396; 633; II:523; III:1099n1;
                IV:286; 846; VII:521;
                VIII:158; 159
33:11 (32:11, S) I:634; II:739; IV:575
33:12 (32:12, S) II:366n7; 522n30; 822; III:773;
                IV:366
33:13 (32:13, S) V:328; 374n5; 522n192
33:14 (32:14, S) II:363; III:1012; V:155
33:15 (32:15, S) II:647; VI:256; 257; IX:627
33:16 (32:16, S) VI:276n13
33:16f (32:16f, S) III:337; VII:975
33:17 (32:17, S) II:523(n39); VI:276n13;
                VII:980
33:18 (32:18, S) II:330; 523; IV:579; V:376;
                VI:194; IX:203; 385; 387
33:18f (32:18f, S) VI:1001; 1002
33:19 (32:19, S) VI:15n23
33:20 (32:20, S) IV:577n1; 583; V:313; VI:196
33:20ff (32:20ff, S) VI:194
33:21 (32:21, S) I:91; II:523(n39); V:259n127;
                IX:363
33:21f (32:21f, S) VI:196
33:22 (32:22, S) II:522n30; IV:579; VI:196;
                IX:385
34 (33, S)   II:417; V:202; VIII:554n66
34 (Title) (34:1, M)
(33:1, S)   IV:755, n1
34:1 (34:2, M) (33:2(1),
S)   II:758; 787; VII:697
34:2 (34:3, M) (33:3, S) VI:647; 892
34:3 (34:4, M) (33:4, S) II:786(n136); 787; VII:770;
                VIII:606
34:4 (34:5, M) (33:5(4),
S)   II:787(n143); V:843n12;
                VI:1000

34:6 (34:7, M) (33:7(6),
  S)   III:141; 143; 500; 899;
                    VII:970n16; 977
34:7 (34:8, M) (33:8, S) VI:1001; 1002; IX:203
34:8 (34:9, M) (33:9(8),
  S)   I:676n9; IV:366; IX:486;
                    487n20; 488; 489
34:9 (34:10, M)
  (33:10(9), S)   I:95; II:690; VIII:421n169; 595;
                    IX:203
34:10 (34:11, M)
  (33:11, S)   III:660; VI:325; 889
34:11 (34:12, M)
  (33:12, S)   I:389(n8); IX:202
34:12 (34:13, M)
  (33:13(12), S)   III:45(n9); 49; 702; V:326; 342
34:13 (34:14, M)
  (33:14(13), S)   I:721; II:953; VII:700
34:13ff (34:14ff, M)
  (33:14ff(13ff), S) III:478
34:13-17 (34:14-18,
  M) (33:14-18, S) III:480n36
34:14 (34:15, M)
  (33:15(14), S)   II:230; 407; IV:1055; IX:202
34:14f (34:15f, M)
  (33:15f, S)   I:14
34:15 (34:16, M)
  (33:16(15), S)   III:126; V:376; 378; 557
34:15ff (34:16ff, M)
  (33:16ff, S)   IV:711n66
34:16 (34:17, M)
  (33:17(16), S)   IV:682; V:171; VI:773; 777;
                    778
34:17 (34:18, M)
  (33:18(17), S)   III:141; 143; 899; VI:1001
34:18 (34:19, M)
  (33:19(18), S)   III:606; 612; VI:362; 401n438;
                    VII:922; 977; VIII:10;
                    IX:630
34:19 (34:20, M)
  (33:20(19), S)   III:141; 142; V:908n22;
                    VI:1001; 1002
34:20 (34:21, M)
  (33:21, S)   VII:921, n13; 923; IX:237
34:21 (34:22, M)
  (33:22, S)   IV:686; 687; VI:550
34:21f (34:22f, M)
  (33:22f, S)   V:561n13
34:22 (34:23, M)
  (33:23, S)   IV:333; V:661; VI:193
35:1ff (34:1ff, S) V:297
35:2 (34:2, S)   V:293; 313
35:3 (34:3, S)   II:229; VI:993; 995n18
35:5 (34:5, S)   V:50
35:5f (34:5f, S)   II:11(n79)
35:6 (34:6, S)   VII:430n50
35:7 (34:7, S)   V:593; 594(n5); IX:99
35:8 (34:8, S)   I:675; VII:354n88
35:9 (34:9, S)   I:676; VI:892; IX:641n147
35:9f (34:9f, S)   IX:623
35:10 (34:10, S)   III:351; VI:39; 889; 892
35:11 (34:11, S)   IV:483

35:11ff (34:11ff, S) I:641
35:12 (34:12, S)   II:341n3; IV:928; 929n27;
                    VI:550(n26)
35:13 (34:13, S)   III:825; IV:927; VII:58n13; 60;
                    VIII:7n19
35:13f (34:13f, S) VIII:7
35:14 (34:14, S)   I:455; V:943n7; VI:313;
                    VII:451; 716
35:15 (34:15, S)   VII:960
35:16 (34:16, S)   I:641; IV:798; VIII:564
35:17 (34:17, S)   IV:738
35:18 (34:18, S)   VI:537; VII:802n22
35:19 (34:19, S)   II:167; IV:686; 687; 692
35:20 (34:20, S)   II:95; 407n37; 418
35:22 (34:22, S)   II:46n18
35:23 (34:23, S)   II:46n18; 223
35:24 (34:24, S)   II:196; 485
35:25 (34:25, S)   VI:158
35:26 (34:26, S)   II:319
35:26f (34:26f, S) I:189
35:27 (34:27, S)   I:20; II:403; 407; 587;
                    III:45(n8); IV:543
35:28 (34:28, S)   II:787
36:1 (36:2, M)
  (35:2(1), S)   I:321; III:612n22; VI:681n184;
                    IX:204; 213
36:2 (36:3, M)
  (36:3(2), S)   I:117n7; II:233; IV:686
36:3 (36:4, M) (35:4, S) IV:686
36:4 (36:5, M)
  (35:5(4), S)   V:53
36:5 (36:6, M) (35:6(5),
  S)   II:95; IV:903; IX:384
36:6 (36:7, M) (35:7(6),
  S)   III:614n4; V:482, n85
36:7 (36:8, M)
  (35:8, S)   VII:395
36:8 (36:9, M) (35:9(8),
  S)   II:919n59; IV:546; VI:159n2;
                    193
36:8f (36:9f, M) (35:9f,
  S)   II:845n94
36:9 (36:10, M)
  (35:10(9), S)   II:792(n188); 844(n87); 846;
                    850, (n142); IV:23; VI:114;
                    139; VIII:321; 322; IX:319;
                    351n338
36:9a (36:10a, M)
  (35:10a(9a), S)   V:324
36:9b (36:10b, M)
  (35:10b(9b), S)   V:324
36:10 (36:11, M)
  (35:11(10), S)   I:698; II:196; 479(n25); IV:877;
                    IX:384
36:11 (36:12, M)
  (35:12, S)   VIII:526
36:12 (36:13, M)
  (35:13, S)   VIII:300
37 (36, S)   III:573; IV:1044; VI:198n155;
                    325; 897
37:1 (36:1, S)   II:883; III:478n32; V:395
37:2 (36:2, S)   IV:66

39:12f (39:13f, M)
(38:13f, S)   V:27
39:13 (39:14, M)
(38:14, S)   I:223; VIII:504n4; IX:664, n3
40 (39, S)   II:710; III:186; IV:1044;
                   V:202
40:1 (40:2, M)(39:2, S) IV:578n1; VI:194
40:2 (40:3, M)(39:3, S) IX:625
40:3 (40:4, M)
(39:4(3), S)   II:522n30, n31, (n32); 523;
                   V:203; VI:192; VII:697;
                   VIII:493; 499n71
40:4 (40:5, M)(39:5(4),
S)   II:708; IV:366; V:262
40:5 (40:6, M)(39:6(5),
S)   I:28n48; 66; 71n8; II:97; III:35;
                   181n4; 351; IV:286; VI:281
40:6 (40:7, M)(39:7(6),
S)   I:270(n9); 476; II:741; III:48;
                   239; VI:55, (n19);
                   VII:1058n363; IX:68
40:6f (40:7f, M)(39:7f,
S)   IX:67
40:6-8 (40:7-9, M)
(39:7-9, S)   III:56; **VII:649;** 811n74
40:6ff (40:7ff, M)
(39:7ff(6ff), S)   II:794(n207); III:183; 275;
                   V:203
40:7 (40:8, M)(39:8(7),
S)   I:617; 747
40:8 (40:9, M)(39:9(8),
S)   I:631n20, (n25); II:743; III:53;
                   239; 609; 786; 787; 788n16;
                   VI:469; 474; VII:908
40:9 (40:10, M)
(39:10(9), S)   I:700; II:710; 712(n59); III:239;
                   529
40:9f (40:10f, M)
(39:10f, S)   II:196; VII:802
40:10 (40:11, M)
(39:11(10), S)   II:479n28; 480(n46); 708;
                   III:529; 970; VI:537; IX:384
40:10f (40:11f, M)
(39:11f, S)   II:479n35; V:160n17
40:11 (40:12, M)
(39:12, S)   II:479(n25), (n31); IX:384
40:12 (40:13, M)
(39:13, S)   III:606; VI:281; 731
40:12f (40:13f, M)
(39:13f, S)   VI:1002; 1003
40:13 (40:14, M)
(39:14(13), S)   II:739; VI:1001
40:14 (40:15, M)
(39:15(14), S)   III:46n18
40:16 (40:17, M)
(39:17(16), S)   I:28(n48); II:790n186; 893;
                   VI:193n139; IX:363
40:17 (40:18, M)
(39:18(17), S)   VI:39; 889; 892
41:1 (41:2, M)
(40:2(1), S)   IV:364; 365; VI:115n15;
                   550(n25); 1002

41:2 (41:3, M)(40:3(2),
S)   IV:365; VII:980n56; IX:621;
                   622n63
41:3 (41:4, M)(40:4(3),
S)   V:115; VIII:310n17
41:4 (41:5, M)(40:5(4),
S)   III:202; 203; V:114n28; IX:378,
                   n45
41:5 (41:6, M)(40:6, S) III:32
41:6 (41:7, M)(40:7, S) IV:4n5
41:8 (41:9, M)(40:9(8),
S)   I:607
41:9 (41:10, M)
(40:10(9), S)   I:477n6; II:407n37; 749;
                   III:666n17; IV:173; VI:628;
                   VII:140n311; IX:157n91
41:10 (41:11, M)
(40:11, S)   VIII:236; IX:378, n45
41:11 (41:12, M)
(40:12(11), S)   III:45n15; 700n13
41:11f (41:12f, M)
(40:12f, S)   I:30n55
41:12 (41:13, M)
(40:13(12), S)   I:601; V:839
41:13 (41:14, M)
(40:14(13), S)   I:233n1; 335; II:764; VI:186
42 (41, S)   II:787(n140)
42-83 (42-82, S)   III:1071
42-89 (41-88, S)   V:396
42 (Title) (42:1, M)
(41:1, S)   VIII:346
42:1 (42:2, M)(41:2, S) VI:447n789; VIII:322
42:2 (42:3, M)(41:3(2),
S)   I:95; II:227; 785(n123); 850;
                   V:325; VI:773; IX:290
42:4 (42:5, M)(41:5(4),
S)   III:35; V:219; 627; VII:369;
                   VIII:198; IX:282; 409; 620
42:5 (42:6, M)(41:6(5),
S)   II:786; IV:323; 579; VI:196;
                   VII:977; 1022; IX:622; 641
42:6 (42:7, M)(41:7, S) VI:609; IX:140n241
42:7 (42:8, M)(41:8, S) I:538; IX:280
42:8 (42:9, M)(41:9, S) IX:384
42:9 (42:10, M)
(41:10(9), S)   II:785(n123); III:140; 202;
                   V:943; VII:451
42:10 (42:11, M)
(41:11, S)   VII:936
42:11 (42:12, M)
(41:12(11), S)   IV:323; 579; VI:196; VII:977;
                   1022; IX:622
43:1 (42:1, S)   II:366n7; 642; VI:1000
43:3 (42:3, S)   II:937n75; V:98; 695n306;
                   VII:309; 383; IX:320; 322
43:4 (42:4, S)   VIII:496n48
43:5 (42:5, S)   IV:323; 579; VI:196; VII:977;
                   1022; IX:622
44 (43, S)   IV:686n10; 981, n26
44:1 (44:2, M)(43:2(1),
S)   I:486; II:637
44:2-4 (44:3-5, M)

VIII:616; 618; IX:201

47:3 (47:4, M) (46:4, S) VI:627; VIII:40

47:4 (47:5, M) (46:5(4),
S)   II:254n2; III:774

47:5 (47:6, M) (46:6, S) VII:79; 84; IX:281; 283

47:6 (47:7, M) (46:7, S) II:788n161; VII:84; VIII:494

47:6f (47:7f, M) (46:7f,
S)   VIII:502

47:7 (47:8, M) (46:8, S) I:469(n24); V:891

47:8 (47:9, M) (46:9(8),
S)   I:571; III:163; 441

47:9 (47:10, M) (46:10,
S)   II:367, n11

48 (47, S)   I:164; VII:311; VIII:495

48 (Title) (48:1, M)
(47:1, S)   VII:7

48:1 (48:2, M) (47:2, S) VI:524; 533

48:2 (48:3, M) (47:3(2),
S)   I:579; III:116n362; V:180n47;
                      482; 505; VI:524; VII:294;
                      310; 317n119

48:2f (48:3f, M) (47:3f,
S)   VIII:617n21

48:3 (48:4, M) (47:4, S) VII:317

48:5 (48:6, M) (47:6(5),
S)   III:34; VII:67

48:6 (48:7, M) (47:7(6),
S)   IV:9; IX:669

48:7 (48:8, M) (47:8, S) VI:360

48:8 (48:9, M) (47:9(8),
S)   V:324; VI:524; 533

48:9 (48:10, M) (47:10,
S)   IX:384

48:10 (48:11, M)
(47:11(10), S)   II:37; V:257; VI:284

48:10-12 (48:11-13,
M) (47:11-13, S)   III:930(n25)

48:12 (48:13, M)
(47:13, S)   VI:953n7; VII:294

48:13 (48:14, M)
(47:14, S)   VIII:154

49 (48, S)   VI:325; IX:645; 655

49:1 (49:2 M) (48:2(1),
S)   II:853n164; V:158;
                      VIII:581n90

49:1f (49:2f, M) (48:2f,
S)   IX:285

49:2 (49:3, M) (48:3, S) VI:888; VIII:346; 581n90;
                      IX:473

49:4 (49:5, M) (48:5, S) V:748; 749; VII:481n135

49:5 (49:6, M) (48:6, S) VI:550, (n25)

49:6 (49:7, M) (48:7, S) I:321; IV:333n14; VI:191; 324

49:7 (49:8, M) (48:8(7),
S)   I:252, n2; III:317; 646; IV:330;
                      333n14; 341n12

49:7b (49:8b, M)
(48:8b, S)   II:854

49:7f (49:8f, M)
(48:8f, S)   IV:333n14; IX:645

49:7ff (49:8ff, M)
(48:8ff, S)   II:846(n101); IV:333

49:8 (49:9, M) (48:9(8),

S)   III:303; IV:331; 335; 349n1;
                      VIII:172

49:8a (49:9a, M)
(48:9a, S)   IV:333n14

49:9 (49:10, M)
(48:10(9), S)   II:854; V:326; VIII:51; IX:99

49:10 (49:11, M)
(48:11, S)   VII:495

49:11 (49:12, M)
(48:12, S)   I:276n25; V:253

49:12 (49:13, M)
(48:13(12), S)   IV:962

49:13 (49:14, M)
(48:14(13), S)   I:321; II:738; 755n3; IV:963,
                      n2; V:51; VI:191n131; 749;
                      VII:342; 345

49:14 (49:15, M)
(48:15, S)   V:718; IX:420n22

49:15 (49:16, M)
(48:16, S)   IV:333; VI:572n39; VII:425n15

49:16 (49:17, M)
(48:17, S)   II:238; 848; IV:333

49:16f (49:17f, M)
(48:17f, S)   VI:325

49:19 (49:20, M)
(48:20(19), S)   V:324

49:20 (49:21, M)
(48:21(20), S)   IV:962; VII:425n15

50 (49, S)   II:793; III:186; 239; V:661n30;
                      IX:284

50:1 (49:1, S)   III:81

50:1-3 (49:1-3, S)   V:877

50:2 (49:2, S)   III:553, n65; VII:310

50:3 (49:3, S)   V:861; IX:284

50:4 (49:4, S)   IX:479n61

50:4-6 (49:4-6, S)   IX:284

50:5 (49:5, S)   II:108; 480(n38); V:491, (n18);
                      IX:387

50:7 (49:7, S)   IV:511; 512

50:7-23 (49:7-23, S) IX:284

50:8ff (49:8ff, S)   III:183; 239; V:203

50:9 (49:9, S)   IX:51

50:11 (49:11, S)   I:698(n36); 700; V:510

50:12 (49:12, S)   V:158; 890

50:13 (49:13, S)   IX:622

50:14 (49:14, S)   II:793(n205); III:183; 184;
                      V:178; 561n14; IX:61; 409,
                      n23

50:14f (49:14f, S)   IV:761

50:15 (49:15, S)   II:793(n205); III:141; 142; 498;
                      499

50:16 (49:16, S)   V:610; VII:282n24; 697

50:16f (49:16f, S)   I:321

50:16-23 (49:16-23, S) IX:356

50:17 (49:17, S)   IV:687; V:610

50:18 (49:18, S)   IV:597n19; 730; V:367

50:19 (49:19, S)   VI:264

50:20 (49:20, S)   IV:3; 644n16

50:21 (49:21, S)   V:839; 841; VI:778

50:22 (49:22, S)   III:86; IV:253n22; 949

50:23 (49:23, S)   II:27; 793; V:53; 92n187; 96;
                      977; IX:61

51 (50, S)

II:792(n187); III:200; 968; **IV:988**; VI:980n19; VII:908; IX:363n31

51-147 (50-146, S)

VII:295n17

51 (Title) (51:1f, M)
(50:1f, S)

VI:808

51:1 (51:3, M) (50:3(1), S)

II:479(n31); 481(n55); V:160n17; 161; VI:276, n13; VIII:16; IX:378, n45, n46; 384, (n84)

51:1-17 (51:3-19, M)
(50:3-19, S)

VI:984

51:2 (51:4, M) (50:4, S) I:721; III:417(n24); IV:943; 945

51:3 (51:5, M) (50:5, S) I:277; 698; IV:644n16

51:4 (51:6, M) (50:6(4), S)

I:277-278; II:213; 215; IV:988; V:686

51:4a (51:6a, M)
(50:6a, S)

I:277

51:5 (51:7, M) (50:7, S) I:117n7; 291; 295; V:646; VII:760; IX:669

51:6 (51:8, M) (50:8(6), S)

I:235; 277; II:61; 213; III:969; VII:487

51:7 (51:9, M) (50:9, S) I:537; II:427; III:812, n5; IV:247; 301; VI:977; 978; 980; VIII:320

51:7f (51:9f, M) (50:9f, S)

III:202

51:8 (51:10, M) (50:10, S)

VIII:8; 24; IX:623

51:9 (51:11, M)
(50:11(9), S)

III:969; VI:778; VII:720

51:10 (51:12, M)
(50:12(10), S)

I:540; III:414; 453; 607; 613; 1015; 1027; IV:345n25; 988; 1001; VI:362; 365; VII:908, n37; 909; 910; 919; IX:628

51:10f (51:12f, M)
(50:12f, S)

I:103; VI:365

51:11 (51:13, M)
(50:13, S)

I:91; 95, n31; 103; 114; VI:363; 778; 992

51:12 (51:14, M)
(50:14, S)

I:19; II:167; VI:362; 397; 699n12; VII:653; 655

51:13 (51:15, M)
(50:15(13), S)

II:137; V:53; 93; VII:729

51:14 (51:16, M)
(50:16, S)

VI:1000

51:15 (51:17, M)
(50:17, S)

I:63; 64; V:203

51:16 (51:18, M)
(50:18(16), S)

I:540; II:741; IV:982n28

51:16f (51:18f, M)
(50:18f, S)

III:183; 186; IV:1093

51:16ff (51:18ff, M)
(50:18ff(16ff), S)

II:738; 794(n207); III:239; IV:143; V:203

51:16-19
(51:18-21, M)

(50:18-21, S)

51:17 (51:19, M)
(50:19(17), S)

51:18 (51:20, M)
(50:20(18), S)

51:19 (51:21, M)
(50:21(19), S)

52 (51, S)

52:1 (52:3, M)
(51:3, S)

52:2 (52:4, M)
(51:4(2), S)

52:3 (52:5, M)
(51:5, S)

52:4 (52:6, M)
(51:6(4), S)

52:5 (52:7, M)
(51:7, S)

52:6 (52:8, M)
(51:8(6), S)

52:7 (52:9, M)
(51:9(7), S)

52:8 (52:10, M)
(51:10(8), S)

52:9 (52:11, M)
(51:11(9), S)

53:1 (53:2, M)
(52:2(1), S)

53:2 (53:3, M)
(52:3(2), S)

53:3 (53:4, M)
(52:4, S)

53:4 (53:5, M)
(52:5(4), S)

53:5 (53:6, M)
(52:6(5), S)

53:6 (53:7, M)
(52:7, S)

54 ((53, S)
54 (Title)
(54:1f, M) (53:1f, S)

54:1 (54:3, M)
(53:3, S)

54:2 (54:4, M)
(53:4, S)

54:3 (54:5, M)
(53:5, S)

54:5 (54:7, M)
(53:7, S)

54:6 (54:8, M)
(53:8, S)

54:6f (54:8f, M)
(53:8f, S)

54:7 (54:9, M)
(53:9(7), S)

VII:811n74

I:540; III:182; 183; 184; 187; 190; 607; IV:761; VI:261n38; 362; 397n402; VII:922; VIII:8; 13; 16; 24; IX:630

II:654; 743; 744; VII:296

II:53; 193; III:186
VI:198n155

III:646

III:646; IV:285

I:23n15; 153; 154; VI:297n72; VII:895n64

I:721

VIII:51; 268n62

I:659

II:286; 523; VI:191; 324; VIII:154

II:522n30, (n32)

IV:584; IX:485

I:598; VII:908; IX:99

V:325; 522n192

IX:490

II:692; III:499

I:456; III:5; VII:422; IX:198

III:358n17; VII:719; 724; IX:363
II:794

VIII:493

III:1070; V:257; 259n126; 261; 277; VII:974; 976(n39)

II:785(n118); 786n129

VIII:165

II:792

II:794(n210)

V:258

II:786n139; 792; III:141; 143;

VI:698n8

55 (54, S)   VIII:493

55:1 (55:2, M)

  (54:2(1), S)   II:785(n118); V:559

55:2 (55:3, M)

  (54:3(2), S)   II:787; III:141; IV:318; 321n29;
                          590n12

55:3f (55:4f, M)

  (54:4f(3f), S)   II:812

55:4 (55:5, M)

  (54:5(4), S)   III:606; 612; IX:641n150;
                          669n22

55:5 (55:6, M)

  (54:6(5), S)   III:5; VII:430n48; IX:199

55:6 (55:7, M)

  (54:7, S)   VI:67(n49)

55:8 (55:9, M)

  (54:9(8), S)   II:58; VI:360; VII:970; 971

55:9 (55:10, M)

  (54:10(9), S)   II:46n18

55:11 (55:12, M)

  (54:12, S)   VI:360

55:13 (55:14, M)

  (54:14(13), S)   I:697n31; 718

55:16 (55:17, M)

  (54:17(16), S)   III:499; 900

55:17 (55:18, M)

  (54:18, S)   I:66; II:786; 793; 801n262;
                          VIII:218; IX:281

55:18 (55:19, M)

  (54:19, S)   IV:333

55:19 (55:20, M)

  (54:20(19), S)   I:200n10; 252; VIII:8

55:20 (55:21, M)

  (54:21(20), S)   I:605; II:115n42; V:738

55:21 (55:22, M)

  (54:22, S)   VI:771; VII:697

55:22 (55:23, M)

  (54:23(22), S)   IV:590; 591n17; VI:992; VII:67

55:23 (55:24, M)

  (54:24, S)   IX:99

56 (Title)

  (56:1, M) (55:1, S)   VII:7n20

56:1 (56:2, M)

  (55:2(1), S)   III:140; IV:655n33; V:942;
                          IX:378n45

56:2 (56:3, M)

  (55:3(2), S)   V:942; VIII:304; 617

56:3 (56:4, M)

  (55:4, S)   VI:192

56:4 (56:5, M)

  (55:5, S)   II:786; VII:107

56:5 (56:6, M)

  (55:6(5), S)   II:97

56:6 (56:7, M)

  (55:7, S)   VI:194; VIII:147

56:7 (56:8, M)

  (55:8, S)   V:401; VII:970n14

56:8 (56:9, M)

  (55:9(8), S)   I:70; 620; II:854n165; VIII:154

56:10 (56:11, M)

  (55:11, S)   I:70

56:11 (56:12, M)

  (55:12, S)   V:424n302

56:12 (56:13, M)

  (55:13(12), S)   II:51

56:13 (56:14, M)

  (55:14(13), S)   I:455, n4; II:853; 854; VI:1001;
                          1002; IX:319; 320; 322

57 (Title)

  (57:1, M) (56:1, S)   VII:7n20

57:1 (57:2, M)

  (56:2(1), S)   II:522n31; VI:193; VII:396;
                          IX:378n45

57:2 (57:3, M)

  (56:3(2), S)   II:654; III:499

57:3 (57:3, M)

  (56:4(3), S)   I:401, n22; III:499; V:942;
                          IX:384

57:4 (57:5, M)

  (56:5(4), S)   I:721; IV:126n215; 525; V:293;
                          VI:997, n26

57:5 (57:6, M)

  (56:6(5), S)   II:242; 244; VIII:606

57:6 (57:7, M)

  (56:7(6), S)   II:706; V:594n5; VI:626

57:7 (57:8, M)

  (56:8(7), S)   I:163; II:363; 788n155;
                          VIII:493; 499; IX:626n72

57:8 (57:9, M)

  (56:9, S)   II:238n22; VIII:494

57:9 (57:10, M)

  (56:10, S)   VIII:493; 494

57:10 (57:11, M)

  (56:11(10), S)   IV:903; IX:384

57:11 (57:12, M)

  (56:12(11), S)   II:242; 244; VIII:606

58 (57, S)   III:1074

58:1 (58:2, M)

  (57:2, M)   III:83n80; VI:186n103

58:2 (58:3, M)

  (57:3, S)   VI:556n70

58:3 (58:4, M)

  (57:4(3), S)   I:265; V:646; VI:235(n37)

58:4 (58:5, M)

  (57:5(4), S)   III:334, n3; 335; V:190; 392;
                          411; 546; 556n125; 572

58:4f (58:5f, M)

  (57:5f(4f), S)   VI:236(n41)

58:5 (58:6, M)

  (57:6, S)   III:801n28; VII:483

58:6 (58:7, M)

  (57:7(6), S)   VI:74n5

58:6ff (58:7ff, M)

  (57:7ff, S)   II:792

58:8 (58:9, M)

  (57:9(8), S)   II:465

58:9 (58:10, M)

  (57:10, S)   V:392n60

58:10 (58:11, M)

  (57:11(10), S)   II:445; VI:627, n34

59 (58, S)   III:1102

59:1 (59:2, M)

  (58:2, S)   IV:332; 333

59:2 (59:3, M)
   (58:3, S)   VI:1001; VII:976(n39)
59:4 (59:5, M)
   (58:5(4), S)   I:334; 335; II:900n28
59:5 (59:6, M)
   (58:6(5), S)   II:602
59:6 (59:7, M)
   (58:7(6), S)   II:955
59:6f (59:7f, M)
   (58:7f, S)   III:1103
59:7 (59:8, M)
   (58:8, S)   I:447; VI:997
59:8 (59:9, M)
   (58:9(8), S)   I:661; IV:797n4
59:9 (59:10, M)
   (58:10(9), S) III:906
59:10 (59:11, M)
   (58:11(10), S) II:26, n2; 480(n46); IX:89; 155;
               156n86; 384
59:11 (59:12, M)
   (58:12(11), S) V:262; 313
59:12 (59:13, M)
   (58:13, S)   I:68; VIII:526
59:12f (59:13f, M)
   (58:13f, S)   I:68n12; VIII:65
59:13 (59:14, M)
   (58:14(13), S) I:68; II:47
59:14 (59:15, M)
   (58:15, S)   III:1103
59:15 (59:16, M)
   (58:16, S)   I:731, n13
59:16 (59:17, M)
   (58:17(16), S) II:294; 480(n46); III:141; 143;
               VIII:493
59:17 (59:18, M)
   (58:18(17), S) V:591; IX:384
60 (59, S)   IV:981n26
60 (Title)
   (60:1f, M) (59:1f, S) II:164; VIII:7n20
60:2 (60:4, M)
   (59:4(2), S)   III:203; VII:66
60:3 (60:5, M)
   (59:5, S)   V:437; VI:139n38; 150(n19);
               159(n3); 369n176; 595n87;
               VII:66
60:4 (60:6, M)
   (59:6, S)   III:168; VII:266n6, n7; 269;
               IX:203
60:5 (60:7, M)
   (59:7, S)   I:30n52; II:26; 37;
               VII:976(n39); IX:682
60:6 (60:8, M)
   (59:8, S)   VII:370n8
60:7 (60:9, M)
   (59:9, S)   VII:493
60:8 (60:10, M)
   (59:10(8), S) IV:301; VIII:40
60:9 (60:11, M)
   (59:11(9), S) V:98
60:10 (60:12, M)
   (59:12(10), S) V:98
60:11 (60:13, M)

   (59:13(11), S)
61 (60, S)   VIII:493
61:1 (61:2, M)
   (60:2, S)   II:785(n118)
61:2 (61:3, M)
   (60:3(2), S)   III:499; V:98; VII:610n16
61:3 (61:4, M)
   (60:4, S)   II:522n31; 523(n35);
               VI:192n136; 954, n9
61:4 (61:5, M)
   (60:5(4), S) I:200n10; V:27; 843; VI:193;
               VII:383
61:5 (61:6, M)
   (60:6, S)   II:795; IX:203
61:7 (61:8, M)
   (60:8, S)   IX:238; 384
61:8 (61:9, M)
   (60:9, S)   II:787; 788n161; 794(n210);
               VIII:494
62:1 (62:2, M)
   (61:2, S)   VIII:40
62:2 (62:3, M)
   (61:3, S)   VII:67; 1013
62:3 (62:4, M)
   (61:4, S)   IV:256n10, n11
62:4 (62:5, M)
   (61:5, S)   III:609; VII:697; VIII:230n32;
               IX:598
62:5 (62:6, M)
   (61:6(5), S) IV:583; 584; VIII:40; IX:622
62:6 (62:7, M)
   (61:7, S)   VII:1013
62:7 (62:8, M)
   (61:8, S)   II:178; VI:193; VII:610n16
62:8 (62:9, M)
   (61:9, S)   II:786; 897
62:9 (62:10, M)
   (61:10(9), S) II:896; IV:521; VIII:346;
               IX:597
62:10 (62:11, M)
   (61:11, S)   VI:191; VIII:168
62:11 (62:12, M)
   (61:12(11), S) III:906
62:12 (62:13, M)
   (61:13(12), S) II:46n18; 167; 178; 647(n35);
               VI:643n3; IX:384
63 (62, S)   II:241
63:1 (63:2, M)
   (62:2(1), S) II:227; 228n11; 849(n123);
               III:89; V:176; VII:107;
               IX:622; 623
63:1ff (63:2ff, M)
   (62:2ff, S)   II:792(n188)
63:2 (63:3, M)
   (62:3(2), S) I:95; II:241; V:325; 326; 333,
               n94
63:2a (63:3a, M)
   (63:3a(2a), S) V:333
63:3 (63:4, M)
   (62:4, S)   II:480(n46); 787(n141); III:89;
               IX:384
63:4 (63:5, M)

   III:141; IV:521

(62:5, S)   II:787; 790(n182); V:259n126;   65:10 (65:11, M)
                     260n131; 262; IX:426   (64:11(10), S)   IV:546
63:5 (63:6, M)   65:11 (65:12, M)
   (62:6(5), S)   I:644; VI:129; IX:619   (64:12, S)   VI:128; VII:626; IX:490
63:8 (63:9, M)   65:12 (65:13, M)
   (62:9(8), S)   II:37; III:823n7   (64:13, S)   V:305
63:9 (63:10, M)   65:13 (65:14, M)
   (62:10(9), S)   II:677; III:641n10   (64:14, S)   II:788n155; VI:281; VIII:493
63:10 (63:11, M)   66 (65, S)   II:794
   (62:11, S)   I:64   66:2 (65:2, S)   II:241; 788n161; VIII:172n17;
63:11 (63:12, M)   493; 494
   (62:12, S)   IX:363   66:3 (65:3, S)   II:640; VI:276n13; IX:201
64 (63, S)   V:491n19   66:4 (65:4, S)   II:788n161; 789; VIII:494
64:1 (64:2, M)   66:5 (65:5, S)   II:640; VI:643; IX:201
   (63:2, S)   IX:204; 617   66:6 (65:6, S)   VII:729
64:2 (64:3, M)   66:7 (65:7, S)   II:47; VI:126; VIII:607
   (63:3, S)   VI:278   66:8 (65:8, S)   II:787; VIII:493; IX:282
64:3 (64:4, M)   66:9 (65:9, S)   V:114n28; VI:626; VII:67;
   (63:4(3), S)   I:721; IV:126n215; V:633;   VIII:154
                     VI:638; 997   66:10 (65:10, S)   II:257; VI:949
64:4 (64:5, M)   66:11 (65:11, S)   I:553n1; III:141; 143
   (63:5(4), S)   III:968; V:368   66:12 (65:12, S)   V:820
64:5 (64:6, M)   66:13 (65:13, S)   II:795n220
   (63:6(5), S)   III:913n2; 961; IV:93; V:593;   66:14 (65:14, S)   II:795n220; III:141
                     594(n5); VII:341   66:16 (65:16, S)   IX:203
64:6 (64:7, M)   66:18 (65:18, S)   IV:724n110; V:328
   (63:7(6), S)   II:656; IV:965n8; IX:626   67 (66, S)   VIII:493
64:7 (64:8, M)   67:1 (67:2, M)
   (63:8(7), S)   I:608; VIII:606   (66:2(1), S)   II:757n7; VI:778; IX:9; 320;
64:8 (64:9, M)   378n48
   (63:9(8), S)   I:721; IV:915; VII:343   67:2 (67:3, M)
64:9 (64:10, M)   (66:3(2), S)   IV:32n11; VII:977
   (63:10(9), S)   I:63; II:642; IV:915; VI:460   67:3 (67:4, M)
64:10 (64:11, M)   (66:4(3), S)   IV:32n11
   (63:11, S)   IX:363   67:4 (67:5, M)
65:1 (65:2, M)   (66:5(4), S)   II:366(n9); V:98
   (64:2, S)   310; VIII:493   67:5 (67:6, M)
65:2 (65:3, M)   (66:6(5), S)   II:764n2; IV:37
   (64:3, S)   VII:106   67:6 (67:7, M)
65:3 (65:4, M)   (66:7(6), S)   II:756
   (64:4, S)   III:302; 304; 315, (n73),   68 (67, S)   VI:891n51; VII:1085n543
                     VII:187(n4)   68:1 (68:2, M)
65:3ff (65:4ff, M)   (67:2, S)   IV:687
   (64;4ff, S)   V:401   68:2 (68:3, M)
65:4 (65:5, M)   (67:3, S)   I:396; VI:935
   (64:5(4), S)   II:195; III:33; 35; IV:15; 155;   68:3 (68:4, M)
                     366; VII:385; IX:201   (67:4, S)   II:787(n147)
65:5 (65:6, M)   68:4 (68:5, M)
   (64:6(5), S)   II:522n30, n31; VII:1013   (67:5(4), S)   I:163; II:787n146; V:257;
65:6 (65:7, M)   264n144; 505n66
   (64:7(6), S)   II:704; III:811n3; 1009; V:304;   68:5 (68:6, M)
                     305; 480   (67:6(5), S)   II:60n4; V:488n4; 963n102;
65:6ff (65:7ff, M)   966n118; 974; VIII:198; 494;
   (64:7ff(6ff), S) IV:1013   IX:446; 460
65:7 (65:8, M)   68:6 (68:7, M)
   (64:8(7), S)   VII:595n2; 887, (n9); VIII:322;   (67:7(6), S)   I:30n58; IV:739n7; VI:126;
                     323n59; IX:246   VIII:352
65:8 (65:9, M)   68:6f (68:7f, M)
   (64:9(8), S)   V:104; VII:887n9   (67:7f, S)   VI:891n51
65:9 (65:10, M)   68:7 (68:8, M)
   (64:10(9), S)   II:602; 704; III:1009; VI:281;   (67:8, S)   VI:487(n19), (n27), 499(n8)
                     287; VIII:496n51   68:7-23 (68:8-24, M)

(67:8-24, S)
68:8 (68:9, M)
  (67:9, S)
68:9 (68:10, M)
  (67:10, S)
68:10 (68:11, M)
  (67:11, S)
68:11 (68:12, M)
  (67:12(11), S)

68:13 (68:14, M)
  (67:14(13), S)
68:14 (68:15, M)
  (67:15(14), S)
68:15 (68:16, M)
  (67:16, S)
68:16 (68:17, M)
  (67:17(16), S)

68:17 (68:18, M)
  (67:18, S)

68:18 (68:19, M)
  (67:19(18), S)

68:19 (68:20, M)
  (67:20, S)
68:20 (68:21, M)
  (67:21(20), S)
68:21 (68:22, M)
  (67:22, S)
68:24 (68:25, M)
  (67:25(24), S)
68:25 (68:26, M)
  (67:26, S)
68:26 (68:27, M)
  (68:27(26), S)
68:27 (68:28, M)
  (67:28, S)
68:28 (68:29, M)
  (67:29(28), S)
68:29 (68:30, M)
  (67:30, S)
68:30 (68:31, M)
  (67:31(30), S)

68:31 (68:32, M)
  (67:32(31), S)
68:32ff (68:33ff, M)
  (67:33ff, S)
68:33 (68:34, M)
  (67:34, S)

68:34 (68:35, M)
  (67:35(34), S)

68:35 (68:36, M)
  (68:36(35), S)
68:36 (68:37, M)
  (67:37, S)
69 (68, S)

VII:198

VII:198, n12; 283n6

VI:698, n7; VII:282n4

II:873; VI:891n51; 892; IX:490

II:708; 709; 712(n59); 713;
  IV:91

IV:557n21

III:408n18; V:539

V:482

II:739; 741n16; VI:290n15; 303;
  VII:294n3; 310; 388; VIII:51

I:82n44; 377n4; VII:310;
  IX:467

I:196; 521; II:99; 764; IV:870;
  V:525, n223; VII:388;
  VIII:605, n27

II:46n18

III:82; V:109; 112; VII:970

I:117n7

V:328

V:831; VIII:493

II:758; III:527

III:527; 821n14

II:286; III:634

VII:311

II:256; 624n8; 751n54; III:528;
  VII:803; IX:14n10

II:745n13; VII:803n25

II:294

V:522n192; VI:577n73;
  VIII:418

II:243; 421; IV:542; V:511;
  512; IX:283

III:33; 35

IX:201
II:793; 880; V:289n8;

VI:892(n58)

69:1 (69:2, M)
  (68:2, S)
69:2 (69:3, M)
  (68:3, S)

69:3 (69:4, M)
  (68:4(3), S)

69:4 (69:5, M)
  (68:5(4), S)

69:5 (69:6, M)
  (68:6(5), S)
69:6 (69:7, M)
  (68:7(6), S)

69:7 (69:8, M)
  (68:8(7), S)
69:8 (69:9, M)
  (68:9(8), S)
69:8-10 (69:9-11, M)
  (68:9-11, S)
69:9 (69:10, M)
  (68:10(9), S)

69:10 (69:11, M)
  (68:11(10), S)

69:11 (69:12, M)
  (68:12, S)
69:12 (69:13, M)
  (68:13, S)
69:13 (69:14, M)
  (68:14(13), S)

69:14 (69:15, M)
  (68:15(14), S)
69:15 (69:16, M)
  (68:16, S)
69:16 (69:17, M)
  (68:17(16), S)

69:17 (69:18, M)
  (68:18(17), S)
69:18 (69:19, M)
  (68:19, S)
69:19 (69:20, M)
  (68:20(19), S)
69:19f (69:20f, M)
  (68:20f(19f), S)
69:20 (69:21, M)
  (68:21(20), S)

69:21 (69:22, M)
  (68:22(21), S)

69:22 (69:23, M)
  (68:23(22), S)

I:538; VII:976(n39); VIII:322

I:518n6; VIII:581, n91, n92;
  582n102

III:500; IV:579; VII:428;
  VIII:280n66

II:167; 229; IV:686; 687;
  VI:281

I:700; III:968; IV:692

II:522n30, (n31), n31; 790n186;
  VI:193n139; 726

V:239; VIII:265n40

V:8; 9; 12; VIII:341

IV:487

I:265n2; II:161; 878;
  III:102n243; 239; 726n10;
  IV:677; V:122; 239; 240

III:723n10; IV:925; 927; 928;
  V:239; VII:743

V:748(n20); VII:60

VIII:493

II:479n28; 743; 744; VI:276,
  n13; IX:384, (n84)

IV:686; VI:118; 1000; VIII:322

VI:158; 159n4; VII:881

II:479(n31); 481; V:160n17;
  VI:276, n13; IX:384(n84);
  485

III:142; 969; VII:605

VI:560(n97)

I:700; III:140; IX:617

III:723n10

IV:323; V:239; 789; VII:920;
  922

II:107; 226n1; V:164; 288, (n1);
  289; 635n30; VI:160;
  VII:459; 923n27; VIII:82

II:169; V:593; VII:341; 342;

73:9 (72:9, S)   V:509; 943; VII:697
73:10 (72:10, S)   IX:526
73:11 (72:11, S)   I:698(n36); 700; VII:493
73:13 (72:13, S)   II:213; VIII:320n42
73:13ff (72:13ff, S) III:1076
73:14 (72:14, S)   IV:798
73:15 (72:15, S)   IV:41n50; V:973; VIII:352
73:17 (72:17, S)   VIII:51n15; 55
73:20 (72:20, S)   V:221; 229
73:21 (72:21, S)   II:883; III:464; 606; 612;
                    IV:911; VII:596
73:22 (72:22, S)   I:697n32; II:883
73:23 (72:23, S)   III:911; VII:780
73:23f (72:23f, S) IV:1014
73:23ff (72:23ff, S) I:466; II:848
73:23-26
  (72:23-26, S)   VI:325
73:23-28
  (72:23-28, S)   V:239
73:24 (72:24, S)   I:634; IV:15; V:98; 101n22;
                    508(n81); VI:572n39;
                    VII:780; VIII:172n17
73:25 (72:25, S)   I:322; II:845n94
73:25f (72:25f, S) II:792(n188); 823; IV:712
73:25-28
  (72:25-28, S)   VI:153n41; VII:496
73:26 (72:26, S)   III:607; VII:108; 129n248;
                    IX:623n67; 631n89; 632
73:27 (72:27, S)   I:396; VI:584; 587
73:28 (72:28, S)   I:70; IV:516; VI:193;
                    VII:294n1
74 (73, S)   IV:981n26; VI:814
74:1 (73:1, S)   II:427; V:399n128; 409;
                    VI:487(n27); 499(n8);
                    500n11; 690; VIII:51
74:1-8 (73:1-8, S) V:398
74:2 (73:2, S)   III:504; 507; 528; 773; 1007;
                    IV:148; 333; 675; V:406;
                    VII:309; 388; 805; 829n199
74:3 (73:3, S)   III:140; VI:814; VIII:52; 526;
                    613
74:3-8 (73:3-8, S) VI:814
74:4 (73:4, S)   III:646; IV:687; 1091; VII:210,
                    n64; 219, n135
74:7 (73:7, S)   VI:814; VII:383; 388
74:8 (73:8, S)   VII:805n31; 810
74:9 (73:9, S)   III:970; VI:808; **813-814;**
                    VII:210n64; 211; 219
74:10 (73:10, S)   VIII:51
74:11 (73:11, S)   III:824; VII:720; VIII:52
74:12 (73:12, S)   II:637; VII:976
74:12ff (73:12ff, S) VII:976; VIII:319
74:13 (73:13, S)   VII:924n31
74:13a (73:13a, S) V:576
74:13f (73:13f, S) II:283; V:572; VII:429;
                    VIII:319
74:14 (73:14, S)   VIII:418
74:15 (73:15, S)   VI:598
74:16 (73:16, S)   IV:1124; VII:429
74:17 (73:17, S)   VI:256; 257
74:18 (73:18, S)   III:1028; V:257; VIII:51
74:19 (73:19, S)   VI:67(n51); 892

74:20 (73:20, S)   VII:428
74:21 (73:21, S)   VI:889; 892; VII:720; VIII:9
74:22 (73:22, S)   V:239
74:23 (73:23, S)   IV:687
75:1 (75:2, M)
  (74:2(1), S)   I:719n4; II:786n138; V:214
75:2 (75:3, M)
  (74:3(2), S)   III:35; 458
75:3 (75:4, M)
  (74:4, S)   IV:1014; V:137n2; VII:610; 733
75:4 (75:5, M)
  (74:5(4), S)   III:670; VII:613n44; VIII:607
75:5 (75:6, M)
  (74:6(5), S)   III:32; 670; VIII:302; 603
75:5a (75:6a, M)
  (74:6a, S)   VIII:603
75:5b (75:6b, M)
  (74:6b, S)   VIII:603
75:6 (75:7, M)
  (74:7(6), S)   V:104
75:7 (75:8, M)
  (74:8, S)   VIII:8; 607
75:7f (75:8f, M)
  (74:8f, S)   VI:150
75:8 (75:9, M)
  (74:9(8), S)   III:168; V:165, n29; 437;
                    VI:139, (n38); 149, n17; 150,
                    n20, n22; 151; 156; 595n87

75:10 (75:11, M)
  (74:11, S)   VIII:607
76 (75, S)   VI:892; VIII:493
76:1 (76:2, M)
  (75:2(1), S)   I:719; IV:539
76:2 (76:3, M)
  (75:3(2), S)   V:155; VII:294; 299; 309; 320;
                    VIII:198
76:3 (76:4, M)
  (75:4(3), S)   III:906; V:293; VI:996
76:3f (76:4f, M)
  (75:4f(3f), S)   VII:921
76:5 (76:6, M)
  (75:6, S)   III:606; VII:895n66; VIII:301
76:6 (76:7, M)
  (75:7(6), S)   II:624; III:337
76:7 (76:8, M)
  (75:8, S)   V:396
76:9 (76:10, M)
  (75:10, S)   III:930; VI:648; 892
76:10 (76:11, M)
  (75:11(10), S)   V:304; VI:647
76:12 (76:13, M)
  (75:13(12), S)   III:32n21; V:732; VI:361
77:2 (77:3, M)
  (76:3(2), S)   III:142; V:789
77:3 (77:4, M)
  (76:4, S)   II:786; 787; VI:361
77:5 (77:6, M)
  (76:6(5), S)   I:208; II:95
77:6 (77:7, M)
  (76:7, S)   VI:361
77:7 (77:8, M)
  (76:8(7), S)   I:200n10; II:738

77:8 (77:9, M)
(76:9, S)   II:426; IV:91; VIII:51
77:9 (77:10, M)
(76:10, S)   II:481(n54); V:405; 408;
                         VII:881; IX:384
77:11 (77:12, M)
(76:12(11), S)   II:640; III:35; VI:638
77:12 (77:13, M)
(76:13, S)   V:55; VI:643
77:13 (77:14, M)
(76:14(13), S)   II:291; IV:538
77:13ff (77:14ff, M)
(76:14ff, S)   V:55
77:14 (77:15, M)
(76:15(14), S)   I:697n34; 718; II:291; III:35;
                         VI:460; 638
77:15 (77:16, M)
(76:16, S)   IV:333
77:15f (77:16f, M)
(76:16f, S)   II:292
77:15ff (77:16ff, M)
(76:16ff, S)   V:49
77:16 (77:17, M)
(76:17(16), S)   V:324; 333; VIII:319
                         IX:198n47; 669n22
77:16ff (77:17ff, M)
(76:17ff, S)   I:505n5; III:406n20
77:16-20 (77:17-21,
M) (76:17-21, S)   IX:283
77:18 (77:19, M)
(76:19, S)   I:505(n4); IV:905; V:49;
                         VII:66; 198n12; IX:280
77:19 (77:20, M)
(76:20(19), S)   I:212; III:402n2; 406n20; V:49;
                         VI:627; VIII:317; 323n60
77:19f (77:20f, M)
(76:20f, S)   VIII:319
77:20 (77:21, M)
(76:21(20), S)   V:98; VI:487(n27); 499(n8); 690
78 (77, S)   II:47n19; VI:127; VII:308
78:1 (77:1, S)   IV:1057
78:2 (77:2, S)   III:885n62; 974; V:748; 757;
                         VI:832; 834; VII:699
78:4 (77:4, S)   I:66; III:35; 970
78:5 (77:5, S)   IV:486; VIII:154
78:5ff (77:5ff, S)   VII:492n188
78:7 (77:7, S)   VI:192n134
78:8 (77:8, S)   IV:840; VI:126; 186; 362;
                         VII:404; 406; 779; IX:630
78:10 (77:10, S)   I:631n16; III:46n31; V:51
78:11 (77:11, S)   II:26; 654; III:35
78:12 (77:12, S)   III:35; VI:638
78:13 (77:13, S)   VIII:319
78:14 (77:14, S)   IV:905; V:98; IX:320
78:15 (77:15, S)   VI:136(n8); 159(n2); VII:959
78:15f (77:15f, S)   VIII:318
78:15-20
(77:15-20, S)   VI:97n28
78:17 (77:17, S)   II:658; VI:126
78:17b (77:17b, S)   VI:127n9
78:17f (77:17f, S)   VI:27

78:18 (77:18, S)   II:785; V:581; VI:32
78:18a (17:18a, S)   VI:127n9
78:19 (77:19, S)   IV:3
78:19f (77:19f, S)   II:705
78:20 (77:20, S)   VII:107; IX:623n67
78:21 (77:21, S)   V:409
78:22 (77:22, S)   II:434; 522n30; 531; VI:187;
                         188n117; 191; 192; 197n149;
                         VII:977
78:23 (77:23, S)   III:176; 177(n52)
78:23f (77:23f, S)   IV:905
78:24 (77:24, S)   I:477; 643; II:935; IV:462; 465;
                         V:527n238
78:24a (77:24a, S)   IV:462
78:24b (77:24b, S)   IV:462; 463
78:25 (77:25, S)   I:643; IV:462(n1); VI:132
78:25a (77:25a, S)   IV:462; 464
78:25ff (77:25ff, S)   III:750n63
78:26 (77:26, S)   V:469
78:27 (77:27, S)   VII:107; 108n78; IX:623n67
78:31 (77:31, S)   V:396; 398
78:32 (77:32, S)   III:35; VI:186n107; 187n114;
                         191; 215n314
78:32ff (77:32ff, S)   VI:188n117
78:33 (77:33, S)   VII:562
78:35 (77:35, S)   III:88; IV:335; 351; 675
78:36 (77:36, S)   IX:598
78:37 (77:37, S)   VI:186; 204; VII:779
78:38 (77:38, S)   III:302; 304; 315; V:407; 410;
                         412; VI:280; VII:720
78:38-41
(77:38-41, S)   V:407
78:39 (77:39, S)   II:850, (n133); IV:675;
                         V:406n181; VI:360; 570;
                         VII:107; 115; VIII:504n5;
                         IX:472
78:40 (77:40, S)   II:658; VI:126
78:40f (77:40f, S)   VI:27
78:41 (77:41, S)   I:95; VII:724
78:42 (77:42, S)   IV:333
78:43 (77:43, S)   VII:210(n65); 212; 218
78:44 (77:44, S)   VI:598; VII:715n7
78:47 (77:47, S)   VII:453; 758
78:48 (77:48, S)   VI:934; 935; VII:744
78:49 (77:49, S)   I:79(n25); 446; III:141;
                         V:393n69; 396; 400; 409; 410;
                         VI:550; VIII:496n51
78:50 (77:50, S)   II:849(n117); VII:744
78:51 (77:51, S)   I:485
78:52 (77:52, S)   VI:690
78:52f (77:52f, S)   VI:487(n27); 499(n8)
78:53 (77:53, S)   V:98; IX:204
78:54 (77:54, S)   III:1007
78:55 (77:55, S)   III:769; 774; V:843
78:56 (77:56, S)   VI:127n9
78:58 (77:58, S)   V:403
78:60 (77:60, S)   VII:383
78:62 (77:60, S)   III:774; VII:744
78:64 (77:64, S)   IX:450n94
78:65 (77:65, S)   III:435
78:67 (77:67, S)   IV:169

	VI:891, n52; VIII:348, n83; 495		VIII:496n51; IX:467
82:1 (81:1, S)	III:96; 517n40; VII:643; VIII:347; 348; 617n21	84:11 (84:12, M) (83:12(11), S)	III:81n70; VI:571; VIII:73; 594, n14; IX:379; 380; 386; 389
82:2f (81:2f, S)	III:930		
82:3 (81:3, S)	II:212; VI:888; 896; VIII:9	84:12 (84:13, M)	
82:3f (81:3f, S)	IX:446n52	(83:13(12), S)	IV:366; IV:192
82:4 (81:4, S)	I:328n83; VI:1001	85 (84, S)	II:403; IV:981n26
82:5 (81:5, S)	I:697n32; VII:66; 424n10; 428; 430n52	85:1 (85:2, M) (84:2, S)	VII:719; 724
82:6 (81:6, S)	III:96; 100n213; 104; IV:112; VII:338; VIII:347; 348; 616; 617n21	85:2 (85:3, M) (84:3(2), S)	III:557; 558n6
82:6f (81:6f, S)	III:83n79; V:966	85:3 (85:4, M) (84:4, S)	III:627; VII:720
82:7 (81:7, S)	V:966n116; VIII:348	85:4 (85:5, M)	
82:8 (81:8, S)	III:774; 777	(84:5, S)	V:398; VII:720; 724
83 (82, S)	IV:981n26	85:5 (85:6, M)	
83:2 (83:3, M)		(84:6, S)	III:1078n205; V:405
(82:3(2), S)	II:955; IV:687	85:6 (85:7, M)	
83:3 (83:4, M)		(84:7, S)	V:398
(82:4(3), S)	I:717; V:724n13	85:7 (85:8, M)	
83:5 (83:6, M)		(84:8(7), S)	II:28n8; 479(n28); 480n48
(82:6(5), S)	II:126	85:8 (85:9, M)	
83:6f (83:7f, M)		(84:9(8), S)	II:408; III:82; V:491(n18), n21
(82:7f, S)	VII:286n33	85:8f (85:9f, M)	
83:11 (83:12, M)		(85:9f, S)	II:480(n41)
(82:12, S)	VIII:154	85:9 (85:10, M)	
83:12 (83:13, M)		(84:10(9), S)	II:408; IX:203
(82:13, S)	VII:532(n24)	85:10 (85:11, M)	
83:14 (83:15, M)		(84:11, S)	II:479(n25), (n29), n35; IX:125n122; 384
(82:15, S)	V:480; VI:942n73	85:10a (85:11a, M)	
83:15 (83:16, M)		(84:11a, S)	IX:126n135
(82:16(15), S)	V:399, n130; 411	85:10b (85:11b, M)	
83:16 (83:17, M)		(84:11b, S)	IX:126n135
(82:17, S)	II:790n186; VI:287	85:10f (85:11f, M)	VII:491; IX:402
83:17 (83:18, M)		(84:11f, S)	
(82:18, S)	I:200	85:11 (85:12, M)	I:236
84 (83, S)	IV:254n3	(84:12, S)	
84:1 (84:2, M)		85:12 (85:13, M)	IX:490
(83:2, S)	VII:383	(84:13, S)	
84:2 (84:3, M)		86 (85, S)	II:785
(83:3, S)	II:849(n123); III:607; VI:66; VII:107; IX:363; 622; 623; 632	86:1 (85:1, S)	VI:39; 889; 892
		86:1f (85:1f, S)	VI:889n24
		86:2 (85:2, S)	V:491n21
84:3 (84:4, M)		86:3 (85:3, S)	IX:378, n45
(83:4, S)	VI:66, n37; VII:731, n11	86:4 (85:4, S)	VIII:135; IX:640n143
84:4 (84:5, M)		86:5 (85:5, S)	II:483n96; 589, n1; III:499; V:491n22; IX:383, n81; 486
(83:5(4), S)	I:200		
84:6 (84:7, M)		86:6 (85:6, S)	II:785(n118); IX:281
(83:7, S)	III:324(n5), VIII:198	86:7 (85:7, S)	III:141
84:6f (84:7f, M)		86:8 (85:8, S)	II:642; III:351
(83:7f(6f), S)	III:726n10	86:9 (85:9, S)	V:272
84:7 (84:8, M)		86:10 (85:10, S)	III:35; IV:538
(83:8(7), S)	II:285; 293; 430; V:333; VI:720n104; VII:311; VIII:198n76	86:11 (85:11, S)	I:236; V:53; 98; 943; VI:188; 190n127; 571; IX:627
		86:12 (85:12, S)	V:257; VIII:498n66
84:8 (84:9, M)		86:13 (85:13, S)	IV:539; VI:1001; 1002; IX:384; 655n227
(83:9, S)	II:785(n118)		
84:9 (84:10, M)		86:14 (85:14, S)	II:485; III:528; VII:803, n25; VIII:165; 301; 526
(83:10(9), S)	V:313; IX:502; 503		
84:10 (84:11, M)		86:15 (85:15, S)	I:249; II:483n96; IV:376(n18);
(83:11(10), S)	I:320; IV:150; 168; VII:396;		

89:17 (89:18, M)
  (88:18(17), S)

89:17f (89:18f, M)
  (88:18f, S)

89:18 (89:19, M)
  (88:19, S)

89:19 (89:20, M)
  (88:20, S)

89:19f (89:20f, M)
  (88:20f, S)

89:19ff (89:20ff, M)
  (88:20ff, S)

89:19-37
  (89:20-38, M)
  (88:20-38, S)

89:20 (89:21, M)
  (88:21, S)

89:21 (89:22, M)
  (88:22, S)

89:22 (89:23, M)
  (88:23, S)

89:23 (89:24, M)
  (88:24, S)

89:24 (89:25, M)
  (88:25(24), S)

89:26 (89:27, M)
  (88:27(26), S)

89:26f (89:27f, M)
  (88:27f, S)

89:27 (89:28, M)
  (88:28(27), S)

89:27a (89:28a, M)
  (88:28a, S)

89:27b (89:28b, M)
  (88:28b, S)

89:27f (89:28f, M)
  (88:28f, S)

89:28 (89:29, M)
  (88:29, S)

89:28f (89:29f, M)
  (88:29f, S)

89:29 (89:30, M)
  (88:30, S)

89:30 (89:31, M)
  (88:31, S)

89:31 (89:32, M)
  (88:32(31), S)

89:32 (89:33, M)
  (88:33(32), S)

89:33 (89:34, M)
  (88:34(33), S)

89:34 (89:35, M)
  (88:35(34), S)

VIII:607; IX:363

II:744; VIII:366

III:646

I:95

IV:159; V:490n16; 687n249;
    VIII:350; 607

VIII:370n255

IX:505

VIII:350

V:664; IX:498; 499; 503

I:375

VIII:346

IV:686

I:601; V:258; VII:775

III:89; 497; 499; V:974;
    979n209; VI:95n9; VIII:350

VIII:349

I:577; **VI:874,** n19; 875;
    880n58; 881n58; VIII:154;
    350; 362n188; 369n248;
    370n255; 617

VI:878

VI:878

I:30n53; V:966n118

II:479(n35); VI:185; IX:385

VIII:367n233

III:162; V:503; VII:540n12;
    VIII:154

VI:571; VIII:341

I:605n1

I:117n7; II:602; III:312;
    IV:518; V:618; VI:967

I:153; II:479n35; IX:384

I:605; V:738; VI:579;
    VII:695n39; VIII:158;

89:35 (89:36, M)
  (88:36, S)

89:36 (89:37, M)
  (88:37, S)

89:37 (89:38, M)
  (88:38(37), S)

89:37b (89:38b, M)
  (88:38b, S)

89:38 (89:39, M)
  (88:39, S)

89:39 (89:40, M)
  (89:40(39), S)

89:41 (89:42, M)
  (88:42(41), S)

89:42 (89:43, M)
  (88:43, S)

89:44 (89:45, M)
  (88:45, S)

89:45 (89:46, M)
  (88:46, S)

89:46 (89:47, M)
  (88:47(46), S)

89:47 (89:48, M)
  (88:48, S)

89:48 (89:49, M)
  (88:49(48), S)

89:49 (89:50, M)
  (88:50(49), S)

89:50 (89:51, M)
  (88:51(50), S)

89:51 (89:52, M)
  (88:52, S)

89:52 (89:53, M)
  (88:53, S)

90 (89, S)

90:1 (89:1, S)

90:2 (89:2, S)

90:3 (89:3, S)
90:3a (89:3a, S)
90:3b (89:3b, S)
90:4 (89:4, S)

90:6 (89:6, S)
90:7 (89:7, S)
90:7ff (89:7ff, S)
90:7-11 (89:7-11, S)
90:8 (89:8, S)
90:9f (89:9f, S)
90:10 (89:10, S)

IX:598n42

I:382

III:162; VII:540n12;
    VIII:367n233

II:363(n6); IV:483; 495; V:510;
    VI:878; IX:446n53

VIII:369n248

IX:502; 503

II:106; V:664n47;
    VIII:367n233

V:48

VIII:607

III:414

VII:689n21; IX:586

III:88; 969; V:405; 412; 446;
    VI:935; VIII:52

III:1017n104; VIII:581, n90

II:846(n103); 850(n133);
    853n164; V:326; VII:980n56

I:146; II:46n18; 479n22, (n35);
    IX:384; 385n86

III:825; IV:675; V:664n47;
    VI:537

IX:502; 533n276

I:335, VI:186

II:785; 850(n133); III:1076;
    IV:344; **V:968**

II:430; VI:809

I:201; II:363(n5); III:811n3;
    1007; 1009, n70; V:480; 968;
    VI:257; 258; 686; IX:667; 669

IV:135; 1014; VIII:11; 12
VII:716n3
VII:716n3
I:202n15; II:950;
    III:1076(n198); IV:1124;
    VII:265; IX:467; 468; 469;
    471

V:1031
V:401; 404
IV:903
V:444
V:404; VIII:154
V:401
II:644; 851; III:828; VI:647,

	n13
90:11 (89:11, S)	V:409
90:12 (89:12, S)	VII:487, n159
90:13 (89:13, S)	V:778n25; VII:724
90:14 (89:14, S)	II:480n48; VI:129; VIII:493; IX:363; 384
90:15 (89:15, S)	V:326; 910; VIII:8
90:16 (89:16, S)	II:638; V:98; 968
90:17 (89:17, S)	II:363(n7); 649(n46); III:553; VI:643; IX:426
91 ((90, S)	III:200; VIII:617n21
91:1 (90:1, S)	I:503; V:510
91:1ff (90:1ff, S)	II:522n30
91:2 (90:2, S)	II:522n30, (n32); VI:192; 752
91:3 (90:3, S)	VI:1001
91:4 (90:4, S)	V:293; 296; 297; 313; VI:193; VII:399; IX:204
91:5 (90:5, S)	I:608
91:5f (90:5f, S)	I:503; VIII:120n41; IX:200
91:6 (90:6, S)	II:11; 12; 19; V:943; VII:424n10
91:8 (90:8, S)	IV:974
91:9 (90:0, S)	II:522n30; VI:192n136; 752
91:10 (90:10, S)	II:683; IV:518; VI:918n6; 927n61
91:11 (90:11, S)	II:545; V:50; IX:240
91:11a (90:11a, S)	VI:628
91:11b (90:11b, S)	VI:628
91:11f (90:11f, S)	V:64; 98; VI:35; 750; 752
91:12 (90:12, S)	I:185; VI:628; 745; 748; 751; IX:430
91:13 (90:13, S)	IV:252n11; 253n21; V:571; 572; 573; **579**; 941; 943; VII:924
91:14 (90:14, S)	I:22n8; 28n43; II:522
91:15 (90:15, S)	III:143; 499; VII:775
91:16 (90:16, S)	VI:129
92 (91, S)	VII:16; VIII:495
92 (Title) (92:1, M)	
(91:1, S)	VII:5
92:1 (92:2, M)	
(91:2, S)	V:257; VII:16; 34n2; VIII:494
92:2 (92:3, M)	
(91:3, S)	I:63; II:787; IX:384
92:3 (92:4, M)	
(91:4, S)	VIII:494n42
92:4 (92:5, M)	
(91:5(4), S)	II:642; III:32; 635; VI:460
92:4f (92:5f, M)	
(91:5f, S)	I:20
92:5 (92:6, M)	
(91:6(5), S)	II:97; 642; IX:363n31
92:6 (92:7, M)	
(91:7, S)	I:276n25
92:7 (92:8, M)	
(91:8(7), S)	I:200; III:635, n3
92:8 (92:9, M)	
(91:9, S)	VIII:617
92:8f (92:9f, M)	
(91:9f, S)	II:846(n101)
92:9 (92:10, M)	
(91:10(9), S)	III:635, n3
92:10 (92:11, M)	

(91:11, S)	VIII:133
92:12 (92:13, M)	
(91:13, S)	VI:281
92:14 (92:15, M)	
(91:15, S)	VI:281
92:15 (92:16, M)	
(91:16, S)	I:63
93 ((92, S)	I:569; III:1017n104; V:862; VIII:219n23; 495
93:1 (92:1, S)	I:571; II:319; III:1009; IV:157n61; VII:67; 610, n13; 613n44
93:1-3 (92:1-3, S)	VI:598n24
93:2 (92:2, S)	II:363; 705; III:163
93:3 (92:3, S)	VIII:503n99
93:3f (92:3f, S)	VIII:319; IX:280
93:4 (92:4, S)	III:35; VIII:322
93:5 (92:5, S)	VI:185n100
94 (93, S)	VIII:495
94:1 (93:1, S)	III:1078; V:877; VII:7
94:2 (93:2, S)	III:891; V:401; VIII:300; 526; 606
94:3 (93:3, S)	III:646
94:4 (93:4, S)	VIII:302
94:5 (93:5, S)	III:774; VI:890; VIII:7
94:6 (93:6, S)	V:10; IX:445; 447n64
94:7 (93:7, S)	IV:834; V:325
94:8 (93:8, S)	III:726n10; IV:834
94:9 (93:9, S)	III:1012; IV:974; V:376; 547; 549; VI:256; 257; VII:542; VIII:496n51
94:10 (93:10, S)	I:700; II:137; V:606, n53; 610; VII:493
94:11 (93:11, S)	I:697; II:97; 523; IV:521; 522; 846
94:12 (93:12, S)	IV:366; 1046; V:606; 610; 618
94:13 (93:13, S)	VI:647n13; IX:97
94:14 (93:14, S)	I:448; III:774; IV:54; VIII:139
94:15 (93:15, S)	II:196
94:17 (93:17, S)	V:844; VII:540n15
94:18 (93:18, S)	V:114n28; VII:67; IX:384; 625
94:19 (93:19, S)	III:609; V:789
94:20 (93:20, S)	III:161; VI:257
94:21 (93:21, S)	III:622
94:22 (93:22, S)	VI:193
94:23 (93:23, S)	II:792(n189)
95 (94, S)	V:1016; VI:126; 127; VII:34; IX:363
95-99 (94-98, S)	V:862
95 (Title)	I:177
(94 (Title), S)	
95:1 (94:1, S)	II:710
95:1-5 (94:1-5, S)	III:1011
95:2 (94:2, S)	V:219; VI:773; VIII:494; IX:89
95:3 (94:3, S)	I:677n2; IV:538
95:4 (94:4, S)	I:448; V:480
95:4f (94:4f, S)	VI:603n69
95:5 (94:5, S)	III:1012; VI:256; 257
95:6 (94:6, S)	I:739; II:789n179; III:726n10; VI:761n29
95:7 (94:7, S)	VI:236(n41); 487(n27); 499(n9); 500(n10), (n12); VII:34; 271;

(101:7b, S)	VII:106n61
102:7 (102:8, M)	
(101:8, S)	VII:731
102:8 (102:9, M)	
(101:9, S)	V:401
102:10 (102:11, M)	
(101:11(10), S)	V:396; 409
102:10f (102:11f, M)	
(101:11, S)	V:401
102:11 (102:12, M)	
(101:12, S)	VII:395; 396
102:12 (102:13, M)	
(101:13, S)	IV:575; 682
102:13 (102:14, M)	
(101:15(13), S)	II:481(n53); IX:378
102:14 (102:15, M)	
(101:15(14), S)	II:738; V:160(n18); VI:611n35; IX:377, n36
102:15 (102:16, M)	
(101:16(15), S)	II:244; V:257; 272
102:16 (102:17, M)	
(101:17(16), S)	V:333; IX:377n41
102:17 (102:18, M)	
(101:18, S)	VIII:10; IX:377n41
102:19 (102:20, M)	
(101:20, S)	V:522n192
102:20 (102:21, M)	
(101:21(20), S)	II:60n4; IV:328
102:21 (102:22, M)	
(101:22, S)	I:63; 67n25; VIII:347
102:22 (102:23, M)	
(101:23(22), S)	II:268; VII:316; VIII:194n50
102:23 (102:24, M)	
(101:24, S)	V:401
102:24 (102:25, M)	
(101:25, S)	I:663n6; V:515
102:25 (102:26, M)	
(101:26(25), S)	I:481; II:638n9; III:1029; IX:427
102:25f (102:26f, M)	
(101:25f, S)	III:1009; V:515
102:26 (102:27, M)	
(101:27(26), S)	IV:757n10; V:515n135; 718; 720; 1007n373
102:26f (102:27f, M)	
(101:27f, S)	V:509n87
102:26-28	
(102:27-29, M)	
(101:27-29, S)	III:1011; VIII:464
102:26ff	
(102:27ff, M)	
(101:27ff, S)	I:201
102:27 (102:28, M)	
(101:28, S)	III:1063n121; V:512n103
102:28 (102:29, M)	
(101:29, S)	VII:388
103 (102, S)	II:792 (n187); IV:760n1; IX:203n73
103f (102f, S)	VIII:200
103:1 (102:1, S)	I:91
103:1f (102:1f, S)	II:787; IX:622
103:2 (102:2, S)	II:655

103:3 (102:3, S)	III:202; 203; IV:1093; V:401
103:4 (102:4, S)	IV:333; 1093; VII:626; IX:99; 384
103:5 (102:5, S)	III:451; VI:129
103:6 (102:6, S)	I:159; II:196; 486; III:53; 927; VI:460
103:6ff (102:6ff, S)	III:930
103:7 (102:7, S)	V:52
103:8 (102:8, S)	II:480n50; 481n53; 485; IV:376(n18); 587; V:160n17; 161; 405; 411; 422n288; VII:557(n56); IX:378(n52); 383, n81
103:8ff (102:8ff, S)	III:573
103:9 (102:9, S)	V:405; 434; VIII:52
103:9ff (102:9ff, S)	V:433
103:11 (102:11, S)	II:195; 480(n37); IX:203; 384
103:13 (102:13, S)	I:30n58; II:480n50; V:646; 970; 1008n378; VIII:352; IX:203; 212
103:14 (102:14, S)	I:700; IV:675; VI:258; 260; IX:472; 473
103:16 (102:16, S)	IV:760n1; VI:369n177; VIII:200
103:17 (102:17, S)	II:195; 480(n37); 483n95; IX:203; 384
103:19 (102:19, S)	I:570(n29); II:47; 705; III:162; 884n60; V:522n188
103:20 (102:20, S)	I:79(n25); VI:460; IX:282
103:21 (102:21, S)	II:743; III:53; IV:230
103:21a (102:21a, S)	VIII:503n99
103:22 (102:22, S)	II:47; 638n9; 787; III:1012; IX:622
104 (103, S)	II:47n19; 537; III:574; 1011; 1013; IV:610; 1013; V:890; 893; VI:603n69; VII:485
104:1 (103:1, S)	II:319; 787; III:553n65; IV:542; V:219; VII:689(n20); IX:319; 622; 632
104:2 (103:2, S)	III:1008; IV:22; 248; V:502(n40); 503(n51); VII:689n21; IX:319; 320
104:2-9 (103:2-9, S)	VIII:319
104:3 (103:3, S)	III:1009; IV:905; V:503; 505; 942; VIII:419n151
104:4 (103:4, S)	IV:26; 230; VI:463; 935; 936; 941; 947; 951n2; VIII:464
104:7 (103:7, S)	II:624; VII:67; VIII:319n38; IX:283
104:8 (103:8, S)	VIII:200
104:9 (103:9, S)	VIII:154
104:11 (103:11, S)	II:58; 159(n1)
104:12 (103:12, S)	VII:388; IX:281
104:13 (103:13, S)	II:638n9; III:614; VI:159(n1)
104:14 (103:14, S)	III:1012n79
104:15 (103:15, S)	III:298; 611; IV:243n13; V:162; 438n390; VII:655; IX:363; 626
104:16 (103:16, S)	IV:140; VII:541
104:17 (103:17, S)	VII:388; 731
104:18 (103:18, S)	VI:192n136
104:19 (103:19, S)	III:459; IV:640; VIII:38

104:19-23
  (103:19-23, S)   III:1013
104:20 (103:20, S)   IV:1123
104:22 (103:22, S)   VIII:194n50
104:24 (103:24, S)   II:638n9; III:1012; 1028;
                     IV:543; VI:287; VII:489
104:25 (103:25, S)   II:873; IV:649
104:25f (103:25f, S) II:283
104:26 (103:26, S)   V:629, n17; 572; 576n105;
                     VI:256; 257
104:27 (103:27, S)   III:462; VI:194n143; 725
104:27f (103:27f, S) III:1011
104:28 (103:28, S)   V:891; IX:490, n3
104:29 (103:29, S)   III:1011; VI:361; VII:716n3;
                     723; IX:472; n5; 629; 631
104:29f (103:29f, S) II:536n3; 850(n127), n130;
                     VI:366
104:30 (103:30, S)   III:451; 1030; VI:362; 363;
                     386n304
104:31 (103:31, S)   II:638n9
104:32 (103:32, S)   V:480; VII:66n7; 198n12;
                     VIII:406
104:34 (103:34, S)   IX:366n57
104:35 (103:35, S)   I:264; 321; II:786; 787; IX:622
105 (104, S)   II:47n19; IX:591
105-107 (104-106, S) I:264
105:1 (104:1, S)   I:66; 718; II:787(n142); III:499;
                     701n18; 214n43; 262;
                     IX:409n23

105:1-15
  (104:1-15, S)   II:797; IX:504n56
105:2 (104:2, S)   II:787; III:35; VIII:493; 499
105:3 (104:3, S)   II:786(n137); 790n186; V:262
105:4 (104:4, S)   II:790n186; III:913;
                     VI:193n139; 773
105:5 (104:5, S)   III:35; VII:696; VIII:118
105:5-9 (104:5-9, S) III:931
105:6 (104:6, S)   IV:155; V:663n43
105:7-11
  (104:7-11, S)   **IX:504-505**
105:8 (104:8, S)   II:126; IV:675
105:8f (104:8f, S)   II:132
105:9 (104:9, S)   II:105
105:9-11
  (104:9-11, S)   III:773
105:10 (104:10, S)   II:126
105:11 (104:11, S)   II:774
105:11ff (104:11ff, S) V:843
105:12-15
  (104:12-15, S)   IX:504
105:14 (104:14, S)   I:510; III:140
105:15 (104:15, S)   VI:808; IX:502; 504; 517
105:16 (104:16, S)   II:883n3; III:140n2; VI:15
105:16ff (104:16ff, S) VI:15(n23)
105:17 (104:17, S)   VI:160
105:18 (104:18, S)   VI:996n21; VIII:7
105:19 (104:19, S)   IV:98; VI:949
105:20 (104:20, S)   IV:328
105:21 (104:21, S)   III:1060; V:129
105:22 (104:22, S)   V:611n86; VII:492; 527;
                     IX:622n63
105:25 (104:25, S)   IV:686; V:661; VII:729

105:26 (104:26, S)   IV:154; 155; 169; V:663n44
105:27 (104:27, S)   VII:210(n65); 212; 218
105:28 (104:28, S)   VI:126; VII:429; 440n153
105:29 (104:29, S)   VI:598; VII:715n7
105:32 (104:32, S)   VI:935
105:33 (104:33, S)   VII:752(n16)
105:36 (104:36, S)   I:485
105:38 (104:38, S)   V:104
105:39 (104:39, S)   IV:905
105:40 (104:40, S)   I:477; 643; II:785(n119); 935;
                     VI:129
105:40b (104:40b, S) IV:462
105:41 (104:41, S)   VI:97n28; 598; VIII:318
105:42 (104:42, S)   I:91; II:268; V:663n43
105:43 (104:43, S)   IV:155; 183
105:45 (104:45, S)   IV:1046(n92)
106 (105, S)   II:47n19; IX:504n56
106:1 (105:1, S)   II:797; V:214n43; VIII:495n45;
                     IX:409n23; 485
106:1ff (105:1ff, S) III:931(n26)
106:3 (105:3, S)   II:200n41; IV:365; VI:469
106:4 (105:4, S)   II:579; 602; 743; 744; IV:675;
                     VII:977
106:5 (105:5, S)   II:366n7; III:774; IV:155; 183;
                     VII:772; IX:490
106:6 (105:6, S)   I:158; VII:772; VIII:224n62
106:7 (105:7, S)   III:35; IX:384; 385n86
106:8 (105:8, S)   I:697n34
106:9 (105:9, S)   II:624; V:98; VIII:319; 323
106:9-11
  (105:9-11, S)   VIII:319
106:10 (105:10, S)   IV:333; 686; VII:976; 977n44
106:12 (105:12, S)   IV:93; VI:186n107; 187; 191;
                     197, n149
106:13 (105:13, S)   II:642; IV:577n1; 583; VI:194
106:14 (105:14, S)   III:170; VI:27; VII:761n12
106:15 (105:15, S)   I:193; VI:132n3
106:16 (105:16, S)   I:94; 102n51
106:17 (105:17, S)   VI:158; VII:805
106:19 (105:19, S)   VII:282n5
106:20 (105:20, S)   I:251; V:191; 192n11
106:21 (105:21, S)   VII:976
106:22 (105:22, S)   III:35
106:23 (105:23, S)   IV:154; 183; V:406; 409;
                     VII:720
106:24 (105:24, S)   IV:93; VI:186n107; 187; 191;
                     197
106:24b (105:24b, S) I:731n11
106:24f (105:24f, S) I:731n11
106:25 (105:25, S)   I:729; 731; VII:374
106:26 (105:26, S)   V:459n19
106:28 (105:28, S)   III:184; IV:814; 892; VIII:59
106:29 (105:29, S)   VI:281
106:30 (105:30, S)   IV:962n1; VII:637n6
106:31 (105:31, S)   II:201; IV:285; 289; 290
106:32 (105:32, S)   V:398; VI:126; VIII:318
106:33 (105:33, S)   VI:126; 364
106:36 (105:36, S)   VI:749n28; VII:342
106:37 (105:37, S)   II:11
106:38 (105:38, S)   VIII:564n25
106:39 (105:39, S)   VI:584
106:40 (105:40, S)   III:774; V:409

	VIII:41n8; 42n12; 156n11; 157; 335; **370**; 395; 407; 462; 609n30; IX:505n58; 508; 514n108; 564n457
110:1 (109:1, S)	I:520; 671n33; II:39; 40; 46n18; 47n24; 814; III:440; 442; 1089; V:514n121; 522n190; 523; 524; 525; 529; 539; 895; 974n155; 979n209; 989; VI:577n73; 629; VII:650; 868; 869n66; VIII:41, n9; 42; 154; **156**, n8; 360; 368n241; 370, n252, n254, n255; 371, n262, n267; 388; 392; 395; 435; 460; 462n421; 464; 483; 484; 485; 487; 609n34; 611; IX:426; 431n42; 505; 508; 530; 533n277; 534n282; 577
110:1a (109:1a, S)	VIII:156
110:1b (109:1b, S)	VIII:388
110:1f (109:1f, S)	II:812
110:2 (109:2, S)	II:299, n52; III:1102; VI:967; VII:308; VIII:350
110:2f (109:2f, S)	VIII:366
110:3 (109:3, S)	I:504, n17; 668; II:948; IV:741n20; VIII:349; 355; 613n57
110:3f (109:3f, S)	IX:505
110:4 (109:4, S)	I:3; III:275; 276; 277n54; IV:237; 339; 497; 568; 569; 570; 575n4; 627; 628; 629; 1080; V:184; 190; VII:299; 301; 302; 308; VIII:370; 388; 389n396; IX:67; 513n95; 569n483
110:5 (109:5, S)	II:948; 952; V:398; 430
110:6 (109:6, S)	VI:166; VII:1045
110:7 (109:7, S)	VIII:607; 613
111 (110, S)	III:931, n26; IX:378n54
111-113 (110-12, S)	I:264
111:1 (110:1, S)	IV:814n113; V:214; VII:802n22; 804; 829n201; VIII:498n66; 609
111:2ff (110:2ff, S)	II:642
111:3 (110:3, S)	IV:542; V:214; 219
111:3b (110:3b, S)	IX:378n54
111:4 (110:4, S)	II:787; III:35; IV:678; V:160n17; 161; VI:460; VII:557(n56); IX:378(n52)
111:5 (110:5, S)	IV:675
111:6 (110:6, S)	III:773
111:7 (110:7, S)	I:236; II:642; VI:185; IX:427
111:8 (110:8, S)	VII:655
111:8a (110:8a, S)	IX:378n54
111:9 (110:9, S)	IV:335; 351; V:271; VI:464; IX:201
111:10 (110:10, S)	VI:183n86; 708; 986; VII:487; 498n205; 890; IX:202; 218; 219
112 (111, S)	IV:711n66; IX:378n54
112:1 (111:1, S)	II:649; III:45n13; IV:366, n36; IX:203

112:3 (111:3, S)	IV:575
112:3b (111:3b, S)	IX:378n54
112:4 (111:4, S)	I:22n5; V:160n17, (n18); VII:428; 431; 441n162; IX:319; 322; 378, (n52)
12:5 (111:5, S)	V:160(n18); IX:377; 485
112:6 (111:6, S)	I:208n2; IV:682; VII:67
112:7 (111:7, S)	II:363; 522(n32); 706; IV:593; VI:191
112:8 (111:8, S)	III:613; V:1007(n373); VI:191n133
112:8a (111:8a, S)	IX:378n54
112:9 (111:9, S)	I:199; II:210; IV:575; VI:37; 39; 40; 910n232; VII:421; VIII:607
112:10 (111:10, S)	I:641
113-118 (112-117, S)	III:733; V:899; IX:682
113:1 (112:1, S)	II:786; V:661n33; 675n122
113:4 (112:4, S)	VIII:603n14
113:4-7 (112:4-7, S)	VIII:10
113:5f (112:5f, S)	IV:655n33; V:507
113:6 (112:6, S)	V:513n119; 522n192
113:6f (112:6f, S)	VIII:9
113:7 (112:7, S)	II:334; VIII:607
114-118 (113-117, S)	VIII:499
114-119 (113-118, S)	I:264
114:1 (113:1, S)	I:549; 726; III:773
114:2 (113:2, S)	I:549; II:564; III:773
114:3 (113:3, S)	V:324; 515n137; VIII:319
114:3f (113:3f, S)	VIII:319n38
114:3-8 (113:3-8, S)	VII:198n12
114:4 (113:4, S)	I:341; VII:401; VIII:346; 353(n114)
114:5 (113:5, S)	VIII:319
114:6 (113:6, S)	I:341; VII:401; VIII:353(n114)
114:7 (113:7, S)	III:86; 1061; V:515n137; VII:66; IX:667; 669n22
114:8 (113:8, S)	VI:97n28, n30; VII:714; VIII:318
115:1 (113:9, S)	II:241(n33); 244; IX:384, (n84)
115:2 (113:10, S)	I:631(n19); III:47(n33)
115:3 (113:11, S)	III:787n9; 1012; V:510; 522n192; VI:460
115:3f (113:11f, S)	III:1013
115:4 (113:12, S)	II:377(n11); 645; VI:150n23
115:4-7 (113:12-15, S)	V:546
115:4-8 (113:12-16, S)	II:377(n25)
115:5a (113:13a, S)	V:376n4
115:5f (113:13f, S)	V:324
115:6 (113:14, S)	V:392; 411; 491(n18)
115:7 (113:15, S)	V:942; IX:302
115:9 (113:17, S)	V:129
115:9-11 (113:17-19, S)	V:313
115:11 (113:19, S)	IX:203
115:13 (113:21, S)	IV:649; V:272; IX:203
115:15-17 (113:23-25, S)	V:503
115:16 (113:24, S)	II:760; V:507; 511; 522n192
115:16f (113:24f, S)	II:847(n108)
115:17 (113:25, S)	IV:892(n10)
115:18 (113:26, S)	IV:1107n11

116 (114f, S)   V:202; 203n16; IX:409
116:1 (114:1, S)   I:28n42; II:785(n122); IX:281
116:3 (114:3, S)   III:141; IV:337; VI:877n40;
                         IX:670
116:4 (114:4, S)   III:499; V:203; 262; VII:980n56
116:5 (114:5, S)   II:186; 481n53; IX:378(n53)
116:6 (114:6, S)   IV:917; VII:517n364; 971n21;
                         977; VIII:8
116:7 (114:7, S)   II:655; IX:622
116:9 (114:9, S)   I:455; V:943; VIII:8; IX:237
116:10 (115:1, S)   II:450; V:20n143; 907n21;
                         VI:189n121; 204n225;
                         VIII:6; 8
116:10-19 (115, S)   III:7
116:11 (115:2, S)   III:7, n19; VI:60; VII:67;
                         IX:597; 601
116:12 (115:3, S)   I:631(n19)
116:13 (115:4, S)   III:499; V:262; 438n390;
                         VI:148; 150n23; 151; VII:977
116:14 (115:5, S)   II:787
116:16 (115:7, S)   V:662
116:17 (115:8, S)   III:184; 499
116:17f (115:8f, S)   II:794(n210), (n211)
116:18 (115:9, S)   II:787
116:19 (115:10, S)   VII:296; 311
117 (116, S)   I:14n9
117:1 (116:1, S)   I:177; II:369; 787(n141);
                         IV:32n12; 37; 52;
                         IX:184n106
117:2 (116:2, S)   IX:384
118 (117, S)   I:14; II:678n6; III:179n85;
                         IV:274n48; 884, n16; V:203,
                         n16; 740n6; VIII:499; IX:683
118:1 (117:1, S)   V:214n43; VIII:495n45;
                         IX:485n15
118:1ff (117:1ff, S)   I:14
118:1-4 (117:1-4, S)   VIII:495
118:2 (117:2, S)   II:221
118:4 (117:4, S)   IX:203
118:6 (117:6, S)   I:628; IX:214
118:7 (117:7, S)   IV:160n84
118:8f (117:8f, S)   VI:193
118:10 (117:10, S)   VI:74n5
118:10-12
   (117:10-12, S)   V:258; 260
118:10ff (117:10ff, S)   VI:74n5
118:12 (117:12, S)   VI:935; VII:166
118:13 (117:13, S)   VI:745
118:14 (117:14, S)   II:788
118:15 (117:15, S)   II:37; III:907n11; VI:460;
                         VII:373; IX:282
118:16 (117:16, S)   II:301n62
118:17 (117:17, S)   II:642
118:17ff (117:17ff, S)   V:204
118:18 (117:18, S)   V:606; 609n69; 624
118:19 (117:19, S)   III:174n18; VI:922n11
118:19f (117:19f, S)   V:71n101
118:20 (117:20, S)   II:676; III:174n18; 178n73; 179;
                         VIII:473n487
118:21 (117:21, S)   V:605n51
118:22 (117:22, S)   I:372; 792; 793; III:179; IV:149;
                         268n3; 271; 272; 273; 274,

                         (n51), n57; 275, n63, n64;
                         276n45; 277; 278; 279; 281;
                         884; 887, n29; V:127, n31;
                         136; 142; 707n406; 712n448a;
                         915n79; VI:98; 189n123; 754;
                         755, n56; VII:353; VIII:444
118:22f (117:22f, S)   I:752; II:260; III:39
118:22ff (117:22ff, S)   II:260n21
118:23 (117:23, S)   I:372; III:35; IV:281n7; V:378;
                         729
118:24 (117:24, S)   IX:683
118:25 (117:25, S)   V:111; VII:976(n39);
                         IX:682-683 (682n2)
118:25f (117:25f, S)   II:670; III:179n85; VII:333
118:26 (117:26, S)   I:578; II:667; 762; 764n8;
                         III:179; IV:274n48; 366n36;
                         V:262; 271; VII:329
118:27 (117:27, S)   IX:9; 10n19
118:28 (117:28, S)   II:787(n144); VII:971; VIII:606
119 (118, S)   II:854; **IV:100**; 135; 137; 140;
                         486; 1043; 1044; V:604; 789;
                         790; 848n33; VI:196; VIII:9;
                         IX:203n73; 237; 322
119:1 (118:1, S)   IV:100; 135; 365; V:52; 82n139;
                         VI:571; VIII:73; 74n36
119:1b (118:1b, S)   V:82n139
119:2 (118:2, S)   II:656, n5; IV:365
119:3 (118:3, S)   VI:571n31
119:3f (118:3f, S)   V:51
119:5 (118:5, S)   V:52; 69; 113n14
119:7f (118:7f, S)   IV:401
119:8 (118:8, S)   II:220
119:9 (118:9, S)   IV:135; 897n14
119:11 (118:11, S)   III:970; VII:908
119:13 (118:13, S)   VII:696
119:14 (118:14, S)   IX:363
119:15 (118:15, S)   IV:974; V:51; 52
119:16 (118:16, S)   IV:135
119:17 (118:17, S)   IV:135; V:661
119:18 (118:18, S)   III:35; IV:100; 135
119:19 (118:19, S)   I:680n12; III:969; V:27; 847,
                         n33; VI:731
119:20 (118:20, S)   III:170; IX:622
119:21 (118:21, S)   II:522n30; 624; VIII:301; 526
119:22 (118:22, S)   VII:353n79
119:23 (118:23, S)   V:661
119:25 (118:25, S)   IV:100; 135
119:26 (118:26, S)   I:70; V:53
119:27 (118:27, S)   III:35; V:51
119:28 (118:28, S)   I:601; II:786; IV:135; IX:622
119:29 (118:29, S)   I:154; IV:135; V:52; 82n139;
                         IX:377
119:29f (118:29f, S)   V:54
119:30 (118:30, S)   IV:150; V:52; 82n139
119:31 (118:31, S)   I:189
119:32 (118:32, S)   V:51; VIII:229; 230, n31; 231
119:33 (118:33, S)   V:51; 53
119:33-38
   (118:33-38, S)   IX:203
119:34 (118:34, S)   II:656; IV:100; VII:890
119:35 (118:35, S)   V:98
119:36 (118:36, S)   III:607; VI:269

119:37 (118:37, S)   V:52; 82n139; VIII:63
119:38 (118:38, S)   IV:100; VI:293; VII:642
119:39-41
  (118:39-41, S)   IX:486
119:41 (118:41, S)   II:479n28; 667; IV:100;
                   VII:1022; IX:384; 385n86
119:42 (118:42, S)   IV:100; 135
119:43 (118:43, S)   IV:93; 135; VI:194; 196n147;
                   VII:697
119:44 (118:44, S)   IV:100; 135
119:45 (118:45, S)   V:72n103; 75n118
119:46 (118:46, S)   V:12
119:49 (118:49, S)   IV:135; 675; VI:196n147
119:50 (118:50, S)   III:141; VIII:11
119:51 (118:51, S)   IV:100; 135; VIII:301; 526
119:52 (118:52, S)   V:790
119:53 (118:53, S)   IV:135
119:54 (118:54, S)   V:842; 843; VI:773
119:55 (118:55, S)   IV:135
119:57 (118:57, S)   IV:100; 135; V:51n30
119:57-64
  (118:57-64, S)   IX:203
119:58 (118:58, S)   II:786; IX:378n47
119:59 (118:59, S)   II:95; V:51n30
119:60 (118:60, S)   IV:135; V:51n30; VIII:230
119:61 (118:61, S)   IV:100; 135
119:63 (118:63, S)   III:801; 802
119:64 (118:64, S)   V:891; VI:284; IX:384
119:65 (118:65, S)   II:654; IV:135; VII:772n35;
                   IX:490
119:65-68
  (118:65-68, S)   IX:486
119:66 (118:66, S)   I:676n4; 700; V:610; VI:187
119:67 (118:67, S)   I:275; V:605n51; 907n21;
                   VIII:6; 8; 9
119:68 (118:68, S)   IX:490
119:69 (118:69, S)   I:154; II:656; VIII:526
119:70 (118:70, S)   IV:135; IX:627
119:71 (118:71, S)   IV:401; V:605n51; 908n26;
                   VIII:8
119:72 (118:72, S)   IV:100; 135; VII:696
119:73 (118:73, S)   II:704; III:1012; IV:401;
                   VI:256, n19; 257
119:74 (118:74, S)   IV:93; 100; 135; VI:194;
                   196n147
119:75 (118:75, S)   V:605n51; VIII:8; 9
119:76 (118:76, S)   V:661; 790
119:77 (118:77, S)   II:667; IV:135
119:78 (118:78, S)   VIII:526
119:79 (118:79, S)   I:698(n36)
119:81 (118:81, S)   II:523(n39); IV:93; 100;
                   VI:194; VII:1022
119:82 (118:82, S)   V:376; 790
119:84 (118:84, S)   II:229; VI:460
119:85 (118:85, S)   IV:135
119:86 (118:86, S)   II:229
119:87 (118:87, S)   VIII:63
119:88 (118:88, S)   VII:696; IX:384, (n84)
119:89 (118:89, S)   I:237; IV:93; 100; 135; V:508
119:90 (118:90, S)   III:1009
119:92 (118:92, S)   VIII:11
119:94 (118:94, S)   VII:976(n39)

119:95 (118:95, S)   VI:194; 726
119:96 (118:96, S)   V:72n103; VIII:65
119:97 (118:97, S)   IV:100
119:98 (118:98, S)   VII:486; 493; 527
119:99 (118:99, S)   II:151(n30)
119:100 (118:100, S)   IV:974n8
119:101 (118:101, S)   IV:100; V:53; VI:551
119:103 (118:103, S)   IV:100; 553
119:104 (118:104, S)   I:152; 154; IV:687; V:52
119:105 (118:105, S)   IV:100; 325; VI:626n31;
                   IX:319; 322
119:106 (118:106, S)   VII:642
119:107 (118:107, S)   IV:100; VIII:6; 8
119:108 (118:108, S)   II:755n3; III:183
119:109 (118:109, S)   I:627n18
119:110 (118:110, S)   V:593; VI:235; VII:342;
                   VIII:154
119:111 (118:111, S)   III:774; 776
119:113 (118:113, S)   IV:687n14
119:114 (118:114, S)   IV:100; V:313; VI:194
119:115 (118:115, S)   II:656
119:116 (118:116, S)   I:189; II:522n30; VI:726
119:120 (118:120, S)   VII:106n61; 108n84; IX:623
119:121 (118:121, S)   III:140; VI:469
119:122 (118:122, S)   II:52n10; 57n2; VIII:526
119:123 (118:123, S)   II:522n30; 523(n39); IV:100;
                   V:376; VII:1022
119:124 (118:124, S)   IX:384(n84)
119:125 (118:125, S)   V:662
119:126 (118:126, S)   III:458; 1099n1; IV:100; VI:634
119:128 (118:128, S)   I:152; IV:687; V:52
119:129 (118:129, S)   II:656; III:35
119:130 (118:130, S)   I:276n25; IV:917; VII:517n364;
                   IX:322
119:133 (118:133, S)   III:1098
119:134 (118:134, S)   IV:333
119:135 (118:135, S)   V:661; IX:320
119:136 (118:136, S)   IV:100; V:108n19; 109, n36;
                   VIII:317
119:139 (118:139, S)   II:878
119:140 (118:140, S)   V:661; VI:949; VII:697
119:143 (118:143, S)   III:141; VII:605; 886
119:147 (118:147, S)   IV:100; VI:194; 196, n147
119:148 (118:148, S)   IX:89
119:149 (118:149, S)   II:480(n36); III:930(n25);
                   IX:281; 384, (n84)
119:150 (118:150, S)   II:332n3
119:151 (118:151, S)   II:330; V:51n30
119:153 (118:153, S)   VIII:11
119:154 (118:154, S)   II:848n112; IV:93; 100; 137;
                   333
119:155 (118:155, S)   IV:372; 373; VII:977; 1022
119:156 (118:156, S)   II:483n96
119:157 (118:157, S)   III:140
119:158 (118:158, S)   VII:890n16
119:159 (118:159, S)   V:325; IX:384, (n84)
119:160 (118:160, S)   I:235f; IV:93; 100
119:161 (118:161, S)   IX:204
119:162 (118:162, S)   IV:100
119:163 (118:163, S)   I:154; 598; IV:100; 687
119:165 (118:165, S)   II:408; V:262; VII:341; 342,
                   n22; 344n31; 357n105

135:3 (134:3, S)	III:544; 553n65; VIII:494	138:5 (137:5, S)	II:241; IV:539
135:4 (134:4, S)	III:773; IV:35; 168; VI:57	138:6 (137:6, S)	I:700; IV:372; VIII:9; 10; 14;
135:5 (134:5, S)	III:1061		603n14
135:6 (134:6, S)	III:47(n33); 1012; V:513n119	138:7 (137:7, S)	III:142; IV:675
135:7 (134:7, S)	IV:906; V:503; VI:360;	138:8 (137:8, S)	II:638; IX:384
	IX:642n156	139 (138, S)	I:700; II:99; III:967; 1012;
135:9 (134:9, S)	VII:210(n65); 212; 218		1076; IV:610; VII:908
135:12 (134:12, S)	III:774; V:680n175; IX:384	139:1 (138:1, S)	I:697; II:257
135:13 (134:13, S)	IV:682	139:2 (138:2, S)	II:96; 97; 337; V:50; 891
135:14 (134:14, S)	IV:54; 55; V:661; 778n25	139:3 (138:3, S)	V:50; 381
135:15 (134:15, S)	II:377(n11)	139:4f (138:4f, S)	I:486
135:15-18		139:5 (138:5, S)	III:1076(n198); IV:1014;
(134:15-18, S)	II:377(n25)		VI:256; 257; 386; 387n307;
135:16f (134:16f, S)	V:324		VII:229
135:17 (134:17, S)	V:546; 549; 942; VI:360;	139:6 (138:6, S)	I:701; III:31; 35; 1076
	IX:302	139:7 (138:7, S)	VI:288; 364; 367n166; 370; 778;
135:20 (134:20, S)	IX:203		VIII:356n134
135:21 (134:21, S)	VII:310	139:8 (138:8, S)	II:847n109; V:229; 507n76; 861
136 (135, S)	**VIII:494-495;** IX:385; 409	139:9 (138:9, S)	VII:385
136:1 (135:1, S)	VIII:495n45; IX:485	139:10 (138:10, S)	V:98
136:1-3 (135:1-3, S)	VIII:494	139:11 (138:11, S)	V:942
136:1ff (135:1ff, S)	II:480(n46)	139:11f (138:11f, S)	VII:429; IX:320
136:2-26		139:12 (138:12, S)	IX:318
(135:2-26, S)	VIII:495n45	139:13 (138:13, S)	II:174; III:1007; 1009;
136:4 (135:4, S)	III:35		IV:148n16; 911
136:4-9 (135:4-9, S)	VIII:494	139:13ff (138:13ff, S)	II:844(n87)
136:5 (135:5, S)	V:511; VII:499n215	139:14 (138:14, S)	II:638n9; 642; III:31; 34; 35; 88;
136:6 (135:6, S)	VII:610; VIII:319; 328		VIII:581n93
136:7 (135:7, S)	IX:356n388	139:15 (138:15, S)	I:666; III:641n10; 960n4; 1009;
136:8f (135:8f, S)	II:565		1011; VIII:581
136:9 (135:9, S)	IV:640; 1123	139:16 (138:16, S)	I:620; 666; 744; IV:1014;
136:10-22			VI:257; 258
(135:10-22, S)	VIII:495	139:17 (138:17, S)	VIII:173
136:13 (135:13, S)	I:184	139:18 (138:18, S)	VII:780
136:13ff (135:13ff, S)	VIII:319	139:19 (138:19, S)	III:86; V:741
136:16b (135:16b, S)	VIII:495	139:20 (138:20, S)	II:96
136:18 (135:18, S)	III:32n23; VIII:495	139:21 (138:21, S)	II:812; IV:687
136:21 (135:21, S)	III:774	139:21f (138:21f, S)	II:814; IV:687n14; 688, n19
136:22 (135:22, S)	III:774; IV:32n12; V:662n41;	139:22 (138:22, S)	VIII:72, n20
	680n175	139:23 (138:23, S)	II:257; VI:31
136:23 (135:23, S)	VIII:10	139:24 (138:24, S)	I:269; V:52; 53; 54; 98
136:23f (135:23f, S)	VIII:495	140 (139, S)	III:334n3; VI:892
136:24 (135:24, S)	IV:332; 333	140:1 (140:2, M)	
136:25 (135:25, S)	VII:106; VIII:495	(139:2, S)	VI:551
136:26 (135:26, S)	VIII:495	140:2 (140:3, M)	
136:26b (135:26b, S)	VIII:495	(139:3(2), S)	I:153; IV:285; 289n18
137 (136, S)	II:792; VII:305	140:3 (140:4, M)	
137:2 (136:2, S)	III:916	(139:4(3), S)	I:721; III:334; V:411; 572; 573;
137:3 (136:3, S)	II:688n6; 788; VII:294		633; VI:552n35; VII:701
137:4 (136:4, S)	II:788; III:1074	140:4 (140:5, M)	
137:5 (136:5, S)	VII:296n20	(139:5, S)	V:392
137:7 (136:7, S)	IV:675; V:711n445;	140:5 (140:6, M)	
	VII:307n91; 312; VIII:346	(139:6(5), S)	V:593; VII:340n7; 341; 342;
137:7-9 (136:7-9, S)	II:792(n190)		345; VIII:154; 300
137:7ff (136:7ff, S)	IV:164n93	140:6 (140:7, M)	II:785(n122); VII:341
137:8 (136:8, S)	IV:365	(139:7, S)	
137:9 (136:9, S)	III:911; IV:365; 915; V:646	140:7 (140:8, M)	
138 (137, S)	VIII:219n23	(139:8, S)	III:89; VII:399; IX:281
138:1 (137:1, S)	II:789; V:214; 876n15;	140:8 (140:9, M)	
	VIII:494; 498n66	(139:9(8), S)	I:288; II:95; VIII:607
138:2 (137:2, S)	I:90; 95; II:789; V:214; IX:384	140:11 (140:12, M)	
138:4 (137:4, S)	V:214	(139:12, S)	VII:1095; IX:97n13

140:12 (140:13, M)		145:8 (144:8, S)	IX:378(n52); 383n81
(139:13, S)	III:927; VI:892	145:9 (144:9, S)	II:638
140:12f (140:13f, M)		145:10 (144:10, S)	II:638n9
(139:13f, S)	II:180	145:11 (144:11, S)	I:570(n29)
140:13 (140:14, M)		145:11f (144:11f, S)	II:245
(139:14, S)	VII:780	145:11ff (144:11ff, S)	I:569
141:2 (140:2, S)	II:794; III:187; 239	145:12 (144:12, S)	II:292; 787(n142); IV:542
141:2ff (140:2ff, S)	VII:697	145:13 (144:13, S)	I:570(n29); II:47; V:891
141:3 (140:3, S)	VII:697	145:14 (144:14, S)	II:642; VI:169
141:4 (140:4, S)	II:744, n12; IV:145; 970n7;	145:15 (144:15, S)	III:462; V:376; VI:194n143
	V:609n69; VI:551; 564	145:15f (144:15f, S)	IV:1013
141:5 (140:5, S)	I:286; 320n31; 321; IX:384	145:16 (144:16, S)	II:743
141:7 (140:7, S)	VII:695	145:17 (144:17, S)	II:186; 642; V:55; 91; 490; 491,
141:8 (140:8, S)	V:376; 711n445; 712n445;		n21; IX:386n96
	IX:620	145:18 (144:18, S)	I:243; II:330
141:9 (140:9, S)	V:593; VII:341; 342	145:19 (144:19, S)	II:743; III:53; IX:203
142 (141, S)	II:785	145:19f (144:19f, S)	VII:977
142:1 (141:1, S)	II:785(n121); IX:282	145:20 (144:20, S)	IX:237
142:2 (141:2, S)	II:786; IX:379	145:21 (144:21, S)	V:257; IX:623
142:3 (141:3, S)	I:700; V:593	146 (145, S)	VIII:495
142:5 (141:5, S)	IV:974	146-150 (145-150, S)	I:264
142:7 (141:7, S)	II:655; VIII:8	146:1 (145:1, S)	IX:622
142:8 (141:8, S)	IV:584	146:3 (145:3, S)	VII:975
143 (142, S)	III:968	146:4 (145:4, S)	II:97; 679; V:892; VI:361;
143:1 (142:1, S)	II:785(n118)		IX:472
143:2 (142:2, S)	II:213; 216; 217; VII:129	146:5 (145:5, S)	IV:366; VI:194n143
143:3 (142:3, S)	VIII:8	146:6 (145:6, S)	I:236; 678; III:884; V:515n129;
143:4 (142:4, S)	II:849(n117); III:612; VI:361		IX:238
143:5 (142:5, S)	II:642; VI:460; 643	146:6-7b	
143:6 (142:6, S)	II:227; 228n11; 790(n184);	(145:6-7b, S)	VIII:495
	IX:622	146:6-9a	
143:7 (142:7, S)	III:969; V:189; 747n16; VI:361;	(145:6-9a, S)	VIII:495
	773	146:6-9 (145:6-9, S)	VIII:495
143:8 (142:8, S)	V:53; IX:622	146:7 (145:7, S)	I:160; II:60n4; III:929n24;
143:10 (142:10, S)	I:95; II:137; III:53; V:98; 100;		IV:328; VI:16
	VI:363	146:7c-9a	
143:11 (142:11, S)	II:479(n25)	(145:7c-9a, S)	VIII:495
143:11f (142:11f, S)	V:660n26	146:8 (145:8, S)	III:918n17; VIII:281; 282; 284
143:12 (142:12, S)	II:480(n36); III:140	146:8ab (145:8ab, S)	VIII:495
144:2 (143:2, S)	V:313; VIII:40	146:9 (145:9, S)	IV:7; V:53; 488n4; IX:237; 446
144:3 (143:3, S)	I:698(n36); IV:148; VII:396;	146:10 (145:10, S)	I:569; 571; VII:314
	VIII:346	147 (146f, S)	V:892, (n58); VII:485
144:4 (143:4, S)	I:130; IV:523; V:189; VII:395	147:1 (146:1, S)	II:715; VIII:494
144:6 (143:6, S)	I:608; VII:418	147:2 (146:2, S)	II:99; 102n12; VII:842n4;
144:7 (143:7, S)	I:401; VIII:322		IX:526
144:8 (143:8, S)	I:154; IX:598	147:3 (146:3, S)	III:202; 203; 728; VII:920; 922;
144:9 (143:9, S)	VIII:493; 499n71		923n23; IX:526
144:10 (143:10, S)	IV:332; 333; VI:550	147:4 (146:4, S)	IV:22; V:253; 266; VI:278
144:11 (143:11, S)	I:154; IX:598	147:5 (146:5, S)	III:1061
144:13 (143:13, S)	VI:281	147:6 (146:6, S)	IV:7; VI:647; 648; 892; VIII:8
144:14 (143:14, S)	V:109: VI:169n2	147:7 (146:7, S)	II:788n159; V:219; VIII:493;
144:15 (143:15, S)	II:822; IV:364; 366		IX:409
145:1 (144:1, S)	II:787(n144); VIII:493; 606	147:8 (146:8, S)	II:704; III:1009; IV:906; V:480
145:4 (144:4, S)	I:66; II:294; 787	147:8f (146:8f, S)	IV:1013
145:4ff (144:4ff, S)	II:642	147:9 (146:9, S)	VIII:346
145:5 (144:5, S)	I:114; II:245; 787; III:35;	147:10 (146:10, S)	III:45n13, (n16); 337
	553n65; IV:542	147:11 (146:11, S)	I:33n68; II:738; IX:203; 385;
145:6 (144:6, S)	II:744; IX:201		387
145:7 (144:7, S)	II:787; IV:679n5; V:309;	147:12 (147:1, S)	II:787(n141); VII:308
	VI:276; 277; VIII:607;	147:14 (147:3, S)	II:403
	IX:490	147:15 (147:4, S)	IV:93; 137; VIII:229; 231
145:7-9 (144:7-9, S)	IX:486	147:15-18	

PROVERBS

4	VII:491		1046n276; IX:623n67
4:1	IV:969; V:609; 637; VIII:343	5:12	IV:687
4:1ff	V:646; 647	5:13	II:151(n130)
4:2	I:14n11; III:702; IV:1045n91	5:14	III:527; V:735; VII:802
4:3	IV:739n7	5:15	VI:138
4:4	II:846(n97); IV:965	5:15f	III:789n18; VIII:322
4:5	VII:489; 890(n19); IX:237	5:16	VI:114
4:5-9	VII:524n406	5:18	VI:114; VIII:322
4:6	I:26n32	5:19	III:558; VI:960, n11; IX:155;
4:6ff	VII:491		381
4:6-9	VII:491; 498	5:20	II:684n1; V:6n33; VII:881
4:7	VII:491; 890(n19)	5:21	V:53; VII:415
4:8	VIII:173	5:21-23	VII:486n153
4:9	VII:626	5:23	VI:276, n13
4:10	II:52; 846(n97); V:50; VI:280;	6:1	V:8; VI:313; VIII:345
	VIII:345	6:1-5	IX:157n97
4:10b	II:851n152	6:2	V:595
4:10c	II:851n152	6:3	V:470; 857(n1); VI:313; 469
4:11	V:52; 53; 88; VII:477; 486; 492	6:4	VIII:551
4:12	VI:749; VII:343	6:5	VII:730n9
4:13	II:846(n98); IV:9; V:609;	6:6	II:883; V:49; 167; VII:485
	VII:491	6:6-11	VI:893
4:14	II:883; IV:364; V:53	6:7	II:46
4:14f	IX:344n271		

4:18	IV:23; V:53; IX:320; 322;		
	344n271		

Back to RSV and M

4:18f	V:54; 94; VII:430n52	6:9	V:167; VIII:551; IX:348n315
4:19	V:53; VI:745; 748; 750; 752n45;	6:10	VIII:550
	753; VII:430n53	6:11	VI:39
4:20	VIII:345		
4:21	VI:114; VII:405n12		

Special S Additions

4:22	II:846(n97); VII:107; 507n293;	6:11a	IX:348n315
	VIII:311n22; IX:623		
4:22f	VII:491		

Back to RSV and M

4:23	II:854; III:609; V:105; **IX:627**	6:12	I:607; V:53
4:24	IV:373; VII:405, n12	6:12-15	IX:598
4:25	V:449	6:13	VII:763n7
4:26	I:738; V:54; 113n14; 449;	6:14	VII:406n18; 718
	VI:470; 628	6:15	III:141
4:27	III:479; V:53; 54	6:16	III:427; IV:686; V:891;
			VIII:218n21

Special S Additions

		6:16ff	V:605n50
		6:16-19	IV:686; **IX:598**
4:27a	V:54; VII:718	6:17	I:721; II:187n8; V:376;
			VIII:301; IX:625

Back to RSV and M

		6:18	III:485
5	VI:586; VII:486n153; 491	6:19	I:400n16; IV:483
5:1	VII:486; VIII:345	6:20	IV:1045n91; 1046; VIII:343
5:1ff	V:6n33	6:20-35	VII:491
5:2	I:697; IV:969; VII:477(n93)	6:21	VI:53n1; 56n23; IX:617
5:3	IV:553n11; V:6n33	6:22	III:434; 606; V:943; VII:491;
5:4	IV:525n5; 527n26; VI:123;		IX:238
	124n8; 997n26	6:23	II:845(n95); 846(n98);
5:5	III:402n2		851(n150); 854; IV:325;
5:5f	V:54		V:52; 605; 911n50; VII:486;
5:6	II:845(n95); 851(n150); 854;		VIII:311n22; IX:322
	V:52; VIII:311n22	6:23-25	VI:419n571
5:7	VII:697	6:24	I:782; II:72(n7); V:6n33;
5:8	IV:373		VII:486n153
5:9	II:487n2; 854n165		
5:11	IV:627; VII:107; 108; 109;		

6:24ff	V:55n36	8:6	V:449; VII:193
6:24-35	VI:586	8:7	I:243; 598
6:25	III:170; IV:943	8:8	VII:405, n14; 484; 718
6:25-35	VII:486n153	8:9	IV:169; V:449; VII:405n14
6:26ff	IV:731	8:10	IV:146; V:605
6:27	III:824; VII:1095	8:11	IV:473n8; VII:494; 507n295
6:27f	VI:935	8:12	I:633; 701; 706n69; IV:969;
6:28	V:942; VII:1095		V:724(n15); VII:484
6:30	III:29; 754; VI:129; 130n7;	8:13	I:154; II:812; IV:686, (n13);
	IX:621		687; V:52; 53; VI:550;
6:31	VI:1001; 1002n6		VII:695; 718; VIII:300; 526;
6:32	IV:730; 731; IX:98; 627		IX:202
6:32f	IV:731	8:14	I:634; VII:489n166; IX:226,
6:33	VIII:302		n37
6:34	II:878; V:395; VII:482n139	8:15f	VII:507n294
6:34f	IV:731	8:16	III:924n8; IV:543
6:35	III:303; 304n13; IV:329; 335	8:17	II:769; IX:116n20; 124n117
7	V:55n36; VI:586; VII:491	8:18	II:408; VII:518n375
7f	V:55n36	8:19	IV:145
7-9	V:55n36	8:20	II:175; 199; 220; 221; V:51; 52;
7:1	VIII:345		943: VI:575n55
7:1a	IX:198	8:21	VII:518n375; IX:389
7:1-5	VII:491	8:21-36	VII:525
7:2	II:851n152; IV:1045n91	8:22	I:668; II:639; III:635; 1007;
7:3	I:770; III:607; 609; 612		1027; IV:136; 1056; V:48; 55;
7:4	V:233; VII:477(n90); 486; 491;		96; VI:879; VII:499n215;
	498		501n234; 507; 525n410;
7:5	I:782; V:6n33; 55n36; VIII:141;		IX:226
	142n14	8:22f	I:482n18; V:529n254
7:5ff	IV:731	8:22-25	VIII:411n76
7:5-23	VII:486n153	8:22-31	V:894; VI:687; **VII:491;** 498;
7:6	V:815		499n215
7:7	VIII:345	8:23	III:1009n68; IV:1111n38;
7:9	VII:491; IX:353(n356)		VI:862n4
7:10	IV:898n16; VII:956n15	8:24	VI:115n15
7:11	I:507	8:25	I:665; 668; IV:741n20;
7:12	IX:586		VI:256(n21); 258;
7:13	VIII:182; 300n44; 302; IX:127;		VII:502n246; IX:667; 669
	141n243	8:26	V:510
7:14	III:181; VII:271(n17)	8:27	II:704; III:1009; 1012;
7:15	III:625		V:502n44; 504(n55); VII:518
7:17	VI:977; 978; 979; VII:458n6,	8:27-29	VIII:319
	n10	8:27ff	VI:603n69
7:18	IX:125n120; 155	8:28	IV:906; V:510
7:20	II:770	8:29	IV:1013; V:738
7:21	V:474n26; VI:235	8:30	IV:136; VII:491, n182; 507n291
7:22	I:211n11; VII:402n8; 936	8:30f	II:773n15; V:629
7:23	VIII:229	8:31	VII:350n62; 491n182; VIII:63
7:25	VI:235	8:32	IV:365
7:27	V:50; 75n116	8:33	V:605; VII:486; 493
8	II:346; VI:586; VII:491; 524	8:34	II:338; IV:365; V:52; 104; 107;
8f	VII:490n180		VIII:141
8:1	IX:226; 281; 285	8:35	II:743; 846(n96); 854; III:62;
8:1ff	II:900n22		V:105; 108; VII:491; IX:202
8:1-21	VII:491	8:36	I:271
8:1-36	VII:517n360	9	VII:491
8:2	V:109n25; VII:491	9:1	V:120; VII:491; 734, n22
8:3	V:104; VIII:493	9:1ff	V:55n36
8:4	V:777n19	9:1-6	VII:498
8:4ff	VI:649	9:2	III:175n37; VII:930n25;
8:5	IV:949n5; V:724(n13); 725;		VIII:209
	726n23	9:3	III:715

9:4	IV:917	10:13	VI:967; VII:1045
9:4f	II:347	10:14	VII:497
9:5	I:644; II:692; VI:16; 139; VII:507n296	10:15	III:1028; V:855n14; VI:39; 324; 325; 523; 954n9; VII:485
9:5f	II:900n22	10:16	II:646
9:6	II:851n152; 854; V:55n36	10:17	II:845(n95); 846(n98);
9:6b	IX:226		851(n150); 854; V:51; 52;
9:7	V:605		605; VI:235(n37); VII:486;
9:7-12	III:479		VIII:311n22
9:8	IV:687; VII:492	10:18	IV:293
9:9	I:718; II:52; V:472; VII:477;	10:19	I:117n7; 363; IV:949; VI:545
	492	10:19f	III:335
9:10	I:636; 698; 700n47; III:125;	10:20	IV:146, n5; V:1026; VI:949
	VI:708; 986; VII:477(n90);	10:21	III:606
	487; 498n205; VIII:421n169;	10:22	IV:318; 590; VI:325
	IX:202	10:23	I:269; 659; IV:962; VI:634;
			VII:497; IX:226; 233n79

Special S Additions

		10:24	II:58
9:10a	IV:965	10:25	VII:970n16; 972
		10:26	V:167n3; 288, (n1), n1

Back to RSV and M

		10:27	IX:202
9:11	II:846(n96); IX:585	10:28	II:185; VI:194n142; IX:363
9:12	VII:494	10:29	V:491; 591; VI:954n9;
9:12b	VI:233n31; 234		IX:198n49
9:13	I:782	10:30	VII:67
9:13ff	V:55n36	10:31	I:721; VII:697n47
9:13-18	VII:491	10:32	II:743; IX:389
9:14	V:120	11:1	I:598; II:743; 896; VII:488
9:15	I:700n47; V:55n36; 113n14;	11:2	V:855n14; VII:487; VIII:9; 301
	VIII:111	11:2a	VII:481
9:16	IV:917; IX:224	11:3	IV:627, n4; V:98; VI:862;
9:16f	II:347		VIII:78
9:18	IV:528; IX:473	11:4	II:175; V:405; 410n199; IX:73
		11:5	I:153; 154; IV:830; V:52; 53;

Special S Additions

			54n34; VI:173; VII:187n6;
9:18a	V:262		190n15; VIII:111
9:18b	V:743	11:6	V:449; VI:1002n6
9:18c	VI:114; 139	11:7	II:532n107; 655; III:647;
9:18d	IX:586		VI:194n142
		11:8	III:431n5; 891n85
		11:8f	VIII:564n25

Back to RSV and M

		11:9	I:320; V:112; 595; VI:526;
10:1	IV:318; 797n2; V:748, n24;		VIII:564; IX:98; 99n25
	VII:460; 494; VIII:343	11:10b	VI:862
10:1-5	VII:138n298	11:12	IV:797; V:631; VI:526; IX:226
10:2	II:196; III:137; VI:1002n6;	11:13	IV:814, n113; V:855n14;
	IX:73		VI:185; 362; 369n177; 453;
10:3	VI:15n23; IX:621		VII:861
10:3-14:23	V:748	11:14	I:633; III:1036; VI:164n20;
10:4	II:91, n11; VI:324; VIII:6		VII:484
10:5	III:434; 643n1; IV:949;	11:15	V:595; VI:5n14
	VII:972; VIII:346; IX:226	11:16	II:243; III:161; V:855n14; 907;
10:6	II:756; III:675; V:855n14;		VI:232; 324; IX:389n116; 409
	VII:697n47; IX:624	11:17	II:479(n27); 485; 487n2; 655;
10:7	IV:679n5; VII:96; 167; IX:238		VII:108; 1046n276; 1048;
10:8	I:562; VII:405; 476n88		IX:623n67
10:8f	II:52	11:18	I:236; VI:470; VII:540
10:9	V:53; 87; 855n14; VII:718	11:18b	IV:697
10:10	II:419; 376; 875	11:20	I:598; II:52; 59; 743; III:607;
10:11	VI:114; VII:486		V:53; 54; VII:488; 718;
10:12	I:25n25; III:558, n8;		VIII:73; IX:627
	IX:154n68; 155; 652	11:21	II:174; IV:6; 697; 711;

	V:855n14; VII:539; 980
11:22	I:782; V:411
11:23	III:169n21
11:24	VII:481; 539
11:25	I:386; II:771; VI:191
11:26	III:675; VII:881; IX:624
11:27	II:743; IX:389
11:28	VI:161; 191; 324
11:29	III:776; VI:360; VII:476n88; IX:224
11:30	II:174; 200; 854; VI:291n26
11:31	I:320; IV:711; 735; VII:190; 972; 995
12:1	IV:687; V:605
12:2	II:743; V:732; IX:225n35; 389
12:3	VI:985; VII:67
12:4	I:782; III:485; VII:453; 626; 630
12:6	V:449; VI:1002n6
12:7	IV:577; 578; V:907
12:8	IV:796; 798; V:631; IX:226
12:9	II:42
12:10	I:698(n36); II:480(n49); 487n2; V:160(n18); VII:550; 551n19; IX:621
12:11	II:230; V:657n4
12:12	III:169n21; VI:985; VII:179
12:13	I:320; IV:193; V:594n5
12:14	III:614; V:855n14; VII:695
12:15	V:53; 449; VII:485; 486
12:16	V:724(n13); VIII:302
12:17	II:185; IV:483
12:18	IV:525n5; VII:494
12:19	I:236; IV:483
12:20	I:631n24; II:407
12:21	VI:128
12:22	I:598; II:743
12:23	I:361; III:161n7; V:724(n15)
12:24	IV:183; IX:80n9
12:25	I:60; IV:590n12; VII:485
12:26	II:229; V:53; VI:234; 236(n42); IX:154
12:28	II:199; V:52; 54; 55n38
13:1	V:605; 724(n14); 725; VII:493; VIII:343
13:2	VI:291n26; VII:695; IX:619; 621
13:3	VIII:141
13:4	IX:622n63
13:5	IV:93; 687; V:876
13:6	V:52; 53; VIII:73n27; IX:238
13:7	II:827; VIII:7
13:7f	VII:485
13:8	III:303; IV:329
13:9	VII:166; 430n53

Special S Additions

13:9a	V:160n17; VI:233n31

Back to RSV and M

13:10	III:479; VI:634; VII:487; 497; VIII:301; 526

13:11	VI:280; VII:179
13:12	II:579; 854
13:13	VI:638; VIII:310; IX:98

Special S Additions

13:13a	V:112; 113n14; VI:643

Back to RSV and M

13:14	II:846(n97), (n100); 854; V:594; VI:114; VII:344; 486; 492; 494; IX:202
13:15	IV:965; V:54n34; IX:379; 380
13:16	I:700, n47; V:724(n13)
13:17	VI:185n96; 1002n6
13:18	V:605; VI:39
13:19	I:700; II:644; III:169n21; IV:372; 962; VII:179
13:19a	VI:235
13:20	VI:312; VII:492
13:21	I:321; II:229
13:21f	IX:202
13:22	III:775; 776; VII:495
13:23	IV:325n17; VI:323; 467; VIII:64
13:24	IV:685; 687; 916; V:605; 855n14; VI:968n14; VIII:343
13:25	VI:129
14:1	VII:476n85; 494
14:2	V:54n34; VI:571; VII:405; IX:202
14:3	VII:494; VIII:302n51
14:4	IV:760n1; IX:51; 52n27
14:5	IV:483; VI:185n95
14:6	I:700; II:769; VII:486; IX:226
14:7	I:188; V:293
14:8	IV:962; V:54n34; 724(n13); VI:235; VII:494
14:9	I:268n2; II:175; 743; III:429; V:561
14:10	VII:485; VIII:302
14:11	VII:370n10
14:12	II:851(n150); V:50; 53; 75n116; 327n67; 449; VIII:51n15
14:13	III:606; IV:318; VII:485
14:14	IV:968
14:15	IV:917; 991; V:724(n13); 725n19; VI:186; 197
14:16	II:523, (n36); VI:191; VII:487, n160
14:17	IV:847n121; V:395; VI:634; VII:482n139; IX:225, n35; 625; 666
14:18	I:700; V:724(n13)
14:20	I:25n25; 27, n36; IV:687; VI:313; 324; 893; VII:485; IX:157n94
14:21	IV:365; IX:377n36
14:22	I:233; II:479(n27); 485n1; III:479; VI:235(n37)
14:23	IV:590; VI:62
14:24	V:724n13; 725; VII:485; 626
14:25	I:233n2; 234; IV:483;

	VI:1002n6	15:27	IV:389; 390n9; VI:270
14:26	II:523; VI:191n131; IX:202; 389	15:27b	IV:687n15
14:27	II:854; III:15n67; V:593; VI:114; VII:344; IX:202	**Special S Additions**	
14:29	V:394; 395; VI:361; 368; VII:482, n139; IX:226; 666	15:28a	V:53
14:29f	IV:377(n24)	**Back to RSV and M**	
14:30	II:849(n124); 878n2; III:606; 1078; VII:107; 108; 277; 482; VIII:311n22	15:29	I:153; II:797; III:126; IV:373; 724n110; VII:487n161
14:31	VI:39; 315n34; 460; 894; VIII:172; IX:377	**Special S Additions**	
14:32	V:493; VI:193	15:29a	V:171
14:33	III:609	**Back to RSV and M**	
14:34	V:239; VIII:607	15:30	VII:485; IX:320n64
14:35	II:743; VIII:534	15:31	VII:486
15:1	V:395; 409; 410; VII:477(n91); 482n139	15:32	IV:685n7; V:605; VIII:141; IX:617
15:2	VII:477(n93); 485	15:33	V:605; VI:648; 708; VII:487; 498n205; VIII:6; 10n24; IX:202
15:3	V:376; VI:558; VII:415; VIII:194; IX:625		
15:4	II:854; VI:361; 369n177	16:1	VII:488; VIII:10n24
15:5	IV:796; 797; V:724(n13); 725; 605; 609; VII:1100; VIII:343	16:2	VI:362; VII:488; IX:630
		16:3	IV:685n7
15:6	II:174; VI:264	16:4	IV:1055
15:7	I:700; VII:477(n93); 485	16:5	II:637; III:427; VII:488; VIII:304; IX:627
15:8	II:59; 743; 797; III:239; VII:487n161	16:6	I:233; II:479n32; III:183; 202; 304; IX:202
15:8f	I:598; VII:488	16:7	I:30n54; II:59; 637; V:52; 53; VII:488
15:9	I:30(n57); II:230; V:53		
15:10	I:718; VII:1100	16:8	I:153; 700; II:916; V:748
15:10b	IV:687n15	16:9	II:523; 642; VII:488; IX:238
15:11	I:4; 396; IX:627	16:10	VI:235; 851n430
15:12	I:23n15; VII:486	16:11	II:896
15:13	VI:361; 368; VII:451; 485; IX:627	16:12	I:269; III:161
		16:13	II:743; IV:93; V:449
15:14	V:449; VII:909	16:14	I:79; III:304; V:395; VII:482n139; 486
15:15	VI:647n11; 902; 913n263; IX:585	16:15	II:52; 59; 743; 853; IV:903
15:16	V:748; VI:325; IX:199n52	16:16	IV:146; IX:226n37
15:16f	II:916	16:17	II:50; 854; V:52; 611; VII:527; VIII:141; 142n17; IX:202
15:17	IV:66; V:21; IX:155		
15:18	IV:377(n24); V:395; VII:479n112	16:18	VI:166; 362; 368; VII:481; VIII:300
Special S Additions		16:19	VI:362; 368; VIII:10; 11; 14; 300; IX:598
15:18a	VII:167	16:20	IV:365; 366; VI:192
Back to RSV and M		16:21	VII:476n88; 486
15:19	V:54	16:22	I:607; II:846(n100); 854; IV:969; 970n7; V:605; VI:114; VII:486
15:20	IV:796; 797, n2; V:631; VII:494; VIII:343		
15:21	IV:961	16:23	IV:949; VII:486; IX:83n1; 84n3
15:22	VII:861	16:25	V:50; 53; 327n67; 449; VIII:111
15:23	III:462; 790	16:26	VII:485; IX:84; 622n63
15:24	II:845(n95); 854; IV:968; V:52; VII:486; 972n27; VIII:311n22	16:26b	VII:406
		16:27	I:607; III:138
15:25	I:601; VIII:300; IX:446, n54; 447	16:28	I:400n16; III:479; IV:325n17; 426; V:410, n205; VII:406; VIII:564; IX:154
15:26	I:122; 598; VII:193; 488	16:29	V:53; VI:24n8
		16:30	II:95; VII:718

16:30a	V:452n2	18:10ff	VI:324
16:30b	V:452n2	18:11	VI:954n9; VII:399
16:31	II:199; III:646; V:52; VII:626	18:12	VI:648; VII:481; VIII:6; 8; 607;
16:32	III:911; IV:377(n24);		IX:627
	V:394n71; 395; 411; VI:361;	18:14	VI:361; 368; 369n177; 370n181;
	523; IX:625		647n13; IX:666
16:33	II:184(n18); III:824; IV:1014	18:15	III:606; IV:969; VII:477(n89);
17:1	II:406; 408; 916; V:748		497; IX:226
17:2	II:46; 48; III:775; IV:595	18:16	IV:530; VII:485
17:3	IV:145; 170; VI:935; 942;	18:17	I:373; II:473; VI:313
	VII:488	18:18	V:452n2
17:4	I:721	18:19	VI:953n7; 954n9
17:5	III:1015n83; VI:315n34; 894;	18:20	III:786; VII:695; IX:625
	VII:550; 551	18:21	I:23n15; 721
17:6	I:156n11; III:646; VII:626, n65;	18:22	I:782; II:743; III:298
	630; VIII:342	18:23	VI:893; IX:379
		18:24	I:25n25; VI:313
	Special S Additions	19:2	I:271
17:6a	III:883	19:3	IV:312; V:393
		19:4	VI:893; IX:157n94
	Back to RSV and M	19:5	IV:483; VII:980
17:7	IX:598	19:6	III:129; 479
17:8	IV:697n4; V:110; 112; VII:485	19:7	IV:687; 969; VI:893;
17:9	I:162, (n4); III:959; V:134;		VII:970n16
	VII:405; IX:154; 155	19:8	II:485; III:606; IX:226
17:9b	IV:687n15	19:9	I:642; IV:483
17:10	I:188; II:625	19:10	VIII:302; IX:74
17:11	I:400n16; 403n34; II:487n2;	19:11	II:485; IV:377(n26); V:744
	VI:126n7	19:12	II:743; III:298; IV:252n19;
17:12	II:95; IV:590; VII:890n21		V:412
17:13	II:168	19:13	I:782; VI:584(n31)
17:14	II:175; VII:570	19:14	I:782; III:775
17:15	II:212; VII:488	19:15	III:434; IX:198n49
17:16	IV:962; VII:486	19:15f	IX:632
		19:16	II:846(n97); III:632; V:51n30;
	Special S Additions		VIII:141; 142n17; IX:237n5
17:16a	IV:400n87; 402; VII:405	19:17	IV:377n26; 711; V:16; IX:377
		19:18	I:634; VIII:301; 302
	Back to RSV and M	19:19	V:395; VII:482n139
17:17	III:141; IV:42; VI:313; IX:154	19:20	I:700; II:51n4; 601n9; V:605;
17:18	IX:224		609; VII:486; 492; 1100
17:20	III:613; IV:400n87; VII:405;	19:21	I:634; II:187n49; IV:575;
	IX:627		VII:488
17:21	IV:833; 834; V:608; VIII:343	19:22	II:479(n27); III:614; VI:893;
17:22	VI:368; 369n177; 370n181		897n100
17:23	II:199; III:824; V:52; 112	19:23	II:601n9; V:234; IX:199n52;
17:25	V:115; VIII:343		202
17:26	III:543	19:24	III:824n1; IX:65
17:27	I:697n32; II:479n32;	19:25	I:700; II:221; V:724(n13)
	IV:377(n24); VI:362; 368;	19:27	III:479; V:605; 609
	VII:482; IX:226	19:28	I:607; IV:482(n25);
17:28	IV:961; VII:477(n89); 485;		VIII:301n5; 302
	496n199	19:29	IV:518; 962
18:2	IX:389	20:1	IV:546; V:162; VI:136n6;
18:3	III:632		VII:486; VIII:301n50; 302
18:4	II:854; VI:114; VII:486; 494	20:2	V:744; IX:63
18:5	II:187(n18); III:30; 543	20:3	II:243; VIII:302
18:6	III:479; V:102	20:4	V:167
18:7	V:595	20:6	II:480n38; 485; VI:185n96
18:8	III:786n2; IX:198n49	20:7	II:174; IV:364; 365; 830; V:637;
18:10	II:642; IV:544; V:258; VI:953;		VII:495; 668n15; 716;
	VIII:607		VIII:353(n114)

20:8	III:162n14		21:20	VII:494
20:9	I:122; III:646; V:876; 881n25		21:21	II:196n14; 199; 479(n27); 769; V:52

Special S Additions

20:9a	III:468; IV:325n17; VII:166		21:22	III:411; 413; VI:523; 954n9; VII:494; 710
20:9b	VII:562		21:23	VIII:151n4; IX:237n5
			21:24	I:227; 508; V:261; 392n62; VIII:301; 302; 304; 526

Back to RSV and M

20:10	III:427; IV:632; VII:488		21:25	V:167
20:11	V:491; VIII:111		21:26	III:479; V:160(n18)
20:12	II:522n30; 639; V:324; 547, n39		21:27	I:598; III:239; IV:970n7; VII:487n161; IX:65n2
20:13	I:23n15; III:427; IV:3n4; 4			
20:14	VI:551n31		21:28	IV:483
20:15	II:639		21:29	VIII:300n44; 302
20:17	I:598; VII:481; IX:605n10		21:30	I:363; VII:489; 497
20:17f	IX:598		21:30f	VII:488
20:18	III:21		22:1	IV:146; 182; V:252; VI:324; IX:389
20:19	IV:814, n113; 921; VII:854n16			
20:20	IV:325n17; VII:166; 430n49, n53; IX:323n79		22:2	VI:39n13; 894
			22:3	II:889; V:724(n13)
20:21	VII:562		22:4	VI:325; 648; VIII:6; IX:202
20:22	II:174f; 195; 479(n33); 522n30; VI:194		22:5	V:53; VII:405; IX:237n5
			22:6	VII:697
20:23	II:896; VII:488; IX:129n157		22:7	II:46; 48
20:24	III:21; IV:949; 1014; V:50; VII:488		22:8	III:132; 298; 479; V:400n137; VIII:302
20:25	IV:989n68; VI:689n6; VII:487n161			

Special S Additions

20:26	VII:484		22:8a	V:376

Back to RSV and M

20:27	II:656; III:786; IV:325, n17; 327n32; VI:364; 453; IX:343n262		22:9	I:386n5; III:298; 299; V:376
			22:10	I:527
			22:10a	VII:861
20:28	II:175; 195; 479(n26); III:162n14; IX:242		22:10b	VII:861
			22:11	I:30(n57); II:59; III:607; V:491; VII:488; 909
20:28b	II:479(n33)			
20:29	III:881; VI:652		22:14	III:479; V:6n33; 393(n67); VIII:292n159
20:30	III:786; IV:829n2; VIII:590			
21:1	V:469			
21:2	II:175; VII:488; IX:627			
21:3	II:196n14; III:183; IV:146; VII:487n161			

Special S Additions

21:4	IV:325n17; VIII:301; 526n10		22:14a	II:21; V:53; VII:405
21:6	II:653; III:15n67; V:594; IX:598			

Back to RSV and M

21:7	II:187(n18)		22:15	IV:898n16; 962; V:609n78; 967; IX:627
21:8	II:639; 642; V:53; 449; VII:406, n18			
			22:16	VI:39
21:9	I:782; III:790; 800; 827; IX:17n31		22:17	VII:492
			22:17-23:10	V:748n22
21:10	IX:377n36		22:17-23:11	III:579n30; VII:480
21:11	III:482; IV:917; V:724(n14); 725; VII:477(n93); 492		22:18	III:609; 787
			22:19	II:522n30; 853; V:53; VII:488
21:14	III:974; VII:485		22:21	I:248
21:15	III:484		22:22	VI:39; 647n11; 889n27
21:16	II:175; 199; IV:528; V:52; VI:235; 236(n42); VII:803		22:22f	VI:1002n6
			22:23	III:814; VI:1002n6
21:17	I:23n15; II:471; V:162; VI:136n6; 893; IX:117; 124n117; 125		22:24	II:700; V:395, n89; 409; VI:312; VII:479n112; IX:155; 156
21:18	II:175; III:303; 431n5; IV:330; VI:88n55		22:25	IV:400; 402; V:53; 474n26; VII:344
21:19	V:411		22:29	IV:1126; V:368; 838

23:1	III:441; IV:949; VIII:210
23:2	IV:525n3, n5; IX:621
23:3	II:854n165
23:4	IV:969
23:5	VI:700
23:6	I:386n5; V:376; VI:556n65; IX:625
23:8	IV:93; 312
23:9	IV:797
23:10	III:720; IX:446, n55
23:10f	IX:446n55
23:11	II:848n112; III:912
23:12	II:706; V:605
23:13	IV:916
23:13f	V:748n22; VI:967; VII:480
23:14	II:846(n98); VI:968n14; 1002n6
23:15	VII:494
23:15f	III:607
23:16	V:449
23:17	I:286; II:883; III:606; IX:202
23:18	II:522(n29); 523; IV:365n33; VI:194n141
23:19	IV:969; VII:477; 486
23:20	IX:622
23:20f	VII:486
23:21	IV:546; VI:888; 893; VIII:550
23:22	III:632
23:23	I:236; VII:486
23:24	VII:477; 494; VIII:343
23:24f	VIII:342
23:26	V:51
23:27	V:6n33; VII:605
23:28	VIII:64
23:29	IV:550
23:31	IV:546; V:164; 942; VI:148n8
23:31ff	IV:731
23:32	III:334; V:571; 572
23:33	V:8; 376; VII:405
23:34	III:1037
23:34ff	IV:731
23:35	V:632
24:1	II:883
24:3	VII:477(n91); 494
24:4	VI:324
24:5	VII:497n203; IX:224
24:6	III:1036
24:7	IV:473n8; 969
24:8	I:288; VII:861
24:9	I:288; IV:970n7
24:11	VI:1002n6
24:12	I:700; II:167; 647(n35); VI:256; 257; 453; 643n3; VII:388; IX:627
24:13	III:330(n68)
24:14	II:522(n29); IV:814n113; VI:194n141
24:16	III:325n23; VI:165n22
24:16f	VI:161
24:17f	I:26n33
24:18	VII:720
24:19	II:883; III:478n32; 485
24:19f	V:395

24:20	IV:325n17; 365n33; 1058; VII:166; 430n53

Special S Additions

24:22c	IV:525; VI:997
24:22e	VIII:236n2

Back to RSV and M

24:23	II:185; V:343n151
24:24	V:393(n68)
24:26	I:700; II:136; IX:126
24:28	II:752; V:811, n84; VI:526
24:28f	VI:389
24:29	I:159; II:637; V:811
(24:44, irregular reference)	
24:30ff	V:167n3
24:31	I:466; II:599
24:32	III:754; IV:145; 170; 989n68; V:605; 611
24:33	II:46; 48; VIII:550
24:34	VI:39
24:34ff	III:479
24:37	II:692
24:38	I:171
25-29	VII:482
25:1	III:950; V:747n14; 748, (n24); 855; VII:460; 482
25:2	IV:731; VIII:172n17
25:5	III:162n14
25:6	IV:530
25:6f	VIII:16
25:7	IV:655n33; VI:772; VIII:7
25:8	IV:528n2; 627; VI:313
25:9	IV:814n113
25:10	II:815

Special S Additions

25:10a	V:51; IX:155

Back to RSV and M

25:11-13	V:748
25:12	VII:494
25:13	VI:185
25:14	I:56; III:646; IV:903; IX:9n15
25:15	IV:377n24; V:112; VII:481
25:16	I:465n3
25:17	VI:313
25:18	IV:482(n25); 483; 510; 525n5
25:19	III:479; V:53
25:20	V:288(n1); 927, n4; VII:276; 453; 1046

Special S Additions

25:20a	V:927n4; VII:277n11

Back to RSV and M

25:21	I:26; II:226; VI:16n31; 21n65; 159
25:21f	II:813; VI:945; VII:1095n5; 1096
25:22	I:26n33; VI:477; VII:1095, n5
25:23	V:393(n68); VI:360; VII:481;

	IX:669	27:23	I:698n36
25:23a	VII:1096	27:26	VIII:172n17
25:24	I:782; III:790; 800; IX:17n31	27:27	II:850n132; 854n165
25:25	I:60; IX:621	28:1	II:523; VI:191
25:26	IV:312; V:104	28:2	V:724(n14); 725
25:27	VIII:172n17	28:3	VII:187(n4)
25:28	III:620; VI:360; 523; 634;	28:4	IV:1045; VII:187(n5)
	VII:879n24	28:4ff	IV:1044n80
26:1	VIII:172	28:5	IV:949; VII:493
26:2	VI:66n37; VII:731, n11	28:5b	VI:550
26:3	III:338; 665; IV:518; VI:967	28:6	V:54n34; 943; VI:324; 571; 893;
26:5	IX:225		VII:405n13
26:6	II:66	28:7	I:507; IV:1045; V:609; VI:312;
26:7	V:855; VI:587n46		VIII:343
26:8	II:243	28:8	IX:377
26:9	IV:546	28:9	I:598; IV:404n109; 1045;
26:10	IV:891n1		VII:487n161
26:11	I:288; III:1101; 1103; IV:304;	28:10	I:14; V:53; VI:234; 236(n42);
	V:855n19; VII:726n22		IX:99
26:12	II:522(n19); VI:194n141;	28:11	I:715; VI:324
	IX:225	28:13	II:797; V:111
26:13	IV:252n11	28:14	II:752; III:613; IV:366
26:15	III:824n1	28:15	IV:309(n13)
26:16	VI:132n3; VII:477n92	28:16	IV:687; IX:585
26:17	VI:701	28:17	III:881
26:18	V:314n10; VI:950	28:18	II:175; V:53; 54n34; VI:571;
26:18f	V:748		VII:405; VIII:72n22; 73
26:19	V:324; 628n14; VI:313	28:19	II:230; V:657n4; VI:39
26:20	I:737; VII:166; 167; 481	28:20	III:479
26:20f	VI:935	28:21	I:171; V:343n151
26:22	I:737; III:786n2; VII:550	28:22	V:376; IX:625
26:23	IV:193, n2	28:23	V:53; IX:388; 389
26:23-28	IX:598	28:24	III:797n1; 801; 804; VII:874n19
26:24	III:609	28:25	II:380n6; VI:192; VIII:526n10;
26:25	II:41; VI:3; 187; 197n149;		IX:622n63
	564(n10), n10; IX:281; 377,	28:26	VI:191; 571; VII:486; 494; 980
	n36; 617	28:27	III:303n12; VII:721n10
26:26	I:268; III:529; VII:743; 861	28:28	VI:280
26:27	VIII:292n159; IX:99	29:1	III:203; 613; V:1029
26:28	III:446; IV:687; VII:695	29:3	I:23n15; VI:312; VIII:343;
27:1	II:598; III:646		IX:125
27:2	V:8n48	29:5	VI:626
27:4	II:487n2; 878; V:395; 409;	29:6	V:594; VII:344
	VII:482n139	29:7	I:700; IV:949; 953; VI:40
27:5	IX:155	29:8	V:395; 410; VII:486
27:6	IX:125; 141n243	29:10	II:831, n5; IV:686; 687; V:491
27:7	V:631; VI:132; VII:481	29:11	V:394n71; 395; 411; VI:361;
27:8	VIII:195		VII:479n112; 486
27:9	II:472; IV:800	29:13	II:606; V:376; VI:460; 894;
27:10	V:960; 1015; IX:154		IX:320n64
27:11	VII:494	29:14	III:162n14; IV:482; IX:444n31
27:12	II:889; V:724(n13)	29:15	I:403n34; IV:916; V:605; 637;
27:13	IV:312; VIII:302		960; VI:234; VII:492; 493
27:14	IX:63; 281	29:17	I:350; III:881; VI:968n14;
27:15	I:782; V:748		VIII:343
27:17	IX:154n70	29:18	IV:365; 1045
27:18	VII:752; VIII:172	29:19	V:608; 1029
27:19	IV:965	29:20	I:699; VI:194n141
27:20	I:721; VI:129; VII:141n318;	29:22	V:395, n89; VII:479n112
	481	29:23	VI:362; 368; 401; VIII:8
27:21	II:256; III:479; VI:942; 951	29:24	IV:687, n15
27:22	IV:515; VII:861	29:25	VI:192; VII:1013n55; IX:198

ECCLESIASTES

1:8	I:230; II:680n5; III:855n1; 989n112; IV:998; V:324; 505n56; VI:129	2:23	I:562; V:393(n70)
		2:24	II:26; 692; VII:492
		2:24-26	VII:492(n189)
1:9	I:477; IV:278n87; 464; 860, n140; V:510; VI:467; 767	2:24ff	VI:136(n7)
		2:26	I:286; 706n69; V:605n49; VI:370; VII:493; IX:628
1:9a	I:230		
1:9f	I:205	3	II:402
1:11	IV:679n5; V:732	3:1	I:204; III:881; V:510; 534(n312); VI:638; IX:585
1:12	VII:460; 463		
1:12-15	VII:492(n189)	3:1-15	VII:492n189; 494
1:13	V:510; 534(n312); VI:550; VII:67n12; 488; VIII:346	3:2	III:1084n232; IX:487n19
		3:2-8	III:458
1:13a	VII:492	3:4	I:660; III:723n6; 845n104; IV:318; VII:401n5
1:14	V:59n51; 96n196; 510; 605n49; VI:360; 370; 460; VII:769n14		
		3:5	I:527
1:15	VII:718; VIII:595	3:8	I:23; IV:685
1:16	III:611; IV:965n7; V:326n61; VII:481n132; 488; VIII:165n2	3:9	VI:63
		3:10f	VII:492
		3:10-14	III:458
1:16-17a	VII:492	3:10-15	VII:492(n189)
1:16f	VII:495	3:11	I:204; III:458; 544n20; 553; 1014; V:892; VI:460; VII:769n14; VIII:51; 52
1:16-18	VII:492(n189)		
1:17	V:605n49; 747(n14); VI:360; IX:628		
		3:13	I:14; 15; VI:136n7
1:18	I:562; 697; 706n69; V:411; VI:276, n13; VII:477(n93); 493; VIII:165n2	3:14	III:889; V:234; IX:202n71
		3:15	II:229
		3:16	VII:179; 492; VIII:200
2:1	IV:523; V:326n60; VII:492	3:16f	VII:492(n189)
2:1-11	VII:492(n189)	3:17	VI:471; 638
2:3	IV:949n5; V:98; 101n22; 510; VII:488; 495	3:19	V:59; 360
		3:19-21	II:851(n146)
2:3a	VII:492	3:19ff	VII:49
2:4	VI:471	3:20	VII:716n3; 723; VIII:200; IX:472
2:4-8	VII:492		
2:5	V:766n3, n9	3:21	III:745n9; VI:360; 368; VII:116n151; IX:629
2:7	VIII:345		
2:8	VI:57	4:1	V:696n311; 778; 789; 817n7; 820, n23; VII:492; VIII:564n26; 568n47
2:9	IV:544; VII:643		
2:10	III:828n7; VII:141n318; 463		
2:11	III:828n7; V:510; 605n49; VI:63; 324n57; 370	4:1-3	VII:492(n189)
		4:2	IV:364; 1111n37; V:892; VII:769n14
2:12	VI:549n23		
2:12a	VII:492, (n189)	4:2f	V:787n113
2:12f	VII:488	4:4	I:363; II:878; V:605n49; VI:370; IX:154n70; 628
2:12ff	VII:49		
2:13	VI:63; IX:322	4:4a	VII:492
2:13f	IX:322	4:4-6	VII:492(n189)
2:13-17	VII:492(n189)	4:5	II:849(n124); VII:106
2:14	VII:482; 488; 494; 495	4:6	III:755n3; V:605n49; VI:299; 370
2:14ff	II:851		
2:14-17	II:851(n146)	4:7	IV:414; VII:492
2:15	VI:62; 63; VII:495	4:7f	VII:492(n189)
2:15f	VII:495	4:8	VI:129; 324n57; VII:141n318
2:16	IV:679n5; VII:482; 488; 494; 495	4:9	III:672; IV:697
		4:10	III:801; VI:161; 165n22
2:17	VI:370	4:12	II:142
2:18	III:828n7; V:907n21	4:13	VI:40n14; 889; 894; VII:484; 495
2:19	III:828n7; VII:484n147		
2:20	III:828n7; VIII:33	4:15	V:941
2:21	I:363; III:828n7; VI:564; VII:488; 495	4:16	V:605n49; VI:360
		5:1 (4:17, M/S)	III:184
2:22	V:605n49; VI:370	5:2 (5:1, M/S)	V:507; 513n119

5:2f (5:1f, M/S)	VI:545		8:1	VII:492; IX:322
5:3 (5:2, M/S)	V:221; 231; VI:276, n13		8:2	V:738
5:5 (5:4, M/S)	II:797		8:3	III:47n43; VI:550n28; VII:562
5:6 (5:5, M/S)	I:77n12; 117; II:470; 849(n124);		8:5	VI:550(n28), n28; VII:494
	IX:100; 632		8:6	VI:638
5:7 (5:6, M/S)	V:221; 231; VI:276, n13;		8:8	II:564; III:497n4; VII:81; 980,
	VII:106			n60
5:8 (5:7, M/S)	III:29; 40n67; VI:638		8:9	II:574
5:8ff (5:7ff, M/S)	VI:136n7		8:10	II:851(n146); VIII:197
5:9 (5:8, M/S)	VI:63		8:11	VI:309; VIII:182
5:11 (5:10, M/S)	I:363; VI:277; 281; IX:184		8:13	VII:395
5:12 (5:11, M/S)	VI:133; 324		8:14	II:647; IV:712; VII:49; IX:89
5:13 (5:12, M/S)	IV:1091; VI:564		8:15	I:14; 15; II:689
5:13-20			8:15f	II:774n38
(5:12-19, M/S)	VI:324		8:16	V:326n60
5:15 ((5:14, M/S)	VI:324n57		8:17	II:639; IV:414; VI:460;
5:16 (5:15, M/S)	IV:1091; VI:63; 360; 370			VII:488; 495
5:17 (5:16, M/S)	V:393, (n70); 410, (n205)		9:1	I:25n24; VII:477; 495
5:18 (5:17, M/S)	I:15		9:1-10	VII:49
6:1	VI:564		9:2	V:461; IX:200
6:2	V:8; 9n52; VI:324n57; 550;		9:2f	II:851(n146)
	VIII:594, n20		9:3	I:508; IV:892(n10); VI:287;
6:3	II:465; V:158; VI:277			549n23; 550n23, (n26)
6:6	VIII:200		9:4	II:522; 843; 850, (n136);
6:7	VI:287; IX:619			III:800; IV:146, n6; 149n18
6:8	VI:40; 63; VII:477(n92); 495		9:5	II:850; IV:679n5; 697; 892(n10)
6:9	V:371; 605n49; VI:370		9:6	I:23; II:850(n136); 878
6:11	VI:545		9:7	IV:318; VI:135n4; 136n7;
6:12	VII:395			VII:909; IX:289
7:1	IV:800n3; V:252; VII:628		9:7f	II:774n38
7:2	III:945n5; VIII:51; 52; 261;		9:7-10	VII:495
	262, n18		9:8	II:472; IV:245, n21; VIII:594
7:3	IV:965; V:393(n70); VI:563;		9:8a	IV:244n15
	564; IX:625		9:8b	IV:244n15
7:3f	IV:318		9:9	II:854n165; V:326n60
7:4	I:659; VII:486		9:10	I:136n11; II:850(n136);
7:5	VII:492			III:746n25; VI:572
7:6	II:625; IX:281			VII:477(n89); VIII:233; IX:381
7:7	I:659; VI:556n70; VII:486		9:11a	VII:494; 495
7:8	IV:376n12; V:395; VI:362; 368;		9:12	V:595; VI:550(n25)
	VIII:51n15; IX:629n85		9:13	II:233
7:8f	IV:378n35		9:13f	VI:523
7:8ff	IV:377(n23)		9:14f	V:171
7:9	II:825; VI:361		9:15	VII:494; **980**
7:11	III:769; 777; V:328; VI:63		9:15f	VI:40n14; 889
7:12	VI:63; VII:280		9:16	VI:893
7:13	II:874; VI:460; VII:718		9:17	II:574; 575
7:14	IX:307		10:1	II:242(n37); 243; IV:800n3;
7:15	IV:379; 572; VI:564;			V:171; VII:96
	VII:770n24		10:2	II:38; IX:625
7:16	VII:527		10:3	III:606; IV:285
7:17	III:458		10:4	VI:361
7:19	VII:494		10:6	VI:324n57; VIII:9; 613
7:20	I:15; 293		10:7	III:855
7:21	II:191; IX:617		10:8	V:855n14; VIII:292n159
7:23	VI:24		10:9	II:334n3; IV:269; VII:959; 962
7:24	I:518n6		10:10	II:286; VI:63; 168; 693; 771;
7:25	I:518n6; IV:970n7; VI:550n23;			VII:497n202
	IX:605, n9		10:12	VII:495; IX:381
7:26	IV:970n7; VI:122; 233n31; 234;		10:13	VI:549n23
	VII:495; 980n58		10:15	VII:424n6
7:28	IX:98		10:16	V:646

10:17	IV:365; VIII:346			IX:89
10:18	VIII:7		12:1-7	V:749n28
10:19	IV:318		12:2	VII:61
10:20	VII:441n157; 909; IX:287n37;		12:3	I:452; VII:67
	627n77		12:4	VII:731; IX:281
11:1	VI:276, n13		12:5	I:147; 209n8; III:5; 837n57;
11:2	VI:550, (n26)			838; 844n95; V:1025; VI:572;
11:3	VIII:193			913; IX:200
11:4	IV:903; VI:370; VIII:141		12:6	IV:335
11:5	V:49; VI:460; IX:297n89; 629		12:7	VI:361; 362; VII:81; 716n3;
11:6	VII:667			723; IX:472, n5
11:7	V:327; VII:424n11; IX:313n11;		12:9	III:896
	319n59		12:9-11	VII:482; 485
11:7f	II:850(n142)		12:10	III:53
11:8	II:851		12:11	III:666; 1080n210; VII:492
11:9	V:51; 370; 943		12:12	II:708n7; 849(n124); III:986
11:10	II:849(n124); IV:962; 963n2;		12:12-14	VII:495n195
	V:393(n70); 628n12; VI:564;		12:13	II:547n4; III:126; VIII:51; 52;
	VII:107			IX:202n71
12:1	III:1008; V:628n12; VI:563;		12:14	III:976; V:59n51; VI:551; 643

CANTICLES (SONG OF SOLOMON)

1:1	I:666; III:900n7; IV:781; VII:460		2:11-13a	VII:485
1:2	IV:866n210; IX:119n45; 125; 127		2:12	II:715n90; VI:66; 70n76;
1:3	I:666; III:1016n94; 1023; IV:23;			382n260; IX:89, n10; 288n41
	V:831; VII:507n294; 937;		2:13	III:703; 712; IV:352n5;
	IX:327			VII:752n7, n9, (n16)
1:4	II:503; V:766n11; IX:365		2:14	I:210n6; II:816n6; VI:67(n53);
1:5	II:738; IV:550; V:977n192;			IX:234n84; 281; 287; 289n52
	VII:57; 307n91; 370; 460		2:15	III:134
1:6	IV:527; 550		2:17	V:189; VII:395
1:7	II:700; III:801; VII:874n19;		3:3	VIII:141
	IX:510n74		3:4	III:991
1:9	I:3; VI:313		3:6	II:77n32; IV:264n8; VII:458
1:10	VI:67(n53)		3:7	VII:460
1:11	VII:660		3:7f	I:292(n79)
1:13	VII:458n6		3:8	III:5; IX:204
1:15	III:408n18; IV:23; VI:67(n53);		3:9	VII:460
	313; IX:100		3:9f	VII:485
1:16	II:187n49		3:10	IV:760n1
2:1	II:76n20; IV:42n53		3:11	VII:460; 626
2:2	IV:350n9; V:791		4:1	VI:67(n53); 70; VII:57;
2:3	IV:58; VI:383n277; VII:395; 840;			VIII:284n102
	VIII:345		4:2	IV:301
2:4	VII:1096		4:4	III:897n2; 916; V:313; VII:698
2:4f	IX:125n118		4:5	IX:509n71
2:7	III:45(n7); 1102; VII:307n91;		4:7	IV:830
	IX:125n118		4:9	III:606n1
2:8	V:863; IX:281		4:12	VI:113
2:9	V:814; 815, n8		4:13	I:446n2; V:766n9
2:9f	IV:464n27; 860n140		4:14	VII:458, n10
2:11	VI:570		4:15	III:991; VI:113; VIII:322

ISAIAH

1:18ff	III:929	2:22	VI:364; VIII:304
1:19	III:46(n30)	3	III:342; VIII:13
1:20	I:269; IV:525n14;	3:1	II:46; III:397; 1061n114;
	VII:696(n42), n42		VII:307; VIII:318
1:21	IV:1117n64; VI:185; 587;	3:1-3	VI:805
	VII:294n1; 312; 315; 813n88	3:1ff	III:929n21; VI:324
1:22	II:255; III:603; VI:935	3:2	VI:806
1:23	II:230; III:754; 797n1; 801; 804;	3:2f	VI:324
	VII:874n19; IX:445; 459	3:3	III:30; VII:483; 706
1:24	II:46; 812; III:1061, n114;	3:4	V:631; 635; 646
	V:410; 861; VI:460;	3:4f	IV:193
	VII:295n17	3:5	VI:745
1:25	IV:183; VI:935; 949; VII:312;	3:6	VII:339n1; 343
	VIII:8; IX:427	3:7	III:201; IX:281n13
1:26	IV:1040; VI:185; 524; VII:315	3:8	IV:1114; VI:10n1; VII:307;
1:27	II:196; 485; III:932; VI:524;		311; 343; VIII:8; 11n25
	VII:972n27	3:9	VI:551
1:27f	IV:1039	3:10	II:647n35; 692
1:28	III:932; VIII:63	3:11	II:645; VI:550, (n26); VIII:24
1:29	IV:146; 149	3:12	IV:365; 914n14; V:646; VI:234;
1:29f	III:1074		236(n42); 642
1:31	I:320n31; VI:398n417; VII:166	3:13	I:776
2	III:928, n16; VIII:13	3:13f	VI:811
2-6	IV:96	3:13-15	III:928
2:1	IV:96; 98	3:14	II:927
2:1-4	III:239	3:15	VI:890
2:2	II:698; 946(n11); 947; V:481;	3:16	IV:915; V:376; 628; VIII:301;
	482n81; 483n93; 486; 862;		607
	896; VI:537; VII:317;	3:16f	VII:294; 311
	VIII:53	3:16ff	III:573
2:2f	III:243; VI:414n539	3:16-4:1	VI:324
2:2-4	II:368; III:574; IV:208; V:862;	3:17	VII:955, n13; VIII:8; 11n25
	VI:537; VII:316; 404n8	3:18	IV:640n21
2:2ff	II:405; III:240; IV:610; 1014;	3:18f	III:881
	VI:511(n76); VIII:254	3:20	II:339; IX:618n52
2:2-5	IV:96; V:483n90	3:23	III:812
2:3	I:63; IV:96; 97; 1040; 1045;	3:24	II:645; III:881; V:304; 305;
	V:53; VI:537		VI:627n39; VII:58; 59; 60n34
2:4	III:923; 924; IV:401n88;	3:26	III:836; 837; VI:42; VIII:8
	V:767(n15); VI:511; 537;	4	III:342
	VII:317	4:1	III:498n8; V:253; 263
2:5	III:357n12; VI:537	4:2	IV:23; 878; VII:315; 979;
2:6	I:267; III:357n12		VIII:605n29; 607
2:6ff	II:945(n3), (n5)	4:2ff	IV:197; 201n25; 203; 204; 205;
2:6-21	V:401; VII:198		206; 207; 209; VI:365n162
2:6-22	V:399	4:3	I:93; 94; 619(n21); II:845n89;
2:8	II:377(n25); 645; III:571;		IV:196; 213; 1014; V:253;
	VI:761(n34)		VII:315
2:10	II:244; III:397; 968;	4:4	I:537; III:430n1; 932n28;
	IV:1108n24; 1121; VI:777;		IV:203; 207; 208; 301;
	IX:204		VI:363; 370; 371n195;
2:11	III:30; 1027; V:862; VIII:8; 10;		399n425; VII:294; 315;
	603; 606		VIII:320
21:11-19	IX:221n7	4:5	III:1008; 1027; IV:905;
2:12	IV:630; VIII:526		VI:399n425; 937; VII:313;
2:17	III:30; VIII:301; 603; 606		314; VIII:198
2:19	II:244; 295; VI:329; 777;	4:5f	VII:314
	VII:963; IX:204	4:6	III:643n1; 961; 969; V:1029;
2:20	I:527; II:377(n25); 789;		VII:396
	IV:521n4	5	V:749
2:21	II:244; VI:329; 777; VII:963;	5:1f	V:403n154
	IX:204	5:1ff	III:929; VI:811

	VI:189; 192; 200n178; 216; 508n54; VII:637
7:10ff	IV:165n94; 205; 206; 209
7:10-17	VIII:344
7:11	I:433; 439n195; 517; II:785(n119); V:831; 832
7:12	II:652; 785(n119); VI:27
7:12f	V:832
7:13	III:95n163; V:1017n6
7:13f	V:832
7:14	III:116n370; 487; IV:161n86; V:254; **831-832;** 833; 836n66; VI:402; VII:760n5, n6; 776; 1087; VIII:363n192
7:14ff	V:646
7:15	IV:170; V:767(n15)
7:15f	IV:149
7:15-17	V:831
7:16	IV:168; IX:198n47
7:17	V:831
7:17-25	VII:198
7:18f	III:572
7:18ff	V:890
7:20	III:675; IV:697
7:21	VI:689
7:23	VIII:193; IX:467
7:24	I:608
7:25	V:941
8	VI:96; 98
8:1	I:743
8:1ff	I:649n9; VII:217
8:1-4	III:572; VIII:344
8:2	IV:482(n25); 483; VI:185
8:3	II:455; V:254; 832, n37; VI:804
8:5ff	III:929n21
8:5-15	VI:198n150
8:6f	VII:317n121; VIII:322; 325n71
8:6-8	IV:161n86
8:7	V:942; VIII:325n73
8:8	IV:161n86; V:831; VII:777; IX:618n52
8:9	I:699; II:368
8:9f	VI:509(n56)
8:10	I:633; IV:161n86; 577; V:831; VII:777
8:11	V:606; VIII:53; IX:427
8:11f	V:689n263
8:12	III:32n21
8:12f	IX:201
8:13	I:111; III:32n21; 1070; VI:183n86; 188(n117); 189; IX:198
8:14	I:372; 793; III:357; IV:271; 273; 276; 277; 278; 281; V:127; 142; VI:5; 95; 98; 166; 746; 747n12; 748, n24; 749; 750; 751; 753n49; 754; 755, n56; VII:296; 307; 327; 341; 343; 344; 345, n39; 352; 353, n81; 610n16; VIII:157
8:14f	VI:541; VII:239n279
8:15	I:372; II:285; V:595; VI:745;

	748; **749;** VII:341; 343
8:16	II:165n1; III:578; 969; IV:401n91; 429; **430,** n117; 1045; 1046; VII:944; 946; VIII:346n73
8:16-18	IV:201; 203; 203f; 205; 206; 207; 209
8:17	II:51n6; 58; 522, (n31); IV:575; 577n1; V:176; VI:5; 6; 194
8:18	III:357(n12); IV:201; V:638; VI:812; VII:210(n65); **216,** n103, n108; 217; 218; 234; 304; 309; VIII:123n60, n61; 252n32
8:19	II:10; III:575; VI:66n41; 67n50; 193n139; 365; 919n16, (n21); IX:302
8:20	IV:1045; VI:920
8:21	V:510; VI:15; VII:344
8:22	III:142; VII:440n153; 607n20, n26
8:22f	VII:605
9:1 (8:23, M/S)	II:370; IV:595; V:48n23; 69; VII:440
9:1f (8:23f, M/S)	IX:344
9:1-7 (8:23-9:6, M/S)	IX:506n62
9:2 (9:1, M/S)	III:17; 443; IV:23; 25; V:324n54; VII:395; 396; 397; 438n136; 441n162; IX:319; 320; 346n292
9:2f (9:1f, M/S)	VII:440
9:2ff (9:1ff, M/S)	III:576; IV:206; V:862n18
9:2-7 (9:1-6, M/S)	II:405n32; III:575; **VIII:349,** n92
9:2-21 (9, M/S)	I:567; 568n18
9:3 (9:2, M/S)	II:366(n9); IV:32; V:438n390; 672n104; IX:363, n30
9:4 (9:3, M/S)	I:258; II:897; 944; III:666; VI:967
9:5 (9:4, M/S)	V:296; 311
9:6 (9:5, M/S)	I:34n73; 57n6; 58n11; 206n33; 634; II:299; 405; 408; III:30n16; 32; 84; IV:205; 206; 209; 530; V:254; 676; 832; 962n98; VIII:7n20; 349; 351; **IX:506;** 508; 524; 525
9:6f (9:5f, M/S)	V:646; IX:493; **506,** n62; 524
9:7 (9:6, M/S)	II:406; 879; III:162; 164; IV:201; 1107n12; 1111; V:611; 767(n15); VIII:7n20; **IX:506;** 524; 569n483; 585
9:7f (9:6f, M/S)	III:931
9:8 (9:7, M/S)	IV:96; 97; V:611
9:9 (9:8, M/S)	VIII:301
9:9f (9:8f, M/S)	VIII:300
9:10 (9:9, M/S)	VII:758
9:11 (9:10, M/S)	II:291n34; VII:294n1
9:11f (9:10f, M/S)	V:400
9:12 (9:11, M/S)	II:507; V:400; 403n155; 405; VII:720; VIII:427n211
9:14 (9:13, M/S)	V:168
9:14f (9:13f, M/S)	III:675; VI:805

9:15 (9:14, M/S)	III:30; 675; VI:805; 806	10:28ff	III:572
9:16 (9:15, M/S)	IV:365; VI:233n32; 234	10:29	IV:5; IX:198n49
9:17 (9:16, M/S)	V:400; VI:550(n30); VIII:564,	10:30	VI:647n11
	n25; IX:446	10:32	V:776n16; 777n24; VII:293;
9:18 (9:17, M/S)	VI:942n73		296
9:19 (9:18, M/S)	V:409	10:33	II:46; 292; III:397; 1061n114;
9:20 (9:19, M/S)	VII:107		IV:1014; VII:772; VIII:8; 24;
9:21 (9:20, M/S)	V:400		301
10:1	VI:564(n11), (n13)	10:34	VI:988n19
10:1ff	VI:324	11	I:567; III:1014; IX:514; 629
10:2	III:927; 929n24; IV:36; VI:39;	11:1	I:640; IV:252n17; V:676; 832;
	889n28; 890; IX:445		VI:967; **986-987** (987n8);
10:3	II:607; III:141		988; 989; VII:1014;
10:4	V:400; 410n201		VIII:479n2; 487; IX:508;
10:5	V:400; 410; 423n300; 890;		512n89; 524
	VI:797; 967	11:1ff	II:405(n31); III:576; IV:209;
10:5f	V:400		V:646; 862n18; VI:511(n76);
10:5ff	II:572; IV:1014; VI:509n60		**IX:508**
10:5-15	V:404	11:1-5	III:931
10:5-19	V:440	11:1-10	VIII:254
10:6	V:424; 941; VI:797;	11:2	I:103; 109n67; 171; 350; 351;
	VIII:564n25		499n23; 633; 698; 706n69;
10:7	I:252; III:607; IX:617		II:299; III:108n281; V:688;
10:7a	IV:953		832; VI:68n56; 69n62;
10:7b	IV:953		116n22; 183n86; 363, n153;
10:7ff	IV:1014		365; 384; 450n827; 874n17;
10:8-16	V:629n18		VII:179; 488; 514n342;
10:10	VI:797		890(n19); VIII:219; IX:199;
10:11	II:377(n11); VI:797; VII:311		513; 524
10:12	IV:953; VI:708; VII:296; 316;	11:3	II:243n38; V:549n50; VI:129;
	VIII:301; 603		VII:504n266; IX:514n107;
10:12ff	III:572		524
10:13	VII:484	11:3f	IX:524
10:13f	VII:499n215	11:3-5	IX:508
10:14	IV:9; V:158; VI:66n41	11:4	I:568n16; IV:205; 206n37; 213;
10:15	V:393n66; 677; VI:967;		526n20, n22; V:688;
	VII:359; VIII:607		709n425; 940, n4; VI:360;
10:16	I:94; II:46n16; III:1061n114		369; 370; 371n195; 552n40;
10:17	VI:934; 937		560n93; 579n4; 888; 889;
10:17ff	VI:942n73		897n102; 997; VII:696; 699;
10:18	II:238; V:480; VII:107; 109;		VIII:10; IX:125n123; 285;
	166; IX:623n69; 632		514n108; 524
10:19	IV:197	11:4f	VI:893
10:19ff	IV:196	11:5	IV:526n20; V:304; 305; 307;
10:20	IV:196; 206; VI:5; VII:970;		496
	973; 978(n51); 979	11:6	IV:309
10:20f	IV:207n38; 986; 987	11:6f	IV:253; V:767(n15)
10:20ff	IV:197; 203; 204; 213	11:6-8	I:141; IX:515n121
10:20-23	IV:207n38	11:6ff	VI:513; 988; VII:121n187; 989;
10:20-25	IV:36		VIII:254
10:21	I:94; III:84; IV:198; 206;	11:6-9	V:862; IX:508; 516; 524
	207n38; 209	11:7	VIII:342n49
10:21f	IV:213	11:8	IV:915; V:571; 573; 579; 631n5;
10:22	IV:196; 198; 204; 207, n38;		767(n15); VI:140n52;
	VII:972; VIII:64		VII:924n34
10:22f	IV:207n38; 210; 213; VIII:64	11:9	I:90; 698; V:479n61; VI:129;
10:23	V:158; VI:464; 638; VIII:64		VIII:322
10:24	V:49n26; VI:967	11:9a	IX:514n107
10:25	IV:651n14	11:10	I:640; II:522; 532n108; IV:37;
10:26	V:49n26		252n17; **VI:986-987**; 988;
10:27	II:897; VII:987; IX:100; 198;		989, n24; VII:269; VIII:480;
	524		487; IX:508; 512n89

11:10ff	VII:239n279	14:4ff	III:151; 851
11:11	II:883n4; III:1007; IV:148; 195;	14:5	I:326; II:897
	196; 203; 835; 859(n138)	14:6	V:394(n76)
11:11f	IX:524	14:7	II:787(n151); VI:5
11:11ff	IV:197; VIII:21	14:8ff	III:239
11:12	I:679; IV:203; VII:208; 220;	14:9	I:147; III:85n91; VII:66; 787;
	269; VIII:131		IX:633
11:13	II:878; 897; III:140	14:9ff	II:847
11:14	I:446n3; 529	14:10	V:747n16
11:15	VI:364n157; VIII:325n75;	14:10ff	VIII:302
	IX:427	14:11	II:244; III:851; VI:572;
11:16	IV:196; 201n25; 203; 204; V:49		VII:96n21; 453
12	V:408	14:12	I:352; IV:27; VI:168; VIII:348,
12:1	II:755n3; VII:720		n85
12:2	II:522n30, (n33); 523; VI:191;	14:12ff	V:482
	VII:970n16; 1013; IX:198;	14:12-15	VII:318; VIII:348n85; 349n94
	204	14:13	I:468; III:162; V:510; 768
12:3	I:21; IV:278; VI:114; 606;	14:13f	IV:887
	VII:534n41; 978	14:14	III:97n179; 352, n43; IV:663n7;
12:4	I:718; II:787(n142); V:262;		903; VIII:617n21
	VIII:493; 606	14:15	III:851; VI:572
12:4-6	VII:316	14:16	III:34
12:5	I:63; V:263; VIII:493	14:17	IV:285; 328; V:158
12:6	I:20; 93; II:787(n148); VII:294;	14:19	I:598; II:446; 465; V:480;
	VIII:606; IX:363		VI:991; VII:1045n269
13	II:945(n5)	14:20	III:851; VII:541; IX:585
13ff	III:574; VIII:428n212	14:21	III:776
13:1	VIII:582n98; IX:482	14:22	IV:195; 196; 197; 198; V:252;
13:1-22	VII:198		253; VII:540; VIII:462
13:2	V:480; 776n16; 777n24;	14:24	IV:575
	VII:208; 220; 269; IX:281	14:25	II:897; V:941; VII:920; 921
13:3	V:398; VI:288; VIII:300	14:26	I:634; V:158
13:4	V:187n6; 400n136; IX:281	14:28	VIII:582n98
13:5	V:158; 398; 400, n136, n140;	14:29	II:897; V:571n76; 572; VI:987;
	423, n300; 435; VII:359n5;		IX:524
	364; IX:100	14:30	II:406; 408; IV:195; 197; 593;
13:6	II:330; 947; V:174; VII:921		VI:5n14; 15; 889; 893n64;
13:7	IX:617		987
13:8	IV:337; IX:624; 670	14:31	V:174; VI:925n44
13:9	II:947; V:158; 396; 398; 399;	14:32	IV:36; 205; 206n37; VI:890;
	409; VIII:459n403		VII:311; 972n27; VIII:10
13:10	III:880; IV:551; V:510;	15:2	VIII:110
	534n318; VII:61; 232;	15:3	V:305; VII:772
	430n48, n49; 440n147;	15:5	III:606
	VIII:450	15:6	VIII:318
13:11	V:158; 399; 409; VIII:300; 306;	15:7	VII:970n16
	307; 526	15:8	VIII:318
13:13	V:398; 400; 409; 509n87	15:9	IV:196; VII:540n14
13:14	VI:233n31; 234; 499n8	16:1	VI:99; VII:286; 293; 315;
13:16	V:646		IX:524
13:17	II:738; IV:292	16:2	I:403n34
13:18	II:480n51	16:3	VI:42; VII:395; 424n5
13:19	VIII:299	16:4	III:1068; V:843; 941
13:20	VII:385n5; 390n6; IX:585	16:4f	IX:508
13:21	II:11; 15; VI:162; VII:401n5	16:5	III:479(n26); III:162; 942;
13:21f	V:156		VII:370n12; IX:508; 524
13:22	IX:592n64	16:6	V:392n62; 404; VIII:302, n54
14	III:840; IV:780	16:8	V:941; VI:42; 233n32; 234(n33)
14:1	II:481(n57); V:849n39; VI:731;	16:9f	IV:254
	736n89; VIII:168	16:10	IV:254
14:4	III:151; 837; V:747n14; 748	16:11	II:954; III:786; VIII:496n48
14:4-6	V:404	16:12	IX:436n1

16:13	IV:96
16:14	II:238; IV:198; 697
16:15	IX:533n276
17:3	II:243; IV:196
17:4	II:238; 242n35; 243; VII:107; 108
17:6	VIII:218
17:7	I:93; III:1005n47; 1012; VI:5
17:8	VI:5
17:10	V:6n33; 403n154; VI:750; 954n9; VII:977; 1013
17:11	III:764; VI:233n32; 235
17:12	VI:277
17:12f	VI:509(n56); VIII:322
17:12-14	VII:316, n112
17:13	II:624; VI:360
17:14	III:759; 760; 776; 777; VI:42
18:1f	I:414n49; III:1036
18:2	I:414; 615(n5); IV:33; V:941
18:3	VII:79; 208; 220
18:4	IV:243; VI:877n40
18:5	VIII:63
18:6	V:510
18:7	II:946(n15); III:140n2; IV:1107n12; 1111; V:862; 941; VII:314; 316; VIII:197; IX:60, n3; 585
19	V:846
19:1	III:441; IV:905; V:505n66; 861; VII:197; 298n33; VIII:406; 418
19:2	II:334
19:3	II:523; VI:362; 365; 368; 919n16, (n21); IX:302
19:4	II:46n16; III:1061n114; V:1028
19:5	VI:598
19:5f	VIII:318
19:6	VII:803
19:7	VII:539
19:8	I:527; VI:42; 43n18
19:9	II:636; VII:960
19:10	II:636; 897
19:11	I:633; IV:846; VII:479n110; 484; 492; 748n2; VIII:346
19:11f	V:748; VII:521n391
19:11-15	VII:489
19:12	VII:483n143
19:13	IV:835n28; VIII:607, n15; IX:246n10
19:13f	VI:234
19:14	I:271n12; III:1060n105; IV:546; VI:234; 361; 362
19:15	VIII:52
19:16	IX:198n49; 199
19:16f	IX:204
19:17	IV:164n93; V:263; IX:198
19:18	III:359n25; V:263; 459
19:19f	VII:211; 213
19:20	III:140; IV:158n70; VI:797; VII:975
19:21	I:719, n4
19:22	II:798n252

19:23	II:266; VI:797
19:24	VI:797; VII:318n125
19:25	III:773; VI:873
20:1	VII:58n14
20:1ff	VI:812
20:2	I:774; III:593; VI:626n29; VII:58; 63n54
20:2ff	V:749(n31)
20:3	V:665n51, n58; 682; VI:812; VII:210(n65); 217, n115; 218; 234; VIII:118; 123; 252n32
20:4	I:189n1
20:5	VI:5
20:6	VI:5; VII:980
21:2	V:371; 777n17; VII:600; VIII:158
21:3	IV:337; VII:562; IX:670
21:3ff	V:332n90
21:4	III:5; VI:234; IX:198n49
21:5	IX:497, n4; 501n48
21:9	III:246n73; VI:162
21:10	I:63; V:728; VIII:347
21:11ff	VI:716
21:13	IV:877
21:14	VIII:318
21:15	VI:233n31; 234(n33)
21:16	II:238; IV:697
21:17	IV:196; V:172
22:1	VII:294n1
22:1-14	VII:311
22:2	IV:572; 892(n8); VII:296n19
22:3	III:720
22:4	V:789; VI:123; 124n12
22:5	V:480; 941; VI:233n32; 234(33); VII:294n1
22:7	IV:145; 177
22:8-11	VI:508n54
22:9	III:960; VI:522
22:11	II:640; III:1006; 1007n57; 1012; 1014; V:456n2; 718
22:12	III:725; 837; 841; VII:60
22:12f	IV:983
22:13	II:689; 693; III:120; 181; V:628n12; VI:136; 140; VII:929n24; IX:363n30; 622
22:14	I:510; III:302; 304; 313; IV:94n105; V:548
22:15	III:750; VII:385; 390n6; 393
22:15ff	VI:890
22:16	I:743; IV:680; VII:371
22:18	V:941; VI:991; VII:625, n61
22:19	V:151; VII:570; VIII:581n87
22:20	V:665n58; 682
22:21	III:357(n9); 906; V:151; 304; 963(n101); VII:296; 625; 688n14
22:22	III:174; 178; 748, n48, n49; 750; V:1017n6; VI:107; VIII:487
22:23	III:161; VI:184; VIII:195
22:24	III:920n33; IV:649; VI:5
22:25	III:920n33; VIII:195
23:1	V:174

27:10f	IX:586	28:22	VI:123; VII:97n23; 724
27:11	III:133; 1007; V:160(n17);	28:23	VI:638; VIII:63; 64, n7
	VI:256; 257; IX:378, n50	28:23ff	IV:91; V:554n100
27:12	III:133; VI:399; 599n33;	28:23-29	III:575; VII:541n18
	610n28; 971		II:648; V:749; VII:484; 489;
27:12f	II:946n17		541
27:13	VII:78; 80; 84; 294n3; 296; 315	28:24	II:636; VII:541
28	VI:96; 98	28:25	VI:978n10; VII:228n199;
28:1	II:243; IV:546; VI:168;		422n17
	VII:625; VIII:300; 526	28:26	V:606; VII:493; 541n18
28:2	VI:278; VIII:322	28:27	V:1029; VI:967; 971
28:3	IV:697; VII:625; VIII:300; 526	28:28	V:941; VI:123
28:4	VI:168; VII:751n3, n5, n6; 752,	28:29	II:679; IV:521n4; V:776n16;
	n8; 753; VIII:235		789; VIII:117; 119
28:4f	II:522	29:1	VII:300
28:5	IV:196; 203; VII:626; 634	29:1f	VII:300
28:6	VI:363; IX:524	29:1-7	VII:312
28:7	II:459; IV:546; VI:234;	29:2	VI:323; VII:605
	VII:197; IX:6	29:2ff	III:929n21
28:7f	I:275	29:4	IV:91; VI:66n41; 67n50; 323;
28:7ff	II:455; V:630; VI:805		365; 368; 919(n16), (n21);
28:8	VI:269n7; VIII:193n45; 199		VIII:8; IX:302
28:9	I:60; V:330n81; VII:493	29:5	V:9; VI:277; 324; VII:660;
28:10	I:275; II:58		IX:57
28:10f	I:724	29:5f	III:575
28:11	II:702n3; III:969; VI:410n508	29:6	II:607; VI:399n425; 935;
28:11f	I:726; IV:52; VII:259		VII:198n14; 772; IX:57; 282;
28:12	I:222; III:46n31		283
28:13	IV:96; 97; 137	29:7	III:140; V:221; VII:295n17;
28:14	III:140n2; IV:96; V:748;		300; 705
	VII:311	29:7f	V:229; VI:509(n56); VII:705;
28:14ff	II:945n7; VI:189		VIII:551
28:14-22	V:398	29:8	II:522; III:659; VII:316
28:15	II:109n23; 126; 522n31;	29:9f	II:455
	VI:192n136; 809n194;	29:10	III:571; 626; 960; 969;
	VII:772; IX:57; 597n39		V:329n74; 378; 557; 1024;
28:15f	VI:198n150		VI:159(n3); 361; 362; 369;
28:16	I:190; 372; 792; II:434; III:64;		805; 806, n174; 809;
	IV:145; 182, n2; 203; 204;		VII:531n20; VIII:280n66;
	205; 206; 207; 213; 271; 272;		IX:629
	274n57; 275, n64; 276; 277;	29:11	I:619n16; VII:945
	278; 279; 281; 887, n29;	29:11f	I:762
	V:127, n31; 142; VI:96; 98;	29:12	I:697(n32)
	189, n123; 192; 195; 197n149;	29:13	II:161; 165n1; 330; 798; III:607;
	199n159; 200n185; 204n218;		612; 866; 1075; IV:52; 524;
	206; 211; 214n303; 216; 754;		VI:834; VII:171; 172; 697;
	755n55, n56; 756; VII:327;		701; VIII:172; 179
	338; 352; 353, n82; VIII:157;	29:14	I:394; III:33; 968; IV:846;
	IX:524		V:609; VII:477(n89), (n90);
28:16a	IV:272; 277; 279		489; 491; 495; 521; 526; 890;
28:16b	IV:272; 275; 277; 279; VI:755		895n65; VIII:161
28:16f	IV:209; 213; 886n24;	29:15	II:117n53; 645; III:960n4; 968;
	VII:736n35		V:325; VII:429
28:17	II:196; 485; III:931; IV:205;	29:16	III:1006n52; 1007n57; 1013;
	206; 207; VI:5		VI:118; 256(n16); 257; 258;
28:18	II:109n23; 522; III:304n19;		260; 467; 471; VII:360; 363;
	IV:577; V:941; IX:57		IX:473
28:19	II:99n3; 522, n28; IV:400n87;	29:16f	III:1006; 1008
	V:330n81; VI:550	29:17	IV:285
28:20	III:823n2; VII:605; 909n39	29:18	V:327n68; 552n77; VIII:279;
28:21	II:637; 640; IV:846n116; V:8;		280n69; 281
	26, n182, n183; 609n77;	29:19	I:93; II:534; VI:129; 889n28;

	893, n64; 900; VIII:6
29:20	I:269
29:21	I:272; VI:747; 748; 750; 751; VIII:154
29:22	III:357n12; IV:334; 1112
29:23	I:111; II:638; 640; V:255; 276; IX:198n47
29:24	I:729; 737; II:407; IV:401; VI:235(n37); 236(n41); 361; IX:629; 630
29:24a	I:729n8
30	V:407
30ff	VII:970
30:1	I:31; 103; 512; 513; 633; IV:41n50; VI:364; 365; VII:531; VIII:168; 351; 352; 353
30:1ff	II:117n53; VI:365
30:1-5	V:403n158
30:2	VI:193
30:3	VI:5; 192n136; IX:588
30:4	IX:89n10
30:6	III:142; IV:252n11; V:284; 571; 572; VI:960n12; VII:605; 607n20
30:7	IV:521n4; V:470; 776n16; VII:223n157
30:8	I:615n4; 617(n7); 743; II:698
30:9	I:31; 631n16; IV:41n50; 96; 1045; VI:10(n2); VIII:351; 352; 353
30:9f	IV:1045
30:10	III:571; V:327; 329n74; 371; VI:809; 812
30:10a	IX:585
30:11	V:53
30:12	I:729; IV:96; VI:5; 191, n133; 192; VII:405n12
30:13f	VI:166
30:14	VI:166; VII:359; 1095
30:15	I:699; II:522(n31); 523(n38), (n40); III:337; IV:521n4; 984n44; 986; 987; 991; 995n91; 996; VI:5; 189; 192; 508n54; VII:600; 720; 975
30:15f	VI:189
30:15-17	VI:198n150
30:15ff	VI:189, n122
30:15-18	IV:207
30:16	III:337
30:17	II:624; IV:198; V:480; VII:220n138; 269
30:18	III:929n23; IV:366; 577; VI:196; VIII:606; IX:378
30:18f	VII:315; IX:378n50
30:18ff	III:929; 930
30:19	III:929n23; IV:37; V:325
30:20	III:141; VI:233n32; 234; 236; VII:314; 605
30:21	V:54; VI:233n31; 234
30:22	II:377(n12); IV:280; 281n5
30:23	VI:132

30:23f	VIII:318
30:23ff	VII:315
30:24	V:283; 284
30:25	VI:162; 954; VII:936
30:26	III:1021n140; V:512; IX:318; 322
30:27	II:692; V:256; 257; 393; 398; 399; 410; 412; 861; VI:284; VII:695n39; IX:586
30:27f	VI:399n425
30:27ff	V:256n102; VIII:406; IX:363n30
30:27-33	V:399
30:28	II:229; IV:521n4; V:394n71; 400; 411; VI:360; 363; 370; VIII:322; IX:618n52
30:29	I:111; VI:95(n8); VII:294n3; 314; 610n16
30:30	I:639; II:244; V:396; 399; 400; VI:398n417; VIII:322
30:30f	IX:282; 283
30:32	VI:5; VIII:496n48
30:33	V:399; VI:364; 398n417; 935
31:1	II:523(n37); VI:5; 191, n133; 192; 277; 508n54
31:1f	VII:489
31:1-3	III:337; V:403n158; VII:495
31:1ff	VI:189n122
31:2	IV:97; VI:551; VIII:158
31:2f	VII:489
31:3	II:850; III:83; VI:364; 365; 393; 369; 417; 508n54; VII:107; 109n93; 126; IX:473; 623; 628; **630**
31:4	I:571; IV:252, n18; V:410; VI:299; 508n54; VII:310; 705; VIII:6
31:5	III:572; V:744; VII:731n13; 972n25
31:6	IV:990
31:7	I:471n2
31:8	VI:995; IX:80n9
31:9	I:657; IV:364; 366; VI:398n417
32:1	IX:509
32:2	II:228n11; VI:360; VII:294n1; 395; 396
32:2a	II:227(n10)
32:2b	II:227
32:3	VI:5
32:4	II:408; IV:243; 400n87
32:5	IV:833; 834; VIII:535n42
32:6	II:228; IV:833; 834; 949, n4; VIII:63; 564, n25; IX:97
32:6f	VI:16n31
32:7	VI:889; 900; VIII:9
32:7f	VII:179
32:8	IV:575
32:9	VI:5; IX:285
32:9-11	II:523(n36); VI:191
32:9ff	VI:192
32:9-14	VI:324
32:10	VI:470

32:11	II:318; 523; III:7n17; IV:318; 593; VI:5; 627n38, n39	34:1-17	VII:198
32:11f	VII:59	34:2	V:400; 409; VII:936
32:12	III:831n1; 834n32; 836; 837; 838; 843	34:2-4	V:400
		34:3	V:493
32:12ff	VI:324	34:4	I:504; 617; 618; II:295; IV:27; V:503; 509n87; 512; 515n135; 534n318, n320; VI:163; 164n20; 948; VII:232 440n147; 686n110; 705; 752(n16); VIII:450
32:13	VII:296n19		
32:13f	VII:312		
32:14	VII:295, n15		
32:15	I:538; II:468; 667; 674n32; 680; V:711n445; VI:68n56; 363; 370; VIII:605n31		
		34:4a	VII:757n60
		34:4b	VII:757, (n60)
32:15f	II:659	34:5	I:354; IV:527n24; 546; V:400; 508
32:15ff	VI:365		
32:17	II:196n14; 405n30; 646; IV:61n5	34:5-8	VII:838n15
		34:6	IV:911n3; V:297; 1025; VII:936, n4
32:18	II:523n34; VI:5; 191n131; 323; 524		
		34:6ff	II:35
32:19	VI:5	34:7	IV:546; 760n2; VI:129
32:20	IV:365	34:8	II:945n6; 948
33	V:547n35	34:9	V:399
33:1	VII:277n11; VIII:158	34:9f	VI:398n417
33:1d	VII:277n11	34:10	VI:937; VII:166
33:2	II:485n102; 522; III:142; VI:5; 196; VII:976; IX:378n50	34:10b	IX:586
		34:11	III:428n12
33:3	IX:198n49	34:13	VII:731
33:4	V:632	34:14	II:11; 15
33:5	VII:488	34:15	V:572; 576
33:6	I:109n67; III:137; IV:388n4; VII:179; 477(n93); 488	34:16	VI:313n11; 364; 370; VII:696(n42)
33:7	II:403(n22); V:777n17, n24; VI:123; 124n12; VII:300n55; IX:198	34:17	III:759; 776; IX:585
		35	V:767(n15)
		35:1	II:227; 228n11
33:7f	IX:198	35:1ff	II:659; VI:619
33:8	IV:149n17; 292; V:49	35:1-7	VI:113n5
33:8ff	II:117n53	35:2	I:787(n150); II:238; 243; 249; IV:542; V:326; 861; VIII:603n11
33:9	VI:42		
33:10	V:677; VIII:606		
33:10f	IV:1114	35:3	I:509; 738; III:913n2; IX:625
33:11	I:188; IV:521n4; V:325; VI:360; VII:563n7; 761n8	35:3f	IX:290
		35:4	II:927; IV:965; V:777n17; 861; VIII:7n20; IX:666
33:11f	VI:936n46		
33:12	III:831n10	35:5	II:718n109; III:37; V:548; 552n77; VII:246, n312; 350; VIII:279; 281, n78; 284; IX:345n277
33:14	I:269; VI:937; VIII:564, n25, n26; IX:204		
33:15	I:153; 559n2; III:919; IV:389; 685n7; 687; V:50; 52; 547; VI:270; 571; VIII:564n25		
		35:5f	III:212; V:552; 772; VIII:280
		35:6	II:227
33:16	VI:99; 184; VIII:613; IX:55n59	35:6f	VIII:318
33:17	III:554	35:7	II:227; VI:113; 116n21
33:18	I:742; VI:953n7; 955n12; VII:748n2; IX:617	35:8	II:100; V:54n34; VI:233n32; 234; 236, (n42)
		35:8f	V:49
33:18f	VII:521n391	35:9	IV:332, n10; VI:549
33:19	I:726; VIII:300n44; 302	35:10	III:675; IV:318; V:115; VI:42n13; VII:315; 600; 603; 719; IX:363
33:20	VI:5; VII:197; 370, n10; 1022; 1023; IX:585		
33:21	IV:530; V:262; **VII:317**	36f	VII:304
33:22	I:569; III:924n8; IV:530; VII:976	36:1	VII:760; IX:589
		36:2	VII:296n20
33:23	VII:209; 220; 269	36:3	V:149
33:24	III:828		
34:1	IX:246	36:6	II:523(n37); VI:967; VII:655

36:7	VI:760n23	38:12	V:133; 147; VII:370; 372n23;
36:9	II:523(n37); IV:649		872, n3
36:10	IX:99	38:13	IX:623
36:13	I:625; IX:281	38:14	V:203; 510; VI:66n41; 67(n50),
36:14	VI:1		n50; 382n260; VII:731n11;
36:14-20	VI:1001		IX:302
36:15	VI:1000	38:15	V:115
36:16	VII:752(n18)	38:16	V:777n17; VI:361, n132
36:19	VI:1001	38:16b	VI:361n132
36:22	V:149; VII:959	38:17	II:738; VI:123n7; 992;
37:1	VII:959		VII:1045; 1046n279; IX:99
37:1ff	VI:811	38:18	I:233; 236; II:485n1; 522n29;
37:2	III:262; V:149		755n3; 847; VI:194n143
37:3	II:473; III:142; V:239; 241;	38:19	I:233; II:175; 196; 755n3;
	430n340; VII:271(n16);		VII:271n15
	IX:667; 670	38:20	II:755n3; VII:772; 971
37:4	III:571; IV:195; 197; 205n36	38:21	III:201; VII:752(n11), (n13);
37:6	I:622		VIII:310n17; 311
37:7	I:60	39:2	II:564
37:10	VI:1	39:6	IV:1107n15; V:862
37:16	III:441; 573; IX:438	39:7	III:853
37:17	V:324	39:8	I:233; II:175; 196
37:18	VI:186n103	40ff	IV:206; V:683; 715
37:19	II:377(n22); IV:269n9	40-55	III:575; IV:859n138;
37:20	IV:1122		V:862(n16)
37:22	IV:96; 797; V:833	40-66	III:576; V:695; VII:492n187;
37:23	I:622; IX:281		IX:130n161
37:24	II:66; IV:145; 146; 177; 544;	40:1	V:777n19
	V:480; 658n14; VIII:51n16	40:1f	V:793; 798; VII:309; 313
37:25	VII:803	40:1ff	III:573; V:789; 791
37:26	I:486; II:947; III:1006; 1007n57	40:2	I:294; II:51; 328; 336n8; V:405;
37:27	V:942		407; 777n19; 798n185; 820;
37:28	V:104		VI:128; VII:705, n25;
37:29	V:548n45; VI:123; VII:944		VIII:10; 11n25; 369n248
37:30	IV:195; VII:220; 231(n213)	40:3	I:58(n11); 625; II:659, n9; 706;
37:31	IV:196		937; IV:193; 867; V:49; 70,
37:31f	IV:197; VII:978n51		n92, n95; 83; 96; VI:470; 615;
37:32	II:879; IV:196; 197; 198; 203;		VII:115; 404n8; IX:281, n12;
	204; 205; VII:970; 973		282; 288n45; 293n70
37:33	I:527; 608	40:3-5	VII:313; 404; 406; 408
37:35	V:665n58; 681n184; 682;	40:3ff	V:486; 861; VIII:16
	703n370; VII:974	40:4	IV:193; V:480; 481; 484n102;
37:36	IV:892n7; VII:1045		VI:287; VII:404; 718; VIII:7
38	III:200	40:4f	V:70n93
38:1	III:946n4; VIII:28; 310n17	40:5	II:242; 248; 709n13; IV:52;
38:1f	**VIII:118**		V:327; 334n101; 347n164;
38:3	I:455n2; III:613; 723; 726n2;		VII:106; 696(n42), n42;
	IV:675; VI:188n118; 571;		697n49; 1022; 1023
	VII:909	40:6	I:625; II:175n3; 237; 850(n133);
38:5	III:723; V:324; VI:571; IX:585		VII:106; 115; VIII:21n64;
38:6	VII:970n16		IX:281, n12; 282; 288n45;
38:7	IV:96; VI:460; VII:220;		386; 623
	231(n213)	40:6f	III:840; 841; IV:430n119
38:8	VII:395; 715n4; IX:677n15	40:7	VI:168, n3; 360; IX:618; 628
38:9	VIII:310, n17; 311	40:8	IV:96; 98; 575
38:9-20	V:202	40:9	I:58n11; 571; II:709(n12); 712,
38:10	I:148; VI:924; 925, n44; 926;		(n59); 713; 716; VII:327;
	VII:695n35		IX:281
38:10-20	III:200	40:9ff	VI:647
38:11	II:847(n108); III:109;	40:10	I:640; II:295; III:402; 635;
	1072n187; V:333; 334(n98);		IV:697; V:861; VII:249;
	VII:1022; 1023		VIII:459n403

40:10f	V:672n104: VI:487(n28)
40:11	I:341; III:556; V:777(n18), n18; 790; 820n23; VI:487, (n23); 489; 500(n9)
40:12	II:896; IV:22 V:480; VIII:319; IX:426
40:12ff	I:706n69; II:382; III:574; IV:610; VII:427n33
40:13	I:699; 705; IV:953; 959; VI:364; 368; VII:518; 765, n28; 766; IX:629
40:13f	VII:489; 763
40:14	I:700; II:27; 136; 169; III:930; 932; V:55; VII:226n175; 765n23, n26; IX:225
40:15	II:897; III:881; IV:285; 902
40:16	III:643n3
40:17	III:87; IV:285; 287n11
40:18	III:82; V:191
40:19	V:191; VII:531n20
40:19f	II:377(n25)
40:20	II:42; IV:149; 168; VII:96n19; 484; 497n202
40:21	VII:890
40:21-31	III:89
40:22	III:1008; V:502(n40), n44; 503(n51); 522n192; VII:372; 642
40:22ff	III:574; IV:610
40:23	III:924n8
40:24	VI:399n425; 452; 990; VII:197; IX:125n123
40:25	I:94; III:351; VIII:606
40:26	I:503; II:244; 293; III:89n109; 402; 880; 906; 1011; 1027; IV:22; 100; V:252; 266; VII:705
40:26ff	I:218n11; III:1012
40:27	III:959; 968; V:50; 669; VI:195
40:28	I:200; 201; III:89; 882; IV:1110n34; V:126n30; VI:15n26; 687; VII:489; IX:225
40:28f	VI:195
40:28ff	III:828
40:29	VI:195
40:29ff	II:317n112
40:30	VI:195; VII:343
40:31	II:522n31; III:89; 828n11; IV:578n1; 584; **VI:195;** VIII:229
41-53	V:682
41:1ff	III:574
41:1-5	V:670n91
41:2	II:178n13; 195
41:2-4	IX:591
41:2ff	IV:1014
41:4	I:1; II:344(n16); 352; 641; 653; III:675n2; 882; 1012; 1063n121; IV:148n15; 1014; VI:865; 867n9
41:7	II:42; VIII:261
41:8	I:8(n14); 28(n44); IV:450n235; V:662; 680(n175), n176, n177; 682; 683, (n199), (n203), n207; 686; 693n291; VII:538; IX:168, n180
41:8f	IV:153(n42); V:662, (n38); 684, n213; 700
41:8-10	IV:37
41:8ff	III:574
41:9	I:375; III:490; IV:148, n15; 163; 169; V:662; 680(n175), n176; 682; 683, (n199), (n203), n207; 693n291
41:9ff	II:344(n16)
41:10	II:195; 293; VI:233n32; 235; VII:775; IX:203
41:11	I:374; 396
41:13	III:911
41:13f	IX:203
41:14	I:94; IV:330; 332; VII:453; 454; 455n23
41:15	V:480
41:15f	IV:281, n5
41:16	II:786(n136); VI:360; 399, n425; VII:197; IX:363n26
41:17	II:228; VI:889; 893n64; 913
41:17f	VIII:318
41:18	II:228, n11; VI:113
41:18f	II:659; V:767(n15)
41:19f	VII:541
41:20	I:94; 698; 712n81; III:1027
41:21	I:569n23; II:330
41:21ff	II:344; III:575
41:21-29	V:670n91
41:22	II:680; IV:953; VIII:51n15
41:22f	V:665n50
41:23	II:680; III:34
41:24	IV:149; 170
41:25	II:344(n14); V:941; IX:524
41:26f	V:665n50
41:27	II:344(n14); 709n11, (n12); 712; 716, n97; V:776n16; 777n24; VI:865; VII:313
41:29	II:645; VI:233n32; 234; 360
42	II:244; V:709; IX:514
42:1	I:67; 102; 103; 184; 339n7; II:57; 738; 739; 740, (n9); 741; III:928n18; 1013; IV:153; 167; 183; 206; V:666n66; 667, n69; 668, (n79); 670n92; 676; 677; 680n175; 681; 682; 683, (n199), (n203), n206, n207; 684; **686-700** (687n249; 693n292, n293, 700n345); 701, n350; 702; 706; VI:294; 363; 370; 406n473; 537; VIII:360; 368, n239, n240, n241; IX:517; 524
42:1f	V:669; IX:285
42:1-3	V:700; 709
42:1ff	V:684; 685n216; 687; 693n292;

	695-697; 698, n328; 699; 709; 712; VI:365
42:1-4	II:740n6; III:932; 933; 942; IV:613; 945; **V:666-673** (669n85; 670n92); 676; 689; 705; 706; 709; VI:384; VII:167; IX:293
42:1-7	V:688
42:2	III:900; 901; IX:281n13
42:2f	V:669, n86; 670n92
42:3	IV:206; V:668; VI:745; VII:167
42:3f	V:667
42:4	II:532; IV:206; 485; 1045; V:262; 274; 668; 669; 670n92; 676; 688; 701n346; VI:194n144; VIII:154; IX:524
42:4d	V:701
42:5	II:367; 862n254; III:82; 574; 882; 933; IV:34; V:504(n55); 516; 941; VI:361, n131; 362; 364; 453; 463; VII:610; IX:629
42:5f	I:34n73
42:5-9	IV:613; V:666n63; 676
42:6	I:72, n22; II:107; 124n73; 133; 195; 344(n16); 367; III:41; 490; 589; 911; 1013; IV:52; 153; 206; V:668; 670n89; 688; 689; 706n403; 709; VII:442n176; VIII:281; IX:321n70; 344; 524
42:6f	VII:428; 442n170; VIII:285; 294
42:6ff	V:11
42:7	I:196n1; III:41; 443; V:99n15; 667; 669; 688; 709n428; VIII:279; 282; IX:345n277; 524
42:8	I:460(n19); II:241; 244; III:573; 1011; V:273
42:9	I:63; 72, n22; III:575; V:665n50; VI:687
42:10	II:788n155; III:449; VIII:493; 499n71
42:11	VI:522; IX:281n13
42:12	I:63, n22; 460(n19); II:244; 713
42:13	II:679; 879; III:109; 297; 404; VI:511n77; VII:922
42:14	I:359; III:617; VI:364; IX:618
42:16	V:53; 709n428; 941; VII:405; VIII:282; IX:345n277
42:16ff	VII:429; IX:320
42:17	VI:191
42:18	V:552n77; VIII:279; 281
42:19	IV:613; V:662; 680n169; 682; 683n207; 684; 685, n215, n219; 693n291; VIII:279; 281
42:19a	V:683n199
42:19b	V:683n200
42:19f	VIII:281n83
42:20	V:548n48

42:21	II:175; 213; IV:1047n97; 1058
42:23	II:680; V:683(n199)
42:23ff	VIII:281n83
42:24	V:51; VI:571n31
42:25	I:697n31; II:468; V:398(n123); IX:617
43	IV:488
43:1	I:698n37; III:490, n6; 1007; 1012; IV:148; 332; V:253; 262; VI:256; 256f; 460; VII:775; IX:203
43:1-3	VII:977
43:1ff	II:344(n14)
43:1-10	V:693n293
43:2	I:538; 752; VII:775
43:3	I:63; 94; III:303; IV:330; 332
43:3f	I:33; VIII:509n14
43:4	III:303; 675; IX:622n63
43:5	VII:775; IX:203
43:5-7	VII:978
43:5ff	VII:421
43:6	IV:41n50; VI:757; VIII:351
43:7	II:242; III:497n2; 1007; 1027; V:279n232; VI:257
43:8	IV:484; V:548n48; 662; 669; VIII:279; 280n69; 281
43:8-13	V:670n91
43:9	I:234; 247; II:195; 213; IV:484; V:186n2
43:9-13	IV:483
43:10	I:698; 704; 712n81; II:399; 400; 432; 739; IV:153(n42); 167; 169; 483n28; 484; V:212n40; 662(n40); 670n92; 681; 682; 683(n199); **686-700** (693n293; 699n336); VI:188; 197; VII:890(n19)
43:10-13	IV:484
43:11	II:344n11; 352(n81); VII:977
43:12	IV:483n28; 484; V:212n40
43:12f	II:352n82
43:13	II:344n12; VIII:254n45
43:14	I:94; IV:330; 332
43:14f	I:569
43:15	I:569n23; III:1007; 1027
43:15ff	II:344(n14)
43:16	V:49; VIII:323n60
43:16-21	VIII:254
43:17	V:584n11; 585
43:18f	III:993; VI:867n8
43:19	III:449; V:49; VI:464; 598; VIII:254n45
43:19f	IV:1014
43:20	I:685; II:228; 755n3; III:991; IV:153(n42); 183; VI:136(n8); VII:731; VIII:318
43:21	I:63n22; 69; 460(n19); 461; III:1007, n57; 1013; V:212n40; VIII:493
43:22-28	V:790
43:23	III:855n1

43:24	VI:701; VII:875	44:20	I:699; VI:233n32; VII:404n7;
43:24f	I:154		IX:599
43:25	II:344; IV:301	44:21	III:1007; 1013; IV:676;
43:26	II:195; 213; IV:676		V:659n23; 662, n38;
43:27	I:274n23; II:662n2; IV:602;		680(n175), n176; 682;
	V:663n42		683(n199); 684; 693n291;
43:28	I:622		VI:257
44	IV:488	44:22	IV:301; 902; 903; 988(n62);
44:1	IV:1121; V:662; 680(n175),		V:662; 669
	n176; 682; 683(n199); 684;	44:22ff	IV:332
	693n291	44:23	II:774; 787(n149), (n151);
44:1f	IV:153(n42); V:662n38		III:700n13; 701n20; V:510;
44:1-5	IV:167n100; VII:664		513n107; 533; VII:78
44:2	III:1007; 1012; IV:988(n63);	44:24	II:344(n12), (n13); III:881;
	V:662; 680(n175), n176,		884n60; 1007; 1008; 1013;
	n177; 682; 683(n199); 684,		IV:330; V:502(n40); 894;
	n213; 693n291; VI:256; 257;		VI:256; 257; VII:610;
	460; IX:203		VIII:63
44:3	I:538; 753n13; II:228; III:991;	44:24ff	IV:100
	VI:68n56; 363; 365n162; 370;	44:25	IV:835; VI:919n16; VII:480;
	VIII:160		483; 495; IX:224; 233n78
44:3ff	II:469	44:26	I:77n12; 633; III:575;
44:4-6	V:670n91		V:664n49; 667n71; 680n169;
44:5	II:368; IV:636n3; V:259;		682; 683(n199); 684n208;
	VII:578n55; 660		685n221; 686; 693n291;
44:5f	VI:867n9		VI:293; VII:315
44:6	**I:1-2;** 3; 569n23; II:343n1;	44:26f	III:1012
	344n11; 345; 351; III:1012;	44:27	VI:598
	1013; IV:332; V:250; 890;	44:28	III:53; 54; VI:470; 488n29;
	1020; VI:865; 867n9; 1000		VII:315; VIII:166n11;
44:7	I:63; 64; III:351; IV:1014		IX:225
44:7f	VIII:254n45	44:28ff	IV:158n69
44:7-9	IV:484	45:1	II:368n15; III:911; VII:744;
44:7ff	III:575		IX:502; **504;** 577
44:7-11	IV:483	45:1ff	I:567; III:572; IV:1014
44:8	I:66; III:5; 86n100; IV:483n28;	45:1-7	IX:321n69; 591
	484; V:212n40; 670n92;	45:2	III:746n33; V:481; VII:404n8
	VI:95(n8); 233n32; 235;	45:3	III:138; 490, n6; 969; 976;
	236(n41)		IV:148; V:262; 368; 370
44:9	III:87; IV:483n28; 484; VI:257	45:3f	I:698n37
44:9f	IX:73	45:4	II:57n2; IV:153(n42); 1014;
44:9-11	IV:484		V:262; 662, n38; 680(n175),
44:9ff	III:87(n107); IV:914n13;		n176; 682; 683(n199); 684;
	VII:360n7		693n291
44:9-20	II:377(n25)	45:4ff	III:574
44:10	VI:257; VII:531n20	45:5	II:344(n11); 352n82
44:11	III:801; IV:484	45:6	III:1080
44:12	III:402; VI:14	45:7	II:405; 408; III:1007, n57; 1008;
44:12ff	II:383		1013; IV:1014; V:126n30;
44:13	IV:746; 752		VI:257n24; VII:153; **429;**
44:13f	III:87n107		IX:317n48; 320; 321, n71
44:15	II:789(n175); III:643n3;	45:8	II:195; 481n72; III:1008;
	VI:760n24		IV:903; VI:977; 978; 980
44:15f	VI:934	45:9	III:1007; 1013; VI:260; 467;
44:16	V:325; VI:934		VII:360; 363
44:17	II:789, (n175); IV:197;	45:9f	V:645; 968n127; 971
	VI:760n24; 761(n34)	45:9-11	VIII:352
44:18	IV:949; 950n7; V:327;	45:10	V:968n127; VI:256(n15); 257;
	VII:890(n19); IX:224; 225		258; 260; IX:473; 669
44:19	II:789(n175), n176; IV:197;	45:11	I:94; II:638; 641; III:1007, n57;
	284n2; VI:760n24; IX:225;		IV:41n50; V:971; VIII:351
	617	45:11f	IX:427

45:12	I:503; III:574; 1008; 1012; 1027; V:502(n40); 510; VII:609n8; 610	47:6	II:481; 897; III:773; V:398(n123)
45:13	II:43; IV:329; 332; 389; VII:310	47:7	IV:949; VII:838; VIII:51n15
45:14	I:211; IV:332, n11; VI:761(n37); VII:315; 316	47:7f	II:346n35
		47:8	I:697; III:612; V:487n2; IX:445
45:14ff	V:11	47:9	III:397; VII:483; IX:445
45:14-25	III:574	47:10	I:699; II:346n35; VI:191; 587n46; VII:477(n93); 480; 483
45:15	I:94; III:88; 120; 572; 969; 1011; 1066n136; VI:234; VII:1012		
45:16	VI:571	47:11	III:141; 302; 303; 304
45:17	I:200; 208; VII:977	47:12	IV:400; VI:248(n129); VII:483; IX:73
45:18	III:574; 1007, n57; 1008; 1009; V:504(n55); VI:256; 257		
		47:13	V:329n74; 504; VI:809; VII:975
45:18ff	I:94; IV:332	47:14	VI:934
45:18-25	IV:37	47:15	VII:971
45:19	III:960n4; VII:538	48:1	V:459
45:20	V:670n91; VII:970	48:2	I:90; VI:191n133; 524; VII:296n19; 309; 310; 655
45:20b	VII:975		
45:20-22	VII:979	48:3	VII:696(n42)
45:20ff	IV:208	48:4	IV:635; V:1028
45:21	III:575; VI:708; VII:977; 1012; VIII:254n45	48:5	II:377(n11)
		48:6	IV:1107
45:22	VII:978	48:6f	V:548
45:23	I:721; 739; II:344(n11); 345; 679; III:595; 1011; V:207; 212n40; 214, n44; 215; 459; 460n21; 541; VII:696(n42); 700	48:7	III:1008; IV:1114; 1120
		48:8	I:699n42; V:548
		48:8ff	II:59
		48:9	V:257; 405
		48:9-11	V:404
		48:10	IV:146, n5; VI:160
45:23f	III:1089; V:670n89	48:11	II:241; 244
45:23-25	II:195; 709n13	48:12	I:2; II:344(n13); 346; 352; n83; III:490; 496; 1012; 1013; IV:153(n42); V:890; VI:865; 867n9
45:24	II:243; 408; 927; III:1013		
45:24f	I:189		
45:25	II:212; 786(n136)		
46:1	VII:921; IX:85		
46:1f	IX:85	48:13	II:37; 295; III:574; 1008; 1009; 1012; IV:100; V:502(n40); VII:610; IX:427
46:1-7	II:377(n25)		
46:2	VI:15n26; VII:921; 970n16; 980		
46:3	IV:196; 197; 198; 201; 204; 205	48:14	I:30; III:53
46:4	IV:7; V:915n83	48:15	III:490; V:111
46:5	III:351; IV:663n7; V:188; 747n16; VI:233n32; 235	48:15f	III:575
		48:16	III:960n4; VI:363; 364; 817n249
46:6	I:426n5; II:789, (n175), n177; 896; VI:760n24; VII:641; IX:436	48:17	II:136, n12; 769; IV:330; 332; V:53; VI:1000; IX:73; 74
46:7	II:42; VII:975	48:18	II:405; VI:597
46:8	IV:676n5; 990, n71; V:777n20; VI:233n32; 235; 236	48:19	I:619n21
		48:20	I:516; II:268; IV:32n12; 332; V:662, n38; 679n166; 680(n175), n176; 682; 683(n200); 684, n208; 693n291; IX:281
46:8f	IV:676		
46:9ff	IV:1014		
46:10	I:63; 634; III:575; 993; VI:460; VII:642; 646; VIII:51n15; 63; 166n11		
		48:20f	VIII:254; 318
		48:21	II:228; IV:859(n138); VI:97n28, n30; 136(n8); VII:960; 961n12
46:11	III:490; 1007n57; 1027; V:111		
46:12	III:607; IV:373		
46:12f	II:195	48:22	II:402n15; 408; 922; IX:363n29; 366n57
46:13	IV:52; 387n113; VII:294; 308; 313; 978		
		49	IX:514
47:1	V:833; VII:430n48	49:1	I:698n37; II:709n13; III:787; IV:148; 153; 154n45; V:668, (n78); 686n228; 688; IX:586
47:1ff	IV:1014		
47:4	I:94; IV:330; 332; V:257		
47:5-9	IX:458	49:1f	V:688; 699

49:1ff	II:346(n38); III:574; IV:1014	49:22f	IV:167n100
49:1-6	IV:154; 613; **V:666-673;** 676	49:23	II:522n30; IV:584; V:604n44;
49:2	I:608; III:969; IV:126n215;		VI:183; 629; 726; 761(n37);
	145; 525; 527; V:667; 669n86;		IX:126n130
	688, n252; 709n425; VI:997,	49:24	VII:980n61
	n26; VII:395; VIII:154;	49:24f	VII:980
	IX:344	49:25	III:400; VII:980n61
49:3	II:254; III:358(n17); V:666;	49:26	I:188; 697n35; III:140; IV:330;
	667n69; 676; 680(n175),		332; 546; VI:138; 1000;
	n176; 682; 683(n200); 684,		VII:107
	n213; 685; 693n291;	50:1	I:403n34; 642; 1101(n25);
	VIII:469n465		VI:160
49:4	III:828; V:672; VI:910n229	50:2	II:228; 473; 624; III:490;
49:5	III:1007; V:591; 668; 669; 682;		IV:331; VI:598; VIII:318;
	683n200); 684; 685n214;		IX:427
	686; 693n291; VI:256; 257	50:3	IV:551; V:509n87; VII:61;
49:5f	III:358(n18); 1013; V:659n23;		VIII:154
	666; 669; 684, n214; 685n214	50:4	I:721; IV:430n117; V:668;
49:6	I:679; II:99; 102n12; 367; 545;		687n240
	709n13; 931; III:589; IV:485;	50:4f	V:548; 667; 668; IX:284
	V:668; 682; 683, (n199),	50:4ff	II:346n38; V:685n216; 686;
	(n203), n207; 684; 685n214;		698n328
	686-700 (693n291; 695n305);	50:4-9	IV:613; **V:666-673;** 676;
	705n390; 706n403; 709; 712;		IX:529n240
	VI:537; VII:442n170, n176;	50:4-10	V:686n226
	978; **1013;** IX:248; 321n70	50:5	V:547n33; 672(n100)
49:6f	V:688; 699	50:6	IV:518; V:634n24; 635n25,
49:7	I:598; III:39; IV:153; 330; 332;		n28; 686n226; VI:778;
	V:666, n63; 670; 671; 673;		VII:869n66; 1045;
	676; 688; VI:185; 1000;		VIII:263n24; 265
	IX:517	50:6f	III:819n5
49:7-13	IV:613	50:7	IV:279; VI:95; 99; 756n58;
49:8	I:221; 222; 628; II:133; 743;		VII:610n16; 611; IX:625
	III:773; V:668; 670n89;	50:7ff	V:672
	695n305; VI:257; 682;	50:8	II:212; 330
	VII:994	50:8f	II:195
49:8f	V:686; VII:977	50:9	I:269; V:718; VII:276; 277; 278;
49:8ff	II:59; V:669		IX:586
49:8-13	V:666n63; 676	50:10	V:259n127; 680n167; 682;
49:9	II:228; V:667; 669		683(n199); 684; 685; **686,**
49:9f	VI:487(n28)		n226; 693n291; VI:191n133;
49:10	II:226; 228; VI:16; 22; 113;		192
	117n25; 136(n8); 163n10;	50:10f	IV:613
	487(n23); VIII:318; 325	50:11	V:314n10; VI:950; VII:454
49:11	V:49; 481; VI:749n26	51:1	II:438n18; IV:271n21, n22;
49:13	II:481(n57); 774; 787(n151);		VI:927; VII:610; IX:669
	V:510; 513n107; 533; 776n14;	51:1f	IX:669
	VI:16; 893; VIII:10; 19;	51:2	III:490; IV:148; 154n50; 166;
	IX:363n26		IX:669
49:14f	VII:313	51:3	II:788(n162); IV:1112n42;
49:15	I:33(n67); II:480n50; IV:642n6;		V:766, n4; 767; 789; VII:315;
	915; V:646; 971n142;		VIII:254; IX:281; 363
	VIII:353(n114)	51:4	II:679; 709n13; III:933;
49:16	VII:326; 660; 948n77; IX:416		IV:33n15; 1045; V:693n293
49:16f	VII:314	51:4f	II:368
49:17	III:411; V:139	51:4ff	III:574
49:18	II:862n255; III:881; IV:1105	51:5	II:195; 291n34; 330; 523(n40);
49:19	VI:158; 169; VII:605; IX:97		679; III:402; IV:584;
49:20	V:546; 547; VII:605; VIII:199		VI:194(n144); VII:1014n59;
49:20f	VII:316		VIII:605n31; IX:427
49:21	V:604n44; IX:445n46; 459	51:6	V:509; 718; VII:611; 978
49:22	III:824; VII:269; VIII:346	51:7	III:607; IV:1045; VI:156;

	IX:203
51:7f	VII:496
51:8	I:663n6; V:672n103; VII:276; 277; 978; IX:586
51:9	I:639; II:291n34; V:470; 572; 576; VIII:319; 418; 605n31; IX:427
51:9f	I:640; VIII:319
51:9ff	I:640; VIII:254
51:10	IV:332; V:49; VI:277; 1001; VIII:319
51:11	III:675; IV:318; V:115; VII:315; 600; 603; 719; IX:363
51:12	I:699; II:752; V:789
51:13	III:140; 1008; 1009; V:394, (n74); 502(n40); IX:198
51:14	VII:642
51:15	II:955; V:257
51:16	II:709n11; V:502(n40); VII:309; 395; 642; 645; 696(n45); IX:434
51:17	III:969; V:165; 398(n123); 399, n133; 400(n134); 407; 437; VI:139(n38); 148n1; 149, (n18); 152n33, n38; 595n87; VII:66; 313
51:17-23	VI:149; VII:308
51:18	V:604n44; 777(n18), n18
51:19	IV:323; V:789; VI:166
51:19ff	V:789
51:20	II:624(n5); III:434; VI:149(n18); 570n30
51:21	IV:546; VI:149n17; 893; VIII:8n22
51:22	V:165; 399, n133; 407; 437; VI:139(n38); 148n1; 149; 150; 152n38
51:23	VII:1045; VIII:7
52	III:550; IV:751n53
52f	VIII:607n12
52:1	I:90; 226; II:319; III:797n43; VI:524; 525; VII:294n1; 296; 310; 314; 315; IX:130n161
52:1f	**IV:271**
52:2	VII:296
52:3	IV:332; 351n14; VI:160; VII:772
52:4	VII:838
52:5	I:621; 622; III:33n30; 992n143; V:174n7; 620
52:6f	II:713
52:7	I:14; 66; 67; 441n211; 571; II:403n22; 409; 707; 708, n9; 709, (n12); 710; 712, (n59); 713; 715n90, n91; 716, n98; 717n105; 719; III:703; V:312, n9; 480; VI:628; VII:314; 594; IX:287; 677
52:7ff	VII:313
52:8	II:716; 787(n150); V:863; VI:771n19; IX:281, n12

52:9	II:787(n150), (n151); IV:332; V:820
52:10	I:640, n2; III:572; 577; IV:52; V:324; 326; 334n101; IX:427
52:10-54:6	IX:674n59
52:11	I:516; II:57; III:428; V:454
52:11f	VIII:254
52:12	III:5; VII:842n4
52:13	V:668; 677, (n136); 681; 682; 683(n199), (n203), n207; 684; **686-700** (692n290; 693n293; 698n328a); 702n356; 704n380; 711, n441; 712n446; VI:110; VII:890n18; VIII:360; 607; 610n41; 613; IX:534n282
52:13-15	V:666; 671n99; 688
52:13ff	III:574; IV:206; 1096n24; V:666n67; 673; 678; 684; 685n217; 687; 688, n254; **695-697** (695n308); 698n328, n328a; 699, n337; 704; 709; 712; VII:987; VIII:407
52:13-53:12	**IV:540; 613; 616; V:666-673** (666n65); **676-677; 689; 692n289; 693-695; 695-697;** 709; 710n434; VI:536; **537-538;** VIII:500n83
52:14	II:242n35; 373; III:31n17; 33n30; 34; 551; IV:746n18; 751n53; 1098; V:370; 677, n135; **688; 689;** 693; 712n446; VI:537; 538; 540; VIII:473n484; IX:96; 524
52:14b	V:677, (n134)
52:14c	V:677
52:14f	V:673; 677
52:15	I:63; 64; III:34; 572; 989n110; V:324; 671; 677; 684; 685; 688; 689; 693; 700n340; 705; 706; 708; 709; 713n454; VI:537; 538; 540; 977; 979; VII:881; 895n64; IX:524
52:15b	III:600
53	I:225; 339, n8; II:266; 278; 853n163; III:142n4; 400n17; 414n2; 536; **550-553** (552n62); 573; 918n22; IV:201; 343n22; 487n35; 516n1; 615n65; 616, n68; 623; 746n20; 829n2; 915n19; 1091; 1093n12; 1094; 1096; **1097; 1098;** V:607n60; 631n4; 667n70; 671; 672; 677; 682; 683n205; 684, n211; 685, n216; 687n251; 688; 689; 690; **691-692** (692n289, n290); **695-700** (695n304; 697n324; 698n328a, n329; 699n331, n338; 700n338); 705n392, n392a; 706, n396, n400; 707, n412; 708; 709, n426; 710;

	304, n142; 339n6; III:296n17;		135(n1); 139; VIII:318; 325
	400; 401; 737; 777; IV:284n2;	55:1f	VI:16
	285; 287; 343; 615; 853, n80;	55:1ff	II:348n59
	854; 1057n152; 1094n12;	55:2	VI:132
	1097; V:39; 565n1; 666; 672;	55:3	II:132; 479(n35); 480n48; 854;
	684; 686, n234; 691, n283,		V:491; 492; VI:185; 308;
	n284; 692; 694; 695n302; 698,		VIII:367n233; 483;
	n329; 702, n356; 705; 706,		IX:385n86; 386
	n397, n399; 707, n404; 708;	55:4	IV:168n100; 485; VII:763n7
	710, n434; 711, n440, n445;	55:4-7	IV:37
	712, n445, n446; 713; 716;	55:5	II:366(n9); IV:32n14
	915, n84; 918; VI:55; 172;	55:6	II:769; 798
	538; 544; VII:533, n33;	55:7	I:287n56; 510; 633; II:481(n56);
	VIII:60n15; 158; IX:60, n3;		IV:990; V:53
	61; 166n162; 524; 620	55:8	II:97; V:96
53:12a	VI:537; 538; 540	55:8f	I:94; 706n69; IV:1014; V:50;
53:12d	V:692		55; 56; IX:530
53:12e	V:692; VI:537; 540; 543, n39,	55:9	IV:965; 968; V:514; 519
	n40; 544, n48, n49	55:10	IV:546; V:503; VII:542n22
54:1	I:625; II:775; 787(n148),	55:10f	II:624; III:575; IV:96; 98; 99;
	(n151); 824; IV:49; VII:337;		100
	366; VIII:342; IX:669; 673,	55:11	II:679; III:47n33; V:110n7;
	n52; 674, n59		111; 114; VII:696(n42)
54:1-6	IX:669	55:12	II:57n2; 137n14; 402n17; 408;
54:2	VII:370		787(n151); IX:369n89
54:4	IX:203; 445; 586n20	55:13	V:252; 257; 263; VII:211n70;
54:4-6	IX:459		220n137
54:4ff	I:654; IV:1101(n25)	56-66	V:675n124
54:5	IV:330; 332; V:257; VI:1000;	56:1	II:196; 200n41; III:577; 919;
	VII:362		IX:5n19
54:5-8	I:33	56:1-7	VII:5
54:6	IV:685, n7; VI:361; 368; IX:666	56:1-8	V:11; VI:730n22; VII:311
54:7	II:481(n57); IV:539; VII:772;	56:2	IV:365; 366n36; VII:5
	IX:586	56:3	I:266; II:768; V:38(n6); 454;
54:8	II:480n48; IV:330; 332;		455
	V:398(n123); 446; VI:1000;	56:3-5	II:766; III:854
	VII:720	56:3ff	II:768n26; V:11
54:8f	IX:386	56:4	II:768; IV:150; 170
54:8-10	V:405; 408	56:5	V:168; 252; 261; 263; 279;
54:9	II:624n5; IX:586		VIII:343
54:9f	VIII:254	56:6	I:29; 266; II:265; 330;
54:10	II:403; 480n48; III:720; VII:66;		IV:150n25; 219; 220n17;
	290n27; 720; IX:386		V:257; 659n23; 662; 676n124;
54:10f	VIII:10		VIII:346
54:11	III:64; 447; VI:893	56:7	I:90; II:59; 743; 793; III:243;
54:11f	IV:269		488; IV:260; V:121, n10;
54:11ff	V:789		891; VII:311; 809
54:11-14	VIII:254	56:8	III:358(n17); V:121n10;
54:11-17	VII:314		VI:487(n26); VII:805; 842n4
54:12	IV:145; 182; 274n57; 473n11	56:10	I:23n15; VIII:279; 281; IX:125;
54:13	II:165; 405; III:121; IV:427n92;		225
	430n117; V:137; VI:834;	56:10f	III:1101
	IX:514n107	56:11	I:215; V:53; VI:132; 270;
54:14	IX:200		488(n29)
54:16	III:1017n104; 1027; IV:1014;	57:1	II:52; 480n38, (n39); IV:974;
	VI:934; IX:96; 99		IX:385n91
54:16f	VII:359	57:3	IV:730; 731n6
54:17	II:205; 738; III:129; IV:62;	57:3f	VII:538
	V:110; 111; 675	57:4	VII:541
55:1	I:126; II:227; 228; 345n23;	57:4ff	IX:599
	350n71; 351n77; III:991;	57:5	II:377(n21); V:776n16; 777n24;
	IV:368; 389; VI:117n25;		VII:930; 931

57:6	II:467; III:182; 760; VII:533; IX:60n3	58:12	V:136
		58:13	I:90; III:53; VI:470; VII:5
57:7-13	VI:587	58:13f	VII:5
57:8	IX:125n118	58:14	III:773n10; V:877; VI:5; VII:696(n42), n42
57:11	II:752; IV:965; IX:595n7		
57:12	II:637; 645; IX:73	59:1	I:559n2; III:823n2; V:549; VII:970n16; 978; IX:427
57:13	III:773n10; VI:360; 399n425		
57:14	V:49; VI:747; 748; 749; VII:341; 343; 405	59:2	VII:720
		59:2-8	VI:749
57:15	I:94; IV:376n13; 378(n37); V:522n192; VI:362; 368; 401; VII:921; 922; VIII:617; IX:666	59:3	I:721; IV:736
		59:4	III:87; 660; VII:760n8; 761n8
		59:5	II:815; V:571; 573; VII:276n8; 959
57:16	II:443; V:406n181; VI:361; 364; 369n177; 378n235; 453; IX:618	59:6	II:645
		59:7	I:174; II:97; 468; V:53; 85; 86; VII:924; IX:625
57:17	I:287; III:607; 969; V:411; VI:270; VII:720	59:7f	I:706
		59:8	I:705; V:85; 116; 942; VI:628; VII:405n13; 718
57:18	V:777n18; 789		
57:18f	II:402n16	59:9	V:943; VI:194; 726; VII:424n5
57:19	II:405; 415; III:1027; IV:373; 374; VII:700	59:9f	VIII:281
		59:9ff	III:931
57:20	I:151; VI:603n66	59:10	VI:745; 748; 749; 753; VII:424n10; 600; VIII:279
57:20f	II:922		
57:21	II:408; IX:363n29	59:11	IV:372; VI:67(n50); 194; 382n260; 726; VII:978
58:1	I:63; 64; 294; III:701n18; IX:281		
		59:12	I:162
58:1b	I:289	59:13	III:613; VI:10n1; VII:188n7; 760n8; IX:599
58:1ff	IV:928; 935		
58:2	II:195; 200n41; 366(n9); III:170; IV:32; V:55	59:14	I:236; IV:372; VII:343
		59:15b-20	VI:509n57
58:2f	II:645	59:16	I:639; II:196; 352n81; 485; IV:974; V:325; VII:655
58:3	IV:927; VIII:7		
58:3ff	IV:931	59:17	I:608; II:195; 196n14; 210; 319; 320n5; V:297; 309, n9; 310; 315; 404; VII:689n19, n21; 1023
58:4	VI:915; 916; VIII:9; IX:281		
58:4b	IV:983		
58:4f	IV:935; VII:63		
58:4ff	IV:935		
58:4-10	VIII:24	59:18	V:398
58:5	II:743; IV:928; 981(n19), (n20); VII:60; 61n47; 62n48; VIII:7; 24	59:19	II:254; V:257; VI:360; VII:266n7; 269; IX:628
		59:19f	VIII:459n403
58:5f	IV:149n21; 170	59:20	II:927; IV:332; V:861; VI:1002; VII:187(n4); 189; 294; 309; 327; **721-722** (721n13)
58:5-7	IV:983		
58:5ff	VIII:7		
58:6	I:154; 510; 511; IV:328; VII:858, n6	59:20f	VI:1003
		59:21	II:107n6; 126; 129; IV:1107n12; 1111; V:730; VI:130; 363, n155; 367; VII:696, (n45)
58:6f	III:545; VI:16(n31); VIII:24		
58:6ff	II:59	60	V:890; VI:525; **VII:313**
58:6-10a	VII:859	60:1	II:717n104; 927; III:990; V:861; VII:313; IX:318; 327n115
58:7	I:503; 774; II:689; III:728n1; V:20; 134; VI:895n83; VII:106; 108		
		60:1f	VI:937
		60:1-3	IX:319
58:7b	VII:540	60:1ff	I:218; III:239; IV:23; V:862
58:8	I:130; II:240n28	60:1-5	IX:322
58:9	I:627n17; 736; II:798; V:861; VII:261; 858; IX:437; 491	60:2	II:717n104; V:327; 334, n101; VII:313; 428n40
		60:2f	VII:313
58:9f	VI:16(n31)	60:3	II:717n104; III:572; IV:168; V:945; VI:571
58:10	VI:937; VIII:6; 8n22; 24		
58:11	III:789; 991; VI:113; VII:775; VIII:322; IX:597n38; 623		
58:11f	VI:606n94	60:3f	VII:317

60:4	IV:372; VI:183
60:5	II:366(n9); III:572; IV:32n14; VI:277; VIII:178; IX:198; 319
60:5-11	VII:315
60:5-16	VI:414n539
60:6	II:709, n15; 712(n59); 713; IV:264n7; VII:1022; 1023
60:7	II:746; IV:219; 220n17; V:121; IX:60n3
60:8	IV:903; 907; VI:67n47
60:9	II:254; VI:194n144
60:10	I:266; II:481n72; 743; IV:219; V:398(n123); 838; VII:314
60:10ff	IV:167n100; VII:317
60:11	VII:314; IX:58
60:11ff	IX:356n392
60:12	I:396
60:13	II:238; III:239; VII:315; VIII:197
60:14	VI:524; 760n23; VII:294; 314; VIII:7
60:15	IV:685, n7; IX:129n157
60:16	I:646; IV:330; VI:323; VII:977
60:17	II:92; 405(n30); 406; 614; 620; VI:678n177; IX:593
60:18	V:253; VII:973; 1022
60:19	IX:319
60:19f	IV:327n30; VI:937; IX:321n72; 322; 356n392
60:20	VI:42; 306
60:21	I:677; II:638; III:773; 780; 783n32; IV:37
60:22	IV:530; 897n13
61	II:348
61:1	I:102; 103; 510; 511; II:426; 709; 712(n59); 716; 718, n109; 719n112; III:203; 212; 215; 612; 701; 712; V:552n77; 668n79; VI:130; 362; 370; 406n473; 893, n64; 906; VII:350; 922; 923; VIII:6; 9; 13; 282; IX:345n277; **501**; 503; 505; 534; 577; 630
61:1f	II:139; 346; VI:833; VII:594; VIII:294; IX:400n244; 517n135
61:1ff	III:573
61:2	II:59; 743; 745; 948; V:790; 806n40; VI:43n22
61:2f	IV:368
61:3	II:472; VI:42; 361; VII:316; 595; 596
61:4	III:451
61:5	I:267; V:8
61:6	III:34; 41n72; 249; 251; IV:230
61:6ff	V:666n67
61:8	II:126; 196; IV:686
61:10	I:655n46; II:196; 319; III:249; 881; IV:1101n26; 1105; VII:977; IX:363
61:10f	II:195
61:11	VII:540; 542n22; VIII:517
62	VII:314
62:1	IV:23
62:2	III:449; V:254; 263; 326; VI:103; VII:315; 326; 696(n42)
62:2f	V:279
62:3	VII:626
62:4	II:738; III:53; IV:147; VII:315
62:4f	I:654
62:5	I:655n46; II:773n14; IV:1101; 1105; VII:366; IX:363; 468
62:6	VII:314; 873n16; VIII:51; IX:243
62:8	I:639; II:243; 812; V:460n21
62:8f	VII:316
62:9	I:90
62:10	IV:37; 485; V:49; 69n89; VII:269
62:11	IV:697; V:861; VI:778; VII:315; 327; 1013n56; VIII:605n31
62:11f	IV:430
62:12	IV:37, 332; VII:315
63	VIII:368n236
63:1	II:94; III:813; VII:1022, n2
63:1-3	V:400
63:1ff	IV:255; 256
63:1-5	VI:509n57
63:1-6	IV:255; V:400n135; 437n388
63:2	V:941
63:2-6	V:943n14
63:3	I:176; IV:255; 256n9; V:398; 941; VI:284n4; 977; 979; 981n24
63:4	II:945n6; IV:331; 332; 335; V:861
63:5	I:639; 640; V:397; 400; 424; VII:655
63:5f	II:346n33; 352n81; IV:256(n8)
63:6	V:398; 941
63:7	I:460n19; II:175; 479n22, (n31); 480(n46), n48; 787; VI:276, n13; IX:385n91
63:7-19	VII:962n17
63:7-64:11	IV:981(n22)
63:7-64:12	IV:981
63:8	IV:41n50; VII:962n17; 971; VIII:352
63:8f	VII:975
63:9	III:142; IV:7; 332; VII:977; VIII:607; IX:625
63:10	I:98n31; II:815; V:857n4; VI:10n1; 364; 371n193; 391n342
63:10f	I:95; 103; 105; 114
63:10ff	I:91
63:11	I:98n31; IV:871n247; VI:363; 494n83; 500n14; 690; VII:962n17; VIII:368n236
63:12	II:244; VIII:319
63:13	VII:343

63:14	V:98; 102n27; VI:363; VII:962n17; VIII:368n236	65:17	I:678; II:586(n4); III:449; 607; 610; 1027; V:509; 515; 557; 862; IX:297n93; 630
63:15	I:359; II:879; V:328; 404; 506n70; 521; VI:277; VII:550n17	65:17-19	IX:363
		65:17-25	VI:59
63:15f	II:480(n50); V:973; VIII:352	65:18	III:1008; 1027; IX:363
63:16	V:978, n207; 981; 1009n384; VI:1001; VIII:351	65:18a	III:1027
		65:19	I:20; II:773; III:725; VII:296; IX:281; 363
63:17	III:773; IV:981; 1014; V:53; 676n124; 1030; VI:234; 236(n42); IX:248	65:19-25	VII:309
63:18	III:776; V:941	65:20	I:272n15; 320; II:846n103; IV:897n14; 915; V:767(n15); VI:129; VII:316; IX:585
63:19	V:253; 263; 502(n43); 507; 521; 529n261; 530n263; VII:66; VIII:368n236	65:21ff	V:862
64:1 (63:19c, M/S)	V:529n261; VII:66; 962	65:22	II:644; 853; IV:155; V:38; 718; 720n2; 767(n15)
64:1f (63:19f, M/S)	V:480	65:23	III:828; IV:183; VII:562
64:2 (64:1, M/S)	IX:3n7	65:25	I:141; IV:253; 309; 312; V:572n81
64:2f (64:1f, M/S)	VII:198n12		
64:3 (64:2, M/S)	VI:194	66	III:239
64:3f (64:2f, M/S)	III:989	66:1	I:679; III:162; 628; IV:885; 890; V:125, n26; 139; 143; 180; 516; 522; VI:630n53
64:4 (64:3, M/S)	I:756n34; II:641; III:989, n113; 1021; IV:577n1; 583; V:176; 324; 334n98; 557, n134, n135	66:1f	III:116n368; 246; VII:309; 464; VIII:204n132; IX:427
64:4f (64:3f, M/S)	VII:962	66:1ff	III:164; 239
64:5 (64:4, M/S)	VI:233n32; 235(n37)	66:2	IV:139n11; VI:362; 368; 370n181; 463; 650; 696n25; 905n186; VII:922; VIII:10; 262; IX:431; 630
64:6 (64:5, M/S)	II:645; IX:57		
64:7 (64:6, M/S)	II:70; III:499; V:262; VII:720		
64:8 (64:7, M/S)	II:638; III:1012; V:955n49; 971; 981; VI:260; VII:360; VIII:351; 352; IX:472	66:3	I:622; IV:150n25; VI:458n19; IX:60n3
64:9 (64:8, M/S)	IV:1108n24; 1122; V:398; 406n180	66:4	I:288; IV:146; 149n21; V:631
64:11 (64:10, M/S)	I:90; II:755n3	66:5	V:253; 274; 333
64:12 (64:11, M/S)	I:359; VIII:8	66:6	II:811; VIII:529; IX:281; 298; 674
65:1	II:687; 769; III:1063	66:6f	IX:674
65:2	I:268; V:53; 93; VI:10n1, n4; 11; 570; IX:431	66:6-9	VIII:363n200
		66:7	II:655; IX:669; 670
65:3	II:11	66:7ff	IX:670
65:4	IV:736; VI:458n19	66:8	V:324; VII:294; 316
65:5	IV:888; V:399, n127; 412	66:9	V:960; VII:880; 881n42; VIII:361
65:6	I:620		
65:6f	III:824	66:10	III:837; V:722; VI:42; IX:363n27; 366
65:7	I:117n7; II:645		
65:8	IV:312n3; V:662; 676n124	66:10ff	V:862
65:9	IV:155; 183; V:662; 676n124	66:10-15	VII:314
65:11	V:967; VII:311; VIII:214n43; 240	66:11	V:104; 108; 777n17; 790; 820; 877
65:12	I:223; 640; IV:150n25; VII:936; IX:130n161	66:12	II:405; V:777n17; 790; VI:597n17; VII:317n120
65:13	II:228; IV:843; VI:16; 135n4	66:13	I:33n67; III:838; IV:642n6; V:646; 777n17; 790; 820; 971n142; 973n153; VII:315; VIII:352
65:13f	IX:363		
65:13-15	V:676n124		
65:13ff	V:662		
65:14	III:606; IV:843; VI:361; 370, n181; VII:922n17	66:14	II:811; III:239; 612; V:393(n67); 398; 411; 676n124; 680n172; VII:171; IX:198n47; 363; 623
65:15	III:448; 449; IV:183; 155; V:254; 279; 460; VI:103; 132, n3		
65:16	I:233n1; 249; 337; 756n34; III:142; 612; VI:185n101	66:15	II:446; 624; V:862; VI:944
65:16-19	VI:42n13	66:15f	VI:398(417); 936

JEREMIAH

2:26	III:89; 575; VI:805; 806
2:26f	V:968; VII:352
2:27	I:31n60; IV:269n9; V:968; VII:272; 724; 970n16
2:27f	VII:975
2:28	III:87(n107); 1074; VII:307; 311
2:29	I:273; 274n23
2:30	II:50; IV:253n19; 523; V:606; 611; 940; VI:805n166; 834n348; IX:198
2:31	IV:96
2:32	III:880; V:832
2:33	I:23n18; IX:125n118
2:35	VII:720
2:35-37	V:403n158
2:36	I:189; II:738
2:37	II:523(n37); III:831n12; V:110n6; 111; 112n12
3	V:973
3:1	IV:645n9; VI:313; 584; VIII:564n25
3:1-4:4	VI:587
3:2	IV:645n9; VI:585; 587; VIII:564n25
3:3	VI:747; 748; 749; IX:625
3:4	I:32; 487; V:834; VIII:351
3:5	V:405; IX:238
3:6	III:88; V:37; VI:584; 587
3:7	IV:154n48
3:8	IV:730; VI:584
3:8f	IV:731
3:9	II:430; IV:269n9; 729; VI:587
3:10	VII:720; 724; IX:628
3:11	II:212; **IX:620**
3:12	I:344n1; V:405; 411; 433; 490n16; VI:571; 776(n45); IX:386, n96
3:12f	II:480n47
3:13	I:154; 274n23; 698; 704; V:6n33; 37; VII:187(n5); IX:284
3:14	I:512; III:1098; IV:41n50; VII:366; 725; VIII:351; 352; IX:290
3:14-18	VII:314n109
3:15	VI:487(n29); 488; VII:314; 493
3:16	II:602; 946(n14); III:162n17; 612; V:263; 557; 862; VII:316
3:17	II:946(n15); III:162; V:279n232; 1023; VI:551; VII:296; 315; 316; 327; IX:630
3:18	II:946(n14); III:773n8; V:862
3:19	I:32; III:159n18; 772; 775; IV:145; 183; V:777n19; **972-973** (972n144, n148); VIII:351; 352; 355
3:19c	V:972n148
3:20	VI:313; VIII:158
3:21	I:158; II:785; III:725; V:52; IX:281

3:21-4:2	IV:981
3:22	III:203; 312; IV:996; V:973; VII:725, n12; VIII:351; 352
3:22b	IV:986
3:23	IV:986; VII:975; IX:599
3:25	IV:1108n16; IX:284
4	II:945n7
4:1	I:32; 598; IV:987
4:3	IV:325n17; 900; VII:539; 541; 547
4:3f	VII:308; 312
4:4	I:29; 540; III:612n21; 613; V:398(n121); 403n155; 405; 407; 412; 556n123; VI:73; 74; **77;** 563; 935; VII:167; IX:628; 633n95
4:5	IV:530; VII:78; 262
4:5ff	III:929n21
4:6	VII:447
4:6f	VIII:199
4:7	VII:447
4:8	III:837; 841; V:173n6; 398(n121); 400; 407; VII:720
4:9	II:459; III:34; V:862; VI:805; 806
4:10	I:384; II:45; 46; 404; III:1059; VI:1
4:11	II:946(n15); VI:368; 399; VII:296; 308
4:12	IV:1114; VI:300; 360
4:13	III:336; IV:903; VII:447
4:14	I:537; II:97; IV:301; VII:308; 977; VIII:320
4:15	IX:281
4:16	IV:372; IX:281
4:17	I:269
4:18	V:50
4:19	III:606; VII:76; 79; IX:617
4:19ff	I:439
4:20	VII:370
4:21	IX:281
4:22	I:276; 704; III:485; V:970n140; VII:477(n89), (n92); 483; VIII:351; 352; IX:233n78
4:23	IX:356n388
4:23f	VII:430n48
4:23-26	V:509
4:24	V:480
4:26	V:398(n121); 409
4:27	VIII:65
4:28	III:836; IV:627; 989; V:469; VI:42; VII:720
4:29	III:968; IV:902; VI:101; VII:447; IX:280
4:30	I:22; 23n17; III:812; 867; 880
4:30f	VII:312
4:31	I:509; II:790(n184); III:141; VI:874; VII:307n93; 600; IX:669
5:1	III:928; VII:296; 311
5:2	V:461
5:3	II:50; IV:515; V:606; 611;

	VI:95; 190; VII:611; 724; VIII:63
5:4	II:284; IV:166; VI:893
5:4f	III:1015; V:52; VI:324
5:4ff	III:120
5:5	II:898; IV:530
5:6	I:287; II:338; IV:309; VI:281; VII:187(n4)
5:7	III:88; IV:730; 731; 985(n47); V:459; VI:585; VIII:110, n8
5:9	II:443; 602
5:10	VIII:65
5:11	VIII:158
5:12	III:1075; IV:161; V:326; VI:15(n24); IX:595n6; 598
5:13	VI:360; IX:628
5:13f	VI:805; 810
5:14	VI:935; VII:696(n45)
5:15	VII:447
5:17	VI:191; VII:752(n10), n15, (n16)
5:18	II:946(n14); VIII:65
5:19	IV:985(n47); V:9; 10
5:20	II:425
5:21	I:220; 276; IV:833; 834; 835; V:327; 548n48
5:22	II:752; IV:1013; V:743; VIII:28; IX:201n62; 669n22
5:22-24	III:1005; 1006
5:23	VI:10(n2)
5:24	IV:1013; VI:133; 300; IX:201n62; 237; 676n12
5:25-31	VI:324
5:26	V:593; 594; VII:730n9
5:26f	VI:324
5:26-31	VI:324
5:28	III:927; 929n24; V:110; 403n157; 488n4; 809; VI:551n31; IX:445
5:29	II:443; 602
5:30	II:450; III:34n35
5:31	VI:798; 805
6:1	V:469; VII:78; 208; 263; 269; 296
6:3	III:917(n14); VII:370
6:4	I:92; VII:395
6:6	III:141
6:6f	VII:311
6:7	IV:518; VI:524
6:8	V:606
6:9	IV:197
6:10	III:1075; IV:512; V:556n123; VI:77; 80n56; 81n69
6:11	IV:403n99; 814n113; 915; V:393n69; 394; 646; VII:803
6:12	IX:427
6:13	III:575n21; IV:649; VI:241; 269; 270; 805; 812
6:13f	VI:805
6:13ff	III:575
6:14	II:402n16; 404, (n28); III:203; IV:161
6:15	II:607; III:461
6:16	I:113; II:769; V:52; IX:639
6:17	VII:78; 414; IX:281
6:19	I:287; III:477
6:20	II:59; 743; V:403(n156); IX:57
6:21	I:490; VII:341; 343, n23
6:22	I:679; II:334; IV:33
6:22f	VII:447
6:23	II:480n51; VII:312
6:24	III:142; IX:669
6:26	III:837; 838; 841; 850n124; IV:739, n7; VI:42, (n9), n9; VII:59; 60
6:27	VI:811
6:27f	VI:935
6:27-29	VII:312
6:27ff	I:561n2; II:257
6:28	V:741; VI:571; VII:405n13; IX:99
6:29	III:659; VI:934
6:30	IV:149n19
7	VIII:197
7:1-15	VII:310
7:2	II:789; VI:760n23
7:3	VIII:197
7:3f	**VII:319**
7:3ff	I:540; III:573
7:4	II:523; IV:93; 161; V:398; VI:191; VII:304; VIII:218, n19; IX:74n9
7:6	III:140; V:845n17; VI:571; IX:446
7:7	III:773; VIII:197
7:8	IV:93; VI:191; IX:73
7:8ff	IV:260
7:9	III:754; IV:99; 1039; V:461; VI:571
7:10	IV:161; V:253; 263; VII:643
7:11	III:243; IV:258; 260, n22; 1040; V:263
7:12	VII:388; VIII:197
7:13	I:218; II:645; IV:1112; V:809
7:14	V:263; VIII:197
7:15	VI:991
7:16	II:683; 798(n249); V:406; VI:811
7:18	II:467; III:88; 1074; IV:63; V:506n69; VI:934; VII:531n22; 532; 705; 709
7:19-22	V:809
7:20	V:398(n121); 409; 410; 412; VIII:197
7:21f	III:183
7:21-28	V:403(n156)
7:22	III:572; IV:1040
7:23	IV:37; V:51; IX:284; 291
7:24	III:478
7:25	II:425; V:665(n52); 676; VI:805
7:25f	III:992
7:26	I:92; IV:167; V:1029; 1030
7:27	V:1026n4
7:28	II:5; V:606, n57; 611; VI:190;

	IX:284
7:29	III:150; 151; V:398(n121); VI:991
7:30	III:498; IV:645n9; V:263; VIII:28
7:30ff	III:929n21
7:31	III:607; V:481n75; VI:935; IX:630
7:32	I:657, n4; II:946(n13); VII:936; VIII:199
7:33	IV:892(n9); VII:1045
7:34	IV:1099n1; IX:281; 291
8:1	II:946(n15); VI:805; 806
8:2	I:28n45; II:33; III:837; 839; 841; V:506(n69)
8:2ff	I:651n22
8:3	IV:149n20; 195; 196; 197; 207; VII:970; VIII:193
8:4	IV:984, n41
8:5	I:287; VII:308; 724
8:6	IV:989; 990; 999n142; V:469; VIII:233
8:7	I:698n36; II:176; III:1011n78; IV:1013; V:104; VI:67; VII:731n11, n14
8:8	IV:97; 523, n1; 1039
8:8f	VII:482; 484
8:10	VI:270; 805
8:10f	VI:805
8:11	II:404(n28); IV:97n110; 161
8:12	VII:344
8:13	VI:752, (n16)
8:13-9:24	IV:847n121; VII:521n389
8:14	VI:137n19; 159(n3)
8:15	I:14; VI:194; VII:562
8:16	VII:198n14; IX:249n26; 281
8:17	V:571; 573; 576
8:18-23	IV:614
8:19	I:569(n23); II:382(n6); IV:372; VII:309; IX:281
8:20	VII:970
8:22	III:201
9:1 (8:23, M/S)	VI:113
9:2 (9:1, M/S)	IV:730; 731
9:2-26 (9, M/S)	III:153
9:3 (9:2, M/S)	I:721
9:3-6 (9:2-5, M/S)	I:698
9:4 (9:3, M/S)	V:663n42
9:5 (9:4, M/S)	I:158; 236; V:632; VII:724
9:7 (9:6, M/S)	II:257; VI:949
9:8 (9:7, M/S)	I:721; II:418
9:9 (9:8, M/S)	II:366(n9); 602; IV:32
9:9ff (9:8ff, M/S)	III:929n21
9:10 (9:9, M/S)	III:150; 151; 153; 725n1; 837, n55; 840; 842n83; IX:281
9:11 (9:10, M/S)	V:155
9:12 (9:11, M/S)	VII:493; 696(n42)
9:14 (9:13, M/S)	III:478; 1058
9:15 (9:14, M/S)	VI:123n7; 124n8; 137n19; 159(n3)
9:17 (9:16, M/S)	III:150; 838; VII:483; 497n202
9:17f (9:16f, M/S)	III:150; 151
9:18 (9:17, M/S)	III:151; 837
9:19 (9:18, M/S)	III:839; 840
9:20 (9:19, M/S)	II:51; 52; III:150; 151; 838; V:554n100; VI:313; VII:696(n42)
9:20f (9:19f, M/S)	III:840
9:22 (9:21, M/S)	II:33; IV:892(n9)
9:23 (9:22, M/S)	VIII:224n61
9:23f (9:22f, M/S)	III:646; 649; 653; 928; VII:496; 526n415
9:24 (9:23, M/S)	II:479(n24), (n25); 482n90; III:53; 928; VII:890(n19); IX:383; 386
9:25 (9:24, M/S)	I:226; 540; II:602; 946(n13)
9:26 (9:25, M/S)	III:607; 612; IV:635; V:556n123; VI:74; 75n17; 77; 78n37; 80n56; 81; VII:109; 129n248; 215; IX:628
10:1-16	I:569n24
10:2	IV:402; V:51n31; 504; VII:211; IX:198n47
10:3	V:51n31
10:3ff	VII:360n7
10:3-9	II:377(n25)
10:6	III:351; V:258
10:6f	IX:201n62
10:7	I:569(n24); II:367; V:272; VII:489
10:8	IV:835; VII:890n16
10:9	VII:482; 484; 497n202
10:10	I:201; III:571; V:399; VII:66
10:10ff	I:569(n24)
10:10-16	II:850(n138)
10:11f	III:1005n48
10:12	III:1008; 1009; 1012; V:502(n40); 890; VII:477(n91); 489; IX:225
10:12f	VII:499n215
10:12-16	III:1013
10:13	IV:902; 906; VI:277; 360
10:14	I:700; IV:835; VI:360
10:15	II:607; III:88; 461; V:631
10:16	II:822; III:773n8; 884n60; 1005n48; V:252; 257; VI:256; 257
10:17	IV:183; VIII:582n102
10:18	III:142
10:20	VII:370
10:21	IV:949; VI:487(n29)
10:22	VII:731; IX:281
10:23	V:50
10:23-25	II:798(n248)
10:24	V:172; 406n180; 408; 607
10:25	II:371; III:100n217; 499; 1063; V:117; 262; 324; 399; 404(n164); 410n201
11:1ff	VI:810
11:2	VII:338
11:2f	II:126
11:4	III:773; VII:642
11:5	I:233n1; 335; III:773; IV:552; VI:186; 293; VII:642

11:6	I:344n1; II:126	13:9f	VII:308
11:7	IV:1108n16	13:10	I:244; II:268; V:110n7; 291;
11:8	VI:551n31		VI:551n31; 690; VII:405
11:9	VII:858	13:10f	V:304
11:10	I:154; 211; II:126; V:291;	13:11	III:646; V:252; 261; 263; 305
	VII:724	13:12	VI:287
11:10f	III:477	13:13	III:162; VI:150(n19); 287; 805;
11:11	III:899		806
11:12	VII:970n16; 975	13:14	II:99
11:13	VII:311; VIII:28	13:15	VIII:300
11:14	II:798(n249); 807	13:16	II:241(n33); 244; VI:194; 745;
11:15	VI:530; VII:106; IX:168n184		748; 753; VII:395; 428
11:16	III:490n6; VI:74; 936; IX:281	13:17	VI:500, (n9); 501n22; VIII:300
11:17	VII:541	13:18	III:411; VII:626; VIII:7
11:18	I:718	13:19	VIII:72, n20
11:18ff	I:440; IV:430(n118)	13:20	VI:690
11:18-21	VI:834n348	13:21	II:602; IV:426, n84; IX:670
11:19	I:341; III:482; IV:285; 289n18;	13:22	I:154; 269; II:32; IV:731
	V:672; VI:551; 690; VII:533;	13:23	IV:402; 987
	930n25; 936	13:24	VI:360; IX:57
11:20	II:175; 219; 257, n8; 445;	13:25	III:760; 776n15; IX:599
	798(n250); III:607; 612; 613;	13:26f	IV:731
	814; IV:911; IX:626	13:27	I:598; IV:730; 731n6
11:21	V:260n134; VI:798	14:1-12	V:1025
11:22	II:602; VI:15(n24)	14:2	III:661; VI:42, n9; 925n44
11:23	II:607; IV:197; 198	14:3	VIII:318
12:1	II:176; V:53; 110; 111	14:4	II:636
12:1-3	II:798(n250)	14:5	III:1060
12:1-5	IV:614	14:6	V:284; VI:360
12:1-6	V:669n87	14:7	I:268; 287; V:257
12:2	IV:911; VI:990; VII:541; 697	14:7-9	II:798(n248); V:406; 809
12:3	I:123; V:672n101; 868n57;	14:8	I:680n12; IV:583; 584; V:847;
	VII:936, n8; IX:627		848; 852n64; VI:631; VII:976
12:4	V:50n29; VI:42	14:9	IV:331; V:263; 847; VII:974
12:5	II:523n36; VI:191; VIII:229	14:10	II:738; V:110; 111; 112n12
12:6	VI:187; 197n149	14:11	I:14
12:7	V:125n27; IX:168n184	14:11f	II:798(n249)
12:7-9	I:32	14:12	I:30n54; II:738; 794; IV:928;
12:7ff	V:671n97		VI:140n50; 996; VIII:63;
12:7-10	III:773		IX:65n2
12:8	IX:281; 282	14:12f	VI:15(n24)
12:9	IV:258; 260n22	14:13	II:45; 46; 398n2; 404; V:326;
12:10	V:942		809; VI:15(n24); 805;
12:11	VIII:154		VIII:197
12:12	II:404(n28); VII:106	14:13f	VI:805; 806
12:13	III:647; 760; V:903n54	14:13ff	III:575
12:14	III:773n8; VI:551; VII:824	14:14	III:607; 701n18; V:260; 261;
12:15	II:481(n57); III:773n8; VII:724		370; VI:784; 798; 799; 805
12:15ff	V:139	14:14f	VI:805; IX:599
12:16	II:137; IV:37; 401; V:48n22;	14:15	III:701n18; V:260; VI:798; 805;
	177n8; 260; 459		996n24; VIII:63; 197
12:17	VII:724	14:15f	VI:15(n24)
13:1	V:304	14:16	V:49; VI:798
13:1ff	V:749(n31)	14:18	VI:15n24; 805
13:2	V:304	14:19	I:14; II:257; III:203; VI:194;
13:4	III:958; V:304; 496		VII:294; 307; 308; 309
13:5	III:958	14:19-22	II:798(n248); V:809
13:6f	V:304	14:20	I:293
13:7	V:110n7; VI:596; VIII:299n40;	14:21	I:126; 246; III:161; 162;
	IX:96		VII:296; 315; 777
13:8	IV:96	14:22	II:377(n20); III:1006; 1013;
13:9	VIII:299; 300		VI:132; 726

	1045; VI:806; VII:486	21:1-10	VII:296n19; 312
18:18ff	III:575; VIII:407	21:2	III:35; V:839n9
18:19	II:175	21:4	V:293; VII:359n5; 745
18:19-23	II:798(n251)	21:5	V:396; 400; 410
18:20	II:790; V:400; 406; VII:720	21:7	II:480n51; IV:197; VI:15(n24);
18:20-23	V:809		996
18:21	VI:15(n24); IX:445, n46	21:8	II:845n95; 854; V:52; 54; 55,
18:22	III:959; IV:257; V:593; 594;		n38; 59; VI:772
	IX:99; 625	21:9	V:54; VI:15(n24); VII:745
18:23	I:490; III:302; 304, n18; V:410;	21:10	VI:776(n45); 934; VII:655
	VI:745; VII:344	21:12	III:927; 942; V:1017n6; VI:563;
19:1	II:567n31; VI:258		935; VII:167
19:2	I:344n1	21:13	V:155
19:3-6	VIII:198n73	21:14	VI:551n31; 935; 936; 942n73
19:4	I:172n6	22:1-5	IX:444n31; 461
19:6	I:657; II:946(n13); VII:936	22:3	III:140; V:488n4; VIII:198n73;
19:7	VII:929n24		IX:445
19:8	V:632n10; VII:451	22:4	III:337n4
19:10	VI:798	22:5	V:125n27; VII:329
19:11	III:1012; VII:296n19	22:6	I:481
19:11a	VI:798	22:7	III:858; IV:177; VI:936
19:12	VIII:198n73	22:8	VII:296n19
19:13	II:467; V:506(n69);	22:8f	VII:307n91
	VII:531n22; 705; 709	22:10	III:725n25; 838n58
19:14	VI:798	22:11f	VIII:194
19:15	V:1029; 1030; VI:522; VII:296,	22:12	VIII:193
	n19; 307	22:13	IV:697
20:1	VI:798	22:15	III:927; 928
20:1ff	I:440	22:16	I:698; VI:39; 913; VIII:9
20:1-7	VII:838	22:17	V:376; VI:269
20:2	I:562; IV:771n60; VI:834n348;	22:18	I:145; III:831n1; 838, n64; 839;
	VIII:33		1060
20:3	III:490n6	22:19	III:840; V:284; VI:991
20:3f	V:254	22:20	I:23(n18); IX:281
20:5	VIII:580n78	22:21	VI:170n2; IX:284
20:6	III:701n18; VI:570; 798; IX:599	22:22	I:23(n18); VI:360; 487(n29);
20:7	I:384; III:910; IV:796; 798		IX:125, n120
20:7-9	IV:614	22:23	IX:377n36; 378n50; 670
20:7ff	I:439; IV:97; VIII:407	22:24	VII:946
20:7-13	II:798(n251)	22:26	VI:991
20:7-18	III:576	22:27	II:778; VII:719
20:8	III:700; 701; V:631	22:28	VI:88; 89; VII:359
20:9	II:719; III:575; 970;	22:29	VIII:218, n19
	V:260n134; 262;	22:30	I:620; 744; III:162; V:110;
	VII:494n191; 880		VIII:517
20:9a	IV:97n111	23:1	VI:500n11; 690
20:9b	IV:97n111	23:1f	VI:500; 690
20:10	II:229; 407n37; 408; III:814;	23:1-4	VI:487(n29)
	VIII:141	23:2	II:443; 601; VI:488(n31); 551;
20:11	II:229; IV:426, n84; 949;		563; 690
	VII:777	23:2f	VI:500(n14)
20:11-13	IV:614	23:3	II:57, n2; IV:32n12; 196; 197;
20:12	IV:911		204; VI:487(n28); 488(n32)
20:13	I:177; II:788n155; VI:39; 893;	23:3ff	IV:205; 209
	896	23:4	I:369; VI:488
20:14ff	I:440; IV:430n120; V:668n75;	23:5	I:352; 568n18; II:187; 946(n13);
	671n97		947; III:932; IV:878;
20:14-18	IV:614		V:687n250; 793n157; VI:988;
20:15	II:707; 712(n59); VIII:345n69		VIII:480; 605n29; IX:524;
20:16	IV:627		568n481
20:18	III:828	23:5f	I:567; **IX:507;** 508
21:1-7	V:398	23:5ff	IV:201n25; 204

25:34-36
  (32:20-22 (34-36), S) VI:487(n29); 488n29; 499n8
25:35 (32:21 (35), S) VII:971; 973; 978(n50); 979
25:38 (32:24 (38), S) IV:196n8; V:392n60; VII:369

**Numbers in Parenthesis throughout remainder
of Jeremiah refer to Septuagint references**

26(33)	VI:806
26(33)-29(36)	VI:812
26(33):1ff	I:440
26(33):2	IX:481
26(33):3	III:477; IV:285; 986(n56); 987; VI:563; VII:720
26(33):3-5	IV:986
26(33):4	IV:1046; V:51
26(33):5	V:665(n52); 676; 679n167; VI:805
26(33):6	V:125n27; VII:296
26(33):6-12	VII:310
26(33):7	VI:812
26(33):7f	VI:805
26(33):7ff	III:575, n21
26(33):8	VI:812
26(33):8-11	VI:834n348
26(33):9	VI:798; VII:296
26(33):11	VI:798; 812
26(33):12	VI:798; VII:296
26(33):13	III:477; IV:1121; V:50; VII:366; 715; IX:284
26(33):14	IX:74
26(33):15	I:243; IV:575
26(33):16	VI:812
26(33):17	III:529, n90; VI:658; VII:803; 804
26(33):18	III:239; VI:798; VII:296
26(33):19	III:477
26(33):20	VI:798
26(33):20ff	IV:486
26(33):20-23	VI:834n348
26(33):23	IV:525; V:14; VIII:346
26(33):24f	II:169
27(34)-29(36)	III:575; V:664
27(34):2ff	V:749(n31)
27(34):3ff	IV:1014
27(34):4	II:233
27(34):5	II:293; III:1005; 1006; 1012; V:890
27(34):6	II:602; 897; V:664
27(34):8	II:897; VI:15(n24)
27(34):9	III:575n21; VI:805; 806; 812; VIII:551
27(34):9f	V:230; VI:805
27(34):10	VI:798
27(34):13	VI:15(n24)
27(34):14	VI:798; 805
27(34):14-16	VI:805
27(34):15	VI:798; 805
27(34):16	VI:798; 805
27(34):18	VI:811; VII:296
27(34):19	III:854n11
27(34):22	VIII:193n45
28(35)	II:404; III:575; IV:167; VI:806; 807
28(35):1	VI:812; VIII:132
28(35):1-17	V:398
28(35):2	II:897
28(35):3	VII:721n8
28(35):3f	VIII:197
28(35):4	II:897
28(35):6	I:233n1; VI:186, n104; 798
28(35):8	VI:798; 805
28(35):8f	VI:807; **840**
28(35):9	I:233; II:404; III:575; 822n1; IV:98; VI:798; 805
28(35):11	II:897; VI:810
28(35):12	IV:96
28(35):14	I:639; II:897
28(35):15	VI:805
28(35):16	VI:805; 810
28(35):17	I:700
29(36)-51(28)	V:843
29(36):1	I:617(n5); VI:658; 812
29(36):2	III:853
29(36):4	II:680
29(36):6	VIII:342
29(36):7	II:402(n19)
29(36):8	III:435; VI:1; 805; 812; VIII:551
29(36):8f	V:230; VI:805
29(36):8-10	VI:805
29(36):9	V:260; 261; VI:798, (n125); 805
29(36):10	II:602; VI:288; 293; 819; VII:313; VIII:194; IX:505
29(36):11	II:405; 523n34, (n40); III:477; 575; IV:285; 286
29(36):13	I:218; II:769; 790n186; VI:193n139; IX:628
29(36):13f	II:798
29(36):14	VIII:193n45; IX:9n15
29(36):17	VI:15(n24); VII:752
29(36):19	V:665(n52); VI:805
29(36):20	II:244
29(36):21	I:634; VI:798
29(36):21f	VI:805
29(36):22	V:460
29(36):23	IV:483; 730; VI:526; 805; IX:481
29(36):25	V:259
29(36):26	II:454; 503; III:1075; IV:360n4; V:259; VI:798
29(36):26f	VI:798; 806
29(36):27	IV:293
29(36):28	IV:373
29(36):30	IV:96
29(36):31	VI:798; 805
29(36):32	II:602
30(37)	III:931
30f(37f)	II:124
30(37):2	I:745n14; IX:481
30(37):3	VII:719
30(37):5	II:404(n28); III:5; IX:198n49; 204; 281
30(37):5f	IX:670
30(37):6	IV:47; VII:971; IX:624

30(37):7	VII:605; IX:586	31(38):23	I:388
30(37):7f	IX:670	31(38):24	II:228
30(37):8	V:9	31(38):25	II:227; 228; IV:546; VI:16, n29
30(37):9	I:369; VIII:254; IX:509	31(38):26	III:434
30(37):10	V:662n35, n41; 677; 679(n156);	31(38):27	II:946(n13); VII:539; 541
	680n175, n176; IX:203	31(38):28	II:338; III:411
30(37):11	V:406n180; 607	31(38):29	II:123n70; 946(n14)
30(37):14	I:23(n18); II:687; V:607;	31(38):29f	III:573; V:646; VIII:291(n150)
	VI:281; VII:610; 1100	31(38):30	I:295n89
30(37):16	II:692; VI:281; IX:63n4	31(38):31	II:106; 946(n13), (n16); 951;
30(37):17	III:203; VII:539		III:448; V:129; 720n13;
30(37):18	VII:725		VIII:64, n5
30(37):19	V:627; VI:264	31(38):31f	II:124; VI:324
30(37):20	II:602; III:140; IV:483	31(38):31-33	VIII:64n5
30(37):21	VII:720; 725; IX:509n67	31(38):31ff	I:174; 540; II:126; 127; 128;
30(37):23	V:399, n130; 410; 411;		129; 130; 133; 468; III:275;
	VI:399n425		449; 576; IV:201n25; 204;
30(37):24	II:946(n11); V:172; 409;		621; 1041; 1079; V:129;
	VI:293; VIII:53		862(n16); VI:534; VII:908
31(38)	II:228; 584; III:282; 931	31(38):31-34	I:304; II:132; III:220; IV:676;
31(38):1	II:946(n15); IX:586		V:720, n13; 767(n15);
31(38):1-3	V:403n154		VI:470; VIII:254
31(38):2	IV:204; VII:562	31(38):32	IV:9; 577; VI:460; 464;
31(38):3	I:32; II:480n48; 503; V:333;		VII:366; IX:430
	IX:386	31(38):33	I:29; 743; 766; 770; II:124; 646;
31(38):4	V:137n1; 627; 833, n45;		III:606; 612; IV:36; 37;
	VII:803; 805		345n25; 497; 965; 966, n12;
31(38):6	III:493; IV:205; VII:294; 310		987; 1001; V:1026;
31(38):7	II:787(n148); IV:197; 204; 205;		IX:274n231; 626
	214; VII:978	31(38):33f	II:129; VII:722
31(38):8	I:679; III:529; V:585; 896n2;	31(38):33ff	III:1015
	VIII:280n71; 282n84	31(38):34	I:145n7; 153; 154; 304; 705;
31(38):9	I:32n66; III:725; IV:41n50;		III:121; 301; 737; IV:427n92;
	V:53; 777; 790; 973, n150;		650n13; V:117; VI:526
	978n206; 1006n365;	31(38):35	VIII:108
	VI:235(n37); 236, (n42);	31(38):35f	III:1005; 1006n53; IV:1013
	873; 874n15; 875; VIII:111;	31(38):35ff	III:1011n78; VII:429n47
	318; 351	31(38):36f	VII:539n10
31(38):10	II:641; IV:160; 281;	31(38):37	III:1005; 1006n53; IV:36
	VI:487(n28); 488(n32);	31(38):38	II:946(n13); VI:524
	IX:237	31(38):38-40	VII:307n91; 314
31(38):11	IV:331; 332n10	31(38):39	IV:182
31(38):12	II:787(n150); VI:16; IX:632	31(38):40	III:337
31(38):13	V:820; VI:42; VII:803; 805	32(39):1ff	IV:98
31(38):14	II:228; IV:546	32(39):2	VII:881n38, n40
31(38):15	III:46n25; 151; 153; 220; 726;	32(39):3	VI:798; VII:312n101
	V:116; 778; VI:834; IX:281	32(39):4	V:325; VI:771n19; VII:980;
31(38):15f	III:725		IX:625
31(38):16	II:647; IV:697	32(39):5	V:110
31(38):16f	II:523(n40)	32(39):6-15	VIII:180n69
31(38):17	II:523n34; IV:365n33	32(39):7	III:925n12; IV:330; V:960
31(38):18	V:116; 607; VII:716n3; 724	32(39):8	III:925n12; VIII:341
31(38):18f	IV:990	32(39):9	III:220; 991
31(38):18-20	V:790; 973, n152; 974	32(39):10	I:744; II:896; IV:483; 512
31(38):18ff	IV:990	32(39):10f	VII:940n13; 945
31(38):19	III:837; 845n105; IV:989;	32(39):12ff	IV:429
	VII:600	32(39):15	III:1027
31(38):20	I:22n12; 32(n66); II:480n50;	32(39):17	I:640; II:293; 398n2; III:959;
	IV:41n50; V:408; 646; 973;		967n24; 1005n48
	VIII:351; 352; 354	32(39):18	III:824; VIII:343; IX:383; 467
31(38):21	III:607; VII:294n1; 720	32(39):19	V:53; 264n144
31(38):22	III:1008; VII:972	32(39):20	III:572; VII:212; IX:473

37(44):10	II:446; IV:197; VII:370	42(49):2-5	III:95n163
37(44):12	VII:307n91	42(49):3	V:53
37(44):14	IX:598	42(49):5	I:234; IV:483; V:459; VI:185
37(44):15	VI:123; VII:886; 887n15	42(49):6	IX:284
37(44):15f	VI:834n348	42(49):7ff	IV:98
37(44):17	II:686	42(49):10	III:411; VII:715
37(44):18	I:158	42(49):11	VII:775; IX:203
37(44):19	V:627; VI:798	42(49):12	II:480n51
37(44):20	II:785(n123); IX:379	42(49):13	II:50; IX:284
38(45):1	V:584n12	42(49):14	IX:281
38(45):1ff	I:440	42(49):15	IV:197; 205n36
38(45):2	VI:15(n24); 996	42(49):16	VI:15(n24)
38(45):4	II:402(n19); 407; VI:808	42(49):17	III:646n6; IV:196; 197; 205n36;
38(45):4-6	VI:834n348		VI:15(n24); VII:970; 978n48;
38(45):6	VI:455; VIII:341		979; VIII:154
38(45):7	II:766; III:854n11	42(49):18	I:450(n6); VII:312; VIII:194
38(45):7-13	I:27n37	42(49):19	IV:196; 197; 205n36; 1108n24
38(45):9	V:449; VI:118(n10)	42(49):21	IX:284
38(45):11	V:718	42(49):22	I:631(n21); VI:15(n24); 996
38(45):12	V:718	43(50):2	VIII:301
38(45):13	II:503	43(50):3	IV:429
38(45):16	III:1005n48; 1072n186	43(50):5	IV:196; 197; 205n36
38(45):18	VII:970n16	43(50):6	IV:916
38(45):19	V:239; 631	43(50):10	V:664
38(45):20	II:845n92; IV:678	43(50):12	VI:936
38(45):21	II:28n9; 29	44(51):3	VI:125
38(45):22	II:407n37; 418; IV:197;	44(51):4	IV:686; V:665(n52); 676;
	VI:626n32		679n167; VI:805
38(45):24-27	IX:598	44(51):6	V:410; 412
38(45):26	II:785(n123); IX:379	44(51):7	III:478; 858; IV:197; 198;
38(45):28	IX:585		205n36; V:646
39(46):3	IV:196; VI:961	44(51):8	III:858; VI:125
39:6	VII:930	44(51):9	II:644; III:478
39:7	VIII:280	44(51):11f	VI:776n45
39:8	VII:810	44(51):12	IV:196; 197; 205n36;
39:10	IV:197; VI:888		VI:15(n24)
39:11	IX:427	44(51):13	II:602; VI:15(n24); VII:312
39:13	II:766; VI:961	44(51):14	II:522; 778; IV:196; 197; 198;
39(46):15	VII:880; 881n40		205n36; V:843; VII:970, n16;
39(46):17	IX:198n47		978n48; 979, n53
39(46):18	VI:191; 192; VII:979	44(51):15	III:528; 529, n90; 530n90;
40(47):3	IX:284		VII:803; 804n27
40(47):4	IV:328	44(51):15ff	VI:814
40(47):6	IV:197; 205n36	44(51):15-18	VI:13n6
40(47):7	VI:888	44(51):17	V:506n69; VII:531n22; IX:485
40(47):10	VII:752n15	44(51):17ff	III:88
40(47):11	IV:195; 197; 205n36	44(51):18	VI:15(n24); 996; VII:531n22
40(47):14	VI:186	44(51):19	VII:531n22
40(47):15	IV:196; 197; 205n36	44(51):21	III:612; IX:630
41(48):1	II:689; VII:539n10	44(51):22	I:598; IX:57
41(48):4	IV:897(n15)	44(51):23	IV:486
41(48):5	III:831n8; 837; VII:303n71;	44(51):25	IV:577; V:204; VI:288;
	305; 661; VIII:110		VII:531n22
41(48):7	VII:930	44(51):26	V:460n21
41(48):8	IV:553n15	44(51):27	VI:15(n24)
41(48):10	IV:197; 205n36	44(51):28	I:697n31; IV:196; 197; 205n36;
41(48):12	VII:706		V:172; VII:970; 979
41(48):15	VII:970n16; 980	44(51):29	II:602; VI:550; VII:215n97;
41(48):16	III:854; IV:196; 197; 205n36;		220; VIII:193n45
	V:584n13	45:1ff (51:31ff, S)	IV:429
42(49):1ff	IV:98	45:4 (51:34, S)	III:411
42(49):2	IV:196; 197; 205n36; V:172	45:4f (51:34f, S)	V:671n97

46(26)	VI:509n60	48(31):37	III:831n8; 837; 841; VII:59,
46(26)-51(31)	IV:165n94; V:11; VI:149		n27; 661; VIII:110
46(26):2	VIII:132	48(31):39	I:254
46(26):3	IV:328; V:296; 313	48(31):40	V:469
46(26):3f	V:296	48(31):41	VII:760; IX:670
46(26):4	V:296; 314	48(31):42	V:584n12
46(26):6	VII:970	48(31):43	IX:204
46(26):7f	VIII:322	48(31):43f	V:594
46(26):9	IV:426, n84	48(31):44	VIII:292n159
46(26):10	II:35; 445; 945n6; IV:546;	48:45	VIII:346
	VII:533; 838n15;	48:47	II:946(n11); VIII:53
	VIII:428n212	49:3 (30:19, S)	III:837; 838; 841; 850n124
46(26):11	V:833	49:4 (30:20, S)	III:137; VI:191
46(26):13	VI:832	49:7 (30:1, S)	V:748; VII:480; 485
46(26):14	I:63; V:763	49:8 (30:2, S)	VII:77; 408n32; IX:586
46(26):15	IV:182	49:9 (30:3, S)	III:755; IV:195; 1125
46(26):16	VI:277	49:10 (30:4, S)	III:960; 967
46(26):17	V:262	49:11 (30:5, S)	IX:446n54
46(26):18	I:569n22; V:177; 257; VII:294	49:12 (30:6, S)	V:165; 437n386; VI:139, (n38);
46(26):21	II:445; IV:697; 761		149; 150
46(26):22	V:573; IX:281	49:13 (30:7, S)	V:241
46(26):23	VI:281	49:14 (30:8, S)	V:330n81
46(26):24	IV:33	49:16 (30:10, S)	III:606; V:629; VII:760;
46(26):25	VI:191; 192		VIII:300; 526
46(26):27	V:676; 680n175; VII:978	49:19 (30:13, S)	II:244; III:351
46(26):27f	V:662n41; IX:203	49:20 (30:14, S)	I:634; IV:285; IX:605
46(26):28	V:607; 676; 680n175; VII:775;	49:21 (30:15, S)	VI:167; IX:198n47; 281
	VIII:65	49:22 (30:16, S)	IX:670
47(29):2	V:173n6; VIII:322; 325n71	49:23 (30:29, S)	VI:550
47(29):3	V:469; VII:727n25; IX:280	49:24 (30:30, S)	IX:670
47(29):4	I:396; IV:197	49:29 (30:24, S)	III:593; VII:370
47(29):4f	IV:196	49:30 (30:25, S)	IV:285
47(29):5	III:831n8; 837n56; IV:196; 197;	49:31 (30:26, S)	VI:5n14
	VII:661; VIII:110, n8	49:32 (30:27, S)	VI:277; 360; VII:215
47(29):6	III:837n56	49:33 (30:28, S)	VII:731
48(31):2	IV:285; V:290	49:35 (25:15, S)	VII:921
48(31):3	V:168	49:36 (25:16, S)	I:791n2; 792(n3); V:503;
48(31):4	IV:879		VI:360; VIII:131
48(31):6	VII:979	49:39 (25:19, S)	II:946(n11); III:838; 850n124;
48(31):7	VI:191		VIII:53
48(31):8	VII:980	50:2 (27:2, S)	I:63, III:970
48(31):10	II:641; VIII:564n26	50(27):3	VII:66
48(31):11	III:1075; VI:5	50(27):4	II:946(n14)
48(31):12	II:946(n13)	50(27):5	II:132; 233; VII:316
48(31):13	II:523	50(27):6	VI:235; 487(n29); 500, n17; 690
48(31):15	I:569n22; V:257; VII:936	50(27):7	I:288; II:195
48(31):16	II:947n22	50(27):8	I:516; II:602; V:576
48(31):17	VI:967	50(27):9	III:528; VII:803
48(31):18	IV:312; IX:96	50(27):11	II:787(n152); III:646; 773n8;
48(31):19	VII:970n16; 979		IV:760n2; VII:401
48(31):20	II:955; V:174; VII:921	50(27):12	II:228n11; IV:642
48(31):26	VIII:301	50(27):13	V:398; 400
48(31):28	VI:67(n49)	50(27):15	II:443; III:701n20; V:398
48(31):29	III:606; VIII:607	50(27):16	VII:540
48(31):29a	VIII:526	50(27):17	VI:234; 690
48(31):29b	VIII:526	50(27):19	IV:195; VI:487(n21), (n28)
48(31):29f	VIII:300	50(27):20	II:946(n14); IV:204; 207
48(31):30	II:645; V:392n62; VIII:302	50(27):22	IX:280
48(31):32	III:757	50(27):23	III:728
48(31):33	IV:254	50(27):25	II:641; III:137; V:400, n136,
48(31):34	IV:879; VIII:318; IX:281		n140; 423, n300; 435; 440;
48(31):36	III:844n96		VII:359; 364; IX:59n14

LAMENTATIONS

	VII:187(n4); VIII:8	3:15	VI:123
1:7	I:659; III:140; 141; VIII:10	3:16	IX:605
1:8	VII:67; VIII:8	3:17	II:406; 408
1:9	III:32; 141; V:789; VIII:10;	3:18	II:522n29
	51n15	3:19	III:141; VI:123
1:10	III:283; 527; VII:714	3:21	III:607; IV:583
1:11	III:362; V:328; VII:724	3:22	III:970; VI:276; IX:384, n83;
1:12	II:948; V:48; 405; VIII:8		385n86
1:12-22	III:839	3:22f	II:480n47
1:13	V:115; VI:935; IX:625	3:23	III:452n1; 1018
1:14	II:338	3:25	II:522n31; IV:583; 584
1:15	III:722; IV:254; 255; V:833	3:26	IV:583; VII:977
1:16	III:465; 825n9; 987; V:789; 793;	3:27	I:596n5; II:898
	VI:388, n314; VII:724; 937;	3:28f	III:970
	IX:54n52; 288n41; 289;	3:30	V:241; VIII:263n22
	525n206	3:31f	VIII:9
1:17	III:140; VII:294; 308	3:32	VI:276n13; IX:384n83
1:18	VI:126; 570	3:32-34	VIII:8
1:19	VII:724	3:33	III:613; VIII:346
1:20	III:140; 142; 606; 786; 787;	3:35	VIII:8
	VI:125	3:36	III:621
1:21	II:786; 944; III:458; 700n15;	3:38	VII:696; 697; IX:289. n52
	V:405; 789	3:39	I:729; 730
1:22	II:786n132, (n133); IV:318	3:40	II:656; V:618
2	VI:808	3:41	I:627n18; II:790n185; IV:7;
2:1	III:838; IV:256n8; V:405;		VIII:603n14
	VI:627; VII:308; 309; 318;	3:42	I:268; 269; III:315
	IX:290; 523n189, n193	3:44	IV:905; V:507
2:2	III:411	3:47	V:409; IX:204
2:4	II:468; V:399; VII:311; 610	3:50	V:328
2:5	VIII:8	3:52	VII:731
2:6	V:396; VII:311; 383; 384n3	3:56	III:969; IV:905
2:8	II:465; IV:632; V:941; VI:42	3:57	IX:203
2:9	IV:1045; V:371; VI:808	3:59	VI:388n315
2:10	I:487; III:832n19; V:305;	3:59f	VI:388n315
	VII:296	3:60f	II:97
2:11	III:609; 612; VIII:280n66;	3:64	II:647(n35); III:825
	IX:626; 641n150	3:65	III:607
2:12	VII:533; IX:620	4:1	III:838
2:13	IV:483; V:789; VII:294; 970n16	4:2	IV:285; VII:308; 359
2:14	V:329; VI:808	4:3	VII:731
2:15	III:718; V:48; 632n10; 891;	4:4	III:728; VII:280
	VII:626	4:5	III:810; VI:183; VII:453
2:16	I:641; VI:158; 726n3	4:6	VII:312; 562; 563
2:17	III:140; 411; VIII:63; 607	4:7	IV:22; 243; 473n8; 557n21;
2:19	II:786; 790n185; 793(n193);		874n1; VI:949
	VI:384n285; VIII:322	4:9	II:446; VI:570
2:20	III:787; V:328; VI:808	4:10	V:160(n18)
2:21	V:104; VI:996; VII:930n25	4:11	II:468; V:400; 410, n201;
2:21f	II:948; III:839; V:405		VIII:59n13; 63
2:22	IV:196; 204; V:604n44; VI:281;	4:12	III:140; VI:197n149
	VII:978n48; 979	4:13	I:154; VI:808
3:1	V:326n60; 400n137; VI:967	4:14	III:447; VII:66
3:1ff	VII:430	4:15	VII:66
3:4	V:718; 720n2; VII:107	4:16	IX:377n43
3:5	III:675	4:17	VII:974
3:6	III:969	4:18	III:458; V:861
3:9	V:49; VI:749	4:20	VI:361; 368; VII:396; IX:99;
3:10	III:960; 969		502; **503-504;** 514n107
3:12	I:601; 608; VII:414	4:21	V:165; VI:149; IX:367n66
3:13	III:334; VIII:345; 353(n114)	4:22	II:602; 933n34; VII:313
3:14	VIII:494	5	IV:981n26

EZEKIEL

3:17	VI:811; VII:414; 696(n42)		VIII:198n78
3:17ff	II:719	6:4-6	II:377(n17)
3:18	VII:720	6:5	VII:1045
3:18f	VI:629n48	6:6	II:659; VIII:198n78; 613
3:18ff	II:845(n91); 851(n149)	6:8	**VII:979**
3:18-21	VII:591; IX:652	6:8f	VII:979
3:19	IV:988; VII:720	6:9	I:598; III:607; 831(n11); 837;
3:20	I:562; II:195n3; VI:469; 470;		841; 845n105; VII:141(n318);
	VII:341; 343		854n14; 922n17
3:22	I:638; IX:427	6:10	II:167
3:22-27	IV:1096	6:11f	VI:15(n24)
3:23	V:330; VII:643	6:12	IV:197; 373; V:398(n122); 400;
3:24	VI:362		VIII:63
3:25f	II:454	6:13	II:377(n17); V:494;
4-24	V:790		VIII:193n45
4:1	IX:416	6:14	IV:162n89; IX:427
4:1-3	VII:217	6:14ff	II:461
4:3	VII:219; VIII:118n35	7:1	IV:96
4:4f	VIII:118n35	7:1ff	III:929n21
4:4ff	II:454	7:1-27	VII:198
4:4-8	IV:1096; V:749(n31)	7:2	I:679; V:862n16; VIII:131;
4:6	VIII:137		IX:91n27
4:7	VI:799n128	7:2ff	II:927
4:9-17	VI:15; 136(n7)	7:3 (7:7, S)	V:53; 403n155
4:10	III:294n6	7:5f, 3f (7:5-8, S)	V:53
4:11	IV:632; 634n10; VIII:318	7:7 (7:4, S)	II:330; 927; 945(n4); 946(n15);
4:12	VII:446		IV:204
4:12f	III:416(n16)	7:8 (7:5, S)	V:398(n122); 399; 409; VIII:63
4:14	I:604; IV:1107n14; 1110;	7:9 (7:6, S)	VIII:261; 268
	VII:106; 697	7:10	II:947; IV:1044; VI:967;
4:15	VII:446		VIII:301; 526
4:16	II:898; IV:590n12; 632; 634n10;	7:11	VI:270, n8
	VI:135n2	7:12	II:927; 946, (n15); III:458;
4:16f	VIII:318		625n5; V:397
5:1	II:896; VI:997n26	7:12-14	VI:277
5:1-17	VII:419	7:14	V:397n106; VII:78; 79
5:2	VI:300; 934; VII:419n6	7:15	II:692; VI:15(n24); VIII:63
5:3-4a	VII:312n101	7:16	IV:204; VI:67(n49); VII:970;
5:5	IV:610; VII:308; 318; VIII:155		979
5:6	VII:312	7:17	IV:736, n2
5:6f	V:51	7:18	III:5; VII:60
5:6ff	III:932	7:19	I:562; III:814; V:405; VI:992;
5:7	V:472; VI:469		VII:341; 343
5:7ff	III:929n21	7:20	III:880; IV:145; VIII:299
5:8	VI:460	7:22	II:606n2
5:9	I:598	7:23	VI:284; 524; VII:307n91
5:10	IV:196; 197; VI:460	7:24	III:776; IV:204; VI:550(n30);
5:10f	VII:312n101		VIII:299
5:11	I:598	7:25	IV:204; VII:886
5:12	VI:15(n24); VII:419n6; VIII:63	7:26	I:60; II:576n2; IV:1045;
5:13	II:879; V:398; 400; 403n155,		VII:492
	n162; 409; 410; VIII:59n13;	7:27	II:319; IV:32n13; 34; V:53
	63	8-11	V:847
5:15	IV:103n128; V:396; 397n114;	8:1	VI:658; VII:811n74; IX:427
	398(n122); 607, n59; 611;	8:1ff	V:330
	VI:460	8:2f	V:196
5:16	III:140n2; VI:15; 551n31	8:2-4	VIII:418n151
5:17	II:676n1; IV:103n128;	8:3	III:904; VI:362; 363; 409;
	VI:15n24; 549; 996		VII:296n20
6:1	IV:96	8:6	I:288
6:2	VI:776(n45); 798; VII:655	8:9	VI:551
6:4	III:431n5; VII:921;	8:10	II:33; 377(n17); IV:521n4;

	V:190		VI:799; VIII:65; IX:281
8:10ff	III:1074n196	11:14-16	VII:811n74
8:11	II:785; IV:264; VI:656n31	11:15	IV:373(n2); VIII:63
8:11f	VI:658	11:16	VII:823
8:12	III:968	11:16f	VII:811n74; 823n151
8:14	III:443; 832n19; 835; 836, n52	11:17	II:57
8:16	V:124n24	11:18	I:598
8:17	IV:797; V:329; VI:128; 233n32;	11:19	I:29; 770; II:849(n121); III:448;
	470		IV:269n10; 890; 988; V:1026;
8:18	V:398(n122); 406; IX:281; 282		VI:362, n142; 365; 370;
9	VII:948n77		VII:107; 108, n84; IX:627;
9:1	II:445; IX:96		628
9:1ff	II:11(n79)	11:19f	III:612n21; 613n1
9:2	IV:550; V:304n6; 305; 307;	11:20	IV:37; V:51
	437n387	11:21	III:172n2; 675; V:50
9:2ff	I:87	11:22f	VII:310; IX:291n61
9:3	II:251; V:304n6; 305; 496	11:23	II:245; V:484n102; VI:524;
9:3a	VII:310		VII:281
9:4	IV:205; 206; 207; 635; 636n3,	11:24	VI:362; 363
	n4, n12; V:650; VI:445n772;	11:25	II:29
	VII:208; 220; 266; 419;	12:1	IV:96
	579n57; 661; **662,** n41; 663,	12:1-11	VII:312
	n46; 664; 951	12:1-16	VIII:118, n35
9:4-6	VII:578, n55	12:2	I:220; 269; V:327; 548n48
9:4ff	VII:214n88	12:3-6	V:749(n31)
9:6	IV:915; 916; V:127; 650; 832;	12:6	VII:217n115; 234; VIII:119;
	VII:208; 220; 579n57; IX:99		252n32
9:8	II:468; IV:196; 197; 205, n36;	12:7	VII:424n5
	207; V:410	12:10ab	VII:312n101
9:9	VII:307n91	12:11	VII:217n115; VIII:252n32
9:10	III:675; V:50	12:12	V:324; VI:460
9:11	IV:550; V:304, n6; 305; 307;	12:13	VII:760
	496	12:15	VII:539
10	III:163	12:16	VI:15(n24)
10:1	III:162; IV:250n66; VII:609	12:17-20	VI:16; 136(n7); VII:312n101
10:1ff	IV:761	12:18	I:562; III:141; 142; VII:66; 67;
10:1-22	IX:438		562
10:2	VI:978n10; VII:310; IX:426	12:18f	VI:135n2
10:3f	IV:905; VI:128	12:19	IV:590n12; VI:299;
10:4	II:251; IV:888		VII:312n101; 768n12
10:5	IX:281; 282; 283	12:20	III:661; VIII:47
10:7	VII:310	12:22	IV:373; V:747n19; 855n12
10:8-11	VI:849	12:23	V:747(n15)
10:9-14	VIII:131	12:27	III:459; V:329; VI:799; 840
10:12	IV:761; VI:284; VII:106; 109	12:28	VI:460
10:14	IV:252	13	II:455
10:17	VI:364n157	13:2	VI:798, n127; IX:627
10:18	II:245; 251	13:2f	VI:805
10:18f	VII:310	13:3	II:609; V:327; VI:361; 696
10:18-22	IX:291n61	13:4	IV:614
10:19	IV:630n1	13:5	II:947; IV:614
10:20	IV:760n1	13:6	I:601; III:1098n1; V:327;
10:21	VIII:131		VI:194
10:22	II:251	13:6f	VI:805; IX:599
11:1	VI:362	13:6ff	IV:522; 524
11:2	IV:285; VI:362; 550; 551;	13:6-9	VI:805
	VII:296n19; 312	13:8	III:701n18; IV:93
11:3	VI:767	13:8f	VI:806
11:4	VI:799	13:9	I:447; 620; 750; 769;
11:5	VI:164n17; 362; IX:630		III:701n18; V:253; 329; 611,
11:6	V:49; VII:296n19; 312		n84
11:13	IV:196; 197; 205, n36; 207;	13:10	II:404(n28); IV:161; VI:234;

16:49f	VIII:299	18:14	IX:198n47
16:51	I:288; VI:280	18:16	VI:16n31
16:51f	II:212	18:17	V:51; VI:647n11
16:52	I:562; IV:962n1; IX:97	18:18	I:154; III:140; 141
16:53	I:287	18:19f	IV:6
16:54	I:562	18:20	IV:709; V:618; VIII:291(n150)
16:55	I:388	18:21	IV:988; VII:720
16:56	VIII:526	18:21-23	IV:988
16:57	V:239	18:21ff	IV:709; 988
16:58	VII:187(n4)	18:23	III:45n15; 62; IV:710; 988
16:59	V:738	18:24	I:154; 295, n87; VI:170;
16:60	II:107n6; IV:675; 916		VII:720
16:61	I:715; IV:400n87; 663; V:53;	18:25	IV:709; V:55; 113n14
	145	18:26	IV:984
16:63	III:304	18:27	IV:988
17	VI:985; IX:508	18:28	VII:187(n4)
17:2	I:178; V:747(n15); 749	18:29	V:55
17:3	IV:145; 557n21; VIII:418n151	18:30	V:53; VII:341
17:4	III:727	18:31	I:274n23; 540; III:607; IV:988;
17:5	VIII:322		V:1026; VI:362; 365; 470;
17:6f	III:757		VII:187(n4)
17:6ff	III:757	18:32	II:854; III:45n15
17:8	IV:530; VIII:322; IX:57	19	II:839; 840
17:9	VI:986; VII:96	19:1-9	III:841
17:9f	V:110n7	19:2	III:839; V:604n44; VI:281
17:11ff	V:749	19:3	IV:401n88
17:13	II:117n50	19:4	VII:760; 944; IX:99
17:15	III:336; V:110n7; 738;	19:5	II:531; VIII:581n88; 582
	VII:970n16; 980	19:6	IV:401n88; V:942
17:16	V:738; VIII:195	19:7	IX:281
17:17	V:145; 585	19:8	VII:760; IX:99
17:18	V:738	19:9	VII:944; IX:281
17:18f	V:463	19:10	III:839; VIII:322
17:19	V:738	19:10ff	I:342
17:20	I:154	19:10-14	III:841
17:21	IV:197; VI:360	19:11	III:757
17:22	III:916; IV:145; VII:294n3; 317	19:11ff	VI:967
17:22f	III:810; VII:291n39	19:12	III:729n8; IV:182; 183
17:22-24	VII:318; IX:508	19:13	III:840n74; IV:1108n24
17:22ff	I:567; IV:66n6	19:14	III:839; IV:145; 182; 183
17:23	III:545n23; 757; IV:630n1;	20:1	VI:658
	VII:388; 389; 395; 396	20:1ff	II:845(n91)
17:24	V:38, (n6); VIII:8; 10; 607;	20:3	VI:658
	IX:508	20:4	II:443; IV:512
18	III:930; IV:988	20:5	III:773; IV:147n7; 169
18:1ff	II:845(n91); 851(n149)	20:5-26	VI:324
18:1-20	VIII:344, n58	20:6	III:159n18; 773; 992n146;
18:2	II:123n70; V:747n19; VIII:344		IV:552
18:2f	V:747(n15)	20:7	VI:749; VII:854n14
18:2-4	I:290	20:8	II:705; V:398(n122); 399;
18:2ff	II:436n7; III:573; V:646		403n155; VII:854n14;
18:4	V:891		VIII:63
18:5ff	IV:988	20:9	V:257
18:7	II:689; V:561; VI:16n31;	20:11	I:718
	VIII:558	20:12	I:90f; VII:5; 215(n95), n97
18:8	I:235	20:13	IV:730n2; VI:469; VII:5;
18:9	I:235; IV:1058; V:51		IX:198
18:10	I:174n14; V:744; VI:470	20:14	V:257
18:11	V:51	20:15	III:159n18; 773; IV:552
18:12	II:377(n17); III:140; V:561n9;	20:16	VII:5
	VI:39; 888	20:17	VIII:65
18:13	I:174	20:18	VII:854, n14

20:20	VII:5; 215(n95), n97	21:31 (21:36, M/S)	I:549; II:536n3; IV:835; V:399;
20:22	V:257		410; 436; VI:935; IX:96; 99
20:24	V:668n78; VII:5	21:31f (21:36f, M/S)	V:399
20:25	III:932	21:32 (21:37, M/S)	IV:678
20:25f	VIII:343	22:2	VII:296n19
20:27	VI:170	22:2f	VII:311
20:28	III:773; V:494; VII:531n22	22:2-4	VI:524
20:29	VII:270	22:3	III:458; VII:296n19
20:30	I:598	22:4	II:330; V:631; 635; VI:170
20:31	I:485; VII:270	22:4f	V:631
20:32	IV:60, n2; 219; 220; 269n9;	22:5	IV:372; V:261; 631
	V:1016; VI:362; IX:246; 630	22:6	VII:738
20:33	I:571; II:295; V:400	22:6-13	VI:324
20:33f	I:640	22:7	III:468; V:487; 488n4;
20:34	II:57		VIII:302; IX:445
20:37	II:108; VI:967	22:8	I:113; VII:5
20:38	I:274n23; IV:145; 147n7; 170	22:9	V:492; VI:470
20:39	VII:854n14	22:10f	VIII:7
20:39f	VII:811n74	22:12	VI:269; VIII:65
20:40	II:602; VII:294n3; VIII:52	22:14	III:606
20:40f	I:33n68; II:57; 738	22:15	II:100
20:41	I:90; 91; 111; II:57, n2; 366(n9)	22:17-22	VI:935
20:42	III:773	22:19	II:57; VII:311; 312
20:43	III:831(n11); 837; 841;	22:20	II:57
	845n105; V:53	22:20f	II:536n3
20:44	IV:970n7; V:53; IX:99	22:21	VI:935
20:46 (21:2, M/S)	VI:798; VII:655	22:24	II:948; V:393n69; 405
20:47 (21:3, M/S)	V:38(n6); VI:942n73; VII:166	22:24-31	VI:324
20:48 (21:4, M/S)	VII:106; 166	22:25	IV:252n19; 253n19; VI:280;
20:49 (21:5, M/S)	V:747n14; 749		806n171; VIII:172
21:2 (21:7, M/S)	I:60; VI:798; VII:296n18	22:25-28	VI:806
21:3 (21:8, M/S)	I:150	22:25-29	VI:324
21:4 (21:9, M/S)	VII:106, n67	22:26	I:89; 604n3; III:303n12;
21:6 (21:11, M/S)	V:115		417(n23); 427; IV:1045;
21:6f (21:11f, M/S)	VII:600		VII:5; VIII:158; 221n41
21:7 (21:12, M/S)	IV:736; VI:361	22:27	IV:309; 389; VI:269
21:8ff (21:13ff, M/S)	V:297	22:28	III:701n18; VI:806
21:9 (21:14, M/S)	VI:798	22:29	III:927; IV:32n13; VI:39; 888;
21:9f (21:14f, M/S)	VI:997n26; VII:665		891
21:10 (21:15, M/S)	VII:665; 929n24; 930n25	22:30	IV:614; VII:668n15; VIII:52
21:12 (21:17, M/S)	III:837; 845n105; V:174	22:31	V:50; 399; 400; 409; 436;
21:13 (21:18, M/S)	II:214		VI:935
21:14 (21:19, M/S)	III:5; VI:799	23	I:23n17; IV:731; V:403;
21:15 (21:20, M/S)	III:606; VI:280; VII:665; 666;		VI:584; 587; VII:296
	936	23:4	V:968
21:19 (21:24, M/S)	VIII:34; IX:427	23:4ff	VII:369n6
21:20-22		23:5	I:23n17; II:660; V:469;
(21:25-27, M/S)	VII:312		VIII:160
21:21 (21:26, M/S)	III:260	23:6	VII:706
21:22 (21:27, M/S)	IX:280	23:6ff	III:337
21:23f (21:28f, M/S)	I:194n8; II:73	23:7	VIII:160; 346
21:24 (21:29, M/S)	I:278n36; V:324; VII:187(n4),	23:9	I:23n17; II:660
	(n5)	23:10	V:252; 261
21:25 (21:30, M/S)	I:117n7; 604; VIII:53	23:11	II:660; V:469; VI:584;
21:26 (21:31, M/S)	VIII:8; 10; 607, n13		VIII:160; IX:99
21:26f (21:31f, M/S)	VII:626	23:12	II:660; VII:706
21:27 (21:32, M/S)	I:269; III:439; V:862n19;	23:13	V:668n78
	VIII:218; IX:507	23:14	IV:663
21:28 (21:33, M/S)	IV:527n24; VI:798; VII:665;	23:15	V:191; 304, n7; VIII:346
	VIII:65	23:17	IX:124n115
21:29 (21:34, M/S)	VIII:53	23:19	VI:584
21:30 (21:35, M/S)	III:1008; 1027	23:20	V:283; 469; VII:107; 108n86;

28:1-10	VII:491; 493	30:16	IX:669n22
28:1-17	V:404	30:18	VIII:299
28:2	II:346(n35); 347n45; III:83;	30:21ff	I:639
	97n179; 120; 613; IV:887;	30:23	IV:281
	V:505n63; VIII:607; IX:627	30:24	VIII:154
28:3	V:611; VII:480	30:26	IV:281
28:3f	VII:484	31:1ff	VII:318
28:4	IX:224	31:2	VI:277; VIII:603
28:5	VIII:607	31:2-4	VII:291n39
28:8	IX:98; 99	31:3	I:481; IV:903
28:11	VII:944	31:4f	VIII:322
28:11-19	III:840; V:482, n88; VII:491;	31:6	III:810; IV:66n6; VI:277; 537;
	493; VIII:348n85		VII:388; 389; 395; 396
28:12	III:837; VII:625; 626	31:7	VI:985; VIII:322; 603
28:12ff	VII:1093	31:8	V:38; 766
28:13	II:919n59; III:1005; 1008;	31:9	II:919n59; V:38; 766
	IV:27n40; V:766; IX:485	31:10	I:481; IV:530; 903; VIII:607
28:13f	V:505n63; 768	31:11	III:85n91
28:13-15	II:392n59	31:12	IV:34; VII:395
28:14	V:942; VI:951	31:13	VI:167
28:14-16	IX:438	31:14	I:481; IV:903; VI:138; VIII:322
28:15	III:1008	31:15	VI:277; VII:430n48; 451
28:16	VI:128; 276, n13; 951	31:16	IV:145; VI:138; 167; IX:281
28:16ff	VII:486	31:17	VII:395
28:17	II:32; III:558n6; 606; VI:991;	31:18	IV:542; VI:75n17; 277;
	VII:318, n126; 480; VIII:607;		VIII:551n43
	IX:99	32	III:840; IX:198n49
28:18	I:154; III:233; IV:882;	32:2	II:283; V:189; 942
	VI:276n13; 277	32:2-10	III:841
28:19	III:33n30	32:5	VII:106; 453
28:21	VI:798	32:6	VI:278
28:22	I:90; II:254	32:7	I:504(n6); VII:61n41
28:24	VII:411, n15	32:7f	IV:551
28:25	I:90; II:366(n9); III:773;	32:9	V:419n271
	IV:32n14; V:662n41;	32:10	II:58; 450; III:33
	680n175	32:12	VII:921; VIII:299
28:26	II:523n34	32:13	III:405
29	IV:780	32:14	VI:570
29:2	VI:798	32:15	VI:300
29:3	II:283	32:16	III:150; 151; 838; 839; 845n99
29:6	VI:967	32:17f	IX:281n11
29:7	VII:655	32:17-32	VII:428
29:9	III:97n179	32:18	III:151
29:10	VI:953n7	32:19-32	III:840; VI:75n17
29:11-13	VIII:136	32:21ff	II:847
29:12	VIII:348n88	32:22	III:529; VII:803
29:14	V:156; VII:720	32:23	II:854n165
29:14f	VIII:9	32:24	I:517; 562; II:854n165
29:15	VIII:607	32:26	I:226; II:854n165
29:16	I:194n8; II:73; 523(n37)	32:27	I:226; V:293; VII:359n5;
29:18f	IV:697		IX:198
29:19	VI:277	32:29	I:226
29:20	IV:221	32:30	I:562; VII:532(n24)
30:1-9	VII:198	32:31f	VI:811
30:2	V:173n6; VI:798	32:32	II:854n165; VI:277
30:3	II:330; 946; IV:905	33-48	V:790
30:4	VI:277	33:1ff	II:845(n91)
30:6	VI:953n7; VIII:299; 300; 526	33:1-9	VI:629n48
30:8	VII:920	33:3	VII:263n8
30:10	VI:277	33:3ff	VII:79
30:11	IV:34	33:4	III:675; IX:624
30:15	V:398; VI:277	33:4f	IX:281

33:6	II:895; VII:263n8		496
33:7	VII:696(n42)	34:23f	I:567; V:664; 681; 682; VI:488;
33:8	II:895		VIII:254; IX:507
33:8f	V:53	34:23ff	IV:209; VI:690
33:9	IV:988	34:23-31	VIII:427n211
33:10	VI:235	34:24	III:1072n188
33:11	IV:988; V:53	34:25	II:109n23; 126; 403; 405; 408;
33:11f	VI:236		VI:549
33:12	IV:988; 990; VI:233n32;	34:26	II:757
	235(n37); VII:921; 970n16	34:27	II:408; 897; VI:5n14
33:12ff	IV:988	34:27f	II:523n34
33:13	I:154; II:523; VI:5; 191	34:28	IX:198
33:14	IV:988; VII:187(n5)	34:29	II:408; V:263; VI:16; IX:57
33:15	II:854	34:31	VI:500n11
33:16	VI:470	35:2	VI:798
33:17	V:55; VIII:346	35:5	III:141; VIII:53
33:18	IV:984	35:10	III:776
33:19	V:988	35:11	II:878; V:394
33:20	V:55	35:12	I:621
33:21	VII:312n101; 978	35:15	III:773
33:21f	II:945	36	II:945(n8); IX:296n84
33:22	VII:881; IX:427	36:1	VI:799
33:23f	VII:811n74	36:3	IV:196; 208; VI:799
33:24	II:438n18; III:773	36:4	V:631; 942
33:25	III:776	36:5	II:878n2; IV:208; V:410
33:25f	III:776	36:6	II:879; V:403n162; VI:799;
33:26	VI:468		IX:57
33:28	VIII:299	36:7	V:459n19
33:30	VI:579	36:8	III:614
33:31	IV:646; VI:270; VII:697;	36:9	III:634; VII:541n17
	811n74	36:10	VIII:52
33:32	IX:281	36:11	III:993; V:156
34	I:773; II:945(n8); III:548n44;	36:12	III:773; 778
	VI:492; 496	36:15	IX:60
34:1ff	III:548n44	36:17	III:427
34:1-10	VI:488(n31)	36:18	II:377(n17)
34:2	VI:798	36:19	I:268
34:2ff	VI:690	36:19ff	IV:281
34:2-10	VI:488(n29)	36:20	V:620
34:3	VII:929n24	36:20ff	I:91
34:4	I:395; III:635; V:632; VI:235;	36:23	I:90; IV:530; V:276
	236; VII:1048n291	36:23ff	V:862(n16)
34:5	V:510; VI:243n73; 691	36:24	VI:690; 980
34:5ff	VI:500n17	36:24ff	III:576
34:6	VI:500(n14); 772	36:24-27	IV:208
34:8	VI:500(n14)	36:24-28	VII:977
34:10	VII:695	36:25	I:537; II:377(n17); III:414;
34:10ff	VI:690		IV:301; VI:977; 978; 980,
34:11	II:601; VI:689n6		n21; 983; VIII:320; 321;
34:11-22	VI:487(n28); 488(n32)		330n114
34:12	II:601; 944; 945n6; IV:209; 905;	36:26	I:540; 770; II:849(n121);
	VI:489; 689n6; VIII:193		III:612n21; 613n1;
34:12f	VII:421; 430n49		IV:269n10; 345n25; 890; 988;
34:13	IV:209		VI:362; 365; 370; 980;
34:15f	VIII:407n35		VII:107; 108, n84; 908;
34:16	I:395; III:928; 930; VI:235; 236;		IX:628
	492n71; 500; VII:720	36:26f	I:95; 103; II:469; V:1026;
34:17	III:946n5		VI:365; 379; 385
34:18	III:295n8; V:942	36:26ff	III:1015
34:20	III:946n5; V:283	36:27	II:540; III:932; V:51; VI:363;
34:22	VII:977		379n243; 980
34:23	I:369; III:556; VI:489n49, n50;	36:29	III:703n28; VI:16; VII:970n16;

	977
36:31	V:53
36:32	I:719
36:33	V:156
36:35	II:919n59; V:766; 767
36:36	III:411; IV:208; VI:690
36:37	VI:690
37	I:790; II:337; 848; 852;
	VI:417n554; VII:118n165;
	120n181; IX:428n21; 623
37:1	VI:362; IX:427
37:1ff	I:419
37:1-14	I:369
37:4	IV:100; VI:799
37:5	II:536; VI:362
37:5f	VI:361; 799
37:6	VI:362; 369
37:7	IX:280; 281
37:9	I:792(n7); II:536(n4); V:510;
	VI:67n43; 363; 364; 442n752;
	799; VIII:131
37:9f	IX:125
37:10	II:676; VI:363; 799; VII:647;
	805
37:11	II:521; 522n29
37:12	VI:799
37:13	IV:681, n5
37:14	II:536; VI:363; 369; 379; 385;
	VIII:155; IX:475n30; 478;
	662
37:16	VII:531n22; VIII:168
37:16f	VI:967
37:18	VIII:346
37:19	II:66
37:22	VI:488
37:22ff	IX:507
37:23	II:377(n17); IV:208; VI:58
37:23f	IV:209
37:24	I:568n18; III:556; 932; IV:208;
	VI:488; 489n50; 496;
	VIII:254
37:24f	I:567; V:664; 681; 682
37:25	III:773; IV:575n4; V:662n41;
	680n175
37:26	II:126; 403; 408
37:26f	IV:580
37:26ff	II:405
37:27	IV:55; VI:533; VII:372; 380;
	388; 389n11; VIII:389n400
37:28	I:90f
38f	I:110; 790, n10; 791; II:945(n8);
	VI:248(n120); 509(n56);
	VII:316n112; VIII:428n219
38:2	VI:798
38:2f	VI:513
38:4	VII:803
38:7	VII:803
38:8	I:468n2; II:408; VI:5n14;
	VIII:53
38:9	IV:905
38:10	IV:285; 286; VI:551
38:11	II:408; VI:5n14

38:12	V:156; 482n79; VII:318
38:14	II:408; V:156; VI:5n14; 799
38:15	I:679; VII:803; VIII:199
38:16	I:90; 111; II:946(n11); 947;
	III:773; VIII:53
38:17	II:66; 946(n14); V:665(n52);
	VI:805; IX:427
38:18	IX:625
38:19	II:879; VI:935
38:19-22	VII:198
38:20	I:678n4; V:480
38:21	I:468n2; IX:198n49
38:22	I:790n1; V:399; 400; VI:936
38:23	VII:537
39	I:117n7
39:1	VI:799
39:2	I:468n2
39:4	I:468n2
39:6	I:790n1; II:408; V:156;
	VI:5n14; 936
39:9	V:293; VI:967
39:10	V:293
39:11	VI:277; VIII:195
39:12	III:416(n18)
39:15	VII:220
39:17	I:468n2; III:181; VII:838n15
39:17f	VII:105
39:17ff	II:34; 35; VI:138
39:17-20	IV:257
39:19	VI:132
39:25	II:481(n57); 879; 884;
	IV:1117n65; VII:716; 720
39:26	I:154; II:408; V:156; VI:5n14;
	IX:198
39:27	I:90; VI:537; VII:720
39:28	II:884; IX:9
39:29	II:468; IV:208; VI:363; VII:720
40	I:117n7; III:344
40ff	I:790; III:240
40-44	III:233; IV:884
40-46	IV:219
40-48	III:239; 302; 303; 306; 309; 576;
	773; IV:632; IX:518n137; 520
40:1	IV:634; VII:307n91; IX:427
40:2	IV:634; V:145; 482n81; 486;
	VII:317
40:2f	VIII:369n250
40:3	I:80n27; VII:666
40:3ff	I:79; II:323n20; IV:634; VI:967
40:4	II:29, n12; V:324; 330
40:5	III:344; VI:967n8
40:5ff	III:343
40:39	I:270n8; II:470; VIII:512n27
40:39-43	VIII:211n22
40:41f	VIII:132
40:43	III:860
40:46	II:330; VII:37; IX:512n87
40:47	IV:595
41:1ff	IV:882n7
41:4	VI:772n24
41:11	VIII:193n45; 198
41:19	IV:251; 252; VI:771

DANIEL

3:44	V:679(n164)
3:45	III:98(n193)
3:46	VI:950n11; VIII:535
3:50	IV:318
3:51-90	IX:413n67
3:52-88	VIII:606
3:52-90	VII:485; VIII:495
3:53	IV:882
3:54	III:161; V:522n190
3:55	III:441; V:327
3:56	VII:610
3:57	II:638n9
3:57ff	II:758
3:57-88	VIII:493
3:57-90	V:890
3:58-73	VIII:495
3:73	IV:906
3:74-81	VIII:495
3:78	VI:598
3:82	VIII:495
3:83-87	**VIII:495**
3:85	V:680n169
3:86	VI:369
3:87	I:770; VIII:10
3:88	III:161; VI:1000; 1001; VII:981
3:89	V:214n43; IX:485

Back to RSV and M

3:24 (3:91, S)	I:99n36; III:33n31; V:328; VII:562
3:25 (3:92, S)	IV:328; V:942; VI:938; VIII:132; 347; 348; 354; IX:100
3:26 (3:93, S)	IV:468n21; V:659n22; 680n169; 681(n193); 678
3:27 (3:94 S)	II:642; V:328; 493; VII:1046; IX:154
3:28 (3:95, S)	II:522; IV:223n23; V:676n125; 677; 678; 680n169; 681(n193); VI:5; 760n25; VII:970n16; 981; 1046; 1048; VIII:158
3:29 (3:96, S)	VI:1001; IX:246
3:30 (3:97, S)	I:380; II:566
4:1 (3:98, S; 3:31, M)	II:407; VI:283; IX:394
4:1ff (3:31ff, M)	III:435
4:2 (3:99, S; 3:32, M)	I:63n22; VI:247; VII:221; VIII:117
4:3 (3:100, S; 3:33, M)	II:565
4:4 (4:1, M)	II:417
4:4-37 (4, M)	II:233; V:890
4:5 (4:2, M)	II:752; III:96; V:221; IX:198, n49; 624
4:6 (4:3, M)	VII:483
4:6f (4:3f M)	I:718
4:8 (4:5, M)	II:819n25; V:512n102; VI:361; 362
4:8f (4:5f, M)	VI:820n271
4:9 (4:6, M)	II:819n25; IV:814; 815
4:10 (4:7, M)	IX:624
4:11 (4:8, M)	IV:903; V:585n15; IX:89, n10
4:12 (4:9, M)	III:810; IV:66n6; VII:106; 388;

	389, n10
4:13 (4:10, M)	I:79, n23; II:14; VII:873n16; VIII:348; 551; IX:624
4:14 (4:11, M)	VI:991; VII:66
4:14a (4:11a, M)	IX:677
4:15 (4:12, M)	VI:986
4:16 (4:13, M)	III:459; IV:685; VI:822n283; VIII:402; **IX:627**
4:17 (4:14, M)	I:79; II:14; 565; 688; III:47n33; 1058; V:516n144; VII:873n16; VIII:348; 402; IX:243

Special S Additions

4:17a	IX:677

Back to RSV and M

4:18 (4:15, M)	VI:820n271; VII:503n253
4:19 (4:16, M)	I:678n4; 724; II:97; III:33, n30; 718; 1058; IV:1018, n6; VI:647; IX:677
4:20 (4:17 M)	IX:89
4:20-22 (4:17-19, M)	VII:291n39
4:21 (4:18, M)	III:810; IV:66n6; VII:388; 389
4:22 (4:19, M)	I:571; VIII:607; IX:89, n10
4:23 (4:20, M)	I:79; II:14; 927; III:459; VIII:348; 616; IX:89n10; 99
4:24 (4:21, M)	III:1058; IX:89, n10; 91n27
4:25 (4:22, M)	III:459; VIII:402
4:26 (4:23, M)	III:459; IV:575; V:509; 537; 539; VI:991
4:26ff (4:23ff, M)	VI:986
4:27 (4:24, M)	I:269; II:196; 486; 589; 645; III:161; IV:332; V:520n179; VI:55n12; 170n2; 284; IX:586
4:27ff (4:24ff, M)	IV:378
4:28 (4:25, M)	VIII:65; IX:89
4:29 (4:26, M)	V:942
4:30 (4:27, M)	III:906; VIII:172
4:31 (4:28, M)	I:631(n19); II:565; V:516n144; VIII:29n14; 65; IX:282; 288n45
4:32 (4:29, M)	III:459; V:890; VIII:402
4:33 (4:30, M)	VII:1045; VIII:58; 63; 402; IX:677

Special S Additions

4:33a	V:516n144
4:33b	IV:1018; V:942; IX:586

Back to RSV and M

4:34 (4:31, M)	I:177; 569n22; IV:334; 335; 352; 354n17; V:516n144; 534n311; VI:288; VIII:51; 65; 526; IX:224; 586
4:35 (4:32, M)	II:294; III:53; VI:460
4:36 (4:33, M)	I:388; IV:746; IX:224
4:37 (4:34, M)	II:642; III:1019; 1027; V:213; 214n43; 516n144; VI:571; IX:198; 586
4:37a (4:34a, M)	II:852: III:35

7:7	III:5; 671; V:734; 942; VI:62; VIII:420; IX:63; 198n49
7:7f	VII:699; VIII:24; 134; 421
7:8	I:366; VIII:402; IX:293
7:9	I:201n12; II:947; III:164; 165; IV:243; 245; 247, n38; 249n51; 250n67; V:330; 509, n86; 718; VI:946; VII:691; VIII:416n118; **417-418** (418n151); 420, n153
7:9f	VI:668; VIII:348; 423
7:9ff	I:109; III:163; V:505(n67)
7:10	I:79; 620; IV:62; 220; 221; 223n21; 225n33; 226; V:509, n86; 532n295; 838; 841; VI:399n418; 597; 939; 975n14; VIII:420; 447n329; IX:467; 469; 471
7:10-13	VII:650
7:11	III:643n3; VII:1045; 1046; VIII:420; IX:293
7:11a	VIII:420n153
7:11b	VIII:420n153
7:11f	V:509n86
7:12	I:481; VIII:420n153
7:12ba	IX:586
7:12bb	IX:585
7:13	I:102n51; 567n13; 585; II:667; 947; III:99n211; 337n8; 442; 850; IV:857n110; 863n187; 868n222; 905; 907; 909; 1015; V:188; 285; 307; 509, n86; 522(n195); 523; 526; 578; 718; 838; 862; 865; 989n278; VII:868; 869n66; VIII:346; 368n241; 371, n262; 402; 404n22, n24; 405n25; 406; 407; 420; 423; 424n186; 425n194; 428n216; 429; 430; 435; 436; 437; 450; 453; 460; 462n421; 463; 477, n517; IX:89, n10; 516
7:13f	IV:273; 617; V:989; VI:823; VII:237; VIII:373n278; **406;** 416n121; 430; 437; 440n291; 464; 465
7:14	I:481; 679n8; II:265, n36; IV:60n3; 223n23; **V:508-509;** 518; 993n289; VIII:172; 420, n153; 422; IX:99; 246; 569n483
7:14a	VIII:421n171
7:15	II:346(n40); VI:361; IX:624
7:16	II:62; IV:401n88
7:16ff	I:571
7:17	VIII:131; 422n173
7:17ff	I:218; V:508
7:18	I:109; VIII:421; 422; IX:569n483
7:19	V:942; VI:62; IX:198
7:20	II:37; VI:168; VIII:422n176
7:21	IV:974; VI:460; 465; VIII:420;

	422, n174, n176, n177
7:21ff	I:109
7:22	II:947; III:165; 458n29; V:718; VII:763; VIII:421; 422n176
7:22a	VIII:422, n174, n176
7:22b	VIII:422n174, n176
7:23	V:942; IX:63
7:24	I:579; III:671; VIII:8; 24; 422n176; IX:63
7:25	II:632n40; 934n52; III:459; IV:1018; VIII:421; 422n176; IX:469
7:25a	VIII:422, n176
7:25b	VIII:422n176
7:25bc	VIII:422
7:25c	VIII:422
7:26	I:481; III:165; VI:975n14; VIII:51
7:26b	VIII:422
7:27	I:102n51; 209n6; 481; 571; II:265, n36; IV:35n20; 37; 223n23; 542; 1015; VI:501, n20; VII:22n176; 925; VIII:40; 41n10; 46; 407; 421; 430; 464
7:27b	VIII:407; 420; 422
7:28	II:346(n40); 450; III:612; IV:746; VIII:151n2, n2(sic.); IX:63
8:1	II:346(n41); 355n107; V:330; 371
8:3	I:341; III:670
8:4	II:743
8:5	II:346(n40)
8:6	V:469
8:7	IX:89
8:8	V:503; VI:360; VIII:131
8:9	VI:62
8:10	I:504; II:295; V:942
8:11	V:112; VIII:348n89
8:11f	V:111
8:11ff	III:239
8:12	I:233; 236; 244; II:175; 196; V:112; VI:190; 992
8:13	I:79(n24); II:660; V:941; 943
8:14	II:934n52; IV:641; 889n36
8:15	V:328
8:15f	I:79(n26)
8:16	IX:281
8:16ff	I:218
8:17	II:946; III:458; VII:570; VIII:53; 65; 418n151; IX:99n18; 676
8:17f	IX:210n108
8:18	II:334; III:5
8:19	V:393, n69; 405; 423; VIII:53; 65; IX:677
8:20	V:328
8:20ff	III:671
8:21	II:507
8:22	VIII:131, n52
8:23	VI:287; 288

8:24	II:63; III:35; IV:35n20; 37; V:111; VII:611; IX:99	9:27	II:286; 660; III:232; 459; 993n150; IV:886; VI:537, n5; VII:562; VIII:52; 64; 65, n4; 66; 204
8:24f	V:110n7		
8:25	II:897; III:613; IV:968; V:111; VII:921; VIII:607		
		10	VI:946
8:26	I:234, n7; 619n16; III:983n86; IV:1108n24; VII:939n1; 944; 946	10:1	I:234; 248; 249; II:29; III:577; IV:530; VI:278; VII:705
		10:2	VI:42
8:27	III:33, n30; VI:641	10:2f	IV:927; 928; VI:42n9; 136(n10)
9	IV:1014; VI:808	10:3	II:472; 690; VI:300; VIII:63; IX:622
9:1	VI:819; VII:539n10; IX:589		
9:1-19	V:205	10:5	I:80n27; II:319; V:304; 307
9:2	I:616(n12); 756; III:218; VI:308; 808	10:6	I:505n2; IV:22; 26; V:585; VI:936; 946; VII:665; 666; 1045; IX:282
9:2f	VI:819		
9:3	III:571; IV:927; 928; 981(n19), (n20); V:510; 516n144; VII:60; 62n48	10:7	II:450; IV:530; IX:198n49
		10:8	IV:197; IX:97, 99, n23
		10:9	VI:772; IX:282
9:4	I:29n49; 39(n95); III:33; V:204; 205; 214n43; VIII:141; IX:383n82; 398n216	10:9f	IX:210n108
		10:10	II:334; III:405
		10:11	I:402n34; II:749, n45; V:435n372; VII:570n5
9:4ff	IV:981(n22)		
9:4-19	IV:981	10:12	IV:927; VIII:7; IX:203
9:5	I:158; 269; V:738; VII:188	10:13	I:79, (n26); 87; 488; IV:35; 39, n37; VI:865; VII:1092n626; VIII:39; 348
9:6	II:286; 366; V:665(n52); 679n167; VI:808		
9:8ff	II:47n23	10:14	II:946, (n11); 947; VIII:53
9:8-11	IV:981	10:15ff	IX:210n108
9:9	I:512; II:481(n55)	10:16	V:190; 196; VII:714; VIII:421, n168
9:10	V:52; 665(n52); 679n167; VI:808		
		10:17	IV:197; VI:364; 368; 453
9:11	I:499n22; 748; V:659n22; 681n183; 738	10:18	V:196; VIII:421, n168
		10:19	II:749, n45; VIII:310; IX:203
9:12	VI:293; VII:312	10:20	I:79; II:507; VII:706
9:13	I:233; 236n11; II:106; 175; 786; VI:190	10:20f	I:488; IV:39, n37; VII:1092n626; VIII:39; 348
9:14	II:338; VI:460	10:21	I:79(n26); 236; 754n17; VI:190
9:15	I:115; 640n1; II:46; VI:324	11:1	III:906
9:16	I:117n7; II:63; 196; 486; V:407; 410; VI:524; VII:296	11:2	II:507; IV:1112n42
		11:3	I:631(n21); II:743; III:53
9:16f	VII:310	11:4	V:503; VIII:131
9:17	IV:1108n24; V:679(n164); IX:9	11:5	II:286
9:18	II:195n3; 483n96; 785; V:160n17; 253; 324; VI:992	11:6	IV:575; VIII:65; IX:677
		11:7	VI:986
9:19	III:315; 498; V:263; VII:294n1	11:8	VII:532n24
9:20	II:785(n123); V:204; 214n43	11:10	V:585; VII:803
9:20-27	VI:819	11:10-13	VII:803, n24
9:21	I:79(n26); V:371; VIII:551; IX:676	11:10-45	V:585
		11:12	VIII:607
9:22	IV:965; 1107n8	11:13	III:459; VIII:51; 52; 65
9:22b	VI:820	11:14	V:739; VI:746; 748; VII:343n23
9:23	VI:817n242; 820	11:15	IV:177
9:24	I:268; 278n36; II:36(n5); III:302; 304n19; VI:524; 808; VII:294n1; 944; VIII:63	11:16	II:743; III:53; 62; VIII:61
		11:17	III:397; V:907; VI:776n45; VIII:28; IX:99
9:24ff	III:993		
9:24-27	VII:19	11:19	VI:746; 748; VII:343n23
9:25	IX:502; **505;** 510n74	11:20	II:947; VI:986
9:25f	IX:500; 502; **505**	11:21	III:769; VI:927n61; VIII:195n53
9:26	II:927; 946; VII:769n15; VIII:51; 65; IX:505; 510, n74		
		11:22	I:639
		11:23	VII:854n15
9:26b	VIII:52	11:24	II:97; III:459; V:585n18

HOSEA

	1040; V:403(n156); VII:23, n182; 142; IX:386; 458n170	9:17	I:218; VI:234; 236(n41)
		10:1	I:342; VI:280
6:7	III:632; V:737; 741	10:2	VI:188
6:9	III:801; VI:194; VIII:564; IX:17n31	10:3	IV:157n60
		10:4	III:927; VI:987n8
6:10	I:93; IV:645(n13)	10:5	VII:173
7:1	III:203; 755; IX:597	10:6	III:861n5
7:1-3	III:483	10:7	V:393n64
7:2	III:483	10:8	III:557; 976; V:483; VI:162; VII:754(n30)
7:3	IV:157n60; IX:497; 498n29; 499n37; 598	10:9	VI:510; VIII:346
7:4	II:906; IV:729; 731n6	10:10	V:606; 611
7:5	V:166; 392	10:12	I:685; 700n50; II:196n14; 210; 480(n37); 853; 932; III:546; IV:861n165; V:606; VII:539; IX:319n60; 386
7:7	III:499; 924n8		
7:8	VII:853		
7:9	I:704		
7:10	IV:990; VIII:8; 300; 526	10:13	I:268; II:523(n37); 692; III:614; VI:191; 276, n13; IX:598
7:11	III:606; V:403n158; VI:67		
7:12	V:606; 611	10:14	III:929n21
7:13	I:274n23; IV:3; 4n5; 331; IX:598; 599	10:15	VI:563
		11:1	I:32, n63; II:382; III:488; 572; IV:41n50; 916; V:652; 970; 972n145; VI:834; VIII:351; 352; 354, n115; 355; 394
7:14	III:1075; IV:981; V:174, n7; 611; VI:133; VIII:110, n7		
7:15	IV:285, n4; 288n13; V:606		
7:16	I:721; II:898; V:393n69; 631	11:1ff	VIII:353
8:1	I:274n23; V:737; VII:78f	11:1-6	V:403n154
8:3	I:14	11:1-7	VIII:354
8:4	II:377(n11); IV:157n60	11:2	III:1075; VIII:354
8:4f	II:382	11:3	I:32, n63; 698; III:203; VIII:354
8:5	V:403n155; 857n3	11:4	I:32(n64); VIII:263n22
8:6	III:447; VI:233n32; 234	11:4a	VIII:354
8:7	V:9n52; VI:360; 367f; IX:628	11:4b	VIII:354
8:8	VI:158; VII:359; 360n14	11:5	III:46n31; IV:990
8:10	II:57; 368; IV:1117n68; IX:510	11:5a	VIII:354
8:11	VI:280	115b	VIII:354
8:12	IV:97; 285; 1039; 1045; 1046; VI:277	11:6	II:692
		11:6a	VIII:354
8:13	II:57; 738; VII:719	11:6b	VIII:354
8:13f	IV:1039	11:7	III:920n33; VIII:354
8:14	III:1012; IV:882n7; VI:936; VIII:198n78	11:8	III:606; IV:627; V:777n20
		11:8f	I:32
9:1	I:23n15; VI:584; IX:363n30	11:9	I:90; 92; III:83; V:400; 405; 407n185; 469; 973
9:2	I:699n41		
9:3	I:109	11:10	IV:252, n18; IX:294
9:3f	III:1074	11:11	I:388; VI:67
9:4	I:93	11:12 (12:1, M/S)	I:93; 700; IV:1118; VI:185n102; VII:187(n4); IX:598
9:5	V:722		
9:6	III:776; 929n21		
9:7	I:103; II:445; 454; 455; 503; III:1075; IV:95; 360n4; VI:130; 276n13; 277; 281; 362; 366; 368; 406n473; 454; IX:629	12:1 (12:2, M/S)	II:112n31; 117; 471; III:660; 861n4; VI:280; 360
		12:3 (12:4, M/S)	V:254; IX:379
		12:3ff (12:4ff, M/S)	V:663n42
		12:4 (12:5, M/S)	III:723; 828n10; IX:378n50
		12:6 (12:7, M/S)	II:479(n24); 482(n90); III:928; IX:386
9:8	VII:405		
9:9	VI:510; IX:96; 99	12:7 (12:8, M/S)	II:896
9:10	I:23(n18); 265; 598; VII:414n4; 751n3, (n4), n4, n5; 752, n8, (n16); 757n52; IX:125n118	12:8 (12:9, M/S)	I:278n37
		12:8f (12:9f, M/S)	I:465
		12:9 (12:10, M/S)	I:659; III:1064; IV:859(n138); VII:370; 373; 380
9:12	V:604n44		
9:15	I:32; IV:686	12:10 (12:11, M/S)	VI:804, n156
9:16	VI:20; 986; VII:757n52; IX:57(n5)	12:11 (12:12, M/S)	II:11n77

JOEL

2:15	II:794(n217); III:131; VII:80
2:15-18	IV:981
2:16	IV:145; 915; VII:829n201
2:17	II:794(n217); 798; III:773; IV:220; V:124n24
2:18	II:884; III:773
2:19	II:471; V:239
2:20	II:645; 657n1; VII:97n23; VIII:301
2:21	II:787(n153); IX:363; 367n66
2:21-27	IX:363
2:22	VII:752(n16); IX:57
2:23	III:991; IV:861n165; V:639; IX:363; 676n12
2:23f	II:468; V:162
2:24	II:471; IV:254
2:26	II:786; III:34; 773
2:27	II:884; III:358(n17); 773
2:28-32 (3, M/S)	II:945
2:28-3:21 (3f, M/S)	II:946
2:28 (3:1, M/S)	I:103; III:435; IV:153n42; 208; V:221; 230; 235, n51; 329; 371; VI:51n45; 370; 654; 799; VII:106; 531n20; VIII:553
2:28f (3:1f, M/S)	II:468; VI:362; 385; 412n521
2:28ff (3:1ff, M/S)	I:105; 538; IV:167n100; 208; VI:399n422; VII:440
2:29 (3:2, M/S)	II:946(n14)
2:30 (3:3, M/S)	V:513n119; 518; VI:50n41; 936; 943; 948; VII:242; VIII:123; 124, n70
2:30f (3:3f, M/S)	V:509n87; VII:216; 430n49; VIII:118
2:30ff (3:3ff, M/S)	I:176
2:31 (3:4, M/S)	II:945(n3); 952; IV:531; 551; V:862n16; VII:61; 729; IX:9; 10; 201
2:32 (3:5, M/S)	II:579; 713; III:497; 499; 501; IV:153n42; 197; 198; 200; 201; 204; 205; 207; 1014; V:205; 209n32; 271; 272; 279, n231; VII:315; 316; 336n281;

	970; 973; 978(n50); 979; 980; 991n108
3 (4, M/S)	VI:509(n56)
3:1 (4:1, M/S)	II:946(n14)
3:1ff (4:1ff, M/S)	III:133
3:2 (4:2, M/S)	III:358(n17); 929; IV:256; 257n13; VI:537
3:2ff (4:2ff, M/S)	III:932n29
3:3 (4:3, M/S)	III:759; 773
3:4 (4:4, M/S)	III:675
3:6 (4:6, M/S)	VII:296; VIII:346
3:7 (4:7, M/S)	III:675; VIII:193
3:8 (4:8, M/S)	IV:372
3:9 (4:9, M/S)	III:701
3:9-12 (4:9-12, M/S)	VII:316
3:10 (4:10, M/S)	II:285; VI:647
3:12 (4:12, M/S)	IV:256; 257n13
3:12ff (4:12ff, M/S)	IV:256n10
3:13 (4:13, M/S)	I:176; III:133; IV:254; 255; 256; V:437n388; 839; 941; 943n14; VI:281
3:13-17 (4:13-17, M/S)	VII:316
3:14 (4:14, M/S)	II:174; 180; 330; 947; IV:256
3:14-16 (4:14-16, M/S)	VII:198
3:15 (4:15, M/S)	I:504(n6); VII:61; 430n49; IX:294
3:15f (4:15f, M/S)	IX:294n77
3:16 (4:16, M/S)	III:358(n17); 773; IV:204; 252n18; VII:310; 316n114; IX:282; 283
3:16f (4:16f, M/S)	VII:314
3:17 (4:17, M/S)	I:266; V:8; VI:524; 525; VII:294; 314; 315; 388
3:18 (4:18, M/S)	I:646; II:945; III:991; IV:278; 860; V:481; 767(n15); VI:59; 113; 596; VII:315; 317; VIII:318; 325n76
3:18f (4:18f, M/S)	VIII:318
3:19 (4:19, M/S)	I:153
3:20 (4:20, M/S)	VII:315
3:21 (4:21, M/S)	II:443; VII:309; 372; 388

AMOS

1	III:929; VII:187(n4)
1:1	IV:96; V:329; VI:686; 689n6; VII:198
1:2	III:1079; **VII:188;** 310; 316n114; IX:281; 282; 294
1:3	VII:720n3; VIII:132
1:3ff	III:1079
1:3-2:3	III:574

1:3-2:16	III:932n29; IV:708
1:4	VI:398(n417); 934; 936
1:6	VII:720n3; 744; VIII:132
1:7	VI:936
1:8	IV:196; 197
1:9	II:111n27; 114(n41); 115; VII:744; VIII:132
1:10	VI:936

1:11	II:480(n50); 481(n54); IV:312n3; 482; V:394, (n74); 470; VII:550n17; VIII:132; IX:99	4:1ff	III:573
		4:2	I:91; II:946(n13); V:293; 460n21
1:12	VI:936	4:4	I:274; VI:280; IX:57
1:13	VII:960; VIII:132	4:5	I:23n15; IV:1047n97; V:204; IX:409
1:14	VI:936; VIII:65		
1:15	VI:570	4:6	IV:982(n33); VIII:194
2	III:929; VII:187(n4)	4:6ff	IV:985; 987
2:1	V:404; VIII:132	4:6-11	V:405
2:1ff	IV:1014	4:6-12	V:400n139; VI:136(n7)
2:2	VI:936; IX:281	4:7	VI:686
2:3	III:924n8	4:7f	VIII:318
2:4	I:211n5; VI:234; VIII:132; IX:599	4:8	IV:982(n33); VIII:218
		4:9	IV:982(n33); VI:951; VII:752(n10), n15
2:4f	VII:312		
2:5	VI:936	4:10	IV:982(n33); V:49n26; 51n31; 392; 411n209; VII:97n23
2:6	III:303n12; IV:1039; VI:39; 890; VIII:132		
		4:11	IV:982(n33); VI:934; 935; 946
2:6ff	III:573; VI:324; 890	4:12	II:706; III:499; IV:162
2:7	I:91; V:255; 942; VI:578; 585; 890; VIII:9	4:13	I:63; III:1007, n57; 1008, n62; V:257; VI:360; VII:427; 429n46; IX:510
2:8	I:270n8; VII:759n2		
2:9	III:772; IV:1039; VI:985	5:1	III:837; IV:97; 204
2:9-11	V:403n154	5:1f	III:840
2:10	III:572; 772; VI:324; 890; VIII:136	5:1ff	III:151; VI:811
		5:2	I:700; III:841; IV:204; 839n56; V:833; VI:165n22
2:11	I:113; IV:6n4; 879		
2:11f	II:455; VI:798n119; 804n164; 805	5:3	III:929n21; IV:198; IX:467
		5:4	II:845n92; 854; III:919; 1075; IV:987; 1059n160; VI:193n139
2:12	IV:879; VI:136		
2:13	V:941		
2:13-16	VII:198	5:4ff	II:757; VI:811
2:14f	VII:980	5:5	IV:987
2:14-16	VI:509	5:6	II:692; III:150; IV:198; 202; 206; VII:166
2:15	III:337		
3:1	IV:97; IX:246	5:7	III:927; IV:1039; V:309; 403n157
3:1b	IV:147n9		
3:1f	IV:709n62	5:7-12	VI:324
3:1ff	III:929	5:8	III:574; IV:22; 610; VII:395; 429; VIII:318; IX:320
3:2	I:698(n37); 700; II:443; IV:147; 148; 162; 708; 1039; V:398; 403n154; VI:509; IX:246		
		5:8f	III:1008n62
		5:10	V:491
		5:10-12	V:403n157
		5:10ff	IV:1039
3:3	I:718	5:11	III:927; IV:145; 183; 708; VI:136(n7); 890
3:3-6	VI:811		
3:4	IX:281	5:12	I:252; III:140; 303; 927; IV:330; 389; V:942; VI:39; VII:187(n4)
3:5	VII:341; 730n9		
3:5f	IV:1014		
3:6	III:141; VI:563; VII:79; IX:302	5:13	II:946(n15); VI:550(n25)
3:7	IV:97; 921; V:611; 665(n52), n58; VI:638; 804n164; 805	5:14	II:845n92; 854; III:840; IV:161n86; 198; 202; 206; VI:550; 551; VII:775
3:8	II:719; III:575; IV:97; 154; 252, n18; VI:798; 810; 811; IX:200		
		5:14f	III:544; IV:987
3:9	III:33; 35	5:15	I:23n15; 388; III:927; IV:197; 198; **202;** 203; 204; 205; 206; 213; 687; 1039; VI:550; IX:378
3:10	III:138; VI:324		
3:12	III:929; IV:202; 204; 253n20; V:546; VIII:210		
		5:16	III:151; 837; 838; 839; 843; 846; VI:42, n9
3:13	IV:510n1		
3:14	II:443	5:16f	III:837; 841
4:1	III:140; IV:97; V:942; VI:39; 136n6; 890	5:16ff	III:929n21

5:18	II:945; 947; III:170; V:398; IX:322	7:13	I:570n28
5:18-20	V:401; 861; VII:198	7:14	II:455; III:575; IV:154; VI:689n6; 804, n158; 809; 813, n212; VII:758; VIII:346, n73
5:18ff	II:945, (n4); III:576		
5:19	IV:251n2; V:573		
5:20	II:945; 947; **VII:430;** IX:322	7:15	IV:154; 987; VI:689, n6; 798; 804
5:21	IV:149n17; 686; V:494; 722		
5:21ff	I:540; III:183; 239; 573; VI:811	7:15f	VI:798
5:21-27	V:403(n156); 494n9	7:16	I:218; IV:1108n24; 1121; VI:798
5:22	I:30n54; II:57; VII:1022, n3; IX:9n15; 57		
		7:16f	VI:810
5:23	II:788(n162); 798n247; VIII:494; 502	7:17	I:109; II:29; III:416(n16); 427; 1074; VI:585; 810
5:24	II:798n247; VIII:322	8:1	II:29; V:330
5:25	II:123(n71); III:182; IV:430; 1040; VII:934n40; VIII:138; IX:65n2; 67	8:1f	IV:94; VII:730n9
		8:1ff	IV:198; 204
		8:2	IV:95; 987; V:327; 329; 406
		8:3	IV:882n7; V:174; VII:66n7; 1045; VIII:194
5:25-27	II:170; VII:374		
5:26	II:382; III:88; 1074; IV:7; 8; VII:3n10; 369; 374; 375n36; VIII:248	8:4	VI:39; 889; 890
		8:4f	VII:3n10
		8:4ff	III:573; 927; IV:1039
5:26f	IV:861n167; VII:374	8:5	II:896; III:137; IV:632; VII:4
5:27	VII:374	8:6	III:303n12; VI:889; VIII:9
6:1	II:523(n36); IV:161n87; 162(n88), n90; VI:5; 191; VII:295	8:7	II:645; IV:708; V:460n21; VIII:526
		8:8	VI:596; 597; VIII:65
6:1-3	IV:982	8:8ff	III:929n21
6:2	IV:162n90	8:9	II:945(n3); IV:551; V:509; VII:61; 430; 440n152
6:3	II:945(n4); IV:162n90		
6:4	III:434; VIII:210	8:9f	VII:198
6:6	II:472; IV:162n88; 800; V:907, n20; IX:497, n4	8:10	II:798n247; III:838; 840; 841n77; IV:739; V:115; VI:42, n9; VII:60; 729; VIII:154
6:7	III:337		
6:8	I:598; V:460n21; 861; VI:300n9; VII:770; VIII:299; 300; 526; IX:622n63		
		8:11	II:227; 946(n13), (n16); VI:15; 16; VII:696n41
6:9	IV:202; 204	8:11f	I:644; IV:97; VIII:322
6:10	III:1070n169; IV:204; V:260; 263; VI:700	8:11ff	II:845
		8:14	I:268n2; IV:162n89; V:48, n22; 90n177; 459; VI:165n22
6:12	II:200; III:614; 927; VI:123		
6:13	III:397; IV:162n99	9:1	IV:202; V:330; VII:198n14; 978n14; 979; 980
6:14	III:140; IV:162(n89), n90; VI:810		
		9:1ff	I:218; IV:94; 198; 204
7-9	II:455; III:575	9:1-4	III:1008n62
7:1	II:29; V:330; VII:540n12	9:2	I:520; II:847n109; III:929(n21); 1076; V:229
7:1ff	III:929n21; IV:94; VI:811		
7:1-6	II:798	9:2-4	III:1006; 1008n62
7:2	IV:202; V:406; 809; VI:811	9:3	II:281n4; 283; V:572; 576
7:3	IV:202n27; 627; 989	9:4	VI:771; VII:655
7:4	II:29; 181; V:330; VI:398(n417); 935; VIII:55; 319n33	9:5	VI:42; 596; 597; VII:66; VIII:65
		9:5f	III:574; 1008n62
7:5	IV:202; V:406; VI:811	9:6	III:1009; 1012; V:503; 522n192; VIII:318
7:5f	V:809		
7:6	IV:627; 989	9:7	II:111n27; III:572; 574; IV:162; 1014; VI:873
7:7	II:29; V:330		
7:8	IV:987; V:329; 406; 749	9:7f	VI:804
7:9	IV:814n107; VIII:59	9:8	I:270; 320; V:376; VIII:51; 52n21
7:10ff	IV:167		
7:10-17	VI:798; 813n213	9:8-15	VIII:427n211
7:12	III:571; V:329; VI:809	9:9	IV:280; VI:399; VII:291n2
7:12f	VI:798, n119		

9:10	II:945(n4)	9:11-15	I:567; V:862n16
9:11	I:199; 567; II:946n10; V:139; VI:162; VII:370; 374; 375n36; 716; VIII:362, n178; 480, n14; 483, n36; IX:524; 525	9:12	III:497; 498; 1079; IV:196; V:263; 271; 481; VI:464
		9:13	II:946(n13), (n16); V:767(n15); VI:59
		9:13ff	II:405(n31)
9:11f	VII:374; 716n6; VIII:254; IX:509	9:14	VI:136(n7)
9:11ff	III:575; 576; IV:198	9:15	III:772n7; VII:541

OBADIAH

1	I:403n37; II:947; III:141; 142; V:330n81	14	II:945n6; III:141; 142; VII:944; 978n48
3	VIII:300; 526	15	II:330; 947; VI:471
4	VIII:301	16	VI:139n38; 150(n19)
5	III:755; IV:258	17	IV:197; 198; 205; 316; VII:971; 973; 978(n50); 979
7	II:403n23; 407n37; 418		
8	V:748; VII:477(n91); 480	17f	VII:316
10	VII:187, (n5); 936	20	III:358(n17); IV:877n14; VII:296
11	I:266; III:759		
12	II:945n6; 947n22; III:141; 142	21	I:569; 570n28; II:443; VII:314; 316; 970n16, n17
13	I:401; VI:925n44		

JONAH

1	III:407; 970	1:13	VI:570
1-4	III:407n8	1:14	II:184n8
1:2	III:701; V:404	1:15	V:393; VII:66; 641
1:3	III:408	1:16	III:408; VIII:323n57
1:4	III:408; VI:360; VII:921	1:17 (2:1, M/S)	III:410; IV:1124; VI:158; VII:29n226; VIII:38
1:4ff	VIII:323n57		
1:5	III:408; 434; VI:467; VII:359; IX:200	1:17b (2:1b, M/S)	VIII:459n405
		1:17-2:1 (2:1f, M/S)	III:786; 787
1:5f	VIII:553n58	1:17-2:10 (2, M/S)	III:408; 409
1:6	III:408; 499	2:2 (2:3, M/S)	III:786; IX:281
1:7	III:759; 763; VI:164	2:2ff (2:3ff, M/S)	II:798
1:9	III:359; 1013; V:516n144; VII:171	2:2-9 (2:3-10, M/S)	V:202
		2:3 (2:4, M/S)	III:613; 786; VI:992
1:10	III:408; IX:199	2:5 (2:6, M/S)	VII:963; VIII:322; IX:619
1:11	III:408; VI:570	2:6 (2:7, M/S)	III:746n33; IX:98; 99
1:12	III:407; 408	2:9 (2:10, M/S)	II:794(n210), (n211); V:203n16;

	VII:973n34; 1022n2; IX:282	4	V:395n86
2:10 (2:11, M/S)	VII:233n230	4:1	IV:318; 529; V:395
3	III:408	4:2	IV:376(n18); 378(n39); 989;
3:2	I:368; III:701; 715		V:160n17; 405; IX:89;
3:4	III:701; VIII:137		378(n52); 383, n81; 384
3:4ff	III:574; VII:62	4:2f	II:798
3:5	III:700; VI:187n115	4:3	II:46; IV:1108n24; 1122
3:5f	VII:60	4:4	IV:318; V:395
3:5ff	IV:928; VII:63	4:5	VII:371; 390; 395
3:5-8	VII:60	4:6	III:81n70; IV:530; VII:395;
3:6	III:443; IV:981n19; VII:59n25		IX:366n61
3:7	I:675; II:690; III:700; VIII:318	4:6f	III:1012
3:7f	IV:981	4:6-8	VIII:38
3:8	II:463; 798; IV:928; 981(n19);	4:7	VII:453
	V:53; VI:551; VII:60, n39;	4:8	II:798; VI:360; 368; IX:666
	720	4:9	II:850; IV:318; 323n1; V:395
3:8-10	IV:989	4:10	V:936; VIII:340; 347
3:9	V:398; 400; VII:720	4:11	III:574; IX:670
3:9f	IV:989; V:53; VII:62n50; 720		

MICAH

1:1	IV:96; 98; 99; V:329; VI:836	2:7	III:357n12; IV:376n14; VI:364;
1:2	IV:485; VI:300n9		367
1:2-4	III:929	2:8	II:408; IV:986n55; VII:922
1:2ff	II:945(n3), n7; III:932n29	2:9	IV:915
1:3	VIII:199	2:10	V:632; IX:100
1:4	V:480; VI:935; VII:66;	2:11	II:229; VI:360; IX:29n98;
	VIII:406		599n52; 629
1:5	VII:296; 311	2:12	II:57n2; III:357(n12); IV:196;
1:5-7	VI:1003n8		197; 201n25; 203; 204; 214;
1:7	II:377(n11); VI:587; VIII:154		VI:496
1:8	III:151; 153; 837; 840; VI:42,	2:12f	I:569(n23)
	n9; 627n38	2:13	IV:201n25; 204
1:8f	VII:325n191	3:1	III:357(n12), n12; V:403n157
1:9	VI:925n44; VII:296; 311	3:1f	III:927
1:10	IV:543	3:2	III:56n15; 927; IV:685; 687;
1:11	III:845n99		VI:550; 551; VII:108
1:12f	III:477	3:3	IV:557n22; VII:108, n78; 745
1:13	I:487; VII:187(n4)	3:4	II:798; 946(n15), (n16); III:899;
1:14	III:778; IV:521n4; IX:597n38		V:862; VI:773; VII:720
1:15	III:776	3:5	I:92; III:575; 701; IV:161;
1:16	IX:445		VI:234; 807
2:1	III:83n81, n82; 478; 828n10;	3:5-7	VI:805
	IV:285; IX:625	3:5ff	II:404; III:575
2:1ff	III:573; VI:324	3:5-8	VI:813n213
2:1-11	VI:324	3:6	V:370; VII:424n5; 427n39
2:2	III:775; 777; VI:890	3:7	V:329; VI:809; IX:629
2:3	IV:285; V:449	3:8	I:66; 103; II:299; III:357(n12),
2:4	III:772; IV:557n20		n12; 928; VI:363; 407n487;
2:5	III:527; 529n90		VII:187(n4)
2:6	IX:29n98	3:9	III:357(n12), n12; 927; V:449;

7:15	III:35; IV:859(n138)		482; V:743; VII:187(n4),
7:16	V:548n48		(n5); 881n43; IX:383
7:17	V:572n81; VII:453n12;	7:19	II:481(n57); VI:992
	IX:126n130; 203	7:20	II:479n35; 480n48; 483n95
7:18	III:617n1; IV:196; 204; 207;		

NAHUM

1-3	III:574		VIII:578n60; 582n102;
1:1	I:681n11; II:752; IV:96		IX:281; 626
1:2	II:443; III:1078; V:397n114;	2:9 (2:10, M/S)	II:238; III:881
	403n162; 404; 405; 407; 660	2:10 (2:11, M/S)	IV:337; IX:624; 669
1:2f	V:432n353	2:11 (2:12, M/S)	V:155; IX:198
1:2ff	IV:376n17; 377	2:12 (2:13, M/S)	IV:253n19; V:155; VI:456; 457
1:2-6	VII:198	2:13 (2:14, M/S)	II:645; VI:278; 995
1:3	IV:905; V:49; 405, n171;	3:1	VIII:108; IX:598
	VI:627; VIII:65	3:1-7	VI:587
1:4	III:1005n47	3:2	IV:518; VII:401n5; IX:280;
1:5	V:480; VII:66		281n11
1:6	V:396; 399; VI:935	3:3	VI:167; VII:665; 1045, n267;
1:7	I:700; II:752; 945n6; III:142;		1046n276
	IV:148; IX:486	3:4	I:515; IV:32n12; VI:248(n129);
1:8	II:229		276, n13; 584; 587, n46; 594;
1:8f	VIII:65		IX:246; 389n116
1:9	IV:285	3:6	I:288; 598; II:33; III:427n7
1:11	IV:285; VI:551	3:7	V:777n21; 789
1:14	VIII:302	3:10	III:759; IV:915
1:15 (2:1, M/S)	I:66; II:403n22; 708n9;	3:11	II:812; IV:546; VI:150(n19);
	712(n59); 715; 716; 795n220;		VII:66; 570
	V:480; VIII:63	3:12	VII:414n4; 751(n4); 752, n8
2:1 (2:2, M/S)	V:496; VII:415	3:13	II:812; VI:936
2:2 (2:3, M/S)	III:357n12; 757; VII:720n2;	3:15	I:559
	VIII:300	3:16	V:469
2:3 (2:4, M/S)	III:337; V:633; VI:935	3:17	VIII:199
2:4 (2:5, M/S)	IV:22; 26	3:18	II:57n2; III:435; VI:488n29;
2:7 (2:8, M/S)	III:838; VI:67(n50); 382n260;		VII:401n4

HABAKKUK

1:1	VI:804	1:5	II:637; 641; III:32; 34, n35; 40;
1:2	VII:974		632; 1006; VI:186
1:3	III:828	1:5-11	V:509n87
1:4	VII:404n5; 718; VIII:52	1:6	III:777; VI:122

1:7	III:5; IX:9
1:8	IV:309; V:469; VII:401n4; VIII:515n46
1:9	VI:270; VIII:65
1:10	V:629, n18; 631
1:11	III:86n100
1:12	VI:95(n8); 256, (n16); 257; VII:611
1:12ff	IV:1014
1:13	II:177n8; III:414; 632; VI:158
1:14	II:823n44
1:15	VIII:65; IX:363
2:1	V:325
2:2	I:743; **VI:820;** VIII:229; 230
2:2f	VIII:230n33
2:3	II:51n6; 58; IV:583; 584; VIII:53; 594; IX:592, n64
2:4	II:177, n8; 187, n55; 191, n72; 739; 741; 845(n92); 865(n289); III:919; IV:1059n160; V:305; VI:190, n125; VII:597; 598; 599; **873;** IX:651n212
2:4b	V:305n17
2:5	I:227; II:57; III:632; IV:253n21; VI:129; VIII:304; IX:619
2:6	I:556n9; II:662n2; V:748
2:7	IV:941
2:8	VII:187, (n4)
2:9	I:157; VI:269
2:11	IV:270; VII:453n15; 858
2:13	IX:666
2:14	VIII:322
2:15	VI:151
2:15f	VI:139; 150

2:16	V:165; VI:132; 139(n38); 149; 150; VII:66
2:17	VI:270; VII:187, (n4)
2:18	II:377(n19); 523; VI:5; 191; 257; 258; IX:73; 599n53
2:18f	II:377(n25)
2:19	IV:941; VI:361
2:20	II:752; III:1070n169
3	V:407; VI:47n19
3:1	VI:804
3:2	I:704; II:30; 330; 459; 641; IV:974; V:287n25; 393; 408n191; IX:55
3:3	460(n18); III:86n100; V:510
3:3ff	I:505n5; III:1006; V:861
3:4	I:22n2; II:243; VII:429; IX:320
3:5	VI:167n2; 628
3:6	V:480; VII:66
3:6ff	III:1005n47
3:7	III:828n10; IV:974n4; VII:370
3:8	V:470
3:9	VI:598
3:9ff	I:608; V:297
3:10	IX:280; 281; 669
3:13	IV:183; V:861; VII:970; 976; 1013; VIII:526; IX:502; 503; 504
3:14	I:286; 508; VII:197
3:15	VIII:317; 322
3:15f	IX:283
3:16	II:945n6; III:142; 609; 787; IV:974n6; VI:26
3:17	III:616; VII:752n15; IX:51
3:18	VII:1013; IX:524; 641n147
3:19	II:788; IV:943, n7; VIII:65

ZEPHANIAH

1	II:945(n3), (n5)
1:1	IV:96; 98; 99
1:2-18	VII:447; VIII:9
1:3	VI:749; VII:342; 344; 345; 346, n43; 347n46
1:4	V:262; VII:296; VIII:197
1:4ff	VII:344n28
1:5	V:459; 506(n69)
1:6	VI:193n139
1:7	II:35; 330; 705; 752; 947; III:495; 1070n169; VII:838n15
1:7ff	VIII:428n212

1:8	VII:533
1:10f	VII:304
1:11	III:603n2
1:12	I:14n12; II:946(n15), (n16); III:632; 1075; VII:312
1:14	II:330; 947; IV:531; VI:122; IX:281
1:14-18	VII:198
1:15	I:346; II:944; 945n6; III:141; 142; IV:905; V:401; 430; VI:26; VII:428n40; 430n49; VIII:281
1:15-18	V:861

1:16	VII:80	3:8	II:57; 879; IV:483; 485; 583;
1:17	VII:105n57; 445n3; VIII:281		584; V:399; 403n162; 410;
1:18	II:879; V:401; VI:935; 936n46;		VI:194; 935; 936n46;
	VII:562; VIII:65		VII:803, n26
2:1	VIII:9	3:8ff	III:932n29
2:1-3	V:401	3:9	II:898; III:499; IV:37; 144;
2:2	V:398; 410, n199; 861; VIII:9		V:255; 260; VII:493
2:3	II:645; 790n186; 948; VI:648;	3:10	II:57n2; IX:57
	VIII:6; **9**	3:11	VIII:300
2:4-15	VIII:9	3:11-13	IV:205
2:5	V:168	3:12	II:752; IV:197; 204; 207; 208;
2:7	II:602; IV:200; 208; VII:719		VI:647; 888; 890; 900;
2:8ff	III:574		VIII:9; 10
2:9	III:773; IV:196; 197; 200; 208	3:12f	VI:648
2:10	VIII:300; 301	3:13	IV:196; 197; 204; 207; VI:470;
2:11	IX:9		IX:198; 598n43, n49
2:13	I:401n23	3:14	II:787n146, (n149), (n152);
2:14	V:156; IX:281; 302		III:700(n12); 701; 702;
2:15	II:523(n36); VIII:300		VII:296; IX:367n66
3:1	IV:332n10; 334; 351n1;	3:14f	VII:294; 316; IX:363n34
	VIII:300	3:14-17	IX:363, n34
3:1-20	V:606n57	3:15	I:162; 569, (n23); III:702;
3:2	II:50; V:606; 611; VI:5; 192		IV:334; VII:314; IX:200
3:3	III:924n8; IV:252n19; 309	3:16	III:26; VII:313
3:3f	VI:805	3:16-18a	IX:363n34
3:4	III:632; IV:1045; VI:406n473;	3:17	I:33n68; II:294; III:451;
	VII:187; VIII:302		VII:314; 972; 976; IX:363
3:4b	IV:1040	3:19	II:57; V:252; VII:978
3:5	III:928	3:19f	II:946(n15); III:646; V:261
3:6	V:49; VIII:526	3:20	II:57; VII:715n4
3:7	II:50; V:606; 611; IX:99		

HAGGAI

1:1	VI:804; VII:37(n12)	2:5	I:103; II:108n16; III:26; VI:363;
1:2	III:459		367; 370
1:3	VI:804	2:6	I:382; 678n5; V:509n87; 515,
1:4-9	VIII:525n2		n134; VII:199, n22; 722;
1:5	III:607; IV:1108n24; VIII:28		IX:297
1:5-11	V:398; 405	2:7	II:368n16; 927
1:6	IV:697; V:172; VI:132	2:7f	VII:315
1:6-11	VI:136(n7)	2:7-9	VII:315
1:9	V:172; VIII:229n28	2:7ff	VI:525
1:10	VII:597	2:9	III:239; 1027; V:734n61;
1:12	I:402n25; IV:196; 197; 205n36;		VI:867n11; VIII:515n46
	VI:804	2:10	VI:804
1:13	I:58(n8), n10; 77n12	2:10-14	VII:306; 309
1:14	IV:196; 197; 205n36; VI:362;	2:11	IV:1045
	IX:629	2:12f	VI:145n2
2:1	VI:804	2:13	IX:620
2:2	IV:197; 205n36	2:13f	IV:645(n12)
2:3	II:243	2:14	II:645

ZECHARIAH

4:11	IV:327		IX:445
4:11-14	II:933	7:11	I:559n2; VI:10n1
4:14	I:679; III:1061; IV:569; 863;	7:12	I:103; IV:1047; V:469; VI:362;
	V:839; VI:826, n320;		805; IX:627
	IX:500-501; 512; 518n137;	7:13	III:899
	520	7:14	I:699; IV:183; VIII:28
5:1	V:329	8:1-6	IV:205
5:1-4	IV:94	8:2	II:884; VII:313
5:2	V:327	8:2f	V:404
5:3	V:460; 461; 466	8:3	V:254; VI:185n97; 524;
5:3f	III:754; IX:598		VII:294n3; 296; 314; 315;
5:4	V:461; VIII:63		317; 372; 380; 388
5:5	II:679; VI:579	8:4	II:846n103; V:767(n15);
5:5ff	I:296; IV:94		VI:967; VII:296; 316
5:6	VI:579	8:5	V:49; 628; VII:316; VIII:342
5:6ff	IV:632	8:6	II:285; 306; 946(n14); III:32;
5:7	III:441		IV:197; 204; 205, n36;
6:1	V:482; 503; 508n84; VI:579		V:730n24
6:1ff	IV:551; VI:367	8:7	VII:970n16, n17; 978
6:1-8	III:337; IV:94; VIII:131	8:8	II:196; VII:296; 316; 372; 380;
6:2	IV:550; 551		388
6:2ff	VI:952	8:9	VI:804
6:4	III:1061; IV:94	8:10	II:407; III:141; IV:697
6:5	I:792(n3); V:503; 838; VI:360	8:11	IV:197; 205n36
6:5f	VI:579	8:12	II:406; III:773; IV:197; 205n36
6:6	IV:550; 551; VI:952	8:13	I:450(n6); III:26; V:254;
6:7	VI:570		VII:970; 978
6:8	V:411; VI:363, n154; VII:315	8:14	IV:627; 989
6:9	VII:314n107	8:15	III:26; VII:296; 313
6:9ff	I:567	8:16	I:234; II:406; 418; III:942;
6:9-15	VII:314, n107; 625n62;		VI:316; IX:601n74
	IX:507-508	8:16f	IV:928
6:10b	VII:314n107	8:17	I:25n29; IV:285; 289; 686
6:11	VII:625; IX:507n65	8:19	II:407; IV:928, n22; 982(n32);
6:11ab	VII:314n107		IX:363
6:12	I:352; 353; IV:878; V:254;	8:20-23	II:368
	VI:69n65; 988; VIII:480;	8:21	II:786; VI:773
	IX:508; 525	8:21f	VI:773
6:12a	VII:314n107	8:22	II:786; III:315; VI:537; VII:316
6:12f	III:240; IX:524	8:23	II:946(n14); III:358n16; 904;
6:13	I:460(n18); II:403; 407n37;		VII:779
	IV:5; VII:314n107; IX:508;	9:1	IX:248
	524	9:2	VII:480
6:13c	VII:625	9:3	III:138; V:49n25
6:14	IV:584; VII:625	9:4	III:778
6:15a	VII:314n107; 315	9:5	II:522
7:1	VIII:132	9:6	I:266; III:411; VIII:300
7:2	II:786; III:315	9:7	IV:37; 204; 208
7:3	IV:928; 982(n32)	9:9	I:578; II:187; 787(n149);
7:5	IV:32n13; 925; 928; 982(n32);		III:337, n8; 338n8; 700(n12);
	1103n41		701; 702; IV:860; V:234;
7:5f	II:690		**284-285** (285n9); 286; 287,
7:5ff	III:239; IV:928		n24; 687n250; VI:39; 647;
7:5b-6	IV:983		649; 893n65; 960; VII:327;
7:6	II:689		978; 1013; VIII:7n20; 342;
7:7	VI:805; 832; VII:307n91;		IX:364; 365, n47; 367n66;
	VIII:35n10		528n236
7:7ff	IV:983	9:9f	I:567n13; II:405; V:862;
7:9	I:234; II:479(n24), (n31); 481;		VI:511(n76); 647; VII:314;
	482n90; III:923; 942;		IX:363; **508**
	V:160(n18); VI:469	9:9ff	V:284
7:10	III:606; V:488n4; 845n17;	9:10	II:405; III:337n4; VI:278;

	599n33; 610n28; 648
9:11	I:175n20; II:115; 132
9:12	VII:805
9:13	V:639; VII:294
9:14	VII:66; 78; 80; 83; 84; 197
9:15	IX:458n169
9:16	II:368; VI:690; VII:266n6
10:1	II:785(n119); 798n252; IX:676
10:2	I:447; III:203; 435; 828n10; V:231; 233; 789; 907n21; VIII:6
10:3	II:602; V:857n3; VI:488, (n29); 500(n9); VIII:28
10:4	VI:642n5; IX:524
10:5	V:49n25; 941
10:6	II:481; VII:720n3; 974; IX:524
10:7	III:606
10:8	II:57; VI:487(n25)
10:10	II:57
10:11	II:945n6; VII:605; VIII:299; 300; 325n75
10:12	III:646; 647
11:1ff	IV:45n77
11:2	V:174
11:3	IV:252n19; IX:281
11:4	III:79; **VII:936**
11:4-14	III:849
11:4-16	VII:936n6
11:4-17	VI:488; VII:936n7
11:4-13:9	III:849n120
11:5	II:764; V:907
11:5f	VI:488(n29)
11:5ff	VI:690
11:6	III:203; VII:936
11:7	VI:647n11; **VII:936**
11:7ff	VI:967
11:7-10	III:556
11:8	I:559; III:823n2
11:9	VII:107; 108n78
11:11	VI:647n11; 898n106; 900
11:12	IV:697; VII:647
11:12f	VII:273; VIII:180
11:13	III:220; 991
11:14	II:106
11:15	VI:277n14; VII:359
11:15-17	III:849n121
11:15ff	VI:488
11:16	II:338; 601; III:766; IV:183; VII:108n78
11:16f	VI:488(n29)
11:17	IV:521n4; VIII:279; IX:290
12ff	II:946
12:1	III:358(n17); 1008; 1009; V:502(n40); VI:256; 257; 361(n131); 362; IX:629
12:1ff	II:945
12:2	VI:150n24; 152n33; VII:66
12:2-6	VII:316
12:3	V:362; 942; 943
12:4	II:450; III:5; IV:360n4; VIII:281n77
12:5	III:617n1

12:6	IV:22; VI:936n46
12:7	VII:315; 970n16; 978
12:7f	V:1017n6
12:8	I:58n11; III:849; VII:316
12:9	IV:48
12:9-13:1	VII:314n106
12:10	II:446; 447; 468f; 945; III:831, n3; 834; 837; 838; 847; **849-850** (850n126); IV:739; V:115; 361; 1017n6; VI:361; 362; 365n162; 370; 446; 488; 874n17; VII:296; **IX:381;** 398n216; 527
12:10f	V:361
12:10ff	I:678; III:841; 848; **850-851;** IV:909; V:697n318; VIII:266n52; IX:250; 527n233
12:10-14	III:839
12:11	I:468; III:836n52; 841n78; 849; 858
12:12	II:446; 447; III:837; 850; 851n128; V:697; 1017n7; VII:237; 238; VIII:437n282
12:12-14	III:838; 849; VII:817n115; IX:246
12:12ff	III:838
12:14	III:847; 851; IV:197; V:862(n16); VII:237; 238; VIII:437n282
13:1	I:537; III:849; 991; IV:301; VI:978n13; VII:296; 534n42; VIII:318; 320
13:1f	II:945
13:1-6	VI:488
13:2	II:377(n11); III:428; IV:207; 678; VI:241; 362; 370; 812; 819n266; VII:842n4
13:2f	**VI:812-813**
13:2ff	III:981; VI:799
13:2-6	VI:806; 809n190; **812-813** (813n209); 818; 821; 822n282; IX:599
13:3	V:963n106; 983; VI:813(n211)
13:4	II:937; III:593; IV:637; VI:969n22; VII:63n54
13:4ff	**VI:812-813**
13:5	V:657n4; VI:813n212
13:6	I:39n91; VII:661n31
13:7	IV:343; 897n15; V:940; VI:488, n35, n37; **492-493** (493n73, n78); 691; **VII:349;** 353n79; 419; 421
13:7b	VI:492; 493
13:7-9	III:849, n121; VII:419
13:8	IV:207; VI:493
13:8f	VI:488; 493
13:9	III:499; IV:207; VI:935; 949
13:9a	VI:493
13:9b	VI:493
14	V:11
14:1ff	II:945(n3)

14:2	IV:205; 736; VIII:428n219	14:10	III:344; IV:254; 575;
14:3	II:679		VII:307n91; 314; 317
14:4	IV:256; V:481; 484n100, n102;	14:11	I:354; 355
	VI:628; VII:281; 960;	14:12	VII:705; VIII:280n66
	VIII:406	14:13	II:450; III:33
14:4f	VII:307n91	14:14	II:366(n9)
14:5	I:79(n24); V:862n16; VII:66n7;	14:16	I:569; II:798(n252); IV:197;
	198; 796, n144; VIII:459n403		208; VII:373; 390
14:6f	IX:322	14:16f	I:569, (n24); IV:278n77;
14:7	II:945; IX:321n72		VII:373; VIII:326n81
14:8	I:753n13; II:679; 945; III:789;	14:16-19	VII:317
	991; V:40; 767(n15); VI:113;	14:17	II:798(n252); III:882; VII:534
	596; 606; VII:317; 534n42;	14:17f	IX:246
	VIII:318; 325n76, n78	14:18f	VII:373; 390
14:9	I:569, (n24); 571; III:98n192;	14:20	III:1037
	1080n211; VII:314	14:21	III:603n2; V:122; VI:895n88

MALACHI

1	IV:179		IX:96; 99
1:1	IV:96	2:9	V:52
1:2	I:34, n71; IV:685	2:10	I:34; 35; III:89; 1008;
1:2f	IV:175; 179; 691; VIII:343		V:969n130; 973; 1002; 1012;
1:3	III:759; 760; IV:685		VIII:351; 352
1:3f	V:404n164	2:11	III:89; VII:312; 542n21;
1:4	V:393(n67); 405; 411		VIII:352
1:6	I:34; III:32n21; V:652; 979;	2:12	III:182; VIII:7
	VIII:345; 352	2:13	II:738; 743; III:726n2; IV:686;
1:7	VIII:214		VII:600
1:8	III:30; VIII:280n73	2:13f	I:784
1:9	II:786; III:315; VI:773;	2:14	I:776; II:116n44; III:801;
	IX:377n37; 378n50		IV:512; 731; VII:874n19
1:10	III:53; VII:745	2:15	II:438n18; IV:195n7; 196;
1:11	III:190; IV:539; V:258;		VI:361; VII:542
	VIII:194; IX:68	2:15f	VI:361
1:12	VIII:214	2:17	II:196; 738; III:544; VI:550
1:13	V:936; IX:57; 65n2	3	II:300
1:14	I:569(n24); 579; II:777; V:258;	3f (3, M/S)	VI:988
	562n15; IX:9; 96; 98; 201	3:1	I:58(n8), n10, (n11); 78n18;
2:2	III:612		83n58; 500(n18); 610;
2:3	II:624(n5); IV:281n6		II:124n72; 930; 931; 933;
2:4f	II:933		936n65; 937; III:45(n9); 103;
2:4ff	IV:1045		593n3; 1061n116; V:49; 70,
2:4-9	IV:235		n96; VI:684; 772; 777; 840
2:5	II:408; 933n37; III:32n21;		VIII:459n403
	V:258; VII:589, n13; 590;	3:1f	II:945; III:929; IV:584; V:104;
	780; IX:199	3:2	372; VI:398(n417); 935; 944;
2:6	I:236; II:407; VII:780		VII:648; VIII:584n114
2:6ff	IV:1045	3:2-4	II:931
2:7	I:58n8, n12; 77n12; VII:696;	3:2ff	III:932n29
	IX:237	3:5	I:626; IV:483; 697; 730; V:263;
2:8	VII:341n16; 343, n23; 344, n30;		460; 461; 861; IX:445; 446

326

I ESDRAS

II ESDRAS

See EZRA; NEHEMIAH

TOBIT

1:1	I:616(n14)	4:6f	VI:894
1:3	II:486n4; 855n170; V:52; VI:469	4:7	II:486n4; VI:895; VII:720; 721n10
1:4	I:512; IV:168; 169; VII:388; VIII:618	4:8	V:171
		4:8ff	III:137; 138
1:8	III:439; VI:735; 736; 740n147; 900; IX:447n57	4:10	II:196; 677; IV:536n33; IX:652
		4:10f	III:187; 241
1:13	III:439; IV:743; 746n20; VIII:618	4:11	II:677; V:789
		4:12	III:192; VI:869; VIII:354
1:14	I:526; VIII:162	4:12f	V:11n65
1:16	II:486n4	4:13	III:446; IV:642; VI:15; VIII:526
1:17	I:774; III:546n32; VI:16n31		
1:17f	III:545	4:14	IV:697; VII:716
1:18	I:622; III:754; V:413(n215)	4:15	I:40n99; IV:546; 685n6
1:21	II:566	4:15a	IV:685
1:22	VII:738	4:16	I:774; II:486n4; 689; III:546n32; VI:16n31; 895
2:1	I:95; VI:45; VIII:210		
2:2	V:327; VIII:209	4:17	II:185; 468; 689
2:5	IV:300; 318	4:18	III:632; V:728
2:9	IV:300; 337(n5)	4:19	I:631(n19); 633; IV:682; V:53; 111; VIII:8
2:10	III:129; 206; VII:731n14; VIII:279; 280	4:20	VIII:162
2:11	II:660n1	4:21	IX:205
2:12	IV:697	5:1	V:985n251
2:13	II:561; 564	5:3	IV:697; IX:435
2:14	II:195n3; 486(n3), n4; IV:697	5:4	VII:643
3:1	III:723; IV:323; VII:600	5:5	VIII:194
3:1-6	V:205	5:6	V:20n143
3:2	I:242; 249; II:185; 642; V:55	5:8	III:618
3:3	I:115	5:9	IX:302
3:3f	VIII:291(n150)	5:10	I:498; II:684n1; V:324; 328; VI:283n26; VII:428
3:4	I:223		
3:5	I:242; 249	5:12	IV:698
3:6	I:456; II:855n177; IV:328n3; VI:368; VII:720	5:14	III:544n19; V:413n217; VI:235, (n37); 986; VII:324; VIII:240
3:7	V:617	5:17	II:739; V:49; 111; 113; VII:982n65; IX:126; 127
3:8	VI:456; 549		
3:10	II:855n177; III:46n20	5:18	III:722
3:11	I:95; 200n10; II:638n9; 764; VII:815	5:19	**VI:88-89**; IX:89
		5:21	II:684n1
3:11-15	V:205	5:22	V:111; 113
3:12	II:793	5:23	III:722
3:13	IV:328n3	6:1	VIII:240
3:15	II:855n177; III:776; IV:736; 738; VII:738	6:2	VI:158
		6:2f	V:638
3:17	III:776; IV:328; V:324; VI:549	6:4	VII:960
4:1	V:617; VIII:162	6:5	VII:960
4:3	II:855n170; VI:369; VIII:172	6:6	V:65n64
4:3-5	V:974	6:8	V:494; 586n19; VI:369
4:5	III:45n13; IV:682; V:52; 54n34; 737	6:8ff	II:12
		6:11	IV:738; VII:738
4:6	I:242; V:111; 112	6:12	II:213n11; III:776

	VII:724; IX:587		
14:6	V:11; VI:234; IX:205	14:10	V:593; VII:981
14:7	I:39n96; 242; II:196; 481n67;	14:10b	V:594n5
	V:214n43; VII:982	14:11	II:196; 486(n3); VI:469
14:8	III:407n8	14:13	III:776
14:9	VIII:141	14:15	I:200; 336

JUDITH

1:9	VI:597	5:10	V:843
1:11	III:351; IX:204	5:11	VII:527n2; VIII:7
1:12	II:443	5:17	IV:686
1:14	III:881	5:18	II:105
2:1	II:443	5:19	II:99
2:2	I:634; IV:814	5:20	I:115; II:46; 601n12; VII:357n105
2:3	VII:109n95	5:21	IV:35n18; V:241
2:5	V:891	5:22	I:731; IV:34; VII:370
2:6	III:625	5:23	III:906; IV:35n18; VIII:354
2:12	II:855n173	5:24	II:46; 601n12
2:13	VIII:61	6:2	IV:697; V:170n3; VII:271(n12)
2:15	IV:182	6:3	III:906
2:16	VIII:34	6:4	VI:169n11
2:25	VI:772	6:5	IV:697
2:27	IV:281	6:7	VI:511n77
2:28	VI:164; IX:199; 204	6:9	VI:169n11
3:1	II:418	6:10	VII:370
3:3	VII:370n8	6:12	IV:8
3:7	VII:625	6:13	V:480; VI:985
3:8	I:720; II:233; IV:61	6:14	IV:328
3:10	VII:449	6:16	VI:660n54
4:1	III:362	6:18	VI:163n13
4:3	VI:767	6:19	V:379; VIII:10; 526
4:5	VI:767; VIII:162	6:20	V:778
4:6	III:266	6:21	VI:660n54
4:7	V:104; VII:605	7:1	III:362; IV:34; V:762
4:8	III:266; VI:660n54; VII:862n14	7:4	I:553
4:9	II:464; VIII:7	7:7	II:601; IV:34
4:9ff	IV:929	7:9	II:46
4:10	IV:697	7:11	II:46; IV:34
4:10ff	IV:981	7:12	V:480; VI:985
4:11	IV:981(n20)	7:13	IV:34
4:12	II:463	7:15	VI:550
4:12f	I:95	7:16	I:455n4
4:14	IV:220; VII:58	7:18	V:585; VII:370
4:15	II:602	7:19	VI:369; IX:666
5:1	III:362; VII:341; 345; VIII:154	7:21	IV:634n10; VI:132
5:2	V:413(n215)	7:23	VI:660n54
5:3	IV:35n18	7:24	II:418
5:5-7	III:1064	7:25	VI:160
5:6	V:843	7:26	IV:34
5:7	I:631n16; V:313; 843; 948	7:27	II:855(n175); 856n183
5:8	V:51; 843; VI:772	7:28	IV:511, n3; V:500; VII:271(n14)
5:9	V:842	7:30	VIII:52

7:32	VIII:10		VII:110
8:1-7	IX:445n45	10:14	IV:974
8:4	IX:445	10:15	VII:370; 981; IX:633
8:4-8	IX:446	10:16	VII:641
8:5	II:793; VII:58; 59; 371; 390n5;	10:18	V:864
	IX:445	10:19	III:30; 35; 632; VII:527n2
8:6	IV:929; 930n40; VII:7; 16;	10:22	IV:17
	IX:445	10:23	III:30
8:8	VI:550; IX:205	11:1	I:777
8:9	VI:550; IX:666	11:2	IV:35n18
8:10	VI:660n54	11:3	II:855(n175); VII:981
8:12	VII:271(n14)	11:4	I:159
8:12ff	VI:199(n169)	11:6	VI:638; VIII:72
8:14	I:517; II:656; 657n8; IV:10;	11:7	II:855n173
	953; 965; 974; V:412(n212)	11:8	III:35; V:725n18; VII:705n24;
8:15	III:47n33		706
8:17	VII:981	11:10	II:46; 442n1
8:18	III:246n73; VII:271(n14)	11:11	V:412(n212)
8:19	VI:166	11:12	IV:1048; VII:591
8:20	I:702; II:529	11:12f	III:264n29
8:22	I:28n44; III:675; VI:750n33;	11:13	III:439
	IX:168n180	11:14	VI:660n54; VII:862n14
8:24	III:919	11:16	VI:639
8:25	IX:368n81; 409; 414n75	11:17	III:124n2; 125; 129
8:25f	VI:26	11:19	I:716
8:25ff	VI:199(n163)	11:20	III:30
8:26	III:191	11:22	IV:35n18
8:27	II:330; 443; III:325(n23);	12:2	VI:120; VII:342
	IV:515; 1021; VI:949	12:4	II:855n173
8:29	IV:590; VI:258; VII:270	12:6	II:679
8:31	VI:54; 132; 300	12:7	I:535; IV:577; VIII:132; 218
8:32	VI:639	12:8	V:53; 69; 113n14; VIII:354
8:33	II:602	12:9f	VI:120
8:34	II:656; VI:643; VIII:58	12:10	III:492; VIII:132; 218
8:35	II:445	12:11	III:368; VI:1
9:1	VII:59n25; IX:445	12:13	II:773n19
9:1-14	V:205	12:15	III:867; 881; VIII:210
9:2	II:445; IV:646; V:948	12:16	VIII:141; 210
9:3	I:171	12:17	II:773n19
9:4	I:184; II:884; IV:646; VIII:354;	12:18	I:682; VII:270
	IX:451n100	12:19	VI:120
9:5	IV:1108n19	13:1	V:838
9:5f	III:1019	13:3	V:104
9:6	I:716; V:839	13:4	II:294; VIII:613; IX:677
9:7	I:702; II:529; VII:922; VIII:607	13:5	III:458n29
9:8	II:292; III:906; VII:383	13:6	III:411; 596
9:9	V:414	13:7	III:458n29; 913
9:11	II:534, n5; III:906; VIII:9	13:10	VI:120
9:12	II:46; 47; 822; III:1019; 1028;	13:11	II:292; VII:271(n16)
	V:511; 516n144	13:13	II:52n10; VI:934; VIII:120
9:13	IV:829	13:14	II:481(n63)
9:14	I:707; III:325(n23); 906	13:15	IV:546; VI:120
10:2	VI:167	13:16	I:384; IV:646; V:50
10:3	II:855n170; IX:445; 511n78	13:17	VII:271(n17)
10:4	III:881	13:18	II:762; 764; III:1019; V:511;
10:5	VI:120, n7; VII:752(n12)		VIII:618
10:6	VI:660n54	13:19	II:529
10:7	III:30	13:20	VIII:10; 603
10:8	VIII:81; 613	14:1	III:917
10:9	VIII:85	14:3	V:296; 313
10:12	III:368	14:6	VI:368
10:13	I:244; II:27; 852; VI:772;	14:10	I:226; VI:73; 200(n179);

	VII:109; VIII:168	16:3	V:482n86
14:11	III:917	16:5	VIII:158
14:13	VIII:52; 182	16:7	I:229; IX:445
14:14	III:954; IV:1018	16:9	I:196
14:16	VII:600	16:11	VIII:9
14:17	IV:34	16:13	III:35; VIII:493n34; 499n71
14:18	III:368	16:14	II:855n172; III:1018; 1019;
15:2	V:185; VI:164; IX:199		1028; VI:368; 381n251; 386;
15:8	V:327; VI:660n54; VII:862n14		388n316
15:9	III:647; VIII:613	16:16	II:294; III:187; 241
15:11	VII:1095; 1096	16:17	II:948; VI:937; VII:453; 454n19
15:12	II:762; V:627	16:19	I:354
15:13	VII:625	16:21	III:459n33
15:14	V:219	16:22	I:701n55; II:855n170
16:1	III:499; 1037	16:24	I:184; III:838
16:1-25	IX:446	16:25	IX:198
16:2	VI:511n77; VII:922		

ADDITIONS TO ESTHER

10:6	I:650n13	14:14	I:700
13:8 (C.1)	II:642	16:2	II:655n9
13:11 (C.22)	II:32	16:3	II:655
14:3 (C.14)	II:823	16:13	II:655
14:10	III:30		

WISDOM OF SOLOMON

1-5	V:820n22		634
1:1	I:387n3; VI:199(n171); VII:460	1:6a	VI:371(n188)
1:1-5	II:474n11	1:6f	VI:388n316
1:2	I:736n1; VI:28; 199(n169),	1:6-8	VII:913
	(n170); IX:7	1:7	I:700; III:351; VI:287; **288;** 368;
1:3	IV:286; VII:406		371; 386; VII:880
1:4	V:153; VII:1047; IX:634	1:7b	VI:288
1:4f	VI:381n256	1:7f	VI:388n320
1:5	I:95; IV:286; VI:610; VI:371,	1:8	II:474n11
	n193; 381n252	1:10	I:736; V:549
1:5f	VI:443	1:11	I:736; IV:4
1:5-10	V:810	1:12	II:854n165; 883; VI:235
1:6	I:736n1; II:614; 615; IV:483;	1:13	I:292; II:856(n193); VI:460;
	911n3; VI:288; 371;		IX:110n26
	VII:500n219; IX:110, n26;	1:14	III:24n17; 881n46; V:168;

5:17-22	V:297; 863	7:10	VII:499n213; IX:322
5:17-23	V:415	7:11f	VII:499n214
5:18	II:319; V:309n9; 315n3;	7:11-14	VII:518n375
	VIII:570, n2	7:12	I:116
5:19	V:313; 493(n5); VIII:570n2	7:13	III:970; IV:401; VII:518n375
5:20	III:881; VI:997n26; VIII:107;	7:13f	VII:500n221
	570n2	7:14	V:610; VII:518n375; 589
5:21	IV:905; VII:414	7:15	I:717; V:97; 98n7
5:22	V:410; 415; VIII:107	7:15ff	VII:523n398
5:23	IV:280; VI:371	7:15-21	V:98n7
6-9	VII:499	7:16	IX:226
6-10	VII:501	7:17	I:700; II:652; III:881; VII:463;
6:1	IV:401n89; VII:893n47		676; IX:601n73
6:1-4	VIII:523	7:17-19	IX:586
6:1-9:18	VII:460	7:18	III:459; VIII:52; IX:586n26
6:2	V:585; VI:278	7:18a	IX:586
6:3	I:633	7:18-21	VII:463; 499
6:4	I:574; VIII:535	7:20	II:97; 873; VI:371; 985;
6:5	VIII:107; 108; 523		VIII:219; IX:266; 275n237
6:6	I:716; II:481(n61)	7:21	V:98n7; VII:499(n215); 676;
6:7	II:46; 47; IV:544; 1010; 1015;		IX:586
	VII:597	7:22	II:655(n8); IV:738n5;
6:9	IV:401; VI:170		VI:292n34; 339; 371n188;
6:11	V:610		IX:226
6:11-13	III:170n31	7:22f	VI:371; VII:500n219; 502n241
6:12	IV:17; V:328; 333; VII:499n213	7:22ff	IX:651n213
6:12ff	VII:524n406	7:22-8:1	VII:499n216
6:12-9:18	VII:499	7:23	I:601; IV:593; VI:371; IX:110
6:13	I:715; II:769; V:328;	7:24	III:414; VI:292n34;
	VII:500(n220); 501n240;		VII:500n219
	IX:88	7:24ff	IX:634
6:14	VII:498n211; 499n213; 518n375	7:25	I:109n67; II:397; IV:645n9;
6:15	IV:593; VIII:78; IX:226n41		V:529n254; VI:370; IX:226
6:15f	VII:498n211	7:25f	II:298; VII:499; IX:421n30;
6:15-21	VII:518n371		422(n31); 477n45
6:16	IX:6	7:26	I:168; 508; II:394n84; 395n95;
6:17-19	V:610		652; 653; 696n2
6:18	I:22n2; 602; VIII:146	7:27	I:523n3, n4; III:451; IV:575;
6:18f	I:40; 41; IX:102		VI:821; VII:500; 515n347;
6:19	VII:499		516n354; IX:168n181
6:20	I:574; III:169n21	7:28	I:30n57; VII:498n211;
6:21	III:163n19; VIII:173		499n213; 500n218
6:22	I:66; 243; III:959; IV:814;	7:29f	IX:324
	VII:499	7:30	VI:927n61
6:23	III:801; VII:499n213	8:1	VI:292n34; VII:500n219
6:24	III:882; VII:982; IX:225	8:2	I:654n38; VII:498n211;
7	IX:422		499n213; IX:125, n120
7:1	VI:875; VII:117n155	8:2f	VII:499
7:1f	VII:110; IX:473; 631	8:2-21	VII:499n216; 524n406
7:1-21	VII:499n216	8:3	II:46; 47; VII:499, n213
7:2	II:684n1; 912; 916; 919;	8:3f	VII:499(n212); 1100
	VIII:550; IX:587; 593n70;	8:4	II:639; IV:814; VII:499;
	619n54		518n371
7:3	III:351; 790; V:938; VI:169	8:5	II:639; VII:499n215; 518n375
7:6	III:351; 881; 889; V:104; 107	8:5f	IX:226
7:7	II:784; VI:371, (n188), n193;	8:6	II:639; IX:226n41
	385; VII:110; 499; 500;	8:7	I:363; 459n10; IX:226
	502n241; 523n398; 524n406;	8:8	I:486; 715; VII:221; 499;
	IX:225		VIII:54n36; 55n39; 119;
7:7f	VI:381n256		IX:587
7:8	III:163n19; 953; VI:324	8:8-21	IX:226
7:9	IV:285	8:9	I:654n38; IV:319; V:790;

12:1	IV:686; VI:370; 386; 388n316; IX:102	13:9	I:203
12:2	I:252n2; II:434; IV:1020; V:171; 172; VI:170; 197n149; VII:913	13:10	II:529; 645; IV:269n9; 892(n11); IX:417n8
		13:10ff	VII:360n7
		13:10-19	II:377(n25)
12:4	V:492; VI:634	13:11	VIII:535, n46, n48, n49
12:5	II:487n2; IV:814; VII:109; 116n147; 550	13:12	IV:195; VIII:535n46, n48
		13:13	II:395
12:6	I:631(n19); VII:109n96	13:14	V:198
12:7	V:638; 677; 678; VIII:354	13:16	II:42; IV:1010; VI:169
12:8	VIII:235	13:18	IV:892(n11); VI:277n14
12:9	VIII:107	14:1	VII:589
12:10	I:116; IV:991; 992; VI:551; VIII:200; 206n142	14:1-14	II:377(n25)
		14:3	IV:1011; 1015; V:49n27; 981; VIII:354n118
12:11	II:752		
12:12	VI:260	14:3ff	III:1037
12:12-14	VIII:107	14:5	I:452; II:638n13; VII:981
12:15	V:561	14:6	I:203; III:882; 890(n79); V:49n27; VII:542; VIII:526
12:16	IV:379		
12:17	III:906; VIII:78	14:7	II:853
12:18	II:589; III:47n33	14:8	IX:102
12:18ff	IV:992	14:9f	IV:686, (n11)
12:19	IV:991; 992; V:678n145; 908; IX:110	14:10	VI:634; VII:796
		14:11	II:606; VI:626; 749n28; VII:342n19
12:19-21	VIII:354		
12:19-27	V:908	14:12	VI:588; VII:342n19
12:20	I:252n2; V:561; 677; 678, n145; 908; VIII:200; IX:587	14:12ff	VI:593n81
		14:14	III:662; 881; 889, n75; VIII:52; 64
12:21	V:678n145; 908		
12:22	II:481(n61); 485; IV:515; V:908; VI:725	14:15	II:171; III:97(n184); IV:813; VIII:173
		14:16	II:373; III:912; IX:587
12:23	I:151; II:854n165; 858; V:633; VII:367n38	14:17	III:157; 817; VII:562; VIII:37; 172; 173
12:24	IV:914; V:633; 646; VI:235; 236(n42)	14:18	I:116; III:157
		14:19	V:189
12:24f	IV:633n5	14:20	VII:173; IX:409n29
12:25f	V:633	14:21	VII:342n19
12:26	II:627n1; IV:1020; V:629; 631; 908	14:22	I:117; 700; VI:235; VII:367n58; IX:188n135
		14:22ff	III:97
12:27	I:469; 702; 707; III:622; V:633; 908	14:23	IV:813
		14:23ff	I:654; VII:367n58
12:27ff	III:586n52	14:24-26	VI:588
13	IX:267n164	14:26	I:490; IV:647; 730
13f	VII:367	14:27	III:157; 477; V:264n144
13-15	I:702	14:27f	VI:588
13:1	I:118; III:1016; IV:522; V:324; 367; VII:367n58; IX:267, n163; 488	14:28	II:858; V:466
		14:29	I:160
		14:30	III:632; V:493(n5)
13:1f	IX:275	14:31	I:150; II:181; V:739; VII:367n38
13:1ff	II:297; 306; 638; III:97; IX:267		
13:2	III:881; VII:676; 681n76; IX:318	15:1	IX:486
		15:1ff	IV:376
13:2f	VII:680n66	15:2	III:906
13:3	III:881	15:2ff	VII:367n58
13:3ff	III:579	15:3	I:702; II:859; III:24; 766; 906
13:4	II:652; IV:949; 951; V:126n30	15:4	III:616; VI:234
13:5	III:544n20; 553; IV:544; V:328; 334; 380, n3, n7	15:4-17	II:377(n25)
		15:5	IV:892
13:6	II:769; IV:572; V:172; VI:235	15:6	II:529
13:6f	VI:236n41	15:7	III:139; VI:118; 256(n14); 257;
13:7	III:544; V:324; 327n68; VI:3		
13:8	I:716		

	VII:363; VIII:176n39; 535, n48, n49	17:1	V:610; VI:235
		17:1ff	VII:431n54
15:7f	VII:360	17:2	IV:33; 35n20; 37; 1011; 1015; 1016
15:8	I:194n4; V:171; VI:256(n14); 257; IX:647n185	17:3	III:5n9; VII:418
15:9	IV:663; VI:256(n14); 257	17:4	IV:780n105; IX:199; 204
15:10	II:529	17:5	IV:584
15:11	I:116; II:536(n2); 653; 858n207; VI:256, (n14); 370; 376n224; 442n752; 452	17:6	V:324; 327n68
		17:7	V:633; 634
		17:8	II:752; IV:1092
15:12	II:854n165; 858; V:628; 722	17:9	V:573; IX:198
15:13	II:62	17:11 (17:10, S)	III:622; IV:15; 483; VII:881; 882n52; **909;** 910
15:14	IV:914; V:646		
15:15	I:452; V:370; 376n4	17:13 (17:12, S)	IX:206
15:16	VI:256(n14); 257; 370	17:14 (17:13, S)	I:147(n7)
15:17	IV:892(n11); VII:173	17:15 (17:14, S)	VIII:120; IX:6
15:18	IV:963	17:16 (17:15, S)	VI:169
15:19	II:587; VIII:240	17:17 (17:16, S)	II:60n4
16	III:324	17:19 (17:18, S)	VII:401; IX:198
16:1	VII:267n38	17:20 (17:19, S)	VII:881
16:1ff-19:12	IV:376n19	17:20f (17:19f, S)	VII:431
16:2	II:655(n8)	17:21 (17:20, S)	I:147(n7)
16:2f	V:26; 448	18:1	IV:365; 746; V:908
16:3	III:324(n9); V:172	18:1-4	VII:431
16:5	V:414; 415; 416; VII:404; VIII:52	18:2	IX:63; 409
		18:3	I:119; V:97; VII:733n11
16:5ff	V:446n433	18:4	I:203; IV:49; VII:442n170; VIII:354; IX:102; 324; 345n283
16:6	I:348; 349; IV:1021; V:172; VII:981		
		18:4ff	IV:633n5
16:6f	V:578	18:5	IV:914; VII:981
16:7	VII:981; 1013	18:6	I:715; VI:200(n178)
16:8	III:477n31; VI:1	18:7	II:58; VII:981
16:10	IV:943; VIII:354	18:9	I:95; II:105; III:123
16:11	II:655(n8); III:324n12; VII:981	18:10	V:160n20; IX:63
16:12	III:129	18:11	II:46; V:907n21; 908
16:13	I:148; II:855; 858; VI:924; 925, n44	18:13	V:204; VI:200n184; VIII:354
		18:14-16	IX:338n223
16:13-15	IX:645	18:15	III:163; IV:527n23; 572; V:511, n91; VI:579n4; 997n26; VIII:37; 46; 107; 570
16:14	II:679; VI:368; 370; 376n224; 924n33; VII:716		
		18:16	V:511n91; VI:287; IX:474n26
16:15	IX:645n172	18:17	V:221; 231; VIII:550n36
16:16	I:639; IV:515; V:26	18:19	I:116; V:221; 231; 908; VIII:550n36
16:17	II:653; III:881; VII:875n32; VIII:120		
		18:20ff	V:416
16:18	III:324n12	18:20-25	V:170; 414
16:19	III:324(n9)	18:21	IV:221; 225; 226; V:293; 416; 424
16:20	I:477; 643; II:910; 916; IV:462n1; 464		
		18:22	II:127; 652; V:413; 414; 940n4; VI:998n31; VII:1047; VIII:40
16:20f	IX:228n50		
16:21	I:631(n23); VIII:354; 535; 582		
16:22	I:700; III:324n12; IV:584; V:26	18:23	VII:960
16:23	III:324(n9)	18:24	III:274n46; 881; VII:690
16:24	I:151; II:655(n8); III:1028; VII:875n32; VIII:535	18:25	V:170n4; 414; VIII:52n23
		19:1	II:487n2; V:414n225; 415; VIII:52
16:24f	VIII:535		
16:25	III:62; VIII:535	19:2	VII:562
16:25f	III:324(n12)	19:3	IV:962f
16:26	VIII:354	19:4	VI:306n3
16:27	I:386	19:5	V:26
16:28	VIII:243; IX:88; 407; 409	19:6	III:1028; V:638; 677; 678;
16:29	II:529; IX:409n29		
17f	IX:323		

SIRACH (ECCLESIASTICUS)

7:19	IX:389n119	10:13	VIII:52; 301
7:20	I:243; IV:698	10:14	III:164n31; 411; 412; 660;
7:22	II:601; V:328		VI:647; 648
7:24	III:298; VII:1046	10:15	VI:986; VIII:10
7:25	I:652n23; II:636; VIII:58; 81	10:18	I:672; III:1027; V:413;
7:27	V:974		VIII:301
7:28	IV:676	10:19	V:737
7:29	II:752; III:30; IV:230; IX:650	10:19f	IX:198
7:30	IV:230	10:22	III:647; VI:894
7:31	I:113; II:253; 752; III:30;	10:23	III:439; VI:894
	IX:198n48	10:24	IX:198
7:32	VI:900(n129); VIII:80	10:25	I:729; 731; IV:220n17
7:33	II:853(n169); IX:389n119; 403,	10:27	VIII:594
	n8	10:28	VI:647; 648; VIII:6; 172
7:34	VIII:594; IX:369n93	10:29	II:212
7:35	II:601; 603	10:30	VI:324; 893
8:4	V:632	11:1	VIII:9
8:6	I:700n49	11:2	V:370
8:8	IV:220n17; V:728; 855	11:4	III:35; 647; 967; IV:797; V:631;
8:9	IV:401; V:728; 977		632; VIII:302
8:9a	IV:400	11:4b	II:639
8:9b	IV:400	11:5	VII:922; IX:83n1
8:10	VI:935	11:7	II:625; 627n1; IV:571; 949n5;
8:11	VIII:302		VI:689n6
8:14	II:243; 743	11:9	I:286; VIII:301
8:15	III:53	11:10	II:230; VI:280; 643
8:16	IV:528n2	11:11	VIII:594
8:17	IV:814n113; 836; VII:585; 586	11:11f	VIII:594
8:18	IV:814n113	11:12	VI:59; VIII:11; 594
8:19	IX:389n119	11:13	III:34, n35; V:685
9:1	III:824; VI:550n23	11:14	II:855; VI:894
9:3	V:594, n5; VI:584n31	11:15	V:52n32
9:3ff	I:782	11:15f	VI:325
9:4	VIII:493	11:16	VI:235; 236
9:5	IV:414; VII:343; 345	11:17	II:744; 748n40; 752; IV:578;
9:6	III:777		V:111, n9
9:7	VI:234; 235	11:17-19	VI:324
9:8	IV:414; V:376; VI:235; 935	11:19	II:689; 769; 856(n184); VI:324
9:9	VI:370, n182; 696n26	11:20	I:127; VIII:644
9:10	IV:897; V:163; IX:487n19	11:20f	III:492n1
9:11	II:883	11:21	II:637; III:35; 40n67;
9:12	II:213; 739; 744; 746n30;		VI:199n166; 894
	VIII:301	11:22	IV:697; VII:179; IX:677
9:13	II:564; V:594; VI:364; 368; 523	11:23	VI:325
9:15	II:97; 909n3; IV:814n113	11:27	II:647; III:577; VIII:65; IX:677
9:16	III:647	11:28	IV:365
9:17	II:636	11:29	V:23n165
10:1	V:608; VIII:28	11:30	VII:417
10:2	IV:230	11:32	I:286; 607, n6; VI:935
10:4	II:565	11:33	III:484; IV:830
10:5	V:112	12:1	II:487(n11); IX:389n119
10:6	I:162; II:637; V:411; VI:634;	12:2	VI:469; VIII:618
	VIII:300	12:3	II:486n4; IX:389
10:7	I:150f; IV:686, (n11), n13;	12:4	VI:894; VII:179
	VIII:526	12:5	VIII:10; 301
10:8	VIII:300; IX:480	12:6	II:446; IV:686, (n11)
10:9	I:680n12; IX:472n4	12:8	II:443; IX:157n96
10:10	VII:270	12:9	IX:157n93
10:11	II:855(n178); III:776; VII:453	12:10	III:334
10:12	I:512; VIII:526	12:11	III:334; VIII:7; 52
10:12f	I:286; VIII:300	12:14	VIII:301
10:12ff	VIII:300	12:15	III:617; IX:677

40:24	VI:1001; 1002, n6
40:26	VII:498n205; VIII:607
40:27	V:766n4, n6, n13
40:28	II:851n152; 858; VI:893
40:28f	II:855(n177)
40:29	II:96; 851n152; 858
40:30	VI:893
41:1	I:676; V:111, n9; 112n12
41:1f	II:856(n189)
41:1-4	VI:893
41:2	II:843(n78); IV:583
41:3	II:752; IV:676
41:3f	II:856(n183)
41:4	II:744
41:5	II:752; V:842; 843
41:7	IV:571
41:11	VII:1046
41:14f	III:970
41:15	IV:835; 836
41:16	IV:146
41:16-42:1	VI:588
41:17	II:908; V:974; VI:584; 588
41:18	I:153
41:19	III:801; VII:874n19; VIII:193n47; 195
41:21	VI:894
41:22	V:370; VI:584(n31); VII:738
41:22b (41:25, S)	V:240n6; 241
41:23 (41:26, S)	III:577
41:24 (41:27, S)	IX:389n119
42:1	III:30; 577
42:1c	IX:389n119
42:2	II:127; 212; IV:1048
42:3	III:801; VII:874n19
42:4	II:896
42:5	V:608; VI:549; IX:63
42:6	VI:551; VII:945
42:7	I:750
42:8	IV:834; 835n25, n26; 962
42:9	IV:388, n2; 590; 685; VIII:550
42:9f	III:982n83
42:10	I:605; V:737; 960; 1021
42:11	III:530; IV:34
42:11c	VI:277
42:13	VII:276
42:15	II:639; 744; 748n40; IV:80; V:326; 333
42:15-43:33	III:1018; VII:498n209
42:16	II:639; VI:284, n4
42:17	III:35; VII:610; VIII:421n169
42:18	V:725(n20); VII:909
42:18ff	I:706n69; III:613
42:19	II:681; III:967
42:20	IV:968
42:21	II:42; VII:498n209; 499n215
42:22	II:639
42:23	II:855n172
42:25	V:326; VII:610
43:1	III:414n3; V:371; 372; VII:609; VII:431n59; IX:323n84
43:1ff	
43:1-33	V:893
43:2	I:68n9; II:639; III:33; 35;

	V:372; VII:227n184; VIII:618
43:2ff	III:643n1
43:4	V:480
43:6	II:31n2; IX:586
43:7	I:203; VIII:65; IX:319
43:8	III:33; 35; VII:227n184; 609; VIII:517
43:9	III:544n20; 553; 881
43:9f	I:503
43:11	III:340; 544n20; 553
43:14	III:177(n52)
43:14f	IV:906
43:15ff	I:706n69
43:16	III:53; V:372; 480; VI:452; VII:67; IX:669n22
43:18	III:34; 544n20; 553; IV:243
43:19	VII:411
43:20	VI:360; 364n159
43:21	VII:166
43:22	III:202; 298
43:23	V:440n399
43:24	III:28; 33
43:25	II:639; III:33; 1028; VIII:117; 120n43
43:26	II:744; V:110n4, n6; 112
43:26ff	V:893
43:27	VII:1004; VIII:65
43:27ff	III:114(n348)
43:28	II:639
43:29	III:35
43:30	VI:281; VIII:523
43:31	II:908; V:333; 364; 366
43:32	II:639; III:967; V:333
43:33	VII:179
44f	II:127
44ff	III:324
44-50	V:977
44:1-8	VI:324
44:1-50:24	IV:439; VII:498n209
44:1-50:26	V:976n176
44:2	III:1027
44:3	I:66; VI:808
44:5	I:750
44:6	VI:324; 325
44:8	II:587
44:10	II:195n3; 481n64; 745; 749
44:13	IV:575
44:14	V:263; VII:1046
44:15	I:70; II:587; IV:33n17
44:16	I:455; II:33; 557, n2; 939n91; III:32; IV:8; 991; 992; VIII:161; 252n32
44:17	I:252; II:186n42; IV:196; V:410; 415; 416; VIII:72
44:17f	III:324n11
44:19	V:976(n184); VI:277
44:20	I:8(n7); II:127; IV:1048; VI:26; 199n162; VII:109; 644; 780n73
44:20f	VII:644
44:21	I:9(n15); III:324n11

48:25	III:967
49:1	IV:553; V:261
49:2	V:907n19
49:3	III:613; V:113n14; VII:179
49:4	IX:512n89
49:5	III:669; IX:512n89
49:6	III:1027; IV:182; V:49; VI:524; VII:320
49:6f	III:218; VI:808
49:7	V:137n1
49:8	II:251; IX:438
49:9	III:979
49:10	II:529; IV:334; V:776n15; 790; VIII:195n53; IX:623
49:11	VII:946
49:11f	IX:512
49:12	II:705; VI:525n56; IX:512n88
49:13	II:334
49:14	II:557, n2; 939n91; III:1027; IV:8; VIII:161
49:14ff	II:557
49:15	II:601
49:16	II:557, n2; III:1028; V:976n176; VIII:410n66; IX:476n34
50	IX:15n18
50:1	II:855n170; III:266
50:1-21	VII:37
50:5	II:253; III:629; VI:525n56
50:5ff	III:274n46
50:6	IV:27; VI:284
50:7	III:340
50:11	I:95; II:253; 319; III:647; VII:690; VIII:65
50:12	IV:557(n21)
50:13	III:527
50:14	III:867; IV:221; VIII:65
50:15	I:176; II:467; VII:533; 1023
50:15-17	VII:532n31
50:16	II:955; VII:79
50:16f	VII:79
50:17	VI:163n13
50:18	IV:557n19; VIII:494n42; IX:281
50:19	III:881
50:19b	VIII:81
50:20	I:186(n2); III:527; 647
50:22	II:481(n62); 743; 758n11; III:32
50:24	IV:334; IX:511, n86
50:25	VIII:218
50:26	IV:833; 834; V:479; VII:44n59;

	91n24
50:27	VII:320; IX:416
50:28	IV:365, n32; VII:527
50:29	III:403n7
51	III:581n34; IV:621; VII:517
51:1	V:214; VII:1013
51:1f	II:348n59
51:1ff	VII:893n44
51:1-12	V:202; 205; VII:517n367
51:2	II:72(n7); IV:333; 334; V:838; VII:1046; 1048
51:3	I:642; II:481(n62); IV:252n19; 334
51:6	I:152; II:72(n7)
51:8	VII:981
51:9	III:24n21; VI:924; 925; 926; 999; IX:281
51:10	V:203; 219; 974; 979(n209), n209; VIII:354
51:11	VI:550(n25)
51:12	IX:511, n86; 521n170

Special S Additions

51:12a-o	IX:385
51:12a-r	VII:37n18
51:12i	VII:37(n18)

Back to RSV and M

51:13	IV:898n16; VI:234(n33)
51:13-22	VII:517n367
51:13-30	VII:498
51:16	V:172; VI:709
51:17	II:900; **VI:709;** 713; VII:516n358
51:17b	VI:709
51:18	II:883
51:19	I:115; VI:42n12; 471; VII:498n207
51:21	III:787
51:22	IV:697
51:23	II:900n22; VII:482; IX:86
51:23ff	II:348n59; V:215; IX:85
51:23-30	VI:649; VII:500n221; 517n360; 518n367
51:24	VIII:594
51:26	II:50; 898; 900n22; V:611; VII:516n358
51:27	I:350; II:900n22; V:172
51:28	II:831n6
51:30	III:458; IV:697

BARUCH

1-3	V:205	3:22	V:324
1:1	I:744	3:23	IV:777n92; 780; 788n152;
1:4	VI:596		V:52; VII:895n65
1:5	IV:929	3:24	VIII:200
1:15-3:8	IV:981	3:27	IV:169; V:52
1:18	IX:286n35	3:28	IV:847n121; V:736
1:19f	V:976n175	3:29	IV:903; V:525n224
1:20	IV:552; 853n65; V:677; 678; 679;	3:29ff	I:706n69
	681(n183)	3:31	V:52
1:21	IX:286n35	3:32	V:126n30; 891; IX:587
1:22	IV:965; 966; VI:550	3:33	III:1018
2:1	VII:642	3:34	IX:243
2:2	I:749	3:34f	IV:22
2:4	V:241	3:37	V:677; 678, n149; 679; 680(n177);
2:5ff	IX:286n35		684n213
2:8	IV:961, n3; VI:550; 773	4:1	I:616n13; II:855n179; IV:136;
2:9	II:338; 639; 646		1048; 1049; VII:509
2:11	I:640; II:291; VII:221; VIII:119	4:2	IV:9
2:12	I:158; VII:188n7	4:3	IX:74
2:13	V:172	4:4	IV:365
2:15	I:702; III:498; V:263	4:5	III:26
2:16	V:379; 549	4:5f	III:325(n23)
2:17	II:219; IV:6; VI:368; VII:550n18	4:6	VI:160n3
2:18	IV:544	4:7	II:11; V:413
2:19	II:221	4:8	I:200; VII:325
2:20	V:637; 677; 678; 679, n167	4:9	V:414n220
2:23	IV:1099n1	4:9-5:9	VII:323n161
2:24	V:677; 678; 679, n167; VII:642	4:10	I:200; VIII:354
2:25	VI:550; 996	4:11	III:725; VI:42n9
2:27	II:589	4:12	IV:1047; 1049; VI:439
2:28	IV:853n65; V:637; 677; 678; 679;	4:13	II:210; V:51
	681(n183); VIII:354	4:14	VIII:354
2:30	II:700	4:16	IV:738
2:31	I:702	4:19	V:639
2:33	V:51; VII:724	4:21	III:25n3; 26; V:639
2:34	V:976n177	4:22	VII:981; 1013, n58
2:35	II:128; 132; VII:642	4:23	III:725; VI:42, n9
3:1	VI:369; VII:605	4:24	VII:981; 982
3:1-8	IV:847n121	4:25	IV:378n40; V:414n220; 639
3:4	IX:286n35	4:27	III:25n3; 26
3:5	IX:678n18	4:28	IV:965; VI:235; 236
3:7	III:499	4:29	VII:981; 982
3:8	I:154; VII:271(n14)	4:30	III:26; V:789; VII:323
3:9	I:702; II:854; 855(n179)	4:34	VI:42
3:9ff	IV:616; VII:895n65	4:35	II:11n82; V:156
3:9-4:4	IV:847n121; VII:509; 521n389	4:36	II:667; VII:323
3:12	VI:114	4:37	VIII:354
3:13	V:51	5:1	II:319; VI:42
3:14	I:702; 706n69; II:855; IV:401;	5:2	II:205
	VII:895n65	5:3	II:29
3:15	VIII:200	5:4	III:125
3:15ff	IV:136	5:6	III:161
3:17	V:633; VIII:52	5:7	V:481; VIII:7
3:20	I:702; V:52	5:9	II:205; 486(n3); VII:768n12
3:20f	VII:890(n19)		

LETTER OF JEREMIAH

Passim	III:97(n183)	36	V:839; VIII:281
4	II:752; IV:5; V:198	37	IX:446n52
4-72	II:377(n25)	38	III:129; V:189
5	V:585	41	I:188
8	III:675; V:832; VII:625	42f	VI:581n9
10	III:335(n6); 336; VII:982n64	49	VII:982
13	IV:258	50	I:702
14	IX:205	53	I:162
17	IV:258	54	VII:981
19	I:188	57	III:756n9; IV:258; VII:982n64
20	IV:550	58	VII:981
22	I:702; IX:205	59	IV:17
23	III:335(n6); 336; VII:666	60	VI:452; IX:9
24	VIII:172	61	IV:906; V:480; 532(n283);
25	III:129		VIII:28; 63
26	IV:892n11	62	V:198
28	I:702	64	I:702
30f	III:826n52	66	II:27; IV:22
31	IV:892n11	70	V:198
33	V:908	71	I:702; VII:96

SUSANNA

Passim	IV:835n26	38	IV:401n88
2	IX:205	39	II:341n4
4	III:365	41	IV:483; VII:805
5	VI:660	42	I:201; III:960; 967
6	III:618	43	IV:510
7	V:942	45	VI:369; 378n236; 381n252,
9	IV:953, n3		(n254)
10	III:626	45-64	IX:598
12	VIII:147	48	III:365, n58; IV:836; V:585
13	V:942	49	IV:510
15	IV:300; VIII:147	50	VI:654; 666n92
16	VIII:147	51ff	III:345
17	IV:300	52	VII:805
21	IV:510	55	I:80(n32); II:225; VII:959
22	III:365, n58; VII:605	56	I:384; VII:718
28	III:365; IV:970n7; VII:803; 805	57	III:365n58; IV:584; 1091
29	VI:660	59	I:80(n32); II:225
30	VII:738	60	II:529(n90); IV:513; VII:805;
32	III:170; 561; VI:129		981
33	V:730	61	IV:513; 514
34	VI:660	62	VI:469; VII:981
36	V:942	63	VI:381(n254); VII:179; 738
37	V:328		

BEL AND THE DRAGON

5	III:246n73; 1019; V:515n130; VII:109n95	27	VII:173
		28	III:365n59; V:585
7	VI:235	30	V:585
8	III:233; VI:700	31	VI:91n73
10	II:379	31f	V:585
14	VII:945	32	VIII:240
15-17	VIII:198n81	34	I:80(n32)
18	IV:539n47	37	I:39(n95)
22	III:233	39	VIII:194
23	VIII:194	41	IV:539n47

PRAYER OF MANASSEH

Passim	IV:1049		992
2ff	III:1018; 1019	9	VIII:603
3	I:10; III:746n27; VII:947n72	9ff	IV:992
5f	V:414; 425n313	10	IV:376n17
7	IV:376n17, (n18); 991n75; 992; VII:552n26	13	III:621; IV:991; 992; V:413; VIII:141
8	I:8(n10); II:186(n40); IV:991;		

I MACCABEES

1:1	II:507, n25	1:25	VI:42; VIII:194
1:2	VII:929n24	1:26	III:271; VI:660, (n53)
1:6	I:184; V:638	1:27	III:443; VI:42
1:8	V:638	1:28	II:319
1:10	I:326; II:507n25; VI:987; IX:589	1:29	V:585; VII:319n130
		1:29-35	VII:321
1:11	I:607n6; VI:79n46	1:32	III:776
1:11-15	VII:321	1:34	I:326
1:14	I:136n8	1:35	VII:319n130; VIII:162
1:15	I:95; 226; 512; II:127; 133; VI:79; 160, n6; 470	1:36	II:72; VI:551
		1:37	IV:736
1:17	V:585	1:38	V:639; VII:319n130
1:20	V:585; VII:319n130; IX:589	1:39	VI:42
1:21	VIII:526	1:39f	VI:42; VII:8
1:22	III:629; 881; VII:625, n64; VIII:211	1:40	VIII:603
		1:41ff	IV:1048
1:23	III:961; 969	1:41-64	VII:321
1:24	VIII:526	1:43	II:738; IV:61; VII:8

1:44	VII:8; 319n130	2:54	I:95; II:878; 884; III:248; 761; V:948
1:45	III:186		
1:46	IV:645n9	2:55	III:292(n58); VI:288
1:47	II:379; III:791	2:56	IV:511
1:48	I:598; IX:633	2:57	I:209n6; III:101; 162; 776; VIII:388n388; 478
1:51	II:614; VI:467		
1:54	II:660; III:182n8; IX:589f	2:58	II:878; 884; 929; 930; IV:8; 440
1:56	VII:960	2:59	VI:199(n167); 200n176, n184; 948; VII:167
1:57	II:127; 739; III:21		
1:59	III:182n8	2:59f	III:979
1:60f	VI:73; 77	2:60	IV:252; 253; VI:1001; 1002
1:61	III:916; V:637	2:61	VI:200n176
1:62	III:791	2:61f	II:529
1:63	I:95; II:51n7; 127; IV:645n9	2:62	I:326; VII:453; IX:204
1:64	V:414n220	2:63	II:97; VII:723
2:1	IV:236(n19); VII:38(n23); 319n130	2:65	V:951n18
		2:67	II:443; 445; VI:471
2:6	I:622; VII:319n130; 320; 321	2:68	III:186
2:7	I:95; VI:524; 909n221; VII:320	2:70	III:837; 838; 847n116
2:10	III:776	3:2	III:822
2:11	III:881	3:4	V:189
2:11f	VII:321n147	3:5	II:656
2:14	VI:42	3:6	V:111; 112n12; VII:596; 981; IX:204
2:15	I:513		
2:18	IV:283; VII:319n130	3:7	VI:123; 126n3
2:19	I:513; IV:61; V:976n174	3:8	V:414
2:20	II:128; V:976n178	3:11	I:704
2:21	II:220	3:14	VII:770
2:22	II:681; IV:61	3:15	II:445; III:364; VIII:354
2:23	III:361n35; 369n82	3:18	III:90; VII:745; 981
2:24	II:883; 884; IV:911n3; V:413; VII:929n24	3:18ff	VI:512n84
		3:19	IV:943
2:26	II:883; 884	3:22	IX:204
2:27	II:127; 128; 130; 884	3:25	IX:204
2:28	V:480	3:26	II:330
2:29ff	VI:242n69	3:28	V:591
2:29-48	VII:38	3:29	I:514
2:30	V:1031	3:30	I:381; III:752; VI:59
2:31	II:546; VII:319n130	3:31	IV:5
2:32-38	VII:8	3:32f	III:784n36
2:33	II:855(n175); IV:1107	3:34	I:631(n24)
2:37	IV:483; IX:446n53	3:35	III:364; IV:195
2:38	VII:7n39	3:36	VIII:354
2:39	VI:42	3:38	VI:862
2:39-41	VII:8; 14(n98)	3:41	III:364
2:40	V:170n3	3:42	I:704; VIII:65
2:41	VIII:452n367	3:43	I:95; III:412
2:42	II:470; III:364; 526; V:491; VII:38n26; 39n27; 803; 805; **IX:14**	3:44	V:160(n22); VII:804
		3:45	V:941; VII:321; VIII:354
		3:47	IV:929; VII:60; 62n48
2:44	I:326; V:413; VII:981	3:48	I:618n12
2:46	V:846; VI:73; 78n35	3:49	III:248; VI:288
2:47	V:112; VIII:354	3:50ff	VII:79
2:48	I:326	3:51	I:95; V:941; VIII:11
2:49	V:412	3:52	IV:285
2:49ff	I:138n19; IV:440	3:58f	I:95
2:50	II:127; 128; 166; 859; 884; IX:637n121	3:59	II:858
		3:60	III:53
2:52	I:8(n7); II:201; 434; IV:285; 289; 290; VI:26; 199n162; 200n182	4:1	IV:182
		4:2	III:361n35; V:97; VIII:354; 365n222
2:53	VII:605	4:4	VII:420

4:5	V:480	5:45	IV:649
4:6	I:631(n23); III:558n1	5:53	V:778
4:7	II:165	5:54	VII:320
4:8	I:171; V:470	5:58	V:762
4:8ff	VI:512n84	5:62	VII:981
4:9	VII:981; VIII:120	5:65	III:411
4:9f	V:976n175	5:68	III:90
4:9-11	II:294	6	VII:18
4:10	II:127; 132; V:510	6:2	II:507n25; III:558n1
4:11	I:702; VII:981	6:8	III:5n9
4:13	VII:79	6:9	III:451
4:18	V:875	6:10	IV:590
4:19	IV:595	6:11	II:564; III:142; IX:485
4:22	I:267	6:12	II:66
4:24	III:544; 553n65; VIII:495n45	6:12f	VII:324n174
4:25	VII:982	6:17	III:489
4:30	V:9n51; 470; 681n184; 703n370; VII:1013; VIII:479	6:18	III:364; VII:745
		6:20	VI:44
4:31	VII:745	6:21	III:822
4:33	VIII:493n34	6:22	II:443
4:35	II:855n177; V:6n32; VI:264	6:23	II:739
4:36	III:454; VII:321	6:24	VII:758
4:36-59	VII:321	6:29	IV:697
4:37	VII:321	6:33	V:470
4:38	VI:814, n220	6:34	I:176
4:40	VII:79	6:35	I:184; IV:144; V:839
4:42	IV:831; 1047	6:37	V:302
4:42ff	IV:1048	6:38	IV:595
4:43	IV:647	6:39	IV:26; VI:935; VII:665
4:43ff	VI:815	6:40	VIII:9
4:44-46	III:980n64	6:44	II:166; VII:981; IX:637n121
4:45	I:633; IV:645n9	6:45	VII:959
4:46	II:455; 569n42; III:577; IV:858n116; VI:385(n292); 814; **815-816** (815n226)	6:47	V:470
		6:48	VII:320
		6:49	VII:18; 745
4:47	III:766; V:175n2	6:50	VIII:33; 141
4:50	IX:1n4	6:53	IV:195; VII:18; 981
4:51	VIII:58	6:54	VIII:194
4:52	IX:590	6:57	VIII:199
4:52ff	VII:533	6:58	II:38; VI:467
4:54	III:454; 1037; VIII:495	6:59	V:51; 413
4:55	V:111, n8	6:60	II:417
4:56	II:773n16; III:454; VII:1023	6:61	V:204
4:57	VII:625, n64	6:62	VIII:158; 199
4:59	II:773n16; III:364; 454; 527	6:63	VII:562
4:60	V:941; VII:320; 321	7:1	VI:44
4:61	VIII:33; 141	7:1-5	VII:38(n21)
5:1	III:454	7:1-22	IX:14
5:3	III:364; VII:596	7:4	III:161
5:4	VII:342; 346n43	7:5	III:249
5:5	VII:745	7:9	III:248
5:10	I:762	7:12	III:526; IV:429; VII:803; 805; IX:22
5:16	III:141		
5:18	VIII:146	7:13	V:491; VII:39n26, n27; **IX:14;** 15
5:19	VI:700		
5:24	V:49	7:13-18	VII:43n52
5:26f	VII:759	7:17	V:491n18
5:27	VIII:28	7:18	I:243; VII:570
5:31	I:478; VII:79	7:19	III:181
5:33	VII:79	7:21	III:248
5:38	VII:417	7:23	III:364
5:39	IV:697	7:26	IV:685

14:37	III:361; VIII:614n8	15:11	IX:32
14:40	III:361; IX:155	15:13	VII:770
14:41	II:455; 739; III:361; 577;	15:15	V:730
	IV:568; 858(n116);	15:16-24	II:100; III:360
	VI:385(n292); 814; **815-816**	15:17	VI:683n2; IX:155
		15:25	VII:745
14:4ff	VII:38n23	15:26	IV:182
14:43	V:263	15:27	VIII:158
14:44	II:561	15:33f	III:778
14:44f	VIII:158	15:40	II:535
14:45	V:735	15:41	VIII:33
14:47	III:361; IX:32	16:2	V:112, n12; VI:1000
14:48	I:750; VII:268;VIII:199n82	16:8	III:227
15:1	III:266	16:11-22	VI:815f
15:1-9	III:360	16:13	VII:44n55
15:2	III:266	16:16	IV:546
15:3	I:388; 631(n17); V:6n32	16:20	III:235n14
15:4	I:631(n24)	16:22	I:704
15:8	IV:1107n12; V:565; IX:587	16:23	VI:643
15:9	III:233	16:24	I:747

II MACCABEES

Passim	II:233	1:24	II:485; IX:486
1:1	VII:319	1:25	I:201; III:363; 477n31; IV:174;
1:1-10	III:364		182; VII:981
1:2	II:127; 132; III:191; IV:675;	1:26	II:57; III:363
	V:681(n186)	1:27	I:702; II:99; 102n12; VII:842n4
1:2-6	V:810	1:29	I:95; VIII:198
1:3	III:53; VII:171	1:30	VIII:493n34; 495
1:4	III:612; VI:460; VII:764n13	1:33	I:68; VI:56
1:5	I:254	1:34	III:227
1:6	VI:54	1:34ff	VIII:199
1:8	II:591n4; VIII:165	1:35	IX:63
1:9	VII:390	1:36	II:663; V:733; VI:539n19
1:10	II:151; VI:659n43; VII:319; 862	2:1	I:756
1:10f	IX:409	2:1ff	III:220n15; IV:1048
1:11	VII:981	2:1-8	III:218
1:11ff	IX:409	2:2	III:881; IV:966n18; VI:235
1:12	I:95; VI:524; 909n221; VII:320	2:3	V:778n26
1:13	III:233	2:4	I:756; V:327; IX:482
1:14	VIII:198n81	2:4f	III:240; V:483
1:15	VIII:165	2:4-7	III:219n9
1:16	II:575; IV:558; VI:95(n6)	2:5	III:173n7
1:18	III:182; VII:390, n4	2:7	II:481, n67; IV:571
1:18ff	VI:934n41	2:7f	VII:842
1:19	I:119; VIII:199	2:8	II:30; 61; 245; III:240; IV:905;
1:19ff	III:186		V:327n66; VIII:199
1:20	II:233	2:8f	VIII:199
1:21	VI:977; 978; 979	2:9	III:233; 454; 531n92; VIII:85
1:22	III:31n18; IX:587	2:13	I:354; III:978n54; 980n73
1:23	IX:303n7	2:17	I:113; II:580; III:250; VII:981

5:10	V:1015	6:24f	VIII:563
5:12	VII:706	6:25	III:462n1; VI:235(n37)
5:12-14	VII:932	6:27f	VIII:563
5:13	IV:897; VI:660; VII:936	6:28	II:33; IV:898n16; VI:694n3;
5:14	VI:160; VII:929n24; VIII:218		VII:194; 603n19
5:15	I:95; V:97	6:30	I:700; IV:354; 355n19; 515;
5:16	VIII:172		V:908; VII:1047; IX:205;
5:17	II:47(n22); IV:630; 965;		368(n78)
	V:412(n212); 414; VI:524;	6:31	II:33; 859; IV:898n16;
	VII:321		VII:603n19
5:18	IV:516	7	III:465; IV:354; VII:937
5:19	IV:169; VIII:204n130	7:1	I:166; IV:518
5:19f	VIII:198	7:1ff	III:987
5:20	I:258; II:47(n22); 655(n8);	7:2	IV:401n88; V:737; 1015
	V:414	7:3	VI:949n4
5:21	IV:630	7:3ff	III:465
5:22	I:549	7:4	I:552(n41); VI:949n4
5:24	II:942(n10); IV:897; VII:706	7:4-8	IV:889n36
5:25	I:95; 452; II:418; VIII:563	7:5	V:778n35, n26
5:26	VI:278; VII:771	7:6	V:680n169; 778n25; VIII:496
5:27	II:690; IV:737; VI:242n69;	7:7	IV:558n23; V:633; VII:771;
	VII:768n12		1046
6	IV:354	7:8	IX:290
6:1	I:523n3; III:364; IV:1048;	7:9	I:209n7; II:852n158; 859, n214;
	V:1015; VI:526		III:881; 886; IV:1049; VI:453
6:1f	I:414n55	7:9ff	VII:48n87
6:1-11	II:508	7:10	V:633
6:2	IV:736; 882(n6); V:17n118;	7:11	II:529; V:510
	264n144; VIII:240	7:13	V:414
6:2-5	VII:321	7:14	II:529; 530n100; 852n158;
6:3	V:854n12		859(n214); VI:725
6:4	I:507; II:508; III:227; 233; 439	7:16	III:47n43; IX:102
6:5	I:166	7:17	III:617
6:6	III:364; V:204; 1015; VII:7; 8	7:18	II:432; III:35n39; V:908;
6:7	VI:122; VII:550		VI:235; 244n87
6:8	I:129; II:507; III:364; VI:168;	7:19	IV:528
	VII:550	7:20	II:529; III:35; 459; IV:679n5
6:9	I:523n3; II:508; 543	7:21	V:778n25, n26; VI:287; IX:226;
6:10	III:916; V:637; VI:73; 77n34		290
6:11	II:752; VI:242n69; VII:7; 8n51;	7:22	VI:368; VII:674n28
	194	7:22f	II:855(n171); IX:654n224
6:12	I:618n11; V:610; 778n26;	7:23	II:852n158; 859n214; III:881;
	VII:596; VIII:243		VI:256, (n14); 257; 260; 369;
6:12ff	III:325(n23)		385n286; 453n2; VII:674n28
6:12-16	IV:45n75	7:24	III:632; IV:364; V:778;
6:12-17	V:908n29		VIII:161
6:13	II:655(n8); VI:173	7:24-29	IV:354
6:14	II:47(n22); III:625n5; V:432;	7:25	VII:981
	VI:308	7:26	VI:1
6:14ff	IV:378	7:27	II:942(n9); V:1015
6:15	II:442n1; 443; VIII:52	7:28	I:702; III:878; 1017
6:16	II:481(n61); V:610	7:29	II:51n7; 481
6:17	II:675; 909n3	7:30	II:66; IV:575
6:18	II:942(n11); VI:881	7:31	III:368
6:19	II:51n7; 855n177	7:32	V:908
6:20	I:675	7:33	I:254; II:858; V:412(n212); 610;
6:21	III:439; V:779; VII:550;		678n148; 680n169; 908
	VIII:28; 563; IX:587	7:34	II:529; IV:630; V:492; 537; 678;
6:22	IV:354; 355n19; IX:110		679n166
6:23	I:147n6; II:942(n11); IV:1089;	7:35	V:374
	VII:716; VIII:524n7; IX:9	7:36	I:209n7; II:852n158; 859;
6:24	I:523n3; II:942(n11)		V:538; 908; VI:165n23

11:8	IV:243; V:296	12:45	IV:328
11:9	II:485	13:1	VI:278
11:10	II:823	13:1-8	VII:38n20
11:12	VII:981	13:2	III:784n36
11:13	III:368; VI:512n84	13:3	V:779; VII:853n11; 982
11:14	IV:329; VI:1	13:4	II:338; 372; V:413
11:15	I:746f; II:66; V:779; IX:74	13:6	III:256n5
11:16	VI:278	13:7	VIII:240
11:17	V:729; IX:482	13:8	I:122
11:19	VI:639	13:9	I:558n1; 559; IX:226
11:20	II:94; IV:595	13:10	IV:1048
11:23	I:631(n17)	13:11	IX:664
11:24	I:129; IV:990n71; VIII:161	13:12	III:725; IV:929; V:778; 779;
11:25	I:387; II:373; VI:526		VIII:218
11:26	I:375	13:13	IV:660(n53); VII:706
11:27	VI:659n43; VII:862	13:14	I:135; 173n12; III:881;
11:29	IX:7		IV:1048; V:778n26; VII:706
11:31	I:115	13:15	IV:943; V:584n12; VI:512n84;
11:32	V:779		881; VII:768n12
11:34	VI:683n2	13:16	VIII:52; IX:199; 204
11:35	VII:738	13:17	IV:174
11:36	III:439	13:18	V:102
11:37	I:717	13:21	IV:814
12:1	II:127	13:23	IV:329; 882(n6); V:779;
12:2	VIII:194		VIII:40; 172; 199
12:3	II:543; V:779	13:24	II:55
12:4	III:45(n8)	13:25	VIII:158
12:6	II:446	14:1	IX:587
12:7	IV:337(n5); VI:527; VII:744	14:2	III:784n36
12:8	VIII:61	14:3	I:95; IV:736; IX:587
12:9	IX:9	14:4	VI:44; VII:625
12:10	V:763; VI:467	14:5	I:633; IV:963; VII:861; 872
12:11f	VII:370	14:6	V:491; VIII:240; IX:14
12:14	I:622; IV:293	14:8	I:360; 727; VI:526; 868; IX:226
12:15	III:881; VI:512n84; IX:587	14:9	IV:1010; IX:110
12:16	III:62; VII:936	14:10	VIII:240
12:18	VIII:194	14:11	VI:949n4
12:20	VIII:34	14:12	II:30
12:21	VIII:195	14:13	VII:420
12:22	V:374; IX:9; 199; 204	14:14	VII:853n11
12:24	I:737	14:14f	II:508
12:25	III:292(n58); VII:981	14:15	VIII:160; IX:9
12:26	VII:1046	14:16	II:908
12:27	VII:705	14:17	VI:883
12:28	III:906	14:18	I:172n6
12:29	VII:449	14:20	I:716; VI:278
12:30	IV:973	14:21	VIII:28
12:31	IX:409	14:22	VIII:34; 199n82
12:32	VI:45	14:23	V:585; VI:634
12:35	III:411; IV:6	14:24	IX:661
12:37	VIII:493n34	14:25	I:650n13; V:779
12:38	IV:7; VII:706	14:26	II:30; IX:226
12:39	V:1015; VII:738; 1046	14:27	II:72(n7)
12:39-45	I:542; V:810	14:28	VII:592n12; VIII:158
12:40	IV:1049; VI:598	14:29	VII:706; VIII:61; 141
12:41	II:224; III:968	14:31	I:716; III:437; 439; VII:706
12:42	I:334; V:778n26; VIII:72	14:33	III:233; IV:882(n6); IX:9
12:43	I:131; II:95; VI:634;	14:35	II:739; VII:388
	VIII:514n40	14:36	I:95; 113; IV:647; VI:767
12:43f	III:187	14:37	IV:973; V:977n198;
12:43ff	VII:48n87		VI:660(n53); VII:862
12:44	VI:62; 725; VIII:514n35	14:38	II:464; III:370n84; 383;

III MACCABEES

2:21	IV:516; V:374	4:21	II:653; III:364; IV:1011; 1015
2:22	VII:69n19; IX:302	5:1	I:557; V:410; VI:290
2:23	VIII:520	5:2	IV:263; V:165n27
2:24	II:624; IV:627; VI:122	5:4	VIII:63
2:25	II:700	5:5	IV:230
2:26	I:210n1; 490; III:62; VIII:165;	5:7	V:979(n210); 1007n371
	194	5:8	I:633; VII:729; IX:9
2:27	I:749; VIII:165	5:9	II:463
2:29	III:645(n10); VII:943; 1046;	5:11	IX:587
	IX:416n5	5:12	I:167; II:47(n22); 653; VIII:165
2:29f	VII:660; 661	5:13	II:26; VIII:526; IX:677, n17
2:30	III:347; IV:813; 828; VI:526	5:14	III:493; 495; VIII:28; IX:677
2:32	VI:1001; 1002	5:16	VIII:210
2:33	VIII:240	5:17	II:773n19; IV:595
3:1	V:410; 412(n212)	5:18	VI:122; 709n43
3:2	V:472	5:19	VIII:52
3:3	IV:973	5:20	V:186; VII:597n2
3:4	VI:526; VII:171	5:22	V:633
3:5	III:867	5:24	III:43n11; VI:278; VII:562
3:7	VIII:240	5:25	IV:557n20; IX:586
3:8	II:507n25; V:778	5:26	II:52n10; VI:695
3:9	I:115	5:27	I:118; II:52; 55; VII:562;
3:10	II:463; VI:641; IX:154		VIII:58
3:11	I:633; 743n5; II:32; V:379	5:28	II:652
3:12	VII:706; VIII:194	5:29	II:463; VIII:165
3:14	VIII:52	5:30	IV:961; 1011; 1015; V:410
3:15	II:589; 590(n8); IV:1090; IX:109	5:31	I:356; 601
3:16	I:95; III:233; IV:963; VII:319;	5:33	VII:596
	VIII:172	5:35	IV:1015; VIII:240; IX:9
3:17	V:859; 864	5:36	II:773n19; V:778n26
3:18	V:104	5:39	III:31n18; VII:738; VIII:210
3:19	I:727; II:655	5:40	IV:141; 990n71
3:20	IV:963; IX:110	5:41	VI:280n7; 726
3:21	I:386; III:232; VI:526; VIII:182	5:42	I:601; 602; II:606; IV:990n71
3:22	II:52	5:43	VII:705; VIII:63
3:23	I:727; VI:526; VII:719	5:44	VII:738; VIII:34; 146; 199n82
3:24	I:549; II:543; IV:1010; VI:3	5:46	VI:278
3:25	VII:769; 770	5:47	V:328; VI:290; IX:226
3:26	VIII:72	5:48	I:210n1
3:28	VIII:240	5:49	VI:726; VII:738; VIII:52;
3:29	VIII:193; IX:266; 587		IX:127; 139n232; 144
3:30	I:743n5; VIII:248	5:51	I:148; II:294; V:160(n21);
4:1	V:875		VI:924; 925; 926; IX:9
4:2	VI:637n21; 949; VII:355	6:1	II:942(n12); III:867; IV:2n9;
4:3	III:837; VIII:194		VII:268; 595
4:4	I:446n2; II:436; VIII:194	6:2	III:1028; 1035; V:160(n22);
4:5	I:171		VIII:618
4:6	III:150; 801	6:2-4	V:979n212; 981
4:6ff	III:150	6:2-15	V:205
4:7	II:503	6:3	I:8(n4); V:9n54; 981
4:8	II:942(n9); III:153; VII:749n4	6:4	I:721; II:481(n68); III:364
4:9	II:896	6:5	I:95; 558; IV:630; VI:909n221
4:10	I:129	6:6	III:660; VI:950n11
4:11	I:136n8; 138n18; VII:589	6:7	II:72(n7)
4:13	V:412(n212)	6:8	III:409(n24), n26; V:981
4:14	III:459; IV:61; VIII:52	6:9	I:598; III:364; 383n118;
4:15	VIII:52		VIII:302; IX:9
4:16	I:604; 605n6; III:439; VI:235;	6:10	VI:1000; 1002; VII:187(4)
	287; IX:226	6:11	VI:1001
4:17	VI:276n12; 467; IX:586	6:12	I:201; II:292
4:18	VIII:195	6:13	III:383n118; VII:271(n12); 981
4:19	VI:3	6:14	IX:9

IV MACCABEES

	VII:534; IX:180
6:29	III:187; IV:334; V:715(n476); 909; VI:88n54; 92
6:30	II:858; III:229
6:31	II:46; V:213, n41
6:32	IV:483
6:33	IV:943
6:34	III:906; V:204; 206n26
6:35	II:917; 924
7:1	V:977
7:3	II:859n213; III:23n12; IV:943
7:4	III:229; IV:943
7:5	IV:360; V:977
7:6	III:125; 229; 248; 809
7:7	IX:307; 308
7:8	II:62; 858; III:158; 252
7:8-15	IX:180
7:9	III:1098; V:977
7:9f	IX:180
7:11	IV:264; V:948
7:13	III:35; VII:110
7:13f	VII:1047
7:14	III:1100; VI:369
7:15	II:858; IV:365; 366; VII:194; VIII:81
7:16	II:858; III:633; V:213; IX:180
7:17	IX:226
7:18	IV:1010; VII:104n52; IX:180, n79
7:19	II:852; 856n196; III:191n3
7:20	V:927n6
7:21	III:596
7:21f	III:125
7:22	I:459; IV:365; 366
7:23	VII:502n243
8:2	III:368
8:3	I:171; VII:603n19; VIII:34
8:4	I:188
8:5	III:35; IV:360; IX:155
8:6	II:655n9
8:7	I:469; 471; VI:526
8:8	IV:990n71
8:9	I:394; III:814; V:410; VI:11
8:10	II:942(n9)
8:11	II:95; III:655n2
8:12	VI:1
8:14	II:181; VII:171
8:16	IX:444n42
8:17	II:655n9; IV:962; V:778n26; VI:3
8:18	I:636; VI:11; VIII:182
8:19	I:227
8:20	II:942(n9)
8:22	I:716; II:181
8:23	III:881
8:26	II:858; VI:3
9:1	II:858; V:737; 1015
9:3	IV:685
9:4	II:481(n58); 858; VII:981
9:5	IV:401n90; IX:198
9:6	II:859; III:368; IV:585; 897; IX:180

9:8	I:136(n11); 138n17; 459; V:909; 936, n4; 937n7
9:9	II:181; III:617
9:10	IX:409n29
9:12	IV:518
9:14	III:728; IV:558n23
9:16	V:204; 206n26
9:17	II:91; IV:558n23; VI:949; VIII:106n2
9:18	I:459; III:368; VI:1; IX:180
9:19	III:662
9:20	VII:109; 166; 1095n2
9:20f	VII:109
9:21	VII:603
9:22	VII:957, n7; IX:102
9:23	I:146; IV:663
9:24	III:228; IV:1011; 1016; VII:534; 705, n25
9:25	III:253
9:26	III:35
9:27	I:717
9:28	III:617; VII:108n84; 109
9:29	VII:179
9:30	VII:179; VIII:526
9:31	II:910n4; 917n47; 919n59
9:32	V:413; 414; VII:188
10:1	I:675; II:859; III:617; V:778n26; VII:981
10:2	I:116n3; 625; VII:539
10:3	I:146; VII:738
10:4	VII:1047
10:5	V:875
10:7	IV:329
10:8	VII:550n18
10:10	I:459; V:610; 909
10:11	III:617; IV:338; VII:188
10:13	IV:360; VI:3; VII:981
10:15	I:146; 168; II:859; IV:365; 366; V:168
10:16	IV:401n90
10:19	V:736; VIII:106n2
10:19f	VII:1047
10:20	IV:558; 560n50; VII:1046; IX:368(n78)
11:2	I:195n4
11:3	V:539; 561
11:5	II:550n19; 858; III:1019; VII:179
11:7	II:529; V:731; VII:1023
11:11	VI:370; VII:1047
11:12	II:470; VI:701
11:14	IV:965
11:15	V:561
11:19	VI:949; VII:550n18
11:20	I:136(n9); 775; III:253; VIII:230
11:26	VI:948
11:27	VI:701
12:1	IV:365; 366
12:3	VI:11; VIII:52
12:4	VI:3; IX:677
12:5	VI:3

MATTHEW

1   I:266n4; IV:1125; VII:464n35;
    776; VIII:376

1f   VIII:363n191

1:1   I:616; **683**; III:288; V:835;
    VIII:485; 486n49; IX:249; 537

1:1ff   II:37; 632

1:1-17   I:141; VII:464; IX:531n266

1:2   I:144; 683

1:2f   II:322n4

1:2-17   I:683

1:2-25   I:683n1

1:3   III:1; 2n8

1:5   III:1; 3, n15

1:6   I:577; III:1, n5; VII:463n30;
    VIII:482

1:6f   VII:464

1:7   IV:434

1:11   I:144; 514

1:12   I:514

1:14   VI:973n1

1:16   V:835n63; VIII:363; 486;
    IX:531; 532n268; 579n546

1:17   I:514; 663; 683; IV:867, n219;
    V:887; VIII:486; IX:531

1:18   I:103; 682; II:684n1; 769;
    III:107(n283); IV:643; V:835,
    (n59); **VI:402;** VIII:380n328;
    IX:531; 537

1:18c   IX:208n104

1:18-25   VIII:486; IX:532n268

1:19   I:363; 632(n53); II:31; 32; 183;
    189; III:46n25; IV:730

1:20   I:103; 776; III:172; 435n14; 436;
    1087, (n255); IV:1099; V:221;
    235; 236; 350; 351; 835; **VI:402;**
    404; VII:272; VIII:486; 553;
    IX:2; 208, n104

1:20f   V:235

1:20ff   I:84

1:20-23   VII:776n55

1:21   I:295; 304; 331; II:715n91;
    III:286n23; 287n28; 289; 487;
    IV:53; V:270; 272; VII:776;
    991; 1001n166; IX:531n267

1:21-25   VIII:363

1:22   I:757; II:67; III:328n45;
    1087(n255); IV:110; 111; 113;
    V:708n424; VI:295, n58;
    831; 832n343

1:23   III:103; 487; V:270; 273;
    834-836; VI:833; VII:760n5;
    776

1:24   I:776; II:334; III:1087, (n255);
    IV:1099; VI:477; VIII:38; 553

1:25   I:705n65; III:487; V:270;
    VI:876n35

2   IV:865n204; 870; 873

2:1   I:352; 577; II:950n43; **IV:358,** n8,
    n9; VII:330

2:2   I:352; 577; II:669; III:375; 376;

2:2ff   IV:28; VI:763n55; 764

2:2-6   V:35n242

2:2-6   IX:532

2:2-16   VI:846

2:3   I:577; IV:870, n238; V:887; 896;
    VII:327; 328n222; 330; 772

2:4   III:271; IV:53; 870n238; V:729;
    VII:864

2:4-6   IV:870

2:5   I:748; 757n40; II:67; VI:831; 832

2:5f   IV:870n238; VI:833

2:6   I:677; II:908; IV:54; 656; VI:494,
    n84

2:7   III:488; IV:358; V:729; IX:1; 591

2:8   I:66; V:638; VI:53; 573; 764

2:9   I:352; 577; V:638; VI:491n59;
    573; VII:648; IX:55n61

2:9f   IV:28

2:10   IX:366; 367, n71; 368

2:11   II:166; III:138; 865; IV:264; 643;
    801n15; V:638; VI:121n21;
    163; 764; VII:458, n7, n8; 772;
    VIII:223

2:12   III:436; V:69; 74; 80; 221; 235;
    236; 350; VIII:553; IX:481

2:12f   VII:272

2:13   I:84; 394; II:334; III:436; 1087,
    (n255); IV:870; V:221; 235;
    236; 350; VIII:553; IX:2

2:13f   IV:643; V:638

2:13-15   IV:870

2:14   VIII:103

2:15   I:757; III:14; 328n45; 488;
    1087(n255); IV:110; 113;
    V:836n67; VI:69n64; 295; 831;
    832n343; 833; 834; VIII:354;
    380, n328; 394

2:16   III:640; IV:358; 870, n238;
    V:342; 419n266; 420; 634, n19;
    637; 729; IX:591

2:17   I:757n40; III:219; 220;
    849n122; IV:110; 1061;
    VI:295; 296; 831; 832n343

2:17f   III:153; VI:833; 834

2:18   III:46n25; 152; 153; 154; 155;
    726; 845n99; V:116; 638; 778;
    819n18; IX:292; 293

2:18ff   IV:925

2:19   III:436; 1087, (n255); V:221;
    235; 350; VII:272; VIII:553;
    IX:2

2:20   II:334; III:384; IV:870; VI:573;
    574; 846; IX:638

2:20f   I:677; IV:643; V:638

2:21   VI:574

2:22   I:590; III:436; IV:595; V:221;
    235; 236; 350; VIII:553;
    IX:208; 481

2:23   I:616; 683n1; 757n40; II:433;
    III:488; IV:110; 456; 874;

4:14	I:757n40; III:328n45; IV:110; VI:295; 830; 831; 832n343
4:14ff	VI:833
4:15	I:677; II:370; V:69; VI:614
4:15f	**VII:440-441**
4:16	I:352; III:17; 443; V:69; **VII:397;** 438n136; IX:344
4:17	I:584; 585; II:715n90; 716n94; 727; 728n59; III:704; 706, n45; 710, (n59); IV:1000n149; 1001, n154; 1002; VI:842
4:18	I:527; V:734; VIII:323n56; IX:531n265
4:18ff	IV:444; 446
4:19	II:156n49; IV:444; V:291
4:21	I:476n1; III:488; VII:772
4:22	V:983
4:23	I:582; 583; II:95; 139; 715n90; 716n94, n96; 720; 726n46; 728n59; III:130; 704, n33; 710(n59); 713; 714; IV:51, n97; V:888; VII:830n210; 832; 833, n222; 834n232
4:23f	IV:1091
4:24	I:563; II:675n1; III:130; V:887; 896; 912; VI:485; VII:883; IX:65
4:25	III:382; VI:614; 617; VII:330
5	V:183; **VI:847,** n417; 906n189
5-7	VI:480; IX:42
5:1	I:519; II:139; 683; III:441; 443; V:484; 485
5:1f	VIII:60n21
5:1ff	VI:847
5:2	VII:699
5:3	I:328; 582; 588; 592; III:523n65; 593; IV:368; 652; 653n22; 718, (n97); V:366; **VI:401;** 649; **904,** n172; 905n186; 906, n188; VII:785n91; VIII:19
5:3b	VI:906n189
5:3f	V:715; VI:327
5:3ff	I:610; II:630n25; III:480; IV:367; 368; 454; 714n72; 1060; VI:20n62; 843
5:3-6	IV:368
5:3-10	IV:657; 716; V:16
5:4	I:662; IV:320; 368; V:790n137; 798; 819n18; VI:30; 42n16; **43**
5:4e	III:647n12
5:5	I:677, n3; III:337; 781; 783; IV:368n45; **VI:649;** 650; **904;** 906
5:6	I:660; II:198; 226, n4; 228; IV:368; VI:12n2; **17-18;** 20
5:7	I:47n132; II:483n92; 484; 485; III:547; V:380; 714; VIII:323
5:7-10	IV:714n72
5:8	I:108; 220; III:425; 613; V:334; 366, (n236), n239
5:8b	VIII:390
5:8f	V:366
5:9	I:47(n130); **II:419;** III:488; V:365; 366; 653; VII:405n14
5:9b	VIII:390
5:10	I:582; 588; 592; II:199; 230; IV:487n37; V:366; 513n113; IX:600n67
5:10f	IV:368
5:10-12	VI:30
5:10ff	I:45
5:11	I:623n13; II:230; IV:294; 1097n36; V:240; 933; VI:152(n35); 562; VIII:439; 442n297; 443; 449; 600n34; IX:600, n67
5:11f	III:829; IV:487; 508; 699; IX:368
5:12	I:20; II:230; 538; IV:588; 699; 714; V:521; 532; 714n467; 916; VI:685; 688; 835; IX:366; 367n71; 600n67
5:13	I:229; 527; II:538; 905; III:397; IV:26; 832; 836n39; **837-839** (839n51, n56); V:759; 944
5:13f	I:678
5:13ff	III:789; IV:452
5:14	III:654; 887; 890; 958; 975, n37; IV:24n27; 326; 327; V:483; 856; VII:327; IX:341; 344
5:14a	IV:26; IX:344
5:14b	V:760
5:14ff	IX:344
5:15	III:331n78; 975; IV:16; 26; 237n25; 326; V:131; 887
5:15f	IV:26
5:16	II:253; 537; 771; III:331(n79); 485n4; 545; 547; 586n6; 975; IV:24n27; 326n20; V:342; 375; 520; 760; 987; 991; VII:249n328; IX:327n119; 341; 344, n271
5:16b	IV:26
5:17	I:758n52; II:156; 348(n55); 668, n14, n15; III:582; IV:126; 338; 503n75; 868n221; 871; 1059; 1062n172; V:718; 719; **VI:293-294** (293n42, n44); 295n60; 832; 847; IX:40
5:17a	VI:294
5:17b	VI:294
5:17f	II:140
5:17-19	VI:662n75
5:17ff	III:327(n37); 936n60; IX:42n183
5:17-20	VI:662n75; IX:36n141; 42n183
5:18	I:130; 678; 760; II:435; 548; 681; 682; IV:1062, n173; V:365; 514n124; **515**
5:18f	IV:1059; IX:42

6:30	VI:205; 207n246; VII:273	7:13bc	VI:922
6:30ff	I:45	7:13f	I:392; 588n79; II:864(n279);
6:31	II:692; IV:591, n14; 592;		III:178n67, n70; 179n80;
	VI:139; 501n19; VII:465;		IV:716; 1002; V:42; 46n12;
	VIII:224		**70-75** (72n102; 75n117,
6:31ff	VI:141		n118); 85n153; 94; 95; 96;
6:32	I:465; II:370; 895; III:888;		VI:749; 921; **922-923**
	V:520, (n180); 538; 987n262,		(922n11; 923n14);
	(n265); 992; VI:140; 501n19		VII:606n15, n17
6:32f	II:893; V:995n300; VI:139	7:14	II:424; 769; 864(n270); V:71,
6:33	I:45; 583; 588; 597; II:198; 201;		n100; 75; VI:922; 923n18,
	IV:591n14; 592; V:31; 236;		n20
	991; VI:18; 19; 20; **870;**	7:15	III:135; **IV:310,** n16;
	VIII:168		311;751n52; V:856; VI:501;
6:33f	VI:327		691; 830; VII:97; 415n2; 754;
6:34	I:465; II:426; 595; 596, n45;		n37; VIII:528
	III:483; IV:592; 593; V:856	7:15ff	III:590; IV:310n16; IX:42n183
7	IV:294n7; 1064n179; VII:754	7:15-20	VII:755n39
7:1	II:483n92; III:331; 923;	7:16	I:220; 704; V:856; VI:423;
	IV:385n98; V:208n27		849n428; 856
7:1f	III:936; 939	7:16a	VII:754, n37
7:1ff	IV:1082	7:16b	**VII:753-755** (755n38)
7:1-5	III:1102	7:16f	III:615; IV:310n16
7:2	I:194n5; III:923; IV:632; 633,	7:16-18	VII:755n40
	n5; 715; V:618	7:16ff	IV:1062; VII:226
7:3	IV:975	7:16-20	V:760; VII:754n32
7:3-5	V:377; 759(n105); VIII:567	7:17	I:10; VI:483; VII:754n34, n37
7:3ff	I:145	7:17-19	**VII:97**
7:4	I:511; 528; III:911; IV:13	7:17ff	III:545
7:5	V:856; VI:869	7:18	VI:554; VII:754n34; IX:58
7:6	I:106; 751n6; III:1102, n6, n7;	7:18f	VIII:528
	1103; 1104; IV:473;	7:19	II:424; III:615; 858; 859;
	V:756(n94); 944; VI:832;		VI:483; 856; 942; VII:754n37
	834; VII:715; 1087n580	7:20	I:704; VI:149; VII:97; 754, n37
7:6a	III:586n6	7:20-23	**VIII:528**
7:7	II:893; III:954n3; **955-956**	7:21	I:587; 588; 610; II:424; 623;
	(955n5); V:75, n117; 856		677; III:54n3; 56; 58;
7:7f	II:769; III:178; 955n9; VIII:224		1084n231, n234; 1086;
7:7-11	II:893		IV:310n16; V:513n111; 520;
7:8	III:911; **955;** IV:7; V:208n27		984; 987n259; 989(n272);
7:9	I:191; III:298n4; IV:269;		995n300; VI:479; 484;
	V:754; 957; VIII:364		VII:754; 999; IX:649n205
7:9-11	V:759, (n105); 991; 992	7:21f	III:1093; V:277
7:9ff	I:192; V:648	7:21-23	III:936; V:995
7:10	**V:579-580**	7:21ff	IV:310; VII:754
7:11	I:11; II:166; 537; V:117;	7:22	I:490; II:952; III:213; 714(n68);
	514n121; 520; 521; 538n17;		1086; V:271; VI:483; **829;**
	638; 986; 987(n265);		856; VII:515n343; **VIII:528**
	989n276; VI:409; 554;	7:22f	II:457; III:936; 937n64;
	VII:348		VII:515n350
7:12	I:46; III:49; 920; IV:535n30;	7:23	I:690n6; 701n55; 703n61; 706;
	1059, n161; 1063; V:73;		II:644; III:1092; IV:1063;
	74n113; 75; 85n153; 752n53;		1086; V:117, n5; 208, n28;
	856; 912n56; VI:315n35; 477;		429
	593; 662n75; 832	7:24	I:220; 362; V:74; 189; 208n27;
7:12f	V:72n107		754; VI:97; 480; IX:234
7:13	I:397; II:65; 424; 677; III:139;	7:24f	II:363n11
	V:71, n100; 72n105; 73; 74;	7:24ff	IV:449; V:131; VI:603n65;
	75n119; 93n188; 96n195;		IX:240
	VI:922n13; 923n18	7:24-27	I:588; III:936; **IV:842-844;**
7:13a	VII:606		V:137; 753n59; 759; VI:97;
7:13b	VI:922; VII:606		99n39; **603;** IX:538n302

7:25	III:64; VI:162; 452		8:17	I:493; 596n6; 757n40; III:130;
7:26	I:220; 362; II:508; V:74; VI:480			204; IV:6; 110; 1091;
7:27	VI:162; 167; 452; 745; 757n69			1094n14; **1097;** 1098, n37;
7:28	II:140; 164; IV:101; 106; V:586;			V:424; 705; 707, (n408); 709;
	VI:18; VIII:60, n21			915n83; VI:295; 296; 830;
7:28f	II:156n49; 348n56; IV:449;			831; 832n343; 833
	IX:932		8:18	V:485
7:29	II:140; 302n68; III:713; VI:702;		8:19	I:213; II:684; V:67
	843, n390; 965; VII:236; 514;		8:19f	I:214
	IX:35n136		8:19ff	I:395
8	II:37; III:404		8:19-22	VII:199; VIII:432n243
8f	VI:847; VIII:290		8:20	III:679; V:534; 852n64; 856;
8:1	V:484			VII:389n11; VIII:394; 405;
8:1ff	III:212			**432-433;** 449n345; 459;
8:2	I:738; II:462; 669; 683; III:424;			477n517
	VI:763		8:21	VI:869
8:2f	III:48		8:21f	III:547; IV:1063; V:982, n235
8:3	II:460; 462; III:424;		8:22	I:213; II:863(n267); III:17;
	VII:554n31; VIII:288n130,			IV:892n12; 893
	n131; IX:430		8:23	V:587n23; VII:199
8:4	I:757n40; II:25; 26; 166; 462;		8:23ff	IV:450
	III:201; 212; 264; 708;		8:23-27	VII:199
	709n52; 865; IV:488n40; 502;		8:24	III:557; VII:70n30; **199;**
	V:763; VIII:505			VIII:553
8:5	II:509; 684; V:794		8:25	II:683; VI:965; VII:989; 990
8:5ff	III:206; 209; 211; VI:958		8:26	II:334; III:210; IV:451n240;
8:5-13	VII:709			VI:205; 207n246;
8:6	I:527; 563; V:637; 638			VII:290n30; IX:666n4
8:7	III:130		8:27	III:38; VII:199; IX:209
8:8	I:330n96; III:294; IV:107;		8:28	III:397; 626; V:69; 74; 80;
	V:637; 638; IX:159; 432			VI:842
8:9	II:270n63; 565; III:210; 294;		8:28-34	VIII:620n49
	IV:535; VI:476; 573; 574;		8:29	I:563; 658; II:17; 19; 669;
	VII:709			III:213; 461, n37; 708(n50);
8:9f	IV:106			900; V:463n7; VI:688, n27;
8:10	I:213; 220; II:509; 769; III:40;			VIII:380n330; IX:675;
	210; 384; V:733;			679n20
	VI:206(n240); 715;		8:30	IV:373
	VIII:435n264		8:31	II:16; V:794n163
8:10ff	III:212; V:847n29		8:32	III:14n61; V:470; VI:456;
8:11	I:9; 352; 587; II:34; 337; 729;			VIII:323n55
	928; III:191; 384n122; 582;		8:33	I:66; VI:530
	825n8; 826; IV:347; 535;		8:34	I:523(n3); III:37; 625;
	V:25; 164; VI:110; 541;			V:794n163; VI:530
	VII:796; VIII:212(n33)		9	II:37; III:404
8:11f	III:782; VI:141n54; 868;		9:1	VI:530
	VII:515n350		9:1ff	III:212; IV:126
8:12	I:582; 587; 642; II:424; 749;		9:1-8	IV:715n77
	III:495; 726, n3, n6; IV:715;		9:2	I:220; 304; III:26; 212; V:342;
	839n56; V:435; 990n282;			639; VI:844; IX:65
	VI:560; VII:439; VIII:365		9:3	II:539
8:13	III:210; V:637; 638;		9:4	III:172, n9, n2(sic.); 612;
	VI:206(n240); VII:726n18;			V:342; VI:562; 844
	VIII:505; IX:432; 679, n29		9:5	IV:908
8:14	I:527; VI:101		9:5ff	IV:122
8:14f	VI:958, n24		9:6	II:565n26; III:327(n39);
8:15	II:154; 334; III:911; VI:958;			IV:908; VIII:405; 459; 460
	VIII:288n130		9:6f	II:334
8:16	I:528; III:130; 207; IV:80; 107;		9:8	II:460; 569; III:37, n44; V:586;
	VI:396; IX:65; 680n39			VIII:405; 459; IX:209; 210
8:16a	VI:541		9:9	I:129; III:443; V:345;
8:11b	VI:541			VIII:98n113

9:10	I:303; 317; 327; II:54n3; III:441; 654; VIII:105n151		713; 714; IV:51n97; 1091; VI:530, n69; 904, n168; VII:830, (n210); 832; 833, n222; 834n232
9:10f	VII:796		
9:11	I:303; III:1093; V:342; VI:965n45	9:36	VI:54; 494; 501; 691; 992; VI:554, n34; VIII:104
9:11f	I:332n114		
9:12	**III:399;** IV:1094n19	9:37f	III:133
9:12f	III:495	9:38	I:528; II:41; III:1086, n252; 1088; V:995n302
9:13	I:303; 328; 330n95; 332n113; II:348(n55); 482; III:48; 181; 184; 488; 546; IV:408; 409n141; 1001n155; VI:20; 573; 662n75; 831n340; 842; VII:23; 142; IX:458n170	10	V:867n49; VI:904
		10:1	I:425(n109); 427; 429; 499; 528; II:325; 566; III:131; 428(n12); 500; 501; IV:1091; VIII:60n21
9:14	II:684; IV:443; 456; 1103n39; VI:140	10:1f	I:428n127
		10:1ff	III:404
9:15	II:671; IV:932; 1099, (n3); 1101; **1103,** n41; 1104; VI:42, n16; VII:772; VIII:365n222	10:2	I:144; 422; 425; 427; 545; II:325; VI:102; 876n31; IX:531n265
9:15a	IV:1103, n39	10:2f	VII:750
9:15b	IV:1103, n39	10:2ff	IV:452n248
9:16	I:529; VI:302; **VII:961**	10:3	III:497; IV:235; VIII:103
9:16f	V:718	10:4	II:884n7; 885n17; 887
9:17	III:448; IV:899n23; VIII:151; 328n96	10:5	I:83; 406(n48); 370; 634; 727; V:66n70; 69; 763; VI:530; VII:91; VIII:60n21
9:18	II:669; 855n175; 862; IV:10; 514; 1107n8; 1112; VI:763, n56; VII:847n25	10:5f	III:582; VII:92; 93; **VIII:436-437**
9:18ff	VI:904n168	10:5ff	IV:452
9:19	II:334	10:6	I:395; III:384; 385; V:129; VI:106; 107; 492; 500, n17; 574; 904n168; VIII:104
9:20	II:322; 684; III:904, n5; IV:1062; V:290		
9:20f	V:586n20	10:6f	VI:574
9:20-22	II:301n60	10:7	I:584; II:331; III:704; 709; 710(n59); 711; 712n60, n61; VI:573; 904n168
9:21	II:539		
9:22	III:26; VII:715; IX:679		
9:23	III:151; 837; 844; V:346; VII:847n25; VIII:261n11	10:7f	I:429; 584; III:714; IV:452; VI:108
9:24	I:660; III:436; 839n72	10:8	I:490; 493; 528; II:167, n2; 335; III:131; 208; 213; 424; 605n8; IV:7n8; 234; 453; 893; 1095; VI:904n168; VII:246
9:25	II:335; 425; III:911; IX:212n122		
9:26	I:677; II:679; V:733	10:8b	V:307
9:27	I:129; II:485(n102); III:901; VIII:287n120; 288n121; (n126); 486	10:8f	VI:273n26
		10:8ff	II:692
		10:9	I:526; II:433; V:307; VI:903n164
9:27ff	V:347		
9:27-31	VIII:289, n137	10:9ff	I:429n129
9:28	II:303; 684; VI:206(n240); 473(n83); VIII:288n121; IX:249	10:10	I:379; II:692; 855n177; 605; IV:698n6; V:69; 311; VI:119n6; **120;** 141; 969, n22; VII:874n26; VIII:35
9:29	IV:561n53; VI:206(n240); VIII:288; 289		
		10:11	I:379; IV:310; VI:530n69
9:29f	V:377	10:11ff	V:22
9:30	III:708n48; V:427; 428; VIII:287	10:12a	V:131
		10:12b	V:131
9:31	I:677	10:12f	I:499; IX:367n64
9:32	IX:65	10:13	I:379, n2; II:413; VII:726
9:33	III:37, n43; 384; IX:2; 532	10:13ff	III:751
9:34	I:528; II:95; 433; 539; III:714(n68); V:714	10:14	I:499n24; II:53n12; V:209n30; VI:530n69
9:35	I:582; 583; II:139; 715n90; 720; III:130; 704n33; 710(n59);	10:14f	VI:629n48

10:15	I:677; IV:715; **V:652-653**		10:29	V:986; 987n263, (n265); 992;
10:16	I:83; 210, n6; 340; 386;			VI:163; VII:732n18
	406(n48); 435n175; II:349;		10:29-31	IV:592; V:991; **VII:731-732**
	III:696; IV:311n18; 499;		10:29ff	IV:1016
	V:29; 33n218; **580;** 752;		10:30	I:461; IV:560
	VI:70; 71; 501; 691; IX:234;		10:31	IX:63
	235		10:31a	VII:731; 732
10:16a	IV:310		10:31b	VII:731; 732
10:16ff	II:327; IV:260n16		10:32	III:936; IV:497n63; 714; V:208,
10:17	I:364; II:169; 433; 504n4;			n27; 211; 218; 513n111; 520;
	IV:516, n3; V:621n160;			VIII:372n268; 442n297;
	634n23; VII:831, n213; 834,			447n329
	n232; **867;** VIII:460n411		10:32f	II:537; III:936, n61; IV:621;
10:17f	V:933; VIII:600n34			V:208n28; 216; 217; 812; 987,
10:17ff	I:45; IV:449; 508; V:916			n259; 989(n272); VIII:439;
10:17-22	VI:444n767			**442;** 460
10:17-23	V:867n49		10:32ff	IV:1060
10:18	I:577; IV:502; 503, n76;		10:32-39	IV:1002
	VII:648; 834; VIII:443n308		10:33	I:469; 470; 471; III:107n282;
10:18ff	I:434(n173)			936; V:217; 513n111; 520;
10:19	IV:591, n15; 592; V:212; 982;			1010n392
	VII:834; VIII:460n411;		10:33ab	I:471
	IX:679		10:34	I:678; II:412; 748n38; **IV:526;**
10:20	I:103n53; V:987n263, (n265);			VI:942
	992; VI:142		10:34f	II:348(n55); 414
10:21	IV:1099n1; V:983; VII:740;		10:34ff	II:668
	IX:163		10:34-37	IX:643
10:21f	V:347		10:35	IV:526; 643; 1099, (n3); V:983;
10:22	II:426; IV:586; 690, n25;			VIII:219
	V:279; 889; VI:194; VII:991;		10:35f	IX:319n56
	VIII:56; 436n273; 443n308		10:36	II:813
10:23	II:230; 585n70; 702n1; III:376;		10:37	I:48n135; 588; IV:643; **690-691**
	384; VI:530; 845; VIII:60,			(690n24); 693; V:982;
	n19, n20; 64n6; **436-437;**			VIII:364; IX:128; **129;** 130;
	442n297; 460, n411			638; 642n157; 644
10:23b	II:230		10:37a	VIII:515
10:23f	V:347		10:37b	VIII:515
10:24	V:347; VIII:436n273		10:37f	I:379
10:24a	IV:442		10:37ff	I:48; IV:488; 560(n48); 621
10:24b	VIII:515		10:38	I:211; 214; IV:6; 494n59;
10:24f	II:152; III:557; 1093; IV:442;			V:916n92; VII:577; 578n49,
	448; V:760			n50, n51; n53
10:25	I:605; II:49; III:487; 496;		10:38f	IV:450n238; VI:144; 152(n35);
	IV:294; VIII:436n273			VII:791n117
10:25a	IV:442		10:39	I:394; 395; II:727; 769; IV:714;
10:25b	IV:442			VI:944; VII:991n105;
10:26	I:703; III:557; 590; V:553n92,			VIII:443n308; IX:130; 608;
	n93; **VII:743,** n8; IX:345n274			642, n156, n157; **643;** 644
10:27	III:704; 705, n40; 709; 713;		10:40	I:404(n38); II:349n60;
	V:553, n93; **VII:441;**			IV:651n16; V:22; 363;
	IX:344-345 (345n274)			VII:1071n447
10:27f	III:557		10:40-42	III:547; IV:651n16; 652; 657;
10:28	I:396; 658; II:567n30; 862n257;			V:16
	III:936; IV:311n18; 344; 347;		10:40ff	I:48; 426; **II:53-54;** IV:652;
	487n37; 714; 716; V:423;			VI:20
	439n397; VI:947;		10:41	II:189; 190; IV:7; 681; 700;
	VII:743(n9); 1058; 1082;			VI:850
	1086; 1087n582; IX:159; 210;		10:41f	II:433; III:351; IV:714; V:274;
	608; 643; **645-646;** 656			275; VIII:224
10:28a	IX:646n176		10:42	I:426; II:168(n3); 349n62; 876;
10:28b	**V:653;** IX:646n176; 647			**IV:649-650; 651-652** (651n16;
10:28ff	VII:731n17; 732n20			652n18); 700; VI:141; 149;

159; VIII:323, n61; IX:530

11	I:612
11:1	I:523(n3); II:139; III:704; 713; VII:833n222; VIII:35, n9; 60
11:1-6	I:609; V:993n290
11:1-24	I:610
11:2	I:83; 417n68; II:642; III:288; IV:456; VII:248n320; 258n388; 856n1; VIII:125; IX:532; 549
11:2ff	I:589; IV:457; VII:350n63
11:2-26	VII:350n62
11:3	II:670; 702; 937; IV:274n48; VI:726; VII:347; VIII:290
11:4	I:219; 220; IV:121; V:342; 343; VI:573n50
11:4f	I:66; VI:959
11:4-6	IX:532
11:4ff	I:219; IV:122; VI:108
11:5	I:370; II:335; 710n26; 715n91; 717; 718, n109, n110; 720; III:212; 424; 714; IV:233; 234; 893n17, n27; V:551n75; 552n77; 715; 772; VI:107; 407n484; 847; **903-904;** 908; VII:246, n312; VIII:19; 287, n119; **290**
11:5f	I:67; 68; 589; II:725; III:589
11:6	III:581; IV:367; 369; 560n45, n46; VI:908n212; VII:341; 343; 344; 345; 349; **350;** 351n70; 352; 353n79; 357; VIII:442
11:7	V:345, n155; VI:573; VII:69
11:7f	I:609
11:7-9	VIII:224
11:7ff	I:538
11:7-19	III:937
11:8	I:577; 591; III:154; 593; IV:249n52; V:345; IX:84; 683n14
11:9	II:719; VI:62; 836; 837; 839; 840; VII:234
11:9-15	I:609
11:10	**I:83;** 389; 610; 748; II:936n65; 937; III:103n256; IV:653; V:70, n96, n97, n98; VI:684; 688; 777; 831n341; 841
11:10ff	**VI:840-841**
11:11	I:587; 672; 776; II:334; III:351; **IV:534-535; 653-654** (654n30); V:993n290; VI:840; VIII:383n358; 474
11:11a	**VI:839-840**
11:11b	IV:653; VI:841
11:11f	I:545
11:11-15	VI:840n372
11:12	I:48; 472; 588; **609-612; 613-614;** II:885
11:12-15	I:472n5
11:13	IV:1059; 1061; VI:829; 832; **839-840;** 841
11:13f	I:610
11:14	I:389; 610; II:52; 670; 719; 937; III:44n5; 593n3; V:496; 553n99; VI:841; VIII:255
11:14f	V:553
11:15	V:552, n79
11:16	I:663; III:443; 848; V:189; 638; 751; 754; VII:715n1; VIII:432n241; IX:154n70
11:16f	III:152n27; 845; V:759(n105)
11:16ff	III:848n118
11:16-19	I:609; V:760; **VII:516**
11:17	III:152, n28; 153; 154; 155; 830; 834; 836; 845, n100; 848; VII:715n1
11:18	II:693; 822; IV:930; 932n60; V:163; VI:140
11:18f	II:669; V:993n290; VIII:17; 103; 212n32; **431-432**
11:19	I:303; 327; II:214; 215; 693; III:154; 581n34; 734; IV:932n60; V:163; 639; VI:135n4; 140; 141, (n53); VII:516, n351, n353; 832; VIII:104; 405; **431-432** (431n237); 433; 449n345; 453; 457n390; 458n399; 459; 477n517; IX:42, n177; 159; 164
11:19a	IX:164n153
11:19c	VIII:432
11:20	V:240; VI:530; 842; **VIII:20;** 125n72
11:20ff	I:219; 220; II:301; IV:122; 1002; V:347; 428
11:20-24	I:610; III:936; IV:503; 714; 715; V:993n290
11:21	III:974; IV:551; 1002; V:717; **VII:61-62** (62n48)
11:21ff	VI:843
11:21-24	VII:516n355
11:22	II:952
11:23	I:148; III:947; IV:1107n15; V:429; 534; VI:577; VIII:608
11:23b	VII:273
11:24	I:677; II:952; VII:273
11:25	I:6(n8); 679; II:803; III:461; 581; 748n47; 886; 945; 1084n232, n233; 1087; IV:344; 454; 652; 654; 840; 920; **921-923;** 1016; 1115n59; V:214; 501; 514n124; 516; 985n251; 993n290; 995; VII:517; 892n40; 893, **n44**(sic.); IX:44n201
11:25f	I:713; II:171; III:973; 1029; V:214; 993n289; VII:516n356; 517
11:25-27	VII:893n44
11:25ff	II:456; III:581n34; IV:621
11:25-30	II:171n16; IV:365n30;

	454n256; 819n140; 920n43;		831n340; 842; VII:23;
	V:947; **992-994** (993n288);		30n231; 142; IX:458n170
	VI:649, n23; **VII:516-517**	12:8	VII:20; 23; VIII:459; 460
	(516n356, n357); 893n44;	12:9	I:523(n3); VII:24n188; 25n199;
	VIII:368n239; 373n276, n281		834n232
11:26	I:6(n7); II:62; 745; 747; 748n40;	12:9ff	II:139; III:212
	IV:344; V:513(n112);	12:9-13	VII:830n210
	984n247	12:9-14	II:462; **VII:24-25**
11:27	I:6(n9); 633; 704; **713,** n83;	12:10	II:561; III:130; 637;
	II:171; 348n58; 568; III:580;		VII:20n157; 25
	591; IV:114, n188; 621; V:74;	12:11	II:334; VI:662(n71); 690;
	80; 214; 363; 520; 889; 989,		VII:25, n198
	n271; 992n288; 993n288,	12:11f	VII:21; 24n197; 25n201; 26,
	n289, n293; VI:496n106;		n203; VIII:364n210; IX:53;
	VII:516n356; 517; VIII:335;		638n130
	366; 371n266; **372-373**	12:12	I:364; II:561; VI:477n99; 478;
	(372n276; 373n282);		723; VII:20n157; 25; IX:63
	374n285; 380; 464n436;	12:13	I:264; II:460; 462, n5; VI:914;
	IX:539n312		VII:24n189; VIII:312
11:27f	VII:517	12:14	VII:25n199
11:27-29	I:610	12:15	I:703; III:130; IV:445
11:28	I:350; 351; VI:908; **IX:86-87**	12:15b	VI:541
	(86n3)	12:15ff	III:207
11:28f	I:350; III:829	12:16	III:708n48
11:28-30	I:713; II:899n21; V:214;	12:16ff	I:102; II:626n17
	993n288, n289, n292; VI:649;	12:17	I:757n40; III:328n45; IV:110;
	VII:516, n357; 517; **IX:85-86;**		VI:295; 296; 830; 831;
	487n22		832n343
11:28ff	II:348(n59); IV:621; 1003; 1060	12:17ff	VI:833
11:29	I:185; 351; 596n5; II:769;	12:18	I:48; **67;** 184; II:739; 740;
	III:337; 613; IV:384n87; 407;		V:446; **700-701** (700n341;
	409; 652; 655; 922; 1062;		701n352); 702, (n360); 704;
	V:895; 993n292; **VI:649;**		710(n429); VI:398; 404;
	VIII:20n59; 25n77; IX:87n5;		VIII:368; 384n365; IX:640
	639-640	12:18c	V:701
11:29a	VII:578	12:18-20	V:700; 707(n408); 709
11:29b	VI:908n213	12:18-21	III:942; V:705; 706; 895;
11:29f	I:556; II:898; 899		VII:167; IX:293
11:30	I:557; IV:1003; VI:719; IX:487	12:19	III:901; VIII:445n315
12	IX:87	12:20	I:528; IV:945; VI:745; VII:167;
12ff	V:993n290		**923**
12:1	III:461; V:68; VI:19; 955;	12:21	II:530n100; 532; V:271; 274;
	VII:20n157; 23n179		700; 707; 708
12:1ff	I:328; 329n93; 330	12:22	III:130; 204; V:343; VIII:287;
12:1-8	VI:19; **VII:23**		288; IX:65
12:1-11	VII:30n231	12:22ff	I:528; IV:1095; VII:235;
12:2	V:342		VIII:289n137
12:3	IV:1059; VI:19; VII:772n33	12:22-25	IX:532
12:3f	VII:772	12:22-38	VII:235n241
12:3ff	I:92	12:23	II:460; III:37; VI:959;
12:4	II:677; III:235; 243; 264;		VII:235n246; VIII:486;
	VII:772n33		IX:532n270
12:4f	VII:21	12:24	I:489; 528; 606, n10;
12:5	I:343; 605; III:235; IV:1059		III:714(n68); VII:330n243;
12:5f	III:264		VIII:365n215; 486; IX:38
12:6	I:793; III:184; 235; 244;	12:25	I:580; II:659; III:172; IV:968;
	263n27; IV:126; 136; 535;		V:131; VI:165n21; 530n69;
	884; 899; VI:62n4; 303;		844
	VII:23; 234; VIII:255; 257	12:25f	VII:651
12:6f	VI:19	12:25ff	IV:715n77
12:7	II:482; III:48; 181; 184; 546;	12:26	V:299n18; 559
	622; IV:408; VI:20; 662n75;	12:27	I:605; II:539; III:202; 714(n68);

	941n2; 943; IV:443; VIII:365, n215; IX:46n215; 91n26
12:28	I:528, n5; 584; 610; II:19; III:212; 589; 1034; IV:718; VI:107; 398; 404; IX:89n11; 90; **91-92** (91n26, n27)
12:28-34	**IX:40**
12:29	I:472; 527; III:210; 400; 401; IV:944; VI:869n4; VII:362
12:29f	V:895
12:30	V:856; VI:397n408; 492n72; 498; 696n27; **VII:420,** n11; VIII:442
12:31	I:103n53; 104n56; 295; 528; VIII:442n301; 451n365; 459n406
12:31b	VIII:459n406
12:31f	I:304; IV:716; VII:755n41; VIII:459
12:32	I:205; 206; 511; 624; II:550; III:107n282; 936; IV:1114n54; 1115n59; VIII:405; 449n345; 453, n372; 459n406
12:32a	VI:397, n408; VIII:459n406
12:32b	VIII:459n406
12:32f	**I:104**
12:33	III:545; VI:479; **VII:97;** IX:3n4
12:33-35	VII:754, n32, n37; 755, n40, n41
12:33ff	IV:310; 1002
12:34	I:16; 452; 672; II:550; 815; III:612; V:427; VI:63; 554; VII:348; 754
12:35	I:528; III:137; VI:555; 561; 562
12:36	I:103n53; 452; II:167; 952; IV:103
12:36f	VI:976
12:37	II:215; 217; III:622
12:38	III:45n8; V:342; VI:847; VII:234(n240); IX:38
12:38f	VIII:449
12:38ff	III:36; 208; 210; 714(n69); VII:234
12:38-42	III:408n14; 409
12:39	I:329; 663; II:893n6; 895n2; **III:408-410;** 590; IV:730; 734; VI:555; 831; VII:230; 233, n227; 234; 235; 236; VIII:439; 449, n349
12:39f	IV:867; **VII:233-234;** 465n38
12:39ff	IV:1002
12:40	I:148; II:424; 948; 950; III:408; 409; 410n28; 613; 787; IV:884n17; 1124, n9; V:772; VI:577n78; VII:29n226; 234, n232; VIII:220; 449; 459; 477n517; IX:450n91
12:40b	VIII:439
12:41	I:362; 663; II:428; III:408, n15; 715; 941n2; 943n4; IV:535;

	899; VI:842; 843; VII:62; 234; 465n38; 516n355
12:41f	III:244n65; 409n22; 936; 951; V:347; VII:465n39; 796; VIII:255; 450n352; IX:537
12:41ff	VI:902
12:42	I:590; 663; 679; II:334; III:1n5; IV:535; 867; 899; VII:234; **465;** 516; VIII:255
12:42f	VI:902
12:43	I:351; II:657n1; III:428(n12); VI:577n84; 905; VIII:203
12:43-45	V:135n2
12:43ff	II:540; IV:576; VII:226
12:44	I:527; II:425; 769; III:867; V:125; VII:726
12:44f	V:125n28
12:45	I:329; 663; II:16; 630; 631; 697; IV:69; V:154; VI:558; 867
12:46f	V:341; VII:647
12:46ff	IV:643
12:47	I:144n3
12:49	II:460; 461; IX:430
12:50	I:144n3; II:461; 537; III:55; 56; 58; IV:121; V:520; 986, (n256); 987n261; 989(n272); VIII:442n299; IX:649n205
13	II:630n25; 632n38; V:718; 755; 757; 761; VII:291n38; 349
13:1	III:441; V:734
13:1f	III:440; 443
13:1-3	VIII:60n21
13:1ff	I:219
13:2	V:586; VII:648
13:3	V:752
13:3f	VII:546
13:3ff	IV:10
13:4	V:68; 734
13:4-8	VI:163
13:5	I:517; VI:170, n3; VII:349
13:6	I:352; **VI:988**
13:7	I:519; VI:456
13:8	III:536; 615
13:9	II:827
13:10	IV:817n133
13:10-13	V:757
13:10-15	VII:894
13:11	I:103n53; 583; 708; IV:108n149; **817-819;** 921; V:150, n14; 513n113; 554; 761; VII:894(n56); **VIII:329**
13:12	II:827; IV:819n138; V:757; VI:59; VII:358
13:13	V:757; VII:892; VIII:451n365
13:13-15	V:554
13:13ff	V:342; VII:351
13:14	I:757n40; IV:110; V:343; VI:306; 830; 833
13:14f	IV:818; V:341; 347; 556; VII:724n10
13:15	I:556; III:204; IV:52; V:378; 1023; 1024; 1025; **VII:727;**

	893; VIII:292n157		VIII:442n297; 461, n414
13:15a	III:613	13:37-39	VI:495; VIII:461n414
13:15b	III:612	13:38	I:582; 587; II:749; III:545, n26;
13:16	I:219; 220; IV:367; 368; V:342;		890; **VI:559-560;** VII:346;
	347; 378; 553; 556		545; VIII:365, n220
13:16f	IV:368; 535; 818; V:343; 347;	13:39	I:84n68; 194n4; 203(n17);
	VI:843		III:133; V:32; VI:559;
13:17	II:189; III:170; IV:103; 681;		VII:158; 160; 346; 546;
	V:342; **347;** VI:833; 843		VIII:66
13:18	V:752; 753	13:39f	VIII:66
13:18f	VII:546	13:40	I:203(n17); III:885; VI:942;
13:18-23	**IV:121-122;** V:756		VII:346; VIII:66
13:19	I:472; 473; 582; 583; 611;	13:40f	IV:714
	III:545n26; 612; IV:121n202;	13:40-43	VIII:461n414
	V:68; 734; 888; VI:549(n22);	13:41	I:84n68; 581; IV:1086; VI:479;
	558; 560; VII:158; 160; 546;		VII:344, n35; 345; **346-347**
	892		(346n41, n43; 347n46); **348;**
13:20	VII:349; 546; 772		356; 357n110; VIII:372;
13:20f	VII:349		442n297; 461, n414;
13:21	III:463; V:299n19; VI:31; 252;		IX:164n151
	988; VII:341; 344; 345; **349**	13:41f	II:190
13:22	I:203; 385; II:920; 925n96;	13:41-43	V:995n300
	III:616; VI:327; 456; VII:546	13:41ff	III:133
13:23	III:536; V:554; VI:483;	13:42	I:527; 642; 658; II:424; III:726;
	VII:546; 892		IV:715; V:429; 945; 946; 947;
13:24	III:545; V:189; 752; 754;		VII:346n44; 347
	VII:545; 546; VIII:163;	13:43	I:582; 587; II:190; 250; 337;
	461n414		IV:24n28; 26; 248n49; V:552,
13:24ff	II:814; V:432n356; VII:351n66		n79; 752; 988n266;
13:24-30	I:585; V:753n59; 759; VIII:104		VIII:461n414
13:25	I:194n4; III:435; VII:546	13:44	I:585; II:769; III:7n16; 137;
13:26	III:615; VI:483; 484;		958; 973; 974; V:438n390;
	VII:347n46; IX:2		752; 754; IX:370
13:26ff	IV:188	13:44-46	I:588; IX:538n307
13:27	II:49; III:545; VII:545; 546;	13:45	II:893; III:537; IV:473n13
	874n27	13:45f	I:585; IV:473; V:752
13:28	III:47n44; VI:476; VII:160	13:46	II:769; IV:473n13; VI:160
13:28f	VII:351n66	13:47-50	I:585; III:936; V:759; VII:97;
13:29	VI:991		VIII:104
13:30	II:60; III:132; 133; 461; 936;	13:48	I:527; III:443; VI:291; 295n60
	VI:717n87; VII:347; 422;	13:49	I:84n68; 203(n17); II:190; 680
	856n1; VIII:518		V:454, n2; 754; VI:558;
13:30b	VIII:461n414		VIII:66; IX:164n151
13:31	III:810; V:515; 752; 754;	13:49f	V:429
	VII:288n13; 546; VIII:163	13:50	I:642; 658; II:424; III:726;
13:31f	I:585; III:810; V:752; VII:289;		IV:715; VI:946; 947
	290-291	13:51	VII:893n42; 894n55, n58; 895
13:31-33	VI:495n98; IX:538n307	13:52	I:528; 587; 742; II:49; III:138;
13:32	III:720; IV:66; 654; VII:289;		448, n6; 750; IV:461;
	545; VIII:518n7; 519n18		V:150n14; **718-719** (719n9,
13:33	I:585; 784; II:905; III:958;		n10); VII:864n27
	966n21; 973; IV:655n35;	13:53	II:140; V:752; VIII:60, n21
	V:752; 754; 759; VIII:220n34	13:53ff	II:139
13:34f	VII:699	13:54	II:139; 155; 303; IV:874;
13:35	I:757n40; III:620; 885n62; 974;		VII:514; 834n232
	1029, n198; IV:110; 818;	13:55	I:144n2; IV:643; VIII:363
	V:757; VI:295; 831; 832,	13:56	VI:722
	n343; 833; 834	13:57	III:995; 997n177; VI:841;
13:36	IV:451; V:586; 756; VII:894n58		VII:343; 344; 345; 349; **350;**
13:36ff	IV:715		358; 740
13:36-43	V:756; VIII:461n414	13:58	II:301; 302; VII:245n306
13:37	III:545; VII:545; 546;	14:1	III:287; 461

16:28	I:581; 589; II:433, n52; 538; 670; V:360; VI:845; 926n52; VII:648; VIII:442n297; 460; 461n414
17:1	I:144; V:485n116; IX:60
17:1ff	I:428n126
17:1-8	VIII:175
17:2	II:249; IV:24n28; 25; 27; 247; 758; VI:776; **VII:666;** IX:343
17:3	V:354; 358n210
17:3f	**II:938-939**
17:4	III:48; 945; VI:965
17:5	II:740; IV:101; 114; 189n17; 248; 250n64; 739; 910n46; V:446; 668n81; 701; VI:847; **VII:400;** VIII:380; IX:298; 343
17:6	VI:163n15; 561n104; 630; 775; IX:209; 210
17:6f	VIII:380
17:7	II:334; IX:212
17:8	V:377
17:9	II:335; 545; 546; V:354; 372, n4; VIII:460
17:10	II:670; 936; VI:869
17:10ff	II:23
17:11	II:933
17:12	II:670; 719; 937; V:707n405; 912n56, n62; **913-916** (913n67, n68); VI:841; VII:894(n56); VIII:460
17:12a	V:914
17:12b	V:914
17:13	I:545; II:937
17:14	I:625n3; 738; II:684
17:14ff	I:428
17:14-21	V:982
17:15	II:485(n102); V:912; 913n67; VI:163; 941; VIII:288n126
17:16	III:131; IX:65
17:17	I:329; 663, n3; IV:582; 1097; V:428; VI:722; VII:407; **718**
17:18	I:493; II:626n19; III:130; V:637; IX:679
17:20	I:220; II:826n58; III:810; 811; IV:108(n150); V:483; VI:205; 206(n242), n203; 207, n246; 715; **VII:289-290** (289n25; 290n28)
17:20a	VII:290n30
17:21	IV:933n73; 934n80; VI:579
17:22	II:169; V:707n405; VII:716n5; IX:426n16
17:22f	VIII:460
17:23	I:430(n132); II:335
17:24	III:1093; IV:283; VI:102; 965n45; VIII:60
17:24f	IV:6
17:24ff	II:500; III:207; IV:1061
17:24-27	III:243; VI:662(n73); VII:30
17:24-18:9	VII:347
17:25	I:265; 577; II:232; VIII:56;

	IX:81n12, n13; 90
17:25f	I:577; VII:351; **VIII:364;** 374n286, n288; 390
17:26	V:887
17:27	I:372; 373; 527; II:769; VI:573, n50; VII:341; 344; 347; 350; **351;** 352; 357; 358
17:27-18:9	VII:347
18	III:752; IV:653n21; 659n52; V:755; 996n303; VI:492n68; 498n125
18:1	I:587; III:752; IV:532; 653; 654; VIII:60n21; IX:679
18:1-3	IV:653n21; VIII:60n21
18:1ff	I:429n129; 430n131
18:1-4	VIII:17n41
18:1-14	VII:347
18:2	III:500; 501; VII:646
18:2ff	V:638; 649; 650
18:3	I:363; 587; II:424; IV:532; 718; 917; 1002; **1003;** 1005; VII:715; VIII:17n41
18:3ff	1:332n116
18:4	I:587; **IV:532-533;** 652; 653n21; 654; 1003; VIII:14n34; **16-17** (17n42)
18:5	II:54; 168(n3); 349n63; III:547; IV:533n18; 653n21; V:271; 277
18:6	I:516; II:433; III:915; **916-917** (916n7); IV:560, n46; 651; 652n19; 653n21; V:421; VI:210(n266); 214(n304); VII:341; 344; 347; **351-352;** 355; IX:75
18:6f	IV:840; VII:344; 347; 357
18:6ff	V:16
18:6-9	VII:347
18:7	I:347; III:890; VII:340; 344; 346; **347-348;** 350; 352; 357n110
18:7a	VII:347
18:7b	VII:347
18:7c	VII:347
18:8	I:209; 392; III:853; 858; 859; IV:560n44; V:434; 436; VI:945; 947
18:8f	II:424; 677; 864(n270), (n277); IV:559n39; 560; 714; 716; V:551n75; VI:327; 945; VII:348; 350; **352,** n72; n73; **IX:75**
18:9	I:527; 583; III:857n1; IV:560n44; V:377; 436; VI:945
18:10	I:82; 86; II:66; 537; III:632; IV:651, n15, n16; 652n19; 653n21, n22; 840; V:275; 341n138; 343; 344; 366; 513(n105); 520; 533; 534n322; 649; 889; 987, n260; 988n266; 989; VI:242n71; 777; VII:347

18:11	I:395; II:669; VII:991n109; VIII:461n415		18:26	IV:379, n48; 387n114; V:889; VI:163; 763; VII:554
18:12	I:510; II:892; V:483; VI:574; 690		18:27	I:511; **IV:380;** V:444; VII:554
18:12f	**VI:242;** 252n163		18:28	V:442; 563; VI:456
18:12-14	V:752; 753n64; 755; 759; VI:490; **492,** n68; 498		18:29	IV:379; V:794n165; VI:163, n15; 763; VII:554
18:12ff	III:752		18:30	III:46n25; IX:244
18:12-24	V:755		18:31	V:342n142; 887
18:12-35	III:937		18:32	I:511; II:271n71; III:500; IV:103n131; V:564; 794n165; VI:554; 561
18:13	II:769; V:754; IX:159; 366; 367n71			
18:13f	VIII:104		18:33	II:483; IV:671n26; VII:554
18:14	II:537; 745; 747; III:54; 56; 329(n59); IV:651; 652n19; 653n21; V:520; 754; 987; 988n266; 992; VI:242n71; 317n43; 492, n66; VII:347; 992		18:34	I:563; IV:380; V:419n266; 425; 428, n333; 429; 430; 434; 435; 438; 442; 444; 447; IX:244
			18:35	III:558; 613; IV:347; 380; V:520(n180); 538, n18; 539n8; 754; 987n260; 988n266; 989(n272); 991; 995; 996n303; VI:171n9; 464; IX:244
18:15	I:663n5; II:432; 474; 625, n12; III:673; 753; VII:992; VIII:505			
			19:1	III:382; VI:614; 617; VIII:60, n21
18:15e	III:647n12			
18:15-17	III:752; VII:160; VIII:221		19:2	III:130
18:15ff	I:145		19:3	II:684; V:888; VI:591, n71
18:15-18	III:752		19:4	I:481; III:1029; VI:462n27; 635
18:15-20	VIII:104		19:5	I:757; III:822, n6; 823; IV:643; V:982
18:16	IV:452n248; 490, n48; 498; VII:648; 698; VIII:221n40		19:6	VI:560n90; 591
			19:6ff	IV:733
18:17	I:223; II:61; 372; III:501; 504; **518-526;** 533; 752; VII:346n43; VIII:103; 104		19:7	I:617; II:545; 548
			19:8	I:481; III:1029; IV:733; VI:724
			19:8b	V:769
18:18	I:109; 449; 679; 742; **II:60-61;** III:752; 753; VI:336; V:513(n118); VI:108		19:9	I:650n14; IV:730; 733, n33; **VI:591-592** (592n74, n75)
			19:10	I:651n17, n20; 652n27; IX:75, n13
18:19	I:679; II:537; 805; **V:519;** 520; 728; 888; 986; 987n260; 988; 989; VI:639; VIII:220; IX:308		19:11	IV:108; 819n138; V:648
			19:11f	I:651n20
18:20	I:430(n133); II:36n1; 349n63; 433; 805; III:505; 809; IV:270; V:274; 275; VI:142(n67); VII:776; 962; VIII:220; IX:308		19:12	I:588; 651; 652; II:765; 767, n18, n19; 768, n27, n29; III:331; 787; 854; 855; IV:643; 737n3; V:648
			19:13	I:427n116; VIII:161; IX:432
18:21	II:432; 683; VI:102		19:13f	V:638
18:21f	II:631, n29; IV:347		19:13-15	V:649
18:21ff	I:47n132		19:13ff	V:649
18:21-35	I:511; II:169(n8); III:936		19:13-19	VIII:17n41
18:22	II:631; 632; 635		19:14	I:510; 588; II:669; IV:654
18:23	I:172; 579; 589; III:47n43; IV:78; 103; V:189; 750n37; 755; 996n303; VII:796; 874n27		19:15	VI:573; 574; VIII:161
			19:16	II:684; 825; 864(n272), (n275)
			19:16ff	II:140
18:23-25	IV:714; V:760; 995		19:16-22	III:593
18:23ff	I:303n136; II:270n65; IV:385n96; V:442; 562; 563		19:17	I:15; 16; II:548; 677; 685; 864(n277); III:49; IV:718; VI:53; 225n362; VIII:144
18:23-24	VI:316n39			
18:23-35	I:585; IV:347; **379-380,** 716; VI:456; **VII:554**		19:18	I:583; II:547; III:755; IV:729; 730n2
			19:19	IV:643; V:989n275; VI:316; VIII:178; IX:130
18:24	I:303n137; V:444; 562; 565			
18:25	III:1086; VI:160		19:20	II:548; VI:905; **VIII:74;** 597; IX:118n36
18:25-34	II:168			

19:20f	II:548	20:13-15	V:442n409
19:21	I:332(n116); II:825; III:49;	20:13-16	VIII:105
	IV:714; V:438; 513(n105);	20:14	VI:868
	VI:903; 905n181; VIII:74,	20:14f	III:47
	n34; 505; 597	20:15	II:561; V:377; VI:476; 555;
19:22	II:855n177; IV:323; VI:327;		VII:416n13; 441
	VII:606; IX:480	20:16	II:698; III:351; 494, n4; 993;
19:23	III:736n61		IV:187; V:74n115; 754; 856;
19:23f	I:587		VI:868, n13
19:23ff	III:331	20:16b	VI:542
19:24	I:582; III:406n1; 593; 594n6;	20:17	II:328; IV:441n198; V:66
	V:513n113; 856; VI:327;	20:17f	I:519
	VII:606	20:18	III:271; V:914n72; VII:864;
19:24f	VIII:74n33		VIII:460
19:25	I:651n20; VI:327	20:19	I:430(n132); II:335; 370; 430;
19:26	II:306; 308		IV:517; **V:634,** n23; 713n459;
19:27	IV:714; VI:19		915n80; VII:581
19:28	I:586; 651n20; 653n29; 688;	20:20	I:191; 192; 193n6; II:684;
	689; II:105; 248; 250; 323;		IV:643; V:728; VI:763;
	326n44; 327; 328; 559n13;		VII:772
	III:161; 165; 351; 384; 385;	20:20ff	III:404; IV:451
	440; 442; 923, n4; VI:152n34;	20:21	I:583; 587; III:49; VIII:212n32
	VIII:212; 390n408; 439;	20:21ff	III:442
	442n297; **447-448** (448n341);	20:22	I:192; V:1001; VI:152; 153n39;
	449n345; 460; 461n413;		845
	IX:673	20:22f	I:545n3; **VI:152**
19:29	I:589; 651n20; II:727; 729;	20:23	I:586; III:351; V:520;
	864(n272), (n274); III:781;		986(n256); 987n260, n261;
	IV:643; 717; V:271; 279; 982;		989(n274); 992
	VI:649; VIII:443n308; 448	20:25	II:85; 370; III:500; 501; VI:529
19:30	II:698; III:993; IV:654; VI:542;	20:25-27	VIII:16
	868	20:25-28	IV:341
20:1	II:49; IV:701; VII:874n27	20:26	II:88; **IV:533-534;** VI:868
20:1ff	III:351; IV:701; **717;** VI:868n13	20:26f	II:278n114; III:45n9; 973;
20:1-6	IV:187		VI:868
20:1-15	VI:476	20:26-28	II:85
20:1-16	I:585; V:752; 753n64; 760	20:27	VI:868
20:2	II:701n11; IV:714; VII:772;	20:28	II:86; 166; 278n114; 669;
	874n27; IX:308, n18		III:401; 640n1; IV:329; 330;
20:3	I:452; VI:56; VII:648; IX:680		341; 342n21; 349; V:706; 710,
20:4	II:188; III:350		n435; 711(n442); 712;
20:5	VI:56; 476		793n160; VI:543; VIII:20;
20:5f	IX:680		288n121; 460; 519n18
20:6	I:452; II:769; VI:56; VII:647;	20:29	III:293; VI:579
	648	20:29f	VIII:288n121; IX:460
20:7	II:188; III:350; IV:701	20:29-31	III:940
20:8	II:167; III:488; IV:698;	20:29-34	VIII:289n137
	V:150n13; VI:868;	20:30	I:129; III:443; 901; V:68; 734;
	VII:874n27		VII:554; VIII:287n120;
20:8ff	II:697		288(n126)
20:9	IX:680, n35	20:30f	VIII:486
20:9f	IV:714	20:31	III:901; V:586; VI:541;
20:10	VI:868		VIII:288n126
20:11	I:733; II:49	20:32	V:68n83; VII:647; 648
20:11f	III:350	20:33	V:377; VI:964n38; 965;
20:12	I:554; II:948; III:348; **349-351;**		VIII:287
	644; VI:868; IX:680	20:34	IV:1097; V:67; 377; VII:554;
20:12a	VI:476		VIII:288, n121, (n131), n133;
20:12b	VI:476		289; IX:432n46
20:13	I:160; II:701; IX:159n113;	21	V:990
	164n148; 308, n18	21f	IV:186
20:13f	II:701n11	21:1	II:332; V:484n100;

22:3	II:669; III:52; 488; 495n6; IV:186
22:3ff	I:655
22:4	II:705; III:181; 488; 495n6; IV:186; V:889; VII:346
22:6	IV:186; V:714n469; VI:835; VIII:306
22:6f	V:754
22:7	I:396; 579; 936; IV:186; V:419n266; 429; 430; 435; 438; 444; VII:328n228; 331, n249; 709n34
22:8	I:379; II:705; III:488; IV:186
22:8ff	II:701
22:9	III:488; IV:186; V:69; **108,** n17; 109n25; VI:573
22:9f	II:769; V:755
22:9ff	I:332(n115)
22:10	III:654, n3; V:69; VI:129; **558**
22:10ff	I:330n98; IV:1104
22:11	I:579; II:319; III:654, n3; V:344
22:11-13	V:755, n79
22:11ff	V:441n406
22:11-14	VI:558
22:12	II:677; 701; III:178; IX:159n113; 164n148
22:13	I:579; 583; 642; 706; II:60; 88; 424; III:726; IV:715; 839n56; V:429; 447; VII:439; IX:429n35
22:14	I:392; 588; 651; **III:494-495** (494n4, n5; 495n6, n8); IV:153; **186-187;** 188; V:856; **VI:542;** VIII:166n13
22:14f	IV:187n10
22:15	IV:106; **V:595-596;** VI:35; 573n50
22:15ff	II:901; IV:261; 449
22:16	II:141n33; 155; III:462; 516; IV:441; 443; V:87; 92n185; 343; VI:54; 780; IX:39
22:17	VI:529; IX:81n12
22:18	I:703; IV:975(n14); VI:35; 565; 844; VIII:568
22:19	IX:66; 81n12
22:21	II:167; III:1058
22:22	III:38
22:23	VII:36
22:23ff	II:139; 630
22:23-33	VII:52n102; IX:36
22:24	I:368; 757n40; IV:110
22:25	V:732
22:26	VIII:221
22:27	V:889; VIII:596
22:28	II:817n5
22:29	I:752; II:304; 306; IV:865; **VI:243-244;** 253, n173
22:30	I:87; II:538; III:61n31; 788; IV:561(n54); V:640; 1018n19
22:31	I:757; IV:110; 893(n25); 1084n287
22:31f	IV:111
22:32	III:101(ń225); 191; 384n122
22:33	II:164; III:921; V:579
22:34	VII:36; 52; IX:38
22:34ff	VII:894n48
22:34-40	VI:316; IX:36
22:35	I:740n3; IV:1088; VI:28; 34
22:36	II:547; 549; IV:535; 1059; VI:868; IX:64
22:36ff	IV:1076
22:37	I:45n124; III:101n227; IX:641
22:37ff	II:139; 140; 554
22:37-40	I:425n107
22:38f	VI:868
22:38-40	**IV:535-536**
22:39	I:45; V:188; VI:306
22:40	I:26; 44; II:549; III:915; **919-921** (919n29); IV:1059; 1063; VI:662n75; 832
22:41	II:687; IX:38
22:41f	IX:530n250
22:41ff	II:39; IV:449
22:41-46	VIII:486
22:42	VI:53; IX:531
22:43	I:103n53; 757; II:540; III:487; IV:110; VI:831
22:44	II:40; 948n24; III:263; 440; IV:237n24; V:895(n31); VIII:156n10
22:45	III:487
23	I:331; 332n110, n113; 741; IV:139; V:99; 124n24; 183; 429n337; VI:18n45; 565n18; 835n351; VII:330; **VIII:293;** 567n44; 568; IX:38; **42-43** (42n184); 449n76
23:1	IV:51; V:991; IX:42n184
23:1-12	VIII:14
23:1-36	I:741
23:2	I:741; III:443; IV:864; VI:662; 871n3; 964n32; VII:690n31; 820, n134; 822n143; 833n227; IX:48
23:2f	**IX:43,** n190; 48
23:3	II:645; 651; VI:478; 479; 480; VIII:144; **IX:43,** n186
23:3-7	IV:864
23:4	I:557; II:900; III:45n7; 718; VI:554n58; VII:856n1; VIII:160; **IX:85**
23:5	III:904; IV:543; V:344; VI:480; 724
23:5ff	I:331(n106); 741; IV:1063
23:6	I:45n126; III:46n21; VI:870; 871n3, n5, n6; VII:820; 833n227
23:6f	I:498; 741; IX:117n33; **128**
23:6-8	V:209
23:6ff	IV:454
23:7	III:488; VI:964, n32
23:7ff	II:655; III:1093
23:8	I:145; II:61; 148; 156; III:488; 1093; IV:919; V:513n111;

708

24:7	I:580; VI:15; 848n425; VII:199, n23
24:8	I:482; VII:346; IX:525; 672, n46
24:9	II:369; IV:188n15; 690, n25; V:271; 279; VIII:436n273; 443n308
24:9f	IV:690
24:9-14	III:145
24:10	I:45(n128); IV:690n25; VI:948; VII:341; 344; 345; **346-347** (346n41); **349;** 352
24:10b	VII:346
24:10-12	VI:247
24:11	II:334; VI:246; 247; 282n20; 855; VII:346
24:11f	I:513; VII:346
24:11ff	IX:42n183
24:12	I:47; 53; III:824; IV:1063; 1086; VI:278; 282; 540; 716; VII:346; 347n46; VIII:519
24:12f	I:45(n128)
24:13	II:426; IV:586; V:867; VI:194; 716; VIII:436n273
24:13f	VII:346
24:14	I:582; 583; II:369; 429; 715n90; 727; 728n59; 729; 928; III:704; 709; 710(n59); IV:188n15; 502; 503, n76; V:158; VI:869; 870n7; VII:348; VIII:55; IX:89n10
24:15	I:106; 757n40; II:660; III:245; 979; 980; IV:110; VI:831; VII:343n24; 648; VIII:204
24:15f	VI:531
24:15ff	I:516
24:15-28	III:145
24:17	V:131
24:18	V:290; 291; VII:726
24:19	V:649; VII:347n50
24:20	III:333(n93); VI:662(n73); VII:21n161; 24n195; 29; 30n230
24:21	I:481; III:885; 1029; IV:1107, n14; 1110; V:430; VII:343n24; 346
24:21f	VII:349
24:21-31	**IV:188-189**
24:22	III:823, n3, n4; IV:188n15; VI:716; VII:346; VIII:434n255
24:22ff	IV:188
24:22-27	V:867
24:23	VIII:150n16; IX:531
24:23f	IX:531
24:23-25	VIII:433n253
24:23-28	III:997n177
24:24	II:334; III:714(n68); 824; IV:139; 513; V:280; VI:246; 247; 282; 830; 847; 856; 948; VII:230; 240; **241,** n288; 260;

	346; IX:530, n255
24:25	VII:357
24:25-51	**VIII:263-264**
24:26	II:658; IV:862; 867; V:688n252; VIII:150n16; 433, n251, n252, n253
24:26f	I:586; II:353; V:866(n46)
24:27	I:352; 505; V:863; 865(n42); **VIII:433-434** (433n251, n253); 457; 459; IX:1
24:28	II:34; V:752n53; 756(n94); 866(n46); VI:166
24:29	IV:551; V:534, n322; VI:163; VII:61n42; 232; **440**
24:29ff	VII:237
24:30	I:678; II:305; 447; 670; III:410n31; 834; 850; 851n128; IV:909; V:361; 367; 513(n105); 522, n195; 697n318; VII:230; **236-238** (237n256, n258, n261, n263; 238n265); 240n283; 343n24; VIII:266n52; 437n282, n283; 442n297; 460; IX:2; 250
24:30a	VII:238n264; VIII:460n412
24:30b	VIII:460, n412
24:30f	VII:236; 796
24:31	I:84n68; 679; III:658n7; IV:188n15; 189; V:516; VII:85; 87; 88; 346; 347; 842; VIII:134
24:32	III:720; IV:406n128; **409**
24:32f	V:759(n105); VII:757
24:33	III:173; 174n8
24:34	I:663
24:34f	I:130
24:35	I:379n2; II:681; 682; III:937n64; IV:105; V:514n124; 515n133; VII:678
24:36	II:952n47; V:520; 989; 992; VIII:372n274; 380
24:37	V:865(n42); VIII:433; **434-435;** 452; 457; 459
24:37f	VIII:433n251
24:37-39	IV:1104; VIII:451n363
24:37ff	IV:386n110; VII:515n350
24:37-41	V:866(n46)
24:38	I:651n15; II:953; III:61n31; IV:591n18; VI:139; 685; VII:140n311; VIII:236; 458n398
24:39	V:865(n42); 889; VI:750; VIII:433; 434, n256; 442n297; 451n365; 459; 477n517
24:40f	I:510; IV:13; VII:346
24:42	II:338; 953; VII:168; VIII:451n360, n365; IX:680
24:42f	VIII:450; IX:680
24:42-44	IV:1104; V:759(n105); IX:679
24:42ff	II:670

VIII:460; IX:678n24

26:45a	III:436
26:47	II:325; III:271; IV:525; V:38; VIII:864; VIII:267n54
26:48	VII:230; **231-232** (232n218); 269; IX:141
26:48f	IX:140n240
26:48-50	IX:141n247, n248
26:49	II:153; 684; III:1093; VI:763n56; 965; IX:141n243, n247, n248; 367
26:50	II:684; 701; V:859; IX:140, n241; 159n113
26:51	II:460; 461; III:270; IV:525; V:551n76; 558; 940; VIII:263; IX:430
26:51f	IV:526n19
26:51ff	IV:451
26:52	I:394; V:558n3; VII:721, n8; VIII:205n141
26:52a	IV:525
26:52b	IV:525, n11; V:443n417
26:52f	I:139n21; VIII:541n92
26:52ff	III:211
26:53	I:6(n9); 84; II:326n45; 806; III:103(n248); IV:68; 69; 1112, n46; V:351; 520; 794; 839; 987n260; 989n273
26:53f	III:208; IV:525n11; V:918n113; 992
26:54	I:752; 758; II:24; III:582; IV:878n16; V:707n405; 708, n424; VI:295; 296, n62
26:55	II:139; III:236; 242; 440; 443; IV:261; 525; 882n8; V:38; VII:760; 772; 822n145; IX:679
26:55f	IV:451
26:56	I:430(n134); 752; 758; III:328(n45); VI:295; 832; 833
26:57	III:270; VII:864; 868
26:58	III:270; 440; 441; IV:373; V:342; VIII:55; 540
26:59	II:430; III:271; IV:514; VII:864; 868
26:60	II:684; IV:489n46; 513; VIII:596
26:61	III:184; 244; IV:338; 883, n15; VII:1058n355; VIII:257
26:62	IV:510
26:62f	III:270
26:63	II:862n255; III:945; IV:294; V:462; **465;** 713; VIII:380; 381
26:63f	V:989n278
26:64	II:297; 306; 352(n91); 670; III:442; 936; IV:237n24; 344; 540; 621; 909; 1107, n9, n12; 1113n49; V:185; 361; 367; 465; 514n121; 522n195; 713n454; 867n50;

	VI:371n195; VIII:435n266; 460, n408; 473; 611; IX:531
26:65	I:623; III:270; IV:489; 1112; 1116; 1118
26:66	II:828; V:563; **VII:868-869**
26:67	III:818n1; 819; VI:775; VIII:265n36
26:67f	**V:635**
26:68	VI:829; IX:529n242; 531
26:69	III:441; IV:874; VII:794
26:69ff	I:430(n135)
26:70	V:117
26:71	III:287; IV:874; VI:921; VII:794
26:72	V:117; 462
26:73	I:244; 248; II:61; IV:650n14; 651n14; VI:483; 484; VII:647
26:74	I:355; 356n2; V:184
26:74f	IX:303
26:75	III:722; IV:105, n144; 677, n10; VI:124, n11, n12
27:1	III:21; 271; VI:659n46; VII:864; IX:680n39
27:2	II:60; III:859n9
27:3	III:271; IV:628; VI:659n46; VII:864
27:3-10	III:997n177
27:4	I:173; II:184n8; 189; V:342; VI:722
27:5	III:235; 246; 865; IV:884; VI:992
27:6	II:561; III:271; 861n3; **865**
27:7	V:2; **14-15**
27:8	III:488; IV:1107n15; VII:273
27:8f	**VIII:180**
27:9	I:756n34; 757n40; II:929; III:193n17; 218n4; 219, n5; 220; 988; **991-992** (991n138); IV:110; VI:295; 296; 831; 832n343; 833; VII:273; 343n24; VIII:180, n68; 365
27:9b-10	III:218, n4; 219n5
27:10	III:1087; VIII:34n6; 180
27:11	I:577; III:376; VII:648; 649; VIII:434n260; IX:529n242
27:12	III:271; 637; V:713; VI:659n46; VII:864
27:13	IV:510
27:14	III:38; 39n53; V:713; VI:723
27:15	III:46n28
27:15ff	IV:261
27:16	III:286; IV:262, n29; VI:964n33; **VII:268**
27:17	III:46n28; 286n18; 376; IX:529n242; 531; 579n546
27:18	I:703n61
27:19	I:785; II:187; III:38; 436; 442; V:221; 235; 236n54; 350; 912; VI:723; VII:272; VIII:553
27:20	I:394; V:587; VI:2; 659n46; VII:864
27:21	III:46n28

28:13	III:755		IX:647n181
28:14	IV:593; VI:2; 475(n92)	28:18b	II:348n57; VIII:372
28:15	II:138; III:376; IV:770;	28:18-20	I:539; VIII:373n277
	1107n15; V:732;	28:19	I:101, n48; 539; II:145, n51;
	VI:475(n92); VII:273		369; III:108; 890; IV:461;
28:16	II:326; **V:485;** VIII:28		**V:274-275;** 276n220; 989;
28:16ff	I:430(n139); III:753; V:355;		990n279; VI:400n430; **401,**
	360n217		**n440;** 434n678; 442;
28:16-20	V:275; VIII:608n24		573(n50); 575; 622n106;
28:17	III:948; V:357; VI:764		VII:348; VIII:223, n48; 225;
28:17b	IV:446		373n277; 380
28:18	I:679; II:171; 538; 568; 684;	28:19b	IV:678n13
	III:103(n252); 116; 782; 1089;	28:19f	I:432; VI:442n752
	1094; V:513(n118); 518,	28:20	I:203(n17); II:145; 349; 545;
	n162; 888; 895; 993n289;		553n32; 824n47; VI:142n67;
	VII:776; VIII:43n19; 486;		VII:776; VIII:66; 144

MARK

1-3	IX:531n261		**VIII:329**
1-7	IX:538n305	1:9	I:539; II:433; III:288;
1:1	I:482; II:719; 727; 728; VI:615;		V:530n273; VI:614
	VIII:379; IX:211; 537	1:9-11	VI:67(n55)
1:2	I:83; 389; 747; II:539; 727n52;	1:9ff	I:538; **VI:400-401;** VIII:333
	936n65; 938; III:103; V:70,	1:10	I:519; II:456n35; III:177;
	n97; VI:684; 688; 777; 830;		V:345; 353; 529n261; 531,
	831n341; 832; 833; 836		n280; 701; VI:142; 404;
1:3	I:625; II:659(n10); III:1086;		**VII:962;** VIII:329n106;
	V:70; VI:479; IX:293		IX:288n41
1:4	I:66; 304; 511; 512; 537; 545;	1:10f	II:456; VI:843; VIII:469
	II:429; 688; III:288n31; 700;	1:11	I:48; 101n49; 339n7; II:740, n7;
	704; 705; 711; **IV:1000-1001**		III:850n123; IV:114; 739;
	(1000n147); V:436; VI:984		V:446; 530; 668n81; **701-702;**
1:4f	VI:615		704; 706, n402; 707(n408);
1:4-11	I:536		710(n429); VIII:335; **367-368**
1:5	I:295; 330(n99); 512; 539;		(368n236); 369; **377,** n310;
	III:382; V:215; VI:398;		**378,** n319; 381; 384n365;
	601-602; 614; 617; 721;		389n396; 394; **IX:298**
	VII:327; 330, (n246)	1:12	I:528; II:658; VI:398; 404;
1:5b	VIII:431n235		449n818
1:6	II:693; 936, n69; III:593;	1:12f	II:658; VI:34; VIII:138n33;
	IV:246; **553-554** (553n15);		471n474
	637; 930; V:306n22; 496, n4,	1:13	I:141; II:85, n9; 626n20; 658;
	n5; VI:56; 140; 602(n52);		III:103(n248); 134;
	838; VII:58; 63, n54;		IV:868n227; 871; V:772;
	VIII:431n235		VI:34; VII:158; 796;
1:7	II:154n41; III:704; 706; IV:335;		**VIII:138-139** (139n34);
	V:290; 311; 814n1; VI:629;		372n268
	VIII:431n235; IX:298	1:14	I:583; II:715n90; 727; 728, n59;
1:7f	VI:837		III:704; V:345
1:8	I:104; 538; 539; 543n69; II:936;	1:14f	II:735; III:706; 710(n59);
	VI:398; 404; 616; 840;		VII:833

1:15	I:584; II:145; 331; 434; 727; 728, n59; III:460; 461n37; 580; IV:628; 1000n147; 1001; 1002, n156; 1003n162; VI:204(n219); 208n258; 211n271; 214(n296), (n299); **294-295;** 296; 716n85; 842; VII:26; VIII:383n357
1:16	I:129; 144; 527(n3); VI:101
1:16ff	III:138; IV:444; 446
1:16-20	VIII:105; IX:129n160
1:17	I:196n3; IV:444; V:291; VI:474
1:18	I:213; 510
1:19	I:144; VI:616
1:20	I:510; III:488; IV:701; V:291; 983n241
1:21	II:95; 139; 677; VI:578; VII:20; 830; 838
1:21f	VII:21; 236
1:21ff	VII:832n218
1:21-28	VII:21n162; 833
1:22	II:140; 164; 569; VI:843, n388, n390; 965; VII:832; 833
1:23	III:116(n370); 428(n12); 900; VII:832n221
1:23ff	VII:833
1:23-27	VII:830(n210)
1:24	I:101; 102n51; 396; II:669; III:104(n261); 287; 708(n50); IV:874; V:117; 118; VII:833; VIII:377; 378; 380; IX:531
1:25	II:626n18; 679; III:210; V:427
1:25f	IV:107
1:26	II:679; IX:294; 303
1:26f	III:428(n12)
1:27	I:223; 528; II:164; 569, n41; III:4n2; 6; 210; 448; VI:843; VII:21n162; 747; 833; VIII:37n2; 42n16
1:28	I:221; II:679
1:29	VI:101; VII:832n221
1:29-31	VI:101
1:29ff	I:784; III:206; V:20; 23
1:30	I:651n18; III:204n30; 655; VII:883
1:30f	VI:958, n24
1:31	I:510; 784; II:85; 334; 684; III:130; 911; VI:958; 959; VIII:288n131, n133; IX:430; 431
1:32	II:318; VI:541; IX:57; 680n39
1:32ff	III:714
1:32-45	IX:538n307
1:33	III:173; V:174; VI:530; 722
1:34	I:511; 527; III:130; IV:1091; V:117; VI:68n57; 396; 485; 541; VIII:380; 381; IX:531
1:35	II:658; III:436; V:484; VIII:203
1:36	VI:102; VII:772
1:37	II:769
1:38	II:429; 668; 679; 718; III:704; 706; 714; VI:530

1:39	II:433; III:704; 714; VII:830, (n210); 832; 833
1:40	I:738; V:794, n164; VI:763
1:40f	III:48
1:40ff	IV:234
1:40-43	V:427n326
1:41	II:460; III:130; 210; V:427, n326; 428n328; VII:554, n31, n33; VIII:288n130; IX:431
1:41ff	VII:246
1:43	I:527; V:427; 428, n328
1:44	I:108n64; II:429; III:208; 264; 429; 708; IV:233; 502; 503, n75; V:763; VI:54; 68n57; VIII:38; 504; 505; IX:66
1:44f	III:708
1:45	II:658; III:703n29; 704; 708n49; 709n53; IV:115n189; 120n201; VIII:203, n123; IX:3
2	IV:1060
2:1	II:66
2:1ff	III:206; IV:621
2:1-12	IV:715n77; **VIII:430-431**
2:1-3:6	**VII:21-22;** 24n193
2:1-3:7a	VIII:452n371
2:2	III:173; **IV:120-121;** 129; VI:722
2:2f	IV:898n17
2:3	VIII:133; IX:57
2:4	II:332n3; III:655
2:4f	V:586
2:5	I:288n58; 295; III:204; IV:344; V:639; VI:206(n240); 844
2:5b	VIII:431
2:5ff	I:493; 511; 512; II:537(n10); IV:1095
2:6	II:96; 539; III:443; 612
2:7	I:623; III:102(n245); 937; IV:106; V:713; VIII:431
2:7-12	IV:345
2:8	I:704; II:96; 539; III:172; 612; V:342; VI:396; 405n470; 844; IX:654n225
2:9	II:334; III:936; V:881; 944
2:10	I:678; 679; 680; II:568; 569; III:327(n39); 937; VIII:373n277; 405; 430; 431n234, n236; 433; 435n264; 452n371; 453; 454n377; 456; 457; 458n399; 459; 477n517
2:10f	III:210
2:10ff	IV:107
2:11	II:334; VIII:504
2:11f	VIII:288n133
2:12	II:334; 460; III:37; 206; V:342; VIII:288n131; IX:209; 210
2:13ff	IV:444
2:13-17	VIII:105
2:14	I:129; 214; 368; IV:234; 444; V:345; VIII:97n93; 105
2:14f	VIII:104

2:14-17	VIII:103	3:1	II:677; 818n10; IV:561n53;
2:15	II:54n3; III:654; 656; 848;		VII:20; 24n194; 832n216,
	VIII:105n151		n219; 834n232; IX:430
2:15f	VIII:98n104	3:1ff	IV:454; 1063; V:713; VII:351;
2:15-17	VIII:105, n151		833
2:15ff	V:20; VI:141(n53); VII:832;	3:1-5	VII:830(n210)
	IX:42, n177	3:1-6	V:714n464; **VII:24;** 25; 26; 33;
2:16	I:317; II:693; V:342n142;		IX:39; 41
	VI:662n68; VII:796; IX:38	3:2	III:130; 637; VII:20, n157; 831;
2:17	I:329n94; II:189; 668; III:204;		VIII:147
	205; 488; IV:717; 1001n155;	3:3	II:334; 462; IX:430
	1002n155; **1095;** V:759;	3:4	III:485n2; 848; VI:477, n99;
	VIII:312; 449n349;		478; VII:20; 21; 25; 26;
	IX:42n177		31n239; 990; **IX:638-639**
2:17a	IX:42n177		(638n131; 639n133)
2:17b	VIII:453	3:5	I:387; II:460; III:613;
2:18	III:848; IV:441; 443; 929; 930;		IV:561n53; 895; V:419; 420;
	932n59; VI:140; IX:41n169		425; 427; 428; 438; 442; 1023,
2:18f	VI:141; VIII:17		n5; 1024; 1026, n3; 1027;
2:18-20	IX:370n100		VII:24; 772; IX:430
2:18ff	III:154; IV:443; 932; 933;	3:5f	V:442
	IX:41, n169; 367n71	3:6	I:394; III:516; V:428; 713;
2:18-22	V:163; IX:41n169		VI:478; VII:24n193; 25n199;
2:19	I:654; II:818n10; 824n47;		IX:36; 37n144; **39,** n153,
	III:554; IV:1103n41; V:754;		n158; **638**
	759; VI:42n16; 140;	3:7	I:213; VI:279; IX:39n155
	VIII:365; IX:591	3:7a	V:713; 714n464; VIII:378n318
2:19a	IV:1103; 1105	3:8	II:510n40; VI:56; 279;
2:19f	IV:1099(n3); 1101; VIII:444;		473(n83); 614; 617; VII:330
	454n378	3:9	III:139; 618; V:586; 653
2:20	II:951; 952n47; IV:932n65; 934;	3:9f	VIII:378n318
	1101; 1103; 1105; V:902n50;	3:10	III:130; IV:519; VI:541; IX:431
	904	3:10f	III:130
2:21	III:448; IV:933; 1061; VI:302;	3:11	III:428(n12); 708(n50); 900;
	974; **VII:961;** 964		V:345; VI:163n14; VIII:378;
2:21f	III:450; IV:898n20; 933n66;		381; IX:531
	1061; **V:718,** n5; 759;	3:12	II:626(n17); III:208; VI:399;
	VII:961n8; VIII:17		478; IX:3; 293
2:22	I:394; 527; II:876; IV:898;	3:13	III:48; 500; 501; V:484;
	899n21, n23; V:163		485n107; VI:400n435
2:23	V:65n64; 69; VI:475(n93);	3:13f	I:584; II:325; IV:450
	VII:20; 547	3:13ff	I:428
2:23f	IV:442; VII:20	3:14	I:429; III:704; 712, (n60);
2:23ff	II:626; VII:351		VI:474; VII:794
2:23-28	**VII:21-22** (22n172); **VIII:452;**	3:14f	III:213; 713n64; 714
	IX:41	3:15	I:527; II:569; III:131, n10
2:23-3:7a	V:713; 714	3:16	V:270; 281; VI:102; 103
2:24	II:561; VII:20; 21	3:16f	VIII:160
2:25	I:343; IV:867; VI:19n52;	3:17	I:144; 640; II:886; V:281, n240;
	VII:772, n33; VIII:452		VI:103n18; VIII:365
2:25f	VIII:255; 482	3:18	I:545; IX:114
2:26	I:477; II:561; 693; III:270n29;	3:19	IV:452
	V:121; VII:21n167; 771;	3:20	II:692; V:23; 586
	772n33; VIII:165	3:20f	V:731n37
2:27	II:70; **VII:22,** n175, n176, n177;	3:20ff	II:18
	VIII:452, n367; IX:639n132	3:21	II:456; 459; 503; III:911; V:730;
2:27f	VI:19; VII:20		VI:844n398
2:28	III:1086; VI:140; **VII:22,** n175,	3:22	I:489; 605; II:456; 539; 652;
	n176, n177; VIII:405; 452,		822; III:154; 714(n68);
	n371; 453; 454n377; 456; 457;		VI:530; VII:235; 330; IX:38
	459	3:22b	V:714
3	V:757	3:22f	I:527

3:22ff	**VII:159-160**	4:10f	IV:451
3:22-30	IX:532	4:10-12	V:555n109, n110; 856;
3:23	III:500; 501; V:752; VII:158		VII:894n51
3:23ff	II:80; IV:715n77	4:10ff	IV:449; V:757
3:24	I:580	4:10-25	V:757n98
3:24f	V:125n27; 131	4:11	II:576; IV:108, n149; 817; 818;
3:25	VI:165n21		819n140; V:554; 555;
3:26	I:368; VII:158; VIII:56; 63		556n118; 757; 758; 889;
3:27	II:79; III:103(n249); 204; 400;		VIII:542; IX:4
	401; IV:868n224; 944; V:759;	4:11f	III:323; 327(n43); 581; 973;
	VI:869n4; **VII:159-160**		IV:802; **817-819** (817n133,
	(159n42); 362; 649n26;		819n140); V:554, n109;
	IX:537; 538n307		555n116; **753;** 756n90;
3:28	I:511; 624; III:107n282;		**757-758** (757n98; 758n101);
	VI:397; VIII:404n22		761; VI:502
3:28f	I:104n56; 294; 622; IV:716;	4:12	I:220; 294; 511; II:425; IV:817;
	VI:408; VII:351n71;		818; V:341; 425; 555n116;
	VIII:439; **442-443; 454**		692n290; 758n101; **VII:727;**
3:28-30	**VI:397-398**		894; VIII:286n117
3:29	I:103n53; 205; 209; 304; 624;	4:13	I:703n61; IV:817n133; V:117;
	II:431; 828; III:107(n282);		699n331; 752; 757; 888
	VI:446n785	4:13ff	IV:818
3:29f	III:154; VI:404	4:13-20	**IV:121-122;** V:755; 756; 757;
3:30	I:606; II:822; III:428(n12);		VI:456
	VI:405n465; 844n398	4:14	III:699; IV:121n202
3:31	I:144n3; III:488; VI:723;	4:14-20	VIII:518
	VII:637	4:15	I:583; II:79; 80; III:699; V:68;
3:31ff	I:144; IV:643; 1002		VI:558; VII:158; **160;** 546
3:31-35	V:586; 757; IX:530n254	4:15ff	IV:122n203
3:32	I:66; 144, n3; III:443; V:731;	4:16	VII:772; IX:367n71
	VI:56	4:17	III:143; 144n8; 146; 147; 463,
3:33ff	I:145		n4; IV:579; V:299n19; VI:31;
3:34	II:461; VI:56		252; 988; VII:340n12; 349
3:34f	VII:742; IX:141	4:19	I:157; 203; 385; II:921; 925n96;
3:35	I:144n3; III:54; 55; 56; 58;		III:170; IV:591n14, n18; 592;
	IV:121; V:986(n256);		VI:56; 327; 456; 578;
	987n261; VI:479; IX:642;		907n204; VII:894
	649n205	4:20	III:616; V:554; VIII:518
4	V:755; 757; 758; IX:4; 59	4:21	III:975, n37; IV:326; V:754;
4:1	III:440; 441; 443; V:485n108		VII:362; VIII:155; IX:344
4:1f	V:755	4:22	III:329n61; 590; 961; 973;
4:1ff	VIII:134		V:553n92; VII:441n157;
4:1-11	**VI:34-36**		743n8; IX:3; 4
4:1-34	V:554; **555**	4:23	I:584; V:552; 754; VII:894
4:2	II:164; IV:931; V:752	4:24	I:219; III:350; IV:632; 633;
4:2-32	I:69		V:344n153; 713n463;
4:3	VIII:335		VII:70n27; VIII:168
4:3-9	V:752; 757; 759; VI:456;	4:24b	VI:715
	VIII:518	4:24f	V:757; 856
4:4	V:68; **VII:160**	4:25	II:827; V:757; VI:59; VII:894
4:4-7	VIII:223	4:25a	VI:715
4:4-8	VI:495n98	4:26	I:219; 527; VI:163n9;
4:5	VI:170; VII:925		VIII:433n251
4:6	**VI:988;** VIII:335	4:26f	VII:546
4:7	I:519; 747n22; II:925; VI:456	4:26-29	I:585; V:752; 754; 759;
4:8	VI:282; VIII:518n7; 519n18;		VI:495n98; IX:538n307
	IX:59	4:27	II:334; III:435
4:9	I:219; V:552, n78, n80;	4:28	III:616; VI:286; IX:59n11
	554n106; 555; 754; 759	4:29	II:172; III:133; 615; V:839; 840
4:10	II:327(n52); 685; 686;	4:30	V:189; 751; 752; VIII:155
	IV:817n133; V:752; 756;	4:30-32	VII:289; **290-291;** IX:538n307
	VI:56; VII:771; 894	4:30ff	**VII:289**

4:31	III:810; IV:654; V:754	5:21ff	III:206
4:31f	III:810; V:759	5:21-43	I:370; 784; VI:456
4:32	I:519; III:720; 757n1; IV:66;	5:22	V:341n136; VI:163, n15; 630;
	V:534; VI:483; 484; **VII:389;**		763; VII:846, n21, n22; 847
	397	5:23	II:697n1; 862, (n246); 864n273;
4:33	**IV:120-121;** 129; V:756, n91;		III:130; V:794; VII:990;
	VIII:378n320		VIII:161; IX:431
4:33f	III:973; IV:794n178; V:756	5:25	I:776; II:322; 540; III:204n30;
4:34	IV:337; 818; V:756, n90; 757;		VI:116n18
	VII:894n58	5:26	II:668; III:204; 206; V:730; 912;
4:35ff	II:154; III:207; **VIII:323**		915n82
4:35-41	III:408	5:27	III:287; 904n4; V:290; 586;
4:36	V:587n22		VI:54
4:37	I:529; IV:276n68; VII:70n30;	5:27f	I:650; IV:693
	199	5:27ff	III:209
4:38	I:394; II:334; 623; III:436;	5:28	III:130; VII:990
	VI:964; 965, n40; VIII:553	5:29	I:703; IV:519; VI:116, n18;
4:39	II:626; IV:107		VII:352n74; 647; 1058
4:40	III:436; 947; VI:206(n241);	5:30	I:704; II:301n61; 539; 680;
	VII:290n30		VI:396; VII:726n19;
4:40f	V:699n331		IX:654n225
4:41	I:223; II:626; III:38;	5:30f	V:586
	VIII:42n16; IX:209; 366	5:31	V:344n153; VII:883
5	III:848; VII:831n212	5:32	VI:478
5:1ff	III:206; IV:681n2; VIII:620n49	5:33	I:66; 243; II:669; V:887; IX:209
5:1-20	V:462n6; VI:456	5:34	II:411; 413; 434; III:211;
5:2	II:540; III:428(n12); 626;		IV:519; V:639;
	IV:681, n2		VI:206(n240); VII:990;
5:3	II:60; 818n10; IV:680; 681, n2		VIII:312; 505, n7
5:3ff	III:660	5:35	I:223; III:1093; VII:847
5:4	II:60	5:35f	I:223
5:5	II:19; 66; III:844; 900;	5:36	I:223; III:210; V:648; 822;
	IV:681n2		VI:204n225; 206(n240);
5:6	IV:373; VI:763n57; VIII:232		VII:847; IX:212; 450n95
5:7	I:563; III:103n250; 116n363;	5:37	I:144; 216; 511; VI:101
	708(n50); 900; IV:512;	5:37ff	II:154
	V:277; **462-463** (462n5);	5:38	I:227; III:842; 844; 846; V:346;
	VIII:335; **377;** 378; 380n330;		821; VII:847
	619; 620n49; IX:294; 531	5:38f	III:722; 832
5:7ff	VI:920	5:39	I:148; VIII:555
5:8	III:428(n12); IV:69n10	5:39ff	V:638
5:9	IV:68; 69n10; V:280	5:40	I:784; III:654n2; IV:643;
5:10	II:806; IV:69n10; V:794, n163		V:982; VI:578; VII:772;
5:11	V:483; 484; VI:721		VIII:288n127
5:12	I:403; IV:69n10; V:794n163	5:41	I:784; II:335; III:130; 210; 911;
5:13	III:428(n12); IV:69n10;		IV:107; IX:430; 431
	V:467n3; 470; VI:396n399;	5:42	I:370; II:322; 450; III:848;
	456; IX:469		V:944; IX:212n122
5:14	I:64; 66; II:433; V:342n143	5:43	I:703; II:692; III:208; 708n48;
5:15	II:822; III:443; IV:68; V:346;		714; V:763; VII:591;
	VII:1102; IX:209		VIII:288n133
5:16	I:66; V:346	6:1	IV:874
5:17	V:794n163; VII:883	6:1ff	VII:832n218
5:18	IV:445; V:794; VII:794, (n133)	6:2	II:67; 139; 301; VI:278; 541;
5:18ff	IV:444		713n70; VII:20; 21; 514; 830;
5:19	I:61n2; 68; 511; II:485;		834n232; IX:430
	III:709n54; 1087; 1093;	6:3	I:144, n2; IV:643; VII:344; 349;
	V:995n302; VI:464;		**350;** 353n79; 355n92; 514;
	VIII:505n7		818; VIII:363; IX:488n74
5:19f	III:709	6:4	V:131; 132; VI:841; VII:736n1;
5:20	III:37; 287; 703n29; 704; 709,		740; VIII:174n25
	n54; VI:473(n83)	6:5	II:301; III:130; 131; 210; 211;

	VI:473, (n83); VII:245n306; VIII:125n72; 161; 288n129; IX:431	6:35	II:683; IV:869; IX:680, n39
		6:35ff	II:34n2; III:207
		6:35-44	VI:691
6:6	III:40; VI:205; 207; 530; VII:554n34; 833	6:36ff	II:692
		6:38	I:703; V:580; VIII:505
6:7	I:83; 417n68; 425(n109); 427; 429; II:566; 569; III:213; 428(n12); 500; 501; IV:452	6:39	IV:246n30; V:763n23; 899n22; VIII:211
		6:41	I:185n1; 477; II:762; 802n279; III:729, n8; 974; V:534; VI:155n62; VIII:163; IX:412n50
6:8	I:526; II:433; 596; V:307; 763; VI:120; 903n164; **969,** n19		
6:8f	V:312n8; 763n26		
6:9	II:319; V:311	6:41ff	V:25
6:10	VIII:203n115	6:43	II:322n5; III:729; VI:302
6:11	I:430; II:429; IV:502; 503; VI:579; **629,** n47, n48; VIII:203n115	6:44	I:362; IX:469
		6:45	V:586f
		6:45ff	III:207; VIII:323
6:12	II:679; III:704; 709; 711; IV:1001n154; 1003	6:45-52	VII:756n50
		6:46	V:484; VIII:33
6:12f	III:714, (n66); IV:452	6:47	V:717n2
6:13	I:230; 231; 232; II:472; III:209; 213n62	6:48	I:563, n16, n17; II:682n4; III:46n20; IV:1124; VIII:133; IX:243, n14
6:14	I:370; 545; 577; II:303; 335; 539; 653; 936n64; V:270; **VI:838;** IX:3		
		6:49	III:901; IX:6; 209
		6:50	II:352(n90); III:26; IX:212
6:14b	II:936n64	6:51	II:460; 539; III:38; VI:62; 763
6:14ff	II:347	6:51f	II:352; 461n4
6:15	I:389; II:936, n64; IV:858(n119), n121, n122; VI:841	6:51b-52	IX:212
		6:52	III:613; IV:950; V:699n331; 1023n5; 1026; 1027, n7; VII:894, n54; 895n62
6:16	V:714		
6:17	I:144; II:60; III:911; IX:244	6:54	I:704
6:17ff	VI:836	6:56	I:493; III:130; V:794; VI:530n69; VII:990; VIII:155; IX:431
6:17-29	VII:865n31		
6:18	II:817n5		
6:19	I:679; II:828	7	II:172; IV:302; VI:662; IX:36
6:19-21	III:138	7:1	IX:38
6:20	I:108n66; 362; II:187; 538; 647; V:587n28; VI:475; VIII:151; IX:208	7:1ff	II:693; IV:1059; VII:822n142; **IX:41;** 46n213; 47
		7:1-23	**VI:661-662;** VII:330; IX:41n170
6:21	II:34; 461n4; 953; VI:475; 868; IX:466n2	7:2	III:797; IV:948; IX:430
		7:2ff	VIII:324
6:22	I:455; 577; III:45n8; 654	7:3	II:140n28; 172; 549n12; III:376; 377; 911; IV:947; V:344n153; VI:654; 660; 916n5; 981n23; VIII:324n67; IX:41n171; 430
6:22f	I:192		
6:23	I:580; V:185		
6:24	I:545; IV:643		
6:24f	I:192	7:3a	VI:981n23
6:25	I:545; 577; III:45n8; VII:566; 772	7:3f	I:546; IV:301; VI:981n23
		7:4	I:530; 545; III:376; 911; VI:149, n11; 871n4; 981, n23, n24
6:26	I:577; III:46n25; IV:323; V:462; VI:542n38; VIII:159		
		7:4a	VI:981n23
6:27	I:577; IX:244	7:5	I:328; 329n93; 331; II:172; 549n12; 687n1; IV:1059; V:945; VI:654; IX:38; 41n171; 430
6:28	IV:643		
6:29	VI:166; 167n3; VIII:155		
6:30	I:422; 425; 427; 428; II:144; III:713n64; VI:483		
6:31	I:350; II:692; VIII:203	7:6	I:748; III:612; 941; IV:50; VI:829; 830; 833; 842; VII:701; VIII:179; 567
6:31ff	II:658		
6:32	IV:869; VIII:203		
6:32-44	V:899	7:6-13	VI:662; VIII:324
6:33	I:582; 704; VI:541	7:7	II:161; IV:524; VII:172
6:34	II:141n33; V:345; 586; VI:494; 501; 691; VII:554, n32, n34	7:8	I:509; 510; 545; II:172; 549n12; III:911, n7; IV:1059; V:199,

	n2; VI:480; 661; VIII:159; 567; IX:40; 186n122
7:8ff	III:582; IV:1063
7:9	I:742; II:70; 172; 549n12, n13; III:1100; VI:293; 661; 662; VIII:144; 159
7:9b	VIII:159
7:9ff	III:864n32
7:9-13	III:866n37
7:10	III:468; IV:110; 111n176; V:982n233; VIII:178
7:10a	IV:643
7:10b	IV:643
7:10ff	**III:865-866**
7:10-13	V:982
7:11	II:166; VIII:178
7:11f	IV:643
7:12	III:866n37; VI:477; VIII:178
7:13	II:171; 549n12, n13, n14; III:1100; IV:112; 844n100; V:199; VI:479(n109); 661; 662; **VII:605-606;** IX:40
7:13f	**VII:605-606**
7:14	III:500; 501; V:586; **VII:605-606;** 893
7:14ff	I:538; 540; **III:787-788;** 1033
7:15	II:570; IV:58; 1002; VI:141; 578; 662; IX:41, n172; 231
7:15b	VI:976
7:15ff	VII:416
7:16	V:552
7:17	II:687n1; V:752; VI:101n11
7:17ff	IX:41
7:17-23	IX:41n172
7:18	IV:950; V:699n331; VI:141; 578; VII:894n51, n54; 895n62
7:18-23	IV:58
7:19	I:642; III:424; 787; 788; VI:578; 662
7:19d	III:1033
7:20ff	III:788
7:20-23	VI:662
7:21	II:97; 699; III:479; 612; 613; VI:272; 556
7:21f	VI:272; IX:41; 231
7:22	I:624; II:917; IV:730; V:377; **VI:272;** 555; 565
7:23	III:479f; VI:562
7:24	I:368; III:48
7:24ff	VII:235
7:24-30	I:784
7:25	II:822; III:428(n12); VI:630; 763
7:26	II:102; 370n19; 509; IX:450n90
7:27	I:511; II:727; III:1104; V:638; 653; 990n282; VI:162n8; IX:450n90
7:27f	II:509
7:27-29	V:772n63
7:28	III:945; 1093; 1104; V:638; 772n63; VI:162n8; VIII:212
7:29	IV:101; VIII:505

7:30	II:769; III:209; V:638
7:31-37	III:396n35; **V:552-553**
7:32	III:130; V:794; VIII:161; 288n129; IX:57; 431
7:32-37	VIII:288n124
7:33	I:527; 448n4; III:130; 209; IV:561n53; V:551; 587; VIII:288n127, n128, n130
7:34	I:185n1; III:210; IV:107; V:427n326; 534; VII:603
7:35	I:221; 719n1; 721; III:206; IV:336; V:449; 552, n85
7:35-37	VI:687n25
7:36	III:208; 703n29; 704; 708, n49; VI:62; VII:591
7:37	III:37; 206; V:772; VI:62n6; 473(n83)
8	**VIII:288-291** (289n141)
8:1	III:500; 501
8:1ff	II:630
8:1-9	V:899
8:2	IV:579; VII:554, n32; VIII:220n32
8:3	II:928n7; IV:373; 925; V:67
8:4	II:658
8:5	II:685
8:6	II:154; 762; III:729; V:763, n23, n27; **IX:411**
8:6ff	V:25
8:7	II:762; VI:157n83; IX:411, n44
8:8	III:729; VI:59(n8); 63
8:9	I:362; IX:469
8:10	IV:595
8:11	III:408n14; 410; V:531; 728; VI:28; 34; 847; VII:52; 230; 234, (n240); 235; 747; IX:37
8:11f	II:893; 906; III:714(n69); VII:354; VIII:449; IX:532
8:11ff	III:36
8:12	I:663; VI:396; 405n470; VII:29n226; VIII:449n347; 450n352; 454n377; 459n405
8:12b	VIII:449n348
8:14	V:772n63
8:15	II:906; V:343n149; VII:52; **591;** VIII:567n45; IX:37; 39
8:16	II:96
8:16-21	II:906; V:699n331
8:17	I:703, n61; 704; II:96; III:613; IV:950; V:1023n5; 1026; 1027, n7; VII:893; 894, n54; 895n62; VIII:289
8:17f	V:1028
8:17ff	VIII:289, n135
8:18	I:220; V:341; 378; 556; VIII:286n117; 289
8:19	I:477; II:322; 425; III:729; IV:682; VI:285n8; 286; IX:469
8:19f	III:729
8:19ff	IV:450
8:20	II:630; VI:302; VIII:458n399;

	IX:469
8:21	IV:950; VII:893; 894, n54; 895n62; VIII:289
8:22	III:130; V:794; VIII:288, n130; IX:57
8:22ff	V:347; VI:118; VIII:289n135, \ n142
8:22-26	III:396n35; VIII:288n124; **289-290**
8:23	II:448n4; III:130; 209; V:377; VI:530; VIII:161; 288, n128; IX:430; 431
8:23f	V:343
8:24ff	III:206
8:25	I:387; III:130; V:377; 889; VIII:155, n2; 161; 287; 288; 290, n144; 456n383; IX:431
8:25f	VIII:288n133
8:26	III:208; 708n48; 714; VI:530
8:27	V:587(n24); VI:530
8:27a	V:66, n71; IX:529n243
8:27b	V:66, n71
8:27f	VI:841
8:27ff	II:347n47
8:27-29	IX:532n273
8:27-30	III:520n53; V:208n28
8:27-33	VIII:378; **444-445; IX:529-530;** 539
8:27-9:29	VII:797
8:27-10:45	VIII:456
8:27-10:52	VII:797n147; IX:529n246
8:28	I:389; 545; II:936; III:220; IV:858(n121), n121, n122; VI:841; **842**
8:29	I:102n51; II:687n1; IV:858n122; V:211; VIII:380
8:29b	IX:529n243
8:29-33	VI:102; IX:298
8:30	II:626; V:763; VII:591
8:31	I:206; 370; II:27; 260; 939; 948, n31; III:271; IV:115n189; 274n48; 343; 758; 884n17; V:707(n405), n406; 713n459; 715; **913-916** (913n68; 914n70; 916n87); VI:296n62; 659n46; 844; VII:329; 330n247; 864; 870n72; VIII:220; 224; 439; 443; 444; **454;** 457, n391; 477n517; IX:37n144; 47; 211
8:31ff	VIII:444
8:32	II:625; IV:15; 115n189; 120n201; V:699n331; 881
8:32a	VIII:378n320
8:32b	VIII:444
8:32f	III:973
8:32b-33	V:881
8:33	II:626; IV:342n17; 343; 344; V:291; 715; VI:36; 102; **VII:158-159;** 162; 348n53; 726n19; VIII:444; 505; IX:232; 529n243; **539;** 557
8:34	I:185; 214; 471; II:669; III:49; 500; 501; V:291; 586; VI:152(n35); VII:577; 578, n44, n51; 579, n57; 771; VIII:179n66; 456; **IX:643; 645**
8:34f	II:886; IX:130
8:34ff	IV:450; 560(n49); 715; V:916
8:34-9:1	VIII:378
8:35	I:394; 395; II:725; 727; 729, n63; 861n241; 874n5; III:52; VII:991; 995n134; VIII:443n308; 453; IX:130; 166n163; 608; **642-644** (642n159; 643n161); **645;** 656
8:35f	IX:608; **645**
8:35ff	IX:646
8:36	I:395; II:888n4; 891; 892n21; III:883n54; 888; IX:642; **645;** 646
8:36b	IX:645n167
8:36f	II:862; VIII:456; IX:642n159
8:37	I:252; IV:341n12; 343; V:856; IX:645, n167
8:38	I:84n68; 109; 190; 303n138; 329; 470; 663; II:248; 919n60; III:103(n248); 107n282; 226; 580; IV:105; 107; 730; 734; 751n52; **V:208,** n27, n28; 216; 812; 866; 987; 989n272, n278; VII:796; VIII:372, n268, n273; 442, n297; **447;** 449n345; **456,** n383; 457; 460; 461n413; 608n24; IX:538n302; 645
8:38f	IV:758
9:1	I:583; 587; 589; 677; II:305; 670; III:18; IV:248; V:359n211; 360; 361n221; 867; VI:412; 437; 845; VIII:453; 456; 461n413
9:1ff	IV:246
9:1-13	VIII:445n318
9:2	IV:758; VI:101; VII:380n68; IX:60
9:2a	IV:869n228
9:2b	IV:869n228
9:2ff	II:249; 456; IV:750; **V:354;** VII:392
9:2-8	IV:758n18; 869; VIII:175
9:2-13	IV:908n36
9:2-29	IX:529n246
9:2b-3	IV:869n228
9:3	I:84n67; 679; III:339; IV:25n30; 243n13; 247; 249; V:311n6; VI:417; **VII:666**
9:3c	IV:246
9:4	II:938n82; III:220n16; IV:908; V:354; VII:771
9:4f	**II:938-939** (939n96); IV:855; 856; 866, n213; V:912n54
9:5	II:153; 623; 938n82; III:945;

	1093; VI:101; 964; 965;	9:24	I:628; III:901; V:638; VI:205;
	VII:378n59; **379-380**		207; VII:772
	(379n60; 380n68); VIII:219	9:25	II:16; 348(n53); 678;
9:6	VIII:554; IX:209		III:428(n12); V:427; 586;
9:7	I:48; 219; II:740n7; 938;		VIII:37n2
	III:850n123; IV:114; 189n17;	9:25f	II:626
	739; 868n225; 869; **908-909;**	9:26	I:625; III:900; VI:278; 541
	V:530; 668n81; **701-702;**	9:27	I:368; 370; II:334; III:911;
	706n402; 707n408;		IX:430; 431
	710(n429); VI:68n57; 417;	9:28	II:687, n1; III:206
	847; **VII:400; 369;**	9:29	III:210; IV:226n36; 933n73;
	378; 381; 384n365; 389;		934n80; VII:290
	445n318; 454n378; IX:298,	9:30	III:48; VI:573
	n96	9:31	I:370; II:948; V:712; 713n459;
9:7a	IV:869n228		715; 716; 914; VI:844;
9:7b	IV:869n228		VI:329; VIII:220; 224; 439;
9:7f	IX:298n99		443; **444,** n309; 455; 457;
9:9	I:370; IV:104n140; 248;		IX:37n144; 211; 430
	893(n22); V:354; 372;	9:32	I:116; V:699n331; 881;
	VI:68n57; VII:591; VIII:439;		IX:209n106; 210
	443; **445; 454;** 457; 473	9:33	II:96; V:23
9:9f	VIII:445n315	9:33f	**V:67;** VI:723
9:9-13	VIII:445n316	9:33-35	IV:532n11
9:10	III:912; IV:101n119; 104n140;	9:33ff	IV:450; V:66n71
	115n189; VII:747;	9:34	II:96
	VIII:380n335	9:35	II:86; 88; 139; 698; 728n59;
9:10b	IV:104n140		III:45n9; 443; 704; VI:868;
9:11	II:23; 687; 936; 937; V:716		VIII:16
9:11f	VI:869	9:36	VII:646; IX:138n229
9:12	I:389; II:933; 936; III:323n4;	9:37	I:404(n38); II:349(n62);
	V:707, (n405), n406, (n408);		III:547; IV:533n18; 651n16;
	712, n448a; 715; **913-916**		VIII:449n349
	(913n68; 914n73; 915n79);	9:38	I:527; 528; II:623; III:714(n68);
	918n109; 924; VIII:445; 457		V:271; 277; VI:964; 965n40
9:12b	V:716; VIII:444; **454**	9:38f	V:277
9:12f	I:749; II:670; 940; 941; IV:864;	9:38ff	I:426; III:213
	V:714; 912n54; 916; VIII:430	9:39	III:468; V:271; 277; VI:483;
9:13	II:938; III:45n7; 593n3; IV:866;		VII:420
	V:686n234; 914;	9:40	V:856; **VII:420,** n11; VIII:442;
	VI:477(n102); 841; VIII:255;		508; IX:129n158
	454n380	9:41	I:394; 426; II:349n63; III:288;
9:14	IV:929n29; VII:747		547; IV:651n16; 652, n18;
9:14ff	I:428; II:302; 310; 457		714; V:271; 274; VI:141; 149;
9:14-29	III:947; V:982; VII:289n25;		159; VIII:323; IX:530, n258
	554n31	9:41ff	IV:714
9:15	I:498; III:5; 6	9:42	II:433; III:656; IV:560; 651;
9:16	VII:747		652, n18, n19; VI:56;
9:17	I:625n3; II:16; 822; VI:964;		210(n268); 214(n306);
	IX:57		VII:347; **351-351** (351n71;
9:17f	VI:350		352n72, n74); IX:75
9:18	III:206; 213	9:42-48	IV:345
9:19	I:329; 359; 663; III:947; IV:451;	9:42-50	IX:647n184
	VI:205; 207; 722; VII:407	9:43	I:658; II:424; 676; 864(n270);
9:19b	V:648		III:852; 853; 860; VI:945;
9:19f	IX:57		947; VII:167; 168; 347; 455;
9:20	VI:163; IX:529n244; 655n226		IX:430
9:21	IX:591	9:43ff	I:658; II:864(n277); IV:559n39;
9:21-24	VII:554n31		560, n42; 561n52; 714; V:434
9:22	I:394; 628; VI:941; VII:554,	9:43-47	V:551n75
	n31; 726n19; VIII:323n55	9:43-48	IV:716; VII:352
9:23	II:303; III:901; 945; V:726	9:43-49	VI:398(n417)
9:23f	VI:204n225; 206(n241)	9:44	VI:945n90; VII:167n5; 347;

10:36	III:49	11:1ff	II:154; IV:448
10:37	I:583; II:248	11:1-10	III:337
10:38	I:192n14; V:291; 436; 437n386;	11:1-11	**V:286**
	699n331; VI:152, n38; 944;	11:1-12:12	VII:756n48
	VII:884n71; 885n77;	11:2	II:60; III:444; IV:336; V:108;
	VIII:444		286; VI:844; 960; VIII:504
10:38f	I:538; 539, n46; 540; 545;	11:3	II:623; III:1093; VI:476
	II:886; **VI:152;** 399n418	11:4	II:60; III:173; V:286; VI:722;
10:39	V:714n472; VI:153n42; 845		960
10:40	I:586; V:345; 986(n256);	11:4f	IV:336
	987n261; 992	11:5	V:286; VI:476; 960; VII:647
10:41ff	V:306n23	11:6	I:510; II:545
10:41-44	VIII:448	11:7	III:444; V:286; VI:960
10:41-45	IX:553n392	11:8	III:831n4; V:587(n25);
10:42	I:478; II:85; 233; 575; III:500;		IX:683n17
	501; 1098; IV:342	11:9	I:589; III:901; 1087; V:286;
10:42-44	VIII:16		IX:684
10:42-45	IV:306; 341; V:715n474;	11:9f	II:762; III:179n85; IV:274n48;
	VI:432		V:271; **IX:683**
10:43	II:88; **IV:533-534;** VI:868;	11:10	I:581; 584; 589; II:669;
	VIII:179n67		III:116n363; IV:867;
10:43f	II:278n114; III:45n9; VI:868		V:286n18; 948; 985n253;
10:43-45	II:85; VIII:448n341		VIII:289n135; 484; 486; 619,
10:43ff	VIII:328		n46; IX:89n10
10:44	II:86; 698; VI:868	11:11	II:677; III:237; 245; V:23;
10:45	I:373; II:86; 166; 278n114; 669;		VII:329n242; IX:680
	III:18n77; IV:329; 330; 341;	11:11ff	VII:756n50
	342-343; 349, n3; 351; 621;	11:12f	VI:20n59
	750; V:25; 74n115; 436n379;	11:12-14	VI:20; **VII:756-757**
	706; 707(n408); 708; 710,	11:12ff	III:208n46
	n435, n436; 711(n442); 712;	11:13	III:461; IV:373; V:286;
	715; 717, n487; 916n88;		VII:756n48, n49
	VI:88n57; 278; 543; **544,** n43,	11:13f	V:435; VI:843
	(n44), n45, n49; VIII:20;	11:14	III:945; V:423n297; 429
	155n6; 156; 405; 438; **448,**	11:15	III:235; VI:69; 870n3;
	n343; 458; 460; 470; 508n9;		VII:329n242; 716
	511, n21; IX:560, n436; 637,	11:15-17	III:243
	n120	11:15ff	III:582
10:45a	VIII:448	11:16	III:243n56; VII:362; IX:63
10:45b	VIII:448; **455**	11:17	I:748; II:369; III:243; 488;
10:46	III:206; 293; 443; V:68; VI:579;		V:121, n10; 715; VI:480;
	VIII:287; 288n121		831n336; 834; 842
10:46ff	III:206; V:347; VIII:289n135	11:18	I:394; II:164; III:271; 921;
10:47	III:287; IV:874; VIII:287;		IV:51; V:587; VII:330; 864;
	288(n126)		867; IX:37n144; 209n106
10:47f	II:485(n102); III:287; **VIII:485;**	11:19	VI:579
	486; IX:249	11:20	VI:988
10:48	II:625; VI:541; VIII:288n126	11:20f	VI:20; 843
10:49	III:26n5; V:68n83; VII:647;	11:20-22	**VII:756-757**
	648; IX:303	11:21	II:153; III:1093; VI:101n11;
10:50	VIII:288n121		964; 965n42
10:51	III:49; 945; 1084n240; 1093;	11:22	II:826n58; VI:204(n230); 206
	VI:473(n83); 962n15; 964;	11:22f	VI:206(n242)
	965	11:22-25	VI:20n57
10:51f	VIII:287; 288	11:23	II:626n20; III:612; 811, n3; 947;
10:52	III:206; 211; 212; V:67;		948; IV:108(n150); V:483;
	VI:206(n240); VII:990;		**VII:389-390** (289n25)
	VIII:288n121, (n131),	11:23f	III:210; VI:204n225
	(n133); 505; IX:432n46	11:24	II:804, n292; VI:206;
11-13	VII:756n48		VII:289n25
11:1	II:332; V:484n102;	11:24f	VII:290
	VII:329n242; 752n9	11:25	I:511; II:169(n8); 537; 805;

	III:331; 558; IV:715; V:421n280; 513(n112); 520; 986; 987, (n265); 991; **VI:171;** VII:289n25; 637
11:25f	I:511; V:986n255; VII:517n366
11:26	II:537; 748n40; V:520; 986n255; VI:171
11:27	III:242; 271; V:895; VI:659n46; VII:329n242; 864; IX:38
11:27ff	I:536; II:347n47, n51
11:28	II:538; 569; VI:474; VII:517n366; 756n47
11:29	II:687; 688; VI:474
11:30	I:364; 538; 545; **V:521,** n184; 530; 531
11:31	II:96; V:733n52; VI:205
11:32	IV:50; 51; V:587(n31); VI:836; IX:208
11:33	VI:474
12:1	IV:254; 255; V:28; 68; 138; VI:842
12:1ff	IV:716; V:28
12:1-9	V:753; VIII:375; **378-379**
12:1-11	V:759; 760
12:1-12	III:781; VI:432; IX:38
12:2	III:461; IV:6; V:728
12:3	I:406n6; III:660
12:4ff	I:404n37
12:5	I:48
12:5f	II:740n7
12:6	I:171; II:439; 697, n1; III:850n123; IV:739n8; VIII:384n365; 596
12:7	II:96; III:781; VIII:391n417
12:7ff	III:328n46
12:8	IV:255; VI:921n6
12:8ff	I:48
12:9	I:396; III:1086; IV:714; VI:476
12:10	I:343; 372; 753; 792; II:434; IV:271; **274-275** (274n49); 884; 887; V:127; 915n79; VII:353n79
12:10f	III:179
12:11	III:39, n61; 1086; IV:281n7; V:729; 995n302
12:12	I:510; 703; III:911; IV:51; V:587; IX:38; 208
12:13	III:516; IV:106; VI:35; **IV:39,** n155
12:13ff	IX:36; 39n158; **81-82**
12:13-17	II:886; VI:35
12:14	I:244; 248; II:561; III:102(n241); V:87; 343, n151; VI:780; 964; IX:81
12:14-17	VIII:97
12:15	I:703n61; V:342; VI:28; 34; 35; 844; VIII:568
12:16	II:387
12:17	II:167; III:38; 102(n238); VIII:29n11; 44; IX:82n17, n18
12:18	I:370; 372; II:687; VII:36; 52

12:18-27	IV:844n103; **VII:52**
12:19	I:746; VI:964; VII:545
12:19f	I:145
12:19-22	I:510
12:20	VII:545
12:21	VII:545
12:22	II:697, n1; V:889; VII:545; VIII:596
12:23	II:337; 817n5
12:24	I:752n8; **VI:243-244;** 252n159
12:24-27	IX:457
12:25	I:83n60; 87; 651, n15; 652; 785; II:337; 538; 866; III:61n31; 1032; IV:893(n24); V:533; 1018n19; VI:146; VII:120n175
12:25f	I:585
12:26	I:581; 616; 757; II:337; III:101(n225); 191; IV:110; 893(n23)
12:26f	VII:236
12:27	II:865; IV:893; **VI:243-244**
12:28	I:558; II:547; 687, n1; IV:1088; V:889; VI:868; VII:52; 747; IX:36; 38
12:28ff	I:44; III:581; IV:1063
12:28-31	V:755n84; VI:316
12:28-34	VI:316n37; IX:36, n140
12:29	II:435; III:98n191; 101(n226); 1087
12:29f	III:101; 941; V:995n302; VI:868
12:29ff	V:172
12:30	III:101n227; 399; 613; 1087; IV:966; V:175; VII:893; IX:134, n191; 152n52; 641
12:30f	IX:129
12:31	II:549; **IV:535-536;** IX:130
12:32	I:244; II:155; 435
12:32f	II:550; III:101
12:33	III:181; IV:535; 966n11; VI:62; VII:893, n43; IX:130; 134n191; 641
12:34	I:587; II:687; 819; IV:374; 959n35; 1063; VIII:184; IX:36
12:35	II:139; III:242; 945; IX:38; **530**
12:35-37	I:577n62; VI:252n160; **VIII:370; 484-485** (484n42); IX:38; 530n250
12:35ff	III:1094; VIII:156; IX:249
12:36	I:757; 793n2; II:814; III:440; 1086f; IV:110; 569; V:522n190; VI:398; 412; 454n7; 629; 831; VIII:482; 483; 608n24
12:36f	III:106n269; 1086; VIII:482
12:37	III:487; **IX:530**
12:38	I:498; II:164; III:46(n21); V:343n149; **VII:690-691**
12:38f	I:331(n106); 741, n14; IX:128; 129

12:38-40	IX:42n184		728, n59; 729; III:338n11;
12:38ff	IX:42		589; 703n29; 704; 713; V:158;
12:39	II:34; V:21; VI:870; 871;		**VI:869-870** (870n7); VII:348
	VII:819n128; 820; 833, n227;	13:11	I:247; III:824; IV:591n14;
	VIII:456		V:813; VI:398; 402; 404;
12:40	I:784; II:803; III:942; IV:7;		444n767; 869; 870; VII:514;
	V:131; 488n3; VI:62; 149;		834; IX:679
	273n26; **IX:448-449** (448n75;	13:12	III:21; IV:1099n1; V:866n48;
	449n77); 461		983; VII:740; IX:159; 163
12:40a	I:741	13:12f	I:145
12:40b	I:741	13:13	II:349n63; III:751n70; 824;
12:41	V:345; VI:328; VII:85		IV:586; 690, n25; V:271;
12:41b	VI:328		866n48; VI:194; VII:894n57;
12:41ff	I:784; III:236; 242		991; VIII:56; 436n273;
12:41-44	VI:328; IX:449		443n308; 450n356; IX:647
12:42	III:866n40; VI:40	13:13b	VII:995n135
12:42-44	IX:451n100	13:14	I:343; 600; II:660; III:245; 824;
12:43	III:500; 501; V:889; VI:844;		IV:950; V:483; 484; VII:648;
	908; IX:449n82		VIII:204
12:43f	IX:449n82	13:14-20	V:866n48
12:44	II:862n252; VI:59;	13:14-27	IX:571
	VIII:597n24; **598**	13:15	V:131
13	I:585; II:353; 354; III:145; 887;	13:16	V:290; 291; VII:726
	IV:187; **V:866-867** (866n48;	13:16f	VII:894n58
	867n49); VI:30; 247, n115;	13:17	III:824
	845, n404; 869n6;	13:18	II:805; VII:29
	VII:440n149; VIII:372n275;	13:19	I:481; III:885; 1028; 1029;
	450n353, n354		IV:1107, n14; V:430
13:1	III:235; IV:246(n31)	13:19-27	**IV:188-189**
13:1f	V:145	13:20	I:362; 627n12; III:823; 824;
13:1ff	IV:885		1087; IV:172; 185; 188;
13:1-23	VIII:450n353		V:995n302; VII:124; 991;
13:2	I:511; IV:338; 883n15; V:346;		995n135
	VI:107; 531; 845;	13:20-23	IV:188
	VIII:450n356	13:21	V:430; VI:203n208, (n213);
13:2f	III:245		VIII:150n16; IX:530n255;
13:3	II:687n1; III:235; 440; 441; 443;		531
	V:484	13:21f	**IX:530**
13:4	V:865n42; VII:232, n220;	13:21-23	VIII:433n253; 450n356
	VIII:64	13:21ff	II:353; IV:188
13:5	VI:246; 247	13:21-27	VIII:55
13:5f	I:183n11; V:866n48	13:22	II:334; III:714(n68); 824;
13:6	II:353, n92; V:277n224;		IV:188; VI:30; 246, n106,
	VI:246; 247, n114;		n107; 247; 830; 886; 943;
	VIII:450n356		VII:230; 240; **241**; 260;
13:6ff	V:291		VIII:335; **IX:530,** n255
13:7	VI:296n62; 513n91;	13:22f	III:589; VIII:595
	VII:199n19; 708; VIII:55;	13:23	V:343n149; 866n48;
	IX:672		VI:246n109
13:7f	V:866n48	13:24	V:430; VII:61; **440;**
13:8	I:482; II:334; VI:848n425;		VIII:450n345
	VII:199; VIII:203; IX:525;	13:24f	VII:232; 887
	672	13:24ff	V:534n319; VII:61; 236n252
13:9	I:577; II:429; 433; 504n4;	13:24-27	V:523n200; 866n48; VIII:55;
	IV:502; 503; V:422; VI:869;		450, n353
	VII:648; 831; 834, n229,	13:24-30	V:867
	n232; **867;** VIII:443n308	13:25	I:504; II:538; V:534; VI:163
13:9-11	V:866n48; VII:648n23;	13:25a	VIII:458n400
	834n233; VIII:450n356	13:26	II:248; IV:909; V:989n278;
13:9ff	IV:450n236		VII:440n149; 796; **VIII:437;**
13:9-13	V:867n49		**450,** n345; 453; 456; 458; 460
13:10	II:23; 369; 425; 715n90; 727;	13:26f	VIII:372

13:27	I:84n68; 679; 792(n3); III:103(n248); IV:188, n14; 189; V:139; 516; 769; VII:842;1092n634; VIII:134; 450n345; 458n400
13:28	II:331; III:720; 757n1; IV:406n128; VII:757(n57)
13:28f	I:703; V:752; 759; VII:757; VIII:566n39
13:28-37	VIII:450n356
13:29	II:331; III:173; 174n8; IV:188; V:754; VII:757(n57)
13:30	I:663; II:585n70; 682; VIII:372n275
13:31	I:678; II:682; IV:107; 838; V:515; 516n141
13:32	I:85; 703n61; 713, n83; III:107n281; IV:344; V:533; 867; 989; 992; VIII:366; 371; **372**, n270, n275; 381; 450; IX:592; 679
13:32f	VIII:55
13:32-37	VIII:450
13:33	II:339; 461, n37; VIII:434n259; 555
13:33-37	IV:1104; V:759; VIII:451n360; IX:243; 680
13:34	II:338; 545; 546; 565; 570; V:29; 754; VII:895
13:34b	VIII:451n360
13:35	II:338; V:131; 755; VIII:451n360; IX:303n5
13:35f	II:935
13:35-37	VI:31
13:36	II:670; VIII:372n270
13:37	II:338
14	VI:903n161
14:1	II:902; III:271; 911; 1096; V:897n7; VII:864; IX:37n144
14:1f	VII:330; 392n16; 867
14:2	II:902; IV:50; 51; VII:571
14:3	I:545; II:472; III:656; IV:801, n12; VII:457n2; 925; IX:139n231
14:3ff	I:232; II:810n16; III:548; V:20
14:3-9	II:727; III:545n27; 850; V:716, n480; VI:903n161; VIII:105; IX:36
14:4	I:396; II:429; III:548
14:4f	IV:801
14:5	III:548; V:716; VI:160; **903**
14:6	I:510; 784; III:829; V:716; VI:903n161
14:6ff	III:548
14:7	II:824n47; III:45n8; VI:477; **903,** n161; 908
14:8	II:727; III:850; IV:14; 801, n13; V:712; 714; 715; 716, n480; VI:478; 903n161
14:9	II:425; 429; 715n90; 727; 728, n59; III:589; 703n29; 704;

	705; 888; 890; IV:676(n6); 682; 882n8; VI:478; 903n161
14:10	II:169; 434n2; VII:864; IX:141
14:10f	III:271
14:11	II:579; VII:647; IX:367
14:12	II:693; 902; III:48; 181; VI:866, n7
14:12ff	III:734; IV:448, n229
14:12-16	V:899
14:13	III:734; VIII:315; 504
14:13ff	VI:844
14:14	II:49; 693; 903n8; III:1093; IV:338; V:897n8; IX:54n46
14:15	II:26; VIII:211
14:16	II:903n8; V:897n8
14:17	III:734
14:17ff	IX:141
14:17-21	VIII:446
14:18	II:693; III:654; 655; 734; VI:844; VII:795; 796; 1057; **VIII:212; 446;** 468n461; IX:141
14:19	VIII:212
14:20	VII:796; VIII:210; **212; 446;** IX:141; 430n36
14:21	I:748; II:68; V:707(n405); 712; 716; VI:573n49; **VIII:446; 455;** 458; 477n517; 504; 506
14:21a	VIII:439; 443
14:21b	VIII:446
14:22	I:477; II:695; 762; III:729; 736n63; **VII:1059**
14:22f	IX:411
14:22-24	V:900; VI:141(n55)
14:22ff	III:734; **735-737;** V:25
14:22-25	III:730; V:716n484; VI:544n43
14:23	III:734; 738n69; VI:155, n70; 154
14:24	I:174; II:133; 468, n2; III:18n77; IV:342; 344; 868; V:74n115; 706; 707(n408); 710, n435; 711; 712; 715; 716, n484; 717; VI:55(n15); 432; 543; **544,** (n44), n49; VIII:255; **510-511**
14:25	I:342; 585; 655n44; 685; II:337; 695n36; III:449; 731; 732; 734; 735; V:164; 359n211; 986(n256); 987n261; VI:141(n54); 142n66; 146n9; 153; 297, n70; VIII:168; 212(n33); 372n270
14:26	III:734; IV:274n48; V:899; VIII:499; 502n96
14:26-30	VI:493n75
14:27	II:665; III:849; IV:343; V:940; VI:252n159; 493, n78; 844; VII:349,n58; 353n79; **421,** n13
14:27f	**VI:492-493;** 497; 501; 844
14:28	I:130; II:335; IV:535; V:361n222; VI:104, n23; **492-493** (493n75)

14:29	V:714n472; VII:347n51; 349; VIII:222n45		VIII:540; IX:343
14:29f	VII:292	14:54f	IX:543n320
14:29-31	VII:349	14:55	II:430; III:21; 271; IV:499; VII:864; 868
14:30	I:469; 471; VI:844; VII:273; VIII:222; 456; IX:303, n4	14:55-59	VII:869n66
14:31	I:328n84; 471; III:19n79; VI:62n6; VII:35; 786; VIII:456	14:55-65	**VII:868-870**
		14:56	III:345; IV:499; V:211
		14:56f	IV:514; 883
		14:57	I:368; VIII:596
14:32-35	VIII:445	14:57f	III:244; 345; VI:107
14:32-42	**VI:36**	14:58	I:793; II:66; 348(n53); 948; 949n32; III:244n62; IV:388; 883, n15; 884n16; 885; 886, n24; 888n31; V:139; 143; 147; 211; 715; 771n53; VI:927n62; VII:382; 869n65; 870n71; 871; 1058n355; VIII:204n134; 220; 454; IX:436
14:33	III:7, n19; VIII:446n322		
14:33f	VI:153		
14:34	II:338; III:14n62; IV:323; VIII:446n322; IX:641		
14:35	I:738; IV:344; 650n14; VI:163; VIII:372n270; IX:677		
14:35ff	III:102(n244)		
14:36	I:6, n7; III:49; 58; IV:343; 344; 470n38; V:437n386; 445; 984, n247; 985n251; 987; 989(n273); 992; 1001; VI:152; VIII:366n277		
		14:59	III:345; IV:499; VII:869n65
		14:60	I:368; IV:510; VII:869n65
		14:60f	II:687, n1; III:270; VII:869n66
		14:61	II:347(n47); 354; 764; V:713, n454; VII:868; 869; **VIII:379;** 380n334; 381; IX:528
14:36-38	VIII:446n322		
14:37	II:338; 435(n4); VI:102; IX:680	14:61f	III:92; V:989n278; **IX:528-529;** 538
14:37f	VIII:372n270		
14:38	II:338; 426; 678; V:917n96; **VI:31;** 36; 396; VII:124; 145; 349	14:62	I:220; II:297; 352; 353; 665; III:442; 580; 937; 1094; IV:344; 540; 909; 1103; V:211; 361; 522, n190; 523; 713n454; 866; 867; VI:493n76; VII:796; 869n66; VIII:370n252; 371; 379; 435n267; **436,** n268; 450; 453; 458; 462n421; 468; 469n462; 608n24; 612; IX:543n326
14:38b	**VI:695-697**		
14:39	IV:115n189		
14:40	I:558n1; 559; V:377; VII:726n18; VIII:445		
14:41	I:328; 350; II:671; 828; V:712; 716; VI:153; 688n27; VIII:22; 372n270; 439; 443; **445-446** (446n322); 455; 458; 468; IX:430; 678		
		14:62c	VIII:381
14:42	II:331; 334; VIII:445; 446n322	14:63	IV:489
14:43	IV:525; V:588; 729; VI:659n46; VII:864; VIII:446n322; IX:141	14:64	I:623; II:828; III:951(n2); V:888; **VII:868-869** (868n52; 869n67); IX:2
14:43-52	VIII:446n322	14:65	III:819; IV:6n5; **V:635,** n26, n27; 900n35; 921n128; VI:775; 829; VII:869n66, n67; VIII:263n24; 264n34, n35; 265, n36, n39, n42; 267n56; 540; IX:529n240
14:44	VII:232n218; 269, n6; IX:140n240; 141		
14:44f	IX:119n42; 140		
14:45	II:153; 684; III:1093; VI:964; IX:140n239, n240		
14:46	I:529; IX:430	14:66	III:270; 640; IX:543n326
14:47	III:270; IV:525; V:551n76; 559; 840; 940; VIII:261	14:67	III:287; IV:874; VII:794
		14:68	I:469; V:117; 208n29; VIII:456; IX:303, n4
14:48	IV:525; VII:760; IX:543n326		
14:49	I:752; 758; III:236; 242; V:707(n405); VI:295	14:69f	V:840
		14:70	I:244; 248; 469; IV:650n14; VIII:456
14:50	I:430(n134); VI:493, n74; VII:349		
		14:71	I:355; 356n2; V:117; 177; 184
14:51	I:216; 773; III:911; IX:132n182	14:72	I:471; 529, n1; IV:105, n144; 677, n10; VIII:222; 456; IX:303, n4
14:51f	IX:132		
14:52	I:773		
14:53	III:270; VI:659n46; VII:864; 868	15:1	II:60; 169; III:271; VI:478; 659n46; VII:864; 870
14:54	III:270; 441n9; IV:373; VI:722;	15:2	I:577; V:211; VIII:436n268;

	IX:528; 529n242; 543n326
15:3	III:271; 637; VII:864
15:4	II:687n1; III:637; IX:543n326
15:5	III:38; V:713
15:6	I:192; 195
15:7	II:60; III:286n18; IV:262, n30; VI:964n33; VII:268; 570
15:8	I:192; 519(n4); 625; V:587; VI:475
15:9	I:577; III:46n28; 376; 945; IX:528; 529n242
15:10	I:703n61; VII:864
15:10f	III:271
15:11	V:587; VII:198; 864
15:11f	III:271
15:12	I:577; III:376; VI:478; IX:528; 529n242
15:13	III:901
15:14	I:625n4; III:901; VI:62; 474
15:15	I:328n84; 632(n53); II:169; IV:517; V:587; 634n23; VI:475(n92); VIII:266n47; IX:375n22
15:16	III:496
15:16ff	IV:246; VII:709
15:16-20	**V:634**
15:17	II:319, n2; III:813; **VII:632**
15:18	I:496; 577; IX:367; 528; 529n242
15:18f	I:498; **VIII:266**
15:19	I:738; III:679; VI:763, n57; VIII:155; 264; 267n56
15:20	II:318; 319; 430; VI:921n6
15:21	I:129; IX:58n10
15:22	VIII:203
15:22f	V:289
15:23	V:164; 635n30; **VII:458-459; 574**
15:24	I:527; III:763; IV:246; VII:458
15:25	VII:439n140; IX:680
15:26	I:577; IX:528; 529n242
15:27	VII:786
15:28	I:753; 758; IV:287; 1087; VII:770n22
15:29	I:623; II:948; 949n32; III:718; IV:338; 882n8; 883, n14, n15; VII:382; 1058n355; VIII:220
15:29f	III:244
15:29ff	VII:255
15:30	VII:989
15:31	IV:798; **V:635;** VII:864; 989
15:32	I:578; III:327n39; 376; 384; V:240; 349; VII:574; 786; **IX:528;** 529n242
15:33	I:677; III:993; IV:882n8; **VII:439;** 459
15:33f	IX:680
15:33-37	VIII:612n54
15:34	I:627; II:429; III:102(n244); IV:344; V:240; 437n386; 701n349; 852n64; VI:36; 153n41; VII:69; IX:294n76
15:35	I:627n15; II:670; V:840; IX:303
15:35f	II:930
15:36	I:511; III:411; **V:288-289** (288n3); 342n143; VI:160; VII:459; 574; VIII:232
15:37	I:510; 627n14; III:901n13; VI:452; IX:294, n76
15:38	III:246; 629; IV:885; VI:767; VII:330; **961,** n15
15:39	II:509; III:849; V:211; 839; VI:452; VII:709; 961n15; VIII:379, n323; IX:294
15:40	I:144n2; IV:373; 643; 650, n12; V:346
15:40f	I:784; IV:461; VIII:183
15:41	II:85
15:42	VII:20n159; 28
15:42-47	VII:20
15:43	I:192; 587; II:58; 526; 771; VI:167n3; 721; VII:1057, n354; VIII:183; IX:169
15:43-45	IX:540
15:44	II:687; III:39; 500; V:717
15:45	I:703; II:167; VI:167, n3; VII:1057n354
15:45f	V:716n480
15:46	III:173; 178n73; 411; IV:268; 269, n6; 680; VI:97; VIII:155
15:47	I:144n2; 430n136; 784; V:345; VIII:183
16	I:66; 208; II:198; 207n58
16:1	I:230; III:846; VII:458
16:1ff	I:784
16:2	I:352; II:434n1; 950; IV:680; VII:20; 29; 32n246
16:3	III:173
16:3f	IV:269
16:4	I:155; V:346
16:5	I:84n67; III:5; 6; IV:27; 429; VII:690n27; 691, n33; IX:211
16:6	II:335; III:5; 6; 287; IV:874; **VI:576;** VIII:203
16:7	I:130; 220; V:357; 361n222; VI:102; 104, n23; 493; VIII:505; IX:211n118
16:8	II:450; III:39; V:355n200; VIII:505; 612; **IX:210-211** (210n115)
16:9	II:630; IV:69; V:727; VI:866; VII:20; IX:2
16:9ff	VI:398n415
16:9-20	IX:210, n114
16:10	I:66; VI:42n16
16:11	V:344; 345, n156; VI:205, n236
16:12	II:702; IV:750; V:359n214; 360n219; IX:5
16:13	I:66
16:14	I:155; II:326; 335; 568; III:614; 654, n3; 781; 783; IV:858(n121); V:240; 345; 360n219; VI:205, n236; VIII:383n357; 596; IX:5;

	210n114	16:17f	VI:438n712
16:15	II:715n90; 727; 729; III:703n29;	16:17-19	IX:531n262
	704; 712n60; 713; 888; 890;	16:18	**V:579;** VI:140n52; VII:876;
	1029; V:895; VI:401n440		VIII:161; IX:431
16:16	I:539; III:951; VI:205;	16:19	II:424; IV:8, n3; 909n42;
	214n291, (n294), (n300)		V:522n190; 524n216; 525,
16:16a	III:753		n216; VII:876; VIII:156
16:16b	I:540; III:753	16:20	I:215; 603; II:67; 679; III:212;
16:16f	VI:210n268		704; 713; 714; IV:118;
16:17	I:215; 528; 722; 726; III:212;		VII:242n295; 259n399; 260;
	450; V:271; **579;**		874; **876**
	VII:242n295; 876		

LUKE

1	II:749; VI:876n35; VIII:21n62		IX:366; 367; 402
1f	II:750n52; 950n42; V:836n66;	1:14-17	II:937
	VI:411; 415	1:15	I:104, (n57); II:693; 719n112;
1:1	I:479n5; II:909; VI:310; 639;		III:787; 1087(n255); IV:531;
	VIII:32-33 (32n3; 33n6)		643; V:163; 164; VI:130;
1:1ff	VII:267		136n11; 140n51; 406n476;
1:1-4	II:909; IV:106; 108; 119;		837; VIII:376; 381
	IX:596	1:15-17	II:719
1:2	I:219; 481; II:171; IV:120; 124;	1:15ff	V:70n94
	789n154; **V:348; 373;**	1:16	III:101n224; 385; IV:1000;
	VI:310n12; VIII:530; **543**		VIII:365
1:3	I:215; 378; 745; II:232; 354;	1:16f	II:938; VI:837; VII:727 .
	IV:641; V:69n90; 889	1:17	I:104(n57); II:190; 300; 706;
1:4	I:506; 704; III:327n40; 639		719; 933; 937n72;
1:4ff	VI:837		III:1087(n255); IV:54;
1:5	**I:4;** 577; 776; III:262; 264; 395;		V:983; VI:10; 407(n487);
	IV:238, n30; V:270;		408n492; 831n341; IX:233
	VII:740n17	1:18	I:703; II:950n42; IV:868n226;
1:5-25	VII:331		V:835
1:6	II:189; 220; 221; 546;	1:18f	VI:723
	III:1087(n255); IV:573n8;	1:19	II:710n28; 719; 721; V:840;
	VI:575		VI:837
1:7	II:950n42; V:835; VII:141n320	1:20	II:427; 433; III:461; VI:205;
1:8	III:249; 262; VIII:543n105		296
1:8ff	VI:825n316	1:21	III:39; IV:50; 51; 885; VI:726
1:9	II:373; 677; III:232; 251;	1:21f	III:232
	1087(n255); **IV:1;** 264n15	1:22	I:704; IV:885; V:351; 372, n4
1:10	IV:50; 51; VI:278; 279; IX:677	1:23	II:950n42; IV:223n22; 226; 227;
1:10f	IV:264n15		VI:50n37; 130
1:11	III:183; 1087, (n255);	1:24	IV:640; V:835; VII:760;
	IV:264n15; V:350; 351; 358,		IX:54n48
	n210; 372n4; VII:648	1:24f	II:950n42
1:11ff	I:84; V:351	1:25	III:1087(n255); V:239; 835;
1:12	IX:209		VI:464; VIII:21
1:13	I:222; II:807; III:487; V:270;	1:26	IV:640; VI:530
	835; VI:723; IX:212	1:26ff	I:84; VI:876n33
1:14	I:20; 682; II:721; VI:541; 837;	1:26-38	VI:402; IX:450

1:27	I:496; IV:238n29; V:129; 270; **834-836;** 1016; VI:402n443; 876; VIII:485; IX:249
1:28	I:500; II:677; 717; 762; III:1087(n255); IV:366n36; V:351; VII:776; IX:360n9; **367;** 391; 392n148; 393
1:28f	I:449n18; VI:402n443
1:29	I:496; 499; II:96
1:30	II:769; V:733; VI:402n443; VII:776; IX:212; 392, n148
1:31	III:487; V:270; 834n54; 835; 836n66; VII:760, n5; VIII:363
1:31f	V:836n66
1:31-33	VI:402n443; IX:533
1:31-35	IX:533n278
1:32	I:194; III:116(n363); 164; 488; 489; IV:531; 867; V:836n66; 948; 985n253; VI:837; VIII:376; 379n323; **381-382;** 448n340; 485; 619; IX:534
1:32f	**VIII:381-382;** 485n47; IX:569n583
1:33	I:199; 581; 590; III:192; IV:1111n38; V:129; VIII:56; 212n32
1:34	I:362; 705n65; V:834n54; VI:402n443; 876
1:34f	VI:402n443
1:34ff	VIII:363n193
1:35	**I:101;** 103; 104, (n57); 670; **II:300;** 307; 311(n87); 681; III:107(n283); 116(n363); 488; IV:754; V:834n54; 835; 985n253; VI:342n32; 402, n443; **405; VII:400;** VIII:370n261; **376-377** (376n307); 379n323; 381, n339, n346; **382;** 619
1:35d	V:835n57
1:36	III:488; IV:238, n29; 640; VII:736n1; 740; 760
1:36f	VI:402n443
1:37	V:730, n24; 888
1:38	II:273; III:1087(n255); VI:402n443; 835; VIII:21
1:39	VI:573; VII:92n29; 566; 772
1:40f	I:449n18
1:40-42	I:500
1:41	I:104, (n57); III:787, n8; V:554; 637; VI:130; 406n476; 408(n489), n489; **VII:402,** n11; IX:303n7
1:41f	VI:835
1:42	II:762; III:615; 787; 903; IV:366n36; IX:303n7
1:43	III:1086; IV:643; IX:533
1:44	I:20; III:787, n8; V:554; 637; **VII:402,** n11; IX:292
1:45	III:1087(n255); IV:367; 369; V:729; VI:203(n214); 205;
	835; VIII:85
1:46	III:1087; IV:543; IX:641
1:46f	I:20; VI:18n43; VIII:21
1:46ff	II:457
1:46-55	V:202; 213; VI:17n43; VIII:21n62; 500n79
1:47	I:20; 21; III:101(n227); VI:405n466; 415; VII:1014n61; 1015
1:48	I:663; II:273; 603n16; IV:367; 1107; 1111; 1121; VIII:16; **21:** 435n266; 528n29
1:49	II:306; III:33n26; IV:531; V:271; VI:464
1:49-55	VI:18n43
1:50	I:663, n6; II:483(n95); IX:212
1:51	I:639; 640; III:612; 907; IV:966; VI:464; **VII:421; VIII:528**
1:51-53	III:907; VII:421
1:51ff	III:723
1:52	III:164; 412; VIII:16; 19; 21; 448n340; 608
1:52f	IV:368
1:53	I:406; III:660; IV:389(n8); VI:18n43; 19; 130; 328; 902n157; 908n215
1:54	I:375; II:483(n95); IV:676, n7; V:679; 680n177; 684n213; 700, n341
1:55	I:199; V:976n178; VII:545
1:56	IV:640; VII:771; VIII:220
1:57	VI:50n37; 130; IX:591
1:58	II:483; III:1087(n255); IV:543; VII:740, n18; 772n35
1:59	III:487; V:270; 638; VI:81; 82
1:60	III:488; 945; IV:643
1:61	VII:740
1:62	III:47n44; 488
1:63	I:191; 743; III:39
1:64	I:721; II:761
1:65	V:887; IX:209
1:66	III:612n19; 1087, (n255); V:638; VII:779; VIII:155; IX:431
1:67	I:104, (n57); V:805; VI:130; 346; 406n476; 408(n489), n489; 829; **835**
1:68	II:605; 764; III:101(n224); 384, n122; IV:53; 351; 352; VI:464; 846
1:68ff	II:457; IV:859; VII:398; 990
1:68-75	II:605n20; VII:1015
1:68-79	II:719; V:213; VIII:500n80; 605n30
1:69	II:334; III:670; 748n50; IV:351; V:129; 679; 681n184; 700, n341; 1017n6; VII:990; VIII:381; 482; 485
1:70	I:198; 199; IV:110; VI:831; VII:700
1:71	II:813; IV:351; 690; IX:430
1:71ff	**VII:990-991**

1:72	I:106; II:132; 483(n95); IV:676, n7; V:976n178; VI:464; VII:772n35	2:10f	**VII:1015**
		2:11	VI:530; VII:274; 1015; VIII:482; **IX:54; 533;** 536; 559n426
1:73	V:177; 461, n28; 961; 976n182; VI:723		
1:73f	VI:1002	2:12	II:769; III:654; V:637; VI:491; **VII:231; IX:53-54**
1:74	II:813; IV:62; 63; 64; VI:561; 1002; IX:430	2:13	I:84; 177; V:537; 538; VI:278; 279; VII:709; 771
1:75	II:199; 210; 862(n244); V:491n24; 493	2:13f	V:351
		2:14	I:85; 364, n3; 679; II:248; 413; 743; 745; **747-751** (747n33; 748n39; 749n46); III:116, n363; 294; IV:262; V:214; 513n118; 519n169; 985n253; 986n254; **VIII:619,** n45, n46, n47; IX:54; 683
1:76	II:937n71; 938; III:116(n363); 488; IV:859; V:70n94; 638; 985n253; VI:688; 777; 835; 836; 837; 840; VIII:382; 619		
1:76-79	II:605n20		
1:77	I:305; 511; 512; 706; IV:53; 351; **VII:991**		
1:78	I:352; 353; II:483(n95); 605, n20; III:101(n226); 112(n314); VI:835; 837; 846; VII:553; 556, n51; 557; **VIII:605**	2:15	I:718; III:1087(n255); V:533; 986n254; VII:231; **IX:54**
		2:15-18	VII:769n20
		2:16	III:654; V:637; VI:491; VII:231; **IX:53-54**
1:78ff	VI:405n467	2:17	I:718; V:221; 638
1:79	I:353; II:412; III:17; 443; V:84; VI:628; **VII:397-398; 440-441;** IX:7n1; 10	2:18	III:39; VI:54
		2:19	I:657n3; III:612; VIII:151, n2; IX:450
		2:20	I:177; 219; V:341; VII:231; 726
1:80	II:31; 950n42; III:384; 913; V:638; VI:405, n466; 415; 713, n69; VIII:518n12; 519n18	2:20-28a	VII:238n275
		2:21	III:787; V:270; VI:50n37; 81; 82; 130; 685; 688; VII:760n6
		2:21b	III:488
2	II:749; VIII:21n62	2:21c	III:488
2:1	II:231, n4; 679; III:395; 657n3; V:158; 729; IX:54	2:21f	II:950n42
		2:21-40	VII:238
2:1f	IV:492n53	2:22	III:429; 1087(n255); IV:864n194; **V:840-841;** VI:50n37; 130; VII:328; 331; 354n90
2:1ff	VI:876n33		
2:1-20	VI:402; **VII:231;** VIII:485; IX:53		
2:2	IX:81n12	2:2ff	IV:1062; VI:876
2:3	V:638; VI:530	2:23	I:747; III:488; 1087(n255); IV:1059; V:841; VI:872; VIII:382n349
2:4	I:519; III:488; V:129; **1016-1017;** VI:530; VIII:381; 482; 485		
		2:23f	VI:873
2:5	I:776; VII:771; VIII:363n193	2:24	III:181; 182; 237; 1087(n255); IV:110; V:841n14; VI:69; VII:331
2:5f	III:245		
2:6	II:950n42; VI:50n37; 130; IX:55n61	2:24f	IV:1062; VII:239n278
		2:25	I:104(n57); 543n68; II:58; 189; 753; III:384; 847n113; V:798; VI:406n475; 835; VII:331
2:7	IV:338; V:19n136; 20n143; 834n55; VI:491; **876-877** (876n32, n35; 877n36); 878; VIII:205; 363; **IX:53-54** (54n48)		
		2:25ff	VII:238; IX:450
		2:25-35	VII:331
2:7-14	VII:769n20	2:26	I:104(n57); 677; III:1087(n255); IV:113; V:342; VI:408n493; 836; IX:481; 533f; 533n276
2:8	V:638; **VI:499;** IX:241; 243		
2:8-16	II:748n38		
2:8-20	VI:485; **490-491**	2:27	II:671; III:245; IV:1062; V:638; VI:54; 415; 478; VIII:204n133
2:9	I:84, n67; II:247; 248; 749; III:1087, (n255); IV:16; 24; V:351; IX:209		
		2:27f	IV:1062
		2:28	II:762
2:10	II:710n28; 718; 721; 750, n52; III:890; IV:53; V:638; VI:541; 837; IX:212; 360n11; 367	2:28ff	II:457
		2:29	II:48; 409n41; 411; III:585; IV:113; 116; 328n3; 1112n45;

	1118; 1120
2:29-32	V:213; 214; 706; 712
2:30	III:245; V:347; n164; 378; VII:1023
2:30f	II:705; IV:52
2:30ff	VIII:543
2:31	IV:50; VI:777
2:32	III:384; 589; IV:52; 54; V:706, n403; 711; VI:405n467; VII:442n176; IX:344
2:32ab	V:706n403
2:33	III:39
2:33f	IV:643
2:34	I:139; 372; II:762; III:327(n42); 385; 654; IV:271; 272; 276; 277; V:425; VI:167; 541; 756n58; 995n17, n19; VII:201; 230; 238-239 (238n274, n275); 259n393; 345; 353; 354n90
2:34f	VI:541; 995-996; VII:238; 239n278
2:34ff	VII:239n279
2:35	II:97; III:590; 612; IV:525n14; VI:541; 996n20; VII:238n274; IX:641
2:35a	VI:995, n17, n18; 996; VII:238n274; 239n280
2:35b	VII:238n275; 239
2:35ff	VII:343
2:36	II:322n4; 862(n244); 950n42; VI:829; 836; IX:249; 450n96; 462
2:36f	I:788; IX:457
2:36-38	VII:331; IX:450-451
2:36ff	IX:463
2:37	II:41; III:236; 237n28; 245; IX:62; 63; 925; 929; VI:836; VIII:204n133; IX:451; 465n241
2:38	II:58; IV:351; 352; 868n226; V:213; 798; VI:836; VII:327; 331; IX:451; 679
2:39	III:1087(n255); IV:1059n162; 1062; VI:530; VII:726; VIII:60
2:40	III:913; V:446; 638; VI:291; 405, n466; 713, n69; VII:514, n339; VIII:43; 518n12; 519n18; IX:392
2:40-52	V:651; VII:514n339
2:41	V:898
2:41ff	IV:1061
2:41-51	V:899
2:41-52	VII:331
2:42	II:322; 373
2:43	I:703; II:950n42; IV:581; V:637; VIII:84
2:44	I:718, n2; II:667; V:69; 105n5; VII:736n1; 740, n19
2:46	II:139n26; 152; 687; III:236; 245; 440; 443; IV:435n152;

	VIII:204n133; 220n32
2:47	II:460; 687; III:946; VI:291; 713; VII:894n54
2:48	IV:643; V:115; 638; VI:474
2:49	II:22; V:122; 987(n260); 988; VII:331; IX:451
2:50	VII:894n54
2:51	III:612; IV:643; VIII:43; 151
2:52	II:942; V:446; 733; VI:712; 713-714 (713n67); 716; VII:514, n339; IX:392
3	VII:464n35
3:1	I:144
3:1f	III:395; IV:193; VI:836
3:1ff	II:31
3:1-6	IV:193
3:2	III:270, n29; 585; IV:113; 116; 492n53; VI:616
3:3	I:304; 330(n99); 537; II:429; 704, n35; 705; 711; VI:614; 615; 617
3:4	I:616; 625; 748; II:659(n10); IV:112; V:70; VI:830; 832; VII:404n8; 407n20, n21
3:4f	V:486
3:5	IV:193; V:70n93; 888; VI:291; VII:406-407 (407n19); VIII:16; 19; 21
3:5f	V:70n93
3:6	IV:193; V:347n164; 888; 895; VII:124; 1023
3:7	I:672; II:815; VII:52; IX:37, n147
3:7f	IX:37n147
3:7-20	IV:193
3:8	III:117; 848; IV:54; 269; 270-271; 1001(n150); V:638; 847n29; 976n183; VI:81; 635
3:9	III:545; IV:1001n150; V:888; VI:399; 722; 942; 988; VII:238n277
3:10	VI:479
3:10-14	IV:1001; V:795; VIII:224
3:11	I:642; VI:477
3:12	II:152; 153n35; VI:479
3:12f	IV:1001; VIII:103; 104
3:13	V:735; VI:635, n7; VIII:35; 102
3:14	I:465; 537; IV:1001; V:592; VI:479; VII:709; 759
3:15	II:96; 937; IV:51; 456n271; 862; 867; VI:726
3:15f	IX:534
3:16	I:104(n57); 538; 539; IV:335; V:311; VI:418n565; 616; 943
3:17	VI:399; 942; 945; VII:168
3:18	II:719; III:706n45; IV:51; 193; V:422; 795; 796n173
3:19	II:474; VI:53; 479(n109); 562
3:19f	VI:615n66
3:20	VIII:168; 381n340
3:21	IV:51; V:529(n261); 889; VI:414(n532); VII:962

3:21b	VIII:381n340		II:769; 830; 832; VIII:207
3:21f	II:456n35; **V:353;** VI:67(n55);	4:17ff	VI:833
	616; IX:298n99	4:18	I:196; 511; 512; II:348; 710n28;
3:22	I:101n49; 104, (n57); 665; 670;		718; III:7n16; 612; 704; 706;
	II:373; 740, n7; IV:114; 739;		712(n60); 714; 1087;
	931; V:530; 531; 668n81; 701,		V:552n77; 790n137; VI:405;
	n349; VI:405; VII:274; 1059;		**407-408;** 906; 908; **VII:923;**
	VIII:368n238; 381; 394		VIII:19; 286; 287; **290;**
3:22a	VIII:381n340		IX:345n277; 534; 555;
3:23	VIII:363		580n547
3:23ff	II:632	4:18a	VI:906
3:23-38	VII:241n289	4:18b	VI:906
3:24	IV:234, n3	4:18ff	II:59; III:706; V:715
3:29	III:286; IV:234	4:19	III:703n29; 704; 706; 1087;
3:31	VII:464n35; VIII:482n31; 485		IV:1119; V:995n302
3:33ff	II:322n4	4:20	I:618; II:168; III:443; V:347;
3:37	II:559		VII:845; VIII:540
3:38	I:141; VI:405n467;	4:21	I:589; 753; 758; III:588; 701;
	VIII:382n351; 389; 404n21;		712; 713; IV:899; 1119;
	486n49		V:547n31; 552; **554;** VI:295;
4:1	I:104, (n57); IV:932; VI:285;		296; VII:274; VIII:290
	404; 406; 614; 615; 616; 617	4:21ff	II:139
4:1f	VI:19	4:22	III:38; IV:106n147; 496;
4:1ff	I:141; VI:34n58		VI:541; 574; 579; 713n70;
4:1-13	**VI:34-36**		VII:241n287; 699; VIII:363;
4:2	II:72n4; IV:871; 931; VI:34;		IX:392; 393
	VIII:64; 596	4:23	II:433; III:131, n11; 204;
4:2f	VIII:139		205n36; IV:874; V:750; 752;
4:3	IV:269; VIII:381		856; VI:473(n83)
4:4	VI:723; VII:699n59	4:23-27	VI:407
4:5	I:580; III:888; IV:1112; V:158;	4:24	II:59; VI:841; 906; VII:740
	486; VII:660; IX:591	4:25	I:244; 337; 677; II:934, n52;
4:5f	V:895		III:177; 384; 745; IV:640;
4:6	II:79; 237; 567; III:48; V:889;		V:438n391; 529n262; 532;
	VI:35; VII:439n146		VI:15n23; VIII:219;
4:7f	VI:764		IX:450n92
4:8	I:747; III:101n227; IV:62; 63;	4:25f	II:935; IX:450
	V:291n13; 995n302	4:25-27	IX:534n282
4:9	III:236; 242; 640; IV:274n60;	4:26	I:776; II:935n55; IX:450, n92
	VII:331; 646; 649;	4:27	III:384; 424; IV:233; VI:831;
	VIII:204n133; 381		906; IX:450n92
4:10	II:545; IX:240	4:28	III:167; V:419; 420; VI:129
4:11	VI:722; 751; **752**	4:28f	VII:345; 350
4:12	IV:110; V:995n302	4:29	V:484; VI:87n51; 921(n5)
4:13	II:80; III:461; V:299n19;	4:30	VI:574
	VI:35, n62; 36; VII:159n38;	4:31	VI:530; VII:23n183
	331n253; 649; VIII:64	4:31ff	IV:446
4:14	II:301; 540; 679; VI:285, n13;	4:32	II:540; IV:106; VI:713n70; 843,
	405; 407(n487); 408n492;		n390
	IX:534	4:33	II:16; 822; III:428(n12); 900;
4:14b	VI:405n464		IX:294
4:15	II:139; 727; VI:405n464; 906;	4:33-36	VII:830n210
	VII:26; 832, n216; 833	4:34	I:101; 102n51; II:669; 702;
4:16	I:343; II:677; 950; III:524n71;		III:708(n50); IV:874; V:117;
	IV:874; VII:23n183;		VII:833
	831n216; 832n216; 835; 838	4:35	II:626n18; VI:992
4:16ff	I:102; II:139; IV:455; VII:830;	4:36	II:301; 540; 569; III:6;
	832, n218; **VIII:539-540**		428(n12); IV:105; VI:843
4:16-20	VII:21	4:37	V:888, n9; VI:53; 579;
4:16-21	VII:21		VIII:203, n116
4:16-30	VI:410; VII:26	4:38	II:686; VI:54; 957n6; 958;
4:17	I:616; 618, n12, n15; 748;		VII:883

4:38f	VI:956; 958
4:39	I:368; II:626; VI:958
4:40	II:318; III:130; IV:1091; VI:485; 541; VIII:161; 288n129; IX:431
4:40f	III:130
4:41	II:626n17; III:708(n50); 900(n9); V:117; 427; VIII:380; 381n337; IX:531n260; 534
4:42	II:658; 829; VI:573
4:43	I:583; II:22; 710n28; 718; 728n59; III:706; VI:530
4:43f	II:715n90; 718; III:712(n60)
4:44	III:704; 706; VII:830; 832, n216, n220
5:1	III:655; **IV:120-121;** V:586; 734; VII:648
5:1f	VIII:323
5:1ff	III:207; IV:444; 446; 452; VI:101
5:2	IV:946n3; V:734; VI:101
5:3	II:139; III:443
5:4	I:517
5:5	II:66; 622; III:828; IV:106; 107; VI:965n40
5:6	VI:278; 279; 477; VII:746; 962
5:7	II:831; III:800; 804n49; V:735; VI:129; VII:762
5:8	I:304; 329; 330; 331; 362; II:623; 679; III:6; IV:444n213; 1002; V:341n136; VI:628
5:9	II:816n1; III:6; V:887; VII:760; IX:212
5:10	III:6; 804; IV:452; 1107; 1111; 1113; VI:101; VIII:435n266; IX:212
5:11	I:213; V:291; VI:907n203; IX:607n23
5:12	I:682; 738; II:40; V:794n164; VI:163, n15; 286; 776
5:12f	III:48
5:13	II:460; VII:554n31; VIII:288n130, n131
5:14	I:108n64; II:840n63; III:264; 708; IV:502; V:763, n26; VI:54
5:15	I:493; III:130; IV:101
5:16	II:658; VIII:203n123
5:17	I:682; 740n3; II:159; 301; III:204; 443; 1087; VI:407(n486); VII:331; IX:432
5:17-26	IV:715n77
5:18f	IX:64
5:19	I:519; VII:771
5:20	VI:844
5:21	II:96; 98; III:102n245; IX:38
5:22	II:96; 97; 98; III:172; V:342; VI:844
5:24	I:678; 679; III:327(n39);
	IV:574; VIII:457
5:25	III:655; VI:574; VII:743n10
5:26	II:255; 450; III:37; 206; IV:6; V:889; VI:129; VII:274; IX:209
5:27	IV:234; V:345, n155
5:28	VI:907n203; IX:607n23
5:29	II:54, n3; III:656; IV:234; V:588; VI:475(n93); VIII:105n151
5:30	I:733; IV:439n191; VI:723; IX:38; 42
5:31	VIII:312
5:32	II:189; 429; 668; III:488; IV:717; 1001, n155; 1002, n155; VI:842; VII:1103
5:33	II:41; 806; 807; IV:443; 929(n29); 930; VI:140; 480; 916n5; VIII:212n32
5:33-39	V:164n18
5:34	II:818n10; IV:1103, n41; VI:477
5:34f	IV:1099(n3); 1101
5:35	IV:1103
5:36	III:448; V:753; **VII:961;** IX:308
5:36-38	V:718
5:38	VIII:151
5:39	III:45n7; V:163, n6; 718; 719; VI:144n77; IX:487
6	IV:1115; VI:111n57
6:1	VII:23n183; IX:430
6:1-5	**VII:23-24**
6:2-4	VI:905n183
6:3	VI:723
6:4	II:677; III:243
6:5	V:741n2; VII:20; 23; VIII:457
6:6	II:818n10; VII:24n187, n188; 26; 833
6:6-10	VII:830n210
6:6-11	VII:25
6:7	III:130; 637; VIII:147; IX:38
6:8	II:97; 334; 462; VI:844; VII:647
6:9	I:17; 394; II:687; III:485n2; VIII:620n50
6:10	II:460; IV:657n42; VI:480
6:11	III:287; IV:963; VI:129; 478
6:11f	IV:657n42
6:12	II:679; 807; III:102(n244); 436; IV:114; 1124; V:484; 485
6:12f	I:428, n127; II:325
6:13	I:428; 429; III:131; IV:172; V:282
6:13ff	IV:234
6:14	V:282; VI:102
6:15	II:887; III:488
6:17	IV:50; 51; 445; V:588; VI:279; VII:331; 647; VIII:203
6:18	III:130; 428(n12); IV:1091; V:582n1; 586n19
6:19	II:301; III:130; 204; 209; V:586; 727; VI:407(n486); 541; 905n182; IX:431; 432

6:20	I:328; 582; 588; 592; III:593; IV:368; 652; 718(n97); V:377; VI:401; **905-906** (905n182; 906n188); VII:785n91
6:20f	VI:591
6:20-22	IV:368
6:20ff	III:660; IV:454; VI:843
6:20-26	VII:347n51
6:21	I:660; 662; II:228; III:722; 726n10; IV:320; 368; 1115; 1116; VI:14n19; **17-18**; 42n16
6:22	I:364; 528; IV:690; V:240; 270n189; 454, n4; 455n5; VI:152(n35); 555, n60; VIII:439; 442n297; 443n307; 449, n345; 456; 457
6:22f	I:48; IV:699; VI:30; IX:600
6:23	III:726n10; IV:699; 714; V:976n174; VI:477(n102); 835; VII:402; VIII:449n345
6:24	II:825; 828; V:798; VI:18; 328; 401
6:24f	I:660; VI:328; 843; 907
6:24-26	VII:347n50
6:25	I:465; 660; 662; III:722; 724; 725n22; IV:1115; VI:18; 42n16; 43; 130
6:26	I:364; V:976n174; 986; VI:477; 855
6:27	I:46; IV:690; 693; V:991; VI:477
6:27f	IV:934n79
6:27ff	I:46; IV:693
6:27-36	IX:130n162
6:28	I:46; 448; 449; II:763; VI:54
6:29	I:264; VIII:260n3; **263;** 264; 266; 267n56
6:30	I:191; 194
6:31	I:46; III:50; 348; IV:1059n161; V:73
6:32	II:818n9; IV:693; 700n17; IX:130; 169; 392; 393
6:32f	I:46
6:32-34	III:350; VIII:103n146; 224
6:32ff	I:303n138; 328; III:42; 348
6:33	I:17; IX:392; 393
6:34	II:530; 534; III:343; **344-345** (344n10); 448; IX:392; 393
6:35	II:534, n5; III:116(n363); 344n11; 345; IV:693; 700; V:985; 987(n265); VI:558; 559n83; VIII:390; 620; IX:393; 487
6:35a	VIII:390n403
6:35f	V:991; IX:488
6:36	IV:380; V:161; 987n262, (n265); VIII:74n34; 390n403
6:36-38	IX:492n1
6:37	III:622; 923; IV:634
6:37f	VIII:292; IX:492
6:38	I:47(n131); 194n5; II:527n71;
6:38a	900n26; III:825; IV:717; VII:69; IX:164n150 IV:632; 634
6:38b	IV:632; 633; 634
6:39	V:100; 752; VIII:286; **292-293**
6:39f	V:755
6:40	I:476; II:152; IV:442; VIII:292n161; 515
6:41	IV:975; V:344n153; VIII:292
6:41f	V:377
6:42	V:344n153; VI:869; VIII:292; 567n41
6:43	**VII:97;** 754n34
6:43f	VII:754
6:43-45	VII:754n32, n36; 755
6:43ff	IV:310; VII:226
6:44	I:704
6:44a	VII:754n37
6:44b	**VII:753-755** (754n27)
6:45	III:613; VI:63; 555n59; 561; 562; VII:754, n27, n37
6:46	III:487; 1086; 1093; V:987n259; VI:480
6:46ff	VII:754
6:47	II:669; VI:479
6:47-49	I:588; **IV:842-843;** VI:97; **603**
6:47ff	VI:603n65
6:48	III:63; 64; 397; V:138; VII:69
6:49	III:63; VI:167; 479
7	VI:630n54
7:1	II:425; IV:50; 51; 105; 335(n20); VI:297
7:1ff	VI:958
7:1-10	VI:743n168; VII:709
7:2	II:509
7:2ff	II:270n63
7:3	I:403n36; 404; III:287; 376; 377; VI:659n46; 661; VII:864n29; 990; IX:90n14
7:4	I:379n3; V:794; VII:566, n11
7:4f	I:48n135
7:5	II:369; 509n36; IV:52; 53; VII:813; 816n111; 818n123; 830
7:6	I:330n96; 404; III:294; IV:373n3; IX:159; 162
7:7	I:380; IV:107; 638; VIII:368n237; IX:432
7:8	VI:574; VII:709; VIII:28
7:9	II:509; III:40; 384; V:586; 847n29; VII:715; VIII:377n315
7:10	I:83; 403n36; II:552n25; III:209; VIII:312; IX:432
7:11	III:488
7:11ff	III:206
7:11-17	I:370; 784; IX:450
7:12	II:332; IV:643; 739; V:821; VI:876n35; 921; VIII:364; IX:449n81; 450
7:13	III:722; 1093(n268); V:822; VII:555

7:14	II:335; 684; VII:647
7:14f	IV:107
7:15	III:212; IV:643; IX:450n93
7:15f	IV:858n121, n125; 868n222
7:15ff	VI:906n192
7:16	II:334; 605; III:101n230; 848; IV:53; 531; VI:841; 846, n411; VII:234n239; IX:209; 534n280
7:17	II:433; 679; IV:101
7:18	I:66n24; III:500
7:18ff	I:589
7:18-35	VIII:377n315
7:19	I:404; II:670; III:1093(n268); VI:723; 726
7:19f	IV:274n48; VIII:290
7:20	I:404; 545; II:348n54; 670; VI:726
7:21	IV:519; 1091; V:343; VI:558; 904n168; 905, n182; VIII:287; IX:393; 679
7:21f	VIII:290
7:21ff	III:129
7:22	I:66; 589; II:710n26; 718; V:341; 342; 343; 551n75; 552n77; 772; VI:407n484; 905, n182; 906; 908; VII:246; VIII:364
7:23	VI:908n212; VII:344; 349; **350;** IX:393n166
7:24	I:83; IV:51; V:345n155; VII:69
7:25	I:591; II:254; III:848; IV:751n52
7:26	VI:836; 840; VII:234
7:27	II:936n65; 937; III:103n256; V:70; VI:684; 777; 841
7:28	I:587; 672; **IV:534-535;** 653; **VI:839-840**
7:29	I:539; 545; II:213; 214; III:723; 848; IV:50; 51; VIII:103
7:29f	V:86n160; IX:36
7:29ff	I:331n104
7:30	I:635; III:848; IV:1088; VIII:159; IX:38, n150
7:31	I:663; V:189
7:31f	III:845
7:31ff	VII:234n239
7:31-35	**VII:516**
7:32	III:152; 153; 154; 443; 722; 845n100; 848
7:33	I:477; 545; II:822; III:121n10; V:163; VI:140
7:33f	II:669; VIII:212n32
7:34	I:303; 317; 327; V:163; VI:135n4; 140; 141, (n53); VIII:104; 456; 457; IX:42, n177; 159; **161**
7:35	II:214, n13; III:92; 848; V:639; VI:713; VII:516, n352; VIII:457n390
7:36	II:686; 687; VII:796; IX:36, n138; 42; 47n222
7:36ff	IV:801, n8; V:20
7:36-50	III:936; IV:621; V:760; **VI:630-631;** VIII:105; **323-324**
7:37	I:327; 334; 335n13; 704; IV:335(n20); 801
7:37ff	I:304
7:37-50	IX:161
7:38	I:230; III:722; IV:801; V:290; 734; VII:647; VIII:328n95; IX:118n36; 122; 127n137; 139; 140n240
7:38ff	I:784
7:39	I:327; 703; 783; III:488; VI:829; 841; 842; IX:534n280
7:39ff	VI:844
7:40	VI:630
7:41	V:562
7:41f	V:759(n105)
7:42	II:168; V:754; IX:396n194
7:42f	IX:393
7:43	III:923; IV:15; V:449
7:44	V:25n177; 343; VIII:324; IX:139n231
7:44-46	VIII:224; **IX:139**
7:45	VII:232n219; VIII:431; IX:118n36; 119n45; 126n126; 138; 139, n231; 679n28
7:45f	VI:630
7:46	I:230; II:472; III:679; IV:801; VI:630n54; IX:139n231
7:47	I:47, (n129); 53; **V:172;** VI:542; 591; IX:118n36; 128; 139; 391
7:47b	V:172
7:47ff	I:304; 511; III:212
7:50	II:411; 413; 434; III:211; VI:573; 590; **VII:990;** 992; 997; VIII:505
8	V:761
8:1	I:583; II:327(n52); 715n90; 718; 728n59; III:704; 705n36; 710(n59); VI:530n69; VII:794
8:1-3	III:796
8:2	I:493; 784; II:630; III:130; 488; IV:69; VI:558
8:2f	I:784; 787; IV:461
8:3	II:85; 154; V:150n13
8:4	II:66; V:752; 755, n84
8:5	IV:839n56; V:68; 534; 944; VI:170
8:6	VI:97; 170; 988n18
8:6ff	II:702n1
8:7	II:925; VI:456
8:7f	VI:170
8:8	V:552; VI:483
8:9	IV:817n133; V:752
8:9f	VII:894; VIII:150n18
8:10	III:327n43; **IV:817-819;** V:554; 556; 761
8:10a	IV:818n134
8:11	IV:121n202; V:752; VII:546

8:11-15	**IV:121-122**; V:756	8:41	V:341n136; 734; 793n160; 794; VI:163, n15; 529; 628; 630; VII:847, n26
8:12	I:583; IV:586; V:68; VI:216n315; 558; VII:158; **160**; 991; 997		
		8:42	II:322, n11; IV:51; 739, n11; VI:456; 876n35; VIII:504
8:12f	VI:210(n268)		
8:13	I:513; III:147; 461; IV:586; V:299n19; VI:31; 214n291, (n302); 252; 724; 988; VII:345; 349; 350n61; 772; VIII:264	8:43	II:862n252; III:206; 397
		8:44	II:684; III:904; V:290; VI:116n18; VII:647
		8:44f	III:130
		8:45	I:469; II:622; IV:51; V:116n18; VI:102; 965n40; VII:771; 883
8:14	I:385; II:863n262; 919, n59; 921; 924; 925; III:171n36; IV:586; 591; VI:170; 327; 328; 456; 578n2; 907, n204; VIII:264	8:46	I:703; 704; II:301
		8:47	I:66; III:206; IV:50; 51; IX:209
		8:48	II:434; VI:573
		8:49	V:729; VII:847, n26
		8:50	V:822; VII:990; IX:212; 450n95
8:15	II:829; III:612; IV:579; 586; V:554	8:51	IV:643; V:637; 982; VII:771
		8:52	III:725n20; 834; 844, n95; 846
8:16	III:557; 975, n37; IV:326, n21; V:343; VI:578; VII:362; IX:343; 344	8:53	III:845
		8:54	III:911; V:637; IX:303
		8:55	VI:415; VII:726; VIII:34; IX:212n122
8:16b	VIII:155n2		
8:17	III:960; 961; 973; V:553n92; VII:441n157; 743n8; IX:4	8:56	II:460; III:708n48; V:763
		9:1	I:420; 425(n109); 428; 429; II:310; 566; III:131; 496; IV:441n198; 1091
8:17a	IX:3		
8:18	II:827; V:344n153		
8:19ff	IV:643	9:1ff	I:429
8:20	I:66; 144n3; II:827; III:45n8; V:341; VII:647	9:1-6	II:719
		9:2	I:429; 583; 584; III:704; 710(n59); 711; 712, (n60); 714
8:21	I:144n3; IV:121; VIII:43; IX:240	9:3	I:526; V:307; VI:120; 121, n17, n18; 903n164; 969
8:21ff	II:827		
8:22f	VIII:323	9:5	II:429; IV:502; 503; VI:629, n47
8:23	VI:308; VII:70n30; 199; VIII:553		
		9:6	II:720; III:131
8:24	II:622; 683; VI:965n40; VIII:323	9:7	II:936; **VI:838**
		9:7f	II:936; VIII:224
8:25	III:38; IX:209	9:7ff	VII:235
8:27	II:319n2; 818n10; 822; III:293; 626; IV:574; 680; IX:591	9:8	I:487; II:936; IV:858n119, n120; VI:841; 842; IX:2
8:28	I:563; II:40; III:708(n50); 900; VI:163n14; VIII:381; 619; 620n49; IX:294	9:9	VI:53
		9:9ff	VI:615n66
		9:10	I:425; 428; III:488
8:29	II:657; III:428(n12); V:763; VII:856n1; 925 IX:241; 591	9:11	I:583; 703; 704; II:55; III:131; VI:541
		9:12	II:948; IV:51; 338; VI:573(n50)
8:30	IV:68	9:13	IV:50; 51; VI:573(n50)
8:31	I:9; 10; II:424; VII:157n30; VIII:37n2	9:14	V:290; VI:871n4; IX:469
		9:15	VI:477
8:31f	V:794n163	9:16	II:762; III:729n8; IX:411n43; 412n50
8:33	V:470; VI:456; VIII:323		
8:34	I:66	9:17	VI:59
8:35	II:769; III:443; V:346; 734; VI:630; VII:1102	9:18	IV:114; V:66; 587
		9:18-27	VIII:20n61
8:36	I:66; VII:990	9:19	I:487; II:936; III:219n13; 220; IV:858n120, (n121); VI:841; 842
8:37	V:794n163; 889; VI:279; VII:883; IX:209		
8:37ff	IV:444	9:20	III:104(n261); VII:690n27; **IX:532**
8:38	II:425; V:794n164; VII:771; 794, n133		
		9:20-22	VIII:20
8:39	III:37; 703n29; 704; 705; 709, n54; V:174	9:21	II:626; V:763
8:40	II:55; V:586; VI:726	9:22	II:22; 27; 260; 335; III:271;

	IV:274n48; V:107; **913-916**
	(914n71, n78); 919n120;
	920n120; VI:659n46;
	VII:348n53; 864; VIII:457;
	IX:47
9:22f	IV:342n17
9:23	I:84n68; 471; II:669; 950;
	III:49; IV:691n27; V:291;
	VII:348n53; 577
9:23ff	**IV:715**
9:23-27	VIII:20
9:24	I:395; II:727; III:52
9:24a	IX:645n170
9:25	I:395; II:891; III:888; IX:608;
	645, n170; **646-647**
9:26	I:69; 109; III:107n282;
	V:107n15; 208n27; 989,
	n272, n278; VI:451(n836);
	VII:650n31; VIII:223; 457;
	462n422
9:27	I:337; 589; V:360; 367; VI:845;
	926n52; VII:648
9:28	V:484
9:28-36	VII:897
9:29	II:249; 373; 702; IV:247;
	248n46; 249, n51; 758(n15);
	VI:776; VII:666
9:30	**II:938-939**
9:30f	**V:354-355**
9:31	II:939; 940; IV:189n16; 248;
	867; 873; V:107, n15; 354;
	707n405; VI:297; 309;
	VII:62n53; 331; 650n31;
	VIII:175; 381; 462n422; 554
9:31f	II:247; 248
9:31ff	V:354
9:32	I:559; IV:248; VI:102;
	VII:771n27; **897;** VIII:554
9:33	II:622; **938-939;** VI:965;
	VIII:554
9:34	VIII:443n308; IX:209, n106;
	210
9:34b	IV:908; V:354n195
9:35	II:740; IV:114; 144; 189;
	V:668n81; 689n261; 701; 710,
	(n429); VI:714; 847;
	VIII:381; IX:298n97
9:36	I:66; II:769; III:107(n281);
	V:354; 372
9:37	II:948
9:37b	VIII:457n394
9:37-43	V:982
9:38	I:625; II:40; IV:739n11;
	VI:876n35
9:39	II:821n39; III:900; IV:735;
	VII:925
9:41	I:131; 663; VII:407
9:42	II:168; 684; III:428(n12); V:637
9:42f	II:626n19
9:43	IV:452; VI:473(n83);
	VIII:288n134
9:43b	III:37

9:44	V:552; 553; 707n405; VIII:155;
	444; 445n315; 457, n387
9:44a	IV:105n144
9:44b	IV:105n144
9:44f	IV:105n144
9:45	I:116; 188; II:685; III:327n43;
	973; IV:108; V:699n331;
	VIII:224
9:46	II:98; 433; IV:532
9:47	II:97; 98; III:612; V:342; 731;
	VI:844
9:48	I:404(n38); III:547; IV:533n18;
	653n21; 654
9:49	II:622; III:714(n68); V:271;
	277; VI:965n40
9:49f	I:426; 427
9:51	IV:9; VI:50, n38; 308; 309; 574;
	776, n47; VII:331; 656;
	VIII:28
9:51ff	V:20; 92n31
9:51-55	V:847n29
9:51-56	VII:91; 92n31
9:51-18:14	IV:50
9:51-19:27	VI:617; VII:331
9:52	I:83; VI:573(n50); 684; 688; 777
9:53	II:52; VI:776, n47; VII:92; 331
9:54	II:886; 934; 935; III:48; V:532;
	VI:942; 943; VII:91
9:54-56	II:935n59
9:55	II:626; 935n60; IV:105n144;
	VII:92
9:56	I:396; II:669, n17; 935n61;
	VI:574; VIII:461n415;
	IX:639
9:56a	VII:991n109
9:57	IV:445; V:67; VI:574
9:57f	IV:444; 450
9:57-62	VIII:224; IX:129n160
9:58	III:679; V:28; 852n64; VI:574;
	VII:389n11; VIII:456; 457;
	IX:55
9:59	III:547; IV:444; 445; VI:869
9:59f	V:982
9:60	I:68; 583; IV:445n214; V:982
9:60ff	IV:444
9:61	IV:445; VI:869
9:61f	I:213; 214; VIII:33
9:62	I:529; 587; 588; V:290; 291;
	343; IX:430; 644
10:1	I:417n68; 427; II:30; 31;
	III:1093(n268); IV:445; 452;
	VI:530n69; 684; 688; 777;
	VII:863n19; VIII:203
10:1ff	II:634; IV:452, n247; VIII:21
10:2	V:995n302
10:3	I:340; 435n175; IV:310;
	VI:499; 501; VIII:504
10:4	I:499; 525; 526; V:68; 307n30;
	311; 312n8; **VI:120-121;**
	903n164
10:5	I:499; II:411
10:5f	II:413

10:5ff	V:23		III:781; IV:1088; VI:28; 34;
10:6	I:351; 499n23; VIII:365		479; IX:38n150
10:7	I:379; 523n1, (n3); II:596;	10:25ff	IV:535n29; 1062
	III:605; IV:698; V:23n165;	10:25-28	V:755n84; VI:316
	730; VI:141; VII:874n26;	10:25-37	V:755n84
	VIII:35; 212n32	10:26f	VI:316n38
10:9	I:68; 490; 493; 584; II:331; 332;	10:27	II:550; III:101n227; VI:696n27
	III:131; IX:89n10	10:27ff	II:549
10:10	V:68n84	10:27-37	IX:161
10:11	I:584; 704; II:331; III:822;	10:28	II:552n25; 864(n271), (n278);
	IX:89n10		IV:1063; V:449; VI:317n43;
10:11f	VI:629n48		479; 480
10:12	I:359; II:952; IV:715	10:28ff	IV:1064
10:13	III:443; IV:551; V:717;	10:29	II:215; III:46n18; VI:316n36
	VII:61-62; 242	10:29ff	**I:46**
10:13-15	IV:715; VII:516n355;	10:29-37	V:847n29
	VIII:377n315	10:30	II:318; 657; IV:15; **261**; V:66;
10:13ff	VI:843		VI:173; 612; VII:328;
10:14	I:359		VIII:160
10:15	I:148; VIII:608	10:30ff	III:547; IV:261n24
10:16	I:426; II:349(n60); III:708;	10:30-35	V:15; VIII:221
	V:556n128; VII:1071n447;	10:30-37	V:752; 760; VII:91; 92
	VIII:159	10:31	V:66
10:17	I:427n115; 430; IV:452; V:271;	10:31f	III:264
	277; VII:772; VIII:42;	10:31ff	V:341n136
	IX:367	10:32	IV:241; VIII:202
10:17f	VII:160	10:33	V:65n64; 69n89; VII:554
10:17-20	VIII:42n16	10:34	I:230; II:472; III:201; 204;
10:18	I:505; II:80; III:103(n249); 213;		213n62; IV:1095;
	426n80; IV:47n84; 130n220;		V:19(n135); 20n143; 25; 164;
	V:345; 346n161; 353; 533;		IX:54n46; 496n3
	540n12; VI:163; 843;	10:34f	V:20
	VII:157; 158, n32;	10:35	I:426n8; 528; II:168
	IX:544n333	10:36	**IV:261**; V:754; 755n84;
10:18-20	II:457		VI:316n36; VIII:221
10:18ff	V:533n308	10:36f	V:15
10:19	I:161; II:310, n86; 566; 569;	10:37	II:483; V:754; VI:477;
	814; III:400n18; V:32; 579;		573(n50); VII:91; 772n35;
	943; VII:158		VIII:505n7
10:20	I:620; **769-770**; II:538; III:213;	10:37a	VI:317n43
	V:281; 513(n106); 521; 532;	10:37b	VI:317n43
	VIII:42; 462n416; IX:366;	10:38	VI:530; IX:165n157
	367	10:38ff	V:20; 23
10:21	I:21; 104, (n57); 679; II:747;	10:38-42	IX:165
	748n40; III:116(n366); 886;	10:39	I:784; III:488; 1093(n268);
	945; 973; 1087; IV:920;		IV:105; VI:630
	V:214; 516n143; 984n247;	10:39f	I:144
	985n251; 995; VI:405, n470;	10:40	I:376; II:85; 87; 154; VI:56;
	408n489; 844; VII:893;		VIII:328n95
	894n54; IX:679	10:40ff	I:332n114
10:21f	V:947; 992; **VII:516-517;**	10:41	III:1093(n268); IV:591; VI:56
	893n44	10:41f	IV:592
10:22	I:633; 704; II:171; 348, n58;	10:42	II:435; III:331; IV:172
	V:36n247; 889; 895; 989,	11	V:69
	n271; 992n288; 993n288;	11:1	II:141n33; 144; 802; 804;
	VIII:372n276; 373n276; 381		IV:442; 456, n264; 930
10:23	V:342; 347; 378; VI:843	11:1-13	III:619; IX:161
10:23f	V:214; 343; 553n89;	11:2	I:6(n8); 111; 499(n20); 584;
	VIII:150n18; IX:534n280		II:537; 667; 669; III:55n11;
10:24	I:577; III:45n8; V:342; 347;		119; V:513n112, n118;
	816n14; VI:833; 843		519n165; 520; VI:410; 545n7;
10:25	I:368; II:424; 864(n274);		VIII:366; 620n50; IX:89n10

11:3	II:590; 597n56; 950; **VII:272**
11:4	I:47(n132); 295; V:562; 563; 565n1; 888; **VI:30-31** (31n41, n44); 561n101
11:5	II:822n41; IX:159, n113; 161; 164n148
11:5ff	III:435; V:20
11:5-8	V:752; 759; **IX:161; 164,** n147; 450n89
11:6	V:69; IX:159; 161
11:7	I:368; III:173; 829; 945; V:638; VII:783n81; IX:159n113; 450
11:8	IX:159; 161; 164n147; 167n177
11:9	**III:955**
11:9f	II:769; VIII:224
11:10	**III:955;** IV:7
11:10ff	I:192
11:11	IV:269; **V:579-580** (579n148)
11:11-13	V:991; 992
11:12	I:101
11:13	I:104(n57); II:166; V:98n6; 117; 513n112; 520; 521; 538n17; 638; 986; 987(n265); 989n276; VI:409; 554
11:14	III:37; VIII:287
11:14ff	VII:235
11:14-23	VIII:377n315; IX:532
11:14-54	VII:235n240
11:15	I:489; III:714(n68)
11:16	III:714(n69); V:531; VI:34; 847; VII:230; 234; 235; VIII:150n18; IX:161n126
11:16ff	VII:235
11:17	I:580; IV:281n9; 968, n5; VI:162; 165n21; 844
11:17f	IV:944
11:17ff	IV:715n77
11:18	I:581; 605; V:299n18
11:19	III:714(n68); 943; IV:443
11:20	I:528; 584; 610; II:20; III:103(n250); 116n369; IV:718; VI:158; 398; 958; VIII:150n18; IX:91n27; 534n280
11:20-22	**III:399-401**
11:21	II:411; III:401; VII:362; IX:241
11:21f	V:713n454a
11:21ff	III:213; V:895
11:22	II:681; III:401; **IV:944;** V:300; 713, n460; VI:6
11:23	VI:492n72; 498; **VII:420,** n10; IX:38; 129n158
11:24	V:125
11:24ff	VII:226
11:25	I:349; III:867
11:26	I:349; II:630; 631; 697; 702n1; IV:69; V:154; VI:558; 867
11:27	III:787; IV:363; 367; 369; V:347; IX:240; 293
11:27f	I:785
11:28	**IV:121;** 368; 369; 643; VIII:145n48; **IX:240**

11:29	I:663; III:36; VI:555; VII:233n227; 234, n240; 235; 236; VIII:150n18
11:29b	VIII:449n348
11:29f	**III:408-410; VII:233-234;** 345; 465n38
11:29ff	VII:234
11:29-32	III:409; VIII:377n315
11:30	I:663; III:408; 409, n23, n26; 410n29, n30; VII:29n226; 234; **VIII:449-450;** 457; 458, n395
11:31	I:590; 663; 679; VI:713; VII:234; **465;** 516; VIII:458n395
11:31f	III:409; 951; VII:465n39; 796
11:32	I:663; II:428; III:408; 715; VI:713; 842; VII:62; 234; 465n38; 516n335; VIII:457
11:33	III:331n78; 960; 975, n37; IV:326, n22, n23; V:343; VI:578; IX:343n261; 344
11:34	IV:326; V:377; **VI:555-556;** VII:416
11:34f	VI:556n64
11:34-36	V:175; VII:416; **441**
11:35	IV:326n23; VI:555; VII:415; **416,** n12
11:36	I:505; IV:326n23; 595; V:174; VI:555; 556; VII:416
11:37	II:686; 687; V:732; IX:36, n138; 42; 161n123
11:37f	I:328
11:37ff	VIII:567n45; IX:42
11:37-44	IX:38
11:37-52	IX:42n184
11:37-12:1	IX:38
11:38	I:530; III:38; IV:301; VI:685
11:39	II:699; III:1093(n268); IV:1109; VI:141; 149; 290; 565; VIII:567n45
11:39f	VI:148; **149;** VIII:567n45
11:39-41	VI:149; IX:41n170
11:39ff	IX:41, n173
11:39-42	I:741
11:40	III:1028; VI:713; **IX:230-231**
11:40f	VI:149n15
11:41	II:486, n9; III:425; VI:870n8; 905n181; IX:399n223
11:41a	IV:382n56
11:42	I:47n133; 509; II:22; 482n90; 682; III:942; **IV:66;** 975; VI:159n2; VIII:567n45; IX:41n168
11:42-52	VI:843
11:43	I:45(n126); 498; 741n14; VI:870; VII:820; 833n227; IX:116n23; 128; 129
11:44	I:741; IV:681, n3; VIII:567n45; IX:35n136
11:45	VIII:305; 307
11:45f	IV:864n197; 1088; IX:38n150

11:45-12:1	IX:38		12:10	I:104(n57); II:431; III:107n282;
11:46	I:741; IX:86			VI:405; **407-408** (408n492,
11:46ff	II:142			n495); **VIII:442-443**
11:46-52	I:741			(443n303); **452-453;** 457,
11:47	IV:681; V:138; VIII:567n45			n388; 458; 459n406
11:47f	V:976n174; VI:835		12:10a	VI:405n465
11:47-51	VI:835		12:11	II:565; VII:831; 834, n230;
11:48	II:645; IV:489; 491			867n47; VIII:44n27; IX:64
11:49	I:428; 756; II:230; III:92; 981;		12:11f	I:434(n173); IV:235n8; VI:142;
	992; IV:110; V:611; VI:713;			VII:514n340; VIII:60n19
	835; VII:329n238; 515		12:12	I:104(n57); II:22; V:987n263,
11:49-51	V:993n288; **VII:515**			(n265); VI:406, n473; 407;
11:50	I:173; 663; III:328n46; 620;			408n492; 444n767; IX:679
	885; 1029		12:13	I:145; III:781
11:50f	I:173; II:895		12:13f	IX:240n24
11:51	I:394; 663; III:182; V:124		12:13ff	I:426n10
11:52	I:186; 583; 587; 706; II:677;		12:13-21	IV:843
	III:747-748; 856; IV:1088;		12:14	III:444; 942n1
	VIII:567n45; IX:38n150; 47,		12:15	II:861n241; 862(n252), (n253);
	n226; 48, n231			VI:59; 140; 271; 907; IX:240
11:52a	III:748		12:15ff	IV:389
11:52b	III:748		12:15-21	IV:591; VI:18
11:53	II:828		12:16	V:752; VI:328
11:54	III:637; V:472; 473; VII:699		12:16ff	I:395; IX:240n24
12:1	II:906; III:705; V:556n119;		12:16-20	III:940; V:759
	944; VIII:567n45; IX:37		12:16-21	III:17; V:752
12:2	V:553n92; 856; **VII:743,** n7, n8;		12:17	II:96; 539; VI:476
	IX:4		12:17f	VII:422
12:2f	III:973; VIII:567n45;		12:18	I:11; 685n8; III:412; V:138;
	IX:345n274			VI:476
12:3	I:372; III:697; 704; **705;**		12:18f	VI:410
	709n55; V:553, n96		12:19	I:350; 465; II:426; 693; 774,
12:3f	**VII:441**			n38; VI:139n44; 140; 328;
12:3ff	VII:743			**IX:640-641**
12:4	III:399; 705; VI:62; 477(n102);		12:19ff	III:101(n235)
	IX:159; 161; 162; **163,** n141;		12:20	I:194; II:861n241; 862(n259);
	167n177; 170; 646n179			III:117; VI:140(n46);
12:4b	IX:646n179			IX:164n150; 231; 608; 638;
12:4f	IV:716; VI:947; VII:1082;			**647**
	IX:163; 210; 217; 608;		12:21	II:431; III:101(n235); 138;
	646-647			V:552n82; 755n85; VI:328;
12:5	I:658; II:424; 567; III:399;			907
	IV:714; V:423; VII:743(n9);		12:22	IV:631; VI:140
	1058n361; IX:646n179		12:22-31	VI:501n19; VII:464
12:6	II:747n35; IV:677n9; V:986;		12:24	IV:975; V:986; VI:542n38
	987n263, (265); VII:731		12:25	II:942
12:6f	V:991; **VII:731-732**		12:26	II:942; IV:657
12:7	VI:542n38		12:27	II:237; IV:415; 975; VII:464
12:7b	VII:731; 732		12:28	IV:631; 561n104; VII:273
12:7c	VII:732		12:28ff	VI:158
12:8	II:747; V:208, n27; 211;		12:29	IV:591n14; **630-631;** VI:139;
	1010n392; VIII:372, n268;			870n8; VII:465
	439; 442; **447;** 457, n388; 458;		12:29ff	VI:141
	IX:567n474		12:30	II:370; III:888; 892n89;
12:8f	I:84; V:217; 987n259;			V:987n262, (n265); 992;
	VI:407n483; VIII:449n345;			VI:140
	IX:164n151; 538n302		12:30f	V:995n300; VI:139
12:9	I:471; III:107n282; V:216; 217;		12:31	I:588; VI:19; 20; 870n8
	VI:405n465; VIII:442n298;		12:32	I:582; 587; II:105; 741; 742;
	447n330; 456n385			III:520; 631; 654; 718; V:75;
12:9a	I:471			987; 988n266; 995n300;
12:9b	I:471			VI:493; 499; **501,** n19

12:33	I:525; 526; II:332; 486, n9; 647; III:138; 796; IV:715; V:720; VI:479; 591; 905n181; VII:277; IX:102
12:33f	III:137; IV:714; V:438; VI:907
12:34	VII:277
12:35	IV:326, n24; 327n32; V:306; 496; VII:168
12:35f	I:589
12:35ff	IV:448
12:35-38	V:866; IX:679
12:35-40	V:496
12:35-59	III:956
12:36	I:648; II:58; **III:956;** IV:337
12:36a	VIII:451n360
12:36-38	VIII:462n422
12:36ff	I:654
12:37	II:84; 338; III:178; 1086; V:20; 25; 306; VIII:448; 451n360; IX:680
12:37b	V:306n23
12:37f	IV:369; IX:243
12:37ff	II:270n64
12:39	II:338; III:755; IX:679
12:39f	IV:1104; V:759
12:39-46	V:866(n46)
12:40	II:338; 706; V:754; VIII:457; IX:679
12:41	V:755; VI:723; VIII:264
12:41ff	VIII:264n32
12:42	III:131; 444; 461; 1086; V:150, n9; 151; VI:140n46; 204; VIII:264; 542
12:42ff	IV:448
12:42-46	IV:547; 714; 1104; VIII:451n360
12:43	II:770; IV:369; V:150
12:44	I:337; III:444; IV:716
12:45	IV:547; V:638; VI:139n44; 140; VIII:263, n26
12:45f	V:150; VIII:268
12:46	III:853; IV:596; 597; V:429; VI:204; 726; VIII:568; IX:679
12:47	III:57; 59; VI:476; 724; VIII:260n3
12:47f	I:703
12:48	I:191; 194; 379; II:892, n2; III:57; **V:173;** VI:62; 476; VIII:163
12:48b	V:856
12:49	I:678; II:667; 668; III:49; V:756; 866; VI:942; 943; **944; VII:884-885** (884n72)
12:49f	I:140; **VI:944; VII:884-885;** VIII:20; 434n258; 444
12:50	I:172n1; 538; 539; 545; V:436; VI:153n40; 399n418; **944;** VII:880n30; **884-885** (884n72, n73; 885n77); VIII:59; 439
12:51	I:678; IV:526; VI:942
12:51ff	II:668; VII:345
12:52	IV:1111; 1113; 1115; VIII:435n266
12:52f	IV:1063; VIII:219
12:53	IV:643; 1099, (n3); VIII:364; IX:319n56
12:54	I:351; III:459; IV:903
12:54f	III:408n14
12:54-56	V:752; 756; 759; VII:230n208; 757; **VIII:567,** n41
12:54ff	III:212
12:55	III:644; VI:452
12:56	I:678n5; 703; II:260; III:460; IV:1115, n59; V:117; 514n124; 534; 754; VI:777; VIII:150n18; 567n41
12:57	II:188
12:58	I:253; 374; III:942; V:67; VI:529; **642;** VIII:504; **539**
12:58f	V:755; 759
12:59	II:168; 697
13	III:859; IX:55n63
13:1	I:66; III:181; 461; IV:1115n59; V:859; VII:535
13:1f	IV:1095
13:1-3	V:899
13:1ff	III:204; IV:715n77
13:1-4	I:303n138
13:1-5	IV:714; 716
13:1-9	VII:26
13:2	I:329; V:565; 734; 910; 912
13:2ff	V:431
13:3	I:394; IV:1002; VI:842; 955n15
13:4	I:329; V:153; 565; 734; 910; VI:162; 955; VII:328
13:5	I:394; IV:1002; VI:842
13:6	III:615; VII:753n20
13:6f	II:671; 769; 892
13:6ff	II:892; V:435
13:6-9	V:752; 754; 759; 813; VI:20; **VII:755-756** (756n44, n45); 757
13:7	I:452; III:858; 859; V:429; 436; VIII:220
13:8	I:510; III:547; 1086; V:432n356; VI:56
13:9	II:427; 433; III:858; 859; V:429n336; 436; VI:483
13:10	VII:21; 26; 831n212; 832, n216
13:10ff	I:784; III:212; IV:454; VII:818; 833; IX:41
13:10-17	I:784; **VII:25-26;** 830(n210)
13:11	I:493; II:16; 18; 80; 427; 822; III:204; V:814n1; VII:159n41; VIII:67
13:12	I:777; VII:159n41; VIII:67
13:12f	I:493
13:13	III:130; VII:159n41; VIII:161; 288n129; IX:431
13:13f	II:626
13:14	II:21; 22; 950; III:130; 945; VII:20; 831; 847

13:15	III:1093(n268); IV:336; V:286; 287; VI:159n4; VII:25; 26; VIII:364n209, n210; 567n41; **IX:53**	13:33f	VI:835
		13:34	III:49; 52; IV:714; V:639; VII:327; 329n236; 842n5
13:15f	VIII:567; IX:638n130	13:34f	V:993n288; **VII:328-329** (329n235); 515
13:16	I:9; 784; II:18; 22; 60; 80; 950; III:400; IV:336, n8; 1095; V:579; VI:959; VII:20; 25; 158; 159; 162; VIII:67	13:35	II:657; 762; 928; IV:274n48; 883n12; V:428n333; 866(n46); VII:329
13:17	I:190; II:254; III:655; VIII:124; 288n134; IX:366; 367	14	III:489n1
		14-18	VI:907
13:17b	VII:26	14:1	VII:21; 26; VIII:147; IX:36, n138; 42; 47n222
13:18	V:189; 751; 754		
13:18f	VII:289; **290-291**	14:1ff	III:955; IV:454; V:20; IX:41
13:19	III:720; 810; V:766n8; VI:163n9; VII:288n13; 289; VIII:518n7; 519n18	14:1-6	VII:25; **26**
		14:2	VIII:315; IX:116n20
		14:3	II:561; III:130; 945; IV:1088; VII:26; IX:38n150
13:19a	VII:290n34	14:3f	VII:20
13:20	V:189	14:4	III:130; IV:9; IX:431
13:20f	I:585	14:5	II:950; V:286; 287; VI:163; VII:20; 21; 24, n197; 25n201; 26; VIII:364; IX:53; 638n130
13:21	II:905; III:958; 973; IV:655n35		
13:21a	VII:290n34		
13:22	V:69n89; VI:473; 530n69; VII:328; 331	14:6	III:945; VI:723
		14:7	III:488; IV:172; V:755; VIII:16; IX:129
13:23	V:71; VII:991; 992n114		
13:23f	I:588n79; IV:716; **VI:922-923**	14:7f	VI:870
13:23ff	I:392; III:725	14:7ff	I:331(n106); III:581; V:21
13:24	I:137, n13; 611; 612; II:677; 893; III:397; 955; V:70; 71; 73; 74; 75, n118; **VII:605-606** (605n13)	14:7-11	VII:26; VIII:7; 16n39
		14:7-24	IV:187
		14:8	I:648; III:488; VI:871n5; IX:303
13:24f	III:178	14:8ff	I:655; VI:871
13:25	II:49; III:173; 174; 945; 955; 956; V:71; 117; VI:923; VII:647	14:8-11	IV:714
		14:9	I:190; II:830; III:488; VII:772; VIII:205; IX:159n113
13:25f	VII:515n350	14:9f	II:698
13:25ff	IV:1105	14:10	I:377n5; II:237; III:488; VI:573(n50); VIII:191n33; 205; IX:159n113; 160n119; 164, n148; 167n177; 303
13:26	II:693; VI:139n43		
13:26f	III:955		
13:27	I:153; 154; II:644; V:117; 429; VII:874n27; 948n80; VIII:506; IX:136n210	14:11	I:330n97; IV:654; VI:328; **VIII:16-17** (16n39); 608; IX:160n119; 164
13:28	I:642; III:725; 726, n6; IV:347; 715; 839n56; V:361; 429	14:12	I:145; II:34; 169; III:488; 496; VI:328; 475(n93); VII:740; IX:159; **160-161;** 303
13:28f	I:587; VI:18; 833n346; 868		
13:29	I:352; II:337; 729; 928; V:20; VIII:458n397	14:12f	IX:303
		14:12-14	III:547; V:21; VI:328; VII:26; IX:160n119; 161
13:30	II:698; VI:868, n14		
13:30b	VI:542	14:12ff	V:20; VI:328
13:31	III:46n18; V:714; VI:573; IX:36n139; 679, n31	14:13	II:54; III:488; V:347; VI:475(n93); 906, n191; 908; VIII:287n119; 288
13:31f	VIII:454		
13:31-33	**VII:273;** 329n233; IX:36	14:13f	VIII:287
13:32	III:204; V:715; VIII:84, n33; 221; 439; 444(n310); 445n315	14:14	I:151; 371; II:169; 190, n65; III:17n72; 902; IV:369; IX:160n119
13:32f	II:949n32		
13:33	I:394; II:22; IV:487; 868n222; V:707n405; 714, n469; VI:573; 574; 841; 843; 844; **VII:273; 328-329** (329n235); 331; VIII:84n33; 221n35; 439; 444n310	14:15	I:477; 587; II:691; 695; IV:367; V:25
		14:15-24	IV:843; VI:328; VII:26
		14:16	III:488; V:755; VI:476
		14:16f	IV:180

14:16ff	I:655n44; II:34; V:20; 25; 442	15:5	VI:492n65; VIII:160
14:16-24	I:588	15:5f	II:769
14:17	II:669; 705; III:488; IX:677	15:5-7	IX:367
14:18a	I:195	15:6	I:394; II:319; III:496, n2;
14:18b	I:195		VI:486; IX:159; 160; 161
14:18f	II:686	15:7	I:303; 329; 507; II:189; 538;
14:18-20	VI:139; VIII:223		III:92n135; IV:347; 717;
14:18ff	II:702		1002; VI:242; 492; VIII:104;
14:19	I:195; II:256		IX:164n151; 364; 367n70
14:20	I:651; 652; II:669	15:8	I:394; 776; II:37; 892; IV:327
14:21	I:66; II:49; **V:68-69;** 108, n18;	15:8f	II:769; VII:991
	347; 428; 430; 435; 438; 442;	15:8ff	I:784; IV:1060
	VI:906, n191; VIII:287,	15:9	II:319; III:496, n2; IX:160; 161
	n119; 288	15:9f	IX:367
14:21-23	IX:161	15:10	I:85; 303; 329; II:747n35;
14:23	I:612; III:178; 1086; **V:68-69;**		IV:347; 1002; VIII:104;
	108; 755		IX:164n151
14:24	I:676; II:34; III:488; IV:187;	15:11ff	I:330n98; 332(n115); IV:621;
	V:754; VI:328;		717; 1060; V:753
	VIII:212(n33)	15:11-32	IV:347; 761; V:759; 947; 990;
14:25-33	V:714		**994-995** (994n294); **VII:554;**
14:26	I:145; 588; IV:643; **690-691**		**794;** VIII:364
	(690n24; 691n27, n30); 693;	15:12	I:184; 529; IV:595; V:983; 984,
	V:983; IX:75n13; 129, n157;		n243
	130n164; 638; 642n155; 644	15:12f	IV:898
14:26f	I:48; IV:450; 560(n48)	15:13	I:507n4; II:863(n261);
14:26ff	IV:442		V:852n64; VII:422
14:27	I:214; 596; II:669; V:291;	15:14	III:398; VIII:597
	VI:152(n35); VII:577;	15:15	III:822; VI:534; 573(n50)
	578n51; IX:58n10	15:16	III:170; 787; VI:18
14:28	III:46n18; 444; V:138; 634n20;	15:17	II:425; 668; IV:701; **V:983-984;**
	VI:869; **955; IX:607**		VI:59
14:28-32	I:588; V:760; VII:291n41	15:17ff	I:331; IV:1002
14:29	III:63; V:346; 634; VI:955	15:18	I:303; 331; II:431; III:92n135;
14:31	I:577; II:538; 667; III:444; 626,		V:512; **519-520; 521,** n184;
	n3; VI:514n93; 869; IX:469		852n64; VI:552; 573
14:32	II:412; 686; VI:724	15:19	I:379; III:488; IV:701; 1062;
14:33	III:796; IV:1002; V:755; 889;		VI:476
	VI:591; 907; 908(n209);	15:20	II:669; 862n252; IV:374;
	VIII:33; IX:607		VII:554; VIII:232; IX:138;
14:34	IV:832; **837-839** (839n50);		139; 144n267
	V:856	15:21	I:303; 331; 379; II:431;
14:34f	I:229; V:759		III:92n135; 488; IV:701n24;
14:35	I:527; V:552		**V:519-520; 521;** VIII:365
15	I:395; **IV:1060;** 1061;	15:21-24	VI:19
	V:984n243; 990; 992; 994,	15:22	II:319; V:311; VII:690;
	n294; 995; IX:487		VIII:399n13; IX:430
15:1	I:303; II:332; 372; VIII:103;	15:22f	IX:144n267
	104	15:23	II:693; III:181; IV:761
15:1f	IV:347; 444; 1060; V:755;	15:23f	II:774
	994n297; VI:19; 141(n53);	15:23ff	V:20
	VIII:105n157; IX:42	15:24	I:394; II:769; 863(n267); 872;
15:1ff	V:755n84		III:17(n76); IV:893; 1062;
15:1-7	VIII:601		VI:500n18; VII:92n26; 690;
15:1-32	VIII:105; 224		991; VIII:365
15:2	I:303; 328; 733; 735; II:57, n2;	15:25	II:332; VI:652; IX:307n14; 308
	693; VII:796; 832; 855; IX:38	15:25ff	I:332n114; IV:1060; V:991
15:3ff	IV:1060; 1062	15:26	III:46n23; 500; V:638
15:4	I:394; II:657; V:483n94; VI:499	15:27	I:145; III:181; IV:761; VIII:312
15:4f	III:556n84	15:28	III:46n25; V:420; 422n209;
15:4-6	VI:490; VII:991		795n166; 817n12; VII:554
15:4-7	VI:490; **492**	15:28ff	I:331(n108)

15:29	II:547; 682; 774; III:945; V:983; VII:794; IX:159; 161
15:29f	VII:796
15:30	I:507; II:669; 862n252; III:181; IV:761; V:984; VI:590; VII:794; VIII:365n212
15:31	V:442n409; 638; 653; 949; 983; 984, n243; 997; VII:794
15:32	I:145; 394; II:22; 769; 774; 863(n267); 872; IV:893; 1062; VI:500n18; VII:690; 991; VIII:365, n312; IX:366; 367; 646(n177)
16	I:157; V:753n61
16:1	II:71; V:149; 150; 755; VI:328; VII:422
16:1ff	VIII:21
16:1-7	IV:390; VII:379n62
16:1-8	V:760
16:1-13	IV:843
16:2	II:167; IV:104; IX:303
16:2ff	V:151
16:3	I:190; III:1086; VI:475
16:4	I:703; VI:475; VII:379n62
16:5	III:500; 1086
16:5-7	IX:164
16:6	II:471; III:443
16:6f	I:744; 764
16:8	I:155; 157; 205; 663; II:587n2; III:1086; 1093(n268); V:150; 734n61; 755n85; VI:475; VIII:365, n220; 515; IX:233n78; 234; 345; 350n323
16:8a	IX:234n82
16:8f	I:156n10
16:9	I:147; 149; 155; 157; 194n5; 209; II:559n13; III:331(n77); 962; IV:388; 390; 714; 716; V:25; VI:328; 907; VII:378-379 (378n60; 379n60, n62); IX:159; 164, n151
16:10	I:152; 157; IV:656; 657; V:172n8
16:10f	IV:388; V:151; VI:204(n231)
16:10-12	IV:657n42; VI:907
16:11	I:152; 157; 249; III:943n2; IV:388; 390; VI:204
16:11b	V:542n27
16:12	I:157; 265
16:13	II:270-271; 827; III:632; IV:690; V:209; VI:158
16:14	IV:796; 799; V:282; VI:149
16:14f	VI:906n193
16:14-18	I:612; VI:328
16:15	I:600; 703; II:190; 214; 215; III:111n307; 612; 613; IV:799; 1061; V:313n8; VIII:568
16:15b	VIII:608
16:16	I:137; 583; 588; 609; 612-613;

	756n28; 760; II:424; 710n26; 718; 719; 728n59; VI:839; 840; 899; 1059; 1061; 1007n9; V:889; VI:832; VII:606; VIII:435n266; IX:534n280
16:16-18	VI:907n202
16:17	I:678; II:548; 682; V:515n138; VI:164; 907
16:17f	IV:1061
16:18	I:650n14; IV:729; 733
16:19	I:152; II:319n2; 774; III:593; 943n2; IV:17; 246
16:19-21	IV:843n85
16:19ff	III:723; 1103; IV:389; 1119n81; V:753; VI:907; 946n96
16:19-26	V:759
16:19-31	I:148; 377n9; III:940; IV:716; V:752; VI:18; 139; 328; 906
16:20	VI:722; 906; 921
16:21	III:170; 1103; VI:18; 162; 328; VIII:212; 323
16:22	I:84; II:424; IV:580; V:99; 976n183; VI:328; 906; VII:781
16:22f	III:825-826; IX:647, n182
16:22ff	I:9; IX:656
16:22-31	V:769n37
16:23	I:147; 148, (n14); 149; 563; II:538; III:16; 826n12; 938n66; IV:373; V:377; 769, n37
16:23b	V:769n39
16:23-26	V:769n39
16:24	I:530; 721; II:228; 485n102; III:826; V:115; 961; 976n183; IX:303
16:24f	V:115
16:24ff	I:9; VIII:323
16:25	III:480; IV:677; 1113n49; 1119; V:115; 638; 799; VI:18; 328
16:26	I:9; 147; 148; V:313n8; 769n39; VII:656
16:27	V:976n183
16:27-31	V:759
16:28	I:145; 563; IV:512; 716; VI:947; VIII:207
16:29	I:756n28; IV:849n1; 864; 865; VI:832
16:30	V:976n183
16:30f	IV:1002
16:31	I:756n28; IV:864; 865; VI:4; 832; 906n195
17	II:670n20; VIII:458n399
17:1	IV:382n56; V:440; VII:344n31; 347-348
17:1f	III:725n23; VII:344; 347; IX:647n184
17:2	III:656; IV:268n3; 269, n4; 651; 652n19; VI:992; VII:347; 351-352; IX:75
17:2-5	VII:347
17:3	II:432; 625

17:3f	I:511; IV:999		437n283; 450; 451; 457; 458, n396, n399
17:4	II:432; 631, n29; VI:722; VII:726	17:24b	VIII:433n251
17:5	I:428; III:1093(n268); VI:715; VII:289n25; VIII:168	17:25	I:663; II:22; 24; 260; IV:274n48; V:707n405;
17:6	I:223; II:826n58; III:810; 1093(n268); IV:381; V:483n95; VI:206(n242), n243; 991; **VII:289-290** (289n25; 290n28); **758,** n3		**913-916** (914n73, n76; 915n78, n83); 918n109; 919n120; 924; VI:869; VIII:444; 456n387; 457n387, n393; 458n398
17:7ff	I:45; II:270n65; 693; IV:1060	17:26	VIII:434, n257; 435; 450; 451; 457; 458, n398, n399
17:7-10	III:936; **IV:718;** V:760		
17:8	II:84; 692; V:306	17:26b	VIII:433n251
17:9	V:152n2; VI:476; VIII:35; IX:392	17:26f	IV:1104; V:866(n46); VIII:434n257; 450
17:10	V:152n2; 562; 563; VI:480; VIII:35	17:26-29	V:759
		17:26-30	V:756; VI:942
17:11	II:69; VII:331	17:26-31	III:481n38
17:11ff	II:805; III:212; VII:246	17:27	I:650; 651; 652; III:61n31; VI:139; VII:140n311; VIII:212n32; 236; 458n398
17:11-19	V:847n29; VII:91; 92		
17:12	III:626; VII:647		
17:12ff	III:206; IV:234	17:27f	II:693
17:13	II:485(n102); 622; III:287; VI:965n40; VIII:288n126; IX:293	17:28	VI:139; VIII:434; 451
		17:28f	VIII:477n517
		17:28-30	VII:434n257
17:14	II:462; III:201; 264; 424; IV:233; V:341n136; 841; VI:573(n50)	17:29	V:532; VI:942
		17:30	II:953; III:580; **VIII:434-435** (434n257); 450; 452; 457; 458, n396, n399
17:14a	VIII:504		
17:14b	VIII:504	17:31	V:290; 291; VII:726
17:15	III:723; V:342; VII:772; IX:293	17:32	IV:682; IX:644
17:15f	II:462	17:33	I:395; II:874; VI:152(n35); VII:991n105; VIII:443n308; IX:129n160; 130; 608; 642, n156; **643-644**
17:16	VI:163, n15; 628; 776; VII:92; IX:411		
17:16b	VI:317n43		
17:17	III:424	17:34f	IV:13
17:17ff	III:208; 212	17:35	V:866(n46)
17:18	I:266; II:769; V:15; VII:91n17; 92	17:37	II:34; V:866(n46); VI:166; VII:842n5; 1057
17:19	I:368; III:211; VI:206n240; VII:990	18	I:626; IV:184; VII:885n77
		18:1	II:22; 25; III:486; V:755n84; VI:723; VIII:434n259
17:20	I:584; II:687; III:118; VII:757; **VIII:149-151** (150n18); IX:89n10	18:1ff	I:784
		18:1-8	III:619; V:752; 760
17:20f	I:585; II:670; VI:997n26; VII:32n247; VIII:148n17; 149n8, n10; **150-151;** IX:364n39; 534n280	18:2	I:171; III:942; IX:212
		18:2-5	IV:380; **IX:449-450;** 458
		18:3	I:375; II:443; 444; IX:451n100
		18:3ff	IX:451
17:20ff	IX:644	18:4	I:171; II:215; III:46n25; IX:212; 591
17:21	III:116(n369); 212; VIII:150n16; 451; IX:534n280		
		18:5	II:426; 443; 444; III:829; VIII:56; **590-591;** IX:450
17:22	II:671; 951; III:116n369; 170; V:342; 343n147; VIII:435; **450-451;** 457; 458, n396, n398	18:6	I:155; 156n10; 157; III:942; 1093(n268); VI:556
17:22ff	IX:647n182	18:6f	VIII:435
17:23	II:229; VIII:150n16; 433n252; 458n396	18:6-8	III:936; IV:380; V:755n85
		18:7	I:627n12; II:54; **IV:187-188;** 189; 368; **380-381** (381n56); 382; 385n96; 386n99; 387n114; VI:464
17:23f	I:586; V:866(n46); VIII:458n397		
17:24	II:951; IV:16; 25; V:534n312; 865n42; VIII:434n257; 435;	18:7f	II:446; IV:188; VI:464; IX:450n89; 458

18:8	I:627; 678; II:769; IV:188; VI:210(n268); 464; **VIII:435;** 457; 458; 477n517; IX:458		
18:8a	IV:381n56; VIII:435	18:31ff	VI:833
18:8b	I:627n12; IV:381; VIII:435, n264	18:32	II:370; **V:634;** VIII:265n41; 305n73; 306
18:9	II:190; IV:368; V:707n406; 755n84; VI:7; VIII:568; IX:42n179	18:33	IV:517; V:621n160
		18:34	I:703; III:973; IV:108; 451; V:699n331; VII:894; VIII:224
18:9ff	I:330, n101; **IX:42**		
18:9-14	III:935n56; IV:347; 621; V:752; 760; VI:328; VIII:16, n40; 103; 104; 105; **264**	18:35	II:332; III:443; V:68; VIII:287
		18:36	VIII:289
		18:37	I:66; II:682; IV:874
18:10	I:519; 520n18	18:38	III:287; VIII:288(n126)
18:10-12	III:940	18:39	VIII:288n126
18:10ff	II:802; 803; III:242; VII:833	18:40	II:332; V:68n83; VII:648; VIII:34n6; 288; 289
18:10-14	VI:18n48		
18:11	I:152; 327n77; II:807; III:237, n29; 723; IV:730; VI:723n9; VII:637; 648; VIII:104, n148; IX:42n180	18:41	III:1093; VI:964n38; 965n43
		18:42f	IX:432n46
		18:43	I:177; IV:50; 51; V:67; VIII:288, (n131), n133; IX:367
18:11f	I:327; III:974		
18:11ff	I:331(n105)	19	VI:907
18:12	IV:925; 929; 930, n30; 931; VII:20; IX:41	19:1f	I:304; VI:610n26; VIII:98
		19:1ff	IV:1062; **VI:617-618;** 906; VII:832
18:13	I:185n1; 186; 329; 330; 331; III:46n19; 237, n28; 315; 713; 834n31; 851n128; IV:373; 1002; V:377n11; 534; VII:647; 648; VIII:262; 266	19:1-10	VI:328; VIII:104, **105**
		19:2	III:488; VI:328; VIII:98n105, n106; 103; 104n148
		19:3	II:942; IV:650, n12; V:342n143; 348
18:13f	IX:130		
18:13ff	I:304	19:3f	V:586
18:14	I:330n97; 332(n112); II:190; III:723; IV:654; 1060; V:735, n65; VII:407n21; **VIII:16-17;** 105; 608	19:4	I:519; **VII:758,** n3
		19:5	II:22; IV:574; VI:844; VIII:202
		19:6	I:330; IX:366; 367
		19:7	I:303; 327; 733; 735; II:678; IV:338; V:731; 732; VIII:104; IX:42
18:14b	IX:42n179		
18:15	V:637; IX:432		
18:15-17	VIII:17n41	19:7-10	VII:992
18:16	III:500; 501	19:8	II:168; III:1093(n268); IV:628; VI:328; 907; VII:648; 659; VIII:98; 99; 102; 134
18:17	I:587; II:424; IV:532n18; 718		
18:18	II:548; III:781; IV:718; VI:905; 907		
		19:8-9a	VI:907n197
18:18-27	VI:328	19:9	I:9; VI:610n26; 991; VIII:104; 365
18:20	II:548(n8); III:755; IV:514; 643; 729; VIII:178		
		19:9b	III:582
18:22	IV:714; V:513(n106); VI:905; VIII:74n32; 597	19:10	I:395; II:669; 892; VI:328; 492, n72; 500; 907n197; VII:991; VIII:104; 407n35; **453;** 456; 457n390; 458; 461n415; IX:42n177; 534n280; **639**
18:22f	VI:328		
18:23	IV:323; VI:328		
18:24	VI:578; 907		
18:25	III:593; 594n6; VI:328; 907; **VII:606**	19:11	I:573n47; 584; II:331; V:755n84; VII:331, n256; VIII:168; IX:647n182
18:27	V:733		
18:28	I:651n18; IV:714; VI:905	19:12	I:580; V:29
18:29	I:589; 651n20; II:727; 729; IV:643; VIII:443n308; IX:75n13	19:12ff	I:429(n130); IV:716; VI:328; 534
		19:13	II:37; III:488; VI:641
18:29f	**IV:715;** 717; 1115; VI:328	19:13ff	II:671
18:30	I:205; 688; II:670; 864(n275); IV:1115n59; IX:89n10	19:14	I:590; III:52; IV:692
		19:15	I:580; VI:642; 779; IX:303
18:31	I:744n7; 748; 749; V:66;	19:16-21	VIII:223
	707(n405), n407; VI:296n61; 832; VII:329(n241); 331; VIII:60, n16; 458		

19:17	II:565; 566; III:351; 783; IV:657; V:172
19:18	VI:483
19:19	III:351
19:20	III:655
19:20ff	III:975
19:21	V:1028; IX:208
19:21f	VIII:155
19:22	II:271n71; VI:554; 561; VII:698
19:23	VI:635, n10; VII:771; VIII:211
19:24	V:839
19:26	II:827
19:27	I:590; II:225; 813; V:429; VII:934n40
19:28	VII:328; 330n242
19:28-38	VII:331
19:29	II:332; III:488; V:484n100
19:30	II:60; 433; III:444; V:286; VI:844; 960
19:30f	IV:336
19:32	I:83; 398n4
19:33	III:1086; IV:336; VI:960
19:35	VI:960
19:36	V:587(n25); VI:573
19:37	I:177; II:301; 303; 332; IV:445; V:342; 484, n100; 889; VI:53; 279; 721; VII:242; IX:293; 367
19:38	I:578; 589; II:248; 538; 670; 749n44; 762; IV:262; 274n48; V:513n118; 985n253; **VIII:619;** n45, n46; IX:528n236; 683
19:38b	II:413; V:519n169
19:39	IV:921
19:39f	II:626
19:40	III:901; IV:269; **270,** n16
19:40ff	IV:1002
19:41	II:332; III:850n126
19:41f	III:725
19:41ff	V:428n333
19:42	I:705; 706; II:413; 953; III:973; IV:262; 1109, n28; V:378; VI:724; VII:332
19:43	II:813; 928; 951; VII:883
19:43f	IV:270n16
19:44	I:511; 705; 706; II:607; III:459; 461; V:639; VII:332
19:45	III:235; VII:331
19:45f	III:243; VII:332
19:46	I:747; III:243; V:121n10; VI:842
19:47	II:950n39; III:236; 242; 271; IV:50; 53; VI:659n45; 868; VII:332; 864
19:48	III:915; **921;** IV:51; V:587(n30); VI:478
20	IV:105n144
20:1	II:718; III:242; 271; IV:51; VI:328; 659n46; VII:332; 771n27
20:3	II:685

20:6	IV:51; 267; V:587(n31); VI:4; 836
20:9	IV:50; 51; 255n5; VI:723; 955n13; IX:591; 592
20:9ff	IV:716
20:10	I:406, n6; III:660
20:11	I:406; III:660; V:631n4
20:11ff	I:404n37
20:12	VIII:222
20:13	III:1086; VI:476; VIII:242n27; 381; 596
20:14	II:96
20:14f	VIII:222
20:15	III:1086; IV:255; 714; VI:476; 921n6
20:17	I:748; IV:271; 281, n9; V:136
20:17f	I:372; IV:278; V:436n377; VI:754; 755n55; VII:345; 348; 353n79, n82
20:18	IV:271; 274; **275-276; 281,** n5, n9; V:425; VI:748; 755; VII:353n79
20:18a	IV:276; 281; VI:163; 164, n18; 170n3
20:18b	VI:162; 164n18
20:19	III:271; 911n1; IV:50; 51; IX:38; 208; 430; 679
20:20	I:482; II:190; 565; IV:9; 105n144; 106; VI:35; VII:147; 568; IX:82
20:20ff	**IX:82**
20:21	II:687; V:87; 90; 343; 449; VI:780
20:22	IX:80
20:23	IV:975; V:726; VI:34; 844; VIII:568
20:24	II:25
20:25	II:167
20:26	III:38; 946; IV:9; 50; 105n144; 106
20:27	VII:36; 52
20:27-40	VII:52n102
20:28	I:746; II:817n5
20:29	**VI:315**
20:32	VIII:596
20:33	II:817n5
20:34	VIII:365; IX:345
20:34f	I:205
20:35	I:380; 651n15; 652n24; III:61n31; IV:893(n26); VIII:241; IX:647n183
20:35f	IX:647
20:36	I:87; V:365; 653; VIII:365; 390; IX:647n183
20:37	II:337; III:101(n225); 191; 1087; IV:865; V:995n302
20:38	III:294
20:40	II:687
20:41	**IX:532**
20:41ff	IX:530n250
20:42	I:616; III:440; IV:110; VI:412; VII:650n31; VIII:462n422;

	499	21:25a	236n252; 886n3; **887**
20:44	III:487	21:25a	VII:887
20:45	IV:51	21:25b	VIII:458n400
20:46	I:331(n106); 498; 741, n14;	21:25f	VII:440, n151
	II:142; III:46(n21), n21;	21:25ff	VII:440
	VI:870; **VII:690-691**	21:26	II:681; V:158; 513(n106);
	(690n29); 820; 833n227;		VI:726; VII:70; 887, n13,
	IX:116n23; 129		n14; IX:210
20:47	III:942; VI:149; IX:448n75;	21:26a	VIII:458n400
	449, n77	21:27	IV:909; VII:236n252; VIII:458
21:1	II:166; III:865; VI:328	21:28	I:186; III:936; IV:335; **352;** 354;
21:1ff	III:236		V:534n311; 814n1;
21:1-4	VI:328; 905n178; IX:449		VII:236n252; 887;
21:2	VI:40; 902n156; 905n179		VIII:458n400
21:3	I:337; V:889; VI:905	21:29	VII:757n56
21:4	II:166; III:865; 866; VIII:598	21:29-31	V:759; VII:757
21:5	I:354; III:235; 867; IV:246n31;	21:31	I:584; II:331n2; VII:757(n58)
	269n5	21:32	I:663
21:6	II:671; 951; IV:338; V:343; 346	21:33	II:682
21:7	II:675; V:865n42; VII:232;	21:34	I:588n1; 559; II:862n252;
	VIII:64		952n47; III:611; 699;
21:8	II:331; III:461; V:291; VI:246;		IV:591n18; 592; V:594n10;
	247; 573; IX:89n10		1023; VIII:372n270
21:9	III:446; VI:513n91; 869;	21:34f	V:494
	VII:199n19; 571; 708	21:34-36	VIII:434; IX:346n287
21:11	VI:848n425; VII:199; 241n289	21:35	I:678; II:681; III:444;
21:12	I:577; II:230; 349n63; V:271;		V:594n10; VI:777
	VI:688; VII:831; 834, n230;	21:36	II:339; III:333(n93); 398; 461;
	867n47; VIII:443n308;		V:1010n392; VII:236n252;
	IX:244; 430		649; VIII:434, n259, n260;
21:13	II:429; IV:502; 503; VII:834		435; 457; 458; 555; IX:680
21:14	III:612; IV:591n15; VII:834;	21:37	II:139; III:236; 488; IV:882n8;
	VIII:155		V:484n100; VII:332
21:15	III:655; IV:504; VI:398n414;	21:37f	III:242
	406, n473; VII:514; 698	21:38	IV:50; 51
21:16	IV:1099n1; VII:740; IX:156;	22:1	II:332; 902; V:898
	159; 160	22:2	III:271; IV:50; 51; VII:864;
21:16b	IX:647		IX:208
21:16f	IX:163	22:3	II:80; 425; 678; III:497;
21:17	IV:690, n25; V:271;		IV:451n243; VI:35n62;
	VIII:443n308		VII:158; **159;** 162; 331n253;
21:17ff	VIII:436n273		332; 439n146
21:18	I:394	22:4	III:271; IV:451n243;
21:18f	IV:504		VII:709n35; 864
21:19	IV:586; VII:366; IX:608; 644;	22:4f	III:271
	647	22:5	VII:647
21:20	II:331; 332; 660; III:245;	22:6	III:462; V:207; 213
	VII:328n228; 332; 708	22:7	II:21; 22; 671; 902; 903; 950;
21:20ff	V:484n98		III:181; V:897n8
21:21	V:445n425	22:7f	II:903n8
21:22	I:748; II:446; 951; V:422;	22:7-14	VI:297n70; IX:411n48; 678n26
	VI:130; 290n21	22:7-18	VI:141n55
21:22f	V:431; 441	22:8	V:897n8; VI:102; 573, (n50)
21:23	I:346; 678; III:146; IV:52;	22:10	VI:578; VII:332
	V:422; 430; 434; 438, n391;	22:10ff	VI:844
	444	22:11	II:49; IV:338; V:19n136;
21:24	I:195; 224n2; II:369; 370;		897n8; IX:54n46
	III:461; IV:525, n14; V:943;	22:13	IV:451n243; V:897n8
	VI:163; 294; 995n16, n16;	22:14	I:428, n123; II:325; VII:711;
	VII:328n228; 332; 698		794; IX:678
21:25	I:678; II:995n1; V:438n391;	22:15	II:693; 911n10; III:170;
	VII:61; 70; 230; 232;		171(n37); 732; 734; V:897n8,

22:44	II:463; 464; V:445; VI:153	23:2f	I:577
22:45	II:807; IV:320; 442; 446;	23:3	I:577; IX:529n242
	VIII:554n64	23:4	IV:51; VI:637; VII:332n258;
22:46	V:920n120; VI:35n62		864n29; VIII:222
22:47	II:332; IX:138	23:5	IV:51; VII:198; 718n5
22:47f	IX:139; 140	23:6	III:902; VII:234
22:48	VIII:438; 443; **446-447;** 456;	23:6-12	VII:332n258
	458; IX:140n241	23:7	I:704; II:565; VII:328; 332n258
22:49	II:538; IV:446, n221; 525;	23:8	II:530; V:342; VII:234; 235,
	V:558n7; 940; VI:56; 995n17		n240; 243; 255; IX:367; 591
22:49f	VIII:260	23:9	IV:101; V:713
22:49ff	III:296	23:10	III:271; 637; VII:647; 864
22:50	III:270; V:558; 940; VIII:263	23:11	IV:17, n3; 27; **V:635;** 707n406;
22:50f	V:551		VII:690n27; 709n34
22:51	II:461; III:206; 296n16; IV:451;	23:12	II:815; VI:723; IX:159;
	VIII:288n130		166n170
22:52	III:271; IV:525; V:38n11;	23:12-16	VII:332n258
	558n7; VI:659n46;	23:13	III:271; 496; IV:51; VI:529;
	VII:709n35; 864n29		VII:864n29
22:53	II:80; 435n4; 460; 461; 568;	23:14	III:637; 943; VII:718n5; 721;
	III:103; 235; 236; 242;		VIII:222; IX:65
	IV:680; 681; V:558; VI:153;	23:14f	VI:637
	VII:159n38; 439; 442n175;	23:15	I:379
	IX:430; 678	23:16	IV:517; **V:621,** n160
22:54	III:270; IV:373; VII:760	23:18	III:901
22:54-71	IX:533n274	23:18-25	VII:332n258
22:55	III:440; VI:941; VII:787	23:19	IV:262; VII:570; IX:244
22:55f	III:441	23:22	**V:621,** n160; VI:637; VIII:222
22:56	IV:446; VI:722; 941; VII:771;	23:23	I:191; 192; III:398; 655; IX:293
	794; IX:343	23:24	I:193; V:587n29; VI:637
22:57	I:777	23:25	II:169; III:59; VII:332n258;
22:58	IV:446		570; IX:244; 540
22:59	I:244; IV:446; VII:794; IX:680	23:26	IV:9n3; V:290; VII:577n43;
22:60f	IX:303		IX:58
22:61	III:1093(n268); IV:105n144;	23:27	III:152; 153; 155; 725; 845n99;
	106; 677, n10		846; 849; VI:278; 279;
22:61b	III:288		VIII:266, n52
22:62	IV:447; VI:124, n11	23:27ff	I:785
22:63	VII:883; VIII:260n3; **265**	23:28	III:153; 722; **725;** 850n126;
22:63f	VIII:264		VI:42n16; VII:332
22:63-65	**V:635**	23:28ff	III:850; IV:1002; VIII:266n52
22:64	VI:829; VIII:260n3; **264-266**	23:29	II:671, n25; 951; III:787;
22:64f	I:623		IV:369
22:66	III:271; IV:53; VI:654;	23:30	III:557; 976; V:483, n96;
	VII:864; 870		VI:162
22:67	VI:203(n213); **IX:532-533**	23:31	**V:38;** 446n430; VI:476
22:67f	II:353; IX:534n280	23:32	II:702; III:484
22:67ff	II:352n91	23:33	III:484; 488; **VIII:203-204**
22:68	II:685	23:34	I:6(n8); 48; 117n7; III:850; 902;
22:69	II:297; III:442; IV:540;		V:713; 715; 813; 985n251;
	1107n12; 1111; 1113, n49;		988; 989n273; VI:88n54;
	V:361; 867n50; 989n278;		397n407; 478; VII:650n28
	VII:650, n28, n31; 797;	23:34a	V:713n455; VII:797
	VIII:381; **435-436;** 440; 457;	23:35	III:104(n261); 376; IV:50; 51;
	462n422; 612		189; 796; **798-799;** V:346;
22:70	**VIII:381;** 436n268		**635; 689;** VII:439n140; 647;
22:71	IV:499; VII:699; 870		VIII:381n341; IX:529n242;
23:1	VI:279		533
23:1ff	VII:718n5; **IX:82**	23:35b	IV:798
23:2	I:578; II:369; III:637; IV:52;	23:36	II:684; IV:798; V:288n3;
	VII:718, n5; 721; 870; IX:81;		VI:160; IX:66
	82; 529n242; 533	23:36f	V:289; 635n30; VII:709

23:37f	I:577	24:10	I:428
23:38	I:744n10; 762; 764; II:508f; III:388; 846	24:11	VI:205, n236; IX:2
		24:12	III:39; IV:447n223; V:343, n150; 346; 814n3; 815; VIII:233n48
23:39	I:623; III:484; 918; VII:989; IX:529n242; 533		
23:39ff	V:425	24:13	IV:446; VI:530; VII:332
23:40	II:625; III:942; IX:212	24:13ff	I:430(n137); IV:750; V:67n79; 355; 356n205
23:41	I:379; II:625; V:912n59; VI:637		
23:42	I:581; 587; II:433; 538; 670; 675; III:287; IV:677; V:770; VIII:212n32; 381n346	24:15	II:331; VII:747
		24:15f	V:359n214
		24:16	I:704; III:911; 973; IV:750; V:378
23:43	I:147; 149; II:538; III:938n66; IV:580; 1113n49; V:765; 769; **770-771** (771n52); 772, n58; VI:415; **VII:273;** 795; IX:647, n182; 656	24:17	V:944; VII:451; 648
		24:18	IV:445; V:851; 853; VII:332
		24:19	I:362; II:300; III:287; IV:54; 102; 868n226; 874; VI:54; 841; 846; 847; VII:239; VIII:54n34; 125; IX:534n280
23:44f	VII:61; 242		
23:45	III:246; 629; IV:882n8; 885; VII:961		
		24:19-21	IX:529n245; 532n273
23:46	I:627n14; III:137; 901; 902; V:772; 985n251; 988; 989n273; VI:415; 452; 453; VII:650n28; 797; VIII:163; IX:294; 303; 431	24:19ff	II:734; **IV:446;** 451
		24:20	III:271; 942n5; VII:864n29
		24:21	II:530; 948; III:384; 902; IV:350; 351; V:714n472; VI:846; VII:273n22; 451; VIII:220
23:47	II:187; VI:637; VII:709; 923; VIII:266; 381		
23:48	III:831n10, n12; 834n31; 845; 846; 849; 850n125; V:345; 346; 587; VIII:262, n16; 264; **266,** n52; 268n61	24:21a	IX:534n280
		24:22	II:459; IX:210n115; 211
		24:23	II:677; 865(n285); V:351; 372, n4; VII:1057
		24:23f	II:769
23:49	I:216; 718; IV:373; IV:446; VII:647	24:25	III:612; IV:272n25; 841; 962; VI:205; 833
23:50	I:15n16; 363	24:25f	II:24; 665; VI:833
23:50f	II:771	24:25-27	V:707n405; IX:534, n280, n282
23:51	I:587; II:650; III:376; VI:530; 643; IX:607n27	24:25ff	IV:411n150
		24:26	II:22; 24; 424; 678; III:328n48; IV:189; V:913, n64; 914n73; 915n83; 919n120; 920n120; 924; 925; 934; VI:296, n62; VII:650n31; VIII:20; 381n342; 462n422; **IX:534**
23:53	III:411		
23:54	II:950; VII:20n159; 28; IX:343		
23:55	IV:681; V:345, n155; VII:1057		
23:55f	I:430n136; III:846		
23:56	II:548; IV:801; VII:21; 458		
24	V:68n80	24:26f	IV:451n242; VII:357
24:1	II:777n11; 950; III:846; IV:680; 801n14; VI:866; VII:20; 29; 458	24:27	I:748; 752; 759; II:662; 663; 665, n12; III:704; IV:864; 865; VI:54; 296; 831n337; 832; 840; VIII:54n34
24:1-4	VI:328		
24:2	I:430(n137); II:769; IV:269; V:346		
		24:28	II:332; VI:530
		24:29	II:678; 948; V:356n205; VI:724
24:3	II:769; VII:1057	24:29f	VII:796
24:4	I:84n67; IV:249; VII:690n27; 691	24:30	I:477; II:762; III:729; 730n16; 741n82; VIII:211; IX:412n50
24:4f	IX:210n115	24:30f	VI:142
24:5	VI:775; IX:210; 211	24:31	I:704; III:174n16; 176n45; 911; IV:8; V:355n201; 359n211; 378; VII:764n13
24:6	IV:677; VII:691		
24:7	II:22; 24; 169; 948; 949; V:707n405; 712; 716; VI:308; VIII:20; 220; 456n387; 457n387, n393; 458; IX:430		
		24:32	I:752; 759; II:666n12; III:174n16; **464;** 612; 747n42; V:67; 707n405; VII:764n13
24:8	I:704; IV:677		
24:9	I:61; 66; II:326; 865(n285); IV:446	24:33	II:326; IV:446; 492n54; VII:332; 771; IX:679
24:9f	IX:451n99	24:34	I:438n185; II:335; III:1093(n268); V:355;

	356n204; 358; VI:103; 104; IX:211n121		747n42; IV:958; 959; VII:764n13; 892; 894n54
24:35	I:704; II:908; III:729; 730n16; V:67; 68n80; VI:142	24:46	I:430n142; IV:189; 596; 893(n22); V:707n405; 913, n64; 914n73; 919n120; 924; 929n33; VI:296; VIII:20
24:36	II:411; III:176n45; V:355; 357; VII:650		
24:36ff	I:430n138; IV:446; V:355	24:46f	III:709(n56)
24:37	V:346; VI:359; 415	24:47	I:305n143; 511; 512; II:369; 425; III:704; 711; 713; 753; IV:492; 873; 1003; 1004; V:271; 278; VI:216n315; VII:332; 335
24:37f	IX:211		
24:38	I:522; II:97; III:612		
24:39	V:341n139; 345; 359n213; VI:147n22; 359; 415; VII:124; 574; 575n24; **VIII:249;** IX:429n35; 430; 630; 647n181; 656		
		24:47f	III:709n51
		24:47-49	VI:50n39
		24:48	IV:446; 455; **492-493**
24:39b	VIII:249	24:48f	I:430(n139); II:310
24:39f	V:357	24:49	I:406; 430n142; II:311(n87); 320; 349; 582; III:444; IV:493; V:987(n260); 989n274; VI:405; 407(n487); VII:335; **VIII:605**
24:39ff	II:335		
24:40	II:25; IX:430		
24:41	III:39; VI:205, n236; IX:211		
24:41ff	II:692; V:357		
24:42	IV:554; 595	24:50	I:186; V:485; IX:430
24:43	VI:142	24:50f	IX:412n50
24:44	I:748; 756, n28; II:22; III:980; IV:106; 864n194; 865; 1059; V:707n405; VI:295; 296; 831n337; 832; VII:794; VIII:499	24:50ff	II:763; V:355
		24:51	II:424; IV:909n42; V:355n201; 524; VI:576n63; VIII:139, n36; 543; 611; IX:60
		24:52	VI:764; VII:332; 772; IX:368
24:44-46	V:707n405	24:52f	III:246
24:44ff	IV:411n150; 451n242; 865; 873; VI:833	24:53	I:177; III:237; VII:331; 332; IX:412n50; 451
24:45	I:752; 759; II:734; III:174n16;		

JOHN

1	III:60; IV:132; VII:525n410		VI:755n56; VIII:375n297; IX:398n209; 575
1-20	IX:132		
1:1	I:406; 482n17, n18, n20, n21; 484n34; III:92(n140); 104n257; 105; 106; 116(n371); 199; 353; 587(n55); **IV:128-130;** 131; 132; 278n89; 611n58; 780n111; V:273; 998; 1002n346; VI:222; 878n45; VII:610n10; 1088n590; IX:112; 165n154; 352n348; 570	1:1-4	III:588n58
		1:1-18	IV:129; **130-136;** VI:687; **IX:315-352**
		1:2	V:998n318
		1:3	II:67; III:103(n247); 587; 884; 1032n209; IV:133n240; V:526; 889; 894; VI:878n45
		1:4	I:245n34; II:841n66; 842n75; 870, (n322); 872; III:259; IV:133; **IX:351-352** (351n333)
1:1f	I:482; III:588; VI:722		
1:1-3	IX:185	1:4b	IX:351
1:1ff	I:711n79; II:353; 423; III:1032; IV:71; 128; 131; 623n94;	1:4f	III:16; IX:165n154
		1:5	II:872; III:116(n371); IV:10; 326; VII:139n303; **443,** n182,

	n183, VIII:290n149; IX:1; 5; 112; 352, n345, n349
1:6	I:404n38; V:270; 729; VIII:356n134; IX:165n154
1:6-8	VII:139n303; IX:352; 566n471
1:7	II:67; 672; III:327n40: IV:127; 498; 500; V:207; VI:208n258; 214(n297); VII:237n257; IX:354n371, n373
1:7f	III:327(n38); IV:498; VII:246n308
1:8	IV:327; IX:165n154
1:9	I:250; II:350(n74); 422, n11; 423; III:882; 889; 894; V:888; 998n315; VI:439n722; VII:422n176; VIII:291; IX:352, n347
1:9-11	IX:351n343
1:9-13	III:588n58
1:10	I:705; 711n79; III:116(n371); 884; 889; 894; VI:750; VII:443n183; IX:351n343; 352n345
1:10f	VIII:290n149
1:10-14	VIII:477
1:11	I:735; IV:13; V:28n191; VII:443n183; IX:352n345
1:11f	VIII:449n349
1:12	II:249; 568; 569; 747n37; 748n38; III:699; IV:6; 724; 739; V:271; 276; 435; 653; VI:203n222; 210(n266); 214(n303), (n304); 222n344; 223; VIII:387; 390; IX:352n349
1:12b	VII:139n303
1:12f	III:895; V:653; 1001n337; VII:421; IX:350n323
1:13	I:172; 378; 665; 671; III:54; 59; 60; 61; IV:740n14; 741n19; V:836; 997n311; VI:438; 439n731; 879n47; **VII:139,** n303; 140n308; VIII:382n354
1:14	I:220; 245n34; 246, n37; 589; II:249; 355(n103); 423; 892; III:116(n371); 117n372; 396n38; 587(n55); 588; 742; IV:90; 129; 131; 134; 135; 738n4; 740, n12, n15; 741; 784; 1083; V:28, n191; 197; 345; 346; 348; 730; 836; 849n43; 997n311; 998; VI:33n54; 224, (n357); 226; **285;** 302, n36; 303n37, n41; **VII:139,** n303; 140n313; 145; 252, n351; 253; 256n371; 381; **385-386** (396n10); IX:399, n226
1:14b	III:244; VI:285
1:14bc	VII:139n305
1:14-17	IX:391
1:15	II:672; III:396n38; 902; IV:498;

	V:207; 290, n9; VI:867n10; 878n44; IX:566n471; 568n479
1:16	I:372; II:355(n103); 430; 937; IV:724; 1083n280; VI:302, n36; 720n104; IX:399n226
1:16f	IX:399
1:16-18	III:588n58
1:17	I:246; 613; 758; II:67; 156n52; 555; 937; IV:134; 872, n254; **1083;** V:28; 364n231; VI:285; **VII:257;** VIII:327; IX:399n224; **566,** n470
1:17a	IV:135; VI:302n36
1:17b	IV:135; VI:302n36
1:18	I:247; 711; II:351n78; 433; 537n1; 908; III:55; 104n257; 105; 107; 825; IV:127; 133; 740; 741; 1083; V:324; 345; 363; 364; 365, n233; 997n311; 998, n316; VI:688; VII:256; VIII:385n373; IX:132; 165n154; 570n491
1:18a	II:908n4
1:19	I:734n26; III:264; 377, n104; IV:241; 500; V:207; 211; 588n36; VI:723; VII:330; 852n28, n30; IX:43; 44n197
1:19ff	II:347(n47); IV:456n271; VII:252n355
1:19-34	V:211
1:19-37	IX:566n471
1:20	I:469; II:937; V:207; 211; IX:567
1:20f	II:347; IX:567n472
1:21	I:389; II:933, n38; 936; 937; III:593n3; IV:857(n115); 858, n122, n124; 859; VI:836; 838; 840; VII:241n288
1:22	III:946
1:23	I:625; II:347; 349n65; 659(n10); 937; III:593n4; IV:110; V:70n92, n95; 83; VI:830; 840; IX:165n154; 293
1:24	VII:765n20; IX:43; 44n197
1:24f	IX:35n136
1:25	II:936; 937; IV:857(n115); 858, n122; 859; VI:836; 838
1:25-33	I:536
1:26	I:538; 539; III:945; V:118; VI:616, n68; VII:637; IX:568n479
1:26f	VIII:329
1:27	I:379; II:154n41; 672; IV:335; V:290, n10; 311; IX:568n479
1:28	VI:614; 615, n63; VII:338n296
1:29	**I:186;** 306; 330n99; 338; 339, n5; 340; 538; II:332; III:104(n261); 894; IV:623; V:40; 341n136; 429; 446; **702;** 708; 710; 711n440; 900; 915n84; 989n277; VI:91n76;

	543, n39, n41; 616; 721;	**VII:753**	
	VII:139n303; 257; 1090n615;	1:47ff	IV:1084
	VIII:329; 468n460;	1:47-51	VIII:468n461
	IX:568n479	1:48	I:703; VI:688; VII:752; **753;**
1:29b	V:702; VI:543n39		IX:303
1:29ff	IV:457; VI:616	1:49	I:578; II:153; III:384; 385;
1:30	II:672; IV:130; V:290, n9;		1093; V:465n9; VI:964;
	VI:878n44; VIII:514		VII:251; 633; VIII:387;
1:31	I:539; II:672; III:327(n38); 385;		468n460; IX:528; 566; 567;
	593n3; VI:616, n68;		569
	VIII:329; IX:5	1:50	IV:536; V:343; VI:214(n298);
1:31ff	V:118		VII:251, n347; 752; **753**
1:31-34	IX:568n479	1:51	I:84; 521; 523; II:85n9;
1:32	I:522; II:456(n35); IV:498; 576;		III:103(n248); 177; IV:131;
	V:344; 345; 529n260; 531,		867; 1107n9; V:351n179; 526;
	n279		529n260; 530; VII:1072n457;
1:32f	VI:68, n56; 616; IX:143n259		VIII:368n236; 372; **468-469**
1:32-34	VI:67(n55)		(468n460, 461; 469n462);
1:33	I:404; 539; V:135n3; VI:438;		477; IX:567, n744
	616, n68; VIII:329; 468n460;	2:1	IV:643
	IX:567	2:1ff	I:648; 656n49; III:207; 741n82;
1:33f	IX:299		848; IV:643n10; VI:135n4;
1:34	II:740; IV:172; 189n18; 498;		VII:246n310; 248; 249n330;
	V:345; 689; n260; 701n350;		251; 252; **VIII:327**
	702; 708; 710; VII:252n355;	2:1-11	**V:163-164**
	VIII:376n305; 386;	2:1-12	III:207n39; VII:246n310;
	IX:298n97; 568n479		247n315
1:35	VII:647; IX:131n171	2:2	III:488
1:35ff	II:153; 156n49; IV:444; 456	2:2b	IX:678n20
1:35-42	VI:101	2:3	IV:643; VI:723; VIII:597
1:36	I:338; 339, n5; 340; V:341n136;	2:4	I:777; II:928; VII:248; **IX:678,**
	702; 708; 900; 989n277;		n25; 679n20
	VII:257; VIII:329; 468n460;	2:5	II:88; IV:643; VI:473; 480
	IX:568n479	2:6	I:108n64; III:377; 429; IV:269;
1:37-41	II:866n19		VIII:327
1:38	II:153; 662; III:389; 1093;	2:6f	VIII:315
	V:343n150; VI:964	2:6-11	V:164n16
	VIII:468n460	2:7ff	I:654n43
1:38f	IV:574	2:8	IV:1121
1:39	II:672; III:389; V:342; 732;	2:9	I:676; II:88; IV:1099(n3);
	IX:680, n35		IX:303
1:40	V:729	2:10	II:787; IV:547; 656, n38;
1:40-46	VI:442n750		1119n79; V:164n16; 888;
1:41	II:769; VI:103; VII:251;		VIII:141; 155; 597
	VIII:387n382; 468n460;	2:11	I:482; 648; II:27; 249; 433;
	IX:566, n467; 567		III:212; IV:131; 451; 459;
1:41f	I:144; III:389		V:276n223; VI:210(n266);
1:42	II:662; III:406; 407, n2; 488;		473(n83); VII:23n183; 243;
	V:341n136; VI:100; 101, n9;		246; 247; 250; 251; 253, n359;
	102; 103		254; 256; VIII:387; IX:5
1:43	III:46n20; IV:444	2:12	I:144; IV:643; V:164n15;
1:44	VI:100; 101; 530		VII:253n359
1:45	I:746, n20; II:769; III:287;	2:13	I:519; II:332; III:377; V:898;
	IV:865; 874; 1082; 1084;		899n24; 901(n43), n43;
	V:836; VI:831n337; 832; 833;		VII:332
	840; VII:251; 255; 363n197;	2:13ff	V:429
	387n382; 468n460; IX:303;	2:13-22	V:899n24; VII:332
	566; **567**	2:14	III:235; 443; VI:69
1:45f	IX:568	2:14f	VI:690
1:45ff	IV:444n211; 446	2:14-17	III:243
1:46	II:672; IV:874; V:342; IX:568	2:14-22	VII:756n47
1:47	II:672; III:385; 387; VI:721;	2:15	II:468; V:429n334; 634n23;

5:2	III:389, n142; VII:328n222; 332; VIII:327n89	
5:2ff	III:209	
5:3	I:490; III:656; 1084n231; V:347; VI:279; VIII:287n119	
5:3f	VIII:327	
5:4	I:522n2; 557; II:433; 830; IV:1092; VIII:312	
5:5	I:493; VIII:139	
5:6	I:703; III:46n25; 656; 681; VIII:312n31; IX:591	
5:7	III:206; VI:685; **VIII:327**	
5:7ff	VIII:327	
5:8	II:334; VI:438n714	
5:8f	III:206	
5:8-12	V:944	
5:9	VIII:288n131; 312, n31	
5:9b	VII:26n208; IX:44n200	
5:9f	VII:21	
5:9b-16	VIII:464	
5:10	II:561; V:713n463	
5:11	VI:473(n83); VIII:312n31	
5:12	VIII:469n462	
5:13	IV:53n101; V:587; 588; VIII:202n108	
5:14	I:288n58; 307; III:204; 212; 235; 242; 327n41; IV:1095; V:175n4	
5:14f	VIII:312, n31	
5:15	I:64; VI:473(n83); VII:852n28	
5:15-18	V:588n36	
5:16	II:230; III:379; VI:473(n83); VII:27n210	
5:17	II:637; 640; IV:1111, n37; 1115; VI:635; **VII:27,** n214, n217; 251; 253; VIII:327	
5:17f	VII:870n70	
5:17-19	VI:225	
5:17ff	VI:224	
5:17-30	**VIII:464-465**	
5:18	III:104, n258; **352-353** (352n47; 353n52); 379; IV:336; 740; V:713; 1002, n346; VI:474; VII:27, n210; 28; VIII:386n379; IX:528n239; 569	
5:18ff	II:399	
5:19	II:304; III:56; 352; 353n54; IV:1084; V:341; 343, n152; 344; 363, n227; 1000, n330; VI:474(n88); VIII:81; **385**	
5:19f	III:118n376	
5:19-21	VII:776	
5:19-23	VIII:374; 385; 464n436, n437	
5:19-30	VIII:385n370	
5:19-47	V:1002; VII:27, n217	
5:20	II:28; 642; III:40; 42; 55; 329(n60); IV:537; V:999; VI:464; VII:247; 248; VIII:385n370; IX:128n150; 134, n192	

5:20f	I:370; VIII:327
5:21	II:335; 856n196; 862(n257); 863(n267); 874; 875; III:18; 48; IV:893(n19), (n23); VI:22; VIII:374n285; IX:567
5:21f	VIII:465
5:21-27	VI:224(n355)
5:22	II:559n13; III:103(n252); 938; 1094; V:887; VIII:385(n369); 469n462
5:22-30	V:998n317
5:23	III:329(n62); V:998n319; VIII:179, n67
5:24	I:333(n125); 523; 671; 712; II:336; 425; 672; 825; 870; 872n332; III:19; 938; IV:107; 128; 724; V:363; 869, n63; VI:210n270; 223; 226; 441; VIII:144; 464n436; 465n440; IX:296; 350n327
5:24f	III:941; VIII:465n441; IX:353n353
5:24ff	IV:724
5:24-29	III:939n69
5:25	II:673; 863(n267); 870, (n326); III:18; IV:893; 1119; V:869; VI:223(n345); VIII:385n371; 387; 464n436; IX:296; 679
5:25f	VIII:464n436
5:25-28	VIII:372n270
5:26	I:711; II:539; 825; 862; 870(n322); IV:740; V:958; VIII:374, n285; 385, (n369); 464n437; IX:567
5:26f	VI:22
5:27	II:568; 871(n327); III:938; VI:474; VIII:385n371; 404n22, n24; 405, n25; 465n441; 466; 468; 469n462
5:27-29	VIII:385n371; 464; 477n517
5:28	III:40; 658; 939n69; IV:681; VI:541; VII:1087n580; IX:296; 679
5:28f	II:336; 870; III:938; 941; V:869n63; VII:140n309; VIII:385n371; 465n441; IX:295
5:29	I:371; 372; II:864(n270), (n278); III:939n69; VI:117; 479; 579; 636; IX:647n183
5:29ff	IV:724
5:30	I:404n43; II:184; 189; 304; III:55; 56; 941; V:363; 998n314; VI:474(n88); VIII:81; 464n436
5:31	I:248; IV:498; 500
5:31ff	III:16
5:31-36	IX:566n471
5:31-37	VI:225n358
5:31-39	IV:498
5:32	IV:498; 500
5:33	I:243; 246; IV:498; 537

5:34	III:329(n59); V:728; VII:997		245; 246; 247
5:35	I:20; II:937n75; III:45n7; 409; 848; IV:327; VI:724; VII:246n308; IX:1; 165n154; 349, n320; 680	6:3	III:440; 441; 443; V:484; VII:795
		6:4	II:332; III:377; V:898; 899n22, n24; 901(n43), n43
5:36	I:6(n7); 27n6; 404(n40); 405; 444n234; II:28; 166; 349n67; 642; III:56n13; 327(n38); 589; IV:498; 500; 537; V:1000n330; VI:474(n88); VII:247; 248; 249; VIII:81; 291; 374n290	6:5	II:672; IV:53n101; V:345; 377; 588
		6:6	VI:28; 473(n83); VII:248, n322
		6:9	V:638; 769n38
		6:10	VI:477; VIII:202n108
		6:11	I:477; III:654; VI:438n714; IX:399n223; 411
5:36f	I:444n236; IV:498; V:998n319	6:12	I:394; VI:130
5:36ff	I:405n45	6:12f	III:729; VI:59; VII:422n21
5:37	I:404(n43); II:374; IV:498; V:340n133; 341; 351n178; 1002n341; IX:296, n88	6:13	II:322
		6:14	II:423; 938n81; III:889; IV:858n125; V:342; VI:473(n83); 841; **845-846;** VII:243; 246; 247; 257; VIII:387
5:37b	V:364		
5:37f	I:711; V:363; 364, n231; VI:443		
5:37ff	V:998		
5:38	I:404(n40); II:539; 820; 826; IV:128; 576; V:1001n337; VI:203n221; 205; VII:249	6:14f	IV:465; 858, n125; 859(n134); 862; V:588n35; 589; VI:847; VII:257n383; IX:529n245; 532n273
5:38a	V:364		
5:39	I:752, n10; 757; II:657; 825; IV:408; 498; V:364n231; 791; VI:223; 478; VIII:82	6:15	I:472; 578; 703; V:484; VI:478; VII:246
		6:16	IX:680n39
5:39f	II:872; IV:1084	6:16ff	VII:246n310; VIII:323
5:39ff	IV:1084	6:16-21	IV:465; VII:257n383
5:39-47	I:759; 766	6:17	IV:10
5:40	II:672; 825; 870n326; III:52; IV:724; VI:144n80; 223(n346)	6:18	VI:452
		6:19	II:332; V:346; IX:209
		6:20	II:352(n90); IX:212
5:41	II:248; III:56; V:728	6:21	III:46n20
5:41ff	III:16	6:22	IV:53n101; V:588; VII:648
5:42	I:53(n152); 703; II:826	6:22ff	I:734
5:43	II:349; 671; IV:6; 623; V:271; 273; 998; 999n323; VI:222n344; 223	6:22-31	IV:465
		6:23	II:332; III:1093(n269); VIII:202; IX:399n223; 411
5:44	II:248; 528; V:209; 728; VI:214n298; 223; VII:852	6:24	IV:53n101; V:588
		6:25	II:153; 769; III:1093; VI:964
5:45	II:528; 531n106; 532; III:637; IV:867, n216, n217; V:869; 998; 1002; VI:210n269	6:26	I:644; 656; II:27; III:944; V:342; VI:22; 225; VII:230; 245; **247;** 248(n319); 249n330
5:45f	II:156	6:26b	II:652
5:45-47	IX:566	6:26f	VI:22n72
5:46	I:744n8; 746, n20; III:58; IV:865; VI:831n337	6:26-51ab	VI:143
		6:27	I:394; 644; II:427; 597n55; 864(n272); 870; V:996; VI:22; 437(n711); VII:949, n83; **VIII:465-466;** 469n462
5:46f	I:759; IV:865; 867; VI:203n221; 205, (n235)		
5:47	I:765; IV:108; 128; 222	6:27b	VIII:466
6	III:378; 588; 727; 731; 741, n82; 742; IV:306; 869; 1083; V:772n63; 1002; VI:22n74; **143-144** (143n74); 156n75, n77; 224; VII:392n16; **VIII:236-237** (237n8, n11)	6:27c	VIII:466
		6:28	I:27n6; II:646; VI:479; VIII:146.
		6:28f	VI:225n361
		6:28-30	VIII:464n437
		6:29	I:404(n40), n43; 644; II:643; 651; III:944; VI:210(n266); VII:247; 249
6:1ff	**VII:244;** 246, n310; 248		
6:1-13	IV:465		
6:2	I:493; III:212; IV:53n101; V:341; 342; 345; 346; 588, n35; VI:473(n83); VII:243;	6:29f	VI:203n221
		6:29ff	I:434

6:30	V:342; VI:223(n350); 225n359; 473(n83); VII:243; 244		1002; VI:225; **VII:138**; 140n309; VIII:363; 378; 469n462; IX:568
6:30f	IV:465; 862; VI:22		
6:30ff	IV:868; VII:257n383	6:43	I:734; III:944
6:31	I:749; II:658; 693; IV:462; **465;** V:976n175; VIII:237n11; 255, n48	6:44	I:370; 371; 404(n43); II:309; 336; 503, n3; 697; 870; 953; 939n69; IV:408; 724; V:869; 998n319; 1000; VI:224(n353); 721; 722
6:31f	VI:22; 147		
6:31ff	I:477; II:658		
6:32	I:250; II:350n74; IV:465; 864; 872; 1083n280; V:527; 542n27; 997; 998; VI:144; VIII:326	6:44f	VI:223(n346)
		6:45	I:749; II:165; 672; III:121; IV:408, n135; V:363; 364; 729; VI:224n353; 831; 832; 834
6:32b	IV:465		
6:32f	IV:465(n28); VIII:465	6:45f	V:341
6:32ff	I:644; IV:465; 872; 873n256; 884n18; V:520n181; VI:847; VII:251	6:46	IV:130; V:341; 363; 364, n230; 730; 998, n315
		6:47	II:825; 870(n325); IV:724; VI:214(n303); 223(n348); VIII:236n6; 237n12
6:32-35	VI:439n722		
6:32-54	III:741		
6:32-59	VIII:237n11	6:48	I:250; 477; II:350(n73); 870; IV:465; VI:143
6:33	I:522; II:855n171; 870; III:104(n261); 894; IV:465; V:527; 998n315; VI:144; 442n755	6:49	II:658; 693; 695; III:14(n61); IV:462; **465**; V:976n175; VI:22
		6:49-58	VIII:237n11
6:33ff	I:522; IV:130	6:50	III:18; 327(n38); IV:465; 724; V:527; VI:144; VII:332
6:34	IV:862		
6:35	I:250; 477; 644; II:226; 350(n73); 672; 855n181; 870; III:318n79; IV:136; 277n73; 465; **VI:21-22;** 143; 144; 210(n266); 214(n303); 223(n346), (n349); 442n755; 606; VII:252n354; VIII:236; 465	6:50f	I:522; II:695; IV:465(n28); V:998n315; VI:144; 442n755; VIII:237n11
		6:50ff	IV:130
		6:51	I:199; 477; 644; II:870, (n326); III:18n77; 117n372; 741; 894; IV:465; V:514n121; 527; 710n435; VI:22; VII:140n309; VIII:237; 469n462; 511
6:36	V:349; VI:443; VII:357n110		
6:37	I:528; II:166; 672; 928; V:1000; VI:223(n346); 224(n353); IX:129n161		
		6:51a	VII:140, n309
6:37a	IX:129n161	6:51b	VI:147n22; VIII:236
6:37b	IX:129n161	6:51c	III:742; VI:22n74; 144; 543; VII:140n309; VIII:236; 237n8, n9, n11; 465n446
6:38	I:522; III:54; 56; 327(n38); V:527; 998n315; VI:474(n88); VIII:469n462		
		6:51ff	III:731; V:218; VII:1059
6:38f	III:55	6:51-58	VI:441; VII:138; 140n309
6:38-40	III:329(n59); V:998n314	6:51	II:870
6:39	I:370; 371; 395; II:61; 166; 870; III:991; V:869; 1000, n331; IX:129n161	6:51b-58	VII:357, n108
		6:51c-58	VI:143, n74; 441n744; VII:139; 140; **VIII:236-237** (237n11); 465n445
6:39f	II:336; 697; 953; III:53; 323(n2); IV:724		
		6:52	VI:527; VIII:466
6:40	I:370; 371; II:825; 870, (n325), n326; III:55; 939n69; V:346; 362; 363; 869; 998n317; VI:223(n348); VII:357; VIII:385; 464n437; IX:129n161	6:52f	VI:22n70; VIII:236
		6:52ff	III:588
		6:53	I:175; II:539; 825; III:742n84; VI:144, n81; 422n592; VIII:236n6; 237, n9, n13; 330; **465-466**; 469n462
6:41	I:734; III:117n372; 378; IV:465(n28); V:527; VI:144	6:53f	VI:22
6:41f	I:522; V:998n315; IX:568	6:53ff	I:644; II:226n5; 695
6:41ff	V:999	6:53-58	III:741
6:42	I:712; IV:643; V:28; 527; 836;	6:54	I:175; 370; 371; II:697; 825; 953; III:939n69; V:869;

VIII:236, n5, n6, n7; 237, n12; 469n462

6:54b   VII:140n309

6:55   I:175; 248; 644; VI:145; 147; 155n72

6:56   I:175; II:543; III:742; IV:576; VI:144n81; VIII:326

6:56b   VIII:237n12

6:56ff VIII:236

6:57   I:404(n40); II:349n67; 862(n257); 870(n322); III:741; V:996n310; 998n319; 999; VI:143; 144; VII:249; VIII:237n12; 374n290

6:58   I:522; II:693; 695; 870(n326); III:14(n61); 117n372; IV:465(n28), n29; V:527; 976n175; 998n315

6:59   II:143; III:741n82; VI:137n26; VII:21; 835; **VIII:467**

6:60   I:712; 734; IV:106; 128; 445; V:756n91; 1028; VI:223(n345); VII:357n107

6:60ff II:144; IV:107; 445; 459

6:60-63 VI:144

6:61   I:734; II:539; VII:140n309; 344; 356; **357**

6:61b   I:734

6:62   I:521; 734; IV:130; 346; **361**; 364; VII:140; 357; VIII:237n11; 467, n453; 469n462; 610; IX:76n15

6:62f   VI:22; 147

6:63   I:644; 757; II:855n180; 856n196; 862(n250), (n258); 867n308; 870; 875; III:741; IV:108; 128; 872n253; VI:144n75; 438; 440; **441-442** (441n744; 442n753); 443; **VII:139-140** (140n308, n309); 357; VIII:330; 467n454; IX:76n15; 296

6:63a   III:742

6:63ab IX:76n15

6:63b   III:742

6:63c   IX:76n15

6:63-65 IV:173

6:64   I:481, n13; 712; 734; IV:173; 447; 452; VI:214(n298); 844; VII:357

6:64f   IV:173

6:55   II:309; 672; IV:108; 172; V:531; VI:223(n346); 224(n353)

6:66   I:734; IV:445; 447; V:218; 290; 291; VII:348n55; 357; 795

6:66-69 IX:568n479

6:67   III:46n18; IV:447n224; VII:348n55

6:67ff II:327

6:68   II:821; 855n180; 862(n250); 867n308; 870; IV:107; 128; 445n216; V:869; VI:102; 441;

IX:296

6:68f   I:734; IV:173; VII:357

6:69   I:101; 102; 112; 712; 713; II:355; III:104(n261); V:211n37; VI:203(n214); 210n263; 214(n293); 227, (n372); VIII:377n313; 387; IX:133

6:70   I:712n81; II:79; 80; 81; 825; **IV:172-174;** VII:162; 253; 357n109; IX:141n242

6:70f   IV:173; 452; VI:844; VII:357; IX:141

6:71   II:327; IV:173; 452(n245); IX:141

7   III:237n29; V:588; 589; VII:392, n16

7:1   III:46n25; 375n99; 379

7:1f   VII:392n18

7:2   II:332; III:377; **VII:391-392** (391n16)

7:3   I:144; 523(n3); II:642; V:345; 346; VI:473(n83); VII:247; 248, n321

7:3-5   VII:248n321

7:3ff   VII:391

7:4   III:960; 975; V:880; VI:475; IX:5

7:5   I:144; V:276n223; 880

7:6   III:460; V:865; VII:248; IX:89n10

7:6ff   V:880

7:7   II:645; III:894; IV:498; 691; 692; VI:557

7:8   I:519, n10; III:460; 975n39; V:880; VI:294; VII:248; 392n16; VIII:383n357

7:9-17 V:769n38

7:10   I:144; 519; III:960; 975; V:880; VII:332; IX:3

7:10f   VII:392n16

7:11   III:378; V:588

7:11f   V:588

7:11-13 III:396; IX:568

7:12   I:735; 736; IV:53n101; V:587; 588; VI:251; IX:44n196

7:13   III:379; V:209n31; 88n36; 881n24; VII:852n28; IX:208; 216n145

7:14   I:519; II:143; III:236; 242; IV:408; V:880; VI:443; VII:27n218; 333; 392, n16, n18

7:14ff II:139; V:588n34; VII:391

7:15   I:764: II:155; III:40; **IV:408;** IX:42n176

7:15-19 V:588

7:15-24 VII:27n218

7:16   II:165n6; VIII:449n349

7:16b   III:58

7:16f   I:712; II:164; III:55

7:17   I:712; III:49; 58; IV:1084;

8:2	II:139n27; III:242; 443; IV:50; V:814n1; VII:392n23
8:2f	III:236
8:3	I:740n2; IV:730; VII:646
8:3f	IV:10
8:4	II:152; IV:729; 734
8:5	II:545; 548; IV:268; 730
8:6	I:743; III:637; 640; V:814n1; VI:28; 34; IX:44n197
8:7	I:327n77; 334; IV:268n12; V:814n1
8:8	I:743; II:826n55; V:814n1
8:9	I:478; II:474; VI:654; VII:914
8:10	I:777; III:636; V:814n1
8:11	I:288n58; IV:734; 1121
8:12	I:214; 250; II:343(n2); 350(n73); 353; 354n97; 826, n55; 870; III:700; 890n83; 894; IV:26; 135n248; 326; 327n30; 498; 1083; V:945; VI:606; VII:28; 252n354; 392, n24; 443; 444; VIII:291; 519n17; IX:344; **350**, n324, n328, n331; 351, n333; 352; 354n373
8:12-10:21	V:589n41
8:13	I:248
8:13f	IV:498; 500
8:13ff	III:16
8:13-18	IV:498
8:14	I:248; II:499; 671; V:28; 118, n11; 852n64; 998n315; VI:441n741; 443; VII:138; VIII:505; 506; 610; IX:297
8:15	III:938; V:869; VII:138; 140, n309
8:16	I:249; 250; 404n43; 444(n236); III:938; V:998n319; 999; 1001
8:16-18	VIII:221
8:17	I:249; 747n24; 749; IV:498; 500; 1084, n287; VII:648
8:18	I:404(n43); 444n236; II:353; IV:498; V:998n319; VI:443n763
8:19	I:444(n236); 703n61; 711; V:28; 118; 999; 1002, n341; VII:248; 249
8:20	II:139; 143; 673; III:236; 242; IV:128; VIII:540; IX:678
8:21	I:295; 296; II:353; III:15n67
8:21f	II:673; VIII:505; 506n11; 610
8:21ff	I:331; V:852n64
8:21-24	III:16
8:21-29	VIII:467n452
8:22	VI:441n745
8:23	I:205; 376; 377; III:640; 885; 894; IV:130; V:118; 514n121; VI:225(n365); 438(n719); VII:138n301; IX:129
8:24	I:295; 296; 307; II:353; 399, n10, n12; 400; III:15n67;
8:24-29	VI:210; 223; VIII:236n6
	II:353
8:25	I:482; II:347(n47); VII:252; VIII:469n462
8:25ff	V:28
8:26	I:248; II:144n47; 425; V:363; 729; 1000n330; VI:53
8:27	I:703
8:28	II:28; 143, n45; 399, n10; 400; III:56; V:711n441; 772; 1000, n330; VI:225; VII:574(n19); VIII:81; **467**; 469n462; **610-611**
8:29	I:456; II:144n47; 349; 353(n94); III:55; 999; 1001; VI:474(n88); VII:776; 779
8:30	VI:210(n266); IX:44
8:30f	VI:222n344
8:30ff	IX:349n321
8:31	II:499; III:378; 619; IV:107; 128; 407; 449; 458; 459; 578; V:1001n337; VI:203n221; 226
8:31f	I:712; 713; VI:227(n372)
8:31ff	II:324; IV:449n234
8:31-36	II:496
8:32	I:245n34; 246; 712n81; II:497; VI:226; 227; 439
8:33	III:16; VII:545
8:33f	I:9
8:34	I:246; 296; 306; 333n129; II:274; 279; 496; III:940; VI:481; 636
8:34a	I:295
8:34-47	III:16
8:35	II:498; III:940; IV:576; V:78; 122, n14; 131; 135n2; 997; 1015
8:35f	II:276; V:122n15; **VIII:374**; 387
8:36	II:498
8:37	II:539; IV:107; 128; VI:144n81; 715n77; VII:545; VIII:326
8:38	IV:130; V:341; 343; 363; 364; 729; 732; 996n309; 1002; VI:474(n88); 481; VII:346; VIII:81
8:38a	V:363
8:38b	V:363
8:38-47	I:671
8:39	II:646; V:638; 1002; VI:481; VII:248n320; VIII:391n417
8:39f	I:9
8:39ff	VIII:146
8:40	I:243; 245; III:451n1; IV:1109; V:363; VI:222; 478; VII:413n36; VIII:405n26
8:41	II:645; 823; III:101n221; V:1002; VI:481; 559; 592; VII:248n320; 346; VIII:391n417
8:41f	III:101(n229)
8:42	I:53(n152); 404(n40); II:671;

	680; 928; III:55; 56; 103; IV:130; V:730n26; 852n64; 996n309; 998n315; 999; 1002; VI:223(n347)		377; VIII:287; **288-291; 465;** IX:567n474
8:42f	II:349(n67)	9:1	I:129; VIII:288; 290, n149
8:42-47	VI:438(n719)	9:1ff	IV:715n77; V:347; VI:119n15; VII:246, n310; 248; IX:43; 44
8:43	I:220; 712; IV:108; 128; V:363; 756n91; VI:223, (n345); IX:277	9:1-34	VI:224
		9:1-41	VI:494; **VII:28;** IX:350n331
8:43f	II:309	9:2	I:308n151; 322n38; 329n89; 493n20; II:153; 685; III:201, n24; 323n4; 1093; V:910; VI:964; VIII:290; 291n153, n154
8:44	**I:245;** 307, n149; 481; 515n3; II:79; 80; 539; III:52; 171; 856; 1029; V:427; 730n25; 1002, n344; VI:223; 225n365; 481; 559; 592; 636; VII:138n301; 158; **162-163** (162n53); 346; 651; 750; IX:277; 479; 600n61; 602n80; 603, n87		
		9:2f	III:327(n41); VIII:290
		9:3	I:308n151; 493n20; II:642; 643; III:329(n60); VI:959; VII:28; 253; IX:3
		9:3b	VIII:291
8:44a	VII:158n33	9:3f	I:444n234; III:204; IV:1095; VII:247; 248; VIII:327
8:44f	**IX:602**	9:4	I:27n6; II:642; 648n39; 953; IV:1123n2; 1125; VIII:221; IX:351
8:45	I:245; VI:222		
8:45f	I:243; VI:203n221; 205(n235)	9:4f	IX:569
8:46	I:245; 306; 335n14; II:474; VI:223	9:5	III:889; 894; 895; IV:1083; VII:28; 392; VIII:291; **IX:350-351** (350n331)
8:47	I:246; III:55; IV:116; 128; V:363; VI:223(n345); 224; 225n365; VII:351; IX:297	9:6	II:448n4; III:209; VI:118; 474; VIII:288n125, n128; 290n147; 327n91
8:47a	VI:559	9:6b	IV:41n51
8:48	II:19; III:379; VII:91, n24	9:6f	VI:438n714; VII:28; VIII:327
8:48f	II:822	9:6ff	VI:119
8:49	II:19; VIII:179	9:7	II:433; 662; III:389; IV:947; VII:333; VIII:327; 505
8:50	II:248; 892; III:56		
8:50a	II:892	9:8	III:443; V:346; VIII:287
8:50b	II:892	9:8f	VIII:291
8:51	I:677; IV:107; 128; 724; V:345; 346; VI:441; VIII:179	9:9	II:352
		9:10	VIII:287
8:51f	II:553n32; IV:107; VI:225(n363); VIII:145	9:11	IV:947; VI:118; 474; VIII:287n118; 288n125, n128; 505n8
8:52	I:677; II:19; 822; III:379; IV:128; 1112; 1116; 1118		
		9:14	VI:474; VII:20; 28n222; VIII:290; 327; IX:44n200
8:52f	III:14(n61); VI:833n346		
8:52-59	I:9	9:14f	VI:118
8:53	IV:537; V:961; 1002; VI:225; 474	9:15	II:687; IV:947; VIII:287n118; 288n128
8:54	II:248; III:92n137; 105n267		
8:54f	V:118; 1002, n341; VII:249	9:16	I:306; 328; 329n93; 331; 332(n119); II:303; III:103; V:730; VI:483; VII:7n42; 28; 230; 245; 246; 247; 964; VIII:144; 290; 291; IX:44
8:55	I:703n61; 711; II:553n32; III:55; IV:128; V:117; 118; 187n6; 188; 1000; VI:223; 225(n364); VIII:144		
		9:17	VI:841; VII:257; VIII:465
8:56	I:20; 21; 759; II:951; V:341n135; 343, n147, n148; 347n164; 352n181; 1002; VIII:387; IX:370	9:18	VI:203; VII:852n28; VIII:287, n118; 291; IX:303
		9:19f	VIII:290
		9:21	II:942
8:57	III:379; V:341n135	9:22	I:528n6; II:142n44; III:379; V:209; 211; 270n189; 454n4; 588n36; **VII:852,** n31; IX:208; 567n474
8:58	I:682; II:353; 399, n12; III:588; IV:130; 741; V:998n315; VI:225; VII:253		
		9:23	II:942
8:59	I:129; III:242; 975; IV:268; V:714(n465); VI:573	9:24	I:331; 332(n119); IX:303
9	II:352; III:379; IV:1083; V:343;		

9:24f	I:328; 329n93
9:25	I:332(n119); VIII:287
9:26	VI:473(n83)
9:27	III:45n8
9:28	II:156; IV:294; 441; **443-444;** 865; IX:566
9:29	III:379; IV:294; 853(n69); 864n193; V:118; VI:441n741; VIII:291
9:29a	IV:443
9:29b	IV:443
9:29f	V:28
9:30	III:40
9:31	I:221; 306; 328; 329n93; 332(n119); III:56; 58; 111n313; 124n2; 125n6; 126; IV:724; VI:479
9:31f	I:331
9:32	I:198; 199; VIII:290
9:33	II:303; III:103; V:730; VI:473(n83); VII:852; VIII:465
9:34	I:295; II:143; 144; V:175n5; 270n189; VII:852; VIII:291; IX:569n489
9:34f	I:528; II:142n44
9:35	VI:210(n266); VII:852; VIII:387; 465, n443; 466; 469n462; IX:567n474
9:35ff	IV:444
9:35-39	VII:852
9:35-41	**VIII:291-292**
9:36	VI:214(n297)
9:37	VII:251; 776n58; VIII:465
9:38	VI:764; VII:251
9:38f	III:106
9:39	I:205; II:349; 671; III:328(n44); 885; 889; 942; V:343; 869; VI:224(n355); VII:251; 351; VIII:287; 291; IX:44
9:39a	VIII:291
9:39b	VIII:291
9:39-41	VII:28; **VIII:290-291**
9:39ff	**VIII:291**
9:40f	VIII:292
9:41	I:295; 307; 331; II:871n327; III:21; IV:1109; VII:254
9:42	IX:45
10	I:134; II:350; III:178; 179; 556n84; 756; VI:492; 494; 495n96, n97; 496; 497; VIII:23n75; **IX:297**
10:1	II:65; III:520; 756; IV:261; VI:495; 496; 499; IX:51n23
10:1f	III:173; 178; 180; VI:495
10:1ff	II:622n16; **IV:261; VI:691**
10:1-5	III:179; VI:495, n100; 496
10:1-18	VI:494; **495-496**
10:1-21	IX:569n489
10:1-29	VI:501
10:1-30	VI:485; **494-497**
10:2	II:678
10:2f	IX:297
10:3	III:179; 488; V:281; VI:490; 495n100; 691; IX:296; 303
10:3f	VI:502; VII:351; IX:293
10:3-5	VI:495; 496
10:3ff	VI:691
10:4	I:528; VI:493n80; **499;** 573; 574; 691; IX:297
10:4f	VI:501
10:5	I:265; VI:496; IX:297
10:6	V:751; **856;** VI:223; 495n100
10:7	II:350(n73); III:173; **178-180** (178n74; 179n75, n80); VI:495; VII:606
10:7f	III:178; 180
10:7ff	VII:252n354
10:7-10	III:179; IV:947; VI:495
10:8	II:672; III:179; 756; IV:261; 623; VI:495; 496; 499; 688
10:9	II:67; 350(n73); 678; 680; 769; III:173; **178-180** (178n74; 179n75, n80); 322n20; V:106; VI:495; 496; VII:252n354; 997
10:9a	III:178
10:9b	III:178
10:9bf	VI:495
10:10	I:395; 405; II:349; 671; 825; 827n62; 870; 871; III:179; 181; 327(n38); 756; VI:62; 496; 499
10:11	II:350n72; 870; III:18n77; 548; IV:311; 342; 623; 872, n252; V:708; 710, n435; 713; 715; VI:439n722; 495; VII:140n309; 252n354; VIII:155, n5, n6; 510; IX:166n162; 638; 644n165
10:11a	VI:495; 496
10:11b	VI:496, n104
10:11-13	VI:490; VIII:156n7
10:11ff	III:555; **VII:421**
10:11-15	IV:947
10:11-17	IV:311
10:11-18	VI:495; 496
10:11b-13	VI:495; 496
10:12	I:472; **IV:311;** 701; V:346; VI:486; 496(n105); 499; VII:421
10:12f	VI:486; 496
10:14	III:548; IV:872, n252; VI:490; 495; 501; 691; IX:129n161
10:14a	VI:495
10:14f	I:711; 712n81; V:1001; VI:496, n106
10:14b-15a	VI:496
10:14b-18	VI:495
10:15	II:870; III:18n77; IV:342; V:708; 710, n435; 713; 715; 1000; VI:496n104; VII:140n309; 248; VIII:155, n6; 510; IX:166n162; 638;

	644n165	10:30ff	III:104
10:15b	VI:496	10:30-39	VI:494
10:15f	IX:76	10:31	I:596; III:379; IV:267n8;
10:16	II:23; 440(n26); III:520;		V:713n461
	548n43; V:363; VI:496, n107;	10:31f	III:548
	499; 502; 691; 722; VII:421;	10:31-33	IV:267; IX:528n239; 569
	IX:296; 297	10:31-36	V:714(n465)
10:17	I:52(n149); 711; II:335; 870;	10:32	II:27; 642; V:1000; VI:53n3;
	III:328n48; IV:342; V:708;		VII:247; 248; 249
	715; 1001; VIII:155; 156n7;	10:32ff	VII:243
	IX:134; 638; 644n165	10:33	III:353; 379; V:713n461;
10:17f	IV:884n17; V:713; 715; 1001;		1002n346; VI:53; 474;
	VI:494n88; 496, n104;		VII:249; 870n70
	VIII:155n4; IX:141n242;	10:33-36	I:623; V:713
	166n162	10:34	I:749; 756n28; IV:1082; 1084,
10:17-19	VII:140n309		n287
10:18	I:185; II:335; 553; 568; III:18;	10:34f	III:92
	V:708; 728; VIII:156n7	10:34ff	I:759; III:100n213
10:18ab	VIII:155	10:35	I:755; 760; IV:112; 128; 336;
10:18c	IV:6		VI:723
10:19	III:378; IV:107n148; 128;	10:36	I:102; 112; 404(n40); II:423;
	VI:495		III:894; V:998n319; 999;
10:19-21	VI:494		VII:870n70; VIII:374n290;
10:19ff	IV:107; 361		379n323; **386**
10:19-29	VI:494; 495	10:36-39	VIII:386
10:20	II:19; 822; III:121(n10);	10:37	I:444n234; II:642; III:549;
	IV:106; 361		VI:395n384; 474(n88)
10:21	II:13n89; 19; III:179n80, n81;	10:37f	V:1000; VI:203n221;
	IV:128; V:377; VI:487n16		214(n296); VII:247
10:22	II:902; III:454; 531n92;	10:38	I:711; 712; 713; II:350(n68);
	VII:328n222; 392n23		543; 642; III:55; 329(n60);
10:22f	VII:333		V:1000, n329; VI:227n372;
10:22-24	VI:494		474(n88)
10:22-39	IX:569n489	10:39	VIII:540; IX:430
10:23	III:234; 236; 242; VII:464	10:40	I:536; VI:614; 615; 617; 868;
10:24	V:209n31; VI:223, (n351); 502;		VIII:202
	IX:569, n484, n485; **640**	10:40-42	IX:566n471
10:24f	V:273; **880**	10:41	I:248; II:672; III:206; VI:483;
10:25	I:444n236; II:27; 349; 642;		VII:245n306, n308; 246n308;
	IV:498; V:271; 276; 999n323;		247
	1000; VI:474(n88); 502;	11	III:848; VI:224; IX:132n180
	VII:247; 248; **VIII:249**;	11:1	VI:530
	IX:569	11:1f	I:144; VII:246
10:25ff	VI:496	11:1ff	III:206; V:23; VII:246n310;
10:25-29	VI:494		248; 252
10:26	VI:214(n298); 224; **501-502**	11:1-44	I:370; 784; IV:681
	(501n23)	11:2	I:230; III:1093(n269); IV:801;
10:26f	VI:501n22		VI:631
10:26-29	VI:494	11:2ff	I:144
10:27	I:711; 712n81; V:363; VI:490;	11:3	IX:128n150; 130; 131n167; 132,
	501; 502; VII:351; IX:296;		n180; 165
	297	11:4	I:493; II:249; III:14n62; 204;
10:28	I:395; 472; IV:189; IX:296		327n41; 329(n62); IV:1095;
10:28f	II:316; IX:430		VI:724; VII:253; VIII:291;
10:29	I:472; II:61; **IV:537**;		385n373; 387; 469n462; 514;
	V:1000n331; VII:964; IX:431		555
10:29b	IV:537n43	11:5	I:53n150; IX:128n150;
10:29f	V:1000		131n167; 134; 165
10:30	I:405; 711; II:350; III:55;	11:6	VIII:202
	103(n255); 353; V:997; 999;	11:8	II:153; III:379; 1093; IV:267;
	1000n329; VI:439n722; 494;		1107n8; 1112; V:714(n465);
	495; VII:776; VIII:416n121		VI:964

11:9	II:948n25; III:885; V:343; VII:392; VIII:221; IX:351n333; 680	11:38	II:539; III:655; IV:681, n4; V:419; 427, n326; 428, n333
		11:38f	IV:269
11:9a	II:953	11:39	I:362; II:592n13; 949n33; III:845; V:821n30; VIII:134; 555
11:9b	II:953		
11:9f	V:945; VI:745; 751; **752-753**; VII:356; IX:349n320; 569		
		11:40	II:249; V:343n148; 346; 349; VI:222n343; VII:253; VIII:236n6; IX:450n95
11:10	II:539; 953; IV:1125		
11:11	III:14n60; V:880; VI:573; **VIII:555**, n74; IX:131; 161n125; 162; 165; 169n191		
		11:41	I:6(n8); 185, nl; 376, n2; IV:269; V:377n11; 514n121; 985n251; 1002n346; 1003; IX:411
11:11f	I:148		
11:11-13	**VIII:555**		
11:12	VII:990; 997	11:41f	I:221; II:803; V:1002; 1003; **VII:603**
11:12f	V:880; **VIII:555**		
11:13	III:14n60; IV:884n17; **VIII:555**	11:42	I:404(n42); II:70; V:586; 587; 589n40, n41; VI:210; 214(n297); 222n343; 227(n370)
11:13f	VIII:555		
11:14	V:209n31; **880-881**		
11:15	IX:366		
11:16	III:19n79; IV:460; VII:795; IX:166n166	11:42ff	VII:251
		11:43	III:901; VI:438n714; IX:295
11:17	III:845; VIII:134; 555	11:44	II:60; 679; IV:336; V:370n1; VI:628n43; IX:429n35
11:18	II:332; VII:328n222; 333		
11:19	III:378; 839n72; 845; 846; V:820; 821, n30; VI:56n25	11:45	III:378; 848; V:342; 345; VI:473(n83); VII:250; VIII:387
11:20	III:440; 626		
11:21f	IX:450n95	11:45ff	IV:107; VII:252
11:22	I:191n2; 192; III:118(n378); IV:1108; 1110	11:45-54	VII:867n51
		11:46	III:839n72; 845; VI:473(n83)
11:23	V:822; 823	11:46ff	IX:43
11:24	II:697; 953; V:869; VI:437n711	11:47	III:271; VI:473(n83); VII:245; 247; 852n30; 864; 867; IX:44
11:24f	V:823		
11:25	I:370; II:336; 350(n73); 865; 870; III:318n79; IV:724; V:81, n134; VI:214(n303); VII:251; VIII:236n6	11:47a	VI:478
		11:48	I:510; II:369; **VIII:204**
		11:48-52	IV:52
		11:49f	III:270
		11:50	II:369; 439(n21); V:917; VI:91n76; VII:867; VIII:511; IX:75; 76
11:25f	III:19; V:869; VI:223(n349); VII:251n348		
11:25-27	VI:222n343	11:50-52	VIII:510
11:25ff	IV:724	11:50ff	VII:140n309
11:26	I:370; VI:203(n211); 226	11:51	II:369; III:269; 270; IV:236n20; V:917; VI:829
11:26f	IX:450n95		
11:27	II:423; 672; III:889; 894; V:211; 465n9; VI:210n263; 214(n293); 227; VIII:387; IX:567; 569	11:51f	III:18n77; V:654; 710n435; VI:492n72; 543n41; VIII:511
		11:52	II:369; 434; 439(n21); 440; IV:739; V:653; 1001n337; VI:501; 502; VII:420; **421**; IX:76
11:28	III:1094; V:859; 865; IX:303		
11:29	II:334		
11:30	III:626; V:1003; VI:530; VIII:202		
		11:54	II:332; 658; V:880; VII:772
11:31	II:679; III:378; 722; 839n72; 845; V:817n4; 820; 821; VII:772	11:55	I:103; 123; 519; II:332; III:377; V:588; 898; 899n24; 901(n43), n43; VI:685; VII:332; 333
11:32	VI:163, n15; 630		
11:33	III:378; 722; 845; V:419; 427, n324, n326; 428; 821; VI:438n714	11:55-57	III:396
		11:56	III:242; VII:648
		11:57	I:703; II:553; III:271; VII:852n30; 864; IX:44
11:34	V:342		
11:36	III:378; IX:128n150; 130; 131n167; 165	12	V:588; 589; VI:630n54
		12-17	II:249
11:37	II:304; III:845; V:377; VI:473(n83)	12:1	II:335; IV:893(n17); V:898; 899n24; **VI:686**

12:1-8	IX:165
12:2	II:34; 84; 85; III:654; VII:771; IX:161n125; 165n157
12:3	I:230; II:472; IV:801; V:495; VI:291; 631; IX:139n231
12:4	IV:452(n245)
12:4ff	III:796
12:5	IV:801; VI:160; 907
12:6	I:596; III:755; 790; V:307n29; VI:907
12:7	II:426; IV:801; VII:925n41; VIII:145
12:8	II:824n47; VI:907
12:9	I:703; II:335; III:378; IV:893(n17); V:586; 588; VII:252n349
12:9ff	V:589n41
12:10	III:271; V:589; VII:864; IX:44n197
12:11	III:378; 848; V:589; VI:210(n266)
12:12	IV:921; V:587n27; 588; VII:332; 333
12:12-19	V:588
12:13	I:578; II:762; III:384; 385; 625; 901; IV:274n48; V:286; 588n39; 996; VII:246; 333; IX:684, n23
12:13-16	VII:333
12:14	I:749; VI:287; VI:961
12:14f	III:444; V:286
12:15	I:578; III:337; V:286; VI:831; 960; VII:327; IX:459n173; 528n236
12:16	I:749; II:248; 249; IV:451; 677; V:287; 711n441; VI:478; 868
12:17	II:335; III:848; IV:496; 497; 893(n17); 921; V:586; 589n40; IX:303
12:17f	V:589n40
12:18	III:626; V:587n27; 589n40; VI:473(n83); VII:246; 247
12:19	III:894; V:291; 346; IX:44n197
12:20	I:519; II:102; III:389; V:13; 589n41; VI:764
12:20f	I:427n116
12:20ff	II:509; 511; **IX:299**
12:20-26	III:1104
12:21	II:683; III:45n8; V:341
12:21f	IX:90n14
12:23	II:248; 249; 673; III:945; V:272, n195; 711n441; **VIII:468;** 469n462; 611; IX:678
12:23ff	I:445(n237); II:249
12:24	III:14n61; 15; 616; 811; V:917; VI:163, n9; VIII:468; IX:59; 130; 644
12:24b	VIII:466
12:24-26	IX:643
12:25	I:205; 214; 395; II:86; 864(n278); 870; III:56; 885; n64; **IV:690-691** (691n30);

	692; 693; V:346; VI:117; 437(n711); VIII:326n82; 443n308; IX:128n150; 129; **130**; 240; 608; 642, n155; **644**
12:25f	IV:450n239
12:26	I:214; II:86; 88; V:79; 80n133; 346; 769; 771; VII:578n44; VIII:179, n65, n66, 506n14; 596; IX:644
12:27	IV:1113; 1119; V:985n251; VI:36; 438n714; VII:69; 989; 997; IX:641, n149, n150; 677, n16
12:27f	I:6(n8); IV:248
12:27ff	IV:1113; V:1002; 1003
12:27-31	III:939
12:28	I:99n35; II:248; 249; **V:272,** n195; 351; 530; 985n251; 999; VI:843; IX:288n47; 299, n101
12:28-30	VII:70n28
12:29	I:640; V:351; 589n40; VII:647; IX:299
12:29f	IX:294
12:30	II:70; IX:299
12:31	I:205; 489, n6; II:79; 80; 871(n327); III:103(n249); 636, n6; 640; 885; 894; 914n8; 939; 941; IV:839n56; 1112; 1119; V:526n228; 589n41; 869; VI:163n11; 224(n355); 225; 530; 559; VII:157; 158n32; 162; 252; VIII:266n52; IX:346n291
12:31f	IX:544n333; **569;** 573
12:31ff	II:31
12:32	I:680; II:503; IV:623; V:711n441; 772; VI:722, n6; VIII:469n462; 506; **610**
12:32f	VI:441n745; VIII:466; 506; 610; IX:76
12:32-34	VII:574(n19)
12:33	IV:884n17; V:917; VI:408n489; VII:247n316; 254n366; 263; **264-265** (265n27, n28)
12:34	I:199; II:24; IV:575; 1082; 1084; V:589n40; 708; 711n441; VI:224; **VIII:467;** 469n462; **610-611;** IX:567n474; **568-569**
12:35	II:539; 826; IV:10; 650n14; 1083; V:945; VI:752n45; VII:392; 443; 444; VIII:292; IX:344; 352n345; 591
12:35f	II:862n55; IX:349; 569
12:36	II:826; III:975; VI:210(n266); 214(n296); 223(n349); VIII:365; IX:345; 349n321; 350
12:36ff	III:975n41
12:37	VI:473(n83); VII:245; 247; 249n331; VIII:292

12:37b	VII:250n342; 252n349
12:37f	I:640; V:708n423
12:37ff	VII:253; 254
12:37-43	VII:251n344
12:37bff	**VII:249-250**
12:38	I:221; 639; III:328n44; 590; 1087; IV:112; 128; V:555n111, n115; 705; 706; 708, n421; 709; VI:208n258; 295; 296; 830; 832; 833; 834; IX:5
12:38f	IV:110
12:39	VI:831; VIII:292
12:39f	V:757
12:40	III:204; 328n44; 613; IV:950; V:341; 342; 378, n16; 380n7; 554; 589n41; 708, n421; 1023; 1024; **1026**; 1027; 1028; VII:392; **727,** n24; 893; 894n53; **VIII:292;** IX:44
12:40b	III:612
12:41	II:248; V:343n148; 352n181; VI:831; VII:387
12:42	I:489; V:209; 211; 212; 454n4; **VII:852;** IX:44; 45
12:42f	VII:852n30
12:43	II:248; V:209; 589n41; VII:852; VIII:515
12:44	V:363; VI:438n714; IX:566
12:44f	V:362; VII:250
12:44ff	III:902; 975
12:44-50	III:975n41; VII:776; IX:350n311; 566
12:45	II:395; V:346; 362; 363; 364; 365, n233; 370; 999; VII:248; 256
12:46	I:405; II:423; 671; III:889; 894; IV:576; 724; VI:223(n349); VII:443; 444; **IX:350-351** (350n331)
12:46f	III:327(n38); 894
12:46-48	I:712; II:871n327
12:47	I:109; 405; 444n235; II:671; III:848; 894; 938; V:363; 869; VI:225(n364); 441; VII:997; VIII:144; IX:240; 296
12:47f	IV:107; 128
12:48	II:697; 870; III:938; 939n69; IV:6; 106; 107; 128; V:869; VI:222n344; VIII:159; IX:240
12:49	I:404(n43); 444n236; II:553; III:56; V:589n41; 998n319; 1000; VI:394n366
12:49a	II:28
12:49f	V:999; 1000n330
12:50	II:553; 870; V:1000
12:50b	II:28
13	III:426; 741; IV:181; 947; VI:631
13-16	IX:135n200
13-17	VI:142n62

13:1	I:53(n151); 205; 377; 523; 711; II:427; 673; 903; III:20; 850; 885; 889; 895; V:118; 898; 899n24; 1000n332; VI:685; VII:248; 392n16; 999n158; VIII:56; 327; IX:114; 130; 134; 678
13:1ff	I:427n116; 711; II:154; **277-278** (278n114); IV:451; V:25
13:1-4	VIII:506
13:2	I:527; II:34; 79; 80; 425; III:612; IV:451n243; 452(n245); VII:439n146
13:2ff	IX:131n173; 135n201
13:3	II:680; III:103, (n252); V:118; 730(n26); 895; 993n293; 998n315, n317; 1000n332; VIII:267n56; 505; 506; IX:430
13:3a	VIII:506n13
13:3f	V:1001n335
13:4	II:34; 334; 903; V:306, n23
13:4f	VIII:23n75
13:4ff	IV:750
13:5	I:478; V:306, n23; VIII:328
13:5f	IV:947
13:6	VI:441
13:6ff	VII:343
13:6-10	V:175n3; VI:474n86; VII:140n312
13:6-11	III:426; VIII:328
13:7	VI:474; IX:568n479
13:8	I:199; II:154; 831; IV:306; 596; 597; 947; VII:795
13:8ff	IV:305
13:9	IX:429n35
13:10	I:382n11; III:426; **IV:305-306**; 947; V:175; VI:441; 631n55
13:10f	III:426
13:11	IV:173; VI:844
13:12	IV:947; VI:474
13:12ff	IV:305; 947
13:12-17	III:426; VIII:23n75
13:12-20	VIII:328
13:13	III:1093; IX:303
13:13f	III:1086
13:14	III:666n17; 1093; V:563; 564n29; VI:631
13:14f	IV:305
13:15	II:33; III:404; VI:474; 482; 631; VIII:249
13:16	I:405n44; 421; 435; II:277; IV:305; 448; 538
13:17	IV:369; VI:479
13:18	I:477; 712n81; 753; 754; III:328n45; IV:172; 173; VI:295; 628; VII:140n311; 253; VIII:236; IX:141
13:18f	IV:172; VI:844; IX:141
13:19	II:353; 399, n10; 400; III:329(n60); IV:1107; 1120; VI:210; 685; 688; VII:357

13:19f	II:353n94		14:1	II:432; III:103(n255); 612;
13:20	IV:6; 305n41; 306n43; V:363;			IV:321; VI:210(n266), n269;
	VI:393n360; VII:1071n447			214(n296); 227; 575;
13:21	IV:496; 497; V:427n324;			VII:250n340; IX:208n104;
	VI:438n714; VIII:468n461;			566; 641
	IX:141		14:1-3	V:805
13:21ff	IV:452		14:1ff	VIII:370n257
13:22	V:343		14:1-4	VIII:207n152
13:23	I:53n150; III:441; 654; 734;		14:1-7	V:997n312
	825; IX:128n150; 131, n169,		14:2	**IV:580-581**; V:78; 79; 80; 121;
	n172; 132n182; 133n189; 170			122; 769; 997; 1001n336;
13:23ff	IX:132			1015; VI:575; VII:379n60;
13:24	IV:174; IX:90n14			VIII:207
13:24f	IX:132		14:2a	V:78, n129
13:24ff	VI:102		14:2b	V:78
13:25	VI:393n357; 394n364; IX:131,		14:2f	II:705; V:79; 80; 82; 83n143;
	n173; 132n182			**132**; 771; VI:437(n711);
13:26	I:530			VII:650; 651n32, n34;
13:26f	IX:141			VIII:202n103; 235; 596
13:27	II:79; 80; 425; 678; III:856;		14:2ff	V:80; 81; 82; 83; 84;
	IV:451n243; 792; VI:478;			VIII:207n154
	636; VII:162; 439n146;		14:2-5	VIII:505
	VIII:506; IX:140n241		14:2-6	V:82
13:27a	IX:141n242		14:3	II:673; IV:13; V:78; 79; 80; 84,
13:27b	IX:141n242			n147; 346; VI:443; 575;
13:27f	IX:45; 638			VII:795; VIII:207; IX:76
13:28	III:654; VI:724		14:4	V:28; **79-80** (80n133); 81;
13:29	III:796; VI:907; VII:392n16			VIII:506n14
13:30	III:396; IX:138n227		14:4f	IV:884n18; **V:78-84**; VIII:505
13:30f	II:680		14:4-6	V:83
13:30-32	VIII:506		14:4ff	V:42; 75; **78-84**
13:31	II:249; IV:1113, n48; 1122;		14:5	V:79; 80; 81
	V:1001; VIII:468n459;		14:5f	I:435
	469n462		14:5-11	VI:443
13:31f	**VIII:468**		14:6	I:246; 247; II:67; 350(n73); 499;
13:32	II:249			865; 870; III:180; 318n79;
13:33	II:673; III:379; IV:650n14;			322n20; IV:455; 498; 623;
	V:639; 852n64; 1005; VI:443;			795; 1083; V:28; 63n59; 77;
	VII:795; VIII:505			**78-84** (80n133; 81n134;
13:33-38	VIII:144n39			82n139, n140; 83n141;
13:34	I:59; 711; II:553; 555; 871;			84n144, n145, n146); 1001;
	III:448; 450; IV:125; 678n13;			1003; VI:227; VII:249;
	VI:228, (n374); 306;			252n354; VIII:224; IX:602
	VIII:144; 327; IX:116n20;		14:6a	V:80
	134; 355n378		14:6b	V:80; 81
13:34f	I:53(n153); III:20; IV:449; 454;		14:7	I:703n61; IV:1107; 1119; V:28;
	1084; V:720; IX:570			80; 84; 117; 119; 362;
13:35	I:711; II:826n52; III:590;			364n229; 1001n337; 1003;
	729n12; IV:1084; VI:228			VII:249
13:36	V:79; 80n133; VIII:506, n14;		14:7-9	I:711; 712
	595-596		14:7ff	IV:884n18; V:80; 81; 82
13:36f	IV:1107n8; 1112n44; 1120;		14:7-10	V:999
	VIII:505		14:8	I:466; 711; V:363
13:36-38	VIII:596		14:8f	V:363; 364; 365n233
13:37	VIII:155; 222n45; 596;		14:8ff	I:28
	IX:166n166		14:9	I:405; II:350; 395;
13:37f	VIII:155; 510			III:103(n255); 486; IV:451;
13:38	I:469; 471; VIII:155; 596;			V:84; 362; 363; 364, n229;
	IX:135, n201; 303			365, n233; 370; 869; VII:256;
14	VI:576			795; VIII:612n55; IX:591
14-16	V:813n95		14:9f	VI:439n722
14ff	V:788n122; 804n28		14:9ff	VII:243; 248; 249

14:10	I:444n236; II:543; 642; III:55; 56; IV:107; 128; 576; V:1000; VI:210; 214(n298); 443; 464; VII:248
14:10a	II:543
14:10b	II:543
14:10f	II:28; V:1000n329
14:10ff	VII:247
14:11	I:711; II:543; 642; V:1000; VI:203n221; 214(n296)
14:12	II:642; III:789n17; IV:537; V:1000n332; VI:474(n88); 482; 575; VII:248; VIII:385
14:12-14	IX:569
14:12-28	V:1003n347
14:13	II:249; III:118(n378); 329(n62); V:271; 769n38; 1001; 1003, n347
14:13f	I:193; II:871(n328); V:276; 1008n380
14:14	V:271
14:15	II:553; n32; 554; VI:223(n347); 225(n364); VIII:144; 145; IX:130
14:15ff	I:53(n153); IV:449; 459; V:119; VI:443n757
14:16	I:192; 199; 247; 435; V:274; 790n136; 800, n1; 804, n28, n29, n30, n31; 805n34; 806, n42; 811; 812; 813, n98; 814; 1001n338; VI:443; VII:776; VIII:375n292; IX:572n503
14:16f	V:804; 812; 813; 814n102; VI:70n76
14:17	I:247; 435; 712; II:540; III:116n371; 895; IV:7; 580n4; V:346; 732; 800; 813; VI:144n81; 442; 444n766; VIII:326; IX:572n502
14:18	I:510; V:362; 488, n8; VI:443; 576
14:18f	V:805
14:18ff	V:362; VI:443n757
14:18-21	V:1001
14:19	II:870n323, (n326); IV:650n14; V:346; 362; 363; 807n47, n49; VIII:612
14:19f	I:712
14:20	I:711; 712; II:350n68, (n70); 543; 952n47; III:808n69; V:362; 1001, n337; 1003, n347; VI:144n81; 442; VIII:326
14:20f	V:1000n329
14:21	II:553, n32; 554; V:362; 1001; VI:223(n347); 225(n364); 908, (n209); VIII:144, n41; 145; IX:130; 134, n191
14:21f	V:363; IX:7
14:21ff	I:53(n150); 711
14:21-24	VI:443n757
14:22	IV:452(n245)
14:22f	IV:884n18
14:22ff	V:362
14:23	II:543; 553n32; III:808n69; 945; IV:128; 580-581; V:238; 362; 732; 1001; VI:142(n67); 473; VIII:145n42; IX:7; 128n150; 130; 134, n191
14:23f	II:554; VI:223(n347); 225(n364); VIII:145
14:24	I:404(n43); II:553n32; IV:107, n148; 128; V:363; 998n319; 1000; VI:442; VIII:145n42
14:25	V:732
14:25f	V:362; VI:443n757
14:26	I:103n54; 405n45; 435; 757; II:143; 144; III:107; IV:346n27; 677; V:100-101 (100n18; 101n26); 271; 274; 800; 804, n31; 811; 812; 813; 814n102; 1001n338; VI:433n672; 439n722; 442; 443; VIII:375n292; IX:163; 572n502, n503
14:27	I:510; II:412, n62; 413; 826n53; III:612; 894; VII:357; IX:370; 641
14:27f	V:805
14:28	I:53(n152); III:352; IV:538; V:997; 999; 1000n332; VI:223(n347); 575; 576; IX:366; 370
14:28a	VI:576; VIII:506
14:28f	II:831
14:28-31	VIII:506n14
14:29	IV:1120; VI:845; VII:357
14:30	I:489; II:79; 831; III:103; 885; 894; VI:36; 559; VII:162; 439n146; 776n58
14:31	I:52; 711; 712, n81; II:334; 545; 553; 831; III:55; 329(n60); V:1001; VI:474(n88); IX:134
15	IV:172; 179; VIII:469n469; IX:162
15:1	I:250; 342; II:350(n73), n74; VI:439n722; VII:1071
15:1ff	I:342; 711; II:543; III:731n21; 757; IV:449n234; V:1001; VII:252n354
15:1-8	II:871
15:1-10	III:654n3; VI:228
15:1-17	IX:569
15:2	I:343; III:414n1; 429n2; 757; 858; IX:59
15:2f	III:426
15:2ff	III:615; 859
15:3	III:426; IV:107; 128; 305; VI:441; VII:140n312
15:4	II:543; III:757; VI:116; VIII:237n12; IX:59
15:4f	III:757; VI:144n81; VIII:326
15:4ff	I:342; 343; III:808n69
15:4-7	IV:576; VI:226(n368)

15:5	I:342; II:304; 350, (n73); 543; III:757; IV:1084; VI:482		225(n365); 438(n719); 441n741; VII:253; IX:114; 129
15:6	I:527; II:424; 543; III:757; 858; 938; IV:173; VI:252; 942, n72	15:20	II:230; 553n32; 554; III:696; IV:107; 128; 448; 538; 682; VI:225(n363); VIII:145
15:7	II:539; 543; 871(n328); III:49; IV:105; 107; 128; 576; V:274; 1001n337; 1003n347; VI:144n81; 908(n209); VIII:326	15:21	II:431; V:271; 279; 1002, n341; VI:477(n102)
15:7ff	II:350n70	15:22	I:295; III:21; IV:1109; V:474; VI:54
15:8	III:323n1, (n2); V:1003n347	15:22-24	I:306f; **VII:138-139**
15:9	I:711; IV:576; V:1000; VIII:143; IX:134	15:23f	IV:691; V:999; 1002n341
15:9f	I:53(n154); V:1001; IX:130	15:24	I:295; II:642; IV:1109; VI:483; VII:247; 250, n334
15:9-17	II:871	15:24ff	VII:254
15:10	II:543; 533, n32; 554; III:55; IV:576; VI:227; VIII:144; IX:165; 166	15:25	I:749; 756n28; II:167; III:328n45; IV:128; 691n30; 692; 1082; 1084; VI:295
15:10-12	IX:570	15:26	I:247; 405n45; 435; III:107; IV:498; V:730; 800; 803; 804, n31; 811; 812; 813; 814n102; 1001n338; VI:442; 443, n759; VIII:330; 375n292; 579; VIII:330; 375n292;
15:10ff	IV:449		
15:11	I:713; II:539; 554; 871(n329); III:329(n59); VI:297; 605; IX:367n70; 370		
15:11-14	III:20		
15:11-17	VI:228	15:26f	IV:459; VI:443; 450n823
15:12	I:711; II:553; 555; 871; III:404; VI:228; IX:134; 166	15:27	I:481; III:704; IV:498; VII:795
		16	IV:1115; VI:576
15:12f	I:711; III:323(n2); 757	16:1	IV:1120; VII:344; 350; 356; 357
15:13	I:53n151; II:826n52; III:18n77; IV:531; V:710, n435; VIII:155; 156; 327; 510; IX:114; 128n150; **166**, n163; 169n189; 638	16:1ff	IV:450
		16:1-4	V:805
		16:2	II:673; IV:65; 1084n287; V:454n4; VI:477(n102); VII:534, n43; **852,** n31; IX:45; 67; 679
15:13ff	IX:162		
15:13-16	**IX:165-166**	16:3	I:712; IV:1084; V:1002, n341; VI:442; 477(n102)
15:13-21	IX:644		
15:14	II:276; 545; 554; V:623; VI:479; IX:116n24; 165	16:4	I:481, n13; II:673; IV:682; 1120; V:806; VI:443; 845; VII:795; 852; IX:678
15:14f	IV:450n235; IX:137; 170		
15:14-16	IX:131	16:5	II:685; IV:1112n45; 1113, n49; 1119; VI:721; VIII:505; 506
15:14ff	IV:449		
15:15	I:63; 718; II:276; IV:1084; V:363; VI:476; VIII:541; IX:163; 165n158, n159; 169; 170n196	16:5-7	VIII:505
		16:6	III:612; IV:320; VI:291; IX:641n149
		16:6f	IV:321
15:15b	IX:165	16:7	I:243; 405n45; 435; V:800; 804, n31; 811; 813; 1001n338; VI:443; 575; 576; VIII:330; 375n292; IX:75; 76n15
15:16	I:712n81; II:871(n328); III:991; IV:172; 174; 444; 449; V:271; 276; 526; 1003, n347; VII:253; IX:165n158, n160		
		16:7a	VI:573n49
		16:7ab	VIII:505
15:16f	IV:173; 174	16:7b	VI:573n49
15:16ff	IV:172; 173; 174	16:7ff	V:119; IX:76
15:17	I:711; II:545; 553; IV:174; IX:134; 165; 570	16:7-11	V:803
		16:8	II:200; 474; 475n12
15:17f	V:710	16:8f	I:307
15:18	III:894; IV:691; VI:878n44	16:8-10	IX:572
15:18f	III:895; IX:371	16:8-11	I:712n81; V:803; 811; 813, n97; 1002; VI:443; VIII:224
15:18ff	IV:321; 449f; VI:226		
15:18-27	VII:357	16:9	VI:210(n266); 214(n302); 443n757
15:18-16:2	VI:444n767		
15:19	I:712n81; III:895; IV:172; 173; 321; V:29; 119; 526; VI:224;	16:9-11	II:474

16:10	II:200; V:341n135; 346; **362;** 1000n332; 1002; VI:908(n209); VIII:506; IX:469
16:11	I:205; 489, n6; II:79; III:103(n249); 885; 894; 939; 941; VI:559; VII:157; 162
16:12	I:596, n1; IV:451; 1120; V:100; 101
16:12f	VI:439n722
16:12-15	IV:346n27; 677n11; VI:443n757
16:13	I:64; 247; II:499; V:98; **100-101** (101n25); 363; 800; 881; VI:438n712; 442; 443; 908(n209); VIII:330
16:13f	V:811; 813; IX:572
16:13-15	I:61; **64;** V:804
16:13ff	III:590
16:14	II:249; III:108; VI:443
16:14f	I:64; II:537(n8); IV:6
16:15	V:997; 999; 1001; VI:908(n209)
16:16	V:715; VIII:612
16:16f	V:341n135; 346; **362**
16:16ff	IV:650n14; V:362
16:16-24	VI:443n757
16:17	III:902; V:1000n332; VIII:505; 506
16:17f	IV:884n18
16:19	III:46n18; V:341n135; 346; **362**
16:19f	VI:908(n209)
16:19ff	IV:451
16:20	III:152; 153; 155; 722; 724, n18; 725, n24; 841; 849n122; 850; IV:320; 321; 932; 1115, n60; VI:908; IX:371
16:20-22	II:871; **IV:321-322; IX:370-371**
16:20ff	IV:320
16:20-23	V:805
16:20-24	II:871(n329)
16:21	I:776; II:434; III:146; 154; 889; IV:320n28; 644n16; V:638; IX:371n105; **678**, n18
16:21f	IV:322
16:22	III:146; 155; 612; IV:320; 322; 1115, n60; 1116; V:341n135, (n138); 362; VI:298; VII:851n21; IX:641n149
16:22-24	I:713
16:23	II:685; 686; 871; 952n47; V:274n210; 276; 362; 1003, n347
16:23a	II:685; 686
16:23f	II:871(n328); V:271; 276
16:23ff	III:118(n378)
16:24	I:192; III:329(n59); IV:7; 1110; 1120; VI:297; 298; 443n757; 605; IX:370; 371
16:24a	II:685n2
16:25	I:64, n29; 681; 713; II:685n2; 871; IV:794; 1120; V:209n31; 751; 854n4; **856;** 999; VI:223;
	IX:679
16:25ff	V:119; 881
16:26	I:192; II:686; 952n47; V:271; 274; 276; VI:54
16:26f	V:276; 1003
16:27	III:103; V:730; 1003; VI:210; 223(n347); 443; IX:116n20; 128n150; 133, n190; 134, n191
16:27f	II:680; V:1003n347
16:27-30	VI:227; VIII:506
16:28	I:405; 510; II:423; III:103; 885; 889; 894; IV:130; V:998n315; 1000n332; VI:575; 576; VII:243
16:29	I:713; II:871; IV:1120; V:209n31; 751; **856;** VI:223; IX:165n159
16:29f	II:685n2
16:29ff	V:881
16:30	I:713; II:538; 680; 685; 686; IV:130; 1110n34; 1118; V:730(n26); 998n315; 1000n332; VI:210; 227
16:30f	VI:214(n298); 222n343
16:32	II:673; IV:1115n60; 1119; V:362n225; 488n8; 708; 1001; VI:493; 501; VII:349; 421, n13; 776; 779; IX:679
16:32f	VI:493n79
16:33	II:413; 541; 826; **III:26-27;** 143; 146; 329(n59); 588; 895; IV:321; 322; 944; V:805; VI:493n79; VII:633; 776; IX:214
17	II:251; III:547; IV:623; 741; 1122; V:813; 1001n339; 1002; 1003; IX:570n490
17:1	I:185n1; 186; 376n2; II:249; 673; III:329(n62); V:514n121; 534; 711n441; 985n251; 1003; VIII:385n373; 387; IX:678
17:1f	III:725n24
17:1ff	IV:451; V:1001; VII:248
17:2	I:362; II:61; 566; 568; V:895; 993n293; 998n317; 1000n331; 1001n335; 1003; VI:908(n209); VII:138; IX:129n161
17:3	I:249; 250; 404(n42); 711; 712; II:871; 872; III:101(n222); 323(n2); IV:872n254; V:869; VI:227(n370); 439; 440; IX:352n350; 565; 566, n470; 569; 570n491
17:3ff	VII:256
17:4	I:27n6; 678; II:28; 249; 643; III:56n13; V:1000, n330; 1001; 1003; VI:474(n88); VII:247; 248; 249; VIII:59n10; 81

17:4ff	I:711
17:5	I:6(n8); 406; 482n17; II:249; III:588; 885; IV:130; 741; 751; 1113n48; 1119; 1122; V:711n441; 985n251; **VI:560**; 685; 687; VII:253
17:6	II:553n32; III:895; IV:128; V:272; 999; 1003; VI:225(n363); 576; VII:250; VIII:145; IX:5
17:6ff	VII:250n341
17:7	IV:1118, n74; V:730; 1003
17:7f	I:712; 713
17:8	I:404(n42); 712; II:680; IV:6; 107; 114n188; 128; V:1000n332; 1003; VI:210; 214(n292); 222n344; 227, (n370)
17:9	V:1003; VI:54
17:10	II:251; V:997; 999
17:11	I:101; 102; 108n66; 392; II:166; 440; III:103, (n255); 329(n59); 889; 895; IV:321; V:31; 135; 271; 272, n199; 956n60; 985n251; 996n310; 999; 1003; VIII:142
17:11f	I:101n48
17:12	I:395; 397; 755; 758; III:328n45; V:272, n199; 999; VI:295; 908(n209); VIII:142, n12, n13; 365; IX:141; 240
17:13	I:101; II:826; 871(n329); III:329(n59); IV:1112n45; 1113, n49; 1119; VI:297; 605; IX:367n70; 370
17:13ff	IV:452
17:13-17	VI:442
17:14	II:351n76; III:895; IV:128; 691; V:29; 119; 135; 1003; VI:224; 225(n365); 438(n719); IX:129; 371
17:14ff	III:426
17:15	I:186; III:333n92; 895; IV:452; VI:225; 226; 549(n22); VII:162; 163; VIII:142; 151n4
17:16	III:895; IV:321; V:29; 31; 119; VI:225(n365); 438(n719)
17:17	I:246; IV:128
17:17-19	I:246; 247
17:18	I:404(n42); II:350n70; 423; III:894; 895; 991; V:31; 33n218; 1001; VI:442n753
17:18f	I:712
17:19	I:111; 112; 246; III:18n77; 20n82; IV:623; V:710n435; VII:140n309; VIII:510
17:20	II:67; 433; IV:174; VI:54; 108; 210(n266); IX:163n142
17:21	I:404(n42); 711; II:350n68; 543; III:808n69; 895; V:272; 985n251; 1000; 1001; VI:210;
	214(n297); 227(n370); VII:421; VIII:82
17:21f	II:440; III:103(n255)
17:21-23	VIII:82n14
17:21ff	III:329(n59)
17:22	II:251; 350n70; 870; V:1003
17:23	I:404(n42); 712, n81; II:434; 440; 543; III:895; V:1001; VIII:82
17:23f	I:711; V:1000; IX:134
17:23ff	I:53(n150)
17:24	I:202; II:61; 251; 336; 870; III:48; 620; 885; 1029; 1032; IV:741; V:79; 346, n162; 364; 984n247; 985n251; 998; 1000, n331; 1003; VI:226; 227; 437(n711); 443; 685; 687; VII:795; VIII:235; IX:76; 129n161
17:24-26	IX:569
17:25	I:108n66; 404(n42); 712; II:188; III:894; V:985n251; 997n310; 1000; 1001; 1002, n341
17:25f	VII:249
17:26	I:711; 718; II:350; 543; V:272; 999; 1000; 1001; 1003; VII:250; IX:5
18-20	VII:254n366
18:1	V:766n8; VI:598; VII:771
18:1f	I:405n46
18:1ff	I:445n237
18:3	III:271; IV:16; 261n28; 326n24; 1100n15; V:294; VI:908(n209); VII:772; 864; VIII:540; IX:44
18:4	IV:173; V:118
18:4ff	VIII:267n56
18:5	II:352n89; III:287; IV:874; VII:748
18:5f	IX:141
18:6	II:352n89; V:290; VI:163
18:7	II:687; III:287; IV:874
18:8	II:352n89; IV:451
18:9	I:395; III:328n45; IV:105; VI:296
18:10	I:424n103; II:503; III:270; 852; IV:451n240; 525; V:343; 551n76; 558, n5; 559; 940
18:11	I:405n46; IV:525; V:437n386; 558n3; 1001; VI:144; **152;** 153n43; 908(n209)
18:12	II:60; IV:261n28; V:588n36; VII:760; VIII:540; IX:466n2
18:12-23	VII:870
18:13	III:270
18:13f	III:270
18:14	II:439(n21); III:18n77; IV:52; V:710n435; 917; VII:140n309; VIII:510; 511; IX:75
18:15	I:718n2; III:270; VII:741n23
18:15f	I:719; II:886n19; IX:131n171;

	132
18:16	I:264; III:173; VI:102; 721; VII:648; IX:132
18:17	IX:135
18:18	VI:475(n92); VIII:540; IX:135n201
18:19	II:164
18:19-24	III:270
18:20	II:139; 143; III:236; 242; 960; 975; V:101n26; 209n31; 880; VII:832n216; **835**
18:20f	**V:879-880**
18:21	II:687
18:22	V:839; VIII:540
18:22f	VIII:266n45; 267
18:23	IV:294; 496; 497; VIII:265n38; 267n56, n57
18:24	II:60; III:270
18:25	I:469
18:25-27	IX:135
18:26	III:270; 852; V:551n76; 558n140, n4 (sic); 766n8; VII:742, n23; 794
18:27	I:469; IX:303
18:28	II:693; 903; IV:646; V:12; 897n8; **899-900** (899n24); VI:156n75
18:28ff	IV:261n28
18:28-37	V:212n40
18:28-19:16	VII:870
18:29	III:637; 941n2; VIII:542; IX:58
18:30	III:945
18:31	II:561; III:923; IV:1082; 1084n288; VII:865; 866
18:32	IV:106; 128; V:917; VI:296; VII:247n316; 254n366; 263; **264-265**
18:33	I:577; III:377
18:35	II:369; III:271; 377; IV:52; VI:474
18:36	I:137n13; 205; 581; III:710n59; 885; 894; IV:1109; V:28; VI:225(n365); VIII:530; **541-542**
18:36b	VIII:542
18:36f	I:139n21
18:36-38	IX:569
18:37	I:220; 246; 405; 577; 578; II:350n75; 352n91; 423; 429; 671; III:327(n38); 885; 889; 894; IV:496; 498; V:211n35; 363; VI:223(n345); 224; 559; VIII:542; IX:296; 297; 350n329
18:38	VIII:222
18:39	I:577; 632(n52); III:377; V:898; 899n24
18:39f	IV:261
18:40	III:901; IV:262
19:1	IV:517, n16; V:621n160; 634
19:1-3	**V:634-635**
19:2	III:679; 813; VII:632, n84;

	VIII:160
19:2ff	VII:709
19:2-5	VIII:266n46
19:3	I:577; III:377; IX:367
19:4	VIII:222
19:5	III:813; VII:632, n84; IX:84
19:6	III:271; 901; VIII:222; 540
19:7	I:759n53; II:826; IV:1082; V:563; 917; 1002; VI:474; VIII:386; IX:528n239; 569
19:7a	IV:1082
19:8	III:38; IX:208
19:9	III:946; V:713
19:10	II:565
19:11	I:295; 378; II:566; V:514n121; 531; 542; VI:151
19:12	I:578; III:901; VI:475; IX:167
19:13	III:389; 442; IV:107n148; VIII:203n126
19:14	V:898; 899, n24; VII:20n159; IX:680
19:14f	I:577
19:15	II:823; III:271; 376n101; 901; IX:158n105
19:17	I:596, n1; 754; II:680; III:389; VI:921n6; VII:238; VIII:203; IX:58n10
19:19	I:577; 744; III:287; 377; IV:874
19:19-22	III:846
19:20	I:343; 744n10; 762; II:332; 509; III:388; 389; VI:921(n6); VII:245; VIII:202, n106
19:21	I:577; III:271; 377
19:21f	I:744
19:23	I:378; II:66; IV:595; VI:475; VIII:127; 134
19:23f	V:286; VII:709
19:24	I:753; 754; 758; III:328n45; **IV:1;** VI:54; 295; 475(n92); VII:962, n19
19:25	I:144; IV:643; V:731; VII:648
19:25-27	IX:678n18
19:25ff	VI:995n18
19:26	I:144n2; 777; II:886n19; IV:643; V:839; VI:102; VIII:335; 364; IX:131; 132; 133n189
19:27	IV:643; IX:678n18; 679n28
19:28	I:754; 758; II:226; III:328n45; V:118; VI:295; VIII:59, n10; 82
19:28-20	V:289
19:29	V:288, n3; VI:129; 160; VII:362; 699; VIII:82n15; IX:66
19:30	II:170; III:679; VI:36; 438n714; 452; VII:633; VIII:59, n10; 267n56; 611
19:31	II:686; III:333n92; VI:156n75; VII:20n159, n160; 28; 574; 923; 1057
19:31-37	VI:628

19:32	I:264; VII:709; 786; 923
19:33	V:342; VII:923; 924n29
19:34	I:172; 175; 540; II:680n4; VI:448n812; 995n18; VII:709; VIII:237n13; 333
19:34b	**VIII:330**
19:34f	IV:498; VI:441
19:35	I:248; 249; II:355n104; III:327n40; 389; 396n38; IV:455; 496; 498; 500; V:345; VI:214(n297); 722; IX:131n171; 132; 133
19:36	I:339; 340; 753; 754; 758; III:328n45; VI:156n75; 295; **VII:923-924** (924n29)
19:36f	IV:109n159
19:37	I:264; 753; 759; II:447; 702; III:663; IV:110; V:361; 697n318; VII:237; 924n28
19:38	I:192; III:333n92; 379; 975; IV:445; 456n267; VII:1057; IX:169; 208
19:38ff	V:716n480
19:39	III:975; VI:868; **VII:458,** n10
19:40	II:60; 373; III:377; IV:262; VII:458; 1057
19:41	III:448; IV:680; V:766n8; VIII:202
19:42	II:332; III:377; VII:20, n159; 28
20	VII:254; 333
20:1	I:784; III:1096; IV:269; VI:866; VII:20; 29; 32n246
20:1-10	VI:102
20:2	III:1093(n269); IV:1110n33; VIII:233; IX:128n150; 131, n70; 170; 210n115
20:2ff	III:523
20:3	I:264
20:3ff	V:815n12
20:3-10	III:39
20:4	I:264; VIII:233; IX:132
20:5	**V:815,** n12
20:5f	V:346
20:6	V:343; 346; 815n11
20:7	III:679
20:8	I:264; IV:446; V:349; IX:132
20:8f	IX:132
20:9	I:755; 759; II:24; IV:893(n22); VII:254
20:10	VI:721
20:11	III:722; V:815; VI:721; VII:648
20:11ff	I:431(n143); 784
20:12	I:84n67; III:440; 679; IV:27; 249; V:346; 351; 815; VI:721; VII:1057
20:13	I:777; III:722; 1093(n269)
20:14	V:290; 343n150; 346; VII:647; 715, n6
20:14f	V:359n214
20:14ff	V:355
20:15	I:596; 777; III:722; 1086
20:16	II:153; III:389, n140, n141;

	1093; VI:962n15; 964; VII:715, n6
20:17	I:145; 521; II:335; III:102; V:996; 1000n332; 1001, n337; 1008n380; VI:405n472; 573; 575; VII:254; VIII:469n462; IX:132; 163; n144
20:18	**I:61;** III:1093n269; V:357; VI:574
20:19	I:430n136; II:335; 411; 673; III:173n2; 174n8; 176; 379; 396; 1096; V:356n203; 357; VII:20; 29; 32n246; 650; IX:208; 680n39
20:19ff	V:355
20:19-23	VI:51n46; VIII:222
20:20	II:25; III:1093n269; V:357; VII:254; VIII:249; IX:367; 430
20:21	I:404(n41); 434; 435; II:411; III:753; 991; V:998n319; 1001; VIII:374n290
20:21ff	I:434
20:21-23	VI:442n750; IX:135n200
20:22	I:103n54; 104; II:536; III:107(n284); 753; IV:7; V:274; VI:142; 405n472; **442;** IX:125
20:22f	VI:438n712; 442; 443, n765
20:23	I:109; 449; 511; 512; II:61; III:752; 753n87; 912; VII:745
20:23a	III:753
20:23b	III:753, n88
20:24	II:328
20:24ff	I:434; IV:446; 459; V:349; 355; VII:247
20:24-29	VIII:222
20:25	I:527; III:1092n269; V:349; 357; VI:205; VII:575; VIII:205n141; 246; 248; IX:429n34; 430
20:25a	VIII:205n141; 249
20:25b	VIII:205n141; 249
20:25ff	II:335
20:26	II:335; 411; 673; III:173n2; 174n8; 176; 1096; V:357; VII:650
20:27	V:349; 357; VI:205; 215; VII:254; IX:430
20:28	II:536n6; III:92(n140); 106; 945; 1086; V:1002n346; VII:633; VIII:155n5
20:29	III:211; 590; IV:368; 369; V:349; 357; VI:223
20:29b	VII:245
20:29f	VII:252n352
20:29ff	VII:252n353
20:30	I:618; 745; VI:473(n83); VII:245; 246, n310; 247; 252; **254-255** (254n365)
20:30f	I:745; 760n54; III:207; IV:741; VII:247, n315; 251, n343;

ACTS

1:6	I:389; 581; II:685; 686; III:386; V:714n472; VIII:255; IX:522; 591	1:22-26	IV:492
		1:23	III:488; 497; VII:646; 649
		1:24	II:30; 614; III:111n307; 613; 1088; IV:174
1:6f	I:432(n153); VIII:381n343		
1:6ff	V:360n217	1:25	I:446; II:88; 327n49; III:217n6; 808n75; V:738; VI:574; **VIII:205;** 207; 208
1:6-11	IX:210n112		
1:7	I:703, n61; II:567; III:461; V:1008n380; VI:723; VIII:39; 157; IX:591; 592, n66		
		1:25a	VIII:205
		1:25b	VIII:205; 207
1:8	I:104(n57); 247; 430(n139); 679; II:310; 311(n87); 681; 697; III:589; 888; 890; IV:7; 446; 455; 492; 493; VI:50; 51; 407(n487); 408n492; VII:91; 93; 335; VIII:605	1:26	I:422; II:326; III:761n9; 763; VI:164; VII:794n134; IX:607
		2	I:724f; II:703; III:389; V:8; VI:49, n32, n33; 52n53; VI:68; 956n17; **IX:296**
1:9	IV:8; 15; 909; V:344; 345; 378; 522n196; 534n315; 772n58; VI:576	2:1	V:185; 186; **VI:50,** n38; 308; 309; VII:647
		2:1ff	I:104; IV:725; V:139; VI:47(n25)
1:9f	**VI:576-577**	2:1-4	**VI:51-52;** 337n8; 346; 414
1:9ff	V:355n201	2:1-13	VI:51, n45; 442n752; IX:432n50
1:10	I:84n67; IV:27; 249; V:351; 530n270; 839; VI:576; VII:690n27		
		2:1-41	VI:52n52
		2:2	III:444; V:353n189; 531; VI:291; 453; VII:335n277; IX:58; 296
1:10f	V:345; 356n204; 524; IX:61		
1:10ff	VI:52n58	2:2f	I:724; V:353n189; VI:411
1:11	I:363; II:424; 675; III:288; IV:8; 874; V:344; 345; 361; 534; 867; VI:576; 577; VII:647; 650n31; VIII:462n422	2:2ff	I:724; 726
		2:3	I:538; 721; III:444; V:353n189; 354n192; VI:398; 947; IX:296
		2:3a	VI:51n49; 453n1
1:11b	IV:140	2:3f	I:725
1:12	II:332; III:488; V:69; 484n100; 485; VII:21; 335	2:3-6	VI:406
		2:4	I:447; 722; 724; 725; 726; II:702; V:31n213; VI:50, n43; 130; 406n476; 408(n488); 410; 849; 851; 852
1:13	II:887; IV:234; VI:102		
1:14	I:144; 785; III:288; 618; IV:643; V:185; 186; VII:794n134		
1:15	IV:53; 441n198; 457; V:270; 588; VI:109; 413	2:4f	I:724
		2:5	I:363; II:753; III:375n99; 379; 847n113; V:153; 534; VII:335
1:15ff	II:326; III:618		
1:16	I:48; 363; 753; 757; 758; II:22; III:288; V:99; VI:295; 408n489; 412; 831; 833; VII:700, n64; 760; VIII:482	2:6	I:722; 725; II:702; VI:49n33; 279; 410; 411n518; VII:764n12; IX:292; 296, n87
		2:7	I:724; II:460; III:40; V:887
		2:8	I:722; 725; III:388; VI:410
1:16ff	II:608	2:8ff	II:512
1:16-20	VIII:482n32	2:9	I:725; III:382n113; VI:51n44
1:17	II:88; III:763; **IV:1-2,** VIII:205n137	2:9f	V:5n29
		2:9-11	II:100; VI:51n44; 411n524; VII:335
1:18	I:156; II:468; IV:698; VII:553; 556, n49		
1:19	I:719; III:488; V:153; VI:973n1; VII:335	2:10	IV:265n1; 595; VI:111
		2:11	I:722; 725; 726; II:702; III:33n26; IV:541; 781; VI:50; 51n44; **742;** IX:296n86
1:20	I:616; 748; II:607; 608; 657; V:153; VIII:482n32; 499; IX:51n23		
		2:11f	II:442(n43)
1:20a	VII:383	2:12	I:724; II:460; III:46n23; 699
1:20b	VII:383	2:12f	V:8; IX:187
1:21	IV:124; V:106; 525n221; IX:591	2:12ff	IV:938
1:21f	I:436; IV:106; 115; 127; 128; 454; V:349n171; VI:644	2:13	I:724; 725; II:703; **VI:51-52;** 350n65; 407n480; 410n510; VII:407
1:21ff	II:616; IV:115		
1:22	I:370; 372; 545; IV:8; 127; 493; VI:619; VII:650n31; 794n134; VIII:462n422	2:14	I:447; III:375n99; V:153; 556n122; 559; VI:50n43; 109;

	VII:335; 648; 794n134;		V:177; 183n71; 381; 462; 497,
	IX:293		n6; VI:831; VII:124n212;
2:14ff	I:433(n162); 725; VI:50		VIII:381n346; 483
2:15	IV:15; 548; 933n69; VI:50n36;	2:30f	VI:833; VIII:335; **367,** n233;
	IX:680, n38		381
2:16	IV:110; VI:831; 833	2:31	I:148; 149; II:433; V:342; 381;
2:16f	I:724		772; VI:833; VII:124;
2:16ff	II:468; 582; VI:849		VIII:483; IX:103; 535; 608;
2:17	II:697; 950; IV:112(n182);		**646-647**
	V:235, n51; 350n175; 371;	2:31f	I:371; VI:415
	518; VI:50n40; 51n45;	2:32	III:288; IV:493; V:356; 524;
	410n507; 654; 849; 851; 852;		887
	VII:124; VIII:553	2:32f	IX:535
2:17f	VI:829; 854	2:32ff	V:525
2:17ff	I:103	2:33	I:104(n57); 219; II:39; 468; 582;
2:17-21	V:279; **VI:410-412;** VII:440		III:108n286; V:353n189; 356;
2:18	II:273; V:708; VI:408(n493)		524; 711n441; VI:405;
2:19	I:176; 376; 678n5; II:538;		408n492; 433n672; 442n751;
	III:640; V:513(n118);		VIII:367; 466; **609-610**
	514n121; VI:50n41; 943;	2:33f	II:424; VIII:156
	VII:240n286; **242;**	2:34	I:520; II:39; III:440; 1086;
	VIII:124-125		1087; IV:110; 237n24; 513;
2:19-21	VI:415		514n121; 522n190; 524;
2:20	I:176; II:675; 952; III:1087;		VII:650n31; VIII:462n442;
	IV:531; VII:61; 430n49; 729;		482; 483
	IX:10	2:34a	VIII:609
2:21	III:497; 500; 1087; V:272;	2:34f	II:814; V:895(n31); IX:533n277
	VII:991n108; 996; IX:536	2:35	V:525; VI:629
2:22	II:67; 301; 425; III:103; 288;	2:36	I:506; 704; II:39; 568(n37);
	386; IV:101; 868n226; 874;		III:103; 288; 328; 386; 918;
	VI:464; 864; VII:230;		1089; 1094; V:129; 887; 895;
	240n286; 242; 243n296;		VI:211(n275); 417; 464;
	VIII:124; 125		VII:292n3; 335; 581; VIII:20;
2:22f	VII:581n2		IX:45; 533n276, n277; **535;**
2:22-24	VI:209(n262); IX:535		536
2:22ff	VII:240	2:37	I:145; 422; III:612; 626; VI:479;
2:22-35	IX:534n282		723; VII:240
2:23	I:328; 635; III:918; IV:1087;	2:37ff	VI:618; IX:535n283
	V:452; 453; 707(n414);	2:38	I:295; 305; 511; 512; 539; 540;
	VII:439n146; IX:45; 431		543(n69); II:167; 429; 688;
2:24	I:370; 719; II:304; III:18; 911;		III:582; IV:7; 1003; 1004;
	IV:336; 337; VI:415; 877n40;		V:271; **276;** 436; VI:216n315;
	926n49; **IX:673;** 674		406n475; 412; **413-414**
2:25	III:1087; IV:110; V:381;		(414n533); 984; VIII:329;
	VI:831; VII:69; VIII:482		IX:355n384; 536
2:25ff	**VII:69**	2:38f	II:582; VI:410
2:25-28	III:747; V:85; 772; VII:29n226;	2:39	II:512; III:101(n226); 500; 501;
	389; IX:646		589; 1087; IV:374; V:638;
2:26	I:21; 721; II:532; 775; III:612;		650; 887; VI:864n11
	V:214; VII:124; 389, n9	2:40	I:633; IV:512; V:795; 796;
2:26f	I:148		820n24; VI:854; **VII:407,**
2:27	I:148; 149; II:424(n17); 433;		n24, n25, n28; 996; 997n142
	V:85; 342; 492; 772;	2:40f	IV:101n118
	VI:578n85; VII:389;	2:41	I:539; II:55; III:766; IV:101;
	VIII:483; IX:103		VI:60; 241n300; 602;
2:27a	VII:124		VII:613; VIII:168; IX:469;
2:28	I:718; II:775; 864n279; V:85;		639; 665
	VI:291; 777	2:42	I:477; II:164; 440; 807; III:619;
2:29	I:145; II:560; IV:680; 1107n15;		729; 730; 731, n22; 737; 809;
	V:209n31; 882; VII:772;		VI:142; IX:169n189
	VIII:483, n33	2:42-47a	VI:154n52
2:30	III:164; 442; 615; 787(n9);	2:42-47	VI:51; 412n523

2:43	III:213; 589; VII:240n286; 242; 335; VIII:124; 125; IX:209; 210; 638n131; 639	3:13ff	V:704
		3:14	I:101; 102; 108n66; 192; 362; 558n1; V:704n380; 707; VII:699n60; IX:375n18; 393
2:44	III:796; 809; IV:457; V:889; VI:214(n307)		
2:44f	III:348	3:15	I:488; II:335; 865; III:288; IV:493; 893(n20); VI:864; VII:613; 1015; IX:105n60
2:44-46	IX:163		
2:45	III:796; VI:160; IX:451		
2:45f	I:426n10	3:15a	V:913
2:46	I:21; 477; II:440; III:246; 613; 618; 729; 730; 731, n22; 737; 803; IV:10; V:130; 186; VI:142; 155n66; VII:335, n277; VIII:204n133; 213n39; IX:451	3:15b	V:913
		3:15ff	IX:45
		3:16	I:433(n166); II:67; III:213; 767; V:277; VI:204(n230); 206; 210(n267); 407(n485); 412(n522); VII:613
		3:17	I:118; 145; VI:397; 636
		3:17-19	VII:581n2
2:47	I:177; III:503; 504; 505; IV:51; VI:60; VII:992n114; 997; VIII:168; IX:392, n147	3:18	I:71; 73; V:704n380; 707(n414), n414; 913; 920; 924; VI:295; 296; 831; 833; 863n9; VII:700; VIII:381n342; IX:535
3	V:701; 707; VI:110		
3f	VI:483		
3:1	I:519; II:801; VI:109; VIII:204n133; IX:677; 680, n38	3:18f	VI:636
		3:18ff	V:916n91
		3:18-22	VI:847
3:1-3	VII:335	3:19	I:295; 305n143; IV:999; 1003; 1004; VI:777; VII:727; 997; **IX:535**
3:1ff	III:131; 213		
3:1-10	III:246; VII:335n277		
3:2	I:191; III:173, n5; 236; 787; IV:643; VI:578	3:19b	IX:665
		3:19-21	IX:664n2; 665
3:2f	II:486	3:19ff	IV:1004
3:4	V:343; 347n163; VII:794n134	3:20	I:367; II:675; III:288; 461; 717; 1094; **VI:863-864** (863n9); **IX:535; 664-665**
3:5	VI:726		
3:6	II:826n60; IV:107; 453; 874; V:271; 277; 466n18; VI:407(n485)		
		3:20f	**I:389-393;** V:867; VI:864n12; VIII:39; IX:665n6
3:6-12	V:944		
3:7	II:334; III:130; VII:613; IX:430; 431	3:21	I:198; 199; 389; 383; II:22; 24; 424; III:582; V:524n208; 525; 531n282; VI:577; 831; 833; IX:591; 665n7
3:8	II:677; VII:335; 647; 794n134		
3:8f	I:177		
3:9	II:457; IV:51	3:21a	IX:665
3:10	I:704; II:450; 486; III:5; 6; 236; 443; VI:130; 724; 921	3:22	I:145; 369; II:938n81; III:1087; IV:110; 270n19; 865; VI:831n337; 841; 845; VIII:255; IX:639n134
3:11	III:5; 6; 236; 488; 911; IV:51; V:484n100; VII:335n277; 464		
		3:22f	IV:858; 868; VI:841
3:11f	VI:410n510	3:22-26	VIII:445n318
3:11ff	I:433(n163)	3:23	IV:53; V:171; IX:639
3:12	II:311; III:40, n65; 386; IV:51; V:341n136; VI:483; 723; VII:181	3:24	**I:71,** n12; 73n29; VI:831; 833; 840
		3:25	I:678; II:106; 133; 765; IV:110; 111; V:976n178; 1017; VI:723; 835; VII:545
3:12-26	VII:52		
3:13	I:339; 469; II:146n54; 266; III:101(n223), (n225); 191; 288; 384n122; V:700, n341; 704, n378, n379, (n380); n385; 705n386; 711n441; 976n178; 977n197; VI:110; 777; 864; VIII:222n43; IX:534n282	3:26	I:369; II:133; 146n54; 266; IV:1004; V:700, n341; 704, n378; 705n386; VI:110; 565; 869; **VII:721;** 997; IX:412n50
		4	V:701; 707; VI:110
		4-19	IV:115
		4:1	III:270; IV:51; 241; VII:36; 53; 709n35; 871
3:13f	II:188; V:707n412; 913; VII:242		
		4:1f	**VII:53**
3:13-15	VI:209(n262)	4:1ff	II:145

	VIII:155; 178; IX:58	5:27	III:270; VII:646; 649
5:3	I:104(n57); II:79; 80; III:612;	5:28	I:173; 632(n53); II:145; 164;
	VI:291; 406n475; 408, n490;		V:271; 278; 762; 764; VI:291;
	VII:161; VIII:178; IX:595n6		VII:327n221; 335
5:3f	IX:58; 600; 601	5:29	I:422; II:22; III:102(n237);
5:4	II:440(n28); 565; III:612; 796;		V:525n221; 950; VI:10; 109;
	VI:160; 252; 562; 639;		746n6
	VIII:155; IX:595n6	5:30	II:335; III:101(n233); 288; 918;
5:4f	IV:725		V:39; 976n174; 977n197;
5:5	V:169; VI:163; IX:209; 210		VII:581n2; IX:45
5:6	IV:898; **VII:597;** IX:57	5:30f	V:356
5:7	I:682; VIII:220; IX:680	5:30ff	VII:53
5:8	II:168	5:31	I:72n19; 295; 305; 488; 511;
5:9	III:173; 1087; VI:32; 406n475;		512; II:39; 145, n53; III:103;
	408, n490; 628; 629; IX:308		1089; IV:1003; 1004;
5:9f	IV:725		V:711n441; VI:211n275;
5:10	II:769; IV:893(n14); 898;		216n315; VII:997; 1015, n64;
	V:169; VI:163, n15; 629		VIII:367; 466; **609-610;**
5:11	III:503; 504; 505; IX:209; 210		IX:396n195
5:12	III:213; 236; 246; V:185; 186;	5:31f	IV:493
	VII:240n286; 335n277; 464;	5:32	I:224; IV:492; 725; VI:10;
	VIII:125; IX:431		408n492; 409; 412; 450n823
5:12ff	VII:240; 242	5:33	I:632(n53); VII:53
5:13	III:822; IV:51; 543; **VIII:184**	5:34	I:368; 420; II:159; 539; IV:51;
5:14	I:776; III:766; VI:214n305;		VI:477; IX:37n143; 45; 46
	279; VIII:168; IX:665	5:34ff	II:145; 885; VI:819n261; IX:45
5:14f	I:433(n166); III:131	5:34-39	VII:871
5:15	I:493; II:310n86; 311n89;	5:35	III:386; VI:635, n7
	III:130; 209; 213;	5:35ff	IV:260
	VI:407n479, (n485); VII:397;	5:36	III:823; VI:4; 826; 837n355
	400; IX:431	5:36f	II:347
5:16	III:131; 428(n12); V:586n19;	5:37	I:513; II:884n9; IV:51; 258n7;
	889; VI:279; VII:335		V:291; VI:4; VII:422;
5:17	I:182; 368; II:880; 887; III:270;		IX:81n12, n14
	271; V:89; VI:130; VII:36;	5:38	I:635; II:643; 650; IV:103; 338;
	794n134; 871		1108; 1121
5:17f	II:145	5:39	II:769; III:117; 121n11; 123;
5:17-42	**VII:53,** n107; 871		176n39; 667; IV:338; **528,** n4
5:18	I:529; VIII:146, n2; IX:430	5:40	III:288; 500; V:271; 278; 762;
5:18-25	IX:244		764; VI:4
5:19	I:85; 196; II:66; III:173n3;	5:41	I:380; IV:508; V:273, n204;
	174n8; 175; 176; 1087;		279; VI:777; VIII:514;
	IV:850n14		IX:368, n84
5:19f	V:352	5:42	I:72n18; II:145; 719; 720;
5:19ff	V:356		III:246; 288; V:130; VII:335;
5:20	II:867n308; III:236; IV:51; 117;		IX:535
	128; VIII:648	6	II:85; 86; 90; 737
5:20f	III:246; VII:335	6f	IV:1068
5:21	III:270; 271; 386; 496;	6:1	I:424n106; 736; 787; II:87; 102,
	VII:794n134; 856n1; 871n80		n12; 509; 510n41; 512, n49;
5:22	I:66; VII:716; VIII:540		**389-390** (310n143); IV:443;
5:22f	II:769		457; 458; VI:281; 406n475;
5:23	III:173; 174n8; VII:648; 856n1;		723; 742; **IX:451,** n103, n104,
	IX:361n12		n105
5:24	III:270; 271; IV:241; VII:53;	6:1f	III:847n113
	709n35	6:1ff	I:376; II:440(n28); IV:115;
5:25	I:66; II:145; III:246; VII:335;		IX:461
	647	6:1-6	**IX:433,** n55
5:25f	IV:51	6:2	I:456; II:85; 326n46; 327;
5:26	III:270; IV:53n100; 241; 268;		III:389; 500; IV:115; 124;
	VII:709n35; 773; 794n134;		VI:279; **VIII:213;** IX:451
	VIII:540; IX:208	6:2ff	II:634

	VI:631; VII:648; VIII:202
7:33f	IV:864; VII:603
7:33ff	VIII:257
7:34	I:221; IV:54; V:341
7:35	I:83; 469; 489; II:538; III:102; 103; 444; 942n1; IV:351; 864; 866n209; 868n226; V:351n177; 358; VI:846; VII:241; 242; 1015; IX:430
7:36	I:677; II:658; IV:864; 868n226; VI:483; VII:240n286; **242;** VIII:124; 125; 138
7:37	I:145; 369; II:936n81; III:386; IV:270n19; 865, n201; 868, n226; VI:831n337; 841; 845; VII:242; VIII:463n427
7:38	I:83; II:658; 855n180; 862(n250); III:504; **IV:138;** 139; 618; 864; 866(n209), n209, n210; VI:106; VII:285; 780n73; 829n199
7:38f	V:976n175
7:39	I:224; 448; III:52; 613; VII:242; 285; 715
7:40	I:677; VI:476
7:40ff	III:100
7:41	II:378; 774; III:181; 182; IX:430
7:41f	III:184
7:41ff	II:658
7:42	I:616; 747; II:170; III:182; 386; IV:62; 63; V:520n174; 533; 538n20; VI:831; 832; 834; VII:709; 715; 934n40; **VIII:138;** IX:66
7:42f	VII:374; 375, n36
7:43	I:514; IV:8; VI:476; 764n59; VII:374; 384; VIII:248; 257n64
7:43f	VII:384; VIII:257n64
7:44	II:658; IV:502; V:363; VI:476; VII:374, **375;** 384; VIII:35; 249; 256; **257,** n64
7:44f	V:976n175
7:44-50	III:246
7:45	III:285; 292; VI:777; VII:375
7:46	II:769; III:192; V:129; VII:375; **384;** IX:392
7:46f	VIII:482
7:47	V:139; VII:384; 463, n30
7:47-50	VIII:257
7:48	III:116(n363); IV:110; 885; 886n24; V:124; 125n25; 153; 154; 985n253; VI:831; 834; VII:464; VIII:620; IX:436
7:48-50	VII:464
7:49	I:679; III:116(n368); 164; 628; IV:885; V:124; 139; 516; 522; VI:630n53; VIII:204n132
7:49f	V:143
7:50	VI:463; IX:431
7:51	I:104(n57); III:612; 613;
7:51f	V:714n469; 976n175
7:52	I:73, n30; II:188; 230; **675;** IV:487; 1112; V:707, n414; VI:833; 835; VII:581n2; VIII:205n135; IX:45
7:53	I:83; II:67n6; 433; IV:618; 866n210; VIII:36; 257; IX:240
7:54	I:641; III:612
7:54-8:2	VII:866
7:55	I:104(n57); II:248; 457; III:288; **V:353,** n187; 517n155; 522n190; 530n270; 534; VI:285; 406; 408n491; VII:648; **650;** 651, n33; **VIII:461-463** (462n419, n421; 463n428); IX:647n182
7:55f	II:457; III:177; V:352; VII:650, n31; VIII:461; 462n416, n422
7:55-8:3	VII:651n33
7:56	II:39; IV:237n24; V:346; 353n187; 530, n268, n270; 867; **VII:650,** n28; 797; 962; VIII:368n236; 383n356; 401; 404n24; **461-463;** 469n462; 477n517
7:57	I:223; II:816n1; III:902; V:186n4; 470; 544n6; 556, n122; VII:878n11; 883; IX:293
7:58	· III:404; 488; IV:489; 490n47; VI:87n53; 921(n5)
7:58f	IV:268
7:59	III:404; 497; 500; V:769; 771; VI:415; VII:650n28; 797; VIII:163; IX:294
7:59f	V:435n373
7:60	I:48; 295; 738; III:14n60; 404; 902; VI:88n54; VII:647; 649; 650n28; 797; VIII:155; IX:293
8	IV:359, n2; 1065n186; VIII:463n428; IX:432
8ff	VII:328
8:1	I:422; 431n149; II:98; 715n90; 739; III:146; 504; 847n113; VI:109n51; 111; VII:333; IX:606n13
8:1ff	I:431; IV:266
8:1-25	VII:91
8:2	II:753; III:837; 846; 847, n116; VI:475(n93)
8:3	I:362; 776; III:504; 847n113; IV:312, n1; IX:244
8:4	II:98; 720; IV:104n139; 116; VII:835n236
8:4f	II:720; 737
8:4-8	II:720
8:4-25	**VII:93**
8:5	I:72n18; III:288; 704; 711;

	VI:530; VII:92n29; 93n34; 835n236; **IX:535**
8:5ff	I:433(n165); II:327
8:5-40	V:707
8:6	IV:53; V:186; 342; 587; VI:483; VII:230; 239
8:7	I:625; II:679; 822; III:131; 213; 428(n12); IX:294
8:8	II:720; IV:122
8:9	II:459; **IV:359;** 541; VI:837n355
8:9f	II:347; **VII:90;** 510n313, n314
8:9ff	II:457; VI:618; VII:235
8:10	II:304; III:488; 972; IV:529; 531n7; **540-541;** 650(n13); VII:90
8:11	II:459; **IV:359;** IX:591
8:12	I:362; 539; 583; 589; II:710n30; 719; 720; 737; III:288; V:278; VI:208n258; 214(n300); 414; IX:535; 536
8:12f	VI:602
8:12ff	V:707, (n411)
8:13	I:433n167; II:311n89; 460; III:618; V:342; VI:214(n292); VII:93; 239
8:13f	VI:214n291
8:14	II:54; IV:104n139; 116; 119; VI:415; VII:333
8:14f	II:737
8:14ff	I:433n169
8:14-17	VI:109; 414; 415
8:14-25	VII:335
8:15	I:104(n57); IV:725; VI:54; 414n532
8:15ff	I:724; IV:7n7
8:16	V:275; VI:412; 602
8:16f	I:543(n69); VIII:329
8:16-18	VI:410
8:17	I:104(n57); IX:432
8:17f	VI:411; **IX:432**
8:17-19	VIII:161
8:17ff	VI:342n29
8:18	VI:408n488; 666n92; IX:66; 480
8:18f	IX:433n52
8:18-20	VI:273n26; 414n532
8:18ff	III:213; 753
8:18-24	VII:93n37
8:19	I:104(n57); II:570; IV:104
8:20	I:397; II:167; VII:858n6; IX:480
8:20f	III:752
8:20ff	IV:725
8:21	III:613; 763; IV:104; 105n140
8:22	I:511; 512; II:41; III:484; 612; IV:999; 1003; 1004
8:22ff	I:48
8:23	I:156; V:345; VI:125; VII:858, n6
8:24	II:41; 681; VI:723; VIII:514
8:25	II:710n29; 720; III:288; 1087;

	IV:512; VI:530; VII:93
8:26	I:85; 368; III:1087; V:66; 352; VI:575
8:26f	VII:335
8:26ff	II:327; VI:618
8:26-40	VIII:20
8:27	I:363; 368; 590; III:854; V:13; VI:573; 574; 764
8:27ff	II:765; 768
8:28	I:343; III:444; VI:830; 832
8:29	II:684; III:822; VI:408(n491)
8:30	I:703; VI:830; 832
8:31	I:519(n4); III:444; V:100; 793, n160; VII:794n134
8:32	I:338; 339, n5; 340; 753; II:816n1; VII:838n12; 937
8:32f	II:665; III:942; IV:1097; V:705; 707; 709
8:32-35	VIII:20
8:33	I:185; 186; 663; 678; VIII:541n87
8:34	II:40; V:666n67; 686; VI:53; 832; 833
8:35	I:72n18; 753; II:710n28; 719; 720; 737; III:288; VII:700n65
8:36	V:66n70; 68n81; 707, (n411); VI:618n84; 619; VIII:329
8:36f	V:211n37
8:36ff	VI:602
8:37	V:211, n37; VI:203n215, n223; 210n263; VIII:381; IX:134n194
8:37f	I:433(n165)
8:38	I:523; VI:618n84; VII:647
8:38f	V:707, (n411); VIII:329
8:39	I:472; III:1087; V:66n70; VI:409; 414n538; IX:370
8:40	II:433; 710n29; 719; 737; 769; V:66n70; VII:835n236
9	VI:863n6
9-10	VI:109
9:1	II:431; 684; III:847n113; IV:312; 458; VI:452
9:1f	III:270; IX:46n219
9:1ff	I:417; 438n182
9:1-18	VIII:224
9:1-19	VI:414
9:2	I:192; 362; II:60; III:468; IV:265; V:48n22; 88; 89; 90n178; VII:335; 828; 830
9:3	II:332; V:356; 531; 538; 542; VI:573; 575; 942; IX:343
9:3ff	VIII:384n366
9:4	I:216; 230; III:666n14; V:1028; VI:163; 169; VIII:306; IX:295
9:4f	VII:1071n447
9:5	III:121, n11; 288; 666n14; 1086; VIII:306; IX:295
9:6	I:368; II:22; III:7n19; 48
9:7	I:216; V:344; 346; VII:647; IX:295, n80

9:8	II:334; V:377; 378; VIII:288; IX:435		n4; V:139; 795; VI:60; 281; 406n475; 408n494; 575; VII:91; IX:216
9:8f	VII:663n47		
9:9	II:693; III:820; IV:929; VI:140; 414(n532); VIII:220; IX:135n202	9:32	I:106; VII:835n236
		9:32ff	III:131; 213
		9:33	III:656
9:10	IV:445; 458; 1125; V:350; 351; 352n181; 357; 372, n4; VIII:553n60	9:34	I:370; III:214; 288; V:277; VI:407(n485); VIII:288n131; IX:536
9:11	III:488; V:68n84; VI:414(n532); VII:394	9:35	VII:728, n32
		9:36	II:486; 663; IV:460n2; 461; VI:286; 477
9:12	V:352n181; 372, n4; VI:414; VIII:161; IX:432	9:36ff	I:787; VIII:554n68
9:13	I:106; II:855n176; IV:232; VI:477(n102); VII:335	9:36-41	**IX:451-452**
		9:37	IV:302; VIII:155
9:14	II:60; 565; 806; III:271; 497, n2; 500; V:279, IX:536	9:38	II:332; V:166; 793, n160; IX:450n95; 452
9:15	I:577; 596; III:386; IV:179; V:278; 919; 920; VI:575; 863n6; VII:335; 364	9:39	I:787; III:722; 846; 847; V:821n32; 839; VI:476; VII:794n134; IX:450n94; 451; 452n108
9:15f	V:919n120		
9:16	I:596; II:22; V:279; 525n221; 904; **919-920** (920n120); 923n142; 933; VIII:514	9:39-41	IX:451n107
		9:40	I:738; V:377; VI:407(n485); 765; VII:726; 1057; VIII:155; 288n127
9:16ff	V:919		
9:17	III:288; IV:459; V:67; 68n80; 351; 356n204; 357; 358; 707, n413; VI:130; 406n476; 410; 412; 413; 414n538; 574; 863n6; VIII:161; IX:432, n49	9:40f	I:370
		9:41	I:106; 368; V:839; IX:303; 430; 431; 452
		9:42	I:719; II:434; VI:203(n217); 211(n272); 214(n292)
9:17f	I:543(n69)	9:43	III:428; V:732; VII:835n236
9:18	III:820; IV:232; V:359n211; 377; VI:413; VIII:288n131	10	I:725; IV:54; VIII:222n42; IX:213
9:19	IV:929; VII:794n134	10f	II:512; IV:1068; VII:710
9:19f	VII:828; 835	10:1	III:488
9:20	I:72n18; III:288; 704; 711; VII:830; 836; VIII:380; 381n337	10:1ff	II:327
		10:2	II:41; 486; 806; IV:53; VI:477; 743; VII:181; 741n22; 794n134; IX:213
9:20ff	VII:835n236		
9:21	II:60; 429; 460; III:271; 327n37; 497, n2; 500; V:279; VII:335; IX:536	10:3	V:351; 372, n4; VI:721; IX:3; 680
		10:3ff	I:85; VII:765n18
9:22	III:337n7; 380; V:89n174; **VII:764;** 836, n244; VIII:381n337	10:4	I:522; II:486, n10; III:1086; IV:676, (n6); IX:209
		10:4ff	IV:725
9:23	II:950n42; III:380; VI:294	10:5	III:497; IV:1121
9:24	I:703; V:708; VI:921; VIII:148, n11	10:6	I:545; V:20; 23; 228n35; 732
		10:7	III:618; VII:181; 710; IX:303
9:25	IV:415; 441; 457; **459;** IX:162	10:8	II:908
9:26	III:337n7; 822; IV:454; 458; VI:28; 203(n214); IX:208	10:9	II:332; 801; V:69n89; VIII:133; IX:680, n38
9:26-30	VII:334n270; 335	10:9-16	VI:413n526
9:27	I:442; III:288; IV:459; V:67; 68n80; 357; 359n214; VII:836	10:10	I:676; II:450; III:45n8; V:352; 357; VI:12; VIII:553n60
9:27f	V:271; 278; 708; 882; VI:209n501	10:10ff	II:457; IV:113
		10:11	I:481n12; III:177; V:346; 530; VII:362; 962; VIII:133; 462n416, n417
9:28	V:106; 708; VI:578; VII:794n134		
9:29	II:102, n12; 509; 511; 512; VII:747; 836n244	10:11f	V:235n53; 372n4
		10:11ff	V:352; 372n4
9:30	I:406; 704	10:12	V:534
9:31	I:104(n57); II:826n53; III:504,	10:13	III:181; V:351n178

10:13-15	VIII:222; IX:298
10:14	I:109; II:693; III:428; 1086; V:888; VI:406; IX:298
10:15	III:424; 797; 809; V:351n178; VI:145n5
10:16	IV:8; VII:362; VIII:222; IX:298
10:17	II:539; V:372; VI:921; VII:765n18
10:18	III:497; V:20; 23; IX:303
10:19	III:172n8; V:372; VI:406; 408(n491); VII:765n18
10:20	III:946n3; 947; 948; VI:414n534; 573; 575; VII:794n134
10:21	V:859
10:22	II:189; 369; 371n24; III:226; 380; IV:52; 496; VI:743; IX:213; 481
10:23	III:496; V:2; 20; VII:794n134
10:23f	VIII:133
10:24	III:496; IV:579n2; VI:726; VII:740; IX:159; 162
10:25	I:166; VI:163, n15; 629; 764; IX:138n229
10:25f	VI:764
10:26	I:433(n163); II:334
10:28	I:109; 267; 362; II:27; 561; 684; III:369n82; 380; 428; 797; 822; V:9; 12; VI:743
10:29	IV:104
10:30	IV:27; 249n53; 933n73; 934n80; V:351; VII:647; VIII:133; IX:680
10:31	I:222; II:486, n10; 807; IV:676
10:32	I:545; III:497; V:20; 23
10:33	IV:1108; VI:477; 723; VIII:38
10:34	I:243; IV:10; VI:780; VII:700n65
10:34f	III:582
10:35	II:59; 199; VI:743; IX:213
10:36	II:67; 413; 718; 719; 720n118; 721; III:288; 1094; IV:120-121; IX:59n16; 536; 560n433
10:36f	II:719
10:36ff	II:720
10:36-43	III:582
10:37	I:545; III:704; 706; VI:614; 619
10:37-41	IV:209(n262)
10:38	I:104(n57); II:18; 79; 301; 655; III:116n370; 204; 213; 288; IV:874; VI:407n486; VII:159, n42; 161; 779; IX:393n165; 534; 555
10:39	III:380; 918; IV:493; V:39; VI:474; VII:335; IX:45
10:40	II:335; V:359n214; IX:7
10:41	I:371; II:335; 693; IV:51; 53; 493; 893(n22); V:67n79; 357; VI:142; VIII:139n38; 212n31
10:42	II:862(n260); III:103; 704; 711;
	713; 943; IV:53; 493; 512; 725; 893(n16); V:453; 707n414; 763; 867; VII:997n143; VIII:367n229; IX:647n182
10:43	I:72; 295; 305; 511; 512; II:199; 433; IV:7; 497; 1004; V:271; 273; VI:210(n266); 214n303; 216n315; 834; VII:997
10:44	I:104(n57); IV:725; VI:50n42; 164n17; 410; 414
10:44f	I:725; VI:411
10:44ff	I:433n169; 543; VI:623; 851
10:44-47	VIII:222n42
10:44-48	VI:413; 414n533; 983n42; IX:432n50
10:45	II:167; 460; 469; IV:53; 1004; VI:81; 215(n312); 743; IX:355n384
10:46	I:722; 724; 725; 726; II:702; IV:543; VI:50n42; 408(n488); 410; 411n518; 829
10:47	IV:2n8; 7; VI:407(n480); 411n518; 413; VIII:222n42
10:47f	VI:413; 414n533; 618; VIII:329
10:48	II:686; V:23; 271; **276;** 650; VI:414; VIII:38
11	VIII:222n42
11:1	II:54; IV:115; 119; 457
11:2	I:519(n12); III:947; VI:81; 479; 723; VII:334; 335
11:3	I:226; II:693; VI:413; 721; 743; VII:855
11:5	I:481n12; II:450; V:352; 357; 372; 530; VI:449n817; 530; VII:362; VIII:133; 553n60
11:5ff	II:457
11:5-12	VII:765n18
11:6	I:539; III:134; IV:975; V:534
11:7	III:181; V:351n178
11:7-9	VIII:222, n42
11:8	I:109; II:428; 1086; IX:298
11:9	III:424; 797; 809; V:351n178; 530; IX:298
11:10	VIII:222
11:12	III:946; 948n11; VI:408(n491); VII:794n134
11:13	I:66; III:497; V:351
11:14	III:710n57; V:130; 650; VII:997
11:15	I:482; 725; VI:411n518; 851
11:15-17	VI:413; VIII:222n42
11:15ff	IV:1004
11:16	I:536; 538; 539; 543n69; III:288; 1092; IV:105; 678; V:530; VI:398; 413; 418n565; 619; VIII:329
11:16b	VI:413
11:16f	VI:410; VIII:329
11:17	I:725; II:167; III:101; 348; 349, n32; IV:2n8; VI:203(n217); 211(n272); 214(n294);

	VII:836n242; VIII:365n221
13:6-12	V:625
13:7	II:895; III:500; IV:116; VII:794n134; 894n54
13:8	**IV:358-359;** VI:212(n278); VII:718
13:8ff	II:311n89
13:9	III:781; VI:130; 286; 406n476; 408, (n490)
13:10	II:79; 80; 199; 814; III:1087; **V:87;** 89; 90; VI:286; 559; 855; 973; VII:161; 162; 718; VIII:233n49; 365
13:11	II:170(n8); III:461; 1087; IV:725; V:343; VI:164; VII:425n16; VIII:287; 288; IX:431; 435
13:12	II:164n5; III:38n45; 288
13:13	VI:56; VII:334; 335
13:14	II:441n39; 677; III:443; VI:743; VII:830; 836n242
13:14f	VII:21; 26
13:15	I:145; 344; 756n28; II:539; III:980n71; IV:51; 57; V:795; VI:832; VII:21; 822n140; 830; 846, n22; 847, n23; VIII:234n5
13:16	I:368; III:386; VI:743n170; 744; VII:198n18; 835n235; IX:213; 430
13:16ff	V:851; VII:365n45
13:16-41	VII:836
13:17	I:639; 677; III:101n224, (n229); 386; IV:52; 53; 179; V:31; 851; 976n175; VIII:608
13:18	II:658; VIII:138; IX:591
13:19	I:677; II:370; 630; III:412
13:20	III:943; VI:831
13:21	I:577; VIII:138; IX:249
13:22	I:577; II:334; 434; III:54; 103; 612; IV:496; 497; VI:479; VIII:482; 484
13:23	II:334; 582; III:103; 288; IV:270n19; VI:864; VII:545; 997n142; 1015; VIII:381; 484
13:24	I:536; 545; III:386; 706; 717; IV:52; 1000; 1001; 1004; V:107; VI:614; 684; 685; 688; 777; 863n9
13:24f	VI:619
13:25	I:379; II:347; 937; IV:336; 1018; V:311; VI:297; 629; 840; VIII:59n11; 81n13; 234
13:25a	VIII:234
13:25b	VIII:234
13:26	I:145; 406; III:632; IV:117; 118; VI:743n170; 744; VII:997, n142; IX:213, n128, n130
13:26-37	VI:209(n262)
13:27	I:116; 343; V:707n414; VI:295; 636; 832; 833; VII:21; 335; 581n2; IX:295
13:27-29	VII:581n2
13:28	I:192; VII:581
13:29	I:748; III:411; V:39; 707n414; VI:296n61; VIII:60
13:30	II:335
13:31	I:438n185; IV:53; 493; 1107; 1108n16; 1121; V:356n204; 358; VII:335
13:32	II:710n29; 720n118; V:795; 976n178; VI:723
13:32f	II:582; 720; VII:274
13:32ff	VIII:540n87
13:33	I:665; 670; 671; 748; II:345(n20); III:288; 781; V:638; 867; VI:307; 417; **VII:274;** VIII:335; **367;** 499; 540n87
13:33f	I:371
13:33-35	VIII:367n232
13:33-36	VIII:381, n336
13:34	V:492; VI:308; 831n336; VII:726n18; VIII:367n233; 483
13:34f	IV:109n160; VI:308
13:34-37	IX:103
13:35	III:747; V:342; 492; VIII:367n233; 482
13:36	I:635; 663; III:14n60; V:976n174; VIII:168; 367n232, n233; **540,** n87
13:36f	VIII:483
13:37	II:335; VIII:540n87
13:38	I:72; 145; 295; 305n143; 511; 512; IV:864n194; VI:216n315; VII:997, n142; VIII:267n233
13:38f	II:218; IX:393n161
13:39	II:216; 541; VI:209; 214n303; 216n315; 744
13:40	II:681; IV:110; VI:831; 834
13:40f	V:795
13:41	II:641; III:40, n65; 632; V:342
13:42	II:427; 433; V:793; VII:21, (n163); 26
13:43	I:215n33; IV:336; 579; VI:2; **743;** VII:750; 828; 835n235; IX:213n128; 392
13:43ff	IX:213
13:44	IV:115; 116; V:12; VII:21, n163; 26; 273; 828n191
13:44ff	VII:835n236
13:45	I:624; II:880; 887; IV:53, n100; V:587; VI:130; VII:836
13:45f	VII:835
13:46	I:379; 448; II:514; 864(n272); 865n290; III:923; IV:53; 54; 115; 117; 119; V:882; VI:869; VII:715; **835-836;** VIII:29
13:46-48	II:866n295
13:47	I:679; II:545; 697; V:705n390; VI:88; VII:997; VIII:157; IX:344

13:48	II:428; 864, (n272); 865n290; III:491; 766; 1087; IV:2; 115; 116; 119; VI:208n258; 744; VIII:28; IX:367; 370	14:16	I:663; II:370; V:85; VI:575
		14:16f	III:589; IV:1016
		14:17	I:17; 511; II:774; III:462; 611; 612; 1032; IV:907; **V:542**; VI:130; VIII:39n21
13:48f	III:288		
13:49	III:1087; IX:63	14:18	III:181; 627; IV:735; V:588
13:50	I:785; II:771; III:380; VI:743n170; 868; IX:213n128	14:19	V:588; VI:2
		14:19ff	VII:835n236
		14:20	III:206; IV:459; VII:794n134
		14:20ff	IV:458
13:51	III:623; VI:629	14:21	II:710n29; 719; 720; IV:461, n2
13:52	IV:458; 459; **VI:291**; 406n475; 408n494; IX:360	14:22	I:587; II:23; 66; 678; III:143; IV:458; 459; 577; 579; 586; 587; V:367n241; 525n221; 796; 933; VI:213(n284); VII:656; 657; 997n143; VIII:20; **IX:640**
14:1	I:682; II:510; 511; 677; III:380; VI:279; 743; 744; VII:830; 835n235; 836		
14:1f	VI:11; 743n170		
14:1ff	III:380; VII:241; 835n236	14:23	II:433; 616; 617; 619; III:504; IV:925; 933; VI:210(n266); 212; 214(n293); 665; 668; VII:773; VIII:163; IX:437
14:2	II:187n57; 411; 511; III:380; 484; IV:457; V:882; VI:11; VII:836; 847; IX:640		
14:3	II:67; III:213; 714; IV:117; 118; 497; V:882; VII:240, n286; 241, n287; 242; 836; VIII:125; IX:392; 430n39; 431; 591	14:25	IV:115; VII:836, n242
		14:26	II:172; 643; VI:297; IX:392; 396n195
		14:27	I:64; III:174; 504; 506; 766; VI:212(n278); 464; VII:779
14:3f	VII:240	14:28	V:172n4; VII:794n134; IX:591
14:4	I:422, n92; VI:279; 644; VII:241n287; 771; 962; VIII:541; IX:187	15	I:424n106; **IV:1065-1067** (1065n187); VI:109; 662; **663**; VII:241n287; 334n271
14:4f	VII:570n9	15:1	II:145; 373; IV:1066; V:945; VI:81; VII:996
14:5	II:511; IV:268; V:470; VIII:305		
14:6	VI:530; VII:241n287; 836n242		
14:6ff	VII:836	15:1f	VI:83(n81)
14:7	II:719; III:461	15:1ff	I:423; 431; V:825; VII:241
14:7ff	III:213	15:1-35	VII:334, n271
14:8	III:443; 787; IV:643; VI:628n43	15:2	I:422; 519(n12); 551(n30); II:894; 896; V:172n4; VI:53; 662; 663; 721; VII:335; 570; 748; VIII:28
14:8-18	II:720		
14:9	II:826n58; IV:268; VI:206; VII:990		
14:9f	I:433(n166)	15:3	III:504; IV:1004n166; VI:477; VII:91; 728
14:10	I:368; V:277; 449; VI:628n43; IX:295		
		15:3-21	VI:83n82
14:11	I:552n37; V:189; 342; 587; 939; VI:483; IX:293; 295	15:4	I:64; 422; II:52n10; III:504; VI:464; 662; 663; VII:335; 779
14:11ff	III:100; V:22		
14:11-15	VI:410n510	15:5	I:182; 368; II:22; IV:104; 864n194; 1066; V:89; 763; VI:81; VIII:144; IX:35n135; 45
14:11-19	IV:53		
14:12	II:908; III:487; IV:87n76		
14:13	II:594n26; III:46n20; 181; 258; **VI:684-685**; 686; 921; VII:794n134	15:6	I:422; IV:104; 105n140; VI:662; 663
		15:7	I:487; 776n1; II:67; 894; 950; IV:117; 119; 174; VI:208n258; 214n298; VII:700; 728; 748
14:13f	V:588		
14:14	I:422, n92; VI:644; VII:750; VIII:541		
14:15	I:362; 433(n163); 678; 679; II:719; 720n118; 735; 862n255; III:100 (n215); 884; 1028; 1029; IV:522; 908; 1004n165; V:514n123; 515; 939; VI:463; 477; VII:728	15:7-9	II:865n290
		15:7ff	IV:1068
		15:8	I:104(n57); III:111n307; 613; IV:497; 725; VI:407(n480)
		15:8f	VI:410; 414
14:15-17	III:586; IV:908n31	15:9	III:349n32; 424; 612; 946, n3; 948n11; VI:145n5;
14:15ff	III:893		

	VIII:206n146
15:10	I:185; 556n9; 596; II:899;
	III:101(n233); IV:1108;
	V:976n174; VI:32; VIII:160
15:11	II:67; IV:1066; VI:203(n215);
	214(n302); 216n315; VII:996;
	IX:392
15:12	I:437; II:67; 908; III:213;
	VI:279; 464; 483n139;
	VII:240n286; 241; 242;
	VIII:125
15:13	III:945
15:14	II:369; 605; 908; III:101n230;
	IV:54; VI:100, n2; 869n5;
	IX:308
15:15	I:747; IV:109n154; 112;
	VI:831; 832; 834; IX:308
15:16	V:139; VI:162; VII:374; 375,
	n35; 378n59; 716, n6;
	VIII:483
15:17	II:894; III:497; 498; 1087;
	V:271; VI:464; VII:375;
	716n7; VIII:483n36
15:18	I:198; II:643
15:19	III:705n43; 923; VII:728
15:20	I:173; II:377; 378; 441n37;
	VI:457-458; 592; VII:593
15:21	I:343; 487; 663; III:704; 705,
	n43; 978n52; IV:405n115;
	864; 1067; VII:21; 821; 830
15:22	I:404; II:907; III:488; 497; 504;
	505; IV:174; VI:279; 663;
	850; VII:750; 794n134
15:22f	I:422; VI:662
15:22ff	II:232
15:23	I:744; II:67; 411; VI:663;
	IX:360n9; 367; 431
15:23ff	IV:1067
15:24	**VII:592**; VIII:243; **IX:640**
15:25	I:48; 404; IV:174; V:185;
	VII:794n134
15:26	V:279; VI:29n35; IX:638
15:27	I:404; IV:101; VII:750
15:28	I:104(n57); 354; 556; V:796;
	VI:406n475; 409; 592;
	VIII:160
15:29	I:48n136; 173; 290n64; II:379;
	411; 901; IV:725; V:912n56;
	VI:457-458; 592; 635;
	VIII:142n14; 151
15:30	VI:279
15:31	I:343; V:796; IX:366
15:32	V:796, n171; VI:848; 849; 850;
	VII:334; 657; 750
15:33	I:404; II:411; VI:475, (n93);
	VII:773; IX:591
15:35	II:145; 702; 720; III:1087;
	IV:116; VII:794n134
15:35f	III:288
15:36	I:71; II:604; III:1087; IV:115;
	VII:726
15:36ff	IV:452

15:37	I:632n52; III:488
15:37f	VII:760
15:38	I:380; 513; II:643; 684
15:39	V:857
15:39f	IX:551n373
15:40	II:172; VII:750; IX:392;
	396n195
15:41	III:504; VII:657
16	V:924
16:1	II:510; 511; III:380; 623;
	IV:458; VI:215(n311);
	VII:750; 836
16:1ff	II:441n38
16:2	IV:496
16:3	II:510; III:380; VI:81;
	VII:794n134; 836; VIII:203
16:4	I:422; II:171; 231; III:923;
	VI:662; **663**; VIII:203;
	IX:240
16:5	III:504; VI:60; 212(n282);
	281n16; VII:613
16:6	I:104(n57); IV:113
16:6f	II:457; III:856; V:351;
	VI:408(n491); 414n534
16:6ff	VIII:232n44
16:7	III:288; IV:115n190; VI:28; 406
16:9	I:628; II:66; III:436; IV:1125;
	V:235; 236; 350; 351; 352;
	356; 372n4; 793; VIII:553n60
16:9f	III:585; V:221; 234; 357; 372
16:10	II:457; 710n29; 719; III:500;
	501; IV:950; V:351; **VII:765**
16:10-17	VII:830
16:11	II:592(n14)
16:11-40	VII:200n28
16:12	VI:530; 533
16:12ff	VIII:305
16:13	II:808n8, n9, n11; III:443;
	VI:602-603; 921; VII:21; 26;
	814, n96; 817n119; 818; 830
16:13f	I:785
16:13ff	II:808
16:14	III:174n16; 612; 704; 766;
	V:554n105; 556n127;
	VI:412(n522); 530; 744;
	VII:764n13; IX:213n128
16:14f	VI:618; IX:451n107
16:15	I:787; III:923; V:23; 130; 650;
	793, n160; VI:210n270; 211;
	214(n309); IX:162n133
16:16	II:16; 808n8; 822; III:626; 1086;
	VI:575n54; 851n430; 918;
	920; VII:817n119
16:16ff	II:311n89
16:17	I:72; II:273; 710n25; 717; 720;
	III:116n363; 708n50; V:85;
	90; VI:920; VII:997;
	VIII:619f; 620n49
16:17ff	II:720
16:18	II:679; III:288; V:271; 277; 763;
	764; VI:407(n485);
	479(n109); VII:726; IX:679

n126; 515; 516; VI:463;
IX:436

17:24f II:42; III:100(n214); IV:1016;
VIII:38

17:25 I:366; II:862n254; III:74n44;
112; 129; 131; 158; V:186;
675n117; 888; VI:453; IX:430

17:25ff V:894

17:26 I:173; 678; II:369; 437; III:461;
V:153; 452n4; 453; VI:463;
777; VII:1072n451;
VIII:38-39 (38n5, n10, n11,
n12; 39n16, n19, n20, n21)

17:26f IV:1016; V:303n5; 452

17:27 II:438n15; 769; 893; III:112;
123; IV:374; VII:890;
VIII:39; IX:417

17:27f III:118n377

17:28 I:684; II:540; 862(n245);
III:718-719; V:653n98;
VI:463n30; 475; VII:740;
VIII:389; IX:417

17:29 II:310n85; III:92n136;
118n377; 123; 172; IV:269;
V:188; 564

17:30 I:66; 118; 119; IV:1003; 1108,
n19; 1116; V:763n28; VI:636;
IX:591

17:30f IV:1016; 1121; IX:188

17:31 I:371; II:198; 539; 952; III:288;
IV:2; 725; V:158, n7; 452n3;
453; 867; VI:204n227;
VII:648; 997n143;
VIII:367n229; 612n47;
IX:551; 647n182

17:31f I:369

17:32 II:441n39; 725; 864n281;
III:699; IV:845; 847n122;
IX:188n134

17:34 I:785; II:702; 777n11; III:699;
766; 822

18:2 II:512; 684; III:380; V:77n126;
VI:767; VII:393; 394;
VIII:34

18:2f V:23; VII:394n13

18:3 V:732; VII:57n9; 382n5;
393-394 (393n6)

18:4 II:94; 510; 511; III:380;
391n152; VI:1; 2; 743, n170;
744; VII:26; 765n16; 830;
835n235; 836, n242

18:4f IX:536

18:4ff II:441n39

18:5 II:816n1; III:288; IV:115; 512;
VII:836; 883, n59

18:5f VII:836

18:6 I:108; 173; 499n24; 624; II:511;
III:425; 675; IV:54; 1107;
1111; 1113; VI:573; 575n54;
629n48; 744; VII:835; 836;
VIII:267n58; 435n266

18:7 I:523(n3); VI:744; VII:814;

830; IX:213n128

18:8 V:130; 650; VI:203(n221); 211;
214(n292), (n300), 618;
VII:794n134; 847

18:9 I:85; 219; III:436; IV:113; 1125;
V:221; 235; 236; 350; 351;
356; 357; 372, n4;
VIII:553n60; IX:212

18:9f II:457; VII:776

18:10 III:484; IV:54; VIII:160

18:11 II:146; III:444; IV:115; 640;
VII:836; VIII:220

18:12 V:186n4

18:12ff VIII:267

18:13 I:625; V:736; VI:744; VII:172

18:14 I:163; 359n2; III:380; IV:104;
IV:558; 973, n9; VII:700n65

18:15 I:632n52; III:942; IV:845;
V:342; VI:53; 54

18:17 VII:847; VIII:267, n53

18:18 I:785; II:777, n11; IV:579;
VI:136n11; VIII:33

18:19 II:94; III:623; VII:830; 836,
n242; 838

18:20 II:686; IX:591

18:21 II:433; III:48; VI:483; VIII:33

18:22 I:500; 519; III:504; IV:667n12;
VII:335

18:22f VII:335

18:23 IV:458; VI:475, (n93); VII:656;
IX:591

18:24 I:362; 752; 759n53; II:512; 876;
III:380; 623; **IV:137**; 456;
457n272; V:89; VII:522

18:24ff I:539n47

18:24-28 III:291

18:25 I:536; 543; 545; II:146; 875;
876; III:288; 291; 639;
IV:137; 456; V:89, n175;
90n175; VI:54; 408n492; 413;
414; 415; 614; 619;
VIII:54n34

18:25f **V:89-90**; 882

18:26 I:787; IV:15; 457; V:89, n175;
90n175; 92n185; 882;
VII:828; 835; 836;
VIII:163n6; IX:457n164

18:27 I:743n5; 744n8; II:55; IV:458;
VI:214(n295); IX:393

18:28 I:752; 759; III:288; 380;
VII:765; 836

19 I:725; III:121n12

19:1 IV:457, n272; 595; VI:575n54

19:1ff I:433n169; 543(n69);
IV:443n205; 456; 457n272;
459

19:1-6 IV:725

19:1-7 **VI:413**; VIII:329

19:2 I:104(n57); IV:7; VI:214(n294);
406n475; 410; 412; 413; 840

19:2ff I:538

19:3 I:539; 540; 545

19:3f	VI:414; 614; 619		233; 412; IV:287n11; 542;
19:3ff	IV:457		596; V:158; **VII:172**
19:4	I:536; 539; 545; II:433; III:288;	19:27f	IV:538
	IV:51; 53; 1000; 1001; 1004;	19:28	III:167; 902; V:68n84; 419; 420;
	VI:210(n266)		VI:285n8; 286
19:5	V:275; VI:414n533; 618	19:29	III:42; V:186n4; 470; VI:130;
19:6	I:104(n57); 499(n20); 722;		699n13; VII:571; 764n12
	II:675; 702; VI:520n42;	19:30	I:632(n53); II:63; IV:53n102;
	408(n488); 410, n506;		VI:529
	411n518; 414n537; 829; 851;	19:31	III:42; V:793; VI:723; IX:159;
	852; VIII:161; IX:432; 433		162
19:7	II:322; IV:456; V:889	19:32	III:505; 513; 902; VII:764n12;
19:8	I:583; IV:640; V:882; VI:2; 54;		765
	VII:836; 838; VIII:220	19:33	II:63; III:46n18; IV:53n102;
19:8f	VII:828		V:588; VI:529; VII:198n18;
19:8-10	VII:836		765; IX:430
19:9	I:513; II:94; III:468; V:48n22;	19:33f	VII:595
	88; 89; 90n175; 454; 1023;	19:34	III:72n33; 902; VII:765;
	1030; VI:11; 279;		IX:295; 680
	VII:828n194; 835; 836, n242	19:34f	IV:538
19:10	II:510; III:288; 380; 1087;	19:35	I:740; IV:53; 882n6; V:588;
	IV:116; VI:744		VI:530
19:11	I:433(n163); VI:464; 483n139;	19:35f	**VII:595**
	644; VII:239; VIII:242;	19:36	V:470; VI:635n7; 636
	IX:431; 432	19:37	I:622n8; III:92n141; 100, n216;
19:11f	IV:693		257
19:11ff	II:310n86; 311n89	19:38	II:820; III:790; IV:103;
19:12	I:253; 493; III:130; 209; 213;		105n140; VII:794n134
	IV:1091; VI:407n479; 558;	19:39	II:895; III:505; IV:337; 1087
	579; 644; VIII:242	19:39f	III:513
19:13	I:72n18; II:822; III:288; 704;	19:40	II:167; III:505; IV:103;
	711; IV:358; 512; V:282; **463**,		VII:273; 570
	n10; 465; VI:407(n485); 558	20	VI:666
19:13ff	II:252; III:213; 397; VI:644	20:1	I:500; III:500; VI:575n54;
19:13-16	V:277		VII:571
19:14	III:272; 704; VI:483	20:1f	V:796
19:15	I:703n62; III:288; 708n50; 945;	20:2	II:508; IV:595
	VI:558; IX:655n226	20:3	I:717; IV:640; VI:475, (n93);
19:16	I:774; II:540; III:1098; VI:558		VIII:220
19:17	II:510; III:380; IV:543; IX:209;	20:4	I:210n1; VII:742
	210; 607n30	20:5	IV:575
19:18	I:64; 512; V:215; 360n216;	20:5f	II:354
	VI:214(n295), (n306); **644**	20:5ff	II:354n101; III:730n15
19:18f	VII:235	20:6	II:630; 902; V:899n26; 901n43;
19:19	I:616; II:635; III:213; 294;		VI:50n34
	VI:636; 644; VIII:178;	20:7	I:477; II:94; 434n1; III:729;
	IX:75; 607, n30; 680, n37		730; 731; 738; 1096; IV:101;
19:20	III:397; 907; 1087; IV:116; 118;		441n198; 457; VI:866;
	VI:204(n230); 281; 282;		VII:20; 29; 32n246
	406n475; 715n77; VIII:518;	20:8	IV:16; 28; 326n24; 1100n15;
	519n18		IX:343n259
19:21	II:23; V:341(n138); VI:297;	20:9	II:94; III:436; 440; 444; 640;
	415; 575; VII:334; 335;		V:637; 650; VI:163; VIII:554
	VIII:155	20:10	III:206; VI:407(n485); IX:637
19:22	II:86, n13; 433; IX:591	20:10ff	I:370
19:23	III:461; V:88; 89; 90n175;	20:11	I:477; 507; 676; III:729; 731;
	VI:54; VII:765		V:817n4
19:24	III:232; 790; IV:882; 885; VI:76	20:12	V:637; 650; 794; 798;
19:25	VI:56		VIII:554n65
19:26	III:100, (216); IV:53, n100;	20:13	VIII:34
	V:588; VI:2; IX:430	20:13f	IV:8
19:27	II:668; III:92n141; 100; 232;	20:13ff	V:66n67

20:14	II:433
20:15	II:592(n14); 702; III:623; VII:273
20:16	III:923; VI:50; VII:335
20:17	III:504; VI:498; 667
20:17-38	VI:665
20:18	V:186; 887; VII:794n134; IX:591
20:18ff	**VII:598**
20:18-35	VI:665
20:19	VI:29n35; VII:773; VIII:22
20:20	II:146; V:130; 822; VII:598; IX:75; 77
20:20f	I:64; 66
20:21	II:145; 432; 510; 511; IV:512; 999; 1003; 1004, n167; VI:204(n228); 210(n266); 212, (n278); IX:536
20:22	II:60; 616n25; IV:1108; VI:408(n491); 415; VII:335
20:22f	VI:414n534; 850
20:23	I:104(n57); III:143; 147; IV:512; VI:404n462; 408(n489), n491
20:24	II:88; 820; IV:7; 102; 512; 726; VI:479; VIII:81; **234;** IX:392, n155; 638
20:24a	VIII:234
20:24b	VIII:234
20:25	I:582; 583; III:704; 710(n59); IV:1108; V:341n138; VI:637; 776; IX:139n232
20:26	I:108; 173; III:425; IV:511; VII:273
20:27	I:64; 635; 636; VII:598
20:27f	V:66n67
20:28	I:104(n57); 175n19; II:615; 616; III:101(n230); 106(n273); 504; 505; 507; 520; IV:310; VI:409; 498; 665; 667; VII:829n199; VIII:157
20:28f	VI:501(n22)
20:28ff	**VI:665**
20:29	I:558; **IV:310**; VI:499; 665; VII:421
20:29f	I:183n11; VI:498; 850
20:30	IV:310; V:291; VI:665; VII:598; 718
20:31	II:339; IV:1022
20:32	I:107, n61; 112; III:781; IV:117; 118; 726; 1108, n19; 1113; 1122; V:139; VII:241n287; VIII:163; 250; 391n417; IX:392, n159
20:33	III:170; 604
20:33ff	IV:453; VII:598
20:34	VII:393; **VIII:540**; IX:429
20:35	I:375; 493; II:22; III:288; 829; 1092; IV:106; 369; 682; V:889; VI:746n6
20:36	I:738; VI:765; VII:794n134; VIII:155; IX:139
20:36f	IX:138
20:37	III:726; IX:138; 139; 141
20:38	V:115; 341n138; VI:776; IX:139n232
21:1ff	II:354n101
21:3	III:847
21:4	II:630; IV:458, n280, n283; 459; VI:404n462; 407n481; 408(n489); 414n534; VII:335
21:5	I:476; 738; II:805; V:638; 650; VI:304n54; 573; 575n54; VII:794n134; VIII:155
21:5f	IX:138
21:6	I:500
21:7	I:500; III:623
21:8	II:737; V:732; VI:663
21:8f	I:431(n144); V:23
21:9	V:834; **VI:829**; 849; IX:451n98
21:9f	VI:404n462
21:10	VI:214(n308); 850; VII:334; IX:46n216
21:10f	VI:848; 849
21:11	II:60; 169; V:306n26; 307; VI:308(n489); 414n534; VII:335; IX:429n35; 430
21:12	I:519(n12); V:793; VII:335
21:13	II:60; III:20; 612; 722; V:279; VII:335, n280; VIII:514
21:14	III:55n12; VI:4
21:15	I:519(n12); II:441n37; VII:334; 335
21:16	I:487; IV:445; 457; 458, n280, n283; V:20; 23; 732; VII:794n134; IX:162n133
21:17	II:55; IV:457; VII:336
21:17-26	VI:663
21:18	II:592(n14); **VI:662-663** (663n77); VII:794n134
21:18ff	IV:1069
21:19	I:500; II:88; 908; VI:464
21:20	II:881; 887; VI:214(n295); 663n79; VII:668; IX:46n214; 665
21:20f	VI:19n53; IX:45
21:21	I:513; II:146; 373; III:638, n3; IV:864; V:945; VI:81; 83n84; VII:667n10
21:23	II:777; VI:308; 483
21:23ff	II:777; VI:136n11
21:24	I:103; 123; II:441n38; III:638, n3; VII:667n10; 668; 794n134; IX:240
21:25	I:173; II:379; IV:1067; VI:214(n295), (n308); **457-458;** 592; VII:593; VIII:144; IX:240
21:26	I:68; 103; 124; 126; II:948; III:237; 246; VI:308; VII:273; 794n134; VIII:508; **IX:66;** 68
21:27	II:512; 630; 950n42; V:345; 588; VI:308; VII:571;

	764n12; VIII:64; IX:430
21:27f	VIII:267
21:27ff	VII:595
21:27-30	III:234
21:27-36	VII:336
21:28	I:628; II:146; 511; III:386n132; 419n50; 809; 902; IV:53; **VIII:204-205** (204n130)
21:29	V:381; VII:794n134
21:30	II:503; III:173; 718; IV:51; V:174; VIII:267n54
21:31	VII:327, n221; 571; 764n12; VIII:267, n54
21:31-33	IX:466n2
21:31ff	IV:407
21:32	VII:709; VIII:261; 267
21:33	II:332; VI:479(n109)
21:34	I:506
21:34f	V:588
21:35	III:237n28; VII:709
21:36	III:902; IV:51; VI:279
21:37	II:509; 561; IX:466n2
21:38	II:347(n47); 658; 659; IV:862, n174; VI:827; VII:278; 279n9; **281**; 378n59; IX:469
21:39	II:40; 770; III:380; V:842n5; VI:534; **VII:267**; 394
21:40	III:237n28; 388; V:275; 817n4; VII:198n18; 648; 709; IX:430
22	III:388; V:357
22:1	I:145; IV:1106n5; 1107n10; 1108; V:948
22:1ff	VII:365n45
22:1-21	VII:836n239
22:2	III:388; V:275
22:3	II:159; 881; 887; III:380; 390; IV:435n151; **V:619**; 1015; 1022; VI:629; 714; VII:273; IX:46, n214, n216, n217
22:4	III:14n62; IV:312; V:88; 89, n174, n175; 90n175; VII:856n1; IX:244
22:5	II:50; 60; III:269; 271; IV:496; VI:575; 654; VII:335; IX:46n219
22:5ff	I:438n182
22:6	II:332; V:356; 538; 542; IX:343
22:6ff	IV:233
22:6-16	VIII:224
22:7	III:666n14; VI:163; VIII:306; IX:295
22:7f	VII:1071n447
22:8	III:288; 1086; IV:874; VIII:306
22:9	V:344; 345; VII:794n134; IX:295; 343
22:10	III:48; 1086; VI:573; 575; VIII:28
22:11	II:248; V:343; IX:343; 435
22:12	II:753; III:380; 847n113; IV:496
22:13	IX:679
22:13f	V:707

22:14	I:705; II:189; III:57; 101(n223); IV:493; 357, n208; 359n214; 707, n413; 977n197; **VI:863-864** (863n6, n7, n8); VII:699, n60; IX:295
22:14f	V:341; 342; VIII:28
22:14-16	VI:863n6
22:15	IV:493; V:888
22:15ff	VI:534n84
22:16	I:295; 305n143; 540; II:806; III:497; 500; IV:303; 1108; VII:997; VIII:331
22:17	II:450; 540; III:246; IV:1125; V:357; 372n4; VI:449n817
22:17f	II:457; V:357; VII:335
22:17ff	II:457
22:18	IV:499; V:357n208
22:19	VI:203(n217); 211(272); 214(n304); VII:828; 831; 834n231; 835; IX:244
22:19f	VII:335
22:20	I:173; II:468; 739; IV:493; 494; 495; 499; IX:241; 606n13
22:21	I:406; IV:373; VI:575
22:21f	VII:700n66
22:22	I:678; II:862; III:437; IV:387n2; IX:293
22:23	III:902n16; VI:992
22:24	I:704; IV:518; VII:709; IX:466n2
22:24f	IV:517
22:25	II:561; III:952; VII:647
22:26	I:66; V:842n5; VI:477
22:26-29	IX:466n2
22:27	VII:709
22:28	**VI:534**
22:29	I:704; II:60; IX:208
22:30	I:506; 632n52; III:271; 380; 637; IV:336; V:729; VII:646; 649; 864, n29; 871
22:30-23:10	VII:871
23	IV:294
23:1	I:17; III:117; IV:1108n16; VI:518; **534**, n82; 757; VII:871; 918
23:1f	III:269
23:1ff	I:145
23:2	III:270; V:839; VII:700; **VIII:267-268**
23:3	III:440; 442; 827; 923; IV:293; 1091; VIII:260n6
23:3b	VIII:267n56
23:4	III:269(n20); IV:293; V:839
23:5	III:269n19; IV:53; 293; VI:529
23:6	II:532; 702; III:923; IV:596; 893(n25); V:454n1; 1022; VII:871; VIII:365; IX:46, n215, n218; 187
23:6ff	VII:36; 53n107; 54n109; IX:45; 46
23:6-9	**VII:53-54**; IX:37n143; 45
23:7	IV:387n2; VI:279; VII:570; 962

23:8	I:80; 370; IV:497n63; V:209; VII:53; 570; IX:45n208	24:7	VII:773; IX:430; 466n2
23:8f	VI:415	24:8	III:637; 943; V:729
23:9	III:121n11; 123; 903; IV:596; VI:637; IX:45	24:10	II:369; III:942; IV:52
		24:11	I:519(n12); 704; II:322; VI:764; 765; VII:335
23:9f	VII:570	24:12	II:94; III:246; V:587; VI:477; VII:323n170; 830; 836; 837
23:10	I:472; II:753; VII:709, n34; 871; IX:208; 466n2	24:13	III:637; IV:1106n5; V:839; VI:53
23:11	II:23; 433; 592(n14); III:26; IV:497; 512; 1125; V:235; 236; 350; 351; 356; 372n4; VI:54; VII:336; VIII:54n34; 553n60	24:14	I:182; 748; 756n28; IV:62; 63; 497n63; V:88-89 (89n175); 90n175; 209; 1015; VI:203(n210); 205; 832
23:12	I:355; 676; II:693; IV:929; VI:140; 475(n92); 477(n102)	24:14-18	I:495
		24:15	I:151; II:58; 190; 432; 532; 824; III:101(n232); IV:725; VI:210n269; VII:997n143; IX:647
23:12ff	II:885		
23:12-15	VII:281		
23:13	VI:475(n92); 477(n102); VIII:138	24:16	I:494; 495, n11; II:538; 824; VI:724; 748; 752; 756-757; VII:918
23:14	I:355; 356; 676; II:693; III:271; IV:929; VI:140; 659n46; VII:864		
		24:16f	VI:909
23:15	II:332; IV:1108; 1121; VI:54; VII:871; IX:7; 466n2	24:17	II:66; 369; 371n24; 486; IV:52; 53; VI:414; 477; IX:68
23:16	I:144	24:18	I:103; 123; III:246; V:587
23:16f	I:66	24:19	III:637; VI:724
23:17	III:500	24:20	I:163; VII:648
23:17-19	IX:466n2	24:20f	VII:871n82
23:17-30	VII:709	24:21	IV:868n226; VII:273; 648; IX:295
23:18	III:500		
23:19	I:66; IX:430	24:22	V:88; 89, n175; 90n175; VI:54; IX:466n2
23:20	III:380; VII:871		
23:21	I:355; II:58; 581; VI:4; VIII:138	24:23	I:367; II:684; VIII:35; 141; 540; IX:114*; 162n136
23:22	V:763n26; 764; IX:7; 446n2	24:24	II:432; VI:204(n228); 210(n266); VII:794n134; IX:536
23:23	III:500; IV:1124; VII:709; IX:680		
23:24	V:839; VII:989n96	24:25	II:194; 199; 342; III:459; 460; 942; IV:11; 725; 1108n17; VI:573
23:25	I:743n5; VIII:248		
23:26	II:411; IX:360n9; 376	24:26	II:530; IV:336; IX:480
23:26ff	IV:407	24:27	II:60; VI:294; IX:373n1; 392, n146; 393n164
23:26-30	VII:871		
23:27	III:380; IV:406; 407; 408n138; VII:709; 760	25:1	I:519(n12); V:899n23; VII:336; VIII:220
23:28	I:632n52; 704	25:2	II:271; V:793; VI:868; VII:864n28, n29; IX:7
23:29	I:379; VI:637; VII:570		
23:30	II:411; 431; III:636; V:764	25:3	III:623n3; V:68; VI:475(n92); 477(n102); VII:336; IX:392; 393n164
23:31	II:66; IV:8; VII:709; VIII:35		
23:32	VI:168n5	25:4	II:433; VI:579; VIII:141
23:33	V:840	25:5	III:637; IX:607n27
23:34	I:343; II:687	25:6	III:442
23:35	III:636; IX:241	25:7	I:557; VI:746; VII:336
24:1	III:270; VI:659n46; IX:7	25:8	II:431; III:235; 246
24:2	I:478; II:68; 369; 412; III:488; 489; 637; IV:52; 1012; VIII:242	25:9	I:519(n12); III:46n28; 945; VII:336; IX:392; 393n164
		25:10	I:161; 704; VII:648
24:3	II:55n2; VII:773; IX:411	25:11	I:160; 195, n4; 379; III:497; 637; IX:393
24:4	II:590; III:855n1; 856; V:793		
24:5	I:182; III:380; 718; IV:874; V:89; 158; VI:870n1; VII:570-571	25:11f	VI:637
		25:12	III:497; VI:575; VII:175
24:6	I:605; III:235; 246; 911; VI:28		

25:13	I:496; 577; III:623	26:13ff	II:464
25:14	I:353; 577	26:14	III:176n39; 388; **666-667;** IV:3;
25:15	II:181; III:271; 623; VI:53;		V:275; 856; 1028; VI:169;
	659n46; VII:336; 864; IX:7		VII:653, n41; VIII:306;
25:16	II:373; III:636; 637; VI:53; 723;		IX:295
	777; VIII:205; IX:393	26:14f	VII:1071n447; VIII:543
25:17	III:442; VI:495(n92)	26:15	III:288; 1086; V:538; VIII:306
25:18	III:636; 941n2; IV:1018;	26:16	II:429; IV:493; V:341; 342;
	VI:562; 637; VII:648; IX:58		356n204; 357, n208; 358;
25:19	II:20; 865(n286); III:288		VI:628; **863-864** (863n6, n7,
25:20	I:632n52; II:894; VII:336		n8); VII:647; 653; VIII:530;
25:21	II:426; III:497; VI:637; VII:175		**542-543** (543n102, n105, n106)
25:21a	VIII:141	26:16f	V:538
25:21b	VIII:141	26:16-18	VII:653n42
25:22	I:632n52	26:17	IV:52; VII:728n29; VIII:543
25:23	VII:773; IX:466n2	26:18	I:112; 295; 305n143; 511; II:79;
25:24	I:577; 625; II:862; V:889;		432; 567; III:174n16; 699;
	VI:53; 279; VII:336		763, n16; 781n27; IV:7; 233;
25:25	I:379; III:497; 923; IV:10;		726; 1004; V:299n16, n18;
	VI:637, n21; VII:175		378; 705n390; 709n428;
25:26	I:506; 577; 744n8; II:170;		VI:204(n228); 210(n266);
	III:943; 1055; 1086		212(n278); 216n315; VII:161;
25:27	IV:141; VII:263; 264		162; 442, n175; **728;** 997;
26	IV:25n31; **VII:652-653**		VIII:369n245; 543; IX:345;
26:1	II:460; 463; VI:55; VIII:508;		356n391
	IX:430	26:18-20	**VII:727-728**
26:1ff	VII:365n45	26:19	I:577; V:356; 357; 372, n4; 538;
26:1-23	IV:361		VI:10; VIII:543
26:2	I:577; IV:370; VII:273	26:20	I:66; 379; II:650; IV:999; 1003;
26:3	II:41; 373; IV:387		VI:635; VII:336; 728
26:4	I:481; II:369; 863n262; IV:52;	26:21	III:246; VI:28; VII:760
	53; 657n41; VII:335; IX:46	26:22	IV:511; 650(n13); 865;
26:4f	IX:46		1108n16; V:730n33; VI:832;
26:5	I:182; 378; 716; II:754;		840; VIII:241
	863(n261); III:44n5; 156;	26:22f	IV:865; 873; V:707n414;
	IV:496; V:89; 1022;		VI:831n337; 833; VII:653;
	VIII:106; IX:35n135; 45		IX:536
26:6	III:923; V:976n178; VI:723;	26:23	I:72; 371; IV:52; 361; V:913;
	VII:647; 652; IX:46n218		916n93; **924;** VI:877; 878n41;
26:6f	II:532; 582		VII:653n42; 997n143;
26:7	I:577; II:103; 322n4; 464;		IX:344n265; 345
	III:623; 624; IV:62; 63;	26:24	I:764; IV:361; 387; 845; IX:293
	IX:250n31	26:24f	VII:1103
26:8	II:337; III:923; IV:893n19;	26:25	I:244; 447; IV:117; 361;
	V:733; VI:205; VII:652		VII:1102
26:9	III:288; IV:874; V:278; VI:637;	26:26	I:577; 791; V:882; VI:4; 53; 635
	VII:653, n41	26:27	I:577; 760; VI:205; 833
26:10	I:106; 742n15; II:565; III:271;	26:28	III:516; V:279; VI:2, n4; 477;
	VI:478; VII:335; IX:46n219;		IX:488; 537n300
	244; 606, n13	26:29	II:776; 777; III:119n380;
26:10-12	VII:653n41		VI:592n74; VII:273
26:11	II:576; VI:62; 407n483;	26:30	I:577
	VII:828; 831; 835	26:31	I:379; VI:632; 637
26:12	II:565; III:271; V:730n33;	26:32	III:497; VI:637, n20
	VII:335; IX:46n219	27:1	III:923; V:270; VII:175; 856n1
26:12ff	I:438n182	27:1ff	II:354n101
26:12-18	VIII:224	27:2	VII:794n134; VIII:203
26:13	I:577; II:948; IV:16; 25; V:68,	27:3	I:48; II:702; III:158; VIII:242;
	n80, n81; 356; 531; 538;		IX:111, n34; 114; 159; **162;**
	542-543; VII:653n42;		163n139
	663n47; 794n134; VIII:515;	27:7	IV:735
	IX:343	27:8	II:332; III:488; IV:735; VI:530;

	VIII:204
27:9	III:293; IV:925; 933; V:817n8; VI:50n34; IX:591
27:9ff	IV:891
27:10	II:888n1; 889; VII:773; **VIII:305;** IX:85; 637
27:11	III:1035; VI:4; VII:709
27:12	I:635; III:623; V:344; VIII:155
27:13	III:911; VIII:166
27:14	I:527; III:488
27:14ff	VIII:553n58
27:15	IX:58
27:16	III:488; IV:735
27:17	I:629; V:302; VI:168; VII:362; IX:58; 208
27:18	VI:475
27:19	VII:362n29
27:20	II:530; III:655; VII:989; IX:10
27:21	II:889; III:673; VI:9; VII:648; **VIII:305,** n71
27:22	IV:1108; 1121; IX:637
27:22ff	VI:850
27:23	I:85; IV:62; 64; 113; 1125; V:235; 350; 351; 356; 372n4; 839; VI:409n501; VIII:553n60
27:23f	V:234; 236
27:23ff	II:457
27:24	II:23; V:840; VII:365n45; IX:212; 393
27:24f	V:351
27:25	III:101(n231); VI:203n207, (n209), (n214); 205
27:26	VI:168
27:27	I:131; II:332n3; IV:1018; IX:63
27:29	II:460; 776; 778; VI:168; VII:407n22; VIII:133; 203; IX:208
27:30	II:460; VI:168
27:31	VII:989
27:31f	VII:709
27:32	III:852; **VI:168**
27:33	IV:10; 15; VI:726; VII:273
27:33f	IV:10; V:793
27:33-38	VI:720n2; IX:411n42
27:34	I:394; VI:163; 720, n3; 721; VII:989
27:35	I:477; III:729, n9; 730n16; IX:411, n42
27:36	IV:15
27:37	V:889; IX:639
27:39	III:825; IV:975
27:40	I:367; II:829n3; VI:173; 452
27:41	IV:336; VI:173; VIII:203
27:42	I:635; VII:709; 856n1
27:43	I:632n53; 637; VI:992
27:43f	VII:989
27:44	IX:85n2
28:1	III:488; VII:989
28:2	I:551; IV:15; VIII:242; IX:111
28:2f	VI:941
28:3	II:815; VI:279
28:3f	IX:430
28:3-6	II:310n86
28:4	I:551; II:181; 862; III:916; V:889; 912; VII:989
28:4b	I:551n32
28:4f	III:133
28:5	III:206; V:912; VI:941
28:6	III:100; IV:893(n14); 990n71; VI:169; 726
28:6b	I:551n32
28:7	II:52n10; V:18; 20; VI:56; 868; VIII:220
28:8	III:656; VI:407(n485); **958,** n27; VII:883; VIII:161; IX:432
28:8f	III:131; 213
28:9	I:493
28:10	VI:724; VIII:160; 179
28:11	III:565n3; IV:640; VIII:220
28:12	VIII:220
28:13	III:623
28:13ff	II:441n39
28:14	II:630; V:793
28:14ff	IV:457
28:15	V:19n134; IX:411
28:16	VII:705n23; 709; 794n134; IX:241
28:17	I:145; II:169; 373; III:496; IV:53; V:1015; VI:482; 868; VII:336; VIII:220; IX:430
28:17ff	VII:365n45
28:18	I:632n53; III:943; VI:637
28:19	II:369; III:497; 637; IV:52; 53
28:20	II:532; III:386; 656; V:341(n138); 793; 817n4
28:21	I:66; 764; VI:562
28:22	I:182; 380; V:89; IX:232
28:23	I:583; 756n28; 759; II:928; III:288; IV:512; 864n194; 865; V:19n137; VI:1; 2; 721; 831n337; 832; 833; 840; VIII:28; 163n6
28:24	III:766; VI:4; 205, n236; IX:187
28:24-28	IX:665n8
28:25	I:104(n57); 757; IV:110; V:976n174; VI:408; 412; 724; 830; 833; VII:835
28:25-27	V:757
28:25ff	V:556
28:26	IV:52; 54; V:343; VII:894n54
28:26f	V:341; 556, n127; VII:893; 894n53, n55
28:27	I:556; III:214; IV:52; 54; V:378; 1023; 1024; 1025; **VII:727;** VIII:292n157
28:27a	III:613
28:27b	III:612
28:28	IV:52; V:557; VII:1023, n12
28:29	VII:748
28:30	II:55; IV:577; V:19n137
28:31	I:583; 589; 756n28; II:146; III:288; 704; 710(n59); 713;

V:209n31; 882; VI:54;
409n501; VII:773, n38;

VIII:54n34; IX:535n289;
536, n294

ROMANS

1	III:586n49; 587; V:442; 443; 444; VII:367; 917
1f	VI:463
1-3	II:203; 442n42; IV:1076; VII:521n393
1ff	II:358
1-5	VI:427n625
1-11	III:1032
1:1	I:438, (n183); 439n189; II:89; 264n25; 268n46; 428; 729; 730n69; 731; 733; III:494; V:454; VI:697; VII:594; IX:46n211; 543, n329; 553
1:1f	II:582n51; VI:832; 833
1:1ff	II:730; 737
1:1-4	V:1009n387
1:2	I:106; 431n148; 751; II:67; 586; VI:832; 833; IX:296
1:2ff	VII:597
1:2-5	III:494
1:3	II:710n30; V:704; 836; VII:124n212; 545; VIII:367; 384; 476; IX:249; 546n343; 555
1:3a	VIII:366n228
1:3f	I:61; II:730; III:105; VI:393n353; **416-417** (417n556, n558); **VII:126;** 143; VIII:335; **366-367; 484,** n39; 485; IX:4; 554; 561; 662n7
1:4	I:72; **114;** 371; 372; II:304; 316; 424; 731; III:903; 1089; IV:130; 353; V:360; **453;** 454n1; VI:418; 425n614; VIII:366n228; 367, n229; 369; 383n356; 384; 484n39
1:5	I:220; 224; 446; II:68; 370; 429; 746n32; III:599n17; IV:7; 453n250; V:278; VI:206; 212; 302; VIII:514; IX:396; 552n383
1:5f	I:551; VI:697
1:5ff	I:432n152
1:6	I:107; III:494; IX:395n186; 553
1:7	I:49; 106; 107; III:494; V:1007; IX:393; 554

1:8	I:72; 502n35; II:68; III:101(n227); 888; VI:206; 212; 219n335; IX:409n28; 412; 413; 551
1:8ff	II:356(n111)
1:9	II:699; 731; 733; IV:62; **64; 491;** 509; 678; 958n34; V:185; 1009n387; VI:435; 477(n101); VII:535n47; 536; VIII:384; IX:649
1:10	II:41; 805; 807; III:59; V:112; **113,** n20, n21; IX:409n27
1:11	II:430; 720; V:140; 341(n138); 344; VI:437n708; **VII:656;** VIII:599; IX:404
1:11f	VI:715
1:11ff	III:332n87
1:12	II:539; V:797n181; VI:213n288
1:13	I:116; II:539; III:49; 615; 856; IV:1108n16; VII:162; VIII:166
1:14	I:410; 548n14; 551; 552; II:304; 513; 515; III:599n17; IV:962; V:565; VII:520n385
1:14f	I:551; V:140
1:15	I:441n211; II:710n28, n31; 720; **VI:697**
1:16	I:190; 552; II:309; 429; 514; 655; 725; 729n65; 731; 732; 867; III:381; IV:353; V:208n27; 532; VI:214n303; 216n315; 869; VII:334; 835; 1002; VIII:447n331; IX:543, n328
1:16f	II:513; 732; 737; 869n318; III:538, n39
1:16ff	II:516; 733
1:17	II:62; 177n12; 191; 203; 205; 206; 251; 430; 864(n271); 865(n289); 869(n315); V:426; 431, n345; 531; VI:190n125; 213n288; 216n315; 426n621; 720n104; 831; IX:4
1:17f	V:426; 433; IX:394n179
1:18	I:156; 242; 243; II:203; 829; III:111n312; 583, n39; IV:382; V:419; 422; 423n298;

	425; 426; 430; 431; 432; 441; 442n408; 531; VI:714; **VII:190,** n14
1:18ff	I:127n2; 292; 326; II:513; III:15; 171; 481; 938; V:423; **426;** 444; VI:593; VIII:206n146
1:18-21	I:259
1:18-23	I:705; V:894
1:18-25	V:894; IX:271n202; **273**
1:18-32	I:257; III:940; V:437; VI:588; VII:520n384; IX:267; 273, n215
1:18-3:20	III:586n49; V:441; VIII:596
1:19	I:243; 719; II:539; III:587; IV:523; V:369, n10; 381; IX:3; 4
1:19a	IV:950; 951
1:19f	III:1032; V:365; VII:521
1:19ff	III:586; IX:273n215
1:19-23	I:156; VII:190n16; IX:267
1:19-32	I:450
1:20	I:121n5; 168; 309; 702n58; 719; II:306; 431; III:123; 587; 875n30; 885; 957n26; 1028; 1029; 1032, n207; IV:948n2; 949n2; **950-951** (950n9); 974; V:323; 328; ᴈ50n174; 369; 379; **380-381** (380n7); 606n53; VI:459n3; 463; VII:252n356; IX:185
1:20f	II:306
1:20ff	VII:521
1:21	I:310; 311; 705; 707; II:97; 513; 823; III:612; 613; IV:522; 523; 740n15; 846; VII:134n279; 367n58; 442; 895; IX:267n163; 413
1:21f	VII:890
1:21-23	VI:243
1:21ff	II:513; IV:962; V:441
1:21-25	VIII:30
1:21-32	III:940
1:22	II:513; III:604; 647n11; IV:832; **845-847; VII:521;** IX:231; 273n221
1:23	I:251; 259; 362; II:378; 393n73; 395; 513n59; III:100(n218); V:192, n11; 444; VII:128n241; IX:104; 417n8
1:24	I:108; 483; II:426n24; 431; 921; III:170; 428; 612; 613; V:928; 1030; VI:151; VII:132; 367n38; 1063, n388
1:24f	V:448
1:24ff	II:170; III:429; V:1026n5; VII:190n16
1:24-28	VIII:48
1:24-31	I:311
1:24-32	I:156; V:895; VI:593n80
1:25	I:199; 243; 259; 337; 702n58; II:764; III:100(n218);

	105n262; 1028; 1029; IV:62; 63; 1111n38; V:444; 735, n65; **VII:173;** 190n16; 442n169; IX:601
1:26	I:190; 259; II:426n24; 431; V:444; 736; **928,** n18; 1030; VII:367n58; 1063n388; IX:273
1:26a	V:928
1:26b	V:928
1:26f	VI:589n57; VII:367n38; IX:273
1:26ff	I:362
1:27	I:510; II:432; III:635; 940; **IV:702;** V:448, (n7); 928; VI:243
1:28	I:707; II:18; 259; 426n24; 431; 823; III:439; IV:958; 1073; V:1030; VI:479; VII:190n16; 367n58; 895; IX:185
1:28f	III:484
1:28ff	IV:702
1:29	I:155; III:485; VI:269n6; **272;** 290n22; 291, n24; 565, n16; VII:571
1:29a	VI:272n21
1:29f	IV:1073
1:29b-31	VI:272n21
1:30	I:277; III:120; 123; 481; IV:4; 684; VI:10; VII:190n16; **VIII:306; 527**
1:31	II:487; 646n28; VI:593n80; VII:895; VIII:525n4
1:32	I:379; 704; II:221; 222; 223; 513; 739; 823; III:15n67; 16; 586; 587; 699; IV:1073; V:444; VI:478; 479(n109); 636, n16; VIII:30n20; IX:138n223
1:32-2:3	**VI:636**
2	I:586; II:770; III:586n49; IV:1072n229; 1073; V:426; VI:693; VII:917`
2:1	II:704; III:923; V:442; IX:273n221
2:1f	IV:1082
2:1-3	VI:636
2:1ff	**VI:636;** VIII:567; IX:273
2:1-11	III:938; IV:719
2:2	I:242; 243; 257
2:3	III:923; IV:287n11; 1004; VI:478; 479(n109); 636; VIII:423n185
2:3-10	III:940
2:4	I:116; 359; 719; III:111; 322; 632; 938; IV:382, n61; 382n74; 384(n79); n79; 1004; 1009; V:102; 425; 432; 442; VI:329; IX:274n223; **487-488;** 491
2:4ff	V:423
2:5	I:257; II:225, n4; 952; III:138; 583; 613; 614; IV:353; 382;

	1009, n2; V:417n253; 422;		917n76; IX:551
	423n295; 424; 425; 430; 431;	2:17	I:351; III:381; 649; V:282;
	432; **438**; 442; 1023; 1028;		VII:130; IX:274; 543n327
	VI:152n33; VII:838n15; 938	2:17ff	III:381; **IV:754-755;** 1072;
2:5f	V:424; VII:1062		1073; V:441
2:5ff	IV:1004	2:17-20	V:282; **IX:231**
2:5-10	I:127	2:17-24	III:57n19
2:5-13	III:17	2:17-29	I:540
2:6	II:167; 649, n49; 897n9; IV:379;	2:18	I:703; 704; 705; II:260n19;
	VII:135n280		747n33; III:57, n19; 638;
2:6ff	**IV:1073**		IX:63, n6, n7; 543n327
2:7	II:649; 661; 864(n272), n273,	2:18ff	II:498; III:382
	(n278); 869(n315); 893;	2:19	V:99; VI:6; VII:442, n176;
	IV:587; 719; 1073; V:430;		VIII:287; **293;** IX:344; 345;
	VII:135n280; VIII:176;		346n292
	224n62; IX:105	2:19f	**V:619-620;** IX:231n65
2:7f	VII:993n115	2:20	I:242; 706; II:152; 158(n66);
2:7ff	I:392		826; IV:754, n5; 755n5; 919;
2:7-10	II:514		1072; V:100; IX:230;
2:8	I:156; 242; II:661, n9, n10, n11;		543n327
	III:167; V:422; 432; 442n408;	2:20ff	IV:1069
	VI:4; 11	2:21	II:145; 158; 497; III:702; 704;
2:8f	I:396; V:422; VII:607, n26;		705; 710; 713; 755; VI:272
	608n28	2:22	I:599; II:378; III:256; IV:729
2:9	II:513n56; 514; III:146; 381;	2:23	II:538; III:649; V:739, n4;
	481; 635; 1073; VII:607n19,		VII:130; IX:543n327
	n20; IX:648	2:24	I:622; 624; V:280; 620; 739n4;
2:9f	II:515; VI:869; 870		VI:831n336
2:10	I:16; III:381; VII:607;	2:25	I:226; IV:1070; V:741; VI:635;
	VIII:176; 224n62		636; IX:46n211; 240
2:10-16	VII:134n277	2:25ff	VI:81
2:11	I:243; IV:1073; V:733; VI:780,	2:25-29	II:516
	n3	2:26	I:225n2; 226; II:221; 223;
2:11-13	IX:273n222		IV:291n24; VI:635;
2:12	I:395; II:542; IV:1074; 1087;		VIII:144n36; IX:240
	IX:274n224; 543n327	2:26f	IX:543n327
2:12a	IV:1070	2:26-29	II:505n6
2:12f	IV:1073	2:27	I:226; 765; II:66; V:741;
2:12ff	II:517; III:587; IV:619n82;		VI:635; VII:130; VIII:60;
	1070; 1073		**IX:272;** 543n327
2:12-16	I:450n5; II:514	2:28	I:542; III:321; 612; IV:27;
2:13	I:220; II:190; 207; 215n18; 217;		**VII:129-130;** 133n270; IX:2
	IV:1072; V:733; VI:479; 480;	2:28f	I:765; III:16; 381; 385; 387;
	IX:273; 274n223		650n39; 1031; **VI:82-83;**
2:13ff	IV:755		732n37; VII:131n260;
2:14	I:453; II:826; IV:509; 1070;		142n330
	1072; VI:479; 635; IX:272;	2:29	I:765; II:587; III:321; 612; 960;
	273-274; 543n327		977; VI:77n32; 81; 83; 428;
2:14f	V:606n53; VIII:30n20;		VII:127; 130
	IX:273n218; 274; 543n327	3	IV:58
2:14ff	II:516; III:586, n49	3:8	**III:902-903**
2:15	I:746; II:646; 699; III:612; 637;	3:1	I:350; VI:62; 81
	IV:287; 508; 509; 1034n31;	3:1f	I:245n34; II:855n180; III:381;
	1050n113; 1073, n233;		IV:1089; VI:688
	V:554n105; VI:724n10; 757;	3:1ff	IV:1073; VII:446
	VII:916-917 (917n77);	3:1-8	VI:693
	IX:185; 273n218; 274	3:2	II:826; III:381; **IV:138;** 139;
2:15a	VII:917n77		1072; VI:204(n226)
2:15b	VII:917n77	3:2-4:19	VI:693
2:16	I:371; II:67; 217; 730; 733; 735;	3:3	I:155; 243; 292n79; III:112;
	952; III:17; 923; 941; 960;		484; IV:300; V:216; 442n408;
	976; V:88; 447; VII:442n168;		VI:204n227; 205; 206n243;

	VI:219(n333)
4:3	I:255; 753; II:207; 434; III:101(n231); IV:110; 289; 290; VI:210
4:3ff	IV:289
4:3-11	VII:789n111
4:4	I:255; IV:291, n29; 696; 700; **720**; V:565; IX:394
4:4f	**IV:290-292**; VI:220
4:5	I:255; II:216n21; 219; 434; III:446; IV:291; 1076; VI:203(n217); 211n273; VII:190; 521
4:5f	II:207; VI:219(n233)
4:5ff	II:215
4:6	I:255; II:651(n58); IV:110; 292; 367; VIII:482
4:7	I:312n159; 511; 512; II:205; IV:1085
4:7f	I:295; **IV:292**; 369
4:7-12	V:460
4:8	I:255; 295; III:1087; IV:292
4:9	I:226; 255; II:207; IV:367; VI:81
4:9ff	III:533; IV:289
4:10	I:226; 255; VI:81
4:11	I:226; 255; II:66; 206; 207; III:1030; V:1005; VI:206; 542; **VII:258**; 895(n64); **949**, n85; 952
4:11f	V:1005
4:11ff	II:430
4:12	I:9; 226; **III:403**; V:961; 1005; VI:81; VII:667n10; 668, n20
4:13	II:207; 582; 583; III:276; 888; V:1005; VII:545; IX:543n327
4:13f	III:781; 785
4:13ff	II:737
4:14	I:454; III:662; IV:1070n211; VI:213; IX:543n327; 553
4:14-16	IX:394
4:15	II:359; 517; 581; III:635; IV:618; 1070, n211; 1073; 1074; V:432; 433; 438; 739; 441; 443; VI:265
4:15f	IX:394n179
4:16	I:485n10; 602; II:430; 582; 583; III:329(n58); IV:619n82; VI:213; 220(n337); 542; VII:545; IX:394
4:16a	IV:291
4:16f	III:328(n51); V:1005
4:16ff	VIII:391
4:16-21	III:617n4
4:17	II:581; 582; 583; 862(n257); 874; III:487; 490; 1010; 1029; IV:892n13; 893(n19); VI:203n209; 210; 310n14; **VIII:157**; IX:550
4:17f	I:559; VI:281n13; 542
4:17ff	II:64
4:17-20	VI:206
4:18	II:430; 531; III:101(n232); 353n52; IV:110; V:728n1; 736; 1005; VI:206; 207; 211n273; VII:389n8; 545
4:19	I:492; IV:894; 895; 975; V:834n50; 1024n9; VI:207; VII:1063
4:20	II:248; 427; 582; III:947; 948n11; VI:205; 207; VII:613
4:20ff	IV:291
4:21	II:306; 581; 582; VI:218n331; 310; 464
4:22	II:207
4:22ff	IV:289
4:23	I:255; 745; 759
4:23f	III:328(n53); 583; IV:291
4:24	I:255; II:581; III:321; IV:893(n20), n22; VI:203(n217); 209; 211n273; 214(n303); IX:550
4:24f	II:335
4:25	I:332(n118); **II:70**; 170; 223; 224; 581; III:18n77; 321; IV:622; V:692; 706, n397; 710, n435; 711; VI:172; VIII:512; IX:395n183
4:25a	V:706n397
5	I:257; 258; II:80; 336; 438; 551, n23; 814; III:16; 342; 445; VII:993; VII:993; VIII:401; 472; IX:395, n183
5-7	I:296
5-8	I:309; II:868n309
5:1	I:328; 333n124, (n135); II:68; 205; 206; 216, n21; 217, n22; 396n100; 414; 415; 826n53; 922; III:1091; V:929; VI:198; 212; VII:994; IX:541; 554
5:1ff	II:358(n135); IX:369; 395n183
5:1-5	VI:434
5:1-11	II:867(n307); VII:417
5:2	I:133, n1; 134, n2; 379; II:67; 250; 426; 532, n107; 825; III:648n35; 650; V:1006; 1011; VI:218; 430; VII:652; VIII:597; IX:395; 413n72; 557n414
5:3	II:259; 538; III:143; 635; 648n35; 650; IV:508; 587; VI:218(n328); VII:922
5:3f	II:258, n14; III:148; VI:30
5:3-5	VII:607; VIII:74n39
5:3ff	VI:21
5:4	I:379; II:824n49; IV:587
5:4f	II:531; 532
5:5	I:49; 50; 51; 105; 190; 255; **256;** II:207; 433; 469, n3; 540; III:612; VI:426(n618); n621; 431n656; VII:556n48; 949; VIII:143n22
5:5f	IX:544
5:6	I:255; 328; 492; III:18n77; 460;

	1090; IV:735n5; V:710n435; VI:714; VII:190; 789; VIII:509; 511; IX:491; 544	5:15	I:141f; 143; 366; II:167; 431; 438, n20; 865n288; V:541n19; VI:60; VIII:404n24; 405; 470; IX:394; 404n18; 551; 552
5:6ff	II:469; III:584; IV:1076		
5:6-11	VII:521		
5:7	III:14; **IV:735;** VIII:184; 509	5:15a	VIII:472
5:7-11	I:309n154	5:15ab	VI:172
5:8	I:49; 127; 255; 309; 328; 332(n120); 492; II:432; III:18n77; 104; 1090; IV:117; V:441; 710n435; VI:426n618; VII:190; 789; 898; VIII:509; 511; IX:544	5:15b	**VI:540-541;** VIII:472
		5:15c	VI:541; 542; VIII:472
		5:15f	VIII:252; IX:404
		5:15ff	V:835n64
		5:16	I:294; II:68; 167; **221-222** (222n8); 429; 438(n20); III:938; 952; V:706; VI:172; 541; 543, n40; 544, n49
5:8f	IV:1120		
5:9	I:174; 255; 256; 257; 258; 309; 328; 379; II:67; 205; 207; 216; 217n22; 224; 538; III:938; IV:722; 1113; 1117; 1120; V:430; 441; 445; 446; 918; VI:1003; VII:993; VIII:370n259		
		5:16ab	VIII:472
		5:17	I:590; II:167; 205; 207; 209; 244; 437; 865n288; III:783; IV:7; VI:60; 63; VII:792; VIII:390n408; IX:394; 551
5:9f	II:203; 205; 826n53; V:445; VII:992; 993; 1018		
		5:17a	VIII:472
		5:17b	VIII:472
5:9ff	I:105	5:17f	II:869(n315); III:15; VI:172
5:10	**I:255-258;** 309; 328; II:67; 207; 415; 814; 864n273; 865; 869(n318); III:18n77; 938; IV:722; V:441; 445; 918; 1009n387; VII:789; 790; 993; VIII:167n16; 335; **384;** IX:394; 544	5:18	I:392; 450; 541; II:68; **221-222;** 224; 336; 360n144; 429; 431; 438; III:445; 938; 952; IV:619; VII:993n118
		5:18a	VIII:472
		5:18ab	VI:541
		5:18b	II:221; VI:541; 542; VIII:472
		5:18f	I:541; V:649; VIII:252
5:10f	IV:1117	5:19	I:175; 223; 224; 310; 328; 332(n120); II:191; 207; 218; 221; 224; III:445; 938; V:706; 917; VI:537n5; 544; IX:167n174; 552n383
5:11	I:257; 258; III:649; IV:7; VII:790; IX:541; 554		
5:12	I:296; 328; 364; II:68; 423; 437, n14; 498; 676; 678; 856n191; III:15, n69; 668; 882; 892; IV:353; V:769; VI:540; 543; VII:762; VIII:41; 472; IX:601		
		5:19a	VI:541; VIII:472
		5:19b	VI:541; 542; 543; VIII:472
		5:20	I:296; II:358(n138); 438n20; 682; III:276; 328(n52); IV:618; 1074; V:620; 740; VI:60; 172, n11; 264; **265;** VII:789; VIII:168; IX:601
5:12b	II:437(n14)		
5:12f	III:889		
5:12-14	II:358(n137)	5:20b	II:359(n139)
5:12ff	I:309; II:517; III:15, n66; 16; 449; IV:622; 867; V:538(n250); VI:159; VIII:472n483	5:20f	V:424n308; IX:395
		5:21	I:296; 312; 590; II:209; 224; 429; 437; 498; 864(n272); 869(n315); III:328(n53); VI:172n11; 265; VII:789; VIII:383n361; IX:542; 554
5:12-19	II:221; IV:342n21		
5:12-21	I:141; 309n154; II:209; 437n13; 542; 867; III:15n69; IV:1121n88; VI:419n572; 541; VII:132n265; 785; **789-792; 1072-1073; VIII:472,** n482		
		5:21a	VI:265
		5:21b	VIII:472
		6	**I:312-313;** 384; 541n57; II:199; 210; 336; 583; 869n316; IV:304n31; 1076; V:194n30; 446; 719; 923; VII:784n90; 790n112; 1072n453; VIII:331
5:13	I:296; 310; II:497; 517; IV:619n82; 1073; 1074; VI:172; 265		
		6f	I:296
5:13f	II:551; III:445; VI:172	6-8	VI:427n625
5:14	I:141; 310; 590; II:437; 438; 439; 517; III:15; IV:619n82; 1070n215; **V:195;** 740; VI:172; VIII:248; **252-253**	6:1	I:296; 313; 333n124; IV:345n24; 722; VI:265; VII:789; 791n117; **IX:396**

	IV:562; 719; VI:431n653; VII:762; VIII:447n331		7:7b	VIII:501n85
6:21a	VIII:55n42		7:7b	II:358
6:21bc	VIII:55n42		7:7ff	III:668n24; IV:618; 755; 1074; V:740; 931; VII:917
6:21f	II:496; IV:1118; 1120; VIII:54n37; 55; 57		7:7-10	I:310
6:21-23	VII:993n115		7:7-12	II:358
6:22	I:113; 296; 313; 333(n128); II:279; 360; 500; 502; 825; 869; III:615; IV:1117; VIII:54n37; 55n42		7:7-23	V:895
			7:7-25	VII:132n266
			7:7-8:1ff	II:358
			7:8	I:296; 310; II:358; 360; 497; 539; 551n22; 862; III:171; 635; IV:6; 893; 1073; V:472n1; 473; **474;** VI:265
6:22f	II:864(n272), (n278); 869; VII:993n115			
6:23	I:296; 309; II:358(n135); 359; 498; 541; 924; III:15n67; 940; 1091; IV:720; **V:592;** VII:762; VIII:383n361; IX:404; 542; 545; 554		7:8a	II:359
			7:8-13	II:552n27
			7:9	I:296; II:551n23; 674; 873;
			7:9a	II:358
			7:9f	I:767; II:359; 551; IV:1074; 1075
7	I:310; 311n157; 766; 767; II:343; **358-362;** 363; **550-552;** 805; 923; **III:50-52** (50n51); 276; 481n39; IV:573n10; 692, n31; 958; 1073n237; 1075; 1076; 1077; VI:435n684; 481n118, n120; 636n17; 637n18; VII:133; 134n277; 357n105; 762; 1065n405		7:9-11	II:498
			7:10	II:359; 429; 497; 551; 769; 869n314; III:16; 18; VI:750; VIII:501n85
			7:10f	II:551n23
			7:11	I:296; 384; II:551, n22; V:473; **474;** VII:356; VIII:501n85
			7:11a	II:359
			7:12	I:106; 751; 768; II:147; 188; 359; 497; 551; 652; 703; III:229; IV:1070; 1110n33
7:1	I:116; 703; III:321; 1097; IV:1055n135; 1070; 1117; IX:543n327; 591			
			7:12f	I:16
7:1-3	II:862(n244)		7:13	I:311; 329; II:359; 497; 551; 652; III:16; 276; 328(n52); 635; IV:1074; V:740; VI:265; VIII:521; IX:2
7:1ff	II:274; IV:1071; 1075; V:760			
7:1-6	III:20; 282n66			
7:2	I:362; 452; 652; II:60; 441(n31); IV:1069; 1070			
			7:13f	VII:133n276
7:2f	IX:457; 462		7:13ff	II:358
7:3	I:362; 788; III:18n78; IV:730; 734; IX:482		7:13-20	**II:359**
			7:14	I:296; 311; II:67n6; III:339; IV:1075; VI:160, n6; 437; VII:133n276; **144**
7:3f	II:496			
7:4	I:655; II:335; 430; III:21; 332(n84); 616; 1090; IV:1075; VII:1067, n414, n415; 1073n465; VIII:56; IX:547		7:14b	II:359
			7:14ff	I:327
			7:14-25	**III:50-52;** IX:649n197
			7:15	I:311; II:359; III:50; 635; IV:683; **692;** VI:478; 481; **636-637** (636n18; 637n18)
7:4-6	III:19			
7:5	I:295; 296; 310; II:274; 430; 431n40; 497; 654; 920; 925n94; III:15n67; 16; 616; **IV:562;** 930; **931; VII:134-135** (135n284); 1067n414			
			7:15a	II:359; VI:637n18
			7:15b	VI:636
			7:16	I:311; II:359; n141; III:50; 52; 549; VI:481; 636
7:5f	II:358; VI:428; 431			
7:6	I:196; 454; 766; II:358; 360; 430; 829; 904; III:20; IV:901; 1117; 1120; 1121; V:719; 720; VI:747n12; VII:686; 785; VIII:168		7:17	296; 311; II:359; 539; III:635; IV:692; 1109, n28; V:153; VI:636n18
			7:17f	II:698
			7:17ff	V:135n2
			7:17-23	VI:436n699
7:7	I:296; 311n156; 703; 707; II:68; 359; 361; 497; 551, n24; III:169n19; 171; IV:1069; 1070, n211; 1073; 1074; V:117; VI:264; VII:762;		7:18	I:313; II:168(n2); 359; 539; 542; III:50; 52; 549; 635; 656; IV:692; V:135, n2; VI:637; **VII:133-134**
			7:18b	II:552n25

8:12f	II:863n261; VII:131; 135n284
8:12-14	VI:426n617
8:12ff	II:869
8:12-39	II:867(n307)
8:13	II:864(n271); 869(n315); III:15n67; 19; 21; IV:561n55; 565; V:931; VI:429; 430; 431; **643-644;** VII:132n267; 785; 1065; VIII:591
8:13f	**VII:131-132**
8:14	II:56; III:903; IV:189; 720; V:1011; VII:792n120; VIII:391, n418
8:14f	IV:189; 509
8:14-16	VI:341n25
8:14ff	IV:918; V:926; VI:877n37; VIII:384n365
8:14-17	VII:792; VIII:390n413; **391-392**
8:15	I:6, n7; 543n69; II:130; 275; 360(n150); 429; 541; 805; 806; III:14n63; 17; 902; IV:7; 189; 470n38; V:350; 984; 1006; VI:221; 429n639; 430; 623; VII:1104; VIII:391n419; 392; n420; 399; IX:214; 216
8:15a	VIII:391
8:15b	VIII:391
8:15f	V:366; VI:427n630; 435n689; 436, n693
8:15-17	VIII:374
8:15ff	V:1006
8:16	I:628; II:336; 360; IV:508; 509, n3; V:653; VI:426, (n618); 427; 436n697, (n700); VIII:389n401; 390n413
8:17	I:671n33; II:250; 254; III:155; 328; 404; 781; 782; 783; 804; 806; IV:114n188; 494n58; 508; V:653; 921; **925-926;** 932; 934; VI:877; VII:135n280; 663; 787; 789; 792; 794; 795; 885n82; VIII:374n288; 391; IX:368n82; **547**
8:17b	VII:797
8:17f	IV:719; VIII:597
8:17ff	IX:368n85
8:18	I:205; 313; 379; 554; II:250; 433; III:461; 583; IV:288; 720; 1115; 1116; V:925; 926n7; 930; 933; 934; VI:724; VIII:597
8:18ff	VIII:392
8:18-30	III:20
8:18-39	II:869(n315)
8:19	I:393; II:56; III:583; IV:189; V:868; VIII:392
8:19f	III:1031
8:19ff	II:336; 435; VIII:391n418
8:19-22	III:1029; VII:601n6; 1003
8:20	I:393n2; II:437; 470; 532; **IV:523;** 1095; V:769; 894;

	VII:389n8; 602; 788n104; VIII:41; IX:104
8:20f	IV:318n25
8:21	II:250; 429; 496; 498; III:1034; IV:335; 352; V:653; VIII:41n5; IX:104
8:21f	IV:1115
8:21ff	III:788; V:515
8:22	II:544; III:893; IV:1107; 1110; V:894; VII:601; **IX:673**
8:22f	II:318
8:22ff	VII:602n16
8:22-27	**VII:601-602**
8:23	I:475; 486; II:56; 275; 336; 361(n153); 539; 584; 820; 825; 867(n303); III:783; IV:176; 335; **352;** 353; 354; 355; V:350; 366; 653; 868; VI:422; 427; 877; **VII:602;** 788, n104; 993; **1061-1062; VIII:399**
8:24	II:218; 530n100; 532; IV:353; V:343; 797n178; VII:993; 994
8:24f	I:393; II:531; 532; V:344; 350, n174; VI:221
8:25	I:51f; II:56; 66; IV:586
8:26	I:375; 376; 491; 628; II:25; 807; VI:421n583; **VII:602;** VIII:514; IX:413
8:26f	II:532; V:813; VI:430; 434n677; VII:600; **602,** n8; VIII:243
8:27	II:656n3; 657; III:51; 107; 111(n307); 612; 613; **VI:430; VII:602;** VIII:514; IX:232, n70
8:27b	VIII:243
8:27f	II:361
8:28	I:17; 49; 50; 52; II:429; III:204; 329; 494; 496; IV:189n19; 1016; VII:788n101; **875,** n32, n34, n35; 922; 993n122; **VIII:166;** 250; IX:134n191; 136n204; 232n70
8:28-30	IV:2; 189
8:28ff	VI:430n644; IX:214
8:28-39	II:336
8:29	I:145; 392; 671n33; 715; II:360(n147); 396; 397; 867; III:18; 332; IV:354; 739; 758; 1016n37; V:435n373; 456, n4; 653; 1009n387; VI:876n29; **877,** n37, n39; 881, n58, n61; VII:650n28; 651n34; **787-788** (788n102); 792; 875, n37; 993; VIII:166; 384; 392, n421; 399n16; IX:556
8:29f	II:250; IV:1016; V:649; VI:877n37; VII:787; **VIII:166-167;** 597
8:30	II:205; 208; 217; 254; 867; III:488; V:456; 925; VII:993;

	VIII:166
8:31	II:361; VIII:508
8:31f	III:117; V:1009n387
8:31ff	I:49; III:584; V:653; IX:370n98
8:31-34	IX:544n333
8:31-39	III:938; IV:722
8:32	I:49n137; 52; II:170; III:18n77; IV:739; V:706, (n399d); 710, n435; 888; VII:783; **785**; 786; 792; VIII:335, **384**, n365; 510, n20; 511; IX:396
8:32-35	III:18n77
8:33	II:207; 218; III:92n137; 496; 636; 637; IV:189, n19; 190
8:33f	I:357; III:938; VIII:501n86
8:34	II:39; 204; 215; 224; 335; III:18; 104(n259); 107; 547; 1089; V:523n204; 691; 706, (n399); 710; 812; VII:292n3; 650, n30; VIII:243; 257; 514; IX:413n72; **544**, n333; 546n345; 552; 562; 570; 573
8:34ff	IV:1076
8:35	I:49; 775; III:146; 147; 1090; IV:526; VI:21; VII:607, n20, n24; VIII:501n86; IX:544, n334; 546
8:35ff	I:52
8:35-39	IV:1016
8:36	III:20n83; 21; 147; VI:691; VII:922n18; 937
8:37	I:49n138; 50; II:68; IV:179; 945
8:37-39	IV:190; VIII:501n86
8:38	I:86; 483; II:544; III:21; V:895; VI:4; VIII:614
8:38f	II:37; 308; 868; III:118(n374); V:310; 771; VIII:614n3
8:39	I:517; II:541; III:1028; 1091; VIII:383n361; **614**; IX:542; 544n334; 554
9	II:484; 744; IV:211; 214; VI:755, n57; VII:353; VIII:64
9-11	I:586; II:516; III:120; 121; **386-388**; 535n99; IV:191n24; 194; **209-214**; 959; 1016; V:1022n1; 1026n5; **1027**; VI:98; 411n520; 693; VII:518; 992; VIII:56n49; 224n64; IX:91n23
9:1	I:243; II:540; 541; IV:508; 509; V:185; VI:426n618; 427n630; VII:916; IX:549n358; 551; 601
9:1ff	II:356(n111); 362n156
9:2	III:612; IV:320; V:115
9:3	I:145; 354, n1; 355; II:359n143; 361n152; 776; 778; III:121; IV:869n230; VI:88n54; VII:126; **741**, n27; 742; VIII:267n58; 508; 511; IX:549

9:3f	II:441(n35), n36
9:3-5	IV:213
9:4	II:130; 380; 583, (n60); 584n61; III:386; IV:65; 755; 1089; V:653; VIII:399
9:4f	**III:105**; 381; 387; IV:1072; 1073; VII:446; IX:403n10
9:5	I:199; 337; II:764; III:105; 106; V:526n225; 889; 894; 976n178; VII:124n212; 127; 128n238; IX:59n16; 541; 546n343
9:6	III:383; 385; 386; 387; 517; IV:57; 112; **VI:169**
9:7	II:539; III:488; V:638; VII:545
9:7f	I:9; IV:57
9:8	II:583; IV:291n24; V:638; 653; VI:429n637; VII:127; 128; 545; VIII:391n417
9:9	III:461; IV:112; 1115n59
9:10	V:976(n185); VII:1072n451
9:11	I:392; IV:179; 211n46; 575; VI:635; VIII:167
9:11f	II:953; III:328n51; 329(n58); 332
9:11ff	I:49n139
9:12	II:651(n58); III:488; IV:110, n173; 179; 656, n38
9:12f	IV:1071n218
9:13	I:49; 748; II:953; III:192; IV:175; 179; 691; VI:831n341; VII:362; VIII:232n41
9:14	I:155; III:111n313; V:733; VII:363
9:15	I:757; IV:110; 355; 865; V:161; VII:550
9:15-18	II:484
9:16	I:638; III:52; VIII:231, n36; **232**, n42
9:17	I:68; 392; 753; II:338; 429; 539; III:329; 332; IV:110; 382; V:271; VII:362; 364
9:17f	V:443n415
9:18	I:637; II:338; 425; III:48; 52; IV:175; V:1023; 1030, n3; VIII:293
9:19	I:636; 637; III:111n313; **IV:572-573**; VII:363, n31
9:19-21	IV:210
9:19ff	**VII:362-364**
9:20	III:121; 945; 1028; **VI:260-261**; 463; VII:363; VIII:423n185
9:20b	VII:364n42
9:20f	VII:363
9:20ff	II:338; III:1038
9:21	II:566; 567; IV:655n35; V:435n370; **VI:118**; 260; VII:363; **VIII:176**, n39
9:21ff	II:428; VII:364, n41
9:22	I:397; 476; II:484; III:48; 52; **IV:382-383** (382n60); 386;

	214(n292); 831
10:16ff	I:221; V:349
10:17	II:68; III:708; IV:109; 119; VI:212; 217(n324); VII:518; IX:543
10:18	III:596; V:158; IX:292n67; 295n83
10:19	I:705; II:442n41; III:329n57; IV:110; 865; 1117n66; V:415n233; 419, n266, n271; VII:895(n64)
10:19ff	IV:1071n218
10:20	II:687; 769; 893; IV:111; VI:831; VIII:185
10:20b	II:893
10:20f	IV:110
10:21	III:387; VI:11; 723; IX:431
11	II:484; 814; III:329; 387; IV:188n15; **211**; 214; V:434; VII:997
11:1	I:448; II:322n4; 362n157; 435; III:386; VII:545; 741n27; IX:46n212; 249
11:1f	II:356(n111); IV:53
11:2	I:448; 715; 753; II:539; 935n58; III:387; IV:110; VIII:243; IX:482
11:2ff	IV:211
11:2-5	II:935
11:3	III:183; 1087; V:714n469; VI:834n348; IX:648
11:3f	IX:478n58
11:4	I:738; 753; II:629; 935n57; III:594; 595; IV:110; 213; IX:469
11:4a	IX:482
11:4b	IX:482
11:4ff	VII:354
11:5	I:205; II:629; III:461; IV:179; 180; 1114
11:5a	IX:478n58
11:5f	VI:220(n337); IX:395
11:6	II:651(n58); IV:213
11:7	II:516; III:387; IV:176; 177; 179; 180; 211; V:1023; 1026; 1027; VIII:212
11:7b	V:1024
11:7f	V:1028; VI:164n19
11:7-10	IV:211; V:1027
11:8	III:626; IV:1107n15; V:341; 342; 378; **557**; 1024; VII:273; 356; VIII:293; IX:478n58
11:8f	IV:1071n218
11:9	II:169; IV:110; V:595; VII:342n20; 344; 345; 352; **354**, n89; 355n90; 356; VIII:209n2; 212; 482
11:10	V:342; 378, n16; VII:354n88; 356; VII:293
11:11	II:442n41; 881; III:329(n57); **VI:164**, n20; **884;** VII:354; 355n90; 992; 997

11:11f	IV:214; VI:172
11:11-24	IV:211
11:12	III:892; IV:212n48; VI:299; **305;** VII:363
11:12-15	VI:329
11:13	II:88; 371; 516; III:295
11:14	II:435; 441n35, n36; 442n41; 881; III:329n57; V:1027; VII:126; 992
11:15	I:258; III:892; IV:15; V:1027; **VI:988;** 989; VII:354; 363
11:15f	IV:211
11:16	I:485; II:362n157; 435; IV:212n49; 655n35; **VI:988-989** (989n21); IX:544n336
11:16a	VI:989, n20
11:16b	III:721n6, n7; VI:989, n20
11:16ff	III:721n5; **VI:988-989**
11:16-21	III:720
11:16-24	IX:271n203
11:17	I:106; II:895; III:804; IV:211n47; **VI:989**
11:17ff	III:387; IV:566n86; V:760; VI:164n20; 989n21; VII:807n40
11:17-24	V:1027
11:18	III:651; 653, n2; 654; V:431
11:19f	III:727
11:19-22	V:1027
11:20	IV:214; VI:205; 212; 218; 221; **VII:651;** VIII:20; 108; IX:213; 232; 234; 235
11:21	V:435; **IX:271**
11:22	III:111; 495; 858; 859; V:342; VI:164, n20; 166; 989; **VIII:108; IX:488;** 491
11:23	III:858; IV:214; V:1027; VI:205; 212
11:23f	III:117; VII:364
11:24	III:858; 859; V:435; 736; VI:989; **IX:271**
11:24b	II:441(n34), n36
11:25	I:116; II:516; 678; III:49; 387; IV:212; **596; 822-823;** V:649; 733; 1023, n5; 1026; 1027; VI:302; IX:232; 234; 235
11:25f	IV:214; 822; IX:90n21; 665
11:25ff	II:516; III:560; VI:850
11:25-32	IV:211
11:26	III:192; V:649; VI:302; 831n336; 1002; **1003;** VII:189; 327; **721-722;** 992; IX:249n27
11:27	I:295; II:129; 130; V:720n13; 730
11:28	I:49n139; 257; II:70; 729n65; 733; 814; III:491; IV:179; V:976n178; **IV:989**
11:28f	IV:823
11:29	III:111; 491; IV:628; 629;

	VII:356; VIII:269; 509; IX:541
14:16	I:624; IX:233n77
14:17	I:583; 586; 643; II:210; **416**; 541; 869; 870; III:788; IV:67; VI:60; 145; 146; 430n650; 431n658; VII:417; VIII:146; 224; IX:369, n89
14:18	I:457; II:260n20; 275; III:1091; VI:756n61; IX:541; 549
14:19	II:230; 411; 416; 432; 694; IV:338; V:145; IX:404
14:19ff	II:694; IV:67
14:20	I:642n1; II:66; 643; 694; III:424; 425n77; IV:338; VI:751; 752; 753; **756-757**; VII:355; 356; VIII:268; 269
14:20f	I:643
14:20ff	II:694
14:21	I:490; III:549; IV:66; V:164; VI:141; 146; 745n3; 746; 751; 752; **753**, n49, n51; 757; VII:125n214; 344; 345; 349; 352; **355**, n91, n96
14:22	II:826n58; III:950; IV:369; VI:218; 219
14:22f	VI:213n288; 310
14:23	I:313; 715; III:947; IV:722; 1077; VI:143n72; 198; 218; 757; VII:355; 356; VIII:269
14:23b	VI:166n31
15	I:139; II:484
15:1	I:491; 492; 596; V:564; VII:356
15:1-3	I:455; III:19; 404; IV:669
15:1ff	II:694; IV:67
15:2	II:694; V:145; VI:316; 317; 724; 754
15:3	IV:669n21; V:122; 240; 242; 564(n29); 918; IX:541; 545; 547
15:4	I:745; 752; 759; 771; II:161; 162; 428; 531; 824, n49; III:328(n53); IV:586; V:796; 797; 798; 823
15:5	III:112(n316); IV:587; 596; 669; V:796; 798n182; 823; IX:233, n75; 553
15:6	V:186; 1008; VII:698; IX:541; 554
15:7	II:429; III:1090; IV:15; 66; 668n17; IX:541; 545; 547
15:7-13	V:213
15:8	I:243; 602; II:88; 583, (n60); 584, n61; 746n32; IV:138; V:976n178; VI:81; 989; VIII:514; IX:541; 555
15:8f	II:484
15:8ff	IV:66
15:9	V:271; VIII:499; 514
15:10	II:367n11; 775; IV:52; 54; 110
15:10f	I:754n19
15:10ff	IV:1071n218
15:11	I:177; II:369; 587n4; III:1087; IV:50; 52
15:12	I:106; 478; II:532, n108; IV:110; VI:831; 989
15:12a	VIII:41n4
15:12b	VIII:41n4
15:12c	VIII:41n4
15:12d	VIII:41n4
15:13	II:314; 412; 417; 532; 922; III:112(n317); VI:61; 291; 310n10; 433(n669); IX:369, n89, n91
15:13f	VI:290n22
15:14	I:18; 707; 708; IV:1022; VI:4; 291
15:14ff	I:64; II:356(n111)
15:15	I:146n10; 744n8; 745; II:86; V:166; VIII:186; IX:396; 403n7
15:15f	III:331(n80)
15:15ff	III:599
15:16	I:105; 106; 107; 111; 112; II:59; 540; 731; 733; 740; 810; III:158; 185; 252; 254; 333(n91); **IV:230-231**; VI:431; VII:535n47; 536; 700; IX:68; 542; 553; 558n420
15:16-20	II:720; IX:542
15:17	II:541; III:649n35; VI:8; 722; IX:542; 552
15:17f	III:650
15:18	I:224; II:371n21; 582; 731; 732; III:252; 635; IV:102; VI:206; 635; VIII:185; IX:542; 555
15:18f	III:213; 214; 589; VI:483n139
15:18-20	I:64
15:19	I:440; II:311, n91; 731; 732; III:1090; IV:117; V:796; VI:297; 423; VII:230; 258; **259-260**; 328n225; 334; VIII:125; IX:542; 543
15:20	II:719; 720n118; 732; III:63, n3; V:140; 278; 282; IX:542
15:20f	III:600; VI:111
15:21	I:64; V:341; 705; 706; 708; 709; VI:831n336; VII:895(n64)
15:22	III:856
15:24	I:552; II:530; IV:596; V:344; VI:131; 573; 671n121
15:25	I:108; VI:573
15:25f	I:106
15:25-31	VII:334
15:26	II:432; III:796n41; 807; 808; IV:283; VI:477; **909**; 912; VII:93n36
15:26f	II:741
15:26-31	VII:334
15:27	II:740; 863n267; III:23; 348; 807; IV:226; **227**; V:564, (n29); 566; VI:414; 437; 909; VII:144; 334; VIII:598
15:27b	VI:909

I CORINTHIANS

	552; 554; **555**
1:3	II:412n64; 414n81; V:1007; IX:554
1:4	II:541; VIII:597; IX:394, n182; 395n185; 403; 407; 555; 561n445
1:4f	IX:409n28; 412; 551
1:4-7	VI:219n335
1:4-9	VIII:501n86
1:5	I:707; 708; II:541; IV:102; V:889; VI:329; VII:522n394; VIII:597
1:5f	VIII:597
1:6	I:603; II:539; III:1090; IV:504, n78; 819n141; IX:543; 555
1:7	II:56; III:583; 1091; VI:426n617; VII:522n394; VIII:597; 600n35; IX:403; 404n14, n15
1:7f	IX:541
1:7-10	**IX:555**
1:8	I:356; 357, n2; 602; 603; II:952; III:1091; V:865; 868; VIII:56; IX:404; 556
1:8ff	III:584
1:9	II:68; 429; 826; III:111(n309); 488; 804; V:1009n387; VI:216(n318); 434; **VIII:384-385;** IX:542
1:10	I:476; 514; 717; II:237; III:1092; IV:846; 958; V:162n2; 271; 278; 795; VII:964; IX:541; 554
1:10f	VIII:498n63
1:10ff	I:183; VI:94; 850
1:11	II:61; III:590; VII:525; IX:451n107
1:11f	VII:520
1:12	IV:137; 456; 1068; VI:100; 111; VII:522; 964, n4; IX:541; 543n326; 553
1:12f	IX:549
1:13	I:442n216; 539; III:18n77; IV:619; 870; **V:275;** 710n435; VI:55; VII:582; 791n117; 1071n443; 1073n460; VIII:509; 512; IX:541, n320
1:13ff	VI:619
1:14	VII:847; IX:412
1:14ff	I:440(n201)
1:15	I:539; III:332n87; **V:275**
1:16	I:485; V:130; 650
1:17	I:403; 406(n48); 441n211; 539n47; 540; 666n7; II:206; 718; 719; 720; 725; 733; III:332(n85); 642(n14); 662; 1090; IV:101; 794; VI:94; VII:354; 519; 520; 522; **575-576;** IX:541; 544; 549; 552
1:17f	VII:519
1:17ff	I:709; III:659n1
1:18	I:71; 395; 441; II:309, n84; III:21; 710; 716n15; 976; IV:117; 118; 845; 847; 920; 1122; VI:426n617; 756; VII:576, n30; 748; 992; **1077**
1:18f	I:312; VII:519n379; 521n389
1:18ff	I:372; II:290n25; 513; III:584; 662; IV:832; **845-847; VII:354;** 526n415; 580; IX:231
1:18-25	IV:822
1:18-31	VII:519n379
1:18-2:5	VII:519; **522**
1:18-2:16	IV:847n121; VII:522
1:18-3:21	VII:517
1:19	I:394; 395; 748; VI:831n336; VII:521; 895; VIII:159
1:19f	I:333n121; IV:922; V:215; VII:517; 521n391
1:20	I:203; 205; 740n2; 742; II:578n18; III:653; 885; IV:777n92; **VII:521,** n390; 685n104; **784**
1:20a	VII:748n2, n3
1:20f	III:892; VI:329
1:21	I:71; 705; II:741; 742; III:586; 587; 716, n15; IV:846, n118; VI:208n258; 214(n303); 216n315; VII:520, n384; 521; 522; 1002
1:21f	III:712; V:162n2
1:22	I:191; II:515; 893; IV:846n120; VII:230; **258-259; 521,** n390; 748n3
1:22f	III:494; 710
1:22-24	II:516
1:22ff	II:441(n39); III:714
1:22-25	VII:519
1:23	II:370; 725; III:704; 711; 716n15; IV:118; 819; 845; V:636; 699n331; VI:329; 425; 755; VII:344; 345; 352; 354; 520n385; **582;** IX:542; 544; 552
1:23f	III:711; 1090; VI:92, n80; 750; VII:520; IX:546n344
1:23-31	IX:557
1:24	I:107; II:304; 305; 514; III:494; 496; 704; 711; 976; IV:819; VI:425; VII:514n342; 521; IX:542
1:24-26	VII:128
1:25	I:491; II:316; 515; III:111; 398; IV:846; VII:354n86; 520
1:25-31	III:649
1:26	III:491, n1; 493n6; 660; IV:655n34; VII:127; 128; VIII:224
1:26f	IV:652; VII:521
1:26-28	IV:175; VIII:224
1:26ff	II:317; 440(n28); III:329n56; 330(n65); 892; IV:846;

	VII:365n47
1:26-29	III:649n38; IV:835n30
1:27	I:190; 491; 492; III:491; 892; VI:910; 911n241; VII:521; 685n104; VIII:224n61
1:27f	III:890; V:114; VIII:224
1:27-29	IV:174; 175
1:27ff	III:1
1:28	I:190; 453; II:541; VII:521
1:28a	VIII:224n61
1:29	I:362; III:649, n35; VI:714; VII:129; 132n265; 521; IX:395
1:30	I:112; 113; II:203n48; 204; 541; III:430; IV:126; 352; 353; 354; 355; VI:88; VIII:224; IX:552; 554; 575n516
1:30f	VII:521
1:31	III:649;1087; IV:409; VI:714; 831n338; IX:395;
2	VII:512; 525; 765
2:1	I:71, n16; II:675; IV:101; 504; 819; 821; VI:94; 426n617; VII:519; 522; VIII:524
2:1ff	I:440(n201)
2:1-5	**II:312;** 313; VI:426n617; 428
2:2	III:642(n14); 923; IV:920; V:118; VI:425; VII:519; **582;** VIII:498n63; 609; IX:542; 544; 552
2:3	I:491; V:107; VII:354n86; 522; IX:213; 214
2:3f	VII:582
2:4	I:71; II:311n91; 732; III:589; 710; 716; IV:101; 102; **VI:8-9;** 94; 311; VII:260n400; 354; 519; 522; IX:213
2:4f	III:213; 712; VI:208n258; 423, n600; 33; VII:522
2:5	III:332(n85); VI:212; VII:520(n386)
2:6	I:203; 205, n31; 453; 489, n7; III:885; 893; IV:819; 847; V:440n400; VI:416n547; 425; VII:128; 519; 576; VIII:76, n57; IX:187
2:6f	IV:819; VII:519n382
2:6-8	IV:820; VI:530; 757n66; VII:581n3
2:66ff	I:709; III:584; 587; 892; 976; IV:822; 824; IX:4n13
2:6-16	**IV:819-822; VI:425-426** (426n615); 428; VII:519; 522; 766; VIII:609n29
2:7	I:199; 202; 366; II:250; III:954; IV:504n78; 819; 820, n144; 821, n148; 847; 1111n38; V:456; VI:425; 426n617; 685; 687; 688; VII:519; 576; IX:593n71
2:7ff	III:976; IV:959
2:7-10	VI:425

2:8	I:205; 489; II:248; III:103; 552; 584; 885; 892; 893; 1086; IV:752; 820; V:35n243; 440, n401; VI:253; 425; **VII:519-520; 581,** n3; 611; VIII:609; IX:346n291
2:8b	III:856
2:9	I:756; II:705; 929; III:612; 981; **988-989** (989n116); V:341; 347; 378, n16; **557;** VI:484; VII:893n44; IX:136n204; 578n540
2:10	I:517; II:67; 657; III:584; IV:821; V:557; 895; VI:32; 425; 426n617; 434n677; VII:1077; VIII:604n24; IX:663
2:10f	VII:765
2:10ff	II:361; 458
2:10-13	VIII:76n55
2:10-16	VII:520
2:11	IV:959; VI:426n617; 435; 436
2:11f	I:703n61; III:584
2:12	I:709; II:822; III:892; IV:7; 967; VI:426n617; 427; IX:375n18; 396; 663
2:12b	VI:425
2:13	I:366; II:165; **953-954;** IV:101; VI:94; 425; 426n617; 433; 437; VII:582
2:13f	VI:349; IX:661
2:13-15	VI:348; 436; VII:519n381
2:13-16	VII:520
2:13-3:3	VI:424n605
2:14	II:54; III:584; 587; 892; 954; IV:832; **845-847;** 959; VI:395n389; 425; VII:521; **IX:663**
2:14f	I:366; III:944; VI:428; VII:1077
2:15	VI:349; VII:520; IX:223n20
2:16	I:705; II:820; III:944; 1087; IV:967n19; VI:437n703; **VII:765-766;** IX:547
2:16a	IV:959
2:16b	IV:959
3	I:647; IV:920
3:1	I:643; 646; II:541; 882; IV:740n15; **919-920;** V:649; VII:517; 519n381; 520(n387); IX:551
3:1f	I:645; VI:711n60; VIII:76n53
3:1-3	VI:424n605; 426n617; 437n703; VII:144
3:1ff	I:709; IV:837
3:1-4	VI:428n633
3:2	I:643; 644n7; IV:1120; V:760; VI:160
3:3	I:364; 514; II:881; 882; III:944; V:945; VI:94n15; VII:128; 135n284; 144; 571; VIII:498n63; IX:662, n13

6:13bf	III:788	7:8f	I:788; IX:452, n112
6:14	I:651n21; II:304; 316; 335;	7:9	II:342; 364; VI:949; VII:358;
	336n17; 338; VI:216(n316);		IX:457
	421; VII:1061; 1062	7:10	I:757; II:356(n114); 820;
6:14ff	I:655		III:1092; IV:106; 107;
6:15	II:305n76; IV:561(n56);		453n253; V:764; VI:454n7;
	564-565; 566; **VII:1070;** 1079;		591; VIII:37n3
	1082; **IX:540;** 548	7:10f	I:651; IV:733
6:15a	VII:1070n438	7:10ff	I:650n14
6:15b	VII:1070	7:10-16	IX:452
6:15f	VI:594; VII:1065	7:11	**I:255-257;** IX:452n110
6:15ff	I:483; 656; IV:565n78	7:11-13	I:510
6:16	I:754n19; III:822; IV:110;	7:12	II:356(n114); 820; III:1092;
	VII:126; 137; 1063		IV:103n129; 106; V:135;
6:16f	I:142n9; 651; 656; IV:565		VII:772
6:17	I:142; II:435; 820(n26); III:107;	7:12f	VII:795
	823, n7; VI:419; **VII:1070**	7:12-15	VI:215(n313)
6:18	I:294; II:431; V:888; VI:479;	7:13	V:135; VII:772
	594; VII:1063	7:14	I:112; 146n10; 483; 543n71;
6:18b	I:651		II:540; III:226; 429; IV:1109,
6:18f	IV:734		n28; V:1004; VI:215(n311);
6:19	I:105; 125; 442; 651n21; II:540;		VII:1070n439
	820; III:228; IV:884n17; 886;	7:14a	I:146n10
	V:126; 133; 144; 760;	7:14c	V:650
	VI:431n658; 432n663; 593;	7:15	I:651n22; II:279; 412n65;
	VII:147n370; 1064; **1065;**		III:488; IX:308; 395n186
	VIII:498n63	7:15c	**II:416**
6:19f	III:247; IV:886	7:15ff	I:652
6:20	**I:125;** 126n1; VII:1064; 1065;	7:16	I:362n10; 777; VII:992
	VIII:178; IX:544	7:17	III:488; 506; 1091; V:88; 944;
7	I:362; 651; 709; II:356; 767,		VIII:35
	n24; III:60n28; 1033;	7:17ff	II:440(n29); 441(n33); III:381;
	IV:490n49; 669; V:649;		VI:515
	IX:452, n109, n110, n111	7:18	I:226; III:488; VI:81
7:1	I:652; 744, n8; 776; III:549;	7:18a	VII:1070n439
	IV:737n3; VI:54;	7:18b	VII:1070n439
	VII:1070n439	7:18f	VI:83
7:2	I:652; 776; II:817n5;	7:18ff	IV:1077
	IV:826n179; VI:594; VII:366	7:19	I:226; II:552, n26; III:990;
7:2-7	IX:452		VI:81; VIII:146
7:3	I:785n35; II:167; IV:972n6;	7:20	III:488; 491, n1; 492n1; 493n6;
	973n10; V:564, n3		IV:56
7:3ff	I:652	7:20ff	II:501
7:4	II:574f; III:60; VII:1063;	7:21	II:272, n89; 501n20; III:488;
	IX:308		VI:910n234
7:5	I:652; 785n35; II:80; 342;	7:21b	II:501n20
	684n1; 901; III:332(n88),	7:21f	VII:408n34
	333(n90); 461; 857n13;	7:22	I:125n1; II:273; 275; III:488;
	IV:933n71, n73; 934n80;		491; 1091; V:760; IX:548
	V:834n52; VI:29; 32;	7:23	**I:125;** II:275n104; III:491;
	221(n341); 724; VII:160; 161;		VIII:178; IX:544
	1070n439; VIII:37	7:24	I:652; III:488; 491, n1; V:732;
7:6	I:717; VIII:37		VII:128n239
7:7	I:652; II:364; 767; 826;	7:25	I:717; II:237; 356(n114); 485;
	III:45n8; 854; VI:594;		820; III:295; 1092; IV:106;
	VII:749; VIII:37; IX:404,		740n15; V:836; VI:175n8;
	n23; 452		204; **VIII:37**
7:7f	I:652, n25; II:356(n114);	7:25-28	IX:452
	VII:1070n439	7:26	I:346; 652; II:60; 544; III:144;
7:8	I:652; III:549; IV:103n129;		146; 491n1; 549
	737n3; IX:452, n112	7:27	I:776; IV:336
7:8b	IX:452n112	7:27a	I:652

7:28	I:785n35; V:836; VII:125; 411n18; 412n28; IX:452n112	
7:28f	I:652; III:144	
7:29	I:652; II:817n5; III:461; IV:188; **VII:596-597**	
7:29-31	II:868; III:860n11; IV:592	
7:29-34	IV:591n18	
7:30	II:830; IX:369	
7:31	I:129; 130; 205; 652; III:625; 885; 893; 895; VI:329; VII:70; **956**	
7:32	III:49; IV:593; VI:756n61	
7:32-34	IV:591; 592; VII:1070n439	
7:32ff	I:455; 652; III:893	
7:32-35	III:1091	
7:33	I:203	
7:34	I:108; III:61; IV:509; V:836; VI:435, n687; VII:125n220; 1063; IX:76; 452n110, n112	
7:35	I:529; 652n27; II:771, n3; VI:724; IX:75, n13; **76**	
7:36	I:785n35; II:364; 574; III:50; 60	
7:36-38	V:836; VI:477	
7:36ff	I:652n23, n24; II:441(n31); **VII:651**	
7:37	II:364; 565; 566; **III:60-61;** 612; 923; VI:54; VII:651	
7:38	I:652n24; II:364	
7:39	I:785n35; II:60; 541; 862(n244); III:14n60; 46n28; 1091; VII:784n85; IX:452, n112; 457; 591	
7:39f	I:652; 788; IX:452	
7:40	I:718; II:237; 356(n114); 820; IV:369; VI:426n618; 427n630; 454n7; IX:452	
7:40a	II:820	
7:40b	IV:669	
8	I:643; II:501; IV:67; VI:94; 753, n47; 757; VII:914	
8-10	III:1033; VII:915n67	
8ff	IV:67; VII:356	
8-14	VII:522	
8:1	I:51, (n144); 701n54; 709; II:694; 826; III:253; IV:669; V:141; VI:54; 94, n16; 426n617; 854; VIII:597; IX:77	
8:1b	**V:141**	
8:1-3	VI:252; 432	
8:1ff	I:709; II:501; VII:355	
8:1-13	II:379	
8:2	II:24	
8:3	I:50, n140; 639; 704; 706; 710, n78; IV:1077; VII:915; IX:136n204	
8:3f	VII:915	
8:4	II:378; 703; III:100; 101; 253; 889; V:514n126; VI:157n87; VII:915; VIII:597; IX:394n182	
8:4-6	I:705; II:378n27	

8:4ff	III:1081n214; **V:1012,** n396
8:5	I:483; 678n5; 681; II:378; III:92(n142); 101; IV:134; 622; V:513, (n118); 514n126; 533; 1012n397
8:5f	III:100; 1091; V:518
8:6	I:679; II:67; 432; 435; III:103(n247); 104; 107; 108, n285; 585; 884; 1030; 1032, n209; IV:130; 619n79; 622; V:212; 514n125; 888; **893-894;** 1007; 1008n379; 1010; 1011n395; 1012, n399; VII:915; IX:394n182; 541; 554
8:7	I:492; 709; II:378; III:253; IV:736; 740n15; 1111; VI:426n617; 757; VII:915, n65; VIII:268; **914;** IX:394n182
8:7ff	II:441(n32); 694
8:7-12	VI:218
8:7-13	**VII:914-915**
8:8	I:643; IV:67; V:840; VI:60; 146; VIII:597
8:9	I:704; 709; II:570; VI:747; 751; **753,** n49; VIII:268
8:9ff	I:492; VII:355n93; VIII:597
8:9-12	VII:914
8:10	I:490; II:379; 430; 693; 826; III:253; 656; V:141; VI:157; 594; 757; VII:355; 914; VIII:210; 268; IX:394n182
8:10f	I:709; VII:915
8:11	I:395; 490; II:70; III:18n77; 1090; V:710n435; VI:753n51; VII:356; 915; 992; 1068; VIII:269; 509
8:11f	II:694; IX:545
8:12	I:313; 492; II:431; 432; III:1091; VI:757; VII:356, n101; 914; 1068; VIII:262; 263; **268-269**
8:12f	VII:915
8:13	I:199; 643; II:694; III:333(n90); VI:165; 753n49; VII:125n214; 344; 350; 351; 352; **355;** 915; VIII:269
9	VI:753; VII:394; 586
9:1	I:220; 423, n96; 438(n184); II:501; 541; 643; III:1091; IV:454; 669; 719; **V:357-358;** VI:419n569
9:1-11	VII:586
9:2	I:446; II:541; III:1091; VII:948; IX:423
9:3	III:944
9:3-5	VI:21n65
9:4	II:692; III:857; VI:141
9:4f	VI:111
9:4-6	II:570
9:4-18	VIII:17

9:5	I:144; 431; 651n18; 652; 776; 785; III:1092; V:649; VI:100; 101; VII:749; IX:452n109; 543n326
9:5f	I:423
9:5-18	VII:630
9:7	I:646n2; II:692; III:520; 615; V:592; VI:641; VII:710; 711
9:7ff	III:857
9:8	I:364; IV:1070; 1077n245; IX:543n327
9:8f	IV:1077
9:8-10	I:263
9:9	I:747; III:990; IV:864n194; 1069(n209); 1070; IX:53n41; 543n327
9:9f	III:583
9:10	I:745; 756; 759; II:530; 831; III:990; V:564
9:11	II:863n267; III:23; 133; 808; VI:265n10; 331n94; 437; VII:144; 546
9:12	I:652; II:501; 566; 731; 732; 831; III:856, n4; 857; 1090; IV:667; VI:753; VII:586-587; IX:543
9:12-18	II:720
9:12-27	III:332(n88)
9:13	II:693; III:182; 184; 230; 232; 235; VII:377; 587
9:13f	VII:586n11
9:14	I:71; 757; II:729, n65; 730; 862(n252); III:605; 857; 1092; VIII:35
9:14f	IV:719
9:15	I:744; III:661; 829; IV:699
9:15f	III:651
9:16	I:346; 432n152; 441n211; II:470; 719; 733; III:647n10; 649n35; 655; IX:392n152
9:16f	II:442(n40); 470
9:16ff	I:333(n136); 639; II:718
9:17	I:639; II:470; 825; IV:699; V:152; VI:204(n226); 635
9:18	II:566; 570; 720n118; 729n65; 731; III:829; IV:699; VIII:155
9:18a	II:729
9:18b	II:729
9:18f	VII:586n11
9:19	II:279; 501; III:673n3; VI:265n7
9:19-21	III:246n72
9:19ff	II:500n19; III:673; IV:668
9:19-22	VII:992
9:20	II:441(n36); 734; III:381; IX:543n327
9:20a	II:441n36
9:20b	II:441n36
9:20f	II:441(n38); 542; IV:1067; VII:835
9:20ff	IV:1072n227; 1077

9:21	II:441n36; IV:1087; IX:545
9:22	I:492; II:441(n32); 442n41; III:673; V:888; VII:355n93; 992
9:22ff	III:332(n87)
9:23	II:70; 442(n40); 729n65; 733; III:804; VI:477
9:24	IV:10; VII:414; VIII:232; IX:185
9:24-26a	VII:629
9:24ff	I:392; 638; VI:755n57; IX:105
9:24-27	I:775; IV:719; V:760; VIII:231-232
9:25	I:137; II:342; IV:7; V:889; VII:629; IX:104
9:25-27	I:495
9:25ff	I:496
9:26	I:166; V:721n7; VI:916-917; VIII:231n36; 590n6
9:26f	VI:917; VIII:591
9:27	I:137; 639; II:258; 280; III:704; 710; IV:668; VI:133; 165; 746; 917; VII:135n282; 1064; VIII:262; 590, n6; 591, n7
10	III:730; 737n68; 738; IV:67; VI:143, n68; 148; 156-158 (156n75, n77); 753, n47; 757; VII:916; VIII:251-252
10:1	III:49; IV:669; V:653; 976n175; VI:593; VIII:253n34
10:1f	I:544; IV:867; 868; 870, n232; V:650; VI:619; VIII:251; 331; 332n122
10:1ff	I:105; 536; III:292; 740; IV:908; VI:838
10:1-4	VIII:237n13
10:1-5	VII:518n376
10:1-11	I:263; 540; VI:266; VIII:251n24
10:1-13	I:542
10:2	I:539; IV:619; 849n1; 870; V:275; VI:146; 418
10:3	I:643; II:693; 695; VI:357n121
10:3f	III:738; 740; IV:130; 464n15; 465n31; 862n177; VI:143; 146; 437; VII:1068n422
10:3ff	IV:465n31
10:4	I:758; III:103; 509, n15; 523; 585; IV:276n70; 277; 548; VI:95; 97; 145; 146n16; 155n72; VIII:213; 326n84; IX:541; 546
10:4b	VI:437
10:4c	IV:271
10:5	II:658; 741; VII:411n20
10:5ff	IV:908; VI:164
10:5-13	VI:143
10:6	III:170; 171; 172; 481; VI:140; VII:761n12; VIII:248; 251-252
10:7	I:748; II:380; 694; III:100, n219; IV:53; V:629-630; VI:139n44; 140; VII:422;

13:4-7	VI:165; 166; **VII:587**; IX:600n63
13:4-13	VI:329
13:5	III:345; 481; IV:289; 591n14; V:419; 857; VII:195; 587n16; IX:162n138
13:6	I:156; 242; IX:366
13:7	II:530; 531; III:558; IV:586; 587; VI:166; 203(n211); 715; **VII:586-587**; IX:162n138
13:8	I:52; 453; 709; 710; IV:575, n2; **VI:165-166** (165n27; 166n29, n31); 168; 830; VIII:23n74; 75n44
13:8f	VI:850
13:8ff	IV:1109n28; V:85n153
13:8-11	IX:406n30
13:8-12	**VI:853-854**
13:9	II:357n127; IV:596; VI:829
13:10	I:453; II:674; IV:596; VIII:75
13:10-12	III:937n64
13:11	I:363; 452; IV:288; **919**; V:649; VIII:76n49; 224; IX:233
13:12	I:50; **178-180**; 220; 639; 704; 706; 610n78; II:357, n127; 375n16; **696-697**; 870; IV:596; 847; 1107n8; 1116; 1123; V:341n138; 343; **344**; 365; 366n237; 760; VI:777; 850; VIII:75
13:12a	II:374
13:12b	II:374
13:12f	II:532
13:13	I:52; 710n78; II:532; 533(n117); 542; IV:531; 575, n2; 587; 1109n28; V:314; VI:165; 207; 213; 219n332; 221; VIII:23n74; 222, n46; IX:406n30
14	II:665; IV:289; V:1006n364; VI:94; 424(n608); 432; **853**; VIII:498n70; IX:295n82
14:1	II:230; 888; VI:423; 427n630; 437; 829; 849; 850; 852; 853; IX:405
14:1a	VI:95
14:1ff	I:440; II:702; III:333(n90); VI:850; VII:131n261
14:1-5	VI:348
14:2	I:722; 726; II:665; IV:882; VI:433n669
14:2f	VI:852
14:2ff	I:722; II:702; VII:522n394
14:3	II:823; V:141; 145; 796, n169; 820; 821; 822; 823; VI:829; 848; 852; 855; 856
14:3f	VI:853; 854
14:3-5	VI:424n610
14:3ff	VI:348
14:4	II:665; III:506; 507; IV:531; V:141; VI:852; VII:914n63
14:4f	III:509; VI:829
14:4ff	I:722
14:5	I:722; 725; II:663; 665; III:45n8; 506; IV:531; V:145; VI:849; 852; IX:128n152
14:6	I:708, n73; II:164; III:585; 592; IV:1109; VI:830; 850; 853; 854
14:7	I:703; VII:593; IX:292; 666
14:7f	I:722; VI:336; 351n69; IX:295
14:8	V:756; VI:514n93; VII:85; IX:292
14:8f	II:770
14:9	I:166; 703; 722; 726; VI:348
14:10	I:722; 726; II:771; III:889; VI:849; VIII:242; IX:295
14:10f	I:722; IX:295
14:11	I:547; 551; 722; 726; VI:348; 852; IX:295
14:11ff	II:357(n123)
14:12	II:888; III:506; 509; V:145; VI:61; 283n29; 424n610; 724; 849; 853; 854
14:13	I:722; II:663; 665; VI:349; 853
14:13ff	I:726; II:805
14:13-19	VI:853
14:14	I:722; III:616; VI:427n630; 430n648; 435; 436; 852; 853
14:14f	IV:959
14:14-16	VI:348; 423
14:14ff	I:722
14:14-17	I:722
14:15	VI:423; 853; VIII:499
14:15f	I:722; II:361n154
14:16	I:336; II:763; III:217; VI:306, n5; 852; VIII:205; IX:411n43
14:16f	I:722; IX:413
14:17	II:704; V:141; VI:853; VII:914n63
14:18	I:440(n204); 724; 725; II:457; IX:412n61; 413n64
14:18-26	VI:423
14:19	I:722; II:458; III:46n29; 506; 639; IV:101; 959; VI:852
14:20	III:484; 699; IV:917; V:649; VI:348; VII:613; VIII:76; IX:230; 234
14:20a	V:649
14:21	I:222; 722; 726; 727n1; 747; 756n28; 757; II:702n3; IV:52; 112; 1071, n217; 1077; VI:410n508
14:22	I:722; 727; II:428; VI:830; **VII:259**
14:22-24	VI:215(n313)
14:23	I:722; II:684; III:506; IV:361; VI:51; 348; 350n65; 852
14:23f	II:678; III:217
14:23ff	II:451
14:24	II:474; III:217; 944
14:24f	V:141; VI:829; 852; 854
14:25	I:66; III:118; 612f; 960; 976; VI:163, n15; 434n677; 630;

	764; 765; 776; 848; 856; VII:442n168; VIII:498n63; IX:3
14:26	I:164; 726; II:164; 662; 684; 826; III:585; V:145; VI:424n610; 724; 853; VIII:499, n73; 500
14:26ff	I:724; II:665
14:26-30	VI:853
14:27	I:722; II:663; 665; IV:596; VI:852; VIII:221
14:27f	I:722; VI:348
14:28	I:722; II:662; 663; 665; III:506
14:28ff	VII:168
14:29	I:348; III:947; VI:348; 849; 855; VIII:221
14:29ff	II:158; VI:851; 854
14:30	II:62; III:444; 585; VI:424n607; 853
14:31	IV:409; V:796; VI:829; 854
14:32	VI:349; 427n630; 435n689; VIII:45
14:33	I:107; II:411; 412; III:112(n315); 446; 506; 507; V:88
14:33a	VII:195
14:33f	III:506; 680; VII:590
14:34	I:656n51; III:506; IV:110; 1077, n245; VIII:43, n23; 46
14:34f	I:787, n55; II:147n61; 441, (n31)
14:35	I:190; 362; II:687; III:45n8; 506; IV:409n143
14:36	II:679; III:625; IV:116
14:37	I:704; 724; 743; 744n8; II:553; 556n39; III:1090; VI:349; 423; 424n605; 437n703; 454n7; 855
14:37ff	I:722
14:38	I:116
14:39	I:724; II:888; VI:427n630; 829; 849; 852; 853; VII:128n239
14:40	I:724; 787n55; III:446
15	I:483n25; 709; II:335; 864n281; 867(n307); 869; III:16; 19; 667; 852; 887; V:359n212; 523; 823; **VI:420-421;** VII:546; VIII:32; **41-42** (41n9); 55; 252n33; 401; 471; 472, n483; 513n29; IX:552
15:1	I:718; II:710n28; 719; 720; 730; 733; 734; 735; IV:13; VI:209; 218; 853n433; VII:652
15:1f	I:441n211; II:720
15:1ff	I:61; 371; 437; II:730; 737; III:584
15:1-11	II:172; VI:910n230; VII:334; VIII:569n55; IX:395n186
15:2	II:172; 380; 710n28; 732; 829; III:396; VI:208n258; 214(n292); VII:993
15:2-5	IX:543n332

15:3	I:295; 312; 332(n118); II:70n24; 171; 172; 173n9; 439; 731; 958; III:18n77; 396; 584n40; 1090; IV:13; 342n16; V:349; 706; 707; 709; 710, n433, n435; VI:55n20; 209; 426n615; VIII:509; 510; 512; 513; IX:509n71; 562
15:3b	IX:509n71
15:3f	I:431n148; 442n214; 752, n11; 759; II:730; III:641; VII:790n114
15:3-5	V:212n39; VII:29n226; 706; VIII:384; 512n24, n26; **IX:543-544** (543n332; 544n332, n333, n335); 546
15:3ff	II:173, n9, n11; 865n286; III:395; 508; IV:342n16; 453; V:349; **358-359;** VIII:512n24
15:3-11	IX:543n332
15:4	II:335; 948; 949; III:395; 641; VI:308; VII:29n226; VIII:220; IX:211
15:4b	VII:29n226
15:5	I:422; II:325n35; 326; 327; IV:25n30; VI:100; 103; 104; 111; VII:292; IX:211; 543n326
15:5-7	IV:342n16
15:5ff	I:220; 438n185; IV:699; V:355; 356n204; 358; 359
15:5-8	VI:104n22
15:6	I:383; 431; II:325n37; 457n43; III:206; VI:51n51; VII:784n85
15:7	I:422, n93; 431; V:360n216; VIII:473
15:7b	I:431n146
15:8	I:438(n184); **II:466-467** (467n21); 697; IV:454n255; V:358; 359n212; VI:90n69
15:8f	I:431
15:8ff	I:423, n96; 430n142; II:457; V:359
15:9	I:308; 309; 437; II:356; III:121; 295; 488; 506; 507; IV:312; 657, n45; VIII:306; 521
15:9f	II:435; IV:573n9; IX:135n202
15:10	I:437; 439; II:360n149; 465; III:295; 649; 650; 660; 829; IV:670; 720; VI:62; **910;** VII:630; 651; 777; VIII:591n13; IX:394n182; 395n186; 396n192; 399n218
15:11	I:437; II:356; III:396; 704; VI:208n258; 209; 214(n292)
15:12	II:335; 441n39; 539; III:704; 711; VIII:498n63; IX:544
15:12f	IV:893(n25)
15:12ff	III:1090
15:12-23	VII:1062
15:14	III:660; 711; 712; 716;

	VI:208n258; 212; VIII:513
15:14f	III:709n51
15:15	II:769; IV:496; **513-514;** VIII:499
15:15a	VIII:513
15:15ff	IV:867
15:15-22	II:337
15:17	I:295; 312; 333(n130); III:660; IV:552; VI:212
15:18	I:395; 541; III:20; VII:784n85; IX:551
15:19	II:364; 531; 532; 863(n265); IX:551
15:20	I:207; 371; 486; II:338; 362n157; 867; III:14n60; 660; IV:681n5; 1109, n33; 1117n70; V:523; 529; VI:877; VII:784n85; VIII:32; 235
15:20-22	II:867
15:20ff	VI:419n572
15:21	I:143; 366; 371; II:68; IV:893(n25); VIII:470; **471-472;** IX:430
15:21b	VIII:405
15:21f	II:438; III:15; 449; VI:419n572; **VII:1072-1073;** VIII:472n482
15:21ff	V:835n64
15:22	I:141; 371; 392; II:70; 541; 542; 874; III:15; IV:619; 622; V:528(n250); 649; VI:540; 541n35; VII:1073n460; VIII:471n476; IX:551; 559n429
15:22b	VIII:32; 471n475
15:22-24	III:17
15:22-28	V:868
15:23	I:207; 486; II:526; 867; V:523; 865; 868; **VIII:31-32;** 56; 471; IX:530f; 544; 547; 553
15:23b	II:16(n119)
15:23f	I:371; V:1010n390
15:23ff	VI:850
15:23-26	II:869(n317)
15:23-28	**VIII:156;** IX:573
15:24	I:86; 454; 484; 578; 581; II:171; 307; 565; 573; III:893; 907; V:533(n303); 888; 895; 993n289; 1007; 1008; VIII:43; 55, n46; 56; 614
15:24-26	VII:162; 1003
15:24ff	V:1010
15:24-28	V:1010
15:24c-27a	VIII:42
15:25	I:590; II:24; 814; IV:237n24; V:529; VI:629; VII:1077n491; VIII:41; 156; 371n264; 611; 614
15:25f	VIII:382n355
15:25-27	VIII:371
15:25ff	I:392; III:1089; V:895(n31)
15:26	I:313; 454; 483; II:304n72; 697; 814; III:14; 15; 18; 907; 1032;

	IV:1117n70; VI:159; VII:158
15:26f	VIII:41
15:27	I:143; II:61; VI:629; VII:1072n454; VIII:41, n10; 42; 156; 405; 471; 609; 614
15:27b	VIII:42n11
15:27f	III:884; **VIII:471-472**
15:28	III:103; 119; 329; 627; 1030; 1090; 1091; IV:1016; V:888; 1007; 1010n390; VI:292n32; VIII:42; **43;** 55; 335; **371-372; 382-383;** 405; 471n473
15:28b	VIII:42
15:28c	VIII:43
15:29	I:542; III:19; VI:420, n579; 477; 619; **VIII:512-513** (513n29); 514n35
15:30	IX:679
15:30-32	IV:719
15:31	I:146n10; II:541; 950; III:20n83; 649n35; 650(n43); V:177n10; 185; VI:91; IX:542; 552; 554
15:32	I:364; II:689n7; 693; III:17; 120; IV:719; V:628n12; VI:140, n45; 146
15:33	V:855; VI:244; **245,** n98; IX:103; 483; 487
15:34	I:119; II:826; III:699; IV:941; VI:140n46, n47; 245; VIII:548n14
15:35	II:441n39; IV:893(n23)
15:35a	VII:128
15:35b	VII:128
15:35f	VII:546
15:35ff	I:483; II:47n19; III:788; V:760; VII:547
15:35-44	VI:146n9; **VII:1060; 1062**
15:35-49	I:377n9
15:35-50	**VI:420-421**
15:35-54	II:869(n320)
15:35-57	IV:352
15:36	II:875n7; III:14n61; 15; VII:546; IX:231
15:36f	VII:546; 1062n385
15:36-38	II:869
15:36ff	III:616n9
15:36-49	VII:128; 129; 1060n375
15:37	II:337; III:811; VII:546; 1084n539; VIII:242
15:37f	II:857n198; VI:421n582
15:37ff	I:774
15:38	III:47; V:529n261; VII:382n7; 545; **1060;** IX:650; 661n4
15:38-49	IX:648n189
15:39	VII:125
15:39ff	VI:421n582
15:40	II:703; V:541; VI:421n584; VII:684n99
15:40b	VII:125n215
15:40f	I:504; II:237
15:40ff	I:681; II:337

15:41	I:504; II:246n54; VII:1060n377; IX:63
15:42	IV:893(n25); VI:417n554; 421; VII:546; IX:105
15:42f	IV:352; 720
15:42-44	VII:788n103; VIII:21
15:42ff	II:337; III:1032; V:359; VII:546
15:42b-43	VIII:501n86
15:43	I:491; II:250; VI:421; VII:546; 792; VIII:21
15:43f	VI:417n551
15:44	IV:248; 353; VI:395n389; 420n575; 421; VII:546; 1060n374; IX:661
15:44a	VI:420n575
15:44ab	VI:421n588
15:44b	I:142; 143; VI:420
15:44-46	VI:437; VII:1068n422; IX:622n11
15:44ff	IV:759
15:44-49	II:869; III:15; VI:159; **IX:662-663**
15:44b-49	I:142
15:45	I:142; 366; II:394n82; 396; 438n17; 537n11; 861n241; 862(n258); 867, (n305); 875; III:990; 1033; IV:353; 751n53; V:529; VI:339n16; 419, n572; 420; 421n585; 422n591; 428; 440n731; **867, n12; VII:1072-1073;** VIII:472; IX:477n52; **478,** n58; 641n150; 649; 654; 662
15:45a	II:438n17; IX:478n58
15:45ab	VI:420n576
15:45b	VI:867; IX:475n30; 478n58; 661n4
15:45-47	IX:650
15:45ff	II:396; 397; 438, n17; 698; III:499; IV:622; V:835n64; VIII:404n24; 472n482
15:45-48	IX:661n4
15:45-49	**I:141-142;** II:542; VIII:405; **471-472**
15:46	I:142; 143; 528, n248; 529; VI:419n572; 420; VII:1060n374; IX:661
15:46a	IX:661
15:46b	V:541
15:46-49	IX:661
15:47	I:142; 366; 679; 680; II:335; 438, n17; IV:353; 644n15; V:522n198; 523; **528-529;** 538n22; 541; **VI:421;** 867; VIII:405; 470; 471; 472; IX:478n54, n58; 662n5
15:47b	IX:477n51; 478n58
15:47f	I:142; IX:555
15:47-49	**IX:477-478**
15:47-54	VII:1061n380
15:48	I:142; V:299n21; 528n249;

	538n16; 540; VIII:471
15:48b	IX:477n51; 663
15:48f	**V:541-542;** VI:421n584; VII:192; IX:478n58
15:49	I:142; II:396, n99; 397n102; III:332n83; IV:248; 249; 354; VI:420; 877n37; VII:1084n536; IX:83n1; 84; 650; 661n4; 662n10
15:49b	II:397
15:49ff	VII:788n104
15:50	I:172; 362; 587; II:335; III:782; 788; IV:720; 963; VI:106n33; 146; 421; **VII:128-129;** 132n265; 993n115; IX:104; 105; 478n58; 662
15:50a	III:781
15:50b	III:781
15:50ff	II:337
15:50-55	V:868; VII:128; 1060n375
15:50-57	II:869(n317)
15:51	II:321; 869; IV:12; 249; **823;** V:352; 868; VII:128; 784n85
15:51f	I:251; II:320n6; III:18; IV:758; 759; VII:783
15:51ff	VI:850
15:51-55	VII:128
15:52	II:697; III:658, n6; IV:893(n23); V:523n204; 529; VII:85; 87; 88; IX:104
15:52a	VIII:224
15:52ff	VI:159
15:53	II:24; 320; IX:104
15:53f	II:321; III:14, n61; 22; 24; IV:352; VII:128; 691; IX:105; 478n58
15:53ff	IV:963
15:54	I:749; II:320; 857n198; IV:112; VI:158; 159
15:54ff	IV:945
15:55	I:148n14; 396; III:18; **667-668;** 746n32; IV:943; VI:831n340
15:55f	II:304n72
15:56	I:309; II:308; 359; 498; III:15n67; 16; 276; 668, n24; IV:1035n36; 1074; 1075; IX:545
15:57	II:67; 359n142; 364; III:667; 668, n24; 1092; VI:159; IX:393; 541; 554
15:58	II:364; 541; 643; III:660; 829; 1091; IV:719; V:300; VI:61; 252; 283n29
16:1	I:106; III:506; 808; VI:54; 477; 909(n217); VIII:35
16:1f	**IV:282-283**
16:1ff	III:796n41
16:1-4	VII:334
16:2	II:434n1; III:136; 138; 738; 796n41; 808; 1096; IV:282n1; V:112; **113-114** (113n22); 731; VI:866; VII:20; 29;

	32n246; VIII:155
16:3	II:66; 432; IV:283; VII:328n225; IX:393; 394n182
16:4	I:379; VI:573; VII:782
16:6	IV:578; VI:573; VIII:242
16:7	II:530; III:46n18; 1090; V:105n5; 341(n138); IX:591
16:8	II:903; VI:50
16:9	II:653; III:174, n10; 655
16:10	II:643; III:1091
16:11	II:56; 411; III:549; VII:795
16:12	III:57n19; 59; IV:1121n87; V:793n161; VI:54; VII:742n29; 795
16:13	I:363; II:338; III:913; V:300; VI:208; 216(n319); 218; 221(n340); **VII:637;** 651
16:14	V:889
16:15	I:106; 108; 485; II:87; 362n157; VI:909n217; VIII:28, n6
16:15-18	VI:451n841

16:16	III:829; **VII:874-875;** VIII:44
16:17	V:859; 868; 933n20; VI:306, n3; **VIII:599,** n29
16:18	I:350; 705n65; IV:509; VI:306; 435
16:19	I:501; 787; II:541; III:506; V:20; 23; VII:394n13; 782
16:20	I:108; 496n2; 501; IX:136n211; 139
16:20b	III:730; IX:136n207
16:21	I:502; 743n3; IX:430
16:22	I:354, n4; II:674; III:737; 738; 752; 1094; **IV:466-472** (469n31); 622; IX:115n16; 118n40; 128; 134n191; **136,** n210, n211; 139
16:22a	IV:467; 470
16:22b	III:731
16:22f	IX:136n207
16:23	VII:778; IX:541; 555
16:23f	VIII:223n47
16:24	VIII:223n47

II CORINTHIANS

1-9	VIII:17n46
1:1	I:423; 438; III:59; 504n4; 506; V:278; VII:742n29; 750; 782; IX:553
1:2	V:1007; IX:554
1:3	II:764; III:112(n318); V:161; 823; 1008, n375; 1009; 1011; IX:412n57; 541; 554; 558n420
1:3f	V:798
1:3ff	I:51(n145); III:111; V:798; 822
1:3-7	VIII:501n86
1:3-11	VII:784n86; 1064n391
1:4	II:430; III:143; V:823; 887; 931
1:4ff	II:356n112; 435; III:143; 144n7; 148; V:933
1:5	II:68; 431; 542; III:143; 806; IV:494n59; V:798n182; 823; 931; 932, n15; 934; VI:60; IX:546; 550
1:5f	III:148
1:5-7	V:798; 930; **931;** VII:1064n392
1:5ff	IV:1097; V:921; 922; 932n11
1:6	II:654; IV:587; V:921; 931; 933; VII:56; 993
1:6a	VIII:514
1:6b	VIII:514

1:6f	V:931
1:7	I:602; II:530; III:806; IV:494n58; V:931; VI:218(n328); VIII:514
1:8	I:559; II:862; III:49; V:931; 932n12; VIII:514; 515
1:8f	III:147
1:8ff	III:333n96; V:931; VI:21
1:8-11	V:798
1:9	I:559; II:337; 862n257, (n259); 874; III:945f; IV:893(n19); VI:6; 7; 8n2
1:9b	VI:6n19
1:10	II:432; 531; III:14n62; IV:863n189; V:798n184; VI:210n269; 561; 724; 1002; VII:993n121
1:11	I:559; II:68; 356(n112); 432; III:651, n45; VI:541; 542; 778; VIII:508; 514; IX:404; 410n34; **413**
1:11b	VIII:514
1:12	I:109n67; **114;** II:398, n6; 531; III:649n35, n37; 651n45; 889; IV:504; VI:62; 430; 724; VII:128; 144; 520n386; 717; 916; IX:395n184; 396

1:12f	III:651n45		742n29; VIII:33
1:12ff	II:356n112	2:14	I:244; 706; 710; II:541; 810,
1:13	I:343; II:530; 531; VIII:56		n12; III:160; 590; V:495, n12;
1:13f	I:704; 705n67		VIII:203; IX:4; 551; 559n429
1:14	II:952; III:649n35; 651, n46;	2:14b	II:810
	1092; IV:596; VI:7; VIII:56	2:14f	**II:809-810**; IX:548
1:15	I:632(n53); II:356; 530; 531;	2:14-16	I:705n67; **V:495**
	826n54; III:650n42; VI:7, n1;	2:14-7:4	III:651
	VII:656; IX:396	2:15	I:395; II:530; IV:1122; V:495;
1:15ff	III:856		VII:992; IX:548n354
1:15-24	VI:700n16; IX:555n405	2:15b	II:810
1:16	III:382	2:15f	IX:549
1:17	I:632n53; V:181n49; 733;	2:16	II:855n181; 867; 869; III:21;
	VII:131		295; V:436n377; 495;
1:18	III:111(n309); VI:204(n233)		993n115
1:18f	III:708	2:17	I:114; II:398; 541; III:604;
1:18ff	II:356(n113)		IV:116; 117; VI:8n2; 221;
1:19	II:68; III:704; **IV:125**; VII:750;		278; 540; IX:551
	VIII:384; IX:551n375	3	I:454; 767; II:130; 251; **IV:869**;
1:19f	II:541; IV:125; IX:551		V:883; VI:430n645
1:20	I:337; II:68; 131; 583n56, (n60);	3:1	I:479; III:651; V:23n165;
	584, n61; VI:833;		VII:594; 897
	IX:551n375	3:1-3	VI:8; **VII:594-595**
1:21	I:337; 603; II:433; 810; IV:25;	3:1ff	III:557; VII:898
	VII:782; 949; IX:494; 541;	3:1-18	II:531
	550	3:2	I:343; VII:594
1:21f	III:108n286; IX:493; 550n364;	3:2f	**I:770**; III:651; V:554n105; 760;
	555-556		VII:897; **IX:548**
1:22	I:475; II:336; 361; 584; 820;	3:3	II:86; III:612; 1090; IV:269;
	825; 867n303; III:612;		551; 967; VII:143
	IV:635n2; 720; VI:422; 445;	3:3a	VII:594
	VII:949; 950n86, n87; 952	3:3b	VII:594
1:23	II:356(n113); III:497; 498, n7;	3:4	II:68; 531; III:101(n232);
	500; IV:491; V:185;		649n37; **VI:8**; 221; 723;
	VIII:267n58; IX:649		IX:550
1:24	I:442n219; III:944; **1097**;	3:4-18	II:130
	VI:212; 218; VII:613; 651;	3:5	IV:288; VII:365n47
	874; 875; IX:370	3:5f	III:295
2:1	II:675	3:6	I:766; II:88; 130; 499;
2:1ff	IV:320; V:822		867(n305); 875; III:16; 321;
2:2	II:774; IV:320		450; 952; IV:620n83; 1075;
2:3	II:675; III:650n42; IV:320;		V:719; VI:417n554; 418,
	VI:6; 7; IX:369		n568; 428; 429n639; 440
2:4	I:703; 744n8; II:66; 80; 826n52;	3:6f	I:766
	III:147; 333(n90); 612;	3:6ff	IV:1075
	IV:320; VI:62; 757; VII:712;	3:6-11	II:866n301; 869n319
	886	3:6-18	II:867
2:5	III:1099; IV:596	3:7	I:454; 767; II:251; III:16; 386;
2:5ff	III:1099n2		560; 952; IV:269; 869;
2:6	II:627; III:1099		VI:421n583; 776;
2:7	III:1099; V:794; 798; VI:62;		VII:950n87; VIII:365
	159	3:7f	II:130
2:8	III:1099	3:7-9	II:87
2:9	I:224; II:259; 429; 433; V:889	3:7ff	I:705n67; **II:251**; V:883
2:10	II:356(n113); VI:777; IX:547	3:7-13	IV:869
2:11	I:116; III:332(n88); IV:961, n4;	3:7-14	**I:454**
	VI:271; **273**; 640n16;	3:7-18	II:397n103; **III:560**; VI:147n17;
	VII:160; 161		**776**
2:12	II:541; 675; 729; 731; III:174;	3:8	II:251; IV:288; 869; VI:418
	1090; 1091; IX:543	3:8-11	III:560
2:12b	VIII:33	3:8-4:6	VI:421n583
2:13	I:367; IV:509; VI:435; VII:125;	3:9	II:204; III:16; 717n17; 952;

	IV:869; VI:60; 428; VIII:521
3:10	II:130; 251; 254; IV:596, n12; VIII:521
3:11	I:454; IV:575
3:11ff	II:356(n113)
3:12	II:531; 824; III:652n48; IV:869; V:883; VI:8; 221; IX:213
3:12f	III:560; IV:869n230
3:12ff	III:557; V:883
3:12-18	I:766
3:13	I:454; 508; III:560; 561; IV:866n212; 869; V:883; VI:724; 776; VIII:56; 155; 365
3:13f	III:328(n53)
3:13ff	IV:758
3:14	I:263; 344; 454; 768; II:130; 541; III:561; 1090; IV:620n83; 869; 898; 961; 1108n16; 1110; 1116; V:719; 1023; 1026; 1027; VI:418; **VII:273-274**; VIII:293n163; IX:551
3:14a	III:560
3:14f	IV:869n230; V:719
3:14-16	I:766; 767
3:14ff	III:589; VI:776
3:15	I:343; III:560; 561; 613; IV:864; 869; 1107n15; V:554n105; VII:274
3:15f	III:557
3:16	III:1087; IV:1005n171; VI:722; **VII:728**, n34
3:16-18	II:868
3:17	II:130; 251; 531; 867; 869; III:107; 1091; **VI:418-419; 422**; 425n614; 443n760; VII:131n262
3:17a	VI:418n566; 419
3:17b	VI:418; 419, n570; 422; VIII:392n420
3:17f	II:499; VI:434
3:18	I:179n9; II:251; 251*; 397, n103; 430, n38; **696-697** (696n2); 869; III:557; 560; 561; IV:756; **758-759**; 792; V:365n234; 883; VI:419n570; 720n104; 776; 877n37; VII:651n34; VIII:369n249; IX:556
3:18-4:6	IX:477n45
4:1	II:88; 251; 485; III:295; 486
4:1ff	III:604
4:2	I:190; 244; II:374; III:557; 603; 605; 651; 960; 976; IV:116; 117; V:726; 888; 944; VI:2; 8n2; 221; 724; VII:897; 916; IX:6
4:3	I:395; II:539; 731; 733; 734; III:557; 560
4:3f	III:21
4:4	I:205, n31; 508; II:79; 395; 430;

	539; 732; III:100; 104(n261); 551; 856; 893; 1090; IV:26; 751n53; 752; 961; V:363; 369; 726; 1027; VI:215(n313); 877n37; VII:160n46; 161; 788; **VIII:293**; 472; IX:343; 346n295; 542; 543; 545
4:4-6	VIII:501n89; **IX:346**; 542
4:5	II:62; 251; III:289; 704; 710; 711; 1091; IV:26; VII:384n4; VIII:264; IX:542; 553, n392
4:6	I:437; 706; 710; 767n19; II:251; 433; III:111; 612; 1029; **IV:25-26**; 967; **VI:133-134**; 776; VII:441; 788; VIII:250; IX:343; 346n295; 542; 545
4:6ff	I:440n200
4:7	II:317, n112; III:137; 147; 651; VII:365; 367; 1063; VIII:521
4:7ff	I:705n67; 710; II:64; 336; III:652; IV:321; VII:784
4:7-11	III:650; VI:21
4:7-12	III:20(n83)
4:7-14	VII:792
4:7-16	II:869n316
4:7-5:10	VII:784
4:7-5:21	VII:791
4:8	III:143; 144; 146; V:932n12; **VII:607**, n20, n26
4:8f	III:146; IV:321; V:932n16; VII:607n25
4:8ff	V:912; VIII:591n13
4:8-16	II:868
4:9	II:64, n3; 230
4:10	II:542; III:147; 332(n86); 819n10; IV:895; V:932, n12, n16; 1024n9; VII:663; 1063; 1064n392
4:10a	III:289
4:10b	III:289
4:10f	II:317n109; 539; 868; III:144; 148; 329(n55); 650; **V:932-933** (933n17); VI:91; 418n568; IX:4
4:10ff	II:336; 699; IV:1097
4:11	I:710; II:170; III:14n61; 22; 147; V:925; 932, n12; VI:420n577; **VII:125-126**; 136; 365; 1064
4:11a	III:289
4:11b	III:289
4:11-14	III:289
4:12	II:356(n113); 539; 654; 869; III:14; 147; 650; VII:1064, n392; VIII:17
4:13	I:749; II:820; III:452; V:209; VI:204n225; 213n288; 214(n292); 265; 426
4:13f	VI:218(n327); 221; 427
4:14	II:335; 337; V:209; 840; VI:216(n316); **VII:783**; 786; 791; 1064n392; 1072n459;

	1073n466
4:14b	III:289
4:14f	VII:789
4:15	III:333(n91); V:888; VI:60; 264; 265, n8; 283; VIII:521; IX:395n188; 413
4:16	I:365; 688n10; II:317n109; 359; 361; 576; 698n2; 699, n5; 869; 950; III:147; 452; 650; V:349; VI:720n104; IX:103
4:16a	III:452
4:16-18	II:336
4:17	I:208; 544; 555; II:250; 427; III:204; 463; 635; IV:719; 1095; 1116; V:26n180; 349; 350n173; 823; VIII:521
4:17f	III:148; V:349
4:17-5:10	II:869n316
4:18	I:208; II:531; 542; III:16; 463; V:343; 344; **349-350** (350n173, n174); 370; VI:133; **VII:415**, n2
4:18b	III:464n6
5	I:257; 258; V:349; VI:682n10
5:1	I:209; 681; II:375; 538; 825; 857n198; III:788; IV:338; V:28n191; 83; 144; **146-147** (147n8); 155; 156; 349; 513n117; 532; 760; **VII:382-383** (382n4, n7; 383n9); 384, n4; 601n4; IX:436
5:1f	V:532; VII:382; IX:650
5:1ff	I:560; V:532n285; VII:383; 546
5:1-5	II:867(n307); 869(n317), (n320); VI:2n6; IX:648n189
5:1-8	III:20
5:1-10	I:774n4; II:869(n315); **V:132-133**; 868; VI:420n580; **VII:1060-1061** (1061n380); 1062; IX:656n232
5:2	II:320; 321; V:155; VII:382; **601**, n4
5:2-4	IV:352; VII:602
5:2ff	IV:248
5:3	I:774; 775; II:318; 319; 321; 769; VII:691; 1061n380; IX:648n189; 656
5:4	I:559; II:318; 321; III:14n61; 22; 45n8; VI:159; **VII:382-383**; 384; 601
5:4-9	VII:784n85
5:5	I:475; 486; II:318; 361; 584; 699; 820; 825; 867n303; III:452; 635; 641n9; IV:25; 720; VI:420n577; 422, n595; 426; 747; VII:791
5:5a	VII:792n119
5:5b	VII:792n119
5:6	II:64; 375; III:27; V:26n180, n181; 30; VI:218(n328); VII:1060; 1061n382; IX:213
5:6-8	VII:788
5:6ff	II:63; 64; III:1091; VI:207n251; IX:213
5:7	I:51; II:66; 336; 374; 542; 870; V:349; 365; 366n237; 945; VI:207n250; 221; 426; 427
5:7b	VI:747n13
5:8	I:149; 503, n3; II:63; 375; 741; 870(n321); III:27; V:769; 771; VII:1060; 1061n382; IX:213
5:9	I:457; II:868; III:20; IV:719; VI:756n61; IX:213; 369n97
5:10	I:371; 392; II:24; 66; 568n38; III:17; 102(n246); 938; 940; 976; IV:719; V:1010n392; VI:635; 724; VII:135n280; 630; 993; 1060; 1062; IX:4; 345; 546; 577n526
5:11	I:256; 704; 705n67; II:530; 539; III:1091; **VI:2**; 221; 724n10; VII:916; IX:4; 213
5:11-15	I:256
5:11-6:10	VI:2n6
5:12	I:256; III:612; 649n35; 650, n39; 651; V:349; 473; VI:777; VII:131; 521; 898; VIII:514
5:12f	VII:883n62
5:13	I:447; II:457; 460; III:821n14; VII:131n261; **1102**
5:14	I:49; 255; 257; III:923; 1090; V:710n435; 888; VI:143n71; VII:556n48; **883-884** (884n63); 1072n451; 1102; VIII:143n22; IX:545; 546
5:14f	I:333(n127); II:439; III:18n77; 19; 952; VI:543; VIII:509; 511; **513**
5:14-17	V:719
5:14-21	**IX:545-546**
5:15	I:255; 257; II:272; 335; 863(n263), (n264); 868(n313); III:332(n83); 333(n91); V:710n435; VIII:509; 510; 513; IX:545; 546
5:16	I:703, n61; 705n67; III:630; IV:1107, n11; 1117; 1118; 1120; V:117; 118; 193n24; **VII:131**; IX:545; 546n343; 344
5:16a	IX:546n343
5:16b	VII:131
5:16f	III:19
5:16ff	III:208
5:17	I:105; 108; 487; 667; II:360; 541; 682; 699; III:449; 453; 952; 1028; 1034; IV:125; V:236; 717; VI:220; 261; 944n82; VIII:157; IX:346n293; 545; 546; 551
5:17f	IX:546n343
5:17ff	I:451

5:17-21	II:336
5:18	**I:255-257**; 258; II:67; 203; III:710n57; 717n17; IV:117; VI:682; VII:874n24; IX:546; 550
5:18f	I:105; II:87; 1090; VI:211; **682**; VIII:157
5:18-20	II:205; 867; IX:546
5:19	I:255; 257, n3; 258; 259; 441; II:541; III:18; 103(n253); 105n267; 321; 710; 892; IV:117; **292**; VI:172; 303; 543; 682; **VIII:157**; IX:551
5:19f	**I:256-257**; IV:117; VII:136; IX:549
5:20	**I:255-256**; 258; 442; II:41; 349n61; 578n21; 731; V:795; **VI:682-683** (682n8, n11); VIII:157n13; 245; 510; **513**, n32; 514
5:20a	VI:683
5:20b	VI:682n11; 683
5:21	I:255; 257; 296; 312; 313; 332(n118); 335n14, n15; 450; 703; II:204; 208; 221; 541; III:18, n77; 321; 328n47; 445; 551(n53); IV:1076; V:196n42; 710n435; 711n441; VI:55n18; 464; VIII:509; **510**; IX:546n346; 551
6:1	I:442; II:54; III:660; V:795; VI:682; 754; VII:874, n22; IX:394; 396
6:2	I:221; 222; 628; 754n19; 757; II:59; 952n49; III:462; IV:110; 1119; 1123; VI:682; 831n336; VII:274; 994
6:3	III:333(n90); 856n4; VI:747; 751; 752; **753-754**
6:3f	II:88
6:3ff	II:89; **VI:909-910**; VII:607n25
6:3-10	VI:910n227; VII:607
6:4	I:346; III:146; 147; IV:587; **VII:607**; 898
6:4f	VII:607n25; VIII:224
6:4ff	IV:587; V:912
6:4-10	II:868; III:651; VI:329; 754
6:5	III:446; 829; IV:925, n2; 933n71; VIII:555; IX:244
6:6	I:124; II:540; IV:384, (n79), n79; VI:431n658; VIII:570; IX:488n26; 491
6:6f	**VIII:570-571**
6:7	I:244; II:210; 317; III:651; IV:117; 118; V:294; 300; VII:515n343; VIII:570
6:7f	II:66; VIII:224
6:7ff	IV:321
6:8	I:248; II:237; VI:250; 253
6:9	I:116; 704; III:20(n83); 21; V:623; VI:91
6:9f	I:442n219
6:10	II:826; 830; III:660; 795; IV:320; 329; 910; VIII:600; IX:369n87; 370, n98
6:11	II:356(n113); III:612; VII:555
6:12	VII:555, n38; **608**
6:13	II:356(n113); **IV:702**; V:638
6:13-7:2	VII:125n219
6:14	II:210; 831; 901; III:798; 801n30; 804; IV:1085; VII:347n46; 442; 750; IX:347
6:14f	VI:215(n313); 732
6:14ff	IV:54; 737; V:1006; 1010; IX:346
6:14-7:1	III:425n7; V:945; VII:442n172; VIII:369n245; IX:216n149; 346n297
6:15	I:607; II:79; VI:215(n312); VII:161; IX:308n16; 548
6:15f	VII:795
6:15ff	II:901
6:16	I:757; II:378; III:101n224, (n236); IV:54; 884n17; 887; V:125n28; 144; **945**; VI:434n677; VII:389n11; VIII:389n400; IX:607n27
6:16b	III:101(n228); V:945
6:16f	III:247; IV:886; VI:831n341
6:16ff	IV:112; 1071n218
6:17	I:757; II:57; III:428; 429n15; 1087; V:454; VI:831n336
6:17f	IV:112
6:18	III:915; V:1009n386; 1010; VIII:389, n400
7:1	**I:114-115**; II:356(n119); 583, (n60); 584n61; III:425n77; IV:509; 737; V:1010, n391; VI:435, n687; VII:125; 1063; VIII:62; IX:216, n149
7:2	I:161; VI:273; VIII:224; IX:102
7:2ff	V:822
7:3	III:19n79; 612; 806; 952; VII:786, n95; 787; 1073n466
7:4	I:442n219; II:531; III:143; 650; 652n48; V:797; 883; VI:60; 291, n24; VIII:514
7:4ff	IX:369n87
7:4-16	IX:370
7:5	I:138; 367; III:143; 147; IV:528; VI:435; VII:125; 132n265; VIII:19; IX:213
7:5f	III:147
7:5ff	VII:384
7:6	V:797, n181; 798; VIII:19
7:6f	V:859; 868
7:7	I:64; II:881; 887; V:116; 797; VIII:508
7:8	IV:628; 629; V:344; VI:724; IX:680
7:8f	IV:320; VII:992n113
7:8-10	IV:628
7:8ff	III:332n86

7:9	II:889; III:329(n56); IV:320; 628; 629; IX:367
7:9f	II:429; IV:999; **1004-1005** (1005n171); VI:159
7:9-11	**IV:320-321**
7:10	II:889; III:15n67; 17; 635; 841; 892; IV:320; 628; 629; 979n11; VII:992
7:10a	III:635
7:11	I:122; II:446; 881; III:635; IV:321; 629; V:419; VI:639; VII:566; 898; IX:213
7:12	I:160; 161; III:1099; V:420; VI:722; **VII:566;** VIII:508
7:13	I:350; IV:509; V:797; VI:62; 435; VII:555; IX:366
7:14	I:190; 243; III:648n35; 649n35; 650; VIII:514
7:15	I:224; II:52; VII:555; 772; IX:213; 214
7:16	III:27; IX:367
8	VII:750n10; IX:394n182; 395
8f	VI:700, n17; VII:334
8:1	III:506; IX:394n182; 395n185; 396
8:1ff	IX:393
8:1-6	II:88
8:1-10	VI:329
8:2	I:387; 517n1; II:258; 429; III:148; VI:60; 63; 302n35; 910; IX:370; 449n80
8:3	IV:496; VIII:515, n45
8:4	I:106; 108; II:41; III:808; IV:283; V:793; VI:909(n217); VII:590
8:4ff	IV:283
8:5	II:530; III:59; 1091
8:6	V:793; VIII:62, n5
8:6ff	III:329n56
8:7	I:708; IV:102; VI:61; 213; 283n29; VII:566
8:7f	I:51n145
8:8	I:727; II:259; VII:567; VIII:37
8:8-10	IX:77
8:9	I:705; II:423; III:18n77; 299; 328(n47); 404; 584; 585; 661; 796n41; IV:130; V:852n64; 895; VI:303; 329; **910;** IX:394n182; 541; 555
8:9ff	II:440(n28)
8:10	I:717; VI:477; VIII:62n5; IX:75
8:10f	III:50; VI:481n123
8:11	III:50; VI:477; 699; VIII:62, n5
8:11f	VI:699
8:12	II:59; III:656; VI:699; IX:449n80
8:13	I:367; III:147; 348
8:13f	**III:348;** VI:63
8:14	I:205; III:348; 461; IV:1114n56; VI:908; VII:93n36; VIII:598; 600n34; IX:449n80
8:15	VI:264; **266**
8:16	VII:566; 567; VIII:508; IX:393
8:16ff	VII:590
8:17	II:52; V:779n28; 793; VII:566
8:18	II:587; 729, n65; 737; III:506; IV:64; VII:750n10; 772
8:19	II:86; III:506; **VI:699-700;** IX:437
8:20	II:86; V:473n13; VI:273; **VII:590,** n20
8:20f	VII:948
8:21	III:1087; IV:1010; V:473n13
8:22	II:256; 530; III:650n42; VI:7; VII:566; 750n10
8:22f	VI:273
8:23	I:422; III:506; 797; 807; IV:283; VII:874, n21, n23; VIII:508; 514, n38; IX:549
8:24	III:506; 650; VI:777; VIII:514
9	VIII:584n116
9:1	I:108; 744n8; II:88; IV:283; VI:53; 62
9:1f	VI:909(n217)
9:2	II:881; III:648n35; VI:699; VII:93n36; VIII:584
9:2f	III:650; VIII:514
9:3	III:649n35; 661; IV:596; VIII:584
9:4	I:190; VII:782; **VIII:584-585**
9:5	I:73n29; 476n3; II:431; 586; IV:282n2; 283; V:793; **VI:273**
9:5f	II:763
9:6	III:133; VII:546
9:6-14	VI:329
9:7	III:298n4; 299, n6; 612
9:8	I:467; II:306; III:116; 332(n81); V:888; VI:60; 283n29; 710; IX:394n182; 396
9:8ff	III:299
9:9	I:199; **VI:40;** 902n155; 910n232; **VII:421**
9:9f	II:210; 486n3
9:10	I:685; VI:281; VII:545; 546; VIII:518
9:11	I:387; II:429; III:635; VI:329; VIII:518n10; IX:413
9:11f	IX:412n61; 413
9:12	I:108; II:570; IV:226; **227,** n39; 283n13; V:215; VI:61, n14; 306n3; 909(n217); VIII:599; 600n34
9:12f	II:88; VIII:599; IX:413
9:13	I:387; II:68; 259; 731; 734; III:808; 1090; **V:215;** VI:206; VIII:46; IX:543
9:14	II:734; VIII:514; 521; IX:394n182
9:15	II:167; 734; V:541n19; IX:393
10-12	VIII:18n48
10-13	I:709; VI:2n6; VII:711n37; VIII:17n46; 108n13

10:1	II:68; 356; 359n143; 589; 590(n6), (n7); III:27; 1090; V:795; VI:650; 777; VII:710; 711n37; VIII:17; 18n48; **19**; 25n77; IX:546
10:1f	V:591
10:1-6	II:589n3; **VII:710**
10:2	II:41; 530; III:27; 649n37; IV:287; 288; VI:8; VIII:184
10:2f	V:945; **VII:130**
10:2ff	**VII:710**
10:3	II:542; IV:287; V:945, n22; VII:126; 134; 146n365
10:3f	IV:528
10:3-6	VII:710; 711n37
10:4	III:412; **IV:287**; V:140; 294; **590-591**; VII:128; 144
10:4ff	V:591
10:5	I:186; 196; 197; 224; 706; 710; II:426; IV:287; 288; 961, n4; VI:297n73; **VIII:614**; IX:548
10:5f	VI:206
10:6	I:223; 224; II:444; 589; VI:297; VII:710
10:7	IV:288; VI:6; 777; VII:131n260; IX:550; 553
10:7f	III:649n37
10:7ff	V:591
10:8	I:190; II:569; 590; III:413; 649n37; 652; 1091; V:140; 145; VII:521; 710
10:8ff	II:531
10:9ff	I:196n4
10:10	I:491; 556; III:398; IV:101; V:859; 868; VI:94; 695n12; VII:354n86; 522; 1063
10:11	II:66; 650; IV:101; 288
10:12	III:651n44; 951; 953; IV:633; 894n4; VII:892; 898; VIII:185
10:12f	III:651; 653; VII:895
10:12ff	IX:86
10:12-16	III:651
10:13	II:427; III:599n20; 651; IV:633; 634; V:76n122; VII:895n69
10:13f	IX:90
10:13ff	III:599
10:13-16	**III:599**
10:13-17	VII:521
10:14	II:465; 731; 733; III:1090; IV:64; IX:90; 543
10:14b	IX:90n16
10:15	I:265; II:427; 530; 824n49; III:648n35; 829; IV:543; VI:63; 206; 212; 218; 715; VIII:518; 519n18
10:15f	II:428
10:15-17	VI:714
10:16	I:265; II:425; 428; 719; III:600
10:17	III:649; 1087
10:18	II:258; III:651; 1091; VII:898
11	IV:1068; IX:231

11:1	I:359; IV:582; IX:231
11:2	I:122; 124n2; 363; 655; **II:881**; 887; III:511; IV:737; 1101; 1104; 1105n50; 1106n57; V:581; **837**; 840; VI:593; VII:711n37; IX:548
11:3	I:122; 124n2; 384; 387; 656; 785; II:551n21; III:15n66, n68; IV:122; 961; V:577n110; **580-581**; 726; VI:252; 253, n173; VII:356; IX:103; 208
11:4	I:244; 264; 359; II:704; 730; 734; III:389; 605; 704; IV:122; 582; V:837; VI:435n689
11:5	I:445; IV:288; VIII:598; IX:404n15
11:6	III:216; IV:102; VI:94; VII:522; IX:4
11:7	I:295; 441n211; II:167; 710n28; 719; 720, n118; 730; 731; III:332n86; VI:477; VIII:17, n45; 608
11:8	II:88; III:506; **V:592**, n3
11:9	VI:306n3; VIII:143; 540n84; 598; **599**; IX:162
11:10	I:243; III:651; IV:719; VII:939n1; IX:546
11:11	I:445; III:111(n307); IV:650n14
11:12	III:652; 858; IV:719; **V:473**; VI:477; 754; VII:521
11:12ff	III:604
11:13	I:417; 445; III:953; 1090; VI:784n20; VII:874n27; 958; IX:549; 553
11:13-15	**VII:957-958**
11:14	II:80; 632; III:40, n71; 589; VII:158n32; 160; 161; 957; 958n8; IX:345
11:14f	II:88
11:15	II:204; IV:531n7; VII:924; 958; VIII:55
11:15b	VIII:268n63
11:16	III:646n5; 650n40; IV:650n14
11:16f	III:652; IX:231
11:16ff	I:440n200; II:531; IV:720
11:17	II:887; III:650n39; 652; IV:669n18; VII:128; 131; VIII:584n117, n118; **585**
11:18	III:650n39; VII:130, n255; 131n260; 521
11:18a	II:887
11:18b	II:887
11:19	I:359; IX:231, n67; 234
11:19f	VI:21n65
11:20	I:186; II:279; IV:582; VI:775
11:21	III:652; VII:130n255; VIII:184; IX:231
11:22	II:441(n34); III:389; **390**; 652; VII:545; 741; 807n42; VIII:224; 521
11:22f	III:652

11:22ff	III:381
11:23	II:89; III:14n62; 20(n83); 147; 829; 1090; V:624; VI:62; VIII:516, n48; 521; IX:244; 549
11:23-25	VII:412
11:23ff	II:17; III:147; IV:321; V:912; 919; VII:365; 608; VIII:305n72; 591n13
11:23-27	VIII:501n86
11:23-29	III:650
11:23-30	III:652
11:23-31	VI:329
11:24	III:381; 939; IV:516; V:735; VII:851n21; VIII:137n21; 138
11:24f	VII:828n194; 835
11:24-33	IX:549
11:25	I:381; II:131; III:821n19; IV:268; 517; 891; V:66n67; VI:479; 971; VIII:30n22; 219
11:26	I:146; 685; II:657; IV:260; V:66n67; 69n89; VI:530n69; 603
11:27	I:775; II:226; III:828n7; 829; IV:925, n2; 933n71; VI:21; VIII:555
11:27ff	IV:1097
11:28	II:950; III:506; 650n39; IV:592
11:29	I:492; VI:950; VII:344; 355, n93; 358
11:29f	VIII:501n86
11:30	I:491; 492; III:648n35; 650; VII:521
11:31	I:199; II:357(n121); 764; III:105n262; V:1007; 1008; IX:558n420; 601
11:32	I:577; VI:530; VIII:148n11
11:33	II:65; IX:430
12	V:352n185; 353; VII:411n17; 412; IX:231
12:1	II:458; 668; III:652; V:235; 352n185; 353; 356; **357**; 372, n4; 373; 770; IX:75; 76
12:1f	IX:549
12:1-3	VII:1060
12:1ff	I:440; II:457; 783; III:495; 508; 820; VII:608
12:1-4	I:440(n204)
12:1-9	VII:521
12:2	I:352n185; 472; 483; 582n73; II:458; 541; V:513, n117; **534-535**; 770; VI:685; VII:412; VIII:219; IX:551
12:2f	II:453; IX:648n189
12:2ff	I:726; II:422n8; 457n44; III:177; **V:352-353**; 357; 517n155
12:3	I:219
12:3f	IV:407; V:535
12:4	I:472; 724; II:422; 561, n1; IV:407; V:352, n185; 765;

	766n7; 769; **770**, n46; VI:572n42; VII:602
12:5	I:440(n205); 491; II:458; III:652; VII:411
12:5ab	VIII:514
12:6	I:243; III:46n18; IV:285n4; 288, (n13); VIII:515; IX:231
12:7	II:16; 17; 80; 457n46; III:204, n31; 819; 820; IV:232; 233n6; V:170; 353; VII:125; 160; 161, n51; 162; **411-412** (411n16; 412n28); 608; VIII:521
12:7f	IV:321
12:7-9	VII:350n61
12:7ff	II:641; 783; 804; III:204; 819n10; IV:1095; 1097
12:7-10	VIII:591
12:8	II:746n32; 806; III:214; 1091; IV:1095; V:775n5; 794; VII:411n21; VIII:222; 515; IX:413
12:8f	III:652; VII:412, n23; VIII:216n4; 217n9
12:8-10	VIII:609
12:8ff	III:214
12:9	I:440(n206); 465n2; 466; 491; III:329(n55); 648n35; 650; IV:846; 847; V:624; VI:21; 418(n568); VII:365; **386-387** (387n6); 388n4; 651; VIII:222; 521; **IX:395**; **545**
12:9a	VII:412; VIII:59
12:9b	VII:411
12:9c	VIII:59
12:9f	II:317; VII:354n86
12:10	I:346; 440n200; 443; 491; 492; II:741; III:146; 819; IV:233n6; VII:411; 412; **608**; VIII:305, n73; 514; IX:546
12:11	II:458; III:652; V:564; VII:898; VIII:598; IX:231
12:11-13	III:652
12:12	I:432n154; 433; 440; II:311; 720; III:213; 635; IV:587; V:888; VI:423n600; 483n139; 635; VII:230; 242, n295; 258; **259-260**; 354n85; 515n343; VIII:125
12:13	I:155; III:506; VIII:515; IX:396
12:14	III:138; V:564; 638; VIII:219
12:14f	VI:273
12:15	II:357n125; VI:62; VIII:508; 511; **IX:648**, n191; 650
12:16	V:726; VI:273n27
12:16-18	V:473n13; VI:909n217
12:17	I:403
12:17f	VI:273
12:18	I:403; II:374; III:402; 403; V:793; 945; VI:436n694; VII:750n10; IX:649n198
12:19	II:541; 746n32; V:140; 145;

	717; VI:8n2; VIII:514;	13:5	I:704; II:260; 542; IV:753;
	IX:551, n368		VI:28; 30n37; 143n72; 212;
12:19-21	VI:593; VIII:17		216(n319); 218; 221(n342);
12:19-13:10	III:944		IX:553
12:20	II:661; 881; III:45n8; 167; 446;	13:5	II:259
	IV:4; V:420n276; VI:94n15;	13:6	I:703; II:530
	VII:571; IX:208	13:7	II:776; 777; III:119n380;
12:20f	VI:593n80		333(n95); 549; VI:479; IX:2
12:21	I:490; 545; II:675;	13:8	I:242; 244
	III:101(n227); 428; 429;	13:9	I:476; 492; II:776; VII:354n86;
	IV:1004; VI:2n6; 42, n15; 43;		IX:367; 370
	594; 636; 722	13:10	II:70; 569; III:413; 1091; V:140;
13:1	IV:490; VI:721; VII:648; 698;		145; 865; **VIII:108**
	VIII:219; 221	13:11	I:476; II:418; III:112(n319);
13:2	VIII:221		V:796; 816n1; VII:778;
13:3	I:491; II:258; 432; 731; IV:753;		IX:233, n74
	846; VII:354n85; 784; IX:549	13:11ff	I:49
13:3f	**II:315**	13:12	I:108; 501; IX:122; 138n226;
13:4	I:491; 627n16; 628; II:304;		139, n236; 144; 145
	305n76; 316; 865(n286); 868;	13:13	I:105; 108; **807**, n63;
	III:651; IV:846; V:453n7;		V:1011n395; VI:434;
	798n182; VII:354n86; 520;		VII:778; VIII:223, n47
	522n395; 581; 783; **784;** 786		

GALATIANS

1	VI:663n78	1:8	I:85; 354; 355; II:710n28; 719;
1f	IV:1068		733; III:589; V:533; VI:682;
1:1	I:364; 414n51; 442, n214; 445;		IX:104
	II:68; 335; IV:893(n20); V:278;	1:8f	I:354n4; III:752; 753; V:736
	VII:334; VIII:37; IX:551; 552;	1:9	II:500n19; 710n29; III:396; IV:14
	553	1:9f	IV:1107n8
1:2	III:506; V:887; VII:782	1:10	I:455; II:277; III:1090; VI:2;
1:3	II:415n89; V:1007; IX:554		IX:549
1:4	I:205; 207; 295; 312; 332(n118);	1:10f	I:442
	II:70n24; 166; 544; III:18n77;	1:11	I:364; II:710n26; 719; 720; 730;
	54; 56; 893; IV:619; 759;		733; 734
	V:706; 710, n435; 1007;	1:11f	I:364
	1008n377; 1010; VI:55n20;	1:12	I:364; II:146n55; 173n11; 730;
	172; 554; VII:407;		734n82; III:583; IV:7; 14;
	VIII:510n15; 512, n27		V:357; 728; IX:186n122; 551;
1:4f	V:1007		552
1:5	I:337; II:248	1:12ff	IV:699
1:6	I:242; 264; II:426; 703; 733;	1:13	I:437; II:230; III:506; 507;
	III:40, n70; 488; 1090;		IV:312; V:89n174; VII:717;
	IV:1066; VIII:161; 498n65;		741n28; VIII:306; 521
	IX:395, n184, n186; 546; 552	1:13f	IV:573n9; VI:82n75; 265;
1:6f	VIII:569		VII:711n37; 741; IX:46, n216
1:6ff	I:442; II:162; VIII:231	1:13-15	IX:46n211
1:6-9	VII:334	1:14	I:308; 438n181; 685; II:172;
1:7	II:731; III:46n18; 1090; VII:729;		549n12; 881; 887; III:383;
	IX:543; 552		**IV:573;** V:1022; VI:62; 712;

3:19b	IV:618; 619	4:1f	II:271n70; III:782; VIII:383n360
3:19f	**IV:618-619**		
3:19ff	IV:870	4:1ff	III:132; IV:912n11; V:653; 1006
3:20	I:450; II:67n6; III:101(n221); IV:618; 619n79		
		4:1-5	I:126
3:20a	IV:618	4:1-7	III:784; V:625n188
3:20b	IV:618	4:1-11	**VII:684-685**
3:21	II:67n6; 202; 308; 583; 874; IV:618; 619; 1072; 1075; VIII:56; IX:543n327	4:2	I:126; III:784n36; V:149n3; 150; 620; VII:684n99; VIII:383n357
3:21ff	IV:618	4:3	I:126; 127n2; II:274; 279; III:784; 887; IV:189; 641; **918-919;** 1075; V:620; 649; VII:30; 670n1; 676n45; 682n78, n79, n82; 683; 684n95, n96; 686; VIII:614n7; IX:475n29
3:22	I:296; 309; 333(n129); 753; 754; II:138n19; 583; V:431; 620; 888; 894; VI:11; 172; 204(n230), n230; 210(n267); 214(n303); 292n32; **VII:746;** IX:552		
3:22f	**VII:746,** n10, n11	4:3-5	VII:684, n97
3:22ff	III:328(n53); IV:1074	4:3ff	VIII:509
3:23	II:427; 674; III:584; V:620; VI:213; 688; **VII:746,** n10	4:4	I:406; 672; 776; II:221; 423; 498; 675; III:584; 585; IV:130; 643n12; V:836; 846n28; 868; 1009n387; VI:294n56; **305;** VII:597; 685; VIII:66n8; **383;** 391; IX:592
3:23f	II:358(n138)		
3:23ff	IV:1109n28; VI:220		
3:23-26	**VI:217**		
3:24	II:216, n21; 217; 359(n139); 427; IV:1030; **V:620,** n151, n154; 624; 625n188; VI:212; VII:746; IX:543n327	4:4f	II:275; 542; VII:1067n414; VIII:335; 355n126; **374-375;** **383;** 386; IX:543n327
3:24f	I:126	4:4-6	VI:434; VIII:**375-376**
3:25	II:675; V:134; VI:213; VIII:168	4:4ff	I:628; III:108
3:25ff	V:653	4:4-7	VIII:374n288; **391-392**
3:26	II:434n54; IV:189; VI:204(n229); 211n271; IX:551	4:5	I:126; 127n2; III:328n47; IV:189; 355; V:1006n363; VII:30; VIII:383n360; 386n376; 391; 399; IX:544
3:26f	I:541; IX:545	4:5-7	VIII:399n16
3:26ff	IV:56	4:5ff	II:275
3:26-29	II:208; **VII:1071;** 1072n454	4:6	I:6, n7, n14; 406, n8; 543n69; II:336; 360; 425; 805; 806; III:612; **902-903;** IV:189; 470n38; V:984; 1006, n364; 1009; VI:419n570; 426; 430; 623; VIII:374n288; **375-376;** 384; 391, n418; 392, n420
3:27	I:539; II:320, n10; 542; 583; III:1090; IV:248n49; 899n28; V:275; VI:619; VII:688; 690n22; IX:547; 550; 551		
3:27f	II:514; V:719; VI:432n662; 908; VII:449	4:6f	II:130; 867n303
3:27-29	**VI:217**	4:7	I:126; III:781; 782; IV:189; VIII:374, n288; 383n361; 391n418
3:28	I:362; 552; 785, n35; II:439; 440n29, n30; 441(n33); 516; 541; 583; III:381; 512; 721; IV:1073; V:846, n29; VI:432(n662); VII:1072n455; 1073n460; VIII:224; IX:552; 558	4:7a	VIII:391
		4:7b	VIII:391
		4:8	I:333(n131), (n132); II:274; 378; III:92(n142); 100(n218); 586; 784; V:117; VII:684n99; **IX:272**
3:28f	II:515; VIII:391		
3:29	I:9; II:514; 583; III:512; 517; 781; 782; 783n30; IV:57; V:639; VII:127; 545; VIII:374n228; 391n417; IX:548	4:8f	I:703n61; 705; II:42; III:100(n217); 121n14; IV:1117; 1118; VII:684
4	IV:918; V:1006, **VII:684-685** (684n94); 686	4:8-10	VII:30; 133
		4:8ff	II:899; III:101; VIII:509
4:1	I:126; III:781; 1086; IV:103n129; **918-919;** V:649; VIII:347n288; IX:591	4:9	I:50; 378; 493; 639; 704; 706; 710, n78; II:274; 275(n105);

	III:46n20; IV:641; 1005n171;
	1075; V:653; **VI:909;**
	VII:677; 678; 683; 684n96;
	685, n101; 726; IX:272;
	475n29
4:10	I:495; II:950; III:461; IV:67;
	641; VII:30n232; 682n78;
	685n101; VIII:148, n14, n17,
	n18; 151
4:11	II:380; III:829; IX:208
4:12	I:161; II:41; 357n131;
	IV:672n29
4:13	I:491n6; 493; II:69; 710n28;
	719; 720; VI:757; VII:125
4:13f	VII:412n28
4:13-15	III:820
4:13ff	III:204
4:13-16	VII:663n47
4:14	I:83; II:52; 448; VI:32, n51;
	VII:125
4:15	IV:232; 367; 496; V:377n12
4:16	I:251; II:813
4:17	II:887; III:323; VI:94n15
4:17f	II:878
4:18	II:887; III:549
4:19	I:666; 668; II:315n102; 542;
	699; IV:644n16; **753-754**
	(754n6); VI:140; 639; 1005;
	VIII:365n217; IX:545, n338;
	556; **673**
4:20	I:251; III:45n8; IX:293
4:21	I:219; 343; II:145; 542; III:49;
	IV:409; 1071; VII:669
4:21ff	III:533
4:21-31	I:263; II:496; 499; V:639;
	VII:285-286; 336-337
4:22	VII:669
4:22f	VII:669
4:22ff	I:9; II:583; IV:566n86
4:22-30	VIII:365
4:22-34	IX:459n173
4:23	V:834n50; **VI:429;** VII:127,
	n230; 128; **131; 131-132;** 285
4:24	I:260; 665; 758; III:583;
	VII:285; 669, n4; VIII:253
4:24f	**I:55**
4:24ff	II:130
4:24-31	**VII:669**
4:25	I:377; 758; II:147; IV:1108;
	1114; 1116n62; V:639;
	VI:418; 525n59; 531;
	VII:285-286; 328n225; **669,**
	n2
4:25a	**VII:285-286** (285n31; 286n35);
	669n4
4:25b	VII:286
4:25f	VI:530; **531;** VII:327n221
4:26	I:376; 377; II:103; 581; IV:644,
	n16; V:29; 514n121; 540n18;
	VII:328n225; 336; 338n297;
	736n33
4:26-31	VII:286

4:27	I:625; II:657; 775; 817n5;
	IV:1071n218; V:639;
	VI:831n336; **IX:673;** 674
4:28	II:581; V:639; VIII:391n417
4:29	IV:116; V:834n50; **VI:429;**
	VII:127, n230; 128; **131**
4:30	I:528; 753; 758; III:781;
	IV:110; 1071n218;
	VIII:391n417
4:31	V:639; VII:337; 345n39
5	III:52
5:1	I:185; II:130; 275n104; 496;
	497; 498; 828; 869; 899;
	VI:216n319; 221n340;
	431n652; VII:638; IX:545
5:1ff	I:442
5:1-5	**VII:663**
5:1-6	IX:545
5:2	IV:103
5:2f	IV:641; VI:81
5:2-4	VI:431n652
5:2ff	II:356(n115); III:854
5:2-6:10	I:50
5:3	II:497; 651; IV:511; 1070;
	V:566; VI:480; 739;
	IX:46n211
5:4	I:454; II:216; 542; III:495;
	VI:168; 218n329, (n330);
	431n652; 756; IX:394; 395;
	543n327; 551
5:4ff	IX:396
5:5	II:56; 207; 208; 532; 867n303;
	III:398; VI:216n315; 221;
	426; 427; 431n652; 433n669;
	VII:993
5:6	I:50; 51; 52; 108; 226;
	II:315n103; 532; 541; 552;
	649; 651; 654; III:185; 397f;
	990; VI:81; **83;** 219; 431,
	n652; VIII:146
5:7	I:244; III:856; VI:4; 9; VII:629;
	VIII:231, n36; 232n44
5:7f	I:639
5:8	III:488; **VI:9**
5:9	II:903; 905; III:857; IV:655,
	n35
5:10	I:144n1; 596; III:942; VI:6; 7;
	VIII:268n63; IX:233
5:11	I:454; II:230; III:704; 711; 854;
	IV:1078n249; V:636; VI:81;
	431n652; VII:344; 352; **354;**
	576
5:12	**III:853-855;** IV:1112n44;
	VI:79n45; VII:417n1;
	VIII:111
5:13	I:50, n141; 108; II:278; 437n14;
	496; 497; 499; III:488; V:473;
	VI:431, n652; **VII:133**
5:13-24	VII:133n270
5:13-25	**VI:431**
5:14	II:147; 435; 497; III:920;
	IV:112; 1073; 1076; V:887;

	VI:220; 292; **293,** n39; 294; 316; 431; IX:130	6	VII:663n45, n47
5:14b	VI:293n40	6:1	I:476; 555n6; II:540; IV:14; VI:29; 172; 221(n341); 424n605; 436; 437n703; 650; VII:127n232; 415
5:14f	III:50		
5:14-18	VI:431		
5:15	VI:158; 431n652	6:1-5	IV:15
5:16	II:374; III:171; IV:103n129; 901; V:944; 945; VI:429; 430n644, n646; 431, n651; 433n669; VII:132; 669; VIII:59	6:2	I:555; 596; II:440; 502; IV:619; 1071; 1076; VI:306; IX:545
		6:3f	VI:221(n342)
		6:4	II:260; 428; III:651; IV:15; 719; 721n107; VII:135(n280); IX:86n9
5:16f	VI:431n652		
5:16-18	VI:431n652	6:4a	II:428
5:16ff	VI:696	6:5	I:555n6; 596; II:428; IX:86
5:17	II:361n153; 922; 923; III:50; 51; 170; 171(n37); 655; **VI:429; 481; VII:133;** 135n284; VIII:59; IX:653	6:6	III:639, n7; 808; IV:116
		6:6-10	II:619
		6:7	III:940; **IV:796,** n2; V:856; VI:244, n85, n90; 252
5:18	II:542; VI:429; 430n646; 431n652; **VII:131-132;** IX:543n327	6:7f	III:15n67; IV:719; VII:546
		6:7ff	II:435; III:133
5:19	I:490; II:645; III:429; VI:244n88; 594; VII:132; IX:3; 346n289	6:8	II:864(n272), (n278); 869, (n315); III:17n75; 940; VI:427; **429-430;** VII:132; 993n115
5:19-21	V:930; VI:593n80; VII:134	6:9	II:233, n6; III:461; 486; 549; VI:477
5:19ff	VII:442; IX:346n290		
5:19-23	VI:431	6:10	I:51; III:460; V:21; **134;** VI:213; 723; 908
5:20	I:183; 514; II:17n120; 380, n3; 541; 661, n8; 815; 880; 881; 882n19; III:167; V:420n276; 456; VI:94n15; VII:571		
		6:11	I:743; 764; V:342; IX:430
		6:11ff	I:502; II:356(n115)
		6:12	II:230; III:46n21; V:636; VI:779; VII:129; 130; 576, n32; IX:542; 544
5:21	I:587; III:781; IV:547; 719; 720; V:188; VI:636; VII:129; 993n115		
		6:12f	IV:641; 1068; VI:81; **VII:130**
5:21b	VI:431	6:13	III:46n18; 649; IV:1070; VII:130; **663;** VIII:144n36; IX:241
5:22	I:18; 50; II:411; 500; 882; 920; III:615; IV:383, n73; 720; 721; **722;** 1076; VI:204n227; 219n332; 431, n655, n656; 594; VII:135n280; IX:346n289; 347; 367n70; 369, n89; 488n26; 491		
		6:13f	II:538
		6:14	I:541; II:321; 868(n311); III:20; 642(n14); 649; 893; 1092; IV:321; VII:127n232; 576; **582;** 686; IX:395; 541; 542
5:22f	II:869	6:15	I:226; II:441(n33); 552, n26; III:449; **989-990;** 1028; 1034; VI:81; 83n79; 261; VII:668; VIII:146
5:23	II:342; 502; IV:1076; VI:650, n30; IX:543n327		
5:24	I:541; II:321; 501; 924n90; III:171; **V:930-931; VII:134-135;** 412n23; **582-583;** IX:553		
		6:16	I:734; 500; II:411; 484, n101; III:387; 517; 598; **600-601;** IV:57; 649; 653; **VII:127;** 667n10; 668, n19; 669, n22; IX:139n234
5:24f	III:50; IV:899n27; VI:429; VII:668		
5:25	II:869; III:50; IV:796; V:931; 944; VI:418n568; 428; 433n669; VII:667n10; 668n17; 669	6:17	I:440n200; 596; II:356; III:289; 404; 644n2; 819n10; 829; IV:637n17; V:919; 932n16; VI:91; VII:578n55; **663,** n46; 664; **1063;** VIII:249n10; IX:417n6
5:25f	II:356(n118)		
5:25ff	I:51(n143)		
5:25-6:10	VI:431	6:18	I:337; IV:509; VI:435; VII:778
5:26	III:496; 662; VII:669		

EPHESIANS

1	I:635; III:57, n17; IV:181; 185; VIII:41; 167n17; 333
1:1	I:144n1; 438; II:68; 541; III:59; VI:214n309; VIII:37; IX:556n410; 558
1:2	II:412n66; V:1007; 1019n23; IX:554
1:3	II:763; 764; V:539, n9; 540; 1008, n375; 1011; VI:437n709; IX:412n57; 558, n420; 559
1:3ff	II:588; III:533
1:3-14	**III:57**; V:1019n23; VIII:501n89; IX:412n57; **559**, n428
1:4	I:108; 202; 392; 635; II:541; III:620; 885; 1029; 1032; **IV:175**; 723; 821n148; 831; VI:685; 688
1:4f	I:49
1:4-6	III:57
1:4ff	IV:189
1:4-12	II:747
1:5	I:438; 635; II:69; 428; 742n1; 747, n34; III:57; V:456; 1019n23; VIII:167; 399; IX:559
1:5f	IV:175
1:6	I:49n137; II:429; 541; 588; IV:175; 179; 191; 354; V:710n429; VIII:384n365; IX:391; 397; 559
1:6f	IX:397
1:7	I:174; 312; 511; 512; II:541; 825; IV:335; 352; 353; 354; 355; VI:172; 216n315; 329; 984n44; VII:994n129; VIII:521; IX:397; 559
1:7f	VII:523
1:7-10	III:57
1:8	II:431; VI:60; 713n71; VII:523; 896n71; IX:233, n79; 234
1:9	I:718; II:541; 747; III:57; 681; IV:12; 820; 821, (n146); VII:523n397
1:9f	IX:559
1:9ff	**VIII:167**
1:10	I:392; 635; 678n5; II:538; 541; III:461, n37; 681; **682, n4**; 884; IV:623; 820; V:152, n5; 153n5; 513, (n118), n119; 514n125; 516; **517-518**; 526; 533n300; 534n322; 541; 888; 1018; VI:304n51; **305**, n55; VII:523n397; VIII:383n357; IX:559
1:10a	VI:305
1:11	I:392; 635; 636; II:541; 653; 747; III:57; 488; **765;** IV:723;

	V:456; 514n125; VI:688; VIII:167
1:11-14	III:57; **IX:559-560**
1:12	II:534f; IX:559n430
1:12b	IX:559n428
1:13	I:244; II:434n54; 541; 583; 732; 825; IV:116; 117; 119; 635n2; V:308n34; VI:208n258; 214(n294); 433n669; VII:950n86; 951n93; 994, n126; 1002; IX:559n428
1:13f	II:584; IV:723; 1120; VI:445; VII:949; 952
1:14	I:112; 475; II:429; III:781; IV:352; 353, n8; 354; 355; VI:422n595; VII:994n129
1:15	I:108; II:434n54; VI:204(n229); 211n271; 212(n278); IX:412n57; 559, n428, n431
1:15ff	I:707; IX:412
1:16	IV:678; VI:477(n101); IX:409n27
1:17	I:706n69; 708; III:104; 585; V:378n18, n19; 1008, n380; 1009; 1011; 1019n23; VI:337n8; 444; VII:523; 526
1:17f	IV:967; VII:523; IX:357n397
1:17ff	III:333n95, n96
1:18	I:107, n61; II:533(n118); **III:401-402;** 491; 492; 511; 612; 781; 783; IV:966n14; V:117; 378; 381; VI:329; 555; VII:994n127, n129; VIII:391n417; IX:332n157; 347
1:19	II:653; 307; 314; 747; **III:401-402;** 907n10; 908; IV:544; V:413; VI:214(n305); VIII:521
1:20	II:39; 335; 541; 653; III:444; 641; 642; 908; IV:237n24; V:522n190; 539; VI:292; VIII:371n264; 614; IX:560
1:20f	II:307; III:707; 1089; 1090; 1096; VII:1075n476; VIII:42n13
1:20-22	VIII:371
1:20ff	II:335; V:895(n31)
1:20-23	III:642; V:517
1:21	I:205; 206; 483; II:565; 652; III:103(n252); 632; 642; V:273; 282; 413; 518; 526n288; 533(n303); 895; VII:1078; VIII:614
1:21-23	V:517n157; VII:1079
1:22	I:423; III:509; 681; 682; IV:623; V:518; VI:304n53; 629; VII:1072n454; 1078; 1079n506; VIII:42, n14; 515,

	n45; 614; IX:557
1:22a	VI:292; VIII:42
1:22b	VI:292
1:22f	III:680; V:895; 896; VI:304
1:23	III:642, n13; IV:623; V:514n125; 889; 895n32; VI:291; **292**; 303n41; **304, n53; VII:1078**
1:23b	III:681
2	V:156
2:1	I:295; 311; II:336; 863(n267); III:17(n76); IV:893; VI:172
2:1f	IX:274
2:1-3	IX:275n235
2:1ff	IV:1117; **VII:793**
2:1-7	III:642
2:1-10	IX:560n433
2:1-11	II:416
2:2	I:165; 205; 207; 224n5; 337(n10); 483; 489; II:16; 18; 79; 539; 565; 567; 653; 925n94; III:100(n218); 642n13; 885; 893; IV:550n9; 1116; V:369; 526n228; 533; 540n11, n14; 944; VI:11; 437n702; 445; 577n84; VII:137; 161; 443n177; 523n400; VIII:365; IX:346n291
2:2f	V:443; VII:137n297
2:3	II:749; 925, n94; III:54; 61; 171, n35; IV:966; V:415n231; 425n316; 435; 438; 639; VI:479; VII:137; 138n297; 717; IX:267; **274-275**
2:3-6	V:435n371
2:4	I:49n138; II:483; VI:329; VII:793n127; IX:396n195; 559; 560
2:4-6	VII:793
2:4-7	VIII:501n89; IX:559; 560n433
2:5	I:489; II:336; 863(n267); 875, n5; III:17(n76); 642; 806; IV:723; 893; VI:172; VII:787; **994; 998**
2:5f	IV:821
2:5-7	VII:994
2:5-8	VII:137n295
2:6	II:541; III:642n13; 806; IV:723; V:29; 539; 540; 925; VII:787; IX:397n200; 559; 560n433
2:6f	III:329(n60)
2:7	I:207; II:541; 681; VI:329; VII:793n128; 994, n127; VIII:521; **IX:491;** 559; 560n433
2:8	II:166; 651n58; IV:2; 723; VII:994; 998
2:8f	III:330(n266); 332; 652; IV:723; IX:400
2:9	II:651n58; III:329(n58); VII:129n247

2:9f	IX:347
2:10	I:16; II:541; 650n50; 705; 706; III:1034; V:21; 944; VI:261; 464; VIII:501n89; IX:559; 560n433
2:11	I:225; 226; III:1031; VI:81; **VII:137;** IX:436
2:11f	I:423; III:121; IV:683
2:11-13	II:925n94
2:11ff	I:548; IV:821(n149)
2:11-17	V:1012
2:11-18	IX:560n433
2:12	I:106; 265; 266; II:130; 370; 532n110; 583; 584n61; 824; III:120; 387; 461; 462; IV:1115n59; 1117, n66; 1122; V:29; **VI:534-535;** VII:137n294; IX:557
2:12-16	VII:1078
2:13	I:174; 175; II:331; 541; IV:374; VI:984n44; IX:557; 560n433
2:13f	VII:1067
2:14	II:415, n92; 718; 747; 815; IV:126; 336; **625**, n5; V:929; VII:137; 1077; VIII:614, n6; IX:557; 560n433
2:14f	II:440; 552; III:349; VI:474
2:14-16	VII:557n40
2:14ff	II:420; III:510; V:312
2:14-17	**II:415**
2:14-18	IX:559; 560n433
2:15	I:259; 365; 366; 453; II:231n5; 415; 440; 552n27; 747; III:329(n59); 425n79; 448; 449; 510; 680; 1034; VI:261; VII:1072n451; 1078; 1083
2:16	I:258; 259, n1; II:415; 416; 718; 815; III:642; IV:625; VII:576; 577, n40; 1067; 1075n480; 1077; 1080
2:17	I:72n23; II:413; 331; 674; 710n28; 718; 719; IV:374; 625; VII:1078; 1087; IX:557
2:18	I:132n5; 133f; II:69; 541; 825; V:1009; 1011; 1012; VI:445; 721; 722; IX:557
2:18f	VII:1085n543
2:19	I:106; III:117(n373); V:2; 29; **134;** 851; 852n64; 853; VI:534; 535; IX:162n136; 163
2:19ff	III:510; V:127n31; 1012
2:19-22	III:247; V:126; VII:736, n34; VIII:501n88; 502n90
2:20	I:105; 109; 423; 441; 792, n2; III:63; 64n8; 523; IV:271; 275; 279; V:147; VI:108; 669n111; 849; 850; 990; VII:353n82; 613n41; 735n30
2:20f	I:792; VI:755n55; 990; VII:856
2:20-22	**IV:275;** V:134; IX:557
2:21	I:105; 106; 107; 792n2; III:63;

	III:641n10; IV:110; 870; VI:291; VII:611; 1085n542
4:8f	VI:291; **VIII:605,** n28
4:8-10	I:521; IX:558
4:8ff	II:424; III:510
4:9	I:680; II:424; **III:641-642;** IV:597; V:526
4:9f	I:523; 680; **V:525-526;** 540; VI:577n78
4:10	III:329(n59); 642n13; V:513; 528; 539; 888; **VI:291-292;** VII:1078n500, n502
4:11	I:423; II:152; 157; 158; 159n67; 737; III:180n88; 639; IV:597; **VI:497-498** (498n122); 849; 850; 854; IX:558
4:11f	II:276n108; III:624
4:11ff	I:105; II:87; IV:275
4:11-16	IV:275; VII:856
4:12	I:108; 476; II:429; 643; III:680; IV:275; VI:990; VII:1078, n501; 1079; VIII:518; IX:558
4:12ff	II:158; III:510
4:13	I:363; 366; 708; II:440n27; 942; 943, n15; III:624; 642; 680; IV:633; 634; 723; V:889; 1009n387; VI:213(n286); **302;** 303n44; 713; 719; 794; 859n8; 1083n529; VIII:76; 384; 518n15; IX:558
4:13f	**IV:918**
4:13ff	III:510
4:14	**II:161-162;** III:332n83; 642; IV:918; **V:103,** n6; 649; 726, n25; 888; **VI:245,** n101; 302
4:15	I:50n140; 251; II:433; III:681; V:889; VI:250; VIII:518n15; 519n18
4:15f	III:680; VII:856; 1078; VIII:518; IX:557; **558**
4:16	I:792n2; II:654; III:350; 510; IV:275; **566,** n85; **597;** 633; 634; V:145; 895; VI:304; 484; 990; **VII:764; 856,** n6; 1076n485; 1077n491; 1078n501; 1079; VIII:518
4:16a	VII:1078n498
4:17	II:370; 541; IV:511; 523; 958; 966; V:944
4:17f	I:118; 119; IV:962; 967
4:17ff	IV:900; VI:639n9
4:17-6:9	V:301
4:18	I:265; 266; II:539; 863n267; III:613; 699; IV:966, n14; V:28; 1023, n5; 1026, n3; 1027; VII:442, n169
4:19	I:490; II:170; 534; III:428; 429; V:1026n5; VI:271; 640n17
4:20	III:584; **IV:410;** 582
4:20f	IV:901
4:21	I:242; II:146; 541; III:289; IV:901

4:22	I:365; 366; 385; II:925, n94; III:171; IV:900; 901; V:719; VII:717; IX:103
4:22f	II:904
4:22-24	V:717
4:22ff	III:448; 449n15
4:23	**IV:900-901;** 958; VI:445
4:23f	IV:897
4:23ff	II:158
4:24	I:242; 365; 366; II:199; 210; 320; III:449; 1034; IV:669n18; 723; 900; 901; V:308n34; 491n24; 493; 719; VI:261; VII:688; 788
4:25	IV:566; VI:316; 317; IX:557n416; 601, n74
4:25-31	VI:593n80
4:26	V:394n78; 419, n266; **421;** VI:715
4:26b	V:421
4:26f	II:81; V:421
4:27	II:79; 80; VII:161; VIII:206
4:28	II:649; III:755, n3; 828; VI:272; VII:97; IX:429
4:29	IV:101; 322; V:145; 888; VI:579; 715; 724; VII:700; IX:397, n202
4:29a	**VII:97**
4:29b	VII:97
4:30	II:426; 541; 952; IV:322, n31; 335; 352; 353; 354; 355; 635n2; V:868; VI:391n342; 433n669; 445; VII:949; 952; 994n129
4:31	I:624; III:167; 484; 903; V:384n6; 420; 421; VI:125
4:32	II:541; III:103(n251); IV:671; VII:556n51; 557; IX:397; **488;** 559
5	I:653n31; 656; IV:844
5:1	**IV:671;** 672; 673; V:1019n23
5:1ff	II:158
5:2	I:49n138; 51n144; 105; II:809; III:18n77; 20n82; 181n4; 182; 184; 185n20; 642; IV:671; V:495; 706; 710, n435; 944; VIII:510; 511; IX:68; 557; 559; 560, n432
5:3	III:429; V:282; **VI:271;** 594; 640n17; VII:97n25
5:3f	VI:593n80
5:3-5	VI:593
5:4	I:191; 360; IV:832; **844-845;** IX:414n77
5:5	I:109; 581; 587; 592; 704; II:380; 825; III:429, n15; 781; 783n30; V:299n16; VI:244n88; 271; 593; 594; 640n17
5:6	I:384; II:674; III:660; IV:101; 844; V:430; 441; 442n408; VI:11, n2; VIII:365

5:7	I:107
5:8	II:541; 925n94; III:699; IV:1118; V:639; 944; 1019n23; VII:442; VIII:365n219; IX:345; 346n292; 350n323
5:8a	IX:348n311
5:8-10	**IX:347**
5:8-11	VII:442
5:9	I:18, 242; II:196; 210; III:615; IV:720; 723; V:308n34
5:9f	II:260
5:10	I:457; II:561; VI:756n61; VIII:77n60; IX:560n432
5:11	II:474, n8; 645; III:616; 699; 804; VII:442; IX:353n358
5:12	I:190; III:960; 976; IX:560n432
5:13	II:474, n8; IX:353n358
5:13f	IX:4
5:14	I:371; 756; II:334; 336; 863(n267); 930; III:16(n76); 219; 437; **990**; 991n133; IV:110; 893; V:524n209; VII:652n40; 653n42; 1020; VIII:225; 500, n81; 501; IX:343; **348**, n311, n312, n315; 357n406; 559; 560, n434; 601n74
5:15	IV:847n123; V:944; VII:523; 668; IX:231
5:16	I:128; II:953; III:460; **VI:554**
5:17	III:58; VI:423; VII:896; **IX:231**
5:18	I:507; IV:548; 939; V:164; VI:291; 423; 433n669; 444
5:18f	VI:140; VIII:498n68
5:18-20	IV:548
5:19	I:164, n2; 165; IV:548n13; VI:437n709; **VIII:498-499** (498n64, n66, n70); 500; IX:414(n78)
5:19a	VIII:499
5:19b	VIII:498n67; 499
5:20	V:271; 274; 1007; 1008, n380; 1010; 1019n23; VIII:498, n67; 514; IX:414, (n78)
5:21	**VIII:45**; 46; 524; IX:217
5:21f	I:785; VIII:45
5:21ff	VII:524n402
5:21-33	VII:1080n512
5:21-6:9	IV:548
5:22	I:363; V:1004n352; IX:217
5:22f	I:362; 656; IV:1104
5:22-24	IV:1106n57; VIII:43
5:22ff	I:653(n30); 656; 776; IV:1105
5:22-32	VII:524n402; **1079-1080**; 1083
5:22-33	VII:1074n469; 1085n548
5:22-6:9	V:1004
5:23	II:439n23; III:509; 680; IV:669n20; VII:1015; **1016**; 1078; 1079, n506; 1080; IX:557
5:23f	III:680
5:23ff	VII:1016n68
5:24	I:363; 656; III:509; VIII:45; **IX:557-558**
5:24f	VIII:44n31
5:25	I:51n142, n144; 363; II:170; III:18n77; 509; 554; 642; V:706; 710, n435; VII:1016; VIII:510; IX:217; 557; 560, n432
5:25f	I:540; III:20n82
5:25-27	**VII:1016**
5:25ff	I:656; II:530; V:1004n352
5:25-32	III:509n16; 510; 511
5:26	I:106; 111; 112; 540; III:425; 429; IV:116n192; 117; 302; **304**; VIII:322; **330**; 331
5:26f	III:332n83
5:26ff	I:541
5:27	I:107; 108; II:254; III:509; IV:304; 831; 1105n50; V:840; VII:1016n67
5:28	I:363; V:564, (n29); VII:137; 1016; 1063; **1079**; IX:217
5:28f	IX:130
5:28ff	IV:692
5:29	I:656; III:509; VII:137; 1016; IX:557
5:29a	IV:692
5:30	IV:566; VII:137n293; 1078; 1079; IX:557n416
5:31	I:372; 656n50; II:435; III:822; 823; IV:643; 823; 1105n50; VI:721; VII:137
5:31f	I:142; 143; 656; IV:1105, n50; IX:5
5:32	I:366; 431; III:509; 898; IV:531; **823**; 825; VII:137; 147n372; 1079; **IX:566**
5:32f	VII:137n293; 145n355; 147n372
5:33	VII:182; VIII:44n31; IX:217
6	I:483; V:302
6:1	I:223; II:188; 541; V:1004n352
6:1-3	V:650; 1004
6:2	II:552; 583n57; IV:643; VI:868; VIII:179
6:3	III:330n67
6:4	V:419, n266; 421; **624**; 1004, n352
6:4a	IV:1021
6:4b	IV:1021
6:5	I:223; 387; II:48; III:613; 1086; VII:137; 772; IX:214; 217
6:5ff	II:273
6:6	I:456; III:275; 280; III:58; IV:973; V:1004n352; VI:292n38; 479; IX:648n191; **649-650**
6:6f	II:280
6:7	III:1091; IV:689; **973**, n7; VII:773
6:8	IV:723; V:728; VI:479

6:8f	II:270
6:9	I:367; II:537; III:355; 1086; V:513, n108; 516; 524; 733; 1004n352; VI:477; 780, n3
6:10	I:146n10; II:313; 541; III:399; 402; 908; V:302; 413; IX:346n288
6:10ff	I:363; II:80; **V:300-302;** 760; VII:442n174; IX:347n299
6:11	II:79; 80; 313; 320; 953; IV:961; V:103, n6; 300; 301n27; 726n25; VI:245n101; VII:161; **652;** 688
6:11ff	II:923; III:399; V:295; VI:216n319
6:12	I:172; 362; 483, n25; 757; II:17; 313; 565; 652; III:642; **914;** 1033; IV:69; 526; 550n9; V:301; 369; 413; 533, (n303); 539; 540, n12, n14; **721;** VI:106n33; 445; 565; 724; VII:137; 442; 924
6:12a	I:483
6:12ff	VII:443n177
6:13	II:953; III:332n88; 635; IV:8; V:300; VI:554; VII:652, n40
6:14	II:210; 320; IV:526n20; **V:307-308; 310;** 496; VII:652; 688
6:14b	V:307
6:14ff	V:294
6:14-17	V:301; VI:561
6:15	II:413; 706; 716(n101); 730; 732; **V:312;** VI:628
6:16	I:608f; II:80; IV:8; V:300; 301; 313; 314n10; VI:212; 549(n22); 559; **950;** VII:161; **167-168**
6:17	IV:113; 116; 118; 126n215; **526, n21;** V:301, n28; 315; VI:444; **VII:1023-1024**
6:18	II:66; 339; 540; 807, n2; III:461; **619-620;** V:888; VI:54; 444; VIII:555; IX:414n79
6:18f	VI:54n9; VIII:514n36
6:18ff	III:333n94; V:301
6:19	I:718; II:730; 733; IV:12; 821; VII:700n65; VIII:514
6:19f	V:883; VIII:513
6:20	II:541; V:883; VI:683; VIII:513n32
6:21	II:89; 541; VI:635
6:22	II:429; III:327n37; 612; V:797
6:23	I:51n142; 500; V:1007; 1019n23; VI:213(n287); VII:772n36
6:23f	**IX:558**
6:24	I:50n140; VII:778; **IX:105;** 136n204, n212

PHILIPPIANS

1:1	I:107; 423; II:89; 91n10; 277n111; 541; 616, n28; 619; III:1036; VI:675; VII:750; 782; 1073n460; IX:552
1:1-3:1a	VII:750n12
1:2	V:1007; IX:554
1:3	III:101(n227); IV:678; V:887; IX:413n71
1:3ff	IX:412
1:4	II:41; 807; VI:477(n101); VII:772n36; VIII:514; IX:369; 409n27
1:5	II:729n65; III:805; IV:1107; 1110
1:6	I:17; II:539; 643; 952; IV:721n107; 722; VI:6, n18, n19; 216; VIII:62, n5; IX:553; 556
1:7	I:603; II:188; 729n65; 733;
	III:612; 807; IV:122; V:424n308; VIII:62n5; 508; IX:233; 395
1:8	IV:491; 753; **VII:556;** 557; IX:601n70
1:9	I:188; 690n2; 706n69; 707; VI:61; 283n29; 756
1:9f	I:708
1:9ff	III:333(n96); VI:291
1:10	I:114; 188; II:260; 398; 427; 952; IV:719; VI:748; **756;** IX:63, n7; 546; 553
1:11	II:68; 210; 430; 588; VI:291, n24; 756; IX:551
1:12	I:632n52; 703; II:675; 729n65; 733; III:857; VI:705n9; 712; 713; **714-715** (715n77)
1:12f	III:329(n55)
1:13	II:43; 541; IX:3; 551

1:14	I:144n1; 145n9; II:541; IV:115; 116; VI:6; 62; 715; VIII:184; IX:214	2	II:558; IX:562n448
		2:1	III:807; V:161; 795; 796; 820; 821; **822-823; VI:434; VII:555-556** (556n51); IX:551
1:15 ˋ	I:71; II:746, n28; III:704; 710; VII:571; IX:542; 543		
1:15ff	VI:111	2:1ff	I:51(n144); II:148; IV:130
1:15-18	VII:629n73; IX:543	2:1-4	**VIII:22;** IX:214
1:15-26	IX:542	2:1-5	II:279; VIII:18
1:16	II:729n65; 733; 746n28; III:654; VIII:157	2:1-11	VIII:18n49
		2:2	I:717; II:826n52; VI:297; IX:233; 666
1:16f	II:746n27		
1:17	I:71; 122; II:334; 661; III:147; IX:542; 543	2:2ff	II:440
		2:3	II:278; 661, n11, n14; 908; III:354; 662; 1035; IV:655; VII:556n51; 1102; VIII:18; **21-22;** 23; 43n25; 174n21
1:18	I:71; 243; IX:369; 370n97; 542; 543		
1:18a	IX:366		
1:19	VI:218(n328); 419n570; 430n650; VII:993; IX:542; 553	2:3a	VIII:524
		2:3b	VIII:524
		2:3f	IV:750; VIII:22n65
1:19f	**V:883**	2:3ff	IV:384n87
1:20	I:190; 393; II:531; 861(n242); 868n312; III:14; IV:543; 1111; 1112; V:883; 888; VII:1064; IX:369n97; 542; 547	2:4	II:661n14; III:354; VII:416
		2:4ff	IV:669
		2:4-11	IV:720n101
		2:5	VIII:18n51; IX:233, n75; 552
		2:5b	II:539n6
1:20-22	II:868	2:5ff	I:335n15; 589; II:423; 589; III:404; 551(n53); 585; IV:289; 1076; VIII:608
1:21	II:360; 868n312; III:21; 673; VII:785; IX:542; 547; 559		
1:21-23	III:20; IX:648n189	2:5-8	V:895; VI:687
1:22	I:180; 718; II:643; 863(n266); 868n312; III:615; IV:719; VII:126	2:5-11	II:279n121; IV:750; V:214n44; 711n444; 712; 1009n388; VI:417n559; VII:533n33; 575n28; 954n7; 956n18; VIII:18n49; 22; 500n83; 608n25; 609; 610; 612n50
1:23	I:149; 196; 774; II:43; 318; 870(n321); 911n10; III:170; 659; IV:337; V:769; 771; 868; VII:536; **783-784** (784n85, n86); 786; 789n107; 878n14; 879; **883-884;** IX:543; 547; 550; 656		
		2:6	**I:473-474;** II:335; 395; III:104(n257), (n258); **353-354** (353n52); 585, n44; IV:745n15; 751n50, n53; 755n5; 758n18; V:197n48; 712n446; VII:157n32; VIII:384; 473n484
1:24	III:20; VI:6n17; VII:126		
1:25	IV:578; VI:6; 212(n283); 712; 713; **714-715** (715n76); 719; IX:369		
		2:6-7a	V:712n445
1:25f	VI:714	2:6f	III:584n43; 661; IV:744; **750-752** (751n48); VII:791n116
1:26	II:541; III:649n35; 651; V:859; 868; VI:61; 722; IX:543; 552		
1:27	I:167; 380; II:440; 729n65; 731; 732; 734; V:341; 920, n125; 938; VI:204(n230); 208n258; 221n340; 435; 445; 518n21; **534;** VII:638; **IX:649;** 654n225	2:6ff	II:279; III:116; 328n48; 634; IV:130; **V:541;** 706n398; VIII:612
		2:6-9	V:711
		2:6-11	III:18; **1088-1089;** VI:209; V:706; **711,** n445; 1011n394; **VIII:18,** n49; 470n472; **500-501** (500n83); 609n27; **IX:553,** n391; 648n189
1:27ff	I:139		
1:27-2:18	IV:750		
1:28	I:137; 397; III:21; 655; V:920; 921; 931; VII:992	2:7	I:225; 680; **278;** 769; III:181n3; 199; 288; 354n59; 584; 782; IV:750n47; V:195; **197-198** (197n47); 711, n444, n445; 712n445, n446; VI:301; 877n37; VII:533n33; 954n4; **956;** VIII:404n24; 405;
1:28f	IX:396		
1:29	II:433; **V:920;** 922n129; 925; 931; 932; VI:212; 219n335; VIII:17n47; 514; IX:546		
1:30	II:539; V:341; **920;** 924; VIII:305		

470n472; 473n484; 500n83

2:7a	V:712n445
2:7b	I:474
2:7f	VI:329
2:7b-8	V:712n445
2:8	I:127; 175; 224; 225; 474; 627n16; II:221; 222n5; 278; 279; III:951; IV:411; 655; 750; V:712n446; 917; 918; VI:21n69; **VII:575;** 957; VIII:18; 223n49; 383n359; IX:214; 552n383
2:8b	V:711n445; 712n445
2:8f	IV:354
2:9	II:335; III:103; 585; V:712n446; VIII:18; 466; 515; **608-609;** 620; IX:396
2:9f	V:273
2:9-11	II:335; 424; III:353; 354; V:712n445; VI:211(n275); 417n557
2:9ff	III:444; 1088; IV:750; V:895; 918
2:10	I:681; 738; III:289; 594; 633; 707; 887n68; 1056n76; 1090; V:271; 513n118; VIII:382n355
2:10b	VI:603n69
2:10f	III:103(n248); 329(n62); 634; IV:751; V:207; 214n44; 711; 1011, n394
2:11	I:721; IV:921; V:212; 214; 215; 1007; VII:700; VIII:372n273
2:11a	VIII:382n355
2:11b	VIII:382; 385
2:12	I:224; 775; II:583; 753; III:635; IV:719; V:859; 868; VI:221; VII:772; 992; IX:213n132; **214,** n134, n135
2:12b	IX:214n134
2:12f	I:50; 639; III:58; 624; VI:707; VII:416; 1002; VIII:241n23
2:13	II:539; 653; 746; 747n33; III:50; 52; 635; IV:720; 1016; VI:216; VII:750; VIII:508; 514; IX:214, n135
2:14	I:736, n2; II:97; III:299; VI:479(n109); 481
2:15	I:209; 663; III:887; 893; IV:326n24; 327; 573; 831, n1; V:653; VI:754n52; **VII:407,** n23, n27, n29; 718; IX:1; 312n5; 343; 345
2:15f	II:590; III:333(n90)
2:16	II:427; 816n1; 867; 952; III:651; 660; 829; IV:117; 118; 128; 719; VI:910n229; VII:629; **VIII:231,** n36; 232n44; 233; IX:369; 546; 553
2:16a	III:185
2:17	I:108; 138; II:467n1; III:159; 182; IV:226; **227;** 228; VI:91;

	92; VII:530n14; **535,** n47; 536; IX:396
2:17a	III:185
2:17b	III:185
2:17f	IX:369
2:19	I:703; II:530; IX:666
2:19f	VI:54
2:20	I:727; IV:591n14; 592; IX:166n162; 666
2:21	IV:591n14; V:888; IX:553
2:22	II:259; 729n65; 733; 737; V:638; 1005; VII:782
2:23	II:530; VI:54n8; 56, n28
2:24	I:144n1; II:43; 541; VI:6
2:25	I:422; IV:230; 231; 283; VII:710; 711n37; 742n29; 874, n21; VIII:540
2:25-30	VII:162
2:26	III:214; V:341(n138)
2:27	II:485; III:14n62; 329(n55); IV:320
2:27f	IV:320
2:28	IV:323; V:341n138; VII:566; IX:367
2:28f	IX:369
2:29	II:57; 541; VII:773
2:30	II:70; 332; 643; III:14n62; 332(n85); IV:226; **227;** V:933n20; VI:306; VIII:599; IX:166n166; **549;** 648
3:1	II:541; V:167; IX:369
3:1a	IX:367, n68
3:1b-4:9	VII:750n12
3:2	III:854n15; 1103; 1104; VII:415n2; 417n1; 446n7; 874n27; VIII:109; **110-111;** 224
3:3	III:517; 649, n35; 650n39; IV:57; 62; **64-65;** VI:7; 81; 83; **428; 430;** VII:127; **131-132;** 447; VIII:110; IX:232; 552
3:3f	III:649, n37; **VI:7; VII:130**
3:3-14	VIII:76
3:4	III:650n39; **VI:8;** VII:735; VIII:516n49
3:4-6	VI:7; 428
3:4ff	I:710
3:4-8	VI:222
3:5	I:685; II:322n4; 441(n34); 890; III:383; 384; 389; **390;** 585; IV:39n36; V:275; 1022; VI:81; VII:741, n27; 807n42; VIII:84n31; IX:46n215; 249
3:5f	VII:446; VIII:501n86; IX:46
3:6	I:291; 308; 309; 327; 438n181; II:202; 357n128; 358; **361-362;** 363; 881; 887; 890; III:506; 507; IV:573; VIII:84n31; 306n81; 521; IX:46n214
3:7	II:362; 890; III:673; VII:446;

4:10ff	II:616; IX:367n68		VI:265n10
4:10-23	VII:750n12	4:15-18	VIII:599
4:11	IV:410; 828; VI:21n67;	4:16	I:381; IX:162
	VII:415; VIII:599	4:17	II:166; III:615; IV:104; VI:264;
4:11-13	I:467; **VI:21**		265
4:12	I:467; IV:655; **828;** 925; V:117;	4:18	I:457; II:59; 809; 828; III:182;
	889; VI:21n69; 61;		185; V:495; 730; VI:61;
	VIII:17n47; 18n48; 597, n24;		294n49; 756n61; VIII:540;
	599		IX:162
4:12f	**VIII:17-18** (18n48)	4:19	III:101(n227); VI:291; 329;
4:13	I:467; II:313; 316; 541; III:398;		IX:552
	IV:720; V:726;	4:20	I:337; II:248; V:1007; 1008n377
	VI:418(n568); VII:784	4:21	I:108; 501; VII:782; IX:552
4:14	III:143; 807; VI:477; VIII:599	4:22	I:501; IV:266; **V:133-134**
4:15	I:482; II:166; 729, n65; 736;	4:23	IV:509; VI:435; VII:778;
	III:506; 808; IV:104;		IX:542; 555

COLOSSIANS

1f	III:120	1:9-2:5	IX:186
1:1	I:423; 438; II:68; III:59;	1:10	I:16; 380; 456; II:732; III:58;
	VII:750; VIII:37; IX:558		616; IV:721n107; V:944;
1:2	I:144n1; 146; II:541;		VII:523; 1075n479;
	V:1007n369; VI:214n309;		1078n501; VIII:518; 519n18
	IX:554; 558, n419	1:11	**II:314;** 429; III:402; 907n10;
1:3	II:807; **V:528;** 1008; VI:54;		908; IV:384; 587; V:936n4;
	VIII:514; IX:558, n419		VII:773; IX:369n96; 370;
1:3f	IX:409n27		413n73
1:4	I:51n142; 108; II:434n54; 541;	1:12	I:107; 112; III:295; 488;
	VI:204(n229); 211n271;		762n13; 763; 781n27;
	212(n278); 219n335;		V:136n4; 299n16; 1009;
	IX:559n431		**IX:347;** 413, n73
1:4f	I:51; II:533(n117);	1:12f	V:1008; 1010
	VI:207(n252); VIII:222	1:12-14	**VIII:369,** n245; **IX:557**
1:5	I:244; II:530n100; 532; 730;	1:12ff	IV:130; IX:357n406
	732; 734; III:655; IV:116;	1:12-20	VI:303
	117; 1109n28; V:532	1:13	I:49n137; 581; 587; II:79; 88n1;
1:6	I:243; 704; 705; II:433; 953;		395; 424; 565; 567; IV:354;
	III:616; V:865; 895; VI:282,		720; V:515n131; 1009;
	n19; 715n77; VII:1076;		VI:561; 879; 1002; **1003;**
	1078n501; VIII:498n63; 518;		VII:439n146; 442; 994n129;
	519n18; IX:396; 413n73		VIII:335; **369;** 384, n365
1:7	I:197; II:89; 737; IV:410n144;	1:13f	VIII:501n88; IX:413n73
	567; VIII:508; IX:558	1:14	I:295; 332(n118); 511; 512;
1:8	I:50; II:61; III:590; VI:431		II:541; 825; IV:335; 352; 353;
1:9	I:191; 618n10; 706n69; II:953;		354; 355; VI:172; 216n315;
	III:58; VI:134n29; 291, n24;		VII:994n129; IX:397, n204
	437n704; VII:523; 896n71;	1:14f	VII:524n401
	VIII:75; 514; IX:234	1:15	I:142, n10; 143; **II:389,** n48;
1:9f	I:708		395; III:551; 893(n90);
1:9-11	IX:232n69		1028; IV:739; 751n53; 752;
1:9ff	III:333(n95)		V:363; 365; 369; 370;

	529n255; VI:687; 876n29, n32; 877n37; 878; 879; 880, n53; 881n58; 882; VIII:22; 354n117; 473, n484; IX:422, n34
1:15a	VII:1074; 1075
1:15f	II:573; IV:623; VI:878n42
1:15-17	IX:185
1:15ff	III:585; 680; IX:413n73; 422n31
1:15-18	V:894
1:15-20	V:517n157; **VI:879-880** (880n54); VII:524n401; 1093; VIII:369n247; **473;** 501, n85, n88; 599; IX:413n73; 421n28
1:15-23	IX:560
1:16	I:86; 259; 483; 678n5; 679; 706; II:67; 432; 538; 565; III:104; 160; 166; 632; 893; 1029; 1032; 1096; IV:130; 622; 642; V:369; 370; 513, (n118); 514n125; 515n131; 516; **517;** 523n206; 533n300, (n303); 534n322; 539; 540n11; 1018; VI:687; **878-880;** VII:1054n339; VIII:614; IX:186n120
1:16a	VII:1074; 1075
1:16b	I:484
1:16c	V:517
1:16d	VII:1074; 1075
1:16f	II:541; III:103(n247); 884; V:517; 888
1:17	III:118; 893(n90); 1090; **VII:897;** n5; 1075; IX:59
1:17a	VI:687; 879
1:17b	VI:687; 879
1:17-18b	VII:1074
1:18	I:371; 423; 484; II:304n72; 338; 439(n23); 867; III:18; 509; 680; IV:566; 681n5; 739; 893(n18); V:517; **VI:877-878;** 879; 880; 881n58; **882;** VII:1067; VIII:599
1:18a	VII:1075; 1076
1:18b	VII:1075
1:18ff	II:335; III:585; 976; VI:304
1:19	I:259; II:539; 741; 742; 750; III:103(n248), n254; IV:623; V:154; VI:217; **303-304** (303n41, n46); VII:1074; 1075; 1077n492
1:19f	II:420; III:119; V:895
1:20	I:174; **258-259;** 392; 678n5; II:67; 410n49; 432; 538; III:426n80; 884; 1090; IV:567; 623; V:513, (n118); 514n125; **517;** 533n300; 534n322; 541; 888; 918; 929; 1018; VI:303, n46; VII:576, n36, n37; IX:397
1:20a	VII:1074; 1075
1:20b	VII:1075
1:20f	VII:1075n479
1:20-22	III:18n77
1:21	I:265; II:645; 814; 925n94; IV:966; V:28; VI:557; VII:1078
1:21f	IV:1117
1:22	I:108; 112; 258; 259, n1; 356; 357, n2; II:67; IV:720; 831; 1113; V:841; 918; VII:136; 137; 1066; 1067; **1075-1076** (1075n480); 1077
1:22ff	III:20n82
1:23	II:88; 364; 533(n118), (n120); 715n90; 730; 732; 733; III:64; 696; 704; 713; 720; 1029; V:513n108; 534; 895; VI:207(n252); 213(n284); 252; 990; **VII:614;** 1076; 1078; VIII:599
1:24	II:435; 542; 641; III:18n77; 20; 143; 147; 148; 404; 509; 806; IV:494n59; 508; 821; 1097, n36; V:930; 931; **933-934** (933n22); VI:91; 307, n4; **VII:136,** n286; 412n28; 663; 1067; 1076, n482; VIII:508; 511; **599-600** (599n33; 600n34); IX:166n163; 368n82; 370; 558
1:24f	IV:822
1:24ff	I:51(n145)
1:25	II:89; 425; III:717n17; IV:112; 117; 821; V:152; 934n22; VI:297; IX:397n201
1:25f	IV:821; IX:4
1:25-27	IV:125; VIII:599
1:25ff	IV:116
1:26	I:199; 202; 207; 663; III:590; 976; IV:820; 821, n147; 822; 1118; IX:4; 593
1:26f	IV:821n148; VII:523; 1076, n485; IX:4; 557
1:27	I:718; II:250; 533(n115); 542; III:48; 976; IV:753; 819; 820; 821, n150; 1118; V:925; VI:329; VIII:521; **IX:556**
1:28	I:71; 72, n28; II:147; 541; III:333(n90); IV:125n213; 821; 1021; V:822; 841; VII:515; 523; **VIII:76;** IX:557
1:28f	VII:764
1:29	I:137; 138; II:312; 539; 653; III:829
2	IV:933; **VII:865-866**
2:1	III:49; V:341n138; VI:55; 776; VII:136
2:1f	I:138
2:2	I:708; III:612; IV:819; 821; 1118; V:797; 821; VI:311; 329; **VII:764;** 895; 896

2:2f	II:741n16; V:1009n381; IX:557	2:13b	VI:172; IX:559n427
2:3	II:536; 539; III:137; 138; 961;	2:13f	III:18n77; **VII:792-793**
	976; IV:623; 822; VII:523;	2:13-15	II:336
	1076n485	2:13-23	IX:186
2:4	III:137; IV:844	2:14	I:186; II:231, n5; 552;
2:5	II:432; IV:509; V:344;		VII:136n292; **576-577**
	VI:204(n228); 210(n266);		(577n39); 785; 793n124;
	212(n282); 304n49; 435; 436;		**IX:435-436** (436n5)
	VII:125n220; 136; 613; **614**;	2:14-17	VII:1075n479
	782; IX:367; 370; 559	2:15	I:483; II:31; 319; 541; 565;
2:5-8	IX:397		III:160; V:533(n303); 883;
2:6	II:541; III:1090; IV:13; 14;		895; VI:304n49;
	V:944; IX:559		VII:137n292; 581n4; 785n92;
2:6f	I:602		1077n491; VIII:614, n7;
2:6-8	IX:186		IX:559, n427
2:6-3:4	**VII:685-686**	2:16	I:638n2; 643, n2; IV:67; 596;
2:7	II:146; III:584; V:148;		641; VI:145; **VII:30;**
	VI:212(n282); 990; **VII:614**;		136n289; VIII:148, n14;
	1071n448; IX:397; 414, n76		IX:186
2:7f	II:364	2:16f	VII:1076
2:8	I:364; 385; II:172; 549n12;	2:16-18	VII:1075
	III:137; 660; 887; IV:641;	2:17	I:250n45; **VII:398**; 686; 1066;
	669n18; 1075; VII:30; 523;		1076n483; VIII:253; IX:558
	678; 683; 684n92; 685, n106;	2:18	I:86; 638n2; II:380; **535-536;**
	686, n107; 1075; VIII:614n7;		III:45n13; 157, n12; IV:642;
	IX:185-187 (186n116, n117);		933n72; 958; V:352n184;
	475n29; 557; 559		372; VI:94, n16; VII:30; 136,
2:8ff	II:441n39		n288; 686n108; 1075n473;
2:9	III:103(n254); 119; 681; V:154;		1076; **VIII:22,** n69; 518n14
	VI:217; 292n35; 303, n41;	2:19	I:792n2; II:439; 536; III:104;
	304; VII:686; 1077, n492;		680; 912; IV:566n82; V:895;
	1078n500; IX:557		VI:704; VII:686n108; **764,**
2:9f	V:895; VI:304		n8; 856n6; 858, n7; **1076;**
2:9ff	IX:397n200		**1077,** n491; 1079; VIII:79n9,
2:9-15	VIII:501n89; IX:186		n11; 518; 519n18
2:10	I:259; 483; II:439; 565;	2:20	I:676; II:231; 863n261;
	III:103(n248); 680; 681;		III:19n79; 20; 680; 887; 893;
	1090; V:533(n303); 895;		IV:641; 1075; VI:134; 146;
	VI:134n29; 291n27; 292, n36;		**VII:30;** 683; 685, n106; 686;
	297; 304n49; 310n17;		**785;** 786; 793; IX:475n29;
	VII:686n108; 1077n491;		559
	IX:557	2:20-3:3	VII:685
2:10f	II:541	2:20-3:4	VII:136n288; VIII:177n48
2:11	II:320; 321; III:321; IV:641;	2:21	I:676; IV:67; VI:146(n7);
	899n28; V:650; VI:81;		VIII:22; IX:186
	VII:136; 143; 1066; **IX:436**;	2:21ff	I:643; IX:186n121
	559, n427; 633n95	2:22	I:364; II:161; 428; VI:134;
2:11f	VI:83, n78		IX:102; 186
2:11-15	I:541	2:22a	III:1033; VI:134n22
2:12	I:105; 112; 545; II:335; 653;	2:22b	VII:136n288
	III:806; VI:204(n230); 209;	2:23	II:820; III:157n12; **159,** n20;
	211n273; 421n589; VII:685;		IV:101, n114; 770n55;
	786; 787; IX:347n301;		VI:131; **133; 134,** n20, n27;
	397n200		146; 725, n17; VII:30n233;
2:12f	I:371n14		136; 1066, n412; **VIII:22;**
2:12ff	I:541; II:336; **VII:792-793**		**177,** n46
2:12-15	VII:685	2:23a	VII:136n288
2:13	I:226; 863(n267); 875, n5;	3:1	I:371n14; 376; 377; II:39; 893;
	III:17(n76); 806; IV:893;		III:442; 806; 1089;
	VII:136; **785,** n92; 786; 787;		IV:237n24; V:522n190;
	IX:397		VI:134; 421n589; 428n632;
2:13a	VI:172; VII:137n292		VII:685; 686; 787; 793n125;

4:5	I:128; II:514(n62); III:460; V:944; VI:724; VII:523		VI:216n319; 291n27; 310, n18, n19; **VII:652;** VIII:75; 508
4:6	I:229; IV:839n49; IX:392; 395n184; 397	4:12f	I:138
4:7	I:197; 718; II:89	4:13	III:828n6; IV:496; VII:1075n479; VIII:508
4:7-17	VII:785n92		
4:8	II:429; III:612; V:797; 821	4:14	I:501; II:511; III:204; IV:1095; VII:742
4:9	I:145; 718; VII:782		
4:10	I:196f; 501; II:546; VI:54	4:15	I:500; 501; III:506; IX:457n163
4:11	I:587; II:511; III:286; V:817n7; 821n29; 822; VI:81; VII:742; 874	4:16	I:343; III:506; V:732; VI:477
		4:17	II:88; 541; IV:13; VI:297
4:12	I:501; II:276; 737; III:59;	4:18	I:502; IV:682; V:424n308; 936; VII:778; IX:430

I THESSALONIANS

1-3	VII:161		864n268; III:100(n217); 101n236; IV:1004n165; 1005n171; V:106, n10; 107n12; VI:204; 209; 721; 722; VII:728
1:1	II:541; III:506; V:990n283; 1007; 1011; VII:750; IX:554n398		
1:2	IV:678; VI:477(n101); 760n22; IX:407; 409n27; 412n55	1:9f	V:1009n387; VIII:471n472; 500n81
1:2f	V:1007; 1010n392		
1:2ff	IX:412	1:10	II:335; IV:719; 893(n20); V:430; 441; 445; 513, n117; 522; 523; VI:561; 1002; **1003;** VII:993; VIII:335; **370;** 382, n348; IX:91n24
1:3	I:51; II:531; 532; 649; III:829; IV:587; 721n107; V:1007n372; VI:207; 213; 219, n332, n335; 910(n233); VII:135(n280); VIII:222; IX:541; 555		
		2:1	III:660; V:106, n10; 107n12; VI:273
1:4	I:49n139; IV:179; V:649	2:1-13	I:411n29
1:5	I:432n154; 440; II:311; 540; 731; 732; 733; 735; III:213; 589; 660; IV:102; 670; VI:218n331; **311;** 418(n568); 423, n600; 433(n669)	2:2	I:137; 138; II:730; 731; III:660; IV:504n79; 670; V:795; 883; 920n123, n124; 923; **924;** 932n12; VIII:305
		2:2ff	V:883
1:5f	IV:102	2:3	III:428; V:795; VI:250; 273
1:6	I:441; II:54; III:143; 144n8; 147; 148; 660; IV:115; 116; 119; 122; 669n20; **670;** 671; 672; VI:214n291; 397; VII:773; IX:367n71; 370	2:3-5	III:604
		2:3ff	III:693
		2:3-7	III:660
		2:4	I:455; II:257; 729n65; 733; III:612; 613; 660; V:152, n2; VI:204(n226); 273; 746; 756n61
1:6b	IV:670		
1:6f	III:148		
1:6-8	I:502n35	2:5	I:556n11; III:428; 818; IV:101; 491; **VI:273;** IX:601n70
1:7	IV:670; **VIII:249-250**		
1:7f	VII:143n341	2:6	II:237; 426
1:8	II:679; III:1087n257; IV:115; 116; VI:204; 206; 209; 211; 212; 723; VIII:203	2:7	I:556; IV:644n16; 919; V:639; VI:682
		2:8	I:51; II:731; 732; 741; V:176, n1; **IX:648**
1:8f	IV:670		
1:9	I:249; 705; II:378; 735;	2:9	I:556n11; II:425; 715n90; 730;

4:13-15	VII:784n85
4:13ff	VI:850
4:13-18	II:869; V:771n56; 868
4:13-5:11	VII:782
4:14	I:442n214; III:18; 20; 289; VI:203; 209; 214(n302); 221; **VII:782-783** (783n81); 784n85; 786
4:14a	III:289
4:14-17	VIII:32
4:15	III:658; 767; 1092; IV:106; V:352; 865; 868; IX:90
4:15-17	VII:783
4:15ff	III:17; 18; 1091; VII:237n259
4:16	I:84; 87; 523; II:16(n119); 541; III:20; 104; **657-659**; V:513n117; 522; 523, n203, n204; VII:85; 87; 88; 261; IX:294; 551
4:16b	VII:782
4:16f	I:371; III:658
4:17	I:166; 377(n10); 380; 472; II:870(n321); III:658; 659; 804; IV:8; 354; 910; V:771; VI:437; VII:783; 784n85; 786; 842; IX:478n55
4:18	V:794; 796n169; 798
5	VII:365n48
5:1	I:744n8; IX:346n287; 592, n66, n67
5:1f	III:461
5:1ff	IV:383; 453n253; V:868
5:2	II:674; 952; III:756n5; IV:1125; VIII:451; IX:346n287; 538n307
5:2-4	III:755; IX:592
5:2ff	IV:566n86
5:3	I:506; II:411; 559n13; V:169, n3; VIII:451n364; **IX:672**
5:4	III:756n5; IV:10; VIII:365n219; 451
5:4f	VII:442; 444n186; IX:346n292
5:4-8	VIII:555
5:5	II:952; 953; IV:939(n15); 1125; 1126; VIII:365; IX:345; **346**; 347; 350n323
5:5-7	IV:1125; 1126
5:6	II:338; III:436; 699; IV:545n3; **547**; 939, (n16), (n18); VI:31; VII:1102n51
5:6-10	III:20
5:7	I:119; III:436; IV:547; 1125
5:8	I:51; 363; 585; II:320; 338; 356; 531; 953; III:699; IV:939, (n20); V:294; 300n24; 309n9; **310**; 314; **315**; 721;

	VI:219n332; VII:652n40; 688; 1024, n13; VIII:222
5:8f	VII:992
5:8ff	III:332(n81)
5:9	II:68; 356; 428; III:1091; V:430; 443; VII:993; VIII:157; IX:644; 651n211
5:9f	III:329(n63); V:445
5:10	I:148; II:339; 864(n271); III:18n77; 436; V:710n435; VI:55; **VII:783**; 784n85; 786; VIII:509; IX:346n287
5:11	**V:141**; 796, n169; 820n25; 821; VI:477
5:12	II:91n10; 541; 619; 907; III:829; IV:1022; V:117; VI:664; **701-702** (702n7, n11)
5:12f	VI:451n841
5:13	II:417; 417f; 907; VI:60; 62n6
5:13a	II:418n2
5:13b	II:418n2
5:14	I:492; II:827; IV:383; 387n114; 1022; V:141; 820; 821; 822; 823; VI:723; VIII:48; IX:666
5:15	I:16; 372; II:168; 230; III:481; V:377
5:15ff	II:356
5:16-18a	VI:422n597
5:17	IX:456
5:17-20	VI:852
5:18	II:541; III:58; IX:413; 414, n78; 552
5:18b	VI:422n597
5:19	I:585; 724; II:876; VI:422; 423, n599; 427n630; 433; **VII:168**
5:19f	VI:422n597
5:19-22	VI:348
5:20	VI:830; VII:168
5:20-22	III:590
5:21	II:260; 375; 829; VI:885
5:21a	II:375; VI:422n597
5:21b	II:375; VI:423n597
5:21f	I:724
5:22	II:375; V:473; VI:423n497; 562
5:23	II:414; 819n24; III:112(n315); 767; 1092; IV:383; 573; 719; V:175; 865; 868; VI:395n387, n389; 422n597; 435, n686, n688; VII:1060; VIII:142; IX:541; 555; 649; 651
5:24	III:488; VI:216(n318); 464
5:26	I:108; 501; IX:138n228; 139, n235; 141
5:27	I:343; IV:512; V:462; 464
5:28	VI:435; VII:778; **IX:393-394**

II THESSALONIANS

3:10-12	II:649		**VII:266; 854-855** (854n18; 855n21); VIII:48
3:10ff	VIII:249		
3:11	II:635; V:944; **VIII:48**	3:14f	VII:854
3:12	I:477; II:541; 692; V:764; 795; 796; VII:773; VIII:46n1	3:15	II:814; III:753n84; IV:1022
		3:16	VII:778; VIII:203
3:12a	VIII:48	3:16a	III:1086
3:13	III:486	3:17	I:502; 743; **VII:259;** IX:430
3:14	I:224; III:753n84; IV:101;	3:18	VII:778

I TIMOTHY

1:1	I:438n188; II:533(n115); VII:1016; 1017; VIII:37; IX:561		VIII:305n73; 306
		1:13f	I:116; 118n11; VI:265
		1:13ff	IV:573n9
1:2	I:727; II:484n100; IV:458; V:639; 1005; VI:213f; VIII:223; IX:396n195; 398; 561, n443	1:14	II:434n54; 541; IV:118; VI:213(n287); VII:772n36; VIII:521; IX:396n195; 398; 561
1:3	II:163; IV:579; V:764, n33; 793n161	1:15	I:308; 328; 379; II:55, n1; 56; 423; 674; III:889; 893; IV:116; 119; 657n44, n45; VI:204(n232), n232; 868n15; VII:995; **IX:560,** n435
1:3f	IV:788; V:765		
1:4	I:664, n4, n8; 665; II:683n4; 894n3; IV:763; 765; 781; 782; 783, n127; **788;** 844; 1019n8; V:153; VI:214; 746n6; VII:527; VIII:54; 312		
		1:15f	III:329n55; IX:135n202
		1:16	II:70; 429; 485; 864(n272); 865(n290); III:330(n66); IV:272; 275; **385;** 844; V:425; VI:204(n218); 211; 214n298; 216; 868n15; VII:995n132; VIII:250; IX:562
1:4ff	II:163		
1:5	I:17; 108; II:894n5; III:425; 613; V:764, n33; VI:250n142; VII:918, n79; VIII:54; **571,** n7		
		1:17	I:210; 337; 579; II:248; III:101(n222); 112(n321); 886; IV:370n52; 385; V:365; 369; 370; VIII:177; IX:104
1:5f	VII:918		
1:6	IV:524; 787n146; VI:213n290		
1:6f	VIII:54		
1:7	I:664, n1, n2; II:159, n5; 163; III:46n24; IV:783; 950	1:18	I:130; II:952; V:639; 765; VI:451; 830; 848; VIII:163; IX:433
1:7ff	VII:183		
1:8	I:664; III:550; IV:1089; V:466n4	1:18f	III:549; **VII:711**
1:8ff	I:664; **V:466**	1:19	I:17; 448; II:824; 826n58; IV:370n52; 891, n1; VI:56; 213; VII:918; VIII:571n8
1:9	I:327; 605; II:191; III:654; IV:1087; V:466; 492; 975n163; VII:190; VIII:47		
		1:19f	I:624
1:9f	VI:593n80; IX:601	1:20	I:624; II:80; 170; III:753; V:169n9; 624n179; 625; VII:161; 162
1:10	II:162(n5), n6; III:655; V:466; VI:249n138; VII:1104n57; VIII:312		
		2:1	II:41; 807; V:795; 889; VI:477(n101); **VIII:244;** IX:414
1:11	II:170; 730; 733; III:112; IV:365; 370, n52; VI:204(n226)		
		2:1f	VIII:514
1:12	II:88; 313; III:1092; V:764n33; VIII:157; IX:397; 398n212; 562	2:1-3:16	I:141
		2:2	I:577; II:49n5; 863(n262); VI:249n135; 250n142; 529; VII:182; 183; 195; VIII:43n24;
1:13	I:116; 118; 623; II:230; 485; III:893; VI:205; 212n280; 482;		

	1095n22; VI:249n137; VIII:244	5:8	I:470; IV:1010; V:134; VI:215(n313); 702; 866; IX:454, n126, n127; 455, n138; 456n153
4:6	I:215; II:89; 162; III:550; IV:782n117; 786; 789n155; 845n109; VI:213; 714; VIII:163n6; IX:561	5:9	I:362; 788; IV:656, n38; IX:451; 455n144; **456-457** (456n152; 457n159); 463
4:6f	IV:786	5:9f	IX:455n144
4:7	I:195; 494; 604; 775; 776; IV:763; 765; 781; 782, n117; **786-788;** VII:182; 527	5:9-13	IX:455n144
		5:10	I:215; 788; III:147; 549; IV:496; 497; V:20; 21; 24; 25n177; 488n5; VI:631; VIII:328n95; IX:456, n150; 457n161; 465
4:7f	I:496; VI:714		
4:7ff	I:137		
4:8	I:775f; II:56; 579; 825; 863(n265); 864(n269); 952; IV:723; 724; 782n117; 1108; 1120; VII:182; 183; 998n155; 1017; 1059	5:10f	III:549
		5:11	I:195; 652; 788; III:45n10; **631,** n1; IV:579; IX:452; **454,** n129, n135, n137; 455n144; 456; **562**
4:8f	IV:118		
4:9	I:379; II:55; IV:119; VI:204(n232)	5:11f	IX:455; 457
		5:11-15	IX:457
4:10	II:56; 532; III:829; V:240; VI:215(n312); VII:184; 1016; **1017**	5:12	I:788; III:942; VI:204n227; 866; VIII:159; IX:448n71; **454-455** (454n136; 455n137); 456
4:11	II:147; V:765		
4:12	I:123; III:632; 633; VI:213(n287); 215(n312); 714; VII:717; VIII:250	5:13	I:452; 788; II:635; 682; IV:410; IX:454n130; 455, n143; **457**
		5:14	I:632n54; 652; 788; II:49; III:655; IV:294; **V:473-474;** IX:391; 455; 457n158
4:13	I:344; II:147; 162; V:796; VI:714		
4:14	II:539; IV:409; VI:451; 654; 666, n92; 714; 830; 848; VII:772n36; VIII:161, n3; IX:406; **433-434** (434n57)	5:14f	VII:161; IX:452
		5:15	II:80; III:655n3; V:292; 473n18; VII:161; IX:455, n142
4:15	VI:709n42; 712; 713; **714;** 715; IX:3	5:16	I:561; 788; III:506; VI:215(n312); VIII:179; IX:454n129; **458**
4:16	II:162; 816n1; IV:723; VI:479(n107); VII:995		
5	IX:457; 463; 464, n225	5:17	I:380; II:162; 617; 620; 828n1; III:829; VI:653n4; **666-667** (666n91); 674n140; **702;** VIII:176; 177n44; IX:456; 457n154
5:1	IV:898; V:796; VI:652n3; 654; 666		
5:1f	V:1005		
5:2	I:123; IV:644; 898; VI:654; 666; IX:457n154	5:17-22	IX:455n144
		5:18	I:379; 753; III:605; IV:110; 698, n5; VI:667, n94; VII:874n26, n27
5:3	**VIII:179; IX:455-456** (456n148, n150)		
5:3ff	I:788; II:93; IX:451n107	5:19	III:637; IV:490; VI:666, n93
5:3-8	IX:455n144	5:19f	III:953; VIII:221
5:3-16	I:195n5; **IX:453-458** (453n115; 455n144)	5:20	II:474; VI:666n93; VIII:221n37; IX:216
5:4	I:788; II:59; 168; IV:410; V:650; VII:181; **IX:453-454** (454n126, n127, n129); 456n153; 462n202	5:21	I:83; III:107(n281); 953; IV:190; 512; VI:451(n836); 477; VIII:144n36; 223; 372n268; IX:241; 562
5:4ff	IX:461	5:22	I:122; 265; 295; III:804; VI:666, n93; VIII:143; 161; **IX:434, n58**
5:5	II:41; 533(n121); IV:579; VIII:179; IX:441n4; 451n100; **454; 456;** 457; 464; 465n241		
		5:23	I:776; III:204; IV:1095; V:165; VI:146n7; VIII:315
5:5ff	I:652	5:24	I:130; 215; 295
5:6	II:863(n267); IV:892n12; IX:452; **454,** n126, n135	5:24f	IV:723
5:7	IV:9; V:765; IX:454, n133	5:25	III:549; 976

6:1	I:379; 622; 624; II:162; 273; 899; V:280; VII:183(n35); VIII:44; 174	6:13	II:862(n257); 874; IV:475; 497n63; **499;** 502; V:210; 211; 212n40; 219; 888; 894; IX:560
6:1f	II:48; III:1086	6:13f	V:765; VIII:144
6:2	I:145; 375; II:147; 655; 899; III:632; V:796, n173; VI:215(n311); VIII:44	6:14	I:502; II:546; 553; 555; III:1092; IV:9; VIII:164; IX:10; 454n133; 561n442
6:3	II:162; 163; 683; IV:109; VII:182; VIII:312; IX:561	6:15	I:578; 590; II:26; III:461; 915n10; 1087; 1088; 1097; IV:365; 370; VIII:177n49
6:4	I:624; II:894; IV:143; 788n152; 844; 1092; **1095;** VI:56; 556	6:16	I:208; 337; II:825; 862; III:14; 25; 138n15; 342; 908, n16; IV:24; **V:136;** 236; 365; VIII:177; IX:347n299; 354n373
6:4f	II:894; IV:1018; 1095		
6:5	I:244; IV:958; VIII:569; IX:103		
6:5f	IV:331n92; VII:182		
6:6	I:467; IV:531; VII:183; 773		
6:6-10	VII:1103	6:17	I:205; II:533(n121); 827; III:117; IV:1108; 1114; V:765, n35; VI:747n12; IX:456n149
6:7	II:61; 422; 827; III:889; IV:768n43; IX:64		
6:8	I:465	6:17-19	VII:1103
6:9	I:397; 632n52; II:426; 925; III:171; IV:962; V:169; 595; VI:32; 173n5; 330; 331	6:17ff	IV:631; VI:330
		6:17-20	IX:241n27
		6:18	I:17; III:549; 809; IX:456n152
6:10	III:480; V:115; 448; VI:249; 252n167; 271n17; 274; 331; 990	6:19	II:427; 647; 864n268; 866; III:63; 550; IV:9; 723; VII:995n132
6:11	I:138; 364; II:210; 230; 650n52; IV:587; V:939; VI:714; VII:182	6:19f	IX:241n27
		6:20	I:605; 709; III:911n7; IV:787n146; 844; V:283; VII:69n21; VIII:163; 164, n10; IX:186n117; 241
6:12	I:137; II:864(n272); 866; III:488; 549; IV:9; 491; 497n63; 499; V:211; 216; VII:995n132		
6:12f	III:550; V:211; **216**	6:21	II:579; V:283; 424n308; VI:56; 213; VII:69n21; 778
6:12-16	VIII:163		

II TIMOTHY

1:1	II:541; 865(n292); 866; III:59; IX:561		VI:445; **VII:1104**
		1:7b	VIII:224
1:2	II:484n100; IV:458; V:1005; VIII:223; IX:396n195; 561, n443	1:7ff	II:317
		1:8	I:190; II:43; 725; 729n65; 733; IV:122; 504; V:208n27; 920; 937; VII:711; 794n134; VIII:447n331
1:3	I:438n188; III:425; IV:62; 64; 678; 958n34; V:1022; VI:757; VII:918		
1:4	V:341(n138); VI:291; IX:360; 370	1:9	I:107n60; 199; 209; II:651n58; III:488; 492; 710n57; IV:723; VI:685; 688; VII:995, n130; VIII:167; IX:398, n209; 561n445
1:5	I:349; II:539; IV:458; 644; VI:4; VIII:571		
1:6	VI:445n777; 451; 666n92; VII:168; 1104n1; VIII:161; 164; IX:406; **433-434**	1:9f	IX:10; **561; 592**
		1:10	I:453; II:732; 733; 861(n242); 864n273; 865; 866(n297); 868; III:14; 18; 19; IV:1113;
1:7	I:28n40; II:311n91; 317; V:236;		

	1119; V:868; VII:995n132; 1016, n65; 1017; 1018; 1021n86; IX:5; 105; 348; 349; 592	2:14	II:437n14; IV:143; 512; 678; 1019n8; VII:716n6; VIII:112
1:11	I:409; II:152; 156n53; 158; 715n90; 730; III:696; 712(n60); V:920; VIII:157; 164; 224	2:15	II:259; IV:117; V:841; VII:565, n10; 874n27; VIII:111; **112;** n4, n11
1:12	I:190; II:426; 952; V:920; VI:4; 211; 214(n293); 216; 445; **VIII:164;** 447n331; IX:241	2:16	I:605; IV:101n115; 787n146; VI:712; 713; 714; 716; VII:190; VIII:112
1:13	II:434n54; 541; V:729; VI:204n233; VIII:164; 250; 312; IX:561	2:16-3:13	VI:716
		2:17	IV:101; 1095; VI:715; 716n79; VIII:312n32; IX:114
1:14	I:105; II:67; III:550; VI:445; **VIII:164;** IX:241	2:18	I:156; 244; 371; II:336; III:19; IV:783; VI:56; 213n290; VII:183; 613n41; 794; 1018; IX:397n200
1:15	VII:722		
1:16	I:190; II:485; V:130; VIII:447n331; **IX:664**	2:18b	VII:190
		2:19	I:156; 620; 706; III:63; 64, n9; 1087; V:271; 282; VII:613n41; **651; 948,** n80
1:17	VII:566		
1:18	II:86; 484; 485; 769; III:1087; V:729n12; VII:995n132; IX:664	2:20	III:64, n9; V:435n370; VII:612; VIII:176n39
2:1	II:541; V:639; IX:561	2:20f	II:428; VII:364; **VIII:176**
2:1f	VII:630; VIII:164	2:21	I:112; II:48; 706; III:430; 1086; VII:612
2:2	II:66; 147; III:293; IV:491; V:937n9; VI:204(n231); VIII:163; 164	2:22	I:108; II:210; 230; 416f; III:171; 425; 497; 500; 613; VII:182; 918
2:3	I:138n17; 139n22; III:549; V:920; **937-938;** VII:630; **711,** n39; 794n134; IX:561	2:23	I:195; 665; II:417; 894; IV:788n152; 832; **844-845** (845n109); V:625
2:3-7	**VII:711-712**	2:23f	IV:528
2:4	I:455; II:863n262; **VI:641,** n2; VII:630; 713; IX:170	2:24	II:165; III:487; IV:919n40; VI:723
		2:24-26	III:752n82
2:4-6	**VII:711-712**	2:25	I:707; IV:1004; **V:625;** VI:650
2:5	I:167; IV:1089; **VII:629-630;** 634	2:25f	**V:594-595**
		2:26	II:80; III:61; VI:715; VII:161
2:6	III:615; 828; IV:10; VII:630	3:1	I:704; II:544; 697; 951; III:462; IV:118; 869; V:868; VI:249; VIII:595
2:7	IV:950; VII:711; 896		
2:8	II:335; 730; 733; IV:682; V:937; VII:545; 630; VIII:484; 485; IX:561		
		3:1ff	**I:18**
2:8ff	II:733	3:1-5	IV:781n117
2:9	II:60; 733; III:117; 484; 696; IV:116; 118; 122; V:937; **VII:612-613**	3:2	I:227; 624; V:492; VI:10; 271n17; VIII:527
		3:2-5	VI:593n80
		3:2-7	IV:469
2:10	I:208; II:250; 541; 866(n300); IV:190; 587; 588; V:931; 937; VI:92; VII:793; 994; 1076n482; VIII:241; IX:561	3:3	II:81; 342n5
		3:4	II:917; 918; 920; 925; IX:134n191; 169
		3:5	I:470; II:316n108; 826n56; IV:755; VII:182
2:10f	IV:118		
2:11	III:19, n79; IV:588; VI:204(n232); VII:786; 787	3:6	I:196; 295; 785; II:925; 926; III:171; IV:782n117; VI:485; **VII:1096;** IX:186n118
2:11f	IV:494n58; VII:767; **793-794;** 795; 995n132		
		3:6f	I:738; IV:410; IX:455
2:11-13	**V:216-217;** VIII:501n87	3:7	I:244; 707
2:11ff	I:470	3:8	I:244; III:193; 981; **990-991** (990n127); IV:865(n208); **869,** n230; 873; 958; 963; VIII:569; IX:103
2:12	I:470; 471; 591; III:806; IV:587; 588; V:926; VII:787; VIII:390n408		
		3:9	IV:869; 963; VI:712; 713; 716
2:13	I:471; V:215n47; VI:205; 208; 216	3:10	**I:128-129;** 129; 215; II:162; 237;

TITUS

PHILEMON

HEBREWS

	888; VI:474; 880; VIII:156;	2:2ff	I:603
	370n255; 583n108; **585,** n123;	2:3	I:219; 482; II:68; III:1092; V:348;
	586, n136; 587, n143; 609;		**VII:996;** VIII:35n12
	IX:59; 185; 420n30; **421-422**	2:3f	III:714; VII:1002
	(421n27, n30; 422n31)	2:4	I:603; 677; III:62; IV:497; **510;**
1:3a	IX:421		V:622n170; VI:415; 446; 485;
1:3f	IX:356		VII:230; **260;** 876
1:3ff	IV:231	2:5	V:159; VI:880; VIII:42
1:4	III:781; IV:231; V:210n33; 273;	2:5ff	I:57; 85; 423
	735; VIII:388n389; 391n417;	2:5-8	IV:676
	IX:64	2:6	I:366; II:605; IV:110; 111; 512;
1:4ff	I:57; 85; III:103(n248)		676n8; V:540n13; VIII:401;
1:5	I:665; 670; II:345n20;		404n24; 405; 461; **464**
	IV:109n160; 111; 339n5;	2:6b	VIII:42
	V:273; 1006n365; 1014;	2:6f	III:551
	VI:880; VII:274; VIII:370n255	2:6-8a	**VIII:175**
1:5a	VI:880	2:6ff	III:1089
1:5ab	VI:880; 881n58	2:7	IV:871; V:735; VIII:175, n26;
1:5b	VI:880		519n18
1:5ff	IV:109n160; 111	2:7b	VIII:42
1:5-13	VIII:370	2:7f	**VIII:42**
1:6	I:670; II:423; III:850;	2:8	I:511; III:884; 1089; IV:1116;
	IV:109n160; 111; V:107; 159;		V:342; 895(n31); VI:629;
	888; VI:765; 876n29; 878n41;		VIII:47; 614
	879; **880,** n54, n56, n57, n58;	2:8b	V:868; VIII:42
	881n58, n59	2:8c	VIII:42
1:7	IV:109n160; 111; 230; 231;	2:8f	V:343
	VI:463; 723; 941; 947	2:9	I:677, n12; III:18n77; 289;
1:8	I:199; 200; 584; III:164; 554n71,		328n48; 1089; IV:676n8; 871;
	n73; V:614n102; VI:723; 970;		V:344; 710n435; 728n1;
	VIII:388, n390		852n64; 916n87; 917; 918;
1:8f	III:105; VIII:370n255; IX:564		930; **934;** VI:543; VII:69;
1:9	I:21; 54(n162); 153; II:199; 472;		633; VIII:42; **175,** n27, n28,
	741; 831; 832; III:92n138; 103;		n29; 510; 519n18; IX:398,
	554n71; IV:691, n29; 1085;		n214, n215
	V:214; 735, n65; IX:555;	2:9a	VIII:41n9
	580n547	2:9f	V:930; 935; VIII:464
1:10	I:201; 481; 679; III:64; 1028;	2:9ff	V:917
	1029; 1032; 1087; V:515;	2:10	I:488; II:68; III:884; IV:189;
	IX:431		411; 412; V:102; 514n125;
1:10f	I:678		563; 678n147; 868; 888; 917;
1:10-12	III:1031; V:527, n242		932; 934; VI:542; 878n41;
1:10ff	I:202		880n57; VII:996; VIII:83;
1:11	V:720		86n3; 235; IX:398n214; 422;
1:11f	V:515		564
1:12	I:251; III:1031; IV:757n10	2:10b	II:67
1:12b	V:516n141	2:10f	VIII:389; 391; IX:565n460
1:13	II:39; 814; III:440; 1089;	2:11	I:103; 112; 190; III:487;
	IV:109n160; 111; 237n24;		IV:726; V:208n27;
	V:522n190; 895(n31); VI:629;		VII:1072n451; VIII:83n26,
	723; VIII:156; 370n255		n27; 447n331
1:14	I:85; 403; II:87; 189; 428; III:781;	2:11ff	I:145
	783; IV:231, n7; VI:446;	2:12	**I:67;** 145; III:513; V:213n42;
	577n84; VII:996;		214; 218; VIII:499
	VIII:391n417	2:12f	IV:110; VI:831n336
2	VIII:41, n9; 42; 464	2:13	IV:339n5; VI:6
2:1	VI:62; VII:405n12; 598; 599;	2:13f	V:638
	VIII:235	2:14	I:112; 172; 453; II:80; 831;
2:1ff	IV:412		III:15; 18; 328n49; 804; 907;
2:2	I:83; 85; 223; 508; 602; IV:112;		IV:871; V:439; 918; 934;
	618; **702;** 866n210; 1078n255;		VI:106n33; 446n781;
	V:740; VIII:35n12; 36; IX:297		**VII:141;** 158; 161; 1059n370

	370n256; 501n89; 612n51; IX:564n457	5:8-10 5:9	IX:563 I:208; 224; III:279; 280, n63;
4:14-10:31	III:276		IV:350n8; 412; V:917; 918;
4:15	I:296; 314; 335n15; 492;		934; VII:274; 996;
	III:278, (n57); 279, n59; 280;		VIII:84n24; 235; IX:67; 422
	462; 482; 551(n53); IV:831;	5:9f	VIII:83
	V:190; 852n64; 917n94;	5:10	III:103; 275; 278(n57); IV:570;
	935-936 (936n6); 938; VI:28;		V:934; VIII:235; IX:564
	33-34 (33n53, n56); 243;	5:10f	VIII:77n61
	VII:159n39; 355	5:11	IV:101; 837; **1126;** VIII:77n61
4:15f	III:279n58	5:11ff	III:451n1
4:16	I:629; II:430; 684; 769; III:161;	5:11-14	VIII:77n61
	282; 462; IV:726; V:424n308;	5:11-6:3	VIII:77n61
	884; 936, n6; VII:773;	5:11-6:20	VIII:235
	IX:396n195; 398	5:12	I:482; 646n1; II:145; 152;
5	IV:920		158(n66); **IV:138;** 139; 140;
5:1	I:295; 313f; II:166, n2;		141; V:564; **VII:612;** 687;
	III:104n260; 181; 182; 277;		VIII:79; IX:591
	444; 865; IV:1079n259;	5:12f	IV:920
	V:934; VI:55n20, n21; 722;	5:12ff	I:643; 646
	IX:67	5:12-6:1	VIII:77
5:1a	VIII:508	5:13	I:188; 646n1; II:198; 831;
5:1b	VIII:512		IV:117n195; V:649
5:1ff	I:677; III:276n52; 277; V:936;	5:14	**I:188;** 775; III:949; **VII:612;**
	IX:67		VIII:77; 79n12
5:1-4	III:275	5:14b	I:188
5:1-9	**I:3**	6	IV:920; 1006n178;
5:1-10	III:279		VIII:587n145
5:2	I:3; 116; 491; III:277; 279; 656;	6ff	I:589
	V:936n6; 938; VI:243;	6:1	I:482; 510; 512; II:645; 651;
	252n163; VII:354n86		III:63; 101(n231); 620;
5:3	I:314; IV:53; 1079; V:563, n26;		IV:109n153; 570; 893; 999;
	VI:55, n20		1004; V:140n10; VI:204; 207;
5:4	I:3; III:488; VIII:175, n32; 241		**209;** 211; 212; VII:612;
5:4f	IX:398n214		VIII:79, n12; 235; IX:58; **564**
5:4-6	III:277; VIII:175n33	6:1f	I:512; 646; IV:920; VI:214n300
5:4-10	IX:565n460	6:2	I:209; 372; 545; II:164; III:942;
5:5	I:665; 670; II:345(n20);		IV:893(n25); V:868;
	III:278(n57); 279; IV:111;		VIII:161; IX:432
	411; VI:723; VII:274; IX:564	6:3	III:451n1; VI:477
5:5f	III:276; VIII:370; **388**	6:4	**I:382;** 383; II:167; 832;
5:6	I:199; III:275; 277n54; IV:111;		III:593n5; IV:462; 726;
	570		V:541, n19; VI:171; IX:355,
5:7	I:140; 221; 222; II:41; 753; 950;		n384; 357n406
	III:279; 280; 297; 398; 903;	6:4f	I:676; VI:415; 446
	IV:412; 670; V:445(n429);	6:4-6	IV:1006; V:428n333
	852n64; 917; 918; VI:33n56;	6:4ff	I:188; 545; IV:304
	36; VII:62n48; 141, n321;	6:5	I:206; 207; 675; 676; II:585;
	772; 989; 996; VIII:83n24;		IV:117; 726; V:350; 541n19
	587; IX:67	6:6	I:138n18; 512; II:32; III:451;
5:7f	I:627n16; III:279n58; VIII:87		IV:411n155; V:215; VI:171;
5:7-9	III:280; VI:33		**VII:584;** VIII:389
5:7ff	IV:410; **V:917-918;** VIII:84n24	6:7	IV:10; VI:138
5:7-10	III:279; VI:33n56; VIII:83n24;	6:7f	II:763
	501n89	6:8	I:449; II:331; III:643, n3;
5:8	I:175; 224; III:276; 279;		IV:1006; VII:754n30;
	IV:390; **410-412;** V:621;		VIII:55
	915n82; 916n87; 917, n103;	6:9	VI:4; VII:996
	918, n109; VIII:84n24;	6:9-15	IV:386n100
	223n49; 388, n390	6:9-20	VIII:596
5:8f	I:3n2; V:934; VI:714; VII:794;	6:10	I:108; 152; II:86; 433;
	VIII:83; 235; IX:67		III:111(n313); IV:386(n106);

7:27	I:3; 314; 383; III:182; 276; 277; 280; 281; 886; IV:53; 647; 1079; V:719n435; 852n64; 936; VI:474; VIII:512; IX:61	8:13	II:132; 331; III:282; 448; 449; 450; IV:898; **V:720,** n13; VI:767; 866; IX:67
		8:13a	V:720n2
7:27f	III:185	8:13b	V:720
7:28	I:492; III:276; 277; 279; 444; 656; IV:112; 339; 1079; V:464; 938; VIII:82; 83; **388, n390**	9	I:102f; IX:61
		9:1	II:132; 221; III:247n77; 277; 278; 897; IV:65; 898; V:720n13; VI:866; VII:142n329; 376; VIII:258
8f	VII:374; 377; VIII:259		
8-10	III:185		
8:1	I:679; II:39; 824; III:161n7; 165; 278(n57); 282; 442; 1089; IV:544; V:514n121; 519; 522; 527; 528; 540n16, n17, n18; VII:375; 377; VIII:156; 257	9:1ff	V:76
		9:1-14	II:131
		9:2	I:477; IV:327; V:126n30; VI:866; VII:379n60; VIII:165; **211**
		9:2f	VII:376, n43
8:1ff	IV:1079n260; V:936; VIII:586n139	9:2ff	**VII:376,** n44; 377
		9:3	I:102; III:278; 630; IV:885n21; V:77n124; VII:376n42
8:1-10:18	VII:398; VIII:257	9:4	**I:3;** IV:264; **465-466; VI:969-970;** IX:439
8:2	I:250; III:247n77; 278; 281; 1087; IV:230; V:124; 540; **VII:375;** 376, n44; 377; 379n60; VIII:258; 609n32		
		9:4f	VII:376n40; IX:439n10
		9:5	II:251; III:323; IV:496; VIII:515n43; **IX:439**
8:3	II:166, n2; III:181; 182; 277; 444; 865	9:6	II:66; III:277n54; IV:63; 65; V:126n30; VI:866; VIII:62
8:3f	III:865	9:6f	III:185; 278; V:78n127
8:4	I:679; II:166; III:276; 277n54; IV:1078; V:519; 528n246	9:7	I:115; 174; 381; III:185; 277; IV:53; VI:982; VII:376; VIII:508; 512
8:5	I:106; 250n45; 679; II:25; 132; III:278; 426n80; IV:62; 63; 110; 620; V:540; VI:476; 532; VII:286n37; **375-376** (376n44); 377; **398;** VIII:61; 249; 256; 257, n64; 258; 585n126; IX:67; 481	9:7f	V:77n124
		9:8	I:757; II:62; III:185; 278; V:42; **75-78** (77n126; 78n127); 84n147; 106, n7; 720n13; VI:446; 767; 866; VII:376, n45, n46; 570; 961
		9:8-10	VIII:258n68
		9:8ff	VII:376n40
8:6	II:33; 132; 584, n65; III:450; IV:226; 619; 620n84; 871; 1090; 1106n2; 1109; 1110n33; VIII:241; 258; IX:64; 67	9:9	II:166, n2; 431; 544; III:185; 278; 461; 865; IV:62; 63; 237; 1115; V:752; VI:145n1; 532; VII:376, n46; 377; 918; VIII:83, (n22); 253
8:6ff	III:186; 448	9:9f	I:540; III:185; IV:1079; VII:130n249
8:6-13	III:275	9:9-11	III:276
8:7	II:132; III:449; 450; IV:572; V:720n13; VI:866; VIII:206; 258	9:9ff	IX:67
8:8	II:675; 951; III:1087; IV:63; 111; 112; **572;** V:129; VI:866; VIII:64	9:10	I:545; 643; II:221; III:278; 462; 655; V:450; VI:145, n1; VII:130n249; 141; 142; 144n343; IX:64; 67
8:8-10	III:1087; VIII:64n5	9:10b	VI:145
8:8ff	II:584; III:449; IV:112; V:129; VI:831n338	9:10-12	V:527n242
8:8-12	II:132; V:720n13	9:11	I:15; III:278, (n57); 281; 897; 1028; 1031; V:527, n242; 535n329; 540; 720n13; 868; VII:142, n329; 375; **376-377** (376n47; 377n48); VIII:77; 258; IX:436; 564
8:9	III:1087; IV:9; 577; V:976n175; VI:464; IX:430		
8:10	II:106; III:384n120; 612; 1087; IV:54; 966, n13; 1078; V:129; 554n105		
8:10b	III:101n228		
8:11	I:705; III:1087; IV:531n7; 650(n13), n13; V:117; VI:534	9:11f	III:185; VIII:257; 258n69; IX:564
8:12	I:153; 314; III:301; IV:676; 1085	9:11ff	II:131; VIII:586n139

9:11-14   V:772
9:12   I:175; 208; 383; II:66; 678; 769;
               III:185; 247n77; 278; 280;
               282; 624n2; 886; IV:350n8;
               351; 352; 355n20; 761;
               V:852n64; 918; VI:982n29;
               VII:375n39; 376; 996n137
9:12a   IV:1079n260
9:12f   I:174; III:247n77; IV:762
9:13   I:103; 108n64; 111n5; III:185;
               278; 426; 809; IV:760; 761;
               762; VI:981; 982n29; IX:67
9:13f   I:175; III:185; **VI:982;** 983;
               VII:142, n326; 918
9:14   I:108; 174; 175; 208; II:132;
               645; 651; 862(n247); III:17;
               185n21; 280; 282; 426; IV:62;
               64; 237; **339,** n4; 345n25; 351;
               831; 893; 1079; V:189; 918;
               VI:446; 767; 983; 984;
               VII:141n321; VIII:84n25;
               IX:67; 564
9:14-28   IX:564
9:15   I:103; 208; 209; II:132; 329;
               584; III:282; 449; 488; 781;
               785; IV:7; 352; 354; 620; 898;
               1080; V:720n13; **740;** VI:866;
               982; VII:375n39
9:15f   V:918
9:15ff   II:131; IV:871
9:15-18   VII:340n8
9:15-22   III:275
9:16   IX:58
9:16f   II:106; 131, n99; 132;
               IX:459n172
9:16ff   IV:620
9:17   II:862(n244); III:397
9:18   I:174; II:132; III:185; 454;
               IV:898; V:720n13; VI:866;
               VIII:258
9:18-20   II:132
9:18ff   I:174; 176
9:18-21   III:277; VI:980n22; **982;** 983
9:19   I:617; II:553; III:813; IV:53;
               111n177; 620; 761; VI:981
9:19f   IV:111n177
9:19ff   II:131
9:20   II:132; 545; 553n30;
               IV:110n161; 111n177;
               VI:982
9:21   I:174; **IV:226;** 227; VI:981;
               VII:362; 376
9:22   I:174; 176; 177; II:538; III:185,
               n21; 277; 424; 426; IV:64;
               237; 1078
9:22f   I:512
9:23   II:538; III:182; 277; 278; 281;
               426; V:513; 528; 540, n16;
               541; VIII:258
9:23f   II:33
9:23ff   IV:871
9:24   I:250; II:424; 678; III:246n73;

247n77; 278; 281; 1031;
               IV:1113; V:527, n242; 528;
               540; 541; 812n91; VI:767;
               777; VII:142n329; 375; 377;
               VIII:249; 258, n69; IX:7;
               436; 564
9:24ff   I:677
9:24-28   III:281
9:25   I:174; 265; 381; II:538; 678;
               III:280
9:25f   I:175; III:185; V:918
9:25ff   I:103
9:26   I:203; 296; 314; 381; 382;
               II:585; III:182; 276; 620; 625;
               885; 1029; IV:411; 1109;
               1113; V:360n219; 918;
               919n114; VIII:159; IX:5n15;
               61
9:26ff   I:333(n126)
9:27   I:364; 382; III:14(n61); 17; 655;
               V:868; 917; **VIII:66**
9:27f   I:381; III:281; V:708n416a;
               VI:544
9:28   I:296; 314; 335n15; 381; II:56;
               III:276; 280; IV:726; 1079;
               1115; V:341; 360; 541; 711,
               n440; 852n64; 868; 918;
               919n114; VI:543; 544, n47;
               VII:996; IX:61; 564
10   II:741n15
10ff   I:138
10:1   I:15; 250n45; II:308; 395; 684;
               III:181; 278; 282; IV:1080,
               V:540; VI:532; 639; 767;
               VII:398; 1066n413; VIII:82,
               n18; 83; 258; 585n126;
               586n139; IX:67
10:1f   I:348; III:278
10:1ff   III:185
10:2   I:314; 382; II:824; III:426;
               IV:62; 63; VII:377; 647; 918;
               VIII:83n22, n24
10:2f   III:278; IX:67
10:3   I:314; 348; 349n4; III:278;
               IV:676(n6); 678; 1080
10:4   I:174; 177; 314; II:308; III:278;
               IV:237; 760; 761; 1079;
               VI:982n29, n32; IX:67
10:5   I:476; II:423; 678; III:48; 181,
               n4; 280; 889; IV:110; V:107;
               VII:141n319; **1058;**
               1071n447; IX:68
10:5ff   III:186; IV:1079, n260; **IX:67**
10:6   II:741; VI:55
10:7   I:617; III:56; V:868; VI:474;
               VIII:84n25; IX:67
10:8   I:377n5; II:471; III:48; 181, n4;
               IV:110; 1078; VI:55(n19)
10:9   III:56; 282; 328(n53); IV:110;
               VI:293; 474; 866; VII:649;
               IX:67
10:10   I:103; 112; 384; III:56; 281;

12	**V:621-623**; IX:77n18	12:18-20	VII:286n37
12:1	I:296; 314; 639n8; II:476n9;	12:18ff	III:36; IV:376n15; VI:942
	III:656; IV:491; 588; 902;	12:18-21	**IX:297**
	V:41, n5; 216; VI:208;	12:18-29	III:276n52
	VII:708; VIII:233	12:19	I:195; IV:112; VII:85; 86; 722;
12:1f	VII:275; IX:565n460		VIII:168; IX:292; 297
12:1ff	I:138; IV:666	12:20	IV:268; VII:591n6; 592; **IX:59**
12:2	I:138n20; 190; 488; II:39;	12:21	IV:620; IX:6
	III:165; 289; 440; 442; 632;	12:22	I:83; 149; II:684; III:282;
	656; 1089; IV:2; 339n5; 411;		IV:620; V:483; 533; 541; **722;**
	412; 582; V:522n190; 622;		769; VI:530; 533; 881;
	918; VI:207; **VII:577;** 612,		VII:286n37; 327; 336; **337;**
	n36; **VIII:86-87** (86n3, n4);		VIII:83; 259; IX:297n91
	IX:564, n459	12:22f	V:29; 1018
12:2f	IV:588; 666; VI:30n38	12:22-24	V:722; VI:531
12:3	V:622; VI:33; VIII:86n4; 87;	12:22ff	I:468
	IX:650	12:23	I:620; II:190; III:513; 530; 943;
12:3f	I:137		V:281; 532; 722; VI:445; 876;
12:4	I:173; 296; 314; VI:724;		880; **881,** n61, n62; VIII:83
	VII:274	12:24	I:8; 175; II:132; III:289;
12:4ff	V:1004		450n17; IV:270; 620; 867;
12:4-13	IV:320		871; 898, n18; 899; VI:866;
12:5	II:94; 474; III:1087; V:797		**981-982;** 983; IX:293n72;
12:5f	V:908n23		564n459
12:5-8	VIII:364	12:25	I:195; 679; V:513; 517n152;
12:6	II:52; III:1087; IV:518, n34;		531, n278; 533; VII:722;
	V:609n70; 622n164;		IX:297n91
	VIII:268; IX:137, n219	12:25a	IX:482
12:7	IV:588; 1005; V:622, n165;	12:25b	IX:482
	IX:66	12:25-29	IX:297
12:7f	**V:622**	12:26	I:382; 678n5; II:581; IV:1116;
12:8	II:831; IX:297n91		V:514n124; 515; 527; 868;
12:9	I:171; II:822n41; 864(n271);		**VII:70;** 198; 199; 722;
	V:622; 1008n379; 1014,		IX:297n91; 564n458
	n412; VI:445; 446; 577n84;	12:26f	VI:831n341
	VII:141; VIII:43	12:27	I:382; II:62; III:590; V:516;
12:10	I:114; II:950; IV:726;		VI:463; 945; VII:70;
	V:622n172; 623; 1010;		VIII:161
	VI:724; IX:75; 77; 78n18	12:27f	VII:199
12:11	I:775; II:167; 200; 419; III:615;	12:28	I:171; 457; 582; 583; 587;
	IV:320; V:623, n173; 865;		II:753; III:280n63; 847n113;
	VI:724; VIII:595; IX:77n18;		939; IV:13; 62; 64; 726;
	368n86		**VII:70;** 773; IX:214; 374n7;
12:12	I:509; 738; IX:430		398n212
12:12f	VII:405n12	12:29	III:112(n322); 939; V:423n297;
12:12ff	II:329		VI:945
12:13	III:214; V:449; VI:446; 628	13	IV:64
12:14	I:113; II:230; 411; 413; IV:646;	13:1	I:146
	V:366; VIII:596	13:1f	V:21
12:14f	II:604; VI:990	13:2	I:83; V:2; 20; **21-22** (22n157);
12:14-16	VI:593		VI:761
12:14ff	I:220	13:2f	III:549; 550
12:15	II:615; IV:646; V:582n1;	13:3	I:196; 197n6; IV:678;
	586n19; VI:124, n13; 541;		V:912n55; VII:856n1;
	542; **990;** VIII:596; IX:399		1058n356, n362
12:16	I:372; 605; 642; II:168; 954;	13:4	I:652; IV:647; 730; 734
	IV:646; VI:875, n22; 881;	13:5	I:367; 465; V:859; VI:271n17;
	VII:577n41; VIII:596		990n26
12:17	II:761; 894n1; 895; III:45n8;	13:6	I:628; III:27; 1087;
	781; 785; IV:304; 628;		VI:477(n102); IX:214
	1006n178; VI:159; VIII:206	13:7	II:907; IV:113; 666; 682;
12:18	II:684; VII:424n3; IX:297		VI:208; VII:717; VIII:55n39

13:8	I:199; 202; III:1031; VII:273; IX:565
13:9	I:602; 643; II:164; 363n8; III:613; 1033; V:2; 31; 945; VI:485; VIII:235; IX:398
13:10	II:569; 693; III:183, n12; 731n21; IV:62; 63; VI:922; VII:375n39; 377, n49
13:10-13	III:282; IX:564n458
13:11	I:174; II:68; 873; VI:55; 922; VII:1057; 1058; 1059n370; IX:64
13:11f	VI:922
13:12	I:112; 175; III:282; 328(n49); IV:54; 55; 255; 411; V:917; 918; VI:87n48; **921-922;** VIII:83n27; IX:565n459, n460
13:12f	I:103
13:12ff	I:106
13:13	II:680; IV:238; 871n246; V:241; VI:922; IX:59
13:14	II:895; V:29; 540; 852; VI:530; 531; 533; **VII:337;** 996n137
13:15	II:68; III:181; 615; V:209;

	210n33; 216; 279; VII:700; IX:61; 67; 414n74
13:15f	III:182; 186; V:127
13:15ff	III:282
13:16	III:808; IV:933
13:17	II:339; 907; IV:103; 104; VI:4; 477; VII:603; 773; VIII:508; 555; IX:650-651
13:18	II:824; III:49; 550; VI:4; 54; VII:717; 918
13:19	I:387; VI:62; 477n101
13:20	I:175; 208; II:132; 413; III:112n315; 274; 450; IV:339n1; 529n1; 871, n247; VI:494; 691; 982; 983; VIII:368n236; IX:565n459
13:20f	II:415
13:21	I:199; 337; 457; 476; II:68; 248; III:57n20; 58; 282; VI:464; 479; IX:564; 565
13:22	I:359; II:66; IV:101; V:795; VII:593; VIII:245
13:23	I:705n65; V:341(n138); VII:772
13:24	I:500; 501; II:907; III:391
13:25	V:424n308; VII:778

JAMES

1:1	**II:102-103** (103n14, n17); 273; 274n97; 276; 277; 323; 411; III:517; 533; IV:1082n278; V:31(n211); 852; VII:996n141; **IX:249-250;** 360n9; 367; 565
1:2	II:230; 259; 926; IV:588; 727; V:299n19; 868; VI:173; 485; IX:368, n80
1:2f	II:258; 259; IV:320; 587; 726; VI:29; 30; 208
1:2-4	IV:588n25
1:2ff	I:52
1:3	I:704; III:635; IV:588; VIII:74
1:3f	VIII:74n39
1:4	II:926; III:767; IV:588; **VIII:74,** n38
1:5	I:386; V:240; 728; VII:524; IX:401
1:6	III:447; 947; 948; 950n4; IV:726; VI:206(n244)
1:6ff	VII:524
1:7	III:1087; IV:7
1:8	I:362; III:447; 947; V:85;

	VI:200n173; VIII:563; IX:665
1:9	VI:911(n239); VIII:19; 605
1:9f	III:652
1:9-11	VIII:21-64
1:10	II:682; VIII:21
1:10f	IV:389(n8); VI:330
1:11	I:352; III:644; V:69n89; 85n154; VI:168; 777; VIII:21
1:12	I:362; II:257; 581; 864(n270); 866n301; IV:7; 369; 588; 727; V:299n19; VI:30; VII:629; **630-631** (630n76); 633; 761n15
1:13	II:214n13; III:111(n313); 480; **VI:29;** IX:64n2
1:13-15	II:923; VII:760
1:14	II:921; III:171; VI:29; VII:761, n13, n15
1:14a	VII:762
1:14f	VII:761
1:15	I:296; 314; III:15n67; 171; **VII:760-762** (761n10)
1:15a	VII:760

1:15b	VII:762	2:6	I:190; II:503; 504n4; III:943; VI:911
1:16	**VI:244**	2:6f	VI:330
1:16-18	VII:760	2:7	I:569n7; 624; III:497; 498; 550;
1:17	I:378; 522, n6; II:166; 167;		553n65; 943n5; V:279; 280;
	III:117; IV:24; V:514n121;		VI:555
	531; 542; 733; 1008n379;	2:8	I:52; 591; 753; IV:1032; 1080,
	1013; VII:399; 444n189;		n266; 1081; 1082; VI:316;
	VIII:75, n42; IX:343;		477; IX:130
	355n386	2:8ff	**IV:1081-1082;** VIII:60
1:17f	**IX:355-356**	2:9	I:295; 314; II:474; V:741, n6;
1:18	I:485; 632; 672n37; II:430; 732;		VI:780
	1028; 1034; IV:116; 117; 119;	2:9f	IV:1081
	726; V:654; **1013-1014**	2:10	II:435; 828; III:351n39;
	(1013n404); VI:261;		IV:1081, n272; VI:883;
	440n731; 881; VII:760;		VIII:144
	761n9; IX:356n390; 652	2:11	IV:111; 729; 730n2; 1081, n272,
1:19	IV:841; V:419; 420; **421;** 432;		n276; V:741, n7
	VI:545n2	2:12	II:502; IV:1080; 1082; V:868;
1:19f	V:421n285		VI:479
1:20	I:362; II:200; III:635; V:395;	2:13	II:481n60; 483; 487; III:653;
	419; 420; 421; VI:650		654; IV:727; VI:477
1:21	II:54; 310; III:484; IV:116; 118;	2:14	I:52; II:826n58; VII:996;
	119; 727; 1081; VI:63; 650;		IX:250
	911n239; VII:996;	2:14ff	I:52; IV:726; 1080; V:217
	IX:650n210; 652	2:14-17	VIII:74n40
1:22	IV:119; VI:479; IX:652	2:15	I:774; III:549; 550
1:23	I:362; 682; 684n11, n15; II:696,	2:16	II:166; 409n41; 411; 434;
	n2; IV:578; VI:479; 776		III:549; 550; IV:1080;
1:23f	I:179n9; IV:975; V:344n153		VI:911n246; VII:1058;
1:25	II:502; 651; IV:369; 578; 727;		VIII:504; 505
	1080, n266; **1081;** 1082, n278;	2:17	II:168(n2); 651; 862(n248);
	V:815; VI:479; 747;		IV:893; VII:717n10
	VII:717n10; VIII:74; 75n41	2:18	II:27n4; 826n58; VI:770n8
1:26	I:385; 721, n3; III:155n1; 613;	2:19	II:19; III:101; 1081n214;
	IV:522; 1081		VI:200n180; 479; 712
1:26f	III:156	2:20	I:452; 703; 708; II:862(n248);
1:27	I:108; 333n121; 502; II:604;		III:44n3; 660; IV:841; 893
	III:147; 425; 549; 550; 893;	2:21	I:9; III:183; V:976n182; IX:61;
	IV:647; 1081; **V:488;** 733;		169n185
	822; 1007n371; VIII:143;	2:21f	IV:588
	IX:448n75; 449n76; 451n100;	2:21ff	IV:450n235
	458, n167, n169	2:21-24	I:9
2:1	II:248; 826n58; III:948n12;	2:22	I:452; V:343; 344; VII:874;
	VI:210(n267); 212; **780,** n3;		**876;** VIII:82
	IX:565	2:22b	VIII:82
2:1ff	IV:1081; VI:911n240	2:23	I:8(n14); 28n44; 753; **II:201,**
2:1-9	VI:330		n43; 434; III:101(n231); 488;
2:2	II:678; III:518; 593; IV:249n53;		IV:110; 289; **290;** VI:295;
	VI:911; VII:798; 800n9;		296; VII:589; VIII:82;
	801n13; 828; 829n199;		IX:159; **167-169**
	837-838	2:24	IV:722; V:342; 343; 344;
2:2f	IV:17; 27; VII:838n256		IX:250
2:2-4	III:948n12; VI:780	2:25	I:83; 528; III:3, n15; 22; 69;
2:3	III:440; 444; VII:647; IX:84		VI:594; VII:417
2:4	II:98; III:943; 947; 948, n12;	2:26	II:862(n248); III:17n76;
	949n18; 950n4; VI:556;		IV:893; VI:446;
	VIII:22		VII:1058n360
2:5	I:52; 582; 583; 587; II:581; 827;	3:1	II:152; 157; III:942; IV:7; 531
	III:660; 781; 948; IV:175;	3:1ff	I:721n3; III:767; IV:727
	727; VI:212; **911,** n241, n245;	3:1-12	I:721; VII:755
	VIII:19; 21; 391n417	3:2	I:362; 363; III:338; 101;
2:5f	IV:389(n8); VI:330		

	VI:883; **VIII:75**		IX:136; 138; 154n68; 159;
3:2f	VII:1058		**167-169**
3:3	III:338; VI:4; VII:1058(n358);	4:4a	III:446n6
	VIII:75	4:5	I:753; 756, n33; II:540; III:660;
3:3-5	II:905; IX:185		**991;** IV:727; 1089n1; **V:156;**
3:4	I:632n42, n53; III:338;		VI:446; 725
	IV:655(n36); V:469n8; **471;**	4:5b	I:756n36
	1028	4:5f	IV:110
3:5	IV:567; 655, n36	4:6	VI:911(n239); VIII:18; **19;** 528,
3:5f	VI:942		n28, n29; IX:397n202; 399
3:5ff	IV:841	4:6a	VI:447n789; VIII:528n28
3:6	I:156; **683-684** (683n5; 684n11,	4:7	II:80; 920; III:425; VI:561;
	n18); III:446; 660n3; 883;		VII:161; VIII:18; 41; 43, n22
	IV:567; VII:1058	4:7-10	IV:4
3:6-12	VIII:75	4:8	I:123; 327; II:331; 925; III:117;
3:7	I:366; III:134; IX:275		425; 613; VIII:19n52; 563;
3:8	III:334; 335; 447; 480		IX:430; 665
3:9	I:448; III:1087; 1088;	4:8ff	I:660
	IV:567n93; V:190; 1007n371;	4:9	I:660; III:722; 724; VI:42n16,
	1009n384		n17; **43;** VII:729n1;
3:9f	II:763; VII:755		VIII:19n52
3:9ff	III:950	4:10	VI:43; 911(n239); **VIII:18-19;**
3:9-12	I:449		608
3:10	II:679; VI:115	4:11	III:923; 939; 943; IV:4; 5
3:10-12	III:335; VII:700	4:11f	**IV:1082;** VIII:567
3:11	VI:115; 124; VII:755	4:11ff	IV:1081
3:12	VI:483; VII:752; 754n31; **755,**	4:12	I:396; III:923; 943; IV:727;
	n42		1082n279; 1089; V:423;
3:12a	VII:755		VI:316; 317; VII:996;
3:12b	VI:115; 124; VII:755		IX:645n171
3:13	III:550; VI:650; 911n239;	4:13	III:673; IV:1108; 1121; VI:475;
	VII:524; 525; 717		573; VII:273, n23
3:13-18	III:653n2	4:13-16	III:652
3:14	I:242; II:661, n11; 826n57; 881;	4:14	II:861(n243); IV:903; V:172;
	III:612; 653; 654; VI:94n15;		VI:724; IX:2
	124; 650; VII:525; IX:601	4:15	I:227; II:862(n259); III:48;
3:15	I:378; 681; II:17; 20;		1090; IV:1011; 1109n28;
	V:514n121; VI:395n389;		VI:475
	VII:525, n407; IX:661; **663**	4:16	I:227; III:653; IV:1109, n28;
3:16	II:661; 881; III:446; VI:94n15;		VI:557
	VII:525	4:17	I:295; 314; V:117; VI:479
3:17	I:122; 378; 681; II:419; 483;	5	I:626
	590; III:950, n3; VI:447; 650;	5:1	II:681; III:722; 724n19; 725;
	VIII:571		IV:389(n8); 1108; 1121;
3:17f	VII:524; 525		V:173; 174; VI:43n19
3:18	II:200; 411; 412; 417; 922;	5:1ff	I:52; III:723
	III:615; VI:477; VII:546	5:1-5	VII:277n13
4:1	II:911; 919; 920; 921; 922;	5:1-6	VI:330
	923n88; III:171n36; IV:567;	5:2	VII:97; **277-278**
	VII:135n284	5:2f	III:335
4:1f	IV:528; **VII:712**	5:3	II:428; 695; 697; 950; III:138;
4:1ff	II:919n58; 920; 924; 925;		334; 725n22; IV:503;
	IV:727		V:868n57; VI:330; 942;
4:2	II:888; 921; 922, n79; III:170;		VII:124; 143; 278
	VI:94n15; 514n92; 515	5:4	II:678; III:132; 864n31; 902;
4:2f	I:192, n13; II:319; 921		1087; IV:270; 385n96; 698;
4:2ff	II:804		V:547n36; 557; VI:330;
4:3	II:919, n60; 920; 921; 922;		VII:874n26
	III:171n36; IV:7	5:4ff	I:627
4:4	I:632n52; II:814; 815; 919n60;	5:5	II:953; III:611; 612; V:868n57;
	920; 922; III:446; 893; 895;		VI:330; **VII:938,** n15; 996;
	IV:730; 734; V:836n73;		IX:454n131

5:6	II:190; III:622; VI:330; 911n240	5:13ff	III:214; IV:1095; 1098
5:7	II:56; III:615; IV:385; 386; 387n114; VII:938n15	5:14	I:230; 231; 232; 493; II:472; III:130; 213n62; 500; 513; 518; 1087; V:271; **VI:664;** VII:838; VIII:598
5:7f	V:866; 868		
5:7ff	IV:727; V:937n8		
5:7-11	**IV:385-386**	5:14f	I:231; V:278
5:8	II:331; III:613; IV:385, n97; VII:656	5:14ff	II:805
		5:15	I:295; 315; 511; II:334; 338; 776, n2; VI:206(n244); 479; VII:990, n101
5:9	III:173; 174n8; 943; 956; IV:385n96; 727; VI:684; VII:603		
		5:15f	II:776
5:10	II:33; III:1087; IV:385; 588; V:271; 714n469; 936n4; **937,** n7; VI:835; VIII:249	5:16	I:315; 493; 512; II:190; 654; 776, n2; 935; III:398; V:215; 939; VI:171n9; 664; VII:990n101; VIII:244; 514
5:10f	III:404		
5:11	III:1087; IV:367; 587; 588; V:161; 342; 937; **VII:557,** n55; VIII:55	5:17	I:364; II:807; 934; 935; IV:640, n24; **V:939;** VIII:219
		5:17f	II:776n2; 934; 935; V:939
5:11a	III:1087	5:18	II:795; III:615; V:529n262; 532
5:12	V:177; **181-182** (181n52, n58; 182n59, n61, n62, n64); 183n71; 461; 516n149; 889; VI:165n23; 686; VIII:569n59	5:19	I:242; 315; V:86; VI:243n77; 249n140; 252n163
		5:19f	VI:243; VII:721n14; 727
		5:20	I:295; 315; 327; 704; III:558; 699; V:86; VI:250n149; 279; VII:996; IX:154n68; **652**
5:13	II:539; V:937; VIII:499		
5:13f	II:776n2	5:20b	IX:652

I PETER

1:1	II:65; 102, n12; **103-104** (103n14); 509n38; III:517; 533; IV:190; V:30; 31(n211); 852; VI:111; IX:563		IV:647; 727; V:532; VI:665n89; VII:995(n133); VIII:141; IX:104f
		1:5	I:674; II:314; 427; 697; III:461; 583; IV:727; V:868; VI:208n255; VII:995; VIII:54
1:1f	II:273; IV:191		
1:2	I:113; 174; 224; 438; 540; 545; II:66; III:108n286; IV:175; 190; 191; 303; V:424n308; 1007n368; 1010; 1011n395; VI:282; 283; 434n678; 447, n794; 981; **983-984;** VIII:223, n49; IX:562; 563n451	1:5ff	IX:346n288
		1:6	I:20; II:230; 259; IV:1116; VI:29; 447; 485; IX:368n80
		1:6f	II:258; III:329; IV:320; 495; 1116; V:922; IX:368
		1:7	II:259; 587; 769; III:583; IV:727; V:868; VI:208(n255); 942; 948; 950n10; VIII:176; IX:562; 652
1:2f	IV:623		
1:3	I:460n17; 673; 674; 675; II:336; 483; 532; 533, (n119); 764; 862; 866; IV:727; V:1008, n375; 1011; **1013;** VI:983n41; VII:995(n133); VIII:331; IX:558n420; 562	1:8	I:20; 54(n160); II:866(n299); III:404n8; IV:1116; V:349; VI:210n266; 212; 214(n305); VIII:23n75; 54; IX:368n80; 563n454
		1:8f	IX:563
1:3f	II:428; III:783	1:9	I:674; IV:727; VI:208n255; VII:995; VIII:54; IX:650n210; 652, n221
1:3-12	VIII:501n89; IX:58		
1:3-4:11	I:672		
1:4	II:434; 538; III:781; 783n30;		

1:9f	IX:562n449
1:10	II:432; 657; 894; III:849; V:816; VI:829; VII:995; IX:399, n219
1:10f	VI:832; 843
1:10-12	II:86; VI:853
1:10ff	V:816n14; 934n25
1:11	I:73n31; 757; II:62; 248; 434; 657; III:461; IV:512; 727; V:708; 919; 925; 930; 932; 934, n25; 935; VI:832; 833; IX:562
1:11f	III:585; 590; VI:447; 833
1:11ff	II:720
1:12	I:64; 85; 175; 403; II:62; 540; 710n29; 720; III:43n7; 170; IV:1118, n73; V:531; 532; 815; 816; VI:718; IX:355n384
1:13	I:673; II:532; 533(n121); III:583; IV:727; 939, (n18), (n20); 967; V:496; 868; 901; VIII:75; IX:58; 399n219; 563
1:13f	IV:939(n15)
1:13-21	**V:901**
1:14	I:118; 119; 224, n3; II:925; III:171; 699; IV:939(n16); 967; V:639
1:15	I:109n67; 114; II:705; III:488; VII:717, (n9)
1:15f	I:101; IV:727; VII:1102n51
1:16	I:106; 112; V:869; VIII:74n36
1:17	I:674; III:497; 500; 939; V:30; 31(n211); 851n62; 852; 853; 869; 901; 995; 1006, n363; VI:780; VII:717; IX:216, n148; 591; 592
1:17ff	V:1010, n393
1:18	I:340; IV:351, n14; 522; V:901(n42); VII:717; 995; IX:104
1:18f	I:102; IV:350; V:901; VI:984n44
1:18-20	IX:5
1:19	I:108; 175; 338; 339n5; 340; 502; IV:831; V:900; IX:562; 563n451
1:20	I:202; 340; 715, n1; II:697; III:18n77; 620; 885; 1029; 1032; IV:190; V:360n219; 868; VI:685; 688; IX:591; 592; 593n71
1:21	I:674; II:67; 248; 335; 432; 531; III:101(n231), (n232); IV:893(n20); VI:204(n228); 208; 209n261; 210n269; 211n273; 214(n305), (n309); IX:563
1:22	I:54n165; 109n67; 123; 146; 224; 244; II:463; 464; III:425; 613; IV:727; VI:983; 984; **VIII:571;** IX:652
1:23	I:672n37; 673; 674; 676; 686; II:732; IV:116, n192; 117; 119; 575, n1; V:654; VII:542n22; 546; VIII:331; IX:104; 563
1:23f	VIII:571
1:23-25	I:672; II:720
1:23ff	I:676
1:24	II:237; VI:168; VII:143
1:24f	IV:575n1
1:25	I:199; 673; II:425; 710n26; 720; III:1087; IV:116; 117; 575
1:25b	I:646
2	I:647; III:251n9; VI:755
2:1	I:792; III:484; IV:4; V:30; VIII:570; 571
2:1f	IV:5; V:649; IX:563n451
2:1ff	II:273
2:1-10	III:250
2:2	I:363; 646; 672; 674, n5; 676; **IV:142;** 143; 659n52; 727; 920; 1117n67; V:30; 637; VII:995; VIII:331; 518, n13; 519n18
2:2f	I:647
2:3	I:647; 676; II:684; III:731n21; 1087; IV:5; V:30; VI:559n83; IX:487n20; 488; 489
2:3ff	V:126
2:4	II:260; IV:190; 275n63; 279; V:127; 733; 901n42; VII:442
2:4f	II:862n251; **IV:276-277** (277n70); 887n29; V:127
2:4-6	IV:275
2:4-7	V:127n31
2:4-8	IV:271; 278
2:4-10	III:247; IV:190; VIII:502n90
2:5	II:59; 68; III:182; 185; **250-251;** 265; 517; **IV:142;** 271; 279; 866n24; 887; V:121; 127; 142; 147; 148n3; VI:98; 437n706; 447; 755; VII:1102n51; VIII:176n36; IX:61; 563
2:5f	V:30
2:5-10	V:853
2:6	I:190; 372; 674; 751n7; 755; 792; II:816n1; IV:190; 272, n27; 277; V:30; VI:98; 204n218; 211; 214n303; 216(n317); 756; VII:327; 348; **353**, n82; VIII:157; 175n34
2:6f	VI:189n123
2:6-8	IV:277; VI:754; 755; **VII:353-354**
2:6-10	VIII:502n90
2:7	I:674; 792; 793; II:260; IV:191; 275n63; V:915n79; VI:11, n4; 214(n305); **VII:353**, n82; **VIII:175-176** (176n36)
2:7a	VII:353
2:7b	VII:353
2:7f	IV:272n27; VI:11; 95; 97; 98; 755; VII:353n79
2:8	I:793; II:428; IV:119; 191; 276; 277, n71; V:443n315; VI:11; 97; 98n35; 716n80; 746; 748; 751; 753n49; **754-756**

	III:332(n85); 481; 488; 781; 783; IV:294; 727; V:377; 557; 918; VII:995(n133); VIII:23
3:10	I:54(n162); 721; II:864(n270); 866n295; 953; III:49; 480n36; V:342; VII:700
3:11	II:230; 411; 417; VI:479
3:12	II:190; III:1087; V:378; 557; 869; VI:479; 777
3:13	II:888; III:484; IV:666
3:13ff	IV:322
3:13-18	III:20
3:14	II:199; 230; IV:368; 495; V:921; 922; IX:214; 600n67
3:14-17	V:922
3:15	I:112; 191; 194; 674; II:533(n118); 539; 706; III:613; IV:103; IX:562; 563, n453
3:16	I:17; 190; II:541; 824; IV:5; VI:650; VII:717(n9); 918; IX:216, n148; 562; 563
3:17	I:17; III:48; 59; 485; V:912n56; 921; 922, n129, n130; IX:368
3:18	**I:131-133** (131n2; 132n6); 151; 295; 315; 332(n118); 381; 589; II:189; 875; III:18n77; 21; 328n47; 707; IV:386n111; V:707; 708; 710n435; 918; 919; 921; 922; VI:55; 447, n800; 448; VII:143; 144n346; 995(n133); VIII:509; IX:544n335; 557n414; 562; 563; 575
3:18b	VI:417
3:18f	**VI:447-448**
3:18ff	III:708
3:18-22	IV:386n111; VI:417n555
3:19	I:148; II:424; 719; III:704; **707-708;** 747, n37; IV:386n111; V:868; 919n116; VI:447; 448; **577-578** (577n75, n78); VII:157n30; IX:244; 300
3:19f	II:559n13; **III:707-708** (707n46); 747; V:772
3:19ff	I:104; 149
3:19-22	VI:69n65
3:20	I:382; II:56; III:707; 747n36; **IV:386;** 587; V:126n30; 426; VI:11, n3; VII:990; VIII:253n34; IX:652
3:20f	I:540; IV:1116; **VIII:331;** 332n122
3:21	I:17; 540; 544; 545; 674; **II:688-689** (688n5); III:417n28; 430; 707; IV:386; 1116; V:444n423; 922; VII:130n249; 143; 918; 995; VIII:249; 253, n34; 330; IX:562
3:21f	V:919
3:22	II:39; 307; 424; 565; III:103(n248); 707; 1090; IV:8n6; 237n24; 727; V:524n216; 525, n222; 533(n303); 895; VI:447n800; 576; 577, n77; 718; VIII:42; IX:61; 544n335; 562; 563; 575
4:1	I:296; III:18n77; 404; 495; 582; 971; V:295; 710n435; 918; 919, n114, n116; 921; 922, n137; VI:436n692; IX:368; 562; 563
4:1a	VII:143
4:1b	VII:143
4:1f	III:20n82; **VII:143;** 144n346; IX:563
4:2	II:862n244; 921; 925; III:58; 171; V:922
4:2f	IX:592
4:3	I:166; 637; II:380, n3; 561; 682; 862n444; 925, n94; III:59; 171; 635; V:165n23; VI:145; 575
4:4	I:507; 623; V:2; 30; VI:447; VIII:233
4:5	II:167; 862(n260); III:943n6; IV:103; 893(n16); VI:448
4:6	I:149; 364; II:424; 429; 710n26; 719; III:747; V:772; 868; VI:435n691; 436n692; **447-448** (448n806); 577n75; 578n87; VII:143; 144n346
4:7	II:86; 331; 463; 804; III:884; IV:939, (n17); V:21; 868; VI:951; **VII:1102-1103;** VIII:55; 56
4:7f	II:486n8; IV:939(n15)
4:7ff	I:55(n167)
4:8	I:295; II:463; 826n52; III:558; IV:939(n19); V:889; VI:279; 686; VII:1103; IX:154n68
4:8f	V:21
4:9	I:736; III:299; 549; 550; V:20; 21
4:9f	III:299; V:21
4:10	II:86; III:550; IV:7; 939(n16); V:151; **VI:485;** IX:399n218; 406
4:10f	**IV:138-139;** IX:563
4:11	I:199; 337; II:68; 86; 248; III:331n79; 333n91; 399; 908; IV:139; V:151; VI:485
4:12	III:40; 147; V:2; 8; 30; 922, n130; **VI:30;** 153; 948; **951**
4:12f	IV:495; V:922; IX:396
4:12-14	**IX:368**
4:12ff	IV:322; 727; IX:653
4:13	I:20; II:248; III:144; 583; 806; IV:494; 495n60; 508; 727; V:823; 868; 922; 930; VI:30; 951; VII:995(n133); IX:366;

II PETER

1:7	I:54n165; 146	2:3a	VI:273
1:8	I:452; 707; III:446; 616; IV:623; V:859; VI:264; 265; IX:565	2:4	I:9; II:16; 17; 427; III:707; VI:578n84; VII:157n30; VIII:142
1:9	I:294; 295; II:816n1; III:429; V:717; VIII:287; 293	2:5	I:487; II:199; III:696; 886; 890; IV:798; VI:11n3; 577n83; IX:241
1:10	I:601; III:492; 495; **IV:180;** VI:479, (n107); 884; VII:565, n10	2:5f	VII:190
		2:6	II:33; III:951; VI:530; VII:191; 716n6; VIII:249; 258
1:11	I:209; 581; 582; 587; II:424; 586; IV:623; V:106; VI:329; VII:1018, n70; IX:565, n464	2:7	I:167; 490; II:189; VI:561; 1002; VII:184; 717
1:12	I:244; IV:677f; V:865; VII:656; **657**	2:8	I:563; II:189; 645; IV:1087; V:370n4; VII:184; IX:653
1:12ff	IV:679n4	2:9	I:151; II:427; 952; **III:814;** IV:727; VI:29n35; 30; 561; 1002; **1003;** VII:181; 184; VIII:142
1:13	I:349; II:185n26; 188; IV:677f; V:133; **VII:384**		
1:13f	V:28n191; 147; VII:382; **384**		
1:14	II:62; VI:111; **VII:384;** IX:565	2:10	I:509; 623; II:251; III:171; 632; 1097; IV:647; V:292; VII:143; VIII:185
1:15	III:185; **IV:679,** 4n; V:107; VI:479; VII:565		
1:16	I:215; 718; IV:542; 763; 765; 781; 784; 786; **789-791** (790n159; 791n164); V:348; 375, n15; 865; VI:262; **VII:527-528;** IX:565	2:10-12	I:623
		2:11	I:84; II:625n15; III:399; 941(n2), n2; V:732; IX:58; 299n100
		2:12	I:166; II:873; IV:141; VI:750; **IX:275-276** (276n246)
1:16-18	**IX:299**	2:12a	IX:103
1:17	I:54(n158); II:248; 434; 739; 740; III:941n2; IV:6; **543;** V:701; 710(n429); 1007; 1010; VI:116; VIII:175; **389;** IX:295	2:12b	**IX:103**
		2:13	I:55n169; 156; 161; 385; 678; II:910; 918; 919n59; 926; 948; III:171n36; IV:698; 830; IX:116n23
1:17a	VIII:389	2:14	I:295; 449; 775; II:926; III:613; IV:730; 734; V:377; 639; VI:273; 640n17; VII:141n318; 657; IX:658
1:17f	IV:784; V:375; VII:527; IX:58; 299n100		
1:18	I:106; V:348; 485; 530; IX:299		
1:19	I:352; 507; 602; II:820; 953; III:612; IV:27; 112; 327; 781; 786; 790; VI:830; IX:1; 312n6; 343	2:15	I:54(n162); 157; 215; 525; 705n67; II:741; IV:698; V:86; VI:250; VIII:233n49
		2:16	I:525; II:474; 476; **1090;** VI:828; 831; 855; IX:295
1:19f	VI:448n808	2:17	IV:903n6; VII:439; VIII:142
1:19-21	IV:784	2:18	I:490; III:171; 699; IV:523; VI:243; VII:143; 717
1:19ff	II:585		
1:20	I:704; 751n7; 755; IV:112; 337; **VI:833**	2:19	II:279; IX:104, n51
		2:20	I:707; II:697; IV:623; 647; VI:265n9; 867; VII:1018; IX:565
1:20f	VI:448n808; 830		
1:21	I:364n6; 757; III:59; IV:790; VI:346; 347; 448; 832; IX:58; 299n100	2:20f	VIII:144n34
		2:21	I:705; 706; II:171; 199; 555; V:86; 87; 90; **VII:726,** n18
2	III:988n108; VIII:185	2:22	I:248; III:1102; 1103; IV:302; **304-305;** V:751; 855; VI:250n146; VII:726; VIII:331
2:1	I:183, n11; 397; 469; **II:48-49; 160;** IV:53; V:456; 824, n2; 825n11, n14; VI:249; 272; 830; 855; VIII:595		
		3	IV:1114; V:516n140, n142; IX:275n241
2:1ff	I:470		
2:1-22	IX:275n243	3:1	I:114; 349; 743n5; II:398; IV:678; 967
2:2	I:215; 490; 624; V:86; 90; VI:272		
2:2a	VI:273n23	3:1-3	**IV:678**
2:3	I:397; 452; III:942; IV:101; 727; 785n139; 789; VI:262; **272-273**	3:2	II:555; IV:678; VI:833;

I JOHN

	VII:993n117; IX:5	3:19	**VI:3**
3:2b	IX:5n18	3:19f	II:355; III:612; **IV:538;** V:654;
3:2f	II:336		VI:3
3:3	I:122; 123; II:532; 533(n121);	3:19ff	II:554n34
	824; V:366	3:19-22	**VII:916**
3:4	I:306; **IV:1086;** VI:482; VII:346	3:20	I:703; III:613; VI:3
3:4f	I:295	3:20f	I:715
3:5	I:186; 295; 296; 305; 306;	3:21	II:824; 871; III:58; 939;
	III:318; 329(n59); IV:336;		IV:538n44; V:881; VI:3; 723
	1086; V:360n219; 364n229;	3:22	I:456; II:553n32; 554; IV:7;
	366; 708; 710; 711, n440;		V:881; VI:227; 482; VIII:145
	IX:5	3:23	II:554n34; 555; V:276; 881;
3:6	I:307; 333n123; 711; 712;		VI:203n221; 211; 214(n297);
	II:336; 543; III:317; 426;		VIII:387; IX:570
	IV:576; V:364n229; 365;	3:23f	VI:227; 228(n375)
	366n236	3:24	II:543; 553n32; 554n34;
3:6b	IV:1086		III:118n376; 808; IV:576;
3:6-10	VI:482n132		967; **V:881;** VI:448; VIII:145
3:7	II:189; 200; V:638; 639; 708;	4:1	II:16; 17; 260; 423; 679; III:889;
	VI:246; VIII:143n22		V:888; VI:830; 855; VIII:595
3:7ff	I:156; 671	4:1-3	VI:830; IX:571
3:7-10	VI:482	4:1ff	III:590; VI:855
3:8	I:295; 306; 481; II:79; 80; 645;	4:1-6	VI:448; IX:600n61; 602n84
	III:103; 329(n59); 1029;	4:2	II:674; VI:224n357; 226; 246;
	IV:336; V:360n219; VI:246;		423; 448n812; VII:140; 141;
	559; VII:158; 163; VIII:387;		252; IX:570; 571; 602n83
	IX:5; 570	4:2f	III:117; V:210, n34; 211n37;
3:9	I:307; 378; 665; 669n21; 671,		217; 218; VI:856; VII:145;
	n34; II:315; 336; III:317;		IX:571, n497; 577n526
	IV:336; V:653; 997n331;	4:3	II:16; 17; 674; III:889; 894;
	VI:439n731; 440n731;		IV:336; 1119; 1120;
	VII:545		V:210n34; VI:246, n103,
3:9f	IV:724; 1086		n104; 449; **IX:571-572**
3:9-24	V:654	4:4	III:894; IV:538; 945; V:639;
3:10	I:53(n154); II:79; 200; IV:740;		VI:246; VIII:82
	V:653; VI:559; VII:162; 346;	4:5	V:29; IX:129
	IX:3	4:6	I:247; 712; II:16; 17; V:526;
3:10f	VI:228(n375)		VI:245; 246; 368n170; 449;
3:11	**I:58-59;** 481; II:576n7; 734n83;		VII:261n412; 351
	IV:1086; V:348	4:7	I:53; 378; 665; 671;
3:12	I:7; II:189; 645; VI:557; 559;		III:112(n320); 317; V:272
	VII:162; 163; 934; IX:391	4:7f	I:53; 711
3:13	III:40; 895; IV:691	4:7-10	II:871
3:13-17	VI:228(n375)	4:7-21	VI:228(n375)
3:14	I:53n155; 333(n125); 523; 671;	4:8	I:711; III:112; 590;
	II:336; 425; 870; III:18; 19;		VII:444n189
	21; 654n3; 938; IV:576; 693;	4:9	II:423; 554n34; 870, (n326);
	V:869; VI:226; 246		III:317; 327(n38); 894;
3:14f	II:871		IV:740; 741, n16;
3:15	II:539; 820n30; 825; 870(n325);		VIII:355n125; **374-375**
	IV:576; 688n17; 692		(374n291); 386; IX:5; 570
3:16	I:53n151; III:18n77; 20n82;	4:9f	I:52; 53n151; 54n162; 711;
	112n320; 318; V:564, (n29);		V:365n233
	710, n435; VIII:511; IX:166,	4:10	I:295; 306; 711; III:18n77; 317;
	n162; 638; 644; 651		318; IV:741n16; V:708; 710,
3:16ab	VIII:155		n435; VIII:75; 386
3:16b	VIII:156	4:11	III:317; V:564, (n29)
3:17	I:53n155; II:166; 168(n2); 543;	4:11ff	I:53(n154)
	III:318; 889; IV:576;	4:12	II:543; V:344; 345; 365, n233;
	VII:577; VIII:143		1001n337; VIII:82; 143
3:18	I:53, (n156); 243; II:650; V:639;	4:12f	II:543
	VII:701; IX:157n95	4:12ff	III:118n376

4:13	II:537n11; 543; III:808; IV:967; VI:448
4:14	I:712; II:355; III:892; 894; IV:498; 741n16; V:342n140; 344; 345; 365n233; 999n320; VI:119n18; VII:1015; 1016; VIII:374n290; 385
4:14f	IV:498
4:15	II:543; IV:336; V:210; VIII:387; IX:570; 571
4:15f	V:1001n337
4:16	I:711; 713; II:355; 543; 826n52; III:68; 118(n376); IV:576; VI:210; 214(n293); 227
4:16a	VIII:75
4:16b	VIII:75
4:16ff	IV:724
4:17	I:205; II:336; 824; 871; 952; III:317; 318; 885; 889; 895; 938; 939; 941; **V:882; VII:778;** VIII:75; 82; IX:216
4:17f	**IX:216**
4:18	I:28n40; II:871; III:817; V:654, n102; **VIII:75;** 81; 82
4:19	I:53, (n150); III:74n43; IX:133n190
4:19a	VIII:75
4:19b	VIII:75
4:19-21	VIII:75
4:20	I:53(n153); IV:692; 693; V:345; 365; VII:444; IX:137n213; 602
4:20f	I:711; II:554; III:317; V:340n126
4:21	VI:228
4:21ff	II:554
5	IV:127n216
5:1	I:665; 671; II:554n34; IV:336; V:997n311; VI:210n263; 214n303; 223(n349); IX:129n161; 570; 571, n495
5:1-3	VI:228(n375)
5:2	II:553n32; IV:740; V:653; 654; VI:227; 478; 482
5:2f	VIII:145
5:3	**I:557-558** (557n3); II:553n32; 554; 555; VIII:145
5:3f	I:59
5:4	I:665; 671; II:554n34; III:588; 895; IV:945; V:314; 869; 997n311; VI:222; 227
5:4f	IV:945
5:5	III:895; IV:336; VI:210n363; 214(n303); 223(n349); VIII:387; **IX:571,** n495
5:5f	IX:570
5:5-11	IV:498
5:6	I:172n1; 715; 247; 540; II:66;
	538; 674; III:318; 731n21; IV:498; VI:144; 448; 984n44; VIII:329; **IX:571**
5:6a	VI:448n812
5:6b	VI:448n812
5:6f	IV:500
5:6-8	VI:448; IX:132
5:6ff	VII:330
5:6-9	VIII:333
5:7	IV:127n216; 498; V:513n109; VIII:221n40
5:7f	III:108; V:1003n349; VI:448; VIII:221; 330
5:8	I:175; II:434; IV:498; 500; V:365; VI:448n812; 984n44; VIII:237n13
5:8b	VIII:221
5:9	IV:500; 537; V:365; VIII:387
5:9f	IV:499
5:9-11	**IV:500**
5:9-12	IX:570
5:10	II:433; 539; IV:499; V:276; VI:208n258; 210(n266), n270; 214(n293); 479; VIII:387; IX:602
5:10a	IV:500
5:10f	IV:498
5:11	II:865(n292); 870(n322); VIII:387
5:11f	II:870(n325)
5:12	II:823; 825; VIII:143n19; 385
5:13	I:745n13; II:355; 825; 870(n325); V:271; 274; 276; VI:210(n266); 214(303); 223(n348); VIII:387
5:14	II:824; 871; III:58; V:881
5:14f	I:221; **V:881**
5:15	I:191n3; 192; 193; II:871(n328)
5:15ff	III:118(n378)
5:16	I:307; 308; 493; II:686; 806; III:426; IV:304; VI:55
5:16f	I:295; III:15n67; VI:725
5:17	I:156; 306; 307
5:18	I:378; 665; 671; II:336; III:654n3; 894; IV:724; 741, n18; V:997n311; VI:559; 879n47; VII:163; VIII:142; 143n20
5:18-20	IX:570
5:18ff	IV:724
5:19	I:155; III:654; 894; VI:559
5:20	I:249; 711; II:543; 865; 870(n322); 928; III:106; **IV:967,** n19; VI:439; **VIII:386;** 387; IX:241; 570; n491
5:21	II:378; III:100; V:639; IX:241

II JOHN

1	I:53n156; 243; 244; 246; **III:1095;** IV:191, n26; V:639; 650n89; VI:671; IX:137n214		246, n103, n105; 715; 855; **VII:140;** IX:570; 571, n497; 572
1-3	I:247	7ff	V:210
2	IV:576	8	II:890n14; III:1095; IV:700; VI:285n8; 286
3	II:484n100; V:996n308; 999n324; 1007n368; VII:778; VIII:223; IX:396n195; 399; 570	9.	**I:130-131;** II:823; III:118n376; IV:576; V:739; 999n325; 1001n337; VI:716, n81; VII:657; VIII:143n19; 385;
4	I:242; II:554; III:1095; V:114n28; 639; 650n89; 945; IX:367	9f	387; IX:570 II:164
5	I:481; 746; II:555; III:448; 449; 450; 1095; IV:1121	10 10f	I:499n26; 500; II:411; IX:58; 65 V:23; VI:670; IX:367n64
6	I:130; 481; II:553n32; 555n35; III:1095; V:945	11 12	II:645; III:804; VI:557 I:632n52; II:66; 530; IV:551;
7	I:130; II:423; 555; 674; 678; 679; III:117; 889; V:210; 218; 869n62; VI:224n357; 226;	13	VI:297; 605; VII:698; IX:370 I:501; III:1095; IV:191, n26; V:639; 650n89

III JOHN

1	I:243; VI:671; IX:137, n214		VII:874; **876**
2	II:776; 777; V:112; **114,** n26; 889; VI:54; VIII:312; **IX:651-652**	9 9f	II:52n10; **VI:670;** 671n121; 882n3 IV:666; V:23; VI:670
3	I:247; IV:496; IX:367	10	I:528; 632n53; II:52n10;
3f	I:242; V:114, n28; 945		III:699; IV:101;
4	II:826n54; V:639		VI:477(n102); 557; 671n121
5	I:53; III:550; V:2; 16; 22; VI:204n231; 477	11	I:17; III:486; IV:666; V:364n229; 365; 366n236
5f	VI:671n121	12	I:247, n39; 248; II:355n104;
5ff	III:549		IV:496; 500; 666;
5-8	VI:670		VI:443n763
6	I:380; 403; IV:496; VI:477; VII:566n12	13 14	IV:551 II:530; V:341(n138); VII:698
7	II:371; 372; 679; V:22; 273; 278; VI:671, n121; VIII:514	15	I:500; 501; II:411; IX:137; 162; **166**
8	I:247; IV:15; V:16; 20; 22; 564;		

JUDE

REVELATION

	264, n23; IX:572	1:13	IV:247, n42; V:188; 196; 307;
1:1f	II:28; VI:850		VI:721; 946; VIII:401;
1:2	II:28; IV:123, n209; 127; 495;		404n24; 461; **463-464**
	499; 500, n68; V:352; VI:849;	1:13-15	VI:997; VIII:37
	IX:572	1:13ff	II:632; III:104; VI:997
1:3	I:110n71; 343; 495; 745; II:28;	1:14	III:679; IV:27; **427;** V:377n13;
	331; III:461; IV:113; 123;		VI:946
	367; 369; V:352; 558; 869;	1:14f	IV:758
	VI:669n111; 830; 849; 853;	1:15	IV:263n4; VI:628n43; 946; 950;
	VIII:144n37; 145		VII:86; VIII:322n54; 324;
1:4	I:87; II:345n21; 398; 411; 632;		IX:292; 294; 296
	674; 821; IV:26; VI:450,	1:16	I:504, n9; II:305; III:911;
	n824, n825, n827; VIII:223;		IV:126n215; 249n51; 527;
	IX:155n79; 399; 572		V:297; 370n1; 709(n425);
1:4b	VI:450n827		VI:579; 765n66; **996-998;**
1:4f	III:107; VI:434n678; VIII:223;		VII:699; IX:1; 430
	372n268	1:16a	VI:997
1:4ff	II:632, n39	1:16b	VI:997
1:5	I:53; 175; 295; 308; 332(n118);	1:16ff	II:632
	489; 577; II:538; III:18; 813;	1:17	I:1; II:351; 355; 698; VI:163;
	IV:123; 127; 336, n9; 495,		169; **630;** 867; VIII:155n2;
	n61; 496; 893(n18); V:212;		IX:210n108; 432n44
	216; VI:529; **878;** 879; 880;	1:17f	I:202; III:342
	881n58; 984n44; VIII:369,	1:18	I:148, n14; 149; II:424;
	n248; 389; **IX:572-573**		537(n10); 865(n286), (n287);
	(573n509)		III:18; 746; 747; 750; IV:681;
1:5a	VIII:224		724; 893(n15); V:772;
1:5b	IV:303; VIII:224		VI:577n78; 928
1:5f	**IX:573**	1:18a	III:746
1:6	I:579; 590; III:249; 264, n30;	1:19	I:745; IV:824
	908; IV:725; V:996n308;	1:20	I:86f; 87; 504; II:617; 633;
	1008n380; VI:473; VIII:224;		IV:327; V:757n99; 853;
	IX:296; 558n420; 573		VI:450; 765n66
1:7	I:337; 678; II:399; 447; 674;	2f	I:86f; II:617; VI:853
	III:663; 834; 848; 850, n127;	2:1	I:504; III:911; IV:327; VI:449;
	IV:126; 909; V:347; 361; 378;		765n66
	523n199; 697n318; VII:237,	2:1ff	III:178
	n261; 238; 796; VIII:266n52;	2:1-3:14	I:745
	437n282; IX:250	2:2	I:446; II:769; III:829; IV:735;
1:8	I:1; II:345; 351; 398; 674;		VI:28; 669n110; IX:602
	III:915; 1087; IV:112; VI:71;	2:2f	IV:588
	VIII:55; 223	2:3	I:651n19; III:828; V:271
1:9	I:583; 587; II:355; III:143; 145;	2:4	I:53; 510; VI:165; 866
	148; 488; 783; IV:123; 127;	2:4f	II:877
	500; 501; 586; 588; V:934;	2:5	II:34; 364n14; 399; 674; III:718;
	VIII:224; IX:572		939; IV:327, n29; 683; 1004;
1:9b	III:289		VI:165; 479; 866; VII:735;
1:9ff	VI:849; **946-947**		**VIII:206**
1:10	II:28; 540; 950; **III:1096;**	2:6	II:827; IV:691, n30; 692; 693;
	IV:113; V:290; 352; 353; 373;		VI:250
	VI:449, n817; 851; VII:29;	2:7	II:695; 840n62; 855n181;
	85; 86; IX:292; 294; 298		864(n270); 866; III:104;
1:10f	II:28		IV:724; 945; **V:40,** n21; 352;
1:10-12	IX:296		558, n141, n142, n143;
1:10-13	IX:298		**769-770** (769n41); 772;
1:11	I:1n3; 618; 745; IX:298		VI:449; 450n822; VII:631;
1:11f	V:344		VIII:352n77
1:12	V:344n153; VII:726n19;	2:8	I:1; 202; II:698; 865(n286);
	776n58; IX:296		IV:893(n15); VI:449; 867
1:12f	IV:327	2:9	I:623; II:79; 827; III:147; 166;
1:12ff	IV:624; VII:86		382; VI:330; 911; VII:161;
1:12-20	IX:573		**828-830** (829n203)

2:9f	III:143; 145	2:26ff	V:1001n340
2:10	II:37; 864(n270); 866, n301;	2:27	VI:494; 501; 945n101; **968-969;**
	III:14; 147; 589; IV:724;		VII:362; 924; VIII:369n248
	725n113; V:352; 912, n58;	2:27a	VI:494n87
	919; VI:30; 204; VII:161;	2:27b	VI:494n87; 501
	629; **630-631** (630n76); 633;	2:27f	II:351
	IX:214; 244	2:28	I:504; IV:6; V:996n308;
2:10b	VI:30		VI:449n821
2:11	I:157; 159n6; 161; III:17;	2:29	V:558; VI:594n85; VIII:371
	IV:945; V:558; 729(n41);	3	I:403
	VI:449	3:1	I:87; 504; II:821; 825;
2:12	II:821; IV:527; V:297;		863(n267); IV:893; V:270;
	VI:996-998		VI:450; 693; 765n66
2:13	I:470; III:166; 912; IV:495;	3:1f	II:862(n248); IX:454n132
	499; 725; V:154; 279; 732;	3:2	II:339; 770; VI:605; VII:653;
	VI:204; 208; 210(n267);		656
	VII:161, n50; 292n4; 347n46;	3:2f	VI:31
	IX:573n509	3:3	I:703; II:338; 928; III:756, n7;
2:14	I:525, n11, n12, n13; II:143;		939; IV:683; 1004; VIII:145;
	144; 164; 379; 694; V:86;		451; IX:538n307; 679; 680
	VI:250; 594; VII:344; 345,	3:3a	III:756n6
	n36; 352n77; **356**	3:4	I:379; IV:249, n52; 250; 725;
2:14f	III:911		736; V:270; VII:691; 795
2:14ff	II:164n5	3:4f	IV:27; 245n25; 249; 724;
2:15	II:164; VI:250; VII:356		VII:691, n35; IX:607n19
2:16	II:34; 399; 674; III:939;	3:5	I:619, (n21); 620; II:864n284;
	IV:126n215; 527; 1004;		IV:250; 945; V:208, n27; 281;
	V:297; VI:514, n92; **996-998;**		769(n41); 996n308;
	VII:699		VI:451(n836); VII:690n26;
2:17	I:477; 703n61; 743; 745;		691; VIII:223; 372n268;
	III:449; 976; IV:27; 250; 462;		IX:164n151
	466; 724; 862n177; 945;	3:6	V:558
	V:281; 558; 769(n41);	3:7	I:101; 102; 249; II:821; III:174;
	VI:449(n820); **IX:606-607**		178; 748, n48; 749; 750;
2:18	IV:263n4; V:377n13;		955(n15); IV:867; VI:107;
	VI:628n43; 947; VIII:335;		**VIII:487**
	370; **371; 389**	3:7ff	**VII:631**
2:19	I:53; II:87; 697; 827; IV:587;	3:8	I:470; 513; II:555n37;
	588; 724; VI:208; 867		III:174n17; 178; 955(n14);
2:20	I:510; 788; II:143; 144; 273;		IV:107; 124; 655; V:279;
	379; 694; III:217; IV:501;		VII:631; 735; VIII:145
	VI:247; 250; 252n161;	3:8b	VII:631
	449n816; 829; 854; 855; 856;	3:9	I:53; 705; II:928; III:382;
	VII:356		VI:473; 629; 765, n66;
2:20f	VI:594		VII:161; **828-830** (828n196);
2:21	III:52; IV:1004; V:425; IX:591		829n203); IX:137n219; 602
2:21f	IV:999; 1004	3:10	I:678; II:555n37; 674; 827;
2:22	III:147; IV:729; 1004		III:136n11; 142n9, n14; 145;
2:22f	III:939; IV:724		IV:124; 586; 588; 724; V:153;
2:23	I:705; II:656n3; 657; III:338;		158; VI:30; 560; VII:161;
	612; 613; 941; **IV:911;** V:639;		386n9; 631; VIII:142; IX:677
	VI:947n101	3:10f	VII:735
2:24	I:517; 556, n9; 709; II:164;	3:11	II:34; 399; 827; III:911; VII:631
	VI:262; VII:161;	3:12	I:523; 746, n17; III:101(n227);
	VIII:604n24		247; 449; IV:724; 887; 889;
2:25	II:34; 827; 928; III:911		945; V:279, n233; 532;
2:25-28	I:671n33		769(n41); 1008n380; VI:473;
2:26	II:566; 643; IV:724; 945;		530; 532; 533; VII:327, n221;
	VIII:56; 146		337; 664; **735-736** (735n32)
2:26f	**VIII:390-391**	3:13	V:558
2:26-28	II:570; V:769(n41); VIII:371;	3:14	I:249; 337; 484; III:1028; 1029;
	389		1032; **IV:125;** 127; 495;

	IX:573n509
3:15	IV:496
3:15f	II:876
3:16	III:939; VII:699
3:17	I:126; 465; 775; VI:908n215; **911;** VIII:287; **293**
3:17a	VI:911
3:17b	VI:911
3:17f	VI:330
3:17ff	III:866n41
3:18	I:126; 190; 774n6; 775; III:333n89; 590; IV:27; 249n57; 725; V:343; 378; VI:911, n248; 942; 948; 950; VII:690n26; VIII:293; IX:5; 607n19
3:19	II:351(n77); 474; III:956; IV:1004; **V:623; IX:128;** 136; **137,** n219
3:19f	II:877
3:20	II:34; 678; 877; III:174; 178; 731n21; 954n3; **956;** IV:724; 725; V:365; VI:721; VII:648; 650; **796;** IX:137
3:20f	VIII:212
3:21	I:671n33; II:351; III:165; 166; 442; 1089; IV:237n24; 945; V:769(n41); 996n308; 1001n340; VII:795
3:22	V:558
4	III:165; 442n14; 1030; IV:761; VI:722; VI:656
4ff	V:352
4:1	I:521; II:23; 28; 538; III:177; IV:113; V:517n155; 522n189; 527n241; 530; VII:85; 86; 776n58; 962; IX:292; 298
4:1f	II:28; III:177; V:352
4:2	II:28; 538; III:165(n36); 177(n65); 654; V:353; VI:449; 851; VII:1089n599
4:2ff	I:341; III:442; V:366
4:3	**III:341-342** (341n9; 342n15, n17); 1030; IV:269; V:371, n6
4:3-7	III:165
4:4	III:166; 167; 444; IV:27; 249; VI:668; VII:631, n81; 690n26; VIII:127; 128; IX:607n19
4:5	I:87; 505; 640; II:632; 633; 821; III:1030; 1031; IV:26; 326n24; VI:450, n824, n828; 579; 947; IX:155n79; 296
4:6	III:342; V:290; 377n13; VI:451n837; 947; VIII:127; 134
4:6f	III:135n9; VIII:134n74
4:6ff	II:873
4:7	IV:252; 761; VI:775; VIII:134
4:7f	IV:760
4:8	I:100; 351; II:345n21; 398; 674; III:915; 1087; IV:761; V:214;

	377n13; VIII:127; 134; 223, n52; 225n71; IX:135n198; 439n13
4:8f	III:165
4:8-11	III:1029
4:9	II:248; 862(n256); III:165; 166; V:522n189; VIII:177; 224n62; IX:399n223; 411n43
4:10	III:165; 166; V:522n189; VI:163, n15; 668; 764; VII:631; 633
4:10f	III:165
4:11	I:379, n1; 397; II:307; III:56; 101(n226); 116n361; 1029; 1086; 1087; 1088; IV:6; V:214; 514n125; 888; VI:668; VIII:178, n50
5	III:1030; 1032; IV:491n51; VI:417n557
5:1	I:618n16; 745; III:165; V:290, n9; 522n189; VI:723; VII:950, n88, n89
5:1ff	II:632; 633; III:442
5:1-5	I:618
5:2	I:379; III:399; 703, n29; 704; 710; IV:335; VII:86; 950
5:3	I:678; 681n2; II:538; V:513(n118); 514n121, n123; 518
5:3f	V:343
5:4	I:379; II:355; 412; 770
5:5	IV:252, n17; 944; VI:668; 989; VII:950; VIII:485n47; 487; IX:249; 573n509
5:5f	I:341
5:5ff	IV:624
5:6	I:87; 341; 619; II:189; 632; 633; 821; III:134; 670, n10; IV:272; V:280; 377n13; 900; VI:450, n824; 668; VII:647; **934;** VIII:134
5:6ff	I:110; II:873
5:7	II:189; III:165; V:522n189; VI:152n32
5:7f	I:618
5:7ff	I:341
5:8	II:806; IV:249n56; 264n12, n15; VI:163, n15; 668; 669; VIII:127; 134; 496n48; 499n74
5:8-10	VI:668
5:8ff	I:341
5:8-14	III:1031
5:9	I:125; 164; 165; 175; 341; 379; 722; II:369n18; 538; III:449, n11; IV:52; V:214; 900; **VII:934;** 950; IX:250
5:9f	IV:725; VI:668
5:10	I:579; 590; III:249; 264, n30; 783; IV:725; V:214; VI:473
5:11	I:461; V:522n189; VI:668; IX:469

5:11ff	I:85
5:12	I:341; 379; II:305; 763; III:135; 399; 1089, (n259); IV:6; 127; V:214; 900; VI:330; VII:524; **934;** VIII:178; IX:293
5:12f	II:248; VIII:178
5:13	I:164; II:763; III:165; 634; 908; 1028; 1029; V:214; 513(n118); 514n123; 518, n161; 522n189; 895; VIII:133
5:14	I:336; II:806; VI:163; 668; 764; VIII:127; 134
6	IX:573n510
6:1	I:640; V:344; VII:950; VIII:134; IX:292; 294
6:1f	IV:872n250
6:1ff	IV:551; V:297
6:1-8	III:338; **VI:952;** VIII:134
6:1-8:1	IV:872n250
6:2	II:679; III:444; IV:27; 250, n63, n65; 944; VII:631
6:3	V:344; VII:664n48; 950
6:3f	VI:514
6:3-8	IV:944
6:4	II:679; III:102(n239); 813; IV:526; VI:952; 996; VII:935
6:4f	III:444
6:5	II:898; IV:551; V:344; VII:950; IX:430
6:5f	VI:15
6:6	I:161; II:471; 898; V:165; VI:848n425; VIII:134
6:7	V:344; VII:950
6:8	I:148n14; II:566; 567; 862n252; III:14(n62); 15; 134; 204; 746n32; IV:945; V:280; VI:15, (n24); 927; **996,** n22, n23, n25; 997; 998
6:8b	II:471
6:9	I:7n7; 149; III:137; 183; IV:123; 127; 500, n66; 501; VI:578n85; **VII:934-935;** 950; **IX:654;** 656
6:9-11	I:8
6:9ff	I:626
6:10	I:101; 102; 173; 249; 627n13; II:48; 399; 444; III:902; V:153; IX:293
6:11	I:350; IV:27; 249; 250, n61; 650n14; V:770n42; VI:294; 572; 605; VII:690n26; 691; IX:591; 592; 654
6:12	I:176; IV:551; V:515n135; 522n189; **VII:61,** n44; 198; 199; 430n49; 440n151; 574; 950
6:12ff	V:431
6:12-17	VIII:206n150
6:13	I:504; 527; IV:27; V:534; VI:163; VII:198; 691; 752; 757
6:14	I:618; III:1031; **V:486,** n120;

	515n135
6:14a	VII:757n60
6:14b	VIII:206, n150
6:15	I:577; V:483n96; VI:329; IX:466n2
6:15f	III:976; V:483; VI:97
6:15ff	V:439
6:16	III:165; 442; V:425; 429, n338; 522n189; VI:162; 777
6:16f	I:341; V:431; 438n393; VI:152n32
6:17	II:674; 952; IV:531; V:417n253; 429n338; 430; 431; VI:165n23; VII:61; 430n49; 648
7	VI:668; IX:249n26; 250; 573n510
7:1	I:679; 791; 792; III:911n4; VI:452; 943; VII:648; VIII:134, n75
7:1ff	II:324, n23
7:1-8	IX:417; 470
7:2	I:352; 596; III:902; **VII:951,** n91; IX:294n73
7:2f	I:161; VII:663; 664
7:3	II:273; IV:635; 636; VI:449n816; VII:951
7:3-8	VII:578n55
7:4	III:384; V:188; IX:469
7:4ff	**II:323-325**
7:4-8	VII:951; **IX:249**
7:5	VII:951n90
7:5ff	II:324n21
7:5-8	IX:469
7:7	IV:235; 237
7:8	VII:951n90
7:8-11	IX:454n132
7:9	I:149; 341; 722; II:226; 324n23; 369n18; IV:27; 50; 52; 249; V:586; 838; VII:648; 690n26; 691; IX:250; 430
7:9f	IX:249
7:9ff	II:324n23
7:9-17	IV:724; 872n250; V:771; VI:494n86
7:10	III:119(n381); 165; 902; VII:997; 998, n148; IX:293
7:10ff	III:442
7:11	VI:163, n15; 630; 668; 764; 776; VII:648; VIII:134
7:12	I:337; II:248; 307; 763; III:101(n226); 399; VII:524; VIII:178; 503n99; IX:399n223; 411n43
7:13	IV:27; 249; VI:668; VII:690n26; 691
7:14	I:174; 175; 341; II:538; 674; **III:144;** 145; 813; 1086; IV:27; 250; 336n8; 725; 946n3; VI:668; 984n44; VII:690n26; 691
7:14f	II:355

7:15	III:116(n364); 165; 247; IV:62; 63; 888; V:533; 535(n326); VII:377; 378n59; 381, n74; 385; 386; 387	9:5	I:563; IV:641, n25, n26; VII:87; VIII:261n14
7:15f	IV:724	9:5b	III:668
7:15ff	IV:249	9:5f	VI:514
7:16	II:226; III:643; VI:22; 163n10	9:6	II:769; III:14; 170; VII:87
7:16f	**VI:22**	9:7	III:338; 668; V:191; VI:514; 775; VII:631
7:17	III:165; IV:318n25; 320; 466; V:100; 377, n13; VI:43n22; 494; VIII:317n24; 325; 326n80	9:7-9	V:309n8
		9:7ff	III:337
		9:8	IV:252
		9:9	III:338; V:309, n8; VI:514; VIII:233; IX:292
8ff	II:821	9:10	I:161; II:567; **III:668;** IV:641
8:1	II:538; V:530; VI:494n86; VII:950	9:10b	III:668
8:2	I:87; III:102(n239); 165n36; VI:450n824, (n825); VII:85; **87;** 648	9:11	**I:4;** 9; 10; 397; 577; II:16; 17; 508; III:389; V:270; 280; VI:749; VII:87
8:2ff	II:632	9:12	VII:87
8:2-14:20	IV:872n250	9:12f	IX:672
8:3	I:110; III:177n56; 183; IV:27; 264	9:13	III:183; 669; VII:87; IX:298
		9:13f	IX:298
8:3f	IV:264n15; 677n9	9:14	I:596; VI:604; VII:85
8:3-5	IV:676n9	9:14f	IV:336; VIII:134
8:3ff	I:626	9:15	II:426; 706; 950; IV:641; VI:603n67; VII:87; 708; VIII:220n33; IX:677
8:4	I:110; 519(n4); IV:264n12; IX:430		
8:5	I:505; 640; II:422; III:183; IV:264; VI:941; VII:199; IX:296	9:16	III:338
		9:16ff	III:135
		9:17	III:135n10; 338; 444; IV:252, n14; V:309; 371; 580, n151; **VI:951-952**
8:6	I:87; VII:85		
8:7	I:176; VI:936; 943; VII:87	9:17f	III:135n10; VI:579; 943
8:7f	VI:604n70	9:17-19	VII:699
8:7ff	I:678; VI:603	9:18	V:580; VI:603n67; 951; VII:87; VIII:220n33
8:7-12	VIII:220n33		
8:8	I:176; V:486; VI:943	9:19	I:161; II:567; III:338; **V:580**
8:8f	VII:87	9:20	II:17; 378; 645; IV:269n9; VI:764n59; VI:347n46; IX:430
8:9	II:819; III:1028; IX:102; 653		
8:10	I:504; IV:26; 326n24; V:534; VI:115; 163; VII:440; VIII:317n24	9:20f	IV:999; 1004; VII:87
		9:21	II:17n120; VI:594
		10:1	**III:341-342** (341n9; 342n15, n16); 399; IV:908; V:533; VI:629; 776; 947; VII:736
8:10f	VI:115; 603; VII:87; VIII:325		
8:11	VI:115; 124, n8	10:1f	VI:628n43
8:12	I:504; II:948; IV:1125; VII:87; 430n49; **440,** n151, n152; VIII:261; IX:1	10:2	I:617; IX:430
		10:3	III:902; IV:252; IX:292; 293; 294; 296
8:13	V:153; VII:85; VIII:325; 605n30; IX:294, n73	10:3f	I:640; II:632; 633
8:13b	IX:292	10:4	I:618; 745; V:531; VII:950; IX:296; 298
9	II:17; III:338		
9:1	I:9; 10; 504; III:746, (n27), n28; V:534; VI:163; VII:87	10:5	I:185; V:534; VII:648; IX:430
		10:5f	V:184n78; IX:430
9:1f	I:10; VI:116n17	10:6	I:678; 679; II:862(n256); III:116(n367); 884; 1028; 1029; V:184; 514n123; 515; IX:591; 592
9:1ff	I:10n6; II:17; III:135; 746; IV:515; VI:927		
9:1-11	VII:157n30; 158n32		
9:2	I:9; 10; 519(n4); VII:61; 87; 440	10:7	I:59n3; II:273; 710n25; 721; 950; IV:123; 501; 824; VI:449n816; 669n111; 849; VII:87; VIII:59
9:3	II:567; III:668; VI:952		
9:3ff	I:10; V:309n8		
9:4	I:161; IV:635; 636; VII:578n55; **951**		
9:4f	VII:87	10:8	I:617; V:531; VII:648;

776n58;VIII:505n8; IX:298; 430

10:8f	IX:298
10:8ff	III:341; IV:888; V:235n53
10:8-11	VII:700
10:9	II:695; III:787n6; VI:124n9
10:9f	I:617; 619; III:787; IV:553; VI:124
10:10	IX:430
10:11	I:577; 722; II:369n18; 370; IV:50; 52; 888; VI:829; 853
11	II:939; VI:531; **VII:336**
11f	V:439
11:1	II:334; III:183; IV:633; **887-888;** VI:765; 849; **967-968**
11:1f	IV:634; 888, n31; VII:336
11:1ff	III:247; IV:888n32
11:1-4	I:619
11:1-13	IV:327n28; VII:336n284
11:2	I:105; 528; II:632n40; 934n52; IV:633; 641; V:943; VI:530, n71; 531; VII:327; 336; IX:469
11:3	II:632n40; 933; 934n52; 936; IV:495; 499; 551; VI:829; 853; 943; VII:61; **62-63** (62n52; 63n56, n60); IX:469
11:3ff	II:933; 938, n82; n89; **939-941;** III:220n16; IV:488n38; 858(n117); 859n127; **863-864** (863n189); 867n214; 872n248; V:912n54
11:3-6	II:940
11:3-12	VI:112
11:4	I:679; III:1087; IV:327; 863; VII:648
11:5	I:161; II:695; 813; 935; IV:863(n189); VI:158; 579; 943; VII:62; 699
11:6	I:176; II:434; 566; 570; 934; 939; III:47n44; 177; 745; 750; IV:863n189; V:529n262; 532; 940; VI:830; 943; VII:380n70; 715; VIII:261; 268; 315; 325
11:6a	VII:62
11:6b	IV:863n189; VII:62
11:7	I:9; 10; II:934; 940; III:134; 135; IV:500; 502; 944; V:714n469; VI:465; 514; VIII:59
11:7-12	III:135
11:8	III:488; 1092; V:68n84; VI:167; 449; 531; VII:336, n283; IX:470
11:8f	VI:166; 167n3
11:8-10	II:940
11:9	I:722; II:369n18; 934n52; 953; IV:50; 52; 680; IX:250
11:9a	VI:167
11:9b	VI:167

11:9ff	II:632n40
11:10	II:166; 774; IV:863n189; V:153; VI:669n111; 829; VII:62; VIII:325; IX:366
11:11	II:434; 537n11; 862(n254); 934n52; 940; 953; VI:164; 449; 628; VII:647; IX:210
11:11f	IV:863
11:12	II:813; 940; IV:724; 909; V:345; 522n196; 525n218; 531; 533; 534n315; 537n15; IX:298
11:12f	VII:66n7
11:13	I:679; IV:595, n11; V:270; 520; VI:162; VII:199; 336n283; IX:470; 679
11:14	VII:87
11:15	I:580; 581; 590; II:538; 750; III:886; 1087; V:214; 530; IX:298; **573**
11:15ff	VII:87
11:16	III:444; VI:163, n15; 630; 668; 764; 776
11:17	I:590; II:345n21; 398; 674; III:915; 1087; IX:399n223; 411
11:17f	II:307; V:214; VI:668; VIII:502
11:18	I:110; II:674; III:461; IV:501; 531; 650(n13); 700; 724; V:272; 279; 420; 421; 423n295; 430; 438, n393; 439; 679n167; VI:449n816; 669n111; 849; 850; VII:582; IX:102; 212n127
11:18b	IX:103
11:19	I:505; 640; II:132n103; 538; III:247; IV:888, n33; V:352n182; 354n192; 527n241; 529n261; 530; 533; VII:199; 375; 377; 386; IX:296
12	II:17; 80; 282; 413; 568; IV:643n12; V:280; 533n308; 581; VIII:206; 363n201
12f	V:581n154
12:1	II:323; 538; IV:27; V:352n182; 354n192; 517n155; 530n269; VI:629; VII:230; 243; 631; VIII:363
12:1ff	II:568; IV:624
12:1-9	I:619n20
12:1-17	VIII:363n201
12:2	I:563, n13; III:902; IX:673
12:3	II:281; 282; 538; 632, n41; III:670; 813; V:352n182; 354n192; 530n269; 533n305; VI:247n118; 952; VII:243; 631; 856n1
12:4	I:504; II:281; V:530n269; 534; VI:603n67; VII:637; 648; VIII:220n33;
12:4a	VII:157n30
12:5	I:472; II:323; III:116(n364);

	165n36; V:638; 688n252; VI:494, n87; 501; **968-969;** VII:157; VIII:363; 369n248; 371; 389; 390n408
12:6	II:632n40; 659; 705n8; 886; 934n52; 935; IV:872n248; VI:159; VII:378n59; VIII:206; IX:469
12:7	II:16; 281; 538; V:517n155; 530n269; 533; VI:514, n92
12:7a	VI:514n92
12:7b	VI:514n92
12:7ff	**V:533**
12:7-12	**VII:157**
12:7-18	IX:544n333
12:8	II:538; 770; III:397; V:533; 540n12; VIII:207
12:9	I:487, n4; 505n3; 606; II:79; 80n49; 281; 282n14; III:488; 636; V:159; 580; VI:163n11; 247, n118; 248, n128; 252n164; VII:158, n32; 161; 162n52
12:9f	V:533; IX:573
12:10	I:374; 583; 589; II:79; 80; 307; 413, n71; 538; 568; 750; III:119(n381); 636; 637; IV:1107n8; 1112; V:439n397; 528; 530; 533; 541; 812n90; VII:157; 161; 997; 998, n148; IX:298; **573**
12:10f	IV:1119
12:10-12	V:214
12:10-ff	II:307
12:11	I:53; 174; 175; III:14; 696; IV:123; 127; 500; 502; 945; V:900; VII:161; IX:128n150; 130n163; 573n509; 638; 653
12:12	II:80, n49; 774; III:148; 168; 461; 1032n208; V:214; 420; 513(n107); 533; VI:163n11; VII:157; 161; 377; 378n52; 386, n9
12:13	II:281; V:342; 530n269; 533; VIII:363n201
12:13-18	VIII:363n200
12:14	II:632n40; 659; 934n52; 935; III:461; IV:641n27; 872n248; VI:777; VIII:206; IX:469
12:14f	V:580
12:15	II:282; V:290; VI:465; 604; 607n2; **608;** VII:699; **VIII:325**
12:16	I:628; 679; II:281; VI:158; 159; VII:698
12:17	II:281; 323n18; 555, n37; III:1095; IV:500; 501; V:420; 439; VI:225n364; 248; 465; 514; VII:161; 545; VIII:145; 325; 363
12:18	VIII:363n199
13	I:515; II:80; III:120; 121n12;

	134; IV:257; VI:151; VII:161; 336, n282; VIII:31; IX:571
13ff	V:441
13:1	I:624; II:632; III:670; V:280; 515n132; VII:631; 856n1
13:1-7	I:619n20; VII:699
13:2	II:80; 281; 308; 568; III:134, n7; 166; IV:252, n14; V:487; VI:628n43; 629
13:3	II:429; III:14n62; 38n46; 41; 131; V:292; VII:934, n43, n44
13:3f	VI:514
13:3ff	III:135
13:4	II:281; 308; 568; III:41; VI:514n92; 764n59; 765
13:4f	III:135
13:4-8	II:886
13:5	I:624; II:568; 632n40; 934n52; IV:641; VI:151; 465; VII:699; IX:293; 469
13:6	I:622; 624; V:280; 524n208; VI:723; **VII:377-378** (378n52, n53; 379n60); 381; 386, n9
13:7	I:110; 722; II:369n18; 566; 568; IV:50; 52; 944; VI:465; 514; VII:161; IX:250
13:7f	VII:346
13:7-10	III:135
13:8	I:341; 619; 620; II:864(n283); III:620; 885; 1029; 1032; V:153; 281; VI:151; 764n59; 765; **VII:934**
13:9	V:558
13:10	I:110; 195; IV:27; 525; 588; 725; V:870; VI:208n253; 996; VII:699n63
13:11	I:341; II:283; III:135; 669; 670, n13; VI:248n122; VII:524
13:11ff	III:134; 135; VI:855
13:11-18	I:619n20; **IX:416-417**
13:12	II:568; III:14n62; 131; V:153; VI:465; 764n59; 765
13:12a	VI:465
13:12b	VI:465
13:12-17	VII:346
13:13	III:714(n68); V:532; VI:856; 943; VII:245
13:13ab	VI:465
13:13f	VI:248; VII:243
13:14	IV:27; 525n14; V:153; VI:248; 476; 996; VII:245; 254n365; **255**
13:14a	VI:465
13:14f	II:388; VI:248
13:14ff	VII:245
13:15	II:388; VI:449; 484; 764n59; 765; VII:524; IX:416
13:15-17	VI:248
13:16	IV:531; **635-637** (635n1);

	650n13; VI:329; 465; 908n216; 911; VII:524; IX:430
13:16f	VII:578n55; 660; 664; 708; IX:416; 417
13:17	I:461; 462; 596; IV:183; V:280; VI:13n10
13:18	I:461; **462-464;** II:819; IV:958; 959; VII:524; **IX:417; 607,** n24
14	IV:257n14; V:441; VI:668
14ff	V:444
14:1	I:341; 596; 746; IV:635; 736; V:279; 996n308; 1001n340; VI:765n66; VII:327; 336; 578n55; 648; 664; 795; IX:470
14:1ff	II:323; IV:724
14:2	I:216; 640; V:531; VIII:322n54; 324; 496n48; IX:292; 294; 298
14:2f	I:486
14:3	I:125f; 149; 164; 165; 680; III:449; **IV:407-408** (408n136); VI:668; 765n66; VIII:134; 325; IX:470
14:4	I:125f; 214; 486, n12; 653, n29; IV:724; 725; 736; 737n3; **V:836;** VIII:505n6
14:4b	VI:494
14:5	II:770; IV:737n3; 831; VII:700; IX:603
14:6	I:59n3; 208; 678; 722; II:369, n18; 710n25, n31; 721; 735n84; III:444; IV:52; IX:250
14:6f	II:735
14:7	I:678; II:674; III:884; IV:724; V:514n123; 515; VI:115; 116n17; 152n32; 463; 765; 766n74; VIII:317n24; 325; IX:212n127; 294, n73; 677; 678n24
14:8	I:514; II:370; III:168, n8; IV:257; 724; V:165; 166, n30; 437, n384; 438; 439; 487(n122); VI:151, n28, n29; 152, n30, n31; 160; 162; 594; 595, n87
14:8-20	II:886
14:9	II:388; 865(n286); IV:257; 635; VI:151n28; 764n59; 765; IX:294, n73; 417; 430
14:9f	I:101; VI:151
14:9-11	VII:660
14:9ff	IV:257; V:439
14:10	I:100; 341; III:168; 226; IV:257; 724; **V:165,** n29; 166; 399n133; 422; 429; 430; 434; 437, n384; 438n393; VI:144; 151, n29; 152, n32; 946; VIII:223; IX:164n151

14:10b	VI:151
14:10f	V:444
14:11	I:351; II:388; IV:257; V:434; VI:764n59; 765; IX:417
14:12	I:110; II:555, n37; III:289; IV:588; VI:204(n230); 208n253, n257; 210(n267); 225n364; VIII:145
14:13	I:110n71; 216; 350; 745; II:541; 648; II:20; 829; IV:27; 367; 368; 369; 724; 1119; V:531; 867n50; VI:449, (n820); 572; VII:34n4; **796;** IX:298
14:14	III:679; IV:27; 250; 255; 256, n9; V:188; VI:399n426; VII:631; VIII:401; 404n24; 461; **463-464;** IX:430
14:14-16	IV:256n9; 910
14:14ff	III:442
14:14-20	IV:255, n6; 257n14; V:869; VI:399n426
14:15	II:674; III:133; 247; 902; IV:888; IX:294n73; 677; 678n24
14:15f	III:132
14:15ff	II:679
14:17	II:538; III:247; IV:255; 256, n9; 888; V:527n241
14:17ff	IV:256n9; 257; 724
14:18	II:566; 567; III:183; IV:256; VI:399n426; 943; IX:294, n73; 303
14:18f	IV:256
14:18ff	V:438n390
14:19	III:168; IV:256, n11; 724; V:165; 422; 439; VI:152n32
14:19f	**IV:255-257;** V:438
14:20	I:109; 176; II:680n4; III:339; IV:256, n8, n9; V:438; 943; IX:470
14:20a	IV:255
14:20b	IV:255
15f	V:431
15ff	II:821
15:1	II:538; 697; III:41; V:422; 437; 517n155; 530n269; VII:243; VIII:59
15:1ff	II:632; IV:724
15:1-16:21	IV:872n250
15:1-20:15	IV:872n250
15:2	II:388; II:944; V:280; VI:947; VII:648; VIII:496n48; 499n74
15:2-4	III:135; 292; IV:724; 872n250
15:3	I:164; 165; 249; 577; II:184; 188; 273; 367; 370; 371; 641; III:41; 915; IV:407; 848n1; 864; **872;** V:90; 681n183; VIII:499n74
15:3f	V:214; VIII:502
15:4	II:222; 370; 928; V:272; 279; 491; VI:765; IX:5; 212n127

	VI:479; VIII:59
17:18	I:514; 516; 577; 580; VI:151
18	I:515; IV:113; VI:43
18:1	II:251; 567; III:102(n239); V:533; IX:356
18:1ff	III:725n22; IV:724
18:2	I:514; II:19; III:398; 428(n12); 902; IV:692; V:155; 531n275; VI:162; 449; VII:354n90; IX:244; 294, n73
18:2f	II:886
18:3	I:577; 678; III:168; 631; V:165; 166; 437, n384; 438; 487n122; VI:139; 144; 151; 152, n31; 248; 330; 594; VII:354n90
18:4	I:308; III:699; 804; IV:54; 55, n103; V:531, n275, n277
18:4f	I:295
18:4-20	IX:298
18:5	I:163; 308; III:822; IV:677; V:519; 534
18:6	II:167f; V:437n384; VI:151; 152, n30
18:7	I:590; III:442; 612; 631; V:342; VI:43; IX:458; 459n173
18:7f	VI:42
18:7ff	I:563
18:8	I:515; II:862n252; 928; 948; III:14(n62); 398; 1087; VI:15; 941; IX:458
18:8ff	II:435(n4)
18:9	I:577; III:631; 725; 834; 845n100; 850n126; 851, n128; VI:594; 951
18:9ff	III:722
18:9-19	I:515n10; II:886
18:10	I:514; II:674; III:399; IV:373; VII:647; VIII:372n270; IX:210; 680
18:11	III:724; 850n126; VI:42n16; 43
18:11ff	III:724n17
18:11-14	III:339
18:11-19	I:515n11
18:12	III:813; 814; IV:246n32; 269, n11; 473; V:38; VII:362
18:13	II:471; III:339; IV:263n3; 264, n15; 801; V:165; VI:690; VII:458n8; 1058; IX:653
18:14	II:770; III:171; IV:17
18:15	III:724; IV:373; V:270; VI:42n16; 43; 330; IX:210
18:16	I:514; III:813; 814; IV:27; 246n32; 269; 273
18:17	II:635; III:1035; IV:373; VI:330; VII:647; VIII:203; IX:458; 680
18:18	I:514; V:188; VI:951
18:18f	III:902
18:19	I:514, n1; III:724; VI:42n16; 43; 330; IX:458; 680
18:20	I:109; 110; II:774; III:942; V:533; VI:669n111; 849; 850
18:21	I:514; 516; III:398; 399; IV:269, n4; V:470-471
18:21f	II:770
18:22	III:844n96; VII:85; 88; IX:292
18:23	II:17n120; IV:327n30; 1099n1, (n3); VI:248; 252n166; IX:1; 1f; 293
18:24	I:110; 173; 515n6; 678; II:770; V:487n122; 714n469; VI:248; 849; 850; VII:935
19	IV:255; 256; 257, n14
19:1	I:264; II:413; 538; 750; V:530; 533; 586; VII:997; 998; IX:292
19:1f	II:307; 413n71; IV:724; V:214
19:1ff	I:85
19:2	I:173; 249; 514; 515; II:188; 273; 444; IV:501; VI:248; 449n816; IX:103; 431(n40)
19:3	I:264
19:4	I:264; 337; III:165; 442; VI:163; 668; 764; VIII:127; 134
19:5	I:177; II:273; III:101(n226); IV:531; 650n13; V:214; 531(n277), n277; VI:449n816; IX:212n127; 291n60; 298
19:6	I:264; 590; 640; II:750; III:915; 1087; V:586; VIII:322n54; 324; IX:292; 294
19:6-8	V:214
19:7	I:20; 776; II:674; IV:1099; 1105; 1106n57; V:214; VI:605; IX:366
19:7f	II:472
19:7ff	I:655
19:8	I:110n71; II:222; III:424n74; IV:27; 246n32
19:9	I:110n71; 249; 341; 745; II:34; III:488; 489n1; IV:123; 368; 369; 724; 1105; VI:849; VIII:212n33
19:9a	IV:123
19:10	I:85; 514; II:355; III:102; IV:123(n210); 500, n67; VI:163, n13, n15; 449, n816; 629; 669, n111; 764; 765, n66; 830
19:10c	IV:501, n69
19:11	I:249; II:198; 538; III:177; 339; 444; 488; IV:27; 127; 250, n65; 872n250; V:525; 527n241; 530; VI:152n32; 513; 514, n92; VII:962
19:11ff	I:505; 626n21; IV:256, n9; V:429; VI:997
19:11-14	III:813
19:11-15	III:336n2
19:11-16	III:338n11; 339; IV:126, n215; 257; V:869; VII:632
19:11-21	V:297; IX:573n511

19:12	III:449; 679; IV:126; V:273; 279; 280; 377n13; VI:947; VII:631; 856n1		501; 635; VI:578n85; 668; 764n59; 765; 995n15; VII:660; 795; IX:417; 430; 470; **573; 654;** 656n231
19:13	I:175; 530; III:134n7; 488; 588; 813; IV:82n58; 123; 124; 125; **126-127** (126n215); V:273; VI:981, n24; VII:690n26; 708	20:4f 20:4-6 20:5	I:149n15; II:866 I:790; VI:513 I:371; II:872; IV:27; VIII:60; IX:470
19:13-15	VIII:375n297; 389n398	20:5f	I:372; VII:1084n532
19:14	II:60; 319; 538; III:339; 424n74; IV:27; 246n32; 249n56; 250, n65; 256n9; V:533; VII:708	20:6	I:110n71; 371; 590; II:566; 831n4; III:17; 264; 283; IV:369; 596; 597, n17; VII:795; IX:470; **573**
19:14a	IV:27		
19:14b	IV:27		
19:15	III:168; 339; 915; IV:126; **255-257;** 527; V:165; 166; 422; 429; 430; 431; 437, n384; 438, n393; 709n425; **940;** 943; VI:152, n32; 494, n87; 501; 579; **VI:968-969; 996-998** (997n29, n30; 998n31); VII:699; VIII:369n248; 371; 389; 390n408	20:7 20:7f 20:7-10 20:8	I:148; IV:336, n8; VII:161; VIII:60; IX:244; 470 VI:927 I:790; VI:531 I:679; 791; 792; II:679; VI:159; 247; 248; 513; 514; VIII:134, n75
		20:8f 20:8-10	**I:789-791;** VI:248; 514 IX:470
19:16	I:341; 577; IV:126; 256n9; V:273; 956n57; VI:514; VII:631; 708; IX:573	20:9	I:53; 110; 792; V:532; VI:398(n417); 530; 945; VII:327
19:17	II:34; III:902; IV:530; VII:648	20:10	I:148; 658; II:424; III:134;
19:17f	II:695		IV:257; V:434; 440; 444; 770;
19:17ff	II:940n105; III:671; IV:257		VI:247; 248; 399n418; 514;
19:17-21	IV:257		855; 946; VII:158; 161; 162;
19:18	IV:531; 650n13; VII:124; IX:466n2		347
		20:10ff	VI:513
19:18f	I:577; III:444	20:11	I:679; III:165; 442; 1031;
19:19	I:486; 577; VI:465; 514; VII:708		IV:27; 250; V:486; 514n124; 515; 516n141, n142; VI:777; VIII:207
19:19a	VII:708		
19:19b	VII:708	20:11ff	I:505; II:16(n119)
19:20	I:148; 658; II:388; 424; III:134; IV:256; 257; VI:248; 399n418; 465; 764n59; 765; 855; 856; 946; VII:243; 254n365; **255;** 660; IX:417	20:11-15 20:12	I:790; III:939; IX:470 I:619; 620; II:864n284; IV:531; 650n13; 724; VII:648; 1084n532
		20:12f	IV:724; VI:152n32
19:21	I:468; III:444; IV:527; **VI:996-998;** VII:124; 699	20:13 20:13f	I:148; IV:893; IX:654 I:149; III:15; 746n32
20	I:489n5; 790n2; VII:789n107; **IX:470-471**	20:14	I:148; 392; 396; 620; III:14; 17; IV:257; V:434; VI:399n418; VII:158
20:1	I:9; 10; 618n15; III:746, (n28); V:533; IX:430	20:14f	I:148; 658; II:424; VI:946
20:1-3	III:746; VI:248n123; VII:745, n8	20:15 21	I:619; II:770; 864n284; IV:257 IV:183; **VI:532-533;** VII:326
20:1ff	VI:514	21f	V:767n19
20:1-10	VII:20n156	21:1	I:678; III:449; 885n64; 1032;
20:2	I:487; II:60; 281; III:911; V:580; 770; VII:161; 162n52; IX:470		V:514n123, n124; 515; 516n142; 517n155; VI:866, n8; VII:381
20:2f	I:148	21:1ff	I:790; VI:513
20:3	I:9; 10; II:424; IV:27; 336; 650n14; VI:247; 248; 927; 946; VII:745; 950; 953; VIII:60; IX:470; 591	21:1-7 21:1-22:5 21:2	IX:573 IX:470 I:363; 515n7; 523; 655; III:116n365; 247; 449; 867;
20:4	I:590; 618n15; II:16(n119); 388; III:163; 165; 289; 443; 783; 923n4; 942; IV:123; 127; 500;		IV:1099(n3); 1105; V:514n121; 532, n298; 770; VI:531; 532; 533; VII:336;

	351; 698; IV:467; VI:867;	22:17	I:655; II:167; 226; 399; 674;
	VIII:55		IV:277n73; 466; 724;
22:14	I:110n71; II:555; 566; 569; 678;		1099(n3); 1105; VI:117; 347;
	864(n270); III:178n70; 1103;		449(n820); **450;** 595;
	IV:369; 946n3; **V:40;** 770,		VIII:325; IX:459
	n42; VI:479; 530; 533; 921;	22:18	IV:123; 496; 499; VIII:160
	VII:327; 690n26; 691;	22:18f	I:618; 744; II:355; VI:669n111;
	VIII:325n77		830; 850; IX:241
22:14f	IX:603	22:19	I:745; II:864(n270); IV:123;
22:15	II:17n120; 380; III:1103; 1104;		596; 597; **V:40;** 770, n42;
	VI:85n14; 479; 595; IX:128;		VI:530; 853; VII:327;
	129; 136; 138		VIII:325n77
22:16	I:504; 685; II:351, (n79);	22:20	I:337; II:399; 674; III:737;
	III:289; 748; IV:17; 27; 499;		IV:471; 499; V:869; IX:459
	624; VI:989; VII:86;	22:21	VII:778; IX:399
	VIII:485n47; 487, n55		

CONTRIBUTORS AND CO-WORKERS

Alswede, Hans, Pastor; b.8.27.1914 Hamburg; Assist. Prof. Hamburg (KH) 1947

Balz, Horst, Prof.; b.3.21.1937 Leipzig; D. Theol. Erlangen 1966; Instructor Kiel 1969; Prof. Kiel 1972, Bochum 1974

τέσσαρες, τέταρτος, τεταρταῖος, τεσσεράκοντα, τεσσερακον-ταετής	VIII:127-139
ὕπνος, ἀφυπνόω, ἐνύπνιον, ἐνυπνιάζομαι, ἔξυπνος, ἐξυπνίζω	VIII:545-556
φοβέω, φοβέομαι, φόβος, δέος	IX:189-197 205-219

Bammel, Ernst (no data at his own request)

Bannach, Horst, Pastor; b.4.14.1912 Allenstein (East Prussia)

Bauernfeind, Otto, Prof.; b.1.14.1889 Behrenhoft, Kr. Greifswald; Lic. Theol. Greifswald 1914; Instructor Greifswald 1922; Assoc. Prof. Greifswald 1928, Tübingen 1931; Prof. Tübingen 1946; d.12.26.1972

ἀναπαύω, ἀνάπαυσις, ἐπαναπαύω	I:350-351
ἁπλοῦς, ἁπλότης	I:386-387
ἀρετή	I:457-461
ἀσέλγεια	I:490
αὐθάδης	I:508-509
καταπαύω, κατάπαυσις	III:627-628
μάταιος, ματαιότης, ματαιόω, μάτην, ματαιολογία, ματαιολόγος	IV:519-524
μάχομαι, μάχη, ἄμαχος, θεομάχος, θεομαχέω	IV:527-528
νήφω, νηφάλιος, ἐκνήφω	IV:936-941
νικάω, νίκη, νῖκος, ὑπερνικάω	IV:942-945
πανουργία, πανοῦργος	V:722-727
πόλεμος, πολεμέω	VI:502-515
ῥαδιούργημα, ῥαδιουργία	VI:972-973
σαπρός, σήπω	VII: 94-97
σής, σητόβρωτος	VII:275-278
στρατεύομαι, στρατεία, στρατιά, στράτευμα, στρατιώτης, συστρατιώτης, στρατηγός, στρατόπεδον, στρατολογέω	VII:701-713
στρουθίον	VII:730-732

τρέχω, δρόμος, πρόδρομος	VIII:226-235
τυγχάνω, ἐντυγχάνω, ὑπερεντυγχάνω, ἔντευξις	VIII:238-245

Baumgärtel, Friedrich, Prof. Emeritus; b.1.14.1888 Plauen (Vogtland); Lic. Theol. Leipzig 1916; Instructor Leipzig 1916; Assoc. Prof. Leipzig 1921; Prof. Rostock 1922, Greifswald 1928, Göttingen 1937, Erlangen 1941

καρδία	III:605-607
πνεῦμα	VI:359-368
σάρξ	VII:105-108
σῶμα	VII:1044-1045

Behm, Johannes, Prof.; b.6.6.1883 Doberan (Mecklenburg-Schwerin); Lic. Theol. Erlangen 1911; Instructor Erlangen 1912; Assist. Prof. Breslau 1913; Assoc. Prof. Königsberg 1916; Prof. Königsberg 1932, Göttingen 1923, Berlin 1935; d.10.13.1948

αἷμα, αἱματεκχυσία	I:172-177
ἄμπελος	I:342-343
ἀνάμνησις, ὑπόμνησις	I:348-349
ἀνατίθημι, προσανατίθημι, ἀνάθημα, ἀνάθεμα, κατάθεμα, ἀναθεματίζω, καταθεματίζω	I:353-356
ἀποφθέγγομαι	I:447
ἀρραβών	I:475
βρῶμα, βρῶσις	I:642-645
γεύομαι	I:675-677
γλῶσσα, ἑτερόγλωσσος	I:719-727
δεῖπνον, δειπνέω	II:34-35
διατίθημι, διαθήκη	II:104-106 124-134
διψάω, δίψος	II:226-227
ἐκχέω, ἐκχύν(ν)ω	II:467-469
ἔξω	II:575-576
ἑρμηνεύω, ἑρμηνεία, ἑρμηνευτής, διερμηνεύω, διερμηνεία, διερμηνευτής	II:661-666
ἐσθίω	II:689-695
ἔσω	II:698-699
θύω, θυσία, θυσιαστήριον	III:180-190
καινός, καινότης, ἀνακαινίζω, ἀνακαινόω, ἀνακαίνωσις, ἐγκαινίζω	III:447-454
καρδία, καρδιογνώστης, σκληροκαρδία	III:608-614
κλάω, κλάσις, κλάσμα	III:726-743
κλῆμα	III:757
κοιλία	III:786-789

κυρόω, ἀκυρόω, προκυρόω   III:1098-1100
μορφή, μορφόω, μόρφωσις,
    μεταμορφόω   IV:742-759
νέος, ἀνανεόω   IV:896-901
νῆστις, νηστεύω, νηστεία   IV:924-935
νοέω, νοῦς, νόημα, ἀνόητος,
    ἄνοια, δυσνόητος, διάνοια,
    διανόημα, ἔννοια, εὐνοέω,
    εὔνοια, κατανοέω,
    μετανοέω, μετάνοια,
    ἀμετανόητος, προνοέω,
    πρόνοια, ὑπονοέω,
    ὑπόνοια, νουθετέω,
    νουθεσία   IV:948-980
        989-1022
παράκλητος   V:800-814

Bertram, Georg, Prof.; b.3.14.1896 Charlottenburg;
Lic. Theol. Berlin 1921; Instructor Berlin 1923; Prof.
Giessen 1925, Frankfurt 1955

ἁμαρτάνω, ἁμάρτημα,
    ἁμαρτία   I:286-289
διψάω   II:227-229
ἔθνος, ἐθνικός   II:364-369
ἔργον, ἐργάζομαι, ἐργάτης,
    ἐργασία, ἐνεργής, ἐνέργεια,
    ἐνεργέω, ἐνέργημα,
    εὐεργεσία, εὐεργετέω,
    εὐεργέτης   II:635-655
ζωή, βίος   II:851-854
ζυγός   II:896-898
θάμβος, θαμβέω, ἔκθαμβος,
    ἐκθαμβέομαι   III:4-7
θαῦμα, θαυμάζω,
    θαυμάσιος, θαυμαστός   III:27-42
θεοσεβής, θεοσέβεια   III:123-128
καλός   III:550-556
κατεργάζομαι   III:634-635
κρεμάννυμι (κρεμάω),
    κρέμαμαι, ἐκκρέμαμαι   III:915-921
κρούω   III:954-957
μακάριος, μακαρίζω,
    μακαρισμός   IV:364-367
μυκτηρίζω, ἐκμυκτηρίζω   IV:796-799
μωρός, μωραίνω, μωρία,
    μωρολογία   IV:832-847
νήπιος, νηπιάζω   IV:912-923
ὁρμή, ὅρμημα, ὁρμάω,
    ἀφορμή   V:467-474
παιδεύω, παιδεία, παιδευτής,
    ἀπαίδευτος, παιδαγωγός   V:596-625
παίζω, ἐμπαίζω,
    ἐμπαιγμονή, ἐμπαιγμός,
    ἐμπαίκτης   V:625-636
παρίστημι, παριστάνω   V:837-839
πᾶς, ἅπας   V:890-892
πατέω, καταπατέω,
    περιπατέω, ἐμπεριπατέω   V:940-943
σαλεύω, σάλος   VII:65-70
σκολιός   VII:403-408
στενός, στενοχωρία,
    στενοχωρέω   VII:604-608

στερεός, στερεόω,
    στερέωμα   VII:609-614
στρέφω, ἀναστρέφω,
    ἀναστροφή, καταστρέφω,
    καταστροφή, διαστρέφω,
    ἀποστρέφω, ἐπιστρέφω,
    ἐπιστροφή, μεταστρέφω   VII:714-729
συνεργός, συνεργέω   VII:871-876
συντρίβω, σύντριμμα   VII:919-925
ὕβρις, ὑβρίζω, ἐνυβρίζω,
    ὑβριστής   VIII:295-307
ὑπερήφανος, ὑπερηφανία   VIII:525-529
ὕψος, ὑψόω, ὑπερυψόω,
    ὕψωμα, ὕψιστος   VIII:602-620
φρήν, ἄφρων, ἀφροσύνη,
    φρονέω, φρόνημα,
    φρόνησις, φρόνιμος   IX:220-235
φυλάσσω, φυλακή   IX:236-244
ὀλιγόψυχος   IX:665-666
ὠδίν, ὠδίνω   IX:667-674

Betz, Johannes, Prof.; b.8.20.1914 Redwitz/Rodach; D.
Theol. Tübingen 1953; Instructor Tübingen 1957;
Assoc. Prof. Bamberg 1958; Prof. Mainz 1963,
Würzburg 1967

Betz, Otto, Prof.; b.6.8.1917 Herrentierbach, Kr.
Crailsheim; D. Theol. Tübingen 1959; Instructor
Tübingen 1961; Prof. Chicago 1962, Tübingen 1967
σικάριος   VII:278-282
στίγμα   VII:657-664
φωνή, φωνέω, συμφωνέω,
    σύμφωνος, συμφωνία,
    συμφώνησις   IX:278-309

Beyer, Hermann Wolfgang, Prof.; b.11.12.1898 Anna-
rode (Mansfelder Gebirgskr.); Lic. Theol. Jena 1925;
Instructor Göttingen 1925; Prof. Greifswald 1926,
Leipzig 1936; d.3.10.1943

βλασφημέω, βλασφημία,
    βλάσφημος   I:621-625
διακονέω, διακονία, διάκονος   II:81-93
ἐπισκέπτομαι, ἐπισκοπέω,
    ἐπισκοπή, ἐπίσκοπος,
    ἀλλοτριεπίσκοπος   II:599-622
ἕτερος   II:702-704
εὐλογέω, εὐλογητός,
    εὐλογία, ἐνευλογέω   II:754-765
θεραπεία, θεραπεύω,
    θεράπων   III:128-132
κανών   III:596-602
κατηχέω   III:638-640
κυβέρνησις   III:1035-1037

Bieder, Werner, Prof.; b.7.21.1911 Basel; D. Theol.
Basel 1940; Instructor Basel 1947; Assoc. Prof.
Basel 1957

πνεῦμα   VI:368-375
ῥίπτω, ἐπιρίπτω, ἀπορίπτω   VI:991-993
σκυθρωπός   VII:450-451

Bietenhard, Hans, Prof.; b.5.31.1916 Gösgen (Switzerland); D. Theol. Basel 1944; Instructor Bern 1947; Assoc. Prof. Bern 1962

| ὄνομα, ὀνομάζω, ἐπονομάζω, ψευδώνυμος | V:242-283 |
| πνίγω, ἀποπνίγω, συμπνίγω, πνικτός | VI:455-458 |

Böhlig, Alexander, Prof.; b.9.2.1912 Dresden; D. Phil. Berlin 1936; D. Theol. Münster 1947; Instructor Munich 1951; Assist. Prof. Munich, Würzburg, Erlangen, 1951; Prof. Halle 1954 (Leipzig 1957); Prof. Tübingen 1964

Boendermaker, Pieter, Prof.; b.8.8.1893 Amsterdam; Doctorate Leyden 1930; Prof. Amsterdam 1946

Bornkamm, Günther, Prof. Emeritus; b.10.8.1905 Görlitz; Lic. Theol. Marburg 1931; Instructor Königsberg 1934; Assist. Prof. Heidelberg 1936, Bethel 1937; Assoc. Prof. Göttingen 1947; Prof. Heidelberg 1949

λάχανον	IV:65-67
λεῖος	IV:193
λεπίς	IV:232-233
ληνός, ὑπολήνιον	IV:254-257
λικμάω	IV:280-281
λύκος	IV:308-311
μυστήριον, μυέω	IV:802-828
πρέσβυς, πρεσβύτερος, πρεσβύτης, συμπρεσβύτερος, πρεσβυτέριον, πρεσβεύω	VI:651-683
σείω, σεισμός	VII:196-200

Braumann, Georg, Pastor; b.5.3.1931 Bochum; D Theol. Münster 1960

| ψῆφος, ψηφίζω, συμψηφίζω (καταψηφίζομαι), συγκαταψηφίζομαι | IX:604-607 |

Braun, Herbert, Prof. Emeritus; b.5.4.1903 Warlubier (West Prussia); Lic. Theol. Halle 1929; Assist. Prof Berlin (KH) 1947; Prof. Berlin (KH) 1949, Mainz 1953

περπερεύομαι	VI:93-95
πλανάω, πλανάομαι, ἀποπλανάω, ἀποπλανάομαι, πλάνη, πλάνος, πλανήτης, πλάνης	VI:228-253
πλάσσω, πλάσμα, πλαστός	VI:254-262
ποιέω, ποίημα, ποίησις, ποιητής	VI:458-484

Büchsel, Hermann Martin Friedrich, Prof.; b.7.2.188? Stükken (Potsdam); Lic. Theol. Halle 1907; Instructor Halle 1911; Assoc. Prof. Greifswald 1916; Prof Rostock 1918; d.5.2.1945

| ἀγοράζω, ἐξαγοράζω | I:124-128 |
| ἀλλάσσω, ἀντάλλαγμα, ἀπ-, δι-, καταλλάσσω, | |

καταλλαγή, ἀποκατ-, μεταλλάσσω	I:251-259
ἀλληγορέω	I:260-263
ἄλλος, ἀλλότριος, ἀπαλλοτριόω, ἀλλογενής, ἀλλόφυλος	I:264-267
ἀντί	I:372-373
ἄνω, ἀνώτερον, ἄνωθεν	I:376-378
ἀρά, καταράομαι, κατάρα, ἐπικατάρατος, ἐπάρατος	I:448-451
βαστάζω	I:596
βοηθέω, βοηθός, βοήθεια	I:628-629
γενεά, γενεαλογία, γενεαλογέω, ἀγενεαλόγητος	I:662-665
γεννάω, γέννημα, γεννητός, ἀρτιγέννητος, ἀναγεννάω	I:665-666 668-675
γίνομαι, γένεσις, γένος, γένημα, ἀπογίνομαι, παλιγγενεσία	I:681-689
δέω (λύω)	II:60-61
δίδωμι, δῶρον, δωρέομαι, δώρημα, δωρεά, δωρεάν, ἀπο-, ἀνταποδίδωμι, ἀνταπόδοσις, ἀνταπόδομα, παραδίδωμι, παράδοσις	II:166-173
εἴδωλον, εἰδωλόθυτον, εἰδωλεῖον, κατείδωλος, εἰδωλολάτρης, εἰδωλολατρία	II:375-380
εἰκῇ	II:380-381
εἰλικρινής, εἰλικρίνεια	II:397-398
εἰμί, ὁ ὤν	II:398-400
ἐλέγχω, ἔλεγξις, ἔλεγχος, ἐλεγμός	II:473-476
ἐριθεία	II:660-661
ἡγέομαι, ἐξηγέομαι, προηγέομαι, διήγησις	II:907-909
θυμός, ἐπιθυμία, ἐπιθυμέω, ἐπιθυμητής, ἐνθυμέομαι, ἐνθύμησις	III:167-172
ἱκετηρία	III:296-297
ἵλεως, ἱλάσκομαι, ἱλασμός, ἱλαστήριον	III:300-301 310-318 319-323
ἱστορέω (ἱστορία)	III:391-396
κατήγορος, κατήγωρ, κατηγορέω, κατηγορία	III:636-637
κάτω, κατωτέρω, κατώτερος	III:640-642
κεῖμαι, ἀνά-, συνανά-, ἀντί-, ἀπό-, ἐπί-, κατά-, παρά-, περί-, πρόκειμαι	III:654-656
κρίνω, κρίσις, κρίμα, κριτής, κριτήριον, κριτικός, ἀνακρίνω, ἀνάκρισις, ἀποκρίνω, ἀνταποκρίνομαι, ἀπόκριμα, ἀπόκρισις, διακρίνω, διάκρισις, ἀδιάκριτος, ἐγκρίνω, κατακρίνω, κατάκριμα, κατάκρισις, ἀκατάκριτος,	

αὐτοκατάκριτος,
πρόκριμα, συγκρίνω III:921-923
933-954
λύω, ἀναλύω, ἀνάλυσις,
ἐπιλύω, ἐπίλυσις,
καταλύω, κατάλυμα,
ἀκατάλυτος, λύτρον, ἀντί-
λυτρον, λυτρόω, λύτρωσις,
λυτρωτής, ἀπολύτρωσις IV:328-356
μονογενής IV:737-741

Bultmann, Rudolf, Prof. b.8.20.1884 Wiefelstede (Olden-
burg); Lic. Theol. Marburg 1910; Instructor Marburg
1912; Assoc. Prof. Breslau 1916; Prof. Giessen 1920,
Marburg 1921; d.7.31.1976

ἀγαλλιάομαι, ἀγαλλίασις I:19-21
ἀγνοέω, ἀγνόημα, ἄγνοια,
ἀγνωσία, ἄγνωστος I:115-121
αἰδώς I:169-171
αἰσχύνω, ἐπαισχύνω,
καταισχύνω, αἰσχύνη,
αἰσχρός, αἰσχρότης I:189-191
ἀλήθεια, ἀληθής, ἀληθινός,
ἀληθεύω I:238-251
ἀναγινώσκω, ἀνάγνωσις I:343-344
ἀνίημι, ἄνεσις I:367
ἀφίημι, ἄφεσις, παρίημι,
πάρεσις I:509-512
γινώσκω, γνῶσις, ἐπιγινώσκω,
ἐπίγνωσις, καταγινώσκω,
ἀκατάγνωστος,
προγινώσκω,
πρόγνωσις, συγγνώμη,
γνώμη, γνωρίζω, γνωστός I:689-719
δηλόω II:61-62
ἔλεος, ἐλεέω, ἐλεήμων,
ἐλεημοσύνη, ἀνέλεος,
ἀνελεήμων II:477-487
ἐλπίς, ἐλπίζω, ἀπ-,
προελπίζω II:517-523
529-535
εὐλαβής, εὐλαβέομαι,
εὐλάβεια II:751-754
εὐφραίνω, εὐφροσύνη II:772-775
ζάω, ζωή, (βιόω, βίος),
ἀναζάω, ζῷον, ζωογονέω,
ζωοποιέω II:832-843
849-851
855-875
θάνατος, θνήσκω,
ἀποθνήσκω,
συναποθνήσκω,
θανατόω, θνητός, ἀθανασία
(ἀθάνατος) III:7-25
ἱλαρός, ἱλαρότης III:297-300
καυχάομαι, καύχημα,
καύχησις, ἐγκαυχάομαι,
κατακαυχάομαι III:645-654
λύπη, λυπέω, ἄλυπος,
περίλυπος, συλλυπέομαι IV:313-324
μεριμνάω, προμεριμνάω,
μέριμνα, ἀμέριμνος IV:589-593

νεκρός, νεκρόω, νέκρωσις IV:892-895
οἰκτίρω, οἰκτιρμός,
οἰκτίρμων V:159-161
πείθω, πεποίθησις,
πειθός, πειθώ, πεισμονή,
πειθαρχέω, ἀπειθής,
ἀπειθέω, ἀπείθεια VI:1-11
πένθος, πενθέω VI:40-43
πιστεύω, πίστις, πιστός,
πιστόω, ἄπιστος,
ἀπιστέω, ἀπιστία,
ὀλιγόπιστος, ὀλιγοπιστία VI:174-182
197-228
φαίνω, φανερός, φανερόω,
φανέρωσις, φαντάζω,
φάντασμα, ἐμφανίζω,
ἐπιφαίνω, ἐπιφανής,
ἐπιφάνεια IX:1-10

Burger, Ewald, Pastor; b.5.18.1905 Stuttgart; D. Theol.
Tübingen 1933; d.6.30.1942

Colpe, Carsten, Prof.; b.7.19.1929 Dresden; D. Phil.
Göttingen 1955; D. Theol. Göttingen 1960; Instructor
Göttingen 1960; Assist. Prof. Göttingen and Ham-
burg 1960; Prof. Göttingen 1962, Berlin (FU) 1969

ὁ υἱὸς τοῦ ἀνθρώπου VIII:400-477

Conzelmann, Hans Georg, Prof.; b.10.27.1915 Tailfingen
(Württemberg); D. Theol. Tübingen 1952; Instructor
Heidelberg 1952; Assoc. Prof. Zurich 1954; Prof.
Zurich 1956, Göttingen 1960

σκότος, σκοτία, σκοτόω,
σκοτίζω, σκοτεινός VII:423-445
συνίημι, σύνεσις, συνετός,
ἀσύνετος VII:888-896
φῶς, φωτίζω, φωτισμός,
φωτεινός, φωσφόρος,
φωστήρ, ἐπιφαύσκω,
ἐπιφώσκω IX:310-358
χαίρω, χαρά, συγχαίρω,
χάρις, χαρίζομαι, χαριτόω,
ἀχάριστος, χάρισμα,
εὐχαριστέω, εὐχαριστία,
εὐχάριστος IX:359-376
387-415
ψεῦδος, ψεύδομαι, ψευδής,
ψεῦσμα, ψεύστης, ἀψευδής,
ἄψευστος IX:594-603

Cullmann, Oscar, Prof. Emeritus; b.2.25.1902 Strassburg; Lic. Theol. Strassburg 1930; Prof. Strassburg
1930, Basel 1938 (Strassburg 1945, Paris 1948)

πέτρα VI:95-99
Πέτρος, Κηφᾶς VI:100-112

Dammann, Ernst, Prof. Emeritus; b.5.6.1904 Pinneberg;
D. Phil. Kiel 1929; Instructor Hamburg 1939; Prof.
Hamburg 1949, Berlin (Humboldt-Univ.) 1957,
Marburg 1962

Debrunner, Albert, Prof.; b.2.8.1884 Basel; D. Phil. Basel 1907; Instructor Zurich 1917; Assoc. Prof. Greifswald 1918; Prof. Bern 1920, Jena 1925, Bern 1935 (Basel 1940); d.2.2.1958

λέγω, λόγος, ῥῆμα, λαλέω   IV:69-77

Deissner, Ernst Ferdinand Kurt, Prof.; b.4.10.1888 Frohse/Elbe; Lic. Theol. Greifswald 1912; Instructor Greifswald 1915; Assoc. Prof. Greifswald 1919; Prof. Greifswald 1920; d.11.6.1942

μετεωρίζομαι   IV:630-631
μέτρον, ἄμετρος, μετρέω   IV:632-634

Delling, Gerhard, Prof. Emeritus; b.5.10.1905 Ossa (Saxony); Lic. Theol. Leipzig 1931; Instructor Greifswald 1948; Prof. Halle 1950

αἰσθάνομαι, αἴσθησις,
    αἰσθητήριον   I:187-188
ἀλαζών, ἀλαζονεία   I:226-227
ἀνεξερεύνητος   I:357
ἀντιλαμβάνομαι, ἀντίλημψις,
    συναντιλαμβάνομαι   I:375-376
ἀποκαραδοκία   I:393
ἀργός, ἀργέω, καταργέω   I:452-454
ἄρτιος, ἐξαρτίζω, καταρτίζω,
    καταρτισμός, κατάρισις   I:475-476
ἄρχω, ἀρχή, ἀπαρχή,
    ἀρχαῖος, ἀρχηγός, ἄρχων   I:478-489
βασκαίνω   I:594-595
βατταλογέω   I:597
γόης   I:737-738
ἐγκομβόομαι   II:339
ἐρευνάω, ἐξερευνάω   II:655-657
ἡμέρα   II:947-953
θριαμβεύω   III:159-160
καιρός, ἄκαιρος, ἀκαιρέω,
    εὔκαιρος, εὐκαιρία,
    πρόσκαιρος   III:455-464
κολοβόω   III:823-824
λαμβάνω, ἀναλαμβάνω,
    ἀνάλημψις, ἐπιλαμβάνω,
    ἀνεπίλημπτος, κατα-,
    μεταλαμβάνω, μετάλημψις,
    παρα-, προ-, προσλαμβάνω,
    πρόσλημψις, ὑπολαμβάνω   IV:5-15
μάγος, μαγεία, μαγεύω   IV:356-359
μήν, νεομηνία   IV:638-642
νύξ   IV:1123-1126
ὀσμή   V:493-495
παρθένος   V:826-837
πίμπλημι, ἐμπίμπλημι,
    πλησμονή   VI:128-134
πλεονάζω, ὑπερπλεονάζω   VI:263-266
πλεονέκτης, πλεονεκτέω,
    πλεονεξία   VI:266-274
πλῆθος, πληθύνω   VI:274-283
πλήρης, πληρόω, πλήρωμα,
    ἀναπληρόω,
    ἀνταναπληρόω,
    ἐκπληρόω, ἐκπλήρωσις,
    συμπληρόω, πληροφορέω,

πληροφορία   VI:283-311
σκόλοψ   VII:409-413
στάσις   VII:568-571
στοιχέω, συστοιχέω,
    στοιχεῖον   VII:666-687
σύζυγος   VII:748-750
συλλαμβάνω   VII:759-762
συμβιβάζω   VII:763-766
τάσσω, τάγμα, ἀνατάσσω,
    ἀποτάσσω, διατάσσω,
    διαταγή, ἐπιταγή,
    προστάσσω, ὑποτάσσω,
    ὑποταγή, ἀνυπότακτος,
    ἄτακτος (ἀτάκτως),
    ἀτακτέω   VIII:27-48
τέλος, τελέω, ἐπιτελέω,
    συντελέω, συντέλεια, παν-
    τελής, τέλειος, τελειότης,
    τελειόω, τελείωσις,
    τελειωτής   VIII:49-87
τρεῖς, τρίς, τρίτος   VIII:216-225
ὕμνος, ὑμνέω, ψάλλω,
    ψαλμός   VIII:489-503
ὑπάλω   VIII:504-506
ὑπεραυξάνω, αὐξάνω   VIII:517-519
ὑπερβάλλω, ὑπερβαλλόντως,
    ὑπερβολή   VIII:520-522
ὑπερέχω, ὑπεροχή   VIII:523-524
χρόνος   IX:581-593
ὥρα   IX:675-681

Denker, Jürgen, Pastor; b.12.24.1942 Potsdam; D. Theol. Kiel 1972

Dihle, Albrecht, Prof.; b.3.28.1923 Kassel; D. Phil. Göttingen 1946; Instructor Göttingen 1950; Prof. Göttingen 1957, Cologne 1958

ψυχή   IX:608-617
    632-635
    656-658
ψυχικός   IX:661
ἀναψύχω, ἀνάψυξις   IX:663-664
ὀλιγόψυχος   IX:665-666

Egg, Gottfried, Pastor; b.5.12.1934 Lauben/b. Memmingen; D. Theol. Erlangen 1966

Egli, Johann Karl, Prof. Emeritus; b.9.22.1891 Vienna; D. Theol. Vienna 1951; Prof. Vienna 1952

Fichtner, Johannes, Prof.; b.7.14.1902 Reichenbach/ OL; Lic. Theol. Breslau 1929; Instructor Greifswald 1930; Prof. Greifswald 1937; Assoc. Prof. Greifswald 1939; Assist. Prof. Bethel 1949; d.7.1.1962

ὀργή, ὀργίζομαι, ὀργίλος,
    παροργίζω, παροργισμός   V:392-412
ὄφις   V:571-576
πλησίον   VI:312-315

Fitzer, Gottfried, Prof. Emeritus; b.5.3.1903 Gross-Bresa, Kr. Breslau; Lic. Theol. Breslau 1928;

Instructor Breslau 1931; Assist. Prof. Erlangen 1948; Prof. Vienna 1949

σκιρτάω	VII:401-402
στίλβω	VII:665-666
σύνδεσμος	VII:856-859
σφραγίς, σφραγίζω, κατα-	
σφραγίζω	VII:939-953
τολμάω, ἀποτολμάω,	
τολμητής, τολμηρός	VIII:181-186
φθάνω, προφθάνω	IX:88-92

Foerster, Werner, Prof. Emeritus; b.7.23.1897 Rheydt; Lic. Theol. Münster 1923; Instructor Münster 1925; Assoc. Prof. Münster 1931; Prof. Münster 1959

ἀήρ	I:165-166
ἄξιος, ἀνάξιος, ἀξιόω,	
καταξιόω	I:379-380
ἀρέσκω, ἀνθρωπάρεσκος,	
ἀρεσκεία, ἀρεστός,	
εὐάρεστος, εὐαρεστέω	I:455-457
ἁρπάζω, ἁρπαγμός	I:472-474
ἀστήρ, ἄστρον	I:503-505
ἀστραπή	I:505
ἄσωτος, ἀσωτία	I:506-507
βδελύσσομαι, βδέλυγμα,	
βδελυκτός	I:598-600
Βεεζεβούλ	I:605-606
Βελιάρ	I:607
βροντή	I:640-641
δαίμων, δαιμόνιον,	
δαιμονίζομαι, δαιμονιώδης,	
δεισιδαίμων, δεισιδαιμονία	II:1-20
δημιουργός	II:62
διαβάλλω, διάβολος	II:71-73
	75-81
δράκων	II:281-283
εἰρήνη, εἰρηνεύω,	
εἰρηνικός, εἰρηνοποιός,	
εἰρηνοποιέω	II:400-402
	406-420
ἔξεστιν, ἐξουσία, ἐξουσιάζω,	
κατεξουσιάζω	II:560-575
ἐπιούσιος	II:590-599
ἐχθρός, ἔχθρα	II:811-815
ἔχιδνα	II:815-816
θηρίον	III:133-135
Ἰησοῦς	III:284-293
κέρας	III:669-671
κλῆρος, κληρόω, προσ-	
κληρόω, ὁλόκληρος,	
ὁλοκληρία, κληρονόμος,	
συγκληρονόμος,	
κληρονομέω,	
κατακληρονομέω,	
κληρονομία	III:758-769
	776-785
κτίζω, κτίσις, κτίσμα,	
κτίστης	III:1000-1035
κύριος, κυρία, κυριακός,	
κυριότης, κυριεύω,	
κατακυριεύω	III:1039-1058
	1081-1098

ὄρος	V:475-487
ὄφις	V:566-571
	576-582
πύθων	VI:917-920
σατανᾶς	VII:151-163
σέβομαι, σεβάζομαι,	
σέβασμα, Σεβαστός,	
εὐσεβής, εὐσέβεια, εὐσεβέω,	
ἀσεβής, ἀσέβεια, ἀσεβέω,	
σεμνός, σεμνότης	VII:168-196
σῴζω, σωτηρία	VII:965-969
	980-1012
σωτήρ	VII:1013-1022
σωτήριος	VII:1023-1024

Fohrer, Georg, Prof.; b.9.6.1915 Krefeld-Uerdingen; D. Phil. Bonn 1939; D. Theol. Marburg 1944; Instructor Marburg 1949; Prof. Marburg 1954, Vienna 1954, Erlangen 1962

Σιών, Ἰερουσαλήμ,	
Ἰεροσόλυμα,	
Ἰεροσολυμίτης	VII:292-319
σοφία, σοφός	VII:476-496
σῴζω, σωτηρία	VII:970-980
σωτήρ	VII:1012-1013
σωτήριος	VII:1022-1023
υἱός, υἱοθεσία	VIII:340-354

Friedrich, Gerhard, Prof.; b.8.20.1908 Jodszen (East Prussia); D. Theol. Tübingen 1939; Assist. Prof. Bethel 1947; Assoc. Prof. Kiel 1953; Prof. Erlangen 1954, Kiel 1968

ἐπαγγέλλω, ἐπαγγελία,	
ἐπάγγελμα,	
προεπαγγέλλομαι	II:576-586
εὐαγγελίζομαι, εὐαγγέλιον,	
προευαγγελίζομαι,	
εὐαγγελιστής	II:707-737
κῆρυξ (ἱεροκῆρυξ),	
κηρύσσω, κήρυγμα,	
προκηρύσσω	III:683-718
προφήτης, προφῆτις,	
προφητεύω, προφητεία,	
προφητικός,	
ψευδοπροφήτης	VI:828-861
σάλπιγξ, σαλπίζω,	
σαλπιστής	VII:71-88

Fritsch, Hermann, Dr.; b.6.8.1913 Hof/Saale; D. Theol. Tübingen 1939; d.10.3.1941

Fuchs, Ernst, Prof. Emeritus; b.6.11.1903 Heilbronn; Lic. Theol. Marburg 1929; Instructor Bonn 1932; Assist. Prof. Tübingen 1949; Prof. Tübingen 1953, Berlin (KH) 1955, Marburg 1961

ἐκτείνω, ἐκτενής,	
(ἐκτενέστερον), ἐκτένεια,	
ὑπερεκτείνω	II:460-465
σήμερον	VII:269-275
σινιάζω	VII:291-292
σκοπός, σκοπέω, κατασκοπέω,	
κατάσκοπος	VII:413-417

Georgacas, Demetrius, Prof.; b.1.30.1908 Siderokastra (Greece); D. Phil. Berlin 1942 (Athens 1932); Prof. Chicago 1948, Salt Lake City 1951, Grand Forks (North Dakota) 1953

Gooding, David Willoughby; b.9.16.1925 Ipswich; Lecturer Durham 1954; Reader Belfast 1959

Goppelt, Leonhard, Prof.; b.11.6.1911 Munich; Lic. Theol. Erlangen 1939; Instructor Erlangen 1946; Assist. Prof. Göttingen 1947, Erlangen 1948, Hamburg 1949; Prof. Hamburg 1954, Munich 1968; d.12.21.1973

πεινάω (λιμός)	VI:12-22
πίνω, πόμα, πόσις, ποτόν,	
πότος, ποτήριον, καταπίνω,	
ποτίζω	VI:135-160
τράπεζα	VIII:209-215
τρώγω	VIII:236-237
τύπος, ἀντίτυπος, τυπικός,	
ὑποτύπωσις	VIII:246-259
ὕδωρ	VIII:314-333

Greeven, Heinrich, Prof. Emeritus; b.10.4.1906 Thorn (West Prussia); Lic. Theol. Greifswald 1930; Instructor Greifswald 1933; Assist. Prof. Heidelberg 1937; Prof. Heidelberg 1948, Bethel 1950, Kiel 1956, Bochum 1964

δέομαι, δέησις, προσδέομαι	II:40-42
ἐρωτάω, ἐπερωτάω,	
ἐπερώτημα	II:685-689
εὐσχήμων	II:770-772
εὔχομαι, εὐχή, προσεύχομαι,	
προσευχή	II:775-784
	800-808
ζητέω, ζήτησις, ἐκζητέω,	
ἐπιζητέω	II:892-896
κατανύσσω, κατάνυξις	II:626
πάλη	V:721
περιστερά, τρυγών	VI:63-72
πλησίον	VI:311-312
	316-318
προσκυνέω, προσκυνητής	VI:758-766
συναναμείγνυμι	VII:852-855

Grether, Oskar, Prof.; b.12.16.1902 Nuremberg; Lic. Theol. Erlangen 1933; Instructor Erlangen 1935; Prof. Erlangen 1944; d.8.3.1949

ὀργή, ὀργίζομαι, ὀργίλος,	
παροργίζω, παροργισμός	V:392-394
	409-412
ὄφις	V:571-573

Grosheide, Frederik Willem, Prof.; b.11.25.1881 Amsterdam; Doctorate Amsterdam 1907; Prof. Amsterdam 1912; d.3.5.1972

Gross, Gustav, Bishop; b.3.9.1864 Karlsruhe; d.2.9.1943

Grundmann, Walter, Prof.; b.10.21.1906 Chemnitz; D. Theol. Tübingen 1931; Prof. Jena 1936

ἀγαθός, ἀγαθοεργέω,	
ἀγαθοποιέω, -ός, -ία,	
ἀγαθωσύνη, φιλάγαθος,	
ἀφιλάγαθος	I: 10-18
ἄγγελος	I: 74-76
ἁμαρτάνω, ἁμάρτημα,	
ἁμαρτία	I: 289-293
	296-302
ἀναγκάζω, ἀναγκαῖος,	
ἀνάγκη	I: 344-347
ἀνέγκλητος	I: 356-357
δεῖ, δέον ἐστί	II: 21-25
δεξιός	II: 37-30
δέχομαι, δοχή, ἀποδέχομαι,	
ἀποδοχή, ἐκ-, ἀπεκ-, εἰσ-,	
προσδέχομαι, δεκτός, ἀπό-,	
εὐπρόσδεκτος	II: 50-59
δῆμος, ἐκδημέω, ἐνδημέω,	
παρεπίδημος	II: 63-65
δόκιμος, ἀδόκιμος, δοκιμή,	
δοκίμιον, δοκιμάζω,	
ἀποδοκιμάζω, δοκιμασία	II: 255-260
δύναμαι, δυνατός, δυνατέω,	
ἀδύνατος, ἀδυνατέω,	
δύναμις, δυνάστης,	
δυναμόω, ἐνδυναμόω	II: 284-317
ἐγκράτεια (ἀκρασία),	
ἐγκρατής (ἀκρατής),	
ἐγκρατεύομαι	II: 339-342
ἕτοιμος, ἑτοιμάζω,	
ἑτοιμασία, προετοιμάζω	II: 704-706
εὔσημος	II: 770
θαρρέω (θαρσέω)	III: 25-27
ἰσχύω, ἰσχυρός, ἰσχύς,	
κατισχύω	III: 397-402
κακός, ἄκακος, κακία,	
κακόω, κακοῦργος,	
κακοήθεια, κακοποιέω,	
κακοποιός, ἐγκακέω,	
ἀνεξίκακος	III: 469-487
καλός	III: 536-550
καρτερέω, προσκαρτερέω,	
προσκαρτέρησις	III: 617-620
κράζω, ἀνακράζω, κραυγή,	
κραυγάζω	III: 898-903
μέγας, μεγαλεῖον,	
μεγαλειότης, μεγαλοπρεπής,	
μεγαλύνω, μεγαλωσύνη,	
μέγεθος	IV: 529-544
μέμφομαι, μεμψίμοιρος,	
ἄμεμπτος, μομφή	IV: 571-574
στέφανος, στεφανόω	VII: 615-636
στήκω, ἵστημι	VII: 636-653
σύν – μετά with Genitive,	
συναποθνήσκω,	
συσταυρόω, συνθάπτω,	
σύμφυτος, συνεγείρω,	
συζάω, συζωοποιέω,	
συμπάσχω, συνδοξάζω	
συγκληρονόμος, σύμμορφος,	
συμμορφίζω, συμβασιλεύω,	
συγκαθίζω	VII: 766-797

ταπεινός, ταπεινόω,
ταπείνωσις, ταπεινόφρων,
ταπεινοφροσύνη VIII: 1-26
χρίω, χριστός, ἀντίχριστος,
χρῖσμα, χριστιανός IX: 493-496
527-580

Gutbrod, Walter, Pastor; b.11.26.1911 Buca (Cameroons); D. Theol. Tübingen 1934; d.7.28.1941

Ἰσραήλ, Ἰσραηλίτης,
Ἰουδαῖος, Ἰουδαία,
Ἰουδαϊκός, ἰουδαΐζω,
Ἰουδαϊσμός, Ἑβραῖος,
ἑβραϊκός, ἑβραΐς,
ἑβραϊστί III: 369-391
νόμος, ἀνομία, ἄνομος,
ἔννομος, νομικός, νόμιμος,
νομοθέτης, νομοθεσία,
νομοθετέω, παρανομία,
παρανομέω IV: 1036-1091

Hammerich, Holger; b.2.22.1940 Kiel

Hanse, Hermann, Pastor; b.9.4.1910 Berlin; Lic. Theol. Halle-Wittenberg 1939; d.2.9.1942

ἔχω, ἀντέχομαι, ἀπέχω,
ἐνέχω, ἔνοχος, κατέχω,
μετέχω, μετοχή, μέτοχος,
νουνεχῶς, συμμέτοχος II: 816-832
λαγχάνω IV: 1-2
λακτίζω IV: 3
λάρυγξ IV: 57-58
λοιδορέω, λοιδορία, λοίδορος,
ἀντιλοιδορέω IV: 293-294

Harder, Günther, Prof. Emeritus; b.1.13.1902 Gross-Breesen; D. Jur. Marburg 1924; Lic. Theol. Berlin 1934; Assist. Prof. Berlin (KH) 1936; Prof. Berlin (KH) 1948

σπουδάζω, σπουδή,
σπουδαῖος VII: 559-568
στηρίζω, ἐπιστηρίζω,
στηριγμός, ἀστήρικτος VII: 653-657
φθείρω, φθορά, φθαρτός,
ἄφθαρτος, ἀφθαρσία,
ἀφθορία, διαφθείρω,
διαφθορά, καταφθείρω IX: 93-106

Hauck, Friedrich, Prof.; b.8.2.1882 Erlangen; Lic. Theol. Erlangen 1921; Instructor Erlangen 1927; Assoc. Prof. Erlangen 1930; Prof. Erlangen 1939; d.2.9.1954

ἁγνός, ἁγνίζω, ἁγνεία,
ἁγνότης, ἁγνισμός I: 122-124
ἅλας I: 228-229
βάλλω, ἐκ-, ἐπιβάλλω I: 526-529
βέβηλος, βεβηλόω I: 604-605
βέλος I: 608-609
δέκα II: 36-37

ἑκών (ἄκων), ἑκούσιος II: 469-470
θερίζω, θερισμός III: 132-133
θησαυρός, θησαυρίζω III: 136-138
καθαρός, καθαρίζω,
καθαίρω, καθαρότης,
ἀκάθαρτος, ἀκαθαρσία,
καθαρισμός, ἐκκαθαίρω,
περικάθαρμα III: 413-417
423-431
καρπός, ἄκαρπος,
καρποφορέω III: 614-616
καταβολή III: 620-621
κοινός, κοινωνός,
κοινωνέω, κοινωνία,
συγκοινωνός, συγκοινωνέω,
κοινωνικός, κοινόω III: 789-809
κόπος, κοπιάω III: 827-830
μακάριος, μακαρίζω,
μακαρισμός IV: 362-364
367-370
μαμωνᾶς IV: 388-390
μαργαρίτης IV: 472-473
μένω, ἐμ-, παρα-, περι-,
προσμένω, μονή, ὑπομένω,
ὑπομονή IV: 574-588
μιαίνω, μίασμα, μιασμός,
ἀμίαντος IV: 644-647
μοιχεύω, μοιχάω, μοιχεία,
μοῖχος, μοιχαλίς IV: 729-735
μολύνω, μολυσμός IV: 736-737
μῶμος, ἄμωμος, ἀμώμητος IV: 829-831
νίπτω, ἄνιπτος IV: 946-948
ὀδύνη, ὀδυνάομαι V: 115
(ὀδύρομαι), ὀδυρμός V: 116
ὀκνηρός V: 166-167
ὅσιος, ὁσίως, ἀνόσιος,
ὁσιότης V: 489-493
ὀφείλω, ὀφειλή, ὀφείλημα,
ὀφειλέτης V: 559-566
παραβολή V: 741-761
παροιμία VI: 854-856
πένης, πενιχρός VI: 37-40
περισσεύω, ὑπερπερισσεύω,
περισσός, ὑπερεκπερισσοῦ,
ὑπερεκπερισσῶς, περισσεία,
περίσσευμα VI: 58-63
πλοῦτος, πλούσιος, πλουτέω,
πλουτίζω VI: 318-332
πορεύομαι, εἰσπορεύομαι,
ἐκπορεύομαι VI: 566-579
πόρνη, πόρνος, πορνεία,
πορνεύω, ἐκπορνεύω VI: 579-595
πραΰς, πραΰτης VI: 645-651
πτωχός, πτωχεία, πτωχεύω VI: 885-887

Heidland, Hans Wolfgang, Prof. and Bishop; b.7.20.1912 Koblenz; D. Theol. Zurich 1935; Prof. Heidelberg 1964

λογίζομαι, λογισμός IV: 284-292
ὀλολύζω V: 173-174
ὀμείρομαι V: 176
ὁμοθυμαδόν V: 185-186
ὄξος V: 288-289

ὀρέγομαι, ὄρεξις   V: 447-448
ὀχύρωμα   V: 590-591
ὀψώνιον   V: 591-592

Hengel, Martin, Prof.; b.12.14.1926 Reutlingen; D. Theol. Tübingen 1959; Instructor Tübingen 1967; Prof. Erlangen 1968, Tübingen 1972

φάτνη   IX: 49-55

Herntrich, Volkmar Martinus, Bishop and Hon. Prof.; b.12.8.1908 Flensburg; D. Theol. Berlin 1931; Instructor Kiel 1932; Assist. Prof. Bethel 1934; Prof. Hamburg (KH) 1949; Hon. Prof. Hamburg (Univ.) 1954; d.9.14.1958

κρίνω   III: 923-933
λεῖμμα, ὑπόλειμμα,
   καταλείπω (κατά-, περί-,
   διάλειμμα)   IV: 196-209

Hermann, Johannes, Prof.; b.12.7.1880 Nossen (Saxony); Lic. Theol. Leipzig 1907; Instructor Vienna 1908; Assist. Prof. Königsberg 1909, Breslau 1910; Assoc. Prof. Breslau 1910; Prof. Rostock 1913, Münster 1922; d.2.6.1960

εὔχομαι, εὐχή   II: 785-800
ἱλάσκομαι, ἱλασμός,
   ἱλαστήριον   III: 301-310
                     318-319
κληρονόμος, συγκληρονόμος,
   κληρονομέω,
   κατακληρονομέω,
   κληρονομία   III: 769-776

Hesse, Franz, Prof.; b.6.11.1917 Loga, Kr. Leer (East Friesland); D. Theol. Erlangen 1949; Instructor Erlangen 1953; Assist. Prof. Marburg 1954; Assoc. Prof. Marburg 1958; Prof. Münster 1960

χρίω, χριστός, ἀντίχριστος,
   χρῖσμα, χριστιανός   IX: 496-509

Hiller, August, Pastor; b.6.27.1897 Tübingen

Horowitz, Charles, Prof.; b.2.12.1892 Landshut; Doctorate Bonn 1962; Instructor Bonn 1956; Prof. Bonn 1965; d.9.8.1969

Horst, Johannes, Prof.; b.2.24.1890 Schmentau (Marienwerder); Doctorate Münster 1931; Assist. Prof. Posen 1930; Prof. Marburg 1948; d.8.24.1956

μακροθυμία, μακροθυμέω,
   μακρόθυμος,
   μακροθύμως   IV: 374-387
μέλος   IV: 555-568
οὖς, ὠτίον, ὠτάριον,
   ἐνωτίζομαι   V: 543-559

Hunzinger, Claus-Hunno, Prof.; b.9.15.1929 Schwerin/ Mecklenburg; D. Theol. Göttingen 1954; Instructor Göttingen 1956; Assoc. Prof. Hamburg 1962; Prof. Hamburg 1968

ῥαντίζω, ῥαντισμός   VI: 976-984
σίναπι   VII: 287-291
συκῆ, σῦκον, ὄλυνθος,
   συκάμινος, συκομορέα,
   συκοφαντέω   VII: 751-759

Jacob, Edmond, Prof.; b.11.1.1909 Beblenheim (Alsace); Doctorate Strassburg 1938; Instructor Strassburg 1945; Prof. Montpellier 1941, Strassburg 1946

ψυχή   IX: 617-631

Jantz, Kurt, Hon. Prof.; b.7.13.1908 Berlin; D. Jur. Erlangen 1935; Instructor Cologne 1962; Hon. Prof. Cologne 1966

Jehle, Arthur, Pastor; b.3.11.1874 Winnenden; d.10.20.1957

Jendreyczyk, Klaus Peter; b.2.28.1914 Elbing; d.8.21.1943

Jeremias, Joachim, Prof. Emeritus; b.9.20.1900 Dresden; D. Phil. Leipzig 1922; Lic. Theol. Leipzig 1923; Instructor Leipzig 1925; Assist. Prof. Riga 1924, Leipzig 1925; Assoc. Prof. Berlin 1928; Prof. Greifswald 1929, Göttingen 1935

Ἀβαδδών   I: 4
Ἀβραάμ   I: 8-9
ἄβυσσος   I: 9-10
Ἀδάμ   I: 141-143
ᾅδης   I: 146-149
αἴρω, ἐπαίρω   I: 185-186
ἀμνός, ἀρήν, ἀρνίον   I: 338-341
ἄνθρωπος, ἀνθρωπινος   I: 364-367
Ἁρ Μαγεδών   I: 468
γέεννα   I: 657-658
γραμματεύς   I: 740-742
γωνία, ἀκρογωνιαῖος,
   κεφαλὴ γωνίας   I: 792-793
Ἠλ(ε)ίας   II: 928-941
θύρα   III: 173-180
Ἰερεμίας   III: 218-221
Ἰωνᾶς   III: 406-410
κλείς   III: 744-753
λίθος, λίθινος   IV: 268-280
Μωυσῆς   IV: 848-873
νύμφη, νυμφίος   IV: 1099-1106
παῖς θεοῦ   V: 677-717
παράδεισος   V: 765-773
πάσχα   V: 896-904
ποιμήν, ἀρχιποίμην,
   ποιμαίνω, ποίμνη, ποίμνιον   VI: 485-502
πολλοί   VI: 536-545
πύλη, πυλών   VI: 921-928
ῥακά   VI: 973-976
Σαμάρεια, Σαμαρίτης,
   Σαμαρῖτις   VII: 88-94

Johnstad, Gunnar; b.9.8.1946 Oslo

de **Jonge,** Marinus, Prof.; b.12.9.1925 Vlissingen; Doctorate Leyden 1953; Assist. Prof. Groningen 1962; Prof. Leyden 1966

| χρίω, χριστός, ἀντίχριστος, χρῖσμα, χριστιανός | IX: 511-517 |
| | 520-521 |

Kasch, Wilhelm F., Prof.; b.2.1.1921 Nordhackstedt (Schleswig); D. Theol. Kiel 1952; Instructor Kiel 1960; Prof. Kiel 1965, Bayreuth 1966 (Erlangen 1968)

πλοῦτος, πλούσιος, πλουτέω, πλουτίζω	VI: 318-332
ῥύομαι	VI: 998-1003
στέγω	VII: 585-587
συγκαλύπτω	VII: 743
συνίστημι, συνιστάνω	VII: 896-898

Katz, Peter, see Walters, Peter Max (adopted name)

Kelber, Gerhard, Pastor; b.5.20.1941 Lindau

| χαρακτήρ | IX: 423 |

Kittel, Gerhard, Prof.; b.9.23.1888 Breslau; Lic. Theol. Kiel 1913; Instructor Kiel 1913; Assist. Prof. Leipzig 1917; Assoc. Prof. Leipzig 1921; Prof. Greifswald 1921, Tübingen 1926, Vienna 1939, Tübingen 1943; d.7.11.1948

ΑΩ	I: 1-3
ἀββᾶ	I: 5-6
Ἅγαρ	I: 55-56
ἄγγελος, ἀρχάγγελος, ἰσάγγελος	I: 80-87
αἴνιγμα (ἔσοπτρον)	I: 178-180
αἰχμάλωτος, αἰχμαλωτίζω, αἰχμαλωτεύω, αἰχμαλωσία, συναιχμάλωτος	I: 195-197
ἀκέραιος	I: 209-210
ἀκολουθέω, ἐξ-, ἐπ-, παρ-, συνακολουθέω	I: 210-216
ἀκούω, ἀκοή, εἰσ-, ἐπ-, παρακούω, παρακοή, ὑπακούω, ὑπακοή, ὑπήκοος	I: 216-225
ἀλήθεια	I: 237-238
ἀναλογία	I: 347-348
ἀρκέω, ἀρκετός, αὐτάρκεια, αὐτάρκης	I: 464-467
αὐγάζω, ἀπαύγασμα	I: 507-508
δεσμός, δέσμιος	II: 43
δόγμα, δογματίζω	II: 230-232
δοκέω, δόξα, δοξάζω, συνδοξάζω, ἔνδοξος, ἐνδοξάζω, παράδοξος	II: 232-237
	242-255
εἶδος, εἰδέα (ἰδέα)	II: 373-375
εἰκών	II: 383-388
	392-397
ἔρημος, ἐρημία, ἐρημόω, ἐρήμωσις	II: 657-660
ἔσοπτρον, κατοπτρίζομαι	II: 696-697
ἔσχατος	II: 697-698

Θαμάρ, Ῥαχάβ, Ῥούθ,

ἡ τοῦ Οὐρίου	III: 1-3
θέατρον, θεατρίζομαι	III: 42-43
(λαλέω) καταλαλέω, καταλαλιά, κατάλαλος	IV: 3-5
λέγω, λόγος, ῥῆμα, λαλέω, λόγιος, λόγιον, ἄλογος, λογικός, λογομαχέω, λογομαχία, ἐκλέγομαι, ἐκλογή, ἐκλεκτός	IV: 100-143
λογεία	IV: 282-283

Kleinknecht, Hermann Martin, Prof.; b.1.12.1907 Marbach; D. Phil. Tübingen 1937; Instructor Halle 1939; Assoc. Prof. Rostock 1944; Prof. Rostock 1947, Berlin (Humboldt-Univ.) 1951; Assoc. Prof. Münster 1953; Prof. Münster 1958; d.3.13.1960

βασιλεύς	I: 564-565
εἰκών	II: 388-390
θεός	III: 65-79
θεῖος, θειότης	III: 122-123
λόγος	IV: 77-91
νόμος, ἀνομία, ἄνομος, ἔννομος, νομικός, νόμιμος, νομοθέτης, νομοθεσία, νομοθετέω, παρανομία, παρανομέω	IV: 1022-1035
ὀργή	V: 382-392
πνεῦμα	VI: 332-359

Knöpp, Wilhelm; b.4.14.1879 Langen, Kr. Offenbach; d.4.3.1949

Köster, Helmut, Prof.; b.12.18.1926 Hamburg; D. Theol. Marburg 1954; Instructor Heidelberg 1956; Assist. Prof. Harvard 1958; Assoc. Prof. Harvard 1959; Prof. Harvard 1963

σπλάγχνον, σπλαγχνίζομαι, εὔσπλαγχνος, πολύσπλαγχνος, ἄσπλαγχνος	VII: 548-559
συνέχω, συνοχή	VII: 877-887
τέμνω, ἀποτομία, ἀπότομος, ἀποτόμως, κατατομή, ὀρθοτομέω	VIII: 106-112
τόπος	VIII: 187-208
ὑπόστασις	VIII: 572-589
φύσις, φυσικός, φυσικῶς	IX: 251-277

Krämer, Helmut, Prof.; b.7.27.1907 Gelsenkirchen; Prof. Bethel 1947

| προφήτης, προφῆτις, προφητεύω, προφητεία, προφητικός, ψευδοπροφήτης | VI: 781-796 |

Kremser, Hubert, Pastor; b.9.22.1914 Ratibor; D. Theol. Hamburg 1959

Kuhn, Karl Georg, Prof. Emeritus; b.3.6.1906 Thaleischweiler (Pfalz.); D. Phil. Tübingen 1931;

Instructor Tübingen 1934; Prof. Tübingen 1942,
Göttingen 1949, Heidelberg 1954

Ἀαρών	I: 3-4
Ἄβελ–Κάϊν	I: 6-8
ἅγιος	I: 97-100
Βαβυλών	I: 514-517
Βαλαάμ	I: 524-525
βασιλεία	I: 571-574
Γὼγ καὶ Μαγώγ	I: 789-791
θεός	III: 92-94
Ἰσραήλ, Ἰουδαῖος,	
Ἑβραῖος	III: 359-369
μαραναθά	IV: 466-472
πανοπλία,	V: 298-300
προσήλυτος	VI: 727-744

Lang, Friedrich, Prof.; b.9.6.1913 Grötzingen; D. Theol.
Tübingen 1950; Prof. Wuppertal 1951; Hon. Prof.
Tübingen 1959; Prof. Tübingen 1962

πῦρ, πυρόω, πύρωσις,	
πύρινος, πυρρός	VI: 928-952
σαίνω	VII: 54-56
σβέννυμι	VII: 165-168
σκύβαλον	VII: 445-447
σκώληξ, σκωληκόβρωτος	VII: 452-457
σωρεύω, ἐπισωρεύω	VII: 1094-1096

Lösch, Stefan, Prof.; b.8.25.1881 Harthausen; D. Phil.
Tübingen 1908; D. Theol. Tübingen 1927; Instructor
Tübingen 1927; Prof. Tübingen 1934; d.10.25.1966

Lohse, Eduard, Bishop and Hon. Prof.; b.2.19.1924
Hamburg; D. Theol. Göttingen 1949; Instructor Mainz
1953; Assist. Prof. Bonn 1955; Assoc. Prof. Kiel 1956;
Prof. Kiel 1962, Göttingen 1964; Hon. Prof. Göttingen
1971

πεντηκοστή	VI: 44-53
πρόσωπον, εὐπροσωπέω,	
προσωπολημψία, προσωπο-	
λήμπτης, προσωπολημπ-	
τέω, ἀπροσωπολήμπτως	VI: 768-780
ῥάββι, ῥαββουνί	VI: 964-965
σάββατον, σαββατισμός,	
παρασκευή	VII: 1-35
Σινᾶ	VII: 282-287
Σιών, Ἰερουσαλήμ,	
Ἰεροσόλυμα,	
Ἰεροσολυμίτης	VII: 319-338
Σολομών	VII: 459-465
συνέδριον	VII: 860-871
υἱός	VIII: 357-362
υἱὸς Δαυίδ	VIII: 478-488
χείρ, χειραγωγέω,	
χειραγωγός, χειρόγραφον,	
χειροποίητος, ἀχειροποίη-	
τος, χειροτονέω	IX: 424-437
Χερουβίν	IX: 438-439
χιλιάς, χίλιοι	IX: 466-471
ψυχή	IX: 635-637
ὡσαννά	IX: 682-684

Lohse, Wolfram, Pastor; b.11.22.1931 Schirgiswalde
(Saxony); D. Theol. Erlangen 1967

Luck, Ulrich, Prof.; b.12.15.1923 Landsberg (Warthe);
D. Theol. Münster 1955; Instructor Münster 1959;
Prof. Bethel 1961

σώφρων, σωφρονέω,	
σωφρονίζω, σωφρονισμός,	
σωφροσύνη	VII: 1097-1104
ὑγιής, ὑγιαίνω	VIII: 308-313
φιλανθρωπία, φιλανθρώπως	IX: 107-117

Lührmann, Dieter, Prof.; b.3.13.1939 Lingen/Ems; D.
Theol. Heidelberg 1964; Instructor Heidelberg 1968;
Prof. Bethel 1974

φαίνω, φανερός, φανερόω,	
φανέρωσις, φαντάζω,	
φάντασμα, ἐμφανίζω,	
ἐπιφαίνω, ἐπιφανής,	
ἐπιφάνεια	IX: 1-10

Mahnke, Hermann; b.10.9.1944 Barmstedt

Manson, Thomas Walter, Prof.; b.7.22.1893 Tynemouth
(England); Prof. Manchester 1936; d.5.1.1958.

Maurer, Christian, Prof.; b.4.30.1913 Arosa; D. Theol.
Zurich 1941; Instructor Zurich 1947; Prof. Bethel
1954, Bern 1966

πολυλογία	VI: 545-546
πράσσω, πρᾶγμα, πραγματεία,	
πραγματεύομαι, διαπραγμα-	
τεύομαι, πράκτωρ, πρᾶξις	VI: 632-644
προέχομαι	VI: 692-693
προσδοκάω, προσδοκία	VI: 725-727
πρόσφατος, προσφάτως	VI: 766-767
ῥίζα, ῥιζόω, ἐκριζόω	VI: 985-991
σκεῦος	VII: 358-367
συναρμολογέω	VII: 855-856
σύνοιδα, συνείδησις	VII: 898-919
σχίζω, σχίσμα	VII: 959-964
τίθημι, ἀθετέω, ἀθέτησις,	
ἐπιτίημι, ἐπίθεσις,	
μετατίθημι, μετάθεσις,	
παρατίθημι, παραθήκη,	
(παρακαταθήκη), προτίθημι,	
πρόθεσις, προστίθημι	VIII: 152-168
ὑπόδικος	VIII: 557-558
φυλή	IX: 245-250

Meyer, Rudolf, Prof.; b.9.8.1909 Leipzig; D. Theol.
Leipzig 1935; Instructor Leipzig 1938; Assist. Prof.
Leipzig 1947; Assoc. Prof. Jena 1947; Prof. Jena 1947

καθαρός, καθαρίζω,	
καθαίρω, καθαρότης,	
ἀκάθαρτος, ἀκαθαρσία,	
καθαρισμός, ἐκκαθαίρω,	
περικάθαρμα	III: 418-423
κόλπος	III: 824-826
ἀπόκρυφος	III: 978-987
λαός	IV: 39-50

λειτουργέω, λειτουργία,　　IV: 222-225
Λευ(ε)ίτης　　　　　　　　IV: 239-241
Μάννα　　　　　　　　　　IV: 462-466
ὄχλος　　　　　　　　　　V: 582-584
　　　　　　　　　　　　585-590
πάροικος, παροικία,
παροικέω　　　　　　　　V: 850-851
περιτέμνω, περιτομή,
ἀπερίτμητος　　　　　　　VI: 72-84
προφήτης, προφῆτις, προ-
φητεύω, προφητεία, προ-
φητικός, ψευδοπροφήτης　VI: 812-828
Σαδδουκαῖος　　　　　　　VII: 35-54
σάρξ　　　　　　　　　　　VII: 110-119
Φαρισαῖος　　　　　　　　IX: 11-35

Michaelis, Wilhelm, Prof.; b.1.26.1896 Darmstadt; Lic. Theol. Berlin 1921; Instructor Berlin 1923; Prof. Bern 1930; d.2.19.1965

κράτος (θεοκρατία), κρατέω,
κραταιός, κραταιόω, κοσμο-
κράτωρ, παντοκράτωρ　　III: 905-915
λέπρα, λεπρός　　　　　　IV: 233-234
λευκός, λευκαίνω　　　　　IV: 241-250
λέων　　　　　　　　　　IV: 251-253
λίβανος, λιβανωτός　　　　IV: 263-264
λιθάζω, καταλιθάζω,
λιθοβολέω　　　　　　　　IV: 267-268
λυμαίνομαι　　　　　　　　IV: 312
λύχνος, λυχνία　　　　　　IV: 324-327
μάχαιρα　　　　　　　　　IV: 524-527
μέλας　　　　　　　　　　IV: 549-551
μέλι　　　　　　　　　　　IV: 552-554
μήτηρ　　　　　　　　　　IV: 642-644
μιμέομαι, μιμητής,
συμμιμητής　　　　　　　IV: 659-674
μύρον, μυρίζω　　　　　　IV: 800-801
ὁδός, ὁδηγός, ὁδηγέω,
μεθοδία, εἴσοδος, ἔξοδος,
διέξοδος, εὐοδόω　　　　V: 42-114
ὁράω, εἶδον, βλέπω,
ὀπτάνομαι, θεάομαι,
θεωρέω, ἀόρατος, ὁρατός,
ὅρασις, ὅραμα, ὀπτασία,
αὐτόπτης, ἐπόπτης,
ἐποπτεύω, ὀφθαλμός,
καθοράω, προοράω,
προεῖδον　　　　　　　　V: 315-382
παρακύπτω　　　　　　　V: 814-816
παρεισάγω, παρείσακτος　V: 824-826
πάσχω, παθητός, προπάσχω,
συμπάσχω, πάθος, πάθημα,
συμπαθής, συμπαθέω,
κακοπαθέω, συγκακοπαθέω,
κακοπάθεια, μετριοπαθέω,
ὁμοιοπαθής, πραϋπάθεια　V: 904-939
πηγή　　　　　　　　　　VI: 112-117
πήρα　　　　　　　　　　VI: 119-121
πικρός, πικρία, πικραίνω,
παραπικραίνω,
παραπικρασμός　　　　　VI: 122-127
πίπτω, πτῶμα, πτῶσις,

ἐκπίπτω, καταπίπτω,
παραπίπτω, παράπτωμα,
περιπίπτω　　　　　　　　VI: 161-173
προχειρίζω　　　　　　　VI: 862-864
πρῶτος, πρῶτον, πρωτοκα-
θεδρία, πρωτοκλισία,
πρωτότοκος, πρωτοτοκεῖα,
πρωτεύω　　　　　　　　VI: 865-882
πύργος　　　　　　　　　VI: 953-956
ῥομφαία　　　　　　　　　VI: 993-998
σκηνή, σκῆνος, σκήνωμα,
σκηνόω, ἐπισκηνόω, κατα-
σκηνόω, σκηνοπηγία,
σκηνοποιός　　　　　　　VII: 368-394
σμύρνα, σμυρνίζω　　　　VII: 457-459
συγγενής, συγγένεια　　　VII: 736-742

Michel, Otto, Prof. Emeritus; b.8.28.1903 Wuppertal-Elberfeld; Lic. Theol. Tübingen 1928; Instructor Halle 1929; Assist. Prof. Tübingen 1940; Prof. Tübingen 1946

ἰός, κατιόομαι　　　　　　III: 334-336
ἵππος　　　　　　　　　　III: 336-339
κάμηλος　　　　　　　　　III: 592-594
καταντάω, ὑπαντάω,
ὑπάντησις　　　　　　　　III: 623-626
κόκκος, κόκκινος　　　　　III: 810-814
κύων, κυνάριον　　　　　III: 1101-1104
Μελχισεδέκ　　　　　　　IV: 568-571
μεταμέλομαι,
ἀμεταμέλητος　　　　　　IV: 626-629
μηλωτή　　　　　　　　　IV: 637-638
μικρός (ἐλάττων,
ἐλάχιστος)　　　　　　　IV: 648-659
μιμνήσκομαι, μνεία, μνήμη,
μνῆμα, μνημεῖον,
μνημονεύω　　　　　　　IV: 675-683
μισέω　　　　　　　　　　IV: 683-694
μόσχος　　　　　　　　　IV: 760-762
ναός　　　　　　　　　　　IV: 880-890
οἶκος, οἰκία, οἰκεῖος, οἰκέω,
οἰκοδόμος, οἰκοδομέω,
οἰκοδομή, ἐποικοδομέω,
συνοικοδομέω, οἰκονόμος,
οἰκονομία, κατοικέω,
οἰκητήριον, κατοικητήριον,
κατοικίζω, οἰκουμένη　　V: 119-159
ὁμολογέω, ἐξομολογέω,
ἀνθομολογέομαι, ὁμολογία,
ὁμολογουμένως　　　　　V: 199-220
ὄνος, ὀνάριον　　　　　　V: 283-287
πῶλος　　　　　　　　　　VI: 959-961
σκορπίζω, διασκορπίζω,
σκορπισμός　　　　　　　VII: 418-422
Σκύθης　　　　　　　　　VII: 447-450
σπένδομαι　　　　　　　VII: 528-536
συγκλείω　　　　　　　　VII: 744-747
σφάζω, σφαγή　　　　　　VII: 925-938
τελώνης　　　　　　　　　VIII: 88-105
φιλοσοφία, φιλόσοφος　　IX: 172-188

Moule, Charles Francis Digby, Prof.; b.12.3.1908 Hangchow (China); Lecturer Cambridge 1947; Prof. Cambridge 1951

Nestle, Erwin, Prof.; b.5.22.1883 Münsingen (Württemberg); D. Phil. Tübingen 1911; d.6.21.1972

Niedlich, Karl-Ulrich, Pastor; b.6.18.1917 Bad Charlottenbrunn

Nock, Arthur Darby, Prof.; b.2.21.1902 Portsmouth (England); Lecturer Harvard 1926; Prof. Harvard 1930; d.1.11.1963

Odeberg, Hugo, Prof. Emeritus; b.5.7.1898 Amal (Sweden); D. Phil. London 1924; Lic. Theol. Uppsala 1929; D. Theol. Uppsala 1932; Assist. Prof. Uppsala 1928; Prof. Lund 1933

Ἐνώχ	II: 556-560
Ἠσαῦ	II: 953-954
Ἰακώβ	III: 191-192
Ἰάννης, Ἰαμβρῆς	III: 192-193
Ἰεζάβελ	III: 217-218

Oepke, Albrecht, Prof.; b.9.10.1881 Arle (East Friesland); Assoc. Prof. Leipzig 1922; Prof. Leipzig 1953; d.12.10.1955

ἀθέμιτος	I: 166
ἄθεσμος	I: 167
ἀνίστημι, ἐξανίστημι, ἀνάστασις, ἐξανάστασις	I: 368-372
ἀπατάω, ἐξαπατάω, ἀπάτη	I: 384-385
ἀποκαθίστημι, ἀποκατάστασις	I: 387-392
ἀπόλλυμι, ἀπώλεια, Ἀπολλύων	I: 394-397
ἄσπιλος	I: 502
ἀστατέω	I: 503
βάπτω, βαπτίζω, βαπτισμός, βάπτισμα, βαπτιστής	I: 529-546
γυμνός, γυμνότης, γυμνάζω, γυμνασία	I: 773-776
γυνή	I: 776-789
διά	II: 65-70
διώκω	II: 229-230
δύω, ἐκδύω, ἀπεκδύω, ἐνδύω, ἐπενδύω, ἀπέκδυσις	II: 318-321
ἐγείρω, ἔγερσις, ἐξεγείρω, γρηγορέω, ἀγρυπνέω	II: 333-339
εἰς	II: 420-434
ἔκστασις, ἐξίστημι	II: 449-460
ἕλκω	II: 503-504
ἐν	II: 537-543
ἐνίστημι	II: 543-544
ἐπιστάτης	II: 622-623
ζέω, ζεστός (χλιαρός, ψυχρός)	II: 875-877
ἰάομαι, ἴασις, ἴαμα, ἰατρός	III: 194-215
καθεύδω	III: 431-437
καθίστημι, ἀκαταστασία, ἀκατάστατος	III: 444-447
καλύπτω, κάλυμμα, ἀνακαλύπτω, κατακαλύπτω,	

ἀποκάλυψις	III: 556-592
κενός, κενόω, κενόδοξος, κενοδοξία	III: 659-662
κρύπτω, ἀποκρύπτω, κρυπτός, κρυφαῖος, κρυφῇ, κρύπτη, ἀπόκρυφος	III: 957-978 987-1000
λάμπω, ἐκλάμπω, περιλάμπω, λαμπάς, λαμπρός	IV: 16-28
λούω, ἀπολούω, λουτρόν	IV: 295-307
μεσίτης, μεσιτεύω	IV: 598-624
νεφέλη, νέφος	IV: 902-910
νόσος, νοσέω, νόσημα (μαλακία, μάστιξ, κακῶς ἔχω)	IV: 1091-1098
ὄναρ	V: 220-238
ὅπλον, ὁπλίζω, πανοπλία, ζώννυμι, διαζώννυμι, περιζώννυμι, ζώνη, θώραξ, ὑποδέω (ὑπόδημα, σανδάλιον), θυρεός, περικεφαλαία	V: 292-298 300-315
παῖς, παιδίον, παιδάριον, τέκνον, τεκνίον, βρέφος	V: 636-654
παρουσία, πάρειμι	V: 858-871

Peisker, Carl Heinz, Rector; b.4.21.1930 Bunzlau (Silesia); D. Theol. Kampen (NL)

Peterson, Erik, Prof.; b.6.7.1890 Hamburg; Lic. Theol. Göttingen 1920; Instructor Göttingen 1920; Prof. Bonn 1924, Rome 1934; d.10.26.1960

ἀλαλάζω	I: 227-228
ἀνεξιχνίαστος	I: 358-359
ἀπάντησις	I: 380-381

Preisker, Herbert, Prof.; b.7.23.1888 Deutsch-Rasselwitz (Upper Silesia); Lic. Theol. Breslau 1915; Instructor Breslau 1924; Assoc. Prof. Breslau 1934, Göttingen 1935; Prof. Breslau 1936, Jena 1947, Halle 1952; d.12.24.1952

ἔγγυος	II: 329
ἐγγύς, ἐγγίζω, προσεγγίζω	II: 330-332
ἔθος	II: 372-373
ἐλλογέω	II: 516-517
ἐμβατεύω	II: 535-536
ἔπαινος	II: 586-588
ἐπιείκεια, ἐπιεικής	II: 588-590
εὑρίσκω	II: 769-770
κλέπτω, κλέπτης	III: 754-756
λεγιών	IV: 68-69
μαίνομαι	IV: 360-361
μακράν, μακρόθεν	IV: 372-374
μέθη, μεθύω, μέθυσος, μεθύσκομαι	IV: 545-548
μισθός, μισθόω, μίσθιος, μισθωτός, μισθαποδότης, μισθαποδοσία, ἀντιμισθία	IV: 695-706 712-728

κορβᾶν, κορβανᾶς III: 860-866
λῃστής IV: 257-262
μανθάνω, καταμανθάνω,
μαθητής, συμμαθητής,
μαθήτρια, μαθητεύω IV: 390-461
πηλός VI: 118-119
ποταμός, ποταμοφόρητος,
'Ιορδάνης VI: 595-623
πρόθυμος, προθυμία VI: 694-700
σημεῖον, σημαίνω, σημειόω,
ἄσημος, ἐπίσημος,
εὔσημος, σύσσημον VII: 200-269
στέλλω, διαστέλλω, διαστολή,
ἐπιστέλλω, ἐπιστολή,
καταστέλλω, καταστολή,
συστέλλω, ὑποστέλλω,
ὑποστολή VII: 588-599
τέρας VIII: 113-126
ὑπηρέτης, ὑπηρετέω VIII: 530-544

Riesenfeld, Harald, Prof.; b.2.8.1913 Freiburg (Br.);
D. Theol. Uppsala 1947; Instructor Uppsala 1947;
Prof. Uppsala 1953

παρά V: 727-736
περί VI: 53-56
τηρέω, τήρησις, παρατηρέω,
παρατήρησις, διατηρέω,
συντηρέω VIII: 140-151
ὑπέρ VIII: 507-516

Risch, Ernst, Prof.; b.10.9.1911 Moscow; D. Phil.
Zurich 1935; Instructor Zurich 1942; Prof. Mainz
1950, Zurich 1952

Rühle, Oskar, Dr.; b.1.3.1901 Niebelsbach (Württemberg); D. Phil. Tübingen 1923

ἀριθμέω, ἀριθμός I: 461-464

Sasse, Hermann, Prof. Emeritus; b.7.17.1895 Sonne-
walde (Niederlausitz); Lic. Theol. Berlin 1923; Assoc.
Prof. Erlangen 1933; Prof. Erlangen 1946, North
Adelaide (South Australia) 1949

ἀΐδιος I: 168
αἰών, αἰώνιος I: 197-209
γῆ, ἐπίγειος I: 677-681
καταχθόνιος III: 633-634
κοσμέω, κόσμος, κόσμιος,
κοσμικός III: 867-898

Schaeder, Hans Heinrich, Prof.; b.1.31.1896 Göttingen;
D. Phil. Breslau 1919; Assoc. Prof. Breslau 1924;
Prof. Königsberg 1926, Leipzig 1930, Berlin 1931,
Göttingen 1946; d.3.13.1957

Ναζαρηνός, Ναζωραῖος IV: 874-879

Schäferdick, Knut, Prof.; b.11.3.1930 Cologne; D. Theol.
Bonn 1958; Instructor Bonn 1966; Prof. Bonn

σατανᾶς VII: 163-165

Schelkle, Karl Hermann, Prof.; b.4.3.1908 Steinhausen,

Kr. Biberach; D. Phil. Tübingen, D. Theol. Bonn,
1941; Instructor Würzburg 1949; Prof. Tübingen 1950

Schiller, Charlotte; b.1.9.1918 Hamburg

Schlichting, Günter, Dean; b.9.6.1911 Zoppot bei Danzig;
D. Theol. Tübingen, 1936

Schlier, Heinrich, Prof. Emeritus and Hon. Prof.;
b.3.31.1900 Neuburg/Donau; Lic. Theol. Marburg
1925; Instructor Jena 1928; Assist. Prof. Marburg
1930, Wuppertal-Elberfeld 1935; Prof. Bonn 1945;
Hon. Prof. Bonn 1952

ᾄδω, ᾠδή I: 163-165
αἰνέω, αἶνος I: 177-178
αἱρέομαι, αἵρεσις, αἱρετικός,
αἱρετίζω, διαιρέω,
διαίρεσις I: 180-185
ἀλείφω I: 229-232
ἀλληλουϊά I: 264
ἀμήν I: 335-338
ἀνατέλλω, ἀνατολή I: 351-353
ἀνέχω, ἀνεκτός, ἀνοχή I: 359-360
ἀνήκει I: 360
ἀρνέομαι I: 469-471
ἀφίστημι, ἀποστασία,
διχοστασία I: 512-514
βάθος I: 517-518
βέβαιος, βεβαιόω, βεβαίωσις I: 600-603
βραχίων I: 639-640
γάλα I: 645-647
γόνυ, γονυπετέω I: 738-740
δάκτυλος II: 20-21
δείκνυμι, ἀναδείκνυμι,
ἀνάδειξις, δειγματίζω,
παραδειγματίζω,
ὑπόδειγμα II: 25-33
διχοτομέω II: 225-226
ἐκκεντέω II: 446-447
ἐκπτύω II: 448-449
ἔλαιον II: 470-473
ἐλεύθερος, ἐλευθερόω,
ἐλευθερία, ἀπελεύθερος II: 487-502
θλίβω, θλῖψις III: 139-148
ἰδιώτης III: 215-217
καθήκω III: 437-440
κάμπτω III: 594-595
κέρδος, κερδαίνω III: 672-673
κεφαλή, ἀνακεφαλαιόομαι III: 673-682
παρρησία, παρρησιάζομαι V: 871-886

Schmid, Lothar, Pastor; b.10.9.1905 Stuttgart; D. Theol.
Tübingen 1932; d.11.5.1961

κέλευσμα III: 656-659
κέντρον III: 663-668

Schmidt, Karl Ludwig, Prof.; b.2.5.1891 Frankfurt;
Lic. Theol. Berlin 1913; Instructor Berlin 1918; Prof.
Giessen 1921, Jena 1925, Bonn 1929, Basel 1935;
d.1.10.1956

ἀγωγή, παράγω, προάγω,

προσάγω, προσαγωγή | I: 128-134
ἀκροβυστία | I: 225-226
ἀπωθέω | I: 448
ἀσφάλεια, ἀσφαλής, |
ἀσφαλῶς, ἀσφαλίζω | I: 506
βασιλεύς, βασιλεία, |
βασίλισσα, βασιλεύω, |
συμβασιλεύω, βασίλειος, |
βασιλικός | I: 574-593
διασπορά | II: 98-104
ἔθνος, ἐθνικός | II: 369-372
θεμέλιος, θεμέλιον, |
θεμελιόω | III: 63-64
θρησκεία, θρῆσκος, |
ἐθελοθρησκεία | III: 155-159
καίω | III: 464-467
καλέω, κλῆσις, κλητός, |
ἀντικαλέω, ἐγκαλέω, |
ἔγκλημα, εἰσκαλέω, |
μετακαλέω, προκαλέω, |
συνκαλέω, ἐπικαλέω, |
προσκαλέω, ἐκκλησία | III: 487-536
κολαφίζω | III: 818-821
κολλάω, προσκολλάω | III: 822-823
κύμβαλον | III: 1037-1039
ὁρίζω, ἀφορίζω, ἀποδιορίζω, |
προορίζω | V: 452-456
πάροικος, παροικία, |
παροικέω | V: 841-850
 | 851-853
παχύνω, πωρόω (πηρόω), |
πώρωσις (πήρωσις), |
σκληρός, σκληρότης, |
σκληροτράχηλος, |
σκληρύνω | V: 1022-1031
πταίω | VI: 883-884
πυγμή, πυκτεύω | VI: 915-917

Schmidt, Martin Anton, Prof.; b.7.20.1919 Wernburg bei. Pössneck (Thuringia); D. Theol. Basel 1951; Instructor Basel 1951; Assist. Prof. Emory Univ. (USA) 1956, San Anselmo (USA) 1958; Assoc. Prof. San Anselmo 1959; Prof. San Anselmo 1961, Basel 1967

πάροικος, παροικία, |
παροικέω | V: 841-850
 | 851-853
παχύνω, πωρόω (πηρόω), |
πώρωσις (πήρωσις), |
σκληρός, σκληρότης, |
σκληροτράχηλος, |
σκληρύνω | V: 1022-1031

Schmitz, Otto, Prof.; b.6.16.1883 Hummeltenberg, Kr. Lennep; Lic. Theol. Berlin 1909; Instructor Berlin 1910; Assist. Prof. Basel 1913; Prof. Münster 1916; Assist. Prof. Bethel 1934, Wuppertal 1945; d.10.20.1957

θρόνος | III: 160-167
παραγγέλλω, παραγγελία | V: 761-765
παρακαλέω, παράκλησις | V: 773-779
 | 788-799

Schneemelcher, Wilhelm, Prof.; b.8.21.1914 Berlin; Lic. Theol. Berlin 1940; Instructor Göttingen 1952; Prof. Bonn 1954

υἱός, υἱοθεσία | VIII: 392-397

Schneider, Carl, Prof. Emeritus; b.12.19.1900 Zwickau; D. Phil. Leipzig 1928; Instructor Leipzig 1930; Prof. Riga 1930, Königsberg 1935, Mainz 1966

καθαιρέω, καθαίρεσις | III: 411-413
κάθημαι, καθίζω, |
καθέζομαι | III: 440-444
κακολογέω | III: 468
καταπέτασμα | III: 628-630
καταστρηνιάω | III: 631
καταφρονέω, καταφρονητής, |
περιφρονέω | III: 631-633
μασάομαι | IV: 514-515
μαστιγόω, μαστίζω, μάστιξ | IV: 515-519
μεσότοιχον | IV: 625
μέτωπον | IV: 635-637
μώλωψ | IV: 829
ῥάβδος, ῥαβδίζω, ῥαβδοῦχος | VI: 966-971

Schneider, Johannes, Prof.; b.9.23.1895 Stadtoldendorf, Kr. Holzminden; D. Rer. Pol. Göttingen 1922; Lic. Theol. Berlin 1927; Instructor Berlin 1930; Prof. Berlin 1935, Berlin (Humboldt-Univ.) 1950; d.5.23.1970

(βαίνω), ἀναβαίνω, κατα- |
βαίνω, μεταβαίνω | I: 518-523
βάσανος, βασανίζω, |
βασανισμός, βασανιστής | I: 561-563
ἔκτρωμα | II: 465-467
ἔρχομαι, ἔλευσις, ἀπ-, δι-, |
εἰσ-, ἐξ-, ἐπ-, παρ-, |
παρεισ-, περι-, προσ-, |
συνέρχομαι | II: 666-684
ἥκω | II: 926-928
ἡλικία | II: 941-943
ἠχέω | II: 954-955
καῦμα, καυματίζω | III: 642-643
καῦσις, καύσων, καυσόομαι, |
καυστηριάζομαι | III: 643-645
κινέω, μετακινέω | III: 718-720
κλάδος | III: 720-722
κολάζω, κόλασις | III: 814-817
(κολακεύω) κολακία | III: 817-818
κονιάω | III: 827
κράσπεδον | III: 904
μάκελλον | IV: 370-372
μέρος | IV: 594-598
μόλις, μόγις | IV: 735-736
ξύλον | V: 37-41
ὀλεθρεύω, ὄλεθρος, |
ὀλοθρευτής, ἐξολοθρεύω | V: 167-171
ὀμνύω | V: 176-185
ὅμοιος, ὁμοιότης, ὁμοιόω, |
ὁμοίωσις, ὁμοίωμα, |
ἀφομοιόω, παρόμοιος, |
παρομοιάζω | V: 186-199
ὄνειδος, ὀνειδίζω, |

ὀνειδισμός   V: 238-242
ὅρκος, ὁρκίζω, ὁρκωμοσία,
  ἐνορκίζω, ἐξορκίζω
  (ἐξορκιστής), ἐπίορκος,
  ἐπιορκέω   V: 457-467
παγίς, παγιδεύω   V: 593-596
παραβαίνω, παράβασις,
  παραβάτης, ἀπαράβατος,
  ὑπερβαίνω   V: 736-744
σταυρός, σταυρόω,
  ἀνασταυρόω   VII: 572-584
στενάζω, στεναγμός,
  συστενάζω   VII: 600-603
συζητέω, συζήτησις,
  συζητητής   VII: 747-748
σχῆμα, μετασχηματίζω   VII: 954-958
τιμή, τιμάω   VIII: 169-180

Schniewind, Julius, Prof.; b.5.28.1883 Elberfeld; Lic.
Theol. Halle 1910; Instructor Halle 1914; Assoc.
Prof. Halle 1921; Prof. Greifswald 1927, Königsberg
1929, Kiel 1935, Halle 1936; d.9.7.1948

ἀγγελία, ἀγγέλλω, ἀν-, ἀπ-,
  δι-, ἐξ-, κατ-, πρόκατ-
  αγγέλλω, καταγγελεύς   I: 56-73
ἐπαγγέλλω, ἐπαγγελία,
  ἐπάγγελμα, προεπαγγέλ-
  λομαι   II: 576-586

Schrage, Wolfgang, Prof.; b.7.30.1928 Hagen-Haspe;
D. Theol. Kiel 1959; Instructor Kiel 1963; Assist.
Prof. Tübingen 1963; Prof. Bonn 1964

συναγωγή, ἐπισυναγωγή,
  ἀρχισυνάγωγος,
  ἀποσυνάγωγος   VII: 798-852
τυφλός, τυφλόω   VIII: 270-294

Schreiber, Johannes, Prof.; b.12.11.1927 Gahlen; D.
Theol. Bonn 1960; Prof. Bochum 1965

Schrenk, Gottlob, Prof. amd Hon. Prof.; b.2.10.1879
Frankfurt; Assist. Prof. Bethel 1913; Prof. Zurich
1923; Hon. Prof. Zurich 1949; d.4.13.1965

ἄδικος, ἀδικία, ἀδικέω,
  ἀδίκημα   I: 149-163
ἀντίδικος   I: 373-375
βάρος, βαρύς, βαρέω   I: 553-561
βιάζομαι, βιαστής   I: 609-614
βίβλος, βιβλίον   I: 615-620
βούλομαι, βουλή, βούλημα   I: 629-637
γράφω, γραφή, γράμμα,
  ἐπι-, προγράφω,
  ὑπόγραμμος   I: 742-773
διαλέγομαι, διαλογίζομαι,
  διαλογισμός   II: 93-98
δίκη, δίκαιος, δικαιοσύνη,
  δικαιόω, δικαίωμα,
  δικαίωσις, δικαιοκρισία   II: 178-225
ἐκδικέω, ἔκδικος, ἐκδίκησις   II: 442-446
ἐντέλλομαι, ἐντολή   II: 544-556
εὐδοκέω, εὐδοκία   II: 738-751

θέλω, θέλημα, θέλησις   III: 44-62
ἱερός, τὸ ἱερόν, ἱερωσύνη,
  ἱερατεύω, ἱεράτευμα,
  ἱερατεία (-ία), ἱερουργέω,
  ἱερόθυτος, ἱεροπρεπής,
  ἱεροσυλέω, ἱερόσυλος,
  ἱερεύς, ἀρχιερεύς   III: 221-283
καταδικάζω, καταδίκη   III: 621-623
ἐκλέγομαι, ἐκλογή,
  ἐκλεκτός   IV: 144
                                                 168-192
λεῖμμα, ὑπόλειμμα, καταλείπω,
  (κατά- περί-, διάλειμμα)   IV: 194-196
                                                 209-214
πατήρ, πατρῷος, πατριά,
  ἀπάτωρ, πατρικός   V: 945-959
                                                 974-1022

Schulz, Siegfried, Prof.; b.6.28.1927 Rummelsburg
(Pomerania); D. Theol. Kiel 1953; Instructor Erlangen
1957; Assoc. Prof. Zurich 1961; Prof. Zurich 1964

πορεύομαι, εἰσπορεύομαι,
  ἐκπορεύομαι   VI: 566-579
πόρνη, πόρνος, πορνεία,
  πορνεύω, ἐκπορνεύω   VI: 579-595
πραΰς, πραΰτης   VI: 645-651
πρόβατον, προβάτιον   VI: 689-692
σκιά, ἀποσκίασμα, ἐπισκιάζω   VII: 394-400
σπέρμα, σπείρω, σπορά,
  σπόρος, σπόριμος   VII: 536-538
                                                 543-547

Schumm, Karl, Pastor; b.1.28.1913 Oberstetten
(Württemberg)

Schweizer, Eduard, Prof.; b.4.18.1913 Basel; D. Theol.
Basel 1938; Instructor Zurich 1941; Prof. Mainz
1946, Bonn 1949, Zurich 1949

πνεῦμα, πνευματικός, πνέω,
  ἐμπνέω, πνοή, ἐκπνέω,
  θεόπνευστος   VI: 389-455
σάρξ, σαρκικός, σάρκινος   VII: 98-105
                                                 108-110
                                                 119-151
σῶμα, σωματικός,
  σύσσωμος   VII: 1024-1044
                                                 1045-1094
υἱός, υἱοθεσία   VIII: 354-357
                                                 363-392
                                                 399
χοϊκός   IX: 472-479
ψυχή, ψυχικός, ἀνάψυξις,
  ἀναψύχω, δίψυχος,
  ὀλιγόψυχος   IX: 637-656
                                                 661-666

Schwen, Paul, Pastor; b.5.19.1879 Bärenstein; Lic.
Theol. Leipzig 1906; d.10.9.1949

Schwerdtfeger, Dieter, Pastor; b.3.5.1920 Halle/Saale

Seesemann, Heinrich, Hon. Prof.; b.5.13.1904 Dorpat;

Lic. Theol. Göttingen 1932; Instructor Göttingen 1935; Assist. Prof. Riga 1935, Berlin 1939, Frankfurt 1950; Hon. Prof.

ὄγκος	V: 41
οἶδα	V: 116-119
οἶνος	V: 162-166
ὀλίγος	V: 171-173
ὅλος, ὁλοτελής	V: 174-176
ὀπίσω, ὄπισθεν	V: 289-292
ὀρφανός	V: 487-488
ὀσφύς	V: 496-497
πάλαι, παλαιός, παλαιότης, παλαιόω	V: 717-720
πανήγυρις	V: 722
παροξύνω, παροξυσμός	V: 857
πατάσσω	V: 939-940
πατέω, καταπατέω, περιπατέω, ἐμπεριπατέω	V: 940-941 943-945
πεῖρα, πειράω, πειράζω, πειρασμός, ἀπείραστος, ἐκπειράζω	VI: 23-36
ποικίλος, πολυποίκιλος	VI: 484-485

Sjöberg, Erik, Dr.; b.4.1.1907 Ovenåker (Sweden); D. Theol. Lund 1939; Instructor Åbo (Finland) 1939; d.12.22.1963

ὀργή, ὀργίζομαι, ὀργίλος, παροργίζω, παροργισμός	V: 412-418
πνεῦμα	VI: 375-389

v.Soden, Hans, Prof.; b.11.4.1881 Dresden; Lic. Theol. Berlin 1906; Instructor Berlin 1910; Assoc. Prof. Breslau 1918; Prof. Breslau 1920, Marburg 1924; d.10.2.1945

ἀδελφός, ἀδελφή, ἀδελφότης, φιλάδελφος, φιλαδελφία, ψευδάδελφος	I: 144-146

Staab, Karl, Prof. Emeritus; b.4.25.1892 Zellingen; D. Theol. Würzburg 1922; Instructor Munich 1925; Prof. Würzburg 1929

Stählin, Gustav, Prof. Emeritus; b.2.28.1900 Nuremberg; D. Phil. Erlangen 1927; Lic. Theol. Erlangen 1928; Instructor Leipzig 1930; Assist. Prof. Madras 1932, Leipzig 1940, Vienna 1943; Prof. Erlangen 1946, Mainz 1952

αἰτέω, αἴτημα, ἀπαιτέω, ἐξαιτέω, παραιτέομαι	I: 191-195
ἁμαρτάνω, ἁμάρτημα, ἁμαρτία	I: 289-302
ἅπαξ, ἐφάπαξ	I: 381-384
ἀσθενής, ἀσθένεια, ἀσθενέω, ἀσθένημα	I: 490-493
ἡδονή, φιλήδονος	II: 909-926
θρηνέω, θρῆνος	III: 148-155
ἴσος, ἰσότης, ἰσότιμος	III: 343-355
κοπετός, κόπτω, ἀποκόπτω, ἐγκοπή, ἐγκόπτω,	

ἐκκόπτω	III: 830-860
μῦθος	IV: 762-795
νῦν (ἄρτι)	IV: 1106-1123
ξένος, ξενία, ξενίζω, ξενοδοχέω, φιλοξενία, φιλόξενος	V: 1-36
ὀργή, ὀργίζομαι, ὀργίλος, παροργίζω, παροργισμός	V: 412-416 417-447
παρακαλέω, παράκλησις	V: 779-793
παραμυθέομαι, παραμυθία, παραμύθιον	V: 816-823
περίψημα	VI: 84-93
προκοπή, προκόπτω	VI: 703-719
προσκόπτω, πρόσκομμα, προσκοπή, ἀπρόσκοπος	VI: 745-758
σάκκος	VII: 56-64
σκάνδαλον, σκανδαλίζω	VII: 339-358
τύπτω	VIII: 260-269
φιλέω, καταφιλέω, φίλημα, φίλος, φίλη, φιλία	IX: 113-171
χήρα	IX: 440-465

Stauffer, Ethelbert, Prof. Emeritus; b.5.8.1902 Friedelsheim; Lic. Theol. Halle-Wittenberg 1929; Instructor Halle-Wittenberg 1930; Prof. Bonn 1934, Erlangen 1948

ἀγαπάω, ἀγάπη, ἀγαπητός	I: 35-55
ἀγών, ἀγωνίζομαι, ἀντ-, ἐπ-, καταγωνίζομαι, ἀγωνία	I: 134-140
ἀθλέω, συναθλέω, ἄθλησις	I: 167-168
βοάω	I: 625-628
βραβεύω, βραβεῖον	I: 637-639
γαμέω, γάμος	I: 648-657
ἐγώ	II: 343-362
ἑδραῖος, ἑδραίωμα	II: 362-364
εἷς	II: 434-442
ἐμφυσάω	II: 536-537
ἐπιτιμάω, ἐπιτιμία	II: 623-627
θεός, θεότης, ἄθεος, θεοδίδακτος, θεῖος, θειότης	III: 90-92 94-121
ἵνα	III: 323-333

Steinwender, Klaus, Dr.; b.9.20.1924 Stolp (Pomerania); D. Jur. Göttingen 1957

Strathmann, Hermann, Prof.; b.8.30.1882 Opherdicke (Westphalia); Lic. Theol. Bonn 1909; Instructor Bonn 1910; Assoc. Prof. Heidelberg 1915; Prof. Rostock 1916, Erlangen 1918; d.11.29.1966

λαός	IV: 29-39 50-57
λατρεύω, λατρεία	IV: 58-65
λειτουργέω, λειτουργία, λειτουργός, λειτουργικός	IV: 215-222 226-231
Λευ(ε)ί, Λευ(ε)ίς	IV: 234-239
Λιβερτῖνοι	IV: 265-266
μάρτυς, μαρτυρέω, μαρτυρία, μαρτύριον, ἐπιμαρτυρέω,	

συμμαρτυρέω, συνεπι-
μαρτυρέω, καταμαρτυρέω,
μαρτύρομαι, διαμαρτύρομαι,
προμαρτύρομαι, ψευδό-
μαρτυς, ψευδομαρτυρέω,
ψευδομαρτυρία   IV: 474-514
πόλις, πολίτης, πολιτεύομαι,
πολιτεία, πολίτευμα   VI: 516-535

Stumpff, Albrecht, Dr.; b.11.23.1908 Zillhausen, Kr.
Balingen; D. Theol. Tübingen 1934; d.6.20.1940

εὐωδία   II: 808-810
ζῆλος, ζηλόω, ζηλωτής,
    παραζηλόω   II: 877-888
ζημία, ζημιόω   II: 888-892
ἴχνος   III: 402-406

Stumpff, Otto; b.12.9.1916 Stuttgart; d.9.9.1943

Traub, Hellmut, Pastor; b.7.13.1904 Dortmund

οὐρανός, οὐράνιος,
    ἐπουράνιος, οὐρανόθεν   V: 497-502
             509-543

Tröger, Karl-Wolfgang, Dr.; b.9.14.1932 Auerbach
(Vogtland); Doctorate Berlin (Humboldt-Univ.) 1967

ψυχή   IX: 658-660

Viering, Fritz, Superintendent; b.11.3.1910 Dortmund;
D. Theol. Tübingen 1938; Instructor Münster 1957;
Assist. Prof. Berlin (KH) 1963

Vogel, Willy, Pastor; b.1.15.1907 Bräunsdorf, Kr.
Chemnitz

Walters, William Peter Max (Katz, Peter), Dr.; b.7.1.1886
Mannheim; d.3.25.1962

ὄχλος   V: 584-585

Wanke, Günther, Dr.; b.8.9.1939 Salzburg; D. Theol.
Vienna 1964; Instructor Erlangen-Nuremberg 1970;
Assist. Prof. Erlangen-Nuremberg 1970

φοβέομαι, φόβος   IX: 197-205

Wanner, Arnold, Pastor; b.7.5.1926 Stuttgart

Weinreich, Otto, Prof.; b.3.13.1886 Karlsruhe; D. Phil.
Heidelberg 1908; Instructor Halle 1914; Assoc. Prof.
Tübingen 1916; Prof. Heidelberg 1918, Tübingen
1921; d.3.26.1972

Weiser, Artur, Prof. Emeritus; b.11.18.1893 Karlsruhe;
Lic. Theol. Heidelberg 1921; Instructor Heidelberg
1922; Assoc. Prof. Heidelberg 1928; Prof. Tübingen
1930

πιστεύω, πίστις, πιστός   VI: 182-196

Weiss, Hans-Friedrich, Dr.; b.10.2.1929 Colditz
(Saxony); D. Theol. Jena 1957; Instructor Jena 1962;
Assist. Prof. Jena 1965

Φαρισαῖος   IX: 35-48

Weiss, Konrad, Prof.; b.7.24.1907 Wüstewaltersdorf;
D. Theol. Berlin 1932; Instructor Berlin 1937; Assoc.
Prof. Rostock 1946; Prof. Rostock 1948

πούς   VI: 624-631
πυρέσσω, πυρετός   VI: 956-959
στόμα   VII: 692-701
ὑπωπιάζω   VIII: 590-591
φέρω, ἀναφέρω, διαφέρω,
    τὰ διαφέροντα, διάφορος
    (ἀδιάφορον), εἰσφέρω,
    προσφέρω, προσφορά,
    συμφέρω, σύμφορος, φόρος,
    φορέω, φορτίον, φορτίζω   IX: 56-87
χρηστός, χρηστότης,
    χρηστεύομαι, χρηστολογία   IX: 483-492

Wilckens, Ulrich, Prof.; b.8.5.1928 Hamburg; D. Theol.
Heidelberg 1956; Instructor Heidelberg 1958; Assist.
Prof. Marburg 1959; Prof. Berlin (KH) 1961, Hamburg
1968

σοφία, σοφός, σοφίζω   VII: 465-476
             496-528
στολή   VII: 687-691
στῦλος   VII: 732-736
ὑποκρίνομαι, συνυποκρίνομαι,
    ὑπόκρισις, ὑποκριτής,
    ἀνυπόκριτος   VIII: 559-571
ὕστερος, ὕστερον, ὑστερέω,
    ἀφυστερέω, ὑστέρημα,
    ὑστέρησις   VIII: 592-601
χάραγμα   IX: 416-417
χαρακτήρ   IX: 418-423

Windfuhr, Walter, Hon. Prof.; b.5.6.1878 Hamburg;
Prof. Hamburg 1919; Hon. Prof. Hamburg 1929;
d.5.22.1970

Windisch, Hans, Prof.; b.4.25.1881 Leipzig; D. Phil.
Leipzig 1906; Lic. Theol. Leipzig 1908; Instructor
Leipzig 1908; Prof. Leyden 1914, Kiel 1924, Halle
1935; d.11.8.1935

ἀσκέω   I: 494-496
ἀσπάζομαι, ἀπασπάζομαι,
    ἀσπασμός   I: 496-502
βάρβαρος   I: 546-553
Ἕλλην, Ἑλλάς, Ἑλληνικός,
    Ἑλληνίς, Ἑλληνιστής,
    Ἑλληνιστί   II: 504-516
ζύμη, ζυμόω, ἄζυμος   II: 902-906
καπηλεύω   III: 603-605

van der Woude, Adam Simon, Prof.; b.10.16.1927
Oosterlittens (Holland); Doctorate Groningen 1957;
Prof. Groningen 1960

χρίω, χριστός, ἀντίχριστος,
    χρῖσμα, χριστιανός   IX: 509-510
             517-520
             521-527

Wülfing, v.Martitz, Peter, Prof.; b.12.9.1930 Berlin; D. Phil. Göttingen 1958; Instructor Cologne 1967; Prof. Cologne

υἱός   VIII: 334-340
                             397-398

Würthwein, Ernst, Prof.; b.9.20.1909 Mannheim; D. Theol. Heidelberg 1934; Instructor Tübingen 1938; Assist. Prof. Tübingen 1946; Assoc. Prof. Tübingen 1948; Prof. Marburg 1954

μισθός, μισθόω, μίσθιος,
    μισθωτός, μισθαποδότης,
    μισθαποδοσία, ἀντιμισθία   IV: 706-712
μετανοέω, μετάνοια   IV: 980-989

Zahrnt, Heinz, Dr.; b.5.31.1915 Kiel; D. Theol. Heidelberg 1948

Zimmerli, Walther, Prof.; b.1.20.1907 Schiers (Switzerland); Lic. Theol. Göttingen 1932; Assoc. Prof. Zurich 1935; Prof. Zurich 1938, Göttingen 1951

παῖς θεοῦ   V: 654-677
χάρις, χαρίζομαι, χαριτόω   IX: 376-387

Zimmermann, Klaus, Pastor; b.10.22.1930 Altenburg (Thuringia)

PRE-HISTORY OF THE THEOLOGICAL DICTIONARY OF THE NEW TESTAMENT

Dictionaries are like watches;
the worst is better than none,
and the best cannot be expected to go quite true.

Samuel Johnson (1709-1784)[1]

1. The Vocabulary of the Complutensian Polyglot and Greek Studies at the Time of the Reformation

a. In the Middle Ages Greek was little known, although intellectual life was much influenced by Greek writers. The Greek philosophers, mathematicians, and astronomers were expounded at the universities but they were read in Latin translation, not in Greek. The Council of Vienne in 1311 recommended the setting up of chairs for the study of the Greek language so that a better understanding of holy scripture might be attained, but theological questions were discussed in terms of the Vulgate, not the Greek text. Since the NT was not known in Greek, no Greek dictionary of the NT was needed.

In 1502 the learned cardinal Ximenes, who had founded the university of Alcala, the Roman Complutum, asked the professors there to prepare an edition of the Bible in several languages. Spanish scholars had been to Italy and studied Greek there. Ximenes also summoned the Greek scholar Demetrius Ducas of Crete to come from Italy to Spain and take part in the work. This man played a great part in editing the Greek text of the polyglot.[2] Opinions differ as to who his fellow-workers were. Since the aim was to bring out a good edition, an attempt was made to consult as many Hebrew and Greek manuscripts as possible. Ximenes managed to borrow some from the Vatican library. The team worked very slowly, so that printing was finished only in 1517. The cardinal saw the work through press but did not live to see the appearance of the book. He died in 1517 at the age of 81. Papal approval for publication was not secured, however, until 1520. The printing numbered 600 copies. It

---

[1]Johnson's own work, *A Dictionary of the English Language: in which the words are deduced from their Originals, and illustrated in their different Significations by Examples from the best Writers. To which are prefixed, a History of the Language, and an English Grammar,* was published in 1755.

[2]F. Delitzsch, *Studien zur Entstehungsgeschichte der Polyglottenbibel des Cardinals Handbuch kl. AW,* II, 1⁴ (1913), 706f.; F. A. Fabricius, *Bibliotheca Graeca,* VI (1798),

reached Germany only later, so that Luther could not use it in his Bible translation.

In regard to the OT the polyglot has the Septuagint with Latin interpretation, the Vulgate, the Hebrew text with brief grammatical notes in the margin, and the Targum Onkelos. It has two columns for the NT, the Greek text and the Vulgate. The sixth volume contains a Greek vocabulary, though this could hardly be called a dictionary. Words without references are assembled on 75 pages of three columns each. Usually only a single Latin word is given for each Greek term. Sometimes a second is added for clarification or differentiation, but no justice is done to the many senses of the NT words. Nor is the list complete; thus we do not find ἀντίχριστος, ἁρπαγμός or ἱλαστήριον.

The editors of the polyglot obviously expected that its readers would know little Greek. To make translation from Greek easier for them, and to make possible comparison with the Vulgate, they arranged the text so that the Greek and Latin text would agree line for line on each page. They also provided each Greek word with a small Latin letter and attached the same letter to the corresponding Latin word in the Vulgate text. The vocabulary was also meant for readers with only a primitive knowledge of Greek. It begins with "α articulus postpositus. neutri generis numeri pluralis. Que." Verbs are not just given in the present tense but also listed alphabetically in their various moods and tenses. Thus we find γεγενημενος, γεγενησθαι, γεγεννηκα, γεγεννημαι, γεγεννημενος, γεγεννησθαι and γεγονα recorded as independent words.

b. Prior to the vocabulary of the Complutensian Polyglot there had been Greek dictionaries in the 15th century, although not for the NT.[3] Greek studies in Italy are commonly attributed to the expulsion of Greek scholars after the fall of Constantinople in 1453. But even before this Greek had been studied in Italy. According to Petrarch (1304-1374), who has been called the "re-awakener of classical antiquity,"[4] there were in Italy in 1360 some eight or nine scholars in Florence, Bologna, Verona, Sulmona, and Mantua who knew Greek.[5] In 1396 Chrysoloras was summoned from Constantinople to Italy. It was he who edited the first Greek grammar of the renaissance which Erasmus and Reuchlin both used to teach Greek. He taught in several Italian cities, led a wandering life, and died in Florence in 1415. Francesco Filelfo (1398-1481), Venetian envoy to Constantinople (1420-1427), learned Greek well. When he returned to Italy, he brought back with him forty Greek writers from Constantinople. Chrysoloras through his labors produced many scholars, e.g., Leonardo Bruni Aretino (1369-1444), Guarino of Verona (1374-1460), and others. Most important is Lorenzo Valla (1407-1457), who in 1433 com-

---

[3]L. Cohn, "Griech. Lexikographie" in K. Brugmann-A. Thumb, *Griech. Grammatik, Handbuch kl. AW*, II, 1⁴ (1913), 706f.; F. A. Fabricius, *Bibliotheca Graeca*, VI (1798), 628-680.

[4]A. Gudeman, *Grundriss der Geschichte der klass. Philologie*² (1909), 171.

[5]F. Paulsen, *Geschichte des gelehrten Unterrichts auf den deutschen Schulen u. Universitäten vom Ausgang des MA bis zur Gegenwart*, I³ (1919), 70.

pared the Vulgate with the Greek text of the NT on a manuscript basis. Theodoros Gaza (1398-1475), born in Salonica, taught in Florence, Ferrara, Rome, and Naples. His γϱαμματικῆς εἰσαγωγῆς βίβλια δ was a favorite textbook which Erasmus used as a foundation. Angelus Politianus (1454-1494), who taught Reuchlin, had already translated Homer's Iliad 2-5 at the age of 16. His work in teaching and translation had a wide influence, giving people the impression of being transported to Greece.[6]

c. In Germany the study of Greek came much later. Reuchlin and Erasmus had to learn Greek elsewhere. It is due to their work, and then to that of Melanchthon and his students, that Greek came to be widely known in Germany. Both directly and indirectly Erasmus was always demanding the study of Greek. In a letter to Anton von Bergen in 1501 he says that Latin culture is mutilated without it. It is especially important that the theologian should learn Greek. The early translators of holy scripture render Greek figures of speech in such a way that even the first sense which native theologians call the literal one cannot be understood without a mastery of Greek.[7] In no case should the theologian be satisfied with unreliable aids. Jerome's translation is not enough; scripture must be quoted according to the sources.[8]

Melanchthon pleads for Greek in the same way as Erasmus. Without it there can be no proper study of either philosophy or theology. Melanchthon summons his students to devote at least some hours to Greek and he will see to it that their time is not wasted. He looks ahead optimistically. The German people will be transformed by the study of Greek. It will become mild and tame in mind and manner whereas previously its barbarian studies made it more like a wild people.[9]

Young students obeyed the summons of their revered teachers. Reuchlin was enthusiastically received when he came to Ingolstadt in 1520 to teach an hour of Hebrew and an hour of Greek every day. The humanist J. Gussubelius in an inspired address presented him to the university as a man with whom no one in Germany could compare. He was not an ordinary man but a god who had been sent in mortal garb to men to lead them out of indolence to industry, out of barbarism to purity of morals, out of darkness to light, out of ignorance to learning. Previously sophistical obduracy and corruption had kept people from the right path. But the golden age was near. Studies were blossoming and

---

[6]O. Kluge, "Die griech. Studien in Renaissance und Humanismus," *Zschr. für Geschichte der Erziehung u. des Unterrichts*, 24 (1934), 7.

[7]P. S. Allen, *Opus Epistolarum Des. Erasmi Roterodami*, I (1906), No. 149, 15ff., p. 352, cf. E. W. Kohls, "Die theol. Lebensaufgabe des Erasmus u. die oberrheinischen Reformatoren," *Arbeiten zur Theologie*, I, 39 (1969), 14.

[8]Erasmus, *Methodus* (ed. A. and U. Holborn [1933], 152, 1ff.; 158, 6ff.; cf. K. A. Meissinger, *Erasmus v. Rotterdam, Veröffentlichungen des Instituts für Reformationsforschung EV München*, I² (1948), 212-215.

[9]Melanchthon, "De corrigendis adolescentiae studiis," CR, XI, 25; cf. Paulsen, *op. cit.*, 119.

Reuchlin was their inspired herald.[10] Students flocked to Reuchlin and filled his lecture-room. In a letter dated 4.12.1520 he said that he had almost 400 students every day when he was teaching Greek and Hebrew.[11] His audience was almost larger than the then student body at Ingolstadt.

Luther in a letter to Spalatin says of Melanchthon that his lecture-room was full and that he attracted theologians in particular.[12] A similar report comes from Leipzig where the Englishman Richard Crocus taught Greek from 1515. He, too, drew a large audience. His students revered him as a messenger from heaven and in an address to the university he himself says that "theologians are so respectful and without pride that even though advanced in years they do not refuse to attend my lectures but follow the example of Cato who learned Greek when he was grayhaired."[13]

The teaching of Greek and the spread of Greek learning were greatly hampered at first by the lack of printed primers and texts. The first printed book in Greek appeared in Italy in 1476. It was the grammar of Constantine Laskaris. German publishers began to use Greek characters only c. 1500. W. Schenk in Erfurt published the *Elementale introductorium in ideoma graecanicum* in 1501. Often Greek words and sentences were left out and had to be filled in later by hand. Reuchlin writes from Ingolstadt that he had to write out the daily assignments for his lectures himself and when Melanchthon lectured on Demosthenes his students had to write out the text. The Greek grammar of Chrysoloras was published in Strassburg in 1515. The grammatical introduction of Theodoros Gaza, which Erasmus translated into Latin to give it wider circulation in Germany, was printed in Basel in 1516. Special note should be taken of Melanchthon's *Institutiones graecae grammaticae*. This work went through 44 impressions in the period 1518-1622.

The first book to be printed wholly in Greek in Germany was the edition of Erasmus' New Testament published by Froben of Basel in 1516. From a publishing point of view this was a masterpiece but from a scholarly point of view it brought no great credit to Erasmus. He had long toyed with the idea of publishing a Greek New Testament. Since he wanted to get this out before the Complutensian Polyglot, he worked under great pressure. In the main Erasmus utilized two 15th century minuscules available to him in Basel, 2^e for the Gospels, 2^{ap} for Acts and the Epistles, and the 12th century MS 1^r for Revelation. The latter unfortunately broke off at 22:16, and, as is well known, Erasmus hastily translated the remaining verses from the Vulgate into Greek. He was helped by Gerbel and especially Oecolampadius, an excellent

[10]L. Geiger, *Johann Reuchlin* (1871), 468, cf. also H. Dibbelt, "Reuchlins griech. Studien," *Das Gymnasium*, 49 (1938), 16-26.
[11]L. Geiger, *Johann Reuchlins Briefwechsel, Bibliothek des litterarischen Vereins in Stuttgart*, 126 (1875), 323.
[12]Paulsen, *op. cit.*, 119.
[13]*Ibid.*, 106.

Hebraist, who in correcting the work also used MS 1[eap], which Erasmus did not rate highly. To the Greek text Erasmus added a new Latin rendering, which in many respects diverged from the Vulgate, and also a commentary with Greek and Latin words. Two introductions precede the text, *Paraclesis ad lectorem pium* and *Methodus*. The work is not just a handy edition of the text but with the introductions, the Greek text, the Latin, and the commentary is a bulky folio volume of some 1000 pages. In the short space of five months Erasmus not only assembled the text but saw the work through the printing, proofreading and publishing. He often ate and slept with the printers in Froben's printing shop so that no time should be lost. Although the first edition of over 12,000 copies contained many errors, it was well received, and three years later a new edition was called for in which most of the errors were corrected. Soon after the appearance of the *Novum Instrumentum*, as Erasmus called his edition, Luther used it for the last chapters of his *Lectures on Romans* (1515-1516) and he later turned to it again in his translation of the Bible.

Since Luther's education was in the scholastic rather than the humanistic tradition, he did not have enough knowledge to translate directly from Greek to German. He certainly had the chance to learn Greek in Erfurt. But he did not study it thoroughly. Thus he acquired only a preliminary knowledge. When the young Melanchthon came from Tübingen to Wittenberg Luther probably took up the study of Greek more intensively. When he translated the NT he knew the Vulgate well. Since Erasmus' NT offered a Latin translation as well as the Greek text, to a large extent he let himself be guided by this in his translation out of the Greek.[14]

On theological grounds Luther attached great value to learning Greek. In his work *An die Ratsherren aller Städte deutschen Landes* in 1524 he asked that as the gospel is dear to us, so we should cleave hard to the languages (WA, 15, 37, 17f.). He then compares them to the sheath which holds the knife of the Spirit, the casket in which the jewel is carried, the vessel which holds the drink, the dish in which the food lies. As the gospel itself shows, they are the baskets in which the bread and fishes and fragments are carried (WA, 15, 38, 8ff.). Luther realizes that one can be a Christian without knowing Hebrew or Greek; one can even be a preacher. He shows, however, that dogmatic errors arise in exposition if the languages are not known. He thus believes that we cannot preserve the gospel properly without the languages (WA, 15, 38, 7f.). He argued, then, that as a knowledge of the languages faded, the gospel and faith and Christianity as a whole declined. Now that they have come back again, they bring such a light and do such great things that the whole

---

[14]Cf. H. Dibbelt, "Hatte Luthers Verdeutschung des NT den griech. Text zur Grundlage?" *Archiv für Reformations-Geschichte*, 38 (1941), 300-330; H. Bornkamm, "Die Vorlagen zur Luthers Übersetzung des NT," ThLZ, 72 (1947), 23-26. Cf. also E. W. Kohls, *Luther oder Erasmus*, I, ThZ Sonderband, 3 (1972), 7-24. Luther on Melanchthon: *at postquam Philippus meus Melanchthon, adolescens corpore, senex venerabili mentis canicie, quo in graecis utor praeceptore, me sic sapere non permisit,* Weimarer Ausgabe, 2, 595, 18-20.

world is astonished and has to confess that we have the gospel almost as clearly and purely as the apostles did and its first purity has been restored (WA, 15, 38, 33f.).

Melanchthon spoke to much the same effect. The proper shaping of the Christian life is a work of the Holy Spirit. If scripture is to be expounded aright, however, knowledge of Greek is absolutely essential (CR, XI, 114f.). Without it one turns to the shadow and does not get at the substance.[15] Melanchthon asked his students to devote at least a few hours to Greek. Those who did would see how a special attention to the language would contribute to an understanding of the sacred mysteries and what a difference there is between the expositor who knows Greek and the one who does not (CR, XI, 25). Since Greek is now learned again, we are in the happy position of being able to speak with the Son of God, the evangelists and the apostles without an interpreter.[16] By the revival of scholarship God has promoted work on the gospel. What is taking place in his day may be compared with the granting of tongues to the apostles on the Day of Pentecost. The languages have contributed to the restoration of theology (CR, XI, 64).

Whereas the reformers welcomed and supported the teaching of Greek, this new subject met with criticism and opposition in some Roman Catholic circles. It was pointed out that the Greeks had been condemned as schismatics by the Catholic Church. To study Greek was to incur a charge of ungodliness. Conrad of Heresbach, when he began to teach Greek in Freiburg in 1521, tells us in his inaugural address that he heard a monk say in a sermon that a new language had lately been found which was called Greek. His hearers were to beware of it, for it was the mother of all heresies. In many hands there was now a book in this language which was given the name of the NT. But this book was full of thorns and serpents.[17] Whether anyone actually said such things, or whether Heresbach was simply describing the situation in the form of an anecdote, need not be decided here. In any case, Erasmus sharply attacked such a view in a letter to John Carondiletus in 1522: *Et ubi sunt interim isti qui negant in literis sacris ullum esse usum Graecarum literarum? Ubi sunt isti cameli verius quam homines, qui blaterant ex Graecis literis nihil aliud oriri quam haereses?*[18]

The first enthusiasm for Greek seems to have soon passed. Melanchthon complains constantly after 1522 that the arts are in decay. In a letter to Helius Eobanus Hessus he exclaims: "Good God, how perverted is the theology of those who want to appear clever by despising scholarship" (CR, I, 613, No. 241). In the *Encomium eloquentiae* he says that there are now many people who deny that the study of rhetoric can be of any profit for theology. This error, which

[15]"De corrigendis adolescentiae studiis," CR, XI, 22.
[16]"De studiis linguae Graecae," CR, XI, 859.
[17]Cf. Paulsen, *op. cit.,* 141 and O. Kluge, *op. cit.,* 12f.
[18]P. S. Allen-H. M. Allen, *Opus Epistolarum Des. Erasmi Roterodami,* V (1924), No. 1334, 833-846, p. 190.

has spread like the plague, has caused many to fight against humanistic studies. But without a knowledge of rhetoric the divine speech itself cannot be properly evaluated (CR, XI, 62). With very strong words Melanchthon inveighs against those who advise inexperienced young people not to study languages. Such people ought to have their tongues cut off (CR, I, 666). If we are wearily to go back from the light of the present to the darkness of the past, there is no quicker way than to give up the study of Greek (CR, XI, 866). The state ought to punish those who mislead young students in this way (CR, XI, 62).

At first Greek was taught only at the large universities. Then it was introduced into the school curriculum. Here, however, it was not pursued intensively. Latin remained the chief foreign language. Greek was taught only at the higher levels. The Brunswick Church Order composed by Bugenhagen in 1528 might be cited in this connection.[19] The Mecklenburg School Order of 1552, which Melanchthon approved, ruled that the higher classes in the bigger schools should have instruction in Greek two hours a week, one hour being devoted to grammar and the other to the reading of Greek authors.

2. New Testament Dictionaries up to H. Cremer

a. Between 1510 and 1568 no fewer than 27 Greek lexicons appeared, often two in the same year.[20] The individual works cannot be easily differentiated but the great number gives evidence of considerable zeal. In the NT field it was some time, however, before an adequate dictionary came out. The otherwise unknown J. Lithocomus published in 1552 a *Lexicon Novi Testamenti et ex parte Veteris* but unfortunately it has not proved possible to find out anything about the author or to consult the work.

The Antwerp Polyglot, also called the Plantinus Polyglot after the publisher, contains a dictionary with the title: *Lexicon graecum et institutiones linguae graecae* (1572), with the long sub-title: *Hoc lexicon graecum diligentia et impensis Christophori Plantini ad sacrorum Bibliorum et simul omnium auctorum graecorum intelligentiam compendio, quanto fieri potuit, maximo confectum, utiliter typis committi posse censemus*. It is meant to cover all Greek authors, so that justice is hardly done to the NT writings.

b. The first attempt to compose a true NT lexicon was made by G. Pasor (1570-1637). Like the Hebraist J. Buxtorff (1564-1629) and the pedagogue J. A. Comenius (1592-1670), Pasor was a student of J. Piscator (1546-1625) in Herborn. He not only studied in Herborn but was also Professor of Theology there from 1607 onwards. He published in 1619 his *Lexicon graeco-latinum in Novum Domini nostri Jesu Christi*

---

[19]E. Sehling, *Die evangelischen Kirchenordnungen des XVI Jhdt.*, VI, 1 (1955), 368.
[20]Cohn, *op. cit.*, 706-709; cf. J. LeLong, *Bibliotheca sacra in binos syllabos distincta*, II (1723), 1197f.

Testamentum. Ubi omnium vocabulorum graecorum themata indicantur et utraque tam themata quam derivata Grammatice resolvuntur. Later he brought out a smaller *Manuale Graecarum vocum Novi Testamenti* and the miniature edition *Syllabus, sive idea graeco-latina omnium NT dictionum, seu dialectorum.*

Herborn, founded in 1584, was then a center of lexical studies.[21] In addition to Pasor, Z. Rosenbach (1595-1638) was at work there as Professor of Medicine and Oriental Languages. Spurred on by Pasor he spent many years preparing dictionaries for the OT and the NT. Unsettled conditions during the Thirty Years War were unfavorable for scholarship, publishing, and the sale of scholarly books, and publication was thus delayed. In 1633 there came out *Moses omniscius sive omniscientia Mosaica, sectionibus VI quam brevissime exhibens supra septies mille Veteris Testamenti voces, secundum rerum locos communes ita dispositas, ut quis inde non tantum omnium autorum scripta accurate resolvere, sed et quaecunque cupit, expedite admodum componere possit.* In this work the words are not arranged alphabetically. As in the lost work of the Alexandrian grammarian Pamphilos or the Onomasticon of Julius Pollux, they are grouped thematically, as is increasingly being demanded today.[22] Materially related words are assembled by Rosenbach in 72 sections. Thus the different words for time are dealt with in c. 11 *De tempore,* parts of the body in c. 31 *De corpore,* and nautical words in c. 52 *De re nautica.* A year later in 1634 NT words were to have been dealt with in a second lexicon. No publisher could be found, however, and only a selection could be issued: *Methodus omniscientiae Christi: cum specimine omniscientiae gentilis et indice corollariorum physicorum Novi Testamenti. Pie doctis lectoribus exhibita, donec opera illa majora, jam diu absoluta, nempe Christus Omniscius et Christus physicus ac medicus.* These indications show what Rosenbach planned and had possibly even outlined. The actual work is in four parts. The first bears the title *Ontologia seu Universalia.* Various word groups are dealt with in 17 chapters with no very obvious principle of arrangement. The individual words are listed without references. Chapters on pronouns, conjunctions, prepositions, adverbs, interjections and numbers are accompanied by others on contrasting pairs such as true and false, good and bad, action and passion. The second part contains 16 chapters of *Physiologia* including *De natura, De mundo, De coelo, De igne, De aqua, De terra* and the various types of plants and animals and the like. In the third part the *Anthropologia* follows in 36 chapters. This deals not only with anthropological terms but also with everything pertaining to human life, e.g., sickness, medicine, dwelling, state, war, trade, conduct. The final part on *Theologia* is very brief. It has only 4 chapters entitled *De Spiritu, Angeli*

---

[21]H. Schlosser, "Die erste Grammatik des nt. lichen Griech. und das erste Septuagints-Wörterbuch," *Festschrift G. Heinrici* (1914), 252-260.

[22]G. Friedrich, "Das bisher noch fehlende Begriffslexikon zum NT," NTSt, 19 (1973), 127-152.

et Daemones, De Deo and *De Religione.*

As a supplement to *Methodus omniscientiae Christi* there was also published the first Septuagint lexicon: *Lexicon breve in LXX interpretes, et libros apocryphos: Methodo Omniscientiae Christi adjunctum, ut studiosi universa S. Biblia Graeca in posterum sibi familiarissima redant.* According to his own statement Rosenbach composed this Septuagint lexicon in the short space of two months on the basis of a concordance which had come out in 1607.

Even Pasor's *Lexicon graeco-latinum* does not follow a strict alphabetical order. Pasor does not group the words by meaning, as Rosenbach does, but puts all the words which have the same stem together and then follows an alphabetical order. He usually starts with the simple form of the verb, then goes on to compounds, and finally deals with the nouns. In an index at the end, the words dealt with are listed alphabetically so that they can be found easily. The meanings of individual terms are lumped together and in many cases are not given very adequately. When a word is used in the transferred sense or as *pars pro toto,* a material paraphrase is given as the meaning. αἷμα might serve as an example: *sanguis* Lk. 13:1; *caedes* Hb. 12:4; *reatus seu poena caedis* Mt. 27:25; *homo* Mt. 27:4; *semen humanum* Ac. 17:26 (vl); *generatio carnalis* Jn. 1:13; *ratio hominis* Mt. 16:17; *homo non renatus* 1 C. 15:50; *homo quicunque* Gl. 1:16; *humana natura* Hb. 2:14; *sacrificium cruentum* Lk. 22:20; *color sanguineus* Ac. 2:20. In compound words Pasor tries to take account of each element in the compound. He does not give every NT reference. The references he does give are in the Greek with a Latin translation. Grammatical questions are often discussed too. On the other hand there are few references to secular authors or the fathers. This is connected with his concept of the NT (→ *infra*).

Some of his etymological derivations are of interest. He traces back many Greek terms to Hebrew stems. αἴγειος comes from αἴξ "goat," which corresponds to Hebrew עֵז. βάπτω is derived from βάω, which comes from בּוא. κεφαλή is related to "to double" because everything in the head is in pairs, two eyes, two ears, two nostrils. In the case of μανθάνω we are referred to למד. τρέφω is connected with טֶרֶף and τρέχω with דֶּרֶך.

As Pasor tells us in the preface, he composed the lexicon in order that young people might come to a better knowledge of the testament of Jesus Christ our Saviour. He rejects philosophers and poets. Homer and his followers say a great deal about the gods but basically they are atheists. *Et uno verbo dicam, ut omnes intelligant: incipiendum esse a Bibliis et in iisdem definendum.* Christ is the focus: *Si Christum discis, satis est si caetera nescis.* Pasor's lexicon enjoyed wide circulation. It was constantly republished for 150 years and reached its thirtieth printing in 1774.

c. In what follows we shall not discuss or even mention all the lexicons that came out after Pasor's[23] but simply deal with the most important and characteristic. C. Schöttgen (1687-1751) began by revising Pasor and considerably enlarging its contents (1716). He brought out his own lexicon in 1746: *Novum Lexicon Graeco-Latinum in Novum D N J C Testamentum*. In this work he aimed at grammatical, historical, and philological exactitude. He refrained from hazardous etymologizing, and did not arrange the words on an etymological principle, but followed the alphabetical order. In spite of the existence of Pasor and other dictionaries, he thought it necessary to write a new work. In contrast to Pasor he gave many references to secular literature. On the other hand he did not give so many Greek quotations from the NT along with his own translations. Schöttgen was convinced that in order to promote understanding of the NT, classical Greek authors must be adduced as well as the OT, the LXX, and the Rabbis. He realized that attention must be paid to Hebrew style in the NT. Having a good knowledge of Hebrew and being well acquainted with the LXX, he had much to offer in illumination of the text. He tried to take Jewish customs and practices into account. Often in his lexicon he referred to his *Horae Hebraicae* in which he had assembled rabbinic examples which helped to bring out the meaning of NT words.

In his treatment of individual words Schöttgen has many subsections so that the articles are clearer and fuller. But he, too, does not give precise meanings. Thus he defines αἷμα in Mt. 16:17 as *natura corrupta* and speaks of the corruption which after the fall has come on man in both reason and will.

J. F. Schleusner in 1792 authored a *Novum Lexicum Graeco-Latinum in Novum Testamentum* in two volumes. This went through several editions. His work is more comprehensive than those of his predecessors. He assembles a good deal of material from the OT, the classical and Hellenistic authors, Josephus, Philo, the Rabbis and the fathers, so that at the time he provided a rich store for further investigation. As he says in the preface, he consulted all existing dictionaries, commentaries, and exegetical monographs. Since he refers to a great number of NT passages, and often gives a brief exposition, his work was for a long time an indispensable aid to exegesis. Schleusner rightly perceived that NT Greek is not that of classical antiquity, so that we are not dealing with Attic Greek but with the popular Macedonian-Alexandrian Greek current in the time of Jesus. The Evangelists and apostles are Semites who have taken over a good deal from the OT. Through examples taken from the OT and the Greek authors he shows that there are strong links to the OT and that the NT contains not a few words unknown to Greeks elsewhere. He combats the view that the NT has the purest and best Greek (→ *infra*). But he also rejects the belief of those who try to understand the NT only in

---

[23]For an instructive survey see W. Grimm, "Kritisch-geschichtliche Übersicht der nt.lichen Verballexika seit der Reformation," ThStKr, 48, 2 (1875), 479-515.

the light of Hebrew and who think that to interpret it there is little need to know Greek (→ *infra*). On the contrary, he tries to show that not infrequently there are in the NT traces of good and pure Greek. At appropriate points he supports this by examples from the Greek authors. Schleusner offers many differentiations of meaning in relation to individual words, though often these have no general validity but acquire an unusual sense from the context. In the case of ἄνθρωπος he distinguishes such meanings as *filius, infans, heros, servus, incola,* and *paganus.* In his instances from the NT he follows the order of the books.

C. G. Bretschneider, who is known by his work *Probabilia de evangelii et epistolarum Joannis apostoli indole et origine* (1820), published his *Lexicon manuale graeco-latinum in libros Novi Testamenti* in 1824. This went through many editions. The author's approach to NT Greek changed from edition to edition. He saw clearly that NT Greek is not classical Greek but koine Greek, or, as he put it, Macedonian Greek. Hence he does not quote the classics but appeals to the pseudepigrapha, Ethiopian Enoch, the Testaments of the Twelve Patriarchs, and the Psalms of Solomon, which hitherto had been little noted. In the main, however, as he himself says, he is governed by the tradition which again and again resorts to the Hebrews and does not pay sufficient regard to the rules of Greek grammar. Later, influenced by Winer's grammar, he pays more attention to Greek authors, especially writers in the koine, and above all Jews who write in Greek like Josephus and Philo, although with some reference to the NT apocrypha as well. Of the older secular writers he turns most often to Homer.

C. A. Wahl, who held posts in Oschatz and Dresden, knew Greek well. After writing two treatises on the grammatical problems of εἰ and εἰς in the NT, he published a NT lexicon in 1822: *Clavis Novi Testamenti philologica usibus scholarum et iuvenum theologiae studiosorum accommodata.* In the foreword he offers a whole list of profane Greek authors whom he has adduced to illustrate the use of Greek. A criticism is that he is not always reliable in his classical quotations, using a compound for the simple form etc.[24] Many of his sections are too broadly conceived, for he first gives the NT passages in Greek, then translates into Latin, and sometimes gives the German as well. He is not content simply to give the exact rendering in the passage concerned but often provides exegetical elucidations and quotations from the commentaries, so that the work becomes very bulky. In individual cases he first adduces NT passages, then the LXX, and finally secular authors. In 1853 he published his *Clavis librorum veteris testamenti apocryphorum philologica.*

C. G. Wilke, originally a Saxon pastor, left the pastorate and took up scholarly work. In 1838 he published his book *Der Urevangelist,* in which he argued for the priority of Mark. His dictionary of the NT came out in 1839-1841 with the title *Clavis Novi Testamenti philologica usibus*

---

[24]Grimm, *op. cit.,* 502.

scholarum et iuvenum theologiae studiosorum accommodata. A second and unaltered edition came out in 1850. The work was very carelessly done.

C. L. W. Grimm, charged to bring out a new edition of Wilke, wrote an almost completely new work. Only a few brief explanations were taken over from Wilke. The result was a new, serviceable, and indispensable tool for NT exegesis. To dissociate himself as much as possible from Wilke, Grimm gave his book the title *Lexicon Graeco-latinum in libros Novi Testamenti.* His concern was to write a work which would enable the student to grasp the meaning of the NT. The work rendered this service for more than 30 years. Grimm gave the etymological derivations of the individual words, explained grammatically significant changes, and set forth the different possibilities of meaning. He did not restrict himself to NT passages but often gave a short history of the terms. Thus we find such phrases as "from Homer on" and "from the time of Herodotus." When no secular instances are discovered, he notes this as in the case of ἀγάπη: *Vox solum biblica et ecclesiastica,* or: *Vox profanis ignota.* The corresponding Hebrew words are given and passages from the LXX are adduced. Instances from Josephus, Philo, and the apostolic fathers are gleaned from his own reading, as he observes in the preface. Although he is at great pains to explain theologically important words correctly, he deliberately avoids any long discussion so as not to go beyond philological limits. Brief bibliographies show where to go for further grammatical, philological, or theological information on the individual terms. The work was republished in 1879, 1888, and — still under Grimm's name — 1903. J. H. Thayer, Professor of NT Exegesis at Harvard, translated it into English in 1886 with some additional material. Since the dictionary was in Greek and Latin, and the knowledge of Latin declined from decade to decade, it finally became unserviceable and was in any case outdated by the discovery of inscriptions and papyri.

3. Theological Dictionaries of the New Testament

In his memorial address for H. Cremer V. Schultze, Dean of the Theological Faculty of Greifswald, said that in Cremer's dictionary we do not merely have a lexical work but also "a biblical theology in lexicographical form."[25] Thus Cremer's work is constantly evaluated contrary to his own desire. Cremer did have a distinctive biblical theology but it was not his concern to write a NT theology arranged alphabetically under the key terms. There have been dictionaries of this kind both before and after him.

a. M. Flacius (1520-1575) composed a dictionary of biblical theology. This came out in 1567 and he called it *Clavis Scripturae Sacrae seu de*

---

[25]V. Schultze, "Rede bei der Gedächtnisfeier" in *August Hermann Cremer, Gedenkblätter* (1904), 21.

sermone Sacrarum Literarum authore Matthia Flacio Illyrico, Pars Prima: in qua singularum vocum atque locutionem S. Scripturae usus ac ratio, Alphabetico ordine, explicatur. Flacius was originally a student of the Venetian humanist Baptista Ignatius, and then followed Luther and Bugenhagen closely. He had all the qualifications for writing a Bible dictionary. In 1544 he became professor of Hebrew in Wittenberg and in 1557 was called to Jena as a ·NT professor. On the title page he says concerning his work: *opus, et maximo annorum aliquot labore ac studio, multisque vigiliis, atque fide singulari, confectum; et maximam quoque S. Theologiae studiosis commoditatem, quicunque candide ac dextre uti eodem voluerint, allaturum: ut simile, in hoc quidem argumenti genere, nullum unquam esse editum, re-ipsa facile sint deprehensuri. Accessit vocum ac phrasium, item locorum S. Scripturae obiter explicatorum, denique etiam rerum, tergeminus Index* (1567). It is astonishing that Flacius was able to write so comprehensive a work in the unsettled conditions of his age.[26]

The first part is a biblical lexicon and theological dictionary, while problems of hermeneutics are dealt with in several excursuses in the second part. W. Dilthey[27] called the first part a concordance, for which preparatory work had been done, but it is more than a concordance. Flacius wrote a comprehensive lexicon in 1344 columns. It deals with theological problems in both the OT and the NT. In alphabetical order biblical terms and expressions are explained. Flacius seeks an understanding of the words because only thus can one get at the meaning and purpose of what is said.[28] For him the words denote the matter. This being so, the expositor has to know them if he is going to understand the sense of scripture (II, 277, 54ff.). The best possible knowledge of the sacred languages of Hebrew and Greek is thus necessary, for without it one is dependent on others and has to guess at the sense (II, 82). Jesus has a threefold name: Jesus, Messiah, Christ. What is more shameful for a teacher and minister of Christ than not to know the names of his Lord and Saviour or to understand what is meant by Jesus, Messiah, and Christ (II, 692, 19ff.)? Through his triumphant title on the cross Christ has declared to us in the three languages of Hebrew, Greek, and Latin who he is. If we do not think it necessary to

[26]He himself moved about a good deal, G. Kawerau, Art. "Flacius," RE³, 6 (1899), 82-89. Because he did not approve of the Augsburg Interim of 1548 he left Wittenberg and went to Hamburg. Finding no printing establishments there, he moved to Magdeburg, where he earned his living as a printing supervisor. He became professor of NT in Jena in 1557 but was dismissed on account of the synergistic controversy in 1561. He wanted to found a Lutheran academy in Regensburg in 1562 but the council, at the instigation of an imperial envoy, refused him protection and so he went to Antwerp. Driven out of Antwerp by war, he sought refuge in Frankfurt in 1567, but the council would not receive him and so he moved to Strassburg, where the *Clavis* appeared. Quotations are from the Basel edition of 1629.

[27]W. Dilthey, *Das natürliche System der Geisteswissenschaften im 17. Jhdt., Gesammelte Schriften,* II (1914), 119.

[28]Cf. G. Moldaenke, *Schriftverständnis und Schriftdeutung im Zeitalter der Reformation, I. Matthias Flacius Illyricus, Forschungen zur Kirchen- und Geistesgeschichte,* 9 (1936).

learn these three languages, through which we are given the possibility of knowing and worshipping God and the Saviour, we heap upon ourselves not only shame and disgrace but guilt as well (II, 692, 6ff.).

Flacius follows the alphabetical order of the Latin, not the Greek words. But it would be a mistake to view his work as a Vulgate lexicon. He does not list many Vulgate words and instead has others which are not in the Vulgate but convey what is in scripture. Sometimes he latinizes Greek words, e.g., adiaphoron, analogia, battologia, plerophoria. The individual articles are grouped according to sense. Flacius pays some attention to etymology, on which he has some odd ideas, and he also traces the change in meaning which some words undergo. His method is first to give the most obvious and natural sense, then to give the transferred sense, and finally to explain difficult expressions. Examples do not follow the sequence of Old and then New Testament but are mixed. Some quotations are given from classical authors and the fathers.

Often the corresponding Hebrew word is given, less often the Greek. This is intentional. For Flacius Hebrew is the original tongue which God gave men at creation and the other languages derive from it. To prove that Greek is dependent on Hebrew he points to similarities in the two alphabets (II, 690, 1-15). A knowledge of Hebrew is essential for an understanding of the NT, since individual words point back to the Hebrew and whole sentences contain Hebraisms. Without a knowledge of Hebrew the NT cannot be expounded or understood (II, 680, 33ff.).

As the head of the implacable Gnesiolutherans, Flacius was one of the chief controversialists of his day. He attacked the Interim severely and was also a heavily engaged champion of pure doctrine in the adiaphoristic, majoristic, Osiandrian, and synergistic disputes. It is not surprising, then, that theologically relevant terms are dealt with very fully in his dictionary. He devotes 24 columns to *imputare* and *imputatio*, 20 to *fides*, 20 to *justitia*, and 17 to *peccatum*. Although he was not a gentle or cautious controversialist, but a pitiless fighter who mounted sharp and often personal attacks, the discussions in his *Clavis* are surprisingly much less aggressive.

b. W. A. Teller (1734-1804), a church councillor in Berlin, wrote a theological dictionary of the NT in German with German words in alphabetical order. In the preface to the first edition of this *Wörterbuch des Neuen Testaments zur Erklärung der christlichen Lehre* (1772) he says that he knew of no index of words "whose author had really sought to explain in a single register the expressions and idioms of our Christian religious books on which a right understanding of the whole of Christianity depends and from which one must extract the core of religion."

While studying theology Teller devoted himself especially to Hebrew, Chaldaic, and Syriac. He also did textual work. When not yet 28 years old he was called to Helmstedt as Professor of Theology, Pastor, and General Superintendent (1761). His *Textbook of the Christian Faith*

(1764) aroused such opposition that his own brother wrote a rejoinder and the book was confiscated in the Electorate of Saxony. Frederick II of Prussia called him to Berlin as a church councillor in 1767. His theological position is typified by an answer he gave to some Jews of the Enlightenment who had thrown off the Mosaic law and who in 1799 asked him as "a noble friend of virtue and honoured friend of humanity" what more they would need than their enlightened faith in God if they were to be accepted into the church without agreeing to those beliefs of Christianity which are contrary to reason. Teller replied that they would have to "accept Christ as the founder of a better moral religion." The baptismal formula could be used: "I baptise thee into the name, or, as it ought really to be translated, the confession of Christ." To make a formal confession of faith would not be necessary. The main thing is that there should actually be faith.[29]

In his dictionary Teller aimed to lead readers who did not know the originals to a point where they could see clearly what they ought to believe and do as Christians. He championed a rational, moral, and inward Christianity freed from everything external. Through the dictionary, as he says in the foreword, he wants to bring more clarity and purity to the system and to distinguish the religion of Jesus from human teachings. Religion is not to be seen as an academic discipline but as the highest wisdom. In the preface to the third edition he tells us what purification from human teachings means. Christ and the apostles took much from the popular ideas of their day. This must be replaced by the religious insights of the present. It is certain that many ideas which belonged to the childhood of NT religion must go now that pure light has spread further and further afield. According to the will of its founder Christianity is simply the highest wisdom leading to ever-increasing felicity.

This is the outlook which underlies Teller's exposition of the individual words of the NT. "To repent" and "do penance" simply means self-amendment. "Atonement" is the union of the Jews with other peoples and of all men in one religion. The kingdom of heaven is the church. According to the common understanding "to rise again" is used in designation of Jesus Christ as the Messiah. The Lord's supper is the meal which Jesus instituted to remind his disciples of his death and passion. The new creature of 2 C. 5:17; Gl. 6:15 is the new and spiritual worshipper who serves God without the intervening material practices of Jewish worship. The spirit of God is a particularly strong impulse toward something, a higher degree of joy, or an extraordinary gift of teaching, prayer, or praise of the divine name in songs and psalms. In the latter sense Greek authors too see the Spirit of God at work in their poets. Revelation is any good thought or religious insight which is fully and clearly grasped by the mind without prior preparation. There is no fear of God. The whole content of religion is to free people from the fear of God

---

[29]W. A. Teller, *Beantwortung des Sendschreibens einiger Hausväter jüdischer Religion* (1799), 45.

and train them in childlike love, respect, and reverence for him. Similarly Teller refuses to recognize the wrath of God. Where "wrath" appears, it is more fitting, and linguistically more accurate, to replace it by "punishment."

Teller's dictionary had considerable influence. Yet it also met with opposition.

c. The Württemberg prelate F. C. Oetinger composed in 1776 a *Biblisches und Emblematisches Wörterbuch, dem Tellerischen Wörterbuch und Anderer falschen Schrifterklärungen entgegen gesetzt.* He relied to a large extent on Bengel, Böhme, and Arndt, and also on various contemporaries. The opponents with whom he took issue were Semler, Teller, Wolff, Leibniz, Basedow, and others. Oetinger quotes many works of his day, both to find support and also in refutation. He follows an alphabetical order in German. For each NT word he gives the Greek and sometimes the Hebrew too. He also includes not only words which would figure in a Bible concordance but others which seem to be especially important for an understanding of the Bible, e.g., Trinity, quintessence, tincture, and triumph. He does not list every possible word or reference but only those in relation to which he can develop his own thoughts. Thus not a single page is devoted to "penitence," "kingdom of heaven," "love," or "prophet," but "crystal" has three pages, "place" and "city of God" have some seven each, and "temple of Ezekiel" thirteen. Under "man" he includes a poem by his friend Fricker which "in a wedding-song summarizes briefly all that can be said about man." Oetinger is not concerned logically to expound the Greek and Hebrew terms but to impart some of the secrets which he has unravelled. In opposition to the wisdom of his day he appeals to the deeper wisdom of the Bible.[30] He does at least realise that one cannot explain everything. Thus what is obscure must be reverently left on one side and words of rich content should be respectfully pondered in the heart after the example of Mary, since only at the end of the days will the whole riches of scripture be laid bare.

The individual articles differ greatly. Note has already been taken of the odd lengths of some of them. In content, too, they are treated very differently. In the case of "sin" Oetinger refers to the terms for sin in the OT. Under "day of Christ" he deals with ἡμέρα, παρουσία, ἀποκάλυψις, ἐπιφάνεια, φανέρωσις and gives the appropriate NT references. Under "blessedness" he has a list of synonymous expressions with NT examples. In this type of article he tries to throw light on the biblical data. In others he diverges from the theme, deals with what others have said, and expounds his own experiences and findings

---

[30]Under "right hand of righteousness" he says that there are some clever folk, not only among naturalists but also among believers, who will not accept any of this, but in the next world they will bewail their shortsightedness and the trust in their own ideas which have led them not to pay sufficient respect to God's word and to ignore the warnings of others, cf. the 1849 edition of J. Hamberger.

not only in theology but also in natural science.

E. Lohmeyer has described Oetinger's dictionary as the unequalled forbear of all theological dictionaries.[31] This judgment is only conditionally true. The dictionary is a unique one with many highpoints but also with many weaknesses. As Oetinger explains in the title, it is a polemical work whose aim is to set precise biblical concepts in confrontation with mounting doubts.[32] In the preface Oetinger accuses Teller of trying to make the gospel easy and practicable by leaving out mysteries he cannot explain and dropping sensory concepts. "He is thus betrayed into a false suprasensoriness. Scripture is full of sensory concepts, especially the NT. This is God's plan, for God is manifested in the flesh, by the resurrection of Jesus everything is set before all creation in bodily and sensory form, and the city of God in Rev. 21:22 is wholly sensory." The incarnation and resurrection of Jesus cause him to give particular emphasis to corporeality. Under the word "body" we find the famous statement which is not usually quoted as Oetinger formulated it: "Corporeality is the end of the works of God, as may be seen clearly from the city of God in Rev. 20." To deny corporeality is in Oetinger's view to deny the basic statements of the Bible and to fall victim to a meaningless suprasensoriness. Spirituality is not achieved by abstracting away corporeality. "If everything corporeal is removed from God, then God is nothing."[33] The fulness of spirituality is manifested in the corresponding corporeality. Oetinger attacks Teller sharply in the article on "Possessed." "Church Councillor Teller boldly expresses his hatred of everything sensory. He does not merely empty out the words of scripture but wrests them simply because he regards the sensory as mere imagination . . . This is to contradict Jesus to his face . . . People of this kind prefer their free thought to the words of Jesus . . . Is it not a judgment that they wallow in the Bible like the sow of 2 Pet. 3:16?"

In many sections Oetinger is not content to present the biblical data. His discussions often take on the character of sermons. In his article on "Reveal" he threatens those who interpret the Bible according to their own abstract ideas: "They are not afraid of their ignorance but they will be silenced when they hear the words: Cast them into outer darkness." In the article on "Man" he has the admonition: "We now find it hard to get a picture of the first man . . . Hence we should be content in weaknesses, afflictions, and anxieties and find our sufficiency in grace, not trying to add a cubit to our stature . . . but receiving daily strength from Jesus." Often he addresses the reader directly as under "City of God, New Jerusalem": "Dear reader, do not be surprised at these unusual consequences of revelation . . . Do not be concerned about the philosophy of this world . . . Cling to the fact that God is

---

[31]E. Lohmeyer, *Das Vater-unser*[4] (1960), 215, n. 8.
[32]*s.v.* "Religionsstreit."
[33]*s.v.* "Offenbaren."

not ashamed to be called your God, for he has prepared a city for you. Be worthy of this by denying worldly lust."

As pastor of Walddorf (1746-1752) Oetinger studied chemistry, or, more accurately, alchemy. He used his work in this field to elucidate his theology. Under "Sea" he writes: "One sees great things in alchemy; without this our concepts are very feeble." He seeks an encompassing harmony of nature and holy scripture. His *philosophia sacra* contains an organic union of the scientific knowledge of alchemy and medicine with the truths of the Bible. With the help of retorts he believed the theologian could achieve a comprehensive knowledge of earthly and heavenly things. Many articles testify to this.

Thus in the article on "Sea" he says that all things are made of salt, even the greatest sweetness, as chemical experiments demonstrate. Pure elements come from pure salt and hell from impure. Pure salt remains to the glory of the sons of God while impure is used to punish the damned. Bodies that cannot be destroyed belong to an unquenchable fire. Salt makes them indestructible. The bodies of the damned are either changed into salt or salted with fire. They can thus resist the effects of consuming fire. In the article on "Cold" he combines Greek etymology with science in defining the soul. Cold comes from ψύχω "to cool," from whose preterite ἔψυχα comes the noun ψυχή "soul." He does not try to explain why the soul should have a cold origin in Greek but learns from chemistry that in saltpetre cold is a special principle, that warmth means sourness, and that both are contained in an alkaline salt. When the cold is separated from the heat it is sweet and gold and silver result. It is clear, then, that creatures are inwardly a cold and hot fire. Since the soul has both in itself at one temperature, one may conjecture that two principles are comprehended in a third and that the soul has more of a sweet than a sour origin. The "Resurrection of Jesus" or resurrection of the dead Oetinger tries to explain also with the help of chemical experiments with balm. The earthly husk remains in the retort while the oil like a spirit flows over in full form without matter. He uses the same illustration to explain what is meant by eating the flesh of the Son of Man and drinking his blood.

In the article on "Sickness" Oetinger has some modern insights. He attacks physicians who are not aware of the origin of illnesses. These begin, "not in the blood or in humours, but in the invisible being." As is now known, the "perverted images of a corrupt imagination" are "the invisible cause of sicknesses. In these images, however, is also the root of sin. If the latter is removed, sickness too is largely removed after the manner of Jesus Christ." Oetinger refers to the healing arts of the Chinese and then concludes: "When all nations camp around the city of God, they will recognize their errors, acknowledge the Jews to be right, and see that in Christ lies the healing of nature and true medicine."

In many articles Oetinger refers to actual events which help to make the statements of the Bible clear. Discussing the three "Angels" of

Rev. 14:6-11, he says concerning the angel with the everlasting gospel who flies in the midst of heaven: "This angel belongs to the time of the third Woe, which is in Europe; hence he is to be sought in Europe . . . His place is Germany in the middle of the lands . . . Bengel with some reason believes that Arndt is meant, for 1. the everlasting gospel had its beginning just about when Arndt lived in 1614, and 2. Arndt's writings agree so closely with the proclamation of this angel. The next angel is probably Spener. Under "Appearance" Oetinger warns against paying heed to faces, mentioning a girl in Herrenberg who was misled in this way. Under "Trinity" he describes how with the earthquake of June 3, 1774 many houses in Guatemala were destroyed along with their inhabitants: "One can see now in Guatemala . . . that God devastates and swallows up mountains and hills."

Often Oetinger draws odd inferences from the biblical data. From God's command that Abraham should be circumcised "one may conjecture that this member was not attached to Adam in the beginning but that like the stomach it will in time be cut off again from the image of God insofar as it represents earthly disorder, 1 Cor. 6:13." But this will happen only at the resurrection. Oetinger also attacks "Laughing": "Jesus never laughed. There is something about laughter, then, which belongs to weaknesses unsuited to the dignity of the first man, and he who walks worthy of Christ will refrain from laughter inasmuch as it is a sign that he is forgetful of the nobility that Christ has won for him. When it is said: 'You will laugh,' this laughter is simply the joy which one confesses with one's bodily members at the things of the Lord. In the present age laughter cannot be regarded as a sin but it lies hard by the practices of fools."

4. New Testament Greek

Cremer's dictionary deals with a problem that has not yet been solved, namely, that of NT Greek.

a. This question was already discussed in the early church.[34] When the NT was becoming known in the Greek world, the educated attached great value to the writing of good Greek. The NT could not compete with the published literary works of the time.[35] Celsus compared the sentences of the Bible with Plato and came to the conclusion that everything was better expressed among the Greeks than in the NT (Orig. Cels., VI, 1). The apostles were uncultured tax-gatherers and

[34]E. Norden, *Die antike Kunstprosa*, II[5] (1958), 521-534; J. Vergote, Art. "Grec biblique" in Dict. Bibl. Suppl., III (1938), 1321-1323.

[35]"To use a non-Attic word was a very serious literary offense and a work not adorned with figures of speech had no claim to a place in literature; in short, writing well or badly distinguished Greeks and barbarians. A public of this kind could only regard the religious documents of the Christians as monstrosities," Norden, *op. cit.*, 516f.

fishermen who could not measure up to Greek philosophers (I, 62). Similar objections were constantly raised. How did the church respond to them?

Two arguments were used in defense of the Greek of the NT. First, it was said that the apostles deliberately used simple speech to make themselves generally understood. The preacher's task is not just to win the clever. Out of love for all men he consciously turns as well to the simple and uneducated, to women and children, even to the uncivilised, in order to convert them. Hence the Christian teacher has to use a language which all can understand and which can captivate all.[36]

The second argument starts with the fact that the apostles themselves were simple people who could not match the skilled speech of the philosophers. Another reason was thus given for the success of primitive Christian preaching. According to Origen, what won people to Christ was not fine speech or oratorical skill, not the art of dialectic or rhetoric, but Christ himself. If Jesus had chosen clever folk to proclaim his teaching, Christianity might have been taken for a philosophical school. But now that uneducated people, fishermen and tax-gatherers, who did not have even the rudiments of learning, have not only spoken to the Jews with shocking boldness about faith in Christ but also preached Jesus successfully to all nations, one has to ask what is the source of the unparalleled power of their words to convince. The only possible conclusion is that a higher than they has been speaking and that he has endowed their words with persuasive force (Orig. Cels., I, 62 [GCS, 2, 113f.]).

Chrysostom uses the same argument.[37] If in a discussion Greeks contend that the apostles were rude and unlearned, one should not try to prove the contrary but trump them and say that they were ἀμαθεῖς καὶ ἀγράμματοι καὶ πένητες καὶ εὐτελεῖς καὶ ἀσύνετοι καὶ ἀφανεῖς. If Paul had been more eloquent than Plato, this would have meant that his success would have been due to his own oratorical skill and not to grace. Although untrained, Paul could convince disciples of Plato. In this way it may be seen that what triumphed in the primitive Christian message was not the power of human wisdom but the power of divine grace.

A third position is taken by Photius.[38] God as the creator of speech has given appropriate words to the disciples of the Logos. Certainly Christ chose as his disciples ignorant men who were more stupid than the fish they caught. When he called them, however, they did not remain fishermen and tax-gatherers but Christ made of the fishermen fishers of men, of the tax-gatherers deliverers of troubled souls, and of the unlearned teachers of the world, filling them with divine and heavenly wisdom so that they could dispute with philosophers (577 CD). If he had

---

[36]Orig. Cels., VI, 1 (GCS, 3, 72); Isidore of Pelusium Ep., IV, 67 (MPG, 78, 1124f.).
[37]Chrys. Hom. in 1 C. 3:4 on 1:10 (MPG, 61, 27f.).
[38]Phot. Ad. Amphilochium Quaestia, 92 (MPG, 101, 577-592).

spoken as a barbarian, how could the apostle have calmed the blood-thirsty Jews or made an impression on the Athenians? God's grace made it possible for the apostles not to say what was unworthy of them but to speak, not like the unlearned, but like those who had undergone technical training. The artistry of Paul is praised in extravagant terms. To depict it fully is like trying to measure the ocean drop by drop (589 B). It is inconceivable that Paul, who by divine inspiration could speak in foreign languages, would not have had a mastery of the generally known Greek tongue (581 D). His words are not just the fruit of training but of supernatural inspiration (589 D).[39]

b. The speech of the NT came in for fresh discussion at the time of the renaissance and reformation. Those who now took offense at NT Greek were not pagan opponents of Christianity but humanistically trained members of the churches who found a difference between classical Greek and that of the NT. The answer of the theologians corresponds in part to the defense of the early church, but other arguments were also used. Already Laurentius Valla, in criticising the Vulgate and comparing it with the Greek MSS of the NT, had pointed out that the NT texts do not offer correct Greek but contain Hebraisms. Erasmus came to the same conclusion.[40] Many errors could be found in the Greek of the apostles. It was irregular and untrained. The apostles did not learn their Greek from the speeches of Demosthenes but from conversation with the people. J. Camerarius, a student of Melanchthon, one of the most significant philologists and editors of his day, professor of Greek and Latin at Leipzig, a cultivated man of many interests, was one of the first who in expounding the NT turned to classical authors rather than the fathers. He confirmed the judgment of the other humanists that NT Greek differs from classical Greek. In his notes on the words, phrases, and constructions used in the NT he was not discussing dogmatic questions but as a philologist drawing attention to lexical, grammatical, and historical problems.

These misled Philippists were opposed by the Gnesiolutheran Flacius, who was merciless and adamant in his battle for pure doctrine. As a humanist Flacius realised that Greek was already in decline in Paul's day. Paul did not address the educated alone but like the prophets, Christ, and the other apostles he intentionally accommodated himself to the capacity and understanding of simple people (II, 514, 41-57). If he avoided ambitious, meretricious, and arrogant loquacity, he did not lack the true oratorical skill which the Holy Spirit had conferred upon him in order that he might present heavenly things more vividly and clearly (II, 512, 26-32, cf. 15, 32-49). The style of Paul is modest and chaste. He avoids adornment or wanton charm. He does not make an elephant out of a flea as the Sophists do (II, 513, 6-13). If he sometimes

---

[39]B. Wyss, "Photius über den Stil des Paulus," *Museum Helveticum,* 12 (1955), 236-251.
[40]Erasmus, Annotationes ad Ac. 10:33, ed. J. Clericus, *Opera omnia,* VI (1705), 476.

claims the right to depart from common forms of speech, this is not barbarism but the freedom which is a mark of the great writer (II, 514, 23-40, cf. also 520, 15-19).

Debate raged for some time on whether the NT is composed in the best Greek of Attic authors or is shot through with Hebraisms. Two groups formed. On the one side were the purists who ascribed to NT Greek the purity and elegance of classical literature; on the other side were the so-called Hebraists or Hellenists who saw and said that the NT writings have a Hebraic tinge.[41] The first purist to take a stand was the philologist S. Pfochen, who worked in Holland. Pfochen wrote a 200-page diatribe *de linguae graecae Novi Testamenti puritate, ubi quam plurimis, qui vulgo finguntur, Hebraismis larva detrahitur, et profanos autores quoque* τὸ κατὰ λέξιν *ita esse loquentos ad oculum demonstratur* (1629) in which he championed in all seriousness the view that the NT has the purity of the classical idiom. If NT Greek is compared with that of profane writers one has to say that no fault can be found with the purity of NT speech. The NT is written in as good Greek as that written by Homer, Demosthenes, and other authors. With the aid of several examples he tries to show that the same words and phrases are used in the NT and classical writers. The English philologist T. Gataker (1574-1655) took issue with this thesis of Pfochen. He pointed out that to find similar words and phrases in the NT and classical authors is not by a long way to prove that the Greek of the NT is classical.

Another group of theologians did not argue philologically but dogmatically. G. Pasor (→ *supra*) in his posthumously published work *Grammatica graeca sacra Novi Testamenti domini nostri Jesu Christi* candidly admits, after discussing the various NT dialects, that not a few Hebraisms may be found in the NT. All the same, he defended the thesis that NT Greek does not fall behind classical Greek in elegance. Since the Bible is inspired, as *lingua sancta* it is superior to all other literature even at the level of speech. He furiously attacks those who claim that the style of the NT is non-Greek. This is completely impossible, since the apostles were instructed by the Holy Spirit: *Facessant illi, qui stylum Novi Testamenti non satis Graecum esse somniabant. Apostoli enim eum edocti fuerunt ab ipso Spiritu Sancto (Ac. 2:4); quo doctore et magistro, quis quaeso unquam disertius aut magis proprie dicere potuit?*[42] J. Himmelius of Jena demanded that grammarians who found fault with the Greek of the NT should first go to school with the Holy Spirit and then change the rules which they laid down. A. Calov (1622-1686) declared: *Quod itaque de soloecismis et barbarismis de sermone agresti ac rustico, et quae id genus alia sunt dicteria, jactatur in scriptores sacros, id non potest non redeundare in ipsum Spiritum Sanctum, qui per ipsum ceu manus suas scripsit.*[43]

---

[41]Winer (Schmiedel), 4-10; Vergote, *op. cit.*, 1323f.; J. Irmscher, "Der Streit um das Bibelgriechisch," *Acta Antiqua Academiae Scientiarum Hungaricae*, 7 (1959), 127-134.
[42]Cf. Schlosser, *op. cit.*, 256f.
[43]Cf. Irmscher, *op. cit.*, 131.

A third group of theologians took a very different tack in dealing with the difficulties of NT Greek. It was seen that the purists were wrong but an attempt was made to counterbalance positively the negative findings of the grammarians. The South German Lutheran Aegidius Hunnius (1550-1603) was aware of the weaknesses of NT diction but he described them as willed by God. Like the fathers he took the view that the incorrectness of speech was planned so that the power of the word would not be attributed to the rhetoric of the NT authors but to the working of the Holy Spirit. T. Beza (1519-1605), originally a humanist, poet, and jurist, became professor of Greek at Lausanne in 1549 and then in 1558 moved to Geneva as professor of Greek and theology. Along with his extensive ecclesiastical activity, which has been more broadly discussed, he worked intensively at the textual criticism, the translation, and the exposition of the NT. He had some understanding of NT Greek and its distinctive character. On the basis of the third edition of the NT of H. Stephanus the Elder, and a collection of several MSS, he published in 1565 a NT text along with the Vulgate, his own translation, and notes, although he does not seem to have used for this purpose Codices D (Cantabrigiensis and Claromontanus) which were in his possession. Beza stressed the simplicity and force of NT speech. Hebraisms did not mar the NT but were the gems with which the apostles adorned their writings. H. Stephanus the Younger (1528-1598), composer of the *Thesaurus linguae graecae*, published his own edition of the NT in 1576. In the preface to this he opposed the view that the NT was written in incorrect Greek. In proof he adduced examples to show that the NT does have some good Greek expressions. The Hebraisms, the thought, gave the NT its force and power. P. Mornaeus (1549-1623), who was called the Huguenot pope, also took issue with the critics of NT Greek. The unadorned style of the NT authors was suited, he thought, to their matter. It was God's will that the apostles should speak and write as in the text. S. Werenfels (1657-1740), NT professor in Basel, opposed the futile squabbling of theologians which often did nothing to advance the truth and had its origin simply in their own pride. In many cases what was being defended was not pure doctrine but a personal position. Regarding the misuse of scripture by exegetes he said: *Hic liber est, in quo sua quaerit dogmata quisque, invenit et pariter dogmata quisque sua.*[44] As regards the debate about NT Greek Werenfels took a middle view in his book *Dissertatio de stilo scriptorum Novi Testamenti*. He did not think the position of the purists was tenable, since in some places the style of the NT is primitive and barbaric. Nevertheless, the Greek of the NT is not to be assessed negatively, but merits more serious attention than the elegant Greek of classical authors.

D. Heinsius (1580-1655), who had an enthusiasm for Greek from early youth, became instructor in poetry at Leyden in 1604 and then professor of Greek in 1605. Drawn into the debates with the Arminians, he devoted

---

[44]Cf. E. Vischer, Art. "Werenfels, Samuel" in RE³, 21, 107.

himself to the NT. His *Exercitationum sacrarum libri XX* (1639) show him to be a grammatically careful exegete. Already in 1627 he had published an *Aristarchus sacer*. In this book he followed Scaliger and tried to show that the NT authors wrote a special Greek which he called Hellenistic. He opposed Pfocher (*supra*), arguing that the Gospels were written in Hellenistic Greek but were Syriac in conception.

The debate between the purists and Hebraists became particularly sharp in Hamburg. J. Jungius (1587-1657), a man of many parts who composed Latin tragedies as a student, became a professor of mathematics at Giessen when only 22, and earned a doctorate in medicine at Padua in 1618, was called as rector to John's Academy in Hamburg in 1628. Conflict arose when he wanted profane authors as well as the Greek NT to be read in the school. In the debate over the issue one of his opponents raised the question: *An Novum Testamentum barbarismis scateat? An Lucae evangelium prae ceteris maiorem Graeci sermonis nitorem habeat?* Although a negative answer was unanimously given, the Hamburg pastors were angry at Jungius. The mere hypothesis that there might be barbarisms in the NT seemed to them to be an attack on the authority of scripture. Jungius was accused of betraying the word of God and called an ungodly man, a blasphemer, and an atheist. In self-defense Jungius wrote a work entitled *Verantwortung wegen desjenigen, was neulich vor und in den Pfingsten wegen des griechischen NT und anderer Schulsachen von öffentlicher Kanzel fürgebracht.*[45] In this work he argued that the language of the NT originated neither in Greece nor with Greeks but with Jews and their associates. The evangelists and apostles spoke Hellenistic, not Greek. Since Jungius wanted his students to learn Greek as it was spoken when Greece was flourishing and not as it was known to Greek Jews who read the OT in Greek in their synagogues (schools) and who should thus be called Hellenists,[46] some pastors accused him of the view that the Holy Spirit could not speak proper Greek. Jungius replied that if it had pleased the Holy Spirit that the evangelists and apostles should write pure Greek unmixed with oriental tongues he could have brought it about that they excelled all Greek orators, but it did not please God to do this but instead to put Greek eloquence to shame with this Hebrew Greek. This rejoinder did not help Jungius at all and in 1638 a judgment was rendered by the theological and philosophical faculty at Wittenberg. It read as follows: "To find solecisms, barbarisms, and incorrect Greek in the speeches and writings of the holy apostles is to do despite to the Holy Spirit who spoke and wrote through them and he who accuses the Holy Spirit of barbarisms . . . commits no little blasphemy."[47] A violent literary feud followed. Jungius

---

[45]Ed. J. Geffcken, *Joachim Jungius. Ueber die Originalsprache des NT vom Jahre 1637* (1863); cf. E. v. Lehe, "Jungius-Archivalien aus dem Staatsarchiv Hamburg," *Beiträge zur Jungius Forschung*, ed. A. Meyer, *Festschr. der Hamburgischen Universität anlässlich ihres zehnjährigen Bestehens* (1929), 62f.

[46]Geffcken, *op. cit.*, 11.

[47]G. E. Guhrauer, *Joachim Jungius und sein Zeitalter* (1850), 114f.

answered with a collection of the views of scholars on the style of the NT. J. Grosse, the chief pastor at St. Katherine's, published a comprehensive work *Trias propositionum theologicarum Graecum Novi Testamenti stilum a barbaris criminationibus vindicantium, et sententiam criticorum Hellenismum propugnantium rectitudini istius nihil derogare, ostendentium* (1640). In this book he tried to show that, while the style of the NT does not correspond to that of classical Greek, nevertheless all the forms of pure Greek are to be found in the NT, and for this reason the school did not need to give instruction in profane authors. Grosse returned to the question in three other works in which he belabored Jungius and his friends more with abuse than solid reasons. Apart from D. Wülfer, a Jena student who supported Jungius in his work *Innocentia Hellenistarum a Triade propositionum (ut vocantur) theologicarum vindicata* (1640), J. Musaeus, Professor of History and Poetry at Jena, was the one who took issue with Grosse in various writings. When a pagan opponent of Christianity argues that the NT contains barbarisms and solecisms, this sounds blasphemous. The situation is different, however, when the same is said by a Christian for whom scripture is an authority. Grosse is confusing young people. The Holy Spirit can address men just as well with a speech lacking in elegance as he can in the most polished speech of a Demosthenes. For the rest, the Holy Spirit probably inspired only the matter, not the individual words. This may be seen from the difference in style in the different books of the NT. Jerome already rejected verbal inspiration. Inspired thoughts are accurately conveyed by the NT authors.

The debate was laid to rest in the 18th century. The OT scholar J. H. Michaelis tried to bring about a compromise in his assessment of the matter in the book *Dissertatio philologica de textu Novi Testamenti graeco* (1707). As an OT scholar he saw clearly that there are Hebraisms in the NT. Nevertheless he still wanted to ascribe a certain purity to the style of the NT. J. A. Ernesti (1707-1781) moved in the same direction. In his work *Institutio interpretis Novi Testamenti* (1761) he championed exact philological exegesis but rejected rationalism. He called the style of the NT Hebraeo-graecus. Words which research elsewhere had not discovered were not coined by the authors but owed their origin to the Holy Spirit. This points forward to a problem which was discussed in the 19th century (→ *infra*).

c. Other ideas were expressed on NT Greek in the 18th century which have found approval in the 19th and 20th centuries. J. G. Hamann (1730-1788) compared the style of the NT writings to that of newspapers and letters (→ *infra*). "It belongs to the unity of divine revelation that the Spirit of God, through the human pen of the holy men who were impelled by him, humbled himself and emptied himself of majesty just as the Son of God, through his servant form and like all creation, is a work of supreme humility . . . Here, too, the principle applies: The voice of the people is the voice of God . . . The style of newspapers and letters belongs to what rhetoricians call a humble manner of speaking and little like it in Greek has survived. The style of the NT books must be assessed accordingly and in this regard they are to some extent original."[48] Hamann knew nothing of the existence of papyri, but he recognised that NT Greek is popular, not literary Greek. He was not led to this conviction by philological studies but by theological considerations. Since God stooped down to man and emptied himself, since the Word became flesh, God's speaking must always be speaking in servant form. The holy scriptures are seen in the most familiar fellowship of impure muses and in ordinary verse to the serious scandalising of all moral pharisees and orthodox scribes and their serpent brood.[49] Hamann does not want the difficulties of the Bible smoothed down or its offense set aside. Strong Christians try to evade the divine ordination of a stone of stumbling and rock of offense and sign of contradiction by new readings, new translations, new dogmas, new homilies, new grammars and new dictionaries.[50] The true theologian is always a philologist of the cross. He will thus affirm the lowliness of scripture.[51]

Important for later developments was what J. G. Herder (1744-1803) said about the needed but still missing NT dictionary. In his *Erläuterungen zum NT aus einer neueröfneten Morgenländischen Quelle* (1775) he had some interesting remarks on what a dictionary should take note of if it was to give a proper exposition of the NT. Christ came when the wall between national modes of thought was no longer standing and there was a fluid sea of mixed ideas and languages. The NT could not have been written in Athenian style.[52] Herder opposed the common practice of adducing quotations and parallels from Xenophon and Polybius to explain the NT, since the meaning of these was often miles apart from what the NT had in view. Scholarly exegetes and commentators who do this sin against Jesus. "Since his crucifixion Jesus has carried no more false sceptres and purple mantels on the one side, and no more drinks of vinegar and crowns of thorns on the other, than those given him by learned exegetes and expositors of the Bible. What filth they have collected, and on the other hand in what water they have again dissolved everything!"[53] To understand the Bible one must not stop with the Greeks. One must survey the whole field, see the great interconnections, and follow the words of Chaldea through later Judaism, Philo, the Septuagint, and on to the church fathers. "In the broken Greek of the apostles flow ideas and series of ideas from all the ends of the earth: Judea, Chaldea, Persia, Egypt, Greece and Rome have all

[48]J. G. Hamann, *Kleeblatt hell. Briefe, 1. Brief*, ed. J. Nadler, *J. G. Hamann, Sämtliche Werke*, II (1950), 171f.

[49]J. G. Hamann, *Beurtheilung der Kreuzzüge des Philologen*, ed. Nadler, *op. cit.*, II (1950), 273.

[50]J. G. Hamann, *Hierophantische Briefe, 4. Brief*, ed. Nadler, III (1951), 150.

[51]Cf. F. Blanke, "Gottessprache und Menschensprache bei J. G. Hamann," *Hamann-Studien* (1956), 84-89.

[52]Ed. B. Suphan, *Herders sämmtliche Werke*, VII (1884), 339f.

[53]*Ibid.*, 350.

helped to shape it. Their Greek was not classical Greek but the language of the uneducated, the untutored, non-greeks." Yet in reality it was "a divine power and a divine wisdom."[54] Herder expressed the hope that from all these sources we should soon get a complete dictionary of the NT.[55]

d. As already indicated earlier, the debate about NT Greek broke out in a new form in the 19th century. It was no longer a question of classical or Semitic Greek. The new issue was whether NT Greek was a unique holy language or the speech of the people which would be a monstrosity to every educated person (→ n. 35). Schleiermacher had some significant thoughts on the matter in his lectures on hermeneutics. He argued that every intellectual revolution has a creative effect on language. Old terminology was often not adequate to express new thoughts or the new relations established by the change. In such a situation a new language had to arise.[56] What is true in general is also true of Christianity. Christianity, being expressed in Greek, necessarily had a creative influence on it and new and unusual usages arose. If Christianity is something new, it has to fashion out of the existing elements a new Greek which emerges out of the total nexus of Christian speech and life.[57] Schleiermacher insists on the language-creating force of Christianity and infers from it that there will be in the NT forms of speech which can be derived from neither Greek nor Hebrew. To discover and assemble these is to find the key to an understanding of language-building in Christianity. "A collection of the various elements in which the language-building force of Christianity is manifested will become a sciagraphy for a NT dogmatics and ethics."[58] Lexicons are needed which will fully present the distinctiveness of the speech of the NT.[59] R. Rothe[60] put it even more sharply. As he saw it, one could appropriately speak in fact of a "language of the Holy Spirit." The divine Spirit at work in revelation fashioned out of the language of the then peoples a unique mode of religious utterance by giving to existing elements and concepts a form corresponding to the subject matter of the Spirit. NT Greek forms the clearest illustration of this process.

What Schleiermacher and Rothe suggested was most explicitly set forth by the Erlangen theologian G. v. Zezschwitz in his work *Profangraecitaet und biblischer Sprachgeist* (1859). The aim of the work was to trace the creative influence of Christianity on the Greek language. The speech-transforming factor of the Spirit, which had manifested itself already in the Greek translation of the OT, achieved its fulness in

[54]*Ibid.*, 354.
[55]*Ibid.*, 351.
[56]F. Schleiermacher, *Hermeneutik und Kritik mit besonderer Beziehung auf das NT*, ed. F. Lücke, *F. Schleiermacher's sämtliche Werke*, I, 7 (1838), 64.
[57]*Ibid.*, 66f.
[58]*Ibid.*, 68.
[59]*Ibid.*, 67.
[60]R. Rothe, *Zur Dogmatik* (1863), 238.

Christianity. The Spirit of the Bible and Christianity raised an undeveloped language to a higher level. No language in the world could better express the message of the Holy Spirit than Greek. "Nevertheless, what a transformation this language had to undergo to become the organ of the Holy Spirit!" What was profane had to be eliminated, what was unsuitably put in the background had to be brought forward, and what was genuinely human had to be transfigured. Only by adopting a Greek which had been thus christianised in its basic concepts could the apostles mediate to a world which in its popular culture was then Greek the language of the Spirit who testified through them. The linguistic transformation was an inner conquest of the spirit of the Greek tongue by the Spirit of Christianity.[61] Zezschwitz exclaims: "If only we had a clavis of biblical Greek which is composed in principle in terms of the distinctive basic thoughts of Christianity!"[62] He was not aware that such a work was already in course of preparation.

5. H. Cremer

a. H. Cremer was the son of a teacher in Unna. His mother Luise, whose maiden name was Josephson, was the daughter of a Jewish merchant, who had been converted to Christianity with his family. When Cremer was a student in Halle, he was stimulated by his teacher Tholuck to the idea of writing a new kind of NT dictionary. Since Tholuck was the initiator of the project, he dedicated the second edition of the work to his beloved teacher on the occasion of his academic jubilee on December 2, 1870, with heartfelt respect and grateful veneration. As Cremer goes on to say in the dedication, the work owed its origin to a remark of Tholuck on a walk in 1855. While still in the middle of his studies Cremer resolved to write a biblical-theological dictionary of the NT. When he moved from Halle to Tübingen, and came to know the bookseller Steinkopf in Stuttgart, he was strengthened in his resolve. Steinkopf met the gifted student halfway, providing him with means so that he could graduate after his first theological examination. Since there would be no question at this stage of an academic career, Cremer entered the pastorate. In 1859 he was called to be pastor of the church of Ostönnen near Unna. There ten years of work produced the dictionary of NT Greek. Cremer did not want to write a specialized lexicon of the NT in the usual sense. He had a vision of something very different from a statistical compilation of NT words in alphabetical order with an interrelating of individual words in their various senses from the grammatical, literary, and other angles. Since Cremer did not intend to handle all the NT words but only those which really promote an understanding of the records of revelation, which have biblical theological content, and which are thus expressions of spiritual, moral, and religious life (preface to the

[61]G. v. Zezschwitz, *Profangraecitaet und biblischer Sprachgeist* (1859), 5.
[62]*Ibid.*, 10.

first edition), Steinkopf wondered whether he could ever publish the work. When Grimm's lexicon came out (→ *supra*), he no longer dared bring out the lexicon. When he had withdrawn, F. A. Perthes in Gotha declared his readiness to publish Cremer's work.

Cremer's dictionary has repeatedly been called a biblical theology in lexical form. Cremer himself protested against this. As the title says, he planned to write a biblical-theological dictionary, not as a dictionary of NT theology, but as a dictionary of biblical Greek. In the preface to the third edition he took up the following position on the matter: "What I am offering, then, is essentially a history of language and concepts, not a biblical theology in lexical, i.e., unscientific form." His concern was to present the distinctive conceptual world with which Christianity reckons (preface to the ninth edition). What he criticised in previous dictionaries was that they did not offer any basic or thorough-going consideration of what Schleiermacher called the language-building force of Christianity (preface to the first edition). If the distinctive concepts of the religion of revelation are to be worked out, the conceptual world of non-biblical Greek must be investigated, the distinction and relation of the biblical understanding must be brought to light, and the point of contact demonstrated (preface to the first edition). To this end Cremer first examined the usage of a given term in classical Greek. Fundamentally he had only a negative interest in this. Since the Greek world represents a rich and full natural life, its language, which derives wholly from this natural world, cannot be taken over as it is by Christianity, which contains the most developed and conscious antithesis to the naturally human (in the pneumatic sense) (preface to the first edition). Classical Greek has to be transformed if it is to be set in the service of the sanctuary. This transformation is accomplished in part by Greek-speaking Judaism which translated the Hebrew Bible into Greek, so that the LXX prepared the way for the NT proclamation of salvation. Cremer thus investigated with great care the usage of the LXX. He studied individual words with great exactness and scholarship, so that in relation to the words he deals with, his dictionary might be called the most penetrating dictionary of the LXX as well (preface to the third edition). But there are still differences between the language of the LXX and that of the NT. Christianity does not just adopt the Greek words. The incarnation of the Word has affected the use of words. Since Greek became the organ of the Spirit of Christ, it underwent a new development. According to Cremer the coming of Jesus has a threefold effect on the Greek language; it has a lifegiving effect, a transforming effect, and a creative effect.

1. Christianity gives life to terms which had already been blunted and eroded by the misuse of language in everyday usage. Such terms receive from Christianity new force, a new imprint, and new energy.

2. Christianity transforms language. It takes existing words which it can use and fills them, as vessels, with the spirit of Christianity. Cremer appeals to a statement by Nägelsbach: "The situation with this

expression (sc. ὁ πέλας, ὁ πλησίον), as with many another in which the pagan and Christian views overlap, is that the ancient word has the sound of a Christian one, is, at it were, a vessel prepared for the Christian concept, but does not reach the same fulness of meaning."[63]

3. The new content of Christian proclamation does not merely transform language; new terms and expressions emerge as well. For this thesis Cremer appeals expressly to Rothe (→ supra). Words which cannot be found in classical literature are attributed to the word-constructing power of the Spirit of Christianity (Preface to the first edition).

As already indicated, Cremer does not deal with every word nor does he follow an alphabetical order, but, like Pasor (→ supra), he adopts an etymological system of grouping. In the first edition Cremer viewed only about 600 terms as the most important expressions of spiritual, moral, and religious life. A whole series of not unimportant words was left out in the first editions.[64] The number of those included rose from edition to edition, by about 120 in the second edition and 300 in the third. The last edition revised by Cremer himself, that of 1902, contained twice as many words as the first, namely, 1251.

b. In his work Cremer tried to combine theory and practice, scholarship and ministry, research and community action. When preparing for the pastorate in Tübingen, he worked on the biblical content of κηρύσσω, κῆρυξ, κήρυγμα in the NT. Before he began to preach, he wanted to know what the NT meant by preaching and the preacher. He believed that the combination of theory and practice would benefit both scholarly and practical work. To do justice to both he deliberately divided up his day into two halves. The morning from 5 a.m. belonged to research, the afternoon to parish activities.

Cremer wrestled with the dogmatic and homiletical question how he could rightly preach penitence and forgiveness to a congregation which was living self-righteously and complacently in open sin. He was a pupil of T. Beck, and the theology of Beck created difficulties for him in the pulpit of this church. Beck rejected the view that the righteousness of Christ is imputed to the believer and that justification is a pronouncing just. Scripture never says that the divine justification takes place through a legal pronouncing of the sinner to be righteous.[65] Beck feared that moral earnestness was sold short by the reformation proclamation of grace. "The way in which grace is usually preached, namely, under the title of justification, is much more harmful than honest preaching of the law."[66] Beck's doctrine of justification is much closer to Trent than to the reformation confessions. "To declare legally

---

[63]C. F. Nägelsbach, Die nachhomerische Theologie des griech. Volksglaubens bis auf Alexander (1857), 239.

[64]E.g., ἀββᾶ, εὐχαριστέω, καυχάομαι, μισθός, περιτομή, σκάνδαλον, σταυρός, σφραγίς, φωτίζω.

[65]J. T. Beck, Erklärung des Briefes Pauli an die Römer (1884), 293.

[66]J. T. Beck, Gedanken aus und nach der Schrift³ (1893), 126.

righteous a guilty or more precisely an ungodly and wicked person" is, he thinks, rejected in scripture as an "abomination to God."[67] Justification is not an imputative act; it is a creative act of divine power. Christ "brings us essential divine righteousness over against what has become essential sin."[68] "The righteousness of divine grace does not merely give believers remission of sins as pardoning grace but also gives them as endowing grace the righteousness which is necessary to life, i.e., righteousness as a gift, i.e., as a new disposition."[69] This essential righteousness works itself out in the life of believers. This outworking is what Cremer did not see in his congregation.

As a true follower of Beck, Cremer stressed very strongly in his preaching the seriousness of penitence. He often spoke very frankly to his people. Thus he said in one sermon: "I will tell you peasants what you want most, to marry money, inherit a lot, and never die."[70] The reaction to this very specific sermon was that in the evening the parsonage windows were broken. Cremer did not just accuse his people of general sins. He was not afraid of bringing notorious sinners under church discipline. Thus he refused communion to one member of the congregation because of fornication. When he visited the man concerned to urge and warn him, the congregation met him with scorn and mockery wherever he was seen and in the taverns the reaction to the pastor's attitude was a scandal such as the village had never previously experienced.[71]

Cremer saw that something must be wrong in his theology. He noted that the proclamation of grace, not the seriousness of law, is the power of penitence. He thus resolved to preach more strongly the gospel of great love to his congregation. He recognised that the note of mercy and joy had been missing in his teacher Beck: "He wants to inculcate respect in us blase and refined folk, but he should also give some thought to the fact that even blase people are very sick."[72] Instead of proclaiming to troubled and assaulted consciences the winning power of the great love of God and the comfort of the gospel, Beck was emphasising the seriousness and discipline of penitence, so that in Cremer's view there was not enough about grace and justification.[73] The preaching needs of his parish and the split with Beck caused Cremer to examine in particular depth the word group δίκαιος, δικαιοσύνη, δικαιόω. He devoted two years to this. His biblical study of the terms led him to see that the reformers were right, not Beck. In his article he insisted firmly that in Pauline usage δικαιοῦν signifies no other than "the judicial activity of God by which man is freed from the guilt and bondage of sin and thereby acknowledged and exhibited as

---

[67]Beck Erklärung, 292.
[68]Beck Gedanken, N. S., p. 67.
[69]Beck Erklärung, 292.
[70]K. Bornhäuser, *In allerlei Gottesdiensten unter allerlei Kanzeln*² (1936), 11.
[71]E. Cremer, *Hermann Cremer* (1912), 45.
[72]E. Cremer, *op. cit.*, 49.
[73]M. Kähler, "Wie Hermann Cremer wurde," BFTh⁸ (1904), 15.

a δίκαιος." As regards δικαιοσύνη he says that "the Pauline concept of righteousness, which in form remains a relation to the divine verdict, has the special content of being the state of the believer established by the divine pardon." What Cremer writes about grace is equally reformed and at odds with the view of Beck. Grace is favor, benevolence, kindness. In particular it is the manifested favor of God to sinful humanity, or to an individual, which, proceeding from freedom, rules out legal claims, and unhindered by guilt, meets sin with forgiveness. These are not the notes that Cremer had learned from Beck. Beck could never forgive his pupil for deviating from his teaching.[74] It was thus, however, that Cremer tried to answer practical problems by biblical study. His pastoral work and his academic work mutually enriched one another. "Therewith I have increasingly learned to admire the sure beat of the evangelical church, which by the way of direct confession of faith has known before us what we have had to establish as truth by our researches. It was important that I should and could test these studies of mine in parish work" (preface to the first edition).

c. In a critical assessment of Cremer's work the following points must be made.

1. Cremer adduces too many quotations from the Greek classics and too few from later Greek witnesses. The vast numbers of papyri were unknown to him when he wrote the first edition. But the first document of this kind had reached Europe in 1778 and others were discovered and in many cases published between 1820 and 1840. Most scholars paid little attention to them. It is worth noting, however, that even before Deissmann some theologians used inscriptions and papyri in studying the biblical text.[75] Cremer listened too carefully to Schleiermacher, Rothe, and von Zezschwitz and too little to Hamann. Hence he did not see the bearing of the new discoveries on his problem.

2. Cremer completely neglected Jewish writings. Although material was available he did not look into the apocrypha, the pseudepigrapha, apocalyptic, or rabbinic literature. The great editions of the Talmud were to hand and comprehensive works had appeared or did appear in his day.[76] But they did not interest him, since they did not seem to him to contribute in any way to an understanding of NT Greek.

3. Cremer did not pay enough regard to the differences between the

---

[74]E. Cremer, "Mitteilung über den Lebensweg und Heimgang von Hermann Cremer" in *August Hermann Cremer, Gedenkblätter* (1904), 128.

[75]Vergote, *op. cit.*, 1328-1330.

[76]J. Lightfoot, *Horae Hebraicae et Talmudicae in IV Evangelistas* (1684); J. G. Meuschen, *Novum Testamentum ex Talmude et Antiquitatibus Hebraeorum illustratum* (1736); C. Schoettgen, *Horae Hebraicae et Talmudicae in universum Novum Testamentum* (*in Theologiam Judaeorum dogmaticum antiquam et orthodoxam de Messia*), I (1733), II (1742); J. Delitzsch, "Talmudstudien," *Zschr. für lutherische Theol. u. Kirche* (1854-1856); Levy, *Chald. Wört.*; J. Buxtorf, *Lexicon chaldaicum talmudicum et rabbinicum . . . Denuo*, ed. B. Fischer (1869); Weber.

individual NT books. He treated the whole of the NT as an undifferentiated unity. When dealing with the Greek, he ought to have seen that there was a great difference between Hebrews and Revelation.

4. Above all it must be stressed that Cremer's whole thrust was a mistaken one. In the main Christianity did not have a constructive influence on language. Christ was not a teacher who brought new insights that had to be put in new words. Nor is Christianity an esoteric teaching which uses a language understood only by initiates. What Jesus has to say about repentance and the gospel may be found already in the OT and Judaism. No new terms are needed to preach the gospel. The new thing that Jesus brought consists in his person, not in a new teaching. Primitive Christian preachers were not disclosing a new view of God; they were proclaiming an event. They declared the gospel, proclaimed God's lordship, testified to what they had seen and heard. Since they were dealing with facts, not with new ideas and revelations, they needed no new terms for their preaching. The word having become flesh, they preached in the very natural speech of ordinary intercourse in their day.[77]

d. For all the criticism of Cremer's work it must be hailed as a great scholarly achievement. Cremer did not write his dictionary in a university town with libraries readily available. He wrote it in the isolation of a Westphalian manse, where he had to rely on his own books bought from his pastor's stipend. Even A. Deissmann, a ruthless critic of Cremer, who had very different ideas concerning the task and method of a NT dictionary, had to admit that in Cremer one finds a serious effort to explain the language of the NT in the light of LXX usage, and that in this effort he was very largely successful.[78] Naturally work had been done on the LXX before Cremer but for the most part it had been inadequate. Most workers had taken as a basis the LXX concordance of Tromm. Of this Deissmann said that the 1718 Tromm had been the father of countless original sins in quotations in the commentaries.[79] Deissmann was no less critical of other aids used in opening up the LXX. He said of Biel-Schleusner that it was a flavorless rehash of Tromm's concordance and if anything is learned from it at all it gives the impression of being a collection of alphabetically related σκάνδαλα.[80] C. A. Wahl's key to the OT Apocrypha fares a little better at Deissmann's hand but it, too, fails to meet the requirements. As concerns LXX study, only Cremer can stand before Deissmann's critical eye. This is worth emphasising.

[77]A. Schlatter, "Die Theol. des NT u. die Dogmatik," BFTh, 13, 2 (1909), 72, cf. Theol. Bücherei, 41 (1969), 248; G. Kittel, "Lexikographia sacra," DTh, 5 (1938), 108f.; G. Friedrich, "Die Problematik eines Theol. Wörterbuchs z. NT," Studia Evangelica, I, TU, 73 (1959), 482f.

[78]A. Deissmann, rev. of H. Cremer, Bibl.-theol. Wörterbuch der nt.lichen Gräzität, ed. J. Kögel[10] (1911), ThLZ, 37 (1912), 521.

[79]A. Deissmann, "Die sprachliche Erforschung der griech. Bibel, ihr gegenwärtiger Stand und ihre Aufgaben," Vorträge der theol. Konferenz zu Giessen, 12 (1898), 12.

[80]Ibid., 14.

6. From Cremer to Kittel

a. The severest critic of Cremer was A. Deissmann.[81] Deissmann attacked the isolating and canonising of the language of the NT[82] which he perceived in Cremer's work. He could find many of the supposed peculiarities of the NT in account books, wills, petitions, private letters, public records, contracts of marriage, letters of divorce, judicial reports, magical texts and horoscopes from papyri of the period. This proves that Christianity had no language-building power. The supposed creations of the apostles and evangelists were inventions of the lexicographers. Deissmann admits that Christianity could transform terms but not that it could construct them. The apostles did not use a language consecrated by sacral usage and they certainly did not use a secret language. They simply spoke as everyone else did in their day, so that they could be understood by anybody. The total of words used in the NT alone was reduced to a minimum by Deissmann. He was able to show that 33 words which Cremer had called biblical could be found on inscriptions or the papyri. H. A. A. Kennedy had counted 4829 words in the NT and described 580 of these as biblical words.[83] Grimm in his *Clavis Novi Testamenti* had noted 253 biblical words. Deissmann, however, estimates them at only about 50. Thus of the 5000 or so words in the NT only about 1%, not 10-12%, are specifically Christian or biblical. If no non-biblical instance of some NT words has yet been found, it is probably a pure accident that no such parallel has as yet been discovered.[84] Deissmann did not merely oppose the idea of biblical words. He also opposed the mistaken concept of a NT Greek constructed from an intermingling of Semitic and Greek linguistic influences.[85] For him there is no Jewish Greek and the number of semitisms in the NT has been much exaggerated. Anything that does not tally with classical Greek has been called a semitism. Through his papyri researches Deissmann was able to show that many things called semitic could be explained in terms of the koine.[86]

A further concern of Deissmann's was to point out that both the preachers and the hearers of the NT message were uneducated people belonging to the lower strata of society. As he sees it, the Bible was the book of the little man. He thus attacks the treatment of non-literary texts as literature.[87] To be sure, there are here and there in the NT erratic blocks from the cultural sphere of the day.[88] On the whole, however, Paul's Greek is not literary but non-literary. It is strongly permeated

---

[81]Deissmann B; Deissmann NB; Deissmann LO; A. Deissmann, *Das Urchr. u. die unteren Schichten*[2] (1908); *Die Urgeschichte des Christentums im Lichte der Sprachforschung* (1910).

[82]Deissmann LO, 335.

[83]H. A. A. Kennedy, *Sources of NT Greek* (1895), 62.

[84]Deissmann Urgeschichte, 43; LO, 61.

[85]Urgeschichte, 4.

[86]A. Thumb, *Die griech. Sprache im Zeitalter des Hell.* (1901), 120f.

[87]Deissmann LO, 335.

[88]Deissmann Urgeschichte, 38.

by the rough terms of popular speech and is perhaps the most brilliant example of the ordinary prose, natural but not inartistic, of a travelled cosmopolitan of imperial Rome.[89] Deissmann cannot deny, of course, that the language of Hebrews is more artistic than that of the papyri and makes some literary impression. He explains this, however, by suggesting that Hebrews opened a new epoch of early Christianity in which Christianity took over the cultural media of the day. "The literary and theological age has begun; the creative age is drawing to its close."[90]

Whereas Deissmann worked for the most part in the field of lexicography and showed that individual words were not uniquely Christian, J. H. Moulton tried to demonstrate from grammar that NT speech corresponds to the koine. He refers to the revolutionary change which discovery of the papyri brought about in our views of NT Greek. Not everything which offends classical Greek in the NT is a semitism. The papyri have finally destroyed the fiction of a special NT Greek. Whereas Cremer and his predecessors saw in biblical Greek the language of the Holy Spirit, Moulton concluded that the Holy Spirit used the language of the people when he addressed men.[91] J. H. Moulton and G. Milligan collected from non-literary documents the material which was most important for the NT. In their *Vocabulary of the Greek Testament* they do not offer an ordinary lexicon but a collection of material from papyri and inscriptions which is relevant for a NT dictionary. The examples are grouped by words alphabetically and dates are given. Sometimes brief notes on the context are added and when it seems necessary an English translation is also given. Secondary literature is listed and at times parallels from the works of antiquity are adduced. The material is designed to demonstrate the koine character of NT Greek.

b. Unaffected by the problems raised by Cremer and Deissmann is the work of E. Preuschen, *Vollständiges Griechisch-Deutsch Handwörterbuch zu den Schriften des NT und der übrigen urchristlichen Literatur* (1901). Preuschen deliberately refrained from linguistic studies and did not adduce the new sources which Deissmann in particular had uncovered for the NT in the form of papyri, ostraca, and inscriptions. Nor did he, like Grimm and Cremer, pay attention to examples from classical Greek. He advanced as a reason for this procedure a desire to avoid too great an enlargement of scope. He was content simply to arrange and translate the biblical references. His lexicon was meant for students and pastors. Instead of examples from the surrounding Greek world he thus adduced texts from the apostolic fathers and early Christianity. To make good the lack of source material he put a good bibliography at the end of each article. This new lexical venture was not well received by the critics. They saw in it a step backwards compared

[89]LO, 54.
[90]Urchr. und die unteren Schichten, 22.
[91]Moulton, 1-6, 26; J. H. Moulton, *A Grammar of NT Greek,* I[5] (1957), 5.

with Grimm. To understand the words of the NT it is not unimportant to know in what relation they stand to the Jewish and Greek worlds. One could not gather from Preuschen's dictionary whether a given word was used already in classical antiquity or whether it belonged to popular speech at the time of the NT.

As Grimm made a totally new book out of the *Clavis* of Wilke, so W. Bauer completely transformed Preuschen in the second edition of 1928. He made some statements of principle in his introduction. He identified himself with the goals of Deissmann and argued that the NT was written by men who spoke the ordinary language of their time in more or less popular fashion.[92] Apart from the papyri, inscriptions, and ostraca he quoted authors such as Polybius, Diodorus Siculus, Strabo, Plutarch, Epictetus, Artemidorus, Pseudo-Apollodorus, Vettius Valens and others who did not follow the Attic mode. He also took into account the representatives of Jewish Hellenism, Philo and Josephus, the Letter of Aristeas and the LXX. He referred, too, to non-canonical Christian works such as the apocryphal Acts, since these are important witnesses to the common speech of the time. Bauer did not merely collect instances from dictionaries and indices. With unflagging zeal he also read the Hellenistic authors, sought parallels, and used them in his Dictionary.

c. Cremer became a friend of A. Schlatter while working with him in Greifswald in the years 1888-1893. He sent the last edition of the Dictionary to him at Tübingen with the remark: *Felici successori.*[93] Schlatter, however, had other commitments and did not accept the offer. Instead J. Kögel, a student of Cremer's, continued work on the Dictionary and Schlatter placed materials he had collected at his disposal. Working hard, Kögel tried to make good the defects which critics had brought to light. He clung to the basic conception of Cremer but sought to correct its onesidedness. In particular he adopted some suggestions of Schlatter. In his work *Die Theologie des NT und die Dogmatik,* Schlatter had made some basic statements about the relation of NT theology to linguistic history. He opposed the view that new terms had been coined in the community: "This contradicts not only the nature of language, which can be understood only when existing linguistic materials are used for new thoughts, but no less so the aim of the messengers of Jesus, who had no interest in a secret language but only that their word should be understood and done."[94] The word structures remained, so that the natural element of speech was not changed. A new language did not emerge through the new thoughts and intentions of the speakers. Kögel took up these hints. He came to the conclusion that Christianity did not create new expressions but laid a new impress on existing expressions. A concern of his was to trace the relation between individual terms and the total thinking. With this basic insight he did not ignore

[92]W. Bauer, "Zur Einführung in das Wörterbuch zum NT," Coni. Neot. 15 (1955), 6.
[93]A. Schlatter, *Erlebtes*[5] (1929), 110.
[94]Schlatter, *op. cit.* (n. 77), 72, cf. *Theol. Bücherei,* 41 (1969), 248f.

the labours of Deissmann but paid them more attention than Cremer had done. To make a place for the inscriptions and papyri he left out many of the classical examples. It was important to him that the NT should be set in its age linguistically. Apart from the inscriptions and papyri he also drew strongly on Philo and rabbinic sayings. He rightly called his work, which was finished in 1910 and came out in 1915, a completely revised and substantially altered edition. Even Deissmann (→ *supra*) took a positive view of his revision. He described Kögel's 10th edition as "in its way a highly meritorious revision" which signals an advance in NT scholarship.[95]

d. Kögel himself observed that the rabbinic element in his new edition was too brief. Hence he wanted to enlist several co-workers for a fresh edition. In 1927 he asked G. Kittel if he would be prepared to take part in such a project. When Kögel died and there was still no one to take charge of the work, Kittel felt it to be his duty not to let the heritage of Kögel be squandered. Yet he also saw that a good deal would have to be radically altered. What was needed was not an improved Cremer but a new one. There had constantly been demanded a NT dictionary which would put the words of the NT in the total context of their development. Herder had conceived of a lexicon which would trace individual words from Chaldea through Judaism to the fathers (*supra*). W. Wrede had asked that NT theology be supplemented by a special history of NT or primitive Christian concepts.[96] Deissmann in particular had clarified programmatically the question of a NT dictionary. The meaning of a word cannot simply be read off from its biblical context. To speak of it scientifically one has to know something of the history of its origin: "The task of scientific lexicography, then, is to reconstruct the history of words from the earliest times for which we have sources . . . to the hour when we find them on the lips or pen of a specific man."[97] Deissmann adds: "He who attempts a NT dictionary without sketching the history and statistics of words and concepts from article to article tears the apostle out of his age, tears the gospel out of history, and blocks off the NT from the light of research."[98] Kittel took note of these and similar demands in projecting the new lexicon. If he retained an etymological structure, this was not out of pious regard for Cremer but corresponded to the scientific discussion of the time. H. Paul had attacked the isolated treatment of individual words in his article on the task of scientific lexicography[99] and demanded that the etymological connection should be brought out clearly, which could hardly be done with an alphabetical arrangement. According to the scientific views of the age an arrangement by roots was to be preferred. This has positive results ac-

[95]Deissmann LO, 16, n. 7.
[96]W. Wrede, *Über Aufgabe und Methode der sog. Nt.lichen Theologie* (1897), 21, n. 1.
[97]Deissmann LO, 342.
[98]*Ibid.*, 347.
[99]H. Paul, "Über die Aufgabe der wissenschaftlichen Lexikographie mit bes. Rücksicht auf das deutsche Wörterbuch," SA Münch. 1894 (1895), 77.

cording to F. Dornseiff: "One can see the imposing growth of the language, learn to know nests of words, the contingent stories of word groups which grow up, spread, and increase from a particular place like great plants."[100] L. W. Weisgerber also described it as the most fruitful way of linguistic research to gather words together into word families and word circles according to the basic etymological principle of common roots.[101] The semantic development of a word could best be presented in this manner. Kittel structured the *Theological Dictionary* according to these principles. When the first fascicle came out it met with the approval of A. Deissmann. In a letter to Kittel dated April 13, 1932 he wrote: "According to my first impression I can heartily congratulate you on this installment. You know how critical I was of Cremer's work in earlier days. It gives me special pleasure, then, that without breaking respectful continuity with Cremer and Kögel you have succeeded in giving to biblical research a work in which powerful traces of the rhythm of modern scholarship may everywhere be seen."

7. Survey: The Present Problem

a. Deissmann's researches carried the day on all fronts. His findings were everywhere accepted and were even worked into the *Wörterbuch der neutestamentlichen Gräzität* (→ *supra*). In the meantime, however, much had changed and doubts arose as to whether Deissmann should be followed blindly. At every point his theses came under criticism.

Deissmann spoke a great deal about the popular speech in which the evangelists and apostles delivered the message of Jesus (→ *supra*). Radermacher, however, had already asked with reason what popular language really is.[102] The people includes members of very different cultural groups. Even the papyri are not uniform. The syntax is strong in some while others break even the simplest rules of grammar. If breaking grammatical rules is being popular, the people numbers only the uneducated.[103] Cremer, too, in his preface to the 9th edition protested against calling the language of the NT popular. The authors may be uneducated folk but they are also people who are not accustomed to putting the language of the streets into writing. We are increasingly inclined to emphasise the difference between the papyri and the NT more strongly than Deissmann and Moulton did and to concede that most of the NT writers had a better education than the majority of those from whom the non-literary sources adduced by Deissmann derive. L. Rydbeck states categorically: "I do not find any truly popular elements in the speech of the NT . . . Between the speech in truly popular papyri and the

[100]F. Dornseiff, "Buchende Synonymik," NJbchKlAlt, 47 (1921), 423.
[101]L. W. Weisberger, *Wortfamilien u. Begriffsgruppen in den idg. Sprachen. Zur Grundlage der ganzheitlichen Sprachauffassung* (1964), 16f.
[102]Radermacher, 6.
[103]E. Schürer in a review of Deissmann LO, ThLZ, 33 (1908), 556.

grammatically correct language of the NT it is hard to trace any connections."[104] If one compares some truly representative papyri letters with any section from the gospels, one will note a big difference both in grammatical and syntactical details and also in sequence of thought and sentence structure. Although Milligan quoted so many parallels from the papyri, he himself believed that the theme of the NT transcended the speech of the usual papyrus letter. He thus warns us against underlining the popular character of even the least literary NT writing so heavily as to lose sight of the dignity and beauty of the subjects dealt with in the NT.[105] Constant demands are being made for a critical approach to Deissmann's statements. Either he overemphasises the non-literary character of the NT or he has too narrow a view of literature. According to A. T. Robertson[106] it would be strange if men like Paul, Luke, and the author of Hebrews had no literary inclinations. To not a few passages in the NT a literary character cannot be denied. Not a few correspond to the literary method of the day.[107] Some are obviously designed to be read by a larger circle, to be copied and circulated, so that they have to be described as literary pieces. Probably authors of the day who did not fall under the art of atticism wrote very much as the authors of the NT did.

If the NT is to be compared with Greek writers of the time, one should turn to technical writers who are unaffected by the new classicism rather than to historians and philosophers who had to pay more attention to questions of taste. Rydbeck refers to the pharmocological prose of Dioscurides, the astronomical of Ptolemy, the mathematical of Nico-machus, the technical of Heronus, and the philosophical of Didymus.[108] Whereas historians and philosophers had literary ambitions, scientific writers had no such goal. They did not stand under the linguistic and stylistic tutelage of rules and taste but were relatively free as regards manner of statement. In their factual prose they made practical use their guide. They imparted facts, described things, and gave reasons for and against. Rydbeck has found noteworthy parallels between the language of these authors and that of the NT. Many grammatical phenomena of the NT which have been called popular occur also in the scientific writers of the Hellenistic imperial age. Rydbeck, then, opposes the method whereby Deissmann and Moulton try to explain the grammatical features of the NT in terms of parallels in popular non-literary texts. The authors of scientific texts should be consulted first.

Deissmann's preference for the papyri can be criticised for another reason. It may be doubted whether Greek papyri from Egypt should be

[104]L. Rydbeck, "Fachprosa, vermeintliche Volkssprache u. NT," *Acta Univ. Upsaliensis, Studia Graeca Upsaliensia*, V (1967), 197f.

[105]G. Milligan, Moult.-Mill., VIII, pp. XIXf.

[106]A. T. Robertson, *A Grammar of the Greek NT in the Light of Historical Research*[3] (1919), 84.

[107]N. Turner, "Modern Issues in Biblical Studies. Philology in NT Studies," *Exp. T.*, 71 (1959/60), 105; also "The Literary Character of NT Greek," *NTSt*, 20 (1974), 107-114.

[108]Rydbeck, *op. cit.*, 14, 75f., 190-193.

recognised as a binding witness to koine Greek in general. It may also be doubted whether a comparison of the papyri with the NT justifies the conclusion that NT Greek is that which was spoken everywhere. It has been pointed out that in Egypt the Greek of the common people was influenced by Egyptian, for even in Hellenistic circles the Egyptian mentality was very much alive. In the papyri, then, we do not have Greek as it was spoken and written elsewhere. We have a Greek influenced by Egyptian. Now in syntax and thought sequence Egyptian is closely related to Hebrew and Aramaic. From this it has been inferred that the presence of non-classical construction is due to Aramaic influence in the NT and to Egyptian influence in the papyri.[109] Other critics of Deissmann have drawn attention to the fact that many Aramaic Jews lived in Egypt who spoke a Greek influenced by the LXX. These Jews shaped the Greek character of the koine in Egypt, so that the Greek of the papyri is not common Greek but Jewish Greek, and the Greek of the papyri does not offer clear testimony to the koine of the age. The papyri and the NT both came under Semitic influence.[110] Radermacher was also of the view that the papyri contain semitisms, so that they are poorly adapted to contradict the Hebraic nature of the NT.[111]

The suspicion has been increasingly voiced, then, that NT Greek is not to be traced back to the koine but that the LXX has had a strong influence through forms and expressions as well as quotations and that in this way it has given the NT its linguistic colouring.[112] Naturally the constant hearing and reading of the LXX could not but affect the speech of the Jews, so that they could not think in authentically Greek terms:[113] "Most (although not all) of the NT writers hebraise in some way, since Aramaic was their mother tongue. To that extent the Greek of the NT is a kind of Jewish Greek."[114] On these grounds a stronger Semitic influence has been estimated than Deissmann allowed for. Many NT expressions for which one or more parallels might be found in the papyri are not thereby shown to be koine Greek. What is possible only on the outer margin of Greek, but is common in the NT, is plainly a semitism if the turn of speech is common in Hebrew or Aramaic.[115] B. M. Metzger argues that to understand the NT it is far more important to know the OT than to know classical Greek. He calls the OT the lexicon one must use for a proper understanding of the NT.[116]

[109]L. T. Lefort, "Pour une grammaire des LXX," *Muséon*, 41 (1928), 158-160; M. V. McKnight, "Is the NT written in 'Holy Ghost' Greek?" *The Bible Translator,* 16 (1965), 90.

[110]C. G. Burney, *The Aramaic Origin of the Fourth Gospel* (1922), 4.

[111]Radermacher, 29.

[112]G. Heinrici, *Der litterarische Charakter der nt.lichen Schriften* (1908), 102.

[113]Bl.-Debr. § 4, 2.

[114]Radermacher, 29.

[115]A. Debrunner's rev. of M. Black, *An Aramaic Approach to the Gospels and Acts* (1946) in ThZ, 3 (1947), 377.

[116]B. M. Metzger, "The Language of the NT" in G. A. Buttrick *et al., The Interpreter's Bible,* 7 (1951), 55, cf. also J. H. Moulton and W. F. Howard, *A Grammar of NT Greek,* II: *Accidence and Word-Formation* (1929), 413-415; C. F. D. Moule, *An Idiom Book of NT*

The astonishing thing about this development is that some NT scholars are not afraid of returning to the 19th century debate and reviving the thesis of a special NT Greek or language of the Holy Spirit (→ *supra*). In a review of the *Theological Dictionary* H. Kittel writes: "A fresh formulation of the principle of a special NT speech can be hazarded. We can no longer say that the Holy Spirit spoke a special Greek in the NT but on the basis of the findings of TDNT thus far we can assert that the NT revelation was a factor in the history of the Greek language. The new life content which it gave to Greek-speaking people left an impress on both the form and content of their speech."[117] N. Turner goes a step further. He does not deny connections between NT Greek and classical and Hellenistic Greek. He also notes semitisms. Nevertheless he concludes that biblical Greek is a distinctive language with its own character. He thinks it quite possible that the old question of a language of the Holy Spirit has new relevance. In his view a period of half a century was needed to assess and integrate the discoveries of Deissmann and Moulton. Today, however, one must agree that not merely the content of the NT writings is unique but also the language in which they are written or translated. We are thus brought back to the problem of the previous century.[118]

b. The issue in discussing the language of the NT is that of classical Greek or hebraisms, of koine or semitisms. It is often assumed that the Jewish and Greek worlds are separated by a deep cleft. More recently, however, students of Judaism[119] have shown repeatedly that in the age of

---

*Greek*² (1953), 4; E. C. Colwell, "Greek Language" in G. A. Buttrick *et al.*, *The Interpreter's Dictionary of the Bible*, II (1962), 485; J. P. Martin, "Theological Wordbooks," *The Bible Translator*, 16 (1965), 5; O. A. Piper, "NT Lexicography: An Unfinished Task," *Festschr. F. W. Gingrich* (1972), 203.

[117]H. Kittel, Rev. of TWNT, *Gnomon*, 11 (1935), 496.

[118]N. Turner, "Syntax" in J. H. Moulton, *A Grammar of NT Greek*, III (1963), 4.

[119]Schürer, II, 59-87; Bousset-Gressm., 473; A. Schlatter, "Die Gesch. u. Heimat des vierten Evangelisten," BFTh, 6, 4 (1902), 9; Schl. Gesch. Isr., 15-40; Gesch. Chr., 41-5; H. Gressmann, "Die Umwandlung der orientalischen Religion unter dem Einfluss hell. Geistes," *Vorträge 1923-24, Vorträge der Bibliothek Warburg* (1926), 175; G. Dalman, *Jesus-Jeschua* (1922), 2-6; Kittel Probleme, 34-38; R. Meyer, "Hellenistisches in der rabb. Anthropologie," BWANT, 4, 22 (1937); S. Liberman, *Greek in Jewish Palestine* (1942); D. Daube, "Rabbinic Methods of Interpretation and Hellenistic Rhetoric," HUCA, 22 (1949), 239-264; V. Tcherikover, *Hellenistic Civilization and the Jews* (1959); B. Lifshitz, "Beiträge zur palästinischen Epigraphik," ZDPV, 78 (1962), 77-79; K. A. Kitchen, "The Aramaic of Daniel" in D. J. Wiseman, T. C. Mitchell *et al.*, *Notes on Some Problems in the Book of Daniel* (1965), 44-50; B. Lifshitz, "Notes d'épigraphie palestinienne," Rev. Bibl., 73 (1966), 248-254; D. Auscher, "Les relations entre la Grèce et la Palestine avant la conquète d'Alexandre," VT, 17 (1967), 8-30; J. A. Fitzmyer, "The Languages of Palestine in the First Century A.D.," *The Catholic Biblical Quarterly*, 32 (1970), 507-518; M. Hengel, *Judt. u. Hell., Wissenschaftliche Untersuchungen zum NT*, 10² (1973); cf. also Zahn Einl., 24-52; J. N. Sevenster, "Do You Know Greek?" *Suppl. Nov. Test.*, 19 (1968).

Hellenism the antitheses between Semite and Greek were not as sharp as they had been before. In the days of Jesus, Palestine was in no sense an island completely sealed off from the surrounding world. As excavations and discoveries of coins have proved, there were trading relations between Greece and Palestine even before Alexander the Great. When Alexander established his empire the boundaries between the peoples and their cultures and languages were broken down increasingly. Judaism could not remain outside this process. The Greek language and Greek knowledge and thought flowed into Palestine. As the Zeno papyri show, Greek was known in the aristocratic circles of Judaism as early as 250 B.C. The Hellenisation of Judaism gathered pace under Antiochus Epiphanes IV (c. 170 B.C.). Jerusalem then became a Greek city. The inhabitants received the title and civil rights of Antiochenes and a gymnasium was founded (1 Macc. 1:14; Jos. Ant., 12, 241) in which Jewish youth appeared in Greek dress and played games in the nude. Priests left their temple services to watch games at the gymnasium (2 Macc. 4:9-14). Since sport was not forbidden in the Torah, gymnastic exercises were not regarded as an offense against the traditional religion. Parallel to the gymnasium a Greek school also opened in Jerusalem. The Maccabeans could not arrest this development. In the 2nd century the view was seriously espoused that the Jews were related to the Spartans. When the high-priest Jason was driven out he went to Sparta hoping to find refuge there on account of this kinship (2 Macc. 5:9). The high-priest Jonathan turned to his brothers in Sparta (1 Macc. 12:6) "to renew the brotherhood which binds you to us and the covenant of friendship" (1 Macc. 12:10). The author of Maccabees reproduces a letter by a king of Sparta in which the Spartan tells the Jews that in a work on the Spartans and the Jews he has found a note that they are brothers and descend from the tribe of Abraham (1 Macc. 12:21). This was how close the relation between the Jews and the Greeks was seen to be. How strongly Hellenism penetrated Palestine may be seen from Palestinian authors who wrote in Greek, e.g., Philo, the old man (FGH, 729) whose topographical knowledge of Jerusalem proves that he was a Palestinian, the unknown Samaritan called Ps. -Eupolemos (FGH, 724), and Eupolemus, who was perhaps the leader of the Jewish embassy to Rome mentioned in 1 Macc. 8:17. All these writers aped the Greeks in their works and tried to combine biblical tradition and Greek culture.

Under Herod Hellenisation made inroads into broad strata of the populace. Although for political reasons the king in many respects acted in the interests of the Jews, at heart he felt himself closer to the Greeks. He surrounded himself with Hellenistic advisers and the Greek author Nicholas of Damascus served as his right hand. He had his sons educated outside the country. Herod promoted Greek culture. He had many theatres built, including a theatre and amphitheatre in Jerusalem in which four kinds of games were held, gymnastic games, musical games, chariot races, and contests with animals. Competitors from outside came to them and they were held every four years in honour of the emperor.

Greek rather than Jewish productions were presented in the theatres. At the time of the games many spectators came to Jerusalem from other lands. Although Jews were opposed to the theatres, they were not frequented by Gentiles alone. Jericho had a theatre as well as Jerusalem. Tiberias had a stadium and games were held in Caesarea every five years following the Olympic cycle. The visits of foreigners to Palestine were not without influence on the inhabitants.

Jerusalem was not just the capital of Palestine but also of the diaspora. Among visitors to the temple at the great feasts were many Jews who had completely or almost completely forgotten their mother tongue in exile. Greeks and Hellenised non-Greeks who had converted to Judaism by circumcision also came to the temple to offer sacrifice. Other non-Jews who felt attracted by monotheism visited the temple to pray. All of them spoke Greek. Many Jews of the diaspora who returned to Palestine at the end of their lives took up residence in Jerusalem so as to be buried in the Holy Land. Having grown up speaking Greek they saw no need to learn Aramaic in old age. Since many did not want to give up Greek even in Jerusalem, special synagogues were built for them in which divine service was held in Greek. How strongly the Greek element had become at home in Palestine may be seen from many inscriptions that have been found. On the outer walls of ossuaries in which the bones of the buried were laid when, after the process of decomposition, space was needed for new corpses, the names of the dead were sometimes inscribed. These inscriptions are sometimes in Greek alone, sometimes in a mixture of Greek and Hebrew. In 1956 the grave of a certain Jason was found which had been dug under Alexander Jannaeus (103-76), was disturbed by an earthquake in the time of Herod, and brought into use again in 31 A.D. In accordance with Greek custom coins and games were put in the grave with the deceased. Good Greek, too, is a summons in Aramaic to mourn the dead man. The epitaph has the name of the dead Jason in Aramaic and then a Greek inscription with the probable text εὐφραίνεστε οἱ ζῶντες [τ]ὸ δέ (λοι)πὸ[ν . . .] πεῖν ὅμα φα[γεῖν].[120] It is to be regarded as very possible that Greek had earned a right of domicile in Jerusalem in NT days.

Knowledge of Greek was not restricted to Jerusalem. It must be assumed that not merely educated people or the inhabitants of large towns could understand and speak it but also those who lived in small towns and villages. Probably several people in Palestine were bilingual from early youth. Those in Palestine who wanted to acquire Greek culture had plenty of opportunity. In East Jordan there had existed from the 3rd century B.C. several Greek cities with Greek-speaking colonists, Greek constitutions, and Greek religion. Gadara was a centre of Greek culture. Once captured by Alexander Jannaeus, it achieved independence after the death of Herod. It produced a string of poets and philosophers (Strabo,

---

[120]Lifshitz Notes, 249; L. Y. Rahmani, "Jason's Tomb," *Israel Exploration Journal,* 17 (1967), 61-100; N. Avigad, "Aramaic Inscr. in the Tomb of Jason," *ibid.*, 101-111.

16, 2, 29) such as the Epicurean Philodemos, the lyric poet Meleagros for whom Gadara was as Attica (Ant. Graec., 7, 417), the satirist Menippos, and the rhetorician Theodoros. The strength of the penetration of Hellenism into Palestine may be judged from the fact that ancient Bethshan, west of Jordan, received the Greek name Scythopolis. Alexander the Great had already set up a Macedonian colony in Samaria. The non-Jewish part of the city became larger when Herod settled army veterans there, so that Greek was undoubtedly spoken in the city. In Galilee, too, there were Gentile cities with Greek culture and language. Since these traded with Greek cities, the common language of commerce inevitably had to be used. Whereas Hasmonean coins were minted with both Greek and Hebrew superscriptions, Herodian and Roman coins bore only Greek superscriptions. When in relation to the problem of paying taxes Jesus asked about the superscription, he presupposed that those whom he questioned could read Greek (Mk. 12:16). After 70 A.D. the Pharisees campaigned against learning Greek but with no success.

How firm a footing Greek secured in Judaism may also be seen from the fact that those who lived in the isolation of Qumran and confronted the non-Jewish world very critically had some knowledge of Greek too. In Cave 4 three fragments of renderings of the Hebrew OT into Greek have been found, probably dating from the 1st century B.C. Further Greek texts have been discovered in Cave 7 (DJD, III, 142-146). The men of Qumran must have regarded it as important to put the OT into Greek or to have Greek texts of the OT. According to Damasc., 14, 9f. (17, 6) the overseer of the camp must know each language according to the tribe. It is surely correct to assume that a mastery of Greek as well as Aramaic was in view.[121] In the Copper Scroll found at Qumran Greek characters occur.[122] If the letters from followers of Bar Kosiba belong to a later time, it is still worth noting that one of the writers wrote in his own hand a Greek letter in which he remarks that at the moment he has no desire to write in Hebrew. This shows that these foes of the Romans not only understood Greek but in their letters preferred Greek to Aramaic and that the recipients of the letters could also read Greek.[123]

It is also worthy of note that quite early Jewish families used Greek names. We find this with leading high-priests who were sympathetic to things Greek, such as Jason and Menelaus. The Hasmoneans, too, bore such names as Alexander, Aristobulus, and Antigonus, while in the Herod family we find Archelaus, Philippus, Antipas and Agrippa. Humbler people followed the same custom. Two disciples of Jesus had Greek names, Andrew and Philip (Mk. 3:18). It is also astonishing how many Greek words found their way into popular Aramaic. Already in Da. 3:5ff.

---

[121]Hengel, op. cit. (→ n. 119), 113.

[122]3 Q 15, col. 1. 4. 12 (DJD, III, 284), cf. E. Ullendorff, "The Greek Letters of the Copper Scroll," VT, 11 (1961), 227f.

[123]Preisigke Sammelbuch, VIII, 9843; Lifshitz Beiträge, 78; Lifshitz, "The Greek Documents from Naḥal Seelim and Naḥal Mishmar," Israel Exploration Journal, 11 (1961), 53-62.

we find Greek loan words for musical instruments, e.g., κίθαρις in 3:5, ψαλτήριον in 3:5, 7, 10, 15, and συμφωνία in 3:5, 15. Many Greek terms also occur in the commercial, military, constitutional, and legal spheres. Familiar Greek loan words in Aramaic are ἀγορά, ἀγών, δῆμος, ἄρχων, βουλή, νόμος and others.[124]

The most astonishing thing is that even Jewish theology could not insulate itself from the Greek world. Greek influence on Qoheleth was demonstrated long ago. If there is no literary connection, the author was clearly affected by Hellenistic influence. In the Wisdom literature the view of the Torah could have been in encounter with Stoic philosophy. Even when alien wisdom is criticised the impact of Hellenistic thought may be seen. Palestinian Judaism was also affected by the transforming and unifying intellectual world of Hellenism, and differences between the diaspora and Palestine were fluid. According to D. Daube the rabbis took over their method of scriptural interpretation from Greek rhetoric.[125] Hillel's theory of the mutual relation of the written law, tradition, and interpretation corresponded to the dominant ideas of Hellenism. The seven rules which he proposed for interpretation, and which are usually regarded as typical products of Jewish thinking, also show the influence of Hellenistic rhetoric according to Daube. Not merely the method of theological work was influenced by Hellenism. Hellenistic anthropology penetrated theology as well.[126] Under the influence of Hellenistic Judaism the rabbis too distinguished between the body and the soul, so that a certain dualism arose which old Hebrew thinking had not known. The rabbis now taught that the body is earthly but the soul is of a heavenly origin and will return to the place from which it has come.

c. Nevertheless, if Judaism was influenced by Hellenism, Hellenism was also influenced by Judaism. According to G. Kittel the essential mark of Hellenism was that Greek form was filled with oriental content.[127] This is palpable in Hellenistic novels but philosophy, too, was affected by Semitism. M. Pohlenz has shown this particularly well.[128] Zeno (336-264), the founder of Stoicism, was a Semite. He came from Kition, a Phoenician city on Cyprus, so that his mother tongue was Phoenician. Only when 22 did he come to Athens. He was accused of putting Greek teaching in a Semitic dress. One might also say that

[124]Krauss Lehnw., cf. G. Zuntz, "Greek Words in the Talmud," *Journal of Semitic Studies*, 1 (1956), 129-140; H. B. Rosén, "Palestinian κοινή in Rabbinic Illustration," *ibid.*, 8 (1963), 56-72; also Str.-B., IV, 405-414; K. Treu, "Die Bedeutung des Griechischen für die Juden im römischen Reich," NF, 15 (1973), 123-144.

[125]Daube, *op. cit.*, 239-264.

[126]Meyer, *op. cit.*; E. Sjöberg → VI, 375, 41ff.

[127]G. Kittel, *Die Religionsgeschichte u. das Urchr.* (1932), 19.

[128]M. Pohlenz, "Stoa und Semitismus," *N. Jbch. Wiss. u. Judendbildung*, 2 (1926), 257-269; also *Die Stoa. Gesch. einer geistigen Bewegung*, I² (1959), 22-110; cf. also U. v. Wilamowitz-Moellendorff, *Der Glaube der Hellenen*, II (1956), 288f. and M. Hadas, *Hell. Kultur* (1963), 126-135.

he offered Semitic teaching in a Greek package. His students and followers were drawn from the Semitic world. In Athens his doctrine was felt to be an alien body. Stoicism was saved from threatened collapse by another Semite, Chrysippus, who was born in the Cilician port of Solai, to which his father, who came from Tarsus, had moved. It has been said that if there had been no Chrysippus, there would have been no Stoicism. This new founder of Stoicism also learned Greek only later and it is said that all his life he never spoke it correctly. The Syrian Poseidonios was also a mediator of eastern ideas.

The Semitic origin of Stoic philosophy may be seen in its teaching. Zeno recognised a transcendent Creator God, a totally non-Greek concept which he brought with him from his homeland. He found in the creative Logos a living and all-directing deity. He felt himself inwardly bound to a higher power which did not just determine the course of the world externally and rule all things for the best but which was decisive for the life of the individual. This Logos, who fashions matter, is also the leader of the individual through life. The rigorism of Stoic ethics has its root in the Semitic origin of the philosophy. The passionate concern of Zeno for justice has been compared to the attitude of the OT prophets. The Greeks, too, knew written and unwritten laws. But for them what a god prescribed was simply what may be known from the world order. Greek ethics rests on the natural will and ability of man, not on a law over man which a god has decreed. For them the idea of Zeus establishing morality by a decalogue would have been unthinkable.[129] The "Thou shalt" of Stoicism reminds us of Semitic ethics. Stoicism has a different view from the Greek one, not only of man's relation to God, but also of his relation to nature, to animals and plants. As Sophocles puts it in his famous chorus (Soph. Ant., 332f.), man is indeed the mightiest of all creatures. Nevertheless, every being has its own destiny in the cosmos. In Stoicism, however, man is the only goal of the universe. Animals and plants are created for his sake. These are notes that remind us of the Bible. Finally Pohlenz points out that Stoicism is affected by the linguistic structure of Semitism. The tenses are not divided into the three sequences of past, present, and future but are used as in the Semitic world. Definite times which express the fact that an action is ongoing or closed are distinguished from indefinite ones in which this is not so.

Semitic influence may be seen in poetry as well as philosophy. The satirist Menippos of Gadara cannot conceal his Semitic origin. The imagination and passion of the Asiatic come to expression in his love poems. He writes in Greek but calls himself a Syrian (Anth. Graec., 7, 417, 5). His burial epigram is worth noting: ἀλλ᾽ εἰ μὲν Σύρος ἐσσί, "Σαλάμ," εἰ δ᾽ οὖν σύ γε Φοῖνιξ, "Αὐδονίς," εἰ δ᾽ Ἕλλην, "Χαῖρε," τὸ δ᾽ αὐτὸ φράσον (Anth. Graec., 7, 419, 7f.). The Greek and Near Eastern worlds are especially fused in Hellenistic novels. The content is

---

[129]Pohlenz Stoa u. Semitismus, 268.

largely oriental but the form and disposition are in accord with the Greek spirit.[130]

d. The reciprocal interaction between the Semitic and the Greek worlds is very great. Nevertheless Judaism is prevented by its fidelity to the law from being sucked into Hellenistic syncretism and in spite of many things in common some distinctions between Hellenism and Judaism remain. In a lexical investigation of the words of the NT one cannot begin with a general assessment and then subjugate all the phenomena to this. Many terms have obviously been given their accent by the OT while others are used in the NT exactly as in Greek. Individual words do not always have the same nuance. Many can be used on the one hand in the Greek sense and on the other in the Semitic. Other words are so strongly put in the foreground in the NT, and filled with so specific a Christian content, that they can be directly described as technical terms of Christian theology, e.g., repentance, Son of Man, Christ, kingdom of God, sin, baptism, righteousness, grace, holiness, love, apostle, or church.[131] The different possibilities make it necessary to ask from case to case what has influenced a word and how it is used in the total context.

e. More recently there has been criticism not merely of the basic conception of Deissmann but also of the design of TDNT. It has been objected that the grouping of words by a common stem has led to an etymologising interpretation which does not do adequate justice to contextual usage, too great importance being attached to the origin of a word. Often a word will move so far away from its original sense that the etymology is more of a hindrance than a help to interpretation.[132] To avoid this danger very different principles of arrangement have been suggested. The alphabetical arrangement of words has long been under fire because it does not do justice to the essence of a word. Material dictionaries have been written in which the concern is onomasiology rather than semasiology, so that the issue is not the meaning of a word but what linguistic media are available to denote a thing or concept. R. Hallig and W. von Wartburg have set up a system of concepts which in their view can serve as the basis of future dictionaries.[133] In philology work is being done according to this system but in the NT only tentative beginnings have been made with this and other systems.[134] Existing dictionaries have also been attacked from the standpoint of linguistics. This new branch of learning is still in process of development. Some basic

[130]R. Merkelbach, *Roman u. Mysterium in der Antike* (1962), 335.

[131]Friedrich Problematik (→ n. 77), 484-486.

[132]J. Barr, *The Semantics of Biblical Language* (1961); G. Friedrich, "Semasiologie u. Lexikologie," ThLZ, 94 (1969), 810f.

[133]R. Hallig and W. von Wartburg, *Begriffssysteme als Grundlage für die Lexikographie. Versuch eines Ordnungsschemas, Deutsche Akademie der Wissenschaften zu Berlin, Veröffentlichungen des Instituts für romanische Sprachwissenschaft*, 19² (1963).

[134]G. Friedrich, "Das bisher noch fehlende Begriffslexikon zum NT," NTSt, 19 (1972/73), 127-152.

essays and monographs on lexicography are available. But many problems still need definitive clarification. It is hard to imagine what a generally recognised dictionary on a linguistic basis will look like. Thus far dictionary articles on a structural semantic basis seem better suited to smaller works than to those which cover the history of language. Perhaps different types of dictionaries will have to be written if the desires of all are to be met.[135]

Every age has its own methods and seeks its own forms. Thus lexicography, like other disciplines even when they have done what they set out to do, is never at its goal but always on the way to new insights. H. Tiktin begins his essay on dictionaries of the future[136] with the words: "All human work is imperfect. Dictionaries are incontestably among the most imperfect of human products. Those who are driven by calling or circumstances to seek help in lexical works should realise how inadequate is that which even the best and most comprehensive of dictionaries can offer the user."

GERHARD FRIEDRICH

(Translated by G. W. Bromiley)

---

[135]"I believe I have shown in the preceding statements that with our present ideas it is not possible to plan a dictionary which can meaningfully set out in a series of cross relations the complex connections of meaning in language. For the moment the time is not ripe for this, since preliminary work will first have to be done," G. Wahrig, "Neue Wege in die Wörterbucharbeit," *Berichte des Instituts für Buchmarktforschung, Special No.* June 1967 (1967), 23; cf. also G. Matoré, *La méthode en lexicographie* (1953); P. Imbs, "Au seuil de la lexicographie," *Cahiers de lexicologie*[2] (1960), 3-17; U. Weinreich, "Lexicographic Definition in Descriptive Semantics," *Problems in Lexicography,* ed. F. W. Householder and S. Saporta, *International Journal of American Linguistics,* 28, 2, Part IV (1962), 25-43; H. A. Gleason, "The Relation of Lexicon and Grammar," *ibid.,* 85-102; K. Malone, "Structural Linguistics and Bilingual Dictionaries," *ibid.,* 111-118; H. C. Conklin, "Lexicographical Treatment of Folk Taxonomies," *ibid.,* 119-121; O. Ducháček, "La structure du lexique et quelques problèmes sémantico-lexicaux," *Revue Roumaine de Linguistique,* 10 (1965), 559-569; A. Rey, "A propos de la définition lexicographique," *Cahiers de lexicologie,* 7 (1965 II), 67-80; also "Les dictionnaires: Forme et contenu," *Cahiers de lexicologie,* 7 (1965 II), 65-102; K. Baldinger, "Sémantique et structure conceptuelle," *ibid.,* 8 (1966), 3-46; J. Rey-Debove, "La définition lexicographique: Recherches sur l'équation sémique," *ibid.,* 71-94; A. Ufimceva, "On Lexico-Semantic Systems of Language," *Zeichen und System der Sprache* III, *Schriften zur Phonetik, Sprachwissenschaft und Kommunikationsforschung,* II (1966), 90-97; J. Filipec, "Zur Theorie und Methode der lexikologischen Forschung," *ibid.,* 154-173; K. Gapka, *Theorien zur Darstellung eines Wortschatzes* (1967); E. Coseriu, "Lexikalische Solidaritäten," *Poetica,* 1 (1967), 293-303; J. Filipec, "Zur Theorie der lexikalischen Synonyme in synchronischer Sicht," *Wissenschaftliche Zschr. der Karl-Marx-Universität Leipzig, Gesellschafts- und sprachwissenschaftliche Reihe,* 17 (1968), 189-198; also "Zur innersprachlichen Konfrontation von semantischen Teilstrukturen im lexikalischen System," *Travaux linguistiques de Prague,* 3 (1968), 105-118; H. Seiler, "Zur Erforschung des lexikalischen Feldes," *Sprache der Gegenwart* 2, *Sprachform, Sprachpflege, Sprachkritik,* ed. H. Moser (1968), 268-286; J. Rey-Debove, "Le domaine du dictionnaire," *Languages,* 5, 19 (1970), 3-34; G.

Stötzel, "Das Abbild des Wortschatzes," *Poetica,* 3 (1970), 1-23; J. and C. Dubois, *Introduction à la lexicographie, le dictionnaire* (1971); M. Kaempfert, "Skizze einer Theorie des religiösen Wortschatzes," *Muttersprache,* 81 (1971), 15-22; L. Zgusta *et al., Manual of Lexicography* (1971); H. Henne, "Semantik u. Lexikographie," *Studia linguistica germanica,* 7 (1972); K. F. Kemper, "Ansätze zu einer sozio-semantischen Theorie des religiösen Wortschatzes," *Linguistica Biblica,* 17/18 (1972), 53-68; G. Wahrig, "Semantische Struktur lexikalischer Einheiten," *Muttersprache,* 82 (1972), 353-363; also "Anleitung zur grammatisch-semantischen Beschreibung lexikalischer Einheiten," *Linguistiche Arbeiten,* 8 (1973).

[136]H. Tiktin, "Wörterbücher der Zukunft," *Germanisch-Romanische Monatsschrift,* 2 (1910), 243f.